MARKETING

4th CANADIAN EDITION

Eric N. Berkowitz
University of Massachusetts

Frederick G. Crane
QMA Consulting Group Limited

Roger A. Kerin
Southern Methodist University

Steven W. Hartley
University of Denver

William Rudelius
University of St. Thomas

Toronto New York Burr Ridge, IL Bangkok Bogotá Caracas
Lisbon London Madrid Mexico City Milan New Delhi
Seoul Singapore Sydney Taipei

McGraw-Hill
Ryerson Limited
A Subsidiary of The ***McGraw-Hill*** *Companies*

MARKETING
Fourth Canadian Edition
Berkowitz, Crane, Kerin, Hartley, and Rudelius

ISBN: 0-07-086045-9

1 2 3 4 5 6 7 8 9 10 GTC 0 9 8 7 6 5 4 3 2 1 0

Printed and bound in the USA.

Publisher/Editorial Director: Evelyn Veitch
Senior Marketing Manager: Jeff MacLean
Marketing Manager: Bill Todd
Sponsoring Editor: Lenore Gray-Spence
Developmental Editor: Elke Price
Copy Editor: Dianne Broad
Production Coordinator: Nicla Dattolico
Cover Design: Sam Tallo/Rebus Creative
Art Direction: Dianna Little
Page Layout: Precision Graphics
Printer: Transcontinental Printing, Inc.

Canadian Cataloguing in Publication Data

Main entry under title:

Marketing

4th Canadian ed.
Includes index.
ISBN 0-07-086045-9

1. Marketing. 2. Marketing – Canada. I. Berkowitz, Eric. N.

HF5415.M293 1999 658.8 C99-932307-5

PREFACE

The Millennium. While *Marketing,* Fourth Canadian Edition, appears at the dynamic dawn of the 21st century, this text also represents our long-standing commitment to a creative, active, and engaging approach to the study of marketing that has been the foundation of our success. The interest in our approach has grown dramatically through the first three editions, putting *Marketing* in the position of the market leader in the introductory textbook market. Hundreds of instructors have become regular users of our materials as students have expressed enthusiasm for the writing style and demonstrated positive learning outcomes. To continue the use and growth of *Marketing* and its features, we are pleased to offer the Fourth Edition as the most comprehensive, up-to-date, and innovative marketing textbook available to you today, and we appreciate the opportunity to explore the exciting field of marketing with you!

DISTINCTIVE FEATURES OF OUR APPROACH

The innovative pedagogical approach we developed through our own classroom experiences was introduced in the first edition in 1991. While each new edition has offered new content, cases, and examples to reflect changes in the marketing discipline and the marketplace, the distinctive features of our approach have remained as the foundation of the text and the supporting supplements. The features which you may recognize from previous editions and which are prominent in this edition include:

- An easy-to-read, high-involvement, interactive writing style that engages students through active learning techniques, timely and interesting examples, and challenging applications.
- A vivid and accurate description of businesses and marketing professionals—through cases, exercises, and testimonials—that allows students to "personalize" marketing and identify possible career interests and role models.
- The use of extended examples, involving people making marketing decisions, that students can easily relate to text concepts and that emphasize a decision-making orientation.
- Comprehensive and integrated coverage of traditional and contemporary scholarly concepts illustrated through relevant practitioner-related literature.
- A rigorous pedagogical framework based on the use of learning objectives, concept checks, key words, chapter summaries, and supportive student supplements such as the Student CD-ROM and the Study Guide.
- A package of support materials to accommodate a wide variety of instructor teaching styles and student learning styles.

Feedback from many instructors and students who have used our text and package in the past has encouraged us to build on these strengths as we developed the fourth edition of *Marketing.*

NEW FEATURES IN THIS EDITION

The new millennium promises exciting, challenging, and unpredictable changes for all of us. The beginning of the 21st century, however, may be particularly dramatic for marketing students, managers, and instructors. The emergence of digital technology and electronic commerce is literally changing everything. Traditional topics such as marketing research, advertising, and distribution are suddenly in the middle of this extraordinary transition. In addition, many new topics and concepts such as disintermediation and rich media are emerging as important additions to the field of marketing.

To build on the strengths of *Marketing* and to incorporate the most recent developments in the field, we solicited detailed evaluations from users and nonusers about content and design issues. The result has been the addition of many new topics and content areas, the revision and retention of important and enduring concepts, and the development of several new design and pedagogical features. Changes in the organization of this edition include:

- A new chapter entitled Interactive Marketing and Electronic Commerce has been added as Chapter 8 to provide coverage of the many new aspects of the digital revolution. The chapter discusses how the new marketspace creates customer value and provides a learning mechanism—the six Cs—to facilitate discussion of online consumer purchasing behaviour.
- Relationship marketing and information technology topics previously covered in Chapter 10 (third edition) have been integrated into the relevant sections of the fourth edition. Sales forecasting topics are now covered in Chapter 9. Collecting and Using Marketing Information (previously Chapter 8) has become Chapter 9. Market Segmentation, Targeting, and Positioning (previously Chapter 9) has become Chapter 10.
- Chapter 17 has been revised and updated to reflect the new concepts and techniques now prevalent in Supply Chain and Logistics Management.
- Direct Marketing has been added to Chapter 19, now titled Integrated Marketing Communications and Direct Marketing. This change is consistent with the growing interest in direct marketing and its importance as an element of the promotional mix.
- Chapter 20 now covers advertising, sales promotion, and public relations as the three elements of the promotion mix that focus primarily on mass communication.
- A new integrated multi-part case at the end of each major part of the text illustrates the concepts of electronic commerce and interactive marketing.

The content of *Marketing* has also been revised to provide complete and current coverage of emerging issues, new marketing terms, trends, and changes in business practices. Examples include:

- brand personality
- banner ads
- bots
- commercial online services
- computer-mediated buying
- corporate Web sites
- disintermediation
- electronic commerce
- emotional intelligence
- extranets
- interactive marketing
- intranets
- ISO 14000
- marketspace
- mass customization
- portals
- reverse logistics
- rich media
- supply chain management
- sustainable development
- vendor-managed inventory
- webcasting
- yield management pricing

In addition, new sections have been added to several chapters. For example, Chapter 1 now contains expanded material on building customer relationships, details of Rollerblade's strategy to reach narrower market segments, and the increasing importance of mass customization. The supply chain and logistics management chapter now includes a section relating marketing channels, logistics, and supply chain management. Chapter 16, Marketing Channels and Wholesaling, contains a new section on Internet marketing channels and Chapter 18, Retailing, now includes a section about online retailing.

Marketplace examples have been updated to reflect the most recent activities of large and small organizations, and to provide relevant, logical illustration of the concepts discussed in the text. Some of these include:

- Rollerblade's introduction of several new products—the Outback™ and the Coyote™—for the rough-road skater and terrain skater segments.
- Clearly Canadian Beverage Corporation's new growth strategy.
- The pricing strategy for the Confederation Bridge, the bridge that links New Brunswick and PEI.
- The efforts to attract tourists to Canada's newest territory, Nunavut.
- P&G's efforts to improve Web advertising through its own advertising investments and by encouraging useful measurement procedures for the industry.
- Using nontraditional marketing research like "cool hunters" to identify key trends likely to sweep popular culture.

Finally, the package of support materials has been expanded to provide more flexibility for instructors as they "customize" their course for the particular need of their students. New features of the package include:

- A student CD-ROM that contains video clips, chapter quizzes, Internet links, and a marketing plan template.
- New videos and cases including America Online, Palm Computing, BMW, Reebok, and Airwalk.
- A text Web site (www.mcgrawhill.ca/college/berkowitz) and software (called PageOut) to allow instructors to easily design a course Web site.

In addition, we have completely revised and updated the instructor's manual, test bank, instructor's CD-ROM, transparencies, PowerPointTM slides, and the study guide.

NEW INTERNET PEDAGOGY

In addition to a new chapter (Chapter 8) on interactive marketing and electronic commerce, we have developed a two-level pedagogy for Internet coverage in *Marketing* and its supplements. The first level is designed to generate student interest and demonstrate a marketing application through short activities described in a Web Link (see the example on the next page) in each chapter.

The second level is designed to challenge students with an issue or problem or question that can be answered using the Internet as a resource. These Internet Exercises (see example on the next page) are located at the end of each chapter and are designed to allow instructors to evaluate students' performance if the exercises are used as assignments.

The third level of our approach to integrate Internet-related marketing topics into a marketing course is through the design of Internet In-Class Activities. These activities are contained in the In-Class Activity Manual, which is part of the Instructor's Survival Kit. The Internet In-Class Activities can be used by instructors

WEB LINK Nunavut's Tourism Initiative

As you read in the chapter opener, Canada's newest territory, Nunavut is trying to bring tourism into the northern region of our country. Go to their web site www.nunavut.com. What do you think of their site? Given they are targeting adventure tourists and eco-tourists, are they providing enough information? Is the message and image they are trying to convey appropriate? Do you think the site would encourage tourists to visit Nunavut?

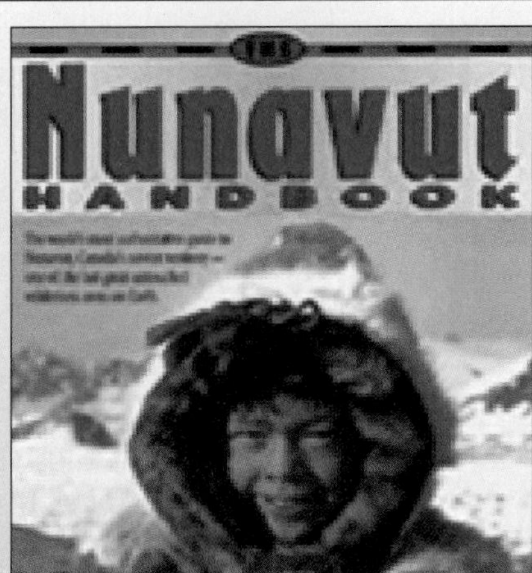

to encourage classroom discussions and student interaction. Examples, some tied to the text, include:

- Comparison Shopping for Personal Digital Assistants
- Testing Your Consultants Aptitude: The Boston Consulting Group Case
- Checking Your Roots . . . If You Really Want to Know!

HELPFUL PEDAGOGICAL FEATURES

Several features facilitate student involvement in the study of marketing. Whenever possible, students are encouraged to take the role of a marketing decision maker or to question the reason for particular marketing actions. Initial inquiries are often posed to students in captions in the margins of the text. In addition, examples of contemporary

INTERNET EXERCISE

Most Web pages accept some form of advertising. If you were to advise your college or university to advertise on the Web, what three Web pages would you recommend? You can use the information at www.adhome.com to help make your recommendation.

1 What is the monthly rate for a full banner ad at each of the Web sites?
2 Describe the profile of the audience for each of the Web sites.
3 Calculate the CPM for each Web site.

WEB SITE	MONTHLY RATE	AUDIENCE PROFILE	CPM
1.			
2.			
3.			

people and organizations, and their marketing decisions, appear in the chapter opening vignettes, the Marketing NewsNet boxes, and the end-of-chapter cases.

The book alerts the reader to special topics with corresponding icons. These include: customer value, global topics, technology, cross-functional topics, and ethics and social responsibility issues.

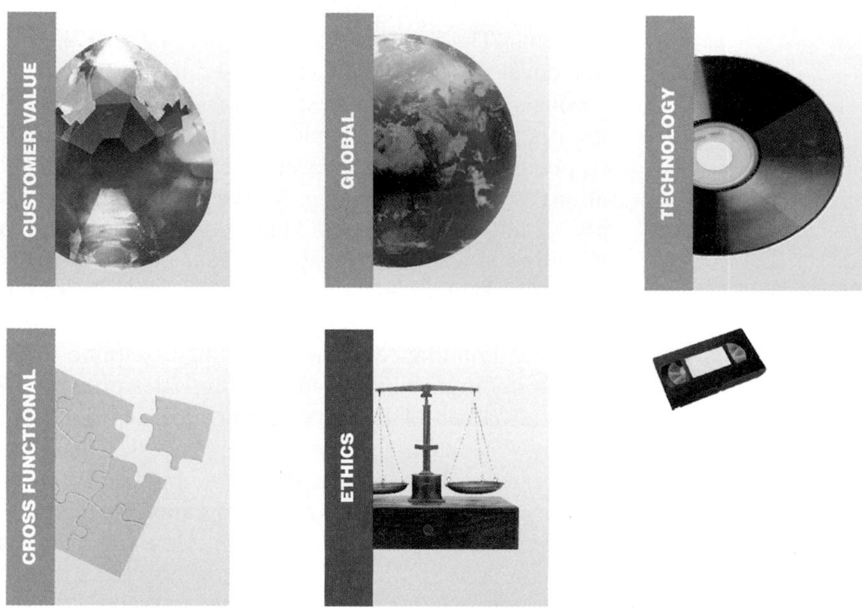

Each chapter uses three reinforcement tools. Learning objectives are presented at the beginning of each chapter to provide readers with a general "map" of the material to follow. At the end of each major section of a chapter, Concept Checks pose two or three questions to test recall and understanding. Finally the Summary and Key Terms and Concepts at the end of each chapter provide further reinforcement of the chapter material.

We believe that the use of these unique learning aids lets students learn about, understand, and integrate the many marketing topics covered in our textbook, and provides an approach that increases the likelihood of an enjoyable and successful experience for students.

THE ORGANIZATION OF THE BOOK

The fourth edition of *Marketing* is divided into five parts. Part I, Initiating the Marketing Process, looks first at what marketing is and how it creates customer value and customer relationships (Chapter 1). Then Chapter 2 provides an overview of the strategic marketing process that occurs in an organization—which provides a framework for the text. Appendix A provides a sample marketing plan as a reference for students. Chapter 3 analyzes the five major environmental factors in our changing marketing environment, while Chapter 4 discusses the significance of ethics and social responsibility in marketing decisions.

Part II, Understanding Buyers and Markets, first describes, in Chapter 5, the nature and scope of world trade and the influence of cultural differences on global marketing practices. Next, Chapter 6 describes how individual consumers reach buying decisions. Finally, because of their important differences from individual consumers, industrial and organizational buyers and how they make purchase decisions are covered in Chapter 7.

In Part III, Targeting Marketing Opportunities, the growing importance of interactive marketing and electronic commerce is discussed in Chapter 8. This chapter emphasizes the key role of the Internet as a means of identifying, understanding, and communicating with target markets. The marketing research function is discussed in Chapter 9, and the process of segmentation and targeting markets and positioning products appears in Chapter 10.

Part IV, Satisfying Marketing Opportunities, covers the four Ps—the marketing mix elements. The product element is divided into the natural chronological sequence of first developing new products and services (Chapter 11) and then managing the existing products (Chapter 12) and services (Chapter 13). Pricing is covered in terms of underlying pricing analysis (Chapter 14), followed by actual price setting (Chapter 15), and Appendix B, Financial Aspects of Marketing. Three chapters address the place (distribution) aspects of marketing: Marketing Channels and Wholesaling (Chapter 16), Supply Chain and Logistics Management (Chapter 17), and Retailing (Chapter 18). Retailing is a separate chapter because of its importance and interest as a career for many of today's students. Promotion is also covered in three chapters. Chapter 19 discusses integrated marketing communications and direct marketing, topics that have grown in importance in the marketing discipline recently. The primary forms of mass market communication—advertising, sales promotion, and public relations—are covered in Chapter 20. Personal selling and sales management is covered in Chapter 21.

Part V, Managing the Marketing Process, expands on Chapter 2 to describe specific techniques and issues related to blending the four marketing mix elements to plan, implement, and control marketing programs (Chapter 22).

The text also offers a new integrated multi-part case at the end of each major part of the text that illustrates the concepts of electronic commerce and interactive marketing.

The book closes with several useful supplemental sections. Appendix C, Career Planning in Marketing, discusses marketing jobs and how to get them, and Appendix D provides Alternate Cases. In addition, a detailed glossary and three indexes (name, URL/company/product, and subject) complete the book.

EXTENSIVE SUPPLEMENTAL RESOURCES

The variety of students, instructors, programs, institutions, and teaching environments who use our text necessitates our providing a comprehensive, integrated, and flexible package of innovative instructional supplements. We assure the quality of the supplements by being involved, as authors or supervisors, in the production of all of the supplements that now accompany our text. To ensure flexibility, we and our publisher have invested extraordinary amounts of time and financial resources to offer every possible instructional aid. These supplements, and several of their unique features, are described below.

Instructor's Manual (Canadian) The Instructor's Manual includes lecture notes, discussions of the Marketing NewsNet boxes, the Web Link boxes, the Ethics and Social Responsibility Alerts, and the Internet Exercises, and answers to the Applying Marketing Concepts and Perspectives questions. Supplemental Lecture Notes are also provided. The fourth edition of the Instructor's Manual also includes teaching suggestions and detailed information about integrating the other supplements.

Transparency Acetates (U.S.) A set of 200 four-colour overhead transparency acetates is available free to adopters. More than 50 percent of these have been developed from information outside the text. In addition, the acetates now include a greater ratio of print advertisements that demonstrate key marketing theories. Several of the ads correspond with the companies that are featured in the video cases, making it possible to teach a more integrated lecture. Each of the transparency acetates from outside of the text is accompanied by lecture notes to assist instructors in integrating the material into their lectures.

PowerPoint® Presentation Slides (Canadian) New to this edition, this software includes a PowerPoint viewer and a set of over 500 PowerPoint slides. The slides include topics not covered in the acetate package and other key concepts covered in the text. Those instructors who have PowerPoint can customize and add to this valuable presentation tool.

Video Case Studies (Canadian) A unique series of contemporary marketing cases is available on videotape cassettes. The video cases feature a variety of organizations and provide balanced coverage of services consumer products, small businesses, Canada 500 firms, and business-to-business examples. America Online, Palm Pilot, BMW, Polaroid Canada, and Rollerblade are just a few of the exciting video cases that are available with the fourth edition.

Video Case and Appendix D Case Teaching Notes (U.S.) This supplement includes teaching notes for the video cases and alternate cases.

Instructor's CD-ROM (Canadian & U.S.) Irwin/McGraw-Hill's new Instructor CD-ROM for Marketing will contain video clips, PowerPoint® slides, and acetates for the text. Great for enhancing class presentations, CD-ROM enables the instructor to show video segments as they pertain to lectures or access the software or electronic slides instantly. The CD-ROM will also include the print supplements and electronic supplements so that the instructor has access to all of the supplements on one disk.

Instructor's Survival Kit and In-Class Activities (U.S.) This U.S. supplement is avaliable in limited quantites to *Marketing,* Fourth Canadian Edition users. Today's students are more likely to learn and be motivated by active, participative experiences than by classic classroom lecture and discussion. While our many other supplements like video cases and transparencies enhance classroom instruction, the Instructor's "Survival Kit" contains three specific elements of special value to today's instructors:

- In-class activities. What we term "in-class" activities have received such extremely positive feedback from our customers—both instructors and students—that we have expanded the number and variety included in the package. These in-class activities may relate to a specific video case or example from the text or may be totally new. For example, some popular activities from our past editions include the "Quick Quiz" on music from Prince's Paisley Park video case, the Coke versus Pepsi taste test, and the "Ethics Quiz." These not only elicit classroom discussion, but also have a learning value in helping students understand marketing.
- "Props" to help run the in-class activities. With the time pressures on today's instructors, our goal is to make their lives simpler. So included in the survival kit are the props to run the activities, such as labels for the Coke versus Pepsi taste test, the "quizzes" for the Paisley Park Quick Quiz (and the right answers), and an example of the America Online direct mail software offer.
- Sample products. *Marketing,* in both the text and supplements, utilizes examples of offerings from both large and small firms that will interest today's students. A number of these are included in the survival kit when they may be new or unusual to students, items such as Breathe Right® Nasal Strips. Also, when appropriate, sample ads are included among our transparencies.

Test Bank (Canadian) Our test bank has been developed and class tested to provide an accurate and exhaustive source of test items for a wide variety of examination styles. It contains more than 3000 questions, categorized by topic and level of learning (definitional, conceptual, or application). The test questions for the Fourth edition are more application oriented. A Test Item Table allows instructors to select questions from any section of a chapter at any of the three levels of learning. The Test Bank includes approximately 10 essay questions, and over 100 multiple-choice questions per chapter, making it one of the most comprehensive test packages on the market.

Computerized Test Bank (Canadian) In addition to the printed format, an electronic version of the test bank is available free to adopters. The program allows instructors to select any of the questions, make changes if desired, or add new questions—and quickly print out a finished set customized to the instructor's course. The program also allows instructors to conduct online testing.

Study Guide (Canadian) The Study Guide enables the students to learn and apply marketing principles instead of simply memorizing facts for an examination. The Study Guide includes chapter outlines for student note-taking, sample tests, critical thinking questions, and flash cards. The new format is based on the results of student focus groups.

Marketing Planning Software (U.S.) Revised for Windows®, the marketing plan software is designed to help students use the strategic marketing process introduced in Chapter 2 and Appendix A and discussed in detail in Chapter 22. The software provides a personal and computer-based tool for involving students in the planning process, and is available on the Instructor's CD-ROM and the *Marketing,* fourth edition, Web site.

Marketing Web Site (Canadian) Visit our new Web site at www.mcgrawhill.ca/college/berkowitz to find an array of features and resources for both instructors and students. The site includes helpful information about the fourth edition of *Marketing,* as well as a link to the Irwin/McGraw-Hill Marketplace, where students and instructors can obtain up-to-the-minute marketing news and information.

PageOut: The Course Web Site Development Center and PageOut Lite This Web page generation software, free to adopters, is designed for professors just beginning to explore Web site options. In just a few minutes, even the most novice computer user can have a course Web site.

Simply type your material into the template provided and PageOut Lite instantly converts it to HTML—a universal Web language. Next, choose your favourite of three easy-to-navigate designs and your Web homepage is created; complete with online syllabus, lecture notes, and bookmarks. You can even include a separate instructor page and an assignment page.

PageOut offers enhanced point-and-click features including a Syllabus Page that applies real-world links to original text material, an automated grade book, and a discussion board where instructors and your students can exchange questions and post announcements.

Online Learning Centre (Canadian) McGraw-Hill Ryerson content and the power of the Web combine to offer you Online Learning Centres—pedagogical features and supplements for McGraw-Hill books on the Internet. Students can simply point-and-click their way to key terms, learning objectives, chapter overviews, PowerPoint slides, exercises, and Web links. And professors profit from the instant access to lecture materials, Instructor's Manuals, test banks, PowerPoint slides, and answers to all exercises in one place.

McGraw-Hill Learning Architecture This unique new Web-based learning system gives instructors ownership over online course administration, study aids and activities, and Internet links to featured companies in many of the McGraw-Hill texts. You can now place course materials online, facilitating the assignment of quizzes and homework—even the tracking of student progress—all from the comfort of your own computer. The system also works to break down traditional instructor/student communication barriers by providing students with an e-mail forum for course topics in addition to auto-graded tests and lecture slide reviews.

DEVELOPMENT OF THIS BOOK

To ensure continuous improvement of our product we have utilized an extensive review and development process for each of our past editions. Building on that history, the fourth edition developmental process included several phases of evaluation and a variety of stakeholder audiences (e.g., students, instructors, etc.). The first phase of the review process asked adopters to suggest improvements to the organization of the text and possible changes to the supplements. The second phase encompassed a more detailed review of each chapter, as the text was used by adopters in the classroom. We also surveyed students to find out what they liked about the book and what changes they would suggest. Finally a group of instructors who do not use the text gave us feedback on the third edition.

ACKNOWLEDGMENTS

Reviewing a book or supplement takes an incredible amount of energy and attention, and we are glad that so many of our colleagues took the time to do it. Their comments have inspired us to do our best.

Reviewers and case authors who have contributed to this edition of the text include:

Cam Gall
Southern Alberta Institute of Technology

Wanda George
St. Mary's University

Malcolm Howe
Niagara College

Henry Klaise
Durham College

John Lille
Centennial College

Shelley Rinehart
University of New Brunswick

John Russell
Lethbridge Community College

Robert Soroka
Dawson College

Vivian Vaupshas
McGill University

The business community also provided great help in making available information that appears in the text and supplements—much of it for the first time in a college or university text. Thanks are due to Alberta Health, BMW Canada, W. K. Buckley Ltd., Canadian Pacific Hotels, Clearly Canadian Beverage Corporation, Dairy Farmers of Canada, Federation des producteurs d'oeufs de consommation du Quebec, Goldfarb Consultants, Gulf Canada, Indigo, Milltronics, Molson Breweries, Nunavut Tourism, Polaroid Canada, Sobey's, Strait Crossing Bridge Ltd., Sympatico, and TSN.

A very special thanks is also extended to Debi Andrus of the University of Calgary for her case contribution to the text. Thank you Debi.

Finally, we acknowledge the professional efforts of the McGraw-Hill Ryerson Higher Education Group Staff. Completion of our book and its many supplements required the attention and commitment of many editorial, production, marketing, and research personnel. Thanks to Elke Price, Associate Editor, for her support and dedication, and to Lenore Gray-Spence, Sponsoring Editor, Kelly Dickson, Manager of Editorial Services, and Dianne Broad, copyeditor. And, finally, thanks to

Evelyn Veitch, Publisher and Editorial Director, for her continued support of this project.

I am responsible for the Canadianization of this text, so any questions or concerns about the book should be directed to me. I would like to thank my co-authors for their input, encouragement, and continued support.

I am dedicating this book to my beautiful wife, Doreen, whose love sustains me; to Erinn, Jacquelyn, and Brenna whose existence uplifts me; to my parents whose guidance enlightens me; and to God whose grace redeems me.

Frederick G. Crane

BRIEF CONTENTS

CONTENTS

PART I

Het is
even
slikken...
...maar dan
ben je wel
mooi van
je hoest af.
Speciaal voor kinderen is er een zoete, zachte hoestsiroop.
Buckley's
HOESTSIROOP
BUCKLEY'S REKENT AF MET HEESHEID EN HOEST.

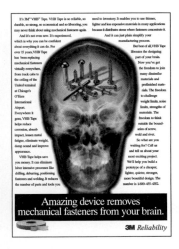

Tom
Hanks
Meg
Ryan
Someone
you pass
on the street
may already
be the love
of your life.
You've
Got
Mail

PART V

MANAGING THE MARKETING PROCESS 565

MARKETING

PART ONE

1 INITIATING THE MARKETING PROCESS

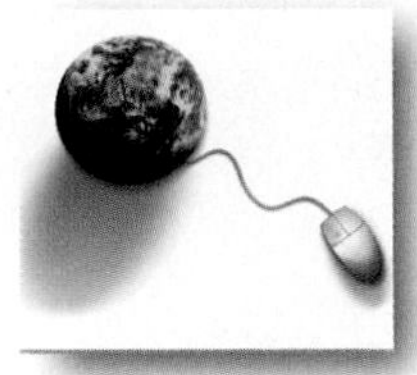

Creating customer value and developing customer relationships. This is the essence of the marketing process described in Part One. Chapter 1 introduces the marketing process by describing the actions of David Samuels as he and Rollerblade, Inc. expand the market for the product and industry created by the company barely a decade ago. Chapter 2 describes how organizations such as Gulf Canada utilize the strategic marketing process to serve their customers. Following Chapter 2 is a sample marketing plan (Appendix A) that illustrates the outcome of the strategic marketing process and provides a reference for students to study and use. In Chapter 3 the dimensions of the business environment and how it has and will change are presented. These changes are described in terms of social, economic, technological, competitive, and regulatory forces. Finally, Chapter 4 provides a framework for including ethical and social responsibility considerations in marketing decisions.

CHAPTER ONE

MARKETING: A FOCUS ON CUSTOMER RELATIONSHIPS AND VALUE

1

AFTER READING THIS CHAPTER YOU SHOULD BE ABLE TO:

- Define marketing and explain the importance of (1) discovering and (2) satisfying consumer needs and wants.
- Distinguish between marketing mix elements and environmental factors.
- Understand how organizations build strong customer relationships using current thinking about customer value and relationship marketing.
- Describe how today's market orientation era differs from prior eras oriented to production and selling.
- Understand the meaning of ethics and social responsibility and how they relate to the individual, organizations, and society.
- Know what is required for marketing to occur and how it creates customer value and utilities for consumers.

NATURE, OUTBACK, AND COYOTES! NATURAL SCIENCE 101?

Well, . . . not quite!

David Samuels and his colleagues have the classic marketing problem of any mind-bending company that has created an entire industry! What do they do for an encore? What do they do to innovate, to provide products that prospective buyers want . . . that build continuing, loyal customer relationships? A big part of the answer *is* nature, outback, and coyotes or—more properly—Nature™, Outback X™, and Coyote™.[1] But that puts us ahead of the Rollerblade® (www.rollerblade.com) story.

The Three-Century-Old Innovation In the early 1700s a Dutch inventor trying to simulate ice skating in the summer created the first roller skates by attaching spools to his shoes. His in-line arrangement was the standard design until 1863 when the first skates with rollers set as two pairs appeared. This design became the standard, and in-line skates virtually disappeared from the market.

In 1980, two hockey-playing brothers found an old pair of in-line skates while browsing through a sporting goods store. Working in their garage, they modified the design to add polyurethane wheels, a moulded boot shell, and a toe brake. They sold their product, which they dubbed "Rollerblade skates," out of the back of their truck to hockey players and skiers as a means of staying in shape during the summer. In the mid-1980s an entrepreneur bought the company from the brothers and then hired marketing executive Mary Horwath to figure out how to market Rollerblade skates.

Understanding the Consumer "When I came here," remembers Horwath, "I knew there had to be a change." By focusing only on serious athletes who used in-line skates to train for other sports, Rollerblade had developed an image as a training product. Conversations with in-line skaters, however, convinced Horwath that using Rollerblade skates:

- Was incredible fun.
- Was a great aerobic workout and made the skater stronger and healthier.
- Was quite different from traditional roller skating, which was practised alone, mostly inside, and by young girls.
- Would have great appeal to people other than just off-season ice hockey skaters and skiers.

Horwath saw her task as changing the image in people's minds—or "repositioning"— Rollerblade skates to highlight the benefits people saw in in-line skating. Using what she called "guerrilla marketing," Horwath used her tiny $280 000 annual marketing budget to gain exposure for Rollerblade skates using inexpensive, nontraditional promotional methods such as "demo vans" loaded with skates that people could try for free.

What a Difference a Decade Makes Fast-forward from the late 1980s to the late 1990s. The marketing problems of David Samuels, senior director of Sports Innovation for Rollerblade, Inc., are a far cry from those faced by Mary Horwath in the late 1980s. As shown in Figure 1–1, she and the company succeeded in popularizing

FIGURE 1–1
Number of in-line skaters in North America. What led to this skyrocketing growth? For some answers, see the text.

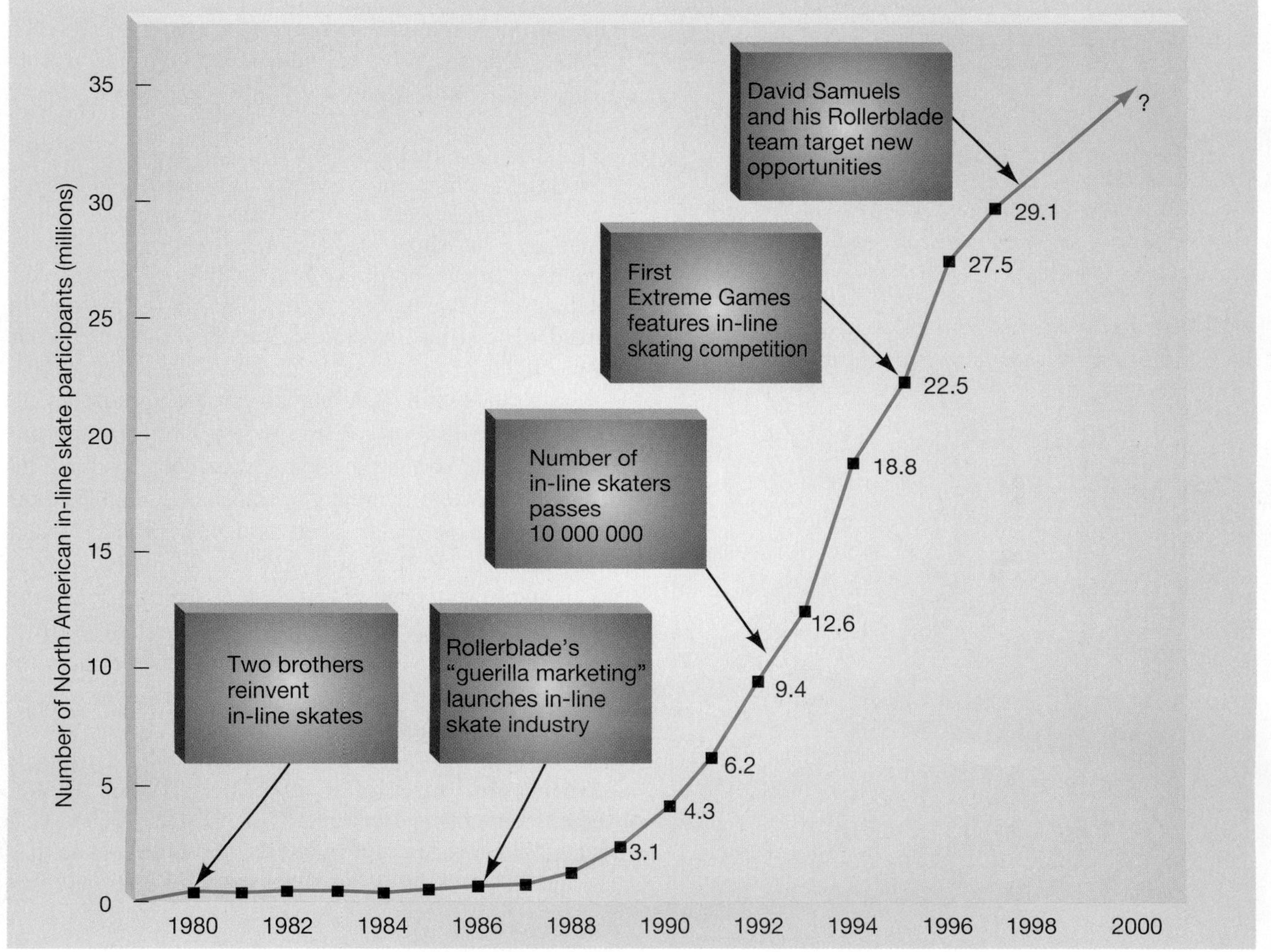

in-line skating—and actually succeeded in launching an entirely new industry, as evidenced by the almost 30 million in-line skaters in North America.

But Rollerblade, Inc.'s success in launching an industry carries its own dangers: competitors. More than 30 of them are facing off with David Samuels and Rollerblade, Inc. as the 21st century starts. Rollerblade, Inc. has 35 percent of the annual industry sales, but faces stiff competition from competitors such as Bauer, which now dominates the in-line hockey segment of the market, especially in Canada.[2] Thus, Samuel's goal is to develop new skating products for current and new segments of buyers, forging strong, loyal customer relationships in the process. This is where breakthrough innovations on Rollerblade, Inc.'s in-line skates such as Nature™, Outback X™, and Coyote™ come in. This situation presents a huge marketing lesson: changing consumer tastes and changing competitive offerings require that organizations search continuously for ways to provide genuine value to customers, or the organizations will die. Thus, the future of organizations such as Rollerblade, Inc. rests on the in-depth understanding of their customers' wants and needs by employees such as David Samuels.

Rollerblade Skates, Marketing, and You What marketing strategy are David Samuels and his Rollerblade marketing team using to try to maintain the skyrocketing growth of in-line skating shown in Figure 1–1? By the time you reach the end of this chapter, you will know the answer to this question.

One key to how well Samuels succeeds lies in the subject of this book: marketing. In this chapter and in the rest of the book we'll introduce you to many of the people, organizations, ideas, activities, and jobs in marketing that have spawned the products and services that have been towering successes, shattering failures, or something in between.

Marketing affects all individuals, all organizations, all industries, and all countries. This text seeks not only to teach you marketing concepts, but also to demonstrate its many applications and how it affects our lives. This knowledge should make you a better consumer, help you in your career, and enable you to be a more informed citizen.

In this chapter and those that follow, you will feel the excitement of marketing. You will be introduced to the dynamic changes that will affect all of us in the future. You will also meet many men and women—like David Samuels and Mary Horwath—whose marketing creativity sometimes achieved brilliant, extraordinary results. And who knows? Somewhere in these pages you may find a career.

WHAT IS MARKETING?

Being a Marketing Expert: Good News–Bad News

In many respects you are a marketing expert already. But just to test your expertise, try the "market expert" questions in Figure 1–2. These questions—some of them easy, others mind-boggling—show the diverse problems marketing executives grapple with every day. You'll find the answers in the next few pages.

The Good News: You Already Have Marketing Experience You are somewhat of an expert because you do many marketing activities every day. You already know many marketing terms, concepts, and principles. For example, would you sell more Sony Walkmans at $500 or $50 each? The answer is $50, of course, so your experience in shopping for products—and maybe even selling them—already gives you great insights into the world of marketing. As a consumer, you've already been involved in thousands of marketing decisions—but mainly on the buying, not the marketing, side.

FIGURE 1–2
The see-if-you're-really-a-marketing-expert test

ANSWER THE QUESTIONS BELOW. THE CORRECT ANSWERS ARE GIVEN LATER IN THE CHAPTER.

1. In a magazine article, a well-known actress said she often "rollerbladed" for fun and exercise. What was Rollerblade, Inc.'s reaction? (*a*) delighted, (*b*) upset, or (*c*) somewhere in between. Why?
2. What is "Polavision"? (*a*) a new breathable contact lens, (*b*) a TV network that competes with Home Box Office, (*c*) special bifocal glasses, (*d*) instant movies, or (*e*) a political newspaper.
3. Right after World War II, International Business Machines Corporation (IBM) commissioned a study to estimate the total market for electronic computers. The study's results were (*a*) less than 10, (*b*) 1000, (*c*) 10 000, (*d*) 100 000, or (*e*) 1 million or more.
4. True or false: Building good customer relationships is a critical marketing issue today, as illustrated by having a loyal Kleenex customer spending more than $1000 during his or her lifetime, in today's dollars.
5. True or false: "Grinding" done by city kids today uses a skateboard with bad wheels or bearings.

The Bad News: Surprises about the Obvious Unfortunately, common sense doesn't always explain some marketing decisions and actions. An actress' saying in a national magazine that she "often rollerbladed" (question 1, Figure 1–2) sounds like great publicity, right? But Rollerblade, Inc. was upset. Legally, Rollerblade® is a trademark registered of Rollerblade, Inc. and, as a brand name, should be used only to identify that firm's products and services. With letters to offenders and advertisements like the one below, Rollerblade, Inc. is trying to protect a precious asset: its brand identity.

Under trademark law, if consumers generally start using a brand name as the generic term to describe the product rather than the source of the product, then the company loses its exclusive rights to the name. "Rollerblade" skates would become "rollerblade"— just another English word to describe all kinds of in-line skating. That fate has already befallen some famous products such as linoleum, aspirin, cellophane, escalator, yo-yo, corn flakes, and trampoline.[3]

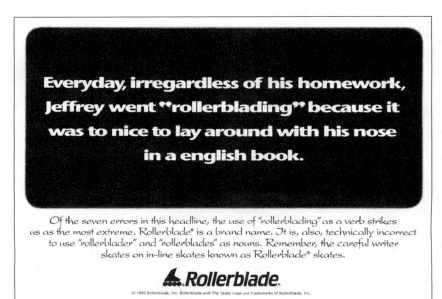

Rollerblade, Inc. ran this ad to communicate a specific message. It's also part of a "reminder" letter sent to people who *slip*. What is the message? For the answer and why it is important, see the text.

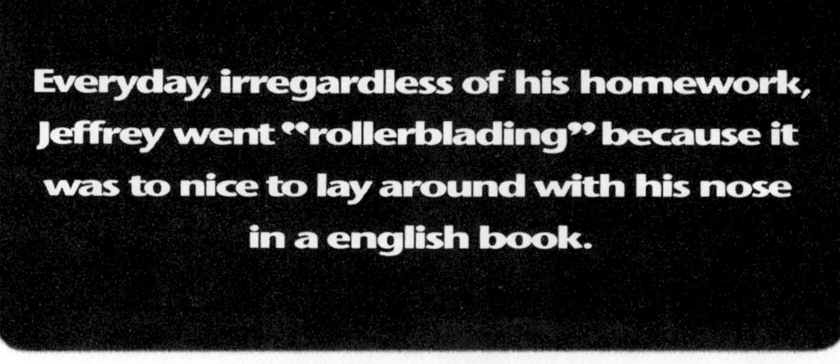

Everyday, irregardless of his homework, Jeffrey went "rollerblading" because it was to nice to lay around with his nose in a english book.
Of the seven errors in this headline, the use of "rollerblading" as a verb strikes us as the most extreme. Rollerblade® is a brand name. It is, also, technically incorrect to use "rollerblader" and "rollerblades" as nouns. Remember, the careful writer skates on in-line skates known as Rollerblade® skates.

www.kimberley-clark.com
www.coca-cola.com

Today firms are spending millions of dollars in both advertising and court cases to protect their important brand names. Examples are Kimberly-Clark's Kleenex tissues and towels and 3M's Scotch tape. Coca-Cola takes dozens of restaurants to court every year for serving another cola drink when the patron asks for a Coca-Cola or even a Coke. Because legal and ethical issues such as the Rollerblade skates trademark problem are so central to many marketing decisions, they are addressed throughout the book.

The point here is that although your common sense usually helps you in analyzing marketing problems, sometimes it can mislead you. This book's in-depth study of marketing augments your common sense with an understanding of marketing concepts to help you assess and make marketing decisions more effectively.

Marketing: Using Exchanges to Satisfy Needs

The American Marketing Association, representing marketing professionals in Canada and the United States, states that "**marketing** is the process of planning and executing the conception, pricing, promotion, and distribution of ideas, goods, and services to create exchanges that satisfy individual and organizational objectives."[4] Many people incorrectly believe that marketing is the same thing as advertising or personal selling; this definition shows marketing to be a far broader activity. Further, this definition stresses the importance of beneficial exchanges that satisfy the objectives of both those who buy and those who sell ideas, goods, and services—whether they be individuals or organizations.

To serve both buyers and sellers, marketing seeks (1) to discover the needs and wants of prospective customers and (2) to satisfy them. These prospective customers include both individuals buying for themselves and their households and organizations that buy for their own use (such as manufacturers) or for resale (such as wholesalers and retailers). The key to achieving these two objectives is the idea of **exchange,** which is the trade of things of value between buyer and seller so that each is better off after the trade. This vital concept of exchange in marketing is covered below in more detail.

The Diverse Factors Influencing Marketing Activities

Although an organization's marketing activity focuses on assessing and satisfying consumer needs, countless other people, groups, and forces interact to shape the nature of its activities (Figure 1–3). Foremost is the organization itself, whose mission and objectives determine what business it is in and what goals it seeks. Within the organization, management is responsible for establishing these goals. The marketing department works closely with a network of other departments and employees to help provide the customer-satisfying products required for the organization to survive and prosper.[5]

Figure 1–3 also shows the key people, groups, and forces outside the organization that influence marketing activities. The marketing department is responsible for facilitating relationships, partnerships, and alliances with the organization's customers, its shareholders (or often representatives of groups served by a non-profit organization), its suppliers, and other organizations. Environmental forces such as social, technological, economic, competitive, and regulatory factors also shape an organization's marketing activities. Finally, an organization's marketing decisions are affected by and, in turn, often have an important impact on society as a whole.

The organization must strike a continual balance among the sometimes differing interests of these individuals and groups. For example, it is not possible to simultaneously provide the lowest-priced and highest-quality products to customers and pay the highest prices to suppliers, highest wages to employees, and maximum dividends to shareholders.

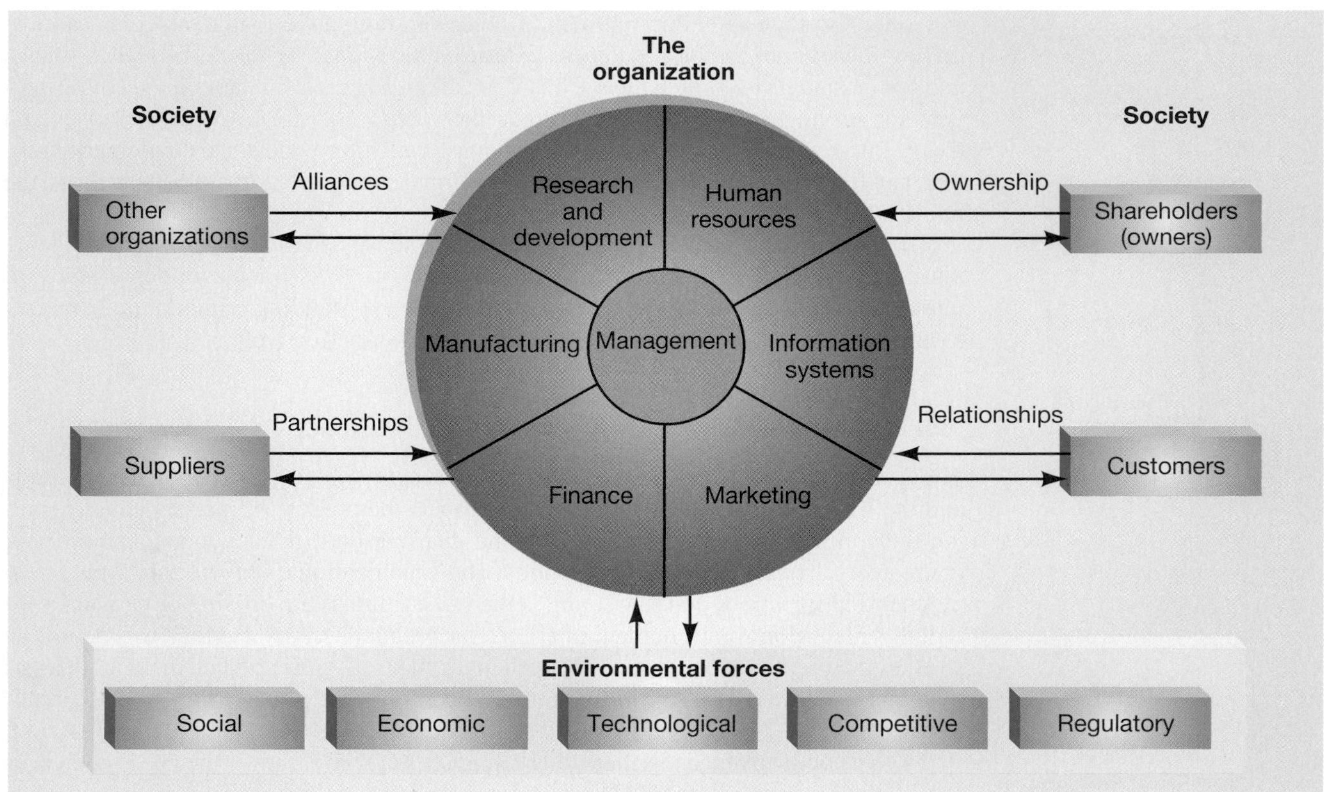

FIGURE 1–3
An organization's marketing department relates to many people, groups, and forces

Requirements for Marketing to Occur

For marketing to occur, at least four factors are required: (1) two or more parties (individuals or organizations) with unsatisfied needs, (2) a desire and ability on their part to be satisfied, (3) a way for the parties to communicate, and (4) something to exchange.

Two or More Parties with Unsatisfied Needs Suppose you've developed an unmet need—a desire for information about how technology is reshaping the workplace and the personal lives of consumers—but you didn't yet know that *Time Digital* magazine existed. Also unknown to you was that several copies of *Time Digital* were sitting on the magazine rack at your nearest supermarket, waiting to be purchased. This is an example of two parties with unmet needs: you, with a need for technology-related information, and your supermarket owner, needing someone to buy a copy of *Time Digital.*

Desire and Ability to Satisfy These Needs Both you and the supermarket owner want to satisfy these unmet needs. Furthermore, you have the money to buy the item and the time to get to the supermarket. The store's owner has not only the desire to sell *Time Digital* but also the ability to do so since it's stocked on the shelves.

A Way for the Parties to Communicate The marketing transaction of buying a copy of *Time Digital* will never occur unless you know the product exists and its location. Similarly, the store owner won't stock the magazine unless there's a market of potential consumers near the supermarket who are likely to buy. When you receive a free sample in the mail or see the magazine on display at the checkout lane, this communications barrier between you (the buyer) and your supermarket (the seller) is overcome.

Something to Exchange Marketing occurs when the transaction takes place and both the buyer and seller exchange something of value. In this case, you exchange your money for the supermarket's *Time Digital.* Both of you have gained something and also given up something, but you are both better off because you have each satisfied your unmet needs. You have the opportunity to read *Time Digital,* but you gave up some money; the store gave up the *Time Digital* but received money, which enables it to remain in business. This exchange process and, of course, the ethical and legal foundations of exchange are central to marketing.[6]

CONCEPT CHECK

1. What is marketing?
2. Marketing focuses on ________ and ________ consumer needs.
3. What four factors are needed for marketing to occur?

HOW MARKETING DISCOVERS AND SATISFIES CONSUMER NEEDS

The importance of discovering and satisfying consumer needs is so critical to understanding marketing that we look at each of these two steps in detail next.

New Coke was not a successful new product.

Discovering Consumer Needs

The first objective in marketing is discovering the needs of prospective consumers. Sound simple? Well, it's not. In the abstract, discovering needs looks easy, but when you get down to the specifics of marketing, problems crop up.

www.polaroid.com

Some Product Disasters With much fanfare, a decade ago, Coca-Cola replaced its 98-year-old Coke with a better-tasting cola called New Coke. Polaroid, flushed with the success of its instant still-photography business, introduced Polavision (question 2, Figure 1–2) as the first instant home movie camera. While Coca-Cola reintroduced its original formula only 79 days after New Coke's launch, Polaroid withdrew its consumer product and tried to redirect it to industrial applications. Both firms lost millions in their failed attempts to introduce new products.

These are two of the best-known product disasters in recent history, but thousands of lesser-known products fail in the marketplace every year. One major reason is that, in each case, the firm miscalculated consumers' wants and needs for these products. In the case of New Coke, Coca-Cola provoked a nationwide uproar from old formula loyalists by failing to understand their bond with the existing product. Polaroid did not anticipate that consumers would prefer the convenience of videotape technology over Polavision.

The solution to preventing such product failures seems embarrassingly obvious. First, find out what consumers need and want. Second, produce what they do need and want and don't produce what they don't need and want. This is much more difficult than it sounds.

www.ibm.com

It is frequently very difficult to get a precise reading on what consumers want and need when they are confronted with revolutionary ideas for new products. Right after World War II, IBM asked a prestigious management consulting firm to estimate the total future market for all electronic computers for all business, scientific, engineering, and government uses (question 3, Figure 1–2). The answer was less than 10! Fortunately, key IBM executives disagreed, so IBM started building electronic computers anyway. Where would IBM be today if it had assumed the market estimate was correct? Most of the firms that bought computers five years after the market study had not actually recognized they were prospective buyers because they had no understanding of what computers could do for them—they didn't recognize their own need for faster information processing.

Consumer Needs and Consumer Wants Should marketing try to satisfy consumer needs or consumer wants? The answer is both! Heated debates rage over this question, and a person's position in the debate usually depends on the definitions of needs and wants and the amount of freedom given to prospective customers to make their own buying decisions.

A *need* occurs when a person feels physiologically deprived of basic necessities such as food, clothing, and shelter. A *want* is a felt need that is shaped by a person's knowledge, culture, and personality. So if you feel hungry, you have developed a basic need and desire to eat something. Let's say you then want to eat an apple or a chocolate bar because, based on your past experience and personality, you know these will satisfy your hunger need. Effective marketing, in the form of creating an awareness of good products at convenient locations, can clearly shape a person's wants. Rollerblade in-line skates are an example.

At issue is whether marketing persuades prospective customers to buy the "wrong" things—say, a chocolate bar rather than an apple to satisfy hunger pangs. Certainly, marketing tries to influence what we buy. A question then arises—at what point do we want government and society to step in to protect consumers? Most consumers would say they want government to protect us from harmful drugs and unsafe cars but not from chocolate bars and soft drinks. The issue is not clear-cut, which is why legal and social issues are central to marketing. Because even psychologists and economists still debate the exact meanings of *need* and *want,* we shall avoid the semantic arguments and use the terms interchangeably in the rest of the book.

As shown in Figure 1–4, discovering needs involves looking carefully at prospective customers, whether they are children buying M&M's candy, university students buying Rollerblade in-line skates, or firms buying Xerox photocopying machines. A principal activity of a firm's marketing department is to carefully scrutinize its consumers to understand what they need, to study industry trends, to examine competitors' products, and to even analyze the needs of a customer's customer.

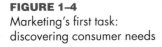

www.xerox.com

What a Market Is Potential consumers make up a **market,** which is (1) people (2) with the desire and (3) with the ability to buy a specific product. All markets ultimately are people. Even when we say a firm bought a Xerox copier, we mean one or several people in the firm decided to buy it. People who are aware of their unmet needs may have the desire to buy the product, but that alone isn't sufficient. People must also have the ability to buy, such as the authority, time, and money. As we saw earlier in the definition of marketing, people may buy, or accept, more than just goods or services. For example, they may buy an idea that results in an action, such as having their blood pressure checked annually or turning down their thermostat to save energy.

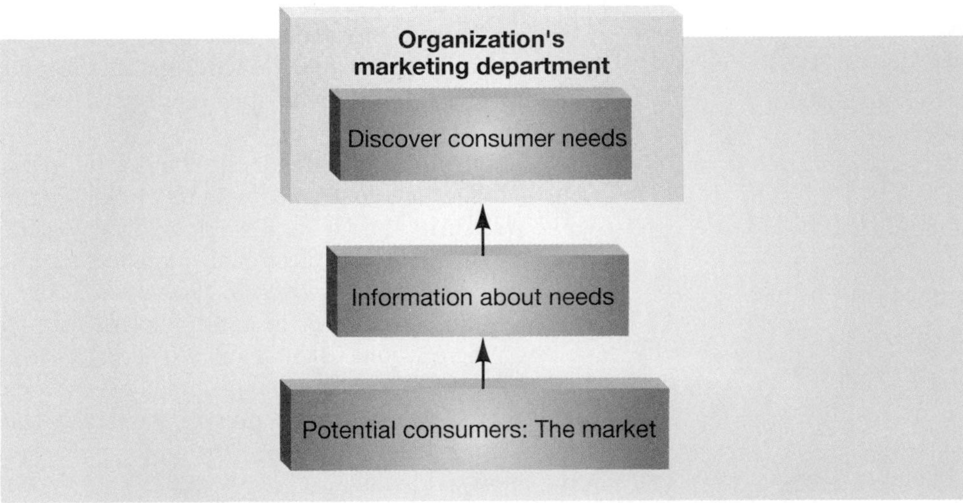

FIGURE 1–4
Marketing's first task: discovering consumer needs

Satisfying Consumer Needs

Marketing doesn't stop with the discovery of consumer needs. Because the organization obviously can't satisfy all consumer needs, it must concentrate its efforts on certain needs of a specific group of potential consumers. This is the **target market**—one or more specific groups of potential consumers toward which an organization directs its marketing program.

The Four Ps: Controllable Marketing Mix Factors Having selected the target market consumers, the firm must take steps to satisfy their needs. Someone in the organization's marketing department, often the marketing manager, must take action and develop a complete marketing program to reach consumers by using a combination of four tools, often called the four Ps—a useful shorthand reference to them first published by Professor E. Jerome McCarthy:[7]

- *Product.* A good, service, or idea to satisfy the consumer's needs.
- *Price.* What is exchanged for the product.
- *Promotion.* A means of communication between the seller and buyer.
- *Place.* A means of getting the product into the consumer's hands.

We'll define each of the four Ps more carefully later in the book, but for now it's important to remember that they are the elements of the marketing mix, or simply the **marketing mix.** These are the marketing manager's controllable factors, the marketing actions of product, price, promotion, and place that he or she can take to solve a marketing problem. The marketing mix elements are called controllable factors because they are under the control of the marketing department in an organization.

The Uncontrollable, Environmental Factors There are a host of factors largely beyond the control of the marketing department and its organization. These factors can be placed into five groups (as shown in Figure 1–3): social, technological, economic, competitive, and regulatory forces. Examples are what consumers themselves want and need, changing technology, the state of the economy in terms of whether it is expanding or contracting, actions that competitors take, and government restrictions. These are the **environmental factors** in a marketing decision, the uncontrollable factors involving social, economic, technological, competitive, and regulatory forces.

Wal-Mart and Lands' End provide customer value using two very different approaches. For their strategies, see the text.

Wal-Mart
www.wal-mart.com

Lands' End Direct Merchants
www.landsend.com

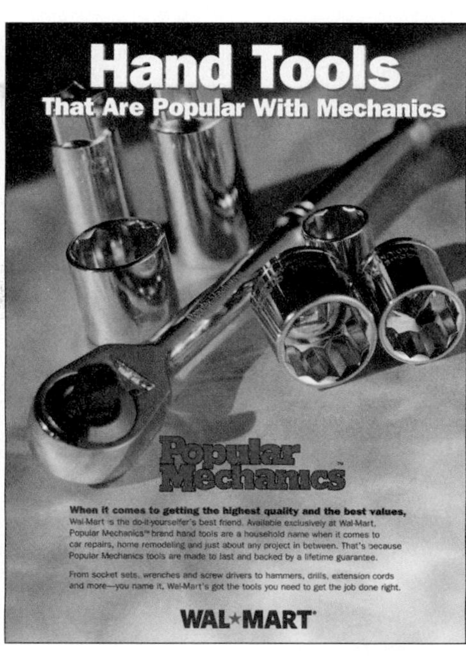

These five forces may serve as accelerators or brakes on marketing, sometimes expanding an organization's marketing opportunities and other times restricting them. These five environmental factors are covered in Chapter 3.

Traditionally, many marketing executives have treated these environmental factors as rigid, absolute constraints that are entirely outside their influence. However, recent studies and marketing successes have shown that a forward-looking, action-oriented firm can often affect some environmental factors. IBM's technical breakthroughs gave birth to the entire digital electronic computer industry, even though initial estimates of demand were low. Cable TV companies have redefined their competition to include telephone companies and vice versa. These technological, competitive, and regulatory factors might have forestalled productive marketing actions had they been seen as completely uncontrollable.

THE MARKETING PROGRAM: HOW CUSTOMER RELATIONSHIPS ARE BUILT

A firm's marketing program connects the firm to its customers. To clarify this link, we shall first discuss the critically important concepts of customer value, customer relationships, and relationship marketing and then illustrate these concepts with the marketing program at Rollerblade.

New Standards in Customer Value and Customer Relationships

Intense competition in today's fast-paced domestic and global markets has caused massive restructuring of many Canadian industries and businesses. Canadian managers are seeking ways to achieve success in this new, more intense level of global competition.[8]

This has prompted many successful firms to focus on "customer value," which has become a critical marketing issue for both sellers and buyers. That firms gain loyal customers by providing unique value is the essence of successful marketing. What is new, however, is a more careful attempt at understanding how a firm's customers perceive value. For our purposes, **customer value** is the unique combination of benefits received by targeted buyers that includes quality, price, convenience, on-time delivery, and both before-sale and after-sale service. The Marketing NewsNet explains how firms actually try to place a dollar value on a loyal, satisfied customer.[9]

Research suggests that firms cannot succeed by being all things to all people.[10] Instead, firms must find ways to build long-term customer relationships to provide unique value that they alone can deliver to targeted markets. Many successful firms have chosen to deliver outstanding customer value with one of three value strategies—best price, best product, or best service.

www.homedepot.com

Companies such as Wal-Mart, Southwest Airlines, Price/Costco, and Dell Computer have all been successful offering consumers the best price. Other companies such as Nike, Starbucks, Microsoft, and Johnson & Johnson claim to provide the best products on the market. Finally, companies such as Lands' End and Home Depot deliver value by providing exceptional service.

But changing tastes can devastate once-successful marketing strategies. Levi Strauss has discovered that today's teens aren't buying its Levi's jeans but prefer the trendier offerings of Old Navy, the Gap, Tommy Hilfiger, MUDD, and JNCO. So in 1999 it closed half of its 22 North American plants and laid off 5900 employees.[11]

Relationship Marketing and the Marketing Program

Meaningful customer relationships are achieved by the firm's identifying creative ways to connect closely to its customers through specific marketing mix actions implemented in its marketing program.

CUSTOMER VALUE

MARKETING NEWSNET

Customer Relationships: Valuing the Retained Customer!

How can a firm put a financial dollar value on good customer relationships with a satisfied customer? The answer: Try to put a dollar value on what a satisfied, loyal, repeat customer spends on the firm's products during a year or a lifetime. Sophisticated firms have learned another marketing lesson: It's a lot cheaper and easier to keep existing customers than try to find new ones!

Frito-Lay, for example, estimates that the average loyal consumer eats 10 kilograms of salty snack chips a year, about $70.00 annually on its snacks such as Lay's and Ruffles potato chips and Doritos and Tostitos tortilla chips. Esso estimates that a loyal customer will spend $700 annually for its branded gasoline, not including candy, snacks, oil, or repair services purchased at its gasoline stations. Kimberly-Clark reports that loyal customers will buy 6.7 boxes of its Kleenex tissues each year and will spend more than $1400 on facial tissue over their lifetime, in today's dollars (question 4, Figure 1–2).

These calculations have focused marketer attention on customer retention. Ford Motor Company has set a target of increasing customer retention—the percentage of Ford owners whose next car is also a Ford—from 60 percent to 80 percent. Why? Ford executives say that each additional percentage point is worth $140 million in profit—a staggering $2.8 billion per year in increased profits if Ford can reach its target!

Relationship Marketing: Easy to Understand The hallmark of developing and maintaining effective customer relationships is today called **relationship marketing,** linking the organization to its individual customers, employees, suppliers, and other partners for their mutual long-term benefits. Note that these mutual long-term benefits between the organization and its customers require links to other vital stakeholders—including suppliers, employees, and "partners" such as wholesalers or retailers in a manufacturer's channel of distribution. In an ideal setting, relationship marketing involves a personal, ongoing relationship between the organization and an individual customer. This is the kind of relationship a rural Canadian family may have had years ago with its local general store.

Relationship Marketing: Difficult to Implement Huge manufacturers find this rigorous standard of relationship marketing difficult to achieve. Today's information technology, along with cutting-edge manufacturing and marketing processes, have led to **mass customization,** tailoring goods or services to the tastes of individual customers in high volumes at a relatively low cost. Thus, you can place an Internet order for all the components of a Dell or IBM computer and have it delivered in four or five days—a configuration tailored to your unique wants. This combines the best features of both mass production and tailoring the firm's product to a single customer's unique wants—what some marketers call strategies to reach "segments of one."

But other forces are working against these kinds of personal relationships between company and customer. One group of researchers has observed that "the number of one-on-one relationship that companies ask consumers to maintain is untenable,"[12] as evidenced by the dozens of credit card and financing offers a typical consumer receives in a year. A decade ago you might have gone to a small store to buy a book or music recording, being helped in your buying decision by a sales clerk or store owner. Today's marketplace, through Internet purchases, often involves bringing the seller and buyer more closely together, eliminating one or more resellers in the channel of distribution. The effect today is that you can use the Internet to buy books directly from amazon.com or download music to your computer from AT&T's a2b. In

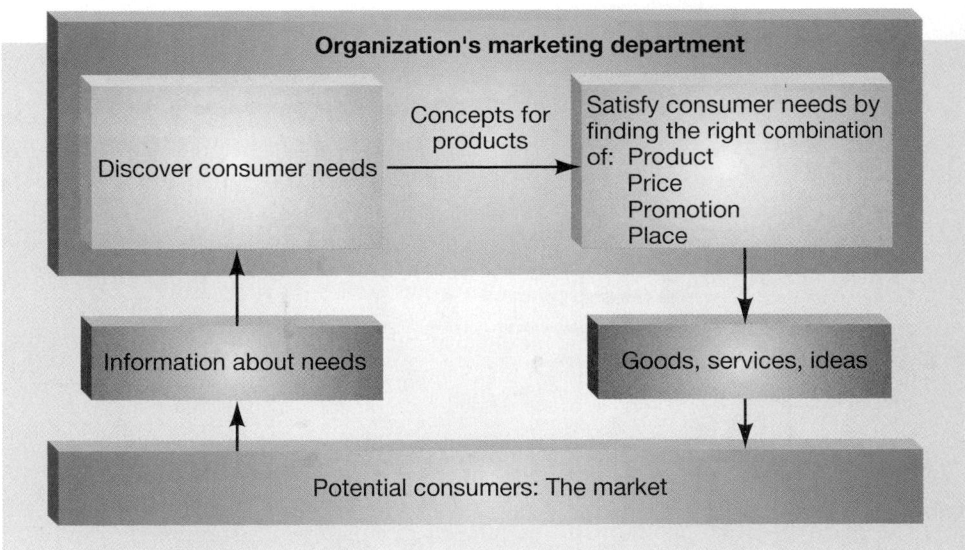

FIGURE 1–5
Marketing's second task: satisfying consumer needs

the process, you may lose the personal, tender-loving-care connection that you once had with your own special book or music store, making it very difficult for stores such as these to really practise relationship marketing.

The Marketing Program

Effective relationship marketing strategies help marketing managers discover what prospective customers need. They must translate this information into some concepts for products the firm might develop (Figure 1–5). These concepts must then be converted into a tangible **marketing program**—a plan that integrates the marketing mix to provide a good, service, or idea to prospective buyers. These prospects then react to the offering favorably (by buying) or unfavorably (by not buying), and the process is repeated. As shown in Figure 1–5, in an effective organization this process is continuous: Consumer needs trigger product concepts that are translated into actual products that stimulate further discovery of consumer needs.

A Marketing Program for Rollerblade

To see some specifics of an actual marketing programs, let's return to the earlier example of David Samuels, Rollerblade, Inc., and their in-line skates. Looking at the in-line skating horizon, David Samuels notes that Rollerblade's long-run strategy is to focus on three areas: (1) expand the market, (2) use the company's strengths in technology, and (3) "stay ahead of the trends." These three areas of focus are intertwined, but each deserves careful scrutiny.

Expanding the Market for Rollerblade Skates In terms of expanding the market, Samuels comments, "Our challenges are to find new venues, new reasons for people to skate." The foundation on which to build marketing programs reaching these new settings rests on two key elements:

- Finding the right benefits—or competitive points of difference (discussed in detail in Chapter 11)—to stress in reaching potential buyers. Three key benefits and points of difference for customers underlie all of Rollerblade's marketing efforts: (1) fun, (2) fitness and health, and (3) excitement.
- Targeting key segments of prospective customers and satisfying them with the specific kinds of Rollerblade brands of skates that they want. In the 1980s this target was 18- to 35-year-old men and women who were active, health- and sports-conscious, and had money to spend on a new sport.

Today, while the fundamental customer benefits remain the same, David Samuels is now trying to reach narrower, more focused segments of customers than in the past. These now vary from children and recreation segments to fitness/performance, in-line hockey, and "aggressive" segments. Let's look at several of these market segments and the products that Samuels and Rollerblade have developed to provide key benefits to satisfy their needs:[13]

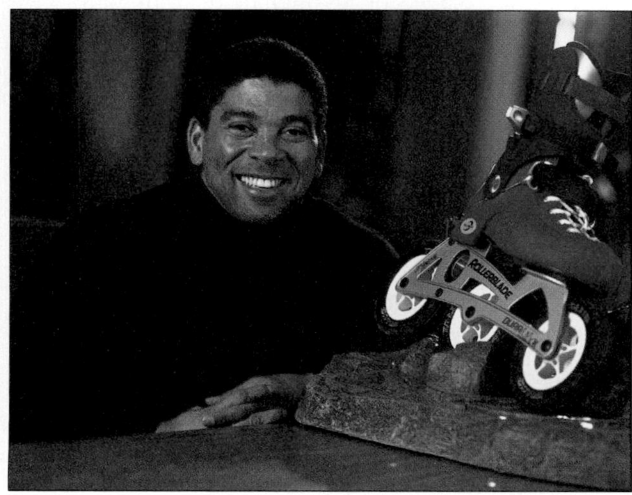

David Samuels and the Coyote™

- *Children segment.* Most parents can't afford to buy a new set of in-line skates each season as their children's feet grow. No problem now! With the Xten-plus™ line, the skate "grows" in four extensions to provide a skate for four sizes of a child's feet.
- *Rough-road skater segment.* Do you skate on country or city roads with bumpy and cracked pavement? If so, then you can try the Outback X™ line, whose air-filled wheels and full-suspension frame can give you a smooth ride over rough roads.
- *Student/transportation segment.* Need an in-line skate to get you from the dorm to your second-hour Econ 101 class but need something to wear in the classroom? The Nature™ line is for you because you can snap the frame/wheels off your skates and sit in class in the hiking boots that are part of the skate.
- *Terrain/"aggressive" segment.* Like to skate down snowless ski hills in the summer? The Coyote™ fills the bill. Its 15-centimetre, pneumatic tires provide a full 2.5 centimetres of shock absorption plus good traction on slick surfaces—an in-line skate for aggressive, all-terrain skating.

Rollerblade has more than 20 lines of skates targeted to different market segments. As illustrated in Figure 1–6 for the Xten-plus™ and Outback X™ brands, most

	MARKETING PROGRAM ACTIVITY TO REACH		
MARKETING MIX ELEMENT	**FAST-GROWING KIDS SEGMENT**	**"ROUGH-ROAD" SEGMENT**	**RATIONALE FOR MARKETING PROGRAM ACTIVITY**
Product	Offer the Xten-plus™, a skate for children that "extends" so that it changes four shoe sizes as the children grow	Offer the Outback X™, a skate with trapped air filled wheels and a full-suspension frame that cushions the ride on rough roads and cracked pavement	Use new-product research, the latest technology, and extensive testing to offer high-quality skates that satisfy the wants and needs of carefully identified customer segments
Price	Priced at $99 a pair	Priced at $199 a pair	Attempt to set prices that provide genuine value to the customer segment that is targeted
Promotion	Use demo vans and blade-mobiles to introduce children to in-line skating while working with Rollerblade dealers to place ads in local newspapers	Feature Rollerblade brand in ESPN in-line sports competitions and magazines such as *Shape, Fitness, Mademoiselle,* and *Inline* and local newspapers	Continue to increase awareness of in-line skating to those new to the sport while offering specific skate designs for more advanced segments wanting them
Place	Distribute the Xten-plus™ through sporting goods stores	Distribute the Outback X™ through specialty in-line sporting goods stores	Make it easy for buyers in the segment to buy at an outlet that is convenient and where they feel comfortable

FIGURE 1–6
Marketing programs for two of Rollerblade, Inc's. skates, targeted at two distinctly different customer segments: fast-growing kids and rough-road skaters

Rollerblade brands require a slightly different marketing program to reach their targeted segments of potential customers.

Exploiting Strengths in Technology In 1995 Rollerblade, Inc. was sold to Nordica, an Italian ski company owned by the Benetton organization. This provided huge technology synergies for the two firms. Examples of exploiting tomorrow's technology—some with Nordica, some on Rollerblade's own—include the following:

- *TriForce™ Technology.* Using Nordica's experience in designing ski boots, Rollerblade used this technology in its skates to support key parts of the foot that generate skating power and then reduce the shock by redistributing the energy out through the toes and heel.
- *Active Brake Technology® (ABT®) system.* Until ABT® brakes arrived, in-line skaters had to lift the toe of their braking foot to force the heel brake onto the road. The ABT® system enables skater to simply slide their braking skate forward, causing the braking device to lower automatically—enabling them to keep all eight wheels on the ground and making skating safer.

Rollerblade's stress on the technology is reflected in the more than 200 patents it holds on key elements of its in-line skate line. The Web Link touches on Rollerblade's strategy on in-line skate products, its technology, and its line of accessories.

Staying Ahead of the Trends Consumer tastes change—and quickly! This is the reason for David Samuels' concerns that Rollerblade stay ahead of trends in the marketplace. Some examples:

- *The Bladerunner® line.* In the 1980s Rollerblade brands of skates were sold through sporting goods stores. But as dozens of new competitors emerged. Rollerblade found that their skates were being sold through mass-merchant chains such as Target and Wal-Mart. Thus, Rollerblade introduced a line of lower-priced skates targeted at customers new to the sport—Bladerunner® by Rollerblade®—to be sold through these outlets.
- *Skates for women in-line skaters.* Half of all in-line skaters today are women. Because the physiology of a woman's foot is different from a man's, this difference can cause problems for women who are serious in-line skaters but skate in a shoe designed mainly for men. Solution: a line of women's in-line skates with a higher arch, narrower heel, and lower cuff to add comfort and protection.
- *Shoes for grinders.* Today's kids love to "grind"—to slide along handrails, curbs, and ledges. To reach this segment Samuels and Rollerblade designed and introduced the RB Grind Shoe™, which features a patented Twin Bar Roller System™ that makes grinding easier and longer lasting on curbs[14] (question 5, Figure 1–2).

Having created a new sport and an entirely new industry, Rollerblade's problems are over, right? Not at all! In a free-market system, success encourages competition and imitations. The Rollerblade case at the end of the chapter lets us look at the marketing strategies that David Samuels and Rollerblade are developing for the next century.

CONCEPT CHECK

1. An organization can't satisfy the needs of all consumers, so it must focus on one or more subgroups, which are its ______.
2. What are the four marketing mix elements that make up the organization's marketing program?
3. What are uncontrollable variables?

WEB LINK What Are the Latest Models in Rollerblade's Product Line?

As described in the text, a key focus of marketing efforts by David Samuels and Rollerblade is to introduce new products that meet the needs of increasingly diverse segments of in-line skaters, such as off-road, rough road, and transportation segments. These skates and accessories for these segments incorporate many of the more than 200 patents held by Rollerblade.

Visit Rollerblade's Web site at www.rollerblade.com. What are the differences in the key features of the Coyote™ and the Outback X™? What are the advantages of the ABT®2 braking system?

HOW MARKETING BECAME SO IMPORTANT

Marketing is a driving force in the modern global economy. To understand why this is so and some related ethical aspects, let us look at (1) the evolution of the market orientation, (2) ethics and social responsibility in marketing, and (3) the breadth and depth of marketing activities.

Evolution of the Market Orientation

Many market-oriented manufacturing organizations have experienced four distinct stages in the life of their firms. We can use the Pillsbury Company as an example.

Production Era Goods were scarce in the early years of North America, so buyers were willing to accept virtually any goods that were produced and make do with them as best they could. French economist J. B. Say described the prevailing business theory of the period: "Production creates its own demand." The central notion was that products would sell themselves, so the major concern of business firms was production, not marketing.

www.pillsbury.com

In 1869, Charles Pillsbury founded his company on the basis of high-quality wheat and the accessibility of cheap water power. Robert Keith, a Pillsbury president, described his company at this stage: "We are professional flour millers. Blessed with a supply of the finest North American wheat, plenty of water power, and excellent milling machinery, we produce flour of the highest quality. Our basic function is to mill quality flour."[15] As shown in Figure 1–7, this production era generally continued in North America through the 1920s.

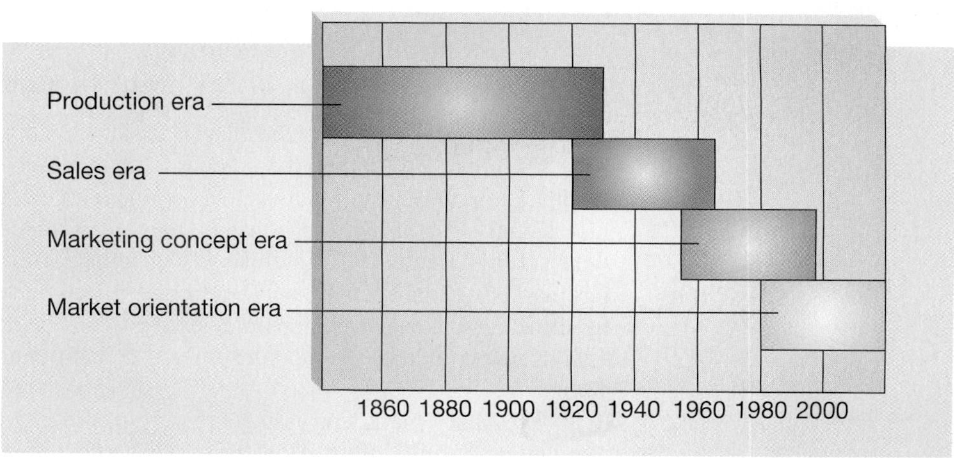

FIGURE 1–7
Four different orientations in the history of North American business

Sales Era About that time, many firms discovered that they could produce more goods than their regular buyers could consume. Competition became more significant, and the problems of reaching the market became more complex. The usual solution was to hire more salespeople to find new markets and consumers. Pillsbury's philosophy at this stage was summed up simply by Keith: "We must hire salespersons to sell it [the flour] just as we hire accountants to keep our books." The role of the Pillsbury salesforce, in simplified terms, was to find consumers for the goods that the firm found it could produce best, given its existing resources. This sales era continued into the 1950s for Pillsbury and into the 1960s for many other firms (see Figure 1–7).

The Marketing Concept Era In the 1960s, marketing became the motivating force in Pillsbury. Since then its policy can be stated as, "We are in the business of satisfying needs and wants of consumers." This is really a brief statement of what has come to be known as the **marketing concept;** the idea is that an organization should (1) strive to satisfy the needs of consumers (2) while also trying to achieve the organization's goals.

The statement of a firm's commitment to satisfying consumer wants and needs that probably launched the marketing concept appeared in a 1952 annual report of General Electric Company:[16] "The concept introduces . . . marketing . . . at the beginning rather than the end of the production cycle and integrates marketing into each phase of the business." This statement had two important points. First, it recognized that sales is just one element of marketing—that marketing includes a much broader range of activities. Second, it changed the point at which marketing ideas are fed into the production cycle from *after* an item is produced to *before* it is designed. Clearly the marketing concept is a focus on the consumer. Unfortunately, although many companies endorsed the marketing concept and defined the purpose of their business as the creation and retention of satisfied customers, implementation of the concept proved to be very difficult.

The Market Orientation Era Many of the implementation issues are now being addressed by the total quality management movement. Firms such as Sony, McDonald's, and Toyota have achieved great success in the marketplace by putting huge effort into implementing the marketing concept, giving their firms what has been called a *market orientation.* An organization that has a **market orientation** focuses its efforts on (1) continuously collecting information about customers' needs and competitors' capabilities, (2) sharing this information across departments, and (3) using the information to create customer value.

A key aspect of this market orientation is that understanding consumers and competitors requires involvement of managers and employees throughout the firm. DuPont, for example, encourages employees to learn about customers' needs by participating in their "Adopt a Customer" program. Similarly, Marriott sends employees to stay in competitors' hotels and assess their facilities and services.[17]

Ethics and Social Responsibility: Balancing the Interests of Different Groups

As organizations have changed their orientation, society's expectations of marketers have also changed. Today, the standards of marketing practice have shifted from an emphasis on producers' interests to consumers' interests. In addition, organizations are increasingly encouraged to consider the social and environmental consequences of their actions. Because the interests of consumers, organizations, and society may differ, marketing managers must often find solutions acceptable to all parties. Guidelines for ethical and socially responsible behaviour can help managers with the complex decisions involved in balancing consumer, organizational, and societal interests.

Ethics Many marketing issues are not specifically addressed by existing laws and regulations. Should information about a firm's customers be sold to other organizations?

ETHICS AND SOCIAL RESPONSIBILITY ALERT

Socially Responsible, Environmentally Friendly, *and* Competitive?

ETHICS

Many organizations today are trying to incorporate social responsibility into their marketing activities. One reason is that socially responsible decisions are likely to have a significant positive impact on society by improving the marketplace and the environment. Another reason is that most of the organization's constituents are taking interest in the issue. Investors now evaluate environmental track records, consumers express interest in environmental issues, and employees often encourage socially responsible behaviour.

Unfortunately, many environmentally friendly products have been costly to produce, and consumers have not been willing to pay a premium for them. As a result, companies often question if they can be socially responsible and competitive.

In the past, policy makers protected the environment through strict environmental regulations even if it eroded competitiveness, while companies tried to appeal to consumers with the often intangible environmental benefits of their products. More recently, some experts have suggested that the solution is innovation that either offsets the cost of improving environmental impact or increases customer value. For example, Scotchbrite Never Rust Wool Soap Pads from 3M—which are made from recycled plastic bottles—are more expensive than competitors' (S.O.S and Brillo) but superior because they don't rust or scratch.

Should companies consider social responsibility in their decision? Must environmentally friendly products be competitively priced?

Should advertising by professional service providers, such as accountants and lawyers, be restricted? Should consumers be responsible for assessing the safety of a product in "normal-use" situations? These, and many other questions, relate to **ethics,** which are the moral principles and values that govern the actions and decisions of an individual or group. Many companies, industries, and professional associations have developed codes of ethics to assist managers.

Social Responsibility While many difficult ethical issues involve only the buyer and seller, others involve society as a whole. For example, suppose you buy batteries for your portable CD player, and, when their charge runs low, you throw them away. Is this just a transaction between you and the battery manufacturer? Not quite! Thrown in a garbage dump, the battery may contaminate the soil, so society will bear a portion of the cost of your behaviour. This example illustrates the issue of **social responsibility,** the idea that organizations are part of a larger society and are accountable to society for their actions. The well-being of society at large should also be recognized in an organization's marketing decisions. In fact, some marketing experts stress the **societal marketing concept,** the view that an organization should discover and satisfy the needs of its consumers in a way that also provides for society's well-being. The difficulty firms face as they attempt to be socially responsible and competitive is discussed in the Ethics and Social Responsibility Alert.[18]

The societal marketing concept is directly related to **macromarketing,** which looks at the aggregate flow of a nation's goods and services to benefit society.[19] Macromarketing addresses broad issues such as whether marketing costs too much, whether advertising is wasteful, and what resource scarcities and pollution side effects result from the marketing system. While macromarketing issues are addressed briefly in this book, the book's main focus is on how an individual organization directs its marketing activities and allocates its resources to benefit its customers, or **micromarketing.** An overview of this approach appears in Chapter 2. Because of the importance of ethical and social responsibility issues in marketing today, they—and related legal and regulatory actions—are discussed throughout this book. In addition, Chapter 4 focuses specifically on issues of ethics and social responsibility.

The Breadth and Depth of Marketing

Marketing today affects every person and organization. To understand this, let's analyze (1) who markets, (2) what they market, (3) who buys and uses what is marketed, (4) who benefits from these marketing activities, and (5) how they benefit.

www.toysrus.com

Who Markets? Every organization markets! It's obvious that business firms involved in manufacturing (Xerox, Heinz, Nike), retailing (Kmart, Toys "Я" Us, The Bay), and providing services (Merrill Lynch, Canadian Broadcasting Corporation, Chicago Cubs, Air Canada, AOL Canada) market their offerings. Today many other types of marketing are also popular. Nonprofit organizations (Winnipeg Ballet, Canadian Red Cross, Canadian Museum of Civilization, your local hospital) also engage in marketing.[20] Your community college or university, for example, probably has a marketing program to attract students, faculty members, and donations. Places (cities, provinces, countries) often use marketing efforts to attract tourists, conventions, or businesses. Chile's "Make the Move" campaign is designed to attract businesses interested in a South American location. Organizations associated with special events or causes use marketing to inform and influence a target audience. These marketing activities range from announcements regarding the Olympics to government agencies encouraging AIDS prevention. Finally, individuals such as political candidates often use

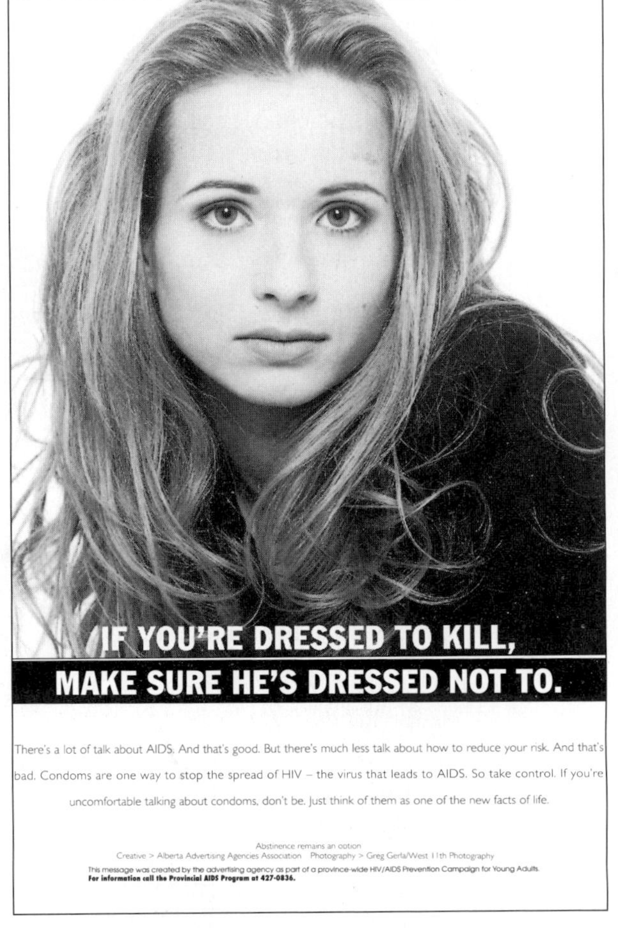

Marketing is used by non-profit organizations, causes, and places.

marketing to gain attention and preference. Celebrities such as Jay Leno, for example, may use marketing activities to increase the size of their "audience," while political candidates such as Jean Chrétien and Paul Martin seek financial support and votes.

What Is Marketed? Goods, services, and ideas are marketed. Goods are physical objects, such as toothpaste, cameras, or computers, that satisfy consumer needs. Services are activities, deeds, or other basic intangibles such as airline trips, financial advice, or telephone calls. Ideas are intangibles such as thoughts about actions or causes. Some of these goods, services, and ideas—such as lawn mowers, dry cleaning, and annual physical examinations—may be bought or accepted by individuals for their own use. Others, such as high-volume office copiers and vending machine repair services, are bought by organizations. Finally, the products marketed in today's global marketplace are increasingly likely to cross a nation's boundaries and involve exports, imports, multinational teams of employees, and international marketing (covered in Chapter 5).[21]

Who Buys and Uses What Is Marketed? Both individuals and organizations buy and use goods and services that are marketed. **Ultimate consumers** are the people—whether 80 years or 8 months old—who use the goods and services purchased for a household. A household may consist of 1 person or 10. (The way one or more of the people in the household buys for it is the topic of consumer behaviour in Chapter 6.) In contrast, **organizational buyers** are units such as manufacturers, retailers, or government agencies that buy goods and services for their own use or for resale. (Organizational buyer behaviour is covered in Chapter 7.) Although the terms *consumers, buyers,* and *customers* are sometimes used for both ultimate consumers and organizations, there is no consistency on this. In this book you will be able to tell from the example whether the buyers are ultimate consumers, organizations, or both.

www.ml.com

Who Benefits? In our free-enterprise society there are three specific groups that benefit from effective marketing: consumers who buy, organizations that sell, and society as a whole. True competition between products and services in the marketplace ensures that we consumers can find value from the best products, the lowest prices, or exceptional service. Providing choices leads to the consumer satisfaction and quality of life that we have come to expect from our economic system.

Organizations that provide need-satisfying products with effective marketing programs—for example, McDonald's, IBM, Avon, and Merrill Lynch—have blossomed, but competition creates problems for ineffective competitors. For example, Wang Computers and DeLorean cars were well-known names a while back but may now be unknown to you. Effective marketing actions result in rewards for organizations that serve consumers and in millions of marketing jobs such as those described in Appendix C.

Finally, effective marketing benefits society. It enhances competition, which, in turn, improves both the quality of products and services and lowers their prices. This makes the countries more competitive in world markets and provides jobs and a higher standard of living for their citizens.

How Do Consumers Benefit? Marketing creates **utility,** the benefits or customer value received by users of the product. This utility is the result of the marketing exchange process. There are four different utilities: form, place, time, and possession. The production of the good or service constitutes *form utility. Place utility* means having the offering available where consumers need it, whereas *time utility* means having it available when needed. *Possession utility* is getting the product to consumers so they can use it.

Thus, marketing provides consumers with place, time, and possession utilities by making the good or service available at the right place and right time for the right consumer.

Although form utility usually arises in manufacturing activity and could be seen as outside the scope of marketing, an organization's marketing activities influence the product features and packaging. Marketing creates its utilities by bridging space (place utility) and hours (time utility) to provide products (form utility) for consumers to own and use (possession utility).

CONCEPT CHECK

1. Like Pillsbury, many firms have gone through four distinct orientations for their business: starting with the ________ era and ending with today's ________ era.
2. What are the two key characteristics of the marketing concept?
3. In this book the term *product* refers to what three things?

SUMMARY

1 Combining personal experience with more formal marketing knowledge will enable us to identify and solve important marketing problems.
2 Marketing is the process of planning and executing the conception, pricing, promotion, and distribution of ideas, goods, and services to create exchanges that satisfy individual and organizational objectives. This definition relates to two primary goals of marketing: (*a*) assessing the needs of consumers and (*b*) satisfying them.
3 For marketing to occur, it is necessary to have (*a*) two or more parties with unmet needs, (*b*) a desire and ability to satisfy them, (*c*) communication between the parties, and (d) something to exchange.
4 Because an organization doesn't have the resources to satisfy the needs of all consumers, it selects a target market of potential customers—a subset of the entire market—on which to focus its marketing program.
5 Four elements in a marketing program designed to satisfy customer needs are product, price, promotion, and place. These elements are called the *marketing mix,* the *four Ps,* or the *controllable variables* because they are under the general control of the marketing department.
6 Environmental factors, also called *uncontrollable variables,* are largely beyond the organization's control. These include social, technological, economic, competitive, and regulatory forces.
7 Building on customer value and relationship marketing concepts, successful firms develop mutually beneficial long-term relationships with their customers.
8 In marketing terms, North American business history is divided into four periods: the production era, the sales era, the marketing concept era, and the current market orientation era.
9 Marketing managers must balance consumer, organizational, and societal interests. This involves issues of ethics and social responsibility.
10 Both profit-making and nonprofit organizations perform marketing activities. They market products, services, and ideas that benefit consumers, organizations, and countries. Marketing creates utilities that give benefits, or customer value, to users.

KEY TERMS AND CONCEPTS

marketing p. 9
exchange p. 9
market p. 12
target market p. 13
marketing mix p. 13
environmental factors p. 13
customer value p. 14
relationship marketing p. 15
mass customization p. 15
marketing program p. 16
marketing concept p. 20
market orientation p. 20
ethics p. 21
social responsibility p. 21
societal marketing concept p. 21
macromarketing p. 21
micromarketing p. 21
ultimate consumers p. 23
organizational buyers p. 23
utility p. 23

INTERNET EXERCISE

Welcome to the opportunity to buy CD-quality music over the Internet! AT&T's a2b music uses revolutionary technology to provide digital downloading of songs and albums from some of the music industry's top artists. Go to the a2b music Web site: www.a2bmusic.com.

1 What do you think of the selection of artists a2b music has?

2 What are the strengths and weaknesses of the online music industry? Is it the future of music retailing?

3 Would *you* buy a CD from your favourite artists over the Internet? Why or why not?

APPLYING MARKETING CONCEPTS AND PERSPECTIVES

1 What consumer wants (or benefits) are met by the following products or services? (*a*) Carnation Instant Breakfast, (*b*) Adidas running shoes, (*c*) Hertz Rent-A-Car, and (*d*) television home shopping programs.

2 Each of the four products or stores in question 1 has substitutes. Respective examples are (*a*) a ham and egg breakfast, (*b*) regular tennis shoes, (*c*) taking a bus, and (*d*) a department store. What consumer benefits might these substitutes have in each case that some consumers might value more highly than those products mentioned in question 1?

3 What are the characteristics (e.g., age, income, education) of the target market customers for the following products or services? (*a*) *National Geographic* magazine, (*b*) *Wired* magazine, (*c*) Toronto Blue Jays baseball team, and (*d*) the Canadian Open tennis tournament.

4 A community college in a metropolitan area wishes to increase its evening-school offerings of business-related courses such as marketing, accounting, finance, and management. Who are the target market customers (students) for these courses?

5 What actions involving the four marketing mix elements might be used to reach the target market in question 4?

6 What environmental factors (uncontrollable variables) must the community college in question 4 consider in designing its marketing program?

7 Polaroid introduced instant still photography, which proved to be a tremendous success. Yet Polavision, its instant movie system, was a total disaster. (*a*) What benefits does each provide to users? (*b*) Which of these do you think contributed to Polavision's failure? (*c*) What research could have been undertaken that might have revealed Polavision's drawbacks?

8 David Samuels and Rollerblade, Inc. are now trying to grow in-line skating—and the company—globally, just as they succeeded in doing in North America. What are the advantages and disadvantages of trying to reach new global markets?

9 Does a firm have the right to "create" wants and try to persuade consumers to buy goods and services they didn't know about earlier? What are examples of "good" and "bad" want creation? Who should decide what is good and bad?

CASE 1–1 ROLLERBLADE, INC.

In the fiercely competitive in-line skate marketplace, what does the future hold for Rollerblade?

As David Samuels, senior director for Sports Innovation at Rollerblade, Inc., explains, innovative technology—in the form of new and better skates—will continue to be key for Rollerblade to stay ahead of the competition. Rollerblade must also find ways to expand the market for in-line skates. "Our challenge is to provide new venues, new reasons for people to skate. There's a lot of growth for us to catch up on in terms of household penetration," says Samuels.

THE SITUATION TODAY

When Rollerblade was founded, it was the only manufacturer of in-line skates in the world. Today the industry has more than 30 competitors, many that sell lower-priced skates than Rollerblade through mass-merchandising chains. Some of the large sporting goods manufacturers, like Nike, that have not traditionally sold in-line skates are now looking for ways to grow and are exploring the in-line skate market. Further, as shown earlier in Figure 1–1, Samuels is concerned that the exploding growth of the in-line skate market seen in the early 1990s is slowing.

THE MARKETING PROGRAM

Expanding the market and continuing to be the leader in product innovation gives Rollerblade a strategic advantage in the marketplace. Yet it is a solid and creative marketing mix that will enable Rollerblade to pass these advantages along to the customer.

The product is the most important "P" in Rollerblade's marketing mix. From introducing the premier braking technology on the market today—ABT brakes—to adding products for new market segments—RB Grind Shoes for the aggressive segment—Rollerblade is always trying to anticipate customer needs and wants. The Grind Shoe, for instance, is a regular athletic shoe with twin roller bars on the instep of the sole, enabling the wearer to slide across railings, curbs, etc.—to "grind." Samuels notes, "Our aggressive segment was doing these tricks on rails with snowboards, skateboards, in-line skates, and bicycles, why not do it while you're walking to school? That's how we came up with the idea." Similarly, the Nature was introduced when Rollerblade discovered students needed something they could skate to class in, and then be able to wear into class. Rollerblade also came out with new product offerings for its kids (Dazzle and Zoom), women (Burner and Viablade, specially contoured to a woman's foot and leg structure), and fitness segments (eSeries) within the last year. Not to mention the far-out Coyote™ and Outback X for the off-road segment.

Rollerblade's promotional strategy continues to set it apart from the competitors, too. Its new print campaign features the ABT braking technology and the tagline "Exercise your soul." The Rollerblade Web site (www.rollerblade.com) is one of the most popular promotional tools with Rollerblade's loyal customers, as it provides chat rooms for aggressive skaters, racers, and fitness skaters.

Since Rollerblade does not have the resources of an industry giant like Nike, it finds ways to communicate with the customer that do not entail huge cash outlays. For example, Rollerblade provides information or product samples to media that, in turn, do in-line-skating features for articles or broadcast programs. It also develops promotional partnerships through sponsoring events and creating sweepstakes with other companies. Recently Rollerblade teamed up with Taco Bell, Curad, Wise Snacks, and Honeywell for joint advertising that benefits the partners but is less expensive for Rollerblade than purchasing nationwide television or radio ads by itself.

Rollerblade also promotes its brands by creating special promotions. Examples are Blade Cross™ competitions at ski hills during the summer to promote the Coyote line and the Blade Fitness™ "workout program on wheels" with a specific curriculum to be used for health club workouts. In addition, Rollerblade receives publicity from its charitable efforts and contributions to silent auctions.

Finally, Rollerblade sponsors a competitive team of aggressive skaters and racers that competes around the world and regularly wins such events as ESPN's X-Games, and has one of the premiere female in-line skate racers as its fitness spokesperson. It is creative and unorthodox approaches such as these that Samuels believes will keep Rollerblade ahead of the competition in the 21st century.

Rollerblade practises an across-the-board strategy when it comes to distribution and price. Samuels says, "Our distribution channels run the gamut. We are everywhere from the large mass market stores to specialty in-line dealers. Additionally, Rollerblade has chosen to hit every single price point possible. We have skates that are at the very high end, as well as skates as low as $79 under the Rollerblade brand. We also take a different brand name called Blade Runner and bring those products to the large mass markets of the world." Giving the lower-priced skates an alternate brand name allows Rollerblade to uphold its high-quality image in the marketplace while still providing an opportunity for beginners to test out the sport.

ISSUES FOR THE FUTURE

Some of the pressing issues in the future are global expansion, creating new segments of skaters, and expanding the product line. As Samuels explains, "Currently, North America makes up over 50 percent of the marketplace worldwide. But Europe has been significant also. Germany is definitely one of the strongest countries for in-line skating." Other areas of growth include Australia and New Zealand, Japan, Mexico, and Korea. Rollerblade hopes to widen its global reach as the company continues to grow.

The youth segment should prove to be one of the most important segments in the future. "One of the biggest changes that's happened to us, and to the world really, is the power of youth. Kids who are anywhere from 10 to 12 years old on up into their twenties have been able to make a significant impact with so little money," explains Samuels. Rollerblade expects young people to continue to shape the recreational sports markets well into the future. Finally, Rollerblade has begun to offer products that are not in-line skates, such as the RB Grind Shoe and accessories like helmets, wrist, elbow, and knee pads, skate bags, and skate tools. Rollerblade will continue to introduce products that respond to consumer needs and desires—constantly working to improve skate comfort, durability, and technologies.

Questions

1 What trends in the environmental forces (social, economic, technological, competitive, and regulatory) identified in Figure 1–3 in the chapter (*a*) work for and (*b*) work against Rollerblade, Inc.'s potential growth in the twenty-first century?

2 What are the differences in marketing goals for Rollerblade, Inc. (*a*) in 1986 when Rollerblade was launched and (*b*) today?

3 How should David Samuels and Rollerblade, Inc. translate the broad goals identified in Question 2 into a specific marketing program for the Nature skate—to integrate product, price, promotion, and place actions? Refer to Figure 1–6 and the text.

4 What are the (*a*) advantages and (*b*) disadvantages of having Rollerblade, Inc. become part of the Benetton sport group? Refer to the text as well as the videocase.

5 In searching for global markets to enter, (*a*) what are some criteria that Rollerblade, Inc. should use to select countries to enter and (*b*) what three or four countries meet these criteria best and are the most likely candidates?

GULF CANADA RESOURCES LIMITED

CHAPTER TWO

LINKING MARKETING AND CORPORATE STRATEGIES

2

AFTER READING THIS CHAPTER YOU SHOULD BE ABLE TO:

- Describe the three organizational levels of strategy and their components.
- Describe how the three organizational levels of strategy relate to each other and how they influence the marketing function.
- Describe the strategic marketing process and its three key phases: planning, implementation, and control.
- Understand how organizations search for new marketing opportunities and select target markets.
- Explain how the marketing mix elements are blended into a cohesive marketing program.
- Describe how marketing control compares actual results with planned objectives and acts on deviations from the plan.

GULF'S STRATEGIES FOR GROWTH IN THE WORLDWIDE OIL AND GAS MARKET

Gulf Canada Resources Limited (www.gulf.ca) is a senior independent oil and natural gas company with four core areas of operation: Canada, including its nine percent interest in the Syncrude Joint Venture; Indonesia, through its 72 percent ownership in Gulf Indonesia Resources; the North Sea, and Australia. The company has an asset base in excess of $5.5 billion that includes proved and probable reserves of more than 1.4 billion barrels of oil, equivalent and substantial ownership of oil and natural gas infrastructure.

Gulf was founded in 1906 in Toronto, and operated as a fully integrated oil company until 1985. After selling its marketing and refining assets, Gulf became solely an exploration and production company. In 1988, the company expanded internationally. In 1997, Gulf furthered its expansion into the North Sea and Australia.

The oil and gas industry is not only highly competitive, but very volatile, given fluctuations in world prices due to oversupply or undersupply situations. Therefore, Gulf, over time, has had to transform itself as a result of changes in market conditions. At present, it is transforming itself from a Western Canadian producer with international assets to a truly worldwide exploration and production company. In order to do so, its strategy, on face, looks simple: work both sides of the street. That is, reduce costs and increase revenues.

It is doing both through a variety of means including cost containment, optimizing production, corporate partnerships, joint ventures, and strategic alliances. For example, there is the creation of Petrovera Resources, a partnership with PanCanadian Petroleum, which focuses on maximizing the value of conventional heavy oil assets for both companies. The goal of the partnership is to optimize the operating cost synergies of the combined companies and to maximize the total asset value. There is the joint venture with Mobil Canada to exploit resources contained in 3.7 million hectares off Canada's East Coast. There is the use of innovative technology to enhance production, and to improve success in exploration. Finally, there is the restructuring of its asset portfolio for fit and synergy, including, if necessary, selling off assets and/or exiting some markets.

By maximizing its expertise in the day-to-day business of production, exploration, and development, Gulf plans to sustain its exploration effort in core areas worldwide, exploit its existing asset base, and continue consolidating its core areas. In addition, it will optimize any opportunities that correspond with Gulf's strategy and assists in Gulf meeting its long-term goals. Richard Auchinleck, Gulf's President and Chief Executive Officer, believes Gulf's overall operational and strategic efforts position the company for increased value and improved financial structure in the near term and the future. Auchinleck believes that for Gulf to be successful it must be smart, fast, innovative, and efficient.[1] And, as you will see in this chapter, these are just a few of the building blocks for an organization's success.

Chapter 2 describes how organizations set their overall direction and link these activities to marketing strategies—the very tasks Gulf Canada faces. In essence, this chapter describes how organizations try to implement the marketing concept to provide genuine value to their customers.

LEVELS OF STRATEGY IN ORGANIZATIONS

This chapter first distinguishes among different kinds of organizations and the various levels within them. It then compares strategies at three different levels in an organization.

Today's Organizations: Kinds and Levels

Large organizations in existence today are often extremely complex. While this is not true for your corner deli or for some of the small businesses highlighted in our textbook cases, all of us deal in some way with huge organizations every day, so it is useful to understand both (1) the two basic kinds of organizations (2) the levels that exist in them, and (3) the Four Building Blocks that are vital to an organization's success.

Kinds of Organizations Today's organizations can be broadly divided into business firms and nonprofit organizations. A *business firm* is a privately owned organization that serves its customers in order to earn a profit. Business firms must earn profits to survive. **Profit** is the reward to a business firm for the risk it undertakes in offering a product for sale; the money left over after a firm's total expenses are subtracted from its total revenues. In contrast to business firms, a *nonprofit organization* is a nongovernmental organization that serves its customers but does not have profit as an organizational goal. For simplicity in the rest of the book, however, the terms *firm, company, corporation,* and *organization* are used to cover both business and nonprofit operations.

Levels in Organizations and How Marketing Links to Them Whether explicit or implicit, organizations have a strategic direction. Marketing not only helps shape this direction but must also help implement it. Figure 2–1 summarizes the focus of this direction at each of the three levels in an organization.

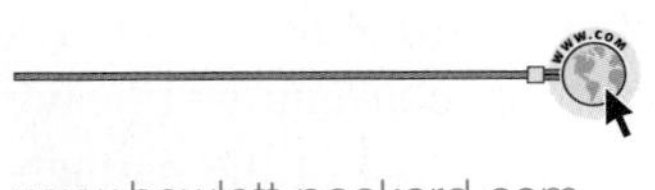

www.hewlett-packard.com

The **corporate level** is where top management directs overall strategy for the entire organization. Multimarket, multiproduct firms such as Hewlett-Packard or Johnson & Johnson really manage a portfolio of businesses, variously termed strategic business units (SBUs), strategic business segments, and product-market units (PMUs).[2]

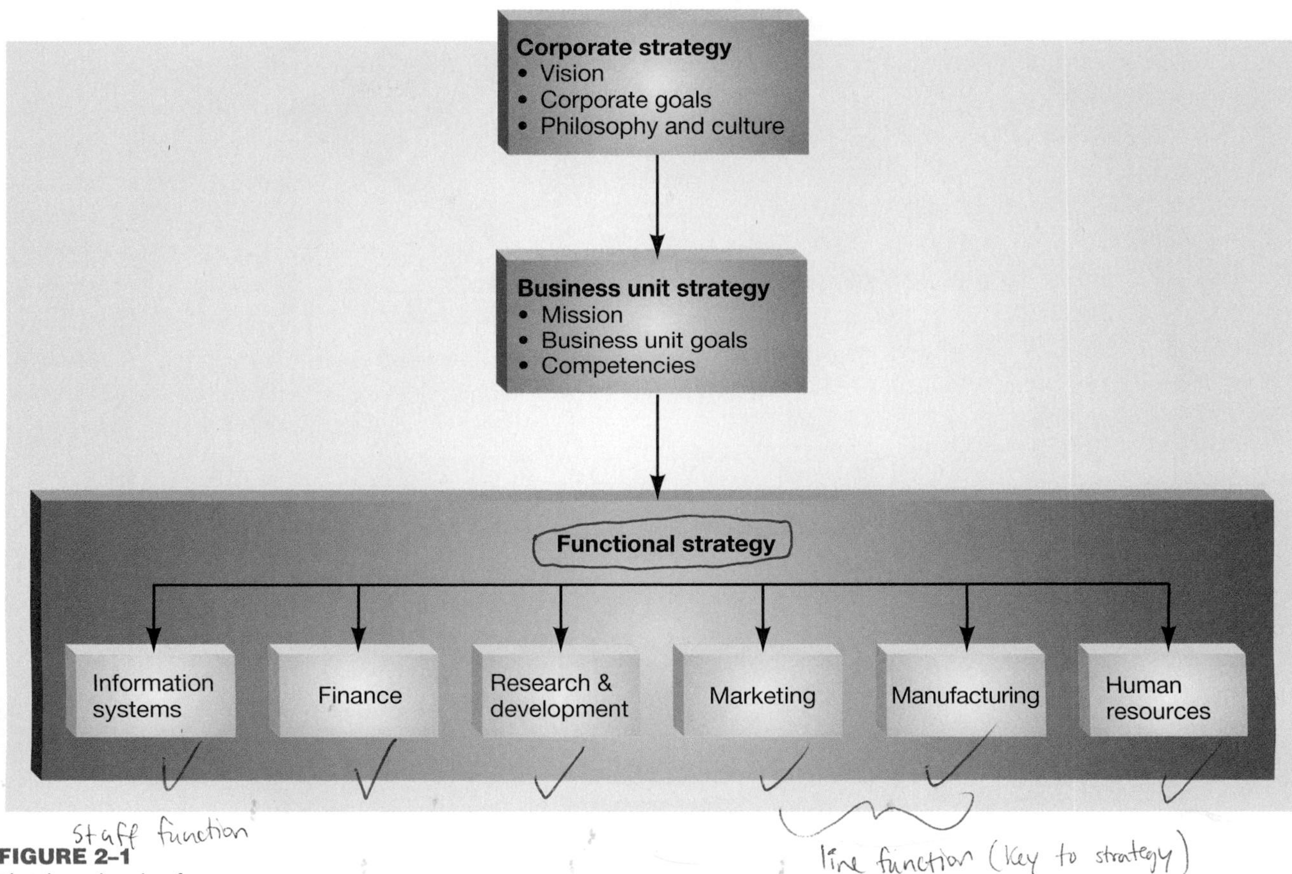

FIGURE 2–1
The three levels of strategy in organizations

The term **business unit** refers to an organization that markets a set of related products to a clearly defined group of customers. The **business unit level** is the level at which business unit managers set the direction for their products and markets. The strategic direction is more specific at the business level of an organization. For less complex firms with a single business focus, such as Pennisula Farms, a Canadian yogurt producer, the corporate and business unit levels may merge.

Each business unit has marketing and other specialized activities (e.g., finance, research and development, or human resource management) at the **functional level,** which is where groups of specialists create value for the organization. The term *department* generally refers to these specialized functions, such as the marketing department or information systems department. At the functional level, the strategic direction becomes more specific and focused. So, just as there is a hierarchy of levels within organizations, there is also a hierarchy of strategic direction set by management at that level.

Marketing has a role at each of these organizational levels. In a larger corporation with multiple business units, the marketing department may be called upon to build a broad corporate image. It may also be called upon to provide comparative analyses of business unit market strengths and opportunities as part of a business portfolio analysis, which is covered later in the chapter. At the business level, the marketing department provides leadership for the other functional activities when applying the marketing concept. But it also must serve as part of a team of functional specialists that develops and implements actual programs at the functional level, which is why cross-functional teams are so vital in today's competitive world. To help develop these programs, the marketing department conducts marketing research and competitive evaluations to identify strategic marketing issues. Armed with an understanding of the marketplace, the marketing department then identifies key target markets and develops specific programs to serve them.

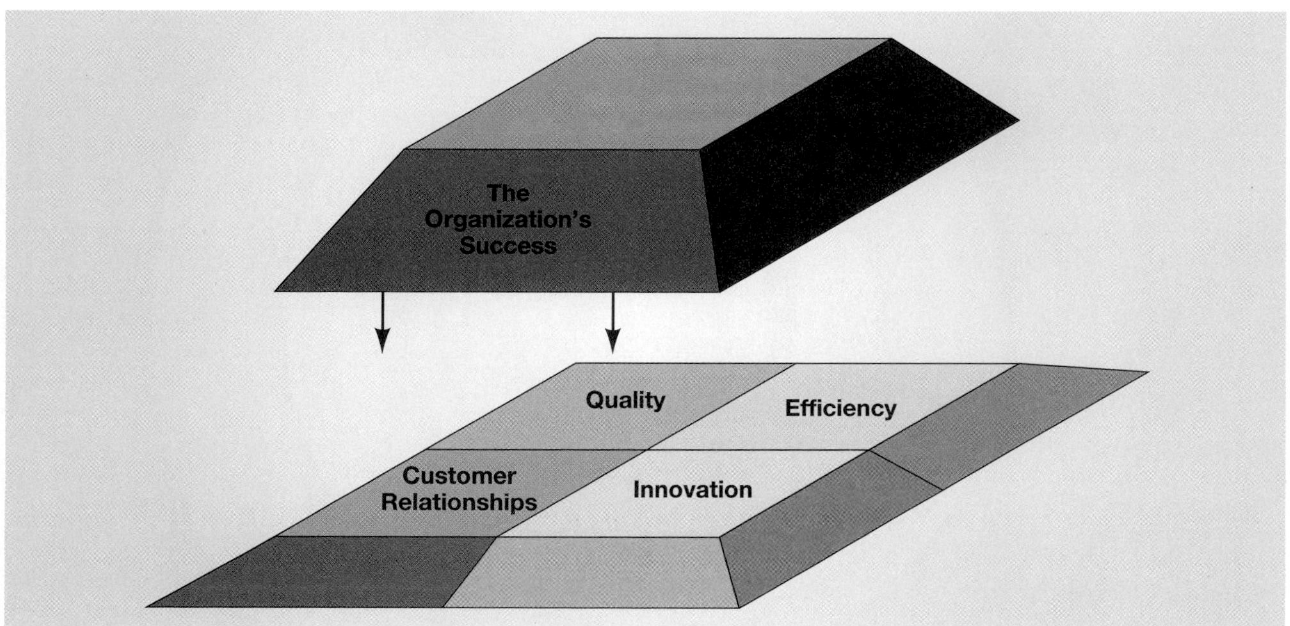

FIGURE 2–2
A combination of customer relationships, innovation, quality, and efficiency are the building blocks for an organization's success

Building Blocks for an Organization's Success Management theorists have attempted to identify key factors that are essential to a firm's success. One such structure appears in Figure 2–2, which identifies four critical factors: (1) customer relationships, to ensure genuine value for customers; (2) innovation, to ensure customers' access to the latest technologies; (3) quality, to ensure an excellence and consistency in what is sold; and (4) efficiency, to lower costs and, hence, the price paid by customers. Note that improving each of these factors at a particular time might cause other factors to decline. Thus, it is a continuing challenge for an organization to strike the right balance among these four "building blocks" that are the foundation for an organization's success.[3]

www.kraft.com

Strategy at the Corporate Level

Complex organizations such as Coca-Cola, Kraft General Foods, and Alcan Aluminium must ask themselves not just what *business* they are in but what *portfolio of businesses* they are in. As shown in Figure 2–1, this portfolio of businesses is often coordinated with a corporate strategy consisting of a common corporate vision, common goals, and a common philosophy that unites them. We will define these terms carefully, but, in actual practice, the terms are not used rigorously and often overlap.

Developing the Corporate Vision A **corporate vision** is a clear word picture of the organization's future, often with an inspirational theme. It sets the overall direction for the organization, describing what it strives to be—stretching the organization, but not beyond the imagination. Even though the terms are often used interchangeably, a vision is something to be pursued, while a mission (discussed later) is something to be accomplished. Ideally, this vision is a short statement that can inspire employees, investors, and customers.

Gulf Canada's vision is to become a premiere international exploration and production company. Similarly, Coca-Cola's vision is simple but effective: "to put a Coke within arm's reach of every consumer in the world."[4] For Coca-Cola this vision really does include the entire world. In fact, in order to make this vision a reality, Coca-Cola actually eliminated the very concept of "domestic" and "international" operating units. With less than 25 percent of its revenues from North American sales, Coca-Cola seems to be actively pursuing its Coke within-an-arm's-reach-of-every-consumer's vision.[5]

Setting Corporate Goals Broadly speaking, a **goal** is a targeted level of performance set in advance of work. Therefore, corporate goals provide strategic performance targets that the entire organization must reach to pursue its vision. Several different types of goals have been identified that business firms can pursue, each of which has some strengths and limitations:

- *Profit.* Classic economic theory assumes a firm seeks to maximize long-run profit, achieving as high a financial return on its investment as possible. One difficulty with this is what is meant by *long run.* A year? Five years? Twenty years? Barbara Thomas, president of Pillsbury Canada, for example, set a five-year goal for the company, referred to as Vision 2000, which calls for the company to triple profits by the end of this decade.[6]
- *Sales revenue.* If profits are acceptable, a firm may elect to maintain or increase its sales level even though profitability may not be maximized. Increased sales revenue may gain promotions for key executives.
- *Market share.* A firm may choose to maintain or increase its market share, sometimes at the expense of greater profits if industry status or prestige is at stake. **Market share** is the ratio of sales revenue of the firm to the total sales revenue of all firms in the industry, including the firm itself.
- *Unit sales.* Sales revenue may be deceiving because of the effects of inflation, so a firm may choose to maintain or increase the number of units it sells, such as cars, cases of breakfast cereal, or TV sets.
- *Quality.* A firm may emphasize the need to maintain or improve the quality of its products and services, especially if quality has been poor in the past.
- *Employee welfare.* A firm may recognize the critical importance of its employees by having an explicit goal stating its commitment to good employment opportunities and working conditions for them.
- *Social responsibility.* A firm may respond to advocates of corporate responsibility and seek to balance conflicting goals of consumers, employees, and shareholders to promote overall welfare of all these groups, even at the expense of profits.

Many private organizations that do not seek profits also exist in Canada. Examples are museums, symphony orchestras, operas, and research institutes. These organizations strive to provide goods or services to consumers with the greatest efficiency and the least cost. The nonprofit organization's survival depends on its meeting the needs of the consumers it serves. Although technically not falling under the definition of "nonprofit organization," government agencies also perform marketing activities in trying to achieve their goal of serving the public good. Such organizations include all levels of federal, provincial, and local government as well as special groups such as city schools, public universities, and public hospitals. As discussed later, marketing is an important activity for nonprofit firms and government agencies, just as it is for profit-making businesses.

Developing a Corporate Philosophy and Culture An organization may also have a **corporate philosophy** that establishes the values and "rules of conduct" for running it.[7] Statements such as "respecting the dignity of all employees" or "being a good citizen of the local community" are examples of corporate philosophies. The Ethics and Social Responsibility Alert describes a critical corporate citizenship issue. An organization's **corporate culture** refers to a system of shared attitudes and behaviours held by the employees that distinguish it from other organizations. Firms around the world are frantically trying to change their corporate cultures in response to

ETHICS

ETHICS AND SOCIAL RESPONSIBILITY ALERT

The Global Dilemma: How to Achieve Sustainable Development

Corporate executives and world leaders are increasingly asked to address the issue of "sustainable development," a term that involves having each country find an ideal balance between protecting its environment and providing its citizens with the additional goods and services necessary to maintain and improve their standard of living.

Eastern Europe and the nations of the former Soviet Union provide an example. Tragically, poisoned air and dead rivers are the legacies of seven decades of communist rule. With more than half of the households of many of these nations below the poverty level, should the immediate goal be a cleaner environment or more food, clothing, housing, and consumer goods? What should the heads of these governments do? What should Western nations do to help? What should Western firms trying to enter these new, growing markets do?

Should the environment or economic growth come first? What are the societal trade-offs?

www.canibm.com

increased global competition. Hewlett-Packard, Apple Computer, 3M, Sony, and Motorola are well known for corporate cultures that stimulate innovation and new product development. IBM Canada has been able to make the transition from a bureaucratic culture to a responsive entrepreneurial culture and as a result has achieved double-digit revenue growth and marketshare leadership in the personal computer sales category. John Wetmore, President and CEO, IBM Canada Ltd. says the company has achieved record domestic sales revenue as a result of its innovation and new product offerings particularly in IBM global services, and e-business products. The company has also hired a record number of people to help continue the company's growth.[8]

CONCEPT CHECK

1. What are the three levels in today's large organizations?
2. What is the difference between corporate vision and corporate goals?

Strategy at the Business Unit Level

The strategic direction for each business unit spells out how it will help the organization accomplish its vision. This business unit strategy has three major components: mission, business unit goals, and competencies. Each component is critical and must be understood if marketing activities are to be relevant.

Defining the Business Unit's Mission This is probably the best-known mission statement anywhere:

> To explore strange new worlds, to seek out new life and new civilizations, to boldly go where no one has gone before.

This is the five-year mission for the Starship Enterprise, as Gene Roddenberry wrote in the "Star Trek" adventure series. The "business unit goals" of the Starship Enterprise vary with each trip, but the competencies centre on advanced technology, strong leadership, and a skilled crew. All these contribute to pursuing the vision of the Starship Enterprise's larger organization, the Federation.

The **business mission** (or **business unit mission**) is a statement that specifies the markets and product lines in which a business will compete. It affects the range of a firm's marketing activities by narrowing or broadening the competitive playing field. In other words, the mission determines the arena in which the business will compete. In many cases, the mission statement is often accompanied by a set of guiding principles that provide meaning and direction for both employees and customers. An example of a mission statement and guiding principles is shown in Figure 2–3. By clearly defining the business mission, marketing activities can be more focused and effective. Moreover, for a business to remain focused and effective, missions must often be redefined as the business itself and/or market conditions change over time.

Specifying the Business Unit's Goals A **business unit goal** is a performance target the business unit seeks to reach in an effort to achieve its mission. Goals measure how well the mission is being accomplished. These goals must be balanced to form a consistent, achievable pattern and should address fundamental issues such as customer satisfaction, innovation, internal processes, and, of course, financial performance.[9] At IBM Canada, customer satisfaction goals are set and tracked the same as financial revenue figures. In fact, customer satisfaction goals are taken so seriously that a percentage of every employee's salary is based on achievement of the customer satisfaction goals set by the business units.[10]

In many cases, business unit goals are called **objectives,** which are specific, measurable performance targets and deadlines. Because there is no consistency in the use of the terms *goals* and *objectives,* the terms are used interchangeably throughout this book.

The use of quantified performance measures and targets can be illustrated by an approach developed by the Boston Consulting Group (BCG), *business portfolio analysis,* that analyzes a firm's business units (called strategic business units, or SBUs, in the BCG analysis) as though they were a collection of separate investments.[11] While used at the business unit level here, this BCG analysis has also been applied at the product line or individual product or brand level. The popularity of this kind of portfolio analysis is shown by the fact that more than 75 percent of the largest firms in North America have used it in some form.

BCG, an internationally known management consulting firm, advises its clients to locate the position of its SBUs on a growth-share matrix (Figure 2–4). The vertical axis is the *market growth rate,* which is the annual rate of growth of the specific market or industry in which a given SBU is competing. This axis in the figure runs from 0 to 20 percent, although in practice it might run even higher. The axis has arbitrarily been divided at 10 percent into high-growth and low-growth areas.

FIGURE 2–3
Mission and guiding principles of the Holiday Inn Burlington

The Holiday Inn Burlington is dedicated to providing quality hospitality product and service. Although we try to anticipate guest concerns before they arise, we understand that every customer is an individual who requires special attention. Therefore,

If a customer has a need or want, we fill it.

If a customer has a question, we find the answer.

If a customer has a concern, we resolve it.

If a customer is lost, we show them the way.

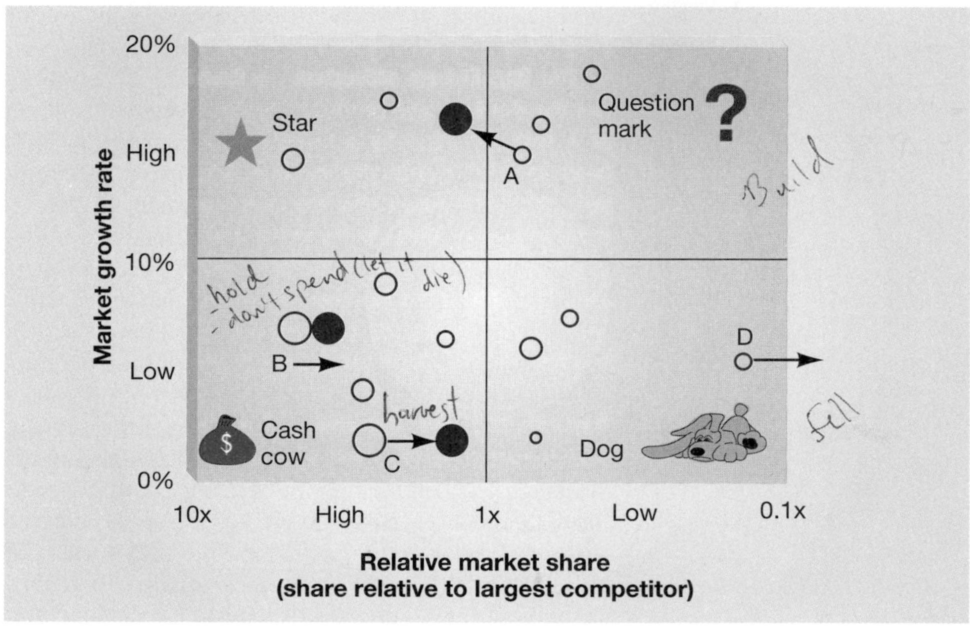

FIGURE 2–4
Boston Consulting Group growth-share matrix for a strong, diversified firm showing some strategic plans

Boston Consulting Group
www.bcg.com

The horizontal axis is the *relative market share,* defined as the sales of the SBU divided by the sales of the largest firm in the industry. A relative market share of 10× (at the left end of the scale) means that the SBU has 10 times the share of its largest competitor, whereas a share 0.1× (at the right end of the scale) means it has only 10 percent of the sales of its largest competitor. The scale is logarithmic and is arbitrarily divided into high and low relative market shares at a value of 1×.

BCG has given specific names and descriptions to the four resulting quadrants in its growth-share matrix based on the amount of cash they generate for or require from the firm:

- Cash cows (lower-left quadrant) are SBUs that typically generate large amounts of cash, far more than they can invest profitably in their own product line. They have a dominant share of a slow-growth market and provide cash to pay large amounts of company overhead and to invest in other SBUs.
- Stars (upper-left quadrant) are SBUs with a high share of high-growth markets that may not generate enough cash to support their own demanding needs for future growth. When their growth slows, they are likely to become cash cows.

- Question marks or problem children (upper-right quadrant) are SBUs with a low share of high-growth markets. They require large injections of cash just to maintain their market share, much less increase it. Their name implies management's dilemma for these SBUs: choosing the right ones to invest in and phasing out the rest.
- Dogs (lower-right quadrant) are SBUs with a low share of low-growth markets. Although they may generate enough cash to sustain themselves, they do not hold the promise of ever becoming real winners for the firm. Dropping SBUs in this quadrant from a business portfolio is generally advocated except when relationships with other SBUs, competitive considerations, or potential strategic alliances exist.[12]

The 14 circles in Figure 2–4 show the current SBUs in a strong, diversified firm. The area of each circle is proportional to the corresponding SBU's annual sales revenue.

The portfolio in Figure 2–4 is a mixed one. On the favourable side, one-half of its SBUs are large and have high market shares, but, unfortunately, the other half are small with low market shares. Because most firms have limited influence on the market

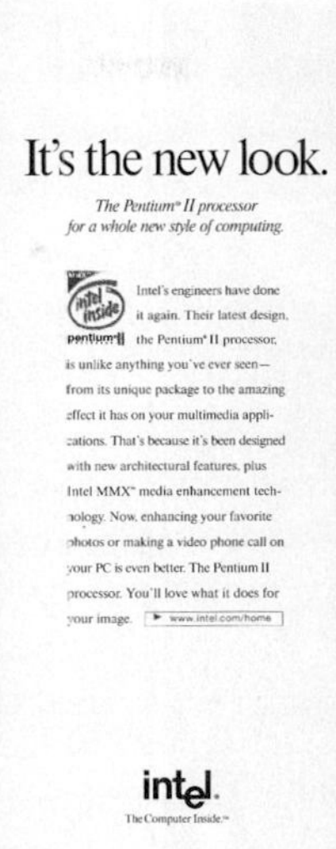

Strategies emerging from a business portfolio analysis: Intel "builds" its chip business while Procter & Gamble "divests" its Duncan Hines cake mix line to Aurora Foods.

growth rate (the factor shown on the vertical axis), their main alternative in a growth-share matrix framework is to try to change the relative market share (the factor on the horizontal axis).

To accomplish this, management makes conscious decisions on what role each SBU should have in the future and either injects or removes cash from it. Four alternative strategies are available for each SBU. The firm can invest more in the SBU to *build* its share (SBU A in Figure 2–3). Or it can invest just enough to *hold* the SBU's share at about its current level (SBU B in the figure). Or it can *harvest* the SBU (SBU C in the figure), trying to milk its short-term cash flow even though it may lose share and become a dog in the longer run. Finally, the firm can *divest* the SBU (SBU D) by phasing it out or actually selling it to gain cash to invest in the remaining SBUs.

The primary strengths of business portfolio analysis include (1) forcing a firm to assess each of its SBUs in terms of its relative market share and industry market growth rate, which, in turn, (2) requires the firm to forecast which SBUs will be cash producers and cash users in the future. Weaknesses are that (1) it is often difficult to get the information needed to locate each SBU on the growth-share matrix, (2) there are other important factors missing from the analysis such as possible synergies among the SBUs when they use the same salesforce or research and development facilities, and (3) there are problems in motivating people in an SBU that has been labelled a dog or even a cash cow and is unlikely to get new resources from the firm to grow and provide opportunities for promotion.[13] In addition, planners have had difficulty incorporating competitive information into portfolio analysis,[14] and formal experiments show the technique may not provide as effective an allocation of resources as more traditional methods of financial analysis.[15]

Specifying the Business Unit's Competencies Whereas the mission defines the scope of the business or business unit and the goals define its strategic performance dimensions, its **business unit competencies**—special capabilities resulting from its personnel, resources, or functional units—determine the means for achieving success.[16] These competencies should be distinctive enough to provide a **competitive advantage,** a unique strength relative to competitors, often based on quality, time, cost, innovation, or customer intimacy; knowing customers better than the competition and building a rock-solid relationship with those customers that the competition *cannot* break.[17]

A competitive advantage from innovation and fast cycle time: Hewlett-Packard's combination colour printer-copier.

For example, if a firm such as 3M or Hewlett-Packard has a goal of generating a specific portion of its sales from new products, it must have a supporting competency in research and development. It must also have a supportive competency to manufacture and market its new products in a timely and effective way. Hewlett-Packard has a truly competitive advantage with its fast cycle time, which allows it to bring innovative products to markets in large volume rapidly.[18]

Another currently popular strategy is to develop a competency in total quality management (TQM). **Quality** here means those features and characteristics of a product that influence its ability to satisfy customer needs. Firms often try to improve quality or reduce new product cycles through **benchmarking**—discovering how others do something better than your own firm so you can imitate or leapfrog competition. Benchmarking often involves studying operations in completely different businesses. When General Mills sought ideas on how to reduce the time to convert its production lines from one cereal to another, it sent a team to observe the pit crews at the Indianapolis 500 race. The result: General Mills cut its plant change-over time by more than half.

www.generalmills.com

If properly done, product quality can lead to a competitive advantage, or at least help a firm remain competitive with other firms that have focused on quality improvement.[19] Understanding and responding to new market opportunities with new products is the driving force for industry change and is one of marketing's more critical challenges. Thus, specific TQM practices of quality training, process improvement, and benchmarking may not produce a competitive advantage by themselves. Rather, as described in the Marketing NewsNet box and earlier in Figure 2–2, quality is only one weapon in a firm's arsenal of strategy initiatives.

CUSTOMER VALUE

MARKETING NEWSNET Quality as One Element of Competitive Advantage

Some quality consultants see a quality strategy as the one solution for all organizations that want to become more competitive; some even claim that quality is just as important as financial results or that it will lead to improved financial performance. A focus on quality has helped make Ford Motor Company ("Quality is Job One") more profitable and has helped propel the Ford Taurus to a bestseller. But a focus on quality has not had the same effect for General Motors' Saturn business unit. Why?

A study of 150 successful organizational turnarounds found that total quality management is not a cure-all and that typical TQM approaches have limited impact. It also noted that poor quality is behind other important causes of business downturn or failure, following high costs, high debt, strategic errors, and bad investments. Indeed, as described earlier in Figure 2–2, high quality must be tied judiciously to customer relationships, innovation, and efficiency to achieve success.

Nonetheless, poor product and service quality can be competitive disadvantages, especially since customers today often demand quality on a par with competition. This is a lesson the North American automobile industry has learned the hard way, and it explains why many organizations with past quality problems are inclined to pursue a quality strategy.

The experience with General Motors' Saturn business illustrates this. Saturn has focused on providing top value to the customers through low defects and excellent, low-pressure service. Unfortunately, Saturn has yet to make reasonable profits after several years of operation, at least in part because of a high cost structure and a product that offers few benefits beyond the competitors' offerings. Successful organizations must emphasize quality—but not as a way to solve more fundamental strategic problems.

Strategy at the Functional Level

The functional departments, such as marketing, respond to the corporate and business strategic directions by creating functional goals, which are simply extensions of the corporate and business goals. At Sears Canada, an example of a functional marketing goal is "to create a new image that emphasizes the soft side of merchandising." To accomplish functional goals requires program plans that spell out very specific marketing objectives with associated actions, responsibilities, and dates. An objective of the new Sears promotional program was to increase customer awareness about its new marketing efforts. Not only have most Canadians heard about the "Softer Side of Sears," many actually sing the new jingle!

However, marketing does not operate by itself in an organization. Successful marketing efforts today are really cross-functional team efforts involving specialists from all the functional units to analyze, implement, and control programs to accomplish the corporate and business strategic directions. The strategic marketing process described in the next section provides the framework for making this happen.

CONCEPT CHECK

1. What is business portfolio analysis?
2. What is a competitive advantage, and why is it important?

THE STRATEGIC MARKETING PROCESS

All approaches to planning try to find answers to these key questions:

1. Where are we now?
2. Where do we want to go?
3. How do we allocate our resources to get to where we want to go?
4. How do we convert our plans into actions?
5. How do our results compare with our plans, and do deviations require new plans and actions?

This same approach is used in the **strategic marketing process,** whereby an organization allocates its marketing mix resources to reach its target markets. This process is divided into three phases: planning, implementation, and control (Figure 2–5).

The strategic marketing process is so central to the activities of most organizations that they formalize it as a **marketing plan,** which is a road map for the marketing activities of an organization for a specified future period of time, such as one year or five years. Appendix A at the end of this chapter provides guidelines for writing a marketing plan and also presents a sample marketing plan for Paradise Kitchens,® Inc., a firm that produces and distributes a line of spicy chilies under the Howlin' Coyote®

FIGURE 2–5
The strategic marketing process

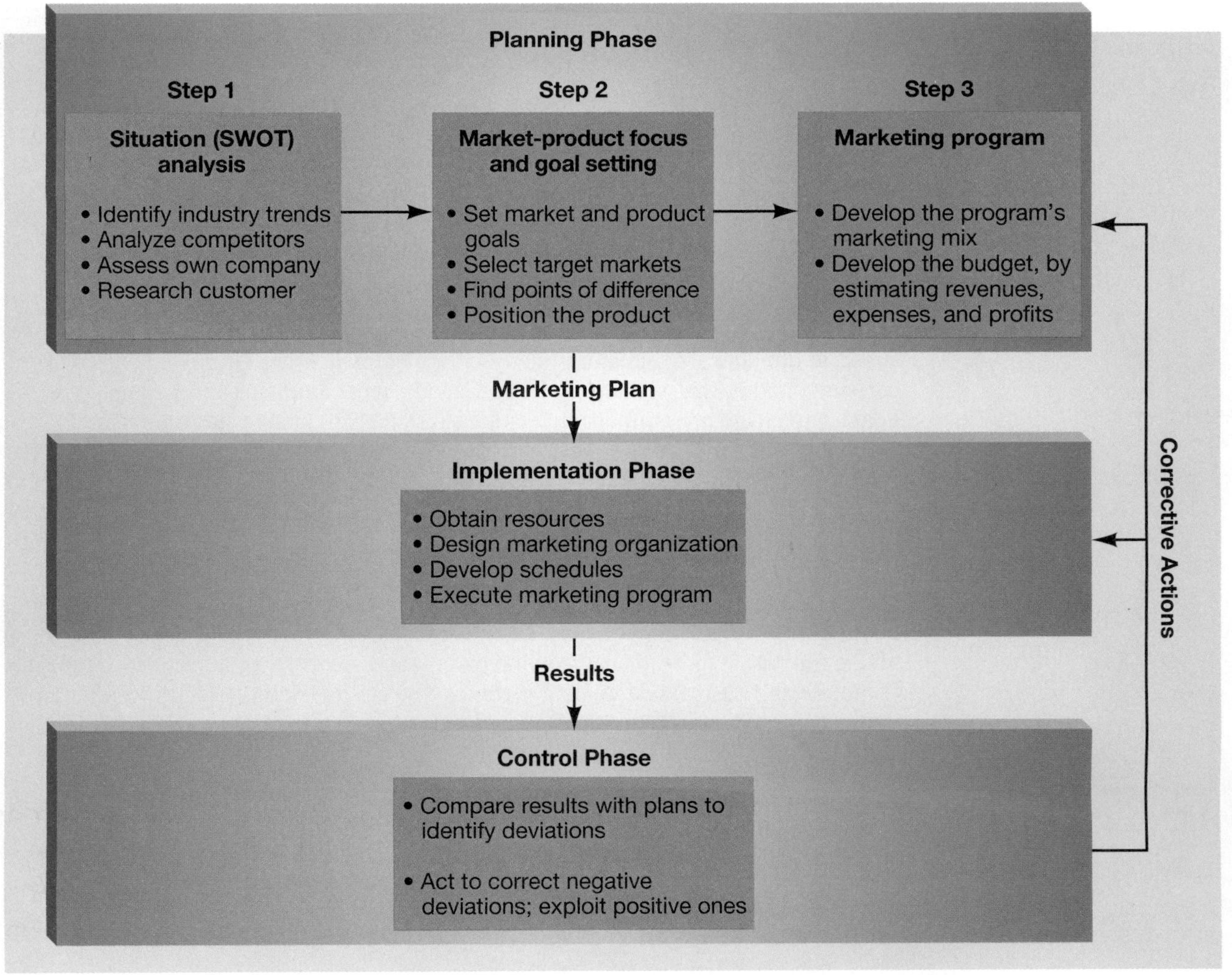

brand name. The sequence of activities that follows parallels the elements of the marketing plan that appears in Appendix A.

The following section gives an overview of the strategic marketing process that places Chapters 3 through 21 in perspective. In Chapter 22 we examine the strategic marketing process again in more depth.

Strategic Marketing Process: The Planning Phase

As shown in Figure 2–5, the planning phase of the strategic marketing process consists of the three steps shown at the top of the figure: (1) situation analysis, (2) market-product focus and goal setting, and (3) the marketing program. Let's use the recent marketing planning experiences of several companies to look at each of these steps.

Step 1: Situation (SWOT) Analysis The essence of the **situation analysis** is taking stock of where the firm or product has been recently, where it is now, and where it is headed in light of the organization's plans and the external factors and trends affecting it. The situation analysis box in Figure 2–5 is the first of the three steps in the planning phase.

An effective short-hand summary of the situation analysis is a **SWOT analysis,** an acronym describing an organization's appraisal of its internal *s*trengths and *w*eaknesses and its external *o*pportunities and *t*hreats. Both the situation and SWOT analyses can be done at the level of the entire organization, the business unit, the product line, or the specific product. As an analysis moves from the level of the entire organization to the specific product, it, of course, becomes far more detailed. For small firms or those with basically a single product line, an analysis at the firm or product level is really the same thing.

Remember Rollerblade, Inc. from Chapter 1? Figure 2–6 shows what a SWOT analysis might look like for that firm. Note that the SWOT table shown has four cells formed by the combination of internal and external factors (the rows) and favourable versus unfavourable factors (the columns) that summarize Rollerblade, Inc.'s strengths, weaknesses, opportunities, and threats.

A more in-depth SWOT analysis might use more detailed checklists of internal and external factors in the table. For example, internal factors might be broken down to in-

FIGURE 2–6
A SWOT analysis for Rollerblade, Inc.

LOCATION OF FACTOR	TYPE OF FACTOR FAVOURABLE	 UNFAVOURABLE
Internal	**Strengths** • Industry leader • Innovative, in products and design • Strong brand awareness • Strong position in sporting goods and specialty outlets	**Weaknesses** • Premium-priced position puts off the "value-conscious" consumer • Limited distribution in mass merchandising outlets.
External	**Opportunities** • Identify new market segments to serve • Develop a brand for the "value-conscious" consumer • Expand distribution globally • Expand accessories line	**Threats** • Fierce competition at both the premium and low-end of market. • Brand name may become a generic term for in-line skates.

clude key elements such as products offered and the effectiveness of the functional areas such as sales or research and development (R&D) that affect marketing activities. Similarly, external factors are often formalized in the SWOT analysis by using the external or environmental factors affecting marketing activities, such as competition, consumer, or technological trends. An example of using these detailed breakdowns of internal and external factors appears in the Paradise Kitchens SWOT in Appendix A. For simplicity, the Rollerblade, Inc.'s SWOT does not contain this level of detail.

A SWOT analysis helps a firm identify the strategy-related factors in these four cells that can have a major effect on the firm. However, all factors in such an analysis are not of equal value, so the ultimate goal is to identify the *critical* factors affecting the firm and then build on vital strengths, correct glaring weaknesses, exploit significant opportunities, and avoid disaster-laden threats. That is a big order. This ultimate goal is not simply to develop the SWOT analysis but to translate the results of the analysis into specific actions to help the firm grow and succeed.

Although the SWOT analysis is a shorthand look at the situation analysis, it is based on an exhaustive study of the four areas shown in Figure 2–5 that are the foundation on which the firm builds its marketing program:

- Identifying trends in the firm's industry.
- Analyzing the firm's competitors.
- Assessing the firm itself.
- Researching the firm's present and prospective customers.

Examples of more in-depth analysis in these four areas appear in the marketing plan in Appendix A and the chapters in this text cited in that plan.

One way for firms to utilize the SWOT results and exhaustive study of their industry, competitors, own firm, and customers is to assess market-product strategies. Four such strategies representing the four combinations of (1) current and new markets and (2) current and new products appear in Figure 2–7.

As Rollerblade, Inc. attempts to increase sales revenue, it must consider all four of the alternative market-product strategies shown in Figure 2–7. For example, it can try to use a strategy of *market penetration*—increasing sales of present products in existing markets, in this case by increasing sales of its present in-line skates to Canadian consumers. There is no change in either the product line or the market served, but increased sales are possible through actions such as better advertising, lower prices, or expanded distribution in retail outlets.

Market development, which for Rollerblade, Inc. means selling existing Rollerblade Inc.'s products to new markets, is a reasonable alternative. Australia and Western European consumers are good candidates as possible new markets.

FIGURE 2–7
Four market-product strategies: alternative ways to expand sales revenue for Rollerblade, Inc.

	PRODUCTS	
MARKETS	**CURRENT**	**NEW**
Current	**Market Penetration** Selling more in-line skates to Canadians	**Product Development** Selling a new product like the Xten-plus to Canadians
New	**Market Development** Selling in-line skates in Australia	**Diversification** Selling in-line skating accessories like helmets and clothing, or entering the bicycle business

WEB LINK Rollerblade, Inc., Market-Product Strategies

Rollerblade, Inc., has chosen to pursue multiple market-product strategies to achieve new sales growth. Go to its Web site (www.rollerblade.com) and check out what the company's current strategies are and what its future plans are likely to be. What do you think about what you have uncovered there?

An expansion strategy using *product development* involves selling a new product to existing markets. As you know from Chapter 1, Rollerblade, Inc. developed the Xtenplus for the children's segment, the Outback X for the rough-road skater, and the Nature line for the student segment as well as the Bladerunner, a lower-priced skate for the value-conscious segment. One problem with a product developent strategy is the possibility of *product cannibalism*—a firm's new product gaining sales by stealing them from its other products.

Diversification involves developing new products and selling them in new markets. This is potentially a high-risk strategy for most firms because the company has neither previous production experience nor marketing experience on which to draw. However, there are varying degrees of diversification. *Related diversification* occurs when new products and markets have something in common with existing operations. For example, Rollerblade, Inc. sells in-line skating accessories including helmets and clothing. *Unrelated diversification* means that the new products and markets have nothing in common with existing operations. In this case, Rollerblade, Inc. might diversify into a completely new area such as the bicycle business. To check out Rollerblade, Inc.'s strategies, go to the Web Link box.

Step 2: Market-product Focus and Goal Setting Finding a focus on what product offerings will be directed toward which customers (step 2 of the planning phase in Figure 2–5) is essential for developing an effective marketing program (step 3). This focus often comes from the firm's using **market segmentation,** which involves aggregating prospective buyers into groups, or segments, that (1) have common needs and (2) will respond similarly to a marketing action. Ideally a firm can use market segmentation to identify the segments on which it will focus its efforts—its target market segments—and develop one or more marketing programs to reach them.

Goal setting here involves setting measurable marketing objectives to be achieved, possibly for a specific market, a specific product or brand, or an entire marketing program. As mentioned earlier, there is a hierarchy of goals and objectives flowing from the corporate strategy set by top management on down to the levels of the marketing managers.

We can illustrate steps 2 and 3 in the planning phase of the strategic marketing process by using the Paradise Kitchens® marketing plan from Appendix A. This firm is trying to expand its line of Howlin' Coyote® spicy chilies from 3 to 20 metropolitan markets during the last half of the 1990s. Stated simply, the five-year marketing plan for Paradise Kitchens specifies these step 2 activities:

- *Set marketing and product goals.* As mentioned later in Chapter 11, the chances of new product success are increased by specifying both market and product goals. Paradise Kitchens® will grow its present markets by expanding brands and flavours, add 17 new metropolitan markets in the next five years, enter the food-service market, and add new products.
- *Select target markets.* Howlin' Coyote® chilies will be targeted at one- to three-person households with annual incomes above $30 000 in which both adults are likely to work outside the home—adventurous consumers wanting premium-quality Mexican food products.

A small business such as Paradise Kitchens has a carefully developed focus for its marketing program.

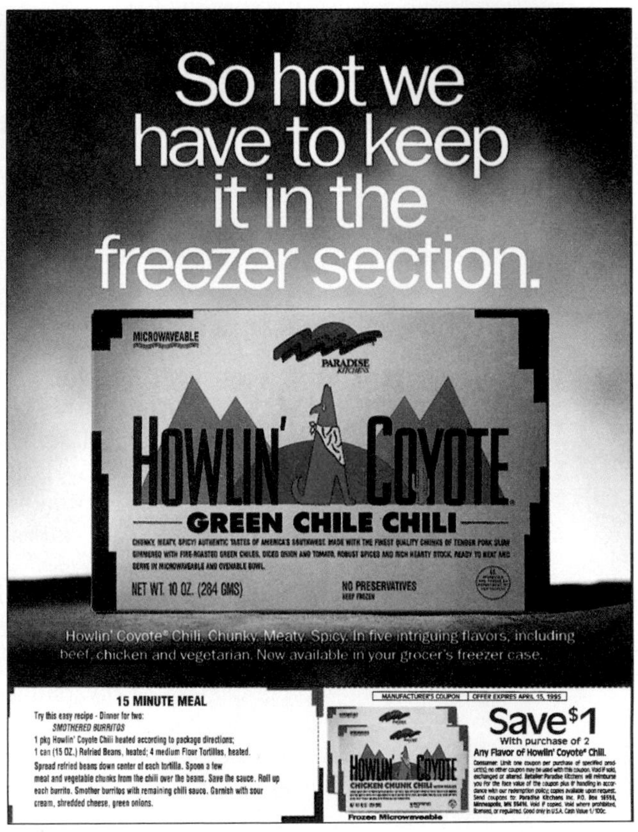

- *Find points of difference.* **Points of difference** are those characteristics of a product that make it superior to competitive substitutes. (Chapter 11 points out that this is the single-most important factor in the success or failure of a new product.) For Howlin' Coyote® chilies these are unique spicy taste; quality, convenience, and a range of flavours; and premium packaging.
- *Position the product.* Howlin' Coyote® chilies will be "positioned" in consumers' minds as "very high-quality, authentic Mexican tasting chilies that can be prepared easily and quickly."

Details in these four elements of step 2 provide a solid foundation to use in developing the marketing program—the next step in the planning phase of the strategic marketing process.

Step 3: Marketing Program Activities in step 2 tell the marketing manager which customers to target and which customer needs the firm's product offerings can satisfy—the *who* and *what* aspects of the strategic marketing process. The *how* aspect, step 3 in the planning phase, involves developing the program's marketing mix and its budget.

Figure 2–8 shows components of each marketing mix element that are combined to provide a cohesive marketing program. For the five-year marketing plan of Paradise Kitchens, these marketing mix activities include the following:

- *Product strategy.* Offer a current line of five Howlin' Coyote® chilies with proprietary flavouring, high-quality ingredients without preservatives, and distinctive packaging that communicates the brand's uniqueness.
- *Price strategy.* Price Howlin' Coyote® chili at $2.99 for a 300 g package, comparable to other frozen offerings and higher than the canned and dried chili varieties.
- *Promotion strategy.* Feature in-store demonstrations to highlight the product's unique qualities, recipes using the brand to stimulate use, and various kinds of cents-off coupons to generate trial and repeat-purchase of the brand.

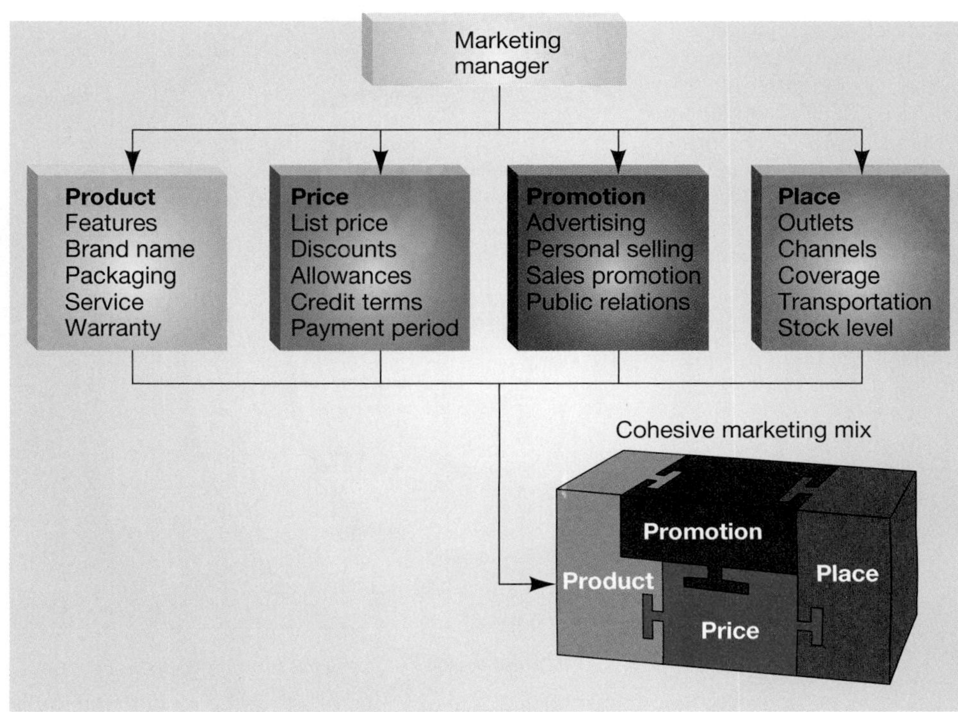

FIGURE 2–8
Elements of the marketing mix that compose a cohesive marketing program

- *Place (distribution) strategy.* Use food distributors with current sales volumes, shifting to brokers as increased sales volumes justify them.

Putting this marketing program into effect requires that the firm commit time and money to it in the form of a budget. The budgeting process starts with a sales forecast based on estimates of units expected to be sold—probably by month, quarter, and year. Estimated expenses for the marketing mix activities comprising the marketing program are estimated and balanced against expected revenues to estimate the program's profitability. This budget is really the "sales" document presented to top management to gain approval for the budgeted resources to implement the marketing program.

CONCEPT CHECK

1. What is the difference between a strength and an opportunity in a SWOT analysis?
2. If Rollerblade, Inc. attempts to enter Australia with its in-line skates, which market-product strategy would it be using?
3. What is market segmentation?

Strategic Marketing Process: The Implementation Phase

As shown in Figure 2–5, the result of the tens or hundreds of hours spent in the planning phase of the strategic marketing process is the firm's marketing plan. Implementation, the second phase of the strategic marketing process, involves carrying out the marketing plan that emerges from the planning phase. If the firm cannot put the marketing plan into effect—in the implementation phase—the planning phase was a waste of time. Figure 2–5 also shows the four components of the implementation phase: (1) obtaining resources, (2) designing the marketing organization, (3) developing schedules, and (4) actually executing the marketing program designed in the planning phase. Eastman Kodak

Want *both* your prints and your pictures online to send them to your family? The solution: Kodak PhotoNet or Picture Disk! This is one of Kodak's steps to fill in its planning gap.

Eastman Kodak Company
www.kodak.com

provides a case example of a firm facing both the implementation and control phases of the strategic marketing process.

Kodak has been known as a rather bureaucratic, paternalistic, slow-moving, and isolated company. But changes have occurred and continue to occur at Kodak. The agent of change is George Fisher, its chief executive officer, who gave up a similar job at spectacularly successful Motorola to try to move Kodak's little yellow boxes and new technologies into the 21st century. His early decisions are classic management and marketing lessons in implementing and controlling the activities of a corporate giant.

Obtaining Resources When George Fisher arrived at Kodak, he observed, "There are textbook types of things that are wrong with this company. Decisions are too slow. People don't take risks."[20] So he pushed some revolutionary and, to him, obvious decisions:

- Focus on Kodak's core business: imaging.
- Serve customer needs better and stress quality.
- Shorten product-development cycles.
- Encourage a more dynamic, risk-taking, fast-decision culture.

Fisher needed financial resources to implement these ideas, however, so he sold or spun off Kodak's health, household-products, and chemicals businesses. The $8 billion he got for these sales provided the resources to enable Kodak to try to implement its strategy to grow its core imaging business.

Designing the Marketing Organization A marketing program needs a marketing organization to implement it. This is especially true for firms such as Kodak that face constantly changing global markets. Figure 2–9 shows the organizational chart of a typical manufacturing firm, giving some details of the marketing department's structure. Four managers of marketing activities are shown to report to the vice president of marketing: product planning, marketing research, sales, and advertising and promotion. Depending on the size of the organization, there may be several product planning managers, each responsible for a separate product line. Also, several regional sales managers and an international sales manager may report to the manager of sales. This marketing organization is responsible for converting marketing plans to reality.

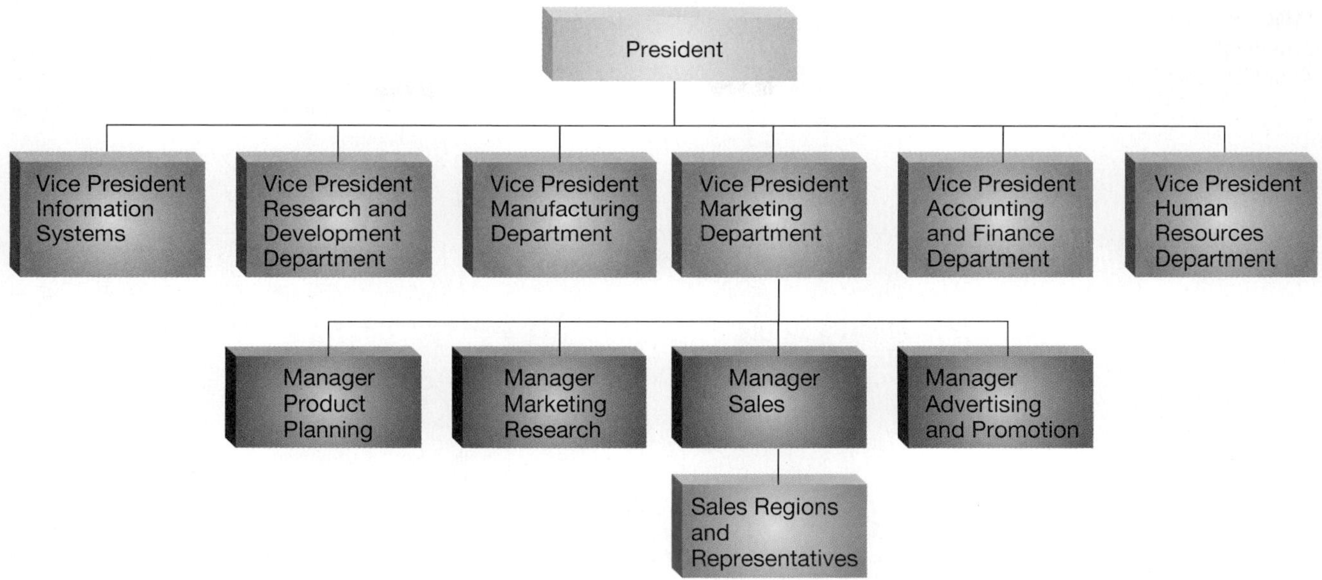

FIGURE 2–9
Organization of a typical manufacturing firm, showing a breakdown of the marketing department

Developing Schedules One key to effective implementation is setting deadlines, which are supported by schedules of important milestones that make the deadlines achievable. "Half the people in the world have yet to take their first picture," says Fisher. So he sees huge opportunities for Kodak in global developing markets and in digital imaging technologies that may replace film in many applications. Some of his deadlines:

- Have 50 000 Kodak Enhance Stations in operation by 2001. Benefiting from Kodak's digital imaging technology, you can blow up your tiny 20-year-old snapshot (not the negative, which you've lost!) into a surprisingly clear 4×6 or 8×10 enlargement.[21]
- Launch PhotoNet—a service that lets you see your photos online—by 1998.[22] This is shown in the ads on the previous page.
- Introduce a high-quality film (the E200) for professional photogaphers—by 1998.[23]
- Introduce by 1996 the "Advantix" Advanced Photographic System (APS), a "smart" film and camera, that lets users get three different picture sizes from the same roll of film.[24]
- Invest $1.1 billion in China by 2002 with three Chinese manufacturers to produce and distribute film and cameras.[25]

To make sure his managers meet the targets in these schedules, Fisher devised a new management compensation structure to tie salary more closely to performance.

Executing the Marketing Program Without effective execution, marketing plans are meaningless pieces of paper. Effective execution requires attention to detail for both marketing strategies and marketing tactics. A **marketing strategy** is the means by which a marketing goal is achieved, usually characterized by a specified target market and a marketing program to reach it. Although the term *strategy* is often used loosely, it implies both the end sought (target market) and the means to achieve it (marketing program).

To implement a marketing program successfully, hundreds of detailed decisions are required, about matters such as advertising copy or the amount for temporary price reductions. These decisions, called **marketing tactics,** are detailed day-to-day operational decisions essential to the overall success of marketing strategies. Compared with marketing strategies, marketing tactics generally involve actions that must be taken right

FIGURE 2–10
Evaluation and control of Kodak's marketing program

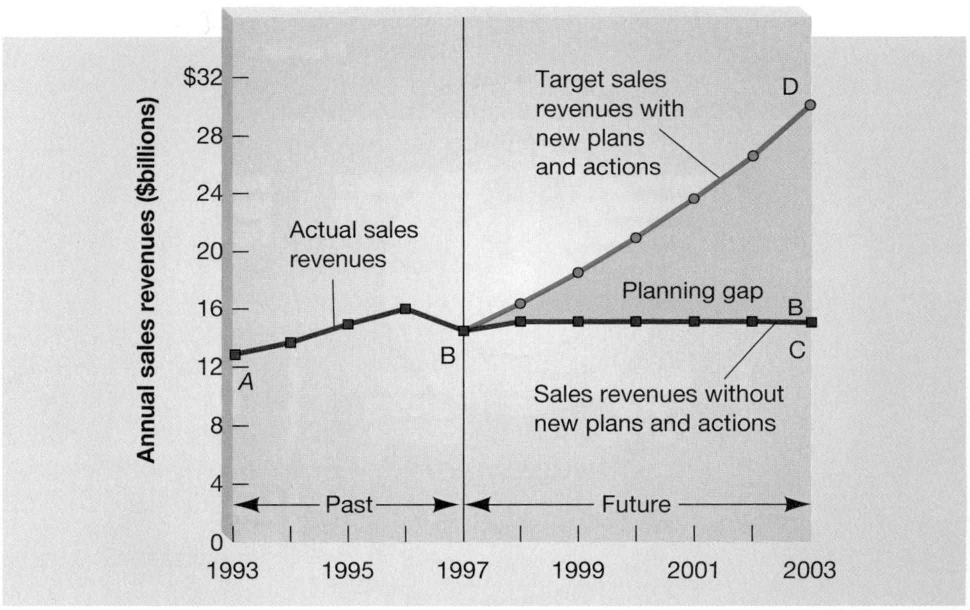

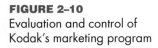

away. We cannot cover many aspects of marketing tactics in detail in a book of this size, and the emphasis here is on marketing strategy—the strategic marketing process. Here are examples of both kinds of decisions Fisher made at Kodak:

www.nikon.com

- Marketing strategy decision: develop a strategic partnership with five Japanese companies (including Fuji, Canon, and Nikon) to develop its smart film and camera—the Advanced Photographic System.
- Marketing tactics decision: assign 10 newly formed teams the responsibility of studying issues such as cycle-time improvement to squeeze excessive time and costs out of Kodak's bloated, slow-moving, new product development process.

Issues that surface at the marketing tactics level can become marketing strategy or corporate strategy issues. There are no precise lines between marketing strategies and marketing tactics because one shades into the other. Clearly, however, effective marketing program implementation requires excruciating concern for details in both marketing strategies and marketing tactics.

Strategic Marketing Process: The Control Phase

The control phase of the strategic marketing process seeks to keep the marketing program moving in the direction set for it (see Figure 2–5). Accomplishing this requires the marketing manager (1) to compare the results of the marketing program with the goals in the written plans to identify deviations and (2) to act on these deviations, correcting negative deviations and exploiting positive ones.

Comparing Results with Plans to Identify Deviations In 1998, as George Fisher looked at the company's sales revenues (from continuing operations) from 1993 through 1997, he didn't like what he saw: the very flat trend, or AB in Figure 2–10. Technological innovations such as digital cameras were redefining the entire amateur photographic market. Also, Fuji started a price war in 1997, cutting some film pack prices by 50 percent and reducing Kodak film sales drastically. This and other factors were inhibiting Kodak's growth opportunities.

Extending the 1993–1997 trend to 2003 (BC in Figure 2–10) showed flat sales revenues, a totally unacceptable, no-growth strategy. Fisher announced that his goal for

Kodak was to increase sales and profits a minimum of 13 percent annually. Applying this annual growth rate gives the target sales revenue line through the year 2003, shown as BD in Figure 2–10. This reveals a huge wedge-shaped shaded gap in the figure. Planners call this the *planning gap,* the difference between the projection of the path to reach a new goal (line BD) and the projection of the path of the results of a plan already in place (line BC).

The ultimate purpose of the firm's marketing program is to "fill in" this planning gap—in Kodak's case, to move its future sales revenue line from the essentially no-growth line BC up to the challenging high-growth target of line BD. Having a challenging series of quantified annual sales revenue targets is not enough. Poor performance could result in actual sales revenues being far less than the targeted levels. This is the essence of evaluation—comparing actual results with planned objectives.

Acting on Deviations When the evaluation shows that actual performance is not up to expectations, a corrective action is usually needed to adjust and improve the program and help it achieve the planned objective. In contrast, comparing results with plans may sometimes reveal that actual performance is far better than the plan called for. In this case the marketing manager wants to uncover the reason for the good performance and act to exploit it.

After only a few months on the job, Fisher recognized the vital importance of fast action and moving new, high-quality Kodak products into the marketplace. This is the reason for the flurry of new and upgraded products released by Kodak in 1995 and 1996. Effective control at Kodak, and all organizations, requires that deviations not only be identified but that positive deviations be exploited and negative ones be corrected. Two recent Kodak "mid-course corrections" to act on deviations from targets illustrate these principles:

- *Exploiting a positive deviation.* The Kodak CopyPrint Stations found spectacular consumer acceptance in enlarging small prints quickly and easily. Kodak exploited this success by not only installing several thousand of these machines around the world but also by quickly designing and introducing even more sophisticated do-it-yourself machines for use by consumers in their local photo shops.
- *Correcting a negative deviation.* In 1997 Kodak blew $100 million launching its Advanced Photographic System (APS) camera and film only to discover that it could not stock store shelves and could not process film at enough locations during the launch. After fixing these problems it relaunched APS successfully in 1998.

The strategic marketing process is discussed in greater detail again in Chapter 22.

CONCEPT CHECK

1. What is the control phase of the strategic marketing process?
2. How do the objectives set for a marketing program in the planning phase relate to the control phase of the strategic marketing process?

SUMMARY

1 Today's large organizations, both business firms and nonprofit organizations, are often divided into three levels. These levels are, from highest to lowest, the corporate, business unit, and functional levels.

2 At the highest level, corporate strategy involves setting the strategic direction for the entire organization, using statements of corporate vision, corporate goals, and corporate philosophy and culture. Four keys to a firm's success are customer responsiveness, innovation, quality, and efficiency.

3 At the business unit level, direction comes from the business unit's mission, goals, and competencies. Concepts such as portfolio analysis, competitive advantage, total quality management, and benchmarking help the business unit achieve its mission and goals.

4 Strategy and direction at the functional level come from having the marketing department work closely with other functional units, such as manufacturing and finance, to achieve the vision, mission, and goals coming from all three organizational levels.

5 The strategic marketing process involves an organization allocating its marketing mix resources to reach its target markets. It has three phases: planning, implementation, and control.

6 The planning phase of the strategic marketing process has three steps, each with more specific elements: situation (SWOT) analysis, market-product focus and goal setting, and marketing program.

7 The implementation phase of the strategic marketing process has four key elements: obtaining resources, designing the marketing organization, developing schedules, and executing the marketing program.

8 The control phase of the strategic marketing process involves comparing results with the planned targets to identify deviations and taking actions to correct negative deviations and exploit positive ones.

KEY TERMS

profit p. 30
corporate level p. 30
business unit p. 31
business unit level p. 31
functional level p. 31
corporate vision p. 32
goal p. 33
market share p. 33
corporate philosophy p. 33
corporate culture p. 33
business (unit) mission p. 35
business unit goal p. 35
objectives p. 35
business unit competencies p. 37
competitive advantage p. 37
quality p. 38
benchmarking p. 38
strategic marketing process p. 40
marketing plan p. 40
situation analysis p. 41
SWOT analysis p. 41
market segmentation p. 43
points of difference p. 44
marketing strategy p. 47
marketing tactics p. 47

INTERNET EXERCISE

Want to own a Ben & Jerry's Franchised Scoop Shop? Every day Ben & Jerry's lovers call the company with great ideas and places for the next perfect Scoop Shop. But the company is very selective in screening locations and qualifying applicants. To see these criteria, visit: www.benjerry.com/scoop/franchise

APPLYING MARKETING CONCEPTS AND PERSPECTIVES

1 (*a*) Explain what a vision statement is. (*b*) Using Coca-Cola as an example from the chapter, explain how it gives a strategic direction to its organization. (*c*) Create a vision statement for your own career.

2 (*a*) How might top management try to change the "corporate culture" of its organization? (*b*) What has George Fisher done at Kodak to change its corporate culture?

3 Using the mission statement shown in Figure 2–3 as a guide, write a plausible mission statement for: (*a*) your college or university's business school and (*b*) Air Canada.

4 Why does a product often start as a question mark and then move counterclockwise around BCG's growth-share matrix shown in Figure 2–4?

5 What organizational or business unit competencies best describe (*a*) your college or university, (*b*) your favourite restaurant, and (*c*) the company that manufactures the computer you own or use most often?

6 What is the main result of each of the three phases of the strategic marketing process? (*a*) planning, (*b*) implementation, and (*c*) control.

7 Select one strength, one weakness, one opportunity, and one threat from the SWOT analysis for Rollerblade, Inc. shown in Figure 2–6, and suggest a specific possible action that might result.

8 Many Canadian liberal arts universities have traditionally offered an undergraduate degree in liberal arts (the product) to full-time 18- to 22–year-old students (the market). How might such a university use the four market-product expansion strategies shown in Figure 2–7 to compete in the year 2000?

9 The goal-setting step in the planning phase of the strategic marketing process sets quantified objectives for use in the control phase. What actions are suggested for a marketing manager if measured results are below objectives? Above objectives?

CASE 2–1 SPECIALIZED BICYCLE COMPONENTS, INC.

The speaker leans forward with both intensity and pride in his voice. "We're in the business of creating a bike that delivers to customers the best possible ride," he explains. "When the customer sees our red 'S,' they say this is the company that understands the cyclist. It's a company of riders. The products they make are the rider's products." The speaker is Chris Murphy, Director of Marketing for Specialized Bicycle Components, Inc.—or just "Specialized" to serious riders.

THE COMPANY

Specialized was founded in 1974 by Mike Sinyard, a cycling enthusiast who sold his VW van for the $1500 startup capital. Mike started out importing hard-to-find "specialized" bike components, but the company began to produce its own bike parts by 1976. Specialized introduced the first major production mountain bike to the world in 1980, revolutionizing the bike industry, and since then has maintained a reputation as the technological leader in the bike and bike accessory market. In fact, since the company's founding, its formal mission statement has remained unchanged: "To give everyone the best ride of their life!"

You probably recognize the Stumpjumper and the Rockhopper, both made by Specialized, as two of the most popular mountain bikes today. The company continues to innovate, with its introduction of a European-style city bike, the Globe. It also sells road bikes and an extensive line of bike accessories, including helmets, water bottles, jerseys, and shoes. As Chris says, "The customer is buying the ride from us, not just the bike."

The first professional mountain bike racing team was created by Specialized in 1983, and Ned Overland, the Team Specialized captain, became the first-ever world champion. Specialized also counts Ned as one of its design consultants. The company banks on the perception, and reality, that this race-proven technology trickles down to the entire line of Specialized bikes and products.

THE ENVIRONMENT

The bike market is driven by innovation and technology, and with the market becoming more crowded and competitive, the fight for the consumer is intense. Specialized divides the bike market into two categories: (1) the independent retailer, and (2) the end-user consumer. While its focus in designing the product is on the end-user consumer, it only sells directly to the retailer, and realizes that a strong relationship with the dealers is a key factor for success.

The end-user consumer is broken down into two target age groups: the 18- to 25-year-old college or university students and the 30- to 40-year-old professional "techies." To differentiate itself from the rest of the market, Specialized positions itself as the innovator in mountain bikes—its models are what the rest of the industry imitates.

Mountain bikes account for approximately two-thirds of total industry bike sales, with road bikes accounting for the other third. The sport of mountain biking experienced a huge surge from 1989 to 1993, but in the mid-1990s sales began to flatten. Does Chris believe this trend will hurt Specialized? "We believe we will see growth in the next six or seven years as the entry level participants trade up—trade their lower end bikes for higher end bikes," he explains.

Specialized began cultivating what was to become an extensive global distribution network as early as 1982. It now boasts subsidiaries in 25 countries in Asia, North America, South America, Europe, and Australia, enabling the red "S" to become a symbol of performance-driven products around the world.

THE ISSUES

How can Specialized stay at the forefront of an industry that now includes more than 20 manufacturers? Strategic placement in the marketplace is one way. Specialized recently designed its own server, the World Ride Web, on the Internet (www.specialized.com/bikes/). The Web site offers international mountain bike trail and road bike trail directories, e-mail access to Specialized engineers, a trail preservation network, and a dealer directory that connects users directly to dealer homepages, in addition to the standard product information. Specialized's new bike, the Globe, appeared on *Seinfeld* and was on display in Gap clothing stores. Specialized believes these nontraditional promotional strategies are helping to keep the Specialized name on the cutting edge and in front of the end-user consumer.

Targeting its other market segment, the dealers, Specialized launched a "Best Ride Tour." It loaded up trailers full of the new models and visited over 30 cities, enabling retailers and shop employees to test-ride the bikes they will be ordering for the coming year—"Ride Before You Buy."

Specialized is also eager to become involved in joint ventures to keep its technological edge. In 1989 it released the Composite wheel, which was a joint venture between Specialized and Du Pont. The wheel is so aerodynamic it actually saves a rider more than 10 minutes over a 160-kilometre ride. Specialized also entered into a distribution relationship with GripShift in 1994, allowing the high-end gear manufacturer access to its extensive dealer network. Why is this beneficial to Specialized? It's another way to support the dealers by providing a top-notch product for its customers that Specialized can support in its marketing efforts.

Specialized sponsors races, provides racer support teams, initiates mountain biking safety programs, and is involved in trail-access advocacy groups all over the world. But, as it was in Specialized's early years, Mike sees a commitment to top quality and design as the most important factor for future success: "Even though we've been around for 20 years, this company still feels like it has something to prove. I expect it will always be that way."

Questions

These questions focus on the three steps of the planning phase of the strategic marketing process.

1 Do a SWOT analysis for Specialized. Use Figure 2–6 in Chapter 2 and Figure 1 in Appendix A as guides. In assessing internal factors (strengths and weaknesses), use the material provided in the case. In assessing external factors (opportunities and threats) augment the case material with what you see happening in the bicycle industry.

2 As part of Step 2 of the planning phase, and using your SWOT analysis, select target markets on which you might focus for present and potential bikers.

3 As part of Step 3 of the planning phase and using your answers in questions 1 and 2 above, outline Specialized's marketing programs for the target market segments you chose.

A SAMPLE MARKETING PLAN

"New ideas are a dime a dozen," observes Arthur R. Kydd, "and so are new products and new technologies." Kydd should know. As chief executive officer of St. Croix Venture Partners, he and his firm have provided the seed money and venture capital to launch more than 60 startup firms in the last 25 years. Today those firms have more than 5000 employees.

Kydd elaborates:

> I get 200 to 300 marketing and business plans a year to look at, and St. Croix provides startup financing for only two or three. What sets a potentially successful idea, product, or tehcnology apart from all the rest is markets and marketing. If you have a real product with a distinctive point of difference that satisfies the needs of customers, you may have a winner. And you get a real feel for this in a well-written marketing or business plan.[1]

This appendix (1) describes what marketing and business plans are—including their purposes and guidelines in writing effective plans, and (2) provides a sample marketing plan.

MARKETING PLANS AND BUSINESS PLANS

After explaining the meanings, purposes, and audiences of marketing plans and business plans, this section describes some writing guidelines for them and what external funders often look for in successful plans.

Marketing and Business Plans: Meanings, Purposes, and Audiences

A *marketing plan* is a road map for the marketing activities of an organization for a specified future period of time, such as one year or five years.[2] It is important to note that no single "generic" marketing plan applies to all organizations and all situations. Rather, the specific format for a marketing plan for an organization depends on the following:

- *The target audience and purpose.* Elements included in a particular marketing plan depend heavily on (1) who the audience is and (2) what its purpose is. A marketing plan for an internal audience seeks to point the direction for future marketing activities and is sent to all individuals in the organization who must implement the plan or who will be affected by it. If the plan is directed to an external audience, such as friends, banks, venture capitalists, or potential investors, for the purpose of raising capital, it has the additional function of being an important sales document. In this case it contains elements such as the strategic plan/focus, organization, structure, and biographies of key personnel that would rarely appear in an internal marketing plan. Also, the financial information is far more detailed when the plan is used to raise capital.
- *The kind and complexity of the organization.* A small neighborhood restaurant has a somewhat different marketing plan than Nestlé, which serves international markets. The restaurant's plan would be relatively simple and directed at serving customers in a local market. In Nestlé's case, because there is a hierarchy of marketing plans, various levels of detail would be used, such as the entire organization, the business unit, or the product line.
- *The industry.* Both the restaurant serving a local market and Medtronic, selling heart pacemakers globally, analyze competition. Not only are their geographic thrusts far different, but the complexities of their offerings and, hence, the time periods likely to be covered by their plans also differ. A one-year marketing plan may be adequate for the restaurant, but Medtronic may need a five-year planning horizon because product-development cycles for complex, new medical devices may be three or four years.

In contrast to a marketing plan, a *business plan* is a road map for the entire organization for a specified future period of time, such as one year or five years.[3] A key difference between a marketing plan and a business plan is that the business plan contains details on the research and development (R&D)/operations/manufacturing activities of the organization. Even for a manufacturing business, the marketing plan is probably 60 or 70 percent of the entire business plan. For businesses like a small restaurant or auto repair shop, their marketing and business plans are virtually identical. The elements of a business plan typically targeted at internal and external audiences appear in the two right-hand columns in Figure A–1.

The Most-Asked Questions by Outside Audiences

Lenders and prospective investors reading a business or marketing plan that is used to seek new capital are probably the toughest audiences to satisfy. Their most-asked questions include the following:

1. Is the business or marketing idea valid?
2. Is there something unique or distinctive about the product or service that separates it from substitutes and competitors?
3. Is there a clear market for the product or service?
4. Are the financial projections realistic and healthy?
5. Are the key management and technical personnel capable, and do they have a track record in the industry in which they must compete?
6. Does the plan clearly describe how those providing capital will get their money back and make a profit?

Rhonda M. Abrahms, author of *The Successful Business Plan,* observes that "within the first five minutes of reading your . . . plan, readers, must perceive that the answers to these questions are favorable."[4] While her comments apply to plans seeking to raise capital, the first five questions just listed apply equally well to plans for internal audiences.

Writing and Style Suggestions

There are no magic one-size-fits-all guidelines for writing successful marketing and business plans. Still, the following writing and style guidelines generally apply:[5]

FIGURE A–1
Elements in typical marketing and business plans targeted at different audiences

Element of the Plan	Marketing Plan		Business Plan	
	For Internal Audience (to Direct Firm)	For External Audience (to Raise Capital)	For Internal Audience (to Direct Firm)	For External Audience (to Raise Capital)
1. Executive summary	✓	✓	✓	✓
2. Description of company		✓		✓
3. Strategic plan/focus		✓		✓
4. Situation analysis	✓	✓	✓	✓
5. Market-product focus	✓	✓	✓	✓
6. Marketing program strategy and tactics	✓	✓	✓	✓
7. R&D and operations program			✓	✓
8. Financial projections	✓	✓	✓	✓
9. Organization structure		✓		✓
10. Implementation plan	✓	✓	✓	✓
11. Evaluation and control	✓		✓	
Appendix A: Biographies of key personnel		✓		✓
Appendix B, etc.: Details on other topics	✓	✓	✓	✓

- Use a direct, professional writing style. Use appropriate business terms without jargon. Present and future tenses with active voice are generally better than past tense and passive voice.
- Be positive and specific to convey potential success. At the same time, avoid superlatives ("terrific," "wonderful,"). Specifics are better than glittering generalities. Use numbers for impact, justifying projections with reasonable quantitative assumptions, where possible.
- Use bullet points for succinctness and emphasis. As with the list you are reading, bullets enable key points to be highlighted effectively and with great efficiency.
- Use "A-level" (the first level) and "B-level" (the second level) headings under the numbered section headings to help readers make easy transitions from one topic to another. This also forces the writer to organize the plan more carefully. Use these headings liberally, at least one every 200 to 300 words.
- Use visuals where appropriate. Photos, illustrations, graphs, and charts enable massive amounts of information to be presented succinctly.
- Shoot for a plan 15 to 35 pages in length, not including financial projections and appendixes. But an uncomplicated small business may require only 15 pages, while a high-technology startup may require more than 35 pages.
- Use care in layout, design, and presentation. Laser or ink-jet printers give a more professional look than do dot matrix printers or typewriters. Use 10 or 11 point type (you are now reading 10.5 point type) in the text. Use a serif type (with "feet," like that you are reading now) in the text because it is easier to read, and sans serif (without "feet") in graphs and charts. A bound report with a nice cover and clear title page adds professionalism.

These guidelines are used, where possible, in the sample marketing plan that follows.

SAMPLE FIVE-YEAR MARKETING PLAN FOR PARADISE KITCHENS,® INC.

To help interpret the marketing plan for Paradise Kitchens,® Inc. that follows, we will describe the company and suggest some guidelines in interpreting the plan.

Background on Paradise Kitchens,® Inc.

With a degree in chemical engineering, Randall F. Peters spent 15 years working for General Foods and Pillsbury with a number of diverse responsibilities: plant operations, R&D, restaurant operations, and new business development. His wife Leah, with degrees in both molecular cellular biology and food science, held various Pillsbury executive positions in new category development and packaged goods and restaurants R&D. Both hobby chefs, Randy and Leah developed and perfected several spicy chili recipes in their own kitchen over a 10-year period. While driving late one night in 1989 they got the inspiration for their registered Howlin' Coyote® brand of chilies and decided to start their own business, Paradise Kitchens, Inc. In its startup years, the company survived on the savings of its cofounders, Randy and Leah. Today Randy serves as president and CEO of Paradise Kitchens, and Leah focuses on R&D and corporate strategy. The first products entered distribution in 1990.

Interpreting the Marketing Plan

The marketing plan that follows for Paradise Kitchens, Inc. which follows is based on an actual plan developed by the company.[6] To protect proprietary information about the company, a number of details and data have been altered, but the basic logic of the plan has been preserved. For example, to keep the plan simpler, it does not include details on a line of spicy salsas developed and marketed.

This sample marketing plan is intended as an *internal* road map to guide marketing activities for the coming five years, during which time the company plans to enter 17 new metropolitan markets.

Notes in the margins next to the Paradise Kitchens plan fall into two categories:

1. *Substantive notes* are shaded blue and elaborate on the significance of an element in the marketing plan and are keyed to chapter references in this text.
2. *Writing style, format, and layout notes* are shaded red and explain the editorial or visual rationale for the element.

A closing word of encouragement! Writing an effective marketing plan is hard—but challenging and satisfying—work. However, dozens of the authors' students have used effective marketing plans they wrote for class in their interviewing portfolio to show prospective employers what they could do and to help them get their first job.

The Table of Contents provides quick access to the topics in the plan, usually organized by section and subsection headings.

Seen by many experts as the single-most important element in the plan, the Executive Summary, with a maximum of two pages, "sells" the documents to readers through its clarity and brevity.

The Company Description highlights the recent history and recent successes of the organization.

The Strategic Focus and Plan sets the strategic direction for the entire organization, a direction with which proposed actions of the marketing plan must be consistent. This section is not included in all marketing plans. See Chapter 2.

The qualitative Mission/Vision statement focuses the activities of Paradise Kitchens for the stakeholder groups to be served. See Chapter 2.

FIVE-YEAR MARKETING PLAN
Paradise Kitchens,® Inc.

Table of Contents

2. Company Description

Paradise Kitchens®, Inc. was started in 1989 by cofounders Randall F. Peters and Leah E. Peters to develop and market Howlin' Coyote® Chili, a unique line of single serve and microwaveable Mexican style frozen chili products. The Howlin' Coyote® line of chili was introduced to a single metropolitan market in 1990. The line was subsequently expanded to two new markets in 1992, and 1994.

To the Company's knowledge, Howlin' Coyote® is the only premium-quality, authentic Mexican style, frozen chili sold in grocery stores. Its high quality has gained fast, widespread acceptance in these markets. In fact, same-store sales doubled in the last year for which data are available. The Company believes the Howlin' Coyote® brand can be extended to other categories of Mexican food products.

Paradise Kitchens believes its high-quality, high-price strategy has proven successful. This marketing plan outlines how the Company will extend its geographic coverage from 3 markets to 20 markets by the year 2003.

3. Strategic Focus and Plan

This section covers three aspects of corporate strategy that influence the marketing plan: (1) the mission/vision, (2) goals, and (3) core competence/sustainable competitive advantage of Paradise Kitchens.

<u>Mission/Vision</u>

The mission and vision of Paradise Kitchens is to market lines of high-quality Mexican food products at premium prices that satisfy consumers in this fast-growing food segment while providing challenging career opportunities for employees and above-average returns to shareholders.

Box explains significance of Marketing Plan element

Box gives writing style, format, and layout guidelines

The Goals section sets both the financial and nonfinancial targets—where possible in quantitative terms—against which the company's performance will be measured. See Chapter 2.

Lists use parallel construction to improve readability—in this case a series of infinitives starting with "To . . .".

Goals

For the coming five years Paradise Kitchens seeks to achieve the following goals:

- Nonfinancial goals
    1. To retain its present image as the highest-quality line of Mexican products in the food categories in which it competes.
    2. To enter 17 new metropolitan markets.
    3. To increase the production and distribution capacity to satisfy future sales while maintaining present quality.
    4. To add a new product line every third year.
    5. To be among the top three chili lines—regardless of packaging (frozen, canned) in one third of the metro markets in which it competes by 2001 and two thirds by 2003.
- Financial goals
    1. To obtain a real (inflation-adjusted) growth in earnings per share of 8 percent per year over time.
    2. To obtain a return on equity of at least 20 percent.
    3. To have a public stock offering by the year 2001.

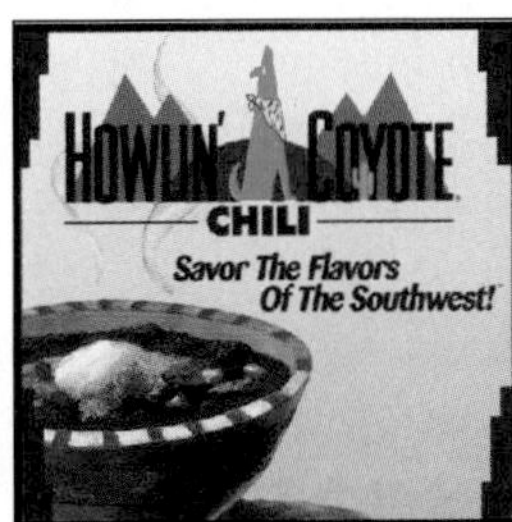

In keeping with the goal of adding a new product line every third year, Paradise Kitchens is introducing a new line of salsas.

Core Competency and Sustainable Competitive Advantage

In terms of core competency, Paradise Kitchens seeks to achieve a unique ability (1) to provide distinctive, high-quality chilies and related products using Mexican recipes that appeal to and excite contemporary tastes for these products and (2) to deliver these products to the customer's table using effective manufacturing and distribution systems that maintain the Company's quality standards.

To translate these core competencies into a sustainable competitive advantage, the Company will work closely with key suppliers and distributors to build the relationships and alliances necessary to satisfy the high taste standards of our customers.

To improve readability, each numbered section usually starts on a new page. (This is not done in this plan to save space.)

The Situation Analysis is a snapshot to answer the question, "Where are we now?" See Chapter 2.

The SWOT Analysis identifies strengths, weaknesses, opportunities, and threats to provide a solid foundation as a springboard to identify subsequent *actions* in the marketing plan. See Chapter 2.

Each long table, graph, or photo is given a figure number and title. It then appears as soon as possible after the first reference in the text, accommodating necessary page breaks. This also avoids breaking long tables like this one in the middle. Short tables or graphs that are less than 3 cm are often inserted in the text without figure numbers because they don't cause serious problems with page breaks.

Effective tables seek to summarize a large amount of information in a short amount of space.

4. Situation Analysis

This situation analysis starts with a snapshot of the current environment in which Paradise Kitchens finds itself by providing a brief SWOT (strengths, weaknesses, opportunities, threats) analysis. After this overview, the analysis probes ever finer levels of detail: industry, competitors, company, and consumers.

SWOT Analysis

Figure 1 shows the internal and external factors affecting the market opportunities for Paradise Kitchens. Stated briefly, this SWOT analysis highlights the great strides taken by the company in the nine years since its products first appeared on grocers'

Figure 1. SWOT Analysis for Paradise Kitchens

Internal Factors	Strengths	Weaknesses
Management	Experienced and entrepreneurial management and board	Small size can restrict options
Offerings	Unique, high-quality, high-price products	Many lower-quality, lower price competitors
Marketing	Distribution in 3 markets with excellent acceptance	No national awareness or distribution
Personnel	Good work force, though small; little turnover	Big gap if key employee leaves
Finance	Excellent growth in sales revenues	Limited resources may restrict growth opportunities when compared to giant competitors
Manufacturing	Sole supplier ensures high quality	Lack economies of scale of huge competitors
R&D	Continuing efforts to ensure quality in delivered products	
External Factors	**Opportunities**	**Threats**
Consumer/Social	Upscale market, likely to be stable; Mexican food category is fast-growing segment	Premium price may limit access to mass markets.
Competitive	Distinctive name and packaging in its markets.	Not patentable; competitors can attempt to duplicate product
Technological	Technical breakthroughs enable smaller food producers to achieve many economies available to large competitors	
Economic	Consumer income is high; convenience important to Canadian households	More households "eating out," and bringing prepared take-out into home
Legal/Regulatory	High government regulatory standards eliminate fly-by-night competitors	

The text discussion of Figure 1 (the SWOT Analysis table) elaborates on its more important elements. This "walks" the reader through the information from the vantage of the plan's writer. (In terse plans this accompanying discussion is sometimes omitted, but is generally desirable to give the reader an understanding of what the company sees as the critical SWOT elements.)

The Industry Analysis section provides the backdrop for the subsequent, more detailed analysis of competition, the company, and the company's customers. Without an in-depth understanding of the industry, the remaining analysis may be misdirected. See Chapter 2.

Even though relatively brief, this in-depth treatment of the Spicy Mexican food industry demonstrates to the plan's readers the company's understanding of the industry in which it competes. It gives both external and internal readers confidence that the company thoroughly understands its own industry.

This summary of sales in the Mexican product category shows it is significant and provides a variety of future opportunities for Paradise Kitchens.

shelves. In the Company's favour internally are its strengths of an experienced management team and board of directors, excellent acceptance of its lines in the three metropolitan markets in which it competes, and a strong manufacturing and distribution system to serve these limited markets. Favourable external factors (opportunities) include the increasing appeal of Mexican foods, the strength of the upscale market for the Company's products, and food-processing technological breakthroughs that make it easier for smaller food producers to compete.

These favourable factors must be balanced against unfavourable ones, the main weakness being the limited size of Paradise Kitchens relative to its competitors in terms of the depth of the management team, available financial resources, and national awareness and distribution of product lines. Threats include the potential danger that the Company's premium prices may limit access to mass markets, no legal patent protection for its foods (although it has registered its Howlin' Coyote® brand), and competition from the "eating-out" and "take-out" markets.

Industry Analysis: Trends in Spicy and Mexican Foods

In the past 10 years, hot-spice consumption has doubled. Currently, Mexican food and ingredients are used in 46 percent of households. Burritos, enchiladas, and taco dinner kits, which had insignificant numbers in 1981, reached between 7 percent and 16 percent of households in 1992. By 1997, volume of Mexican dinner kits in Canada grew by 41 percent over 1996. Experts predict rapid growth in the Mexican food category and huge market potential.[7]

These trends reflect a generally more favourable attitude toward spicy foods. Total spice consumption increased 50 percent from 1983 to 1993, according to the Spice Trade Association. The retail grocery market for Mexican foods (excluding tortilla chips) was more than $4 billion in annual sales in 1994. The Mexican market includes the foods shown in Figure 2.

Figure 2. Foods Included in the Mexican Product Category

Food	1994 Sales ($1 000 000)	% Change from 1993 to 1994
Dry chili mix	$121	6.0%
Canned chili	578	2.3
Salsa and sauces	1438	10.3
Mexican frozen	602	4.5
Mexican foods canned	353	4.4
Peppers	242	2.5
Chilies	90	0.3
Mexican foods dry	1259	5.3
Total	$4681	6.0%

As with the Industry Analysis, the Competitors Analysis demonstrates that the company has a realistic understanding of who its major competitors are and what their marketing strategies are. Again, a realistic assessment gives confidence to both internal and external readers that subsequent marketing actions in the plan rest on a solid foundation. See Chapters 2, 3, and 8.

This page uses a "block" style and does *not* indent each paragraph, although an extra space separates each paragraph. Compare this page with page 44, which has indented paragraphs. Most readers find indented paragraphs in marketing plans and long reports are easier to follow.

Paradise Kitchens addresses the issue of the difficulty and unlikelihood of competitors jumping easily into this niche market.

The Company Analysis provides details of the company's strengths and marketing strategies that will enable it to achieve the mission, vision, and goals identified earlier. See Chapters 2, 9, and 22.

Competitors in Mexican Market

The chili market represents $699 million in annual sales. The products fall primarily into two groups: canned chili (81 percent of sales) and dry chili (17 percent of sales). The remaining 2 percent of sales go to frozen chili products. Besides Howlin' Coyote,® Stouffers and Marie Callender's offer frozen chilies as part of their broad line of frozen dinners and entrees. Major canned chili brands include Hormel, Wolf, Dennison, Stagg, Chili Man, and Castleberry's. Their retail prices range from $1.09 to $1.49.

Bluntly put, the major disadvantage of the segment's dominant product, canned chili, is that it does not taste very good. A taste test described in the October 1990 issue of *Consumer Reports* magazine ranked 26 canned chili products "poor" to "fair" in overall sensory quality. The study concluded, "Chili doesn't have to be hot to be good. But really good chili, hot or mild, doesn't come out of a can."

Dry mix brands include such familiar spice brands as Lawry's, McCormick, French's, and Durkee, along with smaller offerings such as Wick Fowler's and Carroll Shelby's. Their retail prices range from $1.79 to $1.99. The *Consumer Reports* study was more favourable about dry chili mixes, ranking them from "fair" to "very good." The magazine recommended, "If you want good chili, make it with fresh ingredients and one of the seasoning mixes we tested." A major drawback of dry mixes is that they require the preparers to add their own meat, beans, and tomatoes and take more preparation time than canned or frozen chilies.

The *Consumer Reports* study did not include the frozen chili entrees from Stouffer's or Marie Callender's (Howlin' Coyote® was not yet on the market at the time of the test). However, it is fair to say that these products—consisting of ground beef, chili beans, and tomato sauce—are of average quality. Furthermore, they are not singled out for special marketing or promotional programs by their manufacturers. Marie Callender's retails for $2.97, and Stouffer's retails for under $2.00.

While it is feasible for another food company to match Howlin' Coyote® and create a similar product, no known current companies are in a position to quickly match the offerings. Small companies face technical capacity issues. Large companies view the products as too much outside the mainstream of frozen-food retailing to be attracted to the market, at least initially.

Company Analysis

The husband-and-wife team that cofounded Paradise Kitchens, Inc. in 1989 has 44 years of experience between them in the food-processing business. Both have played key roles in the management of the Pillsbury Company. They are being advised by a highly seasoned group of business professionals, who have extensive understanding of the requirements for new product development.

This "introdcutory overview" sentence tells the reader the topics covered in the section—in this case customer characteristics and health and nutrition concerns. While this sentence may be omitted in short memos or plans, it helps readers see where the text is leading. These sentences are used throughout this plan. This text also generally utilizes these introductory overview sentences to aid your comprehension.

The higher-level "A heading" of Customer Analysis has a more dominant typeface and position than the lower-level "B heading" of Customer Characteristics. These headings introduce the reader to the sequence and level of topics covered. The organization of this textbook uses this kind of structure and headings.

Satisfying customers and providing genuine value to them is why organizations exist in a market economy. This section addresses the question of "Who are the customers for Paradise Kitchens's products?" See Chapters 5, 6, 7, and 9.

Currently, Howlin' Coyote® products compete in the chili and Mexican frozen entree segments of the Mexican food market. While the chili obviously competes as a stand-alone product, its exceptional quality means it can complement such dishes as burritos, nachos, and enchiladas and can be readily used as a smothering sauce for pasta, rice, or potatoes. This flexibility of use is relatively rare in the prepared food marketplace.

In its growth strategy, Howlin' Coyote® is retracing a path taken by such enterprising food companies as Snapple Beverages, Celestial Seasonings, and Tombstone Pizza. These companies all broke from the pack of their respective categories and established a new approach. Snapple showed that iced tea and fruit drinks can be fun and highly variable. Celestial Seasonings make tea into a "lifestyle" drink. Tombstone Pizza moved frozen pizza upscale in taste and price, creating the first alternative to "cardboard" home pizzas. Likewise, with Howlin' Coyote® Paradise Kitchens is broadening the postion of frozen chili in a way that can lead to impressive market share for the new product category.

The Company now uses a single outside producer with which it works closely to maintain the consistently high quality required in its products. The greater volume has increased production efficiencies, resulting in a steady decrease in the cost of goods sold.

Customer Analysis

In terms of customer analysis, this section describes (1) the characteristics of customers expected to buy Howlin' Coyote® products and (2) health and nutrition concerns of consumers today.

Customer Characteristics. Demographically, chili products in general are purchased by consumers representing a broad range of socioeconomic backgrounds. Howlin' Coyote® chili is purchased chiefly by consumers who have achieved higher levels of education and whose income is $30 000 and higher. These consumers represent 57 percent of canned and dry mix chili users.

The five Howlin' Coyote® entrees offer a quick, tasty meal with high-quality ingredients.

This section demonstrates the company's insights into a major trend that has a potentially large impact.

Size of headings should give a professional look to the report and not overwhelm the reader. These two headings are too large.

The household buying Howlin' Coyote® has one to three people in it. Among married couples, Howlin' Coyote® is predominantly bought by households in which both spouses work. While women are a majority of the buyers, single men represent a significant segment. Anecdotally, Howlin' Coyote® has heard from fathers of teenaged boys who say they keep a freezer stocked with the chili because the boys devour it.

Because the chili offers a quick way to make a tasty meal, the product's biggest users tend to be those most pressed for time. Howlin' Coyote®'s premium pricing also means that its purchasers are skewed toward the higher end of the income range. Buyers range in age from 25 to 55.

Health and Nutrition Concerns. Coverage of food issues in the media is often erratic and occasionally alarmist. Because consumers are concerned about their diets, studies from organizations of widely varying credibility frequently receive significant attention from the major news organizations. For instance, a study of fat levels of movie popcorn was reported in all the major media. Similarly, studies on the healthfulness of Mexican food have received prominent "play" in print and broadcast reports. The high caloric levels of much Mexican food has been widely reported and often exaggerated.

Less certain is the link between these reports and consumer buying behaviour. Most indications are that while consumers are well-versed in dietary matters, they are not significantly changing their eating patterns. The experience of other food manufacturers is that consumers expect certain foods to be high in calories and are not drawn to those that claim to be low-calorie versions. Low-fat frozen pizza was a flop. Therefore, while Howlin' Coyote® is already lower in calories, fat, and sodium than its competitors, those qualities are not being stressed in its promotions. Instead, in the space and time available for promotions, Howlin' Coyote®'s taste, convenience, and flexibility are stressed.

5. Market-Product Focus

This section describes the five-year marketing and product objectives for Paradise Kitchens and the target markets, points of difference, and positioning of its lines of Howlin' Coyote® chilies.

Marketing and Product Objectives

Howlin' Coyote®'s marketing intent is to take full advantage of its brand potential while building a base from which other revenues sources can be

As noted in Chapter 11, the chances of success for a new product are significantly increased if objectives are set for the product itself and if target market segments are identified for it. This section makes these explicit for Paradise Kitchens. The objectives also serve as the planned targets against which marketing activities are measured in program implementation and control.

A heading should be spaced closer to the text that follows (and that it describes) than the preceding section to avoid confusion for the reader. This rule is *not* followed for the "Target Markets" heading, which now unfortunately appears to "float" between the preceding and following paragraphs.

This section identifies the specific niches or target markets toward which the company's products are directed. When appropriate and when space permits, this section often includes a market-product grid. See Chapter 9.

mined—both in and out of the retail grocery business. These are detailed in four areas below:

- Current markets. Current markets will be grown by expanding brand and flavour distribution at the retail level. In addition, same-store sales will be grown by increasing consumer awareness and repeat purchases. With this increase in same-store sales, the more desirable broker/warehouse distribution channel will become available, increasing efficiency and saving costs.
- New markets. By the end of Year 5, the chili and salsa business will be expanded to a total of 20 metropolitan areas. This will represent 55 percent of food store sales.
- Food service. Food service sales will include chili products and smothering sauces. Sales are expected to reach $583 000 by the end of Year 3 and $1.2 million by the end of Year 5.
- New products. Howlin' Coyote®'s brand presence will be expanded at the retail level through the addition of new products in the frozen-foods section. This will be accomplished through new product concept screening in Year 1 to identify new potential products. These products will be brought to market in Years 2 and 3. Additionally, the brand may be licensed in select categories.

Target Markets

The primary target market for Howlin' Coyote® products is households with one to three people, where often both adults work, with individual income typically above $30 000 per year. These households contain more experienced, adventurous consumers of Mexican food and want premium quality products.

To help buyers see the many different uses for Howlin' Coyote® chili, recipes are even printed on the *inside* of the packages.

An organization cannot grow by offering only "me-too products." The greatest single factor in a new product's failure is the lack of significant "points of difference" that sets it apart from competitors' substitutes. This section makes these points of difference explicit. See Chapter 11.

A positioning strategy helps communicate the company's unique points of difference of its products to prospective customers in a simple, clear way. This section describes this positioning. See Chapters 9 and 11.

Everything that has gone before in the marketing plan sets the stage for the marketing mix actions—the 4 Ps—covered in the marketing program. See Chapters 11 through 21.

The section describes in detail three key elements of the company's product strategy: the product line, its quality and how this is achieved, and its "cutting edge" packaging. See Chapters 11, 12, and 13.

Points of Difference

The "points of difference"—characteristics that make Howlin' Coyote® chilies unique relative to competitors—fall into three important areas:

- Unique taste and convenience. No known competitor offers a high-quality, " authentic" frozen chili in a range of flavours. And no existing chili has the same combination of quick preparation and home-style taste.
- Taste trends. The consumer's palate is increasingly intrigued by hot spices, and Howlin' Coyote® brands offer more "kick" than most other prepared chilies.
- Premium packaging. Howlin' Coyote®'s high-value packaging graphics convey the unique, high-quality product contained inside and the product's nontraditional positioning.

Positioning

In the past chili products have been either convenient or tasty, but not both. Howlin' Coyote® pairs these two desirable characteristics to obtain a positioning in consumers' minds as very high-quality "authentic Mexican tasting" chilies that can be prepared easily and quickly.

6. Marketing Program

The four marketing mix elements of the Howlin' Coyote® chili marketing program are detailed below. Note that "chile" is the vegetable and "chili" is the dish.

Product Strategy

After first summarizing the product line, the approach to product quality and packaging are covered.

Product Line. Howlin' Coyote® chili, retailing for $2.89 for a 300 g serving, is available in five flavours. The five are:

- Green Chile Chili: braised extra-lean pork with fire-roasted green chilies, onions, tomato chunks, bold spices, and jalapeno peppers.
- Red Chile Chili: extra-lean cubed pork, deep-red acho chilies, and sweet onions.
- Beef and Black Bean Chili: lean braised beef with black beans, tomato chunks, and Howlin' Coyote®'s own blend of red chilies and authentic spicing.

Using parallel structure, this bulleted list presents the product line efficiently and crisply.

- Chicken Chunk Chili: hearty chunks of tender chicken, fire-roasted green chilies, black beans, pinto beans, diced onions, and zesty spices.
- Mean Bean Chili: vegetarian, with nine distinctive bean varieties and fire-roasted green chilies, tomato chunks, onion, and a robust blend of spices and rich red chilies.

Unique Product Quality. The flavouring systems of the Howlin' Coyote® chilies are proprietary. The products' tastiness is due to extra care lavished upon the ingredients during production. The ingredients used are of unusually high quality. Meats are low-fat cuts and are fresh, not frozen, to preserve cell structure and moistness. Chilies are fire-roasted for fresher taste, not the canned variety used by more mainstream products. Tomatoes and vegetables are select quality. No preservatives or artificial flavours are used.

A brief caption on photos and sample ads ties them to the text and highlights the reason for being included.

Packaging. Reflecting the "cutting edge" marketing strategy of its producers, Howlin' Coyote® bucks conventional wisdom in packaging. It avoids placing predictable photographs of the product on its containers. (Head to any grocer's freezer and you will be hardpressed to find a product that does not feature a heavily stylized photograph of the contents.) Instead, Howlin' Coyote®'s package communicates the product's out-of-the-ordinary positioning. This approach signals the product's nontraditional qualities: "adventurous" eating with minimal fuss—a frozen meal for people who do not normally enjoy frozen meals.

Howlin' Coyote®'s packages stand out in a supermarket's freezer case.

This Price Strategy section makes the company's price point very clear, along with its price position relative to potential substitutes. When appropriate and when space permits, this section might contain a break-even analysis. See Chapters 14 and 15.

Price Strategy

Howlin' Coyote® Chili is, at $2.89 for a 300 g package, priced comparably to the other frozen offerings and higher than the canned and dried chili varieties. However, the significant taste advantages it has over canned chilies and the convenience advantages over dried chilies justify this pricing strategy.

Elements of the Promotion Strategy are highlighted here with B-headings in terms of the three key promotional activities the company is emphasizing for its product line: in-store demonstrations, recipes featuring its Howlin' Coyote® chilies, and cents-off coupons. See Chapters 19, 20, and 21.

Promotion Strategy

Key promotion programs feature in-store demonstrations, recipes, and cents-off coupons.

In-Store Demonstrations. In-store demonstrations will be conducted to give consumers a chance to try Howlin' Coyote® products and learn about their unique qualities. Demos will be conducted regularly in all markets to increase awareness and trial purchases.

Recipes. Because the products' flexibility of use is a key selling point, recipes will be offered to consumers to stimulate use. The recipes will be given at all in-store demonstrations, on the back of packages, and through a mail-in recipe book offer. In addition, recipes will be included in coupons sent by direct-mail or free-standing inserts. For new markets, recipes will be included on in-pack coupon inserts.

Cents-Off Coupons. To generate trial and repeat-purchase of Howlin' Coyote® products, coupons will be distributed in four ways:

- In Sunday newspaper inserts. Inserts are highly read and will help generate awareness. Coupled with in-store demonstrations, this has been a very successful technique so far.

Photos or sample ads can illustrate key points effectively, even if they are not in color as they appear here.

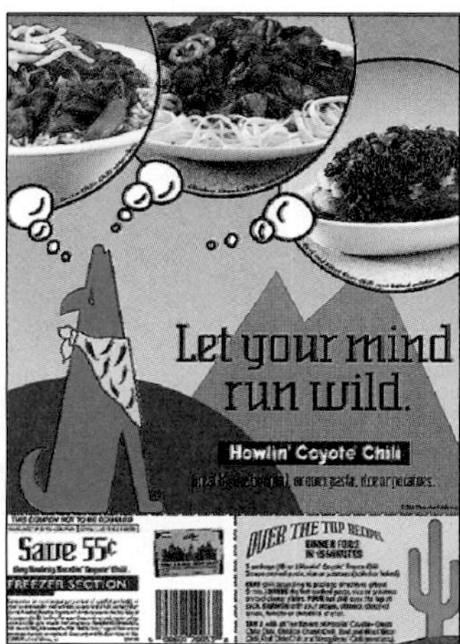

Sunday newspaper inserts encourage consumer trial and provide recipes to show how Howlin' Coyote® chili can be used in summer meals.

Another bulleted list adds many details for the reader, including methods of gaining customer awareness, trial, and repeat purchases as Howlin' Coyote® enters new metropolitan areas. The lack of a space between bulleted items makes it more difficult reading for some readers compared to, say, the bulleted list on page 39.

- In-pack coupons. Inside each box of Howlin' Coyote® chili will be coupons for $1 off two more packages of the chili. These coupons will be included for the first three months the product is shipped to a new market. Doing so encourages repeat purchases by new users.
- Direct-mail chili coupons. Those households that fit the Howlin' Coyote® demographics described above will be mailed coupons. This is likely to be an efficient promotion due to its greater audience selectivity.
- In-store demonstrations. Coupons will be passed out at in-store demonstrations to give an additional incentive to purchase.

The Place Strategy is described here in terms of both (1) the present method and (2) the new one to be used when the increased sales volume makes it feasible. See Chapters 16, 17, and 18.

Place (Distribution) Strategy

Howlin' Coyote® is distributed in its present markets through a food distributor. The distributor buys the product, warehouses it, and then resells and delivers it to grocery retailers on a store-by-store basis. This is typical for products that have moderate sales—compared with, say, staples like milk or bread. As sales grow, we will shift to a more efficient system using a broker who sells the products to retail chains and grocery wholesalers.

All the marketing mix decisions covered in the just-described marketing program have both revenue and expense effects. These are summarized in this section of the marketing plan. See Appendix B.

7. Financial Data and Projections

Note that this section contains no introductory overview sentence. While the sentence is not essential, many readers prefer to see it to avoid the abrupt start with Past Sales Revenues.

Past Sales Revenues

Historically, Howlin' Coyote® has had a steady increase in sales revenues since its introduction in 1990. In 1994, sales jumped spectacularly, due largely to new promotion strategies and the opportunities represented by the products' expansion to Western markets. The trend in sales revenues appears in Figure 3.

Figure 3. Sales Revenues for Paradise Kitchens, Inc.

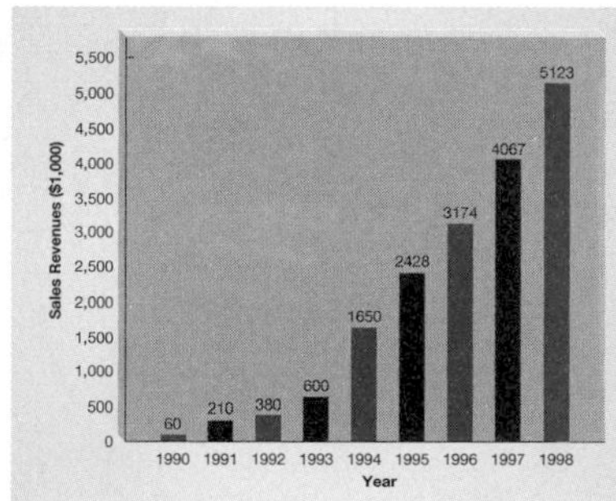

The graph shows more clearly the dramatic growth of sales revenue than data in a table would do.

One key indicator of what future sales will be is to look at what past sales have been. Paradise Kitchens is justifiably proud of the dramatic growth in its past sales revenues and highlights this information. For simplicity, this sample marketing plan omits revenues from the salsa line.

Because this table is very short, it is woven into the text, rather than given a figure number and title.

Because the plan proposes to enter 17 new metropolitan markets in the coming five years (for a total of 20), it is not possible to simply extrapolate the trend in Figure 3. Instead, management's judgment must be used. Methods of making sales forecasts—including the "lost horse technique used here—are discussed in Chapter 8.

The Five-Year Financial Projections section starts with the judgment forecast of cases sold and the resulting net sales. Gross profit and then operating profit—critical for the company's survival—are projected and show the company passes break-even and becomes profitable in Year 2. An actual plan often contains many pages of computer-generated spreadsheet projections, usually shown in an appendix to the plan.

Five-Year Projections

Five-year financial projections for Paradise Kitchens appear below:

			Projections				
Financial Element	Units	Actual 1998	Year1 1999	Year 2 2000	Year 3 2001	Year 4 2002	Year 5 2003
Cases sold	1000	353	684	889	1 249	1 499	1 799
Net sales	$1000	5123	9913	12 884	18 111	21 733	26 080
Gross profit	$1000	2545	4820	6 527	8 831	10 597	12 717
Operating profit (loss)	$1000	339	985	2 906	2 805	3 366	4 039

These projections reflect the continuing growth in number of cases sold (with 8 packages of Howlin' Coyote® chili per case) and increasing production and distribution economies of scale as sales volume increases.

8. Organization

Paradise Kitchens's present organization appears in Figure 4. It shows the four people reporting to the President. Below this level are both the full-time and part-time employees of the Company.

At present Paradise Kitchens operates with full-time employees in only essential positions. It now augments its full-time staff with key advisors, consultants, and subcontractors. As the firm grows, people with special expertise will be added to the staff.

Figure 4. The Paradise Kitchens Organization

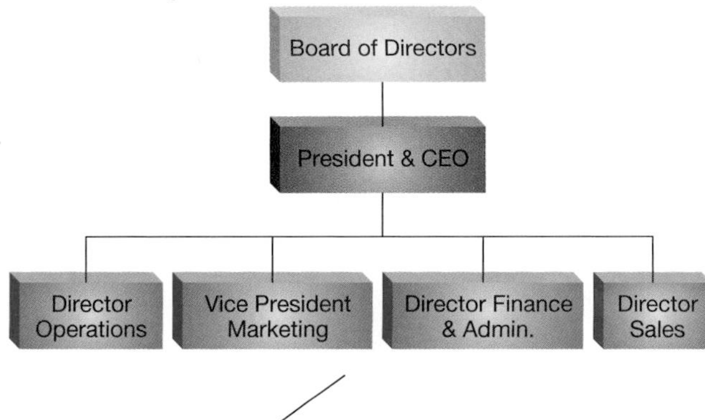

The Organization of Paradise Kitchens appears here. It reflects the bare-bones organizational structure of successful small businesses. Often a more elaborate marketing plan will show the new positions expected to be added as the firm grows. See Chapter 22. Biographical sketches of key personnel often appear as an appendix of a marketing plan targeted at external audiences and used to try to help obtain funding.

The Implementation Plan shows how the company will turn plans into results. Gantt charts are often used to set deadlines and assign responsibilities for the many tactical marketing decisions needed to enter a new market. See Chapter 22.

The essence of Evaluation and Control is comparing actual sales with the targeted values set in the plan and taking appropriate actions. Note that the section briefly describes a contingency plan for alternative actions, depending on how successful the entry into a new market turns out to be. See Chapter 22.

Various appendixes may appear at the end of the plan, depending on the purpose and audience for them. For example, resumes of key personnel or detailed financial spreadsheets often appear in appendixes.

9. Implementation Plan

Introducing Howlin' Coyote® chilies to new metropolitan areas is a complex task and requires that creative promotional activities gain consumer awareness and initial trial among the target market households identified earlier. The anticipated rollout schedule to enter these metropolitan markets appears in Figure 5.

Figure 5. Rollout Schedule to Enter New Markets

Year	New Markets Added	Cumulative Markets	Cumulative Percentage of Market
Today (1998)	2	5	16
Year 1 (1999)	3	8	21
Year 2 (2000)	4	12	29
Year 3 (2001)	2	14	37
Year 4 (2002)	3	17	45
Year 5 (2003)	3	20	53

10. Evaluation and Control

Monthly sales targets in cases have been set for Howlin' Coyote® chili for each metropolitan area. Actual case sales will be compared with these targets and tactical marketing programs modified to reflect the unique sets of factors in each metropolitan area. The speed of the roll-out program will increase or decrease, depending on the Paradise Kitchens's performance in the successive metropolitan markets it enters.

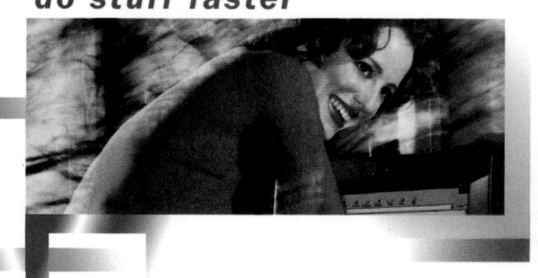

CHAPTER THREE

THE CHANGING MARKETING ENVIRONMENT

3

AFTER READING THIS CHAPTER YOU SHOULD BE ABLE TO:

- Understand how environmental scanning provides information about social, economic, technological, competitive, and regulatory forces.
- Explain how social forces such as demographics and culture and economic forces such as macroeconomic conditions and consumer income affect marketing.
- Describe how technological changes can affect marketing.
- Understand the forms of competition that exist in a market, key components of competition, and the impact of competition on corporate structures.
- Explain the major legislation that ensures competition and regulates the elements of the marketing mix.

THE DIGITAL REVOLUTION IS CHANGING (ALMOST) EVERYTHING!

Digital cameras, digital cable, digital telephones, digital books, personal digital assistants, e-mail, e-zines, e-commerce, the Internet. If any of these products or terms sound familiar to you, then you've already begun to experience one of the biggest changes in the world of marketing—a digital revolution! Changes in technology are transforming the ways we communicate, buy, sell, learn, and work. The shift to a digital era is replacing many existing products with new digital versions that are faster and easier to use. In addition, new products previously impossible to offer consumers are now facilitated through new technology. Computers and access to the Internet are quickly becoming as common in households as televisions and VCRs. As these trends continue we are witnessing a revolution that is changing most aspects of our culture and marketplace.

While many people are trying to adapt to the changes taking place, millions of people under the age of 22—the Net Generation—have grown up with the new technologies, becoming authorities in their use. As the Internet has become the focus of the digital age, the Net Generation has become the first group to use it consistently for entertainment, education, communication, and shopping. The Net Generation is also unique because, through its use of the Net, it has developed a global orientation, has been exposed to a diverse range of topics and opinions, and has developed a preference for interactive communication. These and other differences suggest that the Net Generation will shape new lifestyles, new purchase decision approaches, and new product and service preferences.

Some changes in the marketplace are already evident. Because the Net Generation has not been responsive to unsolicited advertising messages, for example, advertisers are developing unobtrusive campaigns that provide value through entertainment, education, or integration with other transactions. Pepsi follows this approach by offering an interactive experience consisting of games, contests, screen savers, and movie previews at its Web page. Future changes are likely to include a decline in the use of intermediaries such as travel agents, stockbrokers, and real estate agents because the Net Generation relies on the Internet, and Web sites such as Sympatico or Netscape's Netcenter, as a source of information and a means of interacting with sellers.[1]

The Net Generation is clearly changing the marketing environment. It represents a demographic shift, an economic influence, and a force likely to increase the use of digital technologies. Anticipating changes such as these and responding to them often means the difference between marketing success and failure. This chapter describes how the marketing environment has changed in the past and is likely to change in the future.

ENVIRONMENTAL SCANNING IN THE NEW MILLENNIUM

Changes in the marketing environment are a source of opportunities and threats to be managed. The process of continually acquiring information on events occurring outside the organization to identify and interpret potential trends is called **environmental scanning.**

Tracking Environmental Trends

Environmental trends typically arise from five sources: social, economic, technological, competitive, and regulatory forces. As shown in Figure 3–1 and described later in this chapter, these forces affect the marketing activities of a firm in numerous ways.

To illustrate how environmental scanning is used, consider the following trend:[2]

> Coffee industry marketers have observed that the percentage of adults who drink coffee has declined from 75 percent in 1962 to under 50 percent today. Age-specific analysis indicates that coffee consumption declined among all age groups, including 18- to 24-year-olds, despite the perception that young adults are leading a revival in coffee drinking.

What types of businesses are likely to be influenced by this trend? What future would you predict for coffee?

FIGURE 3–1
Environmental forces affecting the organization, as well as its suppliers and customers

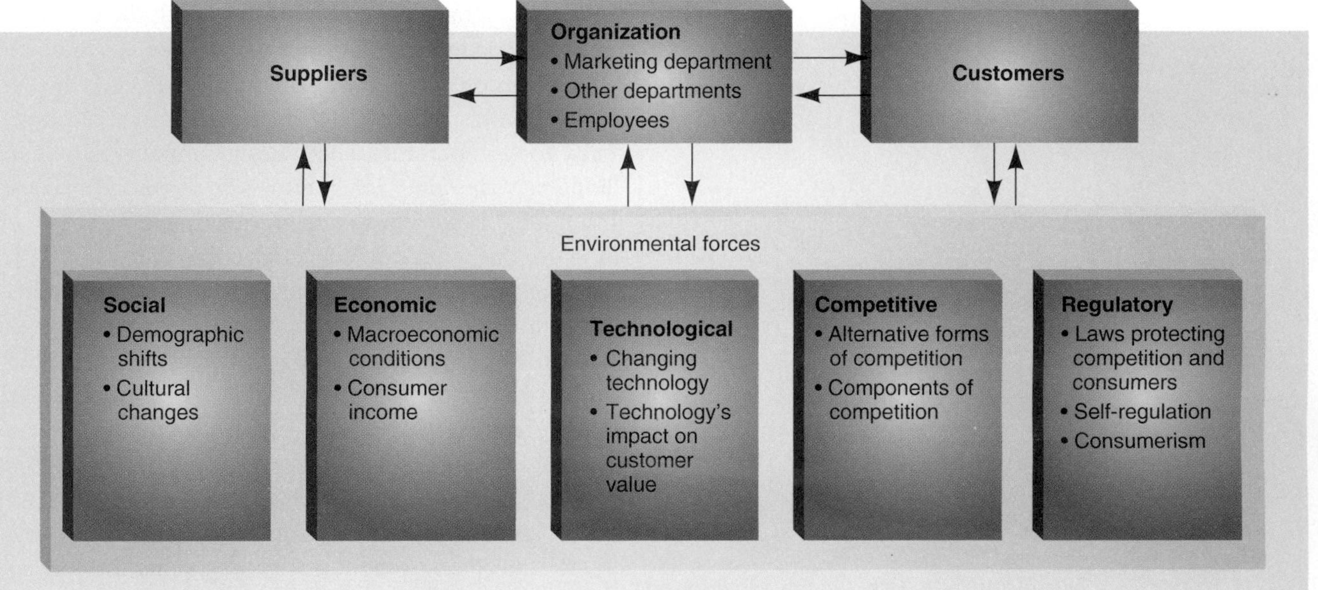

www.starbucks.com

You may have concluded that this trend is likely to influence coffee manufacturers and supermarkets. If so, you are absolutely correct—manufacturers have responded by offering new flavours, and supermarkets have added coffee boutiques and gourmet brands such as Starbucks to try to reverse the trend.[3] Predicting the future of coffee requires assumptions about the number of years the declining trend will continue and the rate of decline in various age groups. Did you consider these issues in your analysis? Because experts make different assumptions, their forecasts range from a 30 percent decline to a 13 percent increase by 2005—a range that probably includes your forecast!

Environmental scanning also involves explaining trends. Why has coffee consumption been declining? One explanation is that consumers are switching from coffee to other beverages such as soft drinks, juices, or water. Another explanation is that preferences have shifted to better-tasting but more expensive types of coffee, and consumers have reduced their use to maintain the same level of expenditure. Identifying and interpreting trends, such as the decline in coffee consumption, and developing explanations, such as those offered in this paragraph, are essential to successful environmental scanning.

An Environmental Scan of Canada

What other trends might affect marketing in the future? A firm conducting an environmental scan of Canada might uncover key trends such as those listed in Figure 3–2 for each of the five environmental factors.[4] Although the list of trends is far from complete, it reveals the breadth of an environmental scan—from population concentration in census metropolitan areas, to the growth of electronic commerce, to the emergence of "network corporations." These trends affect consumers and the businesses and nonprofit organizations that serve them. Trends such as these are covered as the five environmental forces are described in the following pages.

FIGURE 3–2
An environmental scan of Canada

ENVIRONMENTAL FORCE	TREND IDENTIFIED BY AN ENVIRONMENTAL SCAN
Social	• Movement toward "natural" and healthful products and lifestyles • Growing number and importance of older Canadians • Population concentration in census metropolitan areas • Greater desire for product simplicity and honesty in advertising • Greater value placed on education, travel, and leisure
Economic	• Dramatic growth of electronic commerce • Canadian firms adjust to crises in international markets • Public debt levels, high unemployment, and a heavy tax burden persist
Technological	• Increased use of information and communication technology • Growing focus on the Internet as consumers and businesses go online • Expanded computer power and growth of "smart" products • Growing use of electronic money or "e-cash"
Competitive	• New flexible employment agreements and growth of telecommuting • The emergence of fast, responsive "network corporations" • Mergers reduce costs through economies of scale • More international competition from emerging countries
Regulatory	• Increasing emphasis on free trade and deregulation • Greater concern for pollution and global warming • New legislation related to information collection and privacy

SOCIAL FORCES

The **social forces** of the environment include the demographic characteristics of the population, its values, and its behaviour. Changes in these forces can have a dramatic impact on marketing strategy.

Demographics

Demographics is the study of the characteristics of a human population. These characteristics include population size, population growth rate, gender, marital status, education, ethnicity, income, and so forth.

Population Size and Growth The current population of Canada is 31 million, with the population growth rate averaging slightly over one percent per year. The population is expected to be over 35 million by 2011.[5]

Age Waves Because age affects the needs, values, and purchasing habits of consumers, tracking consumers by age groupings is also part of an environmental scan. The size, habits, and relative purchasing power of various age groups is closely examined in an environmental scan.

Canadians are getting older. In 1999 the median age of the population was 35 years, which means 50 percent of the population was below that age but 50 percent was also above 35 years of age. The median age in Canada is projected to be over 40 years by 2011. The forecasted age distribution of Canada's population for 2011 is shown in Figure 3–3.[6] As you can see, over 34 percent of the population will be over the age of 50 by that time. This is a significant demographic trend that indicates the greying of Canada.

The over-50 age group—sometimes called the **mature household**—is a fast-growing age segment in Canada. In recent years, greater marketing attention has been focused on this market because people over 50 years of age control much of the *accumulated wealth* in this country—the value of net assets accumulated by households in the form of real property, financial securities, deposits, and pension assets. Many Canadian companies have responded aggressively to this important market including

FIGURE 3–3
The forcasted age distrbution of the Canadian population for the year 2011

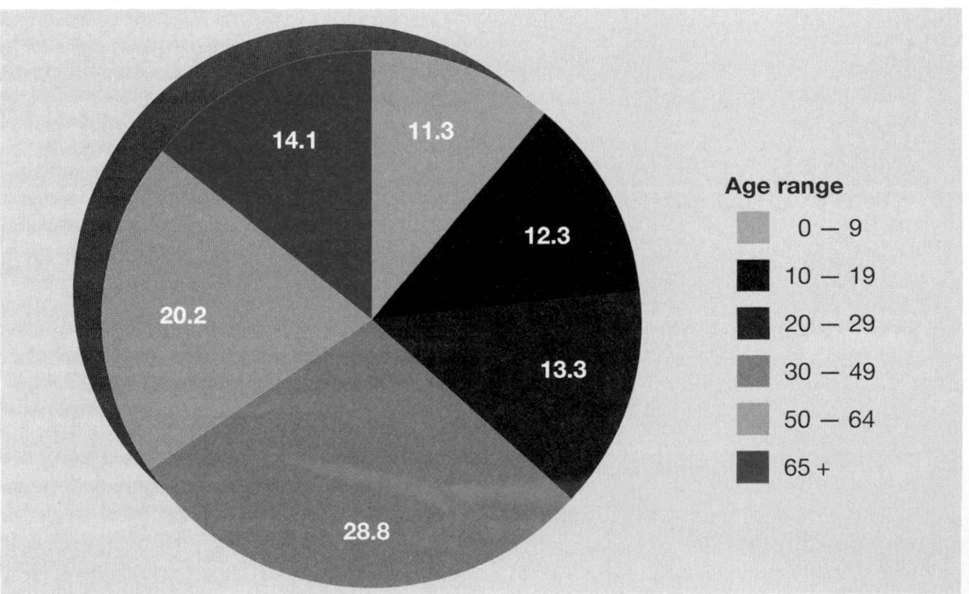

Shouldn't you live some part of your life exactly as you please?
ClubMed

Club Med promotes family vacations to aging baby boomers.

Club Med
www.clubmed.com

developing products and services specific to the mature market such as retirement communities, using older celebrities in ads, and placing larger type on product labels.[7]

A major reason for the greying of Canada is that the **baby boomers**—the generation of children born between 1946 and 1964—are growing older. As millions of boomers have aged, their participation in the workforce and their earnings have increased, making them an important consumer market. It has been estimated that this group accounts for the majority of the purchases in most consumer product and service categories. As the older boomers become part of the mature market, their buying behaviour is changing to reflect greater concern for their children's future and their own retirement. Even the younger boomers are showing greater concern about saving and financial planning.

www.leejeans.com

As a group, boomers are shifting their focus from indulgence and luxury to quality and value.[8] Companies such as Club Med and Lee jeans are refocusing their strategies to a more mature boomer market. Club Med is trying to augment its singles image by promoting family vacations and facilities with child care in addition to vacations that cater to singles and couples, and Lee is responding to an aging baby boomer with loose-fitting jeans and advertising, "You're not a kid anymore."[9]

Generation X is the group of Canadians born between 1965 and 1976. Members of Generation X (Xers) represent about 15 percent of the Canadian population. It is a generation of consumers who are not prone to extravagance and are likely to pursue lifestyles and prefer products and services that are very different from baby boomers. They are also likely to be more demanding consumers. Marketers are very much aware of this group of consumers and are interested in tracking this generation to identify the dominant consumption values of the 21st century.[10]

The **baby boomlet** refers to Canadians born in 1977 and is also described as Generation Y, or the Net Generation (described in the chapter-opening example). The boomlet generation already exerts influence on music, sports, computers, and video game purchases. Later in the 21st century, this group will influence markets, attitudes, and society much like the baby boomers do now and Generation X will do soon.[11]

The Canadian Family The types of families in Canada are changing in both size and structure. The average family size in Canada is three persons. In 1971 one in three Canadian families consisted of the once-typical scenario of a husband working outside the home, with a wife inside the home with their children. Today, only one in seven families fall into this category. The dual-income family is the norm in Canada, representing over 61 percent of all husband-wife families.[12]

About 50 percent of all first marriages in Canada end in divorce. Thus, the single-parent family is becoming more typical and, according to researchers, more acceptable to Canadian society.[13] But the majority of divorced people eventually remarry, giving rise to the **blended family,** one formed by the merging into a single household of two previously separated units. Today, many Canadians are finding themselves as a stepparent, stepchild, stepsibling, or some other member of a blended family. Hallmark Cards specially designs cards and verses for such blended families. Still, many people do not remarry, and single-parent families represent close to 15 percent of all family units in Canada.[14]

Population Shifts Since the mid-1970s there has been a major shift in the Canadian population from rural to urban areas. In fact, over 80 percent of Canadians are urban dwellers.[15] Most Canadians live in **census metropolitan areas** (CMAs), geographic labour market areas having a population of 100 000 persons or more. The top 25 CMAs in Canada include cities such as Toronto, Montreal, Vancouver, Ottawa, and Edmonton, and account for more than 60 percent of the Canadian population. With the concentration of the population in or near CMAs, marketers can reach large segments of the market efficiently and effectively. Some experts have predicted that by the year 2010, most Canadians will be located in seven or eight city-states and be within easy reach of most marketers.[16]

There has not been much of a shift in how the population is distributed across the country. Almost 62 percent of Canadians live in two provinces, Ontario and Quebec. Over the next 10 years, population growth is expected to increase in Ontario, Quebec, Alberta, British Columbia, Manitoba, and Saskatchewan, and either decline or stabilize in the other provinces and territories.

Regional Marketing A recent trend within marketing focuses not only on the shifting of consumers geographically, such as the move from rural to urban areas, but also on the differences in their product preferences based on where they live. This concept has been referred to as **regional marketing,** which is developing marketing plans designed to reflect the specific area differences in taste preferences, perceived needs, or interests. Given the vastness of Canada, many marketers view the country as being composed of regions such as Atlantic Canada, Quebec, Ontario, Western Canada, and British Columbia. In Chapter 10, you will learn more about this approach to the market referred to as *geographic segmentation.*

www.colgate-palmolive.com

Because of differences in economics, topography, and natural resources, consumption patterns in the regions of Canada tend to differ. Some products and brands that sell successfully in one region do not do well in another. Strategies and tactics to sell them may also differ. Colgate-Palmolive found that marketing their Arctic Power "cold water" clothes detergent on an "energy-savings" dimension worked well in Quebec but not in the West where cold-water washing was perceived to be easier on clothes. The company adjusted its marketing strategy accordingly.

Technology has aided marketers in understanding the variations in regional preferences. Computerized cash registers, for example, have allowed companies to coordinate and analyze sales data for geographic regions, determining what does and does not sell well in various regions. Pepsi-Cola can be a market leader in one region while Coca-Cola can be the leader in another. And, with advances in direct marketing approaches (Chapter 19), this focus on regional marketing allows for better targeting of ads and products. Still, the ability to market on a regional basis not only depends on the variance in regional preferences, but also on the sufficiency of size of the region and the cost of localized efforts. Often, regional or localized efforts can be more costly than one simple national effort. But, a better understanding of the geographic regions of Canada and any resultant differences in consumer preferences can lead to more successful marketing. For example, while Harvey's Restaurants sells the same products across Canada, it uses original French-language advertising for Quebec featuring Bernard Fortin, a high-profile and well-liked actor in Quebec. The uniqueness of the campaign has paid off for Harvey's. Sears Canada featured celebrities on the covers of

Benetton is one company that recognizes ethnic diversity in Canada.

its catalogues. For the English catalogue, Michelle Wright graced the front, while Quebec pop singer Julie Masse appeared on the French version. And, finally, Pizza Hut Canada runs a Quebec-specific TV spot for a Quebec-specific product: a medium-size stuffed crust pizza.

Ethnic Diversity While we often think of Canada as consisting of French and English Canadians, close to 3 out of 10 Canadians are of neither French nor British descent. While the majority of the non-British, non-French population are of European descent, there has been growth in other ethnic groups and visible minorities. In fact, close to 70 percent of all immigrants to Canada today are classified as visible minorities, primarily people from China, Southeast Asia, Africa, and India. Hong Kong Chinese and Southeast Asians are the fastest-growing ethnic groups in Canada, representing close to three percent of the Canadian population. Visible minorities are projected to represent close to 18 percent of the Canadian population by the year 2001.[17]

Much of the ethnic population can be found in major metropolitan areas such as Toronto, Vancouver, Montreal, Calgary, and Edmonton. Close to 20 percent of the populations in those areas register their native language as something other than English or French. Marketers have recognized the growing ethnic diversity in Canada. Many companies such as the Royal Bank, Benetton, Ultramar, and Bell Canada are putting "ethnic faces" in mainstream advertising. Many other companies such as Cantel and American Express devote marketing efforts to cater specifically to these ethnic groups, which includes advertising in their language and providing personnel who speak their language. Recently, the Vancouver Grizzlies basketball team has begun targeting Asian-Canadians as part of the marketing effort, capitalizing on Asian fan interest in the NBA.[18]

www.royalbank.com

Culture

A second social force, **culture,** incorporates the set of values, ideas, and attitudes of a homogeneous group of people that are transmitted from one generation to the next. Culture includes both material and abstract elements, so monitoring cultural trends in

Canada is difficult but important for effective marketing. We will deal with noteworthy cultural trends in Canada in this section. Cross-cultural analysis needed for successful global marketing is discussed in Chapter 5.

The Changing Roles of Women and Men One of the most notable changes in Canada over the past three decades has been the change in the roles of women and men in society. These changes have had a significant impact on marketing practices. Distinctions between the traditional gender roles assigned to females and males have become blurred. One of the major trends has been the emergence of women as an integral part of the workforce. Nationally more than 65 percent of women work outside the home. With more women working outside the home, the number of tasks to do is expanding while the time available to do them is shrinking. This phenomenon is often referred to as *time poverty.* As a result, the male spouse has had to assume certain tasks. More men are shopping for groceries and assuming greater roles in child care and housekeeping duties. As consumers' lives become more hectic, supermarkets are finding that one of their hottest-selling categories is frozen, prepared entrees. Stouffer's, whose parent company is Nestlé Canada, says entrees are the fastest-growing segment of the frozen food category in Canada because people are time-poor and need quick, convenient meal solutions.

Marketers are becoming more aware of the necessity not to stereotype female or male behaviour and preferences. *Parents* magazine, for example, has revised its coverage to reflect a growing male readership.[19] Moreover, in an effort to assist consumers in overcoming their time poverty, many marketers offer greater convenience such as express lanes at checkouts, longer store hours, drive-through windows, and delivery services.

Changing Attitudes and Values Culture also includes attitudes and values. In recent years, Canadians have experienced some major attitudinal changes toward work, lifestyles, and consumption. There is a growing sense that the Puritan work ethic of "I live to work" may be redefined as "I work to live." Work is now more likely seen as a means to an end—recreation, leisure, and entertainment. Canadian consumers are placing more emphasis on quality of life as opposed to work, which has contributed to a growth in sales of products such as sports equipment, vacations, electronic entertainment equipment, and easily prepared foods.

There is greater concern for health and well-being, as evidenced by the level of fitness activity and sports participation in Canada. Firms like Nike and Reebok are profiting from this trend. Canadians are also more concerned about their diets, especially because of the linkage between diet and health. Growth in sales of no-fat, or low-fat, and cholesterol-free foods is evidence of this concern. The beverage industry has also seen major changes. Consumers are drinking healthier products including more bottled water and juices as opposed to traditional soft drinks. Canadians buy over 100 million litres of spring water from the grocery stores annually as well as healthful beverages of all kinds. Northpole Beverages Co. of Montreal, for example, sells a fruit-flavoured beverage with ginseng called $E = MC^2$. And Clearly Canadian Beverages of Vancouver markets a new super-oxygenated water called O_2, which is scientifically formulated for active individuals.[20]

Health-conscious Canadians are also buying medical self-diagnostic kits. Lifescan Canada Ltd. of Burnaby, BC, markets a variety of self-testing kits that can monitor cholesterol levels or test for colorectal cancer. The company suggests that well-educated and aging consumers are taking greater responsibility for their health care and are now into self-diagnosis. Planta Dei Plant Medicines Inc. of Nackawic, NB, is also capitalizing on the health-consciousness trend in Canada. The company markets phytopharmaceuticals—medicines made from medicinal plants—via 2000 retail pharmacies across Canada.

Responding to consumer demand for value, Sobeys offers a value-based line of products that come with a low-price guarantee.

www.holidayinn.com

A change in consumption orientation is also apparent. Conspicuous consumption marked much of the past 20 years. Today, and for the foreseeable future, **value consciousness**—or the concern for obtaining the best quality, features, and performance of a product or service for a given price—will drive consumption behaviour. Innovative marketers have responded to this new orientation in numerous ways. Holiday Inn Worldwide has opened Holiday Express Hotels designed to offer comfortable accommodations with room rates lower than Holiday Inns. Sobeys, Inc., one of Canada's top food retailers, now offers consumers its Signal brand of products, which is a private-label, value-based line that comes with a low-price guarantee.[21] Even Canada's major banks are recognizing the value-consciousness trend and are offering consumers credit cards with lower interest rates and value-added enhancements such as frequent flyer programs and cashback offers.[22]

CONCEPT CHECK

1. What is environmental scanning?
2. What is a census metropolitan area?
3. What are the marketing implications of blended families?

ECONOMIC FORCES

Another component of the environmental scan, the **economy,** pertains to the income, expenditures, and resources that affect the cost of running an organization or a household.

We'll consider two aspects of these economic forces: a macroeconomic view of the marketplace and a microeconomic perspective of consumer income.

Macroeconomic Conditions

Of particular concern at the macroeconomic level is the inflationary or recessionary state of the nation's economy, whether actual or perceived, by consumers or businesses. In an inflationary economy, the cost to produce and buy products and services escalates as prices increase. From a marketing standpoint, if prices rise faster than consumer incomes, the number of items consumers can buy decreases.

Whereas inflation is a period of price increases, recession is a time of slow economic activity. Businesses decrease production, unemployment rises, and many consumers have less money to spend. The Canadian economy experienced recessions in the early 1970s, early 1980s, and early 1990s.

Assessing consumer expectations of an inflationary and recessionary economy is an important element of environmental scanning. Consumer spending, which accounts for two-thirds of Canadian economic activity, is affected by expectations of the future. Surveys of consumer expectations are tracked over time by researchers, who ask questions such as "Do you expect to be better or worse off financially a year from now?" Surveyors record the share of positive and negative responses to this question and related ones to develop an index, sometimes called a consumer confidence or consumer sentiment index. The higher the index, the more favourable are consumer expectations. Many firms evaluate such indexes in order to plan production levels. Chrysler, for example, uses such indexes to plan its automobile production levels in order to avoid overproducing cars during a recessionary economy.

Consumer Income

The microeconomic trends in terms of consumer income are important issues for marketers. Having a product that meets the needs of consumers may be of little value if they are unable to purchase it. A consumer's ability to buy is related to income, which consists of gross, disposable, and discretionary components.

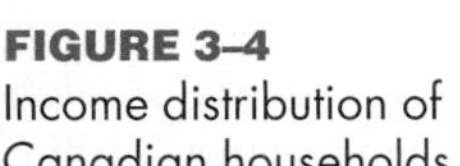

FIGURE 3–4
Income distribution of Canadian households

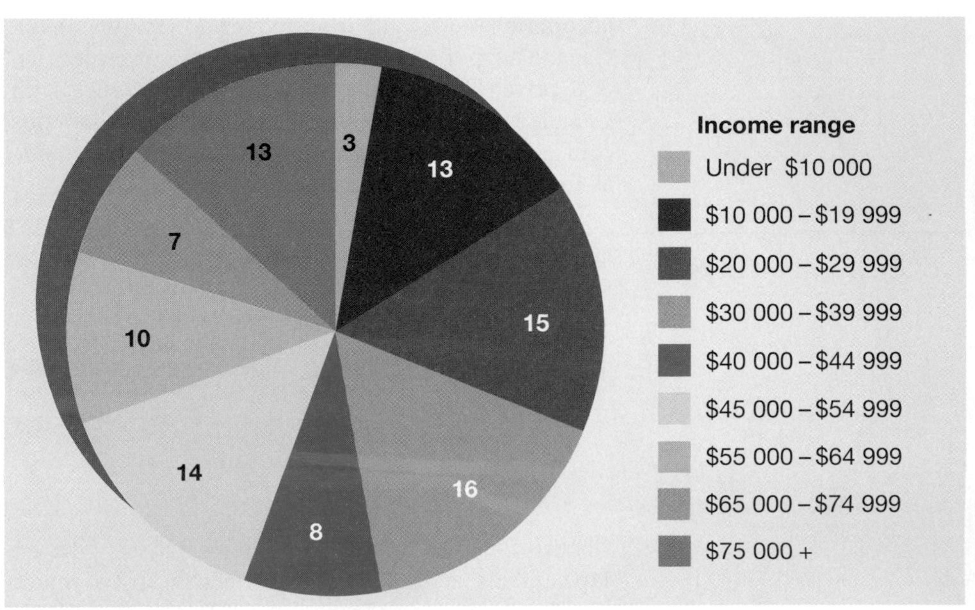

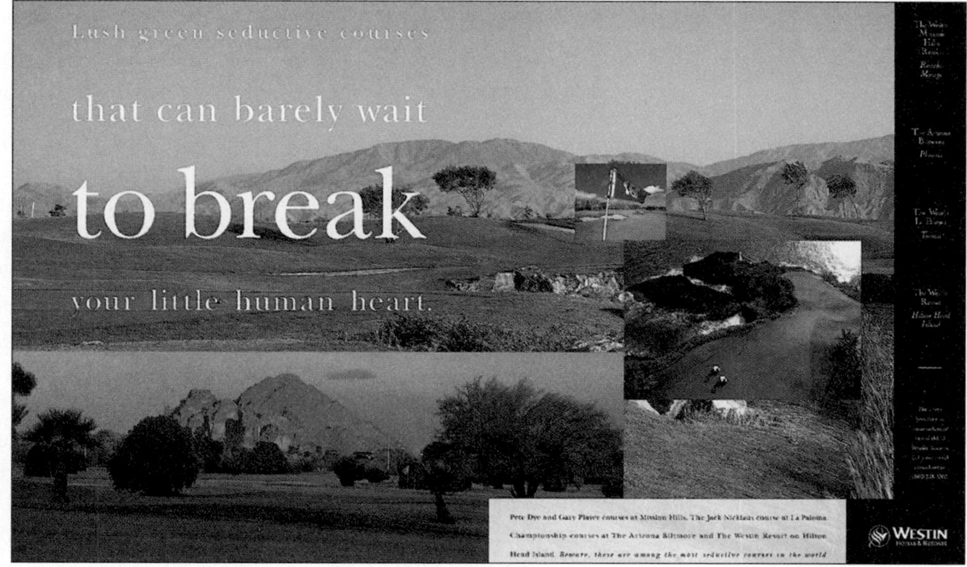

As consumers' discretionary income increases, so does the enjoyment of pleasure travel.

Westin Hotels & Resorts
www.westin.com

Gross Income The total amount of money made in one year by a person, household, or family unit is referred to as **gross income.** Figure 3–4 shows the distribution of annual income among Canadian families.[23] Average gross family income in Canada is slightly over $57 000. But family income in Canada varies by province as well as by the education level and profession of the head(s) of the family. For example, the majority of families earning $75 000 or more are headed by university graduates.

Disposable Income The second income component, **disposable income,** is money a consumer has left after paying taxes to use for necessities such as food, shelter, and clothing. Thus, if taxes rise at a faster rate than does disposable income, consumers must economize. In recent years consumers' allocation of income has shifted. For example, the proportion of disposable income devoted to eating in the home has increased, while the proportion devoted to eating out has decreased. Two environmental factors account for this: the recession of the early 1990s caused people to cut back on expenses such as eating out, and many baby-boom households are in the midst of their child-raising years, causing increased spending on food at home.[24]

Discretionary Income The third component of income is **discretionary income,** the money that remains after paying taxes and necessities. Discretionary income could be used for luxury items such as vacations at a Westin resort. An obvious problem in defining discretionary versus disposable income is determining what is a luxury and what is a necessity. Observation can be a way to make this determination—if a family has Royal Doulton china, Rolex watches, and Lexus automobiles, one could assume that they have, or had, discretionary income. Still, it is important to note that a product defined as a necessity by one individual may be viewed as a luxury by another. For example, some Canadians view an automatic dishwasher as a necessity while others see it as a luxury item.

TECHNOLOGICAL FORCES

Our society is in a period of technological dramatic change. **Technology,** a major environmental force, refers to inventions or innovations from applied science or engineering research. Each new wave of technological innovation can replace existing products and companies. Do you recognize the items pictured on page 84 and what they may replace?

Technology of Tomorrow

Technological change is the result of research, so it is difficult to predict. Some of the most dramatic technological changes occurring now, however, include the following:

1. The declining cost and size, and increasing power, of microprocessors.
2. The convergence of television, personal computer, and telephone technologies, including digital personal communications services (PCS) that provide paging and e-mail on a digital cellphone with a display screen.
3. The pervasive trend toward "connectedness" through the World Wide Web.
4. The emergence of biotechnology.

These trends in technology are seen in today's marketplace. The power of microprocessors has doubled every 18 months for the past 25 years—suggesting that microprocessors at least 10 times more powerful than today's Pentium will be available in just five years (for about $25!). The Internet already offers electronic magazines, shopping, and advertising, and between 20 000 and 25 000 new Web sites are being added each month. Other technologies such as satellite disks, DVD, MP3, HDTV, and voice recognition software are likely to replace or substitute for existing technologies such as cable TV, video tapes, CDs, low-resolution TV, and manual operations such as typing.[25]

Technology's Impact on Customer Value

Advances in technology are having important effects on marketing. First, the cost of technology is plummeting, causing the customer value assessment of technology-based products to focus on other dimensions such as quality, service, and relationships. When Microsoft introduced Windows 95, for example, it gave away 500 000 copies of the software program so customers could try it and later buy upgrades. A similar approach is used by many cellular telephone companies, which charge little or nothing for the telephone if the purchase leads to a cellular service contract.[26]

Technology also provides value through the development of new products. Oldsmobile now offers customers an auto-navigation system that uses satellite signals to help the driver reach any destination. Under development are radarlike collision-avoidance systems that disengage cruise control, reduce the engine speed, and even apply the brakes.[27] Other new products likely to be available soon include a "smart ski" with an embedded microprocessor that will adjust the flexibility of the ski to snow

Technological change leads to new products. What products might be replaced by these innovations?

Examples of a recycling program by Ford and a precycling program by Lever.

conditions; injectable health monitors that will send glucose, oxygen, and other clinical information to a wrist-watch-like monitor; and electronic books that will allow you to download any volume and view it on pages coated with electronic "ink" and embedded electrodes.[28]

Technology can also change existing products and the ways they are produced. Many companies are using technological developments to allow *recycling* products through the manufacturing cycle several times. In Germany, Ford emphasizes that its cars are assembled with parts that can be recycled. The ad above showing a child's toy, exclaims, "I was a car" in the headline. Another approach is *precycling*—efforts by manufacturers to reduce waste by decreasing the amount of packaging they use. The development of new packaging materials, for example, has allowed DuPont to introduce a "minisip" collapsible pouch as an alternative to milk cartons in school lunch programs.[29]

Information Technology

Ultimately, the most important developments for marketers may be those related to information technology. Improved methods of collecting, storing, analyzing, and distributing information about consumers will allow marketers to better understand and serve customers. To provide customized service it is important to know who customers are, their product or service preferences, their individual approach to interacting with the company, and how they make a purchase. MCI has developed a sophisticated customer service system that electronically identifies callers, assesses their account history, and routes priority customers to get first-class treatment within three rings! In the future, smart software may interview customers via E-mail and automatically respond to simple questions, problems, or orders or make connections with a real person to deal with more difficult topics.[30]

In many cases, consumers see and enjoy the benefits of information technology used by marketers. Information technology can often provide customers with improved convenience, speed, accessibility, and efficiency. For example, because of advances in information technology, Canadian banks can offer their customers automated telephone banking (ATB) where a customer can receive cash over the phone by transferring funds to a "smart card," like a debit card.[31] Information technology also allows banking customers to check interest rates 24 hours a day, and even apply for a loan, electronically, in the comfort of their home on a Saturday night. And, for those of you in the stock market, you know you can get instant information about your portfolio thanks to information technology.

COMPETITIVE FORCES

Another component of the environmental scan is competition. **Competition** refers to the alternative firms that could provide a product to satisfy a specific market's needs. There are various forms of competition, and each company must consider its present and potential competitors in designing its marketing strategy.

Alternative Forms of Competition

Four basic forms of competition comprise a continuum: pure competition, monopolistic competition, oligopoly, and monopoly. Chapter 14 contains further discussions on pricing practices under these four forms of competition.

At one end of the continuum is *pure competition,* in which every company has a similar product. Companies that deal in commodities common to agribusiness (for example, wheat, rice, and other grains) often are in a pure competition position in which distribution (in the sense of shipping products) is important but other elements of marketing have little impact.

In the second point on the continuum, *monopolistic competition,* the many sellers compete with their products on a substitutable basis. For example, if the price of coffee rises too much, consumers may switch to tea. Coupons or frequent sales are marketing tactics often used in monopolistic competition.

Oligopoly, a common industry structure, occurs when a few companies control the majority of industry sales. Because there are few sellers in an oligopolistic situation, price competition among firms is not desirable because it would lead to reduced revenue for all producers. Instead, nonprice competition is common, which means competing on other dimensions of the marketing mix such as product quality, distribution, and/or promotion. Canada is sometimes referred to by some economists as the "land of oligopoly," because it has several major industries that can be considered oligopolistic including the airline industry and the banking industry.

The final point on the continuum, *monopoly,* occurs when only one firm sells the product or service. It has been common for producers of goods and services considered essential to a community: water, electricity, or telephone service. Typically, marketing plays a small role in a monopolistic setting because it is regulated by a provincial or the federal government. Government control usually seeks to ensure price protection for the buyer. Historically, there was no competition in the long-distance telephone business in Canada, but deregulation has given rise to new entrants such as MCI, AT&T Canada, and Sprint. Bell Canada and the various provincial telephone companies across Canada now must compete in a different marketing environment, a monopolistic-competitive one. Marketing has now assumed a more important role at the traditional telephone companies. More recent deregulation of the communications industry has now opened the local telephone services market in Canada. For a century, the telephone companies providing local service had a monopoly. This has now ended and local providers, long-distance carriers, and cable TV firms now compete in each other's markets.[32]

www.bell.ca

Components of Competition

In developing a marketing strategy, companies must consider the components that drive competition: entry, bargaining power of buyers and suppliers, existing rivalries (domestic and foreign), and substitution possibilities.[33] Scanning the environment requires a look at all of them. These relate to a firm's marketing mix decisions and may be used to create a barrier to entry, to increase brand awareness, or to intensify a fight for market share.

Entry In considering competition, a firm must assess the likelihood of new entrants. Additional producers increase industry capacity and tend to lower prices. A company scanning its environment must consider the possible **barriers to entry** for other firms, which are business practices or conditions that make it difficult for new firms to enter the market. Barriers to entry can be in the form of capital requirements, promotional expenditures, product identity, distribution access, or switching costs. The higher the expense of the barrier, the more likely it will deter new entrants. For example, IBM once created a switching cost barrier for organizations that considered Apple Computer equipment because IBM had a different programming language for its machines.

Power of Buyers and Suppliers A competitive analysis must consider the power of buyers and sellers. Powerful buyers exist when they are few in number, there are low switching costs, or the product represents a significant share of the buyer's total costs. This last factor leads the buyer to exert significant pressure for price competition. A supplier gains power when the product is critical to the buyer and when it has built up the switching costs.

Existing Competition and Substitutes Competitive pressures among existing firms depend on the rate of industry growth. In slow-growth settings, competition is more heated for any possible gains in market share. High fixed costs also create competitive pressure for firms to fill production capacity. For example, many Canadian universities are increasing their advertising and public relations activities to fill classrooms, which represent a high fixed cost.

The New Look in Canadian Corporations

Competition has had two other important effects on Canadian corporations: (1) the use of the Internet as a way of doing business and (2) the restructuring of corporations.

Competing on the Internet The Internet is changing customers' expectations about convenience, price, quality, and service. As a result, traditional bureaucratic, hierarchical organizations are learning that a new model—the "network organization" or "e-corporation"—is evolving as a new form of competition. These firms combine computers, the Web, and software to change everything about the way they operate. One of the most visible examples of the change is in the brokerage business. Literally, billions of dollars worth of securities are traded through a variety of brokerage firms that offer trading via their Web sites. Schwab had no sales on the Web in 1995. Today, more than $4 billion worth of securities are traded through its Web page every week. This has not gone unnoticed by Schwab's competitors. Merrill Lynch, for example, has now entered the electronic trading business. Firms such as Schwab, Fidelity, and E-Trade offer their customers access to their accounts through the Internet, allow them to obtain research and information, place buy and sell orders, and receive confirmation in real time.

www.ml.com

The Internet is creating a new form of competition that will affect every industry and business. Already over 400 000 companies have created a presence on the Web, and while customers are changing the way they buy, workers and managers are changing too. Sales and service people are becoming consultants accessible by any customer. Managers are becoming coordinators of information, and businesses are beginning to operate with teams specializing in a narrow group of customer's needs. Industries to watch for rapid change include vacation travel, books, music, entertainment, computer hardware, computer software, and information services.[34] Canadian researchers, for example, have a new tool in online information services known as Electric Library Canada. Schools, businesses, and home users can have access to an extensive, full-text collection of current and archived information on virtually any topic without stepping outside.[35]

WEB LINK To Merge or Not to Merge?

Bank of Montreal and the Royal Bank had recently reached an agreement to merge their companies. The banks cited increased competition, particularly, foreign competition from firms such as Citibank, ING, Fidelity, and Wells Fargo, and greater customer demand for better products and services as key reasons behind the merger. However, some competitors, as well as the federal government, didn't believe that the merger was necessary nor beneficial for the marktetplace. So, at the time of writing this Web Link, the merger has appeared to have stalled. Visit the Web site set up by the two banks at www.proposed-merger.com and get the latest news. Why do you think the government turned thumbs down on the deal? What is your opinion on the merger?

Restructuring Corporations Although the process is known by various names—reengineering, streamlining, or **restructuring**—the result is the same: striving for more efficient corporations that can compete globally. For many firms, restructuring means reducing duplicate efforts in multiple company locations, closing or changing unprofitable plants and offices, and often laying off hundreds or thousands of employees. For example, Ford Motor Company recently merged its product development operations, refurbished seven plants, and reduced the number of managers by 20 percent. The result has been an improvement in efficiency—Ford has reduced the amount of time needed to get an engine from design to testing from 24 months to 100 days. Another result, however, has been a huge reduction in the number of middle managers in the workforce. Employers are shifting from a philosophy of unconditional lifetime employment to one of "lifelong employability." This view is based on the idea that employers have an obligation to provide an opportunity of self-improvement and employees have an obligation to take charge of their own careers.[36]

Another approach to restructuring has been through mergers, acquisitions, and takeovers. The past few years have seen numerous well-publicized mega-mergers including Daimler-Chrysler, BMW and Land Rover, Ford and Volvo as well as one major merger in the Canadian banking industry that has apparently stalled at this time. Read the accompanying Web Link to find out more about this not-so-done deal. There have also been many smaller and not so well-known acquisitions including Markham, Ontario-based Yogen Fruz Worldwide Inc.'s acquisition of two Georgia-based ice-cream companies that will provide Yogen access to outlets located in Wal-Mart stores. What is the explanation? In general, firms are striving for market dominance by ensuring control of distribution channels, access to markets, and cost reduction through economies of scale. Businesses are also discovering that information technology will allow effective management of large and complex organizations. Experts debate whether these mergers are good for the economy. While firms that dominate a market might command higher prices, they may also be vulnerable to faster, customer-focused entrepreneurs.[37]

www.yogenfruz.com

CONCEPT CHECK

1. What is the difference between a consumer's disposable and discretionary income?
2. In pure competition there are ____________________ number of sellers.
3. What is a network organization?

REGULATORY FORCES

For any organization, marketing and broader business decisions are constrained, directed, and influenced by regulatory forces. **Regulation** consists of restrictions the provincial and federal laws place on business with respect to the conduct of its activities. Regulation exists to protect companies as well as consumers. Much of the regulation from the federal and provincial levels has been passed to ensure competition and fair business practices. For consumers, the focus of legislation is to protect them from unfair trade practices and ensure their safety.

Protecting Competition and Consumers

Legislation and regulations exist in Canada at all three levels of government—federal, provincial, and municipal—to protect and encourage a competitive environment, which is deemed desirable because it permits the consumer to determine which competitor will succeed and which will fail.

The Competition Act The key legislation designed to protect competition and consumers in Canada is the **Competition Act,** which replaced the Combines Investigation Act. The Combines legislation, in effect since 1923, has been found to be rather ineffectual. The Competition Act was introduced in two stages, in 1975 and 1986. The purpose of the Competition Act is:

> to maintain and encourage competition in Canada in order to promote the efficiency and adaptability of the Canadian economy, in order to expand opportunities for Canadian participation in world markets while at the same time recognizing the role of foreign competition in Canada, in order to ensure that small- and medium-sized enterprises have an equitable opportunity to participate in the Canadian economy and in order to provide consumers with competitive prices and product choices.[38]

In essence, the act is designed to protect and to balance the interests of competitors and consumers. The Bureau of Competition Policy, which is part of the federal department of Consumer and Corporate Affairs, is responsible for administering and enforcing the provisions of the act. The act contains both criminal and noncriminal provisions.

Criminal offences under Part VI of the act include conspiracy (e.g., price-fixing), bid-rigging, discriminatory and predatory pricing, price maintenance, and misleading or deceptive marketing practices such as double-ticketing or bait-and-switch selling.

Noncriminal reviewable matters under Part VIII of the act include mergers, abuse of dominant position, refusal to deal, consignment selling, exclusive dealing, tied selling, market restriction and delivered pricing. The Director of the Bureau of Competition Policy refers these matters to the Competition Tribunal under noncriminal law standards. The tribunal was established when the act took effect and is governed by the Competition Tribunal Act. The tribunal adjudicates all reviewable matters under the act.

Consumer and Corporate Affairs Canada is responsible for most of the legislation affecting business practices in Canada. Figure 3–5 lists the more significant federal legislation that protects competition and consumers in Canada. Marketers must also be cognizant of the fact that, in addition to federal laws and regulations, there are many more at the provincial level. Many provinces have their own departments of consumer affairs in order to administer any such legislation and regulations enacted on the provincial government level.

Unfortunately, the laws and regulations at the provincial level vary from province to province. A marketer may find it necessary to adapt some aspect of the marketing mix or some broader business practice depending on the province. For example, in Quebec there are specific laws dealing with store signage, packaging, and labelling. Additionally, advertising directed toward children is prohibited in Quebec. Many

FIGURE 3–5
Major federal legislation designed to protect competition and consumers

Bank Cost Borrowing Act
Bankruptcy Act
Bills of Exchange Act
Board of Trade Act
Broadcasting Act
Canada Agricultural Products Standards Act
Canada Cooperative Association Act
Canada Corporations Act
Canada Dairy Products Act
Canadian Human Rights Act
Competition Act
Consumer Packaging and Labelling Act
Copyright Act
Criminal Code
Department of Consumer and Corporate Affairs Act
Electricity Inspection Act and Gas Inspection Act
Fish Inspection Act
Food and Drugs Act
Hazardous Products Act
Income Tax Act
Industrial Design Act
Maple Products Industry Act
Motor Vehicle Safety Act
Offical Languages Act
Patent Act
Precious Metals Marketing Act
Small Loans Act
Standards Council of Canada Act
Textile Labelling Act
The Interest Act
Timber Marketing Act
Trade Marks Act
True Labelling Act
Weights and Measures Act
Winding-up Act

provinces, including Quebec, also have consumer protection acts and/or business or trade practices acts.

Self-Regulation

The government has provided much legislation to create a competitive business climate and protect the consumer. An alternative to government control is **self-regulation,** where an industry attempts to police itself. The Canadian Broadcasting Association, whose members include major television networks and radio stations across the country, has a code of ethics that helps govern the conduct of its members in terms of protecting the consumer against deceptive trade practices such as misleading advertising. Similarly, the Advertising Standards Council, the self-regulatory arm of the Canadian Advertising Foundation, has established the Canadian Code of Advertising Standards for its members to follow. The members of this organization consist of major advertising agencies that are responsible for allocating the bulk of advertising dollars in Canada. The Canadian Radio-Television and Telecommunications Commission, the federal agency responsible for licensing and regulating broadcasting in Canada, is in favour of greater industry self-regulation.

www.cdma.org

The Canadian Direct Marketing Association, whose members represent 80 percent of direct-marketing sales in Canada, has mandated that its members comply with the consumers' right to privacy and honour consumers who request not to be contacted by telephone or mail for selling purposes. Critics argue that telemarketers in Canada demonstrate what is wrong with self-regulation efforts: noncompliance by members and enforcement (see the accompanying Ethics and Social Responsibility Alert).

Another well-known self-regulatory group is the Better Business Bureau (BBB). This organization is a voluntary alliance of companies whose goal is to help maintain fair business practices. Although the BBB has no legal power, it does try to use "moral suasion" to get members to comply with its regulations.

Consumerism

Regulation by government and self-regulation by industry help in protecting the consumer in the marketplace. But the consumer can also play a direct and active role. **Consumerism** is a movement to increase the influence, power, and the rights of con-

ETHICS

ETHICS AND SOCIAL RESPONSIBILITY ALERT

All Is Not Right With Telemarketing

Telemarketing does not have a good image with most consumers. In fact, survey after survey shows that the majority of consumers asked feel telemarketing is an invasion of privacy, is an offensive way to market, and a waste of the consumer's time. Why are many Canadians turned off by telemarketers? In some cases, there are telemarketers who engage in illegal and deceptive practices as well unethical behaviour. For example, take the case of a telemarketing company who phones consumers and tells them they have won prizes. The consumers are then asked to pay the shipping and handling costs for the prizes, the cost of which greatly exceeds the real costs of shipping and handling as well as the value of the prize.

In another case, consider telemarketing company representatives who lead consumers to believe they are volunteers requesting donations for a charity. In fact, that are paid fundraisers who are working on commission. What about a telemarketer who uses a telemail program where a consumer receives a direct-mail piece and is asked to phone an 800-number for further information? Unknown to the consumer, the telemarketer uses an automatic number identification or caller ID intrusion system that identifies the incoming caller's number without their knowledge or consent. If the consumer does not buy the product or service initially, the company now has the consumer's telephone number and begins recalling the consumer in an attempt to sell them. The telemarketer also has an opportunity to capture and sell consumers' unlisted telephone numbers.

In many cases, they are telemarketers who are simply guilty of deception, legally, and in other cases, engaging in unethical, but perhaps not illegal practices. This has not only tarnished the image of reputable telemarketers but all other professional marketers. Do you have any personal experiences with a telemarketer who has engaged in an illegal or unethical practice? What can be done about these unethical telemarketers?

sumers in dealing with institutions. Modern consumerism in Canada and the United States really began in the 1960s. U.S. President John F. Kennedy, in a speech entitled "Consumer Bill of Rights," outlined four basic consumer rights: (1) the right to safety, (2) the right to be informed, (3) the right to choose, and (4) the right to be heard. Although not passed as laws, these proclaimed rights serve as the basis for modern consumerism. Shortly after President Kennedy's Consumer Bill of Rights was unveiled in the United States, the Canadian government formed the Department of Consumer and Corporate Affairs, making it the agency responsible for protecting consumers and regulating corporate activities.

Canada also has many independent consumer organizations that advance the cause of consumerism. The Consumers Association of Canada (CAC) is the largest consumer group working on behalf of the Canadian consumer. The CAC serves as a channel for supplying consumers' views to government and industry, providing consumer information, and studying consumer problems and presenting recommended solutions to those problems. In addition to ensuring that the four original consumer rights are protected, the consumer movement of the 1990s also includes consumer demands for environmentally safe products and ethical and socially responsible business practices.

CONCEPT CHECK

1. The ________________ Act is the most important legislation designed to protect competition and consumers in Canada.
2. An alternative to legislation protecting competition and consumers is self-
   ____________.
3. What is consumerism?

SUMMARY

1 The population in Canada is estimated at 31 million. The population is aging, and the number of traditional families as seen in the 1950s is diminishing. The dual-income family is now the norm in Canada and a blended family structure is becoming more common.

2 It is estimated that close to 80 percent of Canadians are urban dwellers, with most living in census metropolitan areas (CMAs). Regional marketing, developing marketing mixes designed to reflect the specific geographic area differences in taste preferences, perceived needs, or interests is something Canadian marketers must consider.

3 Canada is becoming more ethnically diverse, including recent growth in the population of visible minorities.

4 Culture represents abstract values and material possessions. Values are changing toward work, quality of life, the roles of women and men, and consumption.

5 Disposable income is the number of dollars left after taxes. Discretionary income is the money consumers have after purchasing their necessities.

6 Technology increases customer value by reducing the cost of products, providing new products, and improving existing products. The most important new development for marketers may be advances in information technology that allows increasingly customized service.

7 Competition has had two major effects on Canadian corporations: (*a*) the use of the Internet as a way of doing business and (*b*) restructuring through mergers to improve efficiency.

8 For any organization, marketing and broader business decisions are constrained, directed, and influenced by regulatory forces. The most important legislation in Canada designed to protect competition and consumers is the Competition Act.

9 An alternative to government control is self-regulation, where an industry attempts to police itself. The effectiveness of self-regulation is coming under greater scrutiny.

10 The consumer can also play a direct and active role in influencing what happens in the marketplace. Consumerism is a movement to increase the influence, power, and the rights of consumers in dealing with institutions. Modern consumers are demanding more environmentally safe products and ethical and socially responsible business practices.

KEY TERMS AND CONCEPTS

environmental scanning p. 74
social forces p. 76
demographics p. 76
mature household p. 76
baby boomers p. 77
Generation X p. 77
baby boomlet p. 77
blended family p. 78
census metropolitan areas p. 78
regional marketing p. 78
culture p. 79
value consciousness p. 81
economy p. 81
gross income p. 83
disposable income p. 83
discretionary income p. 83
technology p. 83
competition p. 86
barriers to entry p. 87
restructuring p. 88
regulation p. 89
Competition Act p. 89
self-regulation p. 90
consumerism p. 90

INTERNET EXERCISE

Many sources of information might be useful in an environmental scan. One particularly useful Web site is Statistics Canada's site (www.statcan.ca). Statistics Canada is the source for Canadian statistics on Canadian population trends, consumer expenditures, etc. Use this site to help answer the following questions:

1 What is the current (to the minute) population of Canada? What is the projected population of Canada in 2016?

2 How many people are aged 90 and over in Canada? (That's right, 90)

3 How many lone-parent families are there in Canada?

APPLYING MARKETING CONCEPTS AND PERSPECTIVES

1 For many years Gerber's has manufactured baby food in small, single-sized containers. In conducting an environmental scan, identify three trends or factors that might significantly affect this company's future business, and then propose how Gerber's might respond to these changes.
2 Describe the new features you would add to an automobile designed for the mature household. In what magazines would you advertise to appeal to this target market?
3 New technologies are continuously improving and replacing existing products. Although technological change is often difficult to predict, suggest how the following companies and products might be affected by the Internet and digital technologies: (*a*) Kodak cameras and film, (*b*) Canadian Airlines, and (*c*) the Museum of Art.
4 In recent years in the Canadian brewing industry, a couple of large firms that have historically had most of the beer sales (Labatt and Molson) have faced competition from many small regional brands. In terms of the continuum of competition, how would you explain this change?
5 When the Canadian long-distance telephone industry became deregulated, how do you think the role of marketing changed? What elements of the marketing mix are more or less important since the deregulation?
6 The Johnson Company manufactures buttons and pins with slogans and designs. These pins are inexpensive to produce and are sold in retail outlets such as discount stores, hobby shops, and bookstores. Little equipment is needed for a new competitor to enter the market. What strategies should Johnson consider to create effective barriers to entry?
7 Today's consumer is more value-conscious. How could a retail home improvement centre sell the exact same products but still offer the consumer greater perceived value? What specific things could the retailer do?

CASE 3–1 IMAGINATION PILOTS ENTERTAINMENT

What develops critical thinking, problem solving, and math skills; has an original musical score and sound effects; utilizes full-colour graphics; and involves an adventure with the circus? The answer is one of the newest forms of edutainment—a CD-ROM game developed for children called "Where's Waldo?" The game is part of a growing number of offerings from an industry that is rapidly adapting to a wide variety of changes in the business environment. According to the *Hollywood Reporter,* which follows the new developments, "interactive start-ups face new challenges as they stake a claim in a rapidly changing market."

THE COMPANY

The developer of the "Where's Waldo?" game is a fast-growing, entrepreneurial company called Imagination Pilots Entertainment (www.ipilots.com). The founder of the company, Howard Tullman, has focused on developing multimedia entertainment, educational software, and interactive "cinematic" adventures with strong game content. One of the company's first products was the interactive CD-ROM game called *Blown Away,* which was developed as part of a joint venture with MGM/United Artists and released after the movie by the same name. Imagination Pilot's *Blown Away* won the "Game of the Year" award from *Computer Life* magazine, the Gold Medal Invision Award for Best Graphic Design from *New Media* magazine, and the Innovators Software Showcase Award. Other Imagination Pilots products include *Panic in the Park* starring Erika Eleniak; *Virtual Erector Set,* which allows children to build 3-D, real-time models of vehicles; and an adventure game sequel to Arnold Schwarzenegger's movie, *Eraser.*

THE CHANGING ENVIRONMENT

Managers at Imagination Pilots are constantly monitoring social, economic, technological, competitive, and regulatory trends that may influence their business or the CD-ROM game industry. The most obvious trend, for example, is the rapid growth of the software market. Revenues for the packaged software market are expected to grow at an annual rate of 13 percent, reaching $153 billion by 2000. In addition, while many industries are laying off employees, the software industry is a net creator of jobs. A niche within the overall software market is the multimedia software market. Multimedia products combine video, animation, still pictures, voice, music, graphics, and text into a single system, usually on CD-ROM and very often for education or entertainment applications. Sales of CD-ROM titles have doubled each year for the past several years and now exceed $1.2 billion.

Related trends are the increasing penetration of computers into homes due to declining PC prices, and the increasing number of installed CD-ROM drives. According to Tullman, "There are only now becoming enough PC CD-ROM computers in the marketplace, in terms of total units, to permit a number of products to be successful." Although the number has been increasing at an annual rate of 25 percent, the number of worldwide CD-ROM computers was still only a portion of all computers in use. The price of software is also declining while consumer expectations are increasing. Tullman observes that "the price of children's software is decreasing, and continues to decrease even while there is a greater demand for quality . . . the consumer and parents want to pay less for individual games, but they want them to be of high quality."

Increasing competition also represents a challenge for Imagination Pilots. In the children's entertainment category software developers include Electronic Arts, Acclaim Entertainment, Sierra On-Line, Broderbund, Xiphias, and a very large number of relatively small firms. In addition, as growth of computer sales slows in the corporate market, many large firms, including Microsoft, IBM, Compaq, and Apple Computer, are expected to try to develop children's software as a way into the home market. Many new titles are being introduced by both past developers and new entrants—creating a very competitive market.

A final factor that Imagination Pilots and other developers must consider is the possibility of regulation. Concern about the content of some games had led to a discussion about the potential need for a rating system, much like the system used for movies.

THE ISSUES

Imagination Pilots is faced with several key challenges. First, it must attempt to ensure the success of new titles planned for development. Second, it must obtain distribution for existing and future products. Although the two are related, they require attention to very different issues.

Establishing a new title in a cluttered marketplace is likely to be difficult for any software developer. Estimates suggest that from $800 000 to $1.5 million is required to develop a competitive CD-ROM product. As a result, many firms seek partnerships or alliances to spread costs and reduce risk. Recovering the investment may be difficult, however, if sales volume is low or the profit margin of each unit sold is low. Part of Imagination Pilots' strategy is to license rights to existing stories, such as "Where's Waldo?", or movies, such as *Blown Away* and *Eraser.* Tullman believes that the name recognition of licensed titles is important to ensure adequate

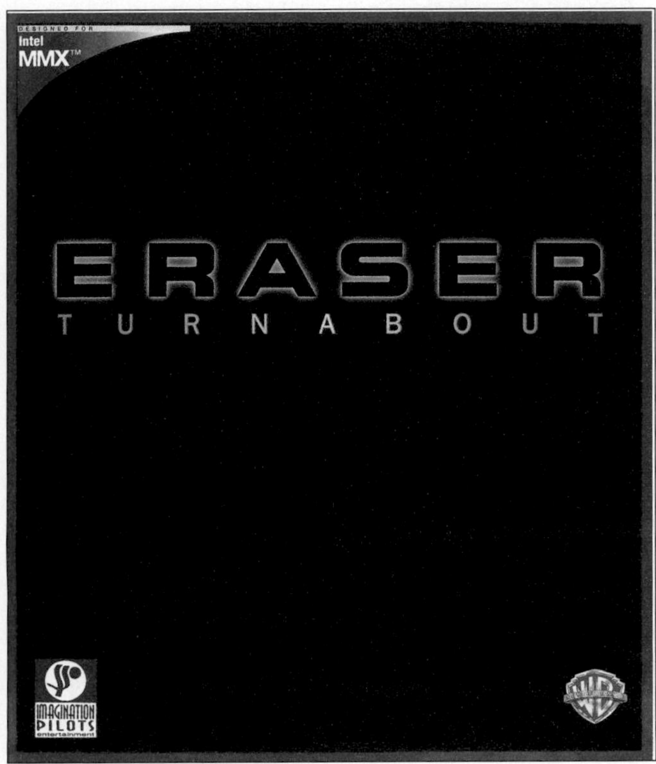

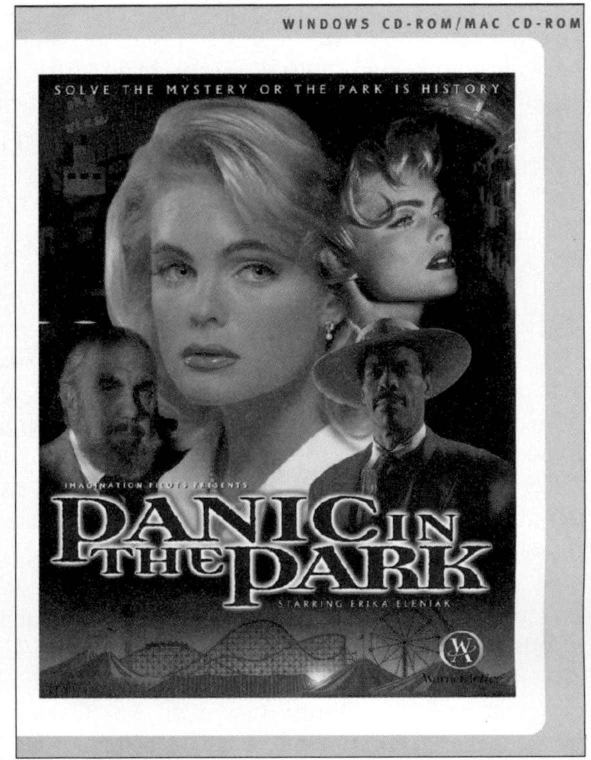

consumer interest. Some developers of children's software have used product line extensions to extend the life of existing titles. Sierra On-Line's *Quest,* for example, is now in its sixth release. New titles will need much more, though, to gain a foothold in the market.

Daniel P. Di Caro, chief operating officer at Imagination Pilots, argues that "distribution is increasingly becoming the most important factor in the success of a product, assuming you have a good product to start with." In the past the traditional channel of distribution was through software specialty stores such as Egghead Software, Babbages, and Software Etc. More recently, sales have increased in computer superstores, department stores such as Sears and Wal-Mart, consumer electronic stores such as Future Shop, and warehouse stores such as Sam's. Their relationship with Warner Music Group provides Imagination Pilots with a strong distribution partner with access to many of these channels. In the future additional channels such as catalogues, interactive television channels, and kiosks may offer the company new distribution opportunities. Imagination Pilots is already testing an online service that makes its games available to the Internet and World Wide Web community!

Questions

1 Conduct an environmental scan for Imagination Pilots Entertainment. How are each of the five environmental forces (social, economic, technological, competitive, and regulatory) likely to influence their multimedia game business?

2 What are the key challenges facing Imagination Pilots? Describe the actions taken by Imagination Pilots to (*a*) ensure the success of, and (*b*) obtain distribution for its games.

3 What are the advantages of making Imagination Pilot's games available online?

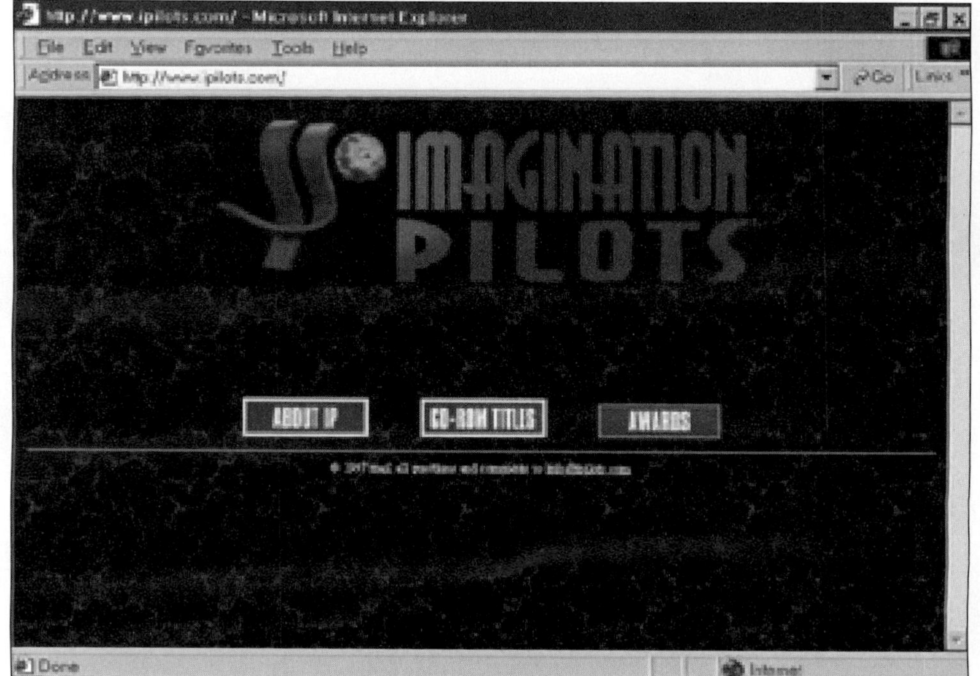

" Planning every run
is the mark of a good skier,
even the run home. So think ahead,
and don't drink and drive."
Brian Stemmle
NATIONAL SKI TEAM MEMBER
Take Care.
MOLSON

CHAPTER FOUR

ETHICS AND SOCIAL RESPONSIBILITY IN MARKETING

4

AFTER READING THIS CHAPTER YOU SHOULD BE ABLE TO:

- Appreciate the nature and significance of ethics in marketing.
- Understand the differences between legal and ethical behaviour in marketing.
- Identify factors that influence ethical and unethical marketing decisions.
- Distinguish among the different concepts of ethics and social responsibility.
- Recognize the importance of ethical and socially responsible consumer behaviour.

AT MOLSON BREWERIES, THERE IS MORE BREWING THAN BEER

Why would a company spend millions of dollars trying to convince people not to abuse its products? Ask Molson Breweries (www.molson.com), one of Canada's largest brewers and a leader in the campaign for the responsible use of alcohol. Molson's "Take Care" program is a multi-million-dollar national communications program that goes beyond conventional "drinking and driving" campaigns. It puts responsible use of alcohol in a broader context—of work, health, and quality of life.

The program includes broadcast, print, and outdoor advertising, promotions tied to Molson sports and entertainment properties across the country, educational initiatives in schools and universities, and support to community and interest groups. Some of their unique initiatives include the *Campus Tour,* where Canadian Indy car driver Patrick Carpentier visits Canadian universities and colleges delivering responsive alcohol use messages. And TAXIGUY (TAXISVP in Quebec) where taxicab transportation is encouraged as an alternative to drinking and driving. A person only needs to call 1-888-TAXIGUY in English Canada, or 1-888-TAXISVP in Quebec, and a participating taxicab company will dispatch a car to pick up the caller. It is an attempt by Molson to move from awareness to social action with respect to responsible use of alcohol.

Molson acts on what it views as an ethical obligation to its customers with its "Take Care" campaign. At the same time, the company is also involved in multifaceted efforts to support the communities in which it operates and to protect our natural environment. Molson has a long history of supporting countless charities and has founded some of Canada's major health, educational, and cultural institutions. Molson has also made the protection of the environment a high priority. For example, over 98 percent of its bottles and 75 percent of its cans are returned to points of sale to be retrieved for reuse or recycling. Molson ensures that its breweries are environmentally efficient throughout all stages of the brewing process, and all its offices have recycling programs.[1]

This chapter focuses on ethics and social responsibility in marketing. You will see how some companies recognize that while ethically and socially responsible behaviour often comes with a price tag, the price for unethical and socially irresponsible behaviour is often much higher. In essence, in this marketplace, companies can "do well by doing good."

NATURE AND SIGNIFICANCE OF MARKETING ETHICS

Ethics are the moral principles and values that govern the actions and decisions of an individual or group.[2] Simply put, ethics serve as guidelines on how to act correctly and justly when faced with moral dilemmas. For marketing managers, ethics concern the application of moral principles and values to marketing decision making.

Ethical/Legal Framework in Marketing

A good starting point for understanding the nature and significance of ethics is the distinction between legality and ethicality of marketing decisions. Figure 4–1 helps you to visualize the relationship between laws and ethics.[3] While ethics deal with personal and moral principles and values, **laws** are society's values and standards that are enforceable in the courts.[4]

FIGURE 4–1
Classifying marketing decisions according to ethical and legal relationships

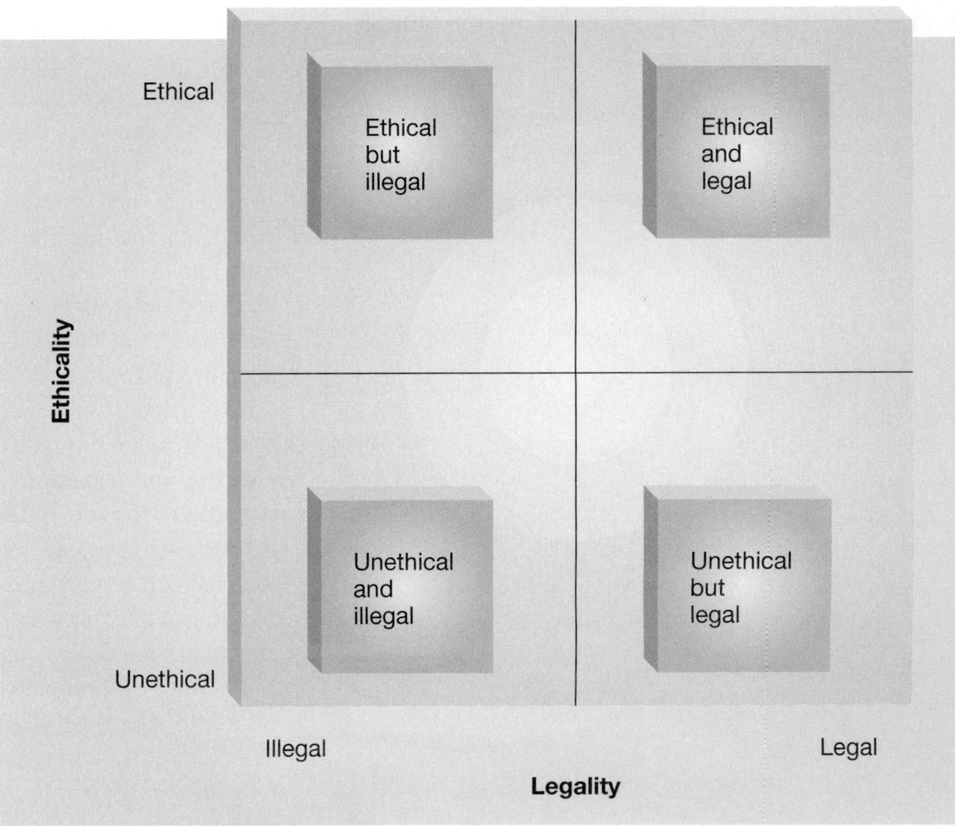

In general, what is illegal is also unethical. For example, deceptive advertising is illegal. It is also unethical, because it conflicts with the moral principles of honesty and fairness. But not all unethical conduct is illegal. For instance, price gouging is usually not illegal, but is often viewed as unethical. Marketing managers often find themselves in many situations where they must make judgments in defining ethical and legal boundaries. For some, the distinction between ethics and laws can sometimes lead to the rationalization that if a behaviour is within legal limits, then it is not really unethical. For example, recently, a group of Canadian business students were surveyed and asked: "Is it okay to charge a higher price than normal when you know the customer really needs the product and will pay the higher price?" Almost 35 percent of the business students who took part in the survey responded "Yes."[5] How would you have answered this question?

Now consider the following situations. After reading each, assign it to the cell in Figure 4–1 that you think best fits the situation along the ethical-legal continuum.

1. Several companies meet and agree to bid-rigging for sealed tendered government contract work. Bid-rigging is illegal under the *Competition Act* since it eliminates free and open competition.
2. A company uses a technique called "slugging" or selling under the guise of research. Once prospective customers agree to take part in the research, the salespeople switch to their sales pitch.
3. A real estate agent sells a high-rise condo unit to a customer, primarily because the customer loves the city view looking out the condo windows. The agent knows that in one year another high-rise will be built, effectively blocking the view so important to the customer. The agent decides not to tell that customer.
4. A company interviews a very qualified female for an industrial sales position. She is more qualified than any males who were interviewed. However, the company knows that some male purchasing agents prefer to deal with a male salesperson, so they hire a less qualified male applicant.

Do these situations fit neatly into Figure 4–1 as clearly defined ethical and legal or unethical and illegal? Some probably do not. As you read further in this chapter, you will be asked again to consider other ethical dilemmas.

Current Perceptions of Ethical Behaviour

There has been much discussion over the possible deterioration of personal morality and ethical standards on a global scale. The news media offer well-publicized examples of personal dishonesty, hypocrisy, cheating, and greed. There also has been a public outcry about the ethical practices of businesspeople. In particular, there is widespread concern over unethical marketing practices such as price-fixing, bribery, deceptive advertising, and unsafe products. Public opinion surveys as well as other research shows that most adults believe the ethical standards of business have declined over the years.[6] One study found that consumers believed advertising practitioners and car salespeople were among the least ethical professions.[7]

There are at least four possible reasons why the state of perceived ethical business conduct is at its present level. First, there is increased pressure on businesspeople to make decisions in a society characterized by diverse value systems.[8] Second, there is a growing tendency for business decisions to be judged publicly by groups with different values and interests. Third, the public's expectations regarding ethical business behaviour have increased. Finally, and most disturbing, ethical business conduct may have declined.

CONCEPT CHECK

1. What are ethics?
2. What are laws?

UNDERSTANDING ETHICAL MARKETING BEHAVIOUR

Researchers have identified numerous factors that influence ethical marketing behaviour.[9] Figure 4–2 presents a framework that shows these factors and their relationships.

Societal Culture and Norms

As described in Chapter 3, *culture* refers to the set of values, ideas, and attitudes of a homogeneous group of people that are transmitted from one generation to the next. Culture also affects ethical relationships between individuals, groups, and the institutions and organizations they create. In this way, culture serves as a socializing force that dictates what is morally right and just. This means that moral standards are relative to particular societies. These standards often reflect the laws and regulations that affect social and economic behaviour, including business practices, which can create moral dilemmas. For example, Levi Strauss decided to end many of its business dealings in China because of what the company called "pervasive human rights abuses." According to its vice president for corporate marketing: "There are wonderful commercial opportunities in China. But when ethical issues collide with commercial appeal, we try to ensure ethics as the trump card. For us, ethical issues precede all others."[10]

www.levistrauss.com

Actions that restrain trade, fix prices, deceive buyers, and result in unsafe products are considered morally wrong in Canada and other countries. However, different cultures view marketing practices differently. Consider the use of another's ideas, copyright, trademark, or patent. These are viewed as intellectual property and unauthorized use is illegal and unethical in Canada.

Outside Canada, however, is another story.[11] Unauthorized use of copyrights, trademarks, and patents is routine in countries such as China, Mexico, and Korea and cost the authorized owners billions of dollars annually. In Korea, for instance, copying is partly rooted in its society's culture. According to international trade officials, many Koreans have the idea that the thoughts of one person should benefit all, and the Korean government rarely prosecutes infringements. Read the accompanying Marketing NewsNet,[12] keeping in mind the ethical-legal framework in Figure 4–1. Would the unauthorized use of copyrighted computer software be considered unethical despite its prevalence?

Business Culture and Industry Practices

Societal culture provides a foundation for understanding moral and ethical behaviour in business activities. *Business cultures* "comprise the effective rules of the game, the boundaries between competitive and unethical behaviour, [and] the codes of conduct in

FIGURE 4–2
A framework for understanding ethical behaviour

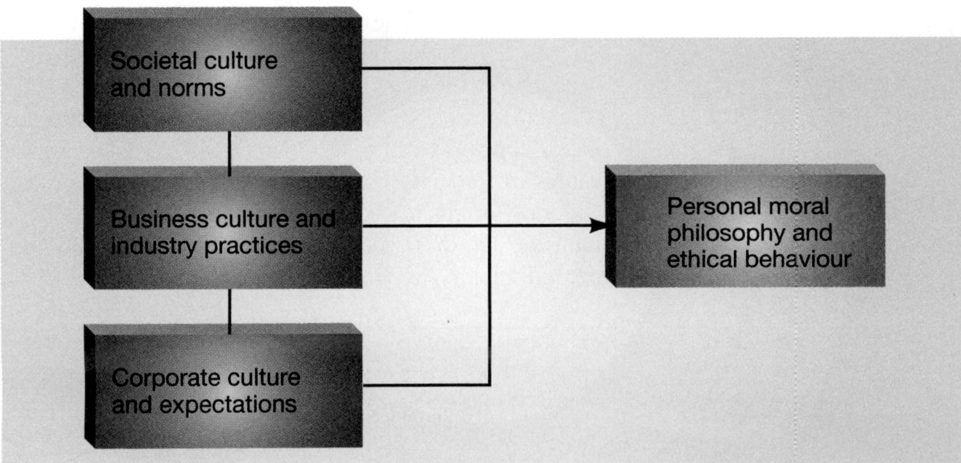

TECHNOLOGY

MARKETING NEWSNET

Software Piracy and Pirates at Home and Abroad

Have you copied a friend's software? If yes, you are among 33 percent of university and college students who acquire software by copying it. And yes, you are a software pirate because unauthorized copying of software is illegal.

The incidence and implications of software piracy are enormous. The Software Publishers Association (SPA) estimates that 4 in every 10 new business software applications installed globally are pirated, that is, copied illegally. The unauthorized copying of business software costs their producers the equivalent of $16 billion in worldwide sales annually.

Software piracy has become widespread in many countries and regions of the world. According to SPA, 77 percent of software in Eastern Europe is pirated, 65 percent in the Middle East and Africa, 62 percent in Latin America, and 39 percent in Western Europe. Countries with the highest piracy rates are Vietnam (98 percent), China (96 percent), Bulgaria (93 percent), and Russia (89 percent). About 25 percent of the software used in Canada has been copied illegally.

Software programs are intellectual property, and their unauthorized use is illegal in many countries. But, for some, their reproduction and distribution is not considered unethical. Indeed, in a recent study of college students, 42 percent consider the practice acceptable behaviour!

business dealings."[13] Consumers have witnessed numerous instances where business cultures in the brokerage (inside trading), insurance (deceptive sales practices), and defence (bribery) industries went awry. Business culture affects ethical conduct both in the exchange relationship between sellers and buyers and in the competitive behaviour among sellers.

Ethics of Exchange The exchange process is central to the marketing concept. Ethical exchanges between sellers and buyers should result in both parties being better off after a transaction.[14]

Prior to the 1960s, the legal concept of **caveat emptor**—let the buyer beware—was pervasive in Canadian business culture. The growth and strength of the consumer movement resulted in this concept becoming an unacceptable marketplace philosophy. A codification of ethics between buyers and sellers was established, with consumers recognizing their rights to safety, to be informed, to choose, and to be heard.

The right to safety manifests itself in industry and federal safety standards for most products sold in Canada. However, even the most vigilant efforts to ensure safe products cannot foresee every possibility. Mattel's experience with its Cabbage Patch Snacktime Kids doll is a case in point.[15] The doll was designed to "eat" plastic french fries, celery, and other tidbits by drawing them into its motorized mouth. Despite exhaustive laboratory and in-home testing, Mattel executives did not consider that a child's hair might become caught in the doll's mouth and cause harm. Unfortunately, this happened. Mattel immediately pulled the dolls from store shelves, refunded buyers, and discontinued the product.

The right to be informed means that marketers have an obligation to give consumers complete and accurate information about products and services. This right also applies to the solicitation of personal information over the Internet and its subsequent use by marketers.[16] For example, a recent survey of Web sites indicated that 92 percent collect personal information such as consumer e-mail addresses, telephone numbers, shopping habits, and financial data. Yet only 14 percent of Web sites inform consumers what is done with this information once obtained. Because consumers often assume that personal information is confidential, it was therefore understandable that subscribers to America Online (AOL) balked when AOL proposed giving member information to partners who could then telemarket to them. AOL backed down.

Relating to the right to choose, today many supermarket chains demand "slotting allowances" from manufacturers, in the form of cash rebates or free goods, to stock new products. This practice could limit the number of new products available to consumers and interfere with their right to choose. One critic of this practice remarked: "If we had had slotting allowances a few years ago, we might not have had granola, herbal tea, or yogurt."[17]

Finally, the right to be heard means that consumers should have access to company and/or public-policy makers regarding comments or complaints about products and services. Many Canadian companies have set up consumer service departments to deal with customer comments and complaints. In fact, it was consumer complaints about late-night and repeated calls by telemarketers that led to greater limitations on telemarketing practices.

Ethics of Competition Business culture also affects ethical behaviour in competition. Two kinds of unethical behaviour are most common: (1) industrial espionage and (2) bribery.

Industrial espionage is the clandestine collection of trade secrets or proprietary information about a company's competitors. Many Canadian and American firms have uncovered espionage in some form, costing them billions of dollars a year.[18] This practice is most prevalent in high-technology industries such as electronics, specialty chemicals, industrial equipment, aerospace, and pharmaceuticals, where technical know-how and secrets separate industry leaders from followers.

www.pg.com

But espionage can occur anywhere—the toy industry and even the ready-to-eat cookie industry! Procter & Gamble charged that competitors photographed its plants and production lines, stole a sample of its cookie dough, and infiltrated a confidential

WEB LINK The Commercial Corruption Perception Index

Commercial corruption in the global marketplace varies widely by country. Transparency International, based in Berlin, Germany, polls employees of multinational firms and institutions and political analysts and annually ranks countries based on the perceived level of corruption.

To obtain the most recent ranking, visit the Transparency International Web site at www.transparency.de.

Scroll to the Corruption Perception Index, and see where Canada stands in the rankings as well as its neighbours, the United States and Mexico. Which country listed in the most recent ranking has the best ranking, and which has the worst ranking?

sales presentation to learn about its technology, recipe, and marketing plan. The competitors paid Procter & Gamble $120 million in damages after a lengthy dispute.[19]

The second form of unethical competitive behaviour is giving and receiving bribes and kickbacks. Bribes and kickbacks are often disguised as gifts, consultant fees, and favours. This practice is more common in business-to-business and government marketing than consumer marketing.

There is also a prevalence of bribery in international marketing, where it is viewed differently in other business cultures. In France and Greece, bribes paid to foreign companies are a tax-deductible expense!

In general, ethical standards are more likely to be compromised in industries experiencing intense competition and in countries in earlier stages of economic development. For example, a recent poll of executives employed by multinational firms revealed that Nigeria, Russia, and Colombia evidenced the least ethical business culture. Denmark, Finland, and Sweden were viewed as having the most ethical business cultures among industrialized countries.[20] Commercial corruption on a worldwide scale is monitored by Transparency International. Visit their Web site described in the accompanying WebLink box, and view the most recent country corruption rankings.

Corporate Culture and Expectations

A third influence on ethical practices is corporate culture. *Corporate culture* reflects the shared values, beliefs, and purpose of employees that affect individual and group behaviour. The culture of a company demonstrates itself in the dress ("We don't wear ties"), sayings ("The IBM Way"), and the manner of work (team efforts) of employees. Corporate culture is also apparent in the expectations for ethical behaviour present in formal codes of ethics and the ethical actions of top management and co-workers.

www.generalmills.com

Codes of Ethics A **code of ethics** is a formal statement of ethical principles and rules of conduct. Ethics codes and committees typically address contributions to government officials and political parties, relations with customers and suppliers, conflicts of interest, and accurate recordkeeping. For example, General Mills provides guidelines for dealing with suppliers, competitors, and customers, and recruits new employees who share these views. However, an ethics code is rarely enough to ensure ethical behaviour. Johnson & Johnson has an ethics code and emphasizes that its employees be just and ethical in their behaviour. But neither of these measures prevented some of its employees from shredding papers to hinder a government probe into the firm's marketing of an acne cream, Retin-A.[21]

The lack of specificity is one of the major reasons for the violation of ethics codes. Employees must often judge whether a specific behaviour is really unethical. The American Marketing Association, representing Canadian and American marketing professionals, has addressed this issue by providing a detailed code of ethics, which all members agree to follow. This code is shown in Figure 4–3.

www.dnb.com

Ethical Behaviour of Management and Co-Workers A second reason for violating ethics codes rests in the perceived behaviour of top management and co-workers.[22] Observing peers and top management and gauging responses to unethical behaviour play an important role in individual actions. For example, what message do employees receive when they see personnel being rewarded for engaging in unethical troubling behaviour and seeing others punished for refusing to engage in unethical behaviour? Clearly, ethical dilemmas often bring personal and professional conflict. In many cases, **whistleblowers,** employees who report unethical or illegal actions of their employers, often face recrimination. Some firms, such as General Dynamics and Dun & Bradstreet, have appointed ethics officers responsible for safeguarding such individuals.[23]

CODE OF ETHICS

Members of the American Marketing Association (AMA) are committed to ethical professional conduct. They have joined together in subscribing to this Code of Ethics embracing the following topics:

Responsibilities of the Marketer

Marketers must accept responsibility for the consequence of their activities and make every effort to ensure that their decisions, recommendations, and actions function to identify, serve, and satisfy all relevant publics: customers, organizations, and society.

Marketers' professional conduct must be guided by:

1. The basic rule of professional ethics: not knowingly to do harm.
2. The adherence to all applicable laws and regulations.
3. The accurate representation of their education, training, and experience.
4. The active support, practice, and promotion of this Code of Ethics.

Honesty and Fairness

Marketers shall uphold and advance the integrity, honor, and dignity of the marketing profession by:

1. Being honest in serving consumers, clients, employees, suppliers, distributors, and the public.
2. Not knowingly participating in conflict of interest without prior notice to all parties involved.
3. Establishing equitable fee schedules including the payment or receipt of usual, customary, and/or legal compensation or marketing exchanges.

Rights and Duties of Parties in the Marketing Exchange Process

Participants in the marketing exchange process should be able to expect that:

1. Products and services offered are safe and fit for their intended uses.
2. Communications about offered products and services are not deceptive.
3. All parties intend to discharge their obligations, financial and otherwise, in good faith.
4. Appropriate internal methods exist for equitable adjustment and/or redress of grievances concerning purchases.

It is understood that the above would include, *but is not limited to,* the following responsibilities of the marketer:

In the area of product development and management

- Disclosure of all substantial risks associated with product or service usage.

FIGURE 4–3
American Marketing Association Code of Ethics

Personal Moral Philosophy and Ethical Behaviour

Ultimately, ethical choices are based on the personal moral philosophy of the decision maker. Moral philosophy is learned through the process of socialization with friends and family, and by formal education. It is also influenced by the societal, business, and corporate culture in which a person finds him- or herself. Moral philosophies are of two types: (1) moral idealism and (2) utilitarianism.[24]

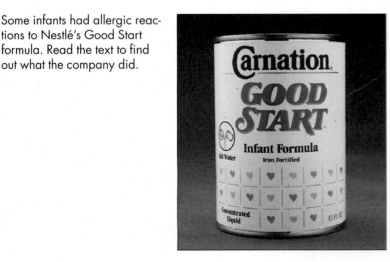

Moral Idealism **Moral idealism** is a personal philosophy that considers certain individual rights or duties as universal (e.g., right to freedom) regardless of the outcome. This philosophy is favoured by moral philosophers and consumer interest groups. This philosophy also applies to ethical duties such as informing the consumer about the safety hazards of a particular product; even conducting a large-scale recall of a deceptive product, regardless of cost, in order to uphold that consumer right to safety.

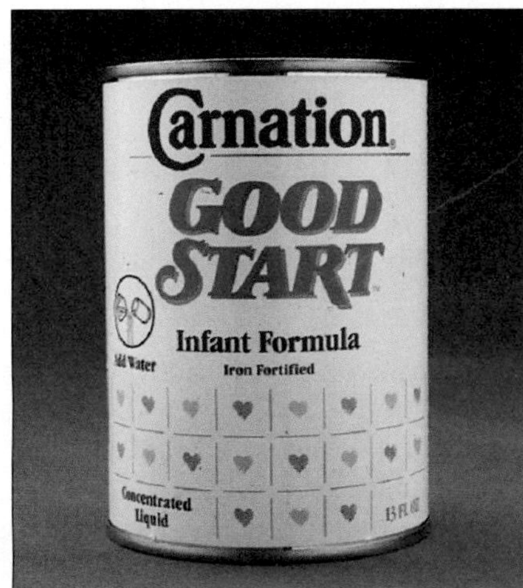

Some infants had allergic reactions to Nestlé's Good Start formula. Read the text to find out what the company did.

Utilitarianism An alternative perspective on moral philosophy is **utilitarianism,** which is a personal moral philosophy that focuses on "the greatest good for the greatest number," by assessing the costs and benefits of the consequences of ethical behaviour. If the benefits exceed the costs, then the behaviour is ethical. If not, then the behaviour is unethical. This philosophy underlies the

FIGURE 4–3 *(CONCLUDED)*

- Identification of any product component substitution that might materially change the product or impact on the buyer's purchase decision.
- Identification of extra-cost added features.

In the area of promotions

- Avoidance of false and misleading advertising.
- Rejection of high-pressure manipulation, or misleading sales tactics.
- Avoidance of sales promotions that use deception or manipulation.

In the area of distribution

- Not manipulating the availability of a product for purpose of exploitation.
- Not using coercion in the marketing channel.
- Not exerting undue influence over the reseller's choice to handle the product.

In the area of pricing

- Not engaging in price fixing.
- Not practising predatory pricing.
- Disclosing the full price associated with any purchase.

In the area of marketing research

- Prohibiting selling or fund raising under the guise of conducting research.
- Maintaining research integrity by avoiding misrepresentation and omission of pertinent research data.
- Treating outside clients and suppliers fairly.

Organizational Relationships

Marketers should be aware of how their behaviour may influence or impact on the behaviour of others in organizational relationships. They should not demand, encourage, or apply coercion to obtain unethical behaviour in their relationships with others, such as employees, suppliers, or customers.

1. Apply confidentiality and anonymity in professional relationships with regard to privileged information.
2. Meet their obligations and responsiblities in contracts and mutual agreements in a timely manner.
3. Avoid taking the work of others, in whole or in part, and represent this work as their own or directly benefit from it without compensation or consent of the originator or owner.
4. Avoid manipulation to take advantage of situations to maximize personal welfare in a way that unfairly deprives or damages the organization or others.

Any AMA members found to be in violation of any provision of this Code of Ethics may have his or her Association membership suspended or revoked.

Source: Reprinted by permission of the American Marketing Association.

www.carnationmilk.com

economic tenets of capitalism and, not surprisingly, is embraced by many business executives and students.[25]

Utilitarian reasoning was apparent in Nestlé Food Corporation's marketing of Good Start infant formula, sold by Nestlé's Carnation Company. The formula, promoted as hypoallergenic, was designed to prevent or reduce colic caused by an infant's allergic reaction to cow's milk—a condition suffered by two percent of babies. However, some severely milk-allergic infants experienced serious side effects after using Good Start, including convulsive vomiting. Physicians and parents charged that the hypoallergenic claim was misleading, and the government investigated the matter. A Nestlé vice president defended the claim and product, saying, "I don't understand why our product should work in 100 percent of cases. If we wanted to say it was foolproof, we would have called it allergy-free. We call it hypo-, or less, allergenic."[26] Nestlé officials seemingly believed that most allergic infants would benefit from Good Start—"the greatest good for the greatest number." However, other views prevailed, and the claim was dropped from the product label.

An appreciation for the nature of ethics, coupled with a basic understanding of why unethical behaviour arises, alerts a person to when and how ethical issues exist in marketing decisions. Ultimately, ethical behaviour rests with the individual, but the consequences affect many.

CONCEPT CHECK

1. What is a caveat emptor?
2. What is a code of ethics?
3. What is meant by moral idealism?

UNDERSTANDING SOCIAL RESPONSIBILITY IN MARKETING

As we saw in Chapter 1, the societal marketing concept stresses marketing's social responsibility by not only satisfying the needs of consumers but also providing for society's welfare. **Social responsibility** means that organizations are part of a larger society and are accountable to that society for their actions. Like ethics, agreement on the nature and scope of social responsibility is often difficult to come by, given the diversity of values present in different societal, business, and organizational cultures.[27]

Concepts of Social Responsibility

Figure 4–4 shows three concepts of social responsibility: (1) profit responsibility, (2) stakeholder responsibility, and (3) societal responsibility.

Profit Responsibility *Profit responsibility* holds that companies have a simple duty—to maximize profits for their owners or stockholders. This view is expressed by Nobel Laureate Milton Friedman, who said, "There is one and only one social responsibility of business—to use its resources and engage in activities designed to increase its profits so long as it stays within the rules of the game, which is to say, engages in open and free competition without deception or fraud."[28] Genzyme, the maker of Ceredase, a drug that treats a genetic illness called Gaucher's disease that affects 20 000 people worldwide, has been criticized for apparently adopting this view in its pricing practices. A Genzyme spokesperson responded by saying that Ceredase profits are below industry standards and that the company freely gives the drug to patients without insurance.[29]

FIGURE 4–4
Three concepts of social responsibility

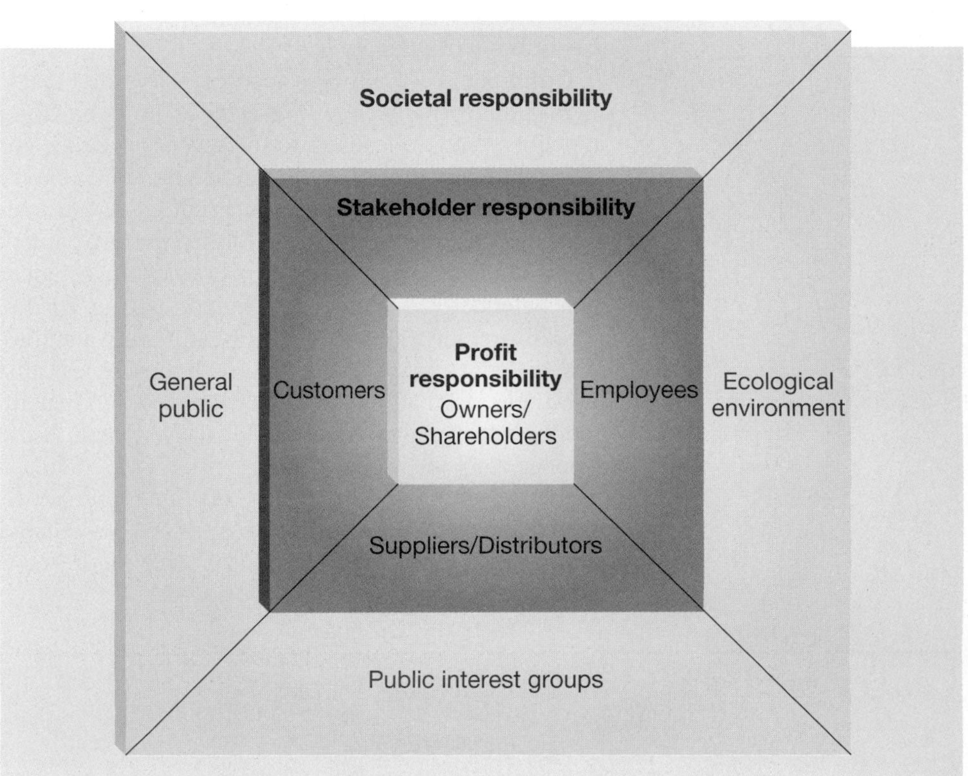

Which of the three concepts of social responsibility do you think Perrier applied when it learned of quality problems with its popular water? Read the text to learn how they responded to this problem and their reasoning.

Stakeholder Responsibility Frequent criticism of the profit view has led to a broader concept of social responsibility. *Stakeholder responsibility* focuses on the obligations an organization has to those who can affect achievement of its objectives. These constituencies include customers, employees, suppliers, and distributors. Source Perrier S.A., the supplier of Perrier bottled water, exercised this responsibility when it recalled 160 million bottles of water in 120 countries after traces of a toxic chemical were found in 13 bottles. The recall cost the company $35 million, and $40 million more was lost in sales. Even though the chemical level was not harmful to humans, Source Perrier's president believed he acted in the best interests of the firm's consumers, distributors, and employees by removing "the least doubt, as minimal as it might be, to weigh on the image of the quality and purity of our product."[30]

Societal Responsibility An even broader concept of social responsibility has emerged in recent years. *Societal responsibility* refers to obligations that organizations have to the (1) preservation of the ecological environment and (2) general public. Concerns about the environment and public welfare are represented by interest and advocacy groups such as Greenpeace, an international environmental organization.

Chapter 3 detailed the growing importance of ecological issues in marketing. Companies have responded to this concern through what is termed **green marketing**—marketing efforts to produce, promote, and reclaim environmentally sensitive products. Green marketing takes many forms.[31] The Canadian aluminum industry recycles nearly two-thirds of all aluminum cans for reuse. The Food and Consumer Products Manufacturers of Canada (formerly GPMC) has a program known as the *Grocery Industry Packaging Stewardship Initiative,* which is designed to promote responsible waste and product recycling. Black Photo of Ontario has factored the environment into everything it does, from product conception to manufacturing, distribution, and sales. And Mercedes-Benz has designed its S-class sedans and 500/600 SEC luxury coupes to be entirely recyclable. These voluntary responses to environmental issues have been implemented with little or no additional cost to comsumers.

Almost 8500 companies around the world have met ISO 14000 standards for environmental quality and green marketing. Japan has the most ISO 14000 certified companies.

ISO 14000
www.iso14000.com

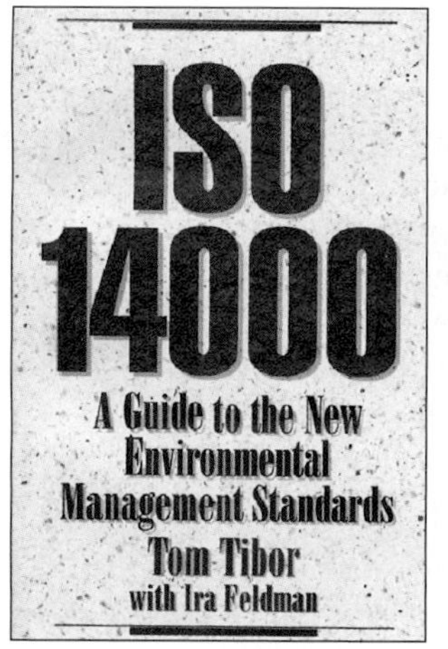

A global undertaking to further green marketing efforts is the ISO 14000 initiative developed by the International Standards Organization (ISO) in Geneva, Switzerland. **ISO 14000** consists of worldwide standards for environmental quality and green marketing practices. These standards have been embraced by about 40 countries, including Canada, members of the European Union, and most Pacific Rim countries.[32]

Socially responsible efforts on behalf of the general public are also becoming more common. A formal practice is **cause-related marketing** (CRM), which occurs when the charitable contributions of a firm are tied directly to the customer revenues produced through the promotion of one of its products.[33] This definition distinguishes CRM from a firm's standard charitable contributions, which are outright donations. For example, Procter & Gamble raises

Marketing and social responsibility programs are often integrated, as is the case with McDonald's. Its concern for ill children is apparent in the opening of another Ronald McDonald House for children and their families.

McDonald's
www.mcdonalds.com

funds for the Special Olympics when consumers purchase selected company products, and MasterCard International linked usage of its card with fundraising for institutions that combat cancer, heart disease, child abuse, drug abuse, and muscular dystrophy. Avon Products, Inc. focuses on different issues in different countries: breast cancer in the United States, Canada, Philippines, Mexico, Venezuela, Malaysia, and Spain; programs for women who care for senior citizens in Japan; emotional and financial support for mothers in Germany; and AIDS in Thailand. CRM programs incorporate all three concepts of social responsibility by addressing public concerns and satisfying customer needs, and enhancing corporate sales and profits.[34]

The Social Audit

www.mcdonalds.com

Converting socially responsible ideas into actions involves careful planning and monitoring of programs. Many companies develop, implement, and evaluate their social responsibility efforts by means of a **social audit,** which is a systematic assessment of a firm's objectives, strategies, and performance in the domain of social responsibility. Frequently, marketing and social responsibility programs are integrated, as is the case with McDonald's. The company's concern for the needs of families with children who are chronically or terminally ill was converted into some 130 Ronald McDonald Houses around the world. These facilities, located near treatment centres, enable families to stay together during the child's care. In this case, McDonald's is contributing to the welfare of a portion of its target market.

A social audit consists of five steps:[35]

1. Recognition of a firm's social expectations and the rationale for engaging in social responsibility endeavours.
2. Identification of social responsibility causes or programs consistent with the company's mission.

3. Determination of organizational objectives and priorities for programs and activities it will undertake.
4. Specification of the type and amount of resources necessary to achieve social responsibility objectives.
5. Evaluation of social responsibility programs and activities undertaken and assessment of future involvement.

Corporate attention to social audits will increase in the 21st century as companies seek to achieve sustainable devleopment and improve the quality of life in a global economy.[36] **Sustainable development** involves conducting business in a way that protects the natural environment while also making economic progress. Ecologically responsible initiatives such as green marketing represent one such initiative. Research initiatives related to working conditions at offshore manufacturing sites that produce goods for North American companies focus on quality-of-life issues. Public opinion surveys show that consumers are concerned about working conditions under which products are made in Asia and Latin America.[37] Companies have responded by imposing closer supervision of offshore manufacturing activities. Reebok, for example, now monitors production of its sporting apparel and equipment to ensure that no child abuse occurs during the production of its products.[38]

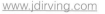

www.reebok.com

Turning the Table: Consumer Ethics and Social Responsibility

Consumers also have an obligation to act ethically and responsibly in the exchange process and in the use and disposition of products. Unfortunately, consumer behaviour is spotty on both counts.

Unethical practices of consumers are a serious concern to marketers.[39] These practices include filing warranty claims after the claim period, misredeeming coupons, making fraudulent returns of merchandise, providing inaccurate information on credit applications, tampering with utility meters, tapping cable TV lines, recording copyrighted music and videocassettes, and submitting phony insurance claims. The cost to marketers in lost sales revenue and prevention expenses is huge. For example, consumers who redeem coupons for unpurchased products or use coupons destined for other products cost manufacturers millions of dollars each year. The record industry alone loses millions of dollars annually due to illegal recording, and many VCR owners make illegal copies of videotapes, costing producers millions of dollars in lost revenue. Electrical utilities lose one to three percent of yearly revenues due to meter tampering.

Consumer purchase, use, and disposition of environmentally sensitive products relate to consumer social responsibility.[40] Research indicates that consumers are generally sensitive to ecological issues. However, research also shows that consumers (1) may be unwilling to sacrifice convenience and pay potentially higher prices to protect the environment and (2) lack the knowledge to make informed decisions dealing with the purchase, use, and disposition of products.[41]

Many marketers suggest that consumers must become aware of and increase their demand for environmentally sensitive products. For example, producers of environmentally certified lumber say the market for "green wood" is very small in Canada. Certified lumber comes from forest companies that use sustainable harvesting practices and produce wood products with the least environmental impact. J. D. Irving Co., a Canadian timber and energy conglomerate, has been pursuing certification of its forest lands. The company suggests that consumers should look for and demand wood products from certified forests. In doing so, consumers could end widespread clear-cutting, chemical spraying, and other destructive forestry practices. "Green wood" products can be easily identified by a trademark product label: a green cross superimposed on a globe.[42]

www.jdirving.com

Ultimately, marketers and consumers are accountable for ethical and socially responsible behaviour. The 21st century will prove to be a testing period for both.

CONCEPT CHECK

1. What is meant by social responsibility?
2. Marketing efforts to produce, promote, and reclaim environmentally sensitive products are called ____________.
3. What is a social audit?

SUMMARY

1 Ethics are the moral principles and values that govern the actions and decisions of an individual or group. Laws are society's values and standards that are enforceable in the courts. Operating according to the law does not necessarily mean that a practice is ethical.

2 Ethical behaviour of businesspeople has come under severe criticism by the public. There are four possible reasons for this criticism: (*a*) increased pressure on businesspeople to make decisions in a society characterized by diverse value systems, (*b*) a growing tendency to have business decisions judged publicly by groups with different values and interests, (*c*) an increase in the public's expectations for ethical behaviour, and (*d*) a possible decline in business ethics.

3 Numerous external factors influence ethical behaviour of businesspeople. These include the following: (*a*) societal culture and norms, (*b*) business culture and industry practices, and (*c*) organizational culture and expectations. Each factor influences the opportunity to engage in ethical or unethical behaviour.

4 Ultimately, ethical choices are based on the personal moral philosophy of the decision maker. Two moral philosophies are most prominent: (*a*) moral idealism and (*b*) utilitarianism.

5 Social responsibility means that organizations are part of a larger society and are accountable to that society for their actions.

6 There are three concepts of social responsibility: (*a*) profit responsibility, (*b*) stakeholder responsibility, and (*c*) societal responsibility.

7 Growing interest in societal responsibility has resulted in systematic efforts to assess a firm's objectives, strategies, and performance in the domain of social responsibility. This practice is called a *social audit.*

8 Consumer ethics and social responsibility are as important as business ethics and social responsibility.

KEY TERMS AND CONCEPTS

ethics p. 98
laws p. 98
caveat emptor p. 101
code of ethics p. 103
whistleblowers p. 103
moral idealism p. 104
utilitarianism p. 104
social responsibility p. 106
green marketing p. 107
ISO 14000 p. 107
cause-related marketing p. 107
social audit p. 108
sustainable development p. 109

INTERNET EXERCISE

Corporate Watch is an online magazine and resource centre committed to monitoring the social, political, economic, and environmental impact of actions taken by global corporations around the world. A wide variety of topics are covered, many of which are also discussed in Chapter 4.

Visit the Corporate Watch Web site at www.corpwatch.com. Choose a topic from Chapter 4 pertaining to social responsibility that interests you, such as sustainable development or green marketing and answer the following questions:

1 Which companies are highlighted from the "Greenwash Awards?"

2 Visit the "Headlines" or "Archives" link. Can you update at least one example in the text related to socially responsible behaviour?

APPLYING MARKETING CONCEPTS AND PERSPECTIVES

1 What concepts of moral philosophy and social responsibility are applicable to the practices of Molson Breweries described in the introduction to this chapter? Why?

2 Where would the following situations fit in Figure 4–1? (*a*) exaggerating the performance of a product to get a sale and (*b*) selling a used automobile knowing it had a major mechanical problem and not telling the buyer.

3 A recent survey of Canadian business students asked, "Is calling your office pretending to be sick in order to take the day off ethical or unethical behaviour?" How would you respond to this question?

4 Compare and contrast moral idealism and utilitarianism as alternative personal moral philosophies.

5 How would you evaluate Milton Friedman's view of the social responsibility of a firm?

6 The text lists several unethical practices of consumers. Can you name others? Why do you think consumers engage in unethical conduct?

7 Cause-related marketing programs have become popular. Describe two such programs that you are familiar with.

CASE 4–1 PRICING IN THE PHARMACEUTICAL INDUSTRY

Canadians spend billions of dollars annually for prescription drugs to treat acute and chronic ailments. The pharmaceutical industry in Canada has often been criticized for its pricing practices. Many public health officials, government departments or agencies, and consumer advocacy groups argue that, in many cases, the industry is simply charging too much money for its products. Pharmaceutical company executives have responded to such criticism by citing large research and development costs, extensive testing requirements to obtain government approval to market the products, and marketplace uncertainties as valid reasons for the prices they charge for their drugs.

FAIR AND REASONABLE PRICING

A central issue in the debate concerning prescription drug pricing relates to what is a "fair and reasonable price." Critics of drug pricing spotlight instances where they believe the prices charged are excessive. For instance, drugs to treat ulcers sell in the range of $1300 to $1400 annually per patient. Drugs that control cholesterol cost patients $1015 to $1265 per year per patient. Persons suffering from high blood pressure pay almost $850 annually to treat this condition. People over the age of 65, many with fixed incomes, bear these costs. For example, 49 percent of the sales of high blood pressure medication are accounted for by the elderly.

Pharmaceutical firms counter critics' charges of excessive pricing using a variety of arguments. They note that the research and development cost of a new medication can be more than $150 million and span a decade of development and testing. Moreover, the risk is very high since most new drugs are never successfully commercialized. In addition, the pharmaceutical industry spends billions annually for marketing the newest drugs to doctors and consumers.

Debate over what is a "fair and reasonable" price for drugs typically focuses on economic versus societal factors, and the relative importance of a firm's stakeholders in setting prices. Often the final pricing decision depends on the individual judgment and moral sensitivity of the managers making the decision.

PROLIFE: PRICING ADL

Issues in the pricing of ADL, a treatment for Alzheimer's disease that affects the elderly, were recently faced by Prolife, a small pharmaceutical company. A task force of company executives was considering the pricing strategy for ADL. Two points of view were expressed: (1) pursuing a high-price strategy designed to recoup the costs of the drug quickly and getting a jump on the competition and (2) pursuing a lower-price strategy to increase the drug's availability to victims of the disease.

Steve Vaughn, an Assistant Product Manager at Prolife, was the principal proponent of a lower-price strategy. He argued that a less aggressive price strategy made sense even though it would take slightly longer to recoup the initial investment in ADL. Having a family member afflicted with Alzheimer's disease, Mr. Vaughn felt that the ability of victims and their families to pay for the drug should be considered when setting the price for ADL. He was overruled, however, by the task force members. Believing that his views deserved attention and action, and that "bottom-line" considerations did not negate his position, he lobbied other task force members and has considered expressing his opinion to senior executives at Prolife. He was cautioned by Bill Compton, a Prolife Senior Product Manager and his mentor, to reconsider his position, noting that Prolife is a business and that "rocking the boat" might not be an advantage to his career at Prolife.

Questions

1 Who are the primary stakeholders who must be considered when setting prices for prescription drugs?
2 How might the personal moral philosophies of moral idealism and utilitarianism be applied to prescription drug pricing in general and in the specific case of ADL?
3 How might the three concepts of social responsibility described in Chapter 4 be applied to prescription pricing in general and in the specific case of ADL?
4 If you were Steve Vaughn, what would you do in this situation?

PART I CASE TECHNOLOGY CHANGING OUR MARKETS AND OUR LIVES

Technological innovation is part of our daily lives, whether or not we are aware of it. We wake to a digital clock radio and take for granted the conveniences provided by appliances manufactured around the globe. The quality of our lives has been improved in a variety of ways. We are able to eat meals cooked quickly in our microwaves. Satellites and digital telecommunication systems allow us to communicate faster and farther than possible just a decade ago. Technology, in its various forms, has touched every aspect of business as well as changed the way in which products are created, manufactured, and purchased. The diffusion of technology theory is a reality and there are many ways in which technology has touched our lives—from changing the way in which we communicate with each other in business to providing convenience in our personal lives. One impetus for recent social and economic metamorphosis is the growth of business on the Internet.

FAST-CHANGING MARKETS

The influence of the Internet on both business and consumer markets is far-reaching. It is pervasive, causing many social, political, economic, and behavioural changes. The ability to facilitate these changes comes from the convergence of technologies: computer, telecommunications, and the Internet. Convergence is the development of the communication infrastructure allowing cable, satellite, or copper wire to be used to transmit phone, Internet, and television services over the same network.[1] The transformation of our world through the digital network is creating great competition among large multinationals, placing pressure on global infrastructures. Governments from around the world are also keeping an eye on this phenomenon and are involved in policy making, trying to determine the extent to which this medium should or should not be regulated. Those countries, companies, and individuals connected to each other through the World Wide Web are faced with more information demands and opportunities than those without access and without skills to access a new world.

Other inventions and innovations such as the automobile, electricity, the telephone, computer chips, and the printing press improved the quality of our lives. The infrastructures in place today evolved from the need to continually innovate and create opportunities for companies. Technological innovation both creates new industries and transforms mature industries. Currently, the convergence of a number of technologies is providing the ability to explore many opportunities for growth. It is also transforming the way in which businesses operate and individuals communicate. The emergence of e-commerce is part of the phenomenon known as the World Wide Web.

UNDERSTANDING E-COMMERCE

The acceptance and adoption of a technology that allows global interaction between organizations and individuals is indeed a phenomenon. E-business, e-commerce, Net shopping, online retailing, Internet diffusion, e-culture, e-age, the virtual world, portals—these are all new terms that are being used by the business press to help to describe new ways of doing business on the Internet.[2]

So what is e-commerce? PricewaterhouseCoopers has been busy following the development of Internet applications. As their clients required assistance in managing their Web sites and exploring efficient, profitable applications of the Internet, PricewaterhouseCoopers acquired expertise in this area. They appear to be clear about what e-business and e-commerce are all about. Their definitions are: "E-Business is using electronic information to improve performance, create value and enable new relationships between business and customers. E-Commerce is marketing, selling and buying of products and services on the Internet."[3]

The Boston Consulting Group, an international consulting firm, believes that online retailing will continue to triple each year, with their estimate of 1998 year-end online retail revenue at US $4.4 billion. The study of 127 online retailers completed by the Boston Consulting Group claims that online retailing is not cannibalizing traditional retail revenue; instead, the Web sites are generating sales that would not necessarily have occurred. A.C. Nielsen estimates that in Canada, 36 percent of Internet users have purchases made over the Net—a 20 percent increase over the number of Internet purchases in 1997.[4]

ONLINE SHOPPING FOR ANYTHING

Shopping online is becoming more popular as more consumers begin to overcome fears of credit-card abuse. The publicity generated by amazon.com, one of the top 10 largest retailing Web sites, has opened the door for other online retailers to benefit from the trust that amazon.com has been able to build with its customer base. The top 10 online retail sites attracting the Canadian consumer are all U.S. based. These

[1]Tom Nicholson, "The Great Technology Race," *Managing Intellectual Property* (July/August, 1998), p. 24.

[2]Andy Riga, "The Web Now Sells Toys to Vegetables," *The Financial Post (National Post)*, (December 10, 1998), p. C10.

[3]http://www.e-business.pwcglobal.com

[4]Andy Riga, "The Web Now Sells Toys to Vegetables," *The Financial Post (National Post)*, (December 10, 1998), p. C10.

include amazon.com, Dell Computer Corp., Lands' End, and Charles Schwab.

Amazon.com has made it difficult for other companies to keep up. Since they opened their cyberspace book store in 1995, little has stopped the Seattle-based company from being considered a pioneer in e-retailing.[5] There was a time when few people felt their credit-card numbers would be safe to use on the Internet. Amazon.com, through their innovative marketing approach and dedication to customer service, have changed that. They used links on major services such as Yahoo!, America Online (AOL), Excite, Netscape Communications, GeoCities, Microsoft, and AltaVista[6] to initially create awareness for their business. Once at the amazon.com site, over time book browsers became online book buyers. amazon.com has continued to grow its product and service portfolio to include CDs, videos, DVDs, and computer software. Recently, they added auctions to enhance their service offering and purchased a 50 percent share in pet.com to expand their retail mix.[7] There is little doubt that e-commerce would not be growing at its current rate had it not been for amazon.com taking the lead and encouraging consumers to consider the Net as a purchasing tool, not just a communication tool.

CANADIAN ONLINE SHOPPING OPPORTUNITIES

A large majority of Canadian companies jumped on the Net only recently—prompting some analysts to claim it may already be too late. With the exception of Toronto's Bid.Com, an early entry in the online auction business, most Canadian companies have been slow to use their Web sites as more than a public relations tool. Late or not, the 1998 Christmas season was profitable for online retailers. It was particularly profitable for Cornucopia, a small Montreal gift store, which received orders not only from across Canada and the United States, but also from places as far away as Saudi Arabia. The Christmas baskets they typically sent included eggnog mix, cranberry cider, cookies and candy. Recipients were family, friends, and business colleagues.[8] About 10 percent of orders came online as some customers preferred to use the Web site to browse and then place the orders directly through the toll-free numbers. Not everyone wants to order online; some people still want to have human contact.

Toys, books, computers, clothes, and investments can now all be purchased online. Not everything is perfect, however, with this particular shopping medium. Although the ability to access Web sites is global, providing customer service and shipping globally is another matter. Two very popular Web sites are eToys and Toys R Us, but unfortunately they do not ship to Canada. This provided Zellers an opportunity to take advantage of this lack of service to the Canadian market. In October 1998, Zellers' parent, the Hudson's Bay Company, took the step into e-commerce. They launched their online toy store featuring 500 toys. Canadian consumers purchasing from U.S.-based sites must be wary. The charges are in U.S. dollars, there can be hefty delivery fees, and there may be minimum purchase limits. All of this makes it prudent for Canadian retailers to take Net shopping seriously.

CHANGING ORGANIZATIONAL BUYING

The Internet hype concerning the ability to generate revenue has been focused on Net shopping. There are, however, ways in which business-to-business transactions can also use this powerful, global communication tool. Online retailing, which is consumer marketing, is a recent marvel with incredible possibilities yet to be realized in that particular market. However, even greater possibilities exist for business-to-business transactions.

MedSite.com is an example of developing a Web-based application for the medical industry. It is preparing to become a "one-stop shop of core supplies for medical professionals."[9] The medical retailer not only sells books, but also offers medical instruments and other supplies. MedSupplies.com is an electronic catalogue with 2000 medical instruments supplied from nearly 100 suppliers. They plan to offer other services such as order tracking, financing, statement checking, and online credit-card applications. The success of Web-based transactions of this type requires a great deal of trust within the medical profession. MedSite.com needs to build strong relationships with their suppliers at the same time as building a reputation of providing security, competitive prices, and exceptional services for doctors and hospitals.

Internet commerce is also transforming the way in which business transactions are managed. Automating organizational purchasing is only one of potentially hundreds of business-to-business applications. These applications are important to industries such as trucking, insurance, and steel. E-Steel has created an independent site that has become a global trading marketplace for buyers and sellers around the world to locate trading partners, send requests, bid and negotiate prices. It is also possible to complete orders online. This concept has also been developed for the paper and textile industries. This virtual marketplace allows companies from around the world to "meet" and conduct business without the expense of international travel. It provides a great equalizer for smaller businesses wanting to compete internationally.[10] Even scientists

[5]Tony Lisanti, "The new stealth competitor," Discount Store News, (March 8, 1999), p. 11.

[6]Amazon.com, *Form 10K*, 1998

[7]Steven M. Zeitchik, "Amazon.com moves into auction, pet marktets," *Publishers Weekly* (April 5, 1999), p. 12.

[8]Andy Riga, "Canada Warms to E-Buying: Orders via Internet Jump For Montreal Firm's Gift Baskets," *The Gazette (Montreal)*, (December 23, 1998), p. D1/D8.

[9]Saroja Girishankar, "Short Online June From Medical Books to Suppliers," *Internetweek*, (April 5, 1999), p. 18.

[10]Christine Larson, "E-valanche," Chief Executive, (Beyond the Internet Supplement, 1999), p. 10-18.

are able to benefit from an electronic venture specifically designed to meet the needs of scientists. Chem Dex was launched in 1997 and developed a multivendor catalogue of specific types of research products and currently handles nearly US $150 million in transactions. The scientific community has found a common place to purchase products such as virus antibodies at the same time as allowing medical suppliers to announce new products and services to their target market.

Electronic ventures are also spreading to the financial services industry. E-loan is an online mortgage company that has successfully taken a traditional company and used technology to provide additional services to its customers. In September 1998, the Royal Bank introduced Canada's first SET (Secure Electronic Transaction) and end-to-end payment service.[11] This service allows Royal's VISA merchants and small businesses that are conducting business online to offer their customers a highly secured payment choice. Future developments may provide the option of digital signatures for cardholders, enhancing the safety of e-commerce.

BUILDING TRUST

Certainly the Internet provides great opportunities for businesses with the strategies and "out-of-the-box" thinking to efficiently reach global markets. There are many advantages to those with the vision to jump onto the Net and find new applications to enhance existing, traditional vehicles of communication and distribution. With these new opportunities, however, come a wide range of issues that must be addressed, since problems are also associated with this opportunity. Issues of trust and privacy surround each transaction on the Net. Not only do customers need to trust the security of the transaction, but they also need to know that their personal information is kept confidential. They do not want to fear that their credit-card numbers are being abused. Since they cannot touch the merchandise, they need to trust the visual representations. The inconvenience and cost of returning goods by mail may outweigh the benefits of being able to shop anywhere, anytime. Online retailers need to trust the buyer. In a business-to-consumer situation, the retailer trusts that the credit cards have not been stolen as they ship their goods. Companies wishing to participate in online ventures need to spend money to ensure that their data-storage systems and networks are protected from hacking or abuse by employees.[12]

Social and political issues raised by Internet commerce affect the growth of e-business as well as individual purchasing behaviour. Governments around the world have hesitated to become involved in monitoring or controlling business practices on the Net. Companies who use the technology for legitimate business purposes understand that Net customers now have a great deal of power because they have access to both more information and products through the Internet. This leads to some interesting social issues as those socioeconomic groups without access to the Internet may become increasingly disenfranchised. E-commerce is changing the way in which consumers and businesses buy goods and services. The virtual marketplace is here.

SITES WORTH A VISIT

http://www.amazon.com
http://www.cornucopia.ca
http://www.e-business.pwcglobal.com
(PricewaterhouseCoopers)
http://shop.hbc.com/toys (Zellers Toyland)

Discussion Questions

1 In your opinion, what relationship does a company's e-business strategy have with its marketing strategy?
2 Can you identify specific uncontrollable, environmental factors that are the result of the growth of e-business? Select an industry and relate how these factors are changing the industry.
3 Relationship marketing is an important concept. What impression do you believe e-business has on a company's relationship with its suppliers and customers?
4 Discuss the ethical and social issues that marketers need to address when considering their e-commerce applications.

[11]Advertising Supplement, "E-comm's Countdown to Ignition," *Canadian-Business,* (February 12, 1999), p. 65–70.
[12]Cal Slemp, "Electronic Commerce Success Is A Matter of Trust," *Network World,* (December 14, 1998), p. 42.

Part Two

2

UNDERSTANDING BUYERS AND MARKETS

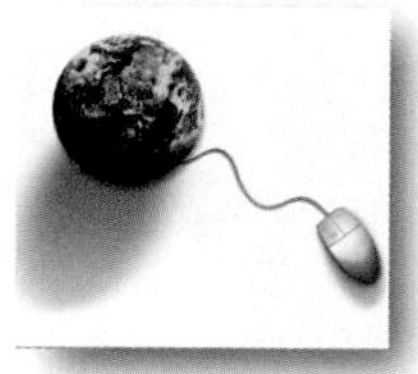

Using local and global perspectives to understand people as individual consumers and as members of companies that become organizational buyers is the focus of Part Two. Chapter 5 describes the nature and scope of world trade and examines the global marketing activities of such companies as 3M, Coca-Cola, Colgate-Palmolive, Ericsson, IKEA, Kodak, L'Oreal, and Volvo. Chapter 6 examines the actions buyers take in purchasing and using products, and explains how and why one product or brand is chosen over another. In Chapter 7 Gary Null, the international business director for a laser-based communication system at Honeywell, helps explain how organizational buyers purchase laser technology and products for their own use or resale. Together these chapters help marketing students understand individual, family, and organizational purchases in a variety of cultural environments.

Het is even slikken...

...maar dan ben je wel mooi van je hoest af.

Speciaal voor kinderen is er een zoete, zachte hoestsiroop.

Buckley's
HOESTSIROOP

BUCKLEY'S REKENT AF MET HEESHEID EN HOEST.

CHAPTER FIVE

GLOBAL MARKETING AND WORLD TRADE

5

AFTER READING THIS CHAPTER YOU SHOULD BE ABLE TO:

- Describe the nature and scope of world trade from a global perspective and its implications for Canada.
- Explain the effects of economic protectionism and the implications of economic integration for global marketing practices.
- Understand the importance of environmental factors (cultural, economic, and political) in shaping global marketing efforts.
- Describe alternative approaches firms use to enter and compete in global markets.
- Identify specific challenges marketers face when crafting worldwide marketing programs.

COMPETING IN THE GLOBAL MARKETPLACE

Canadian marketers cannot ignore the vast potential of global markets. Over 99 percent of the world's population lives outside of Canada and collectively these potential customers possess tremendous purchasing power. Not only are global markets substantial, but many are also growing faster than comparable markets in Canada—a fact not lost on both large and small global-minded Canadian companies.

Successful Canadian marketers have responded to three challenges in the global marketplace. First, they have satisfied the needs of a discriminating global consumer who increasingly purchases goods and services on the basis of value. Ontario-based W. K. Buckley Ltd. (www.buckleys.com) is a small Canadian company that competes effectively in foreign markets with a quality product, a cough-remedy known as Buckley's Mixture. Buckley's famous "tastes bad and it works" positioning theme has struck a resonant chord with global consumers from the United States to Australia, and from Holland to China.[1]

Second, Canadian marketers have capitalized on trends favouring free trade among industrialized nations throughout the world. For example, the North American Free Trade Agreement (NAFTA) has opened up the Mexican market for Canadian companies and many have found opportunities there in a variety of sectors including telecommunications and engineering services. Finally, Canadian marketers have pursued opportunities in the newly emerging democracies in Eastern Europe and the former Soviet Union, including McDonald's Restaurants of Canada Ltd.

Pursuit of global markets by Canadian and foreign marketers ultimately results in world trade. The purpose of this chapter is to describe the nature and scope of world trade and to highlight challenges involved in global marketing.

DYNAMICS OF WORLD TRADE

The dollar value of world trade has more than doubled in the past decade and will exceed $11 trillion in 2002. Manufactured goods and commodities account for 75 percent of world trade. Service industries, including telecommunications, transportation, insurance, education, banking, and tourism, represent the other 25 percent of world trade.

World Trade Flows

All nations and regions of the world do not participate equally in world trade. World trade flows reflect interdependencies among industries, countries, and regions and manifest themselves in country, company, industry, and regional exports and imports.

Global Perspective Figure 5–1 shows the estimated dollar value of exports and imports among North American countries, Western Europe, Asian/Pacific Rim countries, and the rest of the world, including intraregional trade flows.[2] The United States, Western Europe, Canada, and Japan together account for two-thirds of world trade.[3]

Not all trade involves the exchange of money for goods or services. In a world where 70 percent of all countries do not have convertible currencies or where government-owned enterprises lack sufficient cash or credit for imports, other means of payment are used. An estimated 20 percent of world trade involves **countertrade,** the practice of using barter rather than money for making global sales.

Countertrade is popular with many Eastern European nations, Russia, and Asian countries. For example, the Malaysian government recently exchanged 20 000 tons of

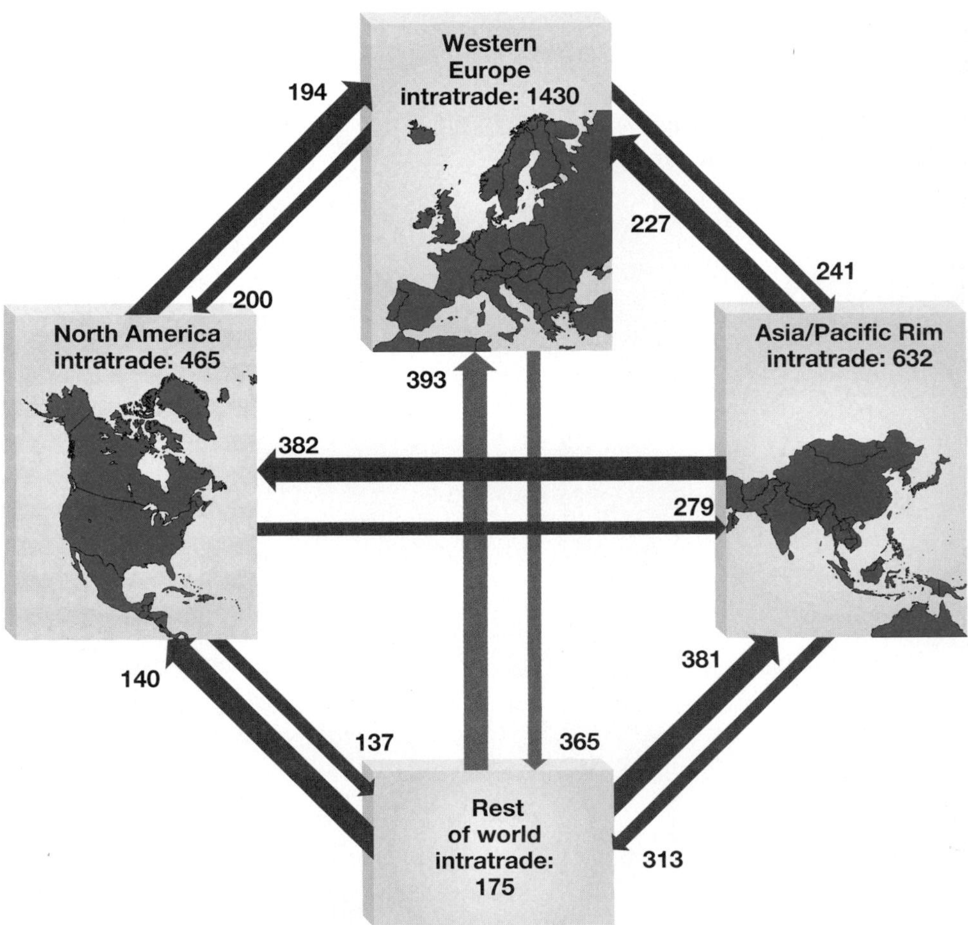

FIGURE 5–1
Illustrative world trade flows (billions of dollars)

www.volvo.com

rice for an equivalent amount of Philippine corn. Volvo of North America delivered automobiles to the Siberian police force when Siberia had no cash to pay for them. It accepted payment in oil, which it then sold for cash to pay for media advertising.[4]

A global perspective on world trade views exports and imports as complementary economic flows: a country's imports affect its exports and exports affect its imports. Every nation's imports arise from the exports of other nations. As the exports of one country increase, its national output and income rise, which, in turn, leads to an increase in the demand for imports. This nation's greater demand for imports stimulates the exports of other countries. Increased demand for exports of other nations energizes their economic activity, resulting in higher national income, which stimulates their demand for imports. In short, imports affect exports and vice versa. This phenomenon is called the **trade feedback effect** and is one argument for free trade among nations.

Canadian Perspective Canada's **gross domestic product** (GDP), the monetary value of all goods and services produced in a country during one year, is valued at almost $900 billion. Canada exports a significant percentage of the goods and services it produces. In fact, it exports over 35 percent of GDP, making it an important trading nation.[5]

The difference between the monetary value of a nation's exports and imports is called the **balance of trade.** When a country's exports exceed its imports, it incurs a surplus in its balance of trade. When imports exceed exports, a deficit has occurred. Canada maintains an overall surplus in its balance of trade at this time.

www.milltronics.com

Almost every Canadian is affected by Canada's trading activity. The effects vary from the products we buy (Samsung computers from Korea, Waterford crystal from Ireland, Lindemans wine from Australia) to those we sell (Moosehead beer to Sweden, Milltronics Ltd.'s measurement devices to New Zealand, Sullivan Entertainment Inc.'s *Anne of Green Gables* videos and merchandise to Japan) and the additional jobs and improved standard of living that can result from world trade.

World trade flows to and from Canada reflect demand and supply interdependencies for goods and services among nations and industries. While Canada trades with dozens of other countries, the three largest importers of Canadian goods and services are the United States (accounting for over 80 percent), Japan, and the European Union (EU). These countries are also the top three exporters to Canada. The EU and Japan enjoy trade surpluses with our country while the United States incurs a trade deficit.[6]

Competitive Advantage of Nations

As companies in many industries find themselves competing against foreign competitors at home and abroad, government policy makers around the world are increasingly asking why some companies and industries in a country succeed globally while others lose ground or fail. Michael Porter suggests a "diamond" to explain a nation's competitive advantage and why some industries and firms become world leaders.[7] He identified four key elements, which appear in Figure 5–2:

1. *Factor conditions.* These reflect a nation's ability to turn its natural resources, education, and infrastructure into a competitive advantage. Consider Holland, which exports 59 percent of the world's cut flowers. The Dutch lead the world in the cut-flower industry because of their research in flower cultivation, packaging, and shipping—not because of their weather.
2. *Demand conditions.* These include both the number and sophistication of domestic customers for an industry's product. Japan's sophisticated consumers demand quality in their TVs and radios, thereby making Japan's producers such as Sony, Sanyo, Matsushita, and Hitachi among the world leaders in the electronics industry.

FIGURE 5–2
Porter's "diamond" of national competitive advantage

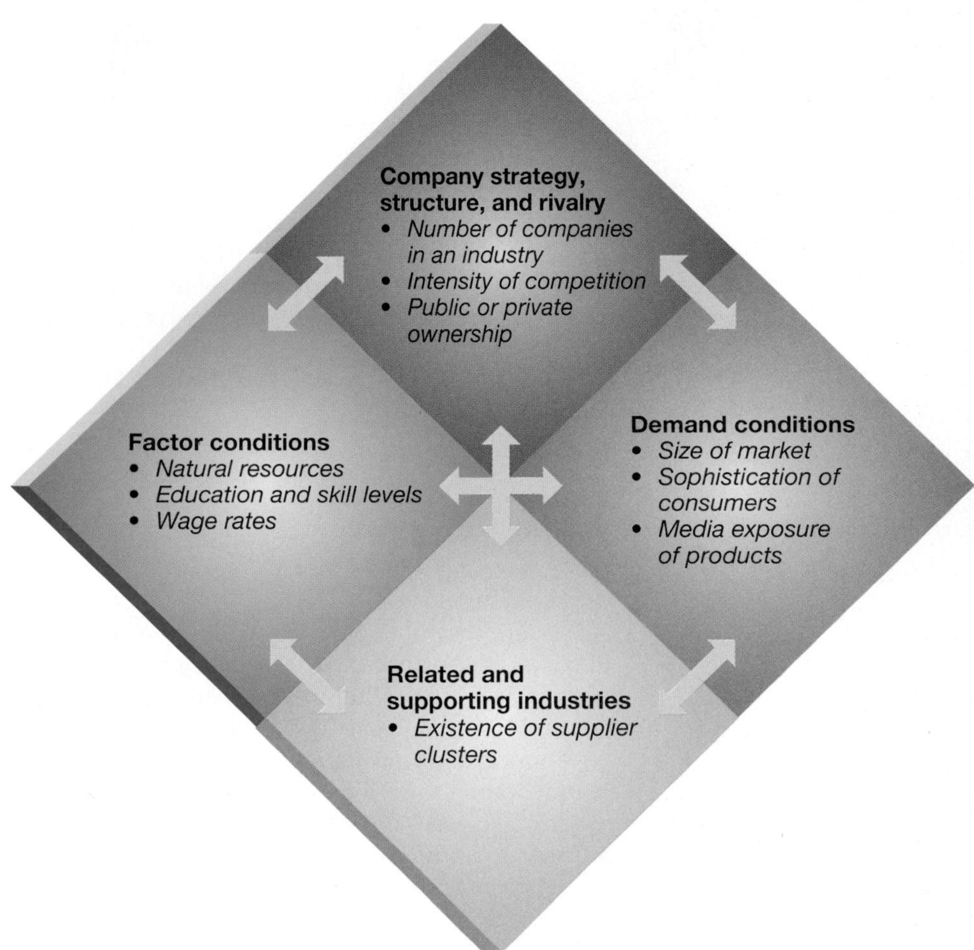

3. *Related and supporting industries.* Firms and industries seeking leadership in global markets need clusters of world-class suppliers that accelerate innovation. The German leadership in scientific and industrial instrumentation relates directly to the cluster of supporting German precision engineering suppliers.
4. *Company strategy, structure, and rivalry.* These factors include the conditions governing the way a nation's businesses are organized and managed, along with the intensity of domestic competition. The Italian shoe industry has become a world leader because of intense domestic competition among firms such as MAB, Bruno Magli, and Rossimoda, which has made shoes for Christian Dior and Anne Klein Couture.

In Porter's study, case histories of firms in more than 100 industries were analyzed. While the strategies employed by the most successful global competitors were different in many respects, a common theme emerged—a firm that succeeds in global markets has first succeeded in intense domestic competition. Hence competitive advantage for global firms grows out of relentless, continuing improvement, innovation, and change.

It is important to note, however, that it is not essential to be a giant company to gain benefits in global markets. Numerous small firms succeed in foreign niche markets or by utilizing unique information, licences, or technology. Ontario-based Milltronics Ltd. developed a non-contacting ultrasonic device for measuring levels of liquids, slurries, and sludges called THE PROBE. It measures levels of liquids as diverse as corn syrup and phenol acids in open or closed vessels by emitting pulses of

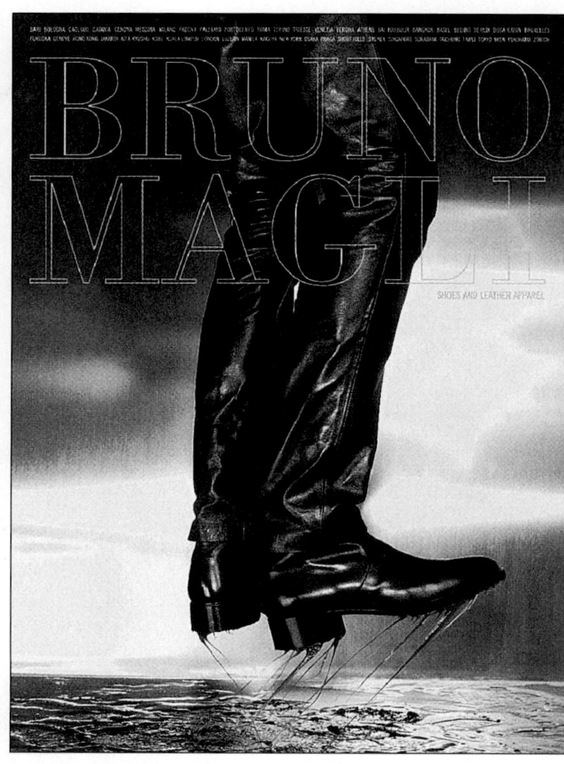

Sony and Bruno Magli have succeeded in the global marketplace as well as in their domestic markets.

high-frequency sound that bounce back to the device. The product has been used in dozens of ways including measuring the amount of milk produced by cows in New Zealand to detecting the depth of snow in Japan. THE PROBE currently accounts for 12 percent of Milltronics' worldwide revenue.

CONCEPT CHECK

1. What is the trade feedback effect?
2. What variables influence why some companies and industries in a country succeed globally while others lose ground or fail?

EMERGENCE OF A BORDERLESS ECONOMIC WORLD

Three trends in the late 20th century have significantly affected world trade. One trend has been a gradual decline of economic protectionism exercised by individual countries. The second trend is apparent in the formal economic integration and free trade among nations. A third trend is evident in global competition among global companies for global consumers.

Decline of Economic Protectionism

Protectionism is the practice of shielding one or more sectors of a country's economy from foreign competition through the use of tariffs or quotas. The principal economic argument for protectionism is that it preserves jobs, protects a nation's political security, discourages economic dependency on other countries, and encourages the

FIGURE 5–3
How protectionism affects world trade

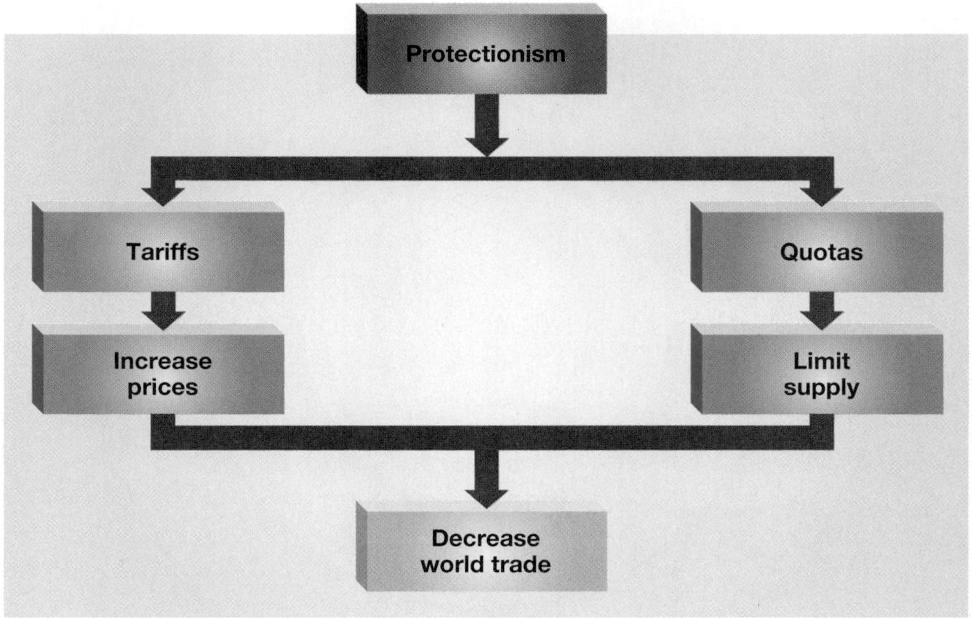

development of domestic industries. Read the accompanying Ethics and Social Responsibility Alert and ask yourself if protectionism has an ethical and social responsibility dimension.[8]

Tariffs and quotas discourage world trade as depicted in Figure 5–3. **Tariffs,** which are a government tax on goods or services entering a country, primarily serve to raise prices on imports. For example, the average tariff on manufactured goods in industrialized countries is four percent.[9]

The effect of tariffs on world trade and consumer prices is substantial. Consider rice exports to Japan. Experts claim that if the Japanese rice market were opened to imports by lowering tariffs, lower prices would save Japanese consumers $8.4 billion annually. Similarly, tariffs imposed on bananas by Western European countries cost

ETHICS

ETHICS AND SOCIAL RESPONSIBILITY ALERT

Global Ethics and Global Economics: The Case of Protectionism

World trade benefits from free and fair trade among nations. Nevertheless, governments of many countries continue to use tariffs and quotas to protect their various domestic industries. Why? Protectionism earns profits for domestic producers and tariff revenue for the government. There is a cost, however. For example, protectionist policies cost Japanese consumers billions annually. Canadian consumers also pay higher prices because of tariffs and other protective restrictions.

Sugar import quotas in the United States, automobile import quotas in many European countries, beer import tariffs in Canada, and rice import tariffs in Japan protect domestic industries but also interfere with world trade for these products. Regional trade agreements, such as those found in the provisions of the European Union and the North American Free Trade Agreement, may also pose a situation whereby member nations can obtain preferential treatment in quotas and tariffs whereas nonmember nations do not.

Protectionism, in its many forms, raises an interesting global ethical question. Is protectionism, no matter how applied, an ethical practice?

consumers $4.2 billion a year. Ecuador (the world's largest banana exporter), Mexico, Guatemala, and Honduras are seeking to end this levy.[10]

A **quota** is a restriction placed on the amount of a product allowed to enter or leave a country. Quotas can be mandated or voluntary and may be legislated or negotiated by governments. Import quotas seek to guarantee domestic industries access to a certain percentage of their domestic market. The best-known quota concerns the mandatory or voluntary limits of foreign automobile sales in many countries. Quotas imposed by European countries make European cars 25 percent more expensive than similar models in Japan, costing European customers $56 billion per year. Less visible quotas apply to the importation of produce and electronics. Ultimately, consumers usually pay higher prices because of quotas.[11]

Every country engages in some form of protectionism. However, protectionism has declined over the past 50 years due in large part to the *General Agreement on Tariffs and Trade (GATT).* This international treaty was intended to limit trade barriers and promote world trade through the reduction of tariffs, which it did. However, GATT did not explicitly address non-tariff trade barriers, such as quotas and world trade in services, which often sparked heated trade disputes between nations.

World Trade Organization
www.wto.org

As a consequence, the major industrialized nations of the world formed the **World Trade Organization** (WTO) to address a broad array of world trade issues. There are 132 WTO member countries, including Canada, which account for more than 90 percent of world trade. The WTO is a permanent institution that sets rules governing trade between its members through panels of trade experts who (1) decide on trade disputes between members and (2) issue binding decisions. The WTO reviews more than 100 disputes annually. For instance, the WTO denied Eastman Kodak's multimillion-dollar damage claim that the Japanese government protected Fuji Photo from import competition. In another decision, the WTO allowed Britain, Ireland, and the European Union to reclassify U.S.-produced local area network (LAN) computer equipment as telecommunications gear. The new classification effectively doubled the import tariff on these U.S. goods.[12]

Rise of Economic Integration

In recent years a number of countries with similar economic goals have formed transnational trade groups or signed trade agreements for the purpose of promoting free trade among member nations and enhancing their individual economies. Three of the best-known examples are the European Union (or simply EU), the North American Free Trade Agreement, and Asian Free Trade Areas.

European Union
www.eurunion.org

European Union In 1993, 12 European countries effectively eliminated most of the barriers to the free flow of goods, services, capital, and labour across their borders. This event, after decades of negotiation, formed a single market composed of 390 million consumers. Original members of the European Union were Great Britain, Ireland, Denmark, Belgium, the Netherlands, Luxembourg, Germany, France, Italy, Greece, Portugal, and Spain. Austria, Finland, and Sweden joined the European Union in 1995, bringing its membership to 15 countries (see Figure 5–4). The Swiss have elected not to join the European Union.

The European Union creates abundant marketing opportunities because firms no longer find it necessary to market their products and services on a nation-by-nation basis. Rather, Pan-European marketing strategies are possible due to greater uniformity in product and packaging standards; fewer regulatory restriction on transportation, advertising, and promotion imposed by countries; and removal of most tariffs that affect pricing practices.[13] For example, Colgate-Palmolive Company now markets its Colgate toothpaste with one formula and package across EU countries at one price. This practice was previously impossible because of different government regulations and tariffs. Europeanwide distribution from fewer locations is also feasible given open

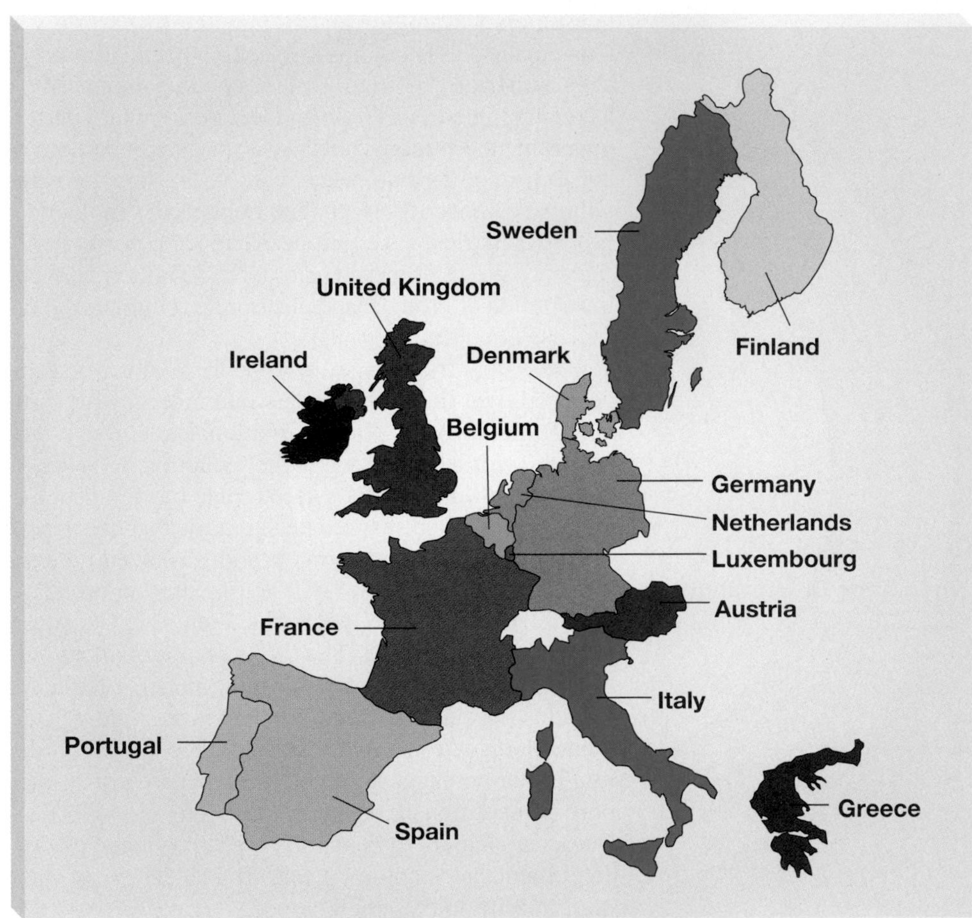

FIGURE 5–4
The countries of the European Union in 2000

borders. French tire maker Michelin recently closed 180 of its European distribution centres and now uses just 20 to serve all EU countries. Pan-European marketing opportunities will benefit further given the issuance of the common currency called the "euro."[14]

NAFTA
http://iepnt1.itaiep.doc.gov/nafta/nafta2.htm

North American Free Trade Agreement The North American Free Trade Agreement (NAFTA) became effective in 1994 and lifted many trade barriers between Canada, the United States and Mexico. This agreement, when coupled with the 1988 U.S.–Canada Free Trade Agreement, established a North American trade arrangement similar to that of the European Union. The reduction of tariffs and other provisions of NAFTA promoted relatively free trade among Canada, the United States, and Mexico and created a marketplace with about 380 million consumers. Negotiations are under way to expand NAFTA to create a 34-country Free Trade Area of the Americas by 2005. This agreement would include Canada, the United States, Mexico, and Latin American and Caribbean countries.[15]

NAFTA has stimulated trade flows among member nations as well as cross-border manufacturing and investment. For example, Whirlpool Corporation's Canadian subsidiary stopped making washing machines in Canada and moved that operation to Ohio. Whirlpool then shifted the production of household garbage compactors, kitchen ranges, and compact dryers to Canada. Ford invested $84 million in its Mexico City manufacturing plant to produce smaller cars and light trucks for global sales.

Asian Free Trade Agreements Efforts to liberalize trade in East Asia—from Japan and the four "Little Dragons" (Hong Kong, Singapore, South Korea, and Taiwan) through Thailand, Malaysia, and Indonesia—are also growing despite an economic downturn in the late 1990s. While the trade agreements are less formal than those underlying the European Union and NAFTA, they have reduced tariffs among countries and promoted trade.[16]

A New Reality: Global Competition among Global Companies for Global Consumers

The emergence of a largely borderless economic world has created a new reality for marketers of all shapes and sizes. Today, world trade is driven by global competition among global companies for global consumers.

Global Competition **Global competition** exists when firms originate, produce, and market their products and services worldwide. The automobile, pharmaceutical, apparel, electronics, aerospace, and telecommunication fields represent well-known industries with sellers and buyers on every continent. Other industries that are increasingly global in scope include soft drinks, cosmetics, ready-to-eat cereals, snack chips, and retailing.

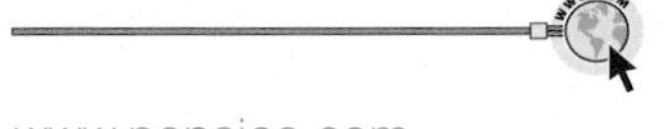

www.pepsico.com

Global competition broadens the competitive landscape for marketers. The familiar "Pepsi Challenge" taste comparison waged by Pepsi-Cola against Coca-Cola in Canada has been repeated around the world, including India and Argentina. Procter & Gamble's Pampers and Kimberly-Clark's Huggies have taken their disposable diaper rivalry from Canada to Western Europe. Boeing and Europe's Airbus Industries can be found vying for lucrative commercial aircraft contracts on virtually every continent.

www.nortelnetworks.com

Collaborative relationships also are becoming a common way to meet the demands of global competition. Global **strategic alliances** are agreements among two or more independent firms to cooperate for the purpose of achieving common goals such as a competitive advantage or customer value creation. For instance, several of the world's largest telecommunication equipment makers, including Ericsson (Sweden), Northern Telecom, now Nortel (Canada), Siemens (Germany), and 3Com and Worldcom (two U.S. firms), have formed Juniper Networks, Inc., an alliance created to build devices to speed global Internet communications. General Mills and Nestlé of Switzerland created Cereal Partners Worldwide for the purpose of fine-tuning Nestlé's European cereal marketing and distributing General Mills cereals worldwide. This global alliance is expected to produce worldwide sales of $1.4 billion by 2000.[17] Another alliance you may be familiar with is Oneworld (www. oneworldalliance.com), a global arrangement between five major airlines including Canadian Airlines, American Airlines, British Airways, Cathay Pacific, and Quantas that is designed to make international air travel easier.

Global Companies Three types of companies populate and compete in the global marketplace: (1) international firms, (2) multinational firms, and (3) transnational firms.[18] All three employ people in different countries, and many have administrative, marketing, and manufacturing operations (often called divisions or subsidiaries) around the world. However, a firm's orientation toward and strategy for global markets and marketing defines the type of company it is or attempts to be.

An *international firm* engages in trade and marketing in different countries as an extension of the marketing strategy in its home country. Generally speaking, these firms market their existing products and services in other countries the same way they do in their home country. Avon, for example, successfully distributes its product line through direct selling in Asia, Europe, and South America, employing virtually the same marketing strategy used in North America.

A *multinational firm* views the world as consisting of unique parts and markets to each part differently. Multinationals use a **multidomestic marketing strategy,** which means that they have as many different product variations, brand names, and advertising programs as countries in which they do business. For example, Lever Europe—a division of Unilever—markets its fabric softener known as Snuggle in Canada in 10 different European countries under seven brand names, including Kuschelweich in Germany, Coccolino in Italy, and Mimosin in France. These products have different packages, different advertising programs, and occasionally different formulas.[19]

A *transnational firm* views the world as one market and emphasizes cultural similarities across countries or universal consumer needs and wants more than differences. Transnational marketers employ a **global marketing strategy**—the practice of standardizing marketing activities when there are cultural similarities and adapting them when cultures differ. This approach benefits marketers by allowing them to realize economies of scale from their production and marketing activities.

www.gillette.com

Global marketing strategies are popular among many business-to-business marketers such as Caterpillar and Komatsu (heavy construction equipment) and Texas Instruments, Intel, Hitachi, and Motorola (semiconductors). Consumer goods marketers such as Timex, Seiko, and Citizen (watches), Coca-Cola and Pepsi-Cola (cola soft drinks), Gillette (personal care products), and McDonald's (fast foods) successfully execute this strategy.

www.ikea.com

Global Consumers Global competition among global companies often focuses on the identification and pursuit of global consumers. **Global consumers** consist of customer groups living in many countries or regions of the world who have similar needs or seek similar features and benefits from products or services.[20] Evidence suggests the emergence of a global middle-income class, a youth market, and an elite segment, each consuming or using a common assortment of products and services regardless of geographic location. A variety of companies have capitalized on the global consumer. Whirlpool, Sony, and IKEA have benefited from the growing global middle-income class desire for kitchen appliances, consumer electronics, and home furnishings, respectively. Levi's, Nike, and Nintendo have tapped the global youth market, as described in the accompanying Marketing NewsNet.[21] DeBeers, Chanel, Gucci, and Rolls Royce successfully cater to the elite segment for luxury goods worldwide.

MARKETING NEWSNET

The Global Teenager: A Market of 240 Million Consumers

GLOBAL

The "global teenager" market consists of 240 million 13- to 19-year-olds in Europe, North and South America, and industrialized nation of Asia who have experienced intense exposure to television (MTV broadcasts in more than 75 countries), movies, travel, and global advertising by companies such as Bennetton, Sony, Nike, and Coca-Cola. The similarities among teens in these countries are greater than their differences. For example, a global study of teenagers' rooms in 25 countries indicated it was difficult, if not impossible, to tell whether the rooms were in Vancouver, Mexico City, Tokyo, or Paris. Why? Teens buy a common gallery of products: Nintendo video games, Tommy Hilfiger apparel, Levi's blue jeans, Nike athletic shoes, Procter & Gamble Cover Girl makeup, and Clearasil facial medicine.

CONCEPT CHECK

1. What is protectionism?
2. The North American Free Trade Agreement was designed to promote free trade among which countries?
3. What is the difference between a multidomestic marketing strategy and a global marketing strategy?

A GLOBAL ENVIRONMENTAL SCAN

Global companies conduct continuing environmental scans of the five sets of environmental factors described earlier in Figure 3–1 (social, economic, technological, competitive, and regulatory forces). This section focuses on three kinds of uncontrollable environmental variables—cultural, economic, and political-regulatory variables—that affect global marketing practices in strikingly different ways than those in domestic markets.

Cultural Diversity

Marketers must be sensitive to the cultural underpinnings of different societies if they are to initiate and consummate mutually beneficial exchange relationships with global consumers. A necessary step in this process is **cross-cultural analysis,** which involves the study of similarities and differences among consumers in two or more nations or societies.[22] A thorough cross-cultural analysis involves an understanding of and an appreciation for the values, customs, symbols, and language of other societies.

Values A society's **values** represent personally or socially preferable modes of conduct or states of existence that are enduring. Understanding and working with these aspects of a society are important factors in successful global marketing. For example,[23]

- McDonald's does not sell hamburgers in its restaurants in India because the cow is considered sacred by almost 85 percent of the population. Instead, McDonald's sells the McMaharajah: two all-mutton patties, special sauce, lettuce, cheese, pickles, onions on a sesame-seed bun.
- Germans have not been overly receptive to the use of credit cards such as Visa or MasterCard and instalment debt to purchase goods and services. Indeed, the German word for debt, *Schuld,* is the same as the German word for guilt.

These examples illustrate how cultural values can influence behaviour in different societies. Cultural values become apparent in the personal values of individuals that affect their attitudes and beliefs and the importance assigned to specific behaviours and attributes of goods and services. These personal values affect consumption-specific values, such as the use of instalment debt by Germans, and product-specific values, such as the importance assigned to credit card interest rates.

Customs **Customs** are the norms and expectations about the way people do things in a specific country. Clearly customs can vary significantly from country to country. For example, 3M Company executives were perplexed when the company's Scotch-Brite floor-cleaning product initially produced lukewarm sales in the Philippines. When a Filipino employee explained that consumers there customarily clean floors by pushing coconut shells around with their feet, 3M changed the shape of the pad to a foot and sales soared! Some other customs are unusual to Canadians. Consider, for example, that in France, men wear more than twice the number of cosmetics than women do and that Japanese women give Japanese men chocolates on Valentine's Day.

Customs also relate to nonverbal behaviour of individuals in different cultural settings.[24] For example, in many European countries it is considered impolite not to have both hands on the table in business meetings. A simple gesture in a commercial such as pointing a finger is perfectly acceptable in western culture, but is perceived as an insult in Middle and Far Eastern countries. Direct eye contact is viewed positively in North and Latin American but negatively in Japan. Casual touching is also inappropriate in Japan, while men hold hands in Middle Eastern countries as a sign of friendship. Business executives in Japan like to hold their opinions, listen longer, and pause before responding in meetings. Sometimes the silence is misread by North American executives as being nonresponsive.

Cultural Symbols **Cultural symbols** are things that represent ideas and concepts. Symbols or symbolism play an important role in cross-cultural analysis because different cultures ascribe different meanings to things. So important is the role of symbols that a field of study, called **semiotics,** has emerged that examines the correspondence between symbols and their role in the assignment of meaning for people. By adroitly using cultural symbols, global marketers can tie positive symbolism to their products and services to enhance their attractiveness to consumers. However, improper use of symbols can spell disaster. A culturally sensitive global marketer will know that[25]

- North Americans are superstitious about the number 13, and Japanese feel the same way about the number 4. *Shi,* the Japanese word for four, is also the word for death. Knowing this, Tiffany & Company sells its fine glassware and china in sets of five, not four, in Japan.
- "Thumbs-up" is a positive sign in Canada. However, in Russia and Poland, this gesture has an offensive meaning when the palm of the hand is shown, as AT&T

learned. The company reversed the gesture depicted in ads, showing the back of the hand, not the palm.

Cultural symbols evoke deep feelings. Just ask executives at Coca-Cola Company's Italian office. In a series of advertisements directed at Italian vacationers, the Eiffel Tower, Empire State Building, and the Tower of Pisa were turned into the familiar Coca-Cola bottle. However, when the white marble columns in the Parthenon that crowns Athens' Acropolis were turned into Coca-Cola bottles, the Greeks were outraged. Greeks refer to the Acropolis as the "holy rock," and a government official said the Parthenon is an "international symbol of excellence" and that "whoever insults the Parthenon insults international culture." Coca-Cola apologized for the ad.[26]

Global markets are also sensitive to the fact that the "country of origin or manufacture" of products and services can symbolize superior or poor quality in some countries. For example, Russian consumers believe products made in Japan and Germany are superior in quality to products from North America and the United Kingdom. Japanese consumers believe Japanese products are superior to those made in Europe and North America.[27]

Language Global marketers should not only know the native tongues of countries in which they market their products and services but also the nuances and idioms of a language. Even though about 100 official languages exist in the world, anthropologists estimate that at least 3000 different languages are spoken. There are 11 official languages spoken in the European Union, and Canada has two official languages (English and French). Seventeen major languages are spoken in India alone.

English, French, and Spanish are the principal languages used in global diplomacy and commerce. However, the best language to communicate with consumers is their own, as any seasoned global marketer will attest to. Unintended meanings of brand names and messages have ranged from the absurd to the obscene[28]:

www.cadburyschweppes.com

- When the advertising agency responsible for launching Procter & Gamble's successful Pert shampoo in Canada realized that the name means "lost" in French, it substituted the brand name Pret, which means "ready."
- In Italy, Cadbury Schweppes, the world's third-largest soft drink manufacturer, realized that its Schweppes Tonic Water brand had to be renamed Schweppes Tonica because "il water" turned out to be the idiom for a bathroom.
- The Vicks brand name common in the United States is German slang for sexual intimacy; therefore, Vicks is called Wicks in Germany.

Experienced global marketers use **back translation,** where a translated word or phrase is retranslated into the original language by a different interpreter to catch errors.[29] For example, IBM's first Japanese translation of its "Solutions for a small planet" advertising message yielded "Answers that make people smaller." The error was caught and corrected. Nevertheless, unintended meanings still occur in the most unlikely situations. A Japanese tire manufacturer found it necessary to publicly apologize in Brunei (a British-protected sultanate on the coast of Borneo) for the tread grooves on one of its tire brands. Some critics claimed the tread resembled a verse from the Koran, the sacred book of the Muslims written in Arabic.

Cultural Ethnocentricity The tendency for people to view their own values, customs, symbols, and language favourably is well known. However, the belief that aspects of one's culture are superior to another's is called *cultural ethnocentricity* and is a sure impediment to successful global marketing.

An outgrowth of cultural ethnocentricity exists in the purchase and use of goods and services produced outside of a country. Global marketers are acutely aware that certain groups within countries disfavour imported products, not on the basis of price, features, or performance, but purely because of their foreign origin. **Consumer ethnocentrism** is the tendency to believe that it is inappropriate, indeed immoral, to purchase foreign-made products.[30] Ethnocentric consumers believe that buying imported products is wrong because such purchases are unpatriotic, harm domestic industries, and cause domestic unemployment.[31]

In Japan, principally a tea-drinking country, Nestlé has converted the market not just to coffee but to instant coffee.

Nestlé
www.nestle.com

Cultural Change Cultures change slowly. Nevertheless, fewer impediments to world trade are likely to accelerate the rate of cultural change in societies around the world. A challenge facing global marketers is to anticipate how cultures are changing, particularly with respect to the purchase and use of goods and services.

An acknowledged master of anticipating cultural change and responding quickly is Nestlé, the world's largest packaged food manufacturer, coffee roaster, and chocolate maker. Nestlé derives 98 percent of its sales outside of its home country, Switzerland, because the company is always among the first to identify changing consumption patterns in diverse cultures. Consider Great Britain and Japan, with two very different cultures but a common passion—tea. Nestlé pioneered coffee marketing in both countries with its Nescafé instant coffee. The cultural preference for tea was changing, and Nestlé capitalized on this change. Today, Britons consume one cup of coffee for every two cups of tea. Thirty years ago, the ratio was one cup of coffee for every six cups of tea. The Japanese are now among the world's heaviest consumers of instant coffee on a per-capita basis. Nestlé is a dominant coffee marketer in both countries.[32]

Economic Considerations

Global marketing is also affected by economic considerations. Therefore, a scan of the global marketplace should include (1) a comparative analysis of the economic development in different countries, (2) an assessment of the economic infrastructure in these countries, (3) measurement of consumer income in different countries, and (4) recognition of a country's currency exchange rates.

Stage of Economic Development

There are more than 200 countries in the world today, each of which is at a slightly different point in terms of its stage of economic development. However, they can be classified into two major groupings that will help the global marketer better understand their needs:

- *Developed* countries have somewhat mixed economies. Private enterprise dominates, although they have substantial public sectors as well. Canada, the United States, Japan, and most of Western Europe can be considered developed.
- *Developing* countries are in the process of moving from an agricultural to an industrial economy. There are two subgroups within the developing category: (1) those that have already made the move and (2) those that remain locked in a preindustrial economy. Countries such as Poland, Hungary, Israel, Venezuela, and South Africa fall into the first group. In the second group are Pakistan, Sri Lanka, Tanzania, and Chad, where living standards are low and improvement will be slow. The economies of developing countries are expected to average five percent annual growth compared with two percent annual growth for developed countries through 2000.

A country's stage of economic development affects and is affected by other economic factors, as described next.

Reader's Digest learned important lessons that apply to most global firms entering foreign markets when it launched its Russian and Hungarian editions. For those lessons, see the text.

Reader's Digest
www.readersdigest.ca

Economic Infrastructure The **economic infrastructure**—a country's communications, transportation, financial, and distribution systems—is a critical consideration in determining whether to try to market to a country's consumers and organizations. Parts of the infrastructure that North Americans or Western Europeans take for granted can be huge problems elsewhere—not only in developing nations but even in countries of Eastern Europe and the former Soviet Union where such an infrastructure is assumed to be in place. Consider, for instance, transportation and distribution systems in these countries. Two-lane roads with horse-drawn carts that limit average speeds to 55 or 65 kilometres per hour are commonplace—and a nightmare for firms requiring prompt truck delivery. Wholesale and retail institutions tend to be small, and a majority are operated by new owner-managers still learning the ways of a free market system. These conditions have prompted firms such as Danone, a French food company, to establish their own wholesale, retail, and delivery systems. Danone delivers its products to 700 shops in Russia and has set up 60 shops-in-shops, where it has its own retail sales associates and cash registers.[33]

The communication infrastructure in these countries, including telecommunication and postal systems, also differ. About one in ten people have a telephone. As for postal systems, *Reader's Digest* learned to send its magazine by registered mail in brown envelopes—or by private delivery services—because attractive packages tend to get "lost" frequently. These problems have led to several billion-dollar investments to upgrade telecommunication and postal systems in these countries.

Even the financial and legal system can cause problems. Formal operating procedures among financial institutions and private properties did not exist under communism and are still limited. As a consequence, it is estimated that two-thirds of the commercial transactions in Russia involve non-monetary forms of payment.[34] The legal red tape involved in obtaining title to buildings and land for manufacturing, wholesaling, and retailing operations also has been a huge problem. Nevertheless, the Coca-Cola Company has invested $750 million from 1991 through 1998 to build bottling and distribution facilities in Russia, Allied Lyons has spent $30 million to build a plant to make Baskin-Robbins ice cream, and Mars recently opened a $200-million candy factory outside Moscow.[35]

Consumer Income and Purchasing Power A global marketer selling consumer goods must also consider what the average per-capita or household income is among a country's consumers and how the income is distributed to determine a nation's

The Coca-Cola Company has made a huge financial investment in bottling and distribution facilities in Russia.

The Coca-Cola Company
www.thecoca-colacompany.com

purchasing power. Per-capita income varies greatly between nations. Average yearly per-capita income in EU countries is $28 000 and is less than $250 in some developing countries such as Vietnam. A country's income distribution is important because it gives a more reliable picture of a country's purchasing power. Generally speaking, as the proportion of middle-income class households in a country increases, the greater a nation's purchasing power tends to be. Figure 5–5 shows the worldwide disparity in the percentage distribution of households by level of purchasing power.[36] In established market economies such as those in North America and Western Europe, 65 percent of households have an annual purchasing capability of $28 000 or more. In comparison, 75 percent of households in the developing countries of South Asia have an annual purchasing power of less than $7000.

Seasoned global marketers recognize that people in developing countries often have government subsidies for food, housing, and health care that supplement their income. Accordingly, people with seemingly low incomes are actually promising customers for a variety of products. For example, a consumer in South Asia earning the equivalent of $350 per year can afford Gillette razors. When that consumer's income rises to $1400, a Sony television becomes affordable, and a new Volkswagen or Nissan can be bought with an annual income of $14 000. In developing countries of Eastern Europe, a $1400 annual income makes a refrigerator affordable, and $2800 brings an automatic washer within reach. These facts have not gone unnoticed by Whirlpool, which now aggressively markets these products in Eastern Europe.

Income growth in developing countries of Asia, Latin America, and Central and Eastern Europe is expected to stimulate world trade well into the next century. The number of consumers in these countries earning the equivalent of $14 000 per year is expected to surpass the number of consumers in North America, Japan, and Western Europe combined by 2005.[37]

Currency Exchange Rates Fluctuations in exchange rates among the world's currencies are of critical importance in global marketing. Such fluctuations affect everyone—from international tourists to global companies.

A **currency exchange rate** is the price of one country's currency expressed in terms of another country's currency, such as the Canadian dollar expressed in Japanese yen or Swiss francs. Failure to consider exchange rates when pricing products for global markets can have dire consequences.[38]

FIGURE 5–5
How purchasing power differs around the world

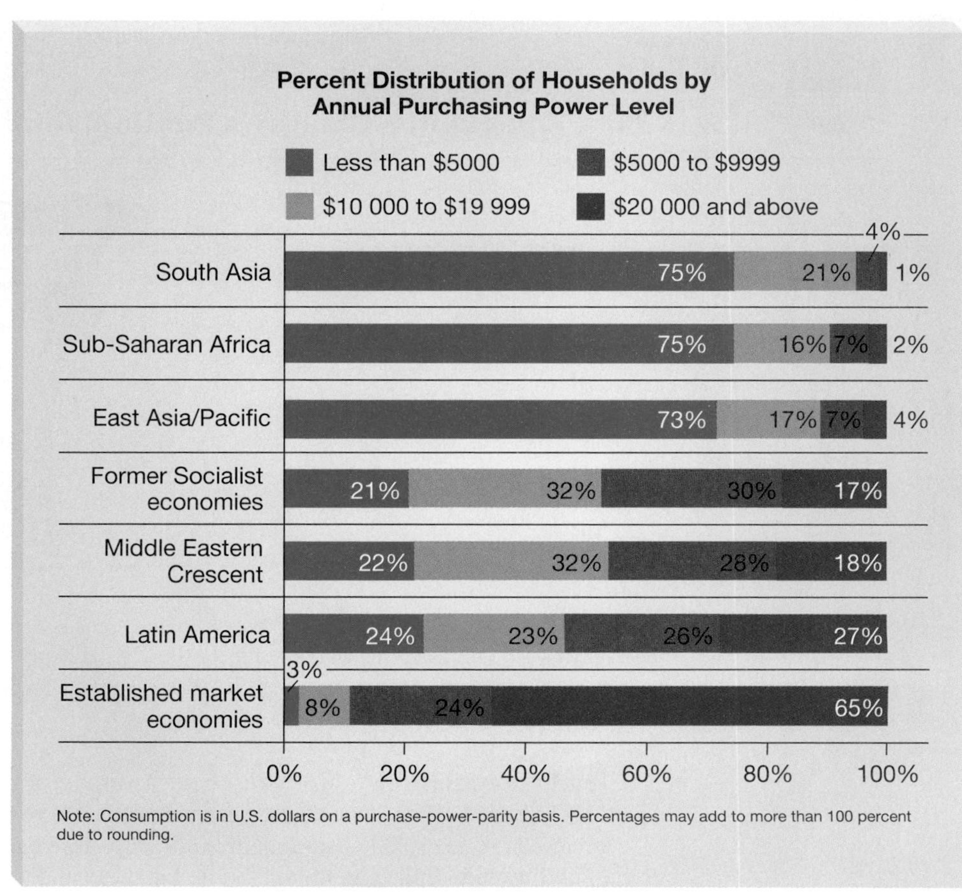

Exchange rate fluctuations have a direct impact on the sales and profits made by global companies. When foreign currencies can buy more Canadian dollars, for example, Canadian products are less expensive for foreign customers. Short-term fluctuations, however, can have a significant effect on the profits of global companies. Hewlett-Packard gained nearly a half million dollars of additional profit through exchange rate fluctuation in one year. On the other hand, Nestlé has lost as much as a million dollars in six months due to fluctuations in the Swiss franc compared with other currencies.[39]

Political-Regulatory Climate

The political and regulatory climate for marketing in a country or region of the world lies not only in identifying the current climate but in determining how long a favourable or unfavourable climate will last. An assessment of a country or regional political-regulatory climate includes an analysis of its political stability and trade regulations.

Political Stability Trade among nations or regions depends on political stability. Billions of dollars have been lost in the Middle East and the former Federal Republic of Yugoslavia as a result of internal political strife and war. Losses such as these encourage careful selection of politically stable countries and regions of the world for trade.

Political stability in a country is affected by numerous factors, including a government's orientation toward foreign companies and trade with other countries. These factors combine to create a political climate that is favourable or unfavourable for marketing and financial investment in a country or region of the world. Marketing managers monitor political stability using a variety of measures and often track country risk

WEB LINK Checking a Country's Political Risk

The political climate in every country is regularly changing. Governments can make new laws or enforce existing policies differently. Numerous consulting firms prepare political risk analyses that incorporate a variety of variables such as the risk of internal turmoil, external conflict, government restrictions on company operations, and tariff and nontariff trade barriers.

The PRS Group maintains multiple databases of country-specific information and projections, including country political risk ratings. These ratings can be accessed at http://www.prsgroup.com/gptop.html. What country has the most favourable business climate and the least favourable business climate?

ratings supplied by agencies such as the PRS Group. Visit the PRS Group Web site shown in the accompanying Web Link and see the most recent political risk ratings for countries.

Trade Regulations Countries have a variety of rules that govern business practices within their borders. These rules can often serve as trade barriers.[40] For example, Japan has some 11 000 trade regulations. Japanese car safety rules effectively require all automobile replacement parts to be Japanese and not North American or European; public health rules make it illegal to sell aspirin or cold medicine without a pharmacist present. The Malaysian government instituted advertising regulations stating that "advertisements must not project or promote an excessively aspirational lifestyle," and Sweden outlaws all advertisements to children.

Trade regulations also appear in free trade agreements among countries. European Union nations abide by some 10 000 rules that specify how goods are to be made and marketed. For instance, the rules for a washing machine's electrical system are detailed on more than 100 typed pages. Regulations related to contacting consumers via telephone, fax, and E-mail without their prior consent and toy advertising to children also exist. The European Union's ISO 9000 quality standards, though not a trade regulation, have the same effect on business practice. **ISO 9000** standards, developed by the International Standards Organization (ISO) in Geneva, Switzerland, refer to standards for registration and certification of a manufacturer's quality management and quality assurance system. Many European companies require suppliers to be ISO 9000 certified as a condition of doing business with them. Certified companies have undergone an on-site audit that includes an inspection of its facilities to ensure that documented quality control procedures are in place and that all employees understand and follow them. More than 100 countries have adopted ISO 9000 standards, and 60 000 certificates have been issued worldwide.[41]

CONCEPT CHECK

1. Semiotics involves the study of ____________________.
2. When foreign currencies can buy more Canadian dollars, are Canadian products more or less expensive for a foreign consumer?

FIGURE 5–6
Alternative global market-entry strategies

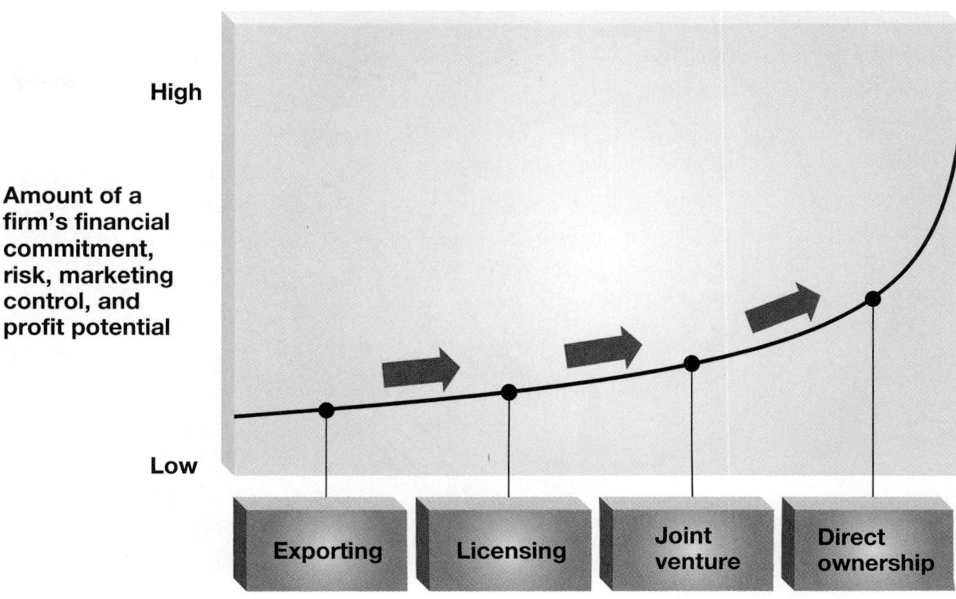

GLOBAL MARKET-ENTRY STRATEGIES

Once a company has decided to enter the global marketplace, it must select a means of market entry. Four general options exist: (1) exporting, (2) licensing, (3) joint venture, and (4) direct investment.[42] As Figure 5–6 demonstrates, the amount of financial commitment, risk, marketing control, and profit potential increases as the firm moves from exporting to direct investment.

Exporting

Exporting is producing goods in one country and selling them in another country. This entry option allows a company to make the least number of changes in terms of its product, its organization, and even its corporate goals. Host countries usually do not like this practice because it provides less local employment than under alternative means of entry.

Indirect exporting is when a firm sells its domestically produced goods in a foreign country through an intermediary. It involves the least amount of commitment and risk but will probably return the least profit. This kind of exporting is ideal for the company that has no overseas contacts but wants to market abroad. The intermediary is often a broker or agent that has the international marketing know-how and the resources necessary for the effort to succeed.

Direct exporting is when a firm sells its domestically produced goods in a foreign country without intermediaries. Most companies become involved in direct exporting when they believe their volume of sales will be sufficiently large and easy to obtain that they do not require intermediaries. For example, the exporter may be approached by foreign buyers that are willing to contract for a large volume of purchases. Direct exporting involves more risk than indirect exporting for the company but also opens the door to increased profits.

Remember W. K. Buckley Ltd. and its cough-remedy product (Buckley's Mixture) from the chapter opener? This company uses an indirect exporting strategy for the Australian market, and a direct exporting strategy for the United States market.[43] Sullican Entertainment Inc. of Toronto, creators of the *Road to Avonlea* television series, also uses an exporting strategy to market the show (a season of 13 episodes is sold as a unit) in over 100 countries including Bolivia, the Czech Republic, and South Korea.[44]

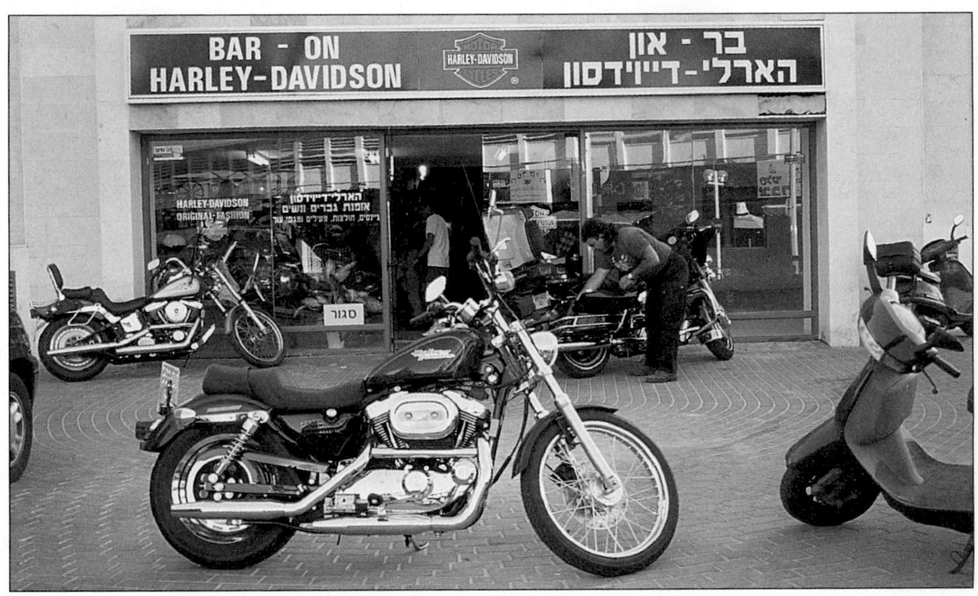

Harley-Davidson, Inc. exports about one fourth of its annual production of heavyweight motorcycles. The company is represented internationally by 577 independent dealers in 55 countries.

Harley-Davidson, Inc.
www.harley-davidson.com

Licensing

Under licensing, a company offers the right to a trademark, patent, trade secret, or other similarly valued items of intellectual property in return for a royalty or a fee. In international marketing, the advantages to the company granting the licence are low risk and a capital-free entry into a foreign country. The licensee gains information that allows it to start with a competitive advantage, and the foreign country gains employment by having the product manufactured locally. W. K. Buckley Ltd. used licensing for entering Holland. Similarly, Clearly Canadian Beverages of Vancouver used licensing to enter several markets, including the United States and Japan.

There are some serious drawbacks to this mode of entry, however. The licensor forgoes control of its product and reduces the potential profits gained from it. In addition, while the relationship lasts, the licensor may be creating its own competition. Some licensees are able to modify the product somehow and enter the market with product and marketing knowledge gained at the expense of the company that got them started. To offset this disadvantage, many companies strive to stay innovative so that the licensee remains dependent on them for improvements and successful operation. Finally, should the licensee prove to be a poor choice, the name or reputation of the company may be harmed.

Two variations of licensing, local manufacturing and local assembly, represent alternative ways to produce a product within the foreign country. With local manufacturing, a Canadian company may contract with a foreign firm to manufacture products according to stated specifications. The product is then sold in the foreign country or exported back to Canada. With local assembly, the Canadian company may contract with a foreign firm to assemble (not manufacture) parts and components that have been shipped to that country. In both cases, the advantage to the foreign country is the employment of its people, and the Canadian firm benefits from the lower wage rates in the foreign country.

A third variation of licensing is franchising. Franchising is one of the fastest-growing market-entry strategies. Franchises include soft-drink, motel, retailing, fast-food, and car rental operation and a variety of business services. McDonald's is a premier global franchiser: more than 70 percent of the company's stores are franchised, and 70 percent of the company's operating income is projected to come from foreign operations in 2001.[45]

McDonald's uses franchising as a market-entry strategy and 70 percent of the company's projected operating income will come from foreign operations in 2001.

McDonald's
www.mcdonalds.com

Joint Venture

When a foreign country and a local firm invest together to create a local business, it is called a **joint venture.** These two companies share ownership, control, and profits of the new company. Investment may be made by having either of the companies buy shares in the other or by creating a third and separate entity. This was done by Caterpillar, Inc., the world's largest manufacturer of earth-moving and construction equipment. It recently created NEVAMASH with its joint-venture partner, Kirovsky Zvod, a large Russian manufacturer of heavy equipment.[46]

The advantages of this option are twofold. First, one company may not have the necessary financial, physical, or managerial resources to enter a foreign market alone. Ford and Volkswagen formed a joint venture to make four-wheel-drive vehicles in Portugal. Second, a government may require or strongly encourage a joint venture before it allows a foreign company to enter its market. This is the case in China. Today, more than 50 000 Chinese–foreign joint ventures operate in China, including W. K. Buckley Ltd and its joint-venture partner.[47]

The disadvantages arise when the two companies disagree about policies or courses of action for their joint venture or when governmental bureaucracy bogs down the effort. For example, Canadian firms often prefer to reinvest earnings gained, whereas some foreign companies may want to spend those earnings. Or a Canadian firm may want to return profits earned to Canada, while the local firm or its government may oppose this—the problem now faced by many potential joint ventures in Eastern Europe, Russia, Latin America, and South Asia.

Direct Investment

www.hyundai.com

www.ey.com

The biggest commitment a company can make when entering the global market is **direct investment,** which entails a domestic firm actually investing in and owning a foreign subsidiary or division.[48] Examples of direct investment are Toyota's automobile plant in Ontario and Hyundai's plant in Quebec. Many Canadian-based companies are also switching to this mode of entry. Alcan Aluminium built a recycling plant in Worrington, England, and Ganong Brothers opened a plant to manufacture chocolates in Thailand.

For many firms, direct investment often follows one of the other three market-entry strategies.[49] For example, Ernst & Young, an international accounting and management consulting firm, entered Hungary first by establishing a joint venture with a local company. Ernst & Young later acquired the company, making it a subsidiary with headquarters in Budapest.

The advantages to direct investment include cost savings, better understanding of local market conditions, and fewer local restrictions. Firms entering foreign markets using direct investment believe that these advantages outweigh the financial commitments and risks involved.

CONCEPT CHECK

1. What mode of entry could a company follow if it has no previous experience in global marketing?
2. How does licensing differ from a joint venture?

CRAFTING A WORLDWIDE MARKETING EFFORT

The choice of a market-entry strategy is a necessary first step for a marketer when joining the community of global companies. The next step involves the challenging task of designing, implementing, and controlling marketing programs worldwide.

Product and Promotion Strategies

Global companies have five strategies for matching products and their promotion efforts to global markets. As Figure 5–7 shows, the strategies focus on whether a company extends or adapts its product and promotion message for consumers in different countries.

A product may be sold globally in one of three ways: (1) in the same form as in its home market, (2) with some adaptations, or (3) as a totally new product[50]:

1. *Product extension.* Selling virtually the same product in other countries is a product extension strategy. It works well for products such as Coca-Cola, Gillette razors, Breathe Right nasal strips, Wrigley's gum, and Levi's jeans. However, it didn't work for Jell-O (a more solid gelatin was preferred to the powder in England) or Duncan Hines cakes (which were seen as too moist and crumbly to eat with tea in England).
2. *Product adaptation.* Changing a product in some way to make it more appropriate for a country's climate or preferences is a product adaptation strategy. Gerber baby food comes in different varieties in different countries. Vegetable and Rabbit Meat is a favourite food in Poland. Freeze-Dried Sardines and Rice is popular in Japan.
3. *Product invention.* Alternatively, companies can invent totally new products designed to satisfy common needs across countries. Black & Decker did this with its Snake Light Flexible Flashlight. Created to address a global need for portable lighting, the product became a bestseller in North America, Europe, Latin America, and Australia and is the most successful new product developed by Black & Decker.

www.blackanddecker.com

FIGURE 5–7
Five product and promotion strategies for global marketing

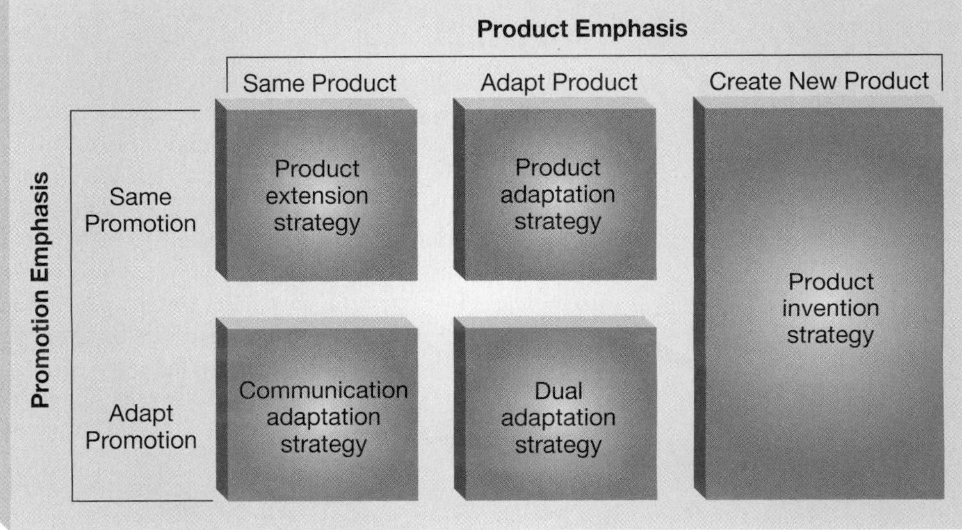

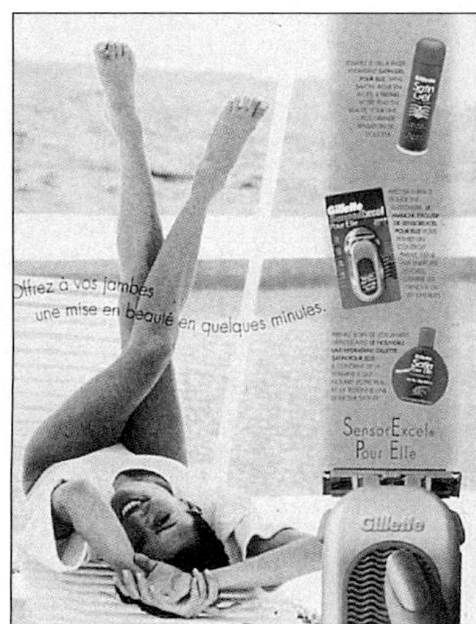

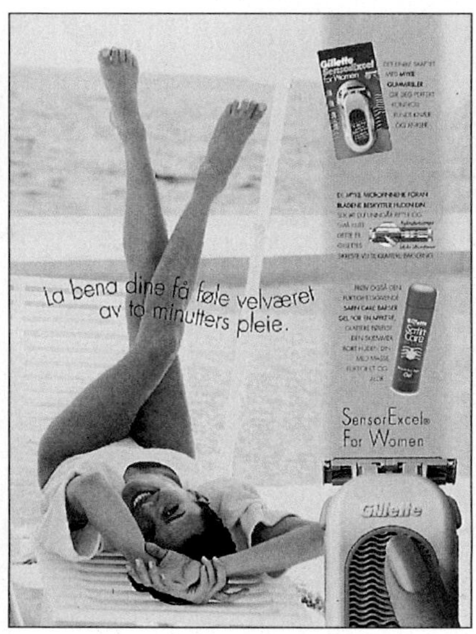

Gillette delivers the same global message whenever possible, as shown in the Sensor for Women ads from France, Norway, and Canada.

The Gillette Company
www.gillette.com

An identical promotion message is used for the product extension and product adaptation strategies around the world. Gillette uses the same global message for its men's toiletries: 'Gillette, the Best a Man Can Get.'

Global companies may also adapt their promotion message. For instance, the same product may be sold in many countries but advertised differently. As an example, L'Oreal, a French health and beauty products marketer, introduced its Golden Beauty brand of sun care products through its Helena Rubenstein subsidiary in Western Europe with a communication adaptation strategy. Recognizing that cultural and buying motive differences related to skin care and tanning exist, Golden Beauty advertising features dark tanning for Northern Europeans, skin protection to avoid wrinkles among Latin Europeans, and beautiful skin for Europeans living along the Mediterranean Sea, even though the products are the same. Other companies use a dual adaptation strategy by modifying both their products and promotion messages. Nestlé does this with Nescafé coffee. Nescafé is marketed using different coffee blends and promotional campaigns to match consumer preferences in different countries.

Distribution Strategy

Distribution is of critical importance in global marketing. The availability and quality of retailers and wholesalers as well as transportation, communication, and warehousing facilities are often determined by a country's stage of economic development. Figure 5–8 outlines the channel through which a product manufactured in one country must travel to reach its destination in another country. The first step involves the seller; its headquarters is the starting point and is responsible for the successful distribution to the ultimate consumer.

The next step is the channel between two nations, moving the product from one country to another. Intermediaries that can handle this responsibility include resident buyers in a foreign country, independent merchant wholesalers who buy and sell the product, or agents who bring buyers and sellers together.

Once the product is in the foreign nation, that country's distribution channels take over.[51] These channels can be very long or surprisingly short, depending on the product line. In Japan, fresh fish go through three intermediaries before getting to a retail outlet. Conversely, shoes only go through one intermediary. In other cases, the channel does not even involve the host country. Procter & Gamble sells its soap door to door in the Philippines because there are no other alternatives in many parts of that country. The sophistication of a country's distribution channels increase as its economic infrastructure

FIGURE 5–8
Channels of distribution in global marketing

develops. Supermarkets facilitate selling products in many nations, but they are not popular or available in many others where culture and lack of refrigeration dictate shopping on a daily rather than a weekly basis. For example, when Coke and Pepsi entered China, both had to create direct-distribution channels, investing in trucks and refrigerator units for small retailers.[52]

Pricing Strategy

Global companies also face many challenges in determining a pricing strategy as part of their worldwide marketing effort. Individual countries, even those with free trade agreements, may impose considerable competitive, political, and legal constraints on the pricing latitude of global companies. Of course, economic factors such as the costs of production, selling, and tariffs, plus transportation and storage costs, also affect global pricing decisions.

Pricing too low or too high can have dire consequences. When prices appear too low in one country, companies can be charged with dumping, a practice subject to severe penalties and fines. **Dumping** is when a firm sells a product in a foreign country below its domestic price or below its actual cost. This is often done to build a company's share of the market by pricing at a competitive level. Another reason is that the products being sold may be surplus or cannot be sold domestically and, therefore, are already a burden to the company. The firm may be glad to sell them at almost any price.

When companies price their products very high in some countries but competitively in others, they face a grey market problem. A **grey market,** also called parallel importing, is a situation where products are sold through unauthorized channels of distribution. A grey market comes about when individuals buy products in a lower-priced country from a manufacturer's authorized retailer, ship them to higher-priced countries, and then sell them below the manufacturer's suggested retail price through unauthorized retailers. Many well-known products have been sold through grey markets, including Olympus cameras, Seiko watches, IBM personal computers, and Mercedes-Benz cars.[53]

CONCEPT CHECK

1. Products may be sold globally in three ways. What are they?
2. What is dumping?

SUMMARY

1 The dollar value of world trade has more than doubled in the past decade and will exceed $11 trillion in 2002. Manufactured goods and commodities account for 75 percent of world trade, while services account for 25 percent.

2 Not all world trade involves the exchange of money for goods or services. About 20 percent of world trade involves countertrade, the practice of using barter rather than money for making global sales.

3 A global perspective on world trade views exports and imports as complementary economic flows. A country's exports affect its imports and vice versa. This phenomenon is called the *trade feedback effect.*

4 Canada is a trading nation, exporting over 35 percent of its gross domestic national product on an annual basis.

5 The reason some companies and some industries in a country succeed globally while others do not lies in their nation's competitive advantage. A nation's competitive advantage arises from specific conditions in a nation that foster success.

6 Three trends in the late twentieth century have significantly affected world trade: (*a*) a gradual decline of economic protectionism, (*b*) an increase in formal economic integration and free trade among nations, and (*c*) global competition among global companies for global consumers.

7 Although global and domestic marketing are based on the same marketing principles, many underlying assumptions must be re-evaluated when a firm pursues global opportunities. A global environmental scan typically considers three kinds of uncontrollable environmental variables. These include cultural diversity, economic conditions, and political-regulatory climate.

8 Four global market-entry strategies are exporting, licensing, joint venture, and direct investment. The relative difficulty of global marketing, as well as the amount of financial commitment, risk, marketing control, and profit potential, increase in moving from exporting to direct investment.

9 Crafting a worldwide marketing effort involves designing, implementing, and controlling a marketing program that standardizes marketing mix elements when there are cultural similarities and adapting them when cultures differ.

KEY TERMS AND CONCEPTS

countertrade p. 120
trade feedback effect p. 121
gross domestic product p. 121
balance of trade p. 121
protectionism p. 123
tariffs p. 124
quota p. 125
World Trade Organization p. 125
global competition p. 127
strategic alliances p. 127
multidomestic marketing strategy p. 128
global marketing strategy p. 128
global consumers p. 128
cross-cultural analysis p. 129
values p. 130
customs p. 130
cultural symbols p. 130
semiotics p. 130
back translation p. 131
consumer ethnocentrism p. 132
economic infrastructure p. 133
currency exchange rate p. 134
ISO 9000 p. 136
exporting p. 137
joint venture p. 139
direct investment p. 139
dumping p. 142
grey market p. 142

INTERNET EXERCISE

As you read in this chapter, Canada is a trading nation. Go to the Department of Foreign Affairs and International trade home page at www.dfait-maeci.gc.ca. Peruse this site. While you are there, find the answers to these questions:

1 What was the value of Canada's exports for the most current fiscal year?

2 What are Canada's priorities in terms of world trade?

3 What is the current status of the Canada-EFTA free trade agreement?

APPLYING MARKETING CONCEPTS AND PERSPECTIVES

1 What is meant by this statement: "Quotas are a hidden tax on consumers, whereas tariffs are a more obvious one"?

2 Is the trade feedback effect described in the text a long-run or short-run view on world trade flows? Explain your answer.

3 Since English is the official language in Australia, some Canadian global companies might select it as an easy market to enter. Others believe that this similarity in language could make it harder to successfully enter that market. Who's right? Why?

4 How successful would a television commercial in Japan be if it featured a husband surprising his wife in her dressing area on Valentine's Day with a small box of chocolates containing four candies? Why?

5 As a novice in global marketing, which alternative for global market-entry strategy would you be likely to start with? Why? What other alternatives do you have for a global market entry?
6 Coca-Cola is sold worldwide. In some countries, Coca-Cola owns the bottling facilities; in others, it has signed contracts with licensees or relies on joint ventures. When selecting a licensee in each country, what factors should Coca-Cola consider?
7 Now that China has taken back control of Hong Kong, what advice would you give to Canadian companies currently doing, or planning to do, business in Hong Kong?

CASE 5–1 CNS, INC., AND 3M: BREATHE RIGHT® NASAL STRIP

"When we first began marketing this product, what was so gratifying, particularly as a physician, were the literally thousands of letters and phone calls we would receive talking about how much better people slept at night. Almost all the letters began with 'thank you, thank you, thank you!' Just three thank you's. It was, 'I haven't gotten a good night's sleep like this in 10 years.'"

What is Dr. Dan Cohen, CEO OF CNS, Inc., talking about? It's Breathe Right® nasal strips, the innovative adhesive pad with a small spring inside that, when attached to the nose, pulls the nasal passages open and makes it easier to breathe. Since its introduction, Breathe Right strips have been coveted by athletes hoping to improve their performance through increased oxygen flow, snorers (and, more often, snorers' spouses) hoping for a sound night's sleep, and allergy and cold sufferers looking for relief for their stuffed noses.

HOW THIS WEIRD-LOOKING STRIP CAME ABOUT

The Breathe Right® strip was invented by Bruce Johnson, who suffered from chronic nasal congestion. At times he would put straws or paper clips up his nose at night to keep his nasal passages open. After tinkering in his workshop for years, he came up with a prototype design for the Breathe Right® strip. He brought the prototype to CNS, which was in the sleep disorders diagnostic equipment business at the time. Dr. Cohen knew instantly the market for the strips would be huge. After the products received government approval and became successful in the market, CNS divested its other interests and went to work marketing the strips full time.

Being a small company, CNS did not have the budget to launch a large-scale marketing campaign. But it got the break it needed when Jerry Rice, the wide receiver for the San Francisco 49ers, wore one of the strips on national TV when the 49ers won the 1995 Superbowl. The entire nation became aware of the product overnight, and demand for the strips increased dramatically. An indication of this national awareness was discussion on TV talk shows and even appearances of the strip in cartoons.

EVERYBODY HAS A NOSE: THE DECISION TO GO INTERNATIONAL

The problems that the Breathe Right® strips solve—snoring, congestion—are not unique to the North American population. Also, with the media being so global today, people around the world were seeing athletes wearing the strip and wondering how they could get their noses on some. CNS decided to take Breathe Right® international. But because it was still a relatively small company and had no experience in the global marketplace, it opted to take on a distribution partner that had extensive global outlets already in place as well as the ability to market the product abroad. 3M, makers of such products as Post-It™ notes and the leader in stick-to-skin products around the world, became the international distributor for Breathe Right® strips.

David Reynolds-Gooch, International Business Manager at 3M, explains that the strips fit in well with 3M's existing adhesive line of first-aid products and are sold in channels with which 3M has extensive leverage: pharmacies, hyper-markets, and food markets. 3M agreed to take control of all the marketing and communication responsibilities in addition to the distribution in return for a percentage of the sales revenue of the strips. The strips are "co-branded" in the international markets: The packages say both Breathe Right® and 3M.

BREATHING RIGHT AROUND THE WORLD

3M introduced the Breathe Right® strip in Japan, then it was rolled out in Europe, and now can be found in more

than 40 countries from Australia to South America. 3M used a similar approach to that used by CNS in North America: Create awareness during the introduction phase through public relations—sports related and otherwise. "The first year we had incredible PR success," remembers Reynolds-Gooch. "We believe we got about $20 million worth of free TV, radio, and print time around the world." This was done through such tactics as having the South African rugby team wear the strips while it won the World Cup of rugby and having pulmonologists and breathing experts describe the benefits of the product on talk shows in Japan, Australia, Europe, and Latin America.

CNS quickly discovered some major differences in marketing the product here and abroad. For instance, as Gary Tschautscher, Vice President of International Marketing at CNS explains, "In the United States and Canada, we positioned and distributed the strips as part of the cough/cold category of products. As we rolled it out globally, suddenly we realized in some countries that section in the store doesn't even exist. So where do you position your product?" Additionally, says Reynolds-Gooch, "There really aren't many large drug chains or pharmacy chains. The stores are independent in most countries by law. So what that means is you have to go through multiple layers of distribution, and ultimately we were able to influence the pharmacists because of the other products 3M distributes in the stores." Finally, there is no couponing in most countries in the world. That vehicle for inducing trial of a new product is not available, and hence a lot more in-store sampling is needed.

BREATHE RIGHT® IN THE TWENTY-FIRST CENTURY

Both CNS and 3M face some issues for the future as Breathe Right strips gain in popularity around the globe. While the athletic segment of the market gets most of the publicity, the snorers are the bulk of the market for the strips internationally. Reynolds-Gooch has identified creating heavy users—those who use the strip every night—as the most important marketing point for the future, ahead of people with seasonal colds or allergies.

Also, many of the markets that have been identified as "hot" new markets throughout the business community may not be appropriate for the Breathe Right strips. For example, Latin America and Asia (especially China) are emerging markets with steadily increasing income levels and large populations, but the average age in these countries is under 30, and people under 30 typically do not have snoring problems with the frequency that older people do.

Questions

1 What are the advantages and disadvantages of CNS taking its Breathe Right® strip into international markets?

2 What advantages does CNS gain by having 3M as its international licensing partner? What are the advantages for 3M?

3 What criteria might CNS and 3M use in selecting countries to enter? Using these criteria, which five or six countries would you enter?

4 Which market segment would you target in entering the international markets—snorers, athletes, people with chronic congestion and allergies, or a new segment?

5 Which marketing mix variables do you think CNS should concentrate on the most to succeed in a global arena? Why?

CHAPTER SIX

CONSUMER BEHAVIOUR

6

AFTER READING THIS CHAPTER YOU SHOULD BE ABLE TO:

- Outline the stages in the consumer decision process.
- Distinguish among three variations of the consumer decision process: routine, limited, and extended problem solving.
- Explain how psychological influences affect consumer behaviour, particularly purchase decision processes.
- Identify major sociocultural influences on consumer behaviour and their effects on purchase decisions.
- Recognize how marketers can use knowledge of consumer behaviour to better understand and influence individual and family purchases.

GETTING TO KNOW THE AUTOMOBILE CUSTOM(H)ER

Who will buy at least half of all new cars in 2001? Who already spends billions on new and used cars and trucks and automotive accessories? Who influences 80 percent of all automotive-buying decisions? Women—yes, women.

Women are a driving force in the Canadian automotive industry. Enlightened automakers have hired women design engineers and marketing executives to help them understand this valuable custom(h)er. What have they learned? First, women prefer "sporty" vehicles that are relatively inexpensive and fun to drive rather than "sports" cars, luxury cars, and full-sized trucks with bigger engines and higher price tags. Second, a vehicle's "feel" is important to women. Sleek exteriors and interior designs that fit proportions of smaller drivers as well as opening ease for doors, trunks, and hoods are equally important.

Third, women approach car buying in a deliberate manner. They approach car buying, usage, and maintenance from a woman's point of view. They often visit auto-buying Web sites to gather information and will shop an average of three dealerships before making a purchase decision. Fourth, while men and women look for the same car features, their priorities differ. Both sexes value dependability most, but more women consider it a higher priority. Women also rank low price, ease of maintenance, and safety higher than men. Men view horsepower and acceleration as being more important than women. Finally, automakers have learned that 66 percent of women dislike the car-buying process.

Recognition of women as purchasers and influencers in car and truck buying has also altered the behaviour of dealers. Many dealers now use a one-price policy and have stopped negotiating a vehicle's price. Industry research indicates that 68 percent of new-car buyers dread the price negotiation process involved in buying a car, and women often refuse to do it at all![1]

This chapter examines **consumer behaviour,** the actions a person takes in purchasing and using products and services, including the mental and social processes that precede and follow these actions. This chapter shows how the behavioural sciences help answer questions such as why people choose one product or brand over another, how they make these choices, and how companies use this knowledge to provide value to consumers.

CONSUMER PURCHASE DECISION PROCESS

Behind the visible act of making a purchase lies an important decision process that must be investigated. The stages a buyer passes through in making choices about which products and services to buy is the **purchase decision process.** This process has the five stages shown in Figure 6–1: (1) problem recognition, (2) information search, (3) alternative evaluation, (4) purchase decision, and (5) postpurchase behaviour.

Problem Recognition: Perceiving a Need

Problem recognition, the initial step in the purchase decision, is perceiving a difference between a person's ideal and actual situations big enough to trigger a decision.[2] This can be as simple as finding an empty milk carton in the refrigerator; noting, as a first-year university student, that your high school clothes are not in the style that other students are wearing; or realizing that your laptop computer may not be working properly.

In marketing, advertisements or salespeople can activate a consumer's decision process by showing the shortcomings of competing (or currently owned) products. For instance, an advertisement for a compact disc (CD) player could stimulate problem recognition because it emphasizes the sound quality of CD players over that of the conventional stereo system you may now own.

Information Search: Seeking Value

After recognizing a problem, a consumer begins to search for information, the next stage in the purchase decision process. First, you may scan your memory for previous experiences with products or brands.[3] This action is called *internal search.* For frequently purchased products such as shampoo, this may be enough. Or a consumer may undertake an *external search* for information.[4] This is especially needed when past experience or knowledge is insufficient, the risk of making a wrong purchase decision is high, and the cost of gathering information is low. The primary sources of external information are: (1) *personal sources,* such as relatives and friends whom the consumer trusts; (2) *public sources,* including various product-rating organizations such as *Consumer Reports,* government agencies, and TV "consumer programs"; and (3) *marketer-dominated sources,* such as information from sellers that include advertising, salespeople, and point-of-purchase displays in stores.

Suppose you consider buying a portable CD player. You will probably tap several of these information sources: friends and relatives, portable CD-player advertisements,

FIGURE 6–1
Purchase decision process

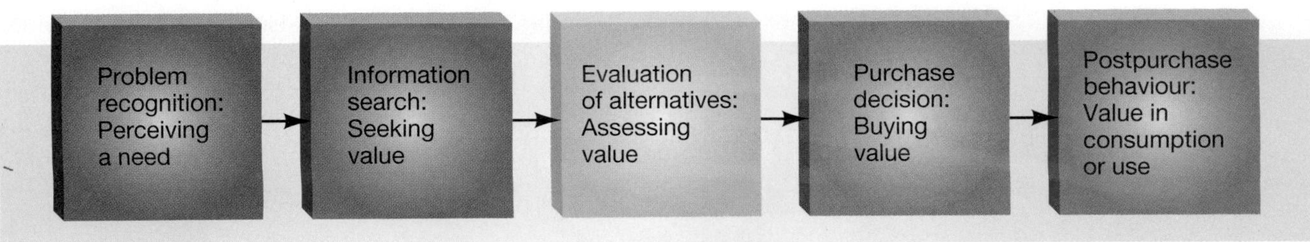

Brand	Model	Price	Headphones	Error Correction	Bumps	Locate Speed
Panasonic	SL-SX500	$150	Very Good	Excellent	Very Good	Excellent
Phillips (A CR best buy)	AZ7383	100	Good	Excellent	Excellent	Very Good
Phillips	AZ7583	120	Good	Very Good	Excellent	Very Good
Sony	D-E409CK	140	Good	Good	Excellent	Good
Aiwa	XP-SP1200	145	Very Good	Fair	Good	Good
Sony	D-E401	100	Good	Good	Very Good	Good
Panasonic	SL-SW505	150	Fair	Excellent	Excellent	Excellent
JVC	XL-P34	80	Good	Excellent	Good	Excellent
Sony	D-ES55	200	Good	Very Good	Good	Fair
Panasonic	SL-S230	80	Good	Good	Very Good	Excellent
Aiwa	XP-570	75	Good	Good	Good	Fair

Rating: Excellent, Very Good, Good, Fair, Poor

FIGURE 6–2
Consumer Reports' evaluation of portable compact disc players (abridged)

Source: "Portable CD Players," Consumer Reports Buying Guide 1998, pp. 70–71

Consumer Reports
www.consumerreports.org

and several stores carrying CD players (for demonstrations). You might study the comparative evaluation of portable CD players that appeared in *Consumer Reports,* published by a product-testing organization, a portion of which appears in Figure 6–2.

Alternative Evaluation: Assessing Value

The information search stage clarifies the problem for the consumer by (1) suggesting criteria to use for the purchase, (2) yielding brand names that might meet the criteria, and (3) developing consumer value perceptions. Based only on the information shown in Figure 6–2, what selection criteria would you use in buying a portable CD player? Would you use price, ease of use, quality of headphones, or some combination of these and other criteria?

For some of you, the information provided may be inadequate because it does not contain all the factors you might consider when evaluating portable CD players. These factors are a consumer's **evaluative criteria,** which represent both the objective attributes of a brand (such as the locate speed) and the subjective ones (such as prestige) you use to compare different products and brands.[5] Firms try to identify and capitalize on both types of criteria to create the best value for the money sought by you and other consumers. These criteria are often displayed in advertisements.

Consumers often have several criteria for evaluating brands. (Didn't you in the preceding exercise?) Knowing this, companies seek to identify the most important evaluative criteria that consumers use when judging brands. For example, among the evaluative criteria shown in the columns of Figure 6–2, suppose that you use three in considering brands of portable CD players: (1) a list price no more than $100, (2) error correction, and the (3) locate speed. These criteria establish the brands in your

evoked set—the group of brands that a consumer would consider acceptable from among all the brands in the product class of which he or she is aware.[6] Your three evaluative criteria result in three models in your evoked set. If these brands don't satisfy you, you can change your evaluation criteria to create a different evoked set of models.

Purchase Decision: Buying Value

Having examined the alternatives in the evoked set, you are almost ready to make a purchase decision. Two choices remain: (1) from whom to buy and (2) when to buy. For a product like a portable CD player, the information search process probably involved visiting retail stores, seeing different brands in catalogues, viewing portable CD-player promotions on a home shopping television channel, or visiting a seller's Web site. The choice of which seller to buy from will depend on such considerations as the terms of sale, your past experience buying from the seller, and the return policy. Often a purchase decision involves a simultaneous evaluation of both product attributes and seller characteristics. For example, you might choose the second-most preferred portable CD player brand at a store with a liberal refund and return policy versus the most preferred brand at a store with more conservative policies.

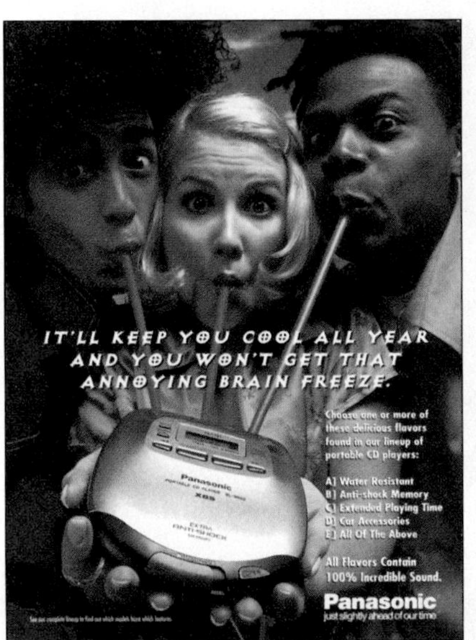

Deciding when to buy is frequently determined by a number of factors. For instance, you might buy sooner if one of your preferred brands is on sale or its manufacturer offers a rebate. Other factors such as the store atmosphere, pleasantness of the shopping experience, salesperson persuasiveness, time pressure, and financial circumstances could also affect whether a purchase decision is made or postponed.[7]

Information technology is expected to revolutionize the consumer purchase decision process in the next decade. Consumer **computer-mediated buying,** or online buying, is the use of Internet technology to seek information, evaluate alternatives, and make purchase decisions.[8] This technology also allows marketers to customize their offering to the specific needs of individuals thereby increasing customer value and satisfaction, as described in the accompanying Marketing NewsNet.[9] The growth of consumer computer-mediated buying and its implications for marketing is detailed in Chapter 8.

Postpurchase Behaviour: Value in Consumption or Use

After buying a product, the consumer compares it with his or her expectations and is either satisfied or dissatisfied. If the consumer is dissatisfied, marketers must decide whether the product was deficient or consumer expectations too high. Product deficiency may require a design change; if expectations are too high, perhaps the company's advertising or the salesperson oversold the product's features.

www.att.com

Sensitivity to a customer's consumption or use experience is extremely important in a consumer's value perception. For example, research on long-distance telephone services provided by MCI, Sprint, and AT&T indicates that satisfaction or dissatisfaction affects consumer value perceptions.[10] Studies show that satisfaction or dissatisfaction affects consumer communications and repeat-purchase behaviour. Satisfied

TECHNOLOGY

MARKETING NEWSNET

Computer-Mediated Buying: Creating Customer Value in Cyberspace

Information technology has changed the way many consumers seek information, evaluate alternatives, and make purchase decisions. Consider just a few ways that inventive marketers use the Internet to create customer value by easing the consumer decision process. The Gap (www.gap.com) provides a virtual dressing room that allows visitors to mix and match outfits. Eddie Bauer Home (www.eddiebauer.com) allows visitors to enter the dimensions of a room, rearrange furniture, and even turn pieces upside down for inspection. Music Boulevard (www.musicblvd.com) lets you listen to featured albums before making a selection.

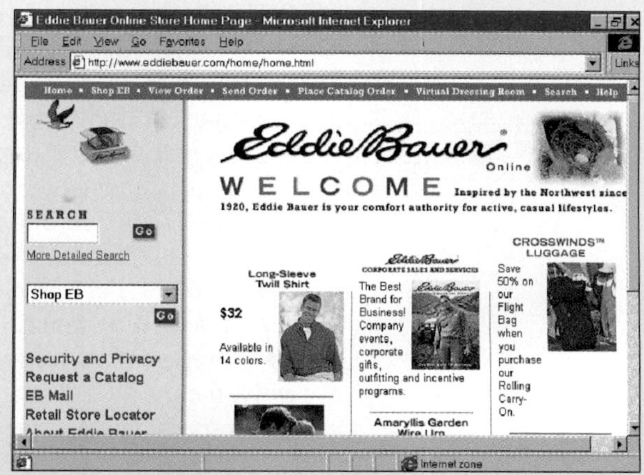

Not interested in clothing, furniture, or music? Then how about car buying? General Motors (www.gmbuypower.com) and Chrysler (www.chrysler.com) allow shoppers to choose options, compare prices, and obtain a price quote via phone or e-mail without ever visiting a dealership. Industry surveys show that a quarter of all new-car buyers use the Internet for "virtual shopping." By 2001, half of all new-car buyers will visit a Web site to gather car information, evaluate choices, and make purchase decisions.

These examples illustrate just a few of the ways computer-mediated buying is creating a more informed consumer. Information technology can create customer value by easing the decision process.

www.nissancanada.com

buyers tell three other people about their experience. Dissatisfied buyers complain to nine people![11] Satisfied buyers also tend to buy from the same seller each time a purchase occasion arises. The financial impact of repeat-purchase behaviour is significant. For example, Ford Motor Company estimates that each time the company increases its number of repeat buyers by one percent, Ford increases its profit by $100 million. Accordingly, firms such as Nissan Canada, Johnson & Johnson, Coca-Cola, and British Airways focus attention on postpurchase behaviour to maximize customer satisfaction and retention.[12] These firms, among many others, now provide toll-free telephone numbers, offer liberal return and refund policies, and engage in staff training to handle complaints, answer questions, and record suggestions. Research has shown that such efforts produce positive postpurchase communications among consumers and contribute to relationship building between sellers and buyers.[13]

Often a consumer is faced with two or more highly attractive alternatives, such as a Panasonic or Sony portable CD player. If you choose the Panasonic, you may think, "Should I have purchased the Sony?" This feeling of postpurchase psychological tension or anxiety is called **cognitive dissonance.** To alleviate it, consumers often attempt to applaud themselves for making the right choice. So after your purchase, you may seek information to confirm your choice by asking friends questions like, "Don't you like my portable CD player?" or by reading ads of the brand you chose. You might even look for negative information about the brand you didn't buy and decide that Sony's error correction, which was rated "good" in Figure 6–2, was actually a deficiency. Firms often use ads or follow-up calls from salespeople in this postpurchase stage to try to convince buyers that they made the right decision. For many years, Buick ran an advertising campaign with the message, "Aren't you really glad you bought a Buick?"

Involvement and Problem-Solving Variations

Sometimes consumers don't engage in the five-step purchase decision process. Instead, they skip or minimize one or more steps depending on the level of **involvement,** the personal, social, and economic significance of the purchase to the consumer.[14] High-involvement purchase occasions typically have at least one of three characteristics—the item to be purchased (1) is expensive, (2) can have serious personal consequences, or (3) could reflect on one's social image. For these occasions, consumers engage in extensive information search, consider many product attributes and brands, form attitudes, and participate in word-of-mouth communication. Low-involvement purchases, such as toothpaste and soap, barely involve most of us, whereas stereo systems and automobiles are very involving. Researchers have identified three general variations in the consumer purchase process based on consumer involvement and product knowledge. Figure 6–3 summarizes some of the important differences between the three problem-solving variations.[15]

Routine Problem Solving For products such as toothpaste and milk, consumers recognize a problem, make a decision, and spend little effort seeking external information and evaluating alternatives. The purchase process for such items is virtually a habit and typifies low-involvement decision making. Routine problem solving is typically the case for low-priced, frequently purchased products. It is estimated that about 50 percent of all purchase occasions are of this kind.

Limited Problem Solving In limited problem solving, consumers typically seek some information or rely on a friend to help them evaluate alternatives. In general, several brands might be evaluated using a moderate number of different attributes. You might use limited problem solving in choosing a toaster, a restaurant for dinner, and other purchase situations in which you have little time or effort to spend. Limited problem solving accounts for about 38 percent of purchase occasions.

Extended Problem Solving In extended problem solving, each of the five stages of the consumer purchase decision process is used in the purchase, including considerable time and effort on external information search and in identifying and evaluating alternatives. Several brands usually are in the evoked set, and these are evaluated on many attributes. Extended problem solving exists in high-involvement purchase situations for items such as automobiles and investments in stocks and bonds. Firms marketing these

	CONSUMER INVOLVEMENT		
	HIGH ←	→	LOW
CHARACTERISTICS OF PURCHASE DECISION PROCESS	**EXTENDED PROBLEM SOLVING**	**LIMITED PROBLEM SOLVING**	**ROUTINE PROBLEM SOLVING**
Number of brands examined	Many	Several	One
Number of sellers considered	Many	Several	Few
Number of product attributes evaluated	Many	Moderate	One
Number of external information sources used	Many	Few	None
Time spent searching	Considerable	Little	Minimal

FIGURE 6–3
Comparison of problem-solving variations

products put significant effort into informing and educating these consumers. Twelve percent of purchase occasions fall into this category.

Situational Influences

Often the purchase situation will affect the purchase decision process. Five **situational influences** have an impact on your purchase decision process: (1) the purchase task, (2) social surroundings, (3) physical surroundings, (4) temporal effects, and (5) antecedent states.[16] The purchase task is the reason for engaging in the decision in the first place. Information searching and evaluating alternatives may differ depending on whether the purchase is a gift, which often involves the social visibility, or for the buyer's own use. Social surroundings, including the other people present when a purchase decision is made, may also affect what is purchased. Physical surroundings such as decor, music, and crowding in retail stores may alter how purchase decisions are made. Temporal effects such as time of day or the amount of time available will influence where consumers have breakfast and lunch and what is ordered. Finally, antecedent states, which include the consumer's mood or the amount of cash on hand, can influence purchase behaviour and choice.

Figure 6–4 shows the many influences that affect the consumer purchase decision process. The decision to buy a product also involves important psychological and sociocultural influences, the two important topics discussed during the remainder of this chapter. Marketing mix influences are described in Chapters 11 through 21.

FIGURE 6–4
Influences on the consumer purchase decision process

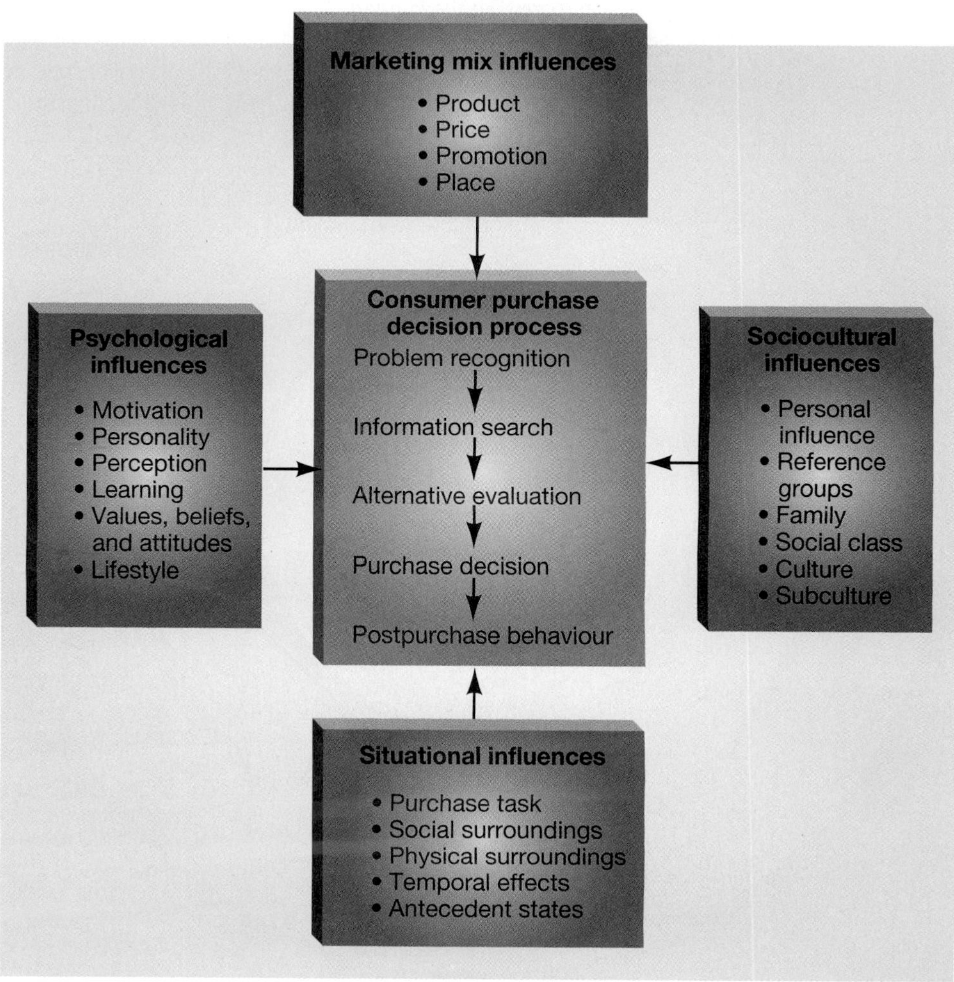

CONCEPT CHECK

1. What is the first step in the consumer purchase decision process?
2. The brands a consumer considers buying out of the set of brands in a product class of which the consumer is aware is called the __________.
3. What is the term for postpurchase anxiety?

PSYCHOLOGICAL INFLUENCES ON CONSUMER BEHAVIOUR

Psychology helps marketers understand why and how consumers behave as they do. In particular, concepts such as motivation and personality; perception; learning; values, beliefs, and attitudes; and lifestyle are useful for interpreting buying processes and directing marketing efforts.

Motivation and Personality

Motivation and personality are two familiar psychological concepts that have specific meanings and marketing implications. They are both used frequently to describe why people do some things and not others.

Motivation **Motivation** is the energizing force that causes behaviour that satisfies a need. Because consumer needs are the focus of the marketing concept, marketers try to arouse these needs.

An individual's needs are boundless. People possess physiological needs for basics such as water, sex, and food. They also have learned needs, including esteem, achievement, and affection. Psychologists point out that these needs are hierarchical; that is, once physiological needs are met, people seek to satisfy their learned needs. Figure 6–5 shows one need hierarchy and classification scheme that contains five need classes.[17] *Physiological needs* are basic to survival and must be satisfied first. A Burger King advertisement featuring a juicy hamburger attempts to activate the need for food.

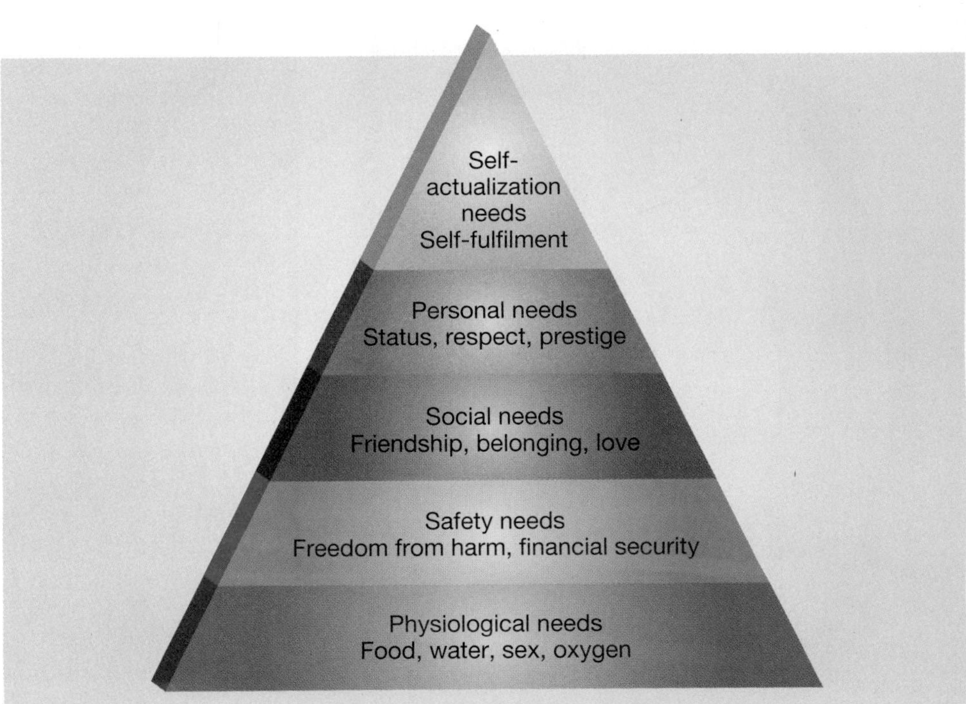

FIGURE 6–5
Hierarchy of needs

Safety needs involve self-preservation and physical well-being. Smoke detector and burglar alarm manufacturers focus on these needs. *Social needs* are concerned with love and friendship. Dating services and fragrance companies try to arouse these needs. *Personal needs* are represented by the need for achievement, status, prestige, and self-respect. The American Express Gold Card and Brooks Brothers Clothiers appeal to these needs. Sometimes firms try to arouse multiple needs to stimulate problem recognition. For example, Michelin combines security with parental love to promote tire replacement. *Self-actualization needs* involve personal fulfilment such as completing your degree.

Personality **Personality** refers to a person's consistent behaviours or responses to recurring situations. Although numerous personality theories exist, most identify key traits—enduring characteristics within a person or in his or her relationship with others. Such traits include assertiveness, extroversion, compliance, dominance, and aggression, among others. Research suggests that compliant people prefer known brand names and use more mouthwash and toilet soaps. In contrast, aggressive types use razors, not electric shavers, apply more cologne and after-shave lotions, and purchase signature goods such as Gucci, Yves St. Laurent, and Donna Karan as an indicator of status.[18] Cross-cultural analysis also suggests that residents of different countries have a **national character,** or a distinct set of personality characteristics common among people of a country or society.[19] For example, Americans and Germans are relatively more assertive than Canadians.

These personality characteristics are often revealed in a person's **self-concept,** which is the way people see themselves and the way they believe others see them.[20] Marketers recognize that people have an actual self-concept and an ideal self-concept. The actual self refers to how people actually see themselves. The ideal self describes how people would like to see themselves. These two self "images" are reflected in the products and brands a person buys including automobiles, home appliances and furnishings, magazines, clothing, grooming and leisure products, and frequently, the stores a person shops. The importance of self-concept is summed up by a senior executive at Barnes & Noble: "People buy books for what the purchase says about them—their taste, their cultivation, their trendiness."[21]

Perception

One person sees a Cadillac as a mark of achievement; another sees it as ostentatious. This is the result of **perception**—the process by which an individual selects, organizes, and interprets information to create a meaningful picture of the world.

Selective Perception Because the average consumer operates in a complex environment, the human brain attempts to organize and interpret information through a filtering process called *selective perception.* The four stages of selective perception are selective exposure, selective attention, selective comprehension, and selective retention. First, consumers are not exposed to all information or messages in the marketplace. In other words, there is *selective exposure.* For example, you may watch CTV, but not CBC television. In doing so, you do not expose yourself to any information broadcast on the CBC network. Because of selective exposure, marketers must work to determine where consumers are most likely to be exposed to information.

www.baton.com

But even if a consumer is exposed to a message, either by accident or design, the consumer may not attend to that message. In general, with *selective attention,* the consumer will only pay attention to messages that are consistent with their attitudes and beliefs and will ignore those that are inconsistent. Consumers are also more likely to attend to messages when they are relevant or of interest to them. For example, a consumer is likely to pay attention to an ad about a product they just bought, or to an ad for a product they are interested in buying.

ETHICS

ETHICS AND SOCIAL RESPONSIBILITY ALERT

The Ethics of Subliminal Messages

For almost 50 years, the topic of subliminal perception and the presence of subliminal messages embedded in commercial communications has sparked debate. To some, the concept of subliminal messages is a hoax. To others, the possibility of a person being influenced without their knowledge is either an exciting or frightening concept. Many experts suggest that the use of subliminal messages by marketers, effective or not, is deceptive and unethical.

But there are marketers who occasionally pursue opportunities to create these messages. For example, Time Warner Interactive's Endorfun, a CD-ROM puzzle game, has a music soundtrack with more than 100 subliminal messages meant to make players feel good about themselves, even if they can't solve the puzzle. One message says, "I am a winner." Puzzle players are informed that subliminal messages exist and instructions on how to turn off the soundtrack are provided.

Do you believe that attempts to implant subliminal messages are a deceptive practice and unethical, regardless of their intent?

Selective comprehension involves interpreting information so that it is consistent with your attitudes and beliefs. A marketer's failure to understand this can have disastrous results. For example, Toro introduced a small, lightweight snowblower called the Snow Pup. Even though the product worked, sales failed to meet expectations. Why? Toro later found out that consumers perceived the name to mean that Snow Pup was a toy or too light to do any serious snow removal. When the product was renamed "Snow Master," sales increased sharply.[22]

Selective retention means that consumers do not remember all the information they see, read, or hear, even minutes after exposure to it. This affects the internal and external information search stage of the purchase decision process. This is why furniture and automobile retailers often give consumers product brochures to take home after they leave the showroom.

Because perception plays such an important role in consumer behaviour, it is not surprising that the topic of subliminal perception is a popular item for discussion. **Subliminal perception** means that you see or hear messages without being aware of them. The presence and effect of subliminal perception on behaviour is a hotly debated issue, with more popular appeal than scientific support. Indeed, evidence suggests that such messages have limited effects on behaviour.[23] If these messages did influence behaviour, would their use be an ethical practice? (See the accompanying Ethics and Social Responsibility Alert.[24])

Perceived Risk Perception plays a major role in the perceived risk in purchasing a product or service. **Perceived risk** represents the anxieties felt because the

Companies use a variety of strategies to reduce consumer-perceived risk.

consumer cannot anticipate the outcomes of a purchase but believes that there may be negative consequences. Examples of possible negative consequences are the size of the financial outlay required to buy the product (Can I afford $200 for those skis?), the risk of physical harm (Is bungee jumping safe?), and the performance of the product (Will the hair colouring work?). A more abstract form is psychosocial (What will my friends say if I wear that sweater?). Perceived risk affects information search because the greater the perceived risk, the more extensive the external search phase is likely to be.

Recognizing the importance of perceived risk, companies develop strategies to reduce the consumer's risk and encourage purchases. These strategies and examples of firms using them include the following:

- Obtaining seals of approval: the Good Housekeeping seal or Canadian Standards Association (CSA) seal.
- Securing endorsements from influential people: Athletes promoting milk consumption.
- Providing free trials of the product: sample packages of Duncan Hines Peanut Butter Cookies mailed by P&G.
- Giving extensive usage instructions: Clairol haircolouring.
- Providing warranties and guarantees: Cadillac's four-year, 80,000-kilometre, Gold Key Bumper-to-Bumper warranty.

Learning

Much consumer behaviour is learned. Consumers learn which information sources to use for information about products and services, which evaluative criteria to use when assessing alternatives, and, more generally, how to make purchase decisions. **Learning** refers to those behaviours that result from (1) repeated experience and (2) thinking.

Behavioural Learning *Behavioural learning* is the process of developing automatic responses to a situation built up through repeated exposure to it. Four variables are central to how consumers learn from repeated experience: drive, cue, response, and reinforcement. A *drive* is a need that moves an individual to action. Drives, such as hunger, might be represented by motives. A *cue* is a stimulus or symbol perceived by consumers. A *response* is the action taken by a consumer to satisfy the drive, and a *reinforcement* is the reward. Being hungry (drive), a consumer sees a cue (a billboard), takes action (buys a hamburger), and receives a reward (it tastes great!).

Marketers use two concepts from behavioural learning theory. *Stimulus generalization* occurs when a response elicited by one stimulus (cue) is generalized to another stimulus. Using the same brand name for different products is an application of this concept, such as Tylenol Cold & Flu and Tylenol P.M. *Stimulus discrimination* refers to a person's ability to perceive differences in stimuli. Consumers' tendency to perceive all light beers as being alike led to Budweiser Light commercials that distinguished among many types of "lights" and Bud Light.

Cognitive Learning Consumers also learn through thinking, reasoning, and mental problem solving without direct experience. This type of learning, called *cognitive learning,* involves making connections between two or more ideas or simply observing the outcomes of others' behaviours and adjusting your own accordingly. Firms also influence this type of learning. Through repetition in advertising, messages such as "Advil is a headache remedy" attempt to link a brand (Advil) and an idea (headache remedy) by showing someone using the brand and finding relief.

Brand Loyalty Learning is also important because it relates to habit formation—the basis of routine problem solving. Furthermore, there is a close link between habits and **brand loyalty,** which is a favourable attitude toward and consistent purchase of a single brand over time. Brand loyalty results from the positive reinforcement of previous actions. So a consumer reduces risk and saves time by consistently purchasing the same brand of shampoo and has favourable results—healthy, shining hair. There is evidence of brand loyalty in many commonly purchased products in Canada and the global marketplace. However, the incidence of brand loyalty appears to be declining in North America, Mexico, European Union nations, and Japan.[25]

Values, Beliefs, and Attitudes

Values, beliefs, and attitudes play a central role in consumer decision making and related marketing actions.

Attitude Formation An **attitude** is a "learned predisposition to respond to an object or class of objects in a consistently favourable or unfavourable way."[26] Attitudes are shaped by our values and beliefs, which are learned. Values vary by level of specificity. We speak of Canadian core values, including material well-being and humanitarianism. We also have personal values, such as thriftiness and ambition. Marketers are concerned with both, but focus mostly on personal values. Personal values affect attitudes by influencing the importance assigned to specific product attributes. Suppose thriftiness is one of your personal values. When you evaluate cars, fuel economy (a product attribute) becomes important. If you believe that a specific car has this attribute, you are likely to have a favourable attitude toward it.

Beliefs also play a part in attitude formation. **Beliefs** are a consumer's subjective perception of *how well* a product or brand performs on different attributes. Beliefs are based on personal experience, advertising, and discussions with other people. Beliefs about product attributes are important because, along with personal values, they create the favourable or unfavourable attitude the consumer has toward certain products and services.

Attitude Change Marketers use three approaches to try to change consumer attitudes toward products and brands, as shown in the following examples.[27]

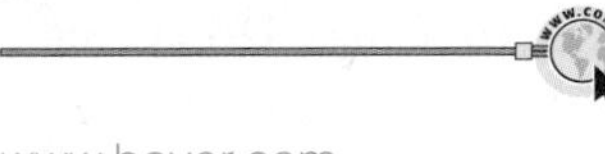

www.bayer.com

1. *Changing beliefs about the extent to which a brand has certain attributes.* To allay consumer concern that aspirin use causes an upset stomach, The Bayer Company successfully promoted the gentleness of its Extra Strength Bayer Plus aspirin.

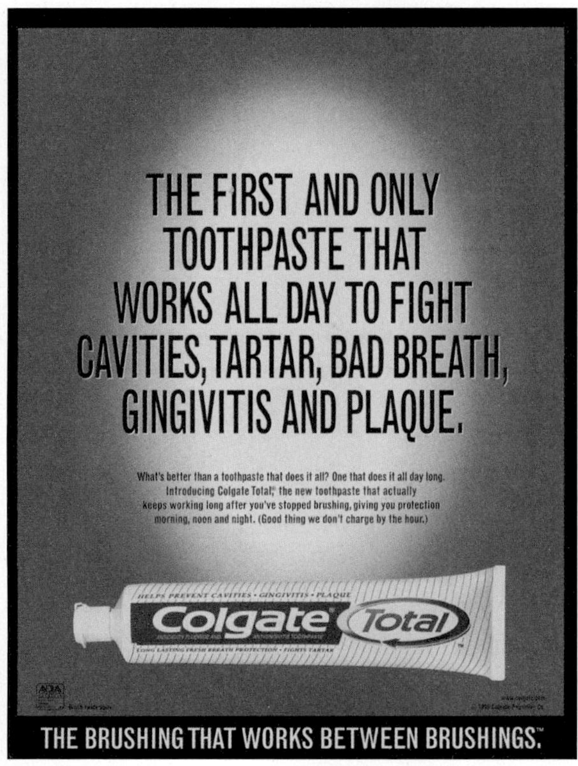

Attitudes toward Colgate toothpaste and Extra Strength Bayer aspirin were successfully changed by these ads. How? Read the text to find out how marketers can change consumer attitudes toward products and brands.

2. *Changing the perceived importance of attributes.* Pepsi-Cola made freshness an important product attribute when it stamped freshness dates on its cans. Prior to doing so, few consumers considered cola freshness an issue. After Pepsi spent about $35 million on advertising and promotion, a consumer survey found that 61 percent of cola drinkers believed freshness dating was an important attribute![28]
3. *Adding new attributes to the product.* Colgate-Palmolive included a new antibacterial ingredient, tricloson, in its Colgate Total toothpaste and spent $140 million marketing the brand. The result? Colgate replaced Crest as the market leader for the first time in 25 years.[29]

Lifestyle

Lifestyle is a mode of living that is identified by how people spend their time and resources (activities), what they consider important in their environment (interests), and what they think of themselves and the world around them (opinions). The analysis of consumer lifestyles (also called *psychographics*) has produced many insights into consumers' behavior. For example, lifestyle analysis has proven useful in segmenting and targeting consumers for new and existing products (see Chapter 10).

Lifestyle analysis typically focuses on identifying consumer profiles. Perhaps the best-known example of this type of analysis is the Values and Lifestyles (VALS) Program developed by SRI International.[30] The VALS Program has identified eight interconnected categories of adult lifestyles based on a person's self-orientation and resources. Self-orientation describes the patterns of attitudes and activities that help people reinforce their social self-image. Three patterns have been uncovered; they are oriented toward principles, status, and action. A person's resources encompass income, education, self-confidence, health, eagerness to buy, intelligence, and energy level. This dimension is a continuum ranging from minimal to abundant.

While the VALS Program is the most widely known lifestyles or psychographics system in North America, it has only been used a few times in Canada for commercial marketing applications. Canada has a few home-grown systems, with the most comprehensive being the Goldfarb Segments.

The Goldfarb Segments Many experts believe that Canadians and Americans differ in terms of values and buying behaviour, and therefore, an indigeneous psychographic system would be more useful for the Canadian marketplace. The Goldfarb Segments were produced as a result of a large-scale sampling of adult Canadians and examining their responses to hundreds of questions concerning their activities, interests, and opinions. After analyzing the data, six lifestyle or psychographic segments were identified and labelled as the Goldfarb Segments. Three of the segments are more traditional in their outlook, two are less traditional, and one segment floats somewhere in between. As you can see in Figure 6–6, the more traditional segments represent 50 percent of the population, the less traditional segments represent 31 percent, and the floating segment represents 19 percent of the population. Figure 6–6 also highlights selected lifestyle and behavioural characteristics of each segment.

CONCEPT CHECK

1. The problem with the Toro Snow Pup was an example of selective ___________.
2. What three attitude-change approaches are most common?
3. What does *lifestyle* mean?

FIGURE 6–6
The Goldfarb Segments

SEGMENT	PERCENT OF POPULATION	CHARACTERISTICS
MORE TRADITIONAL		
Structured	19%	Traditional value structure, religious, satisfied with life as it is; low risk; early followers in terms of product adoption.
Discontented	16%	Not likely to describe themselves as happy with their family life, friends, or work; like package deals and respond to feel-good messages.
Fearful	15%	Quiet, reserved, cautious, afraid; disapprove of biotechnology; and don't understand computers; don't want to be conspicuous in terms of behaviour or consumption.
LESS TRADITIONAL		
Resentful	18%	Loners; want power and money; like expensive things; gamble; prepared to bend rules to suit themselves.
Assured	13%	Leading edge group; self-confident and self-oriented; optimistic; eager to try new experiences, new brands, new ideas; work hard and can also kick back and relax.
FLOATING SEGMENT		
Caring	19%	Family is top priority; value relationships; strong work ethic; give back to society; do not buy things they cannot afford.

SOCIOCULTURAL INFLUENCES ON CONSUMER BEHAVIOUR

Sociocultural influences, which evolve from a consumer's formal and informal relationships with other people, also exert a significant impact on consumer behaviour. These involve personal influence, reference groups, the family, social class, culture, and subculture.

Personal Influence

A consumer's purchases are often influenced by the views, opinions, or behaviours of others. Two aspects of personal influence are important to marketing: opinion leadership and word-of-mouth activity.

www.popularmechanics.com

Opinion Leadership Individuals who exert direct or indirect social influence over others are called **opinion leaders.** Opinion leaders are more likely to be important for products that provide a form of self-expression. Automobiles, clothing, club membership, home video equipment, and PCs are products affected by opinion leaders, but appliances are not.[31] A recent study by *Popular Mechanics* magazine identified 18 million men who influence the purchases of some 85 million consumers for "do-it-yourself" products.[32]

www.chrysler.com

Only a small percentage of adults are considered opinion leaders.[33] Identifying, reaching, and influencing opinion leaders is a major challenge for companies. Some firms use sports figures or celebrities as spokespersons to represent their products, such as Donovan Bailey for Maple Leaf, Brett Favre for Right Guard Sport and Cindy Crawford for Omega watches, in the hope that they are opinion leaders. Others promote their products in media believed to reach opinion leaders. Still others use more direct approaches. For example, Chrysler Corporation recently invited influential community leaders and business executives to test-drive its Dodge Intrepid, Chrysler Concorde, and Eagle Vision models. Some 6000 accepted the offer, and 98 percent said they would recommend their tested car. Chrysler estimated that the number of favourable recommendations totalled 32 000.[34]

Word of Mouth People influencing each other during their face-to-face conversations is called **word of mouth.** Word of mouth is perhaps the most powerful information source for consumers because it typically involves friends viewed as trustworthy.

Firms use sports figures or celebrities as spokespersons to represent their products, such as Brett Favre for Right Guard Sport and Cindy Crawford for Omega watches, in the hope that they are opinion leaders.

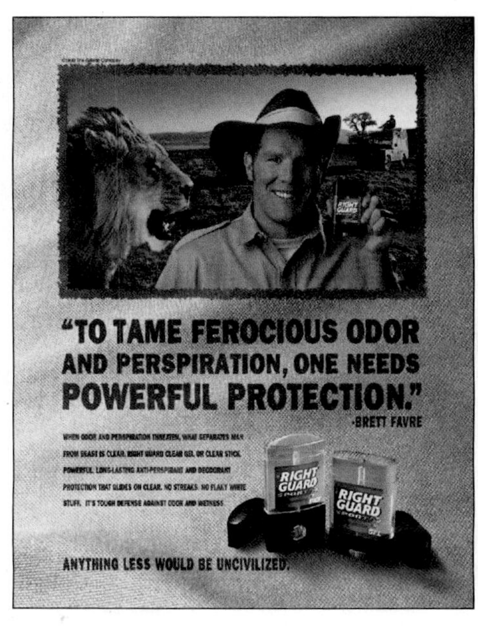

GLOBAL

MARKETING NEWSNET

Psst. Have You Heard . . . ? The Nemesis of Negative Word of Mouth in Global Marketing

Global marketers have learned painfully that word of mouth is a powerful information source in developing countries. Rumours that result in negative word of mouth are particularly common. For example, several food products in Indonesia, including some sold by Nestlé, were rumoured to contain pork, which is prohibited to the 160 million Muslim consumers in that country. Nestlé spent $350 000 in advertising to counteract the rumour. In Russia, Mars, Inc. had to confront the untrue claim that 200 000 Moscow children acquired diabetes from Snickers candy bars. Pabst Blue Ribbon beer was hit by a rumour in China that its beer was poisoned. Actually, a home-brewed beer had been poured into an empty Pabst bottle and resold.

Negative word of mouth has been shown to reduce the credibility of a company's advertising and consumers' intention to buy products. Its effect can be particularly damaging for companies that have recently entered a new country.

A Canadian study found that 70 percent of those surveyed relied on word of mouth when selecting a bank; and 95 percent said they used advice from friends when choosing a physician.[35]

The power of personal influence has prompted firms to promote positive and retard negative word of mouth.[36] For instance, "teaser" advertising campaigns are run in advance of new product introductions to stimulate conversations. Other techniques such as advertising slogans, music, and humour also heighten positive word of mouth. On the other hand, rumours about Kmart (snake eggs in clothing), McDonald's (worms in hamburgers), and Corona Extra beer (contaminated beer) have resulted in negative word of mouth, none of which was based on fact. Overcoming or neutralizing negative word of mouth is difficult and costly. Firms have found that supplying factual information, providing toll-free numbers for consumers to call the company, and giving appropriate product demonstrations also have been helpful. Negative word of mouth is particularly challenging for global marketers as described in the accompanying Marketing NewsNet.[37]

Reference Groups

Reference groups are people to whom an individual looks as a basis for self-appraisal or as a source of personal standards. Reference groups affect consumer purchases because they influence the information, attitudes, and aspiration levels that help set a consumer's standards. For example, one of the first questions one asks others when planning to attend a social occasion is, "What are you going to wear?" Reference groups have an important influence on the purchase of luxury products but not of necessities—reference groups exert a strong influence on the brand chosen when its use or consumption is highly visible to others.[38]

Consumers have many reference groups, but three groups have clear marketing implications. A *membership group* is one to which a person actually belongs, including fraternities, social clubs, and the family. Such groups are easily identifiable and are targeted by firms selling insurance, insignia products, and charter vacations. An *aspiration group* is one that a person wishes to be a member of or wishes to be identified with, such as a professional society. Firms frequently rely on spokespeople or settings associated with their target market's aspiration group in their advertising. A *dissociative group* is one that a person wishes to maintain a distance from because of differences in values or behaviours.

Family Influence

Family influences on consumer behaviour result from three sources: consumer socialization, passage through the family life cycle, and decision making within the family.

Consumer Socialization The process by which people acquire the skills, knowledge, and attitudes necessary to function as consumers is **consumer socialization.**[39] Children learn how to purchase (1) by interacting with adults in purchase situations and (2) through their own purchasing and product usage experiences. Research shows that children evidence brand preferences at age two, and these preferences often last a lifetime.[40] This knowledge has prompted Sony to introduce "My First Sony," a line of portable audio equipment for children; Time, Inc. to launch *Sports Illustrated for Kids;* Polaroid to develop the Cool Cam camcorder for children between ages 9 and 14; and Yahoo! and America Online to create special areas where young audiences can view their children's menu—Yahooligans! and Kids Only, respectively.

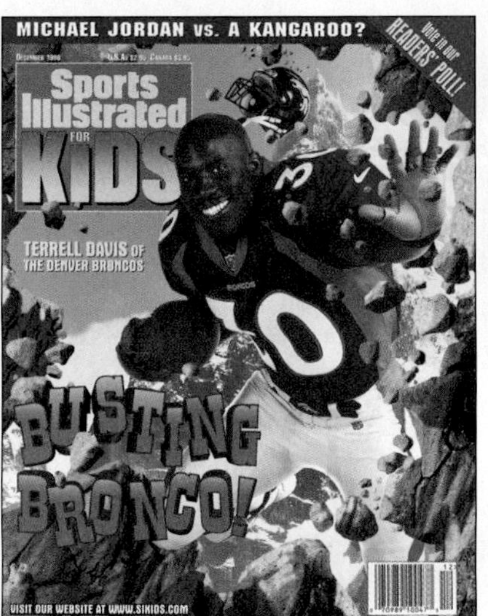

Family Life Cycle Consumers act and purchase differently as they go through life. The **family life cycle** concept describes the distinct phases that a family progresses through from formation to retirement, each phase bringing with it identifiable purchasing behaviours.[41] Figure 6–7 illustrates the traditional progression as well as contemporary variations of the family life cycle, including the prevalence of single-person households with and without children. Young singles' buying preferences are for nondurable items, including prepared foods, clothing, personal care products, and entertainment. They represent a target market for recreational travel, automobile, and consumer electronics firms. Young married couples without children are typically more affluent than young singles because usually both spouses are employed. These couples exhibit preferences for furniture, housewares, and gift items for each other. Young marrieds with children are driven by the needs of their children. They comprise a sizeable market for life insurance, various children's products, and home furnishings. Single parents with children are the least financially secure of households with children. Their buying preferences are affected by a limited economic status and tend toward convenience foods, child care services, and personal care items.

Middle-aged married couples with children are typically better off financially than their younger counterparts. They are a significant market for leisure products and home improvement items and represented the fastest-growing family life cycle stage in the late 1990s. Middle-aged couples without children typically have a large amount of discretionary income. These couples buy better home furnishings, status automobiles, and financial services.

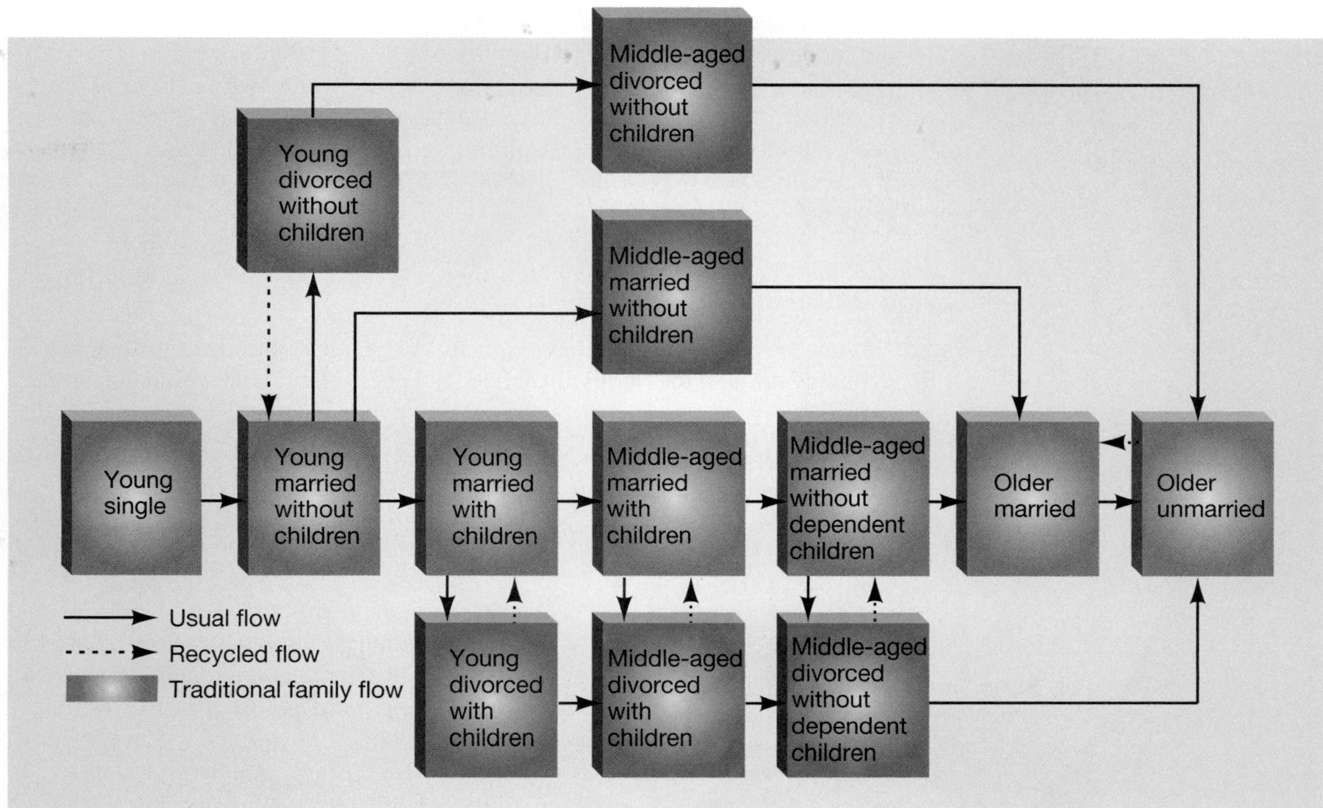

FIGURE 6–7
Modern family life cycle

Persons in the last two phases—older married and older unmarried—are a sizeable market for prescription drugs, medical services, vacation trips, and gifts for younger relatives. These consumers also represent one of the fastest-growing family life cycle stages in the late 1990s.

Family Decision Making A third influence in the decision-making process occurs within the family. Two decision-making styles exist: spouse-dominant and joint decision making. With a joint decision-making style, most decisions are made by both husband and wife. Spouse-dominant decisions are those for which either the husband or the wife is responsible. Research indicates that wives tend to have the most say when purchasing groceries, children's toys, clothing, and medicines. Husbands tend to be more influential in home and car maintenance purchases. Joint decision making is common for cars, vacations, houses, home appliances and electronics, medical care, and long-distance telephone services. As a rule, joint decision making increases with the education of the spouses.[42]

Roles of individual family members in the purchase process are another element of family decision making. Five roles exist: (1) information gatherer, (2) influencer, (3) decision maker, (4) purchaser, and (5) user. Family members assume different roles for different products and services. This knowledge is important to firms.[43] For example, 89 percent of wives either influence or make outright purchases of men's clothing. Knowing this, Haggar Clothing, a men's-wear marketer, now advertises in women's magazines such as *Vanity Fair, Mademoiselle,* and *Redbook.* Even though women are often the grocery decision maker, they are not necessarily the purchaser. More than 40 percent of all food-shopping dollars are spent by male customers. Increasingly, preteens and teenagers are the information gatherers, influencers, decision makers, and purchasers of products and services items for the family, given the prevalence of working parents and single-parent households. Children under 18 currently influence a

The Haggar Clothing Co. recognizes the important role women play in the choice of men's clothing. The company directs a large portion of its advertising toward women because they influence and purchase men's clothing.

Haggar Clothing Co.
www.haggar.com

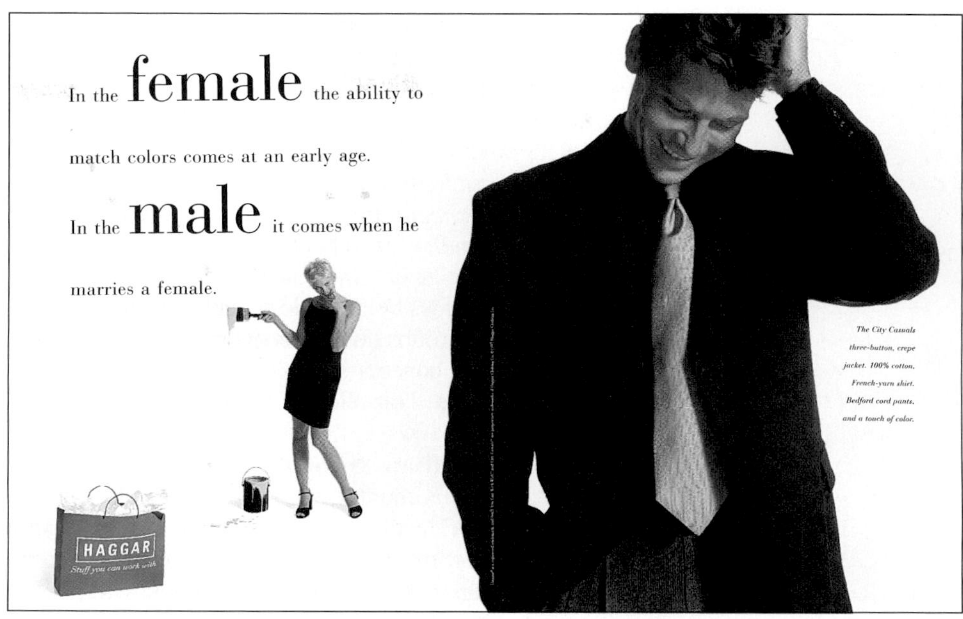

variety of family purchase decisions.[44] This figure helps to explain why, for example, Nabisco, Johnson & Johnson, Apple Computer, Kellogg, P&G, and Oscar Mayer, among countless other companies, advertise in media that reach preteens and teens.

Social Class

A more subtle influence on consumer behaviour than direct contact with others is the social class to which people belong. **Social class** may be defined as the relatively permanent, homogeneous divisions in a society into which people sharing similar values, interests, and behaviour can be grouped. A person's occupation, source of income (not level of income), and education determine his or her social class. Generally speaking, three major social class categories exist—upper, middle, and lower—with subcategories within each. This structure has been observed in Canada, the United States, Great Britain, Western Europe, and Latin America.[45]

To some degree, persons within social classes exhibit common attitudes, lifestyles, and buying behaviours. Compared with the middle classes, people in the lower classes have a more short-term time orientation, are more emotional than rational in their reasoning, think in concrete rather than abstract terms, and see fewer personal opportunities. Members of the upper classes focus on achievements and the future and think in abstract or symbolic terms.

Companies use social class as a basis for identifying and reaching particularly good prospects for their products and services. In general, people in the upper classes are targeted by companies for items such as financial investments, expensive cars, and evening wear. The middle classes represent a target market for home improvement centres, automobile parts stores, and personal hygiene products. Firms also recognize differences in media preferences among classes: lower and working classes prefer sports and scandal magazines, middle classes read fashion, romance, and celebrity (*People*) magazines, and upper classes tend to read literary, travel, and news magazines.

Culture and Subculture

As described in Chapter 3, culture refers to the set of values, ideas, and attitudes that are accepted by a homogeneous group of people and are transmitted to the next generation. This we often refer to as Canadian culture, American culture, British culture, or Japanese culture, etc. (Cultural underpinnings of Canadian buying patterns are described in Chapter 3, whereas Chapter 5 explores the role of culture in global marketing.)

Subgroups within the larger, or national culture, who share unique values, ideas, and attitudes are referred to as **subcultures.** Subcultures can be identified by age (e.g., baby boomers vs. Generation X), geography (e.g., Western Canadian vs. Atlantic Canadian), and ethnicity. Here, we focus on ethnic subcultures.

An *ethnic subculture* is a segment of a larger society whose members are thought, by themselves and/or by others, to have a common origin and to participate in shared activities felt to be culturally significant.[46] Common traits such as customs, language, religious, and values hold ethnic subcultures together. Because of Canada's pluralistic tradition, ethnic groups do not necessarily join the cultural mainstream. Some people have referred to this concept as a *salad bowl* phenomenon, where a potpourri of people mix but do not blend. This allows for the maintenance of subcultural traditions and values.

French-Canadian Subculture There are over seven million French-speaking Canadians in this country, about 25 percent of the population. The overwhelming majority of French Canadians live in Quebec. Research shows that French-speaking Quebecers do exhibit different consumption behaviour from the rest of Canadians.[47] French Quebecers link price to perceived value but will pass on a buy rather than buy on credit. They are more willing to pay higher prices for convenience and premium brands, and they give more credence to advertising than the average Canadian. Metro-Richelieu Inc., a Quebec grocery store chain, says their research shows that 56 percent of Quebecers consult the grocery chain's weekly circulars.

www.metro-richelieu.com

But French Quebecers are cautious of new products and often postpone trial until the product has proven itself. They do exhibit brand loyalty but will switch for specials. They also prefer convenience and health food stores over food warehouses and local grocery stores. French Quebecers are less likely to buy grocery items on impulse and are increasingly calculating in their food purchases. Metro-Richelieu Inc. has responded by offering more discount coupons, weekly specials, and money-saving tips under one plan called EconoMetro. Also, French Quebecers are more concerned with personal grooming and fashion, and more likely to shop in specialized clothing boutiques. Eaton's has shifted its advertising approach in Quebec in an attempt to appeal to Quebecers' heightened fashion sense while recognizing that department stores are not the most popular option for fashion in La Belle Province.

French Quebec has a higher percentage of wine and beer drinkers and more smokers. And, while Quebecers enjoy their beer, Molson says its research indicates that French Quebecers prefer a stronger beer. Accordingly, Molson launched O'Keefe 6.2. Brand (which contains 6.2 percent alcohol) exclusively for the Quebec market. There are fewer golfers, joggers, and gardeners, and the proportion of people who go to movies or entertain at home is also lower. There are, however, more cyclists, skiers, and live theatre fans.

French Quebecers are big buyers of lottery tickets and more likely to subscribe to book clubs, but they make fewer long-distance phone calls. They travel less, whether for business or pleasure. More French Quebec adults hold life insurance policies but they are less likely to have a credit card. They also tend to use credit unions (caisses populaires) more than banks.

Some argue that French Quebec can be characterized by a set of values that are traditional, consistent, and relatively static. But changes are evident. While values are still strong about family life, about having children in a marriage, and about giving them religious training, the use of birth control is on the rise and the marriage rate is below the national average.

Marketers must realize that certain products and other elements of the marketing mix may have to be modified in order to be successful in French Quebec. In addition to cultural differences, there are other issues that marketers must address. Commercial advertising to children is prohibited and greater restrictions exist for alcohol advertising. Provincial regulations also require that labels and packages must be both in French and English, while storefront signage must be in French, not English. Good investigation and analysis of this market is a requirement for all companies wishing to do business there.

Acadian Subculture Many Canadians assume that French Canadians are basically the same. Even though the majority of French-speaking Canadians reside in Quebec, another special group of French-speaking Canadians live outside of Quebec. These people are the Acadians, most of whom live in New Brunswick and are proud of their distinctive heritage. The Acadians are often referred to as the "forgotten French market."

Acadians are different from French Quebecers in many ways. In terms of consumption, Acadians are very fashion-oriented and tend to dine out more often than their French counterparts in Quebec. Acadians are also very price-conscious. They also prefer companies that speak to them in their language, which is slightly different than French Quebecois.

Chinese-Canadian Subculture The Chinese-Canadian market currently represents over three percent of Canada's population, but it is one of the fastest-growing subcultures in Canada. This ethnic group is composed predominantly of immigrants from Hong Kong and Taiwan and is concentrated largely in Toronto and Vancouver.

Chinese Canadians have unique values. While most Canadians value straight-line thinking (logic), the Chinese value circular thinking (what goes around comes around). They value work, family, and education. They have different purchasing patterns and often perceive products differently from other Canadians. This group also appreciates companies that speak to them in their language. For example, many firms produce ads in Mandarin or Cantonese and run them in specialty publications such as the *Sing Tao,* a Toronto newspaper for Chinese readers.

The average Chinese Canadian has a higher income, is better educated, less likely to be unemployed, and is significantly younger than the general Canadian population. Because of these characteristics, many firms see Chinese Canadians as a viable target market for a variety of products. For example, the Royal Bank sees them as good prospects for RSP and mutual fund products, while Cantel markets its cellular phones to this group.

Other Ethnic Subcultures Many other ethnic Canadians can be found in large metropolitan centres or clustered in certain geographic areas. Kitchener-Waterloo has a large German Canadian population, Winnipeg is home to many Ukrainian Canadians, and Toronto has a large number of Italian Canadians. The emerging trend in Canada today is that 70 percent of all immigrants to this country are visible minorities. In addition to Asia, many new Canadians are coming from Africa and India. Marketers must appreciate the fact that these new ethnic Canadians may carry with them distinctive social and cultural behaviour that will affect their buying patterns. Subcultural research and sensitivity can aid organizations in developing effective marketing strategies designed to appeal to these groups. For example, a common misconception is that ethnic Canadians have less spending power than Canadian-born people. However, studies show that arriving immigrants are bringing in large amounts of capital. This is particularly true of immigrants from Hong Kong who have and continue to migrate here due to mainland China's takeover of Hong Kong. Moreover, it has been found that foreign-born Canadians earn more money, comparatively, than native-born Canadians.[48]

CONCEPT CHECK

1. What are the two primary forms of personal influence?
2. Marketers are concerned with which types of reference groups?
3. What is an ethnic subculture?

SUMMARY

1 When a consumer buys a product, it is not an act but a process. There are five steps in the purchase decision process: problem recognition, information search, alternative evaluation, purchase decision, and postpurchase behaviour.
2 Consumers evaluate alternatives on the basis of attributes. Identifying which attributes are most important to consumers, along with understanding consumer beliefs about how a brand performs on those attributes, can make the difference between successful and unsuccessful products.
3 Consumer involvement with what is bought affects whether the purchase decision process involves routine, limited, or extended problem solving. Situational influences also affect the process.
4 Perception is important to marketers because of the selectivity of what a consumer sees or hears, comprehends, and retains.
5 Much of the behaviour that consumers exhibit is learned. Consumers learn from repeated experience and reasoning. Brand loyalty is a result of learning.
6 Attitudes are learned predispositions to respond to an object or class of objects in a consistently favourable or unfavourable way. Attitudes are based on a person's values and beliefs concerning the attributes of objects.
7 Lifestyle is a mode of living reflected in a person's activities, interests, and opinions of himself or herself and the world.
8 Personal influence takes two forms: opinion leadership and word-of-mouth activity. A specific type of personal influence exists in the form of reference groups.
9 Family influences on consumer behaviour result from three sources: consumer socialization, family life cycle, and decision making within the household.
10 Within Canada there are social classes and subcultures that affect a consumer's values and behaviour. Marketers must be sensitive to these sociocultural influences when developing a marketing mix.

KEY TERMS AND CONCEPTS

consumer behaviour p. 148
purchase decision process p. 148
evaluative criteria p. 149
evoked set p. 150
computer-mediated buying p. 150
cognitive dissonance p. 151
involvement p. 152
situational influences p. 153
motivation p. 154
personality p. 155
national character p. 155
self-concept p. 155
perception p. 155
subliminal perception p. 156
perceived risk p. 156
learning p. 157
brand loyalty p. 158
attitude p. 158
beliefs p. 158
lifestyle p. 159
opinion leaders p. 161
word of mouth p. 161
reference groups p. 162
consumer socialization p. 163
family life cycle p. 163
social class p. 165
subcultures p. 166

INTERNET EXERCISE

A customer's consumption or use experience with products and services is extremely important in determining value perceptions. Furthermore, postpurchase experiences can lead to positive or negative word of mouth and influence the likelihood of repeat-purchase behaviour.

Service Intelligence, Inc. maintains a Web site (www.serviceintelligence.com) that catalogues customer stories of unpleasant and pleasant experiences with airlines, banks, retailers, and other businesses. Visit their Web site, click Customer Service Heroes & Horror Stories, and answer the following questions:

1 Are there more "horror" stories than "hero" stories?
2 Choose two particular businesses, such as airlines and banks. What is the most frequently mentioned complaint customers have for each business?

APPLYING MARKETING CONCEPTS AND PERSPECTIVES

1 Review Figure 6–2 in the text, which shows the CD-player attributes identified by *Consumer Reports.* Which attributes are important to you? What other attributes might you consider? Which brand would you prefer?

2 Suppose research at Apple Computer reveals that prospective buyers are anxious about buying PCs for home use. What strategies might you recommend to the company to reduce consumer anxiety?

3 A Porsche salesperson was taking orders on new cars because he was unable to satisfy the demand with the limited number of cars in the showroom and lot. Several persons had backed out of the contract within two weeks of signing the order. What explanation can you give for this behaviour, and what remedies would you recommend?

4 Which social class would you associate with each of the following items or actions: (*a*) tennis club membership, (*b*) an arrangement of plastic flowers in the kitchen, (*c*) *True Romance* magazine, (*d*) *MacLean's* magazine, (*e*) formally dressing for dinner frequently, and (*f*) being a member of a bowling team.

5 Assign one or more levels of the hierarchy of needs and the motives described in Figure 6–5 to the following products: (*a*) life insurance, (*b*) cosmetics, (*c*) *The Financial Post,* and (*d*) hamburgers.

6 With which stage in the family life cycle would the purchase of the following products and services be most closely identified: (*a*) bedroom furniture, (*b*) life insurance, (*c*) a Caribbean cruise, (*d*) a house mortgage, and (*e*) children's toys?

7 "The greater the perceived risk in a purchase situation, the more likely that cognitive dissonance will result." Does this statement have any basis given the discussion in the text? Why?

CASE 6–1 THREE SISTERS CAFE

Three Sisters Cafe is a medium-sized (120 seats), upscale restaurant that had been in business for five years. The owners, three sisters, are happy with the restaurant's performance but would like to do better. They believe their customers like the restaurant and repeat business is very good. In a highly competitive market, however, the sisters feel they must find ways to attract more business. After much discussion and debate, the three sisters decided to hire a local consulting firm to conduct some consumer research. Basically, the three sisters wanted to know (1) the attributes that a licensed sit-down restaurant must possess in order for consumers to patronize an establishment; (2) how well Three Sisters Cafe measured up on those attributes; and (3) consumers' satisfaction and dissatisfaction with Three Sisters Cafe. A telephone survey of restaurant goers was conducted. A person had to have dined out in the last four weeks to be part of the survey. A total of 320 respondents participated. Of this total, 140 had dined at Three Sisters Cafe at least once in the previous four weeks.

CONSUMER RESEARCH FINDINGS

First, consumer awareness levels were obtained for the licensed sit-down restaurants in the area. It was particularly important to examine consumer awareness of a business or brand since awareness is a necessary prerequisite to purchase. A restaurant with low awareness levels may mean consumers will not think of that particular restaurant when they consider dining out. Three Sisters Cafe had an overall awareness score of 60 percent. In other words, 60 percent of consumers surveyed were aware of Three Sisters Cafe. Many of its competitors had lower awareness scores, ranging from 25 percent to 55 percent. One nearby competitor, however, had the highest awareness score at 85 percent.

The consulting firm uncovered the attributes required by consumers in order to patronize a licensed sit-down restaurant. Exhibit 1 depicts what respondents believed to be the "ideal" attributes making up such an establishment. It was derived by examining the percentage of those who, on the dimension under consideration, rated the attributes as "Very Important or Must Have It." The element was considered to be an ideal element if 70 percent or more respondents indicated it to be very important or a must-have. There were no differences between users of Three Sisters Cafe and nonusers in terms of the ideal attributes that a restaurant must have in order to patronize. Exhibit 1 also shows how Three Sisters Cafe was rated by users on those ideal attributes.

The consulting firm also examined customer satisfaction with Three Sisters Cafe. The analysis revealed that 87 percent of users were satisfied with their experience while 13 percent were dissatisfied. Of those who were dissatisfied, 70 percent stated food quality to be the reason for their dissatisfaction, while 30 percent stated high prices was their reason for dissatisfaction. All three sisters reviewed the findings and wondered about the ratings their restaurant received, as well as the awareness scores and the satisfaction data. They realized the key issue now is what to do with the information.

Questions

1 Which attributes (evaluative criteria) do you think are most critical in the consumers' assessment of value when selecting a restaurant?

2 What is the relationship between a consumer's awareness of given restaurants and his or her evoked set of choice?

3 What do you think about the consumers' satisfaction levels with Three Sisters Cafe? Do you think this is a problem area they need to address? Why or why not?

EXHIBIT 1

Attributes a restaurant must possess and how users rate Three Sisters Cafe on those attributes

	IDEAL ATTRIBUTES (% MENTIONING AS VERY IMPORTANT OR MUST HAVE IT, ALL RESPONDENTS)	USERS' RATINGS OF THREE SISTERS (% RATING IT AS VERY GOOD/EXCELLENT ON THAT ATTRIBUTE)
Good food	95.0%	66.0%
Atmosphere	90.0	84.0
Efficient service	83.0	82.0
Friendly service	80.0	77.0
Comfortable seating	78.0	87.0
Decor	77.0	92.0
Good prices	76.0	26.0
Table presentation	75.0	85.0
Good wine list	73.0	76.0
	N = 320	N = 140

Gbps WDM INNOVATION Gbps

Gbps WDM INNOVA

ION

Honeywell
OPTOELECTRONICS
RS232
FIBRE OPTIC MODEM

CHAPTER SEVEN

ORGANIZATIONAL MARKETS AND BUYER BEHAVIOUR

7

AFTER READING THIS CHAPTER YOU SHOULD BE ABLE TO:

- Distinguish among industrial, reseller, and government markets.
- Recognize key characteristics of organizational buying that make it different from consumer buying.
- Understand how types of buying situations influence organizational purchasing.
- Recognize similarities and differences in industrial and reseller purchase behaviour.

LASER TECHNOLOGY IS BRIGHT AT HONEYWELL

Gary Null views light very differently from most people. He pictures a world where information is processed at the speed of light and electricity is converted to light with unprecedented efficiency.

As the International Business Development Director at Honeywell (www.honeywell.com), MICRO SWITCH Division, Null shares responsibility for the global launch of Honeywell's newest innovation, the *V*ertical *C*avity *S*urface *E*mitting *L*aser or VCSEL (pronounced "Vik-Sel"). VCSEL is emerging as the light source of choice for high-speed short-wavelength communication systems. Numerous other potential applications exist in computer networks and consumer, industrial, and office products.

Successful commercialization of this innovative laser technology depends on a coordinated worldwide team effort that draws on the talents of MICRO SWITCH design and application engineers and marketing and sales professionals. Their efforts focus on demonstrating the performance, cost, and reliability advantages of the VCSEL over existing technology to a diverse set of organizational buyers around the world. It also requires knowing which people influence the purchasing decision; what factors they consider when choosing suppliers, technology, and products; and when, where, and how buying decisions are made in Asian, European, and Latin American business cultures.

Null believes Honeywell, MICRO SWITCH Division, is poised to capture a significant share of the multi-billion-dollar global market for laser technology and products. Ultimate success will depend on continued product development that creates customer value and effective marketing to an ever-increasing number of industrial buyers of laser technology in a worldwide marketplace.[1]

The challenge facing Null of marketing to organizations is often encountered by both small, start-up corporations and large, well-established companies such as Honeywell. Important issues in marketing to organizations are examined in this chapter, which analyzes types of organizational buyers, key characteristics of organizational buying, and some typical buying decisions.

THE NATURE AND SIZE OF ORGANIZATIONAL MARKETS

Gary Null and Honeywell's MICRO SWITCH Division engage in business marketing. **Business marketing** is the marketing of goods and services to commercial enterprises, government, and other profit and nonprofit organizations for use in the creation of goods and services that they then produce and market to other business customers, as well as individuals and ultimate consumers.[2] Because many Canadian business school graduates take jobs in firms that engage in business marketing, it is important to understand the fundamental characteristics of organizational buyers and their buying behaviour.

Organizational buyers are those manufacturers, retailers, and government agencies that buy goods and services for their own use or for resale. For example, all these organizations buy computers and telephone services for their own use. However, manufacturers buy raw materials and parts that they reprocess into the finished goods they sell, whereas retailers resell goods they buy without reprocessing them. Organizational buyers include all the buyers in a nation except the ultimate consumers. These organizational buyers purchase and lease tremendous volumes of capital equipment, raw materials, manufactured parts, supplies, and business services. In fact, because they often buy raw materials and parts, process them, and sell the upgraded product several times before it is purchased by the final organizational buyer or ultimate consumer, the aggregate purchases of organizational buyers in a year are far greater than those of ultimate consumers.

Organizational buyers are divided into three markets: (1) industrial, (2) resellers, and (3) government markets.

Industrial Markets

There are thousands of firms in the industrial, or business, market in Canada. **Industrial firms** in some way reprocess a good or service they buy before selling it again to the next buyer. This is certainly true of a steel mill that converts iron ore into steel. It is also true (if you stretch your imagination) of a firm selling services, such as a bank that takes money from its depositors, reprocesses it, and "sells" it as loans to its commercial borrowers.

There has been a marked shift in the scope and nature of the industrial marketplace. Service industries are growing and currently make the greatest contribution to Canada's gross domestic product (GDP). Because of the importance of service firms, service marketing is discussed in detail in Chapter 13. Industrial firms and primary industries currently contribute less than 25 percent to Canada's GDP. Nevertheless, primary industries (e.g., farming, mining, fishing, and forestry) and the manufacturing sector are important components of Canada's economy. There are about 40 000 manufacturers in Canada whose estimated value of shipments are over $450 billion.[3]

Reseller Markets

Wholesalers and retailers who buy physical products and resell them again without any reprocessing are **resellers.** Over 200 000 retailers and over 65 000 wholesalers are currently operating in Canada. In Chapters 16 through 18 we see how manufacturers

Printed in English, the Moscow Yellow Pages lists more than 22 000 industrial, trade, joint venture, and government office telephone numbers and addresses. Read the text to find out how firms in Germany, Russia, and the United States work together to produce, promote, and distribute this directory.

Moscow Yellow Pages
www.russia.net/country/moscow-yellow-pages.html

use wholesalers and retailers in their distribution ("place") strategies as channels through which their products reach ultimate consumers. In this chapter we look at resellers mainly as organizational buyers in terms of (1) how they make their own buying decisions and (2) which products they choose to carry.

Government Markets

www.canada.gc.ca

Government units are the federal, provincial, and local agencies that buy goods and services for the constituents they serve. Their annual purchases vary in size from the billions of dollars for a federal department such as National Defence to millions or thousands of dollars for a local university or school. The bulk of the buying at the federal government level is done by the Department of Supply and Services Canada. Most provincial governments have a government services department that does the buying on the provincial level. Hundreds of government departments, including agencies and Crown corporations such as CN and the Royal Canadian Mint, must purchase goods and services to operate. The federal government is a large organizational consumer making total purchases of goods and services in excess of $170 billion annually.[4]

Global Organizational Markets

www.nortelnetworks.com

Industrial, reseller, and government markets also exist on a global scale. In fact, many of Canada's top exporters including Nortel, Noranda, Abitibi-Price and Pratt & Whitney, focus on organizational customers, not ultimate consumers.

Most world trade involves manufacturers, resellers, and government agencies buying goods and services for their own use or for resale to others. The exchange relationships often involve numerous transactions spanning the globe. For example, Honeywell, MICRO SWITCH Division sells its fibre-optic technology and products to manufacturers of data communication systems worldwide, through electronic component resellers in more than 20 countries, and directly to national governments in Europe and elsewhere. Europe's Airbus Industrie, the world's largest aircraft manufacturer, sells its passenger airplanes to Air Canada, which flies Canadian businesspeople to Asia. A North American firm solicits advertising for and a publisher in Germany prints the Moscow Yellow Pages on behalf of the Moscow city government and telephone system for resale to businesses through Moscow stores, hotels, and international trade centres.

MEASURING DOMESTIC AND GLOBAL INDUSTRIAL, RESELLER, AND GOVERNMENT MARKETS

The measurement of industrial, reseller, and government markets is an important first step for a firm interested in gauging the size of one, two, or all three of these markets in Canada and around the world. This task has been made easier with the **North American Industry Classification System (NAICS).**[5] NAICS provides common industry definitions for Canada, Mexico, and the United States, which facilitate the measurement of economic activity in the three member countries of the North American Free Trade Agreement (NAFTA). NAICS replaced the Standard Industrial Classification (SIC) system, a version of which has been in place for more than 50 years in the three NAFTA member countries. The SIC neither permitted comparability across countries nor accurately measured new or emerging industries. Furthermore, NAICS is consistent with the International Standard Industrial Classification of All Economic Activities, published by the United Nations, to facilitate measurement of global economic activity.

The NAICS groups economic activity to permit studies of market share, demand for goods and services, import competition in domestic markets, and similar studies. NAICS designates industries with a numerical code in a defined structure. A six-digit coding system is used. The first two digits designate a sector of the economy, the third digit designates a subsector, and the fourth digit represents an industry group. The fifth digit designates a specific industry and is the most detailed level at which comparable data is available for Canada, Mexico, and the United States. The sixth digit designates individual country-level national industries. Figure 7–1 presents an abbreviated breakdown within the Information Industries Sector (code 51) to illustrate the classification scheme.

The NAICS permits a firm to find the NAICS codes of its present customers and then obtain NAICS-coded lists for similar firms. Also, it is possible to monitor NAICS categories to determine the growth in various sectors and industries to identify promising marketing opportunities. However, NAICS codes, like the earlier SIC codes, have important limitations. The NAICS assigns one code to each organization based on its major economic activity, so large firms that engage in many different activities are still given only one NAICS code. A second limitation is that five-digit national industry codes are not available for all three countries because the respective governments will not reveal data when too few organizations exist in a category. Despite these limitations, development of NAICS represents yet another effort toward economic integration in North America and the world.

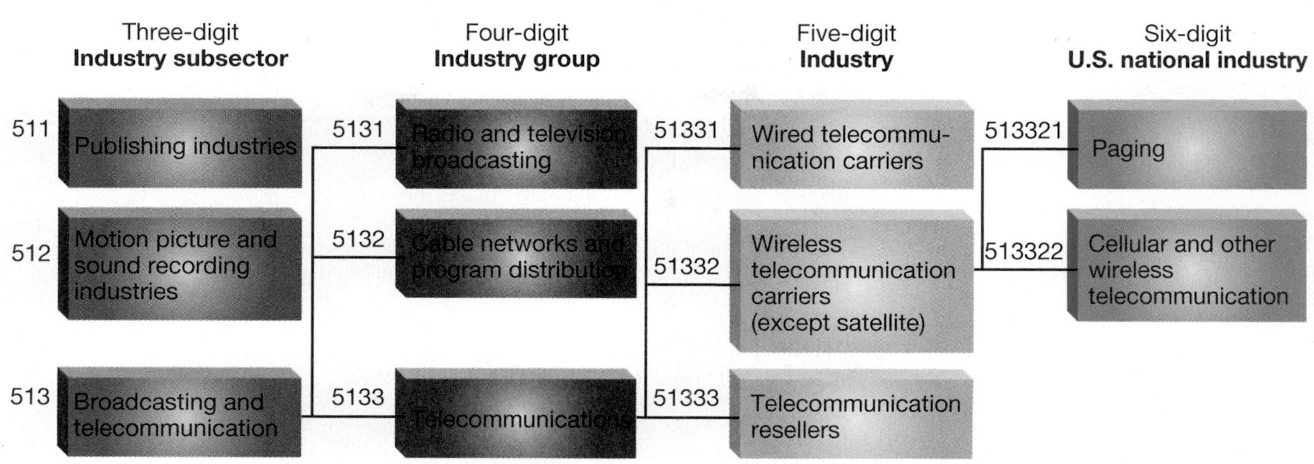

FIGURE 7–1
NAICS breakdown for information industries sector: NAICS code 51 (abbreviated)

CONCEPT CHECK

1. What are the three main types of organizational buyers?
2. What is the North American Industry Classification System (NAICS)?

CHARACTERISTICS OF ORGANIZATIONAL BUYING

Organizations are different from individuals, so buying for an organization is different from buying for yourself or your family.[6] True, in both cases the objective in making the purchase is to solve the buyer's problem—to satisfy a need or want. But unique objectives and policies of an organization put special constraints on how it makes buying decisions. Understanding the characteristics of organizational buying is essential in designing effective marketing programs to reach these buyers.

Organizational buying behaviour is the decision-making process that organizations use to establish the need for products and services and identify, evaluate, and choose among alternative brands and suppliers. Key characteristics of organizational buying behaviour are listed in Figure 7–2 and discussed next.[7]

Demand Characteristics

Consumer demand for products and services is affected by their price and availability and by consumers' personal tastes and discretionary income. By comparison, industrial demand is derived. **Derived demand** means that the demand for industrial products and services is driven by, or derived from, demand for consumer products and services. For example, the demand for MacMillan Bloedel's pulp and paper products is based on consumer demand for newspapers, Domino's "keep warm" pizza-to-go boxes, Federal Express packages, and disposable diapers. Derived demand is often based on expectations of future consumer demand. For instance, Whirlpool purchases parts for its washers and dryers in anticipation of consumer demand, which is affected by the replacement cycle for these products and by consumer income.

www.macmillanbloedel.com

FIGURE 7–2
Key characteristics of organizational buying behaviour

MARKET CHARACTERISTICS
- Demand for industrial products and services is derived.
- Few customers typically exist, and their purchase orders are large.

PRODUCT OR SERVICE CHARACTERISTICS
- Products or services are technical in nature and purchased on the basis of specifications.
- There is a predominance of raw and semi-finished goods purchased.
- Heavy emphasis is placed on delivery time, technical assistance, postsale service, and financing assistance.

BUYING PROCESS CHARACTERISTICS
- Technically qualified and professional buyers exist and follow established purchasing policies and procedures.
- Buying objectives and criteria are typically spelled out, as are procedures for evaluating sellers and products (services).
- Multiple buying influences exist, and multiple parties participate in purchase decisions.
- Reciprocal arrangements exist, and negotiation between buyers and sellers is commonplace.
- Online buying over the Internet is widespread.

OTHER MARKETING MIX CHARACTERISTICS
- Direct selling to organizational buyers is the rule, and physical distribution is very important.
- Advertising and other forms of promotion are technical in nature.
- Price is often negotiated, evaluated as part of broader seller and product (service) qualities, typically inelastic owing to derived demand, and frequently affected by trade and quantity discounts.

As demand for the products that comprise the Information Superhighway grows, so too will the demand for the technology that makes them possible. Read the accompanying Marketing NewsNet to see how companies that produce microchips and microprocessors will benefit from the merging of telecommunications, information, and data networks on the Information Superhighway.[8]

Size of the Order or Purchase

The size of the purchase involved in organizational buying is typically much larger than that in consumer buying. The dollar value of a single purchase made by an organization often runs into the thousands or millions of dollars. For example, Motorola was recently awarded an $88 million contract to install a cellular phone system in Brazil.[9] With so much money at stake, most organizations place constraints on their buyers in the form of purchasing policies or procedures. Buyers must often get competitive bids from at least three prospective suppliers when the order is above a specific amount, such as $5000. When the order is above an even higher amount, such as $50 000, it may require the review and approval of a vice president or even the president of the company. Knowing how the size of the order affects buying practices is important in determining who participates in the purchase decision and makes the final decision, and also the length of time required to arrive at a purchase agreement.

Number of Potential Buyers

Firms selling consumer products or services often try to reach thousands or millions of individuals or households. For example, your local supermarket or bank probably serves thousands of people, and Quaker Oats tries to reach over 10 million Canadian

GLOBAL

MARKETING NEWSNET

The Global Information Superhighway Is Paved with Silicon Chips

The 21st century will witness the merging of telecommunications, information, and data networks into what has been labelled the "Information Superhighway." As new products and applications emerge for use by businesses and consumers alike, demand for microchips (the small piece of silicon that holds a complex electronic circuit) and demand for microprocessors (a miniature computer consisting of one or more microchips) will expand dramatically.

Companies that produce microchips and microprocessors will benefit from the demand derived from the sale of a multitude of products and technologies that comprise the Information Superhighway. Powerful microprocessors and multimedia graphics software will boost demand for DRAMS (dynamic random-access memory chips), a business dominated by Korean and Japanese firms. Demand for digital-signal-processing chips that speed up video and graphics will boost the fortunes of Texas Instruments and SGS-Thomson. Demand for multimedia chips will grow as telephone and cable TV companies begin buying video services and set-top boxes to deliver movies and interactive games to homes.

"The Information Highway will be paved with silicon," says an executive at Texas Instruments, and microchip demand will be driven by the telecommunication, information, and data networks that travel the highway.

households with its breakfast cereals and probably succeeds in selling to a third or half of these in any given year. In contrast, firms selling to organizations are often restricted to far fewer buyers. Gulfstream Aerospace Corporation can sell its business jets to a few thousand organizations throughout the world, and B. F. Goodrich sells its original equipment tires to fewer than 10 car manufacturers.

Organizational Buying Objectives

Organizations buy products and services for one main reason: to help them achieve their objectives. For business firms the buying objective is usually to increase profits through reducing costs or increasing revenues. Southland Corporation buys automated inventory systems to increase the number of products that can be sold through its 7-Eleven outlets and to keep them fresh. Nissan Motor Company switched its advertising agency because it expects the new agency to devise a more effective ad campaign to help it sell more cars and increase revenues. To improve executive decision making, many firms buy advanced computer systems to process data. The objectives of nonprofit firms and government agencies are usually to meet the needs of the groups they serve. Thus, a hospital buys a high-technology diagnostic device to serve its patients

Sylvania focuses on buyers' objective of reducing costs to improve profits.

Sylvania
www.sylvania.com

better. Understanding buying objectives is a necessary first step in marketing to organizations. Recognizing the high costs of energy, Sylvania promotes to prospective buyers cost savings and increased profits made possible by its fluorescent lights.

Organizational Buying Criteria

In making a purchase the buying organization must weigh key buying criteria that apply to the potential supplier and what it wants to sell. **Organizational buying criteria** are the objective attributes of the supplier's products and services and the capabilities of the supplier itself. These criteria serve the same purpose as the evaluative criteria used by consumers and described in Chapter 6. Seven of the most commonly used criteria are (1) price, (2) ability to meet the quality specifications required for the item, (3) ability to meet required delivery schedules, (4) technical capability, (5) warranties and claim policies in the event of poor performance, (6) past performance on previous contracts, and (7) production facilities and capacity.[10] Suppliers that meet or exceed these criteria create customer value.

Organizational buyers who purchase products and services in a global marketplace often supplement their buying criteria with supplier ISO 9000 certification. As described in Chapter 5, ISO 9000 certification means that a supplier has undergone an on-site audit to ensure that a quality management and quality assurance system is in place. 3M, which buys and markets its products globally, has 80 percent of its manufacturing and service facilities ISO 9000 certified. According to the company's director of quality control, certification also gives 3M confidence in the consistent quality of its suppliers' manufacturing systems and products.[11]

Many organizational buyers today are transforming their buying criteria into specific requirements that are communicated to prospective suppliers. This practice,

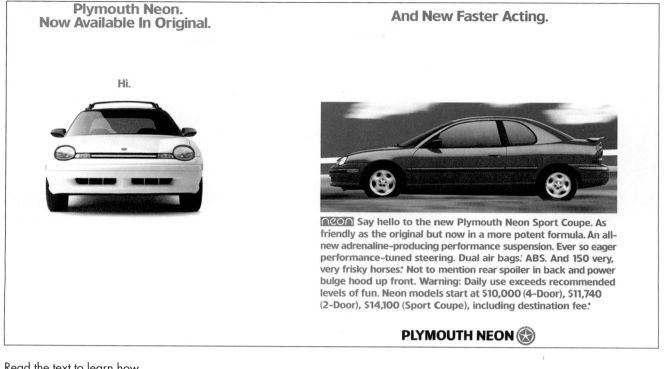

Read the text to learn how Johnson Controls, Inc., the seat supplier for Neon, played an important role in making the Neon a success.

Johnson Controls, Inc.
www.jci.com

called **reverse marketing,** involves the deliberate effort by organizational buyers to build relationships that shape suppliers' products, services, and capabilities to fit a buyer's needs and those of its customers.[12] For example, consider the case of Johnson Controls, Inc., the supplier of seats for Chrysler's small car, the Plymouth Neon.[13] Johnson was able to meet Chrysler's cost target but not its safety, weight, and comfort requirements. After five 11-hour days, Johnson and Chrysler engineering and marketing staffs jointly worked out the technical details to satisfy Chrysler's performance requirements at a price acceptable to both parties. Ongoing reverse marketing efforts also exist. Harley-Davidson expects even its long-term suppliers to provide written plans of their efforts to improve quality, and it monitors the progress of these suppliers toward achieving these goals.

With many Canadian manufacturers adopting a "just-in-time" (JIT) inventory system that reduces the inventory of production parts to those to be used within hours or days, on-time delivery is becoming an even more important buying criterion and, in some instances, a requirement. Caterpillar trains its key suppliers at its Quality Institute in JIT inventory systems and conducts supplier seminars on how to diagnose, correct, and implement continuous quality improvement programs.[14] The just-in-time inventory system is discussed further in Chapter 17.

Buyer-Seller Relationships and Supply Partnerships

Another distinction between organizational and consumer buying behaviour lies in the nature of the relationship between organizational buyers and suppliers. Specifically, organizational buying is more likely to involve complex and lengthy negotiations concerning delivery schedules, price, technical specifications, warranties, and claim policies. These negotiations can last for more than a year. This was the case when a customer recently purchased a $49 million Cray Research T90 supercomputer that performs up to 60 million calculations per second.[15]

ETHICS

ETHICS AND SOCIAL RESPONSIBILITY ALERT

Scratching Each Other's Back: The Ethics of Reciprocity in Organizational Buying

Reciprocity, the buying practice in which two organizations agree to purchase each other's products and services, is frowned upon in many countries because it restricts the normal operation of the free market. Reciprocal buying practices do exist, however, in a variety of forms, including certain types of countertrade arrangements in international marketing. Furthermore, the extent to which reciprocity is viewed as an ethical issue varies across cultures. In many Asian countries, for instance, reciprocity is often a positive and widespread practice.

Reciprocity is occasionally addressed in the ethics code of companies. For instance, the Quaker Oats Company's code of ethics states:

> In many instances, Quaker may purchase goods and/or services from a supplier who buys products or services from us. This practice is normal and acceptable, but suppliers may not be asked to buy our products and services in order to become or continue to be a supplier.

Do you think reciprocal buying is unethical?

www.canada.gc.ca

Reciprocal arrangements also exist in organizational buying. **Reciprocity** is an industrial buying practice in which two organizations agree to purchase each other's products and services. Consumer and Corporate Affairs Canada frowns on reciprocal buying because it restricts the normal operation of the free market. However, the practice exists and can limit the flexibility of organizational buyers in choosing alternative suppliers. Regardless of the legality of reciprocal buying, do you believe this practice is ethical? (See the accompanying Ethics and Social Responsibility Alert.)[16]

Long-term relationships are also prevalent.[17] As an example, Scandinavian Airlines System recently announced the purchase of 35 Boeing 737–600 airliners with an option to buy another 35 in the future for a total expenditure of $3.3 billion. With aircraft deliveries beginning in late 1998 and continuing into the 21st century, Scandinavian Airlines cited its desire for a long-term relationship with "a professional and solid supplier" such as Boeing.[18] Dana Corporation is presently engaged in a 10-year, $2.8 billion contract to supply Mack Trucks with axles, clutches, and frame assemblies.

In some cases, buyer-seller relationships develop into supply partnerships.[19] A **supply partnership** exists when a buyer and its supplier adopt mutually beneficial objectives, policies, and procedures for the purpose of lowering the cost and/or increasing the value of products and services delivered to the ultimate consumer. Intel, the world's largest manufacturer of microprocessors and the "computer inside" most personal computers, is a case in point. Intel supports its suppliers by offering them quality management programs and by investing in supplier equipment that produces fewer product defects and boosts supplier productivity. Suppliers, in turn, provide Intel with consistent high-quality products at a lower cost for its customers, the makers of personal computers, and finally you, the ultimate customer. Retailers, too, are forging partnerships with their suppliers. Wal-Mart and Kmart have such a relationship with Procter & Gamble for ordering and replenishing P&G's products in their stores. By using computerized cash register scanning equipment and direct electronic linkages to P&G, these retailers can tell P&G what merchandise is needed, along with how much, when, and to which store to deliver it on a daily basis. Because supply partnerships also involve the physical distribution of goods, they are again discussed in Chapter 17 in the context of supply chains.

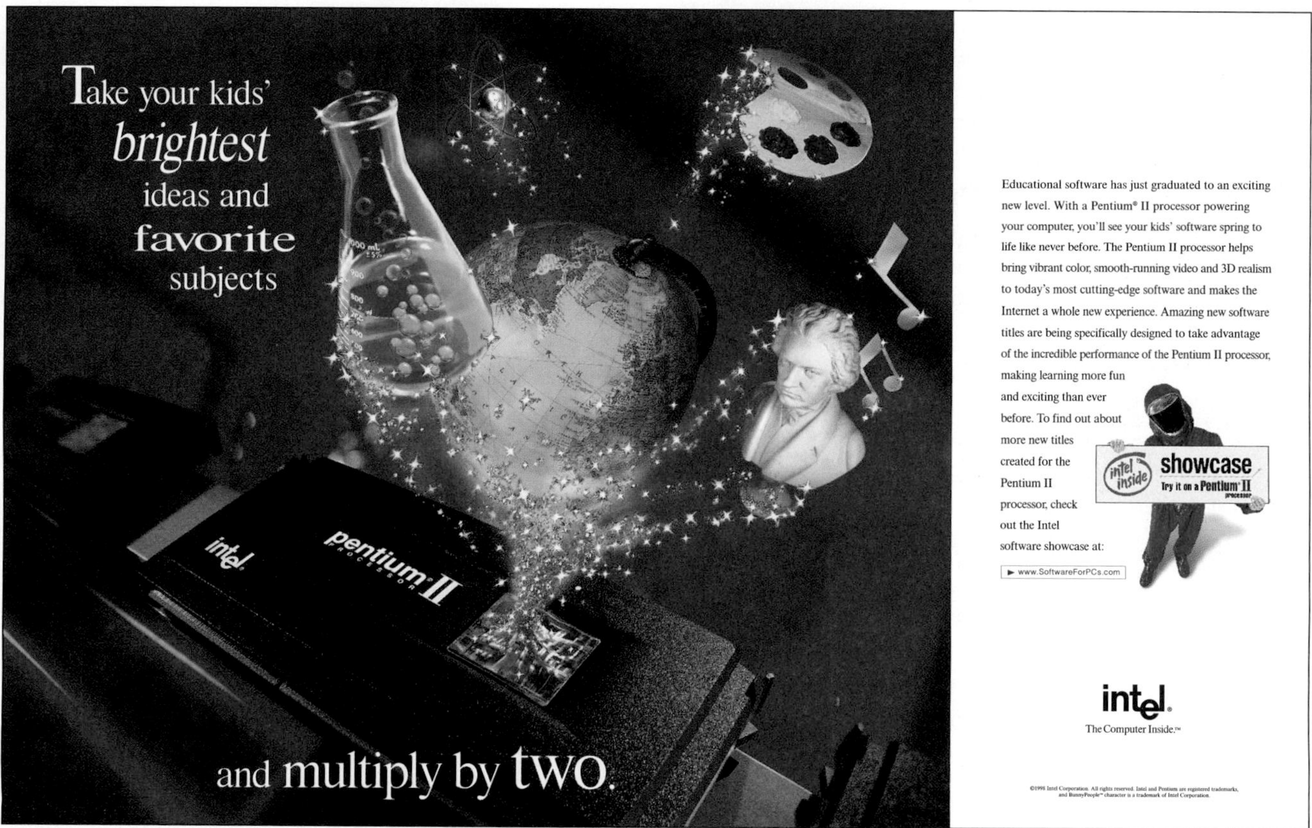

Supply partnerships are an important reason for Intel's success in the computer industry.

Intel Corporation
www.intel.com

Online Buying in Organizational Markets

A final distinction between organizational and consumer buyer behaviour resides in the use of Internet/World Wide Web technology in the purchase process. Although lacking the visibility of consumer online shopping, business-to-business electronic commerce is huge. In fact, organizational buyers account for 80 percent of the total dollar value of all online transactions. It is expected that North American and European organizational buyers alone will purchase about $560 billion worth of products and services online by 2002.[20]

The popularity of online buying will grow in the 21st century for two reasons. First, organizational buyers depend heavily on timely supplier information that describes product availability, technical specifications, application uses, price, and delivery schedules. This information can be conveyed quickly via Internet/World Wide Web technology. Second, business marketers have found that this technology can reduce marketing costs, particularly sales and advertising expense, for many types of products and services. For these reasons, online buying is prominent in all three kinds of organizational markets.[21]

An ambitious online buying initiative is the Trading Process Network (TPN) operated by General Electric (GE) Information Services. TPN is a service that enables GE buyers to post requests for quotes, negotiate, and place orders with global suppliers. GE expects to buy more than $7 billion in products and services in 2000 and estimates that the cost of purchasing and supplies has declined by 20 percent because of TPN. GE's success prompted a number of other large firms—such as Hewlett-Packard, 3M, Consolidated Edison, and Textron Automotive—and some 1400 small and medium-sized manufacturers to join TPN for the purpose of improving and expanding online buying with their suppliers and customers.[22] Visit the TPN Web site shown in the accompanying Web Link to appreciate the process and benefits of online buying and selling in organizational markets. Chapter 8 expands on the role of electronic commerce in marketing and its importance for business and consumer marketers.

The Buying Centre: A Cross-Functional Group

For routine purchases with a small dollar value, a single buyer or purchasing manager often makes the purchase decision alone. In many instances, however, several people in the organization participate in the buying process. The individuals in this group, called a **buying centre,** share common goals, risks, and knowledge important to a purchase decision. For most large multistore chain resellers, such as Sears, 7-Eleven convenience stores, Kmart, or Safeway, the buying centre is highly formalized and is called a *buying committee.* However, most industrial firms or government units use informal groups of people or call meetings to arrive at buying decisions.

The importance of the buying centre requires that a firm marketing to many industrial firms and government units understand the structure, technical and business functions represented, and behaviour of these groups. One researcher has suggested four questions to provide guidance in understanding the buying centre in these organizations:[23] Which individuals are in the buying centre for the product or service? What is the relative influence of each member of the group? What are the buying criteria of each member? How does each member of the group perceive our firm, our products and services, and our salespeople?

WEB LINK

The GE Trading Process Network Demonstrates the Process and Benefits of Online Buying and Selling in Organizational Markets

You only have to visit the General Electric Information Services Trading Process Network Web site (www.tpn.geis.com) to appreciate how online buying and selling for organizations actually works. General Electric Information Services has created a virtual marketplace where buyers and sellers can exchange information, products, and services effectively and efficiently.

To learn about the process and benefits of online buying and selling, go to the GE TPN™ Web site and click Getting Started. You will see the buying and selling process and benefits prominently listed. How does the buying process compare with the description in your text? What are the benefits of online buying?

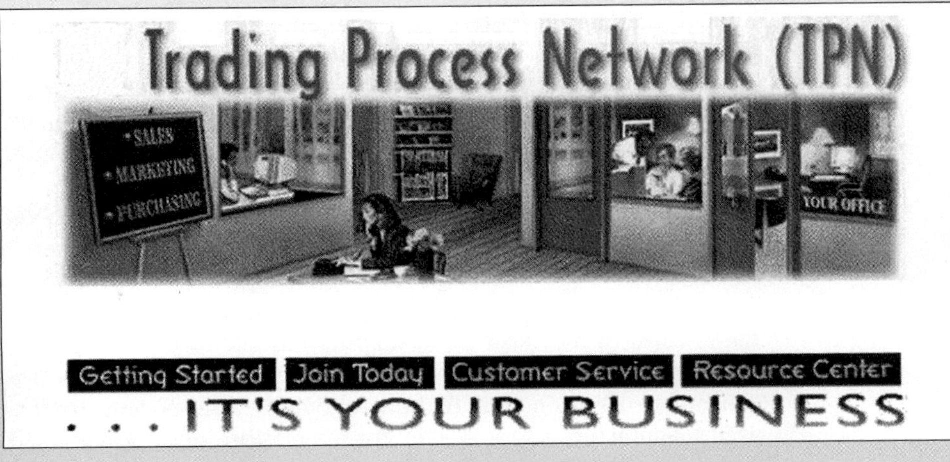

Answers to these questions are difficult to come by, particularly when dealing with industrial firms, resellers, and governments outside Canada.[24] For example, Canadian firms are often frustrated by the fact that Japanese buyers "ask a thousand questions" but give few answers, sometimes rely on third-party individuals to convey views on proposals, are prone to not "talk business," and often say yes to be courteous when they mean no. Firms in the global chemical industry recognize that production engineering personnel have a great deal of influence in Hungarian buying groups, while purchasing agents in the Canadian chemical industry have relatively more influence in buying decisions.

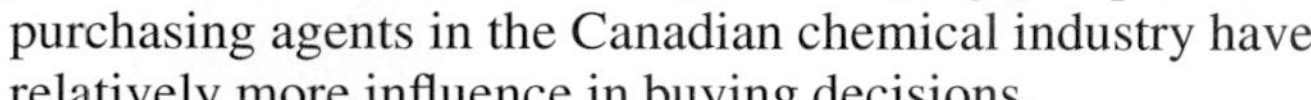

People in the Buying Centre The composition of the buying centre in a given organization depends on the specific item being bought. Although a buyer or purchasing manager is almost always a member of the buying centre, individuals from other functional areas are included, depending on what is to be purchased. In buying a million-dollar machine tool, the president (because of the size of the purchase) and the production vice president or manager would probably be members. For key components to be incorporated in a final manufactured product, a cross-functional group of individuals from research and development (R&D), engineering, and quality control are likely to be added. For new word-processing equipment, experienced secretaries who will use the equipment would be members. Still, a major question in penetrating the buying centre is finding and reaching the people who will initiate, influence, and actually make the buying decision.[25]

Roles in the Buying Centre Researchers have identified five specific roles that an individual in a buying centre can play.[26] In some purchases the same person may perform two or more of these roles.

- *Users* are the people in the organization who actually use the product or service, such as a secretary who will use a new word processor.
- *Influencers* affect the buying decision, usually by helping define the specifications for what is bought. The information systems manager would be a key influencer in the purchase of a new mainframe computer.
- *Buyers* have formal authority and responsibility to select the supplier and negotiate the terms of the contract. The purchasing manager probably would perform this role in the purchase of a mainframe computer.
- *Deciders* have the formal or informal power to select or approve the supplier that receives the contract. Whereas in routine orders the decider is usually the buyer or purchasing manager, in important technical purchases it is more likely to be someone from R&D, engineering, or quality control. The decider for a key component being incorporated in a final manufactured product might be any of these three people.
- *Gatekeepers* control the flow of information in the buying centre. Purchasing personnel, technical experts, and secretaries can all keep salespeople or information from reaching people performing the other four roles.

Stages in an Organizational Buying Decision

As shown in Figure 7–3 (and covered in Chapter 6), the five stages a student might use in buying a portable compact disc (CD) player also apply to organizational purchases. However, comparing the two right-hand columns in Figure 7–3 reveals some key differences. For example, when a portable CD player manufacturer buys headphones for

STAGE IN THE BUYING DECISION PROCESS	CONSUMER PURCHASE: PORTABLE CD PLAYER FOR A STUDENT	ORGANIZATIONAL PURCHASE: HEADPHONES FOR A CD PLAYER
Problem recognition	Student doesn't like the sound of the stereo system now owned and desires a portable CD player.	Marketing research and sales departments observe that competitors are including headphones on their models. The firm decides to include headphones on their own new models, which will be purchased from an outside supplier.
Information search	Student uses past experience, that of friends, ads, and *Consumer Reports* to collect information and uncover alternatives.	Design and production engineers draft specifications for headphones. The purchasing department identifies suppliers of CD player headphones.
Alternative evaluation	Alternative portable CD players are evaluated on the basis of important attributes desired in a CD player and several stores are visited.	Purchasing and engineering personnel visit with suppliers and assess (1) facilities, (2) capacity, (3) quality control, and (4) financial status. They drop any suppliers not satisfactory on these factors.
Purchase decision	A specific brand of portable CD player is selected, the price is paid, and the student leaves the store.	They use (1) quality, (2) price, (3) delivery, and (4) technical capability as key buying criteria to select a supplier. Then they negotiate terms and award a contract.
Postpurchase behaviour	Student reevaluates the purchase decision, may return the portable CD player to the store if it is unsatisfactory, and looks for supportive information to justify the purchase.	They evaluate suppliers using a formal vendor rating system and notify supplier if phones do not meet its quality standard. If problem is not corrected, they drop the firm as a future supplier.

FIGURE 7–3
Comparing the stages in consumer and organizational purchases

its units from a supplier, more individuals are involved, supplier capability becomes more important, and the postpurchase evaluation behaviour is more formalized. The headphone-buying decision illustrated is typical of the steps in a purchase made by an organization.[27] Later in the chapter we will analyze more complex purchases made by an industrial organization.

Types of Buying Situations

The number of people in the buying centre and the length and complexity of the steps in the buying process largely depend on the specific buying situation. Researchers who have studied organizational buying identify three types of buying situations, which they have termed **buy classes.**[28] These buy classes vary from the routine reorder, or **straight rebuy,** to the completely new purchase, termed **new buy.** In between these extremes is the **modified rebuy.** Some examples will clarify the differences:

- *Straight rebuy.* Here the buyer or purchasing manager reorders an existing product or service from the list of acceptable suppliers, probably without even checking with users or influencers from the engineering, production, or quality control departments. Office supplies and maintenance services are usually obtained as straight rebuys. Online buying is often used for straight rebuys.
- *Modified rebuy.* In this buying situation the users, influencers, or deciders in the buying centre want to change the product specifications, price, delivery schedule, or supplier. Although the item purchased is largely the same as with the straight rebuy, the changes usually necessitate enlarging the buying centre to include people outside the purchasing department.

	BUY-CLASS SITUATION	
BUYING CENTRE DIMENSION	**NEW BUY**	**STRAIGHT/MODIFIED REBUY**
People involved	Many	Few
Decision time	Long	Short
Problem definition	Uncertain	Well defined
Buying objective	Good solution	Low-price supplier
Suppliers considered	New/present	Present
Buying influence	Technical/operating personnel	Purchasing agent

FIGURE 7–4
How the buying situation affects buying centre behaviour

- *New buy.* Here the organization is a first-time buyer of the product or service. This involves greater potential risks in the purchase, so the buying centre is enlarged to include all those who have a stake in the new buy. The purchase of laser technology and products from Honeywell, MICRO SWITCH Division, represents a new buy for many companies.

Figure 7–4 summarizes how buy classes affect buying centre tendencies in different ways.[29]

The marketing strategies of sellers facing each of these three buying situations can vary greatly because the importance of personnel from functional areas such as purchasing, engineering, production, and R&D often varies with (1) the type of buying situation and (2) the stage of the purchasing process.[30] If it is a new buy for the manufacturer, you should be prepared to act as a consultant to the buyer, work with technical personnel, and expect a long time for a buying decision to be reached. However, if the manufacturer has bought the component part from you before (a straight or modified rebuy), you might emphasize a competitive price and a reliable supply in meetings with the purchasing agent.

CONCEPT CHECK

1. What one department is almost always represented by a person in the buying centre?
2. What are the three types of buying situations or buy classes?

AN ORGANIZATIONAL NEW BUY DECISION

New buy purchase decisions are ones where the most purchasing expertise is needed and where both the benefits of good decisions and penalties of bad ones are likely to be greatest. This means that effective communication among people in the buying centre is especially important. Tracing the stages in the buying decisions made by a manufacturer highlights some of the important aspects of organizational buying. It also illustrates the challenges involved in marketing to organizations.

An Industrial Purchase: Machine Vision Systems

Machine vision is becoming widely regarded as one of the keys to the factory of the future. The chief elements of a machine vision system are its optics, light source, camera, video processor, and computer software. Vision systems are mainly used for product inspection. They are also becoming important as one of the chief elements in the information feedback loop of systems that control manufacturing processes. Vision systems, selling in the price range of $5000, are mostly sold to original equipment manufacturers (OEMs) who incorporate them in still larger industrial automation systems, which sell for $50 000 to $100 000.

Finding productive applications for machine vision involves the constant search for technology and designs that satisfy user needs. The buying process for machine vision components and assemblies is frequently a new buy because many machine vision systems contain elements that require some custom design. Let's track five purchasing stages that a company such as the Industrial Automation Division of Siemens, a large German industrial firm, would follow when purchasing components and assemblies for the machine vision systems it produces and installs.

Problem Recognition Sales engineers constantly canvass industrial automation equipment users and manufacturers such as Ford Motor Company, Grumman Aircraft, and many Asian and European firms for leads on upcoming industrial automation projects. They also keep these firms current on Siemens' technology, products, and services. When a firm needing a machine vision capability identifies a project that would benefit from Siemens' expertise, company engineers typically work with the firm to determine the kind of system required to meet the customer's need.

After a contract is won, project personnel must often make a **make-buy decision**—an evaluation of whether components and assemblies will be purchased from outside suppliers or built by the company itself. (Siemens' produces many components and assemblies.) When these items are to be purchased from outside suppliers, the company engages in a thorough supplier search and evaluation process.

www.siemens.com

Information Search Companies such as Siemens employ a sophisticated process for identifying outside suppliers of components and assemblies. For standard items such as connectors, printed circuit boards, and components such as resistors and capacitors, the purchasing agent consults the company's purchasing databank, which contains information on hundreds of suppliers and thousands of products. All products in the databank have been prenegotiated as to price, quality, and delivery time, and many have been assessed using **value analysis**—a systematic appraisal of the design, quality, and performance of a product to reduce purchasing costs.

For one-of-a-kind components or assemblies such as new optics, cameras, and light sources, the company relies on its engineers to keep current on new developments in product technology. This information is often found in technical journals and industry magazines or at international trade shows where suppliers display their most recent innovations. In some instances, supplier representatives might be asked to make presentations to the buying centre at Siemens. Such a group often consists of a project engineer; several design, system, and manufacturing engineers; and a purchasing agent.

Alternative Evaluation Three main buying criteria are used to select suppliers: price, performance, and delivery. Other important criteria include assurance that a supplier will not go out of business during the contractual period, assurance that the supplier will meet product quality and performance specifications, and service during the contractual period. Typically, two or three suppliers for each standard component and assembly are identified from a **bidders list**—a list of firms believed to be qualified to supply a given item. This list is generated from the company's purchasing databank as well as from engineering inputs. Specific items that are unique or one-of-a-kind may be obtained from a single supplier after careful evaluation by the buying centre.

Firms selected from the bidders list are sent a quotation request from the purchasing agent, describing the desired quantity, delivery date(s), and specifications of the components or assemblies. Suppliers are expected to respond to bid requests within 30 days.

The purchase of machine vision systems involves a lengthy organizational buying process.

Purchase Decision Unlike the short purchase stage in a consumer purchase, the period from supplier selection to order placement to product delivery can take several weeks or even months. Even after bids for components and assemblies are submitted, further negotiation concerning price, performance, and delivery terms is likely. Sometimes conditions related to warranties, indemnities, and payment schedules must be agreed on.

The purchase decision is further complicated by the fact that two or more suppliers of the same item might be awarded contracts. This practice can occur when large orders are requested. Furthermore, suppliers who are not chosen are informed why their bids were not selected.

Postpurchase Behaviour As in the consumer purchase decision process, postpurchase evaluation occurs in the industrial purchase decision process, but it is formalized and often more sophisticated. All items purchased are examined in a formal product acceptance process. The performance of the supplier is also monitored and recorded. Performance on past contracts determines a supplier's chances of being asked to bid on future purchases, and poor performance may result in a supplier's name being dropped from the bidders list.

The preceding example of an organizational purchase suggests four lessons for marketers to increase their chances of selling products and services to organizations. Firms selling to organizations must (1) understand the organization's needs, (2) be included on the bidders list, (3) find the right people in the buying centre, and (4) provide value to the organizational buyer.

CONCEPT CHECK

1. What is a make-buy decision?
2. What is a bidders list?

SUMMARY

1 Organizational buyers are divided into three different markets: industrial, reseller, and government.

2 Measuring industrial, reseller, and government markets is an important first step for firms interested in gauging the size of one, two, or all three markets. The North American Industry Classification System (NAICS) is a convenient starting point to begin this process.

3 Many aspects of organizational buying behaviour are different from consumer buying behaviour. Some key differences between the two include demand characteristics, size of the order or purchase, number of potential buyers, buying objectives, buying criteria, buyer-seller relationships and partnerships, online buying, and multiple buying influences within companies.

4 The buying centre concept is central to understanding organizational buying behaviour. Knowing who composes the buying centre and the roles they play in making purchase decisions is important in marketing to organizations. The buying centre usually includes a person from the purchasing department and possibly representatives from R&D, engineering, and production, depending on what is being purchased. These people can play one or more of five roles in a purchase decision: user, influencer, buyer, decider, or gatekeeper.

5 The three types of buying situations, or buy classes, are the straight rebuy, the modified rebuy, and the new buy. These form a scale ranging from a routine reorder to a totally new purchase.

6 The stages in an organizational buying decision are the same as those for consumer buying decisions: problem recognition, information search, alternative evaluation, purchase decision, and postpurchase behaviour. An example of an organizational purchase described is the purchase of machine vision technology components by an electronics manufacturer.

7 To market more effectively to organizations, a firm must try to understand the organization's needs, get on the right bidders list, reach the right people in the buying centre, and provide value to organizational buyers.

KEY TERMS AND CONCEPTS

business marketing p. 174
organizational buyers p. 174
industrial firms p. 174
resellers p. 174
government units p. 175
North American Industry Classification System (NAICS) p. 176
organizational buying behaviour p. 177
derived demand p. 177
organizational buying criteria p. 180
reverse marketing p. 181
reciprocity p. 182
supply partnership p. 182
buying centre p. 184
buy classes p. 186
straight rebuy p. 186
new buy p. 186
modified rebuy p. 186
make-buy decision p. 188
value analysis p. 188
bidders list p. 188

INTERNET EXERCISE

The North American Industry Classification System (NAICS) structures 24 industrial sectors into their component industries. The NAICS can be accessed at www.statcan.ca/naics. A person only has to click NAICS codes to obtain industry breakdowns.

You have been hired by a large industrial firm as a market analyst. Your first assignment is to identify the kinds of companies and services that fall into the Arts, Entertainment, and Recreation industry sector (code 71) and make a presentation to senior management. Your immediate supervisor advises you that senior management would be interested in the following information:

1 How many three-, four-, five-, and six-digit industries exist in the Arts, Entertainment, and Recreation industry sector?

2 How is the performing arts, spectator sports, and related industries subsector (code 711) structured? That is, how would you display this subsector using the framework shown in Figure 7–1?

APPLYING MARKETING CONCEPTS AND PERSPECTIVES

1 Describe the major differences among industrial firms, resellers, and government units in Canada.
2 Explain how the North American Industry Classification System (NAICS) might be helpful in understanding industrial, reseller, and government markets, and discuss the limitations inherent in this system.
3 List and discuss the key characteristics of organizational buying that make it different from consumer buying.
4 What is a buying centre? Describe the roles assumed by people in a buying centre and what useful questions should be raised to guide any analysis of the structure and behaviour of a buying centre.
5 Effective marketing is of increasing importance in today's competitive environment. How can firms more effectively market to organizations?
6 A firm that is marketing multimillion-dollar wastewater treatment systems to cities has been unable to sell a new type of system. To date, the firm's marketing efforts have been directed to city purchasing departments to be included on approved bidders lists. Talks with city-employed personnel have indicated that the new system is very different from current systems and therefore city sanitary and sewer department engineers, directors of these two departments, and city council members are unfamiliar with the workings of the system. Consulting engineers, hired by cities to work on the engineering and design features of these systems and paid on a percentage of system cost, are also reluctant to favour the new system. (*a*) What roles do the various individuals play in the purchase process for a wastewater treatment system? (*b*) How could the firm improve the marketing effort behind the new system?

CASE 7–1 ENERGY PERFORMANCE SYSTEMS, INC.

"What we need," says David Ostlie matter-of-factly, "is just one electric utility to say 'yes'—to try our technology. Then the Whole-Tree Energy™ technology will speak for itself." David Ostlie is president of Energy Performance Systems, Inc. (EPS), a firm he founded in 1988 to produce environmentally clean, cheap electricity by growing, harvesting, transporting, drying, burning *whole* hardwood trees (trunks, branches, and all) in either (1) old retrofitted coal and oil (fossil fuel) power plants or (2) new power plants.

THE IDEA

Dave Ostlie points to three key features that make the EPS-owned and patented Whole-Tree Energy™ (WTE) technology unique:

1 Using *whole* hardwood trees. The use of whole trees saves a tremendous amount of time and energy over using wood chips—a common form for wood burned to produce electricity. "Hardwood trees" here means all broadleaf trees—mainly species such as cottonwood, aspen, birch, maple, and poplar (essentially all trees but conifers).
2 Drying the whole trees. Moisture is the culprit that leads to incomplete wood combustion and reduced energy output, resulting in emissions that lead to air pollution and acid rain. So the WTE process dries the trees to remove about 70 percent of the moisture prior to combustion, using waste heat from the combustion process itself.
3 Three-stage combustion. The whole trees burn at three levels in the furnace: (*a*) as trees in a three-metre-deep, mid-level pile, (*b*) as wood char that falls and is burned on a grate below the pile, and (*c*) as volatile gases (gasified wood) above the pile that burns cleanly like natural gas. The result is an incredibly *environmentally clean,* efficient combustion process.

The simplicity of the technology is a big plus compared to many of the current alternative energy technologies being studied around the world.

THE COMPANY

EPS is based on the Whole-Tree Energy™ technology and owns U.S., Canadian, European, and Japanese patents. The WTE™ technology has been scaled up in four successive tests that have demonstrated the feasibility of large-scale power production from sustained burning of whole trees. The mission of EPS: to commercialize the Whole-Tree Energy™ technology.

THE ISSUES

In assessing the Whole-Tree Energy™ technology, three critical issues soon emerge: (1) the environment and pollution, (2) jobs and economic development, and (3) buying interest of utilities.

The Environment and Pollution

Conventional coal-fired power plants, the staple for utilities, produce large volumes of SO_2, NO_x, ash, and extra CO_2 that contribute to air pollution, acid rain, and global warming. Based on test results, a WTE™ plant produces far less pollution than comparable fossil-fuel plants. Compared to a coal plant, the following levels of pollution have been demonstrated for a WTE™ plant:

- SO_2—less than $^1/_{400}$ of that for coal (on a fuel comparison basis) because wood contains virtually no sulphur.
- NOx—approximately $^1/_{10}$ of that for coal due to the naturally low nitrogen content of wood fuel and the multi-stage WTE™ combustion process.
- Ash—less than $^1/_{10}$ of that for coal. The ash produced can be returned to the forest or sold as a fertilizer. Coal ash is considered a hazardous waste and must be stored indefinitely in specially designed storage ponds.
- Extra CO_2—Coal plants release enormous amounts of CO_2 to the atmosphere by burning the remnants of prehistoric plant life—coal—in large quantities. The rapidly increasing level of atmospheric CO_2 due to the burning of fossil fuels is a significant cause of global climate change. In contrast, using biomass—including trees—as a fuel results in no net addition of CO_2 to the atmosphere because the amount of CO_2 removed over the life of the tree is equal to that released by the tree, regardless of the tree's end use.

The net effect of burning a renewable biomass—trees—instead of fossil fuels will be a reduction in air pollution, acid rain, and global warming.

Jobs and Economic Development

WTE™ plants will burn (1) hardwoods that are unsalable (not wanted by other forest product firms), (2) fast-growing energy trees raised on plantations that can be harvested as often as every five to six years and add agricultural jobs, and (3) waste wood left over by other forest product firms. Harvesting overage hardwoods actually stimulates forest regeneration and often provides better habitat for wildlife. Reports indicate that there is plenty of hardwood overage, not wanted by the logging, paper, and pulp industries and should be harvested.

A 100 megawatt WTE™ plant—providing enough electricity for a city of 100 000 people—will provide over 600 jobs in growing, harvesting, and transporting whole trees and in the plant producing electricity. In the search for local jobs, this is a huge benefit for economic development organizations trying to increase local employment.

Buying Interest of Utilities

To avoid more electrical blackouts, utilities must add new electrical generating capacity. For EPS, this provides an opportunity, either (1) by retrofitting to use in WTE™ some coal and oil-fired plants that are operated infrequently because of their pollution problems or (2) by building new plants to use the WTE™ technology.

In an electric utility, capacity planners project the demand for electricity by industrial, commercial, and residential users and assess the utility's ability to supply the demand. The chief executive officer makes the recommendation to add new capacity, a decision reviewed by

Cost of producing electricity using four different fuels, cents/kilowatt-hour

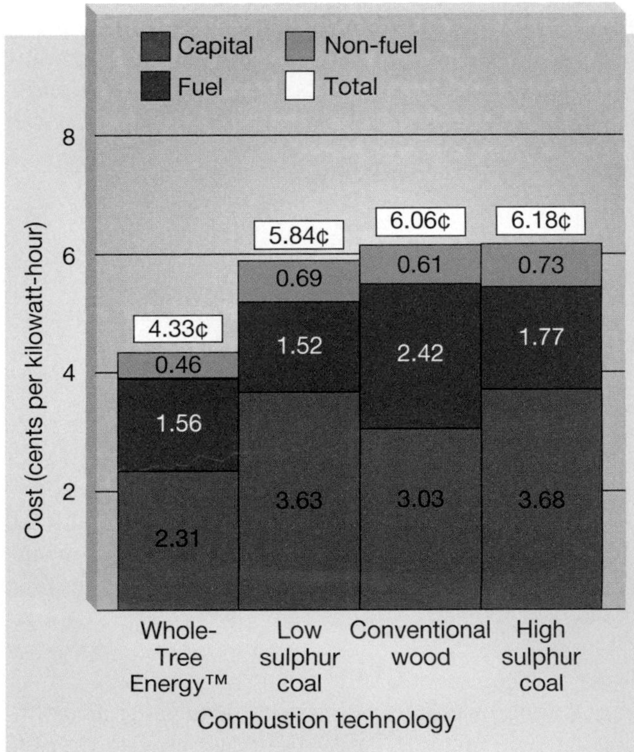

Source: Research Triangle Institute, Electric Power Research Institute and Energy Performance Systems, Inc.

the board of directors. The vice president of power supply probably recommends the technology to be used and the site for the new power plant.

As Ostlie talks to prospective utility customers about the WTE™ technology, six concerns emerge that are covered below.

1 Can enough heat be generated by burning wood to produce electricity? "All the skeptics said we couldn't get a high enough temperature by burning wood," says Ostlie. "But in one recent heat-release test we produced values higher than those of state-of-the-art coal plants."

2 Can whole trees be loaded, transported, and dried? Forestry experts told Ostlie he couldn't load and transport whole trees on a truck because the branches wouldn't compress. So he hired a logger and did it. The WTE™ technology calls for large-scale drying of whole trees in an air-supported dome like those used in a sports stadium.

3 Are there enough trees available at reasonable cost to support commercial-size power plants? To support such a power plant, only about 0.1 percent of the land in a 70-kilometre radius of the plant would be harvested each year. Residential biomass and waste wood from pulp and timber mill operations are potential fuel sources, as are natural stands. Ultimately, much of the tree resource may come from short-rotation, hybrid tree plantations that provide farmers with an alternative cash crop.

4 What are the environmental benefits of WTE™ for utilities? Besides being increasingly sensitive to environmental concerns, a utility retrofitting a polluting electric power plant with Whole-Tree Energy™ can gain over a million dollars a year in SO_2 credits"—an incentive for a utility to offset power produced by its high-pollution plants with electricity produced by non-polluting plants.

5 What will it cost to build a retrofitted or new WTE™ power plant? A major appeal of the WTE™ process is its simplicity relative to, say, coal-fired power plants. To retrofit an existing 100 megawatt coal plant, it will cost about $35 million—thereby putting back into production an existing plant that is of little value. To build a new 100-megawatt WTE™ plant would take about $100 million, about 25 to 30 percent less than a new fossil fuel plant.

6 What will the cost be of electricity produced by a WTE™ plant? A recent feasibility study evaluating the WTE™ technology estimated that a WTE™ power plant could produce a kilowatt-hour of electricity for 20 to 40 percent less than today's fossil fuel plants (see figure).

"It's not far away, but we've still got to make that first sale," adds Dave Ostlie.

Questions

1 In a utility's decision whether to buy and use the WTE™ technology (*a*) who comprises the buying centre and (*b*) what aspects of the buying decision does each look at?

2 What are some of the key elements EPS should have in developing its strategy to market WTE™ to prospective utility buyers?

3 As a concerned citizen, (*a*) what do you see as the key benefits of the WTE™ technology and (*b*) what do you personally see as the potential "show stoppers" for WTE™—the critical things that can prevent it from being commercialized and becoming a reality?

4 A new product or technology like WTE™ requires educating a number of key groups, or "influencers," about the technology. Excluding the electric utilities themselves, (*a*) what groups, or market segments, should EPS try to reach, (*b*) what key benefits should be emphasized to each, and (*c*) what promotional methods or media should EPS use to reach each segment?

PART II CASE BUYING BEHAVIOUR ONLINE: UNLIMITED SHOPPING ANYTIME

The Internet is changing buying behaviour. Both consumers and organizational buyers have access to a very different shopping experience and this is putting pressure on retailers to examine their store environments and consider the possibilities of online storefronts as an alternative to traditional shopping. Using technology to create online storefronts has provided consumers with an abundance of options when they are in the shopping mood. The Internet is changing business designs by substituting manual labour—allowing customers to compare, order, and customize their service options and, in theory, providing cost efficiencies. There is an opportunity, if tapped, for companies to improve the one-to-one relationship with their company base to add value to customer interactions.[1] Companies such as amazon.com and E-trade, in their respective industries have been putting pressure on companies within their industries and others to move ahead with e-commerce even though there are pitfalls as well as great windfalls for those using the technology effectively.

THE ONLINE CONSUMER

The explosion of Internet shopping opportunities is causing both businesses and consumers to change. Consumer buying behaviour has been studied within the context of traditional Main Street experiences. With the increase in online shopping, consumers have more choices and the balance of power in the buying relationship is changing.[2] International Data Corporation (IDC), a technology research firm, believes that online buyers will emerge as an important consumer group.[3] A research survey to compare online buyers and non-buyers was conducted that uncovered interesting information to better understand those choosing to buy online. Retailers will need to better understand this group of online users choosing in order to better serve them. Online buyers appear to differ from their non-buying counterparts in attitudes and behaviours rather than demographics. Gender is not an issue as an online buyer is as likely to be male as female. Online buyers are well educated and have a high income. They are more occupied by the Internet, price-sensitive, heavier users of news and information, and concerned about easy navigation. The table below demonstrates the high usage rates of the Internet by the online buyers when compared with non-buyers.

Canadian online shoppers spend more money at U.S. Web sites than at Canadian sites.[4] A study done by IBM Canada for the Retail Council of Canada discovered that Canadian online buyers spent 63 percent of their online money at U.S. sites.

ONLINE ACTIVITIES

	ONLINE BUYERS	ONLINE NON-BUYERS
Read news	78%	59%
Read about other non-news information, such as cultural activities and community events	71%	53%
Browse Web sites to gather information on products or services you might buy	70%	60%
Gather information on recreation or vacation ideas	69%	64%
Look up the weather	63%	47%
Make investments, adjust personal finance plans, conduct home banking	54%	44%
Gather information on business or investment opportunities, personal finance	32%	27%
Make reservations for recreations or vacation plans	27%	25%

Source: International Data Corporation, 1998

[1]Richard Christner, "The Internet Growth Path," *Telephony*, (April 12, 1999), p. 46.
[2]James Lucas, "The Critical Shopping Experience," *Marketing Management*, (Spring 1999), p. 60-62.
[3]Barry Parr, "Online Nation: The Buyers," Proprietary Research Study, *International Data Corporation*, 1999.
[4]Marina Strauss, "U.S. Web sites Click with Canadian Shoppers," *Globe and Mail*, (Tuesday, June 15, 1999), p. B1/B13.

The value of the Canadian Internet spending for 1998 was estimated at $688 million, a 56 percent increase from 1997.

BUILDING A NEW SHOPPING EXPERIENCE

One of the top Web sites for online shopping is amazon.com.[5] The hype generated by amazon.com has provided the impetus for other retailers, both traditional and online, to look closely at the benefits of investing in e-commerce. Even with the extraordinary growth of online expenditures, security and privacy remain important issues for online buyers. These sophisticated buyers want to know that their personal information is kept confidential and that their transactions are secure.[6] Amazon.com has been successful in providing a level of security as well as convenience to overcome the fears of a particular group of online users and claim the status of becoming a major threat to traditional book, music, and video retailers.

Since its incorporation in 1994 and the opening of its online store front in July 1995, amazon.com has grown to be considered one of the Internet's number one retailers of books, music, and video.[7] The amazon.com site offers more than 4.7 million book, music CD, video, DVD, computer, and other titles. The 1-Click ordering, personalized shopping services, direct shipping worldwide, and easy-to-use search and browse features have satisfied a growing customer base to earn amazon.com the distinction of capturing 16 percent of Web users for visits to the site.

The founder and CEO of amazon.com, Jeff Bezos, identified the opportunity to create a cyberstore and did research to determine the most attractive product category. Mr. Bezos looked at 20 different product categories and he chose books, "primarily because there are more items in the book category than in any other category by far—more than three million in-print books worldwide."[8] Unlike shopping for clothing, shopping for books does not require trying on the clothes or feeling the fabric, making it more attractive for a less traditional shopping experience.

The attraction of the amazon.com site can be attributed to the design of the site combined with the effective use of technology to develop relationships with both its customer base as well as search engine providers. Customer service is important to online buyers and amazon.com has paid attention to important attributes to enhance the online shopping experience for its visitors. The content and design of the site combined with their customer service program makes amazon.com an online retail leader. The site contains personalized content, and ongoing changes and additions increase the return rate of online users.

MAKING ONLINE BUYING SAFE AND SECURE

Security has been addressed with the use of specialized software encrypting all of the customer's personal information, including credit-card number, name and address. This protects against improper use of this information as it travels over the Net. With security handled, amazon.com has focused on personalizing its products and services by greeting customers by name and providing instant recommendations, bestseller and chart-topper listings, personal notification services, and purchase pattern filtering. Once the virtual shopping cart has been filled and an order placed, customers receive a personalized message to confirm their order and when to expect delivery. Should an item be out of stock, the customer is notified and informed about future availability. The company then attempts to ship orders within 24 hours. The return policy is generous, allowing the customer to return merchandise within 30 days as long as the original packaging is intact. A CD, DVD or VHS tape, can only be returned if it is unopened.

The thoroughness of addressing security, content, and ease-of-use issues is part of an attempt to encourage repeat visits and ultimately purchases. For this reason, amazon.com considers customer service an important component in its e-commerce strategy. Customer service not only includes creating a hassle-free order-processing system but also extends to more traditional and familiar activities. There are a number of email addresses for shoppers to use to request information. In addition, customer service representatives can be reached 24 hours a day, 7 days a week in case a customer has an urgent question or prefers to order by phone instead of online.

Building brand awareness with the book-buying public has been a priority for amazon.com. The company has taken steps, as it continues to add services and product categories to its portfolio, to carefully construct a shopping experience that satisfies the needs of online shoppers. Another aspect of brand building has taken place with its Associates Program.[9] There are approximately 200,000 Web sites enrolled in the Associates Program, including Yahoo! Inc., America Online, Inc., Excite, Inc., Netscape Communications Corporation, Geocities, Microsoft Corporation, and AltaVista Company. The presence of amazon.com is broadened through the Associates Program, enabling associated Web sites to provide products and services on behalf of amazon.com. This association is part of the business-to-business aspect of e-commerce.

[5]Andy Riga, "The Web Now Sells Toys to Vegetables," *The Financial Post (National Post),* (December 10, 1998), p. C10.
[6]Marina Strauss, "U.S. Web sites Click with Canadian Shoppers," *Globe and Mail,* (Tuesday, June 15, 1999), p. B1/B13.
[7]Amazon.com, Form 10-K, (1998), p. 3.
[8]Anthony B. Perkins, "The Angler: Amazon.com has come a long way since going public," *The Red Herring,* (March, 1999), www.herring.com/mag/issue 64.

[9]Amazon.com, Form 10-K, (1998), p. 5.

BUSINESS-TO-BUSINESS ONLINE

In 1998, the Internet market for Canada was estimated at $5.3 billion with the majority of that revenue generated from business-to-business interactions. In fact, business-to-business online spending climbed 192 percent to $4.6 billion, making up 86 percent of online sales.[10] The growth of consumer spending at a range of online retail sites is amazing but will be dwarfed by the growth of business-to-business activity on the Net in the future. Companies are finding innovative uses for Web-based applications in managing business-to-business relationships and costs. E-commerce is having an impact on the way in which manufacturers, distributors, and resellers conduct business with each other. In a study on distribution done by Evans Research Corporation, the greatest changes that are occurring are in the area of online support.[11] There is a great deal of activity in building online catalogues, making it possible for resellers to order from their Web sites. Other applications include customer databases and online technical support. This provides an alternative for adding value to the customer on a 24-hour basis. It is less expensive to order from the Net than to have a salesperson take it. Ordering online is possible for existing customers who enter the password-protected environment when it is convenient to them. The password is used to identify the user and links to that particular user's purchase rates, providing a level of customization that is important to the supplier.

The Internet also has far-reaching effects on distribution. Using a secure Web site, companies can link to customers and suppliers, shortening the whole supply chain and removing costs. The business relationship will change dramatically, taking administrative tasks away from salespeople and purchasing managers so that business problems can be tackled more effectively.[12]

As amazon.com is using technology to form strategic alliances with associated Web sites, Ford Motor Co. plans to use the Internet to boldly enter the market for used car parts.[13] Ford is the first of the big three U.S. automakers to take advantage of the power of the Internet to provide a channel to sell used parts from junkyards to body shops, insurance companies, and retailers. This recycling project is estimated to generate US $1 billion new revenue for Ford. Ford will use the Internet and act as a broker to bring together buyers and sellers of used parts, creating an opportunity to cost-effectively recycle plastics and metals and save on making new parts. "I see this as Ford looking at an opportunity and realizing the Internet is a wonderful tool to put customers together with the products they're looking for," explains Chris Denove, an analyst at J.D. Power and Associates.[14] Ford is also exploring the possibility of moving its worldwide vehicle design program to a virtual private network and using the Net for procurement purposes.

A number of studies have been completed to determine the level of participation in web-based business-to-business interactions. A study done by Penton Research Services discovered that half of organizational purchasing decision-makers were using the Internet in the job and 86 per cent expected to be using the Web in the job over the next five years.[15]

When reading the business press and browsing the Web, it appears that e-commerce is a North American phenomenon. However, it is a global phenomenon. The use of electronic purchasing is spreading worldwide. Globally, the Organization of Economic Cooperation and Development (OECD) estimates global e-commerce activity at US $26 billion and believes that the volume will rise to US $1 trillion between 2003 and 2005. Another study, the 1998 Survey of Chief Information Executives, included six major industries in 25 countries and concludes that there could be a 300 per cent growth in e-commerce over the next two years.

ONLINE SELLERS BEWARE

With the promise of increased use of cyberstores and online purchasing systems, there is however also an increased risk of fraud, which companies must consider before entering this communication channel. An estimate of as much as five to six percent of the average Internet retailer's transactions involve consumer fraud.[16] Malls and stores have an advantage over their online counterparts because with person-to-person transactions that do not include cash, a signature and identification is required. However, tracking the identity of Net shoppers is almost impossible if they do not provide truthful personal information. An email address does not help to reveal the identity of a customer or whether the credit card they are using is their own. With the risk of credit card fraud higher for e-commerce transactions, companies must be cautious and evaluate their purchase processes to minimize the risk of getting caught by consumer fraud.

The opportunity to generate revenue through the Internet has changed the way in which consumers shop. The number of transactions over the Internet will continue to grow, as will the purchasing of goods and services by both consumers and organizations. The main benefit of shopping on the Net is the

[10]Marina Strauss, "U.S. Web sites Click with Canadian Shoppers," *The Globe and Mail,* (Tuesday, June 15, 1999), p. B13.

[11]Deborah Rowe, "The e-commerce relationship," *Computer Dealer News,* (April 16, 1999), p. 23-24.

[12]Anonymous, "Internet to play bigger role in distribution," *Purchasing,* (April 22, 1999), p. 47-50.

[13]Bob Wallace, "Ford Will Use Net to Sell Used Parts," *ComputerWorld,* (May 3, 1999), p. 6.

[14]IBID.

[15]Wallys W. Conhaim, "The buisness-to-business marketplace," *Link-up,* (January/February, 1999), p. 5, 12.

[16]Cecile B. Corral, "Online security, payment services aid e-tailers stung by fraud," (April 19, 1999), p. 20-25.

24-hour, 7-day-a-week access that traditional shopping cannot provide. The acceptance of e-shopping will continue to shape consumer buying behaviour and business opportunities.

Discussion Questions

1 Discuss the principles of consumer buying behaviour and how they apply to the online shopper. Highlight any similarities as well as differences.

2 Based on what you know about consumers and what motivates them to make purchase choices, explain the high growth rates in online shopping.

3 Why do you think business-to-business online transactions are predicted to generate considerably greater revenue opportunities than the consumer online shopping revenues? What opportunities do you believe exist for online business-to-business.

4 In your opinion, do you believe that online shopping will replace traditional shopping? Why or why not? Support your answer with consumer behaviour theory.

PART THREE

3

TARGETING MARKETING OPPORTUNITIES

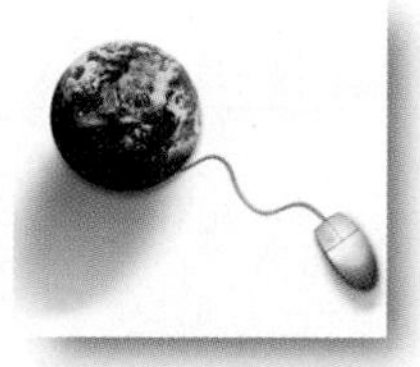

Part Three focuses on targeting marketing opportunities. Chapter 8 illuminates the revolutionary change in marketing opportunities made possible through electronic commerce. Developments in interactive marketing and electronic commerce have captured the eye and imagination of marketers because of the innovative ways value can be created for consumers in this new exchange environment. Chapter 9 describes how people with similar wants and needs become the target of marketing opportunities. This chapter details how information about prospective consumers is linked to marketing strategy and decisive actions and how information technology improves this process. Finally, Chapter 10 describes how Reebok International, New Balance, and Vans design shoes to satisfy different customers and covers the steps a firm uses in segmenting and targeting a market and then positioning its offering in the marketplace. The chapter also shows how the application of segmentation, targeting, and positioning were used by Apple Computer in the launch of its iMac line of personal computers.

MY SYMPATICO · SITE INDEX · COMMUNICATE · SHOPPING · S

Shopping

CLICK NOW REGISTER ON LINE

Shopping

IN THIS SECTION

- Stores + Services
- Advisories + FAQ's
- Forums
- Add Your Store

TOOLS + RESOURCES

- Buyer's Guide
- Compare Prices
- Credit Cards
- Currency Converter
- Present Picker
- Product Reviews
- Service Charges

CANADA TOLL FREE

- Appliances
- Computers
- Garden Tools
- Music

Or enter a keyword

SEARCH

"Buy books online in Canada. **Visit Indigo.ca**" AD

FEATURED

ONLINE VENDORS SERVING CANADIANS

Auction (7)
» CLICKABID
Automotive (4)
Books + Magazines (6)
» INDIGO
Business + Finance (11)
» E*TRADE CANADA
Children (4)
Computers + Electronics (5)
Department Store (3)
Entertainment (4)

Fashion + Beauty (15)
Food + Drink (7)
» HILLEBRAND ESTATES
Gifts + Flowers (5)
Hobbies + Sports (3)
» GARDEN CRAZY
» SPORTMART
Miscellaneous (3)
Travel (1)
» TRAVELOCITY

(#) = Indicates the number of vendors in the category

Suggestions or comments? EMail Us!

HOT D

Vista 35 price!

Look co Sympat gear!

Online busines Get list

EXPLORE SYMPATICO.CA -- CANADA'S HOME ON THE INTERNET

in sympatico shopping: Advisories + FAQ's - Forums - Add Your Store

CHAPTER EIGHT

INTERACTIVE MARKETING AND ELECTRONIC COMMERCE

8

AFTER READING THIS CHAPTER YOU SHOULD BE ABLE TO:

- Understand what electronic commerce and interactive marketing are and how they create customer value.
- Distinguish among the different types of electronic networks that make electronic commerce and interactive marketing possible.
- Identify online consumers and their purchasing behaviours.
- Recognize why certain types of products and services are particularly suited for electronic commerce.
- Explain how companies create a presence in the electronic marketspace through different kinds of Web sites and different forms of online advertising.
- Describe how companies benefit from electronic commerce and interactive marketing.

www.aol.ca

SYMPATICO™—"CANADA'S HOME ON THE INTERNET"

If you needed information for a term paper this week, would you really have to go to the library? If you needed to buy a new shirt for the pub crawl on the weekend, do you really have to go to the mall? A revolutionary change in technology has now made it possible for you to accomplish both of these tasks from the comfort and security of your home. Welcome to the world of electronic information and commerce. And there are plenty of companies out there that want to bring that world to you.

Sympatico™ (www.sympatico.ca) is one of Canada's largest online (Internet) service providers. Founded in partnership with the provincial telco companies (MTT, NBTel, Island Tel, NewTel, SaskTel, Bell, LINO, NorthwesTel, Northern Tel, MTS), Sympatico™ provides Canadians access to the global electronic community. A subscriber to the service can send and receive electronic mail (e-mail) to millions of Internet users with absolutely no long distance charges; gain access to the World Wide Web (www) and all the information that is located there including text, pictures, sound, and video (especially for that term paper); join discussion groups and newsgroups and stay informed about a variety of topics from cars to cancer, weaving to weather; and, of course, you can do a lot of electronic shopping including choosing that new shirt.

Sympatico™ is clearly the market leader, well ahead of other providers such as AOL Canada and Sprint. And Canadians are flocking to the electronic community, with close to 30 percent of Canadian households now accessing the Internet and World Wide Web. Businesses, of course, have responded to this trend toward electronic information and commerce, and for some, the electronic world of commerce is their future.[1]

The purpose of this chapter is to describe the nature and scope of electronic commerce, online consumer and purchasing behaviours, and interactive marketing practices.

THE NEW MARKETSPACE AND ELECTRONIC COMMERCE

Consumers and businesses populate two parallel and complementary markets today. One is the traditional marketplace, where buyers and sellers engage in exchange relationships in a material environment mostly inhabited by people, facilities (stores and offices), and physical objects. The other is the **marketspace,** an information- and communication-based electronic exchange environment mostly occupied by sophisticated computer and telecommunication technologies and digitized offerings. You enter the marketspace whenever you access the World Wide Web or log onto a commercial online service such as Sympatico. But the marketspace is broader than "the Web." It is electronic commerce in its many forms. **Electronic commerce** is "any activity that uses some form of electronic communication in the inventory, exchange, advertisement, distribution, and payment of goods and services."[2]

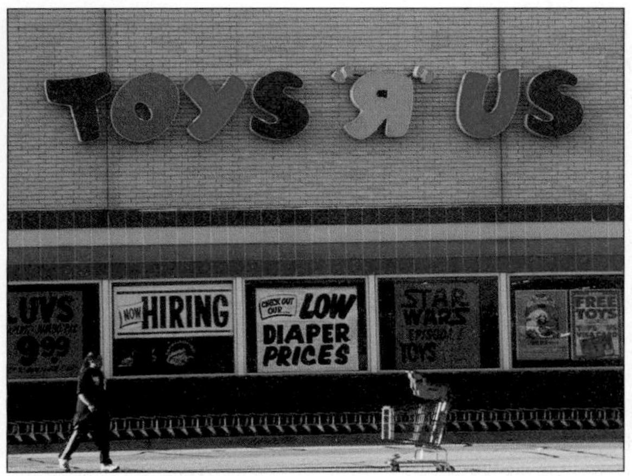

Toys "Я" Us has a significant presence in both the traditional marketplace and the new marketspace.

Toys "Я" Us
www.tru.com

Electronic commerce has existed for many years, and consumers benefit from it every day. Consider the familiar chore of grocery shopping. Each time a checkout clerk at the local supermarket scans your grocery items, precise data on what was purchased are electronically transmitted to the store's warehouse and to suppliers who replenish the store's stocks. Suppose you pay for your purchase with an ATM or debit card. You swipe the card through a transaction terminal, which reads the information on the card's magnetic strip. Enter your personal identification number (PIN), and the terminal routes the transaction through an ATM network back to your bank for authorization against your chequing account. Funds are then electronically transferred from your bank to the supermarket's bank. The transaction is completed in a few seconds. Now comes the hard part—preparing a meal!

Your grocery transaction, eased by electronic point-of-sale scanning and payment equipment and systems, was made possible by proprietary computer and telecommunication networks devised and managed solely for companies that owned and used them. These networks dominated electronic commerce until 1996—a year etched in ancient history. The World Wide Web burst upon the scene that year, and a new era of electronic commerce and interactive marketing was born.

Interactive marketing involves buyer–seller electronic communications in a computer-mediated environment in which the buyer controls the kind and amount of information received from the seller. Interactive marketing, made possible by the Internet, the World Wide Web, and commercial online services, has numerous applications and presents new opportunities for customer value creation.

The Nature and Scope of Electronic Commerce

Electronic commerce today consists of a family of electronic networks, each with a different application. These applications illustrate the varied nature and broad scope of electronic commerce and interactive marketing.

Business-to-Consumer Electronic Commerce The most widely visible application of electronic commerce exists in business-to-consumer interactive marketing, involving the Internet, the World Wide Web, and commercial online services. Many people view these three as being the same. They are not.[3]

The **Internet** is an integrated global network of computers that gives users access to information and documents. Anyone with a personal computer, a modem, and proper software can access the Internet free and can obtain and share information with others via e-mail, electronic messages transmitted to and from Internet host computers. More than 250 million people are projected to have access to the Internet in 2005. The Internet is a network upon which the system known as the World Wide Web runs.

The **World Wide Web (WWW)** is a part of the Internet that supports a retrieval system that formats information and documents into Web pages. The "Web" uses hypertext markup language (html) to format documents to be viewed by users with a browser program, such as Netscape's Navigator or Microsoft's Internet Explorer. A hypertext transfer protocol (http) is the means by which documents are actually delivered from a Web site to a user's computer. A Uniform Resource Locator (URL) identifies each site, a location in the marketspace akin to the traditional marketplace street address. The typical URL for a business might be http://www.yourcompany.com; for an organization, http://www.yourorganization.org; and a government agency, http://www.youragency.gc.ca. If you haven't already done so, visit the Web site for this book at http://www.mcgrawhill.ca.

www.prodigy.com

Systems that offer much of the popular appeal of the World Wide Web, but are not dependent on the Internet, are commercial online services. **Commercial online services** offer electronic information and marketing services to subscribers who are charged a monthly fee. As mentioned in the chapter opener, Sympatico is one of the largest and most popular commercial online services providers in the country, competing against other providers such as AOL Canada and Prodigy. Sympatico provides subscribers with news, entertainment, e-mail, Internet access, and online shopping opportunities. Its subscribers can order thousands of products and services from hundreds of companies. They can buy and sell investments through distant brokerage services; do their banking with a local bank; and make airline, hotel, and car rental reservations without leaving their home.

Business-to-consumer electronic commerce activity has skyrocketed since 1996, due in large part to the World Wide Web and commercial online services.[4] It is expected that at least one-half of all Canadian households will be buying something online in 2002.

Business Support Functions Many companies have adapted Internet-based technology internally to support their external electronic commerce initiatives. An **Intranet** is an Internet/Web-based network used within the boundaries of an organization. It is essentially a private Internet that may or may not be connected to the public Internet. Those that are connected are protected by "firewalls" from outside intrusion ("hacking") by millions of Internet users.

www.elililly.com

Intranets serve primarily as a business support function network and facilitate the internal, electronic exchange of corporate data and files. By 2001, an estimated 133 million companies in North America and Europe will have Intranets.[5] The pharmaceutical giant Eli Lilly & Co. operates an extensive Intranet known as ELVIS (Eli Lilly Virtual Information System). Employees can access internal job postings, corporate policies and handbooks, and a daily news summary on scientific and competitive developments in the global pharmaceutical industry. Marketing and sales information is also transmitted to field offices and employees in more than 120 countries instantaneously and electronically to better serve Eli Lilly customers.[6] The use of Intranets for selling and sales management is discussed further in Chapter 21.

Business-to-Business Electronic Commerce The largest application of electronic commerce exists in the realm of business-to-business interactive marketing. As described in Chapter 7, online buying between businesses accounts for a large percentage of the dollar value of all online transactions in North America.

Business-to-business electronic commerce comes in two forms. **Electronic data interchanges (EDI)** combine proprietary computer and telecommunication technologies to exchange electronic invoices, payments, and information between businesses, such as suppliers, manufacturers, and retailers. When linked with store scanning equipment and systems, EDI provides a seamless electronic link from a retail checkout counter to suppliers and manufacturers. Wal-Mart and Procter & Gamble pioneered the use of EDI in the 1980s. Today, EDI is commonly used in retail, apparel, transportation, pharmaceutical, grocery, health care, and insurance industries, as well as by local, provincial, and federal government agencies. Almost all of the companies listed in the Financial Post 500 use EDI, which is an indispensable electronic network for supply chain and logistics management as described in Chapter 17. At Hewlett-Packard, for example, one million EDI transactions are made every month.[7]

www.hewlett-packard.com

A second form of business-to-business electronic commerce is an Extranet, an extension of a company's Intranet. An **Extranet** is an Internet/Web-based network that permits private business-to-business communication between a company and its suppliers, distributors, and other partners (such as advertising agencies). Extranets are less expensive and more flexible to operate than EDI because of their connection with the public Internet. General Electric's Trading Process Network (TPN) highlighted in Chapter 7 is an example of an Extranet. Another is the Automotive Network Exchange (ANX), a collaborative effort among General Motors, Ford, and Daimler Chrysler, which is described later in Chapter 17. TPN and AMX represent virtual business communities populated by an array of companies sharing information and doing business with each other electronically in the new marketspace.

EDI and Extranets will account for the bulk of Canadian electronic commerce expenditures for goods and services into the 21st century.[8]

The fusion of Internet, Intranet, and Extranet Web-based technologies common in electronic commerce will create the "e-corporation or virtual organization" of the next decade. Apparel maker VF Corporation is already on its way toward becoming an e-corporation, as described in the accompanying Marketing NewsNet.[9]

Marketing.com: Electronic Commerce and Customer Value Creation

Despite the widespread attention given the new marketspace and electronic commerce, its economic significance is small compared with the traditional marketplace. Electronic commerce is expected to represent less than 10 percent of total Canadian consumer and industrial goods and services expenditures in 2001, and less than one percent of global expenditures. Why then has electronic commerce and interactive marketing captured the eye and imagination of marketers?

Marketers believe that the possibilities for customer value creation are greater in marketspace than the traditional marketplace.[10] Remember from Chapter 1 that marketing creates time, place, form, and possession utilities for customers, thereby providing value. In marketspace, the provision of direct, on-demand information is possible from marketers *anywhere* to customers *anywhere* at *any time*. Why? Geographical constraints and operating hours do not exist in marketspace. For example, Recreational Equipment (www.rei.com), an outdoor gear marketer, reports that 35 percent of its orders are placed between 10:00 P.M. and 7:00 A.M., long after and before retail stores are open for business. Twenty percent of amazon.com book sales are from buyers who live outside North America. Possession utility—getting a product or service to consumers so they can own or use it—is accelerated. Airline, car rental, and lodging electronic reservation systems such as Travelocity (www.travelocity.com) allow comparison shopping for the lowest fares, rents, and rates and almost immediate access to and confirmation of travel arrangements and accommodations.

TECHNOLOGY

MARKETING NEWSNET

The Twenty-First Century E-Corporation Is Virtually Here

Electronic commerce and e-corporations continue to evolve with new Internet, Intranet, and Extranet applications. Increasingly, companies are focusing on creating seamless streams of information between corporate functions (manufacturing, sales, marketing, finance, human resources); suppliers, partners, and distributors; and the ultimate customer. Computer software for the different forms of electronic commerce, called e-ware, that makes it easier for businesses to market products and services via the Web (Internet), to get the most out of customer and competitive data (Intranet), and to manage relationships with suppliers and customers (Extranet) represents the next evolutionary phase of electronic commerce and the e-corporation.

VF Corporation, the maker of Lee, Wrangler, Britannia, and Rustler jeans; Timber Creek khakis; Healthtex clothes for kids; Jantzen bathing suits; and JanSport backpacks, has taken the lead in stitching together an e-corporation with e-ware. The company has invested more than $70 million in computer software alone to link functions, people, and companies for the purpose of getting the right information, in the right form, to the right place, at the right time. According to a senior VF executive, "If we pull this off, no one else will be close" in integrating data across operations. Another executive replied, "Knock on wood."

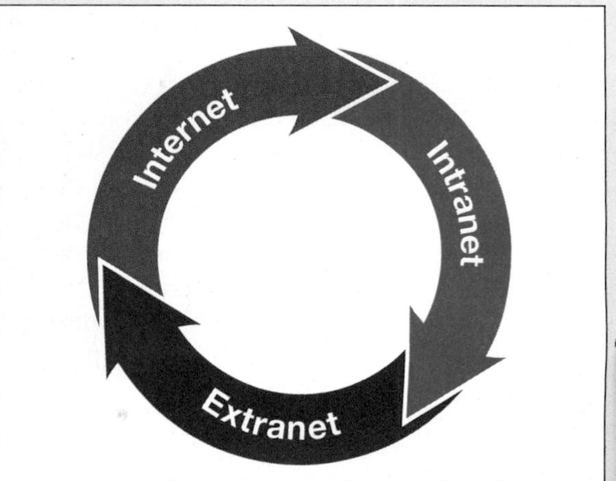

The greatest marketspace opportunity for marketers, however, lies in its potential for creating form utility. Interactive two-way Internet/Web-based communication capabilities in marketspace invite consumers to tell marketers exactly what their requirements are, making customization of a product or service to fit the buyer's exact needs possible. For instance, bluefly.com, an apparel company, encourages customers to develop their own catalogue free of unwanted items. Consumers can specify the brands, clothing category, and sizes right for their needs. Bluefly.com will instantaneously create a personalized catalogue just for them.

CONCEPT CHECK

1. What is electronic commerce?
2. How can electronic commerce create customer value?

ONLINE CONSUMERS AND BUYING BEHAVIOUR IN THE NEW MARKETSPACE

Who are online consumers, and what do they buy? Why do they choose to purchase products and services in the new marketspace rather than or in addition to the traditional marketplace? Answers to these questions are important to marketers today and offer clues to the future growth of electronic commerce and interactive marketing.

The Online Consumer

Many labels are given online consumers—cybershoppers, Netizens, and e-shoppers—suggesting they are a homogeneous segment of the population. They are not, but as a group, they do differ demographically from the general population.

Online Consumer Profile Online consumers differ from the general population in one important respect: they own or have access to a computer. About 30 percent of Canadian households have a computer in the home with Internet/Web access, although access is often possible at work and/or school. As a country, Canada ranks third in the world in terms of its percentage of population with access to the Internet/Web.[11]

As a group, online consumers tend to be better educated, younger, and more affluent than the general population, which makes them an attractive market.[12] The majority are married and male, although the number of online women consumers has increased rapidly. Currently, about 50 percent of adult Canadian women now have access to the Internet/Web. Income is clearly the driving factor with respect to Internet/Web use. Over 70 percent of Canadian households with income over $60 000 have access while only 30 percent of households with income under $20 000 have access. There is also some regionality involved in Intranet/Web use, with British Columbians having the highest usage and Quebecers having the lowest.

Research indicates that about 60 percent of Canadian Internet/Web users have sought product or service information online before making a purchase. For example, new car buyers will visit numerous Web sites before making a purchase design. But research also indicates that less than 20 percent of those using the Internet/Web have actually made a purchase online.

Online Consumer Psychographics Not all Internet/Web users use the technology the same way, nor are they all likely to be online buyers. SRI International, the same research firm that developed the Values and Lifestyles (VALS) Program described in Chapter 6, has identified 10 distinct Internet/Web user profiles, called iVALS segments, which illustrate how diverse Internet/Web users can be (Figure 8–1).[13]

Internet/Web users differ along two dimensions: (1) how heavily and enthusiastically they use the Internet and (2) the reason for usage.[14] Wizards are the most active and skilled Internet users and possess sophisticated technical skills. Mostly male and relatively young, Wizards are likely to be active online consumers, especially for products such as computers, software, and technical information. At the other extreme are Immigrants. They are skeptical of the Internet and do not use it willingly, often only if

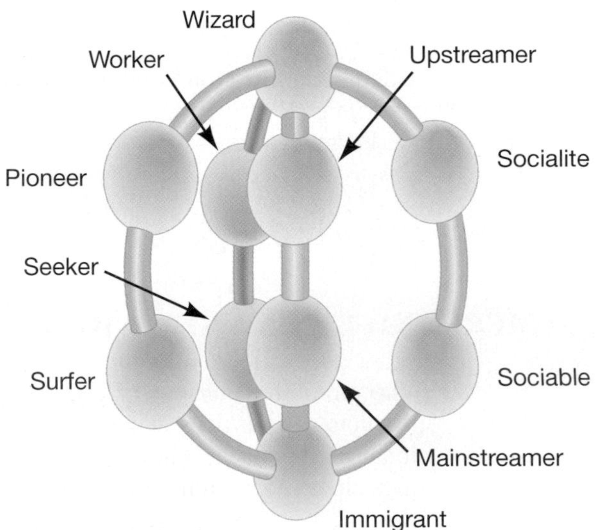

FIGURE 8–1
iVALS Internet user segments
Source: SRI Consulting.

forced to do so at school or at work. Immigrants have limited technical skills and are among the least promising online consumers.

The remaining eight segments fall between these extremes. Pioneers and Surfers are attracted to the Internet because of its recreational possibilities. They visit Web sites for the enjoyment of seeing what's there and, like recreational shoppers, are good prospects for online buying. Socialites and Sociables are among the youngest Internet users and value the social aspects of the Internet. They are heavy users of chat rooms and online communities where they can meet new people.

Workers and Seekers use the Internet mostly as a professional tool. Workers are mainly upscale, professional males who use the Internet as a source for research and industry information. Seekers are also professionally oriented and seek to improve their productivity through Internet use. University professors, students, and consultants populate these categories because of their information-intensive needs and visit Web sites that provide news, information summaries, and directories. Finally, Upstreamers and Mainstreamers are generalists. They use the Internet for a combination of personal and professional reasons. Like Workers and Seekers, they rely on the Internet to help them in their careers. And like Pioneers and Surfers, they enjoy browsing the Internet and use it for personal tasks such as online banking, investing, and shopping.

Do any of these iVALS consumer profiles fit you? Take a break and visit the SRI International Web site listed in the accompanying Web Link. Complete the short questionnaire, and find out which iVALS segment best describes your Internet/Web activity and usage.

Online Consumer Purchasing Behaviour

Much still needs to be learned about online consumer purchase behaviour in the new marketspace. While research has documented the most frequently purchased products and services bought online, marketers also need to know why these items are popular and why consumers prefer to shop and buy in the new marketspace.

What Online Consumers Buy Six general product and service categories appear to be particularly suited for electronic commerce.[15] One category consists of items for which product information is an important part of the purchase decision, but prepurchase trial is not necessarily critical. Items such as computers, computer accessories, and consumer electronics sold by dell.com and egghead.com fall into this category. So do books, which accounts for the sales growth of amazon.com and Barnes & Noble (www.barnesandnoble.com). Both booksellers publish short reviews of new books that visitors to their Web sites can read before making a purchase decision. According to an authority on electronic commerce, "You've read the reviews, you want it, you don't need to try it on."[16] A second category includes items for which audio or video demonstration is important. This category consists of CDs and videos sold by columbiahouse.com, cdnow.com, and towerrecords.com. The third category contains items that can be delivered digitally, including computer software, travel reservations and confirmations, brokerage services, and electronic ticketing. Popular Web sites for these items include travelocity.com, ticketmaster.com, and schwab.com.

Unique items, such as collectibles, specialty goods, and foods and gifts, represent a fourth category. Collectible auction houses (www.auctions-on-line.com and www.eworldauction.com), wine merchant Virtual Vineyards (www.virtualvin.com), and flower and gift marketer 1-800-Flowers (www.1800flowers.com) sell these products. A fifth category includes items that are regularly purchased and where convenience is very important. Many consumer-packaged goods, such as grocery products, fall into this category, which has benefited peapod.com and netgrocer.com, two online grocers. A final category of items consists of highly standardized products and services for which information about price is important. Certain kinds of insurance (auto and homeowners), home improvement products, casual apparel, and toys comprise this

WEB LINK What iVALS Type Are You?

Are you curious about how you stack up as an Internet user? If you are, complete the short iVALS questionnaire developed by SRI International at http://www.future.sri.com:80/vals/ivals/segs.html, and find out.

In addition to obtaining your profile, you can examine the characteristics of your and other profiles in greater detail.

category. These categories dominate online consumer shopping today and for the foreseeable future, as shown in Figure 8–2.[17]

Why Consumers Buy Online: The Six Cs Marketers emphasize the customer value creation possibilities in the new marketspace. However, consumers typically refer to six reasons why they prefer to buy online (also called the six Cs): convenience, cost, choice, customization, communication, and control (Figure 8–3).

Online buying is *convenient*. Consumers can visit Wal-Mart at www.wal-mart.com to scan and order from among 80 000 displayed products without fighting traffic, finding a parking space, walking through long aisles, and standing in store check-out lines. Alternatively, online consumers can use **bots,** electronic shopping agents or robots that comb Web sites, to compare prices and product or service features. In either instance, an online consumer has never ventured from his or her PC monitor. Consumer *cost* is a second reason for buying online. Recent research indicates that almost 90 percent of the 30 most popular items bought online can be purchased at the same price or cheaper than in retail stores.[18] A consumer's cost of external search, including time

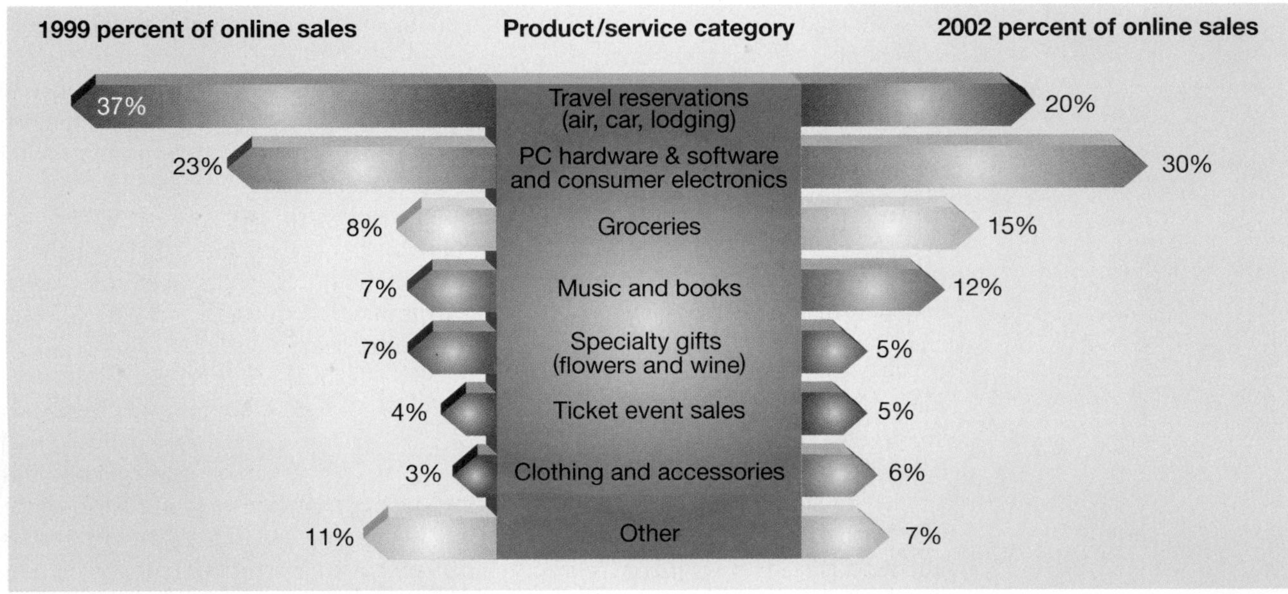

FIGURE 8–2
Online consumer sales by product/service category: 1999 and 2002

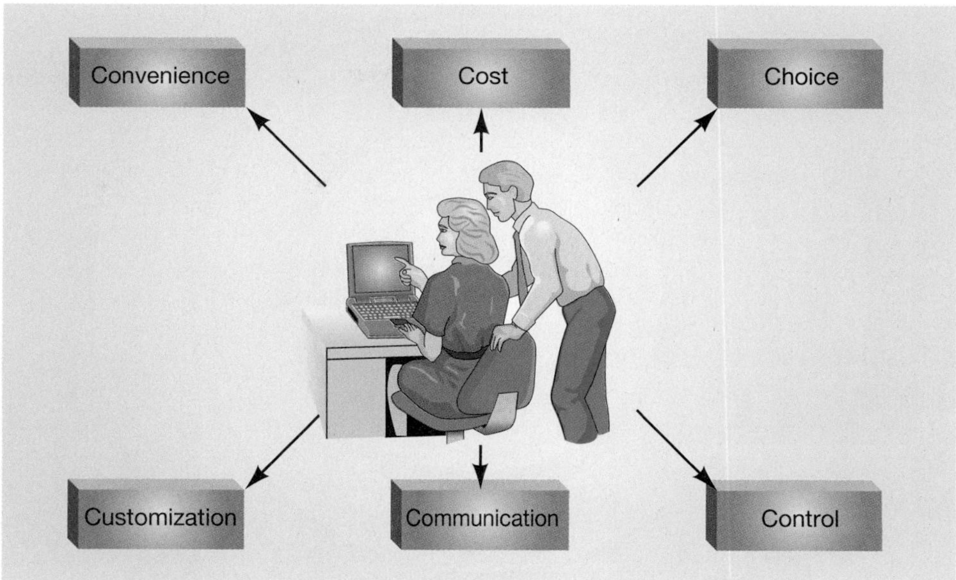

FIGURE 8–3
Why consumers buy online

spent and often the hassle of shopping, is also reduced. Shopping convenience and external search costs are two major reasons for the growth of online buying among women, particularly for those who work outside the home.[19]

Choice and *customization* opportunities are two additional reasons consumers buy online. Consumers desiring selection can avail themselves of numerous Web sites for almost any product or service they want. For instance, online buyers of consumer electronics can shop individual manufacturers such as Bose (www.bose.com) or Sony (www.sony.com) or visit iqvc.com, a general merchant with more than 100 000 products. Even with a broad selection, some consumers prefer one-of-a-kind items that fit their specific needs. Consider, for instance, buying a Barbie doll for a child. Online buyers can shop etoys.com and choose a Barbie doll from 117 versions available. On the other hand, a visit to Mattel at www.barbie.com allows buyers to design their own doll. They can specify the doll's skin tone, eye and hair colour, hairstyle, clothes, accessories, and give her a name. Fill out a questionnaire, and a computer-generated personality profile for Barbie is prepared.[20]

Online consumers also welcome the interactive *communication* capabilities of Internet/Web-based technologies that allow them to engage in an electronic dialogue with marketers. These "push" technologies send information to online consumers automatically according to their expressed preferences. Garden Escapes, Inc. (www.garden.com), which provides visitors with a computer-aided design for home landscaping, is a case in point.[21] Through state-of-the-art garden design techniques and working with plants and shrubs appropriate to particular geographical regions, online gardeners can create and then see what their finished landscape will look like instantaneously. If it meets with their approval, items can be purchased, with delivery scheduled in time for the best planting.

The sixth reason consumers prefer to buy online is the *control* it gives them over their purchase decision process. Online buyers are empowered consumers. They deftly use Internet/Web-based technology to seek information, evaluate alternatives, and make purchase decisions on their own terms and conditions. Online buyers regularly engage **portals** and "search engines," which are electronic gateways to the World Wide Web that supply a broad array of news and entertainment, information resources, and shopping services.[22] Well-known portals include Yahoo!, Infoseek, Snap, Excite, Lycos, Microsoft's Internet Start, and Netscape's Netcenter. To evaluate alternatives, consumers visit comparison-shopping Web sites such as comparenet.com

ETHICS

ETHICS AND SOCIAL RESPONSIBILITY ALERT

Sweet and Sour Cookies in the New Marketspace

Privacy and security are two key reasons consumers are leery of online shopping. An Angus Reid report (www.angusreid.ca) shows that Canadians are concerned about giving out personal and credit card information online, and very concerned about someone being able to track where they go as they travel online. Canadians are also concerned about the government enforcing laws and regulations pertaining to the Internet.

The privacy and security concerns of online buyers are related to the "cookies" described in the text and how those cookies can be used or misused. The Canadian Direct Marketing Association (CDMA) introduced new regulations regarding online marketing by its members. One regulation pertains to protecting consumers' privacy. Consumers must be informed if information is being collected on them when they visit Web sites, and how this information will be used. Consumers must also be able to decline to have such information collected, or transfered for marketing purposes. The CDMA says members who break these regulations face public censure to expulsion from the CDMA.

Do you think that government or self-regulation is the best way to deal with issues of privacy and security in the new marketplace?

and price.com or employ bots such as Yahoo! Shopping and Excite's Product Finder, which provide product descriptions and prices for a wide variety of brands and models. The result of these activities is a more informed and discerning shopper. In the words of one marketing consultant, "In the marketspace, the customer is in charge."[23]

Even though consumers have many reasons for buying online, a segment of Internet/Web users refrain from making purchases for privacy and security reasons as described in the accompanying Ethics and Social Responsibility Alert.[24] Those consumers are concerned about a rarely mentioned seventh "C"—cookies. **Cookies** are computer files that a marketer can download onto the computer of an online shopper who visits the marketer's Web site.[25] Cookies allow the marketer's Web site to monitor an online shopper's "clickstream"—the way that person navigates through the Web, record a user's visit, track visits to other Web sites, and store and retrieve this information in the future. Cookies also contain information provided by visitors, such as expressed product preferences, personal data, and financial information, including credit card numbers. Clearly, cookies make possible customized and personalized content for online shoppers. The controversy surrounding cookies is summed up by an authority on the technology: "At best a cookie makes for a user-friendly Web world: like a doorman or salesclerk who knows who you are. At worst, cookies represent a potential loss of privacy."[26]

CONCEPT CHECK

1. Which iVALS segment is the least promising group for online buying? Why?
2. Why is it that travel reservations account for such a large percentage of online buying?
3. What are the six reasons consumers prefer to buy online?

INTERACTIVE MARKETING IN THE NEW MARKETSPACE

Interactive communication between buyers and sellers and consumer control over what, where, when, and how information is exchanged in the new marketspace have significant implications for marketing practice. Even though the fundamental tasks of marketing refined in the traditional marketplace still apply—creating customer value by providing the right product, at the right time, at the right place, at the right price—the setting is very different.[27] A challenge for marketers in the new marketplace is to have an electronic presence that attracts the attention and interaction of the online consumer and makes a profit.

Creating a Presence in the New Marketspace

Marketers create a presence in the new marketspace through their Web sites and online advertising.

Corporate and Marketing Web Sites Companies employ two major types of Web sites, each with a different purpose.[28] A **corporate Web site** is designed to accommodate interactive communication initiated by a company's employees, investors, suppliers, and customers. These sites provide information about the company such as its history, mission and corporate values, products and services, and annual report. Many contain recent news releases and offer opportunities for visitors to ask questions and make comments through e-mail. More advanced Web sites provide interactive entertainment features such as games to keep a visitor's attention. Corporate Web sites are not specifically designed to promote and sell a company's products or services; however, some do. Rather, they serve to build relationships with customers and other important constituencies. Visit the Gillette Company (www.gillette.com) and Gulfstream Aerospace Corporation, a leading manufacturer of business jets (www.gulfstreamaircraft.com), to see the similarity of corporate Web sites across different industries.

A **marketing Web site** is designed to engage consumers in interactive communication or dialogue that will result in the sale of a company's product or service or move the consumer closer to a purchase. In contrast to corporate Web sites, marketing Web sites initiate interactive communication with prospective buyers. These sites outnumber corporate Web sites by a wide margin.

Marketing Web sites come in two general forms: (1) transactional sites and (2) promotional sites. Transactional Web sites are essentially electronic storefronts, such as those operated by amazon.com and cdnow. They focus principally on converting an online browser into an online buyer. Many provide access to human service representatives to assist in making purchases. For example, two-thirds of the sales through Dell Computer's Web site (www.dell.com) involve human sales representatives.[29] These sites also can be used for customer research and feedback. Canadian Airlines is a case in point. Its Web site (www.canadianairlines.com) is used to interview frequent flyers to determine their travel preferences and buying habits in addition to performing other functions. A truly multifunctional transactional Web site is operated by Cisco Systems,

TECHNOLOGY

MARKETING NEWSNET

Cisco Systems Makes Its Living on the Net

When it comes to electronic commerce, no one understands it better than Cisco Systems. The reason? Cisco's business is electronic commerce. The company sells 80 percent of the networking products that make the Internet, and most corporate Intranets and Extranets, work.

Cisco generates almost 60 percent of its sales, or about $10 million per day, through its Web site, Cisco Connection Online (www.cisco.com). At last count, Cisco accounted for roughly one-third of all North American revenues generated by electronic commerce. Cisco's Web site blends technical support with every step in selling and servicing its products, all of which are custom-built to a customer's specifications. For example, Cisco's Configuration Agent software walks customers through the dozens of components that typically go into one of its products. Its Status Agent software lets customers track the progress of their orders online. Overall, 7 out of 10 customer requests for technical support are filled electronically—at satisfaction rates that eclipse those involving human interaction.

the company that sells 80 percent of the networking products that make the Internet, and corporate Intranets and Extranets, work. Read the accompanying Marketing NewsNet to see how its Web site—Cisco Connection Online—blends technical support with every step in selling and servicing its products before and after a transaction.[30]

Promotional Web sites have a very different purpose than transactional sites. They promote a company's products and services and provide information on how items can be used and where they can be purchased. They often engage the visitor in an interactive experience involving games, contests, and quizzes with electronic coupons and other gifts as prizes. Procter & Gamble maintains separate Web sites for 24 of its leading brands, including Pringles potato chips (www.pringles.com), Vidal Sasson hair products (www.vidalsasson.com), Scope mouthwash (www.scope-mouthwash.com), and Pampers diapers (www.pampers.com).[31] Promotional sites can be effective in generating interest in and trial of a company's products and services.[32] General Motors reports that 80 percent of the people visiting a Saturn store first visited the brand's Web site (www.saturn.com). The Metropolitan Life Insurance Web site (www.metlife.com) is a proven vehicle for qualifying prospective buyers of its insurance and financial services.

Marketing Web sites can be expensive to develop and maintain, particularly with the growing use of sophisticated interactive and experiential activities and eye-catching animation and three-dimensional graphics. The average marketing Web site costs $1 million to develop and takes one year to launch. The cost of creating a transaction-based Web site is about 10 times that of a promotional Web site.[33]

Having a corporate or marketing Web site does not, by itself, guarantee that online consumers will ever visit it. While a Web site can be invaluable in conveying information, creating product involvement, and even making sales, online consumers must first be attracted to the site. Attracting online consumers is difficult in an increasingly cluttered marketspace where 100 000 Web sites are added to the World Wide Web and commercial online services each week. Advertising plays an important role in the new marketspace just as it does in the traditional marketspace. In fact, companies prominently advertise

Print advertisements are frequently used to create awareness of and interest in corporate and marketing Web sites.

their Web sites using conventional print and broadcast media and direct mail, in addition to using online advertising.

Online Advertising A primary objective of online advertising is to generate sales directly and quickly through a marketer's transactional Web site.[34] However, because most companies operate both in the new marketspace and the traditional marketplace, other objectives for online advertising exist. Creating awareness and a favourable image of a company and its products and services are frequently stated objectives for corporate Web sites. Online advertising is also used to support a company's traditional sales channel, including retail stores and building customer relationships. This is the objective of the Clinique division of Estee Lauder Companies, which markets cosmetics through department stores. Clinique reports that 80 percent of current customers who visit its Web site (www.clinique.com) later purchase a product at a retail store; 37 percent of non-Clinique buyers make a Clinique purchase after visiting the site.[35]

Companies have adopted two approaches for placing online advertising. One approach focuses on buying space on a heavily trafficked Web portal, such as Yahoo!, or a commercial online service such as Sympatico. The second involves buying space on commercially sponsored **Web communities**—Web sites that cater to a particular group of individuals who share a common interest. Members of the Web communities are prime targets for advertisements linked with the topic of the site. For instance, iVillage.com, the Women's Network, is a Web community for women and includes topics such as career management, personal finances, parenting, relationships, beauty, and health. Avon and Charles Schwab Investments are among the many companies that advertise on iVillage.com.

Companies have several options when deciding which type of advertisement to use. The most common form of advertisement are *banner ads*—strip ads that usually contain a company or product name or some kind of promotional offer. Online consumers merely

Banner ads are a popular form of online advertising.

need to click on the ad to visit either a company's corporate or marketing Web site. Over 50 percent of online advertising in Canada consists of banner ads. The typical monthly space cost for a banner ad is $10 000. And, according to AC Nielsen's Canadian Internet Survey (www.acnielsen.ca), banner ads do get consumers' attention. Their study revealed that over 50 percent of online Canadian consumers say they have clicked on a banner ad.[36] The second most common form of online advertising consists of *sponsorships*.[37] These ads are typically integrated with a Web community site. For example, Schering-Plough's allergy remedy, Claritin, is a sponsor of the OnHealth Network's Web site (www.onhealth.com). This site provides health and fitness information for adults and families.

Two other types of ads account for most of the remaining kinds of online advertising. *Key word ads* are linked to Web portals or search engines such as Yahoo! or Excite. Whenever a customer initiates a search using a certain key word, an ad for a product related to that word will appear. Miller Brewing Company, for instance, purchased the key word "beer" on Yahoo! Every online consumer who searches Yahoo! using that word sees an advertisement for Miller Genuine Draft Beer. *Interstitials* or *intermercials* are similar to television ads because they often incorporate video and audio features. An interstitial appears automatically on the computer screen in the time interval after the user clicks on a Web site and before it appears on the screen just as television ads appear in the time interval between programs. Recent research suggests that interstitial ads are twice as effective at generating brand awareness as banner ads.[38] Industry analysts project that by 2002, 50 percent of ads will be banners, 25 percent will be sponsorships, and 25 will be interstitials.[39]

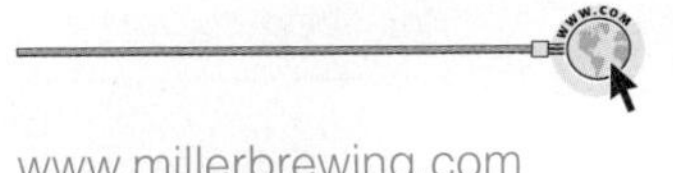

www.millerbrewing.com

Many companies today have supplemented their online advertising with **webcasting**—the practice of pushing out corporate and marketing Web site information to online consumers rather than waiting for them to find the site on their own.[40] Webcasting services, such as Pointcast (www.pointcast.com), automatically deliver customized information to an online consumer's computer, including news, entertainment, and company product and service information, based on their preferences.[41] Webcasting is likely to improve the effectiveness of online advertising. Why? According to one authority on electronic commerce: "Now instead of waiting for Web surfers to stumble onto their sites and banner ads, marketers can send animated ads directly to the desktops of target customers. . . . Merchants can now approach live sales prospects and not just couch potatoes."[42]

How Companies Benefit from Electronic Commerce and Interactive Marketing

Interactive marketing and electronic commerce have profoundly changed the exchange relationship between customers and companies. Continual advances in interactive digital technology and development of new marketing applications promise even more change in the future.

The Gap has found its Web site to be an important source of incremental sales.

Gap
www.gap.com

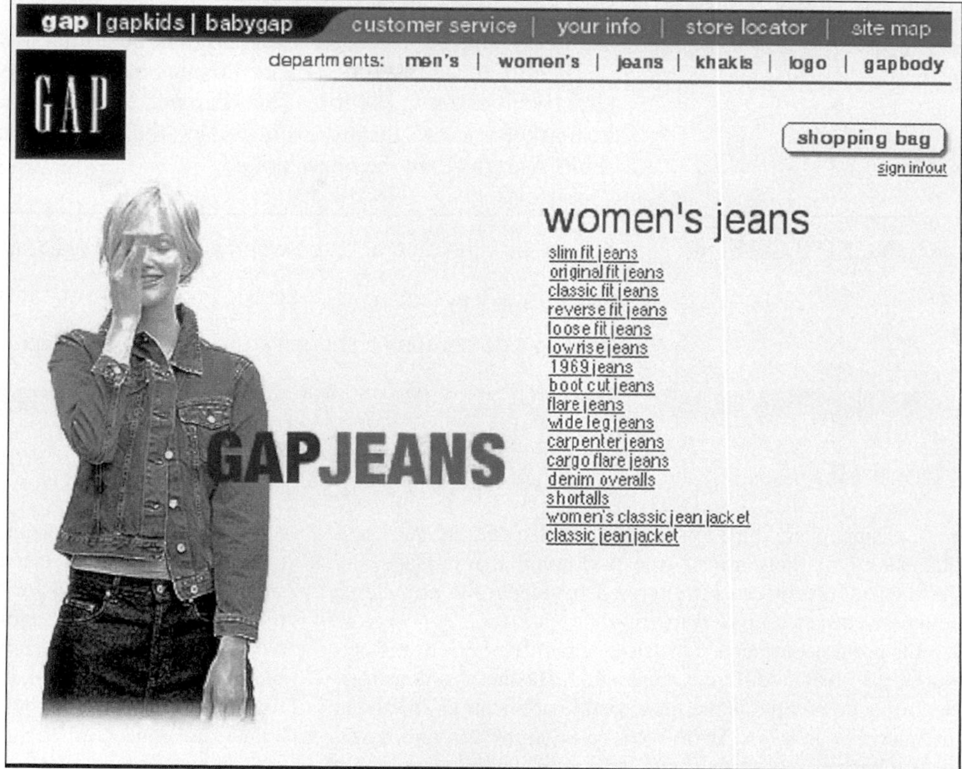

Marketers recognize the customer value creation potential in the new marketspace. However, electronic commerce and interactive marketing can provide numerous other benefits to companies. Notably, electronic commerce has already been shown to lower costs. Cost savings in inventory handling, order processing, and communications made possible by corporate Intranets, Extranets, and electronic data interchanges are huge. For example, the cost to process an order using an Extranet is $1.50. The same order using paper, including administrative costs, is $40.00—a savings of 96 percent![43] Similarly, online marketers are not burdened by the cost of building and operating retail stores. This fact has led many retailers to set up Web sites. The Gap, for instance, generates more sales volume from its Web site at (www.gap.com) than any one of its stores except one.[44]

The technology of electronic commerce and interactive marketing allows for greater flexibility in managing elements of the marketing mix. For example, online marketers routinely adjust prices in response to changing environmental conditions, purchase situations, and purchase behaviours of online buyers.[45] For example, amazon.com can offer different prices and deals to its customers depending on how and what they purchased in the past. And, as mentioned earlier in the chapter, online marketers can monitor an online shopper's clickstream to examine closely the customer's behaviour. If the visitor behaves like a price-sensitive shopper—perhaps by comparing many different products—that person may be offered a lower price. The life of an advertisement is also shortened in marketspace. Many advertisements in marketspace have a life of four hours in any 24-hour period and are adjusted to a particular online buyer's purchase behaviour. In short, customization can apply to price and promotion elements of the marketing mix, not just products and services described earlier.

Finally, because the new marketspace has no geographical boundaries, marketers can benefit from its global reach. An online consumer from Toronto can access Marks & Spencer, the well-known British department store at (www.marks-and-spencer.co.uk) to shop for clothing as easily as a person living near London's Piccadilly

Square. Large and small consumer and business-to-business marketers alike have found that this benefit has broadened their customer base.

Despite these benefits, few companies have mastered electronic commerce and interactive marketing.[46] More often than not, marketers have found the pathway to profit in marketspace to be more illusionary than real because of higher costs and lower profit margins than they anticipated.[47]

CONCEPT CHECK

1. What is the difference between a corporate Web site and a marketing Web site?
2. Why is webcasting expected to improve the effectiveness of online advertising?
3. How do companies benefit from electronic commerce and interactive marketing?

SUMMARY

1 Consumers and businesses populate two parallel and complementary markets today—the traditional marketplace and the new marketspace characterized by electronic commerce networks and interactive marketing.

2 Electronic commerce consists of a family of electronic networks, each with a different application. Business-to-consumer electronic commerce is the most visible application, involving the Internet, the World Wide Web, and commercial online services. Corporate electronic networks such as the Intranet are used to perform internal company functions, while electronic data interchanges (EDI) and Extranets are used for business-to-business electronic commerce.

3 Electronic commerce creates time, place, possession, and form utility in novel ways, resulting in customer value.

4 Online consumers differ demographically from the general population. They tend to be better educated, younger, and more affluent than the general population. The majority are married and male. They also exhibit distinct psychographic profiles.

5 Six general product and service categories appear to be particularly suited for electronic commerce. However, travel reservations, PC hardware and software, and consumer electronics account for the majority of online consumer purchases.

6 Consumers typically refer to six reasons they prefer to buy online: convenience, cost, choice, customization, communication, and control over the purchase process. However, consumers are concerned about privacy and security when making online purchases.

7 Marketers create a presence in the new marketspace through Web sites and online advertising. Web sites come in two forms: corporate Web sites and marketing Web sites. Marketing Web sites are of two types: (*a*) transactional sites and (*b*) promotional sites. The principal form of online advertising is banner ads.

8 Electronic commerce and interactive marketing not only provide novel opportunities for customer value creation but also result in cost savings, marketing mix flexibility, and global exposure.

KEY TERMS AND CONCEPTS

marketspace p. 202
electronic commerce p. 202
interactive marketing p. 202
Internet p. 203
World Wide Web (WWW) p. 203
commercial online services p. 203
Intranet p. 203
electronic data interchange (EDI) p. 204
Extranet p. 204
bots p. 208
portals p. 209
cookies p. 210
corporate Web site p. 211
marketing Web site p. 211
Web communities p. 213
webcasting p. 214

INTERNET EXERCISE

What are the most recent statistics and trends in interactive marketing and electronic commerce? Look no further than Nua Internet Surveys (Nua), an online service that abstracts up-to-date research on Internet/Web usage and applications from around the world. Nua conveniently organizes research by business, social, technical, demographic, and geographic categories for easy inspection.

Visit the Nua Web site at www.nua.ie/surveys. Your assignment is as follows:

1 Choose a topic covered in the chapter that interests you, such as the demographics of Internet/Web users. Compare and contrast the most recent research published in Nua with information contained in the chapter. Don't be surprised if you find differences!

2 Choose two regions of the world, such as North America and Europe. How does Internet/Web usage and electronic commerce differ between the two regions based on the most recent research?

APPLYING MARKETING CONCEPTS AND PERSPECTIVES

1 How do marketers use the Internet, Intranets, electronic data interchanges (EDI), and Extranets to create customer value through electronic commerce?

2 By mid-1999, only about 20 percent of Internet/Web users had actually purchased something online. Have you made an online purchase? If so, why do you think so many people who have access to the Internet and the World Wide Web are not also online buyers? If not, why are you reluctant to do so? Do you think that electronic commerce benefits consumers even if they don't make a purchase?

3 Compared to the marketplace, the marketspace offers marketers opportunities to create greater time, place, form, and possession utility. How do you think electronic commerce rates in terms of creating these values? Take a shopping trip at a virtual retailer of your choice (don't buy anything unless you really want to), or choose from one of the companies listed below. Then compare the time, place, form, and possession utility provided by the virtual retailer with that you enjoyed during a non-electronic experience shopping for the same product category. Here are some sites you might like to visit: www.aircanada.com; www.jango.com; www.dell.com.

4 Visit each of the following Web sites: www.singles.com; www.wsnbc.com; www.schwab.com; www.virualemporium.com; www.gateway.com. Which of the iVALS segments would be most attracted to each of these sites? Why?

5 Suppose you are planning to open an electronic store on the World Wide Web. How likely would a Web site featuring each of the following product categories be to succeed? Why?

a High-priced, high-fashion women's shoe salon.

b An energy comparison shopping service where consumers can shop for the best gas and electricity rates.

c Video rental service.

6 Visit Internet bookseller www.amazon.com or www.barnesandnoble.com. As you tour the company's Web site, think about how shopping for books online compares with a trip to your university bookstore to buy books. Specifically, compare your shopping experiences with respect to each of the six Cs of electronic commerce.

7 Suppose you are planning to buy a new car, so you decide to visit www.autobytel. Based on your experience visiting that site, do you feel you would enjoy more or less control in negotiating with the dealer when you actually purchase your vehicle?

8 Visit the Web site for your university or community college. Based on your visit, would you conclude that the site is a corporate or a marketing site? Why? If it is a marketing Web site, is it a transactional site or a promotional site? Why?

9 Visit a Web community such as www.women.com or www.parents.com. What companies/products advertise on the community's Web site? Why do you think those companies/products chose the Web community as an advertising venue? Do you think the choice was a good one? Why?

10 One of the benefits that electronic commerce and interactive marketing provides for companies is the ability to obtain consumer information that can be used to more effectively manage the marketing mix. Catalina Marketing Corporation, for example, creates profiles of its online customers' product category and brand preferences and use this information to generate personalized coupons. Some consumers, however, worry about their privacy as companies like Catalina create highly detailed customer databases. Visit Catalina's Web site at www.valuepage.com to determine what information you must provide to obtain your own customized coupons. Is the added value of the coupons worth the price of the information you must reveal to get it? Why or why not?

CASE 8–1 AMERICA ONLINE, INC.

"America Online started as a vision of Steve Case to provide basic e-mail and bulletin board communication services," says Wendy Brown, vice president of commerce strategy at America Online (AOL). This, of course, was several years before the commercialization of the World Wide Web (WWW) and the Internet. Over the years, AOL has added a variety of communication services, information "channels," shopping opportunities, and personalization features. Today, AOL has become the convenient tool that, according to Brown, "people use to be able to manage their lives, stay in touch with others, buy things, and learn."

THE COMPANY

Meyer Berlow, senior vice president of interactive marketing, says, "the important thing to understand about our business model is that we have a dual income stream. We have subscriber revenues and we have other revenues, namely advertising and e-commerce." To maintain its revenue growth, AOL has had to address several key challenges—attracting new subscribers and managing its "access" capabilities.

The essence of AOL's growth strategy is to be the easiest and most convenient Internet online service. To increase the number of subscribers, AOL has developed several programs to get its software in the hands of potential customers. For example, AOL has mailed disks to computer users, shrinkwrapped copies with computer magazines, and placed freestanding displays in selected retailers. In addition, AOL has offered up to 100 free hours to potential customers to encourage them to explore the service during a one trial-month period. To ensure that installation was easy, the software was designed so that trial users of AOL's service only need to "point and click" and the software installs itself. To make the access and navigation of its online service easy, AOL designed a well-organized, graphical interface to allow users to quickly seek and select items of their choice. These and other design features were critical in converting trial users to paying subscribers.

AOL has also grown through key acquisitions and alliances. In 1997, AOL purchased Internet pioneer CompuServe, which increased its subscription-based Internet services by 2 million users. In 1998, AOL's acquisition of the leading Internet browser, Netscape, brought an additional 15 million subscribers to the company. "Our merger with Netscape provides us with another world-class brand, a fast-growing portal, innovative talent, and cutting-edge technologies," said Steve Case. AOL also entered into strategic alliances with Sun Microsystems to provide software for e-commerce, telco companies to provide convenient and affordable high-speed telephone and cable TV access to millions of Internet PC users across North America, and DirectTV, Philips Electronics, and others to provide Internet access via television in the future.

To manage growth, AOL has had to revise how to predict and deal with unexpected demand for its service.

When AOL switched from usage (time spent) to flat-rate (monthly fee) pricing a few years ago, it created an "access crisis" that made the nightly news. Demand temporarily surged beyond AOL's capacity and caused subscribers to receive unwanted busy signals. Companies and other users who relied on AOL for e-mail service had to wait hours before gaining access. AOL failed "to estimate what kind of pent-up demand there was among our members," Brown said. That challenge has since been resolved, as AOL spent millions of dollars to add computer and communications connectivity capacity.

AOL has now become the largest online service in the world with over 17 million "members" or paid subscribers who connect to the service an average of 55 minutes per day. Millions more access its Web site, www.aol.com. In 1998, about 16 percent of AOL's $2.6 billion in revenues came from advertising and e-commerce, a substantial increase from 9 percent in 1996.

E-COMMERCE AT AOL

Nearly nine million North American households had shopped via the Internet in 1998, generating almost $8 billion in online retail sales, according to a report from Forrester Research, Inc. By 2003, more than 50 million North American households will shop online, producing over $108 billion in revenues. "The Internet is the first medium that really solves the marketers dilemma. It lets consumers seek information about a particular brand and then be able to buy it quickly, thereby simplifying the entire purchase process," says Berlow.

The potential of e-commerce became clear during the 1998 holiday season when AOL members spent $1.2 billion online. During this period, almost 1.25 million AOL members made their first purchase online. AOL estimates that 84% of its present members "window-shopped" and 44% bought merchandise through AOL or aol.com. Members who shopped online were very satisfied with the experience. They said they appreciated AOL's ease-of-use, convenience, and security of their online transactions, not to mention the great values offered by many of its retail partners. Moreover, research indicates that once members shop online, they developed an e-commerce habit by purchasing one to three items during the first three months alone.

This success was largely due to the 110 merchants and "e-tailers" (such as Eddie Bauer, J. Crew, Toys "Я" Us, Macy's, Barnes and Noble, Digital Chef, etc.) AOL partnered with to enhance AOL's Shopping Channel. AOL's goals regarding its foray into the exciting world of e-commerce were to offer consumers "one-stop shopping" convenience, branded products and services, and value pricing. What are AOL shoppers buying? Based on traffic averages to AOL Shopping Channel departments, the Toys, Kids, and Babies category held the number-one

spot, followed closely by apparel. The average AOL holiday shopper purchased two items online every week during the holiday shopping season and spent about $54. Since interactive marketing and e-commerce are growing rapidly, AOL continues to attract e-tailers, other mass merchandisers, and service providers to sell their wares through AOL. Recent agreements with Unilever, Visa (credit cards), Citibank, etrade (brokerage), Hertz Car Rental, eBay (online auctions), and *The Financial Times* (news) are among many companies partnering with AOL in long-term relationships.

ENSURING THE FUTURE OF E-COMMERCE

While the future of e-commerce looks bright, AOL faces several important issues. According to a Boston Consulting Group study, retailers must continue to offer consumers compelling reasons to shop online. Further advances in convenience, cost, choice, customization, communication, and control must be made for more consumers to change their shopping behaviour. With respect to *convenience,* "portals" are expected to be the primary means consumers will use to access and browse the Internet. While AOL is positioned to be one of the principal Internet portals, it will need to promote and defend its leading presence against the efforts by Disney, Microsoft, Yahoo!, and other formidable competitors.

In terms of *cost,* the expected increase in online advertising and competition from "free" portals, such as Yahoo!, means AOL must continue to provide added value. Consumers should benefit by reduced costs for product and services purchased online because they can order directly from the manufacturers, retailers, or service providers. Moreover, they can search the Internet for the best price for the products and services they desire. However, AOL and its retailer partners must resolve any channel conflicts that may arise as a result of selling online directly to consumers. Specifically, some potential AOL retail partners may hesitate or choose not to sell online because it might cannibalize sales through existing channels, alienate existing distribution partners, and, more important, lower margins for all in the channel. AOL retail partners who chose to sell online may be able to charge a premium if they provide superior service, enhanced features, and a strong brand presence not found on other online portals' or retailers' Web sites.

Giving consumers *choice* in their Internet experience will continue to be critical. As a portal, AOL must continue to expand the choices available to its subscribers, both in terms of the types (shopping, e-mail, messaging, news, etc.) and depth (number of retail partners for each shopping category) of the services offered. These retail partners must provide AOL members with a broad array of goods and services available for browsing or purchase online. To date, AOL has offered the most comprehensive array of top brand names and it must continue to do so.

As Dell Computer, Mattel, and other companies have demonstrated, "build-to-order" systems allow customers to *customize* their product and service purchases with the feature set they want and at a price they can afford. For AOL and its partners, the continued integration of manufacturing, database, customer service, and fulfillment or service delivery systems must provide consumers with the customization they desire. In addition, *communications* issues must be resolved. Cable modems, digital subscriber lines (DSL), fiber optics, and other technologies need to become more readily available to consumers. AOL's alliances with telecommunication companies and acquisitions of Personalogic and When.com are a start but more needs to be done.

Finally, online consumers want to *control* the personal and financial data that is gathered during an online visit or transaction. Specifically, they want to know whether their data is safeguarded, how it is used by e-tailers, and if it is disclosed to other organizations for marketing purposes. Consumers also want the ability to restrict access to morally objectionable Web sites and "chat rooms" and to protect their computers from "viruses." International Data Corporation estimates the market for Internet security software to reach $7.4 billion by 2002. While AOL has taken a lead in investing in its "Parental Control" and "Privacy" programs, additional efforts may be required as international e-commerce grows and demands for a "safer" Internet increase. Overall, consumers seem to be—as was the case with ATM machines—becoming more and more comfortable with shopping online, which is—at least on AOL—safer than handing over your credit card at a restaurant.

Questions

1 How has the vision or mission of AOL changed from the early 1980s to the present?

2 How does AOL facilitate online shopping or e-commerce? What are the advantages and disadvantages of using AOL for online shopping versus the more traditional method you may use?

3 What challenges has AOL overcome to attract both consumers and retailer partners to engage in e-commerce? What challenges do they still need to overcome?

4 What are the six "C's" of e-commerce and what is AOL's marketing strategy in each of these areas?

CHAPTER NINE

TURNING MARKETING INFORMATION INTO ACTION

9

AFTER READING THIS CHAPTER YOU SHOULD BE ABLE TO:

- Know what marketing research is and does.
- Explain the different types of marketing research.
- Understand the stages in the marketing research process.
- Know when and how to collect secondary data.
- Explain the use of surveys, experiments, and observation in marketing research.
- Identify ethical issues in the marketing research process.
- Understand how information technology enables information systems to be used that link massive amounts of marketing information to meaningful marketing actions.
- Recognize alternative methods to forecast sales and use the lost-horse and linear trend extrapolation methods to make a simple forecast.

LISTENING TO CONSUMERS EARLY: TRYING TO REDUCE MOVIE RISKS!

"Blockbuster movies" are essential for today's fiercely competitive world of filmmaking—examples being movies such as *Titanic* (opposite page), *Star Wars Episode I: The Phantom Menace, Shoeless Joe, Teenie Weenies,* and *3000!*

What's in a Movie Name? Can't remember those last three movies—even after scratching your head? Well, it turns out marketing research on moviegoers in test screenings discovered they had problems with those names, too. Here's the title these three movies started with, where they wound up, and the reason:

- *Shoeless Joe* became *Field of Dreams* because audiences thought Kevin Costner might be playing a homeless person.
- *Teenie Weenies* became *Honey, I Shrunk the Kids* when moviegoers couldn't relate the original title to what they saw in the movie.
- *3000* became *Pretty Woman* when audiences didn't have a clue what the number meant. Hint: It was the number of dollars to spend an evening with Julia Roberts.[1]

Filmmakers want movie titles that are concise, attention-getting, capture the essence of the film, and have no legal restrictions—basically the same factors that make a good brand name.

How Filmmakers Try to Reduce Risk Is research on movie titles expensive? Very! But the greater expense is selecting a bad title that can kill a movie and cost the studio millions of dollars. So with today's big budget films costing almost $70 million to produce and market,[2] how can movie studios reduce their risk of losses? One part of reducing risk: Use marketing research to recruit people to attend sneak previews (test screenings) of a forthcoming movie and then ask them questions that might bring about improvements in the final edit of the movie.

Without reading ahead, think about answers to these questions:

- Whom would you recruit for these test screenings?
- What questions would you ask them to help you in editing or modifying the title or parts of the film?

While *Field of Dreams* and *Star Wars Episode I: The Phantom Menace* have little else in common, they—like virtually every major movie produced today—use test screenings to obtain the key reactions of consumers likely to be in the target market. Figure 9–1 summarizes some of the key questions that are used in these test screenings, both to select the people for the screenings and to obtain key reactions of those sitting in the screenings.

Here are some examples of changes to movies that have resulted from this kind of marketing research:

- *Making the plot move faster.* Disney cut a duet by Pocahontas and John Smith in *Pocahontas* because it got in the way of the action and confused test audiences.[3]
- *Reaching a market segment more effectively.* More action footage was added for Kevin Costner when preview screening showed young males were less enthusiastic about *The Bodyguard* than young females.[4]
- *Changing an ending. Fatal Attraction* had probably the most commercially successful "ending-switch" of all time. In its sneak previews, audiences liked everything but the ending, which had Alex (Glenn Close) committing suicide and managing to frame Dan (Michael Douglas) as her murderer by leaving his fingerprints on the knife she used. The studio shot $1.3 million of new scenes for the ending that regular audiences eventually saw.[5]

Sometimes studios get the pleasant news in test screenings that a movie or plot "works" with an audience. This was the case when James Cameron, writer-director of *Titanic,* sat in on the first test screening of his $200 million epic and watched the audience go wild, a huge relief after months of bad vibes.[6] Because the first two weeks of attendance after a movie's release often determine its success or failure today, marketing research on names and plots are even more important than in the past.[7]

FIGURE 9–1
Marketing research questions asked in test screenings of movies, and how they are used

POINT WHEN ASKED	KEY QUESTIONS	USE OF QUESTION(S)
Before the test screening	• How old are you? • How frequently do you pay to see movies? • What movies have you seen in the last three months?	Decide if person fits profile of target audience for movie. If yes, invite to test screening. If not, don't invite.
After the test screening	• What do you think of the title? What title would you suggest?	Change movie title.
	• Were any characters too distasteful? Who? How?	Change aspects of some characters.
	• Did any scenes offend you? Which ones? How?	Change scenes.
	• How did you like the ending? If you didn't like it, how would you change it?	Change or clarify ending.
	• Would you recommend the movie to a friend?	Overall indicator of liking and/or satisfaction with movie.

Besides test screenings, motion picture firms also use marketing research to do concept tests of proposed plots and to design and test the $17-million marketing campaigns that support a typical movie's launch.[8] These examples show how marketing research is linked to marketing strategy and decisive actions, the main topic of this chapter. Marketing research is often used to help a firm develop sales forecasts, the final topic in the chapter.

WHAT MARKETING RESEARCH IS AND DOES

Marketing research is the process of defining a marketing problem or opportunity, systematically collecting and analyzing information, and recommending actions to improve an organization's marketing activities.[9]

A Means of Reducing Risk and Uncertainty Assessing the needs and wants of consumers and providing information to help design an organization's marketing program to satisfy them is the principal role that marketing research performs. This means that marketing research attempts to identify and define both marketing problems and opportunities and to generate and evaluate marketing actions. Although marketing research can provide few answers with complete assurance, it can reduce risk and uncertainty to increase the likelihood of the success of marketing decisions. It is a great help to the marketing managers who must make final decisions. Conducted properly, marketing research can solve most marketing-related problems that an executive might have. However, marketing research should not be designed to simply replace an executive's good sense, experience, or intuition but rather should be used in conjunction with those skills and as a way of taking out some of the guesswork in the marketing decision-making process.

TYPES OF MARKETING RESEARCH

To understand the variety of research activity, it is helpful to categorize different types of marketing research. Marketing research is often classified on the basis of either technique or function. Surveys, experiments, and observation are a few research techniques with which you may be familiar. However, categorizing research by its purpose or function shows how the nature of the marketing problem influences the choice of research techniques. The nature of the problem will determine whether the research is (1) exploratory, (2) descriptive, or (3) causal.

Exploratory Research

Exploratory research is preliminary research conducted to clarify the scope and nature of the marketing problem. It is generally carried out to provide the researcher with a better understanding of the dimensions of the problem. Exploratory research is often conducted with the expectation that subsequent and more conclusive research will follow. For example, the Dairy Farmers of Canada, an association representing dairy producers in the country, wanted to discover why milk consumption was declining in Canada.

www.milk.org

They conducted a search of existing literature on milk consumption, talked to experts in the field, and even conducted preliminary interviews with consumers to get ideas about why consumers were drinking less milk. This exploratory research helped the association to crystallize the problem, and identify issues for more detailed follow-up research. We examine exploratory research as an integral component of the basic marketing research process later in the chapter.

The Dairy Farmers of Canada conducted three types of marketing research in an effort to solve the decline in milk consumption problem. For details read the text.

Descriptive Research

Descriptive research is research designed to describe basic characteristics of a given population or to profile particular marketing situations. Unlike exploratory research, with descriptive research the researcher has a general understanding of the marketing problem and is seeking conclusive data that answers the questions necessary to determine a particular course of action. Examples of descriptive research would include profiling product purchasers (e.g., the Canadian health food store shopper), describing the size and characteristics of markets (e.g., the Canadian pizza restaurant market), detailing product usage patterns (e.g., ATM usage by Canadian bank consumers), or outlining consumer attitudes toward particular brands (e.g., Canadian attitudes toward national, private, and generic brands).

Magazines, radio stations, and television stations almost always do descriptive research to identify the characteristics of their audiences in order to present it to prospective advertisers. As a follow-up to its exploratory research, the Dairy Farmers of Canada conducted descriptive research to determine the demographic characteristics of milk consumers, current usage patterns, and consumer attitudes toward milk consumption.

Causal Research

Causal research is research designed to identify cause-and-effect relationships among variables. In general, exploratory and descriptive research normally precede causal research. With causal research there is typically an expectation about the relationship to be explained, such as predicting the influence of a price change on product demand. In general, researchers attempt to establish that one event (e.g., a price change) will produce another event (e.g., a change in demand). Typical causal research studies examine the effect of advertising on sales; the relationship between price and perceived quality of a product; and the impact of a new package on product sales. When the Dairy Farmers of Canada conducted their descriptive research on milk consumers, they discovered many believed milk was too fattening and too high in cholesterol. The association felt that these beliefs might be related to the overall decline in milk consumption in Canada. To test this assumption, the association ran a television advertising campaign to demonstrate that milk was a healthful product and essential to a person's diet. In their tracking studies, they found that the ad campaign did change consumer attitudes toward milk which, in turn, was causally related to a subsequent increase in milk consumption. We refer to causal research later in this chapter when we deal with experiments as a basic research technique.

CONCEPT CHECK

1. What is marketing research?
2. What is the difference between exploratory, descriptive, and causal research?

THE MARKETING RESEARCH PROCESS

Marketing research should always be conducted based on the scientific method, a process of systematically collecting, organizing and analyzing data in an unbiased, objective manner. Marketing research must meet two basic principles of the scientific method—reliability and validity. *Reliability* refers to the ability to replicate research results under identical environmental conditions. In other words, if a research project were to be conducted for the second, third, or fourth time, the results should be the same. Marketers need to have reliable information to make effective decisions. If results of a study are not reliable, the research can do more harm than no research at all. *Validity* involves the notion of whether the research measured what was intended to be measured. In other words, does the research tell marketers what they needed to know? You should keep the concepts of reliability and validity in mind as we discuss the marketing research process.

Figure 9–2 outlines the basic marketing research process. The figure is perhaps an oversimplification of the process since marketing research does not always follow such a neat and ordered sequence of activities. However, all marketing research consists of four basic stages: (1) defining the problem, (2) determining the research design, (3) collecting and analyzing data, and (4) drawing conclusions and preparing a report.

In reviewing Figure 9–2 you can see that the researcher has a number of decisions and choices to make during the stages of the process. For example, the red boxes in Figure 9–2 indicate stages in the process where a choice of one or more techniques or methods must be made. The dotted line indicates the researcher's choice to bypass the exploratory research stage of the process.

PROBLEM DEFINITION

The first step in the marketing research process is to properly define the scope and nature of the marketing problem to be investigated. In general, the term *problem* suggests that something has gone wrong. In reality, to the marketing researcher, the word *problem* may also mean something to explore or an opportunity to define, or a current marketing situation to monitor or evaluate. Sometimes the problem is obvious, but in other cases, the problem may be more difficult to identify and define. In either case, the marketing researcher must fully understand and properly identify the problem at hand.

www.oceanspray.com

The marketing research process is often initiated by the marketing manager who will approach the marketing researcher with a problem that requires information for decision making. For example, suppose you were the marketing manager for cranberry juice at Ocean Spray. You want to know if Asian consumers would buy cranberry juice when they have never heard of cranberries. You also have other problems. The word "cranberry" isn't part of any foreign language so you would have to find a name for it and its juice. Also, if you were going to take the product to Asia you have to find a way to encourage consumers there to try the new product.[10] The marketing researcher has to fully understand these problems. The researcher must also remember that the best place to begin a research project is at the end. In other words, the researcher must know what is to be accomplished through the research process. In this case, as the marketing manager what you really want to know is: Is there a market opportunity in Asia for cranberry juice? If so, how can it be exploited?

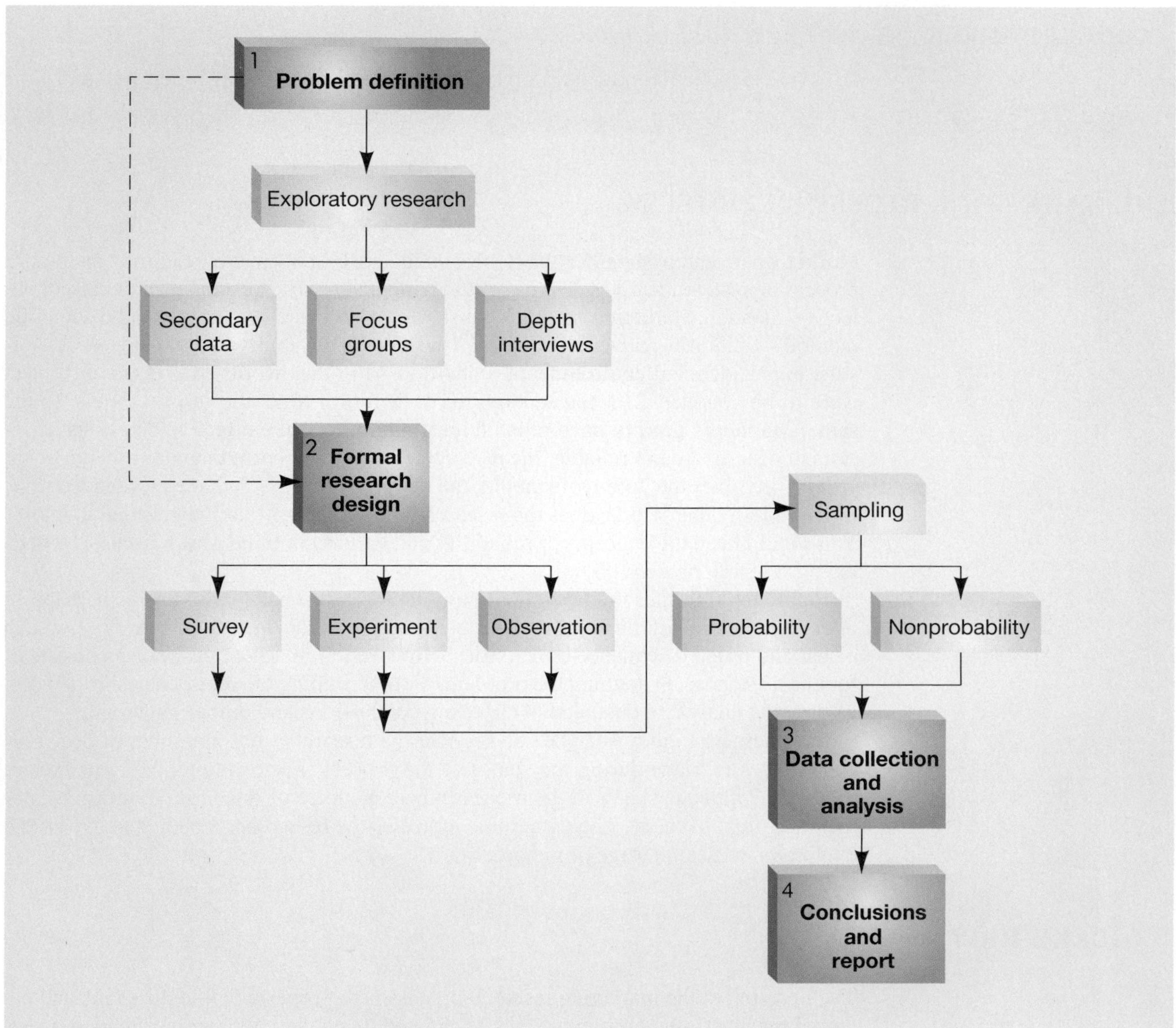

FIGURE 9–2
The basic marketing research process

Note: Red boxes indicate stages in the process where a choice of one or more techniques or methods must be made. The dotted line indicates the researcher's choice to by-pass the exploratory research stage of the process.

Proper problem definition is critical since research based on incorrect problem definition will be a waste of resources. Good marketing researchers adhere to the old adage "a problem well defined is a problem half-solved." If the research problem is clear, the chances of collecting the necessary information to solve the problem are increased.

CONCEPT CHECK

1. What is reliability and validity?
2. What are the four basic stages in the marketing research process?

Exploratory Research

Your colleague, the marketing researcher at Ocean Spray, has to make a decision early on in the marketing research process. Should exploratory research be conducted in an attempt to help answer the question: Is there a market opportunity in Asia for cranberry juice? As

Should Ocean Spray introduce cranberry juice in Asia when consumers there have never heard of cranberries? See the text.

we saw earlier in the chapter, exploratory research is preliminary research conducted to clarify the scope and nature of the marketing problem. In general, it is designed to provide the researcher with a better understanding of the dimensions of the problem and is often conducted with the expectation that subsequent and more conclusive research may follow.

Most researchers will usually conduct some basic exploratory research during the early stage of the research process. The extent of the exploratory research will depend on the magnitude of the problem as well as its complexity. If the researcher decides to conduct exploratory research, he or she has three basic techniques to choose from: (1) secondary data analysis, (2) focus groups, and (3) depth interviews.

Secondary Data Exploratory research almost always involves the use of **secondary data** (or historical data)—data previously collected and assembled for some project other than the one at hand. **Primary data,** on the other hand, are data gathered and assembled specifically for the project at hand. As a rule, researchers gather secondary data before collecting primary data. In general, secondary data can be obtained more quickly and at a lower cost compared to primary data. However, there can be problems with secondary data. The required information may not exist, and if it does, it may not be current or particularly pertinent to the problem at hand. Still, most researchers agree that investigating secondary data sources can save researchers from "reinventing the wheel."

Researchers examine secondary data both inside and outside the organization. Internal secondary data include financial statements, research reports, customer letters, and customer lists. What did your colleague in marketing research at Ocean Spray discover during the secondary data search efforts? She was able to discover that Ocean Spray did attempt to introduce a bland cranberry juice in Japan—named "Cranby"—and it fizzled and was pulled off the market. As a marketing manager this

www.statcan.ca

does provide some background information, but you still have more questions than answers about the possible marketing opportunity in Asia.

Sources of external secondary data can be wide and varied. One key source, for example, is the federal government with data made available through Statistics Canada or local libraries. Statistics Canada completes the *Census of Canada* once every decade and updates certain census data every few years. The census provides detailed information on Canadian households. Statistics Canada also prepares annual or biannual reports including the *Family Expenditure Guide,* which gives a detailed breakdown of how families spend their money. These basic sources of information are used by manufacturers and retailers to identify characteristics and trends of ultimate consumers.

Statistics Canada produces many other census reports that are vital to business firms selling goods and services to organizations. Such reports include the *Census of Manufacturers,* which lists the number and size of manufacturing firms by industry group as well as other information including values of shipments and wages paid.

A marketing researcher can obtain from Statistics Canada their annual *Marketing Research Handbook* or the *Canada Year Book,* which includes a summary of key information often necessary to aid marketing decision making. Statistics Canada also has a database system known as CANSIM (Canadian Socio-Economic Information Management System), which marketers can access directly in order to examine aggregate data.

In addition to government-supplied data, trade associations, universities, and business periodicals provide detailed data of value. For example, one business periodical, *Sales and Marketing Management,* publishes special issues each year that provide useful data for firms selling both consumer and industrial products. The most famous publication by *S&MM* is their *Annual Survey of Buying Power. The Financial Post* produces a publication called *Canadian Markets,* which provides demographic information and data on consumer spending power in provinces, cities, and towns across the country.

Companies such as Compusearch and A. C. Nielson offer both standard and customized information services to other firms on a subscription, or for-fee, basis. Compusearch can provide information on any geographic area of any size in Canada which highlights population, income, and retail expenditure trends in that area. Figure 9–3 shows some of the secondary data sources available to the marketer in Canada. There are also hundreds of useful online databanks and specialized data services such as Dow Jones, Dialog, and Infoglobe. The Web Link box provides examples.

Getting back to our marketing researcher at Ocean Spray and the cranberry juice in Asia question, she discovers some external secondary data, specifically a study on Taiwan consumers that shows increased consumption of juice beverages. Still, the study is not specific to cranberry juice, and is about four years old. As marketing manager, you realize you still have a high degree of uncertainty about the possible marketing opportunity in Asia. So you ask your colleague in marketing research to continue the exploratory stage of the marketing process.

Focus Groups A very popular exploratory research technique designed to obtain primary data is the use of focus groups. **Focus groups** are informal interview sessions in which 6 to 10 persons, relevant to the research project, are brought together in a room with a moderator to discuss topics surrounding the marketing research problem. The moderator poses questions and encourages the individuals to answer in their own words and to discuss the issues with each other. Often, the focus-group sessions are watched by observers through one-way mirrors and/or the sessions are videotaped. Of course, participants should be informed they are being observed and/or taped. Focus-group sessions often provide the marketer with valuable information for decision making or can uncover other issues that should be researched in a more quantitative fashion.

Britain's Lewis Woolf Griptight, a manufacturer of infant and toddler products, conducted focus groups about possible brand names for their products before bringing a new product line to market. U.K. consumers turned thumbs down on using "Griptight"

SELECTED GUIDES, INDEXES, AND DIRECTORIES

Business Periodical Index
Canadian Almanac and Directory
Canadian Business Index
Canadian News Index
Canadian Periodical Index
Canadian Statistics Index
Canadian Trade Index
Directory of Associations in Canada
Fraser's Canadian Trade Directory
Predicasts Index
Scott's Directories
Standards Periodical Directory
Ulrich's International Periodicals Directory

SELECTED PERIODICALS AND NEWSPAPERS

Advertising Age
Adweek
American Demographics
Business Horizons
Canadian Business
Canadian Consumer
Forbes
Fortune
Harvard Business Review
Journal of Advertising
Journal of Advertising Research
Journal of Consumer Research
Journal of Marketing
Journal of Marketing Management
Journal of Marketing Research
Journal of Personal Selling and Sales Management
Journal of Retailing
Journal of Small Business
Marketing Magazine
Marketing & Media Decisions
Marketing News
Progressive Grocer
Sales and Marketing Management
The Globe and Mail
The Financial Post
The Financial Post Magazine
The Wall Street Journal

SELECTED STATISTICS CANADA PUBLICATIONS

Annual Retail Trade
Canadian Economic Observer
Canada Yearbook
Family Expenditure Guide
Market Research Handbook
Statistics Canada Catalogue

SELECTED TRADE SOURCES

A. C. Nielson
Compusearch
Conference Board of Canada
Dun & Bradstreet
Financial Post Publishing
Find/SVP
Gale Research
MacLean Hunter Research Bureau
Predicasts International
R. L. Polk

SELECTED DATABASES

CANSIM (Statistics Canada)
Dialog
Dow Jones
Infoglobe
Infomart
The Source

FIGURE 9–3
Sources of secondary data in Canada

as a brand name for kids' products because they thought it sounded like "a carpet glue, a denture fixative, a kind of tire." So the firm called its product line by the name "Kiddiwinks™"—a British word for children.[11]

Depth Interviews Another exploratory research technique used to obtain primary data involves the use of depth interviews. **Depth interviews** are detailed individual interviews with people relevant to the research project. The researcher questions the individual at length in a free-flowing conversational style in order to discover information that may help solve the marketing problem being investigated. Sometimes these interviews can take a few hours and they are often recorded on audio- or videotape.

Hamburger Helper didn't fare too well with consumers when General Mills first introduced it. Initial instructions called for cooking a half pound of hamburger separately from the noodles, which were later mixed with the hamburger. Depth interviews revealed that consumers didn't think the recipe called for enough meat and that they didn't want the hassle of cooking in two different pots. So the Hamburger Helper product manager changed the recipe to call for a full pound of meat and to allow users to prepare it in one dish; this converted a potential failure into a success.

WEB LINK Online Databases Useful in Marketing

Information in online databases available through the Internet divide into two categories: (1) indexes to articles in publications, which are accessed through keyword searches, and (2) statistical and directory data on households, products, and companies.

Online databases of indexes, abstracts, and full-text information from journals and periodicals include:

- Lexis-Nexis' Academic Universe, which gives full-text information from more than 650 periodicals and abstracts from more than 1000 sources. (www.lexis-nexis.com)
- ProQuest databases from UMI, Inc., which contain academic articles from more than 800 management, marketing, and business periodicals and journals. (www.umi.com)
- General BusinessFile ASAP from Information Access Company, which contains references, abstracts, and full-text articles from more than 1000 business and industry publications. (www.library.iacnet.com)

Statistical and directory information about households, products, and companies through online databases include:

- Moody's Business and Financial Information, which gives data on more than 23 000 domestic and international public companies that are traded on the NYSE, AMEX, and NASDAQ stock exchanges. (www.fisonline.com)
- Dow Jones Interactive from Dow Jones & Company (publisher of *The Wall Street Journal*), which provides up-to-the-minute business news; secondary research reports on companies, industries, and countries; and up to 25 years of historical pricing on thousands of securities. (www.dowjones.com)
- Statistics Canada, which provides census data and detailed information on Canadian households, as well as industrial and retail trade information. (www. statcan.ca)

Some of these sites are accessible only if a subscription fee has been paid by an organization. To check out these sites, access your college or university Web site, click on the icon for your library, and then click on these or other useful databases to which your institution subscribes.

Researchers have also become creative in devising other exploratory research techniques. For example, finding "the next big thing" for consumers has become the obsession in many industries.[12] In order to unearth the next big thing, marketing researchers have developed some unusual techniques sometimes referred to as "fuzzy front-end" methods. These techniques are designed to identify elusive consumer tastes or trends far before typical consumers have recognized them themselves. For example, having consumers take a photo of themselves every time they snack resulted in General Mills' Homestyle "Pop Secret" popcorn, which delivers the real butter and bursts of salt in microwave popcorn consumers thought they could only get from the stovetop variety.[13]

This is a snapshot of YOU! Show and tell us more about you -- what you like to do, wear, listen to, read, say.
And don't worry, we can't draw either!!

First Name: Lindsay

Where am I??? a dance floor

What's my attitude? / What am I saying? Let's have a good time! I'm happy, smiling, & out going!

Music/CD/tape I'm listening to: Gettin' Jiggy With It, Funk Phenomenon, Miami or DMB, Indigo Girls, Violent Femmes, Barenaked Ladies

What I like to do (hobbies/activities, etc.): dance, sing, Pom Pon, listen to music, shop, hang out with friends, write, study english & history

My favorite magazine: Teen

My favorite brand of jeans: Blue Comet

ALSO: give me a face, hair, shoes and a design/logo on my shirt and something I always have with me!

Other unusual techniques are also being used to try to spot trends early. For example, Teenage Research Unlimited had teenagers complete a drawing to help discover what teenagers like, wear, listen to, and read.[14] Wet Seal hires "cool hunters," people with

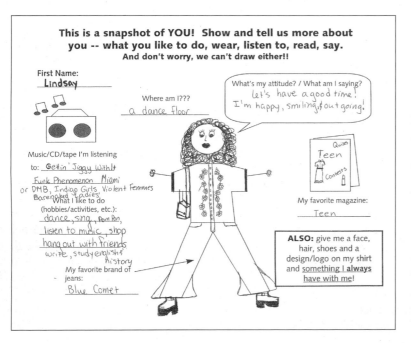

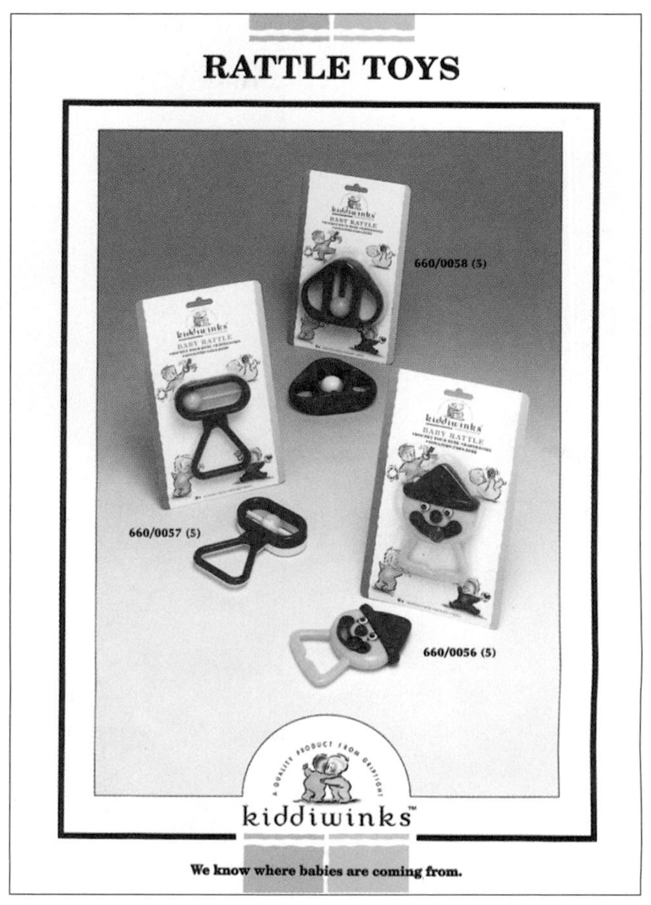

Focus groups in Britain give thumbs down on one brand name and thumbs up to another. Read the text.

tastes far ahead of the curve, to identify the "next big things" likely to sweep popular culture. In doing so, Wet Seal anticipated teenage girls' fashion picks such as slip dresses and hooded sweaters with zippers.[15]

CONCEPT CHECK

1. What are secondary data?
2. What are focus groups?

FORMAL RESEARCH DESIGN

After identifying and clarifying the marketing problem, with or without exploratory research, the researcher must determine the basic framework for finding a solution to the problem. At the formal research design stage, the researcher produces a plan that outlines the method and procedures for collecting and analyzing the required information. The plan includes the objectives of the research; the sources of information to be used; the research methods (e.g., survey, experiment); the sampling plan; and the schedule and cost of the research.

In selecting basic research methods, the researcher must make decisions. In general, the objectives of the research, the available data sources, the nature of the information required, and timing and cost considerations will determine which research method

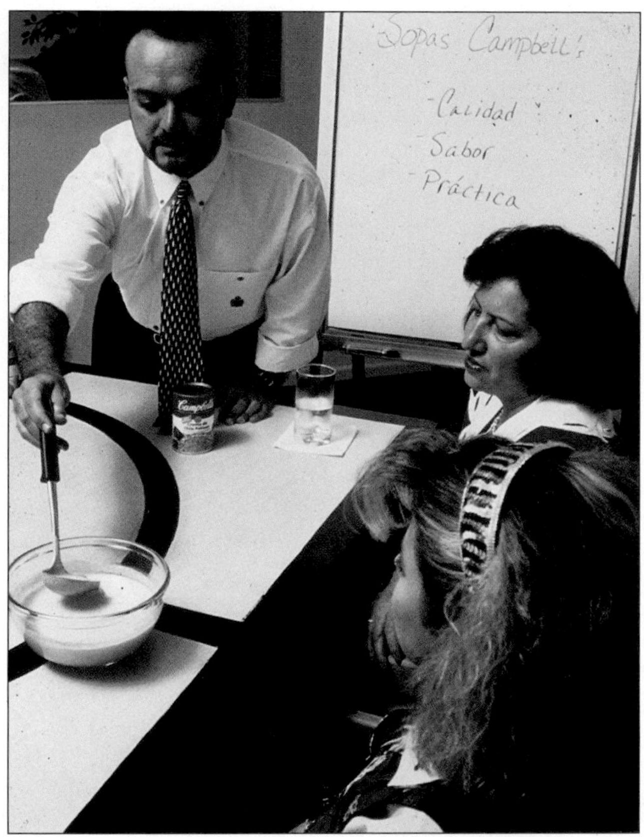

Focus groups enable a moderator to obtain information from 6–10 people at the same time.

will be chosen. The basic methods the researcher can choose for descriptive and causal research include: (1) survey, (2) experiment, and (3) observation.

Survey

The most common research method of generating new or primary data is the use of surveys. A **survey** is a research technique used to generate data by asking people questions and recording their responses on a questionnaire. Surveys can be conducted by mail, telephone, or personal interview. In choosing between the three alternatives, the marketing researcher has to make important trade-offs (as shown in Figure 9–4) to balance cost against the expected quality of the information obtained. The figure shows that personal interviews have a major advantage of enabling the interviewer to be flexible in asking probing questions or getting reactions to visual materials. In contrast, mail surveys usually have the lowest cost per completed survey of the three data collection procedures. Telephone surveys lie between the other two technologies in terms of flexibility and cost.

Sometimes marketers will survey over time the same sample of people, commonly known as a survey *panel.* A panel can consist of a sample of consumers, stores, or experts from which researchers can take a series of measurements. For example, a consumer's switch from one brand of breakfast cereal to another can be measured with panel data. The use of panels is becoming more popular with marketers as they attempt to obtain ongoing information about their constituents. Panel data are often incorporated into information systems, which are discussed later in the chapter.

When marketers decide to use surveys to ask questions, they assume that: (1) the right questions are being asked, (2) people will understand the questions being asked, (3) people know the answers to the questions, (4) people will answer the questions truth-

FIGURE 9–4
Comparison of mail, telephone, and personal interview surveys

BASIS OF COMPARISON	MAIL SURVEYS	TELEPHONE SURVEYS	PERSONAL INTERVIEW SURVEYS
Cost per completed survey	Usually the least expensive, assuming adequate return rate	Moderately expensive, assuming reasonable completion rate	Most expensive, because of interviewer's time and travel expenses
Ability to probe and ask complex questions	Little, since self-administered format must be short and simple	Some, since interviewer can probe and elaborate on questions to a degree	Much, since interviewer can show visual materials, gain rapport, and probe
Opportunity for interviewer to bias results	None, since form is completed without interviewer	Some, because of voice inflection of interviewer	Significant, because of voice and facial expressions of interviewer
Anonymity given to respondent	Complete, since no signature is required	Some, because of telephone contact	Little, because of face-to-face contact

fully, and (5) the researchers themselves will understand the answers provided. Marketers must not only concern themselves with asking the right questions but also with how to properly word those questions. Proper phrasing of a question is vital in uncovering useful marketing information.

Figure 9–5 shows typical problems to guard against in wording questions to obtain meaningful answers from respondents. For example, in a question of whether you eat

FIGURE 9–5
Typical problems in wording questions

PROBLEM	SAMPLE QUESTION	EXPLANATION
Leading question	Why do you like Wendy's fresh meat hamburgers better than those of competitors made with frozen meat?	Consumer is led to make statements favouring Wendy's hamburgers
Ambiguous question	Do you eat at fast-food restaurants regularly? ☐ Yes ☐ No	What is meant by word *regularly*—once a day, once a month, or what?
Unanswerable question	What was the occasion for your eating your first hamburger?	Who can remember the answer? Does it matter?
Two questions in one	Do you eat Wendy's hamburgers and chili? ☐ Yes ☐ No	How do you answer if you eat Wendy's hamburgers but not chili?
Nonexhaustive question	Where do you live? ☐ At home ☐ In dormitory	What do you check if you live in an apartment?
Nonmutually exclusive answers	What is your age? ☐ Under 20 ☐ 20-40 ☐ 40 and over	What answer does a 40-year-old check?

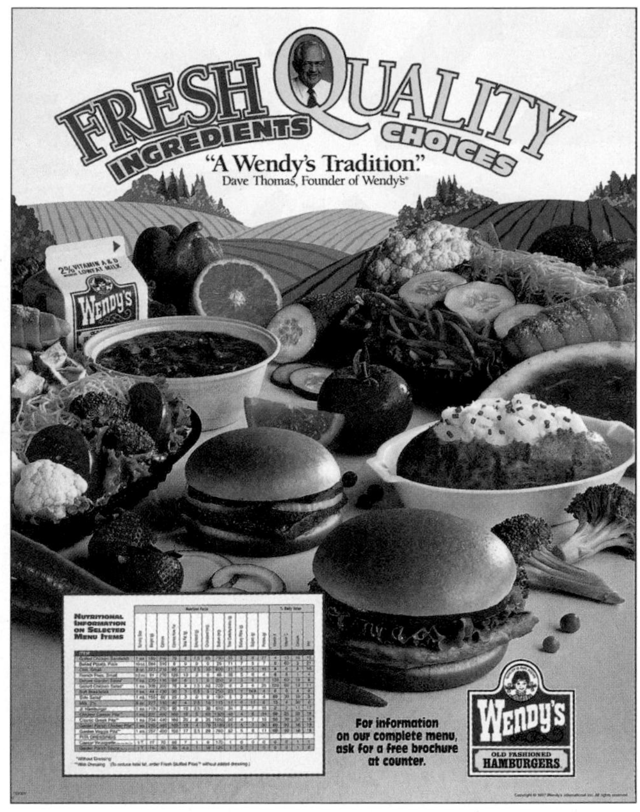

Wendy's changes continuously in response to changing customer wants, while keeping its "Fresh Ingredients, Quality Choices" image.

Wendy's Restaurant
www.wendys.com

at fast-food restaurants regularly, the word regularly is ambiguous. Two people might answer "yes" to the question, but one might mean "once a day" while the other means "once or twice a year." Both answers appear as "yes" to the researcher who tabulates them, but they suggest that dramatically different marketing actions be directed to each of these two prospective consumers. Therefore, it is essential that marketing research questions be worded precisely so that all respondents interpret the same question similarly. Marketing researchers must also take great care not to use "leading" questions (wording questions in a way to ensure a particular response), which can lead to a very distorted picture of the respondents' actual feelings or opinions.

In Figure 9–6 we can see the number of different formats that questions can take in a survey instrument. The questions presented are taken from a Wendy's survey that assessed fast-food preferences among present and prospective consumers. Question 1 is an example of an *open-end question,* which the respondent can answer in his or her own words. In contrast, questions in which the respondent simply checks an answer are *closed-end* or *fixed alternative questions.* Question 2 is an example of the simplest fixed alternative question, a *dichotomous question* that allows only a "yes" or "no" answer. A fixed alternative question with three or more choices uses a scale. Question 5 is an example of a question that uses a *semantic differential scale,* a seven-point scale in which the opposite ends have one- or two-word adjectives that have opposite meanings. For example, depending on how clean the respondent feels that Wendy's is, he or she would check the left-hand space on the scale, the right-hand space, or one of the five intervening points. Question 6 uses a *Likert scale,* in which the respondent is asked to indicate the extent to which he or she agrees or disagrees with a statement.

FIGURE 9–6
Sample questions from Wendy's survey

1 What things are most important to you when you decide to eat out and go to a restaurant?

____

____

____

____

____

____

2 Have you eaten fast-food restaurant food in the past three months?
☐ Yes ☐ No

3 If you answered "yes" to Question 2, how often do you eat fast food?
☐ Once a week or more ☐ Two or three times a month ☐ Once a month or less

4 How important is it to you that a fast-food restaurant satisfy you on the following characteristics? Check the box that describes your feelings.

CHARACTERISTIC	VERY IMPORTANT	SOMEWHAT IMPORTANT	IMPORTANT	UNIMPORTANT	SOMEWHAT UNIMPORTANT	VERY UNIMPORTANT
Taste of food	☐	☐	☐	☐	☐	☐
Cleanliness	☐	☐	☐	☐	☐	☐
Price	☐	☐	☐	☐	☐	☐
Variety on menu	☐	☐	☐	☐	☐	☐

5 Check the space on the scale below that describes how you feel about Wendy's on the characteristics shown.

CHARACTERISTIC	CHECK THE SPACE DESCRIBING HOW WENDY'S IS		
Taste of food	Tasty	_ _ _ _ _ _ _ _ _	Not tasty
Cleanliness	Clean	_ _ _ _ _ _ _ _ _	Not clean
Price	Inexpensive	_ _ _ _ _ _ _ _ _	Expensive
Variety on menu	Wide	_ _ _ _ _ _ _ _ _	Narrow

The questionnaire in Figure 9–6 is an excerpt of a precisely worded survey that provides valuable information to the marketing researcher at Wendy's. Questions 1 to 8 inform him or her about the likes and dislikes in eating out, frequency of eating out at fast-food restaurants generally and at Wendy's specifically, and sources of information used in making decisions about fast-food restaurants. Question 9 gives details about the personal characteristics of the respondent's household, which can be used in trying to segment the fast-food market, a topic discussed in Chapter 10.

Surveys of distributors—retailers and wholesalers in the marketing channel—are also very important for manufacturers. A reason given for the success of many Japanese consumer products in Canada such as Sony Walkmans and Toyota automobiles, is the stress that Japanese marketers place on obtaining accurate information from their distributors.

www.labatt.com

Electronic technology has revolutionized the traditional concept of surveys.[16] Today, respondents can walk up to a kiosk in a shopping centre, read questions off a screen, and key their answers into a computer on a touch screen. Labatt Breweries Ltd. uses an interactive kiosk in the shape of a beer can and rewards customers with coupons as a

FIGURE 9–6
(concluded)

6 Check the box that describes your agreement with the statement.

STATEMENT	STRONGLY AGREE	AGREE	DON'T KNOW	DISAGREE	STRONGLY DISAGREE
Adults like to take their families to fast-food restaurants.	☐	☐	☐	☐	☐
Our children have a say in where the family eats.	☐	☐	☐	☐	☐

7 How important is this information about fast-food restaurants?

SOURCE OF INFORMATION	VERY IMPORTANT SOURCE	SOMEWHAT IMPORTANT SOURCE	NOT AN IMPORTANT SOURCE
Television	☐	☐	☐
Newspapers	☐	☐	☐
Billboards	☐	☐	☐
Mail	☐	☐	☐

8 In the past three months, how often have you eaten at each of these three fast-food restaurants?

RESTAURANT	ONCE A WEEK OR MORE	TWO OR THREE TIMES A MONTH	ONCE A MONTH OR LESS
Burger King	☐	☐	☐
McDonald's	☐	☐	☐
Wendy's	☐	☐	☐

9 Please answer the following questions about you and your household.

a Are you ☐ Male ☐ Female

b Are you ☐ Single ☐ Married ☐ Other (widowed, divorced)

c How many children under age 18 live in your home?
☐ 0 ☐ 1 ☐ 2 ☐ 3 ☐ 4 ☐ 5 or more

d What is your age?
☐ 24 or under ☐ 25-39 ☐ 40 or over

e What is your approximate total annual household income?
☐ Less than $15 000 ☐ $15 000-$30 000 ☐ More than $30 000

thank-you for completing an electronic survey.[17] Even fully automated systems exist for conducting surveys by telephone. An automated voice questions respondents over the telephone, who key their replies on a touch-tone telephone.

Experiment

Another method that can be used by marketing researchers to generate primary data is the experiment. Marketing experiments offer the potential for establishing cause-and-effect relationships (causal research). An **experiment** involves the manipulation of an independent variable (cause) and the measurement of its effect on the dependent variable (effect) under controlled conditions.

In marketing experiments the independent variables are often one or more of the marketing mix variables, such as product features, price, or promotion used. An ideal dependent variable usually is a change in purchases of an individual, household, or entire organization. If actual purchases cannot be used as a dependent variable, factors that are believed to be highly related to purchases, such as preferences in a taste test or intentions to buy, are used.

A successful test market led to the national rollout of Shoppers Drug Mart's Life brand cola.

A potential difficulty with experiments is that an extraneous (or outside) variable can distort the results of an experiment and affect the dependent variable.

Experiments can be conducted in the field or in a laboratory. In *field experiments,* the research is conducted in the real world such as in a store, bank or on the street, wherever the behaviour being studied occurs naturally. Field experiments can be expensive but are a good way to determine people's reactions to changes in the elements of the marketing mix. Test marketing is probably the most common form of field experiments. Shoppers Drug Mart used taste tests in the field to determine how consumers felt about its Life Brand Cola, compared to the national brands such as Pepsi and Coke. The tests revealed that 33 percent of the consumers who participated liked Life Brand better than the competitive colas. Shoppers Drug Mart then put the product on the shelves of stores in Atlantic Canada to test the market's response to the product. A successful test market there led to a national rollout of the product in Shoppers stores across Canada.[18] Remember your problem as marketing manager for cranberry juice at Ocean Spray? You wanted to know if Asian consumers would buy cranberry juice when they had never tasted cranberries? Perhaps your marketing research colleague might recommend taste tests in Asia to gauge consumers' responses to the product.

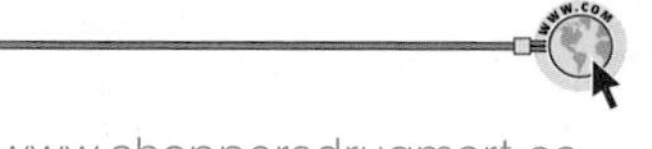

www.shoppersdrugmart.ca

Because marketers cannot control all the conditions in the field, they sometimes turn to a laboratory setting. Laboratories are not the real world but do offer highly controlled environments. Unlike in the field, the marketer has control over all the factors that may play a role in impacting on the behaviour under investigation. For example, in a field experiment the marketer may wish to examine the impact of a price reduction on sales of a particular product. The competition, however, may see the price reduction and offer their own price deal, thus interfering with the possible results of the field experiment. This does not occur in a lab setting. Many companies are using laboratory settings where they can control conditions but can do so in a real-world fashion such as simulated supermarkets or test stores. Here they can experiment with changes in isle displays, packaging changes or other variables that may affect buyer behaviour without the fear of other extraneous factors influencing the results.

Observation

Another basic research method used to obtain primary data is observation. In general, **observation** involves watching, either mechanically or in person, how people behave. In some circumstances, the speed of events or the number of events being observed make mechanical or electronic observation more appropriate than personal observation. Retailers, for example, can use electronic cameras to count the number of customers entering or leaving a store.

A classic form of mechanical observation is A. C. Nielsen's "people meter," which is attached to television sets in selected households in Canada and the United States in order

How can Fisher-Price do marketing research on young children who can't even fill out a questionnaire? For the answer, see the text.

Fisher-Price
www.fisherprice.com

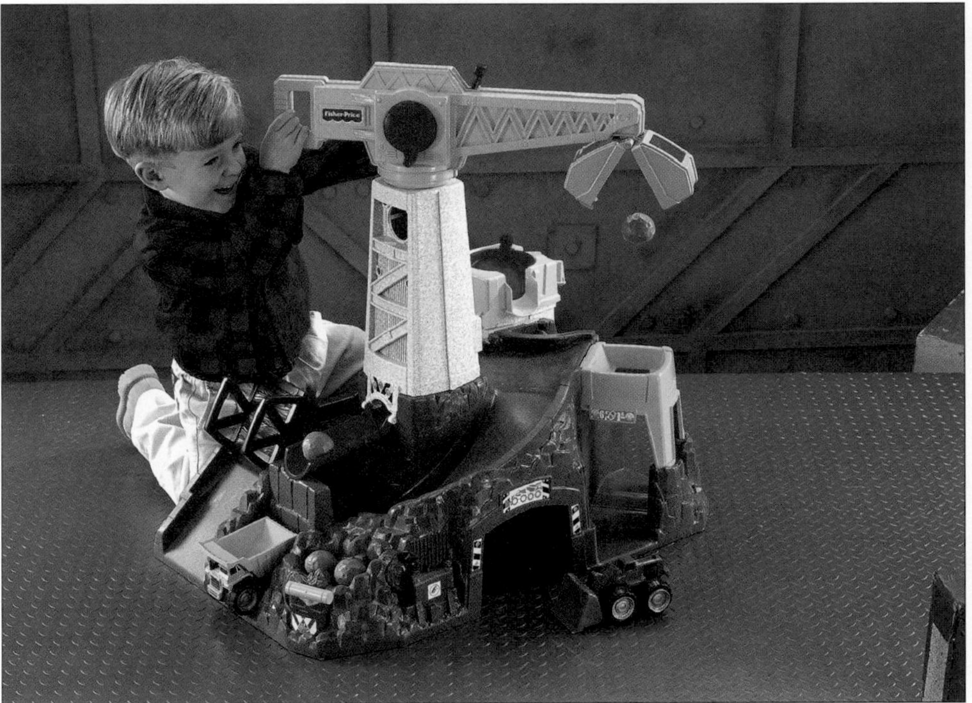

to determine the size of audiences watching television programs delivered by the networks. When a household member watches TV, he or she is supposed to push a button on the box and push it again when viewing stops. The people meter is supposed to measure who in the household is watching what program on every TV set owned.

But people meters have limitations—as with all observational data collected mechanically. Critics aren't so sure the devices are measuring what they are supposed to. They are concerned that household members, especially teenagers and the elderly, find it annoying to hit the button every time they start or stop watching TV. A "passive people meter" is now being tested that can be worn on a pin or watch to measure both TV viewing and radio listening at home, at work, or in the car and is intended to address some of the concerns about the traditional people meter.[19]

www.pg.com

Marketers also rely on personal observations to collect primary data. For example, Proctor & Gamble observes how consumers bake cakes in its Duncan Hines kitchens to see if the baking instructions on the cake mix box are understood and followed correctly. Chrysler watches how drivers sit behind the wheel of a car to see if they can turn or operate the radio and air-conditioning buttons easily. Fisher-Price uses its licensed nursery schools to observe children use and abuse toys in order to develop better products.

Personal observation is both useful and flexible, but it can be costly and unreliable, especially when different observers report different conclusions in watching the same activities. Also, although observation can reveal what people do, it cannot determine why they do it, such as why they are buying or not buying a product. To determine why consumers behave as they do, marketing researchers must talk with consumers and record their responses. This is usually accomplished through the use of surveys.

Is There an Optimal Research Design?

In short, there is no optimal research design. A researcher may choose among a variety of alternative methods for solving a particular marketing problem. A good marketing researcher understands that there is likely to be more than one way to tackle the problem. The ability to select the most appropriate research design develops with experience.

Inexperienced researchers often embrace the survey method as the best design because they are most familiar with this method. More experienced researchers, on the other hand, recognize the value of other methods and can often put together creative research designs that can solve marketing problems more quickly and less expensively. Experienced researchers often note that proper definition of the marketing plays a central role in determining the most appropriate research design.

Sampling

Although sampling is an inherent component of the research design stage, it is a distinctive aspect of the research process. The researcher's sampling plan indicates who is to be sampled, how large a sample is needed, and how sampling units will be selected. Rarely does a research project involve a complete census of every person in the research population. This is because of the time and cost involved in conducting a census. Thus, sampling is used. **Sampling** is the process of gathering data from a proportion of the total population rather than from all members (census) of that particular population. A *sample,* then, is a subset from a larger population.

If proper statistical procedures are followed, a researcher does not need to select every member in a population, because a properly selected sample should be representative of the population as a whole. However, errors can and do occur in sampling and thus the reliability of the data obtained through sampling can sometimes become an issue. Thus, the first and most critical sampling question for researchers to ask is: Who is to be sampled?

Another key question concerns the sample size: How big should the sample be? As mentioned, it is usually unrealistic to expect a census of the research population be conducted. In general, larger samples are more precise than smaller ones, but proper sampling can allow a smaller proportion of the total population to provide a reliable measure of the whole.

The final question in the sampling plan concerns how to select the sampling units. There are two basic sampling techniques: probability and nonprobability sampling. **Probability sampling** involves precise rules to select the sample such that each element of the population has a specific known chance of being selected. For example, if your university wants to know how last year's 1000 graduates are doing, it can put their names in a bowl and randomly select 100 names of graduates to contact. The chance of being selected—100/1000 or 0.10—is known in advance, and all graduates have an equal chance of being contacted. This procedure helps select a sample (100 graduates) that should be representative of the entire population (the 1000 graduates) and allows conclusions to be drawn about the entire population.

Nonprobability sampling involves the use of arbitrary judgment by the marketing researcher to select the sample so that the chance of selecting a particular element of the population is either unknown or zero. If your university decided to talk to 100 of last year's graduates but only those who lived closest to the university, many class members would be arbitrarily eliminated. This has introduced a bias, or possible lack of representativeness, which may make it dangerous to draw conclusions about the entire population of the graduating class. Nonprobability samples are often used when time and budgets are limited and are most often used for exploratory research purposes. In general, marketing researchers use data from such samples with caution.

CONCEPT CHECK

1. What is a survey?
2. Which research method offers the potential for establishing cause-and-effect relationships?
3. What is sampling?

DATA COLLECTION AND ANALYSIS

Once the research design has been formalized, the process of gathering or collecting data begins. Sometimes referred to as fieldwork, data collection at this stage of the research process includes all the activities that the researcher (and staff) undertakes, to obtain data from the identified sources or respondents. Since there are several research methods that could be used by the researcher, this means there may be multiple ways to collect the data. For example, with the survey method, data may be collected by telephone, mail, or personal interview.

However the data are collected, it is important to minimize errors in the process. Most research experts agree that the data collection stage of the research process is one of the major sources of error in marketing research. Some of the errors that occur are a result of a variety of problems ranging from failure to select the right respondents to incorrect recording of observations. Competent and well-trained researchers inside the organization or those employed by outside research companies can go a long way in ensuring proper data collection.

The next step for the marketing researcher is data analysis. Mark Twain once observed, "Collecting data is like collecting garbage. You've got to know what you're going to do with the stuff before you collect it." In essence, the marketing researcher must know *why* the data are being collected and *how* to analyze it effectively in order for it to have any value in decision making.

The level of analysis conducted on the data depends on the nature of the research and the information needed to provide a solution to the marketing problem. For survey data, frequency analysis is completed—calculating the responses question by question. The researcher may then wish to identify patterns in the data or examine how data pertaining to some questions may relate to data obtained from asking other questions. Probably the most widely used technique for organizing and analyzing marketing data is cross-tabulation. This method is particularly useful for market segmentation analysis and is discussed in Chapter 10.

CONCLUSIONS AND REPORT

At this stage of the process, the marketing researcher, often in conjunction with marketing management, must review the analysis and ask: What does this information tell us? A critical aspect of the marketing researcher's job is to interpret the information and make conclusions with regard to managerial decision making. The researcher must prepare a report to communicate the research findings. Included in this report should be suggestions for actions which might be taken by the organization to solve the marketing problem.

The researcher must be careful not to overwhelm management with technical terminology. Rather the report should highlight in a clear and concise manner the important results and conclusions. Ultimately, the marketing researcher and management must work closely together to ensure proper interpretation of the research results. In addition, management must make a commitment to act—to make decisions based on the research and their good judgment and knowledge of the situation. In other words, someone must "make something happen" to see that a solution to the marketing problems gets implemented. Failure to act on the research findings creates an appearance that the marketing research effort is of little value. Finally, once implemented, the proposed solution should be monitored to ensure intended results do occur.

ETHICAL ISSUES IN THE MARKETING RESEARCH PROCESS

Ethical issues can arise in marketing researchers' relationships with all parties involved in the research process, including respondents, the general public, their organizations, and/or their clients. Professional marketing researchers must make ethical decisions

ETHICS

ETHICS AND SOCIAL RESPONSIBILITY ALERT

What is "Truth" in Reporting Survey Results?

Doctors were surveyed to find out what brand of butter substitute they recommend for their patients concerned about cholesterol. The results:

- Recommend no particular brand: 80%
- Recommend Brand A: 5%
- Recommend Brand B: 4%

No other brand is recommended by more than 2 percent of the doctors. The firm owning brand A runs an ad that states: "More doctors recommend brand A than any other brand." Is this ethical? Why or why not? What kind of ethical guideline, if any, should be used to address this issue?

regarding the collecting, using, and reporting of research data. Examples of unethical behaviour include failure to report problems with research results because of incomplete data, reporting only favourable but not unfavourable results, using deception to collect information, and breaching the confidentiality of respondents and/or their personal data if anonymity or nondisclosure was guaranteed.[20] The Ethics and Social Responsibility Alert box shows a classic example of an ethical issue in marketing research, the incomplete reporting of data collected.[21] Also, as you read in Chapter 8, many companies collect clickstream data on consumers when those consumers visit their web sites and sometimes use this data for marketing purposes without the knowledge and consent of the consumer.

www.camro.org

Using formal statements on ethical policies and instituting rewards and punishments can help ensure that ethical behaviour is the norm in marketing research. For example, the Professional Marketing Research Society of Canada (PMRS) and the Canadian Association of Marketing Research Organizations (CAMRO) have codes of ethics or rules of conduct to which their members must adhere. However, unethical or inappropriate behaviour by individuals or organizations cannot be regulated away. As mentioned in Chapter 4, ethical behaviour rests with the individual, but the consequences affect many.

INFORMATION TECHNOLOGY AND MARKETING ACTIONS

Today's marketing managers can be drowned in such a flood of information that they have difficulty making effective, timely decisions. The solution: Find ways to manage the information properly. While a decade ago managers talked about "manufacturing information systems" or "marketing information systems," the lines of separation of information among the various departments in a firm are now disappearing. So today, all generally fall under the broader term of **information technology,** which involves designing and managing computer and communication networks to provide an information system to satisfy an organization's needs for data storage, processing, and access.

Key Elements of an Information System Figure 9–7 shows how marketing researchers and managers use information technology to frame questions that provide answers that enable them to take marketing actions. At the bottom of Figure 9–7 the marketer queries the databases in the information system with marketing questions needing answers. These questions go through models of the relationships among the data contained in the databases to be able to access the key bits of information needed. The

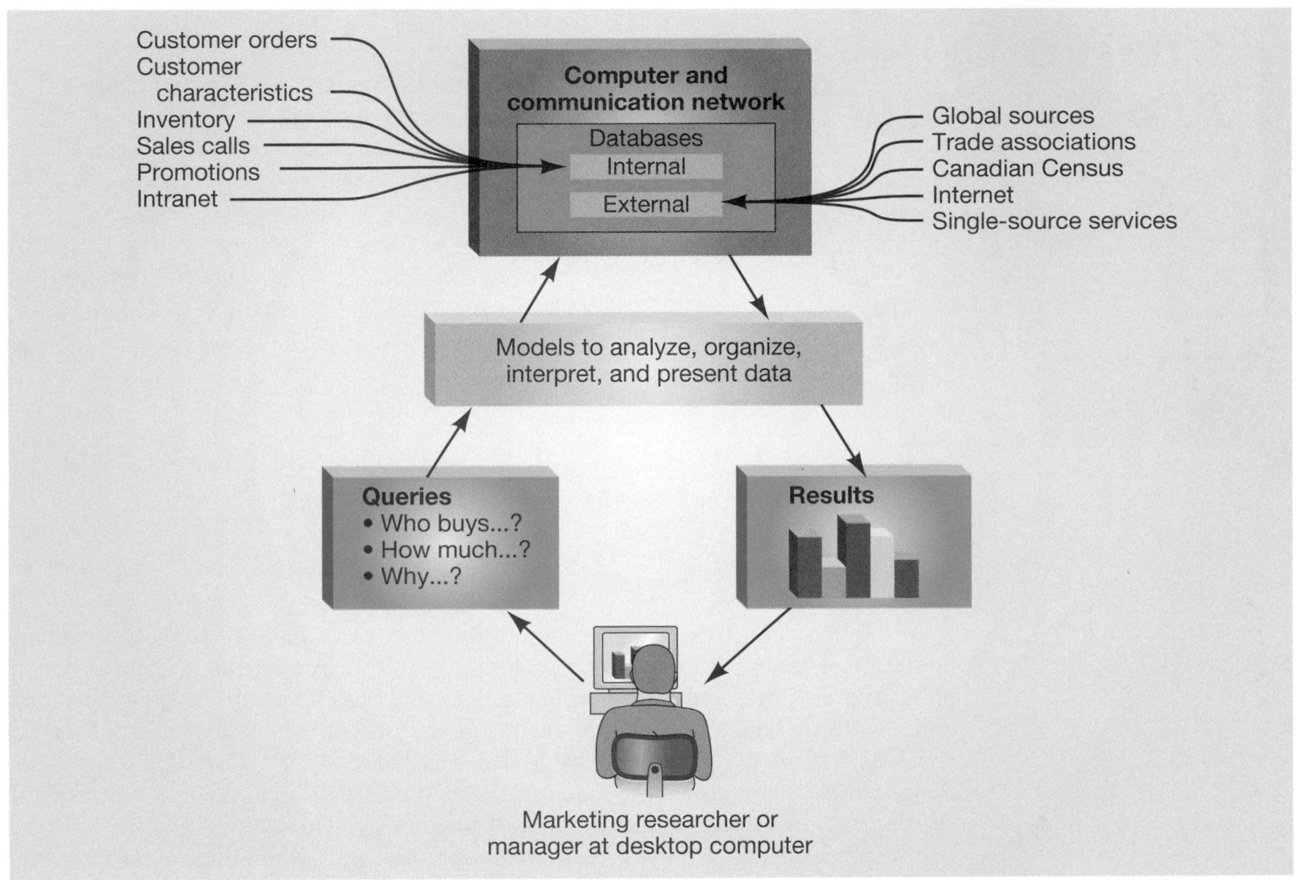

FIGURE 9–7
How marketing researchers and managers use information technology to turn information into action

databases form the core of the computer and communication networks that collect and store millions of bits of information. These databases range from internal sources like customer orders and characteristics to external ones that are available from the Internet, Statistics Canada, and trade associations. After the search of the databases, the models select the pertinent data—often summarizing them in tables and graphics for easy interpretation.

Querying the Information System What kind of questions might the marketer ask the information system? Here are some examples:

1. What are the demographic characteristics of our present customers?
2. How do these demographic characteristics vary by kind of product purchased from our line?
3. What kinds of TV programs and magazines do these customers watch or read?
4. If we advertise on a specific TV program, how many of our existing customers and prospective new ones are we likely to reach?
5. What incremental sales revenue can we expect from this TV ad?

Note that these questions are progressively more complex and move subtly from asking questions about known facts to making sophisticated "what if" projections. For example, the first two questions have exact answers that are available from the firm's internal records. The third question may require calculating the relationship between data in different databases. The last two questions require making assumptions to build hypothetical models about the relationships between different marketing variables—models that are self-correcting as new data become available.

An information system such as this permits a marketing manager to reach decisions using *sensitivity analysis,* asking "what if" questions to determine how changes in a factor such as price or advertising affect marketing results such as sales revenues or profits.[22]

Peopleless Marketing Actions With today's information systems, some marketing actions require a lot of people input. Other actions require almost none. Catalogue companies such as Lands' End, Fingerhut, and Spiegel use sophisticated "data mining"—hunting through the computer databases for tiny nuggets of information about customers—to reach them more efficiently. For example, Fingerhut studies about 3500 variables over the lifetime of a consumer's relationship; it found that customers who had changed residences are three times as likely as regular customers to buy tables, fax machines, and decorative products but no more likely to buy jewellery or footwear. So Fingerhut has created a catalogue targeted at consumers who have recently moved—a somewhat people-intensive marketing action.[23]

Today's information technology and systems have also made some marketing actions possible with almost no people involved. For example, "mass customization" has enabled Levi's retail clerks to ask a customer a few questions, take computer measurements, and deliver a personal pair of jeans in about three weeks. Custom Foot retail outlets do the same for shoes—requiring a lot of computer power and only a little people power.[24] And you can place an Internet order for your preferred configuration of a Dell computer that goes directly to its production line, resulting in the delivery of this computer within a week—all with few Dell marketers involved.

MARKET AND SALES FORECASTING

Forecasting or estimating the actual size of a market is often a key goal in a marketing research study. Good sales forecasts are important for a firm as it schedules production.[25] We will discuss (1) some basic forecasting terms, (2) two major approaches to forecasting, and (3) specific forecasting techniques.

Basic Forecasting Terms

Unfortunately, there are no standard definitions for some forecasting concepts, so it's necessary to take care in defining the terms used.

Market or Industry Potential The term **market potential,** or **industry potential,** refers to the maximum total sales of a product by all firms to a segment under specified environmental conditions and marketing efforts of the firms. For example, the market potential for cake mix sales to Canadian consumers in 2003 might be two million cases—what Pillsbury, Betty Crocker, Duncan Hines, and other cake mix producers would sell to Canadian consumers under the assumptions that (1) past patterns of dessert consumption continue and (2) the same level of promotional effort continues relative to other desserts. If one of these assumptions proves false, the estimate of market potential will be wrong. For example, if Canadian consumers suddenly become more concerned about eating refined sugar and shift their dessert preferences from cakes to fresh fruits, the estimate of market potential will be too high.

Sales or Company Forecast What one firm expects to sell under specified conditions for the uncontrollable and controllable factors that affect the forecast is the **sales forecast,** or **company forecast.** For example, Duncan Hines might develop its sales forecast of one million cases of cake mix for Canadian consumers in 2003, assuming past dessert preferences continue and the same relative level of promotional expenditures among it, Pillsbury, and Betty Crocker. If Betty Crocker suddenly cuts its promotional spending in half, Duncan Hines' old sales forecast will probably be too low.

FIGURE 9–8
Percentage of Canadian population, personal income, and retail sales in selected provinces, 1999

	POPULATION	PERSONAL INCOME	RETAIL SALES
PROVINCES	% OF CDN. TOTAL	% OF CDN. TOTAL	% OF CDN. TOTAL
Newfoundland	1.8	1.3	1.6
Quebec	24.2	21.7	23.1
Ontario	37.7	40.6	37.5
British Columbia	13.2	12.8	13.4

With both market potential estimates and sales forecasts, it is necessary to specify some significant details: the product involved (all cake mixes, only white cake mixes, or only Bundt cakes mixes); the time period (month, quarter, or year); the segment (Canada, Western Canada, upper-income buyer, or single-person households); controllable marketing factors (price and level of promotional support); uncontrollable factors (consumer tastes and actions of competitors); and the units of measurement (number of cases sold or total sales revenues).

Two Basic Approaches to Forecasting

A marketing manager rarely wants a single number for an annual forecast, such as 5000 units or $75 million in sales revenue. Rather the manager wants this total subdivided into elements the manager works with, such as sales by product line or sales by market segment. The two basic approaches to sales forecasting are (1) subdividing the total sales forecast (top-down forecast) or (2) building the total sales forecast by summing up the components (buildup forecast).

Top-down Forecast A **top-down forecast** involves subdividing an aggregate forecast into its principal components. A shoe manufacturer can use a top-down forecast to estimate the percentage of total shoe sales in a province and develop province-by-province forecasts for shoe sales for the coming year. *Canadian Markets,* published by the Financial Post, and *Sales and Marketing Management* magazine are sources that are widely used for top-down forecasting information.

For example, as shown in Figure 9–8, the province of Ontario has 37.7 percent of the Canadian population, 40.6 percent of the personal income in Canada, and 37.5 percent of Canadian retail sales.[26] If the shoe manufacturers wanted to use a single factor related to expected shoe sales, it would choose the factor that has been closely related to shoe sales historically, in this case the percentage of Canadian retail sales found in Ontario. The top-down forecast would then be that 37.5 percent of the firm's sales would be made in the province of Ontario.

A single factor is rarely a true indicator of sales opportunity in a given market. So, sometimes multiple factors are considered when making forecasts. The Buying Power Index (BPI) developed by *Sales and Marketing Management* magazine gives weights of 0.2, 0.5, and 0.3, respectively, to the three previously mentioned factors, as follows.

$$\begin{aligned} \text{BPI} &= (0.2 \times \text{Percentage of national population in area}) + (0.5 \times \text{Percentage of national personal income in area}) + (0.3 \times \text{Percentage of national retail sales in area}) \\ &= (0.2 \times 37.7) + (0.5 \times 40.6) + (0.3 \times 37.5) \\ &= 7.54 + 20.30 + 11.25 \\ &= 39.1 = 39.1\% \end{aligned}$$

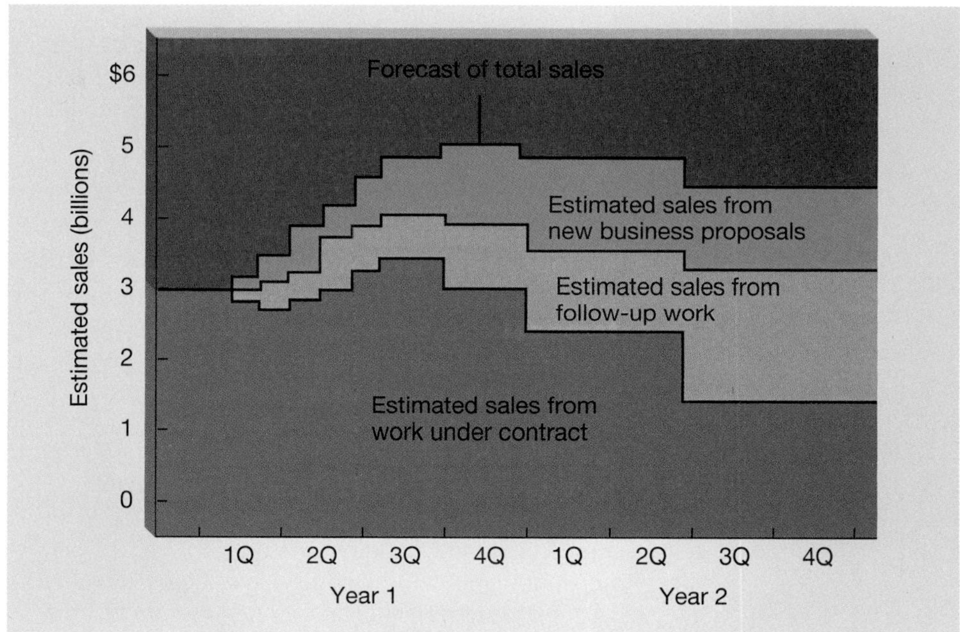

FIGURE 9–9
Buildup approach to a two-year sales forecast for Boeing's aerospace department

Thus, the BPI forecasts that 39.1 percent of the firm's shoe sales will occur in Ontario, which is higher than if retail sales alone were used for the forecast. A marketer could also obtain data on retail sales and family expenditures from Statistics Canada and use this information to make sales forecasts.

Buildup Forecast A **buildup forecast** involves summing the sales forecasts of each of the components to arrive at the total forecast. It is a widely used method when there are identifiable components such as products, product lines, or market segments in the forecasting problem.

Figure 9–9 shows how Boeing's aerospace department uses the buildup approach to develop a sales forecast involving three broad categories of projects or products: (1) work currently under contract that can be forecast precisely, (2) follow-up work that is likely to result from current contracts, and (3) new business that results from Boeing's proposals for new business, which is difficult to forecast. Each of these three forecasts is the sum of a number of individual products or projects, which for simplicity are not shown. In turn, forecasts for each of the three kinds of business can be summed to give the total sales forecast for the entire department. Increasingly, with more detailed information available on all customers and segments in given markets, annual forecasting for Canadian firms has been transformed from a top-down forecast to a more buildup-oriented process.[27]

Specific Sales Forecasting Techniques

Broadly speaking, three main sales forecasting techniques are available that can lead to the forecasts used in the top-down or buildup approaches. Ordered from least costly in terms of both time and money to most costly, these are (1) judgments of the decision maker, (2) surveys of knowledgeable groups, and (3) statistical methods.

Judgments of the Decision Maker Probably 99.9 percent of all sales forecasts are judgments of the person who must act on the results of the forecast—the individual decision maker. An example is the forecasts of likely sales, and hence the quantity to order, for the 13 000 items stocked in a typical supermarket that must be forecast by the stock clerk or manager. A **direct forecast** involves estimating the value to be forecast without any intervening steps. Examples appear in your daily life: How many litres of milk should I buy? How much time should I allow to drive to the game? How much money should I get out of the automated teller machine? Your mind may go through some intervening steps but so quickly you're unaware of it.

So in estimating the amount of money to get from the automated teller machine, you probably made some unconscious (or conscious) intervening estimates (such as counting the cash in your pocket or the special events you need cash for) to obtain your direct estimate. Lost-horse forecasting does this in a more structured way. A **lost-horse forecast** involves starting with the last known value of the item being forecast, listing the factors that could affect the forecast, assessing whether they have a positive or negative impact, and making the final forecast. The technique gets its name from how you'd find a lost horse: go to where it was last seen, put yourself in its shoes, consider those factors that could affect where you might go (to the pond if you're thirsty, the hayfield if you're hungry, and so on), and go there. For example, a product manager for Wilson's tennis rackets in 1998 who needed to make a sales forecast through 2000 would start with the known value of 1998 sales and list the positive factors (more tennis courts, more TV publicity) and the negative ones (competition from other sports, high prices of graphite and ceramic rackets) to arrive at the final series of annual sales forecasts.

Surveys of Knowledgeable Groups If you wonder what your firm's sales will be next year, ask people who are likely to know something about future sales. Four common groups that are surveyed to develop sales forecasts are prospective buyers, the firm's salesforce, its executives, and experts.

A **survey of buyers' intentions forecast** involves asking prospective customers whether they are likely to buy the product during some future time period. For industrial products with few prospective buyers who are able and willing to predict their future buying behaviour, this can be effective. For example, there are probably only a few hundred customers in the entire world for Boeing's largest airplanes, so Boeing simply surveys these prospects to develop its sales forecasts and production schedules.

A **salesforce survey forecast** involves asking the firm's salespeople to estimate sales during a coming period. Because these people are in contact with customers and are likely to know what customers like and dislike, there is logic to this approach. However, salespeople can be unreliable forecasters—painting too rosy a picture if they are enthusiastic about a new product and too grim a forecast if their sales quota is based on it.

A **jury of executive opinion forecast** involves asking knowledgeable executives inside the firm—such as vice presidents of marketing, research and development, finance, and production—about likely sales during a coming period. Although this approach is fast and includes judgments from diverse functional areas, it can be biased by a dominant executive whose judgments are deferred to by the others. Also, the technique raises questions about how valuable judgments are from executives who rarely come in contact with customers—such as vice presidents of finance and production.

A **survey of experts forecast** involves asking experts on a topic to make a judgment about some future event. For example, 20 electronics and TV experts might be asked when a 25-inch high-definition television (HDTV) set might sell to consumers for less than $1000. One form of a survey of experts forecast is a *technological forecast,* which involves estimating when breakthroughs in basic science will occur. In 1963, experts used a technological forecast to estimate the year by which a limited degree of weather control would occur. Their estimate: 1990! While this technological forecast looks silly today, the technique is valuable in helping managers make new product development decisions.

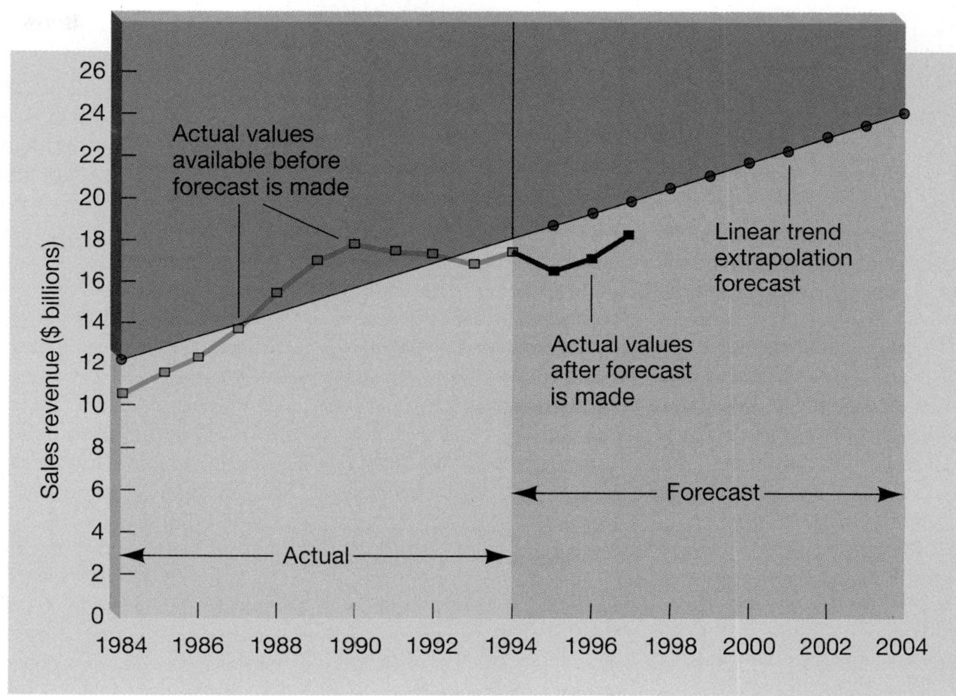

FIGURE 9–10
Linear trend extrapolation of sales revenues of Xerox, made at the start of 1995

www.xerox.com

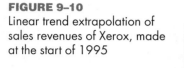

Statistical Methods The best-known statistical method of forecasting is **trend extrapolation,** which involves extending a pattern observed in past data into the future. When the pattern is described with a straight line, it is *linear trend extrapolation.* Suppose that in early 1995 you were a sales forecaster for the Xerox Corporation and had actual sales revenues running from 1984 to 1994 (Figure 9–10). Using linear trend extrapolation, you draw a line to fit the past data and project it into the future to give the forecast values shown for 1995 to 2004.

If in 1997 you want to compare your forecasts with actual results, you are in for a surprise—illustrating the strength and weakness of trend extrapolation. Trend extrapolation assumes that the underlying relationships in the past will continue into the future, which is the basis of the method's key strength: simplicity. If this assumption proves correct, you have an accurate forecast. However, if this proves wrong, the forecast is likely to be wrong. In this case your forecasts from 1995 through 1997 were too high, largely because of fierce competition in the photocopying industry.

In practice, marketing managers often use several of the forecasting techniques to estimate the size of markets important to them. Also, they often do three separate forecasts based on different sets of assumptions: (1) "best case" with optimistic assumptions, (2) "worst case" with pessimistic ones, and (3) "most likely case" with most reasonable assumptions.

CONCEPT CHECK

1. What is the difference between the top-down and buildup approaches to forecasting sales?
2. How do you make a lost-horse forecast?
3. What is linear trend extrapolation?

SUMMARY

1 Marketing research is the process of defining a marketing problem or opportunity, systematically collecting and analyzing information, and recommending actions to improve an organization's marketing activities. Marketing research assists in decision making.

2 There are three basic types of marketing research: (1) exploratory research—preliminary research conducted to clarify the scope and nature of the marketing problem, (2) descriptive research—research designed to describe basic characteristics of a given population or to profile particular marketing situations, and (3) causal research—research designed to identify cause-and-effect relationships among variables.

3 All marketing research consists of four basic stages: (1) defining the problem, (2) determining the research design, (3) collecting and analyzing data, and (4) drawing conclusions and preparing a report.

4 The first stage of the marketing research process—problem definition—is critical since research based on incorrect problem definition will be a waste of resources.

5 If the researcher decides to conduct exploratory research in the early stages of the marketing research process, he or she has three basic techniques to choose from: (1) secondary data analysis, (2) focus groups, and (3) depth interviews.

6 Secondary data (or historical data) are data previously collected and assembled for some project other than the one at hand, whereas primary data are data gathered and assembled specifically for the project at hand.

7 At the formal research design stage, the researcher produces a plan that outlines the methods and procedures for collecting and analyzing the required information. The plan includes the objectives of the research; the sources of information to be used; the research methods; the sampling plan; and the schedule and cost of the research.

8 The basic methods the researcher can choose from for descriptive and causal research at the formal research design stage include: (1) survey, (2) experiment, and (3) observation. A survey is a research technique used to generate data by asking people questions and recording their responses on a questionnaire. An experiment involves the manipulation of an independent variable (cause) and measuring its effect on the dependent variable (effect) under controlled conditions. Observation involves watching, either mechanically or in person, how people actually behave.

9 Sampling—the process of gathering data from a proportion of the total population rather than from all members (census) of that particular population—is an inherent component of the research design stage. The researcher's sampling plan indicates who is to be sampled, how large a sample is needed, and how sampling units will be selected.

10 The third stage of the marketing research process is data collection and analysis. Sometimes referred to as fieldwork, data collection at this stage of the research process includes all the activities that the researcher (and staff) undertakes to obtain data from the identified sources or respondents. Once the data is collected, the marketing researcher must analyze and transform it into valuable information for decision making.

11 In the final stage of the process, the marketing researcher must take conclusions and prepare a research report. Included in this report should be suggestions for actions that might be taken by the organization that will solve the marketing problem.

12 Professional marketing researchers have to make ethical decisions in the collecting, using and reporting of research.

13 Information technology enables massive amounts of marketing data to be stored, processed, and accessed. Today's information systems can be queried to guide decisions and even programmed to make ordering decisions.

14 Two basic approaches to forecasting sales are the top-down and buildup methods. Three forecasting techniques are judgments of individuals, surveys of knowledgeable groups, and statistical methods.

KEY TERMS AND CONCEPTS

marketing research p. 223
secondary data p. 227
primary data p. 227
focus groups p. 228
depth interviews p. 229
survey p. 232
experiment p. 236
observation p. 237
sampling p. 239
probability sampling p. 239
nonprobability sampling p. 239
information technology p. 241
market or industry potential p. 243
sales or company forecast p. 243
top-down forecast p. 244
buildup forecast p. 245
direct forecast p. 246
lost-horse forecast p. 246
survey of buyers' intentions forecast p. 246
salesforce survey forecast p. 246
jury of executive opinion forecast p. 246
survey of experts forecast p. 246
trend extrapolation p. 247

INTERNET EXERCISE

WorldOpinion calls its Web site "the world's market research Web site." To check out the latest marketing research news, jobs that are available, and details of more than 8500 research locations in 99 countries, go to www.worldopinion.com and do the following:

1 Click on the "Latest research news" banner on WorldOpinion's home page to read about the current news and issues facing the market research industry. Then, click on a topic of interest under "This week's news."

2 Under the "Research resources" banner, click on the "Links to major researchers' sites" link. Scroll down the Web page to obtain information on the following market research firms:

a. Click on the "Gallup" link to go to its home page. Then, click on the link that is specified to find out how The Gallup Organization conducts its polls.

b. Click on the "Abt Associates, Inc." and "Market Facts, Inc." links (or other firms of interest) to identify the market research positions currently available.

APPLYING MARKETING CONCEPTS AND PERSPECTIVES

1 Is it possible to make effective marketing decisions without marketing research?

2 Why is the problem definition stage of the marketing research process probably the most important stage?

3 You plan to open an ice-cream shop in your town. What type of exploratory research would you conduct to help determine its feasibility? You find the exploratory research doesn't answer all your questions. You decide to do a survey to determine whether you should open the shop. What kind of questions will you ask? Who do you ask?

4 Suppose you are trying to determine the top three favourite department stores in your area. You show customers at a shopping mall a list of department stores and ask them to rank their three favourite stores from 1 to 3 (with 1 being the favourite). What problems can go wrong with the survey?

5 Your university bookstore wants to find out how students feel about the store's merchandise, prices, and customer service. What type of marketing research would you recommend to the store?

6 Before the people meter, Nielson obtained TV rating data by using "audimeters" attached to TV sets. These devices measured (1) if the TV set was turned on and (2) if so, to which channel. What are the limitations of this mechanical observation method?

7 You are a marketing researcher observing what people do when selecting bread in a supermarket. You are behind a one-way mirror and none of the customers know they are being observed. During the course of the day, you observe several people shoplifting a smaller snack product near the bread section. You know personally two of the shoplifters you see. What are the ethical problems you face in this situation?

8 You plan to open a new rent-a-car business. You have drafted a survey you want to distribute to airline passengers. The survey will be left at the airports and respondents will mail the surveys back in a prepaid envelope. Some of the questions you plan to use are shown below. Use Figure 9-5 to (*a*) identify the problem with each question and (*b*) correct it. **Note:** Some questions may have more than one problem.

a. Do you own your own car or usually rent one? ____ Yes ____ No

b. What is your age? ____ 21–30 ____30–40 ____41–50 ____50+

c. How much did you spend on rental cars last year? ____$100 or less ____$101–$400 ____$401–$800 ____$800–$1000 ____$1000 or more

d. What is a good daily rental car rate? ________

9 Suppose you are to make a sales forecast using a top-down approach to estimate the percentage of a manufacturer's total Canadian sales going to each of the 10 provinces. You plan to use only a single factor—percentage of Canadian population, percentage of personal income, or percentage of retail sales. Which of the three factors would you use if your sales forecast were for each of the following manufacturers, and why? (*a*) Sifto salt, (*b*) Christian Dior dresses, and (*c*) Columbia records.

10 Which of the following variables would linear trend extrapolation be more accurate for? (*a*) Annual population of Canada or (*b*) annual sales of cars produced in Canada by General Motors. Why?

CASE 9–1 BOOKWORMS, INC.

Late one August morning, Nancy Klein, co-owner of Bookworms, Inc., sat at her desk near the back wall of a cluttered office. With some irritation, she had just concluded that her nearby calculator could help no more. "What we still need," she thought to herself, "are estimates of demand and market share . . . but at least we have two weeks to get them."

Klein's office was located in the rear of Bookworms, Inc., an 1800-square-metre bookstore specializing in quality paperbacks. The store carries more than 10 000 titles and sold more than $520 000 worth of books last year. Titles were stocked in 18 categories, ranging from art, biography, and cooking to religion, sports, and travel.

Bookworms, Inc. was located in a small business district across the street from the boundary of Verdoon University (VU). VU currently enrolled about 12 000 undergraduate and graduate students majoring in the liberal arts, the sciences, and the professions. Despite national trends in enrollment, the VU admissions office had predicted that the number of entering students would grow at about one percent per year through the 1990s. The surrounding community, a city of about 350 000, was projected to grow at about twice that rate.

Bookworms, Inc. carried no texts, even though many of its customers were VU students. Both Klein and her partner, Susan Berman, felt that the VU bookstore had simply too firm a grip on the textbook market in terms of price, location, and reputation. Bookworms also carried no classical records, as of two months ago. Klein recalled with discomfort the $15 000 or so they had lost on the venture. "Another mistake like that and the bank will be running Bookworms," she thought. "And, despite what Susan thinks, the copy service could just be that final mistake."

The idea for a copy service had come from Susan Berman. She had seen the candy store next door to Bookworms (under the same roof) go out of business in July. She had immediately asked the building's owner, Ed Anderson, about the future of the 800-square-metre space. Upon learning it was available, she had met with Klein to discuss her idea for the copy service. She had spoken excitedly about the opportunity: "It can't help but make money. I could work there part-time and the rest of the time we could hire students. We could call it 'Copycats' and even use a sign with the same kind of letters we do in 'Bookworms.' I'm sure we could get Ed to knock the wall out between the two stores, if you think it would be a good idea. Probably we could rent most of the copying equipment, so there's not much risk."

Klein was not so sure. A conversation yesterday with Anderson had disclosed his desire for a five-year lease (with an option to renew) at $1000 per month. He had promised to hold the offer open for two weeks before attempting to lease the space to anyone else. Representatives from copying-equipment firms had estimated that charges would run between $200 and $2000 per month, depending on equipment, service, and whether the equipment was bought or leased. The copy service would also have other fixed costs in terms of utility expenses, interest, insurance, and the inventory (and perhaps equipment). Klein concluded that the service would begin to make a profit at about 20 000 copies per month under the best-case assumptions, and at about 60 000 copies per month under the worst-case assumptions.

Further informal investigation had identified two major competitors. One was the copy centre located in the Krismann Library on the west side of the campus, a kilometre away. The other was a private firm, Kinko's, located on the south side of the campus, also one kilometre away. Both offered service while you wait, on several machines. The library's price was about ½ cent per copy higher than Kinko's. Both offered collating, binding, colour copying, and other services, all on a seven-days-a-week schedule.

Actually, investigation had discovered that a third major "competitor" consisted of the VU departmental machines scattered throughout the campus. Most faculty and administrative copying was done on these machines, but students were allowed the use of some, at cost. In addition, at least 20 self-service machines could be found in the library and in nearby drugstores, grocery stores, and banks.

Moving aside a stack of books on her desk, Nancy Klein picked up the telephone and dialled her partner. When Berman answered, Klein asked, "Susan, have you any idea how many copies a student might make in a semester? I mean, according to my figure, we would break even somewhere between 20 000 and 60 000 copies per month. I don't know if this is half the market or what."

"You know, I have no idea," Berman answered. "I suppose when I was going to school I probably made 10 copies a month—for articles, class notes, old tests, and so on."

"Same here," Klein said. "But some graduate students must have done that many each week. You know, I think we ought to do some marketing research before we go much further on this. What do you think?"

"Sure. Only it can't take much more time or money. What do you have in mind, Nancy?"

"Well, we could easily interview our customers as they leave the store and ask them how many copies they've made in the past week or so. Of course, we'd have to make sure they were students."

"What about a telephone survey?" Berman asked. "That way we can have a random sample. We would still ask about the number of copies, but now we would know for sure they would be students."

"Or what about interviewing students in the union cafeteria? There's always a good-sized line there around noon, as I remember, and this might be even quicker."

"Boy, I just don't know. Why don't I come in this afternoon and we can talk about it some more?"

"Good idea," Klein responded. "Between the two of us, we should be able to come up with something."

Questions

1 What sources of information should Klein and Berman use?
2 How should Klein and Berman gather data?
3 What questions should they ask?
4 How should they sample?

D.L.
K-SWISS
K-SWISS

MARKET SEGMENTATION, TARGETING, AND POSITIONING

10

AFTER READING THIS CHAPTER YOU SHOULD BE ABLE TO:

- Explain what market segmentation is, when to use it, and the five steps involved in segmentation.
- Recognize the different dimensions used to segment consumer and organizational markets.
- Develop a market-product grid to use in segmenting and targeting a market.
- Interpret a cross tabulation to analyze market segments.
- Understand how marketing managers position products in the marketplace.

SNEAKERS STORY: FROM LITTLE SKIRMISHES TO ALL-OUT WAR

What do you need in the sneaker business to stand out from the pack when consumers are faced—literally—with a "wall" of athletic shoes, like that shown on the opposite page?

This is the $12 billion dollar question for sneaker manufacturers around the world. The $12 billion is the estimated size of the global market for "sneakers," a term that includes all kinds of athletic shoes. To answer this question, sneaker manufacturers are searching for new market segments of consumers and ways to differentiate their products from everyone else's! This search for market segments applies to all sneaker manufacturers from the giants such as Nike and Reebok to smaller competitors such as New Balance and Vans.

Quick Quiz Vans? Without peeking at the answers in the Marketing NewsNet[1] box on page 255, try to connect the age of the average consumer of the brand in the right column below to the appropriate brand (in alphabetical order) in the left column:

SNEAKER BRAND	CONSUMER'S AVERAGE AGE
New Balance	15
Nike	25
Reebok	33
Vans	42

Hint: "Shredders" are a key target market for one of the brands. Using age to segment markets is just one alternative available to sneaker manufacturers, as discussed later in the chapter.

The Sneaker Turmoil The "walls" of sneakers in sporting goods and mass merchandiser stores across the nation are just one symptom of the turmoil in the industry. And times are gone when sneaker manufacturers give superstars such as Michael and Shaq—if you need last names, you're not a basketball fan—$15 million or

$30 million to use their name as a brand. Here are some other elements in the sneaker turmoil:

- Sales of men's sneakers are flat—not growing—and sales of high-tech basketball shoes are languishing.
- In 1994, sales of athletic footwear (sneakers) to women age 12 and older passed those of men in that age group for the first time.
- Kids are turning from buying 10 to 15 pairs of sneakers a year to "wearing brown"—wearing brown boots or casual shoes, a trend that may accelerate when Michael Jordan's signature brands are less fashionable now that he has retired from basketball.[2]
- Pressed by public outcry, firms such as Nike and Reebok joined together to approve a monitoring system and code of conduct to curtail use of sweatshop labour abroad.[3]

Reebok's marketing research shows that while about 1 out of every 30 Canadian girls were involved in sports in 1971, the ratio today is 1 in 3! Thus, Reebok has given special emphasis to the female segment. Reebok's strategy, designing shoes to satisfy needs of different customers, illustrates successful market segmentation, the main topic of this chapter. The intense competition in sneakers also explains why Reebok's segmentation strategy includes non-sneaker products, as discussed in detail in the next few pages. The Marketing NewsNet box on the following page also describes how small firms such as Vans and New Balance have succeeded using segmentation strategies to reach special groups of customers.

After discussing why markets need to be segmented, this chapter covers the steps a firm uses in segmenting and targeting a market and then positioning its offering to the marketplace.

WHY SEGMENT MARKETS?

www.reebok.com

A business firm segments its markets so it can respond more effectively to the wants of groups of prospective buyers and thus increase its sales and profits. Nonprofit organizations also segment the clients they serve to satisfy client needs more effectively while achieving the organization's goals. Let's use the dilemma of sneaker buyers finding their ideal Reebok shoes to describe (1) what market segmentation is and (2) when it is necessary to segment markets.

What Market Segmentation Means

People have different needs and wants, even though it would be easier for marketers if they didn't. **Market segmentation** involves aggregating prospective buyers into groups that (1) have common needs and (2) will respond similarly to a marketing action. The groups that result from this process are **market segments,** a relatively homogeneous collection of prospective buyers.

The existence of different market segments has caused firms to use a marketing strategy of **product differentiation,** a strategy that has come to have two different but related meanings. In its broadest sense, product differentiation involves a firm's using different marketing mix activities, such as product features and advertising, to help consumers perceive the product as being different and better than competing products. The perceived differences may involve physical features or nonphysical ones, such as image or price.

In a narrower sense, product differentiation involves a firm's selling two or more products with different features targeted to different market segments. A firm can get into trouble when its different products blend together in consumers' minds and don't reach distinct market segments successfully. The Reebok example discussed below

CUSTOMER VALUE

MARKETING NEWSNET

Shoe Segments for the Little Guys: Shredders versus Boomers

"It's not a lot of bucks," comments Lee Dancie, "considering one small mistake . . ." You can complete his sentence when you hear what he does for a living.

A top racer in the sport of street luge, Dancie earns less than $35 000 a year in endorsements and prizes lying on a two-metre-long skateboard racing down hills at more than 110 kilometres an hour while dragging his feet on the concrete for control. But life has changed for Dancie: Vans, Inc., a sneaker manufacturer, now pays him a salary, supplies his Vans shoes, and sponsors him in competitions.

Never heard of Vans shoes? Well, maybe you're a bit too old, as suggested by the answers to the quiz questions from the first page of the chapter:

SNEAKER BRAND	CONSUMER'S AVERAGE AGE
Vans	15
Nike	25
Reebok	33
New Balance	42

The recent successes of Vans and New Balance brands in their niche market segments are indicators of the revolutionary competition that has emerged in the sneaker market going into the 21st century. A look at their strategies also provides road maps for how small companies can succeed against giant competitors by responding effectively to needs of smaller segments of consumers.

Vans

Vans has targeted the rising wave of young athletes, often in the perilous world of board-riding sports. "Shredders," "riders," or simply "skaters" to their peers, the youth who wear Vans ride their skateboards down handrails, their snowboards down mountain trails, and their stunt bikes down slippery, muddy hills. In the next three years, these markets are expected to double. With $250 million in sales in 1998, Vans encourages its athletes—most of whom frown on Nike and Reebok shoes—to help it design its shoes and low-key ads. Selling for about $35 less than a pair of Nikes at retail, Vans had a breakthrough when the Footlocker chain started featuring the Vans line in its more than 1000 outlets.

New Balance

Talk about boring: How about using a marketing strategy that includes moderate prices, extra-wide shoe widths available, links with podiatrists who insert foot supports in the extra-wide shoes—all actions targeted at serving the weightier (!) baby boomers. This is New Balance, whose $980 million of 1998 sales included customers such as Steve Jobs and Dustin Hoffman. Its $5.6 million advertising budget was less than one percent of Nike's $1.5 billion and Reebok's $595 million. And you don't see well-known athletes in New Balance ads because, as its president says, "We'd just as soon pass the $10 to $15 a pair we need in a superstar endorsement to the customer."

Stay tuned for the future for Vans and New Balance! Now that they have demonstrated the importance of the shredder and boomer segments, Nike and Reebok are moving more aggressively to reach those customers.

shows how the company is using both market segmentation and product differentiation strategies.

Segmentation: Linking Needs to Actions The definition of market segmentation first stresses the importance of aggregating—or grouping—people or organizations in a market according to the similarity of their needs and the benefits they are looking for in making a purchase. Second, such needs and benefits must be related to specific, tangible marketing actions the firm can take. These actions may involve separate products or other aspects of the marketing mix such as price, advertising or personal selling activities, or distribution strategies—the four Ps (product, price, promotion, place).

The process of segmenting a market and selecting specific segments as targets is the link between the various buyers' needs and the organization's marketing program

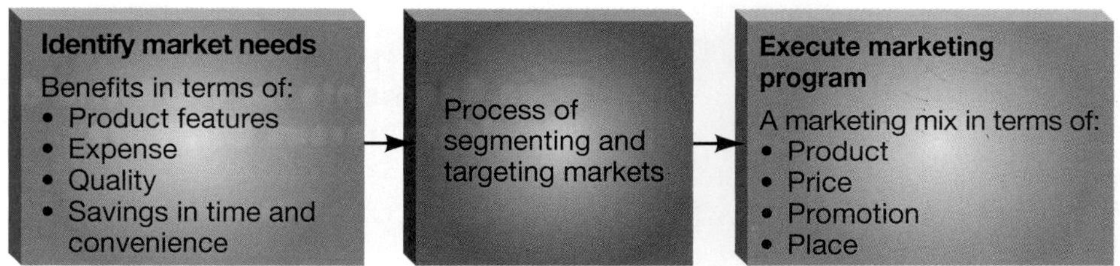

FIGURE 10–1
Market segmentation links market needs to an organization's marketing program

(Figure 10–1). Market segmentation is only a means to an end: In an economist's terms, it relates supply (the organization's actions) to demand (customer needs). A basic test of the usefulness of the segmentation process is whether it leads to tangible marketing actions to increase sales and profitability.

How Reebok's Segmentation Strategy Developed In 1979 Paul Fireman, who had dropped out of university to run his family's business, wandered through an international trade fair and saw Reebok's custom track shoes. He bought the North American licence from the British manufacturer and started producing top-of-the-line running shoes at about the time the running boom had peaked.

In a brilliant marketing decision, Fireman introduced the first soft-leather aerobic-dance shoe—the Reebok "Freestyle"—in 1982. The flamboyant colours of these Reebok designer sneakers captured the attention of aerobic-dance instructors and students alike. Figure 10–2 shows Reebok introduced a variety of shoes, from tennis shoes, children's shoes ("Weeboks"), and basketball shoes in 1984 to Step Trainers in 1991.[4]

A $4-billion-a-year sneaker business has a huge appetite and need for revenues. So in 1993 Reebok introduced its athletic clothing lines—including the Greg Norman Collection, and in 1997 it launched a line of Greg Norman golf shoes.[5] Choosing a product differentiation strategy stressing technology, in 1997 Reebok launched a line of "DMX-enhanced" running shoes that its ads said was "the best running shoe in the

FIGURE 10–2
Market-product grid showing how 10 different styles of Reebok shoes reach segments of customers with different needs

MARKET SEGMENT		PRODUCT									
GENERAL	GROUP WITH NEED	RUNNING SHOES (1981)	AEROBIC SHOES (1982)	TENNIS SHOES (1984)	BASKETBALL SHOES (1984)	CHILDREN'S SHOES (1984)	WALKING SHOES (1986)	CROSS-TRAINERS SHOES (1988)	STEP-TRAINERS SHOES (1991)	ATHLETIC CLOTHING (1993)	GOLF SHOES (1997)
Performance-conscious consumers (athletes)	Runners	P						P			
	Aerobic dancers		P					P			
	Tennis players			P				P			
	Basketball players				P			P			
	Step exercisers							S	P		
	Golfers									P	P
Fashion-conscious consumers (nonathletes)	Comfort- and style-conscious	S	S	S	S		S	S		S	
	Walkers	S	S	S	S		P	P		S	
	Children					P					

Key: P = Primary market; S = Secondary market

history of the world" and gave extra cushioning by distributing air through six chambers in the shoe to create extra cushioning.[6]

What segmentation strategy will Reebok use to take it into the 21st century? Only Reebok knows, but it will certainly involve trying to differentiate its products more clearly from its global competitors and perhaps target segments such as shredders, baby boomers, and global consumers.

Using Market-Product Grids A **market-product grid** is a framework to relate the segments of a market to products offered or potential marketing actions by the firm. The grid in Figure 10–2 shows different markets of sneaker users as rows in the grid, while the columns show the different shoe products (or marketing actions) chosen by Reebok, so each cell in a market-product grid can show the estimated market size of a given product sold to a specific market segment.

The lightly shaded cells in Figure 10–2, labelled P, represent the primary market segment that Reebok targeted when it introduced each shoe. The darker shaded cells, labelled S, represent the secondary market segments that also started buying the shoe. In some cases, Reebok discovered that large numbers of people in a segment not originally targeted for a style of shoe bought it anyway. In fact, as many as 75 to 80 percent of the running shoes and aerobic-dance shoes are bought by non-athletes represented by the (1) comfort- and style-conscious and (2) walker segments shown in Figure 10–2—although walkers may object to being labelled "non-athletes." When this trend became apparent to Reebok in 1986, it introduced its walking shoes targeted directly at the walker segment.

Figure 10–2 also suggests one of the potential dangers of a firm's using market segmentation: subdividing an entire market into two or more segments, thereby increasing the competition from other firms that focus their efforts on a single segment. Notice that Reebok's strategy is to reach both the performance (athletes) and fashion (non-athletes) segments. To reach each segment more effectively, in the 1990s Reebok divided its operations into two separate units: "Technology," targeted at athletes, performance-oriented consumers, and children, and "Lifestyle," targeted at style-conscious consumers.

When to Segment Markets

A business firm goes to the trouble and expense of segmenting its markets when this increases its sales revenue, profit, and ROI. When its expenses more than offset the potentially increased revenues from segmentation, it should not attempt to segment its market. The specific situations that illustrate this point are the cases of (1) one product and multiple market segments, (2) multiple products and multiple market segments, and (3) "segments of one," or mass customization.

One Product and Multiple Market Segments When a firm produces only a single product or service and attempts to sell it to two or more market segments, it avoids the extra costs of developing and producing additional versions of the product, which often entail extremely high research, engineering, and manufacturing expenses. In this case, the incremental costs of taking the product into new product segments are typically those of a separate promotional campaign or a new channel of distribution. Although these expenses can be high, they are rarely as large as those for developing an entirely new product.

Magazines and movies are single products frequently directed to two or more distinct market segments. *Time* magazine, for example, now publishes more than 100 international editions, each targeted at its own geographic and demographic segments and its own mix of advertisements. Movie companies often run different TV commercials featuring different aspects of a newly released film (love, or drama, or spectacular scenery) that are targeted to different market segments. Although multiple TV commercials for movies and separate covers or advertisements for magazines are expensive, they are minor compared with the costs of producing an entirely new movie or magazine for another market segment. Even computer software companies often market single products to multiple market segments. For example, Ottawa-based Cognos Incorporated markets its business intelligence software product—PowerPlay—to a variety of business segments, in Canada and abroad.

Multiple Products and Multiple Market Segments Reebok's different styles of shoes, each targeted at a different type of user, are an example of multiple products aimed at multiple markets. Manufacturing these different styles of shoes is clearly more expensive than producing one but seems worthwhile if it serves customers' needs better, doesn't reduce quality or increase price, and adds to the sales revenues and profits.

Marketing experts are increasingly stressing the need for what they call "two-tier marketing strategies" for the 21st century.[7] Affluent Canadians, about a fifth of the population in the country, have seen their incomes increase over the past two decades while middle-class and working-class Canadians have seen their incomes stagnate or even decline in terms of real buying power. The result is that many firms are now offering different products or services to high-end and low-end segments:

- Gap's Banana Republic chain sells blue jeans for $58, while its Old Navy stores sell a slightly different version for $22.
- General Motors' Saturn unit not only sells its no-haggling-on-price new cars but is aggressively marketing its "pre-owned" cars to reduce customer fears about buying a used car.

www.disney.com

- The Walt Disney Company is carefully marketing two distinct Winnie-the Poohs—such as the original line-drawn figures on fine china sold at upscale department stores and a cartoon-like Pooh on polyester bedsheets sold at Zellers and Wal-Mart—and these Poohs don't play together on the shelves of the same retailer.

www.costco.com

The lines between customer segments often blur, however, as shown by the Cadillacs and Mercedes in Wal-Mart and Price/Costco parking lots.

The key to successful product differentiation and market segmentation strategies is to assess how they provide the organization with **synergy,** the increased customer value achieved through performing organizational functions more efficiently. The "increased customer value" can take many forms: more products, improved quality on existing products, lower prices, easier access to product through improved distribution, and so on. But the ultimate criterion is that customers should be better off as a result of the increased synergy.

Some car manufacturers have failed to achieve expected synergies as they offered many models and options to try to reach diverse market segments. They have concluded that the costs of developing, producing, marketing, and servicing dozens of slightly different models probably outweigh the higher prices that consumers are willing to pay for the wider array of choices. This is why General Motors recently reduced the number of basic car platforms from 12 to 5—a "car platform" being small front-wheel drive cars or large rear-wheel drive cars.

Segments of One: Mass Customization Canadian marketers are rediscovering today what their ancestors running the corner butcher shop or general store knew a century ago: Every customer is unique and has unique wants and needs. Economies of scale in manufacturing and marketing during the past century made mass-produced goods so affordable that most customers were willing to compromise their individual tastes and settle for standardized products. Today's information technology and flexible manufacturing and marketing processes have made mass customization possible, tailoring goods or services to the tastes of individual customers in high volumes and at a relatively low cost.

Paris Miki, the Japanese eyewear retailer with the most outlets in the world, is a case study of effective mass customization that enables customers to help design their own eyeglasses. Paris Miki spent five years developing a system—called the Eye Tailor—that eliminates the need for the customer to try on countless pairs of eyeglasses to find the right one. The system takes a digital photo of the customer's face, analyzes its key features, and collects statements from the customer about the kind of look desired. Working with the optician on details, customers receive a photo-quality picture of themselves with the proposed eyeglass design. A technician in the store grinds the lenses and assembles them to the frames within an hour.[8]

In the Paris Miki system, customers gain the benefits from information technology, flexible production, and personal choice to satisfy an individual customer's wants and needs.

CONCEPT CHECK

1. Market segmentation involves aggregating prospective buyers into groups that have two key characteristics. What are they?
2. What is product differentiation?
3. The process of segmenting and targeting markets is a bridge between what two marketing activities?

STEPS IN SEGMENTING AND TARGETING MARKETS

The process of segmenting a market and then selecting and reaching the target segments is divided into the five steps discussed in this section, as shown in Figure 10–3. Segmenting a market is not a science—it requires large doses of common sense and managerial judgment.

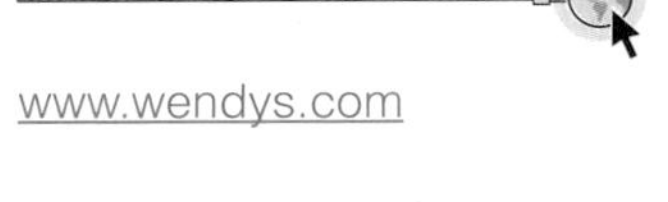

www.wendys.com

Market segmentation and target markets can be abstract topics, so put on your entrepreneur's hat to experience the process. Suppose you own a Wendy's fast-food restaurant next to a large urban university that offers both day and evening classes. Your restaurant specializes in the Wendy's basics: hamburgers, french fries, Frosty milkshakes, and chili. Even though you are part of a chain and have some restrictions on menu and decor, you are free to set your hours of business and to undertake local advertising. How can market segmentation help?

Form Prospective Buyers into Segments

Grouping prospective buyers into meaningful segments involves meeting some specific criteria for segmentation and finding specific variables to segment the consumer or industrial market being analyzed.[9]

FIGURE 10–3
The process of segmenting and targeting markets involves five key steps

Criteria to Use in Forming the Segments A marketing manager should develop segments for a market that meet five principal criteria:

- *Potential for increased profit and ROI.* The best segmentation approach is the one that maximizes the opportunity for future profit and ROI. If this potential is maximized through no segmentation, don't segment. For non-profit organizations, the analogous criterion is the potential for serving client users more effectively.
- *Similarity of needs of potential buyers within a segment.* Potential buyers within a segment should be similar in terms of a marketing activity, such as product features sought or advertising media used.
- *Difference of needs of buyers among segments.* If the needs of the various segments aren't appreciably different, combine them into fewer segments. A different segment usually requires a different marketing action that, in turn, means greater costs. If increased revenues don't offset extra costs, combine segments and reduce the number of marketing actions.
- *Feasibility of a marketing action to reach a segment.* Reaching a segment requires a simple but effective marketing action. If no such action exists, don't segment.
- *Simplicity and cost of assigning potential buyers to segments.* A marketing manager must be able to put a market segmentation plan into effect. This means being able to recognize the characteristics of potential buyers and then assigning them to a segment without encountering excessive costs.

Ways to Segment Consumer Markets Figure 10–4 shows the main dimensions used to segment Canadian consumer markets. These include geographic, demographic, psychographic, and behavioural segmentation.[10] By examining Figure 10–4, you can also see that a number of variables can be used within each dimension for segmentation purposes. What you should remember is that segmenting markets is not a pure science—it requires large doses of common sense and managerial judgment. A marketer may have to use several dimensions and multiple variables within each dimension to form proper market segments. Let's take a look at how some marketers might segment consumer markets using the information in Figure 10–4.

www.colgate-palmolive.com

- *Geographic Segmentation.* Using geographic segmentation, a marketer segments based on where consumers live. Geographic variables such as countries, regions, provinces, counties, cities, or even neighbourhoods could be used. Marketers often find Canadians differ in terms of needs or preferences based on the region in which they live. Remember, the concept of regional marketing from Chapter 3? This is a form of geographic segmentation. For example, Colgate-Palmolive markets Arctic Power, its cold-water detergent, on an energy-cost-saving dimension in Quebec, but as a clothes saver (cold-water washing is easier on clothes) in Western Canada.
- *Demographic Segmentation.* One of the most common ways to segment consumer markets is to use demographic segmentation, or segmenting a market based on population characteristics. This approach segments consumers according to variables such as age, gender, income, education, occupation, and so forth. Cyanamid Canada Inc. uses age as a segmentation variable, producing and marketing its vitamins to various age groups including children, young adults, and older Canadians. Centrum Select, for instance, is specifically designed for adults over 50. Trimark Investments of Ontario segments the financial services market by gender, targeting males and females with different products and different advertising campaigns. General Electric uses family size as a segmentation variable, targeting smaller families with compact microwaves and larger families with extra-large refrigerators. You should note, however, that a single demographic variable may not be sufficient in understanding and segmenting a given market. Thus, many marketers combine a number of demographic variables that

MAIN DIMENSIONS	VARIABLES	TYPICAL BREAKDOWNS
Geographic segmentation	Region	Atlantic, Quebec, Ontario, Prairies, British Columbia
	City or census metropolitan area (CMA) size	Under 5000; 5000–19 999; 20 000–49 000; 50 000–99 999; 100 000–249 000; 250 000–499 999; 500 000–999 000; 1 000 000–3 999 999; 4 000 000+
	Density	Urban; suburban; rural
	Climate	East; West
Demographic segmentation	Age	Infant; under 6; 6–11; 12–17; 18–24; 25–34; 35–49; 50–64; 65+
	Gender	Male; female
	Family size	1–2; 3–4; 5+
	Stage of family life cycle	Young single; young married, no children; young married, youngest child under 6; young married, youngest child 6 or older; older married, with children; older married, no children under 18; older single; other older married
	Income	Under $10 000; $10 000–19 999; $20 000–29 999; $30 000–39 999; $40 000–54 999; $55 000–74 999; $75 000+
	Occupation	Professional; managerial; clerical; sales; labourers; students; retired; housewives; unemployed
	Education	Grade school or less; some high school; high school graduate; some college; college graduate
	Race	White; Black; Asian; Native; other
	Home ownership	Own home; rent home
Psychographic segmentation	Personality	Gregarious; compulsive; extroverted; introverted
	Lifestyle (GoldFarb Segments)	Structured; discontented; fearful; assured; resentful; caring
Behavioural segmentation	Benefits sought	Quality; service; low price
	Usage rate	Light user; medium user; heavy user
	User status	Non-user; ex-user; prospect; first-time user; regular user
	Loyalty status	None, medium, strong

FIGURE 10–4
Segmentation variables and breakdowns for Canadian consumer markets

might clearly distinguish one segment from another. For example, cosmetics companies such as Clinique combine gender, income, and occupation in order to examine market segments for different lines of cosmetic products.

- *Psychographic Segmentation.* Marketers use psychographic segmentation when they segment markets according to personality or lifestyle. It has been found that people who share the same demographic characteristics can have very different psychographic profiles. As we saw in Chapter 6, personality traits have been linked to product preferences and brand choice. In addition, a person's lifestyle (his or her activities, interests, and opinions) also affects the types of products, and the particular brands of products that may be purchased. Remember the Goldfarb Segments from Chapter 6? Members of the discontented segment like package deals when they buy because they do not want to make decisions.[11] On the other hand, those in the resentful segment like expensive brands and they don't worry about price.[12]
- *Behavioural Segmentation.* When marketers use consumers' behaviour with or toward a product to segment the market, they are using behavioural segmentation. A powerful form of behavioural segmentation is to divide the market according to the benefits consumers seek from a product category. Using *benefits sought,* the marketer examines the major benefits consumers look for in the product category, the kinds of consumers who look for each benefit, and the

Lactantia Purfiltre for a market segment looking for a fresher, longer-lasting milk.

major brands that deliver each benefit. For example, Ontario-based Ault Foods examined the fluid milk market and discovered a segment who was looking for a fresher-tasting, longer-lasting product and who were prepared to pay a premium price for a product that would deliver those benefits. In response, Ault developed Lactantia PurFiltre milk for this consumer segment.[13]

Another behavioural segmentation variable often used by marketers is **usage rate**—quantity consumed or patronage during a specific period, which varies significantly among different customer groups. Air Canada, for example, focuses on usage rate for its frequent-flyer program, which is designed to encourage passengers to use its airline repeatedly. Usage rate is sometimes referred to in terms of the **80/20 rule,** a concept that suggests that 80 percent of a firm's sales are obtained from 20 percent of its customers. The percentages in the 80/20 rule are not really fixed; rather, the rule suggests that a small fraction of customers provide a large fraction of sales. For example, Air Canada pays special attention to the business travel segment that comprises only 20 percent of the airline seats but 40 percent of overall revenues.[14]

www.aircanada.ca

Research shows that the fast-food market can also be segmented into light, medium, or heavy users. For every $1.00 spent by a light user in a fast-food restaurant, each heavy user spends over $5.00. This is the reason for the emphasis in almost all marketing strategies on effective ways to reach heavy users of products and services. Thus, as a Wendy's restaurant owner you want to keep the heavy-user segment constantly in mind. With advances in information technology, marketers are now able to conduct detailed segmentation studies. Some Canadian telecommunications companies, for example, can now segment based on more than 100 criteria, from calling patterns to promotional response.

Now, in determining one or two variables to segment the market for your Wendy's restaurant, very broadly we find two main markets: students and non-students. To segment the students, we could try a variety of demographic variables such as age, gender, year in school, or university major, or psychographic variables such as personality or lifestyle. But none of these variables really meets the five criteria listed previously—particularly the fourth criterion about leading to a feasible marketing action to

What variables might Savin use to segment the organizational markets for its answer to "digital document handling" problems? For the possible answer and related marketing actions, see the text.

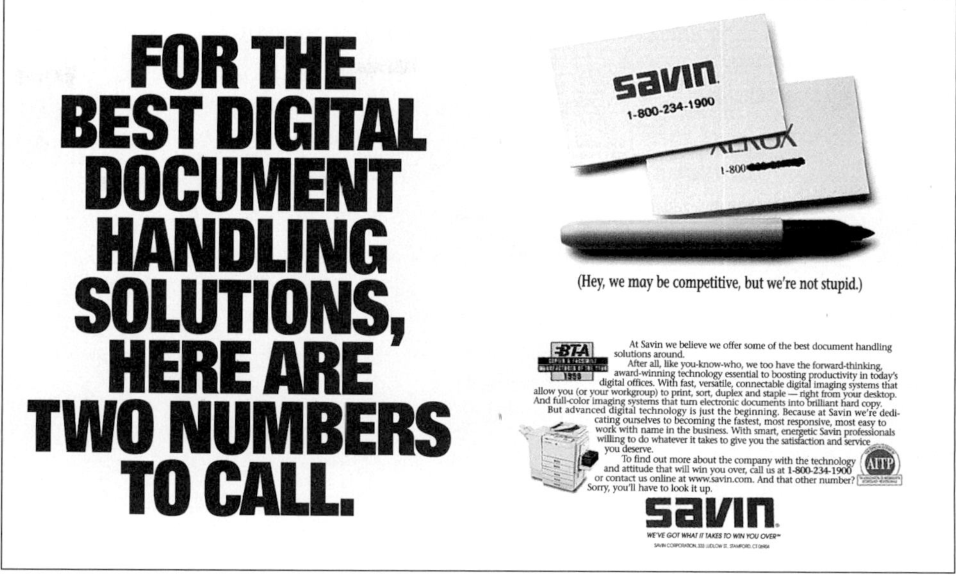

reach the various segments. Four student segments that *do* meet these criteria include the following:

- Students living in dormitories (residence halls, fraternity houses).
- Students living near the university in apartments.
- Day commuter students living outside the area.
- Night commuter students living outside the area.

These segmentation variables are really a combination of where the student lives and the time he or she is on campus (and near your restaurant). For non-students who might be customers, similar variables might be used:

- Faculty and staff members at the university.
- People who live in the area but aren't connected with the university.
- People who work in the area but aren't connected with the university.

DILBERT **by Scott Adams**

FIGURE 10–5
Dimensions used to segment Canadian organizational markets

MAIN DIMENSIONS	VARIABLES	TYPICAL BREAKDOWNS
Geographic segmentation	Region	Atlantic, Quebec, Ontario, Prairies, British Columbia
	Location	In CMA; not in CMA
Demographic segmentation	NAICS code	2-digit; 3-digit; 4-digit; 5-digit; 6-digit categories
	Number of Employees	1–19; 20–99; 100–249; 250+
	Annual Sales Volume	Less than $1 million; $1–10 million; $10–100 million; over $100 million
Behavioural segmentation	Benefits sought	Quality; customer service; low price
	Usage rate	Light user; medium user; heavy user
	User status	Non-user; ex-user; prospect; first-time user; regular user
	Loyalty status	None, medium, strong
	Purchase method	Centralized; decentralized; Individual; group
	Type of buy	New buy; modified rebuy; straight rebuy

Ways to Segment Organizational Markets Variables for segmenting organizational markets are shown in Figure 10–5. A product manager at Savin responsible for its new digital imaging systems might use a number of these segmentation variables, as follows:

- *Geographic segmentation.* The product manager might segment based on region or actual location of the potential customer. Firms located in a census metropolitan area (CMA) might receive a personal sales call, whereas those outside the CMA might be contacted by phone.
- *Demographic segmentation.* Firms might be categorized by the North American Industry Classification System (NAICS). Manufacturers, for example, with global customers might have different digital imaging needs than do retailers or lawyers serving local customers.
- *Behavioural segmentation.* The market might also be segmented based on benefits sought. Savin may decide to focus on firms looking for quality product and good customer service as opposed to those looking for simply low prices. The product manager might also segment the market based on usage rate, recognizing that larger, more globally oriented firms are more likely to be heavy users.

Form Products to Be Sold into Groups

As important as grouping customers into segments is finding a means of grouping the products you're selling into meaningful categories. If the firm has only one product or service, this isn't a problem, but when it has dozens or hundreds, these must be grouped in some way so buyers can relate to them. This is why department stores and supermarkets are organized into product groups, with the departments or aisles containing related merchandise. Likewise, manufacturers have product lines that are the groupings they use in the catalogues sent to customers.

What are the groupings for your restaurant? It could be the item purchased, such as a Frosty, chili, hamburgers, and French fries, but this is where judgment—the qualitative aspect of marketing—comes in. Students really buy an eating experience, or a meal that satisfies a need at a particular time of day, so the product grouping can be defined by meal or time of day as breakfast, lunch, between-meal snack, dinner, and after-dinner snack. These groupings are more closely related to the way purchases are actually made and permit you to market the entire meal, not just your french fries or Frosties.

Develop a Market-Product Grid and Estimate Size of Markets

Developing a market-product grid means labelling the markets (or horizontal rows) and products (or vertical columns), as shown in Figure 10–6. In addition, the size of the market in each cell, or the market-product combination, must be estimated. For your restaurant this involves estimating the number of, or sales revenue obtained from, each kind of meal that can reasonably be expected to be sold to each market segment. This is a form of the usage rate analysis discussed earlier in the chapter.

The market sizes in Figure 10–6 may be simple "guesstimates" if you don't have time for formal marketing research (as discussed in Chapter 9). But even such crude estimates of the size of specific markets using a market-product grid are far better than the usual estimates of the entire market.

Select Target Markets

A firm must take care to choose its target market segments carefully. If it chooses too narrow a group of segments, it may fail to reach the volume of sales and profits it needs. If it selects too broad a group of segments, it may spread its marketing efforts so thin that the extra expenses more than offset the increased sales and profits.

Criteria to Use in Choosing the Target Segments Two different kinds of criteria are present in the market segmentation process: (1) those to use in dividing the market into segments (discussed earlier) and (2) those to use in actually choosing the target segments. Even experienced marketing executives often confuse these two

FIGURE 10–6
Selecting a target market for your fast-food restaurant next to an urban university (target market is shaded)

	PRODUCTS: MEALS				
MARKETS	BREAK-FAST	LUNCH	BETWEEN-MEAL SNACK	DINNER	AFTER-DINNER SNACK
STUDENT					
Dormitory	0	1	3	0	3
Apartment	1	3	3	1	1
Day commuter	0	3	2	1	0
Night commuter	0	0	1	3	2
NON-STUDENT					
Faculty or staff	0	3	1	1	0
Live in area	0	1	2	2	1
Work in area	1	3	0	1	0

Key: 3 = Large market; 2 = Medium market; 1 = Small market; 0 = No market.

different sets of criteria. The five criteria to use in actually selecting the target segments apply to your Wendy's restaurant in this way:

- *Size.* The estimated size of the market in the segment is an important factor in deciding whether it's worth going after. There is really no market for breakfasts among campus students (Figure 10–6), so why devote any marketing effort toward reaching a small or non-existent market?
- *Expected growth.* Although the size of the market in the segment may be small now, perhaps it is growing significantly or is expected to grow in the future. Night commuters may not look important now, but with the decline in traditional day students in many universities, the evening adult education programs are expected to expand in the future. Thus, the future market among night commuters is probably more encouraging than the current picture shown in Figure 10–6.
- *Competitive position.* Is there a lot of competition in the segment now or is there likely to be in the future? The less the competition, the more attractive the segment is. For example, if the university dormitories announce a new policy of "no meals on weekends," this segment is suddenly more promising for your restaurant.
- *Cost of reaching the segment.* A segment that is inaccessible to a firm's marketing actions should not be pursued. For example, the few non-students who live in the area may not be economically reachable with ads in newspapers or other media. As a result, do not waste money trying to advertise to them.
- *Compatibility with the organization's objectives and resources.* If your restaurant doesn't have the cooking equipment to make breakfasts and has a policy against spending more money on restaurant equipment, then don't try to reach the breakfast segment.

As is often the case in marketing decisions, a particular segment may appear attractive according to some criteria and very unattractive according to others.

Choose the Segments Ultimately, a marketing executive has to use these criteria to choose the segments for special marketing efforts. As shown in Figure 10–6, let's assume you've written off the breakfast market for two reasons: too small market size and incompatibility with your objectives and resources. In terms of competitive position and cost of reaching the segment, you choose to focus on the four student segments and not the three non-student segments (although you're certainly not going to turn away business from the nonstudent segments). This combination of market-product segments—your target market—is shaded in Figure 10–6.

Wendy's can target different market segments with different advertising programs.

Take Marketing Actions to Reach Target Markets

The purpose of developing a market-product grid is to trigger marketing actions to increase revenues and profits. This means that someone must develop and execute an action plan.

www.burgerking.com

Your Wendy's Segmentation Strategy With your Wendy's restaurant you've already reached one significant decision: There is a limited market for breakfast, so you won't open for business until 10:30 A.M. In fact, Wendy's first attempt at a breakfast menu was a disaster and was discontinued in 1986. Wendy's evaluates possible new menu items continuously, not only to compete with McDonald's and Burger King but also with a complex array of supermarkets, convenience stores, and gas stations that sell reheatable packaged foods as well as new "easy-lunch" products.

Another essential decision is where and what meals to advertise to reach specific market segments. An ad in the student newspaper could reach all the student segments, but you might consider this "shotgun approach" too expensive and want a more focused "rifle approach" to reach smaller segments. If you choose three segments for special actions (Figure 10–7), advertising actions to reach them might include:

- *Day commuters* (an entire market segment). Run ads inside commuter buses and put flyers under the windshield wipers of cars in parking lots used by day commuters. These ads and flyers promote all the meals at your restaurant to a single segment of students—a horizontal cut through the market-product grid.
- *Between-meals snacks* (directed to all four student markets). To promote eating during this downtime for your restaurant, offer "Ten percent off all purchases between 2:00 and 4:30 P.M. during winter quarter." This ad promotes a single meal to all four student segments—a vertical cut through the market-product grid.
- *Dinners to night commuters.* The most focused of all three campaigns, this ad promotes a single meal to a single student segment. The campaign might consist of a windshield flyer offering a free Frosty with the coupon when the person buys a hamburger and french fries.

FIGURE 10–7
Advertising actions to reach specific student segments

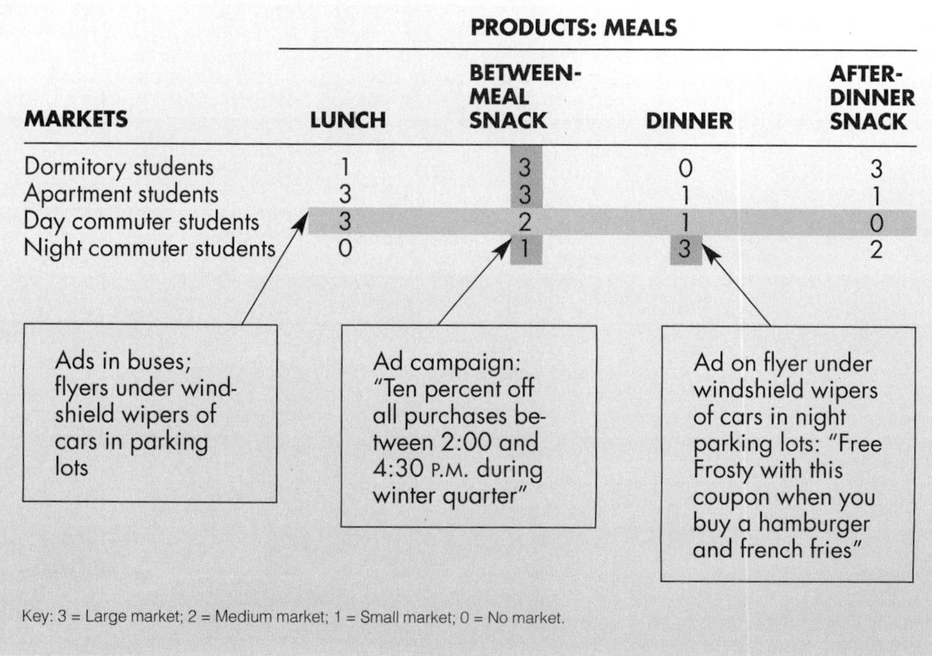

Depending on how your advertising actions work, you can repeat, modify, or drop them and design new campaigns for other segments you feel warrant the effort. This example of advertising your Wendy's restaurant is just a small piece of a complete marketing program using all the elements of the marketing mix.

Apple's Ever-Changing Segmentation Strategy Steven Jobs, John Scully, Michael Spindler, Gilbert Amelio, and—deja vu!—Steven Jobs! Apple Computer came full circle in 1997 with the return of Steve Jobs. Each of these Apple CEOs presided over some of the most innovative and questionable market-product decisions during their tenure.[15]

Steven Jobs and Stephen Wozniak didn't realize they were developing today's multibillion-dollar PC industry when they invented the Apple I in a garage on April Fool's Day, 1976. Typical of young companies, Apple focused on its products and had little concern for its markets. When IBM—"Big Blue"—entered the PC market in 1981, Apple was forced to become a "real company," much to the chagrin of its creative young engineers who were likened to "Boy Scouts without adult supervision."

With the introduction of the IBM PC, Big Blue quickly dominated the market, having licensed its operating system from Microsoft. Apple lost significant market share, and many experts predicted it wouldn't survive. Jobs realized that Apple needed to "grow up" and therefore sought professional marketing expertise. Enter John Scully, who concluded that Apple needed to update its market-product strategies. His solution was to differentiate Apple's line of computers more clearly and to target them at important market niches.

The succession of Apple CEOs after Scully also sought to formalize and give cohesiveness to Apple's market segmentation strategy and to target specific Apple machines

What market segments for Apple's computers are represented by these products? The Marketing NewsNet box and text discussion provide insights into Apple's market segmentation strategy.

Apple Computer
www.apple.com

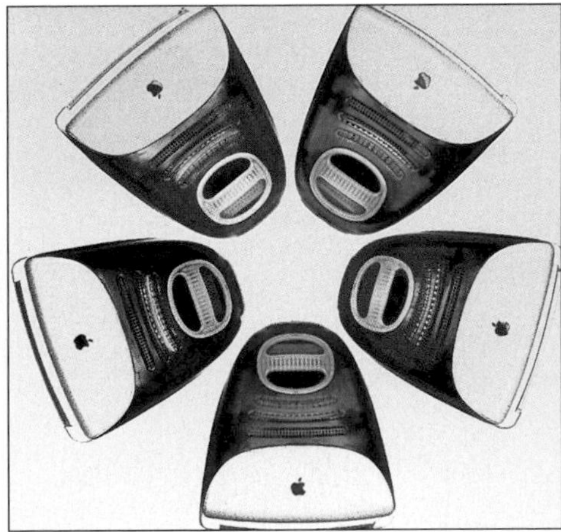

CUSTOMER VALUE

MARKETING NEWSNET

Apple's Segmentation Strategy: Search for the Right Niches

"Camp Runamok" was the nickname some computer industry wags gave to Apple Computer in the early 1980s because the entrepreneurial company had no coherent series of product lines directed at identifiable market segments. And as Apple's history indicates, this moniker was well deserved!

Today, Apple has targeted its various lines of Macintosh computers at specific market segments, as shown below. Because the market-product grid shifts as a firm's strategy changes, the one shown here is based on Apple's product line in early 1999. This market-product grid is a simplification because each "product" is really a series of Macintosh computers in that line. Each series has computers specifically configured to the desires of the customer, such as PowerPC processor speed, amount of memory, an add-on graphics card, drive type and speed/size, and kind of connection for Internet and intranet access. There is also an overlap of likely market segments from one product line to another.

Nevertheless, the grid suggests a market-product strategy for Apple's product lines: iMacs (*Business Week*'s 1998 Product of the Year) for the consumer and educational market segments; Power Mac G3s for users who need more speed; PowerBooks for those who need portability; and servers for Internet developers and network users. And now: a "business" iMac, a new Mac OS X operating system, a new G4 PowerPC processor, faster Internet connections, and a consumer iMac portable, called "iBook."

MARKETS			PRODUCTS (PERSONAL COMPUTERS)			
SECTOR		SEGMENT	POWER MACINTOSH G3	POWERBOOK G3	IMAC	POWER MACINTOSH G3 SERVER
Consumer/household		Family/games			✓	
Education	Primary through OAC	Students			✓	
		Faculty/administration	✓	✓		✓
	Community college and university	Students	✓	✓	✓	
		Faculty/administration	✓	✓		✓
Commercial	Small business	Owners/employees	✓	✓	✓	✓
	Large business	Administration/technical	✓	✓		✓
	Design and publishing	Media/graphics/Internet	✓	✓		✓
		Desktop publishing	✓	✓		✓

to particular market segments. With varying degrees of success, the core product strategy continued to be the innovation of Apple's line of Macintosh computers.

Upon Steve Jobs' return to Apple in 1997, he detailed his vision for a reincarnated Apple. He announced the controversial "Think Different" advertising campaign and described upcoming new Macs. He deleted many models from Apple's existing line and announced Apple would also sell computers direct via The Apple Store over the Internet and the phone, patterning the site after Dell Computer.

In 1998 Apple re-targeted the consumer and education markets by introducing the iMac—the most innovative PC ever created according to many PC and business analysts. The iMac, initially priced at $1800, was fast, Internet-ready, easy-to-use, and the first PC to eliminate the 3.5-inch floppy drive for storage. Instead, other storage options were developed by Imation, Iomega, and other third-party vendors. By the end of 1998, more than 800 000 units had been sold, making the iMac the greatest PC product launch ever.[16] In early 1999, Apple introduced iMacs in five "fruit" flavours. And, in late 1999, it introduced the portable iMac, called iBook, with an innovation called *airport,* which is a PC version of the cordless phone.

As in most segmentation situations, a single Apple product does not fit into an exclusive market niche. Rather, there is overlap among products in the product line and also among the markets to which they are directed. But a market segmentation strategy enables Apple to offer different products to meet the needs of the different market segments, as shown in the Marketing NewsNet box on the previous page. What does Steve Jobs have in store for Apple? Here are some of his plans:

- Presenting its new, faster, value-priced Power Macintosh G3s based on the radically translucent blue design of the iMac.
- Increasing its market share by adding new retail outlets and selling through its own Apple Store.
- Positioning the Mac as the best game platform—a growing market segment—due to its superior graphics compared to its PC rivals.

Market-product challenges for Apple to overcome include:

- Maintaining the sales momentum of its consumer iMacs and introducing a business iMac, networkable PC.
- Reducing the price differential between Apple's Power Macs and PowerBooks and their PC counterparts.
- Web initiative: Quicktime TV for Web video and Sherlock 2, an upgraded search engine.

Stay tuned to see if Steve Jobs and these market-product strategies will enable the Apple "phoenix" to rise from its own ashes!

CONCEPT CHECK

1. What are some of the variables used to segment consumer markets?
2. What are some criteria used to decide which segments to choose for targets?
3. Why is usage rate important in segmentation studies?

ANALYZING MARKET SEGMENTS USING CROSS TABULATIONS

To do a more precise market segmentation analysis of your Wendy's restaurant, suppose you survey fast-food patrons throughout the metropolitan area where your restaurant is located, using the questionnaire shown in Figure 9–6. You want to use this information as best you can to study the market's segments and develop your strategy. Probably the most widely used approach today in marketing is to develop and interpret cross tabulations of data obtained by questionnaires.

Developing Cross Tabulations

A **cross tabulation,** or "cross tab," is a method of presenting and relating data having two or more variables. It is used to analyze and discover relationships in the data. Two important aspects of cross tabulations are deciding which of two variables to pair together to help understand the situation and forming the resulting cross tabulations.

Pairing the Questions Marketers pair two questions to understand marketing relationships and to find effective marketing actions. The Wendy's questionnaire in

Figure 9–6 gives many questions that might be paired to understand the fast-food business better and help reach a decision about marketing actions to increase revenues. For example, if you want to study your hypothesis that as the age of the head of household increases, patronage of fast-food restaurants declines, you can cross tabulate questions 9*d* and 3.

Forming Cross Tabulations Using the answers to question 3 as the column headings and the answers to question 9*d* as the row headings gives a cross tabulation, as shown in Figure 10–8, using the answers 586 respondents gave to both questions. The figure shows two forms of the cross tabulation:

- The raw data or answers to the specific questions are shown in Figure 10–8A. For example, this cross tab shows that 144 households whose head was 24 years or younger ate at fast-food restaurants once a week or more.
- Answers on a percentage basis, with the percentages running horizontally, are shown in Figure 10–8B. Of the 215 households headed by someone 24 years or younger, 67.0 percent ate at a fast-food restaurant at least once a week and only 8.8 percent ate there once a month or less.

Two other forms of cross tabulation using the raw data shown in Figure 10–8A are as described in problem 7 at the end of the chapter.

Interpreting Cross Tabulations

A careful analysis of Figure 10–8 shows that patronage of fast-food restaurants is related to the age of the head of the household. Note that as the age of the head of the household increases, fast-food restaurant patronage declines, as shown by the boxed percentages on the diagonal in Figure 10–8B. This means that if you want to reach the heavy-user segment, you should direct your marketing efforts to the segment that is 24 years old or younger.

FIGURE 10–8
Two forms of a cross tabulation relating age of head of household to fast-food restaurant patronage

A. ABSOLUTE FREQUENCIES

AGE OF HEAD OF HOUSEHOLD (YEARS)	FREQUENCY			
	ONCE A WEEK OR MORE	2 OR 3 TIMES A MONTH	ONCE A MONTH OR LESS	TOTAL
24 or less	144	52	19	215
25 to 39	46	58	29	133
40 or over	82	69	87	238
Total	272	179	135	586

B. ROW PERCENTAGES: RUNNING PERCENTAGES HORIZONTALLY

AGE OF HEAD OF HOUSEHOLD (YEARS)	FREQUENCY			
	ONCE A WEEK OR MORE	2 OR 3 TIMES A MONTH	ONCE A MONTH OR LESS	TOTAL
24 or less	67.0%	24.2%	8.8%	100.0%
25 to 39	34.6	43.6	21.8	100.0
40 or over	34.4	29.0	36.6	100.0
Total	46.4%	30.6%	23.0%	100.0%

As discussed earlier in the chapter, there are various ways to segment a consumer market besides according to age. For example, you could make subsequent cross tabulations to analyze patronage related to where students live and the meals they eat to obtain more precise information for the market-product grid in Figure 10–6.

Value of Cross Tabulations

Probably the most widely used technique for organizing and presenting marketing data, cross tabulations have some important advantages. The simple format permits direct interpretation and an easy means of communicating data to management. They have great flexibility and can be used to summarize experimental, observational, and questionnaire data. Also, cross tabulations may be easily generated by today's personal computers.

Cross tabulations also have some disadvantages. For example, they can be misleading if the percentages are based on too small a number of observations. Also, cross tabulations can hide some relations because each typically only shows two or three variables. Balancing both advantages and disadvantages, more marketing decisions are probably made using cross tabulations than any other method of analyzing data.

The ultimate value of cross tabulations to a marketing manager lies in obtaining a better understanding of the wants and needs of buyers and targeting key segments. This enables a marketing manager to "position" the offering in the minds of buyers, the topic discussed next.

POSITIONING THE PRODUCT

When a company offers a product commercially, a decision critical to its long-term success is how to position it in the market on introduction. **Product positioning** refers to the place an offering occupies in consumers' minds on important attributes relative to competitive offerings.

Two Approaches to Product Positioning

There are several approaches to positioning a new product in the market. Head-to-head positioning involves competing directly with competitors on similar product attributes in the same target market. Using this strategy, Dollar competes directly with Avis and Hertz, and Volvo pits its turbo-charged cars against Porsche.

Differentiation positioning involves seeking a less competitive, smaller market niche in which to locate a brand. As shown in the Web Link box, Buy.com is positioning itself as having the "lowest prices on Earth" to buyers on the Internet. SoyaWorld Inc. of Vancouver positions its soy beverage product, called So Good, to appeal to a small niche segment of the market that is looking for an alternative to cow's milk. Companies also follow a differentiation strategy among brands within their own product line to try to minimize cannibalization of a brand's sales or shares.

Product Positioning Using Perceptual Maps

A key to positioning a product effectively is the perceptions of consumers. In determining a brand's position and the preferences of consumers, companies obtain three types of data from consumers:

1. Evaluations of the important attributes for a product class.
2. Judgments of existing brands with the important attributes.
3. Ratings of an "ideal" brand's attributes.

From these data, it is possible to develop a **perceptual map,** a means of displaying or graphing in two dimensions the location of products or brands in the minds of consumers. The example illustrates how a manager can use perceptual maps to see

A sense of style as refined
as your sense of business.
PARK AVENUE BY BUICK

couture
AURORA
DEFY CONVENTION
aerodynamic steel skin · carved haunches · sculpted tail · V8/250hp
Oldsmobile

To which market segments are these General Motors cars targeted? Do potential buyers see them as the same or different? For the company's position dilemma and strategy, see the text and Figure 10–9.

how consumers perceive competing products or brands and then take actions to try to change the product offering and the image it projects to consumers.

GM's Positioning for 1990 By the 1980s General Motors (GM) was concerned that the image of its five main models of cars—Chevrolet, Pontiac, Oldsmobile, Buick, and Cadillac—had so blurred in the minds of Canadian consumers that they could not distinguish one brand from another. So in 1982 GM interviewed consumers and developed the perceptual map shown in Figure 10–9A. Note that the two dimensions on the perceptual map are (1) low price versus high price and (2) family/conservative versus

WEB LINK "The Lowest Prices on Earth": The Most Precise Positioning Statement Ever?

Here's an idea for a new business: Sell dollar bills for 85 cents!

The only problem is Scott Blum, CEO of Buy.com, is pretty much doing it already by selling consumer products at or below cost. He is trying to position the company as being synonymous with low price—as shown by Buy.com's tag line: "the lowest prices on Earth." Blum's strategy is described in more detail at the start of Chapter 18.

As discussed in the text, product positioning refers to the place an offering occupies in a consumer's mind. In Buy.com's case, this means the *absolute* lowest prices. Sound crazy? Visit the www.Buy.com Web site, and see for yourself. Compare its prices with those of other Internet sellers. Are they the lowest?

If Buy.com isn't an active Web site when you read this, it probably *was* a crazy idea!

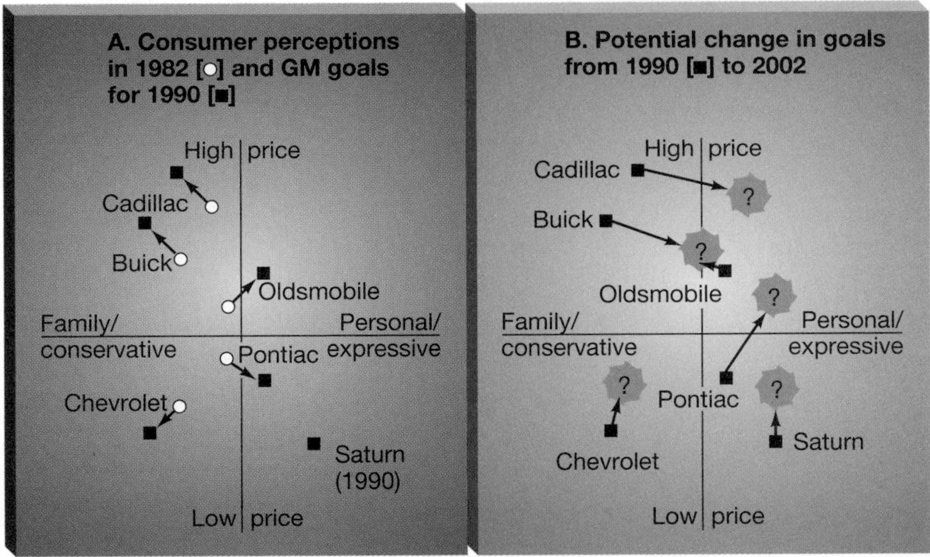

FIGURE 10–9
GM's strategy to reposition its major car brands from 1982 to 1990 to . . . 2002(?)

personal/expressive appeal. Figure 10–9A shows that GM indeed had a problem. Although there was some variation in the vertical dimension (consumers' perception of price), there was little difference in the horizontal dimension (family/conservative appeal versus personal/expressive appeal). Then GM set new goals for where it wanted its models to be when its small car Saturn would be introduced (which turned out to be 1990). This involves **repositioning** the models, or changing the place an offering occupies in a consumer's mind relative to competitive offerings.

Figure 10–9A highlights the special 1980s problem GM faced in having its divisions sell nearly identical cars to nearly identical market segments: Pontiac went head-to-head with Chevrolet for younger buyers and Buick and Oldsmobile did the same for the sixtyish segment. So divisions were cannibalizing each others' sales. The figure shows that its 1990 goals included the following:

- Position Saturn as a low-priced, stylish import-fighter.
- Try to reposition Pontiac as a more personal/expressive (stylish) car and Chevrolet as a more family/conservative car.
- Try to reposition Buick as a higher priced, family/conservative car and Oldsmobile as a more stylish car.

Things didn't work out quite the way GM expected. One problem was the sudden 1990s love affair Canadians had with minivans, pickup trucks, and sports utility vehicles.

GM's Positioning for 2002 In the late 1990s GM embarked on several strategies that accentuated the importance of making some difficult product repositioning decisions. It invested about $4 billion in its "four-country strategy" that involved building virtually identical new car production plants in Argentina, Poland, China, and Thailand—plus a fifth and newer plant in Brazil.[17] GM also announced major reorganizations to combine its five marketing divisions into one and to consolidate engineering operations—all directed at reducing the development time for GM cars and trucks and to improve their marketing.[18] The problem: All these actions didn't directly address the fact that from 1992 to 1997 GM's market share was falling in all car and truck categories except for small cars—where profits are lowest.

Cadillac is an example of GM's positioning dilemma. Cadillac's basic problem: The average Cadillac buyer is 63! So it's clear that Cadillac must find ways to compete with foreign rivals such as Lexus, Mercedes, and BMW to attract younger luxury-car buyers without destroying its classic image and losing its present buyers. One strategy: The Cadillac Escalade sport-utility vehicle.[19]

We can look at GM's designs and advertising for its current lines and assess where GM wants the models to be positioned in, say, the year 2002. Figure 10–9B is just such a projection. One thing is certain. Canadians of all ages want more stylish cars and are moving to the right in the positioning matrix in Figure 10–9B—especially as minivans and pickup trucks take over more of the "family/conservative" end of the scale.

Gazing into our own crystal ball and those of reporters close to GM, Figure 10–9B suggests possible GM repositioning strategies for 2002:

- Cadillac—move in the direction of more personal/expressiveness to attract younger buyers.
- Buick and Oldsmobile—GM-watchers are betting these two divisions will merge, with a positioning between their 1990 locations.[20]
- Pontiac—add price, power, and sportiness to reach younger buyers now driving foreign cars.
- Chevrolet—keep it conservative and a bit more pricey to distinguish the brand from Pontiac and Saturn.
- Saturn—GM's "orphan"; Saturn achieved huge customer acceptance and loyalty when launched, but billions of dollars in the early 1990s were pumped into new models intended to revive the stodgy images of Oldsmobile and Buick, leaving Saturn with an empty new-model cupboard; watch for pricier Saturn models—perhaps a compact sedan and larger sports utility vehicle.[21]

Are these positioning projections correct? Read today's GM ads and see for yourself. Your personal car-buying decisions will affect the outcome as well.

CONCEPT CHECK

1. What is cross tabulation?
2. What are some advantages of cross tabulations?
3. Why do marketers use perceptual maps in product positioning decisions?

SUMMARY

1 Market segmentation is aggregating prospective buyers into groups that have common needs and will respond similarly to a marketing action.

2 A straightforward approach to segmenting, targeting, and reaching a market involves five steps: (*a*) form prospective buyers into segments by characteristics such as their needs, (*b*) form products to be sold into groups, (*c*) develop a market-product grid and estimate size of markets, (*d*) select target markets, and (*e*) take marketing actions to reach the target markets.

3 The main dimensions used to segment Canadian consumer markets include geographic, demographic, psychographic, and behavioural segmentation. A number of variables within each dimension can be used for segmentation purposes. For example, using demographic segmentation, a marketer can use age, gender, education, or income as segmenting variables. Organizational markets can be segmented on geographic, demographic, and behavioural dimensions. Typical variables used to segment organizational markets include NAICS codes and size of firm.

4 Criteria used (*a*) to segment markets and (*b*) to choose target segments are related but different. The former includes potential to increase profits, similarity of needs of buyers within a segment, difference of needs among segments, and feasibility of a resulting marketing action. The latter includes market size, expected growth, the competitive position of the firm's offering in the segment, and the cost of reaching the segment.

5 A market-product grid is a useful way to display what products can be directed at which market segments, but the grid must lead to marketing actions for the segmentation process to be worthwhile.

6 Cross tabulations are widely used today in market segmentation studies to identify needs of various customer segments and the actions to reach them.

7 A company can position a product head-to-head against the competition or seek a differentiated position. A concern with positioning is often to avoid cannibalization of the existing product line. In positioning, a firm often uses consumer judgments in the form of perceptual maps to locate its product relative to competing ones.

KEY TERMS AND CONCEPTS

market segmentation p. 254
market segments p. 254
product differentiation p. 254
market-product grid p. 257
synergy p. 258
usage rate p. 262
80/20 rule p. 262
cross tabulation p. 270
product positioning p. 272
perceptual map p. 272
repositioning p. 274

INTERNET EXERCISE

In its two-decade history, Apple computer has initiated a series of creative market segmentation strategies, with new product lines targeted at specific market segments. For a continuing update of Apple's strategies, go to www.apple-history.com and click on the "Intro" and "History" menu options. As you read the narrative, identify the various market-product strategies Apple has employed, compared to those described in the text and the Marketing NewsNet box. Given Apple's recent turnaround, do you think Apple can continue its comeback in the 21st century? Do you believe Apple can survive as a "niche" PC marketer? Why or why not?

APPLYING MARKETING CONCEPTS AND PERSPECTIVES

1 What variables might be used to segment these consumer markets? (*a*) lawnmowers, (*b*) frozen dinners, (*c*) dry breakfast cereals, and (*d*) soft drinks.

2 What variables might be used to segment these industrial markets? (*a*) industrial sweepers, (*b*) photocopiers, (*c*) computerized production control systems, and (*d*) car rental agencies.

3 In Figure 10–6 the dormitory market segment includes students living in university-owned residence halls. What market needs are common to these students that justify combining them into a single segment in studying the market for your Wendy's restaurant?

4 You may disagree with the estimates of market size given for the rows in the market-product grid in Figure 10–6. Estimate the market size, and give a brief justification for these market segments: (*a*) dormitory students, (*b*) day commuters, and (*c*) people who work in the area.

5 Suppose you want to increase revenues from your fast-food restaurant shown in Figure 10–7 even further. What advertising actions might you take to increase revenues from (*a*) dormitory students, (*b*) dinners, and (*c*) after-dinner snacks from night commuters?

6 Look back at Figure 9–6. Which questions would you pair to form a cross tabulation to uncover the following relationships? (*a*) frequency of fast-food restaurant patronage and restaurant characteristics important to the customer, (*b*) age of the head of household and source of information used about fast-food restaurants, (*c*) frequency of patronage of Wendy's and source of information used about fast-food restaurants, or (*d*) how much children have to say about where the family eats and number of children in the household.

7 Look back at Figure 10–8A. (*a*) Run the percentages vertically and tell what they mean. (*b*) Express all numbers in the table as a percentage of the total number of people sampled (586) and tell what the percentages mean.

8 In Figure 10–8, (*a*) what might be other names for the three patronage levels shown in the columns? (*b*) Which is likely to be of special interest to Wendy's and why?

CASE 10–1 CANTEL

INTRODUCTION

Rogers Cantel Mobile Communications Inc. (Cantel) (www.rogers.com), owns and operates Canada's largest and only nationally licensed wireless (cellular) telephone company. It also operates a national paging service, a wireless data communications service, and a chain of retail service centres for the sale and service of wireless equipment. Cantel competes with the cellular subsidiaries of the "wireline" companies such as Bell

Canada, Maritime Tel & Tel, Alberta Government Telephone, or BC Tel, which also offer conventional telephone services via telephone wires. Cantel has spent over $1.5 billion on high-quality mobile facilities from coast to coast to provide cellular service to its customers.

HOW CELLULAR PHONES WORK

A cellular phone uses radio signals instead of wires to transmit calls. The cellular networks are connected to the public wireline phone system allowing cellular users to make calls to, or receive calls from, virtually any other phone in the world. As a cellular network service provider, Cantel has erected hundreds of transmitters across the country; each transmitter serves an area called a "cell." As a cellular subscriber uses a phone in a moving car, or walks down the street, a switching computer "hands off" the call from one cell to another without interruption of the call.

CANTEL

Cantel first launched cellular service in July 1985 in Montreal and Toronto. In July 1987 Cantel was the first cellular company to complete continuous coverage of the 1200-kilometre corridor from Windsor, Ontario, through to Quebec City. This corridor has since almost doubled in length and now extends 2000 kilometres through to the Atlantic coast, making it the longest cellular corridor in North America. Cantel's cellular network covers cities and corridors in all 10 Canadian provinces. Today more than 93 percent of the Canadian population has access to Cantel service.

In less than 10 years, cellular penetration in Canada went from 0 to 9 percent. In 1995, Cantel had over one million cellular subscribers and over 200 000 paging subscribers. Cantel expects wireless penetration to triple in the next five years. In 1996 Cantel began offering its customers digital personal communications services (PCS)—an innovative and superior technology for transmitting and receiving data. The service includes paging, e-mail, mobile faxing, and voice mail. Cantel also offers international cellular service that allows its customers to make and receive calls in over 40 countries. A long-term strategic alliance with AT&T Canada, including a co-branding agreement, also provides Cantel an opportunity to provide seamless availability of its services, including digital PCS throughout Canada and the United States.

In an effort to further penetrate the market, Cantel offers an all-in-one cellular service program called Amigo for as low as $19.95 per month. The package includes a lightweight cellular phone and a choice between two different calling plans.

Questions

1 Segment the market for cellular phone subscribers.

2 Who are the key target segments for cellular phones?

3 How should Cantel position its cellular service in those target segments?

PART III CASE BOOK BUYERS AND THEIR CHOICES

Internet users and Internet buyers are of particular interest to companies developing products and services because their behaviour is more than a passing curiosity. Segmenting a market to determine the common needs of a prospective group of buyers is done by marketing professionals to develop appropriate marketing action plans designed for that specific group of buyers. The phenomenon of the Internet and its many applications for reaching a worldwide audience have created opportunities to apply market segmentation principles to Internet users. With this revolutionary communication vehicle, companies are learning that it may be possible to put technology to use for the purpose of encouraging consumers to purchase online. There is tremendous interest to learn more about Internet users—specifically those predisposed to purchasing online. In exploring the population of Internet users, there is increasing fascination in identifying differences or similarities among online users in terms of buying behaviour, personality or lifestyle, characteristics, and geography.

SEGMENTING ONLINE BUYERS

The Internet had created a new marketspace,[1] creating a land of opportunity for those companies that can successfully harness the benefits of cyberspace. This new borderless, virtual medium is changing the way companies look at their customers, particularly geographically. Geography and other accepted segmentation criteria may not be appropriate for marketing in cyberspace.

Defining useful segmentation criteria to understand Internet users is being done by a group of companies interested in developing data-capture tools designed to catch, interpret, and act on web-site behaviour.[2] With advanced data-mining applications, it is now possible to collect information about purchase behaviour on the Internet to monitor post-purchase activities of Net buyers. MatchLogic is a marketing services firm providing companies using e-commerce with specialized databases designed to collect user data for very different purposes. The company can collect information about users' computers as well as track web activity. For example, by monitoring user clicks, one database is able to collect when ads are clicked, information is requested, or purchases made. MatchLogic also collects information for companies wanting to know the effectiveness of their web advertising. A third database is one that contains "self-reported" data. With the use of incentives such as a sweepstakes, web-site users can voluntarily register, and this information is used to build demographic profiles by combining age, geography, and income. Companies can then design advertising campaigns for a specific target group usinge these profiles.[3]

Combining Internet technology with sophisticated data-mining techniques, companies will be able to move towards a more customer-oriented approach.[4] Companies that are savvy about Internet users and their preferences will do well. Knowing where to find their potential target consumers on the Net is also important. The steady stream of research on Net users and purchasers is finding that the Internet is losing the male-dominated, computer-jock focus. The Web is not necessarily a mass-market tool. A recent study found that women account for more than half of new Internet users.[5] Narrowly targeted web-sites such as SeniorNet and Bluemountain.com (electronic greeting cards) have a good handle on the needs of their audience and have been successfully creating loyal Net users and purchasers.

Segmenting markets helps companies earn better margins by providing an understanding of the differences that drive purchase behaviour, customer value, and disposition to pay. Technological innovation has created opportunities for growth in a mature retail segment—books. Technology has changed customer value perceptions in this market segment in two ways. First, amazon.com has become the best-known brand due to its creation of the digital bookshelf. Second, within the book-buying market, specific segments are well suited to using technology to generate increased interest in a specific genre.

A BOOK BUYER IS A BOOK BUYER BY ANY OTHER NAME

The retail industry as a whole has been buoyed over the last two years in part by the increase in growth of a specific retail category—book superstores. Amazon.com created a market for the digital bookshelf, thereby changing the way consumers shop for and purchase books. Although there has been a change in how a segment of the populations buys its books, the brick-and-mortar book sellers have yet to be put out of business. Barnes and Noble and Borders, both of which are U.S.

[1]Jeffrey F. Rayport and John J. Sviokla, "Managing In the Marketspace," *Harvard Business Review* (November-December 1994), pp. 141-53.

[2]Clinton Wilder, "Web Data—Tapping the Pipeline—Web Sites Can Offer a Wealth of Customer Data; Smart Companies are Mining, Analyzing, and Acting On It for Competitive Advantage," *Information Week* (March 15 1999), p. 38.

[3]IBID.

[4]Christopher C. Nadherny, "Technology and direct marketing leadership," *Direct Marketing,* (November 1998), p. 42-45.

[5]Roger O. Crockett, "A Web That Looks Like The World," *Business Week* E.BIZ, (March 22, 1999), p. EB46-47.

retailers, as well as Canadian booksellers Chapters and Indigo, now have both storefronts as well as Web sites. These major book retailers have been under increased pressure ever since Amazon.com demonstrated that a group of consumers was prepared to shop for and purchase books online. With consumers using the Internet to shop for books, the competition for the book buyer has become more intense, both in-store and online.

Book superstores can now be classified as traditional and electronic. Spending on books through traditional bookstores was estimated at US $12.4 billion in 1998, up from US $11.9 billion with expectations that growth will continue to increase to US $14.5 billion by 2002.[6] This is a significant increase in a mature retail category, proving that books are good business both for virtual sellers like Amazon.com as well as conventional brick-and-mortar stores. Retailers selling both online and in-store will be able to capitalize on both channels of distribution, thereby integrating their marketing efforts. Amazon.com is being credited to a large extent with this growth in book buying. It is likely that amazon.com and its continued growth as a virtual seller has been a contributor to the interest in book buying, and examination of increased growth in use of technology has created a different type of book reader and purchaser.

Amazon.com knows its customers: "Our customers need to have three things: a computer, access to the Internet, and a credit card," says Bill Curry, spokesman for amazon.com. "A lot of demographic segments fall out when you have those requirements," he adds.[7] Although purchasing books may not have broad appeal, the three requirements may not thwart the typical instore book buyer, but having all three requirements does not necessarily encourage buying books through cyberspace.

THE REAL SHOPPING EXPERIENCE

Are there differences between online book buyers and those who still want the conventional book-buying experience? People typically go into a bookstore to shop, buy, browse, touch, meet people, and drink cappuccino.[8] A recent study examined the differences between the two groups of book buyers. The typical bookstore book buyer is 42 years old with a median annual income of US $39 000, as just as likely to be married or not, and 60 percent of them do not have children at home. "Women (53%) are slightly more likely than men (47%) to buy books. The online shopper, on the other hand, is slightly more likely to be male than female (51 percent male versus 49 percent female)."[9] Online book buyers tend to have higher-than-average incomes, with 44 percent earning between US $35 000 and US $75 000, and 36 percent have incomes of US $75 000 and higher. The remainder of online book buyers has annual incomes less than US $35 000.

Within the book business, a trend has been occurring within certain genres that is changing the demand of books within that particular genre. The concept of reader involvement accounts for book publishers creating demand for their authors' books. The Net is being used in a number of book categories to spread the word about popular authors and characters. Publishers that encourage readers to involve them in their favourite topic genre have drawn science-fiction and romance readers to the Net. Mystery readers, however, seem to be using the Net more than any other type of reader. "Mystery readers are generally very 'wired' and Internet savvy," says Kat Berman, director of online business for Penguin Putnam.[10] Mystery readers are an important segment of the book-reading public. They are considered heavy readers and very author-loyal. Mystery.com is an important place for mystery readers to gain more information about their favourite authors and to participate in interactive mystery stories. 'Mystery Monday" is an interactive chat room on iVillage.com, a Web site designed for and visited predominantly by women. This is a new promotion medium for publishers who are taking advantage of the interest in online book buying created by Amazon.com. It is an innovative way to promote new authors and increase the demand for books—regardless of how it is purchased. Avon Twilight is using consumer coupons to discount their mystery series. And Really Great Books, a small niche publisher, is offering a draw for a free book monthly at its Web site. Visitors to their Web site (www.reallygreatbooks.com) must provide their name and other information to qualify for the incentive. The company plans to use this to create a database designed for direct marketing campaigns.

Amazon.com has taken advantage of a number of trends in book selling, book publishing, and changing buying behaviour to realize incredible growth in revenue from its virtual stores. Amazon.com is best known for its pioneering in online book selling, but it has also expanded its service offerings to include music and videos. Expansion of its customer base is critical to amazon.com as they battle competition from both the online commerce market and traditional retailers wanting to grab a share of the increased market growth of books, CDs, and video.[11] In understanding the online book buyer, amazon.com has been able to develop an understanding of online buying behaviour that can be used when expanding into other complementary product categories.

[6]Marcia Mogelonsky, "Book biz boon," *American Demographics,* (March 1999), p. 16-17.

[7]IBID.

[8]Bob Metcalfe, "A glutton for punishment: Back with more predictions on the future of the Internet," *InfoWorld,* (April 12, 1999), p. 118.

[9]Marcia Mogelonsky, "Book biz boon," *American Demographics,* (March 1999), p. 16-17.

[10]James A. Matin, "Spinning a New Web," *Publishers Weekly,* "(April 26, 1999), p. 36.

[11]Amazon.com, Form 10K, 1998.

SITES WORTH A VISIT

www.women.com
www.seniornet.com
www.connect.gc.ca
www.bluemountain.com
www.shopnchek.com

Discussion Questions

1 Explain how you would segment the women's clothing market. Does your description of the various segments apply for women shopping online? Why or why not?

2 Describe the important variables in segmenting online book buyers? Compare these variables to variables used to segment book buyers shopping at traditional brick-and-mortar stores.

3 Visit the site www.connect.gc.ca. Based on what you see at the site, who is the target market? How does this Web site fit within the marketing program of the Canadian federal government?

4 In your opinion, what are the important segmentation variables for understanding the needs of online shoppers? How would you use this knowledge to encourage online purchasing?

Part Four

4 SATISFYING MARKETING OPPORTUNITIES

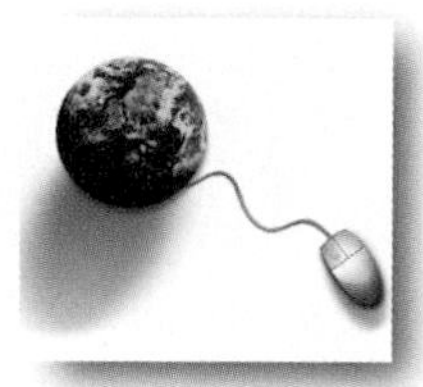

Part Four covers the unique combination of products, price, place, and promotion that results in an offering for potential customers. How products and services are developed and managed is the focus of Chapters 11, 12, and 13. Pricing is covered in Chapters 14 and 15 and Appendix B. Three chapters address the place (distribution) element, which includes retailing innovations. Finally, three promotion chapters cover topics ranging from Taco Bell's integrated marketing communication program, to Claritin's interactive Web advertising, to Joan Rothman's efforts to sell Dun & Bradstreet's database products and services.

CHAPTER ELEVEN

DEVELOPING NEW PRODUCTS AND SERVICES

11

AFTER READING THIS CHAPTER YOU SHOULD BE ABLE TO:

- Understand the ways in which consumer and industrial products can be classified and marketed.
- Explain the implications of alternative ways of viewing "newness" in new products.
- Analyze the factors contributing to a product's success or failure.
- Recognize and understand the purposes of each step of the new-product process.

A NEW-PRODUCT LESSON FROM 3M: A BETTER PRODUCT *AND* A CREATIVE WAY TO GET THAT MESSAGE TO TARGET BUYERS

3M's (www.3m.com) Todd DiMartini knows that "having a better mousetrap"—or in his case a better industrial adhesive—isn't enough! He knows he also has to get prospective buyers to make the effort to learn about the adhesive, understand its benefits, and think about ways to actually apply it. Here's a quick-take on the marketing issues he faced recently:

- *The product?* A revolutionary 3M VHB™ (for "very high bonding") tape made with high-strength structural adhesives that can make a continuous bond on cars and airplanes stronger than spot welds or rivets.
- *The target market?* Mechanical engineers responsible for the designs of everything from trucks and cars to ceilings in buildings.
- *The marketing task?* To get the target mechanical engineers to seriously consider the 3M VHB tape adhesive and actually use it in applications where they normally use screws or rivets.

Todd DiMartini and his marketing staff developed the advertisement shown on the opposite page that ran in design engineering magazines.[1] Note the detailed text, which stresses the VHB tape's points of difference to prospective users. How can DiMartini and his team rework the ad to make it even more effective in getting design engineers to consider VHB tape and actually specify it in their designs? The answer appears later in Chapter 11 and illustrates the team creativity needed for new-product success.

A brief look at 3M's adhesives technologies provides us with insights into how its new products enable 3M to find synergies to design multiple products for multiple markets (discussed in Chapters 10 and 22). In the 1950s,

3M developed an acrylate adhesive, for example, that made possible the introduction of its Scotch™ Magic™ Tape that you can write on with a pen or pencil. 3M's search for creative products led it into the research that makes it a world leader today in adhesives technology.

3M's research has led to dozens of revolutionary 3M adhesive products, including the following:

- 3M™ Post-It® Notes. The adhesive enables you to stick and unstick that note to your friend over and over again.
- 3M™ Nexcare™ Waterproof Bandages with Tattoo Designs. This is a bandage that combines superior, waterproof wound protection with popular designs that children want to wear.
- Scotch™ Pop-up Tape. This is the latest version of the tape everyone uses to wrap gifts and mend well-worn pages in textbooks.
- 3M™ Latitude™ Drug-in-Adhesive technology. This has led to breakthrough advances in delivery of pharmaceuticals, including the Minitran™ (nitroglycerin) transdermal delivery system, which is the smallest daily nitroglycerin patch in the world.[2]

Note the technology common to all these new products: 3M's ability to coat a variety of adhesives with strikingly different characteristics onto a continuous surface.

The essence of marketing is in developing products such as a new, technologically advanced adhesive to meet buyer needs. A **product** is a good, service, or idea consisting of a bundle of tangible and intangible attributes that satisfies consumers and is received in exchange for money or some other unit of value. Tangible attributes include physical characteristics such as colour or sweetness, and intangible attributes include becoming healthier or wealthier. Hence, a product includes the breakfast cereal you eat, the accountant who fills out your tax return, or the Canadian Red Cross, which provides you self-satisfaction when you donate your blood. In many instances we exchange money to obtain the product, whereas in other instances we exchange our time and other valuables, such as our blood.

The life of a company often depends on how it conceives, produces, and markets new products. This is the exact reason that 3M encourages its researchers to spend up to 15 percent of their time on projects of their own choosing—"bootlegging time" they call it. This strategy contributes to more than 500 3M patents a year.[3] In this chapter we discuss the decisions involved in developing and marketing new products and services. Chapters 12 and 13 cover the process of managing existing products and services, respectively.

THE VARIATIONS OF PRODUCTS

A product varies in terms of whether it is a consumer or industrial good. For most organizations the product decision is not made in isolation because companies often offer a range of products. To better appreciate the product decision, let's first define some terms pertaining to products.

Product Line and Product Mix

www.polaroid.com

A **product line** is a group of products that are closely related because they satisfy a class of needs, are used together, are sold to the same customer group, are distributed through the same type of outlets, or fall within a given price range.[4] Polaroid Canada has two major product lines consisting of cameras and film; Nike's product lines are

Nike's striking ads gain attention for its product lines of shoes and clothing.

Nike, Inc.
www.nike.com

www.sickkids.on.ca

shoes and clothing; the Toronto Hospital for Sick Children product lines consist of inpatient hospital care, outpatient physician services, and medical research. Each product line has its own marketing strategy.

Within each product line is the *product item,* a specific product as noted by a unique brand, size, or price. For example, Downy softener for clothes comes in 360-mL and 700-mL sizes; each size is considered a separate item and assigned a distinct ordering code, or *stock-keeping unit (SKU)*.

The third way to look at products is by the **product mix,** or the number of product lines offered by a company. Cray Research has a single product line consisting of supercomputers, which are sold mostly to governments and large businesses. Pillsbury Canada, however, has many product lines consisting of Green Giant canned and frozen vegetables, Pillsbury refrigerated baked goods, Prima Pasta, Old El Paso Mexican foods, and Underwood meat spreads.

Classifying Products

Both the federal government and companies classify products, but for different purposes. The government's classification method helps it collect information on industrial activity. Companies classify products to help develop similar marketing strategies for the wide range of products offered. Two major ways to classify products are by degree of product tangibility and type of user.

Degree of Tangibility Classification by degree of tangibility divides products into one of three categories. First is a *nondurable good,* an item consumed in one or a few uses, such as food products and fuel. A *durable good* is one that usually lasts over an extended number of uses, such as appliances, automobiles, and stereo equipment. *Services* are defined as activities, deeds, or other basic tangibles offered for sale to consumers in exchange for money or something else of value. According to this classification, government data indicate that Canada has a service economy, the reason for a separate chapter (Chapter 13) on the topic.

This classification method also provides direction for marketing actions. Nondurable products such as Wrigley's gum are purchased frequently and at relatively low cost. Advertising is important to remind consumers of the item's existence, and wide distribution in retail outlets is essential. A consumer wanting Wrigley's Spearmint Gum would most likely purchase another brand of spearmint gum if Wrigley's were not available. Durable products, however, generally cost more than nondurable goods and last longer, so consumers usually deliberate longer before purchasing them. Therefore, personal selling is an important component in durable-product marketing because it assists in answering consumer questions and concerns.

www.cdnair.ca

Marketing is increasingly being used with services. Services are intangibles, so a major goal in marketing is to make the benefits of purchasing the product real to consumers. Thus, Canadian Airlines shows the fun of a spring vacation or the joy of seeing grandparents. People who provide the service are often the key to its success in the market because consumers often evaluate the product by the service provider they meet—the Hertz reservation clerk, the receptionist at the university admissions office, or the nurse in the doctor's office.

Type of User The second major type of product classification is according to the user. **Consumer goods** are products purchased by the ultimate consumer, whereas **industrial goods** are products used in the production of other products for ultimate consumers. In many instances the differences are distinct: Oil of Olay face moisturizer and Bass shoes are clearly consumer products, whereas Cray computers and high-tension steel springs are industrial goods used in producing other products or services.

There are difficulties, however, with this classification because some products can be considered both consumer and industrial items. A Compaq computer can be sold to consumers as a final product or to industrial firms for office use. Each classification results in

No woman skier flies down a mountain like Picabo Street. At the 1994 Olympics in Lillehammer, her daring and skill made her the toast of international skiing and won her a silver medal in the Downhill, and four years later in Nagano, she topped herself by capturing an Olympic gold medal in the Super G. Picabo's chosen timepiece has long demonstrated the same combination of style and substance. In addition to being strikingly attractive, its legendary Oyster case, along with its Triplock winding crown and crystal, protects the complex mechanical movement under the most rigorous conditions. And in Picabo's case, those conditions can be very rigorous indeed.
ROLEX
PICABO STREET ATTACKS THE MOUNTAIN WITH A HEADLONG STYLE THAT IS AN ELECTRIFYING COMBINATION OF STRENGTH AND GRACE.
IT'S ALSO A PRETTY FAIR DESCRIPTION OF HER ROLEX.
Lady Yacht-Master
Officially Certified Swiss Chronometer
For the name and location of an Official Rolex Jeweler near you, please call 1-800-36ROLEX. Rolex, ♛, Oyster Perpetual, Triplock and Lady Yacht-Master are trademarks.

The Rolex brand of watch is an example of a specialty good.

Rolex
www.rolex.com

different marketing actions. Viewed as a consumer product, the Compaq would be sold through computer stores. As an industrial product, the Compaq might be sold by a salesperson offering discounts for multiple purchases. Classifying by the type of user focuses on the market and the user's purchase behaviour, which determine the marketing mix strategy.

CLASSIFYING CONSUMER AND INDUSTRIAL GOODS

Because the buyer is the key to marketing, consumer and industrial product classifications are discussed in greater detail.

Classification of Consumer Goods

Convenience, shopping, specialty, and unsought products are the four types of consumer goods. They differ in terms of (1) effort the consumer spends on the decision, (2) attributes used in purchase, and (3) frequency of purchase.

Convenience goods are items that the consumer purchases frequently, conveniently, and with a minimum of shopping effort. **Shopping goods** are items for which the consumer compares several alternatives on criteria, such as price, quality, or style. **Specialty goods** are items, such as Tiffany sterling silver, that a consumer makes a special effort to search out and buy. **Unsought goods** are items that the consumer either does not know about or knows about but does not initially want. Figure 11–1 shows how the classification of a consumer product into one of these four types results in different aspects of the marketing mix being stressed. Different degrees of brand loyalty and amounts of shopping effort are displayed by the consumer for a product in each of the four classes.

The manner in which a consumer good is classified depends on the individual. One person may view a camera as a shopping good and visit several stores before deciding on a brand, whereas a friend may view cameras as a specialty good and will only buy a Nikon.

The product classification of a consumer good can change the longer a product is on the market. When first introduced, the Litton microwave oven was unique, a specialty

FIGURE 11–1
Classification of consumer goods

BASIS OF COMPARISON	TYPE OF CONSUMER GOOD: CONVENIENCE	SHOPPING	SPECIALTY	UNSOUGHT
Product	Toothpaste, cake mix, hand soap, laundry detergent	Cameras, TVs, briefcases, clothing	Rolls Royce cars, Rolex watches	Burial insurance, thesaurus
Price	Relatively inexpensive	Fairly expensive	Usually very expensive	Varies
Place (distribution)	Widespread; many outlets	Large number of selective outlets	Very limited	Often limited
Promotion	Price, availability, and awareness stressed	Differentiation from competitors stressed	Uniqueness of brand and status stressed	Awareness is essential
Brand loyalty of consumers	Aware of brand, but will accept substitutes	Prefer specific brands, but will accept substitutes	Very brand loyal; will not accept substitutes	Will accept substitutes
Purchase behaviour of consumers	Frequent purchases; little time and effort spent shopping; routine decision	Infrequent purchases; comparison shopping; uses decision time	Infrequent purchases; extensive time spent to decide and get the item	Very infrequent purchases, some comparison shopping

good. Now there are competing brands on the market, and microwaves are a shopping good for many consumers.

Classification of Industrial Goods

A major characteristic of industrial goods is that their sales are often the result of *derived demand;* that is, sales of industrial products frequently result (or are derived) from the sale of consumer goods. For example, if consumer demand for Fords (a consumer product) increases, the company may increase its demand for paint-spraying equipment (an industrial product). Industrial goods are classified not only on the attributes the consumer uses but also on how the item is to be used. Thus, industrial products may be classified as production or support goods.

Production Goods Items used in the manufacturing process that become part of the final product are **production goods.** These include raw materials such as grain or lumber, as well as component parts. For example, a company that manufactures door hinges used by GM in its car doors is producing a component part. As noted in Chapter 7, the marketing of production goods is based on factors such as price, quality, delivery, and service. Marketers of these products tend to sell directly to industrial users.

Support Goods The second class of industrial goods is **support goods,** which are items used to assist in producing other goods and services. Support goods include installations, accessory equipment, supplies, and services.

- *Installations* consist of buildings and fixed equipment. Because a significant amount of capital is required to purchase installations, the industrial buyer deals directly with construction companies and manufacturers through sales representatives. The pricing of installations is often by competitive bidding.
- *Accessory equipment* includes tools and office equipment and is usually purchased in small-order sizes by buyers. As a result, instead of dealing directly with buyers, sellers of industrial accessories use distributors to contact a large number of buyers.
- *Supplies* are similar to consumer convenience goods and consist of products such as stationery, paper clips, and brooms. These are purchased with little effort, using the straight rebuy decision sequence discussed in Chapter 7. Price and delivery are key factors considered by the buyers of supplies.
- *Services* are intangible activities to assist the industrial buyer. This category can include maintenance and repair services and advisory services such as tax or legal counsel. The reputation of the seller of services is a major factor in marketing these industrial goods.

CONCEPT CHECK

1. Explain the difference between product mix and product line.
2. What are the four main types of consumer goods?
3. To which type of good (industrial or consumer) does the term *derived demand* generally apply?

NEW PRODUCTS AND WHY THEY FAIL

New products are the lifeblood of a company and keep it growing, but the financial risks are large. Before discussing how new products reach the stage of commercialization when they are available to the consumer, we'll begin by looking at *what* a new product is.

When Nintendo cancelled Sony's contract to provide parts, Sony got even—big time! The retaliation: Sony's new product, PlayStation.

Sony Corporation
www.sony.com

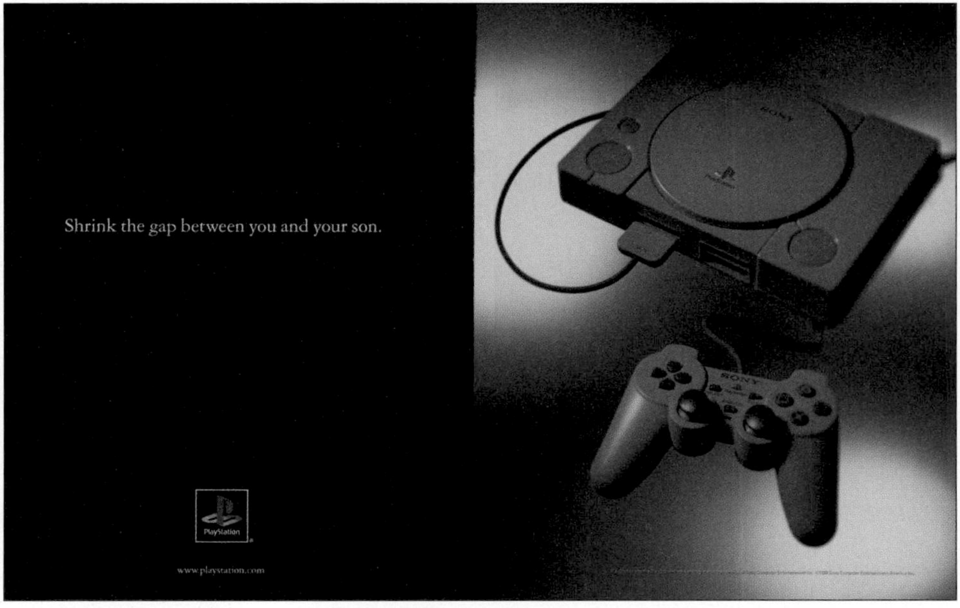

What Is a New Product?

The term *new* is difficult to define. Does changing the colour of a laundry detergent mean it is a new product, as a new hot-air appliance that cooks like a regular oven but with the speed of a microwave would be considered new? There are several ways to view the newness of a product.

Newness Compared with Existing Products If a product is functionally different from existing offerings, it can be defined as new. The microwave oven and automobile were once functionally new, but for most products the innovation is more a modification of an old product than a dramatic functional change.

Breathe Right® strips: What kind of innovation are they and what does this mean for marketing strategy? For the answers see the text and Figure 11–2.

Breathe Right®
www.breatheright.com

Newness in Legal Terms Consumer and Corporate Affairs Canada (CCAC) has determined that a product can be called "new" for only up to 12 months.

Newness from the Company's Perspective Successful companies are starting to view newness and innovation in their products at three levels. At the lowest level, which usually involves the least risk, is a product line extension. This is an incremental improvement of an exciting or important product for the company, such as Frosted Cheerios or Diet Cherry Coke or Sensor for Women—extensions of the basic Cheerios or Diet Coke or men's Sensor product lines, respectively. At the next level is a significant jump in the innovation or technology, such as Sony's leap from the micro tape recorder to the Walkman. The third level is true innovation, a truly revolutionary new product, like the first Apple computer in 1976. Sometimes strange circumstances cause a company to introduce a new product; Sony developed its widely successful PlayStation video game system because Nintendo cancelled a parts contract with Sony—suddenly putting Sony into a new line of products.[5] Effective new product programs in large firms deal at all three levels.

Newness from the Consumer's Perspective A fourth way to define new products is in terms of their effects on consumption. This approach classifies new products according to the degree of learning required by the consumer, as shown in Figure 11–2.

With *continuous innovation,* no new behaviours must be learned. Examples include Pillsbury's Toaster Strudel that competes with Kellogg's Pop Tarts, Mercedez-Benz Canada Inc.'s SLK convertible sportscar, Cadbury Chocolate Canada's TimeOut Candy bar, Nestle Canada's Parlour Signature line of premium ice cream, and Breathe Right nasal strips targeted toward athletes and people who snore. These innovations do not require people to change their behaviour to adopt these products. With consumer products requiring minimal consumer education, effective marketing depends on generating awareness and having strong distribution in appropriate outlets.

With *dynamically continuous innovation,* only minor changes in behaviour are required for use. An example is built-in, fold-down child seats such as those available in

FIGURE 11–2
Consumption effects define newness

LOW ← DEGREE OF CHANGE BEHAVIOUR AND LEARNING NEEDED BY CONSUMER → HIGH

BASIS OF COMPARISON	CONTINUOUS INNOVATION	DYNAMICALLY CONTINUOUS INNOVATION	DISCONTINUOUS INNOVATION
Definition	Requires no new learning by consumers	Disrupts consumer's normal routine but does not require totally new learning	Establishes new consumption patterns among consumers
Examples	Sensor and New Improved Tide	Electric toothbrush, compact disc player, and automatic flash unit for cameras	VCR, Jet Stream Oven, and home computer
Marketing emphasis	Generate awareness among consumers and obtain widespread distribution	Advertise benefits to consumers, stressing point of differentiation and consumer advantage	Educate consumers through product trial and personal selling

Chrysler minivans. Built-in car seats for children require only minor bits of education and changes in behaviour, so the marketing strategy is to *educate* prospective buyers on their benefits, advantages, and proper use.

A *discontinuous innovation* involves making the consumer learn entirely new consumption patterns in order to use the product. After decades of voice-recognition research, IBM introduced its ViaVoice Gold. If you are using ViaVoice Gold you are able to speak to your computer and watch your own words appear on your computer screen and you can also open Windows programs with your voice. The risk that IBM faces in introducing this discontinuous innovation is that people will have to learn new behaviours in producing word-processed memos and reports, which—along with potential technical glitches in the computer's ability to recognize your unique voice sounds—may restrict acceptance and sales of this new product.[6] Hence, marketing efforts for discontinuous innovations involve not only gaining consumer awareness but also educating consumers on both the benefits and proper use of the innovative product. Personal selling and creative advertising are often needed to achieve this consumer education—activities that can cost millions of dollars for some discontinuous innovations.

www.ibm.ca

Why Products Fail

The thousands of product failures that occur every year cost Canadian businesses millions of dollars. Recent research summarized in Figure 11–3 suggests that it takes about 3000 raw unwritten ideas to produce a single commercially successful new product.[7] To learn marketing lessons and convert potential failures to successes, we can analyze why new products fail and then study several failures in detail. As we go through the new-product process later in the chapter, we can identify ways such failures might have been avoided—admitting that hindsight is clearer than foresight.

FIGURE 11–3
What it takes to launch one commercially successful new product

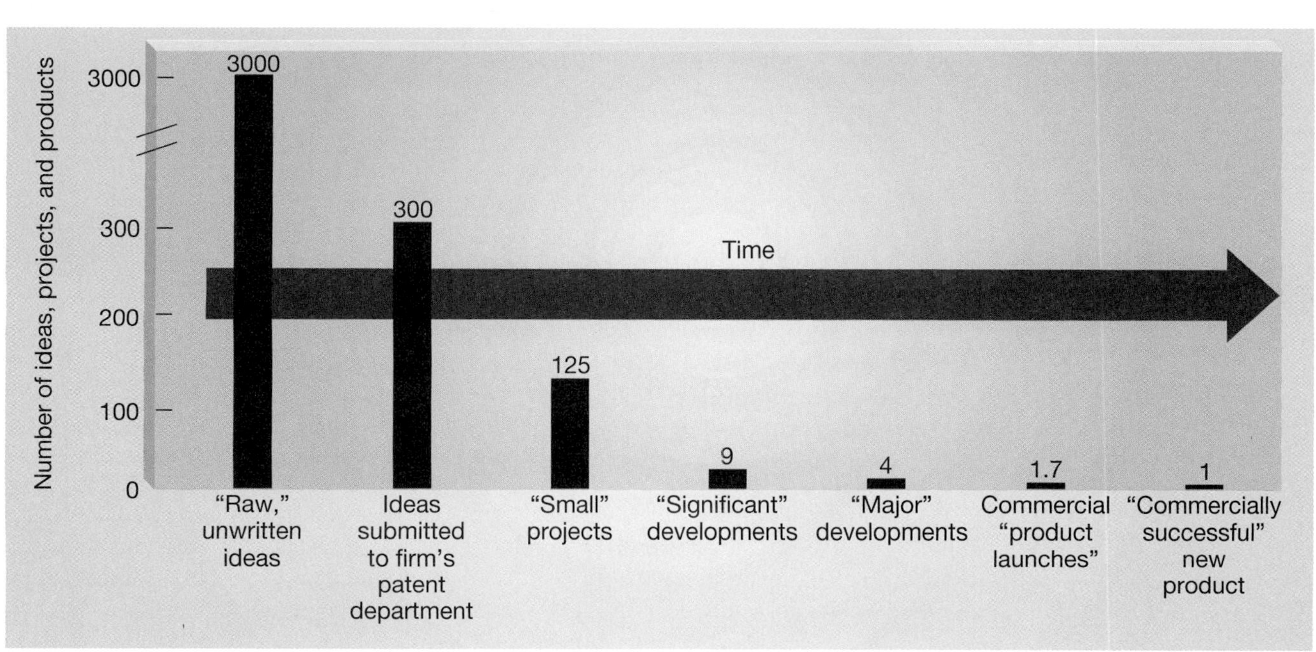

New product success or failure? For the special problems these products face, see the text.

Marketing Reasons for New-Product Failures Both marketing and nonmarketing factors contribute to new-product failures, as shown in the accompanying Marketing NewsNet box.[8] Using the research results from several studies[9] on new-product success and failure and also those described in the Marketing NewsNet box, we can identify seven critical marketing factors—sometimes overlapping—that often separate new product winners and losers:

www.generalmills.com

1. *Insignificant "point of difference."* Shown as the most important factor in the Marketing NewsNet box, a distinctive "point of difference" is essential for a new product to defeat competitive ones—through having superior characteristics that deliver unique benefits to the user. In the mid-1990s General Mills introduced "Fingos," a sweetened cereal flake about the size of a corn chip. Consumers were supposed to snack on them dry, but they didn't.[10] The point of difference was not important enough to get consumers to give up competing snacks such as popcorn, potato chips, or Cheerios from the box late at night.
2. *Incomplete market and product definition before product development starts.* Ideally, a new product needs a precise **protocol,** a statement that, before product development begins, identifies (1) a well-defined target market; (2) specific customers' needs, wants, and preferences; and (3) what the product will be and do. Without this precision, loads of money disappear as research and development (R&D) tries to design a vague product for a phantom market. This combines factors 2 and 5 in the Marketing NewsNet box. Apple Computer's hand-sized Newton computer that intended to help keep the user organized fizzled badly because no clear protocol existed. In contrast, the Palm Pilot is wildly successful because it was designed from the outset to link to desktop computers.[11]
3. *Too little market attractiveness.* Shown as factor 8 in the Marketing NewsNet, market attractiveness refers to the ideal situation every new product manager looks for: a large target market with high growth and real buyer need. But often, when looking for ideal market niches, the target market is too small and competitive to warrant the R&D, production, and marketing expenses necessary to reach it. In the early 1990s Kodak discontinued its Ultralife lithium battery. Seen as a major breakthrough because of its 10-year shelf life, the battery was touted as lasting twice as long as an alkaline battery. Yet the product was only available in the 9-volt size, which accounts for less than 10 percent of the batteries sold in North America.

CUSTOMER VALUE

MARKETING NEWSNET

What Separates New-Product Winners and Losers

What makes some products winners and others losers? Knowing this answer is a key to a new-product strategy. R. G. Cooper and E. J. Kleinschmidt studied 203 new industrial products to find the answers shown below.

The researchers defined the "product success rate" of new products as the percentage of products that reached the company's own profitability criteria. Product "winners" are the best 20 percent of performers and "losers" are the worst 20 percent. For example, for the first factor in the table below, 98 percent of the winners had a major point of difference compared with only 18 percent of the losers.

Note that the table below includes both marketing and nonmarketing factors. Most of the marketing factors below tie directly to the reasons cited in the text for new-product failures that are taken from a number of research studies. These include having a point of difference and a well-defined product before actual development starts (a product protocol).

FACTOR AFFECTING PRODUCT SUCCESS RATE	PRODUCT "WINNERS" (BEST 20%)	PRODUCT "LOSERS" (WORST 20%)	% DIFFERENCE (WINNERS–LOSERS)
1. Point of difference, or uniquely superior product	98%	18%	80%
2. Well-defined product before actual development starts	85	26	59
3. Synergy, or fit, with firm's R&D, engineering, and manufacturing capabilities	80	29	51
4. Quality of execution of technological activities	76	30	46
5. Quality of execution of activities before actual development starts	75	31	44
6. Synergy, or fit, with marketing mix activities	71	31	40
7. Quality of execution of marketing mix activities	71	32	39
8. Market attractiveness, ones with large markets, high growth, significant buyer need	74	43	31

4. *Poor execution of the marketing mix.* Coca-Cola thought its Minute Maid Squeeze-Fresh frozen orange juice concentrate in a squeeze bottle was a hit. The idea was that consumers could make one glass of juice at a time, and the concentrate stayed fresh in the refrigerator for over a month. After two test markets, the product was finished. Consumers loved the idea, but the product was messy to use, and the advertising and packaging didn't educate them effectively on how much concentrate to mix.
5. *Poor product quality on critical factors.* Overlapping somewhat with point 1, this factor stresses that poor quality on one or two critical factors can kill the product, even though the general quality is high. For example, the Japanese, like the British, drive on the left side of the road. Until 1996 North American carmakers sent Japan few right-drive cars—unlike German carmakers who exported right-drive models in a number of their brands.[12]
6. *Bad timing.* The product is introduced too soon, too late, or at a time when consumer tastes are shifting dramatically. Coaches of baseball teams are increasingly

FIGURE 11–4
Why did these new products fail?

As explained in detail in the text, new products often fail because of one or a combination of seven reasons. Look at the two products described below, and try to identify which reason explains why they failed in the marketplace:

- Del Monte's Barbecue Ketchup that contained finely chopped onions and was aimed at the heavy ketchup-eating segment.
- Mennen's Real deodorant, a cream-like antiperspirant developed for women, that was applied like a roll-on.

Compare your insights with those in the text.

concerned about the use of aluminum baseball bats that can rocket a baseball at a pitcher's head. Small wonder that Worth's "Copperhead ACX" bat is causing concern among these coaches. The ACX enlarges the bat's "sweet spot" using a piezoelectric circuit that automatically dampens vibrations and lengthens a batter's hits.[13]

7. *No economical access to buyers.* Grocery products provide an example. Today's mega-supermarkets carry 30 000 different products (meaning they carry 30 000 different SKUs). With about 34 new food products introduced each day, the fight for shelf space is tremendous in terms of costs for advertising, distribution, and shelf space.[14] Because shelf space is judged in terms of sales per square foot, Thirsty Dog! (a zesty beef-flavoured, vitamin-enriched, mineral-loaded, lightly carbonated bottled water for your dog) must displace an existing product on the supermarket shelves. Many small manufacturers simply do not have the money to gain effective exposure for their products.

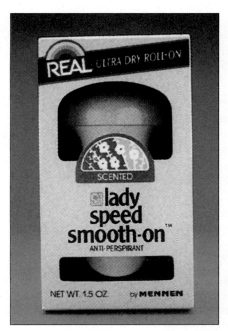

A Look at Some Failures Before reading further, study the product failures described in Figure 11–4, and try to identify which of the eight reasons is the most likely explanation for their failure. The two examples are discussed in greater detail below.

www.delmonte.com

Del Monte aimed its Barbecue Ketchup to the heavy ketchup-using segment—children and teenagers. The problem is that most consumers in this segment hate onions, so the product's difference—onions mixed with regular ketchup—worked against it. As a result, the target market was too small. The product was subsequently reintroduced as a gourmet sauce for meat cooked on outdoor grills.

Poor execution of the marketing mix hurt Real, Mennen's deodorant. The product was introduced with a $19 million advertising campaign. One problem, though, was that customers found that if they twisted the dispenser too hard, too much cream came out, creating an instant mess. Also, the name Real gave little indication of the product or its benefits.

Developing successful new products may sometimes involve luck, but more often it involves having a product that really meets a need and has significant points of difference over competitive products. The likelihood of success is improved by paying attention to the early steps of the new-product process described in the next section of the text.

CONCEPT CHECK

1. From a consumer's viewpoint, what kind of innovation would an improved electric toothbrush be?
2. What does "insignificant point of difference" mean as a reason for new-product failure?

THE NEW-PRODUCT PROCESS

Companies such as General Electric, Sony, or Procter & Gamble take a sequence of steps before their products are ready for market. Figure 11–5 shows the seven stages of the **new-product process,** the sequence of activities a firm uses to identify business opportunities and convert them to a saleable good or service. This sequence begins with new-product strategy development and ends with commercialization.

New-Product Strategy Development

For companies, **new-product strategy development** involves defining the role for a new product in terms of the firm's overall corporate objectives. This step in the new-product process has been added by many companies recently to provide a needed focus for ideas and concepts developed in later stages.

Objectives of the Stage: Identify Markets and Strategic Roles During this new-product strategy development stage the company uses the environmental scanning process described in Chapter 3 to identify trends that pose either opportunities or threats. Relevant company strengths and weaknesses are also identified. The outcome of new-product strategy development is not only new-product ideas but identifying markets for which new products will be developed and strategic roles new products might serve—the vital protocol activity explained earlier in the discussion of the Marketing NewsNet on new-product winners and losers.

Booz, Allen & Hamilton, Inc., an international consulting firm, asked firms what strategic role was served by their most successful recent product. These roles, shown in Figure 11–6, help define the direction of new-product development and divide into externally and internally driven factors.

Henry C. Yuen is an example of using an externally driven action to pre-empt a market segment (Figure 11–6). Not your typical TV couch potato, Yuen tried to tape a baseball game and got only snow. Unlike the rest of us who might just have mumbled, Yuen took his PhD degree in mathematics and co-invented "VCR Plus"—the device millions of TV fans use to set their VCRs by punching in numbers from newspaper listings.[15]

FIGURE 11–5
Stages in the new-product process

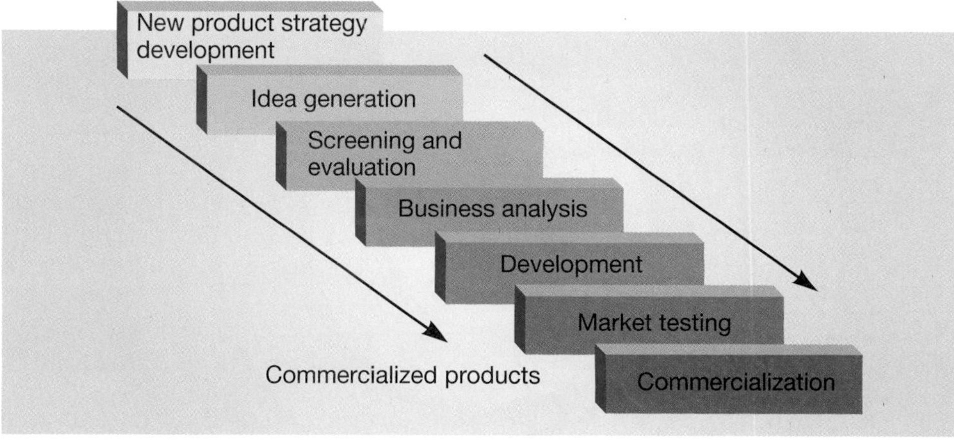

FIGURE 11–6
Strategic roles of most successful new products

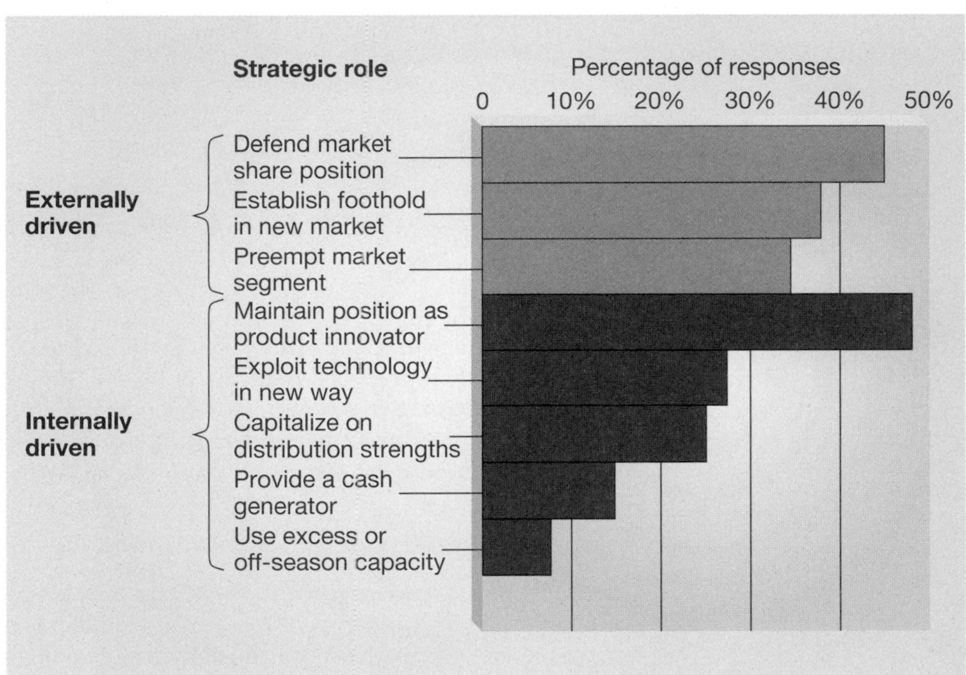

Cross-Functional Teams Another key to 3M's success in new-product development is its use of *cross-functional teams,* a small number of people from different departments in an organization who are mutually accountable to a common set of performance goals. Teams are especially important in new-product development so that individuals from R&D, marketing, manufacturing, finance, and so forth can simultaneously search together in a constructive environment for new product and market opportunities. In the past, 3M and other firms often utilized these department people in sequence—possibly resulting in R&D designing new products that the manufacturing department couldn't produce economically and that the marketing department couldn't sell.[16]

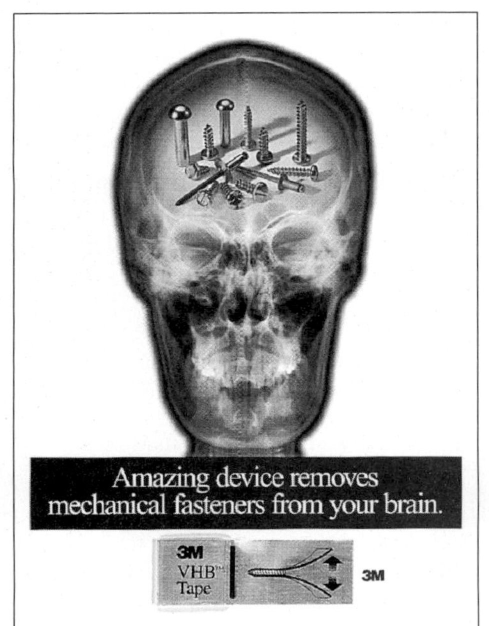

The VHB pull-apart challenge for design engineers; note the actual pull-apart films in the bottom of the ad

One 3M cross-functional team studied creative ways to get the attention of design engineers to find uses for its VHB tape—the example that started the chapter. The team came up with the idea of putting an actual piece of VHB tape between two pieces of film in the ad itself. The resulting ad (shown at left) then challenged engineers reading it to pull the film apart—and also to note their design problem on another part of the ad and to fax it to 3M.

3M's experiences suggest some conclusions about today's style of teamwork:

- Teams are ongoing, not just a one-shot effort.
- Teamwork takes time because the members have to learn about each other and find a comfort level.
- Team members can—and do—disagree, and that's okay.
- Teams can be informal or formal, depending on the task that needs doing.
- Teams need "champions," individuals willing and able to carry messages and requests to management and to move the project forward.

Because program and product champions are so important in marketing, they are discussed again in Chapter 22.

Idea Generation

Developing a pool of concepts as candidates for new products, or **idea generation,** must build on the previous stage's results. New-product ideas are generated by consumers, employees, basic R&D, and competitors.

Customer Suggestions Companies often analyze consumer complaints or problems to discover new-product opportunities. They also pose complaints to a sample of consumers, who are asked to suggest products with such deficiencies in order to identify new product opportunities. Listening to growing concerns about cholesterol and fat in its food, McDonald's reformulated its shakes with a low-fat mixture and introduced a low-fat hamburger.

Annette Pappas and Nita Metairie listened to women complain about runs or holes in their pantyhose for several years. Their solution: a three-legged pantyhose product called "Pantyhose Garment With Spare Leg Portion." The wearer inserts her legs into two of the leg openings in the conventional manner and the remaining unused leg portion is then gathered and the toe end is tucked into a pocket near the top of the pantyhose. If a run or hole develops in one of the leg portions being worn, the leg of the wearer can be placed into the undamaged spare leg portion.[17] Will it be a hit? Consumers will decide.

Employee and Co-Worker Suggestions Employees may be encouraged to suggest new product ideas through suggestion boxes or contests. The idea for General Mills's $500 million-a-year Nature Valley Granola Bars came when one of its marketing managers observed co-workers bringing granola to work in plastic bags.

Research and Development Breakthroughs Another source of new products is a firm's basic research, but the costs can be huge. As described in the Marketing NewsNet box,[18] Sony is the acknowledged world leader in new-product development in electronics. Its scientists and engineers produce an average of four new products each business day. Sony's research and development breakthroughs have led to innovative products, and its ability to manufacture and market those products has made it a legend in the electronics industry, popularizing VCRs, the Walkman, and digital video discs (DVDs).

"R.P. Fetchem" dog toy

Not all R&D labs have Sony's genius for moving electronic breakthroughs into the marketplace. Take Xerox Corporation's Palo Alto Research Center (PARC). In maybe the greatest electronic fumble of all time, by 1979 PARC had what's in your computer system now—graphical user interfaces, mice, windows and pull-down menus, laser printers, and distributed computing. Concerned with aggressive competition from Japan in its core photocopier business, Xerox didn't even bother to patent these breakthroughs. Apple Computer's Steven Jobs visited PARC in 1979, adapted many of the ideas for the Macintosh, and the rest is history.[19]

Even getting R&D breakthroughs into the marketplace—which PARC never did—doesn't guarantee success. Eye-popping high-definition television (HDTV) is making its grand entrance on the stage of Canadian consumer electronics—at initial prices of $5000 to $12 000.[20] While the TV picture is far better than on your analog TV set, is HDTV worth the improvement? As you read this, hundreds of manufacturers and retailers are also wondering. You, and millions of consumers like you, hold the answer.

TECHNOLOGY

MARKETING NEWSNET

The World Consumer Electronics Champ: And Its Name Is . . .?

The "battle for the living room" begins this company's 21st century. To win, it will have to keep linking technology and entertainment, content and hardware, digital insides and perfectly cool plastic outsides, in a new new new digital dance, daily. Late in the 20th century, it was already a nearly $70 billion concern polled as one of the world's "most respected brands" and known—along with Coke, Nike, and MTV—as one of the four most creative companies in the world. Yet its army of engineers work in an "eel's bedroom." Heard enough to know? It is Sony.

This Japan-based company with tentacles around the world made transistor history early on, launched the likes of Walkman and PlayStation, and came up with designs that said "wow" and wormed their way into consumers' hearts. But in a society that has gone from abacus to analog to digital in about one generation, you have to reinvent and reintegrate yourself regularly. Walkman, Handycam, Discman—keep running!

Under the new CEO, Nobuyuki Idei, who came out of marketing, Sony is attempting just that. Under way now: perfecting product to win the DVD (digital video disk) war, launching satellite broadcast service, making management more international at the same time, taking risks that can't always be market-researched, creating products that are lifestyle-exciting, computerizing mixes of video and audio, whatever!

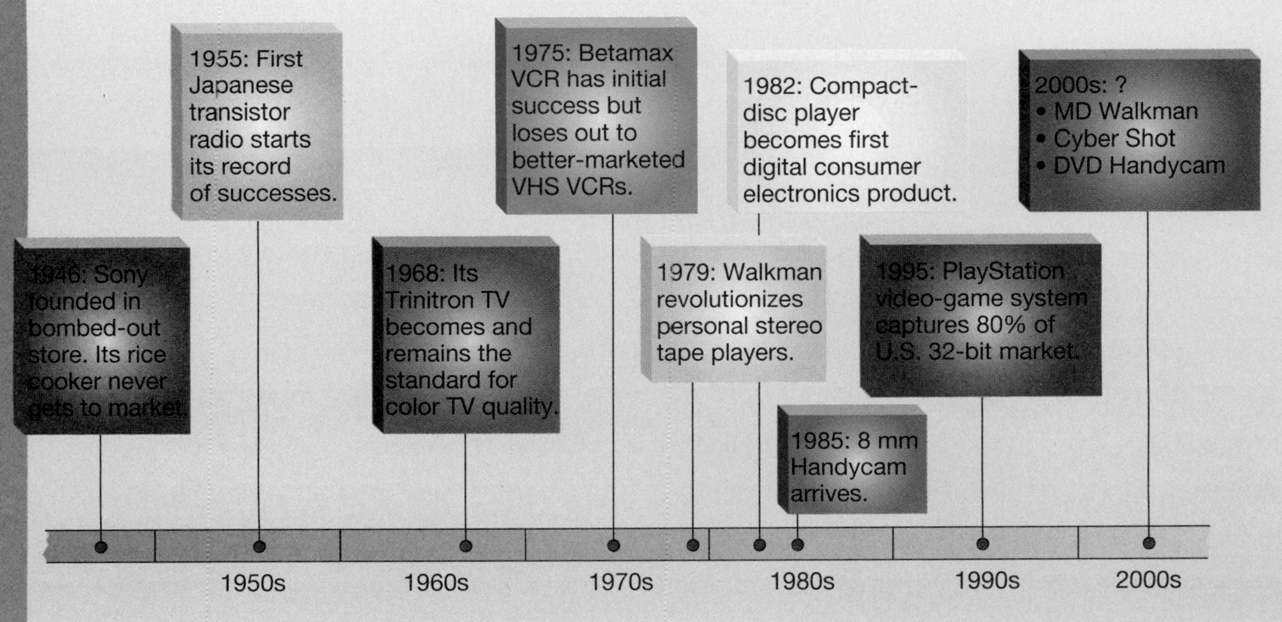

Professional R&D laboratories also provide new-product ideas. Labs at Arthur D. Little helped put the crunch in Cap'n Crunch cereal and the flavour in Carnation Instant Breakfast. Because broccoli is increasingly believed to contain cancer-fighting properties, Little's labs are trying to find ways to make the vegetable more appealing to today's consumers. Some ideas now in test: sweetened broccoli-based vegetable juices and a chocolate-flavoured powdered broccoli-juice drink mix. An idea sent back to the drawing boards: broccoli cereal.[21]

Competitive Products New-product ideas can also be found by analyzing the competition. A six-person intelligence team from the Marriott Corporation spent six

A year's worth of consumer interviews went into the development of Sun Chips.

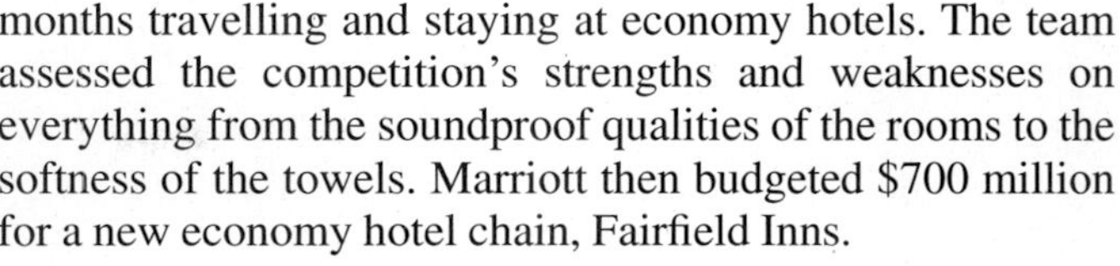

months travelling and staying at economy hotels. The team assessed the competition's strengths and weaknesses on everything from the soundproof qualities of the rooms to the softness of the towels. Marriott then budgeted $700 million for a new economy hotel chain, Fairfield Inns.

Screening and Evaluation

The third stage of the new product process is **screening and evaluation,** which involves internal and external evaluations of the new-product ideas to eliminate those that warrant no further effort.

www.ralstonpurina.com

Internal Approach Internally, the firm evaluates the technical feasibility of the proposal and whether the idea meets the objectives defined in the new-product strategy development step. In the 1990s Penn Racquet Sports, a large producer of tennis balls, faced flat sales because of a decade-long lull in recreational tennis. What to do? Penn Racquet employees observed that many used tennis balls are given as a toy to the family dog. So in 1998 the company designed and introduced R.P. Fetchem—a dye-free "natural felt fetch toy" that looks remarkably like . . . a tennis ball! One difference: The balls carry the Ralston Purina logo because of a licensing agreement with the giant dog-food producer.[22]

Tiny Magnetic Poetry, Inc. has a limited budget for customer research. But, as shown in the Web Link box, that has not restricted employees from extending the product line from magnetic words for refrigerator doors to electronic ones for the Internet.[23]

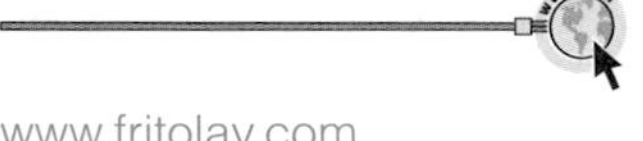

www.fritolay.com

External Approach Concept tests are external evaluations that consist of preliminary testing of the new-product idea (rather than the actual product) with consumers. Concept tests usually rely on written descriptions of the product but may be augmented with sketches, mockups, or promotional literature. Several key questions are asked during concept testing: How does the customer perceive the product? Who would use it? How would it be used?

Frito-Lay spent a year interviewing 10 000 consumers about the concept of a multigrain snack chip. The company experimented with 50 different shapes before settling on a thin, rectangular chip with ridges and a slightly salty, nutty flavour. The product, Sun Chips, is highly successful.

CONCEPT CHECK

1. What step in the new-product process has been added in recent years?
2. What are four sources of new-product ideas?
3. What is the difference between internal and external screening and evaluation approaches used by a firm in the new-product process?

Business Analysis

Business analysis involves specifying the features of the product and the marketing strategy needed to commercialize it and making necessary financial projections. This is the last checkpoint before significant capital is invested in creating a prototype of the product. Economic analysis, marketing strategy review, and legal examination of the proposed product are conducted at this stage. It is at this point that the product is analyzed relative to the firm's marketing and technological synergies, two criteria noted in the Marketing NewsNet shown earlier in the chapter.

WEB LINK ElectroMagnetic Poetry: From Fridge . . . to . . . Cyberspace

Brand and product line extensions, like adding Diet Coke to the Coke line or Frosted Cheerios to the Cheerios line, are well-established marketing strategies. But if you start with Magnetic Poetry—the words on a strip with magnetic backing mainly found on refrigerators—where do you go next?

It turns out the company has taken Magnetic Poetry into more than 50 items. The "Original Edition" has given birth to the Flip Series (words on both sides of the tiles), Kids Edition, Gardener Edition, and Really Big Words Edition. Pretty tame? Then consider Accessory Editions for car bumpers (Bumper Poet), your coffee mug (Magnetic Poetry), or your lunch box (Poetry Case). Or World Series will let you do foreign language sentences. Or you can paint your walls with Poetry Paint that makes any surface hold magnets, a surface that can be painted or papered over if you want.

For the computer segment, there's ElectroMagnetic Poetry, an application that can also be used as a screen saver. Word tiles will float by on your computer screen that your mouse clicks can grab and arrange. If your newly created poem is too good to lose, you can save it, print it, or paste it into an e-mail note to a friend.

To see these new product line extensions, check out: www.magneticpoetry.com

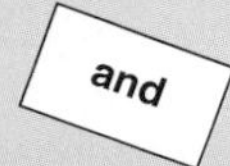

The marketing strategy review studies the new-product idea in relation to the marketing program to support it. The proposed product is assessed to determine whether it will help or hurt sales of existing products. Likewise, the product is examined to assess whether it can be sold through existing channels or if new outlets will be needed. Profit projections involve estimating the number of units expected to be sold but also the costs of R&D, production, and marketing.

As an important aspect of the business analysis, the proposed new product is studied to determine whether it can be protected with a patent or copyright. An attractive new-product proposal is one in which the technology, product, or brand cannot easily be copied.

Development

Product ideas that survive the business analysis proceed to actual **development,** turning the idea on paper into a prototype. This results in a demonstrable, producible product in hand. Outsiders seldom understand the technical complexities of the development stage, which involves not only manufacturing the product but also performing laboratory and consumer tests to ensure that it meets the standards set. Design of the product becomes an important element.

Liquid Tide, introduced by P&G, looks like a simple modification of its original Tide detergent. However, P&G sees this product as a technological breakthrough: the first detergent without phosphates that cleans as well as existing phosphate detergents. To achieve this breakthrough, P&G spent 400 000 hours and combined technologies from its laboratories in three countries. The new ingredient in Liquid Tide that helps suspend the dirt in wash water came out of the P&G research lab in North America. The cleaning agents in the product came from P&G scientists in Japan. Water-softening technology came from P&G's lab in Belgium. In a blind test consumers preferred Liquid Tide nine to one over the detergent of their choice.

The prototype product is tested in the laboratory to see if it achieves the physical standards set for it if used the way it is intended. But safety tests are also critical for when the product isn't used as planned. To make sure seven-year-olds can't bite

ETHICS

ETHICS AND SOCIAL RESPONSIBILITY ALERT

Sports Utilities versus Cars: Godzilla Meets a Chimp?

Make car wrecks safer? This sounds sort of stupid. But . . . the problem is death! The high and heavy pickups, vans, and especially sport utility vehicles (SUVs) are now involved in an increasing number of highway deaths. When one huge vehicle meets a bitty little car, the larger, higher one smashes the smaller one's passenger compartment, instead of going head-to-head at bumper level. The people in the cars, unfortunately, are more likely to be killed in such accidents.

The problem is also money. These mega-vehicles now account for a large percentage of Canadian automakers sales and profits. Improving the smaller cars—with side air bags and steel supports—is cheaper than lowering the frame or adding a crumple zone for the frame of the bigger vehicle. Nothing is easy. And consumers love the power of these hefty vehicles that are about 1000 kilograms heavier than a compact car.

But changes are on the way. Mercedes Benz has completely redesigned its M-class SUV. Mercedes engineers addressed the compatibility of their SUV with smaller cars so the Mercedes SUV frame and bumper is as much as 20 centimetres lower than its competitors' SUV models. This makes the bumpers of Mercedes SUVs and those of small cars more likely to meet in a crash, dramatically increasing the safety for small-car passengers.

Who should crush the crashes here? The federal government? The insurance companies? The vehicle manufacturers? Consumers?

Barbie's head off and choke, Mattel clamps her foot in steel jaws in a test stand and then pulls on her head with a wire. Similarly, car manufacturers have done extensive safety tests by crashing their cars into concrete walls. As mentioned in the Ethics and Social Responsibility Alert box, consumer groups are increasingly concerned about what happens when a pickup truck or sport utility vehicle hits a small car when their bumpers don't line up.[24] Auto industry tests are identifying some feasible, but costly, solutions.

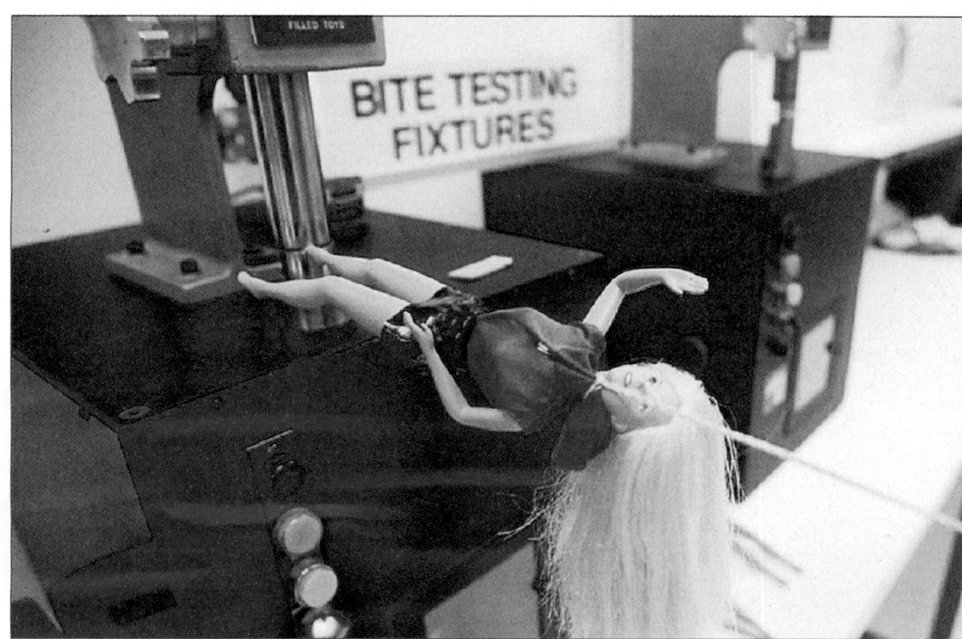

Mattel's laboratory testing subjects its toys and dolls, like Barbie here, to extreme tests to ensure quality and protect children.

Why do you want General Electric to pass the "bird strike test" on its new GE90 jet engine? For the answer, see the text.

Industrial products often have special, exacting test requirements. For example, jet engines for commercial aircraft have to pass a "bird strike test" and have minimal engine damage when carcasses of ducks or gulls are fired into the whirling jet engine operating on a test stand. Why this weird field test? To simulate the conditions that might occur when your plane ingests an unfortunate seagull or duck standing around on the runway at takeoff. General Electric's huge new GE90 is used to power Boeing 777 commercial jets. As a result of tests like these, GE engineers redesigned the GE 90's jet engine blades, and it passed its next bird strike test with flying colours.[25]

Market Testing

The **market testing** stage of the new-product process involves exposing actual products to prospective consumers under realistic purchase conditions to see if they will buy. Often a product is developed, tested, refined, and then tested again to get consumer reactions through either test marketing or purchase laboratories.

Test Marketing Test marketing involves offering a product for sale on a limited basis in a defined area. This test is done to determine whether consumers will actually buy the product and to try different ways of marketing it. Only about a third of the products test marketed do well enough to go on to the next phase. These market tests are usually conducted in cities that are viewed as being representative of Canadian consumers.

In examining the commercial viability of the new product, companies measure sales in the test area, often with *store audits* that measure the sales in grocery stores and the number of cases ordered by a store from the wholesaler. This gives the company an indication of potential sales volume and market share in the test area. Market tests are also used to check other elements of the marketing mix besides the product itself such as price, level of advertising support, and distribution. Representativeness of the test market to the target market for the product is very important so that results can be projected. Market tests also are time consuming and expensive because production lines as well as promotion and sales programs must be set up. Costs can run over a million dollars. Market tests also reveal plans to competitors, sometimes enabling them to get a product into national distribution first. Although Hunt-Wesson got its Prima Salsa Tomato Sauce into the test market first, Chesebrough-Pond's Ragu Extra Thick & Zesty beat it into national introduction. Competitors can also try to sabotage test markets. With such problems, some firms skip test markets completely or use simulated test markets.

Simulated Test Markets Because of the time, cost, and confidentiality problems of test markets, manufacturers often turn to *simulated* (or *laboratory*) *test markets* (*STM*), a technique that simulates a full-scale test market but in a limited fashion. STMs are often run in shopping malls, where consumers are questioned to identify who uses the product class being tested. Willing participants are questioned on usage, reasons for purchase, and important product attributes. Qualified persons are then shown TV commercials or print ads for the test product along with competitors' advertising and are given money to make a decision to buy or not buy a package of the product (or the competitors') from a real or simulated store environment. If the test product is not purchased, the consumer may receive it as a free sample and be interviewed later for reactions.

When Test Markets Don't Work Test marketing is a valuable step in the new-product process, but not all products can use it. Testing a service beyond the concept level is very difficult because the service is intangible and consumers can't see what they are buying. Similarly, test markets for expensive consumer products such as cars or VCRs or costly industrial products such as jet engines or computers are impractical. For these products consumer reactions to mockup designs or one-of-a-kind prototypes are all that is feasible.

An extreme example: In 1984 car designer Tom Matano took his marketing director for a spin in his new roadster prototype. "People in Porsches were chasing us and a guy was running next to us on the sidewalk, asking questions," Matano recalls. The marketing director became a believer and helped introduce the Mazda Miata, whose half-million cars sold make it one of the most popular sports cars ever—and a launching pad into the 21st century.

Commercialization

Finally, the product is brought to the point of **commercialization**—positioning and launching it in full-scale production and sales. Companies proceed very carefully at the commercialization stage because this is the most expensive stage for most new products, especially consumer products.

Increasing the Success Rate of New Products In recent years, companies have begun to recognize that speed is important in bringing a new product to market. Recent studies have shown that high-tech products coming to market on time are far more profitable than those arriving late. As a result, some companies—such as Sony, Nortel, Honda, Bell Canada, and Hewlett-Packard—have overlapped the sequence of stages described in this chapter. With this approach, termed *parallel development* (the simultaneous development by cross-functional teams of both the product and the production process), marketing, manufacturing, and R&D personnel stay with the product from conception to production. The results are a significant reduction in new-product development times. Honda has cut car development from five years to three, while Hewlett-Packard has reduced the development time for computer printers from 54 months to 22.

www.nortelnetworks.com

Space on supermarket shelves is so limited that retailers often charge manufacturers slotting fees and failure fees.

The Risks and Uncertainties of the Commercialization Stage The job is far from over when the new product gets to the commercialization stage. In fact, disasters still often occur. Some examples include the following:

- The high quality of the 5 or 50 prototypes that were handcrafted in the R&D lab with lots of tender loving care can't be replicated on the mass-production lines.
- Costs have gone so far beyond original budgets that customers won't buy the product at the new price point that must be set to make a profit.
- Buyers can't understand the benefits of the new product without extensive, costly education activities—necessitating new training of the sales force and distributors, along with new videos and infomercials.
- Competitors introduce their new product a few weeks before the firm's own product hits the market, making the product obsolete before potential customers ever see it.

The last point in the list—bad timing—gives new-product managers nightmares. IBM, for example, killed several laptop computer prototypes because competitors introduced better, more advanced machines to the market before IBM.

Grocery products have special problems at the commercialization stage. Because space is so limited on supermarket shelves, many require manufacturers to pay a **slotting fee,** a payment a manufacturer makes to place a new item on a retailer's shelf. This can run to several million dollars for a single product. But there's even another potential expense. If a new grocery product does not achieve a predetermined sales target, some retailers require a **failure fee,** a penalty payment by a manufacturer to compensate the retailer for sales its valuable shelf space never made. To minimize the financial risk of a new product failure, many grocery product manufacturers use *regional rollouts,* introducing the product sequentially into specific geographical areas of Canada to allow production levels and marketing activities to build up gradually.

Effective cross-functional teams at Hewlett-Packard have reduced new-product development times significantly.

Figure 11–7 identifies the purpose of each stage of the new-product process and the kinds of marketing information and methods used. The figure also suggests information that might help avoid some new product failures. Although using the new-product process does not guarantee successful products, it does increase a firm's success rate.

FIGURE 11–7
Marketing information and methods used in the new-product process

STAGE OF PROCESS	PURPOSE OF STAGE	MARKETING INFORMATION AND METHODS USED
New-product strategy development	Identify new-product niches to reach in light of company objectives	Company objectives; assessment of firm's current strengths and weaknesses in terms of market and product
Idea generation	Develop concepts for possible products	Ideas from employees and co-workers, consumers, R&D, and competitors; methods of brainstorming and focus groups
Screening and evaluation	Separates good product ideas from bad ones inexpensively	Screening criteria, concept tests, and weighted point systems
Business analysis	Identify the product's features and its marketing strategy, and make financial projections	Product's key features, anticipated marketing mix strategy; economic, marketing, production, legal, and profitability analyses
Development	Create the prototype product, and test it in the laboratory and on consumers	Laboratory and consumer tests on product prototypes
Market testing	Test product and marketing strategy in the marketplace on a limited scale	Test markets, simulated test markets (STMs)
Commercialization	Position and offer product in the marketplace	Perceptual maps, product positioning, regional rollouts

CONCEPT CHECK

1. How does the development stage of the new-product process involve testing the product inside and outside the firm?
2. What is a test market?
3. What is commercialization of a new product?

SUMMARY

1 A product is a good, service, or idea consisting of a bundle of tangible and intangible attributes that satisfies consumers and is received in exchange for money or some other unit of value. A company's product decisions involve the product item, product line, and range of its product mix.

2 Products can be classified by tangibility and by user. By degree of tangibility, products divide into nondurable goods, durable goods, and services. By user, the major distinctions are consumer or industrial goods. Consumer goods consist of convenience, shopping, and specialty products. Industrial goods are for either production or support.

3 There are several ways to define a new product, such as the degree of distinction from existing products, a time base specified by the CCAC, a company perspective, or effect on a consumer's usage pattern.

4 In terms of its effect on a consumer's use of a product, a discontinuous innovation represents the greatest change and a continuous innovation the least. A dynamically continuous innovation is disruptive but not totally new.

5 The failure of a new product is usually attributable to one of seven marketing reasons: insignificant point of difference, incomplete market and product definition before product development begins, too little market attractiveness, poor execution of the marketing mix, poor product quality on critical factors, bad timing, and no economical access to buyers.

6 The new-product process consists of seven stages. Objectives for new products are determined in the first stage, new-product strategy development; this is followed by idea generation, screening and evaluation, business analysis, development, market testing, and commercialization.

7 Ideas for new products come from several sources, including consumers, employees, R&D laboratories, and competitors.

8 Screening and evaluation can be done internally or externally.

9 Business analysis involves defining the features of the new product, a marketing strategy to introduce it, and a financial forecast.

10 Development involves not only producing a prototype product but also testing it in the lab and on consumers to see that it meets the standards set for it.

11 In market testing new products, companies often rely on market tests to see that consumers will actually buy the product when it's offered for sale and that other marketing mix factors are working. Products surviving this stage are commercialized—taken to market.

KEY TERMS AND CONCEPTS

product p. 286
product line p. 286
product mix p. 287
consumer goods p. 288
industrial goods p. 288
convenience goods p. 289
shopping goods p. 289
specialty goods p. 289
unsought goods p. 289
production goods p. 290
support goods p. 290
protocol p. 294
new-product process p. 297
new-product strategy development p. 297
idea generation p. 299
screening and evaluation p. 301
business analysis p. 301
development p. 302
market testing p. 304
commercialization p. 305
slotting fee p. 306
failure fee p. 306

INTERNET EXERCISE

Jalepeno soda? Aerosol mustard? These are just two of the more than 60 000 failed consumer products on the shelves of the New Product Showcase and Learning Center. You probably can't visit the Showcase personally to learn important new-product lessons like executives from firms such as Procter & Gamble and Kraft do, but you can visit its Web site (www.showlearn.com). Study several of the failed products on the Web site and try to identify which of the reasons discussed earlier in the chapter explain the failures—shown as "Bob's Favourite Flops" (www. showlearn.com/favflops). Or check out "Rising Stars" (www.showlearn.com/risingstar)—products seen as about to take off into fame and fortune.

APPLYING MARKETING CONCEPTS AND PERSPECTIVES

1 Products can be classified as either consumer or industrial goods. How would you classify the following products: (*a*) Johnson's baby shampoo, (*b*) a Black & Decker two-speed drill, and (*c*) an arc welder?

2 Are products such as Nature Valley Granola bars and Eddie Bauer hiking boots convenience, shopping, specialty, or unsought goods?

3 Based on your answer to problem 2, how would the marketing actions differ for each product and the classification to which you assigned it?

4 In terms of the behavioural effect on consumers, how would a PC, such as a Macintosh PowerBook or an IBM ThinkPad, be classified? In light of this classification, what actions would you suggest to the manufacturers of these products to increase their sales in the market?

5 Several alternative definitions were presented for a new product. How would a company's marketing strategy be affected if it used (*a*) the legal definition or (*b*) a behavioural definition?

6 What methods would you suggest to assess the potential commercial success for the following new products: (*a*) a new, improved ketchup, (*b*) a three-dimensional television system that took the company 10 years to develop, and (*c*) a new children's toy on which the company holds a patent?

7 Look back at Figure 11–6, which outlines the roles for new products. If a company followed the role of defending market share position, what type of positioning strategy might be implemented?

8 Concept testing is an important step in the new-product process. Outline the concept tests for (*a*) an electrically powered car and (*b*) a new loan payment system for automobiles that is based on a variable rate interest. What are the differences in developing concept tests for products as opposed to services?

CASE 11–1 PALM COMPUTING, INC.

Developing new products often requires a complicated and challenging sequence of activities. "It's not as simple as taking what the customer wants and creating a product," says Joe Sipher, director—Wireless Products at Palm Computing, Inc., a subsidiary of 3Com Corp. "If we did that, we would have ended up with something like Apple Computer's Newton, which was a failure because it incorporated too many features into the product." While this perspective seems counter-intuitive, it has proven highly successful for Palm Computing, the market leader for personal digital assistants (PDA).

THE COMPANY

The original PalmPilot inventors, Jeff Hawkins and Donna Dubinsky, started out developing personal computing connectivity and shorthand software for other

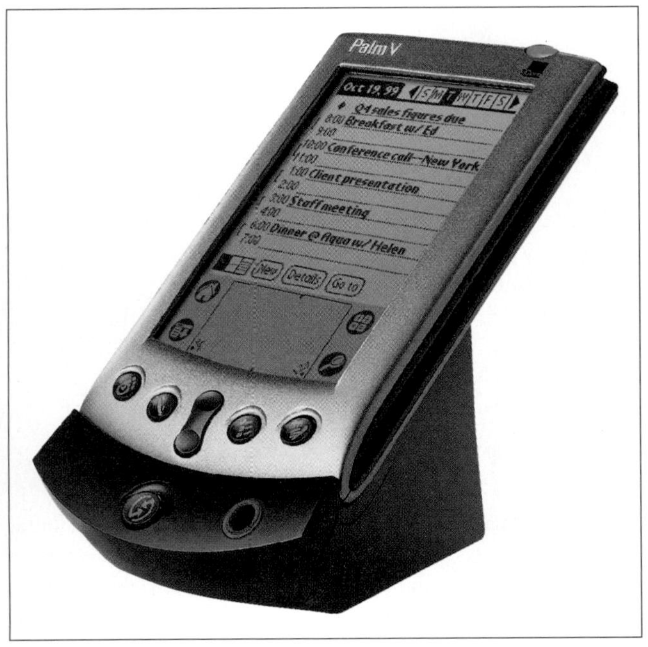

PDA manufacturers in the spring of 1994. According to Dubinsky, "We started out as an applications software company. We worked with Casio, Sharp, Hewlett-Packard, Apple, and others—everybody who was working in the field at that time. But none of the platforms were compelling. Most thought a PDA should be a smaller version of a laptop computer." Although Palm Computing was the leading software developer for these PDA entrants, sales were too low to keep the company running. "The reasons why early handheld computers failed were because they had too many features, making them too big, too slow, too heavy, and too expensive," explains Andrea Butter, vice president of marketing.

Palm Computing managers saw a dismal future in being the leading applications provider for a nonexistent market. However, as Butter states, "We felt we knew what customers wanted to do in handheld computing and one day an investor challenged us and said, 'If you know how to do it, why don't you do it?'" They accepted the challenge and today Palm Computing is the market share leader in the PDA industry. To provide additional funding and technology for the PalmPilot, U.S. Robotics, a leading modem manufacturer, acquired Palm Computing in 1995, which in turn was acquired in 1997 by 3Com Corp, a leading manufacturer of information access products and network system solutions.

During 1998, Palm Computing sold 1.3 million units. By 2000, Palm Computing's sales are expected to reach 1.8 million units in a total PDA market of 2.7 million units.

THE POSITIONING DILEMMA

Defining this type of product has been a challenge. These products have been referred to as information appliances, smart handheld computers, personal information managers, and personal digital assistants (PDA). Physically, these products have a thin, panel-like body (like the "communicator" from the original Star Trek series) measuring about 12 cm × 8 cm × 1 cm. They typically do not have keyboards or keypads; instead, they use a pen or stylus and handwriting recognition software to allow users to store addresses and telephone numbers, enter appointments on a calendar, make notes and to-do lists, and interface with personal computers to transfer e-mail and other data. Hawkins and Dubinsky viewed PDAs as digital replacements for paper-based systems, such as DayTimers, Rolodexes, and Post-it® Notes.

PALM COMPUTING'S NEW PRODUCT PROCESS

Hawkins used his own experience with the "GRiDPad," the first handheld computer developed in the mid-1980s, and "Graffiti," a shorthand-type of handwriting recognition software developed for other entrants in the PDA market, to design the original PalmPilot. Hawkins' R&D consisted of carrying a rectangular block of wood in his shirt pocket with "function buttons" glued to it. When people asked him if he was free for lunch, he would take out his "connected organizer," tap on a "button," and observe their reactions. Hawkins tried several variations before settling on a final design: the PalmPilot would only have four function buttons (calendar, addresses and phone numbers, to-do lists, and memos) because those were the most frequently used applications. In addition, Palm Computing conducted a survey among customers of Casio's "Zoomer" PDA. The most important finding was that 90 percent used a personal computer. As a result, the new PalmPilot would also include PC connectivity. Finally, the PalmPilot would only be sold in computer and office supply stores because their salespeople were perceived to have greater skills in selling technology-based products.

The original PalmPilot was launched in 1996 at Demo'96, a trade show whose attendees were technology opinion leaders. The PalmPilot was the "media darling of the show" and sales took off from there. The original PalmPilot has since been retired. The current PalmPilot Connected Organizer product line consists of the PalmPilot Professional ($149), the Palm III ($249), the Palm IIIx ($369), the Palm V ($449), and the Palm VII ($599). Each of these models has the same minimalist design as the original.

COMPETITION AND THE PDA MARKET

When Windows CE 1.0 came out in 1997, Dubinsky recalls, "We said, 'Oh-oh, it's all over for us now.'" But it turned out that consumers weren't interested in devices that were positioned between PDAs and personal computers. In 1998, International Data Corp. reported that Windows CE devices held only a 15 percent market share, but may garner a 55 percent share by 2002. Hardware manufacturers, such as Hewlett-Packard, Casio, Philips, etc., have partnered with Microsoft and are enthusiastic about newer versions of this OS software and other innovations in battery and memory technology that allow them to offer more features such as colour touch-screens for graphics, charts, and other presentations, slimmed down versions of Microsoft's popular Word and Excel programs, the familiar Windows-like interface, and Internet searching and paging via a PC card interface in their products. However, these products are still pricey, sluggish, and consume more power than those from Palm Computing. At the low end of the market, companies such as Casio and Royal have introduced single-function PDA devices at $99 or less. Finally, Palm Computing faces competition from Web-based personal information managers (PIM), which perform identical functions as the PalmPilot. These organizers are stored at one's Internet service provider and accessed via browsers, such as Netscape or Internet Explorer, or portals, such as Yahoo! or America Online (AOL).

THE FUTURE OF PALM COMPUTING

Palm Computing has responded by introducing two new products: the Palm IIIx and Palm V. Both compete with Windows CE-based systems. Both products offer better screen contrast and faster processors, but no changes in the Palm OS, the "operating system" software that gives these PDAs their handwriting recognition, time management, database (address and telephone number), and note-taking functionality. The Palm IIIx offers twice the memory as previous models while the Palm V has a sleeker, slimmer design, recessed buttons, and lithium instead of AAA batteries for 10 hours of life. Palm Computing also encouraged third-party software developers to extend the Palm OS's functionality to include e-mail, Internet search, expense recording, and even e-commerce applications. To further expand its share of the PDA market, Palm Computing has licensed its OS to other original equipment manufacturers (OEM) for their private-label brands, such as IBM's "WorkPad" PDA and Qualcomm's "pdQ," a combination PDA organizer and cellular telephone. Finally, Palm Computing has encouraged others to develop accessories for the Palm Connected Organizer product line.

Palm Computing's Palm VII, introduced in mid-1999, could revolutionize the PDA marketplace. The Palm VII is targeted at the rapidly growing wireless and mobile market, which has an estimated potential market of 21 million subscribers by 2002. The $599 Palm VII is positioned between a two-way pager and a laptop computer with wireless Internet access, and is virtually identical to the Palm III except for the wireless antenna that connects users to the proprietary Palm.net "Web clipping" service. E-Trade, Ticketmaster, The Weather Channel, Yahoo!, and other Palm.net content partners optimized content for the memory and small screen of Palm VII. In addition, users can send and receive short e-mail messages through Palm.net's iMessenger service. Future Palm Computing PDAs may include full Internet Web site access and e-mail messaging.

Questions

1 Which of the steps in the new product process discussed in Chapter 11 did Palm Computing use to develop the PalmPilot? What activities did Palm Computing use in each step?

2 What are the characteristics of the PalmPilot target market?

3 What kinds of learning or behavioural changes were required by consumers who purchased the PalmPilot?

4 What are the key "points of difference" of the PalmPilot when compared to substitute products?

5 How would you rate the PalmPilot on the following reasons for success or failure: significant points of difference; size of market; product quality; market timing; and access to consumers?

FRUIT & BERRIES
CLEARLY CANADIAN
11 FL. OZ. / 325 mL
BLACKBERRY
CLEARLY CANADIAN
RASPBERRY CREAM
CLEARLY CANADIAN
CARBONATED MINERAL WATER
CLEARLY CANADIAN
PEACH MANGO
CLEARLY CANADIAN
Sparkling Water Beverage
With Natural Peach & Mango Flavour
Natural Water Imported from Canada
11 FL. OZ. / 325 mL
WILD CHERRY
CLEARLY CANADIAN
TANGERINE
CLEARLY CANADIAN
STRAWBERRY MELON
CLEARLY CANADIAN
Sparkling Water Beverage
With Natural Strawberry & Melon Flavour
Natural Water Imported from Canada
11 FL. OZ. / 325 mL

CHAPTER TWELVE

MANAGING PRODUCTS AND BRANDS

12

AFTER READING THIS CHAPTER YOU SHOULD BE ABLE TO:

- Explain the product life cycle concept and relate a marketing strategy to each stage.
- Recognize the differences in product life cycles for various products and their implications for marketing decisions.
- Understand alternative approaches to managing a product's life cycle.
- Describe elements of brand personality and brand equity and the criteria used when selecting a good brand name.
- Explain the rationale for alternative brand name strategies employed by companies.
- Understand the benefits of packaging and warranties in the marketing of a product.

THE ROAD TO GROWTH

Many industry analysts credit Clearly Canadian Beverage Corporation (www.clearly.ca) of Vancouver with pioneering the alternative beverage industry in 1988 when it began marketing its premium-priced, single-serve sparkling flavoured water to North American consumers. To date, the company has sold more than 1.4 billion bottles of Clearly Canadian. The company is now focused on selling the next billion bottles of Clearly Canadian products. To achieve that goal, the company will need to continue to follow its pioneer spirit and innovate in order to stay current with consumers' needs and ahead of its competition.

Like Clearly Canadian itself, the alternative beverage market has grown dramatically over the past decade. The alternative beverage market is now valued at over $7.7 billion. Clearly Canadian Sparkling Flavoured Water, the product that started the whole phenomenon, continues to be a market leader. But now new products have also emerged such as ready-to-drink teas, sports beverages, and still waters. The industry players now range from those who began as small, entrepreneurial companies like Clearly Canadian, to major beverage companies, which are using their distribution and marketing muscle to garner their share of the alternative beverage market.

Despite the entry of the major global beverage companies and the crowded space on store shelves, new entrants, new products and even new categories of alternative beverages continue to emerge and keep the market dynamic. Experimentation and innovation, according to Doug Mason, president and CEO of Clearly Canadian, remain the key factors to success in the category. The company sees its road to growth as involving a diversified product portfolio, new manufacturing capability, and an expanded distribution system. The company will focus on building premium niche brands and building volume for non-Clearly Canadian products. But the Clearly Canadian line will continue to expand with new flavours, innovative packaging, and new sizes.

In its effort to diversify its product portfolio, Clearly Canadian introduced two new products. Clearly Canadian O+2, an oxygen-enhanced beverage for active adults, and Battery, an energy drink that energizes and fuels the body. These products enter the existing portfolio which includes the core brand, Clearly Canadian Sparkling Flavoured Water; Cascade Clear, a still bottled water; Fruit Fresher, a noncarbonated fruit drink for children that is fortified with vitamins; Orbitz, a texturally enhanced beverage with flavoured gel spheres suspended in the bottle; and REfresher, a light-tasting, fruit-flavoured, noncarbonated beverage for young adults. To continue down the road to growth, the company will expand its geographic reach and continue to build more efficiency into its overall costs, particularly in the areas of production and distribution.[1]

This chapter shows how the actions taken by Clearly Canadian Beverage Corporation are typical of those made by successful marketers in managing products and brands in competitive marketing environments.

PRODUCT LIFE CYCLE

Products, like people, have been viewed as having a life cycle. The concept of the **product life cycle** describes the stages a new product goes through in the marketplace: introduction, growth, maturity, and decline (Figure 12–1).[2] There are two curves shown in this figure, total industry sales revenue and total industry profit, which represent the sum of sales revenue and profit of all firms producing the product. The reasons for the changes in each curve and the marketing decisions involved are discussed in the following pages.

Introduction Stage

The introduction stage of the product life cycle occurs when a product is first introduced to its intended target market. During this period, sales grow slowly, and profit is minimal. The lack of profit is often the result of large investment costs in product development, such as the $1 billion spent by Gillette to develop and launch the MACH 3 razor shaving system. The marketing objective for the company at this stage is to create consumer awareness and stimulate trial—the initial purchase of a product by a consumer.

Companies often spend heavily on advertising and other promotion tools to build awareness among consumers in the introduction stage. For example, Frito-Lay spent $30 million to promote its SunChips multigrain snacks to consumers and retailers, and Gillette budgeted $300 million in advertising alone to introduce the MACH 3 razor to consumers.[3] These expenditures are often made to stimulate *primary demand,* or desire for the product class (such as multigrain snack chips), rather than for a specific brand since there are no competitors with the same product. As competitors introduce their own products and the product progresses along its life cycle, company attention is focused on creating *selective demand,* or demand for a specific brand.

Other marketing mix variables also are important at this stage. Gaining distribution is often a challenge because channel intermediaries may be hesitant to carry a new product. Moreover, in this stage a company often restricts the number of variations of the product to ensure control of product quality. For example, SunChips originally came in only two flavours and Gillette currently offers only a single version of the MACH 3 razor.

During introduction, pricing can be either high or low. A high initial price may be used as part of a *skimming* strategy to help the company recover the costs of development as well as capitalize on the price insensitivity of early buyers. 3M is a master of this strategy. According to a 3M manager, "We hit fast, price high, and get the heck out when the me-too products pour in."[4] High prices also tend to attract competitors more

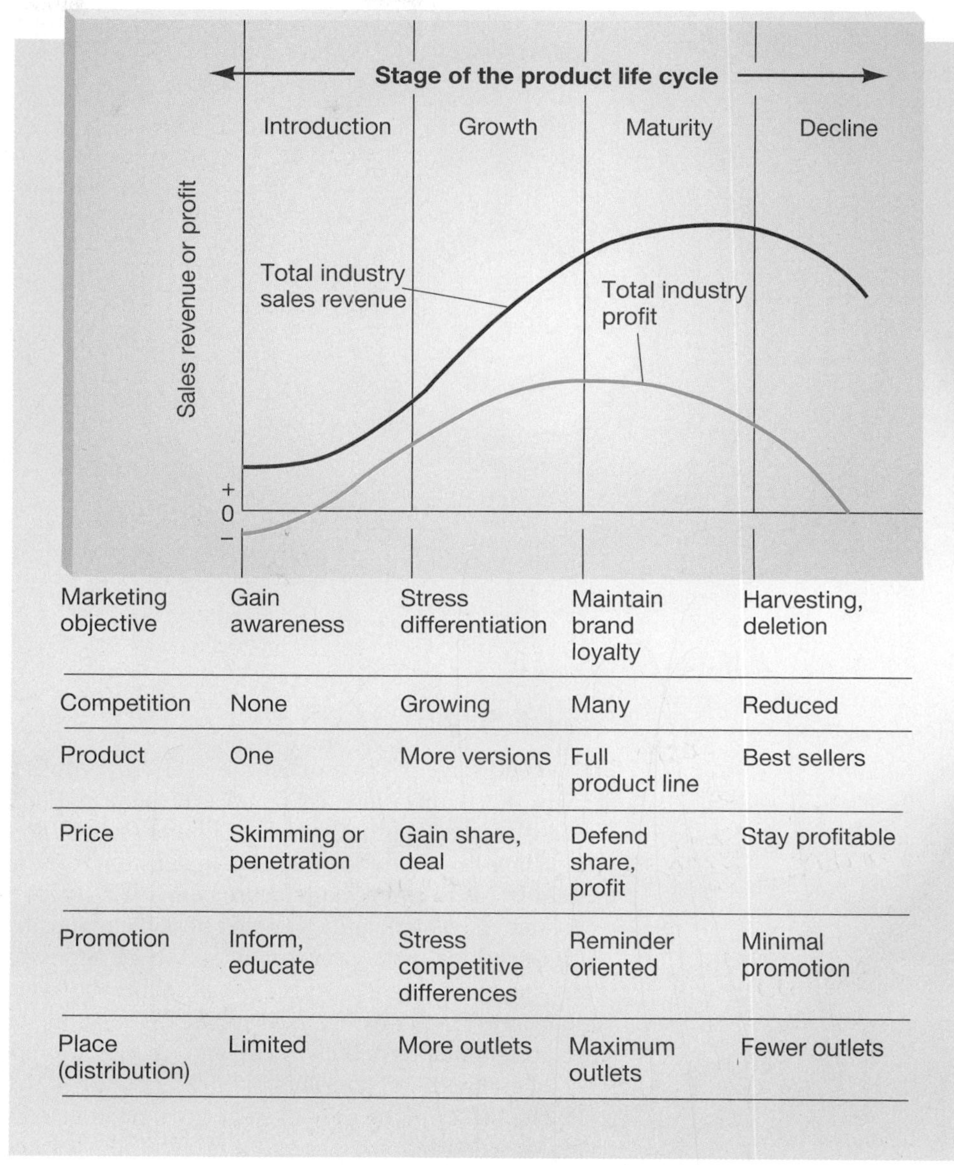

	Introduction	Growth	Maturity	Decline
Marketing objective	Gain awareness	Stress differentiation	Maintain brand loyalty	Harvesting, deletion
Competition	None	Growing	Many	Reduced
Product	One	More versions	Full product line	Best sellers
Price	Skimming or penetration	Gain share, deal	Defend share, profit	Stay profitable
Promotion	Inform, educate	Stress competitive differences	Reminder oriented	Minimal promotion
Place (distribution)	Limited	More outlets	Maximum outlets	Fewer outlets

FIGURE 12–1
How stages of the product life cycle relate to a firm's marketing objectives and marketing mix actions

eager to enter the market because they see the opportunity for profit. To discourage competitive entry, a company can price low, referred to as *penetration pricing.* This pricing strategy also helps build unit volume, but a company must closely monitor costs. These and other pricing techniques are covered in depth in Chapter 15.

Figure 12–2 charts the stand-alone fax machine product life cycle for business use from the early 1970s through 1999.[5] As shown, sales grew slowly in the 1970s and early 1980s after Xerox pioneered the first lightweight portable fax machine that sent and received documents. Fax machines were originally sold direct to businesses through company salespeople and were premium priced. The average price for a fax machine in 1980 was $12 700. By today's standards, those fax machines were primitive. They contained mechanical parts, not electronic circuitry, and offered few of the features seen in today's models.

Several product classes are in the introductory stage of the product life cycle. These include high-definition television (HDTV), electric vehicles, and digital cameras and camcorders.

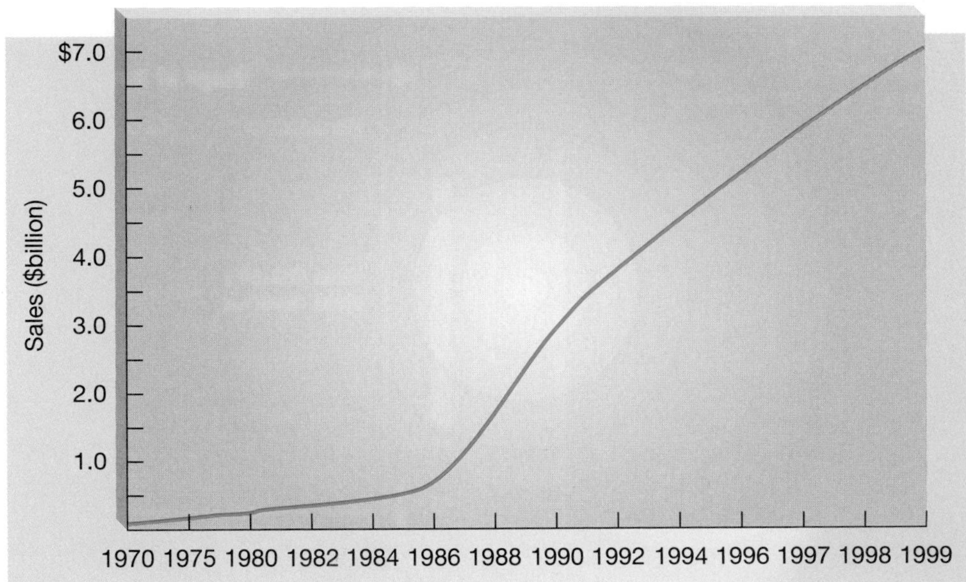

FIGURE 12–2
Product life cycle for the stand-alone fax machine for business use: 1970–1999

Growth Stage

The second stage of the product life cycle, growth, is characterized by rapid increases in sales. It is in this stage that competitors appear. For example, Figure 12–2 shows the dramatic increase in sales of fax machines from 1986 to 1990. The number of companies selling fax machines was also increasing, from one in the early 1970s to four in the late 1970s to seven manufacturers in 1983, which sold nine brands. By 1990 there were some 25 manufacturers and 60 possible brands from which to choose.

The result of more competitors and more aggressive pricing is that profit usually peaks during the growth stage. For instance, the average price for a fax machine declined from $3300 in 1985 to $1500 in 1990. At this point the emphasis of advertising shifts to stimulating selective demand, in which product benefits are compared with those of competitors' offerings.

www.alberto-culver.com

Product sales in the growth stage grow at an increasing rate because of new people trying or using the product and a growing proportion of *repeat purchasers*—people who tried the product, were satisfied, and bought again. As a product moves through the life cycle, the ratio of repeat to trial purchasers grows. Failure to achieve substantial repeat purchasers usually means an early death for a product. Alberto-Culver introduced Mr. Culver's Sparklers, which were solid air fresheners that looked like stained glass. The product moved quickly from the introduction to the growth stage, but then sales plummeted. The problem was there were almost no repeat purchasers because buyers treated the product like cheap window decorations, left them there, and didn't buy new ones. Durable fax machines meant that replacement purchases were rare; however, it was common for more than one machine to populate a business as their use became more widespread. In 1995, there was one fax machine for every eight people in a business.

Changes start to appear in the product during the growth stage. To help differentiate a company's brand from those of its competitors, an improved version or new features are added to the original design, and product proliferation occurs. Changes in fax machines included (1) models with built-in telephones; (2) models that used plain, rather than thermal, paper for copies; (3) models that integrated telex for electronic mail purposes; and (4) models that allowed for secure (confidential) transmissions. For SunChips and Clearly Canadian, new flavours and package sizes were added during the growth stage.

In the growth stage it is important to gain as much distribution for the product as possible. In the retail store, for example, this often means that competing companies fight for display and shelf space. Expanded distribution in the fax industry is an example. In 1986, early in the growth stage, only 11 percent of office machine dealers carried this equipment. By the mid-1990s, more than 70 percent of these dealers carried fax equipment, distribution was expanded to other stores selling electronic equipment, and the fight continues for which brands will be displayed.

Numerous product classes or industries are in the growth stage of the product life cycle. Examples include disposable 35-mm cameras, cellular telephones, and laptop computers.

Maturity Stage

The third stage, maturity, is characterized by a slowing of total industry sales or product class revenue. Also, marginal competitors begin to leave the market. Most consumers who would buy the product are either repeat purchasers of the item or have tried and abandoned it. Sales increase at a decreasing rate in the maturity stage as fewer new buyers enter the market. Profit declines because there is fierce price competition among many sellers and the cost of gaining new buyers at this stage increases.

Marketing attention in the maturity stage is often directed toward holding market share through further product differentiation and finding new buyers. For example, fax machine manufacturers developed models suitable for small and home businesses, which today represent a substantial portion of industry sales. Still, a major factor in a company's strategy in this stage is to reduce overall marketing cost by improving promotional and distribution efficiency.

Stand-alone fax machines for business use approached the maturity stage in the early 1990s. By 1998, more than 80 percent of industry sales were captured by six producers (Brother, Canon, Hewlett-Packard, Muratec, Panasonic, and Sharp), reflecting

Electric vehicles and digital cameras and camcorders are in the introductory stage of the product life cycle. Honda and Canon are two early marketers of these products.

Honda
www.honda.com
Canon
www.canondv.com

TECHNOLOGY

MARKETING NEWSNET Will the Upstart Internet Bury the Familiar Fax?

Technological substitution often causes the decline stage in the product life cycle. Will the Internet and E-mail replace fax machines?

This question has caused heated debates. Even though sales of Internet host computers are in the growth stage of the product life cycle (see the graph), fax machine sales continue to grow as well. Industry analysts estimate that there are more than 125 million E-mail user accounts worldwide. However, the growth of E-mail has not affected faxing because the two technologies do not directly compete for the same messaging applications.

E-mail is used for text messages and faxing is predominately used for communicating formatted documents by business users. Fax usage is expected to increase through 2000, and sales of stand-alone fax machines are expected to increase into the 21st century. Internet technology may eventually replace facsimile technology, but not in the foreseeable future.

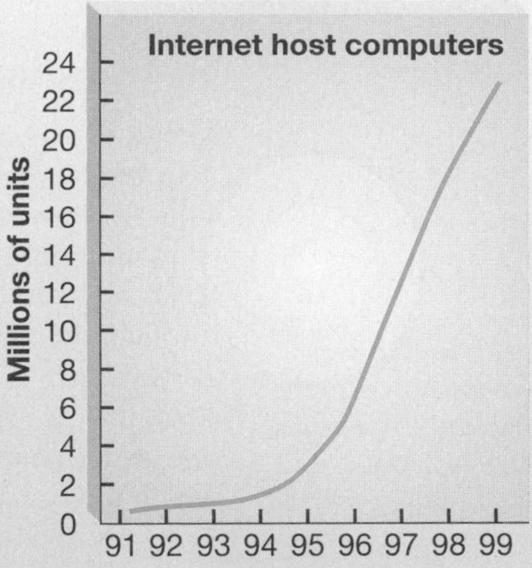

the departure of many marginal competitors. Industry sales had slowed in the late 1990s compared with triple-digit average annual dollar sales increases in the late 1980s. By 1999, there were an estimated 30 million stand-alone fax machines for business use installed throughout the world.

Numerous product classes and industries are in the maturity stage of their product life cycle. These include carbonated soft drinks, automobiles, and TVs.

Decline Stage

The decline stage occurs when sales and profits begin to drop. Frequently, a product enters this stage not because of any wrong strategy on the part of the company but because of environmental changes. Technological innovation often precedes the decline stage as newer technologies replace older technologies. The word-processing capability of personal computers pushed typewriters into decline. Compact discs did the same to cassette tapes in the prerecorded music industry.

Will Internet technology and e-mail spell doom for fax machines? The accompanying Marketing NewsNet offers one perspective on this question.[6] Products in the decline stage tend to consume a disproportionate share of management time and financial resources relative to their potential future worth. A company will follow one of two strategies to handle a declining product: deletion or harvesting.

Deletion Product *deletion,* or dropping the product from the company's product line, is the most drastic strategy. Because a residual core of consumers still consume or use a product even in the decline stage, product elimination decisions are not taken lightly. When Coca-Cola decided to drop what is now known as Classic Coke, consumer objection was so intense that the company brought the product back.

Harvesting A second strategy, *harvesting,* is when a company retains the product but reduces marketing support costs. The product continues to be offered, but salespeople do not allocate time in selling nor are advertising dollars spent. The purpose of harvesting is to maintain the ability to meet customer requests. For example, Gillette continues to sell its Liquid Paper correction fluid for use with typewriters in the era of word-processing equipment.

Some Dimensions of the Product Life Cycle

Some important aspects of product life cycles are (1) their length, (2) the shape of their curves, and (3) how they vary with different levels of the products.

Length of the Product Life Cycle There is no exact time that a product takes to move through its life cycle. As a rule, consumer products have shorter life cycles than industrial products. For example, many new consumer food products such as SunChips move from the introduction stage to maturity in 18 months. The availability of mass communication vehicles informs consumers faster and shortens life cycles. Also, the rate of technological change tends to shorten product life cycles as new product innovation replaces existing products.

The Shape of the Product Life Cycle The product life-cycle curve shown in Figure 12–1 is the *generalized life cycle,* but not all products have the same shape to their curve. In fact, there are several different life-cycle curves, each type suggesting different marketing strategies. Figure 12–3 shows the shape of life-cycle curves for four different types of products: high learning, low learning, fashion, and fad products.

A *high learning product* is one for which significant education of the customer is required and there is an extended introductory period (Figure 12–3A). Products such as home computers had this type of life-cycle curve because consumers have to understand the benefits of purchasing the product or be educated in a new way of performing a familiar task. Convection ovens, for example, necessitate that the consumer learn a new way of cooking and alter familiar recipes.

FIGURE 12–3
Alternative product life cycles

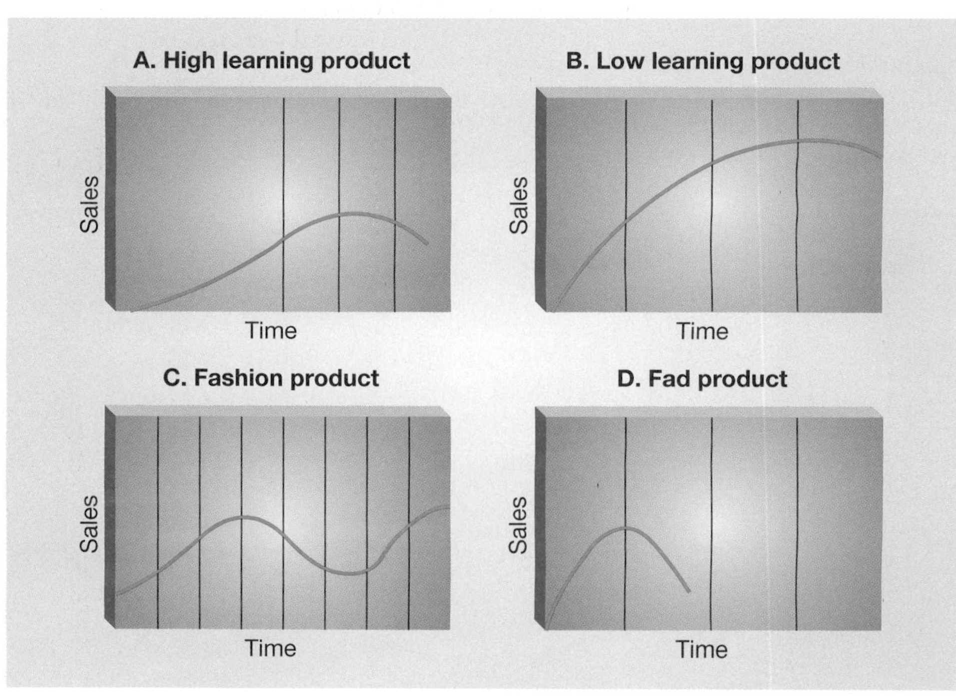

In contrast, for a *low learning product* sales begin immediately because little learning is required by the consumer, and the benefits of purchase are readily understood (Figure 12–3B). This product often can be easily imitated by competitors, so the marketing strategy is to broaden distribution quickly. In this way, as competitors rapidly enter, most retail outlets already have the innovator's product. It is also important to have the manufacturing capacity to meet demand. A recent example of a successful low learning product is Gillette's MACH 3 razor. Introduced in mid-1998, MACH 3 is projected to record $1 billion in sales before 2001.[7]

A *fashion product* (Figure 12–3C), such as hemline lengths on skirts or lapel widths on sports jackets, is introduced, declines, and then seems to return. Life cycles for fashion products most often appear in women's and men's clothing styles. The length of the cycles may be years or decades.

A *fad,* such as wall walkers or toe socks, experiences rapid sales on introduction and then an equally rapid decline (Figure 12–3D). These products are typically novelties. They include car tattoos, described as the first removable and reusable graphics for automobiles, and vinyl dresses, fleece bikinis, and an AstroTurf miniskirt.[8]

The Product Level: Class, Form, and Brand The product life shown in Figure 12–1 is a total industry or product class curve. Yet, in managing a product it is important to often distinguish among the multiple life cycles (class, form, and brand) that may exist. **Product class** refers to the entire product category or industry, such as video games shown in Figure 12–4A.[9] **Product form** pertains to variations within the class. For video games, product form exists in the computing capability of game players such as 8-, 16- and 32/64-bit machines. Game players have a life cycle of their own and typically move from the introduction stage to maturity in five years. A final type of life-cycle curve can represent a video-game brand such as Nintendo, Sony, or Sega. Sales of these brands are driven by the purchase of their game players and the number and quality of their games. Expect the video-game product class, product form, and brand life cycles to change again in 2000 following Sega's introduction of its Dreamcast 128-bit machine and Sony's new PlayStation.[10]

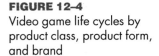

FIGURE 12–4
Video game life cycles by product class, product form, and brand

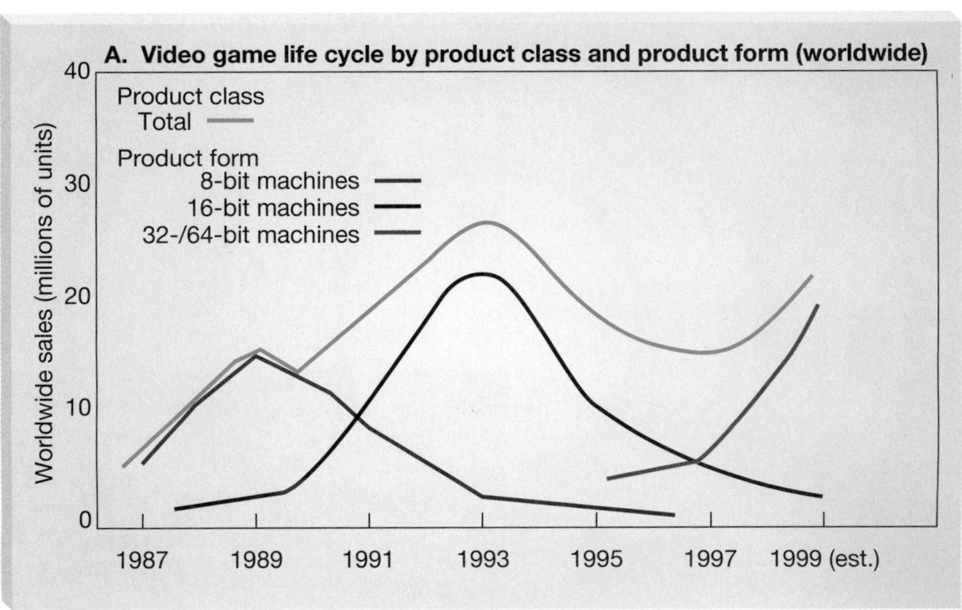

FIGURE 12–5
Five categories and profiles of product adapters

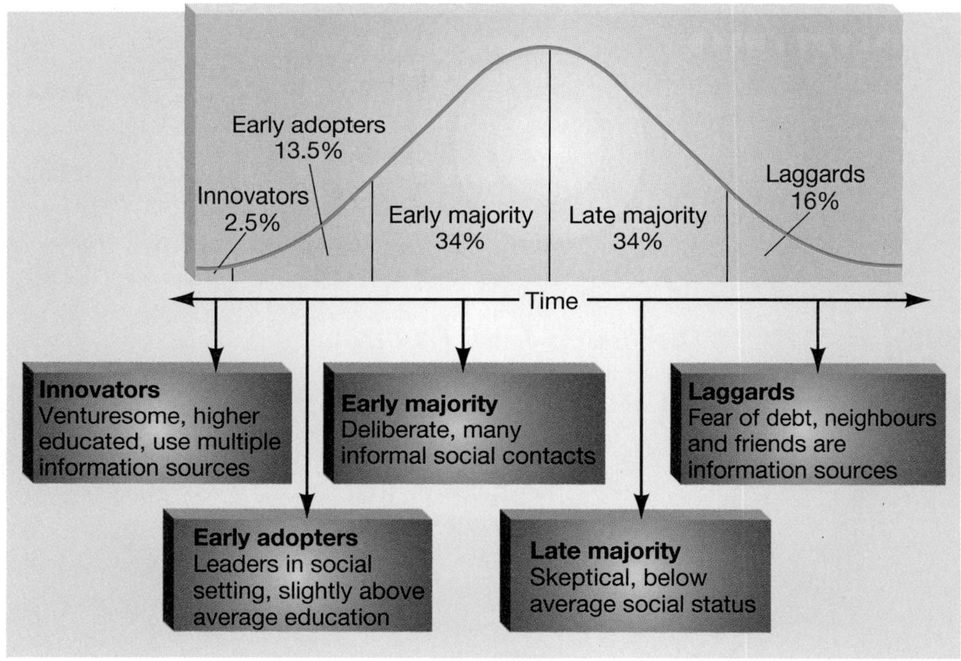

The Life Cycle and Consumers The life cycle of a product depends on sales to consumers. Not all consumers rush to buy a product in the introductory stage, and the shapes of the life-cycle curves indicate that most sales occur after the product has been on the market for some time. In essence, a product diffuses, or spreads, through the population, a concept called the *diffusion of innovation.*[11]

Some people are attracted to a product early, while others buy it only after they see their friends with the item. Figure 12–5 shows the consumer population divided into five categories of product adopters based on when they adopt a new product. Brief profiles accompany each category. For any product to be successful, it must be purchased by innovators and early adopters. This is why manufacturers of new pharmaceuticals try to gain adoption by leading hospitals, clinics, and physicians that are widely respected in the medical field. Once accepted by innovators and early adopters, the adoption of new products moves on to the early majority, late majority, and laggard categories.

Several factors affect whether a consumer will adopt a new product. Common reasons for resisting a product in the introduction stage are usage barriers (the product is not compatible with existing habits), value barriers (the product provides no incentive to change), risk barriers (physical, economic, or social), and psychological barriers (cultural differences or image).[12]

www.maybelline.com

Companies attempt to overcome these barriers in numerous ways. They provide warranties, money-back guarantees, extensive usage instructions, demonstrations, and free samples to stimulate initial trial of new products. For example, software developers offer demonstrations downloaded from the Internet. Maybelline allows consumers to browse through the Cover Girl Color Match system on its Web site to find out how certain makeup products will look. In-store and mailed samples are one of the most popular means to gain consumer trial. In fact, many companies and consumers alike consider a sample to be the best way to evaluate a new product. For example, some Ontario winemakers from the Niagara region believe that sampling (via taste testing) is critical in order for a new wine product to be successful in a crowded and competitive Canadian market.[13]

CONCEPT CHECK

1. Advertising plays a major role in the ________________ stage of the product life cycle, and ________________ plays a major role in maturity.
2. How do high learning and low learning products differ?
3. What does the life cycle for a fashion product look like?

MANAGING THE PRODUCT LIFE CYCLE

An important task for a firm is to manage its products through the successive stages of their life cycles. This section discusses the role of the product manager, who is usually responsible for this, and analyzes three ways to manage a product through its life cycle: modifying the product, modifying the market, and repositioning the product.

Role of a Product Manager

www.pillsbury.com

The product manager (sometimes called *brand manager*) manages the marketing efforts for a close-knit family of products or brands.[14] Introduced by P&G in 1928, the product manager style of marketing organization is used by consumer goods firms such as General Mills and Frito-Lay and by industrial firms such as Intel and Hewlett-Packard. Pillsbury Canada and General Motors of Canada also use product managers. All product managers are responsible for managing existing products through the stages of the life cycle, and some are also responsible for developing new products. Product managers' marketing responsibilities include developing and executing a marketing program for the product line described in an annual marketing plan and approving ad copy, media selection, and package design. The role of product managers in planning, implementing, and controlling marketing strategy is covered in depth in Chapter 22.

Modifying the Product

Product modification involves altering a product's characteristic, such as its quality, performance, or appearance, to try to increase and extend the product's sales. Wrinkle-free cotton slacks sold by Levi Strauss revitalized sales of men's casual pants and now account for 60 percent of the men's cotton pants product class sales. Iced tea, in dry mix or ready-to-serve formats, has enjoyed a revival in recent years. But a new modification of iced tea, frozen iced tea, is showing impressive sales increases. The Minute Maid Company of Canada Inc., which markets Nestea frozen iced tea, calls it the biggest new product it launched in the 1990s.[15]

New features, packages, or scents can be used to change a product's characteristics and give the sense of a revised product. Procter & Gamble revamped Pantene shampoo and conditioner with a new vitamin formula and relaunched the brand with a multimillion-dollar advertising and promotion campaign. The result? Pantene, a brand first introduced in the 1940s, became the top-selling shampoo and conditioner in an industry with more than 1000 competitors.[16]

Modifying the Market

With **market modification** strategies, a company tries to increase a product's use among existing customers, create new use situations, or find new customers.

Increasing Use Promoting more frequent usage has been a strategy of Campbell Soup Company. Since soup consumption rises in the winter and declines during the summer, the company now advertises more heavily in warm months to encourage consumers to think of soup as more than a cold-weather food. Similarly, The Florida Orange Growers Association advocates drinking orange juice throughout the day rather than for breakfast only.

Creating New Use Situation Finding new uses for an existing product has been the strategy behind Woolite, a laundry soap. Originally intended for the hand washing of woollen material, Woolite now promotes itself for use with all fine clothing items. Mars, Inc. suggests a new-use situation when it markets its M&M's candy as a replacement for chocolate chips in baked goods.

Finding New Users Harley-Davidson has successfully marketed its cruiser motorcycle to women. Women now represent nine percent of its customers compared with only two percent in 1985. Sony and Nintendo have expanded their user base by developing video games specially designed for children under 13 years old.[17]

Repositioning the Product

Often a company decides to reposition its product or product line in an attempt to bolster sales. *Product repositioning* is changing the place a product occupies in a consumer's mind relative to competitive products. A firm can reposition a product by changing one or more of the four marketing mix elements. Four factors that trigger a repositioning action are discussed next.

Reacting to a Competitor's Position One reason to reposition a product is because a competitor's entrenched position is adversely affecting sales and market share. Procter & Gamble repositioned its venerable Ivory soap bar in response to the success of Lever 2000, sold by Lever Brothers. Lever 2000, a bar soap that moisturizes, deodorizes, and kills bacteria, eroded P&G's dominance of the bar soap market. P&G responded with its own triple-threat soap called New Ivory Ultra Safe Skin Care Soap. The problem? The new Ivory doesn't float![18]

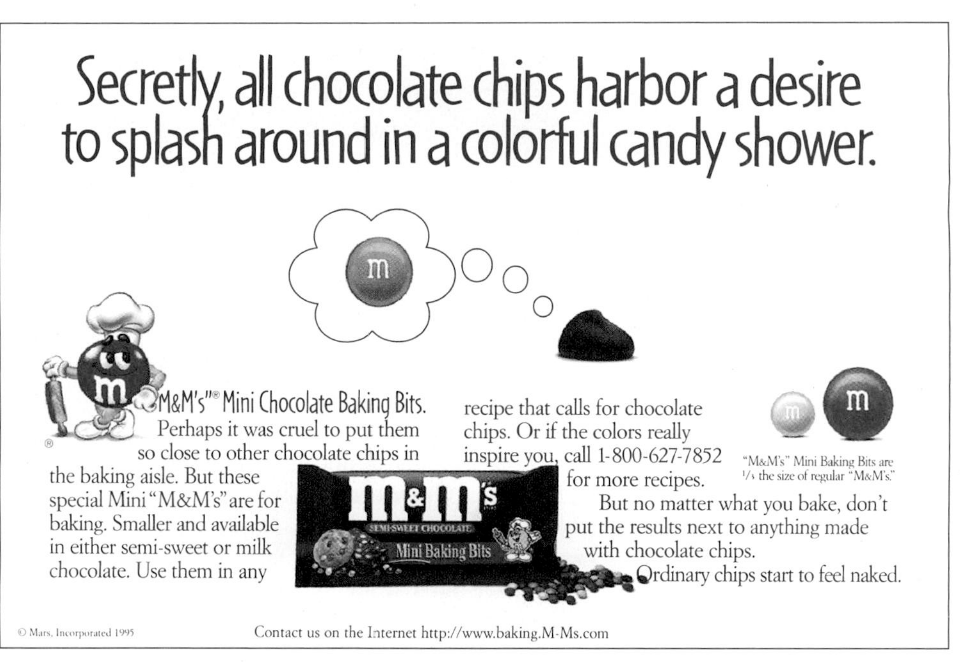

Mars, Inc. successfully extends the life cycle of its M&M's candy by finding new use situations.

Reaching a New Market When Unilever introduced iced tea in Britain in the mid-1990s, sales were disappointing. British consumers viewed it as leftover hot tea, not suitable for drinking. The company made its tea carbonated and repositioned it as a cold soft drink to compete as a carbonated beverage and sales improved. New Balance, Inc. has repositioned its athletic shoes for aging baby boomers. Instead of competing head-on against Nike, Reebok, and Fila, the company offers an expansive range of widths tailored for an older consumer's higher weight and networks with podiatrists who use the wide models to insert foot-support devices.[19]

Catching a Rising Trend Changing consumer trends can also lead to repositioning. Consumer interest in "functional foods" is an example.[20] These foods offer health and dietary benefits beyond nutrition. A number of products have capitalized on this trend. Quaker Oats now makes a government-approved claim that oatmeal, as part of a low saturated fat, low cholesterol diet, may reduce the risk of heart disease. Calcium-enriched products, such as Nutri-Grain bars, Tropicana juice, and Uncle Ben's Calcium Plus rice, focus on healthy bone structure for children and adults.

www.hbc.com

Changing the Value Offered In repositioning a product, a company can decide to change the value it offers buyers and trade up or down. **Trading up** involves adding value to the product (or line) through additional features or higher quality materials. Michelin has done this with its "run-flat" tire that can travel up to 70 kilometres after suffering total air loss. Dog food manufacturers, such as Ralston Purina, also have traded up by offering super premium foods based on "life-stage nutrition." Mass merchandisers, such as Sears Canada and The Bay can trade up by adding a designer clothes section to their store.

Trading down involves reducing the number of features, quality, or price. For example, airlines have added more seats, thus reducing leg room, and eliminated extras, such as snack service and food portions. Trading down often exists when companies engage in **downsizing**—reducing the content of packages without changing package size and maintaining or increasing the package price. Firms have been criticized for this practice, as described in the accompanying Ethics and Social Responsibility Alert.[21]

CONCEPT CHECK

1. How does a product manager help manage a product's life cycle?
2. What does "creating new use situations" mean in managing a product's life cycle?
3. Explain the difference between trading up and trading down in repositioning.

BRANDING

A basic decision in marketing products is **branding,** in which an organization uses a name, phrase, design, symbols, or combination of these to identify its products and distinguish them from those of competitors. A **brand name** is any word, "device" (design, sound, shape, or colour), or combination of these used to distinguish a seller's goods or services. Some brand names can be spoken, such as Clearly Canadian or Rollerblade. Other brand names cannot be spoken, such as the rainbow-coloured apple (the *logotype* or *logo*) that Apple Computer puts on its machines and in its ads. A **trade name** is a commercial, legal name under which a company does business. The Campbell Soup Company is the trade name of that firm.

A **trademark** identifies that a firm has legally registered its brand name or trade name so the firm has its exclusive use, thereby preventing others from using it.

ETHICS

ETHICS AND SOCIAL RESPONSIBILITY ALERT

Consumers Are Paying More for Less in Downsized Packages

For more than 30 years, Starkist put 6.5 ounces of tuna into its regular-sized can. Today, Starkist puts 6.125 ounces of tuna into its can but charges the same price. Colgate-Palmolive's Ajax king-size laundry detergent package has remained the same size, but the contents have been cut from 61 ounces to 55 ounces, and the package price increased from $2.59 to $2.79. Procter & Gamble cut the number of Pampers disposable diapers in its packages while leaving the price the same. The price of Mennen Speed Stick deodorant has not changed, but it now comes in a larger package with 2.25 ounces of deodorant versus 2.5 ounces in the previous, smaller package.

Consumer advocates charge that "downsizing" packages while maintaining or increasing prices is a subtle and unannounced way of taking advantage of consumers' buying habits. Manufacturers argue that this practice is a way of keeping prices from rising beyond psychological barriers for their products.

Is downsizing an unethical practice if manufacturers do not inform consumers that the package contents are less than they were previously?

In Canada, trademarks are registered under the Trademarks Act with Consumer and Corporate Affairs Canada. A well-known trademark can help a company advertise its offerings to customers and develop their brand loyalty. Figure 12–6 shows examples of well-known trademarks.

Because a good trademark can help sell a product, *product counterfeiting,* which involves low-cost copies of popular brands not manufactured by the original producer, has been a growing problem. Counterfeit products can steal sales from the original manufacturer or hurt the company's reputation.

Trademark protection is a significant issue in global marketing. For instance, the transformation of the Soviet Union into individual countries has meant that many firms, such as Xerox, have had to reregister trademarks in each of the republics to prohibit misuse and generic use ("xeroxing") of their trademarks by competitors and consumers.

Consumers may benefit most from branding. Recognizing competing products by distinct trademarks allows them to be more efficient shoppers. Consumers can recognize and avoid products with which they are dissatisfied, while becoming loyal to other, more satisfying brands. As discussed in Chapter 6, brand loyalty often eases consumers' decision making by eliminating the need for an external search. CanWest Global TV System uses a single brand "Global," which it says makes it easier for viewers to identify the network's stations and to find the schedule they have.

Brand Personality and Brand Equity

Product managers recognize that brands offer more than product identification and a means to distinguish their products from competitors. Successful and established brands take on a **brand personality,** a set of human characteristics associated with a brand name.[22] Research shows that consumers often assign personality qualities to products—traditional, romantic, rugged, sophisticated, rebellious—and choose brands that are consistent with their own or desired self-image. Marketers can and do imbue a brand with a personality through advertising that depicts a certain user or usage situation and conveys certain emotions or feelings to be associated with the brand. For example, the personality traits associated with Coca-Cola are real, and cool; with Pepsi, young, exciting, and hip; and with Dr. Pepper, nonconforming, unique, and fun.

FIGURE 12–6
Examples of well-known trademarks, brand names, and trade names

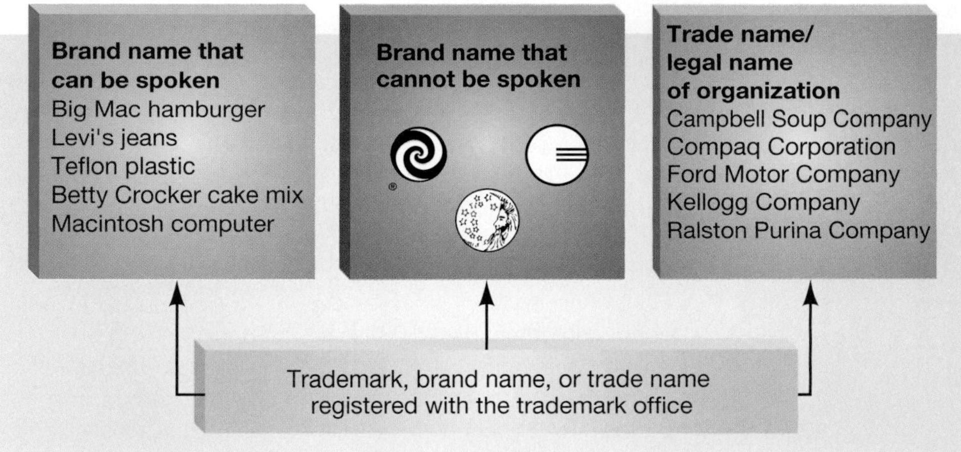

A good brand name is of such importance to a company that it has led to a concept called **brand equity,** the added value a given brand name gives to a product beyond the functional benefits provided.[23] This value has two distinct advantages. First, brand equity provides a competitive advantage, such as the Sunkist label that implies quality fruit and the Gatorade name that defines sport drinks. A second advantage is that consumers are often willing to pay a higher price for a product with brand equity. Brand equity, in this instance, is represented by the premium a consumer will pay for one brand over another when the functional benefits provided are identical. Intel microchips, Bose audio systems, Duracell batteries, Microsoft computer software, and Louis Vuitton luggage all enjoy a price premium arising from brand equity.

Licensing

The value of brand equity is evident in the strategy of licensing. **Licensing** is a contractual agreement whereby a company allows another firm to use its brand name, patent, trade secret, or other property for a royalty or a fee. Licensing can be very profitable to a licensor and a licensee as annual worldwide retail sales of licensed products exceed $110 billion.[24] Playboy has earned more than $260 million licensing its name for merchandise ranging from shoes in North America to wallpaper in Europe and cooking classes in Brazil. Murjani has sold more than $500 million of clothing worldwide bearing the Coca-Cola logo.

Licensing also assists companies in entering global markets with minimal risk. Frito-Lay licensed Elite Foods in Israel to produce and market Frito-Lay's Ruffles potato chips and Chee-tos cheese-flavoured corn puffs. These brands capture a significant percent of the salty snack market in Israel.

Picking a Good Brand Name

We take brand names such as Dial, Sanyo, Porsche, and Adidas for granted, but it is often a difficult and expensive process to choose a good name. Companies will spend between $25 000 and $100 000 to identify and test a new brand name.[25] For instance, Intel spent $45 000 for the Pentium name given its family of microchips.[26] There are five criteria mentioned most often when selecting a good brand name.[27]

- The name should suggest the product benefits. For example, Accutron (watches), Easy Off (oven cleaner), Glass Plus (glass cleaner), Cling-Free (antistatic cloth for drying clothes), Powerbook (laptop computer), and Tidy Bowl (toilet bowl cleaner) all clearly describe the benefits of purchasing the product.

Ruffles and Chee-tos are in Israel now, and more Frito-Lay snack items may follow. Entry into Israel was made possible through a licensing agreement with Elite Foods in Israel.

Elite Company
www.elite.co.il

- The name should be memorable, distinctive, and positive. In the auto industry, when a competitor has a memorable name, others quickly imitate. When Ford named a car the Mustang, Pintos, Colts, and Broncos soon followed. The Thunderbird name led to the Phoenix, Eagle, Sunbird, and Firebird.
- The name should fit the company or product image. Sharp is a name that can apply to audio and video equipment. Excedrin, Anacin, and Nuprin are scientific-sounding names, good for an analgesic. However, naming a personal computer PCjr, as IBM did with its first computer for home use, neither fit the company nor the product. PCjr, sounded like a toy and stalled IBM's initial entry into the home-use market.
- The name should have no legal or regulatory restrictions. Legal restrictions produce trademark infringement suits, and regulatory restrictions arise through improper use of words.[28] Increasingly, brand names need a corresponding address on the Internet. This further complicates name selection because more than two million domains are already registered.
- Finally, the name should be simple (such as Bold laundry detergent, Sure deodorant, and Bic pens) and should be emotional (such as Joy and Obsession perfumes). In the development of names for international use, having a nonmeaningful brand name has been considered a benefit. A name such as Esso does not have any prior impressions or undesirable images among a diverse world population of different languages and cultures. The 7Up name is another matter. In Shanghai, China, the phrase means "death through drinking" in the local dialect, and sales have suffered as a result.[29]

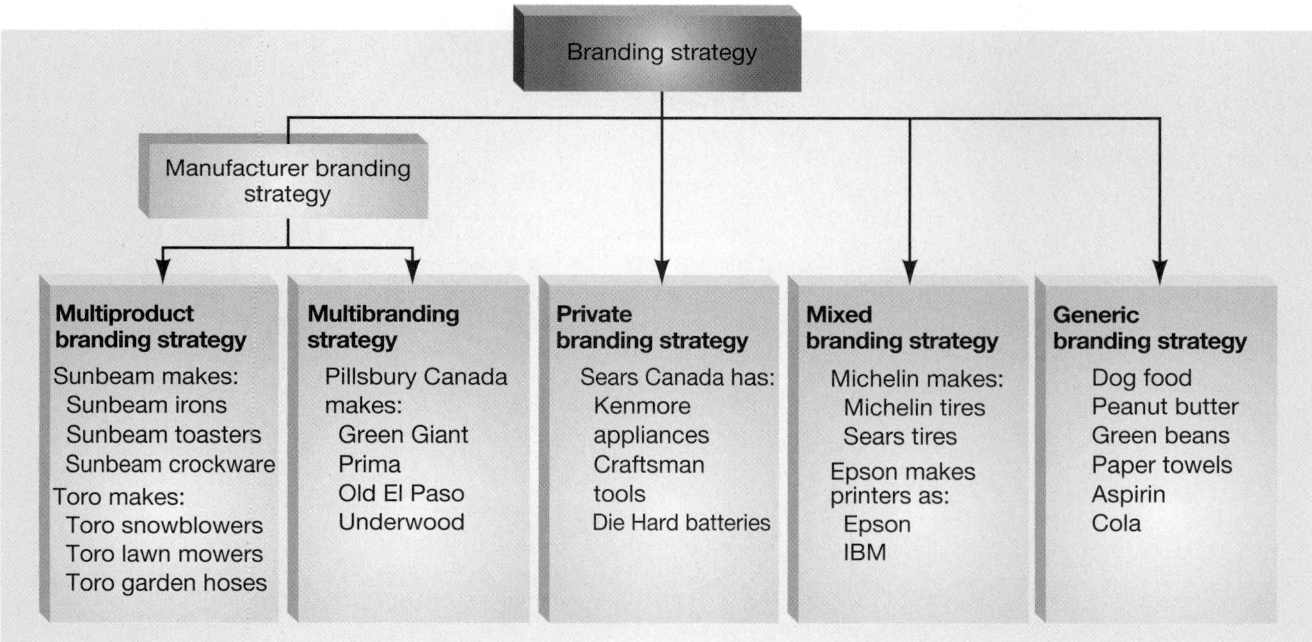

FIGURE 12–7
Alternative branding strategies

Branding Strategies

In deciding to brand a product, companies have several possible strategies, including manufacturer branding, reseller branding, or mixed branding approaches.

Manufacturer Branding With **manufacturer branding,** the producer dictates the brand name using either a multiproduct or multibrand approach. **Multiproduct branding** is when a company uses one name for all its products. This approach is often referred to as a *blanket* or *family* branding strategy (Figure 12–7).

There are several advantages to multiproduct branding. Capitalizing again on brand equity, consumers who have a good experience with the product will transfer this favourable attitude to other items in the product class with the same name. Therefore, this brand strategy makes possible *line extensions,* the practice of using a current brand name to enter a new market segment in its product class. Campbell Soup Company effectively employs a multiproduct branding strategy with soup line extensions. It offers regular Campbell soup, home-cooking style, and chunky varieties and more than 100 soup flavours. This strategy can also result in lower advertising and promotion costs because the same name is used on all products, thus raising the level of brand awareness.

Some companies employ *subbranding,* which combines a family brand with a new brand. For example, ThinkPad is a subbrand to the IBM name.

www.johnsonjohnson.com

A strong brand equity also allows for *brand extension,* the practice of using a current brand name to enter a completely different product class.[30] For instance, the equity in the Tylenol name as a trusted pain reliever allowed Johnson & Johnson to successfully extend this name to Tylenol Cold & Flu and Tylenol PM, a sleep aid. Fisher-Price, an established name in children's toys, was able to extend this name to children's shampoo and conditioners and baby bath and lotion products.

However, there is a risk with brand extensions. Too many uses for one brand name can dilute the meaning of a brand for consumers. Marketing experts claim this has happened to the Arm & Hammer brand given its use for toothpaste, laundry detergent, gum, cat litter, air freshener, carpet deodorizer, and anti-perspirant.[31]

Louis Vuitton. Writing.
New York Beverly Hills Aspen Atlanta Bal Harbour Shops Boca Raton Boston Carmel Chicago Dallas Denver Fairfax Square Houston King of Prussia Las Vegas Los Angeles Manhasset Miami Palm Beach Riverside Square San Diego San Francisco Scottsdale Seattle Short Hills Somerset Collection South Coast Plaza Banff Montreal Toronto Vancouver Calgary Edmonton Bermuda Puerto Rico
Sold exclusively in Louis Vuitton shops & select department stores in major cities in North & Latin America.
1.800.285.2255
LOUIS VUITTON

The strong brand equity of Louis Vuitton makes possible successful brand extensions, including fashion writing instruments.

Louis Vuitton
www.louisvuitton.com

A recent variation on brand extensions is the practice of **co-branding,** the pairing of two brand names of two manufacturers for joint-marketing purposes. Co-branding benefits firms by allowing them to enter new product classes, capitalize on an already established brand name in a product class, or reach new market segments. Second Cup of Toronto co-brands with Air Canada while rival Starbucks co-brands with Canadian Airlines. Rogers Cantel Communications and AT&T Canada Inc. also co-brand, offering consumers seamless wireless telecommunications throughout North America.[32]

An alternative manufacturer's branding strategy, **multibranding,** involves giving each product a distinct name. Multibranding is a useful strategy when each brand is intended for a different market segment. P&G makes Camay soap for those concerned with soft skin and Safeguard for those who want deodorant protection. Black & Decker markets its line of tools for the household do-it-yourselfer segment with the Black & Decker name, but uses the DeWalt name for its professional tool line. Disney uses the Miramax and Touchstone Pictures names for films directed at adults and its Disney name for children's films.

Multibranding strategies become more complex in the global marketplace. As an example, P&G uses multiple brand names for the same product when competing internationally. For instance, PertPlus shampoo is sold as Rejoice in Hong Kong, PertPlus in the Middle East, and Vidal Sassoon in the United Kingdom. However, international branding strategies do differ. In Japan, where corporate names are important, P&G markets the company's name prominently with the brand name of the product.

Compared with the multiproduct approach, promotional costs tend to be higher with multibranding. The company must generate awareness among consumers and retailers for each new brand name without the benefit of any previous impressions. The advantages of this approach are that each brand is unique to each market segment and there is no risk that a product failure will affect other products in the line.

The multibranding approach in Europe is slowly being replaced by **euro-branding,** the strategy of using the same brand name for the same product across all countries in the

Black & Decker uses a multibranding strategy to reach different market segments. Black & Decker markets its line of tools for the do-it-yourselfer market with the Black & Decker name, but uses the DeWalt name for its professional tool line.

Black & Decker
www.blackanddecker.com

European Union. This strategy has many of the benefits linked with multiproduct branding in addition to making Pan-European advertising and promotion programs possible.

Private Branding A company uses **private branding,** often called *private labelling* or *reseller branding,* when it manufactures products but sells them under the brand name of a wholesaler or retailer. Radio Shack, Sears, and Kmart are large retailers that have their own brand names. And recently, Zellers launched its Truly private brand hoping to foster the same customer loyalty as Loblaw's very successful President's Choice private brand.[33]

Matsushita of Japan manufactures VCRs for Magnavox, GE, Sylvania, and Curtis Mathes. The advantage to the manufacturer is that promotional costs are shifted to the retailer or other company, and the manufacturer can often sell more units through others than by itself. There is a risk, though, because the manufacturer's sales depend heavily on the efforts of others.

Mixed Branding A compromise between manufacturer and private branding is **mixed branding,** where a firm markets products under its own name and that of a reseller because the segment attracted to the reseller is different from their own market. Sanyo and Toshiba manufacture television sets for Sears as well as for themselves. This process is similar to Michelin's, which manufactures tires for Sears as well as under its own name. Kodak uses a mixed branding approach in Japan to increase its sales of 35-mm film. In addition to selling its Kodak brand, the company now makes "COOP" private-label film for the Japanese Consumer Cooperative Union, which is a group of 2500 stores. Priced significantly below its Kodak brand, the private label seeks to attract the price-sensitive Japanese consumer.[34]

Generic Branding An alternative branding approach is the **generic brand,** which is a no-brand product such as dog food, peanut butter, or green beans. There is no identification other than a description of the contents. The major appeal is that the price is up to one third less than that of branded items. Generic brands account for less than one percent of total grocery sales. The limited appeal of generics has been attributed to the popularity of private brands and greater promotional efforts for manufacturer brand-name items. Consumers who use generics see these products as being as good as brand-name items, and, in light of what they expect, users of these products are relatively pleased with their purchases.

PACKAGING

The **packaging** component of a product refers to any container in which it is offered for sale and on which information is communicated. To a great extent, the customer's first exposure to a product is the package, and it is an expensive and important part of the marketing strategy. For Pez Candy, Inc., the character head-on-a-stick plastic container that dispenses a miniature brick candy, is the central element of its marketing strategy as described in the accompanying Marketing NewsNet.[35]

CUSTOMER VALUE

MARKETING NEWSNET

Creating Customer Value through Packaging: Pez Heads Dispense More Than Candy

Customer value can assume numerous forms. For Pez Candy, Inc., customer value manifests itself in some 250 Pez character candy dispensers. Each 99 cent refillable dispenser ejects tasty candy tablets in a variety of flavours that delight preteens and teens alike.

Pez was formulated in 1927 by Austrian food mogul Edward Haas III and successfully sold in Europe as an adult breath mint. Pez, which comes from the German word for peppermint, *pfefferminz,* was originally packaged in a hygienic, headless plastic dispenser. Pez first appeared in North America in 1953 with a headless dispenser, marketed to adults. After conducting extensive marketing research, Pez was repositioned with fruit flavours, repackaged with licensed character heads on top of the dispenser, and remarketed as a children's product in the mid-1950s. Since then, most top-level licensed characters and hundreds of other characters have become Pez heads. Consumers eat more than one billion Pez tablets annually, and company sales growth exceeds that of the candy industry as a whole.

The unique Pez package dispenses a "use experience" for its customers beyond the candy itself, namely, fun. And fun translates into a 98 percent awareness level for Pez among teenagers and 89 percent among mothers with children. Pez has not advertised its product for years. With that kind of awareness, who needs advertising?

Creating Customer Value through Packaging

Today's packaging costs Canadian companies billions of dollars, and an estimated 10 cents of every dollar spent by a consumer goes to packaging. Despite the cost, packaging is essential because packages provide important benefits for the manufacturer, retailer, and ultimate consumer.

Communication Benefits A major benefit of packaging is the information on it conveyed to the consumer, such as directions on how to use the product and the composition of the product, which is needed to satisfy legal requirements of product disclosure. Other information consists of seals and symbols, either government required or commercial seals of approval (such as the Good Housekeeping seal or the CSA seal).

Functional Benefits Packaging often plays an important functional role, such as convenience, protection, or storage. Quaker State has changed its oil containers to eliminate the need for a separate spout, and Borden has changed the shape of its Elmer's Wonder Bond adhesive to prevent clogging of the spout.

The convenience dimension of packaging is becoming increasingly important. Kraft Miracle Whip salad dressing and Del Monte ketchup are sold in squeeze bottles, microwave popcorn has been a major market success, and Folgers coffee is now packaged in single-serving portions.

Consumer protection has become an important function of packaging, including the development of tamper-resistant containers. Today, companies commonly use safety seals or pop-tops that reveal previous opening. Nevertheless, no package is truly tamper resistant.

Perceptual Benefits A third component of packaging is the perception created in the consumer's mind. Just Born Inc., a candy manufacturer of such brands as Jolly Joes and Mike and Ike Treats, discovered the importance of this component of packaging.

Can you name this soft drink brand?

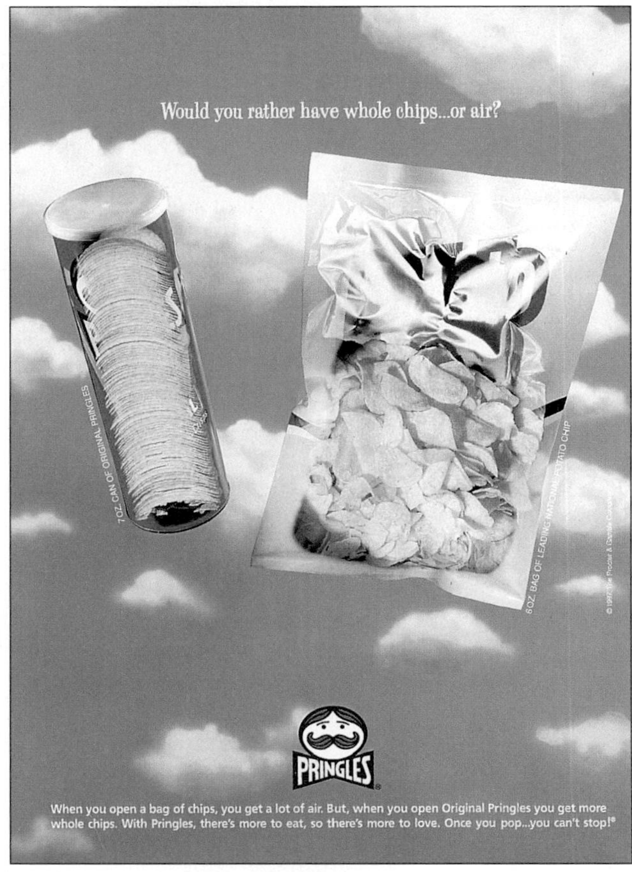

The unique cylindrical packaging for Pringles provides both functional and perceptual benefits and serves as a major point of difference for the snack chip.

Pringles
www.pringles.com

For many years the brands were sold in old-fashioned black and white packages, but when the packaging was changed to four colour, with animated grape and cherry characters, sales increased 25 percent. Coca-Cola brought back its famous pale-green, contoured bottle to attract consumers who remember drinking soft drinks from glass bottles, not from aluminum cans and large plastic bottles. A worldwide sales increase of 8 percent was linked to the new-old bottle.[36]

A package can connote status, economy, and product quality. Procter & Gamble's Original Pringles, with its unique cylindrical packaging, offers uniform chips, minimal breakage, freshness, and better value for the money than flex-bag packages for chips.

In the past, the colour of packages was selected subjectively. For example, the famous Campbell's soup can was the inspiration of a company executive who liked Cornell University's red and white football uniforms. Today, there is greater recognition that colour affects consumers' perceptions.[37] Owens-Corning judged the pink colour of its fibre insulation to be so important that the colour was given trademark status by the courts.

Global Trends in Packaging

Two global trends in packaging originating in the mid-1990s will continue into the 21st century. One trend involves the environmental effects of packaging, the other focuses on packaging health and safety concerns.

Environmental Sensitivity Because of widespread worldwide concern about the growth of solid waste and the shortage of viable landfill sites, the amount, composition, and disposal of packaging material continues to receive much attention.[38] Recycling packaging material is a major thrust. Procter & Gamble now uses recycled cardboard in 70 percent of its paper packaging and is packaging Tide, Cheer, Era, and Dash detergents in jugs that contain 25 percent recycled plastic. Spic and Span liquid cleaner is packaged in 100 percent recycled material. Other firms, such as the large U.K. retailer Sainsbury, emphasize the use of less packaging material. Sainsbury examines every product it sells to ensure that each uses only the minimum material necessary for shipping and display. Not surprisingly, when ARCO, one of the world's largest petrochemical firms, announced that its new packaging material would reduce packaging volume by 40 percent compared with corrugated paper shipping containers, the news was favourably received by manufacturers and retailers alike.

European countries have been trendsetters concerning packaging guidelines and environmental sensitivity. Many of these guidelines now exist in provisions governing trade to and within the European Union. In Germany, for instance, 80 percent of packaging material must be collected, and 80 percent of this amount must be recycled or reused to reduce solid waste in landfills. Canadian firms marketing in Europe have responded to these guidelines, and ultimately benefitted Canadian consumers.

Increasingly, firms are using life-cycle analysis (LCA) to examine the environmental effect of their packaging at every stage from raw material sources and production through distribution and disposal. A classic use of LCA was the decision by McDonald's to abandon the polystyrene clam-shells it used to package its hamburger. LCA indicated that the environment would be better served if the amount of solid waste packaging was reduced than if the polystyrene shells were recycled. McDonald's elected to package its hamburgers in a light wrap made of paper and polyethylene and eliminate the polystyrene package altogether.

Health and Safety Concerns A second trend involves the growing health and safety concerns of packaging materials. Today, a majority of North American and European consumers believe companies should make sure products and their packages are safe, regardless of the cost, and companies are responding to this view in numerous ways.[39] Most butane lighters sold today, such as those made by BIC, contain a child-resistant safety latch to prevent misuse and accidental fire. Child-proof caps on pharmaceutical products and household cleaners and sealed lids on food packages are now common. New packaging technology and materials that extend a product's *shelf life* (the time a product can be stored) and prevent spoilage continue to be developed with special applications for less developed countries.

PRODUCT WARRANTY

A final component for product consideration is the **warranty,** which is a statement indicating the liability of the manufacturer for product deficiencies. There are various degrees of product warranties with different implications for manufacturers and customers.[40]

The Variations of a Warranty

Some companies offer *express warranties,* which are written statements of liabilities. In recent years the government has required greater disclosure on express warranties to indicate whether the warranty is a limited-coverage or full-coverage alternative. A *limited-coverage warranty* specifically states the bounds of coverage and, more important, areas of noncoverage, whereas a *full warranty* has no limits of noncoverage. Cadillac is a company that boldly touts its warranty coverage. Also, in an effort to improve its image with Canadian consumers, Hyundai automobiles offer what it claims to be the best warranty in the industry.

With greater frequency, manufacturers are being held to *implied warranties,* which assign responsibility for product deficiencies to the manufacturer. Studies show that warranties are important and affect a consumer's product evaluation. Brands that have limited warranties tend to receive less positive evaluations compared with full-warranty items.

The Growing Importance of Warranties

Warranties are important in light of increasing product liability claims. In the early part of this century the courts protected companies, but the trend now is toward "strict liability" rulings, where a manufacturer is liable for any product defect, whether it followed reasonable research standards or not. This issue is hotly contested by companies and consumer advocates.

Warranties represent much more to the buyer than just protection from negative consequences—they can hold a significant marketing advantage for the producer. Sears has built a strong reputation for its Craftsman tool line with a simple warranty: if you break a tool, it's replaced with no questions asked. Zippo has an equally simple guarantee: "If it ever fails, we'll fix it free."

CONCEPT CHECK

1. How does a generic brand differ from a private brand?
2. Explain the role of packaging in terms of perception.
3. What is the difference between an expressed and an implied warranty?

SUMMARY

1 Products have a finite life cycle consisting of four stages: introduction, growth, maturity, and decline. The marketing objectives for each stage differ.

2 In the introductory stage the need is to establish primary demand, whereas the growth stage requires selective demand strategies. In the maturity stage the need is to maintain market share; the decline stage necessitates a deletion or harvesting strategy.

3 There are various shapes to the product life cycle. High learning products have a long introductory period, and low learning products rapidly enter the growth stage. There are also different curves for fashions and fads. Different product life-cycle curves can exist for the product class, product form, and brand.

4 In managing a product's life cycle, changes can be made in the product itself or in the target market. Product modification approaches include changes in the quality, performance, or appearance. Market modification approaches entail increasing a product's use among existing customers, creating new use situations, or finding new users.

5 Product repositioning can come about by reacting to a competitor's position, reaching a new market, capitalizing on a rising trend, or changing the value offered in a product.

6 Branding enables a firm to distinguish its product in the marketplace from those of its competitors. Successful and established brands take on a brand personality, a set of human characteristics associated with a brand name. A good brand name should suggest the product benefits, be memorable, fit the company or product image, be free of legal restrictions, and be simple and emotional. A good brand name is of such importance that it has led to a concept of brand equity, the added value a given brand name gives to a product beyond the functional benefits provided.

7 Licensing of a brand name is being used by many companies. The company allows the name to be used without having to manufacture the product.

8 Manufacturers can follow one of three branding strategies: a manufacturer's brand, a reseller brand, or a mixed brand approach. With a manufacturer's branding approach, the company can use the same brand name for all products in the line (multiproduct, or family, branding) or can give products different brands (multibranding).

9 A reseller, or private, brand is used when a firm manufactures a product but sells it under the brand name of a wholesaler or retailer. A generic brand is a product with no identification of manufacturer or reseller that is offered on the basis of price appeal.

10 Packaging provides communication, functional, and perceptual benefits. The two global emerging trends in packaging are greater concerns regarding the environmental impact and the health and safety of packaging materials.

11 The warranty, a statement of a manufacturer's liability for product deficiencies, is an important aspect of a manufacturer's product strategy.

KEY TERMS AND CONCEPTS

product life cycle p. 314
product class p. 320
product form p. 320
product modification p. 322
market modification p. 322
trading up p. 324
trading down p. 324
downsizing p. 324
branding p. 324
brand name p. 324
trade name p. 324
trademark p. 324
brand personality p. 325
brand equity p. 326
licensing p. 326
manufacturer branding p. 328
multiproduct branding p. 328
co-branding p. 329
multibranding p. 329
euro-branding p. 329
private branding p. 330
mixed branding p. 330
generic brand p. 331
packaging p. 331
warranty p. 334

INTERNET EXERCISE

New Product News provides a central Internet location on the latest new products. It provides a forum for companies to present their most recent new products. New Product News is updated daily with company press releases from the entire world. Some 30 product categories with one or more new products are typically listed by New Product News each day. A unique feature of New Product News is that a company Web site address that can be accessed immediately follows each new product description.

Visit the New Product News Web site at www.newproductnews.com and go to "new items this week." Your assignment is outlined below:

1 Identify and describe how a new product listed promotes more frequent usage, creates a new use situation, reaches a new market or new users, or changes the value offered to consumers.

2 Identify and describe a new product that is branded using a family branding strategy, a subbranding strategy, or a brand extension strategy.

APPLYING MARKETING CONCEPTS AND PERSPECTIVES

1 Listed here are three different products in various stages of the product life cycle. What marketing strategies would you suggest to these companies? (*a*) GTE cellular telephone company—growth stage, (*b*) Mountain Stream tap-water purifying systems—introductory stage, and (*c*) hand-held manual can openers—decline stage.

2 It has often been suggested that products are intentionally made to break down or wear out. Is this strategy a planned product modification approach?

3 The product manager of GE is reviewing the penetration of garbage compactors in Canadian homes. After more than two decades in existence, this product is in relatively few homes. What problems can account for this poor acceptance? What is the shape of the garbage compactor life cycle?

4 For several years Ferrari has been known as the manufacturer of expensive luxury automobiles. The company plans to attract the major segment of the car-buying market who purchase medium-priced automobiles. As Ferrari considers this trading-down strategy, what branding strategy would you recommend? What are the trade-offs to consider with your strategy?

5 The nature of product warranties has changed as the court system reassesses the meaning of warranties. How does the regulatory trend toward warranties affect product development?

CASE 12–1 POLAROID CANADA

When Polaroid (www.polaroid.com) first introduced instant photography in 1947, it was a remarkable breakthrough in consumer photography. Polaroid prints were of comparable quality to other camera systems of the time, but the unique aspect of Polaroid pictures was that they developed instantly.

Instant photography became very popular with consumers and very profitable for Polaroid. However, in the 1980s the advent of newer technology and a changing and more sophisticated consumer began to change the marketplace. New, compact, fully automatic 35-mm cameras provided high-quality prints never before achieved with easy-to-use cameras. Meanwhile, rapidly declining processing time—to as low as one hour—further contributed to the popularity of 35-mm cameras. This development began to undermine Polaroid's competitive advantage: immediacy.

In the late 1980s, 35-mm cameras and film became the standard in consumer photography for traditional photographic uses. The new 35-mm prints forced comparisons with instant pictures and consumers perceived that there were some differences in terms of colour and resolution. In addition, an instant print was typically twice as expensive as a 35-mm print. As the photographic marketplace changed, Polaroid remained committed to the instant segment even though instant photography's competitive advantage of immediacy was slowly eroding. With the advent of 35-mm point-and-shoot cameras, there was a concern that consumers would be less likely to use Polaroid instant cameras in traditional photographic situations since they now had more camera options.

The key issue facing Polaroid in the 1990s was how to make "instant" important to consumers once again. Polaroid had to begin to reposition the camera and rejuvenate what consumers saw as a mature brand.

Questions

1 How can Polaroid revitalize their instant photography business?

2 Who should Polaroid target?

3 What message should Polaroid communicate to the target(s)?

THE

Nunavut HANDBOOK

The world's most authoritative guide to Nunavut, Canada's newest territory — one of the last great untouched wilderness areas on Earth.

Travelling in Canada's Arctic

CHAPTER THIRTEEN

MANAGING SERVICES

13

AFTER READING THIS CHAPTER YOU SHOULD BE ABLE TO:

- Describe four unique elements of services.
- Explain the service continuum.
- Understand the way in which consumers purchase and evaluate services.
- Understand the important role of internal marketing in service organizations.
- Explain the special nature of the marketing mix for services.

NUNAVUT IS LOOKING FOR TOURISTS

Canada's third and newest territory is putting out the welcome mat, hoping to make it a hot (or is that a cold) destination for tourists. Nunavut (www.nunavut.com) is a sprawling region of tundra, Arctic islands, frozen fjords, and lakes. It doesn't have a lot of people—less than 25 000—but covers over two million square kilometres, or about 20 percent of the area of Canada. That makes it about the size of Britian, France, Germany, Italy, and Spain combined. There is plenty to see and do: North America's northernmost national part on Ellesmere Island; sheer cliffs on Baffin Island; kayak expeditions into artic fjords; wildlife ranging from polar bears to musk ox to caribou. Travellers to Nunavut can also refer to the 1999 *Nunavut Handbook* for information. The Handbook is a travel guide written by over 50 writers, mostly northern and many Inuit. The northerners who know the land, wildlife, and history are the best sources for travel information.

The tourism industry is truly global in scope and is fiercely competitive. As a country, Canada depends heavily on tourism to keep its economy strong. Nunavut also believes that tourism can help bolster its territorial economy. Nunavut will focus on two small niche segments of the tourism market: adventure tourists, those seeking activities such as dog-sledding, snowmobiling, kayaking, hunting and fishing, and eco-tourists, those who are intersted in the wildlife.

However, there are a few major obstacles in the way of developing a tourist trade in Nunavut. One is the high cost of getting there. Its towns are only accessible by air, except for a few cruise-ship stops, and air fares are high because of the lack of competition in the region. The other problem is that hotel and restaurant availability is limited and unsophisticated. Iqaluit, the capital, has about 175 hotel rooms, and some quality dining choices. But most of the other towns offer only one lodging place, with the prospect of shared bedrooms and bathrooms.

According to Nunavut Tourism's executive director, Madeleine Redfern, "Our short-term goal is not to raise the number of tourists, but to raise the quality of what we offer to match the expectations of those who do come." Perhaps Nunavut can take solace in the fact that tourists are increasingly visiting remote destination spots around the world, including the Antarctic. So why wouldn't they consider the top of the North American continent to view polar bears or take an igloo-building lesson![1]

The tourism industry illustrates that the marketing of services is unique and challenging, particularly the matching of demand and capacity. In this chapter, we will discuss how services differ from traditional products (goods), how service consumers make purchase decisions, and the important aspects of developing and managing the marketing mix for services.

THE SERVICE ECONOMY

As defined in Chapter 1, **services** are activities, deeds, or other basic intangibles offered for sale to consumers in exchange for money or something else of value. One services-marketing expert suggests that services permeate every aspect of our lives.[2] We use transportation services when we travel; we use restaurant services to feed us and hotels to put roofs over our heads. At home, we rely on services such as electricity and telephones. At work, we need postal, courier, and maintenance services to keep our workplaces running. We use the services of hairstylists to maintain our personal self-image. Our employers use public relations and advertising firms to maintain their corporate images. Lawyers, physicians, dentists, stockbrokers, and insurance agents look after our personal and financial health. In our leisure time, we use a variety of services ranging from cinemas to theme parks for amusement and relaxation. And when we do buy goods, such as a new car or a washing machine, we rely on services to keep them running and repair them when they break down.

Services have become one of the most important components of the Canadian as well as world economy. The services sector now accounts for close to 60 percent of global gross national product, and with many service firms operating internationally, exports of services are also increasing. In Canada, over 60 cents out of every consumer dollar is spent on buying services. More than 7 out of 10 Canadians work in the service sector. In other words, more Canadians are doing things (performing services) than making things (producing goods). Experts predict that nearly all new employment in the future will be created by the service sector. They suggest that if current trends continue, almost all Canadians will be working in services by 2025.[3] Much of this employment is expected to be created by small service companies, particularly those offering personal, professional, and informational services. In fact, one of the fastest-growing segments of the Canadian services economy is information technology services, which includes computer training. And, of course, the Internet is now the new frontier for many newly emerging services such as people locator services and financial advisory services.

THE UNIQUENESS OF SERVICES

www.royalbank.com

As we noted in Chapter 11, when consumers buy products they are purchasing a bundle of tangible and intangible attributes that deliver value and satisfaction. In general, it is very difficult to define a pure good or a pure service. A pure good implies that the consumer obtains benefits from the good alone without any added value from service; conversely, a pure service assumes there is no "goods" element to the service that the customer receives. In reality, most services contain some goods element. For example, at McDonald's you receive a hamburger; at the Royal Bank you are provided with a bank statement. And most goods offer some service—even if it is only delivery. In fact, many goods-producing firms are adding service offerings as a way to differentiate their products from those of their competitors.

Why do many services emphasize their tangible benefits? The answer appears in the text.

Canadian Pacific Hotels
www.cphotels.ca

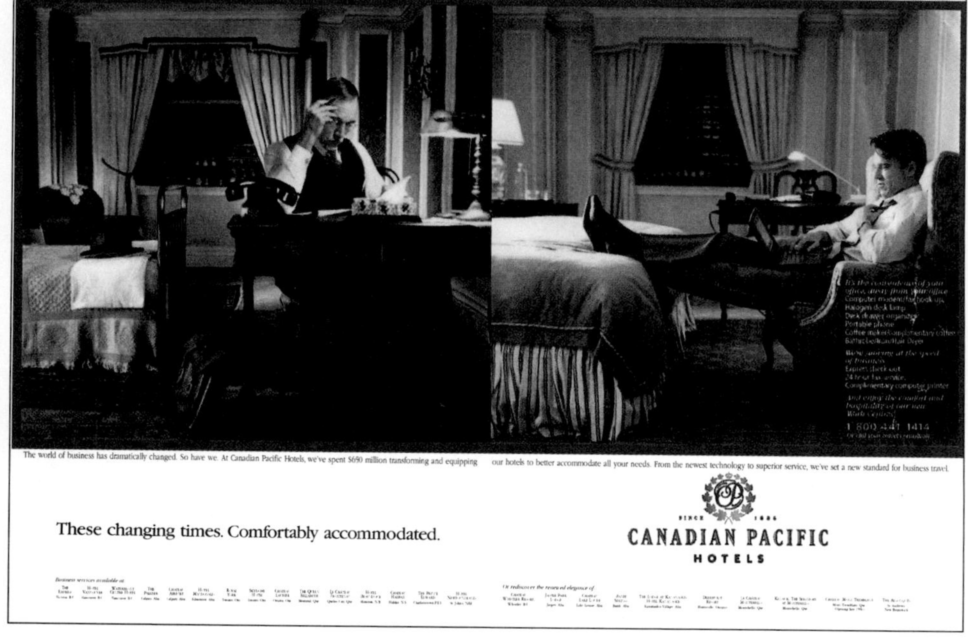

But there are certain commonalities between *services as products* that set them apart from tangible goods. The four unique elements to services are intangibility, inconsistency, inseparability, and inventory. These elements are sometimes referred to as the **four I's of services.**

Intangibility Services are intangible; that is, they can't be held, touched, or seen before the purchase decision. In contrast, before purchasing a traditional product, a consumer can touch a box of laundry detergent, kick the tire of an automobile, or sample a new breakfast cereal. A major marketing need for services is to make them tangible or show the benefits of using a service. American Express emphasizes the gifts available to cardholders through its Membership Rewards program; and a leading insurance company says, "You're in Good Hands with Allstate"; and Canadian Pacific Hotels tells business travellers that they'll have the convenience of their offices away from their offices, including computer hook-ups and portable phones.

Inconsistency Developing, pricing, promoting, and delivering services is challenging because the quality of a service is often inconsistent. Since services depend on the people who provide them, their quality varies with each person's capabilities and day-to-day job performance. Inconsistency is much more of a problem with services than it is with tangible goods. Tangible products can be good or bad in terms of quality, but with modern production lines the quality will at least be consistent. On the other hand, the Toronto Maple Leafs hockey team may look like potential Stanley Cup winners on one day, but lose by 10 goals the next day. Or a cello player with the Vancouver Symphony may not be feeling well and give a less-than-average performance. Whether the service involves tax assistance at Ernst & Young or guest relations at the Sheraton, organizations attempt to reduce inconsistency through standardization and training. Standardization through automation is becoming increasingly popular in many service industries including banking. Marathon Buildings Group of Toronto uses both highly trained personnel and technology to ensure that the tenants in their office buildings receive prompt and effective customer service.

Inseparability A third difference between services and goods is inseparability. There are two dimensions to inseparability. The first is inseparability of production and consumption. Whereas goods are first produced, then sold, and then consumed, services are

People and technology play an important role in delivering many services.

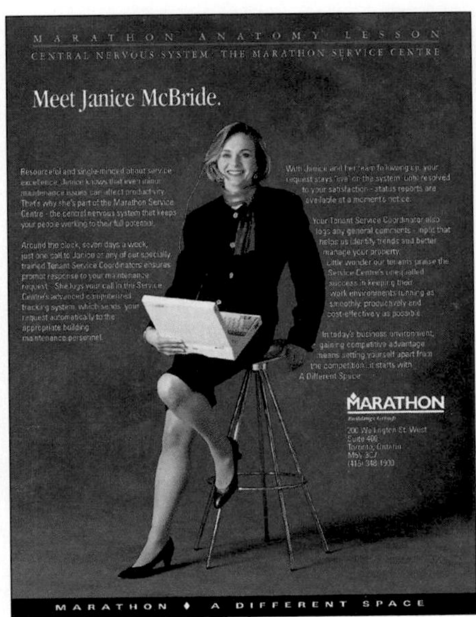

sold first, and then produced and consumed simultaneously. For example, you can buy a ticket at the Canadian Airlines ticket office, then fly and consume in-flight service as it is being produced. The second dimension of inseparability is that, in most cases, the consumer cannot (and does not) separate the deliverer of the service from the service itself. For example, to receive an education, a person may attend a university. The quality of the education may be high, but if the student has difficulty interacting with instructors, finds counselling services poor, or does not receive adequate library or computer assistance, he or she may not be satisfied with the educational experience. In short, a student's evaluations of education will be influenced primarily by the perceptions of instructors, counsellors, librarians, and other people at the university responsible for delivering the education.

The amount of interaction between the consumer and the service deliverer or provider depends on the extent to which the consumer must be physically present to receive the service. Some services such as golf lessons and medical diagnoses require the customer to participate in the delivery process. Other services, such as car repair or dry cleaning, that process tangible objects require less involvement from the customer. Finally, many services such as banking, and insurance can now be delivered electronically, often requiring no face-to-face customer interaction.

Inventory Inventory of services is different from that of goods. Inventory problems exist with goods because many items are perishable and because costs are associated with handling inventory. With services, inventory carrying costs are more subjective and are related to **idle production capacity,** which is when the service provider is available but there is no demand. The inventory cost of a service is the cost of paying the person used to provide the service along with any needed equipment. If a physician is paid to see patients but no one schedules an appointment, the fixed cost of the idle physician's salary is a high inventory carrying cost. In some service businesses, however, the provider of the service is on commission (the Merrill Lynch stockbroker) or is a part-time employee (a counterperson at McDonald's). In these businesses, inventory carrying costs can be significantly lower or non-existent because the idle production capacity can be cut back by reducing hours or having no salary to pay because of the commission compensation system.

Figure 13–1 shows a scale of inventory carrying costs represented on the high side by airlines and hospitals and on the low end by real estate agencies and hair salons. The inventory carrying costs of airlines is high because of high-salaried pilots and very expensive equipment. In contrast, real estate agencies and hair salons work on commission and need little expensive equipment to conduct business.

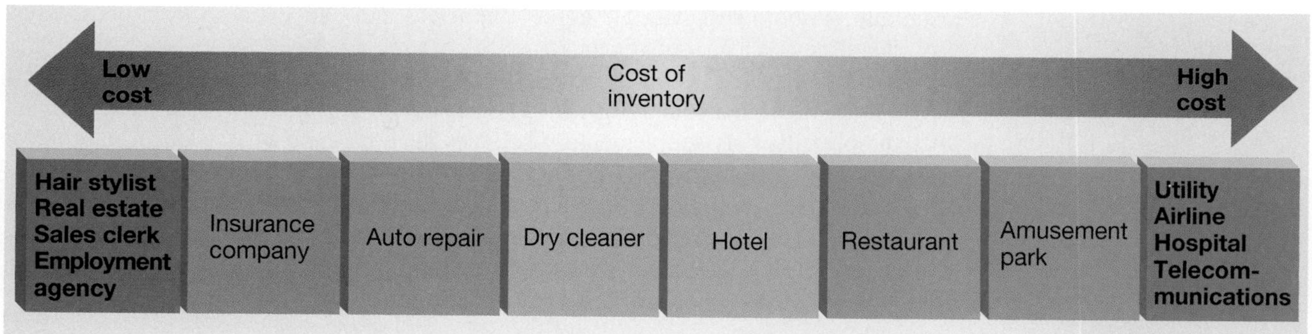

FIGURE 13–1
Inventory carrying costs of services

The Service Continuum

The four I's differentiate services from goods in most cases, but as we mentioned earlier, most products sold cannot be defined as pure goods or pure services. For example, does IBM Canada sell goods or services? While the company sells computers and software, a major component of its business is information technology services. Does McLean Hunter provide only goods when it publishes *Marketing* magazine, or does it consider itself a service because it presents up-to-date Canadian business information? As companies look at what they bring to the market, there is a range from tangible to the intangible or good-dominant to service-dominant offerings referred to as the **service continuum** (Figure 13–2).

Teaching, nursing, and the theatre are intangible, service-dominant activities, and intangibility, inconsistency, inseparability, and inventory are major concerns in their marketing. Salt, neckties, and dog food are tangible goods, and the problems represented by the four I's are not relevant in their marketing. However, some businesses are a mix of intangible-service and tangible-good factors. A clothing tailor provides a service but also a good, the finished suit. How pleasant, courteous, and attentive the tailor is to the customer is an important component of the service, and how well the clothes fit is an important part of the good. As shown in Figure 13–2, a fast-food

FIGURE 13–2
Service continuum

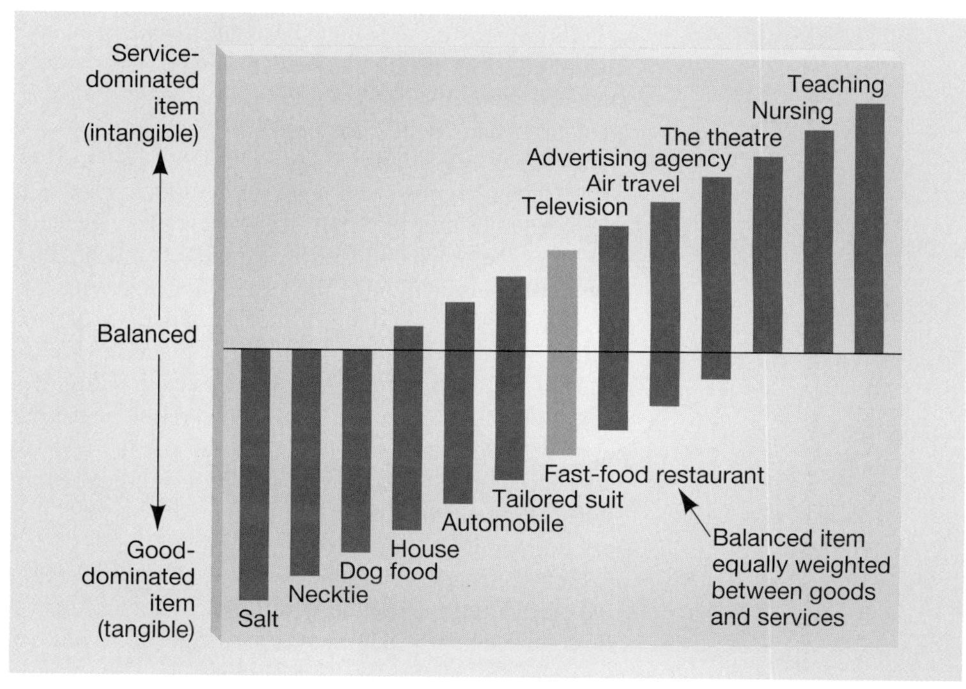

restaurant is about half tangible goods (the food) and half intangible services (courtesy, cleanliness, speed, convenience).

For many service businesses today it is useful to distinguish between their core service and their supplementary services. A core service offering such as a bank account, for example, also has supplementary services such as deposit assistance, parking or drive-through availability, ATMs, and monthly statements. Supplementary services often allow service providers to differentiate their offering from competitors, and they may add value for consumers. While there are many potential supplementary services, key categories of supplementary services include information delivery, consultation, order taking, billing procedures, and payment options.[4]

CONCEPT CHECK

1. What are the four I's of services?
2. Would inventory carrying costs for an accounting firm employing chartered accountants be (*a*) high, (*b*) low, or (*c*) nonexistent?
3. To eliminate inconsistencies, organizations rely on _______ and _______.

HOW CONSUMERS PURCHASE SERVICES

Universities, hospitals, hotels, and lawyers are facing an increasingly competitive environment. Successful service organizations, like successful goods-producing firms, must understand how the consumer makes a purchase decision and a postpurchase evaluation. Service companies will be better able to position themselves effectively if they understand why a consumer chooses to use a particular service. Moreover, by understanding the consumer's postpurchase evaluation process, service companies can identify sources of customer satisfaction or dissatisfaction.

Purchasing a Service

Because of their intangible nature, it is generally more difficult for consumers to evaluate services before purchase than it is to evaluate goods (see Figure 13–3). Tangible goods such as clothes, jewellery and furniture have *search* qualities, such as colour, size, and style, which can be determined before purchase. But rarely can a consumer inspect, try out, or test a service in advance. This is because some services such as restaurants and child care have *experience* qualities, which can only be discerned after purchase or consumption. Other services provided by specialized professionals such as medical diagnosis and legal services have *credence* qualities, or characteristics that the consumer may find impossible to evaluate even after purchase and consumption.[5]

The experience and credence qualities of services forces consumers to make a prepurchase examination of the service by assessing the tangible characteristics that are part of, or surround, the service.[6] In other words, consumers will evaluate what they cannot see by what they can see. For example, you might consider the actual appearance of the dentist's office, or its physical location when making a judgment about the possible quality of dental services that might be supplied there. Many service organizations go to great lengths to ensure that the tangible aspects of the services convey the appropriate image and serve as surrogate indicators of the intangible service to be provided. Proper management of the tangible aspects of services is sometimes called *impression management.*

Service marketers must also recognize that because of the uncertainty created by experience and credence qualities, consumers turn to personal sources of information such as early adopters, opinion leaders, and reference group members during

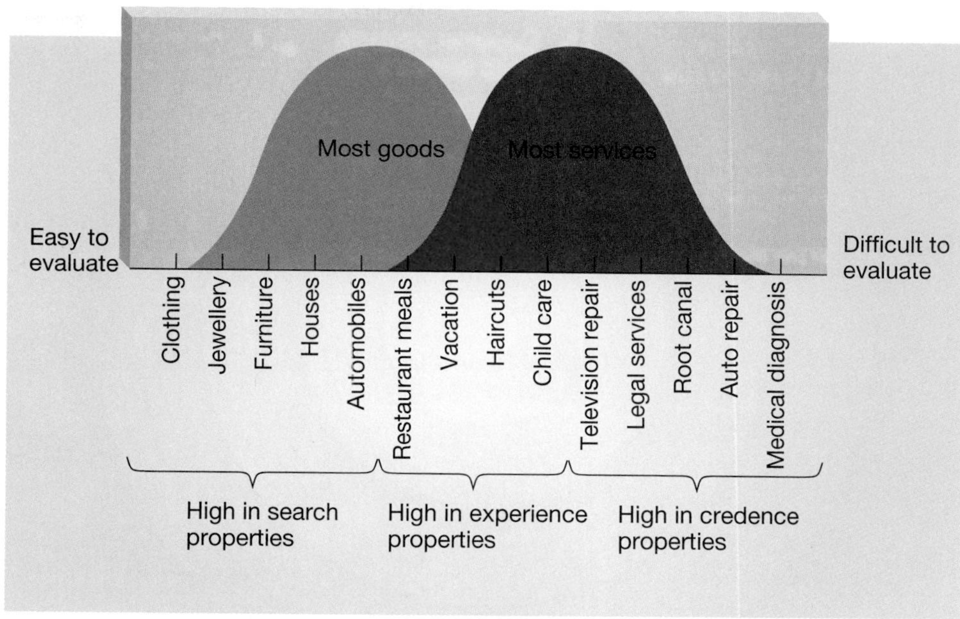

FIGURE 13–3
Services are more difficult to evaluate than goods before a purchase

the purchase decision process.[7] Accordingly, services marketers must ensure customer satisfaction in order to ensure positive word-of-mouth referral.

Customer Contact Audit

To better understand the service purchasing process, service firms can develop a **customer contact audit**—a flowchart of the points of interaction between consumer and service provider.[8] These points of interaction are often referred to as contact points or service encounter elements. Constructing a customer contact audit is particularly important in high-contact services such as educational institutions, health care, and even automobile rental agencies. Figure 13–4 illustrates a consumer contact audit for renting a car from Hertz. The interactions identified in a customer contact audit often serve as the basis for developing better services and delivering them more efficiently and effectively.

When a customer decides to rent a car he or she (1) contacts the rental company (see Figure 13–4). A customer service representative receives the information (2) and checks the availability of the car at the desired location. When a customer arrives at the rental site (3), the reservation system is again accessed, and the customer provides information regarding payment, address, and driver's licence (4). A car is assigned to the customer (5), who proceeds by bus to the car pickup (6). On return to the rental location (7), the car is parked and the customer checks in (8), providing information on mileage, gas consumption, and damages (9). A bill is subsequently prepared (10).

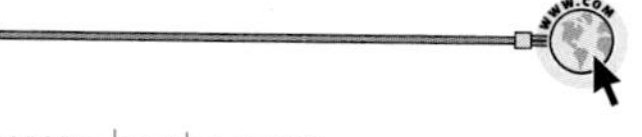

www.hertz.com

Each of the setps numbered 1 to 10 is a customer contact point where the tangible aspects of Hertz service are seen by the customer. Figure 13–4, however, also shows a series of steps lettered A to E that involve two levels of inspections on the automobile. These steps are essential in providing a car that runs, but they are not points of customer interation. To be successful, Hertz must create a competitve advantage in the sequence of interactions with the customer. In essence, Hertz must attempt to deliver the car in a seamless and timely manner, limiting the amount of time and effort required on the part of the customer. The customer contact audit is one tool that may help create that competitive advantage for Hertz or any other service firm.

FIGURE 13–4
Customer contact in car rental (green shaded boxes indicate customer activity)

Source: Adapted from W. Earl Sasser, R. Paul Olsen, and D. Daryl Wyckoff, *Management of Service Operations: Text, Cases, and Readings* (Boston: Allyn & Bacon, 1978).

The Hertz Corporation
www.hertz.com

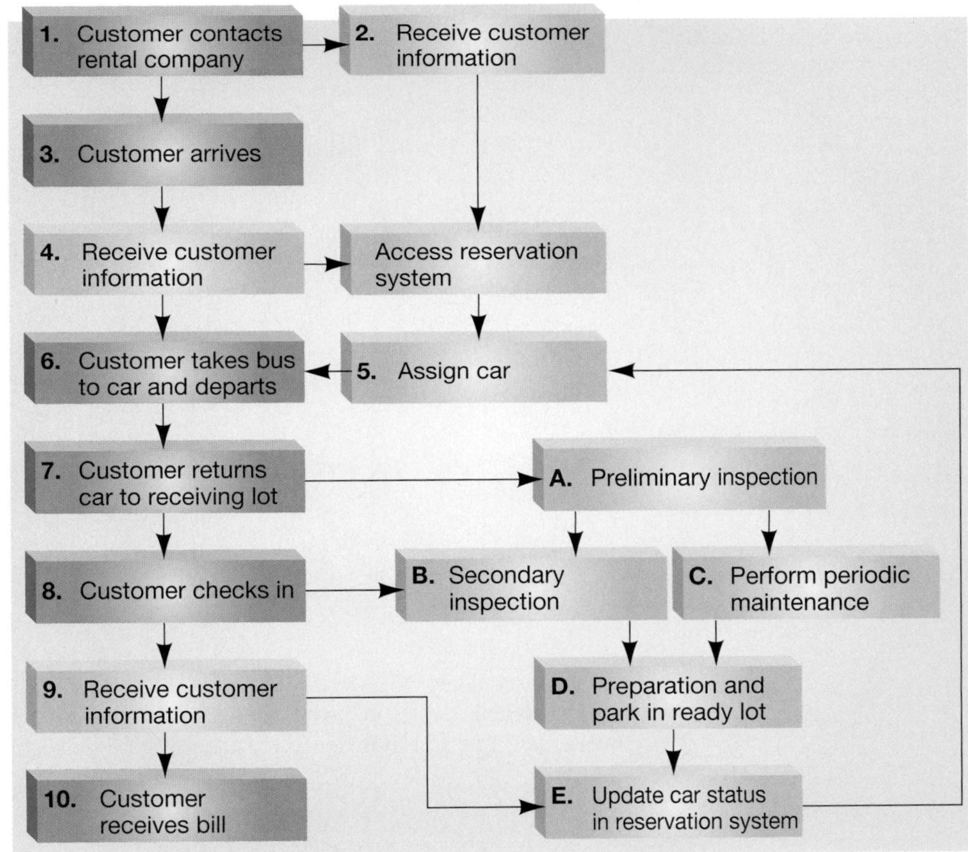

Postpurchase Evaluation

Once a consumer tries a service, how is it evaluated? The primary method is by comparing expectations about the service offering with the actual experience a consumer has with the service.[9] Differences between a consumer's expectations and experience are often identified through **gap analysis.** This type of analysis asks consumers to assess their expectations and experiences on various dimensions of service quality. Expectations are influenced by word-of-mouth communications, personal needs, past experience, and marketing communications activities, while actual experiences are determined by the way an organization delivers the service.

One popular instrument developed by researchers to measure service quality and to conduct gap analysis is called SERVQUAL.[10] Researchers measure consumers' expectations and their actual service experience using a multi-item instrument. Consumers are asked to rate the importance of various dimensions of service quality and to score the service in terms of their expectations and actual experience. SERVQUAL provides the services marketer with a consumer rating of service quality and an indication of where improvements can be made.

Researchers using SERVQUAL have found that consumers judge service quality along five key dimensions: tangibles, reliability, responsiveness, assurance, and empathy (see Figure 13–5).[11] However, the relative importance of these various dimensions of service quality has been found to vary by type of service.[12]

Service marketers must understand what dimensions consumers use in judging service quality, recognize the relative importance of each dimension, find out how they rate in terms of service quality, and take actions to deliver service quality that is consistent with consumer expectations. As a consumer, you play an important role in

ETHICS

ETHICS AND SOCIAL RESPONSIBILITY ALERT

The Consumers' Role in Improving Service Quality

Research has shown that many consumers are reluctant to provide feedback to service firms about the quality of their services. In fact, current studies show that only 5 to 10 percent of service customers offered direct feedback to service firms that might be important in improving service quality.

Most services marketers want to know if customers are happy or satisfied with the services provided, and many try a variety of methods (e.g., customer response or comment cards) to obtain or encourage answers regarding perceived service quality. However, most consumers do not take the time to respond, even if they are dissatisfied. Instead, consumers, if unhappy, will simply not return and will switch providers. Moreover, while they will not take the time to tell the organization about their dissatisfaction, they will take the time to tell their friends and co-workers.

The question is, why? If you have a problem with a service firm—whether it is inconvenient hours or rude employees—wouldn't it be better to tell the firm? Is it ethical for you to complain to your friends without informing the firm?

ensuring that service firms deliver service quality. However, as the Ethics and Social Responsibility box points out, sometimes consumers do not provide the feedback necessary to improve service quality.[13]

There are benefits to the customer and the service provider when service quality is improved. For the customer, improved service quality increases the likelihood that you will return to the same provider that offers the benefits of continuity of a single provider, customized service potential, reduced stress due to repetitive purchase process, and an absence of switching costs. For the service provider, retaining existing customers is much less costly than attracting new customers, and repeat customers are clearly more profitable over time.

FIGURE 13–5
Dimensions of service quality

DIMENSION	DEFINITION	QUESTIONS USED TO ASSESS
Tangibles	Appearance of physical facilities, equipment, personnel, and communications materials.	Do our employees dress appropriately?
Reliability	Ability to perform the promised service dependably and accurately.	Did we perform the service right the first time?
Responsiveness	Willingness to help customers and provide prompt service.	Do our employees provide you with prompt service?
Assurance	Respectful, considerate personnel who listen to customers and answer their questions.	Do our employees treat you courteously? Do they answer all your questions?
Empathy	Knowing the customer and understanding their needs. Approachable and available.	Do our employees understand your needs? Are our operating hours convenient for you?

Service firms see service quality as a basis for relationship marketing. And recent surveys have indicated that consumers concur. In fact, these same surveys indicate that many customers are intersted in being "relationship customers," provided, of course, that the relationship is balanced in terms of loyalty, benefits, and respect for privacy.[14]

CONCEPT CHECK

1. What are the differences between search, experience, and credence qualities?
2. What is gap analysis?
3. An instrument or approach used to measure service quality is ________________.

MANAGING THE MARKETING OF SERVICES

Just as the unique aspects of services necessitate changes in the consumer's purchase process, the marketing management process requires special adaptation.[15] In services marketing, the employee often plays a central role in attracting, building, and maintaining relationships with customers.[16] This aspect of services marketing has led to a concept called internal marketing.[17]

Internal marketing is based on the notion that in order for a service organization to serve its customers well, it must care for and treat its employees like valued customers. In short, it must focus on its employees (or its "internal market") before successful marketing efforts can be directed at customers.[18] Internal marketing involves creating an organizational climate in general, and jobs in particular, that lead to the right service personnel performing the service in the right way. The organization must train and motivate all its employees to work together to provide service quality and customer satisfaction. Research has shown that service organizations that want to be truly customer-oriented must be employee-oriented.[19]

In addition to employees, services organizations must also focus on the proper management of the marketing mix. Let's now discuss the special nature of the marketing mix for services.

Product (Service)

To a large extent, the concepts of the product component of the marketing mix discussed in Chapters 11 and 12 apply equally to Cheerios (a good) and to Royal Bank Visa (a service). Yet there are three aspects of the good/service element of the mix that warrant special attention: exclusivity, brand name, and capacity management.

Exclusivity Chapter 11 pointed out that one favourable dimension in a new product (a good) is its ability to be patented. Remember that a patent gives the manufacturer of a good exclusive rights to its production. A major difference between products and services is that services cannot be patented. Hence the creator of a successful fast-food chain could quickly discover the concept being copied by others. Domino's Pizza, for example, has seen competitors copy the quick delivery advantage that propelled the company to success.

Branding An important aspect of marketing goods is the branding strategy used. However, because services are intangible and, therefore, more difficult to describe, the brand name or identifying logo of the service organization is particularly important when a consumer makes a purchase decision. Many companies in the Canadian financial services industry, such as banks, trust companies, brokerage firms, and insurance

Logos create service identities.

companies, use branding in order to distinguish themselves in the minds of the consumers. Canada Trust, Bank of Montreal, and the Royal Bank are three prime examples. Strong brand names and symbols are important for service marketers, not only for differentiation purposes but also for conveying an image of quality. A service firm with a well-established brand reputation will also find it easier to market new services than firms without such brand reputations.[20]

Take a look at the figures at the top of this page to determine how successful some companies have been in branding their service by name, logo, or symbol.

Capacity Management Most services have a limited capacity due to the inseparability of the service from the service provider and the perishable nature of the service. For example, a patient must be in the hospital at the same time as the surgeon to "buy" an appendectomy, and only one patient can be helped at that time. Similarly, no additional surgery can be conducted tomorrow because of an unused operating room or an available surgeon today—the service capacity is lost if it is not used. So the service component of the mix must be integrated with efforts to influence consumer demand.[21] This is referred to as **capacity management.**

FIGURE 13–6
Managing capacity in a hotel

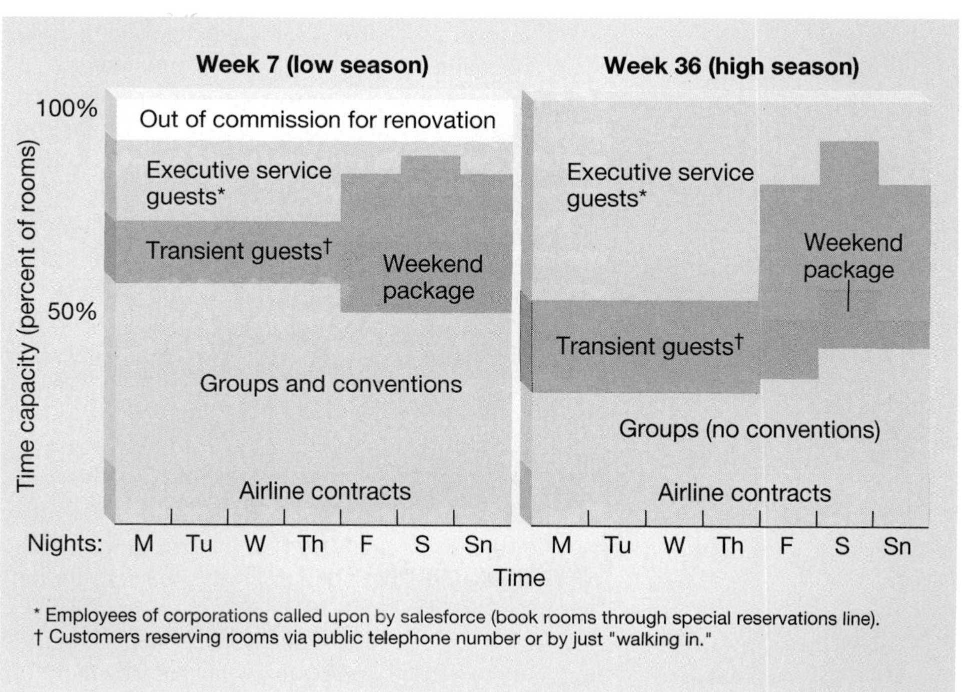

WEB LINK Nunavut's Tourism Initiative

As you read in the chapter opener, Canada's newest territory, Nunavut is trying to attract tourism to the northern region of our country. Go to their web site www.nunavut.com. What do you think of their site? Given they are targeting adventure tourists and eco-tourists, are they providing enough information? Is the message and image they are trying to convey appropriate? Do you think the site would encourage tourists to visit Nunavut?.

Service organizations must manage the availability of the offering so that (1) demand matches capacity over the duration of the demand cycle (for example, one day, week, month, year) and (2) the organization's assets are used in ways that will maximize the return on investment (ROI).[22] Figure 13–6 shows how a hotel tries to manage its capacity during the high and low seasons. Differing price structures are assigned to each segment of consumers to help moderate or adjust demand for the service. Airline contracts fill a fixed number of rooms throughout the year. In the slow season, when more rooms are available, tour packages at appealing prices are used to attract groups or conventions, such as an offer for seven nights at a reduced price. Weekend packages are also offered to buyers. In the high-demand season, groups are less desirable because more individual guests will be available and willing to pay higher prices.

Pricing

In service industries, *price* is often referred to in many ways. Hospitals refer to charges; consultants, lawyers, physicians, and accountants to fees; airlines to fares; and hotels to rates.

Role of Pricing In services marketing, pricing plays two essential roles: (1) to affect consumer perceptions and (2) to be used in capacity management. Because of the intangible nature of services, price is often perceived by consumers as a possible indicator of the quality of the service. For example, would you be willing to risk a $10 dental surgery? Or a $50 divorce lawyer? In many instances, there may be few other available cues for the customer to use to judge a service, so price becomes very important as a quality indicator.[23]

The capacity management role of price is very important to a number of service operations including movie theatres, hairstylists, restaurants, hotels, and airlines. Many service businesses use **off-peak pricing,** which consists of charging different prices during different times of the day or days of the week to reflect variations in demand for the service. For example, airlines offer discounts for weekend travel, and movie theatres offer matinee prices.

Place (Distribution)

Place or distribution is a major factor in developing a service marketing strategy because of the inseparability of services from the producer. Rarely are intermediaries involved in the distribution of a service; the distribution site and the service deliverer are the tangible components of the service.

Historically, in professional services marketing, little attention was paid to distribution. But increased competition has forced many professional firms to consider the

www.deloittetouche.com

value of convenient distribution. Hairstyling chains, legal firms, and accounting firms such as Deloitte & Touche all use multiple locations for the distribution of services. In the banking industry, customers of participating banks using the Interac system can access any one of thousands of automated teller machines across Canada.

Service marketers are also recognizing the potential of the electronic marketplace or marketspace. The Internet, for example, is now used by many service organizations as an alternative distribution channel. More and more often, customers are moving from face-to-face contacts with suppliers in fixed locations to "anywhere, anytime" marketspace transactions.[24]

Promotion

The value of promotion, especially advertising, for many services is to show consumers the benefits of purchasing the service. For example, advertising can be an effective way to demonstrate attributes such as availability, location, consistent quality, efficient and courteous service, and assurances of satisfaction.[25] While many service firms are using the Internet as an alternative distribution channel, they are also using it as an advertising medium. Many community colleges and universities, for example, have their own web sites and well-designed home pages to convey their messages to prospective students. Tourism marketers are also finding the Internet a valuable tool in reaching their prospective target markets. Use the Web Link to check out Nunavut Tourism's web site.

Public relations is an important promotional tool for services firms. It is particularly useful in conveying a proper image and in helping to support a firm's positioning strategy. Public relations tools such as events sponsorship or public-service activities are very popular among service firms. This is particularly true for professional services companies, which are often restricted in the use of advertising by their professional governing bodies.

Personal selling also plays an important role in services marketing. It has been said that when a consumer buys a service, they are buying the person selling the service. Personal selling is valuable not only in attracting customers but also in retaining them. Increasingly, many service marketers are following the path set by packaged-goods firms, that is, they are developing integrated marketing communications plans.[26]

SERVICES IN THE FUTURE

What can we expect from the services industry in the future? New and better services, of course, and an unprecedented variety of suppliers—changes that will largely be driven by deregulation, technological development, and consumer interests.

Deregulation in telecommunications, financial services, professional services, and other service industries has led to a greater variety of services, and in some cases, to a convergence of many of the suppliers of services. Many financial services suppliers, for example, are moving toward a one-stop-shopping environment where consumers can obtain loans, credit cards, mortgages, and insurance all under one roof. Other businesses we traditionally think of as manufacturers are adding services. General Motors Canada, Ford Canada, and General Electric, for example, now offer consumer loans, credit cards, mortgages, commercial loans, and insurance.

www.ford.ca

Technological advances are also changing many service industries. Perhaps the most dramatic is the trend toward Internet-based services such as banking, travel and vacation planning, and even personalized shopping. For example, egift offers to wrap and ship "great gifts for everyone" at a discount! The Internet is now capable of offering movies, software, video games, music, and virtually all digital information electronically for a fee. Other businesses are using technology to change the way they operate. Many airlines, for example, are offering electronic versions of traditional

CUSTOMER VALUE

MARKETING NEWSNET

Delivering Customer Satisfaction

Many service experts agree that in order for services firms to grow and prosper in the future, they must focus on delivering customer satisfaction. From the customers' perspective, satisfaction occurs when a service firm meets or exceeds customer expectations. So the starting point in designing efforts to deliver customer satisfaction is determining customers' expectations about the service. To accomplish this, service firms must spend time listening to customers to find out what they want and then deliver it. This is the most fundamental step that service firms can take to ensure customer satisfaction.

In general, service marketing experts suggest that customers expect service companies to keep their promises (reliability), to offer honest communications materials and clean, comfortable facilities (tangibles), to provide prompt service (responsiveness), to be competent and courteous (assurance) and to provide caring, individualized attention (empathy). What is most important, according to experts, is that service firms focus on delivering a highly reliable service. Research shows that little else matters to customers when service is unreliable. Friendly staff and sincere apologies do not compensate for unreliable service. Although most customers appreciate an apology, the apology does not erase the memory of that service.

The goal, then, is to focus on no mistakes in the first place. An internal "double-checking" system ensures that if a mistake does occur, it gets corrected *before* it reaches the customer. By focusing on "zero defects" (mistakes), service firms can move toward "zero defections"—no lost customers due to dissatisfaction.

paper tickets called E-tickets and new technology-driven services such as OnStar, a 24-hour-a-day emergency service for automobiles, are quickly becoming available to a large number of consumers. Future readers of this book may simply use their computer and a cable, telephone, or satellite connection to read assigned pages or to download a copy of the book. In fact, you may have to decide whether to download it to your computer or to your new E-book, a notebook-sized, battery-powered device with a high-resolution screen that can hold thousands of pages.[27]

Other changes in services are being driven by changes in consumer interests. Experts suggest that "time will be the currency of the future." Consumers will search for new services that reduce the time needed to go to the post office, bank, or supermarket or to prepare food, clean clothes, or maintain their homes. Consumers will put increased demand on services companies, expecting greater choice, convenience, information, responsiveness, and access. Technology will play a key role in satisfying those demands. Many banking customers, for example, prefer to visit their bank as little as possible and many are now doing more business by phone. It is very possible that an all-telephone or completely virtual bank is on the horizon for Canadian consumers. Consumers will have a choice to do everything electronically or to deal with a real person 24 hours a day, every day of the year for all their financial needs including loans and mortgages.

Still, experts suggest that many services organizations are currently failing to satisfy their customers. They argue that customers are often overheard saying, "if this is a service economy, where the heck's the service?" Unless services marketers start today to focus on delivering customer satisfaction, experts predict service companies will be facing increased numbers of aggravated, stressed, and unhappy consumers in the future.[28] The Marketing NewsNet discusses how service firms can better deliver customer satisfaction.[29]

CONCEPT CHECK

1. Matching demand with capacity is the focus of _______ management.
2. What factors will influence future changes in services?

____

SUMMARY

1 Services are activities, deeds, or other basic intangibles offered for sale to consumers in exchange for money or something else of value. Services have become one of the most important components of the Canadian and world economy.
2 Services share four commonalities that set them apart from goods: intangibility, inconsistency, inseparability, and inventory.
3 Intangibility refers to the difficulty in communicating service benefits. Inconsistency refers to the difficulty of providing the same level of quality each time a service is purchased. Inseparability means services are produced and consumed simultaneously and that consumers cannot separate the service deliverer from the service itself. Inventory costs for services are related to the cost of maintaining production capacity.
4 Many companies are not clearly service-based or goods-based organizations. As companies look at what they bring to the market, there is a range from tangible to the intangible or goods-dominant to service-dominant offerings referred to as the service continuum.
5 Consumers can evaluate goods by the search properties, but must evaluate services by their experience and credence properties.
6 A customer contact audit is a flowchart of the points of interaction between a service provider and its customers.
7 A gap analysis determines if consumers' expectations are different from their actual experiences. Gap analysis usually measures dimensions of service quality including: tangibles, reliability, responsiveness, assurance, and empathy.
8 Internal marketing is based on the notion that in order for a service organization to serve its customers well, it must care for and treat its employees like valued customers. In short, it must focus on its employees, or internal market, before successful programs can be directed at customers.
9 Because services are intangible, branding a service is particularly important in order to differentiate the service and to convey an image of quality. The brand name or identifying logo helps "tangiblize" the service for the consumer.
10 The inseparability of production and consumption of services means capacity management is important in services marketing. Capacity management involves smoothing demand to meet capacity.
11 The intangible nature of services makes price an important cue to service quality.
12 Distribution is important as a tangible component of a service offering. Technology is allowing service firms to expand their distribution including the use of marketspace.
13 Promotion is important in services marketing in order to demonstrate to consumers the benefits of purchasing a service.
14 Three factors are driving changes in the services industry: deregulation, technology, and consumer interests.

KEY TERMS AND CONCEPTS

services p. 340
four I's of services p. 341
idle production capacity p. 342
service continuum p. 343
customer contact audit p. 345
gap analysis p. 346
internal marketing p. 348
capacity management p. 349
off-peak pricing p. 350

INTERNET EXERCISE

The *Journal of Services Marketing* is a comprehensive source of information for anyone interested in the latest services marketing concepts, cases, trends, application, and strategies. Go to the *Journal*'s home page (http://www.mcb.co.uk/jsm.htm), click on "click here to view current and previous contents pages," and use the search function to investigate one of the following topics: relationship marketing, implications of the Internet for services marketing, or the advertising of services.

1 How many articles are available regarding the topic you selected?
2 Describe three insights you obtained from the summaries of the articles.

APPLYING MARKETING CONCEPTS AND PERSPECTIVES

1 Explain how the four I's of services would apply to a branch office of the Royal Bank.

2 Idle production capacity may be related to inventory or capacity management. How would the pricing component of the marketing mix reduce idle production capacity for (*a*) a car wash, (*b*) a stage theater group, and (*c*) a university?

3 What are the search, experience, and credence properties of an airline for the business traveler and pleasure traveler? What qualities are most important to each group?

4 This chapter showed that consumers judge service quality along five key dimensions: tangibles, reliability, responsiveness, assurance, and empathy. Indicate the "one" dimension that is most important to you in judging service quality of each of the following services: (a) physicians, (b) banking, (c) car rental companies, and (d) dry cleaning.

5 The text suggests that internal marketing is necessary before a successful marketing effort can be directed at consumers. Why is this particularly true for service organizations?

6 Outline the capacity management strategies that an airline must consider.

7 Draw the channel of distribution for the following services: (*a*) a restaurant, (*b*) a hospital, and (*c*) a hotel.

8 How does off-peak pricing influence demand for services?

9 In recent years, many service businesses have begun to provide their employees with uniforms. Explain the rationale behind this strategy in terms of the concepts discussed in this chapter.

10 Look at the service continuum in Figure 13–2. Explain how the following points in the continuum differ in terms of consistency: (*a*) salt, (*b*) automobile, (*c*) advertising agency, and (*d*) teaching.

CASE 13–1 NATIONAL HOCKEY LEAGUE

The National Hockey League (www.nhl.com) traces its beginnings to November 22, 1917, and as such is the second-oldest league of four major team sports in North America, with only professional baseball predating it. Throughout its history, the NHL has been recognized for its ideas and innovations. For example, the NHL was the first major sports league to introduce a play-off system, one that has been adopted by all other major sports.

However, historically, the NHL and many of the team owners had a negative mindset toward marketing. Marketing was actually considered unseemly. The general approach was to simply open the doors at the arenas and wait for customers to come. But with NHL costs, particularly player salaries on the rise, the NHL needed a bigger audience, both at the games and on television. The league now fully embraces marketing and it starts at the top. NHL Commissioner Gary Bettman, the former vice-president of the NBA (National Basketball Association) leads the marketing effort of the NHL.

The league is heavily involved in product licensing. It even has an on-line or cyberspace store where fans can purchase official NHL merchandise. Fans can also obtain an NHL mastercard complete with the logo of their favourite team. Corporate involvement and sponsorship in the NHL is also a priority with the league. Several teams have built new arenas and have attracted major corporate sponsors to be associated with the new complexes (e.g., General Motors Place, home of the Vancouver Canucks, and the Molson Centre, home to the Montreal Canadiens, the Air Canada Centre, home to the Toronto Maple Leafs).

The NHL has also penetrated the European television market with ESPN broadcasting NHL games on prime-time Swedish TV. Europe is also seen as a good market for licensing. In an effort to improve the entertainment value of the game for television viewers, the league has worked to improve how the games are televised, from the use of different camera angles to a computer-enhanced puck that is easier to follow.

Marketing professional hockey in the United States became a little easier in 1993–94 when entertainment giants Disney and Blockbuster Entertainment bought the league's Anaheim and Miami franchises. Blockbuster now offers NHL merchandise in its video outlets across Canada and the United States. Cross-marketing possibilities with Disney appear endless. For example, the Mighty Ducks arena, The Pond, is close to Disneyland, so vacation packages and other tie-ins with the theme park are being utilized.

The NHL believes that other strong franchises in the US including Denver and Phoenix are helping to sell the game to a new generation of fans. Strong fan support and media interest in the United States has led to the awarding of new franchises in Nashville, Atlanta, Columbus, and St. Paul. The NHL believes a strong presence in the United States market will ensure the league's long-term prosperity.

By the year 2000, only six teams will be Canadian-based, with the other 24 teams being located across the

United States. The NHL believes hockey is clearly an international game with only soccer being played in more countries. It hopes that with great players and great teams, consumers around the world will support and patronize professional hockey as a wholesome form of entertainment.

Questions

1 What is the "product" that the National Hockey League is really marketing to prospective fans?

2 Who is the NHL competing with in terms of fan attendance?

3 How does marketing "hockey" differ from marketing a consumer product like breakfast cereal?

CHAPTER FOURTEEN

PRICING: RELATING OBJECTIVES TO REVENUES AND COSTS

14

AFTER READING THIS CHAPTER YOU SHOULD BE ABLE TO:

- Identify the elements that make up a price.
- Recognize the constraints on a firm's pricing latitude and the objectives a firm has in setting prices.
- Explain what a demand curve is and how it affects a firm's total and marginal revenue.
- Recognize what price elasticity of demand means to a manager facing a pricing decision.
- Explain the role of costs in pricing decisions.
- Calculate a break-even point for various combinations of price, fixed cost, and unit variable cost.

HERE'S A PRICING PROBLEM FOR YOU!

Imagine you are part of the management team for Strait Crossing Bridge Ltd. (SCBL), a subsidiary company of Strait Crossing Development Inc. You know—the company that built the Confederation Bridge (www.confederationbridge.com), the bridge that joins Borden-Carleton, Prince Edward Island and Cape Jourimain, New Brunswick? Yeah, that one. It's 12.9 kilometres long and is the longest bridge over ice-covered waters in the world. And, it just cost you $1 billion to build it. Now you must determine what price to charge users who might want to cross it.

Well, you have many things to ponder. First, you must consider what it is that you are offering customers. You have a pretty good handle on that. Your bridge carries two lanes of traffic 24 hours a day, seven days a week, and it takes approximately 10 minutes to cross at normal travelling speed, which is, by the way, 80 km/hour. So, compared to ferry service, which often involves a wait and a much longer travel time to cross, you feel consumers will want to use the bridge. But how many customers and how often are two key questions. In this case, things aren't so clear. You do know, however, that consumer demand for your product clearly affects the price that can be charged.

So, you hire a consulting firm that does some demand estimates for you. The problem is, you must consider the type of user for the bridge, or more specifically, the type of vehicle being driven across the bridge. Why? Because traffic volume is made up of a variety of different vehicles from passenger cars and buses to recreational vehicles and motorcycles. And, some vehicles, particularly heavy trucks, put more wear and tear on the bridge, and therefore you believe that these types of vehicles should pay more to use the bridge. So, now you try to crunch some numbers: traffic volume by type of vehicle.

But wait a minute, before you can set prices to make some revenue projections, you must consult the federal government of Canada. The federal government through its regulatory agency, Transport Canada, has the power to dictate the price you charge, or in the case, the toll users will pay. You are told that the base rate for tolls by vehicle type must be developed based on previous ferry-service revenue data plus the rate of inflation. With all this information, you must come up with a pricing strategy for the bridge—a pricing strategy that will cover your capital and operating costs as well as provide some long-run profits for the firm. Wow, it is a pricing problem![1]

Welcome to the facinating—and intense—world of pricing, where myriad forces come together in the specific price prospective buyers are asked to pay. This chapter and Chapter 15 cover important factors used in setting prices. By the way, the toll rate for a passenger-vehicle, round trip is $35 and is collected on exiting PEI. If you are riding a motorcycle, it is a little cheaper at $14.25. But if you're driving a tractor trailer, you pay $50.75.

NATURE AND IMPORTANCE OF PRICE

The price paid for goods and services goes by many names. You pay *tuition* for your education, *rent* for an apartment, *interest* on a bank credit card, and a *premium* for car insurance. Your dentist or physician charges you a *fee,* a professional or social organization charges *dues,* and operators of the Confederation Bridge charge you a "fare" or a "toll" to use their bridge. In business, a consultant may require a *retainer* for services rendered, an executive is given a *salary,* a salesperson receives a *commission,* and a worker is paid a *wage.* Of course, what you pay for clothes or a haircut is termed a *price.*

What Is a Price?

www.shell.ca

These examples highlight the many varied ways that price plays a part in our daily lives. From a marketing viewpoint, **price** is the money or other considerations (including other goods and services) exchanged for the ownership or use of a good or service. For example, Shell Oil recently exchanged one million pest-control devices for sugar from a Caribbean country, and Wilkinson Sword exchanged some of its knives for advertising used to promote its razor blades. This practice of exchanging goods and services for other goods and services rather than for money is called **barter.** These transactions account for billions of dollars annually in domestic and international trade.

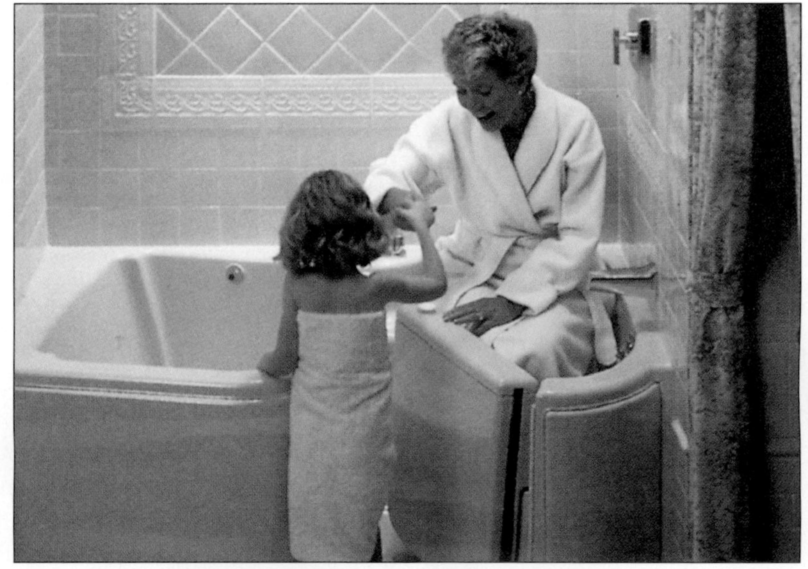

How do consumers relate value to price, as in the new Kohler walk-in bathtub that is safe for children and elderly alike? For a discussion of this important issue, see the text.

Kohler Company
www.kohler.com

For most products and services, money is exchanged, although the amount is not always the same as the list or quoted price, because of the discounts, allowances, and extra fees shown in Figure 14–1. Suppose you decide to buy a Lamborghini Diablo SV because its 510-horsepower engine moves you from 0 to 80 km/hr in 3.9 seconds. The list price is $255 000. As a vehicle incentive for buying within the year you receive $20 000 off the list price. You agree to pay half down and the other half when the car is delivered, which results in a financing fee of $19 000. To ship the car from Italy you will pay a $6000 destination charge. You are given a trade-in allowance of $1000 for your 1990 Honda Civic DX, which is the *Kelley Blue Book* (www.kbb.com) value of your car.[2]

Applying the "price equation" (as shown in Figure 14–1) to your purchase, your price is:

Price = List price – Incentives and allowances + Extra fees
= $255 000 – ($20 000 + $1000) + ($19 000 + 6000)
= $259 000

Your monthly payment is $2400. Are you still interested? Perhaps you might look at the Dodge Viper GTS Coupe (www2.4adodge.com/viper/) to compare prices. Figure 14–1 also illustrates how the price equation applies to a variety of different products and services.

Price as an Indicator of Value

From a consumer's standpoint, price is often used to indicate value when it is paired with the perceived benefits of a product or service. Specifically, **value** can be defined as the ratio of perceived benefits to price, or:[3]

$$\text{Value} = \frac{\text{Perceived benefits}}{\text{Price}}$$

This relationship shows that for a given price, as perceived benefits increase, value increases. Also, for a given price, value decreases when perceived benefits decrease.

FIGURE 14–1
The price of four different purchases

ITEM PURCHASED	PRICE	= LIST PRICE	– INCENTIVES AND ALLOWANCES	+ EXTRA FEES
	PRICE EQUATION			
New car bought by an individual	Final price	= List price	– Vehicle incentive Cash discount Trade-ins	+ Financing charges Special accessories Destination charges
Term in college bought by a student	Tuition	= Published tuition	– Scholarship Other financial aid Discounts for number of credits taken	+ Special activity fees
Bank loan obtained by a small business	Principal and interest	= Amount of loan sought	– Allowance for collateral	+ Premium for uncertain creditworthiness
Merchandise bought from a wholesaler by a retailer	Invoice price	= List price	– Quantity discount Cash discount Seasonal discount Functional or trade discount	+ Penalty for late payment

Creative marketers engage in **value-pricing,** the practice of simultaneously increasing product and service benefits and maintaining or decreasing price.

For some products, price influences the perception of overall quality, and ultimately value, to consumers.[4] For example, in a survey of home furnishing buyers, 84 percent agreed with the following statement: "The higher the price, the higher the quality." For computer software it has been shown that consumers believe a low price implies poor quality.[5]

Consumer value assessments are often comparative. Here value involves the judgment by a consumer of the worth and desirability of a product or service relative to substitutes that satisfy the same need. In this instance a "reference value" emerges, which involves comparing the costs and benefits of substitute items.[6] For example, Kohler recently introduced a walk-in bathtub that is safe for children and the elderly. Although priced higher than conventional step-in bathtubs, it has proven very successful because buyers place great "value" on the extra safety.

Price in the Marketing Mix

Pricing is also a critical decision made by a marketing executive because price has a direct effect on a firm's profits. This is apparent from a firm's **profit equation:**

Profit = Total revenue – Total cost

or

Profit = (Unit price × Quantity sold) – Total cost

What makes this relationship even more important is that price affects the quantity sold, as illustrated with demand curves later in this chapter. Furthermore, since the quantity sold sometimes affects a firm's costs because of efficiency of production, price also indirectly affects costs. Thus, pricing decisions influence both total revenue and total cost, which makes pricing one of the most important decisions marketing executives face.

The importance of price in the marketing mix necessitates an understanding of six major steps involved in the process organizations go through in setting prices (Figure 14–2):

- Identify pricing constraints and objectives.
- Estimate demand and revenue.
- Determine cost, volume, and profit relationships.
- Select an approximate price level.
- Set list or quoted price.
- Make special adjustments to list or quoted price.

The first three steps are covered in this chapter and the last three in Chapter 15.

STEP 1: IDENTIFYING PRICING CONSTRAINTS AND OBJECTIVES

To define a problem, it is important to consider both the objectives and constraints that narrow the range of alternatives available to solve it. These same principles apply in solving a pricing problem. Let's first review the pricing constraints so that we can better understand the nature of pricing alternatives.

Identifying Pricing Constraints

Factors that limit the latitude of prices a firm may set are **pricing constraints.** Consumer demand for the product clearly affects the price that can be charged. Other constraints on price vary from factors within the organization to competitive factors

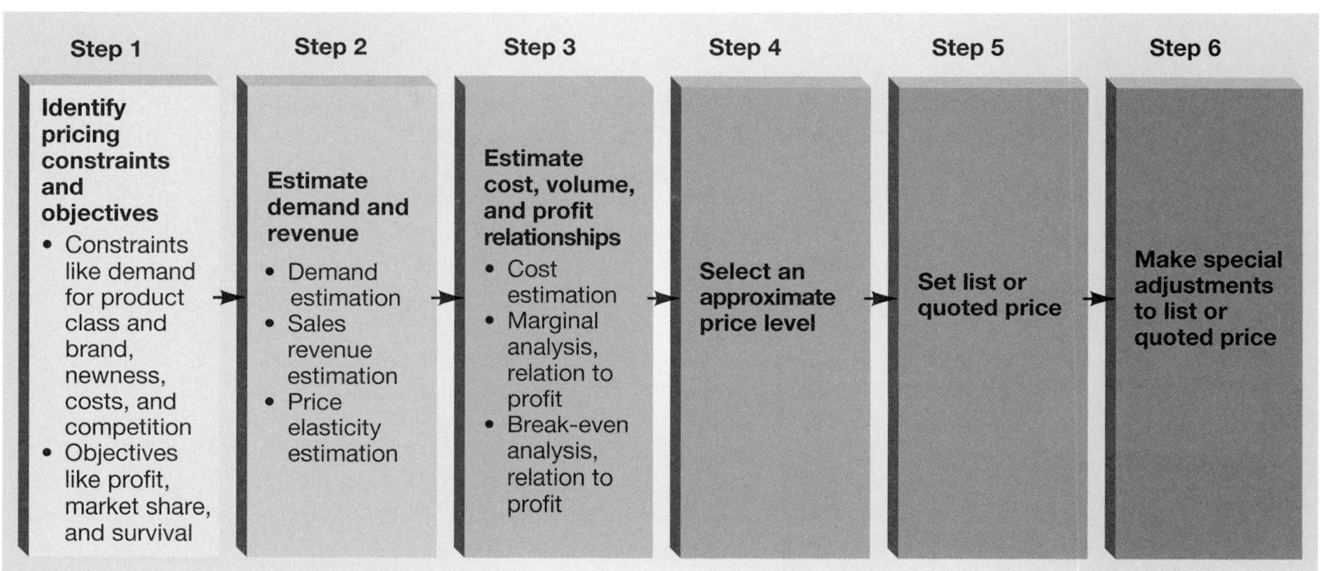

FIGURE 14–2
Steps in setting price

outside the organization. Legal and regulatory constraints on pricing are discussed in Chapter 15.

Demand for the Product Class, Product, and Brand The number of potential buyers for the product class (such as cars), product (sports cars), and brand (Dodge Viper) clearly affects the price a seller can charge. So does whether the item is a luxury—like a Viper—or a necessity—like bread and a roof over your head. In fact, when a consumer is in urgent need of a particular necessity, a marketer may command a premium price. In this case, there may be ethical issues involved (see the accompanying Ethics and Social Responsibility Alert).[7] The nature of demand is discussed further later in this chapter.

Newness of the Product: Stage in the Product Life Cycle The newer a product and the earlier it is in its life cycle, the higher is the price that can usually be charged. Willing to spend up to $1000 for a new electronic book? The high initial price is possible because of patents and limited competition early in its product life cycle. By the time you read this, the price will probably be much lower.[8]

Sometimes—when nostalgia or fad factors come into play—prices may rise later in the product life cycle. As described in the Web Link box, collectibles such as specific Beanie Babies or old sneakers can experience skyrocketing prices.[9] Publishing competitive prices on the Internet for the same or similar brands of products has revolutionized the access to price comparisons for both "collectors" and buyers of more traditional products.

www.sony.com

Single Product versus a Product Line When Sony introduced its CD player, not only was it unique and in the introductory stage of its product life cycle but also it was the *only* CD player Sony sold, so the firm had great latitude in setting a price. Now, with a wide range of Sony CD products and technologies, the price of individual models has to be consistent with the others based on features provided and meaningful price differentials that communicate value to consumers.

Cost of Producing and Marketing the Product In the long run, a firm's price must cover all the costs of producing and marketing a product. If the price doesn't cover the cost, the firm will fail, so in the long term a firm's costs set a floor under its

ETHICS

ETHICS AND SOCIAL RESPONSIBILITY ALERT

Getting an Unfair Premium Price?

The drug Clozapine is one of the most significant advances in antipsychotic drugs in two decades. But few of the people who really need this drug get it since the drug costs about $9000 a year. Pharmaceutical companies have been accused of price-gouging with respect to this drug and critical life-saving drugs, such as those used in AIDS treatment.

Some consumer advocates argue that many industries have a tendency to command premium prices for necessary products or services knowing that consumers usually have little choice but to pay them. Oil companies, for example, are often criticized for raising prices on home-heating oil during the cold Canadian winters. The oil companies argue it is simply a supply-and-demand issue. Many consumers, however, feel they are being gouged unfairly because oil companies realize the consumer has little choice but to pay the price. Price-gouging claims are also levied against major airlines during peak travel periods. Individual companies are sometimes accused of price gouging during shortages. For example, during water shortages bottled water suppliers have sometimes increased the price of their product by two to three times its original price. University students often report paying high and unfair prices for off-campus housing when demand is high, and supply is low.

The practice of commanding premium prices for luxuries and necessities appears to be gaining acceptability with marketers. A recent survey of Canadian MBA students found that 30 percent of them stated they would charge higher than normal prices if they believed the consumer would pay the higher price.

Is the use of premium pricing for necessities fair? Is it ethical? What should be done about this practice?

price. The operators of the Confederation Bridge are clearly conscious of the fact that the total cost of providing their bridge service must not exceed total revenue, otherwise they cannot succeed.

www.sears.ca

Cost of Changing Prices and Time Period They Apply If Canadian Airlines asks General Electric (GE) to provide spare jet engines to power the new Boeing 737 it just bought, GE can easily set a new price for the engines to reflect its latest information since only one buyer has to be informed. But if Sears Canada decides that sweater prices are too low in its winter catalogues after thousands of catalogues have

Are these real "collectibles" or "trashables?" The text describes factors that affect a product's price. And you can check the Web Link box to see if those old Beanie Babies or Nikes in your attic have value!

WEB LINK Pricing 101: $5900 for a 1969 Used Hotwheels Volkswagen Van or a Beanie Baby "Cubbie" for $6400?

Prices of "collectibles"—such as toys or old sneakers—are set by demand and supply forces discussed in this chapter. And for fads, the prices can fluctuate wildly. Some other recent collectibles prices, besides those mentioned above:

- Zip, a cat, Beanie Baby: $3150 (if it has black paws).
- 1985 Nike Dunks, high-top, blue-and-black basketball shoes: $3200.
- Mint-in-package *Star Wars* "Empire Strikes Back" Hans Solo figure: $350.

To get a feel for prices of some of these collectibles, visit:

- www.ebay.com
- www.thebeaniemom.com.

Marathon runner Malcolm East now wishes he had done a little more research on sneaker prices. At his wife's insistence he threw out six pairs of old shoes—that he now thinks would have fetched $19 000!

Want in on the collectibles business? Invest in an action figure from the next *Star Wars* movie—but don't take it out of its box!

been mailed to customers, it has a big problem, so it must consider the cost of changing prices and the time period for which they apply in developing the price list for its catalogue items. A recent study of four supermarket chains found the average annual cost of these price changes was $148 241, which represents 0.70 percent of revenues and an astounding 35.2 percent of net margins.[10] In actual practice, research indicates that most firms change the price for their major products once a year.[11]

Type of Competitive Markets The seller's price is constrained by the type of market in which it competes. Economists generally delineate four types of competitive markets: pure monopoly, oligopoly, monopolistic competition, and pure competition. Figure 14–3 shows that the type of competition dramatically influences the latitude of price competition and, in turn, the nature of product differentiation and

	TYPE OF COMPETITIVE MARKET			
STRATEGIES AVAILABLE	**PURE MONOPOLY (One seller who sets the price for a unique product)**	**OLIGOPOLY (Few sellers who are sensitive to each other's prices)**	**MONOPOLISTIC COMPETITION (Many sellers who compete on nonprice factors)**	**PURE COMPETITION (Many sellers who follow the market price for identical, commodity products)**
Price competition	None: sole seller sets price	Some: price leader or follower of competitors	Some: compete over range of prices	Almost none: market sets price
Product differentiation	None: no other producers	Various: depends on industry	Some: differentiate products from competitors'	None: products are identical
Extent of advertising	Little: purpose is to increase demand for product class	Some: purpose is to inform but avoid price competition	Much: purpose is to differentiate firm's products from competitors'	Little: purpose is to inform prospects that seller's products are available

FIGURE 14–3
Pricing, product, and advertising strategies available to firms in four types of competitive markets

extent of advertising. A firm must recognize the general type of competitive market it is in to understand the latitude of both its price and non-price strategies. For example, prices can be significantly affected by four competitive situations:

www.johnsonandjohnson.com

- *Pure monopoly.* In 1994 Johnson & Johnson (J&J) revolutionized the treatment of coronary heart diseases by introducing the "stent"—a tiny mesh tube "spring" that props clogged arteries open. Initially a monopolist, J&J stuck with its early $2235 price and achieved $1.4 billion in sales and 91 percent market share by the end of 1996. But its reluctance to give price reductions for large-volume purchases to hospitals antagonized them. When competitors introduced an improved stent at lower prices, J&J's market share plummeted to eight percent two years later.[12]
- *Oligopoly.* The few sellers of aluminum (Alcan, Alcoa) or mainframe computers try to avoid price competition because it can lead to disastrous price wars in which all lose money. Yet firms in such industries stay aware of a competitor's price cuts or increases and may follow suit. The products can be undifferentiated (aluminum) or differentiated (mainframe computers), and informative advertising that avoids head-to-head price competition is used.
- *Monopolistic competition.* Dozens of regional, private brands of peanut butter compete with national brands like Skippy and Jif. Both price competition (regional, private brands being lower than national brands) and non-price competition (product features and advertising) exist.
- *Pure competition.* Hundreds of local grain elevators sell corn whose price per bushel is set by the marketplace. Within strains, the corn is identical, so advertising only informs buyers that the seller's corn is available.

Competitors' Prices A firm must know or anticipate what specific price its present and potential competitors are charging now or will charge. When the NutraSweet Company planned the market introduction of Simplesse® all natural fat substitute, it had to consider the price of fat replacements already available as well as potential competitors, including Procter & Gamble's Olestra, Pfizer Inc.'s VeriLo, and the Stellar brand made by A. E. Staley Company.

Identifying Pricing Objectives

www.heinz.com

Expectations that specify the role of price in an organization's marketing and strategic plans are **pricing objectives.** To the extent possible, these organizational pricing objectives are also carried to lower levels in the organization, such as in setting objectives for marketing managers responsible for an individual brand. H. J. Heinz, for example, has specific pricing objectives for its Heinz ketchup brand that vary by country. Chapter 2 discussed six broad objectives that an organization may pursue, which tie in directly to the organization's pricing policies.

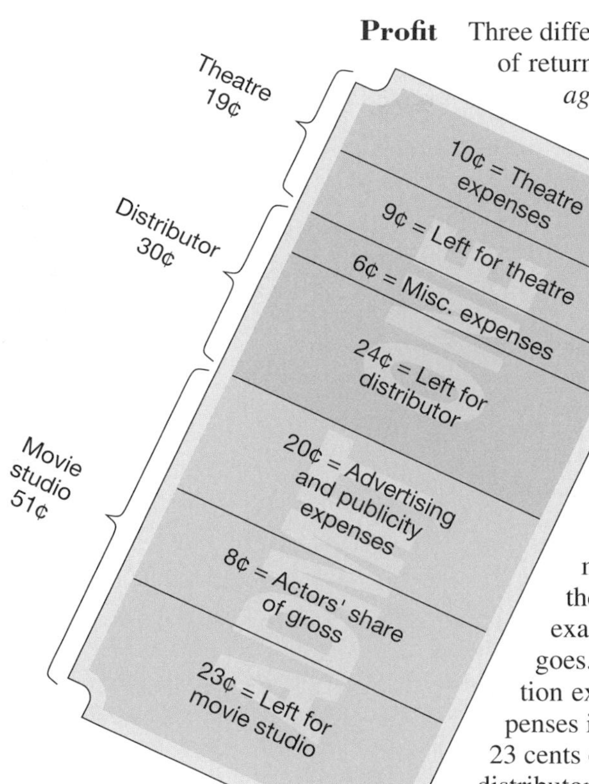

FIGURE 14–4
Where each dollar of your movie ticket goes

Profit Three different objectives relate to a firm's profit, usually measured in terms of return on investment (ROI) or return on assets. One objective is *managing for long-run profits,* which is followed by many Japanese firms that are willing to forgo immediate profit in cars, TV sets, or computers to develop quality products that can penetrate competitive markets in the future. A *maximizing current profit* objective, such as during this quarter or year, is common in many firms because the targets can be set and performance measured quickly. Canadian firms are sometimes criticized for this short-run orientation. A *target return* objective involves a firm such as Irving Oil or Mohawk setting a goal (such as 20 percent) for pretax ROI. These three profit objectives have different implications for a firm's pricing objectives.

Another profit consideration for firms such as movie studios and manufacturers, discussed in more depth in Chapter 15, is to ensure that those firms in their channels of distribution make adequate profits. Without profits for these channel members, the movie studio or manufacturer is cut off from its customers. For example, Figure 14–4 shows where each dollar of your movie ticket goes. The 23 cents the movie studio gets must cover both its production expenses and its profit—a big order if it's the $200 million of expenses it took to produce *Titanic.* While the studio would like more than 23 cents of your dollar, it settles for this amount to make sure theatres and distributors are satisfied and willing to handle their movies.[13]

Sales Given that a firm's profit is high enough for it to remain in business, its objectives may be to increase sales revenue. The hope is that the increase in sales revenue will in turn lead to increases in market share and profit. Cutting price on one product in a firm's line may increase its sales revenue but reduce those of related products. Objectives related to sales revenue or unit sales have the advantage of being translated easily into meaningful targets for marketing managers responsible for a product line or brand—far more easily than with an ROI target, for example.

www.labatt.com

Market Share Market share is the ratio of the firm's sales revenues or unit sales to those of the industry (competitors plus the firm itself). Companies often pursue a market share objective when industry sales are relatively flat or declining. Molson and Labatt Breweries have adopted this objective in the beer market while Pepsi-Cola Canada and Coca-Cola Canada battle for market share in the soft drink category.[14] But although increased market share is the primary goal of some firms, others see it as a means to an end: increasing sales and profits.

Unit Volume Many firms use unit volume, the quantity produced or sold, as a pricing objective. These firms often sell multiple products at very different prices and are sensitive to matching production capacity with unit volume. Using unit volume as an objective, however, can sometimes be misleading from a profit standpoint. Volume can be increased by employing sales incentives (such as lowering prices, giving rebates, or offering lower interest rates). By doing this the company chooses to lower profits in the short run to quickly sell its product. This happened when Fiat offered $1600 rebates and zero-interest financing in Italy on its $10 000 Uno compact car.[15]

Survival In some instances, profits, sales, and market share are less important objectives of the firm than mere survival. Continental Airlines has struggled to attract passengers with low fares, no-penalty advance-booking policies, and aggressive promotions to improve the firm's cash flow. This pricing objective has helped Continental to stay alive in the competitive airline industry.

Social Responsibility A firm may forgo higher profit on sales and follow a pricing objective that recognizes its obligations to customers and society in general. Medtronics followed this pricing policy when it introduced the world's first heart pacemaker. Gerber supplies a specially formulated product free of charge to children who cannot tolerate foods based on cow's milk. Government agencies, which set many prices for services they offer, use social responsibility as a primary pricing objective.

CONCEPT CHECK

1. What factors impact the list price to determine the final price?
2. How does the type of competitive market a firm is in affect its latitude in setting price?

STEP 2: ESTIMATING DEMAND AND REVENUE

Basic to setting a product's price is the extent of customer demand for it. Marketing executives must also translate this estimate of customer demand into estimates of revenues the firm expects to receive.

Fundamentals of Estimating Demand

www.newsweek.com

Newsweek decided to conduct a pricing experiment at newsstands in 11 cities.[16] In one city, newsstand buyers paid \$2.25. In five cities, newsstand buyers paid the regular \$2.00 price. In another city, the price was \$1.50, and in four other cities it was only \$1.00. By comparison, the regular newsstand price for *Time* was \$1.95. Why did *Newsweek* conduct the experiment? According to a *Newsweek* executive, at that time, "We wanted to figure out what the demand curve for our magazine at the newsstand is." And you thought that demand curves only existed to confuse you on a test in basic economics!

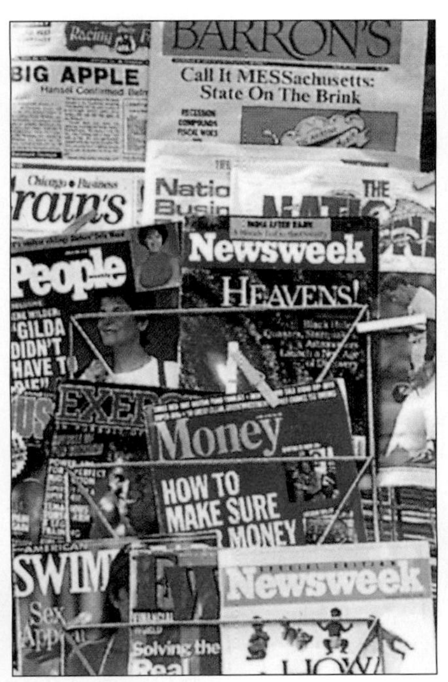

The Demand Curve A **demand curve** shows a maximum number of products consumers will buy at a given price. Demand curve D_1 in Figure 14–5 shows the newsstand demand for *Newsweek* under existing conditions. Note that as price falls, people buy more. But price is not the complete story in estimating demand. Economists stress three other key factors:

1. *Consumer tastes.* As we saw in Chapter 3, these depend on many factors such as demographics, culture, and technology. Because consumer tastes can change quickly, up-to-date marketing research is essential.
2. *Price and availability of other products.* As the price of close substitute products falls (the price of *Time*) and their availability increases, the demand for a product declines (the demand for *Newsweek*).
3. *Consumer income.* In general, as real consumer income (allowing for inflation) increases, demand for a product also increases.

The first of these two factors influences what consumers *want* to buy, and the third affects what they *can* buy. Along with price, these are often called **demand factors,** or factors that determine consumers' willingness and ability to pay for goods and services. As discussed earlier in Chapters 9 and 11, it is often very difficult to estimate demand for new products, especially because consumer likes and dislikes are often so difficult to read clearly. For example, Campbell Soup spent seven years and $75 million on a supersecret project to produce a line of Intelligent Quisine (IQ) food products. The company expected that its line of 41 breakfasts, lunches, dinners, and snacks would be the first foods "scientifically proven to lower high levels of cholesterol, blood sugar, and blood pressure."[17] After 15 months in a test market, Campbell Soup yanked the entire IQ line when it fell far short of expectations because customers found the line too pricey and lacking in variety.

Movement Along versus Shift of a Demand Curve Demand curve D_1 in Figure 14–5 shows that as the price is lowered from $2 to $1.50, the quantity demanded increases from 3 million (Q_1) to 4.5 million (Q_2) units per year. This is an example of a movement along a demand curve and assumes that other factors (consumer tastes, price and availability of substitutes, and consumer income) remain unchanged.

What if some of these factors change? For example, if advertising causes more people to want *Newsweek,* newsstand distribution is increased, and consumer incomes double, then the demand increases. This is shown in Figure 14–5 as a shift of the demand curve to the right, from D_1 to D_2. This increased demand means that more *Newsweek* magazines are wanted for a given price: At a price of $2, the demand is 6 million units per year (Q_3) on D_2 rather than 3 million units per year (Q_1) on D_1.

Fundamentals of Estimating Revenue

While economists may talk about "demand curves," marketing executives are more likely to speak in terms of "revenues generated." Demand curves lead directly to three

FIGURE 14–5
Illustrative demand curves for *Newsweek* magazine

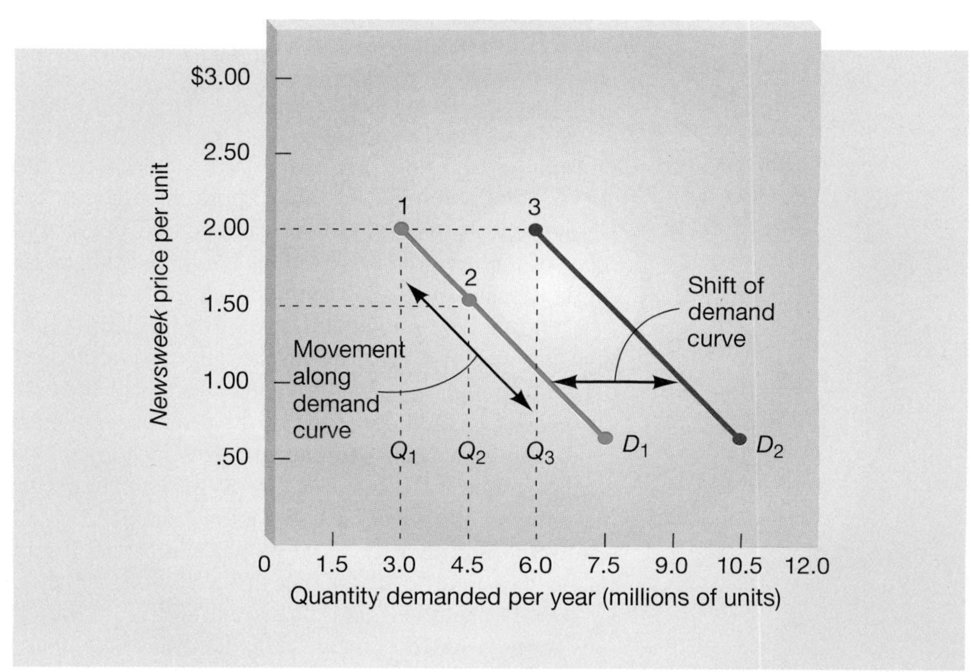

FIGURE 14–6
Fundamental revenue concepts

Total revenue (*TR*) is the total money received from the sale of a product. If:

TR = Total revenue
P = Unit price of the product
Q = Quantity of the product sold

then:

$$TR = P \times Q$$

Average revenue (*AR*) is the average amount of money received for selling one unit of the product, or simply the price of that unit. Average revenue is the total revenue divided by the quantity sold:

$$AR = \frac{TR}{Q} = P$$

Marginal revenue (*MR*) is the change in total revenue obtained by selling one additional unit:

$$MR = \frac{\text{Change in TR}}{\text{1 unit increase in Q}} = \frac{\Delta TR}{\Delta Q} = \text{slope of TR curve}$$

related revenue concepts critical to pricing decisions: **total revenue, average revenue,** and **marginal revenue** (Figure 14–6).

Demand Curves and Revenue Figure 14–7A again shows the demand curve for *Newsweek,* but it is now extended to intersect both the price and quantity axes. The demand curve shows that as price is changed, the quantity of *Newsweek* magazines sold increases. This relationship holds whether the price is increased from \$2.50 to \$3.00 on the demand curve or is reduced from \$1 to \$0 on the curve. In the former case the market demands no *Newsweek* magazines, whereas in the latter case nine million could be given away at \$0 per unit.

It is likely that if *Newsweek* was given away, more than nine million would be demanded. This fact illustrates two important points. First, it can be dangerous to extend a demand curve beyond the range of prices for which it really applies. Second, most demand curves are rounded (or convex) to the origin, thereby avoiding an unrealistic picture of what demand looks like when a straight-line curve intersects either the price axis or the quantity axis.

Figure 14–7B shows the total revenue curve for *Newsweek* calculated from the demand curve shown in Figure 14–7A. The total revenue curve is developed by simply multiplying the unit price times the quantity for each of the points on the demand curve. Total revenue starts at \$0 (point *A*), reaches a maximum of \$6 750 000 at point *D,* and returns to \$0 at point *G.* This shows that as price is reduced in the *A*-to-*D* segment of the curve, total revenues are increased. However, cutting price in the *D*-to-*G* segment results in a decline in total revenue.

Marginal revenue, which is the slope of the total revenue curve, is positive but decreasing when the price lies in the range from \$3 to above \$1.50 per unit. Below \$1.50 per unit, though, marginal revenue is actually negative, so the extra quantity of magazines sold is more than offset by the decrease in the price per unit.

For any downward-sloping, straight-line demand curve, the marginal revenue curve always falls at a rate twice as fast as the demand curve. As shown in Figure 14–7A, the marginal revenue becomes \$0 per unit at a quantity sold of 4.5 million units—the very point at which total revenue is maximum (see Figure 14–7B). A rational marketing manager would never operate in the region of the demand curve in which marginal revenue is negative. This means that in Figure 14–7A this manager would set prices only in the *A*-to-*D* segment of the demand curve.

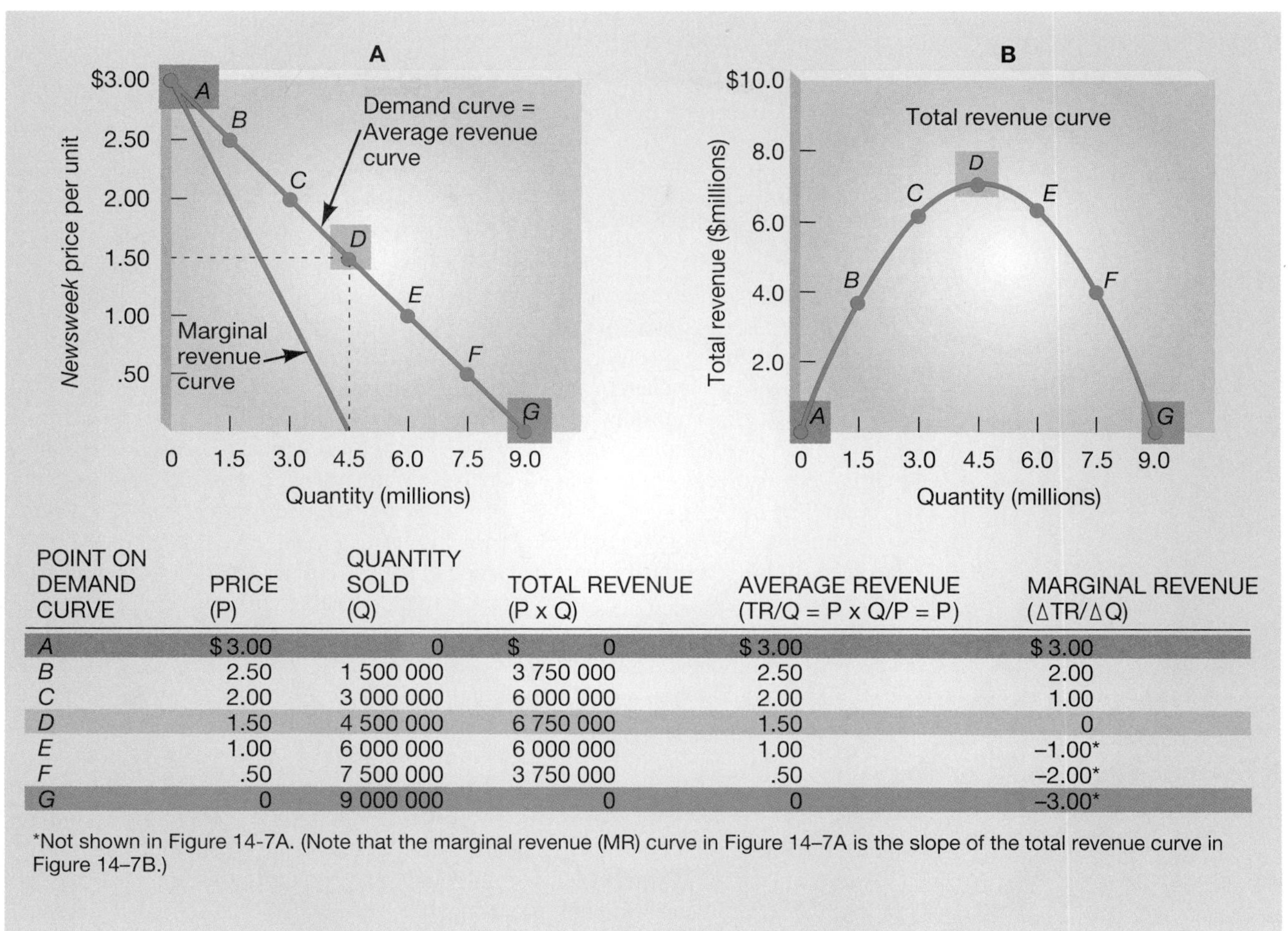

POINT ON DEMAND CURVE	PRICE (P)	QUANTITY SOLD (Q)	TOTAL REVENUE (P x Q)	AVERAGE REVENUE (TR/Q = P x Q/P = P)	MARGINAL REVENUE (ΔTR/ΔQ)
A	$3.00	0	$ 0	$3.00	$3.00
B	2.50	1 500 000	3 750 000	2.50	2.00
C	2.00	3 000 000	6 000 000	2.00	1.00
D	1.50	4 500 000	6 750 000	1.50	0
E	1.00	6 000 000	6 000 000	1.00	–1.00*
F	.50	7 500 000	3 750 000	.50	–2.00*
G	0	9 000 000	0	0	–3.00*

*Not shown in Figure 14-7A. (Note that the marginal revenue (MR) curve in Figure 14–7A is the slope of the total revenue curve in Figure 14–7B.)

FIGURE 14–7
How a downward-sloping demand curve affects total, average, and marginal revenue.

What price did *Newsweek* select after conducting its experiment? It kept the price at $2.00. However, through expanded newsstand distribution and more aggressive advertising, *Newsweek* was later able to shift its demand curve to the right and charge a price of $2.50 without affecting its newsstand volume.

Price Elasticity of Demand With a downward-sloping demand curve, we have been concerned with the responsiveness of demand to price changes. This can be conveniently measured by **price elasticity of demand,** or the percentage change in quantity demanded relative to a percentage change in price. Price elasticity of demand (E) is expressed as follows:

$$E = \frac{\text{Percentage change in quantity demanded}}{\text{Percentage change in price}}$$

Because quantity demanded usually decreases as price increases, price elasticity of demand is usually a negative number. However, for the sake of simplicity and by convention, elasticity figures are shown as positive numbers.

Price elasticity of demand assumes three forms: elastic demand, inelastic demand, and unitary demand elasticity. *Elastic demand* exists when a small percentage decrease in price produces a larger percentage increase in quantity demanded. Price elasticity is greater than 1 with elastic demand. *Inelastic demand* exists when a small percentage decrease in price produces a smaller percentage increase in quantity demanded. With inelastic demand, price elasticity is less than 1. *Unitary demand* exists when the percentage change in price is identical to the percentage change in quantity demanded. In this instance, price elasticity is equal to 1.

Price elasticity of demand is determined by a number of factors. First, the more substitutes a product or service has, the more likely it is to be price elastic. For example, butter has many possible substitutes in a meal and is price elastic, but gasoline has almost no substitutes and is price inelastic. Second, products and services considered to be necessities are price inelastic. For example, open-heart surgery is price inelastic, whereas airline tickets for a vacation are price elastic. Third, items that require a large cash outlay compared with a person's disposable income are price elastic. Accordingly, cars and yachts are price elastic; books and movie tickets tend to be price inelastic.

Price elasticity is important to marketing managers because of its relationship to total revenue. For example, with elastic demand, total revenue increases when price decreases, but decreases when price increases. With inelastic demand, total revenue increases when price increases and decreases when price decreases. Finally, with unitary demand total revenue is unaffected by a slight price change.

Because of this relationship between price elasticity and a firm's total revenue, it is important that marketing managers recognize that price elasticity of demand is not the same over all possible prices of a product. Figure 14–7B illustrates this point using the *Newsweek* demand curve shown in Figure 14–7A. As the price decreases from $2.50 to $2, total revenue increases, indicating an elastic demand. However, when the price decreases from $1 to 50 cents, total revenue declines, indicating an inelastic demand. Unitary demand elasticity exists at a price of $1.50.

Price Elasticities for Brands and Product Classes Marketing executives also recognize that the price elasticity of demand is not always the same for product classes (such as stereo receivers) and brands within a product class (such as Sony and Marantz). For example, marketing experiments on brands of cola, coffee, and snack and specialty foods generally show elasticities of 1.5 to 2.5, indicating they are price

What are the marketing secrets of the entrepreneur who entered the frozen-entree fray, against the advice of experts? For the answer, see the text and the Marketing NewsNet box.

Michelina's Frozen Foods
www.michelinas.com

elastic. By comparison, entire product classes of fruits and vegetables have elasticities of about 0.8—they are price inelastic.[18]

Recently, the price elasticity of demand for cigarettes has become a hotly debated public health issue and a matter of corporate ethics and social responsibility. Research generally shows that cigarettes are price inelastic.[19] However, price elasticity differs by the age of the smoker. Because 12- to 17-year-olds often have limited "spending money," this group is very price elastic in its demand for cigarettes. As a result, many legislators recommend even higher taxes on cigarettes to increase their prices significantly, with the goal of reducing teenage smoking. Thus, price elasticity is not only a relevant concept for marketing managers, but it is also important for public policy affecting pricing practices.

CONCEPT CHECK

1. What is the difference between a movement along and a shift of a demand curve?
2. What does it mean if a product has a price elasticity of demand that is greater than 1?

STEP 3: ESTIMATING COST, VOLUME, AND PROFIT RELATIONSHIPS

While revenues are the moneys received by the firm from selling its products or services to customers, costs or expenses are the moneys the firm pays out to its employees and suppliers. Marketing managers often use marginal analysis and break-even analysis to relate revenues and costs at various levels of units sold, topics covered in this section.

The Importance of Controlling Costs

The profit equation described at the beginning of the chapter showed that Profit = Total revenue – Total cost. Therefore, understanding the role and behaviour of costs is critical for all marketing decisions, particularly pricing decisions. Four cost concepts are important in pricing decisions: **total cost, fixed cost, variable cost,** and **marginal cost** (Figure 14–8).

FIGURE 14–8
Fundamental cost concepts

Total cost (*TC*) is the total expense incurred by a firm in producing and marketing the product. Total cost is the sum of fixed cost and variable cost.

Fixed cost (*FC*) is the sum of the expenses of the firm that are stable and do not change with the quantity of product that is produced and sold. Examples of fixed costs are rent on the building, executive salaries, and insurance.

Variable cost (*VC*) is the sum of the expenses of the firm that vary directly with the quantity of product that is produced and sold. For example, as the quantity sold doubles, the variable cost doubles. Examples are the direct labour and direct materials used in producing the product and the sales commissions that are tied directly to the quantity sold. As mentioned above:

$$TC = FC + VC$$

Variable cost expressed on a per unit basis is called *unit variable cost* (*UVC*).

Marginal cost (*MC*) is the change in total cost that results from producing and marketing one additional unit:

$$MC = \frac{\text{Change in TC}}{\text{1 unit increase in Q}} \quad \frac{\Delta TC}{\Delta Q} = \text{slope of TC curve}$$

CUSTOMER VALUE

MARKETING NEWSNET

The Secrets of a Food Entrepreneur: Pay Attention to Detail and Control Costs

"I think I'm well liked by my employees," he says, "but I'm a [soft expletive] on quality. If the pasta is a little mushy, I get a lot of upset."

The speaker is Jeno Paulucci, chief executive officer of Lugino's foods and called one of the most accomplished food entrepreneur in recent times by *Fortune* magazine. Across five decades and through three huge new-food businesses, Paulucci's secrets have remained consistent: (1) a passion for detail and (2) low, low overhead to control costs. The effect has been to provide genuine value to customers that, in turn, has resulted in huge success for his three separate businesses, described here.

Chun King Foods. In 1945 Paulucci began selling Chinese food. Chun King took off when GIs returning from World War II sought the convenience—and customer value—of easy-to-prepare dinners. In 1966 Paulucci sold Chun King to what was then R. J. Reynolds for $88 million.

Jenos. He took the cash and started producing pizzas and pizza rolls. How did Paulucci get the idea for pizza rolls? His response: "I had to do something with my egg roll machines"—a low-cost way of utilizing his leftover Chun King equipment. By 1972 Jeno's was a leader in frozen pizza and frozen hot snacks. But Paulucci got bored with the business and sold it to Pillsbury for $210 million in 1985. Paulucci's quality concern: "The pies got smaller, with more artificial ingredients. I didn't like making food that way."

Luginos. In 1990, against the judgment of experts, Paulucci entered the overcrowded frozen-entree fray, competing with giant brands such as Stouffer, Healthy Choice, and Weight Watchers. Paulucci was unfazed and observes, "All those big companies with all their overhead—I knew if we paid attention to the little things our plan would work." Two examples: (1) Paulucci packs the pasta in his Michelina's Italian dinners separately from the sauce to improve flavour, and (2) he sells his Italian dinners for about half the price of competitors—by controlling his costs.

His credo: "Gold is in the details"—which applies to customer value, costs, and prices.

Many firms go bankrupt because their costs get out of control, causing their total costs to exceed their total revenues over an extended period of time. This is why sophisticated marketing managers make pricing decisions that balance both their revenues and costs. An example, described in the Marketing NewsNet box, is that of an entrepreneur who has achieved spectacular success in three different food businesses by controlling costs and attending to critical details that ensure that his products provide genuine value to customers. Controlling costs carefully has enabled him to sell his Michelina's Italian dinners at prices well below those of his competitors.[20]

Marginal Analysis and Profit Maximization

A basic idea in business, economics, and indeed everyday life is marginal analysis. In personal terms, marginal analysis means that people will continue to do something as long as the incremental return exceeds the incremental cost. This same idea holds true in marketing and pricing decisions. In this setting, **marginal analysis** means that as long as revenue received from the sale of an additional product (marginal revenue) is greater than the additional cost of production and selling it (marginal cost), a firm will expand its output of that product.[21]

Marginal analysis is central to the concept of maximizing profits. In Figure 14–9A, marginal revenue and marginal cost are graphed. Marginal cost starts out high at lower quantity levels, decreases to a minimum through production and marketing efficiencies, and then rises again due to the inefficiencies of overworked labour and equipment. Marginal revenue follows a downward slope. In Figure 14–9B, total cost and total revenue curves corresponding to the marginal cost and marginal revenue curves

FIGURE 14–9
Profit maximization pricing

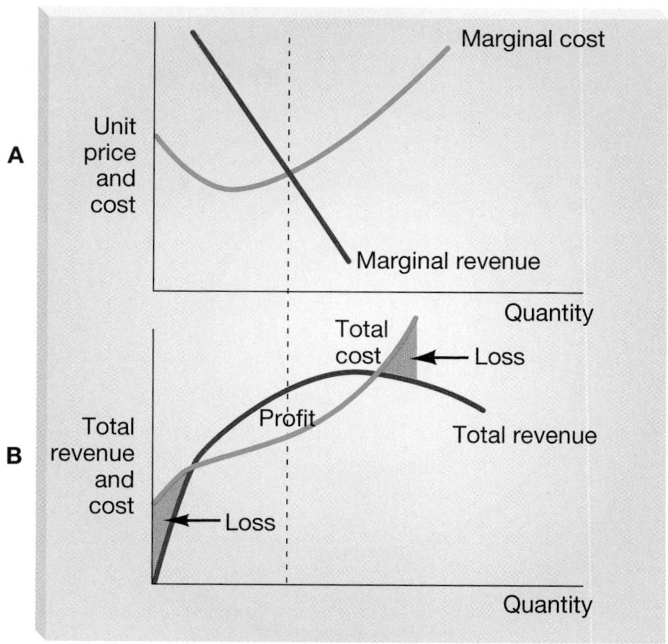

are graphed. Total cost initially rises as quantity increases but increases at the slowest rate at the quantity where marginal cost is lowest. The total revenue curve increases to a maximum and then starts to decline, as shown in Figure 14–9B.

The message of marginal analysis, then, is to operate up to the quantity and price level where marginal revenue equals marginal cost (MR = MC). Up to the output quantity at which MR = MC, each increase in total revenue resulting from selling one additional unit exceeds the increase in the total cost of producing and marketing that unit. Beyond the point at which MR = MC, however, the increase in total revenue from selling one more unit is less than the cost of producing and marketing that unit. At the quantity at which MR = MC, the total revenue curve lies farthest above the total cost curve, they are parallel, and profit is a maximum.

Break-Even Analysis

Marketing managers often employ a simpler approach for looking at cost, volume, and profit relationships, which is also based on the profit equation. **Break-even analysis** is a technique that analyzes the relationship between total revenue and total cost to determine profitability at various levels of output. The **break-even point** (BEP) is the quantity at which total revenue and total cost are equal and beyond which profit occurs. In terms of the definitions in Figure 14–8:

$$BEP_{\text{Quantity}} = \frac{\text{Fixed cost}}{\text{Unit price} - \text{Unit variable cost}}$$

Calculating a Break-Even Point Consider, for example, a corn farmer who wishes to identify how many bushels of corn he must sell to cover his fixed cost at a given price. Suppose the farmer had a fixed cost (FC) of $2000 (for real estate taxes, interest on a bank loan, and other fixed expenses) and a unit variable cost (UVC) of $1 per bushel (for labor, corn seed, herbicides, and pesticides). If the price (P) is $2 per bushel, his break-even quantity is 2000 bushels:

$$BEP_{\text{Quantity}} = \frac{FC}{P - UVC} = \frac{\$2000}{\$2 - \$1} = 2000 \text{ bushels}$$

The shaded row in Figure 14–10 shows that the break-even quantity at a price of $2 per bushel is 2000 bushels since, at this quantity, total revenue equals total cost. At less

QUANTITY SOLD (Q)	PRICE PER BUSHEL (P)	TOTAL REVENUE (TR) (P × Q)	UNIT VARIABLE COST (UVC)	TOTAL VARIABLE COSTS (TVC) (UVC × Q)	FIXED COST (FC)	TOTAL COST (TC) (FC + VC)	PROFIT (TR – TC)
0	$2	$ 0	$1	$ 0	$2 000	$2 000	–$2 000
1 000	2	2 000	1	1 000	2 000	3 000	–1 000
2 000	2	4 000	1	2 000	2 000	4 000	0
3 000	2	6 000	1	3 000	2 000	5 000	1 000
4 000	2	8 000	1	4 000	2 000	6 000	2 000
5 000	2	10 000	1	5 000	2 000	7 000	3 000
6 000	2	12 000	1	6 000	2 000	8 000	4 000

FIGURE 14–10
Calculating a break-even point

than 2000 bushels the farmer incurs a loss, and at more than 2000 bushels he makes a profit. Figure 14–11 shows a graphic presentation of the break-even analysis, called a **break-even chart.**

Applications of Break-Even Analysis Because of its simplicity, break-even analysis is used extensively in marketing, most frequently to study the impact on profit of changes in price, fixed cost, and variable cost. The mechanics of break-even analysis are the basis of the widely used electronic spreadsheets offered by computer programs such as Microsoft *Excel* that permit managers to answer hypothetical "what if . . ." questions about the effect of changes in price and cost on their profit.

An example will show the power of break-even analysis. As described in Figure 14–12, if an electronic calculator manufacturer automates its production, thereby increasing fixed cost and reducing variable cost by substituting machines for workers, this increases the break-even point from 333 333 to 500 000 units per year.

But what about the impact of the higher level of fixed cost on profit? Remember, profit at any output quantity is given by:

$$\text{Profit} = \text{Total revenue} - \text{Total cost}$$
$$= (P \times Q) - [FC + (UVC \times Q)]$$

FIGURE 14–11
Break-even analysis chart

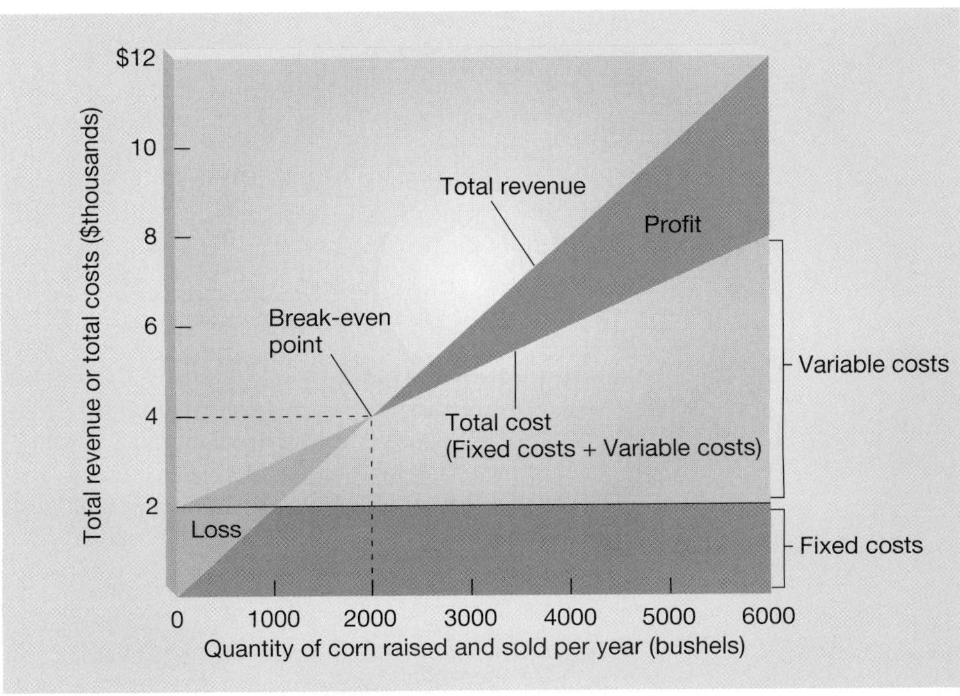

FIGURE 14–12
The cost trade-off: fixed versus variable costs

Executives in virtually every mass-production industry—from locomotives and cars to electronic calculators and breakfast cereals—are searching for ways to increase quality and reduce production costs to remain competitive in world markets. Increasingly they are substituting robots, automation, and computer-controlled manufacturing systems for blue- and white-collar workers.

To understand the implications of this on the break-even point and profit, consider this example of an electronic calculator manufacturer:

BEFORE AUTOMATION			AFTER AUTOMATION		
P	=	$10 per unit	P	=	$10 per unit
FC	=	$1 000 000	FC	=	$4 000 000
UVC	=	$7 per unit	UVC	=	$2 per unit
$BEP_{Quantity}$	=	$\frac{FC}{P - UVC}$	$BEP_{Quantity}$	=	$\frac{FC}{P - UVC}$
	=	$\frac{\$1\,000\,000}{\$10 - \$7}$		=	$\frac{\$4\,000\,000}{\$10 - \$2}$
	=	333 333 units		=	500 000 units

The automation increases the fixed cost and increases the break-even quantity from 333,333 to 500,000 units per year. So if annual sales fall within this range, the calculator manufacturer will incur a loss with the automated plant, whereas it would have made a profit if it had not automated.

But what about its potential profit if it sells one million units a year? Look carefully at the two break-even charts below, and see the text to check your conclusions:

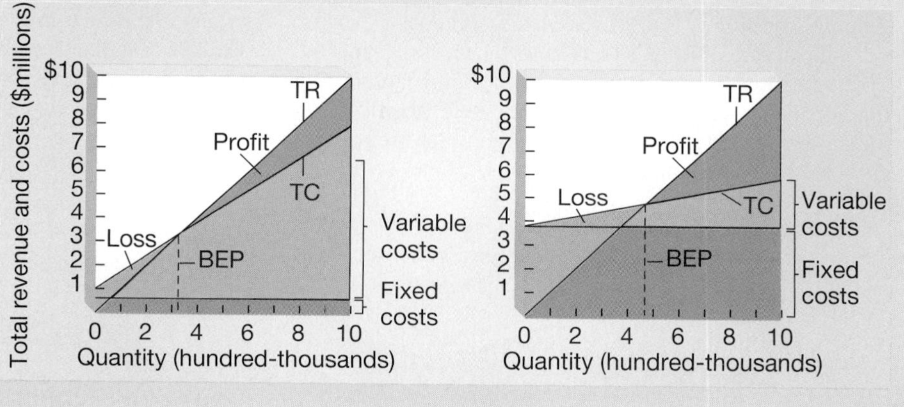

So profit at 1 million units of sales before automation is:

$$\begin{aligned}\text{Profit} &= (P \times Q) - [FC + (UVC \times Q)] \\ &= (\$10 \times 1\,000\,000) - [\$1\,000\,000 + (\$7 \times 1\,000\,000)] \\ &= \$10\,000\,000 - \$8\,000\,000 \\ &= \$2\,000\,000\end{aligned}$$

After automation, profit is:

$$\begin{aligned}\text{Profit} &= (P \times Q) - [FC + (UVC \times Q)] \\ &= (\$10 \times 1\,000\,000) - [\$4\,000\,000 + (\$2 \times 1\,000\,000)] \\ &= \$10\,000\,000 - \$6\,000\,000 \\ &= \$4\,000\,000\end{aligned}$$

Automation, by adding to fixed cost, increases profit by $2 million at one million units of sales. Thus, as the quantity sold increases for the automated plant, the potential increase or leverage on profit is tremendous. This is why with large production and sales volumes, automated plants for GM cars or Texas Instruments calculators produce large profits. Also, firms in other industries, such as airline, railway, and hotel and motel industries, that require a high fixed cost can reap large profits when they go even slightly beyond the break-even point.

CONCEPT CHECK

1. What is the difference between fixed cost and variable cost?
2. What is a break-even point?

SUMMARY

1 Price is the money or other considerations exchanged for the ownership or use of a product or service. Although price typically involves money, the amount exchanged is often different from the list or quoted price because of allowances and extra fees.

2 Consumers use price as an indicator of value when it is paired with the perceived benefits of a good or service. Sometimes price influences consumer perceptions of quality itself and at other times consumers make value assessments by comparing the costs and benefits of substitute items.

3 Pricing constraints such as demand, product newness, costs, competitors, other products sold by the firm, and the type of competitive market restrict a firm's pricing latitude.

4 Pricing objectives, which specify the role of price in a firm's marketing strategy, may include pricing for profit, sales revenue, market share, unit sales, survival, or some socially responsible price level.

5 A demand curve shows the maximum number of products consumers will buy at a given price and for a given set of (*a*) consumer tastes, (*b*) price and availability of other products, and (*c*) consumer income. When any of these change, there is a shift of the demand curve.

6 Important revenue concepts include total revenue, average revenue, and marginal revenue.

7 Price elasticity of demand measures the sensitivity of units sold to a change in price. When demand is elastic, a reduction in price is more than offset by an increase in units sold, so that total revenue increases.

8 It is necessary to consider cost behaviour when making pricing decisions. Important cost concepts include total cost, variable cost, fixed cost, and marginal cost.

9 Break-even analysis shows the relationship between total revenue and total cost at various quantities of output for given conditions of price, fixed cost, and variable cost. The break-even point is where total revenue and total cost are equal.

KEY TERMS AND CONCEPTS

price p. 358
barter p. 358
value p. 359
value-pricing p. 360
profit equation p. 360
pricing constraints p. 360
pricing objectives p. 364
demand curve p. 366
demand factors p. 367
total revenue p. 368
average revenue p. 368
marginal revenue p. 368
price elasticity of demand p. 369
total cost p. 371
fixed cost p. 371
variable cost p. 371
marginal cost p. 371
marginal analysis p. 372
break-even analysis p. 373
break-even point p. 373
break-even chart p. 373

INTERNET EXERCISE

Want to check out the options and prices on your next car? First, write down the features you want in a car. Then, check out these three Web sites:

- General Motors: www.gmbuypower.com
- Ford: www.buyerconnection.com
- An independent car buying service: www.autobytel.com

After you have printed the price quotes for the cars you desire from the above Web sites, call or visit a local dealer and get a quote for the cars with the same features. Compare the prices and experiences of buying a car from the Internet and the traditional car dealer. What are the similarities and differences, if any, in negotiating the list prices, vehicle incentives, trade-in allowances, financing, warranties, accessories (or option packages), destination charges, etc. of the cars you want?[22]

APPLYING MARKETING CONCEPTS AND PERSPECTIVES

1 How would the price equation apply to the purchase price of (*a*) gasoline, (*b*) an airline ticket, and (*c*) a chequing account?

2 What would be your response to the statement, "Profit maximization is the only legitimate pricing objective for the firm"?

3 How is a downward-sloping demand curve related to total revenue and marginal revenue?

4 A marketing executive once said, "If the price elasticity of demand for your product is inelastic, then your price is probably too low." What is this executive saying in terms of the economic principles discussed in this chapter?

5 A marketing manager reduced the price on a brand of cereal by 10 percent and observed a 25 percent increase in quantity sold. The manager then thought that if the price were reduced by another 20 percent, a 50 percent increase in quantity sold would occur. What would be your response to the marketing manager's reasoning?

6 A student theatre group at a university has developed a demand schedule that shows the relationship between ticket prices and demand based on a student survey, as follows:

TICKET PRICE	NUMBER OF STUDENTS WHO WOULD BUY
$1	300
2	250
3	200
4	150
5	100

(*a*) Graph the demand curve and the total revenue curve based on these data. What ticket price might be set based on this analysis? (*b*) What other factors should be considered before the final price is set?

7 Touché Toiletries, Inc. has developed an addition to its Lizardman Cologne line tentatively branded Ode d'Toade Cologne. Unit variable costs are 45 cents for a 60-mL bottle, and heavy advertising expenditures in the first year would result in total fixed costs of $900 000. Ode d'Toade Cologne is priced at $7.50 for a 60-mL bottle. How many bottles of Ode d'Toade must be sold to break even?

8 Suppose that marketing executives for Touché Toiletries reduced the price to $6.50 for a 60-mL bottle of Ode d'Toade and the fixed costs were $1 100 000. Suppose further that the unit variable cost remained at 45 cents for a 60-mL bottle. (*a*) How many bottles must be sold to break even? (*b*) What dollar profit level would Ode d'Toade achieve if 200 000 bottles were sold?

9 Executives of Random Recordings, Inc. produced an album entitled *Sunshine/Moonshine* by the Starshine Sisters Band. The cost and price information was as follows:

Album cover	$	1.00 per album
Songwriter's royalties		0.30 per album
Recording artists' royalties		0.70 per album
Direct material and labour costs to produce the album		1.00 per album
Fixed cost of producing an album (advertising, studio fee, etc.)	100 000.00	
Selling price		7.00 per album

(*a*) Prepare a chart like that in Figure 14–11 showing total cost, fixed cost, and total revenue for album quantity sold levels starting at 10 000 albums through 100 000 albums at 10 000 album intervals, that is, 10 000, 20 000, 30 000, and so on.
(*b*) What is the break-even point for the album?

CASE 14–1 WASHBURN INTERNATIONAL, INC.

"The relationship between musicians and their guitars is something really extraordinary—and is a fairly strange one," says Brady Breen in a carefully understated tone of voice. Breen has the experience to know. He's production manager of Washburn International (www.washburn.com), one of the most prestigious guitar manufacturers in the world. Washburn's instruments range from one-of-a-kind, custom-made acoustic and electric guitars and basses to less expensive, mass-produced ones.

THE COMPANY AND ITS HISTORY

The modern Washburn International started in 1977 when a small firm bought the century-old Washburn brand name and a small inventory of guitars, parts, and promotional supplies. At that time annual revenues of the company were $300 000 for the sale of about 2500 guitars. Washburn's first catalogue, appearing in 1978, told a frightening truth:

> Our designs are translated by Japan's most experienced craftsmen, assuring the consistent quality and craftmanship for which they are known.

At that time the North American guitar-making craft was at an all-time low. Guitars made by Japanese firms such as Ibane and Yamaha were in use by an increasing number of professionals.

Times have changed for Washburn. Today the company sells about 250 000 guitars a year. Annual sales exceed $50 million. All this resulted from Washburn's aggressive marketing strategies to develop product lines with different price points targeted at musicians in distinctly different market segments.

THE PRODUCTS AND MARKET SEGMENTS

Arguably the most trendsetting guitar developed by the modern Washburn company appeared in 1980. This was the Festival Series of cutaway, thin-bodied flattops, with built-in bridge pickups and controls, which went on to become the virtual standard for live performances. John Lodge of the Moody Blues endorsed the 12-string version—his gleaming white guitar appearing in both concerts and ads for years. In the time since the Festival Series appeared, countless rock and country stars have used these instruments including Bob Dylan, Dolly Parton, Greg Allman, John Jorgenson, and George Harrison.

Until 1991 all Washburn guitars were manufactured in Asia. That year Washburn started building its high-end guitars in North America. Today Washburn marketing executives divide its product line into four levels. From high-end to low-end these are:

- One-of-a-kind, custom units.
- Batch-custom units.
- Mass-customized units.
- Mass-produced units.

The one-of-a-kind custom units are for the many stars that use Washburn instruments. The mass-produced units targeted at first-time buyers are still manufactured in Asian factories.

PRICING ISSUES

Setting prices for its various lines presents a continuing challenge for Washburn. Not only do the prices have to reflect the changing tastes of its various segments of musicians, but the prices must also be competitive with the prices set for guitars manufactured and marketed globally. In fact, Washburn and other well-known guitar manufacturers have a prestige-niche strategy. For Washburn this involves endorsements by internationally known musicians who play its instruments and lend their names to lines of Washburn signature guitars. This has the effect of reducing the price elasticity or price sensitivity for these guitars. Stars playing Washburn guitars like Nuno Bettencourt, David Gilmour of Pink Floyd, Joe Perry of Aerosmith, and Darryl Jones of the Rolling Stones have their own lines of signature guitars—the "batch-custom" units mentioned earlier.

Joe Baksha, Washburn's executive vice president, is responsible for reviewing and approving prices for the company's lines of guitars. Setting a sales target of 2000 units for a new line of guitars, he is considering a suggested retail price of $329 per unit for customers at one of the hundreds of retail outlets carrying the Washburn line. For planning purposes, Baksha estimates half of the final retail price will be the price Washburn nets when it sells its guitar to the wholesalers and dealers in its channel of distribution.

Looking at Washburn's financial data for its present North American plant, Baksha estimates that this line of guitars must bear these fixed costs:

Rent and taxes	= $12 000
Depreciation of equipment	= $ 4000
Management and quality control program	= $20 000

In addition, he estimates the variable costs for each unit to be:

Direct materials = $25/unit
Direct labour = 8 hours/unit @ $14/hour

Carefully kept production records at Washburn's North American plant make Baksha believe that these are reasonable estimates. He explains, "Before we begin a production run, we have a good feel for what our costs will be. The North American-built N-4, for example, simply costs more than one of our foreign-produced Mercury or Wing series electrics."

Caught in the global competition for guitar sales, Washburn searches for ways to reduce and control costs. After much agonizing, the company decided to move to Nashville, Tennessee. In this home of country music, Washburn expects to lower its manufacturing costs because there are many skilled workers in the region, and its fixed costs will be reduced by avoiding some of the expenses of having a big city location. Specifically, Washburn projects that it will reduce its rent and taxes expense by 40 percent and the wage rate it pays by 15 percent in relocating from its current plant to Nashville.

Questions

1 What factors are most likely to affect the demand for the lines of Washburn guitars (*a*) bought by a first-time guitar buyer and (*b*) bought by a sophisticated musician who wants a signature model signed by David Gilmour or Joe Perry?

2 For Washburn what are examples of (*a*) shifting the demand curve to the right to get a higher price for a guitar line (movement *of* the demand curve) and (*b*) pricing decisions involving moving *along* a demand curve?

3 In Washburn's current plant what is the break-even point for the new line of guitars if the retail price is (*a*) $329, (*b*) $359, and (*c*) $299? Also, (*d*) if Washburn achieves the sales target of 2000 units at the $329 retail price, what will its profit be?

4 Assume that Washburn moves its production to Nashville and that the costs are reduced as projected in the case. Then, what will be the (*a*) new break-even point at a $329 retail price for this line of guitars and (*b*) the new profit if it sells 2000 units?

5 If for competitive reasons, Washburn eventually has to move all its production back to Asia, (*a*) which specific costs might be lowered and (*b*) what additional costs might it expect to incur?

CHAPTER FIFTEEN

PRICING: ARRIVING AT THE FINAL PRICE

15

AFTER READING THIS CHAPTER YOU SHOULD BE ABLE TO:

- Understand how to establish the initial "approximate price level" using demand-oriented, cost-oriented, profit-oriented, and competition-oriented approaches.
- Identify the major factors considered in deriving a final list or quoted price from the approximate price level.
- Describe adjustments made to the approximate price level based on geography, discounts, and allowances.
- Prepare basic financial analyses useful in evaluating alternative prices and arriving at the final sales price.
- Describe the principal laws and regulations affecting pricing practices.

GILLETTE KNOWS THE VALUE OF A GREAT SHAVE

How much is a close and comfortable shave worth? Ask The Gillette Company (www.gillette.com), the world leader in shaving technology and marketing. Gillette commands 71 percent of the North American and European markets for shaving razors and blades and captures 91 percent of the market for blades in Latin America and 69 percent in India.

Product innovation that benefits the customer is a critical ingredient in Gillette's success. Gillette's breakthrough MACH 3 shaving system is an example. MACH 3 is the first and only shaving system with three progressively aligned blades that provide men with a closer shave in fewer strokes with less irritation. According to Gillette's consumer tests, men preferred MACH 3 nearly two-to-one over the company's hugely successful SensorExcel shaving system introduced in 1994, and by a still larger margin over rival products.

Such innovation naturally translates into the price customers are willing to pay. Gillette's pricing research indicated men would pay 45 percent more for the MACH 3 than they paid for the SensorExcel given the shaving benefit provided. Gillette ultimately chose a 35 percent price premium over SensorExcel and supported the 1998 launch of MACH 3 with a first-year marketing support budget of $300 million—the largest marketing effort in the company's history. MACH 3 is scheduled to be marketed in 100 countries by 2000 and expected to log $1.8 billion in annual worldwide sales.[1]

The marketing success of MACH 3 illustrates the imaginative commercialization of shaving technology at a price point that creates value for the consumer. In addition to understanding consumer demand, cost, competition, and profit considerations played a role in Gillette's pricing decisions as will be discussed later.

This chapter describes how companies such as Gillette select an approximate price level, highlights important

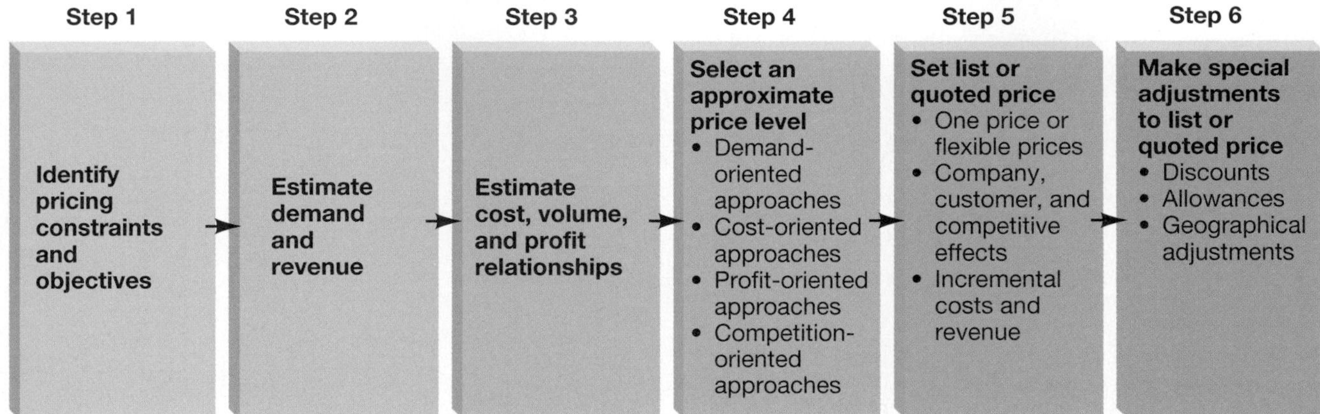

FIGURE 15–1
Steps in setting price

considerations in setting a list or quoted price, and identifies various price adjustments that can be made to prices set by the firm—the last three steps an organization uses in setting price (Figure 15–1). In addition, an overview of legal and regulatory aspects of pricing is provided.

STEP 4: SELECT AN APPROXIMATE PRICE LEVEL

A key to a marketing manager's setting a final price for a product is to find an "approximate price level" to use as a reasonable starting point. Four common approaches to helping find this approximate price level are (1) demand-oriented, (2) cost-oriented, (3) profit-oriented, and (4) competition-oriented approaches (Figure 15–2). Although these approaches are discussed separately below, some of them overlap, and an effective marketing manager will consider several in searching for an approximate price level.

Demand-Oriented Approaches

Demand-oriented approaches weigh factors underlying expected customer tastes and preferences more heavily than such factors as cost, profit, and competition when selecting a price level.

Skimming Pricing A firm introducing a new or innovative product can use **skimming pricing,** setting the highest initial price that customers really desiring the product are willing to pay. These customers are not very price sensitive because they weigh the new product's price, quality, and ability to satisfy their needs against the same characteristics of substitutes. As the demand of these customers is satisfied, the firm lowers the price to attract another, more price-sensitive segment. Thus, skimming pricing gets its name from skimming successive layers of "cream," or customer segments, as prices are lowered in a series of steps.

Skimming pricing is an effective strategy when (1) enough prospective customers are willing to buy the product immediately at the high initial price to make these sales profitable, (2) the high initial price will not attract competitors, (3) lowering price has only a minor effect on increasing the sales volume and reducing the unit costs, and (4) customers interpret the high price as signifying high quality. These four conditions are most likely to exist when the new product is protected by patents or copyrights or its uniqueness is understood and valued by customers. Gillette adopted a skimming strategy for the MACH 3 shaving system since many of these conditions

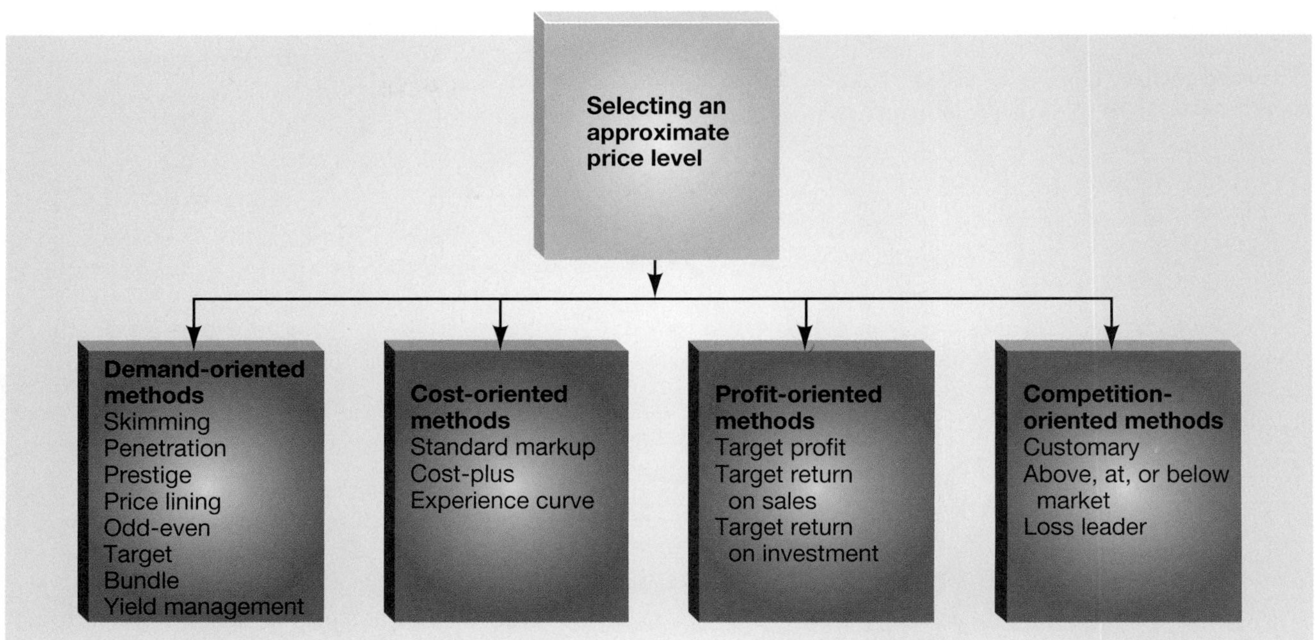

FIGURE 15–2
Four approaches for selecting an approximate price level

applied, including patent protection. The MACH 3 shaving system has some 35 patents that protect its product and manufacturing process technology.[2]

Penetration Pricing Setting a low initial price on a new product to appeal immediately to the mass market is **penetration pricing,** the exact opposite of skimming pricing. Sony Corporation consciously chose a penetration strategy when it introduced its PlayStation video-game player. Sony's penetration strategy was designed to quickly gain market share, attract price-sensitive consumers, discourage competitors from entering the market, and according to a company executive, "achieve a massive mass market," which it did.[3]

www.sony.com

The conditions favouring penetration pricing are the reverse of those supporting skimming pricing: (1) many segments of the market are price sensitive, (2) a low initial price discourages competitors from entering the market, and (3) unit production and marketing costs fall dramatically as production volumes increase. A firm using penetration pricing may (1) maintain the initial price for a time to gain profit lost from its low introductory level, or (2) lower the price further, counting on the new volume to generate the necessary profit. Sony chose the second approach for its video-game player. Sony slashed the price of PlayStation to half of its original price 18 months after its introduction.[4]

In some situations penetration pricing may follow skimming pricing. A company might initially price a product high to attract price-insensitive consumers and recoup initial research and development costs and introductory promotional expenditures. Once this is done, penetration pricing is used to appeal to a broader segment of the population and increase market share.[5]

Prestige Pricing As noted in Chapter 14, consumers may use price as a measure of the quality or prestige of an item so that as price is lowered beyond some point, demand for the item actually falls. **Prestige pricing** involves setting a high price so that status-conscious consumers will be attracted to the product and buy it (Figure 15–3A). The demand curve slopes downward and to the right between points *A* and *B* but turns back to the left between points *B* and *C* because demand is actually reduced between points *B*

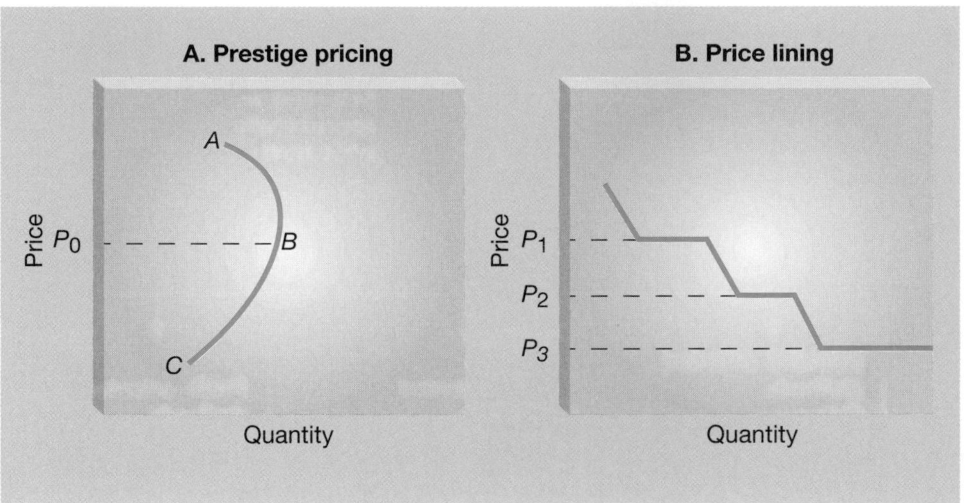

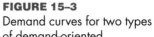

FIGURE 15–3
Demand curves for two types of demand-oriented approaches

and *C*. From *A* to *B* buyers see the lowering of price as a bargain and buy more; from *B* to *C* they become dubious about the quality and prestige and buy less. A marketing manager's pricing strategy here is to stay above price P_o (the initial price).

Rolls-Royce cars, diamonds, perfumes, fine china, Swiss watches, and crystal have an element of prestige pricing appeal in them and may sell worse at lower prices than at higher ones.[6] The recent success of Swiss watchmaker TAG Heuer is an example. The company raised the average price of its watches from $250 to $1,000, and its sales volume increased sevenfold![7]

Price Lining Often a firm that is selling not just a single product but a line of products may price them at a number of different specific pricing points, which is called **price lining.** For example, a discount department store manager may price a line of women's dresses at $59, $79, and $99. As shown in Figure 15–3B, this assumes that demand is elastic at each of these price points but inelastic between these price points. In some instances all the items might be purchased for the same cost and then marked up at different percentages to achieve these price points based on colour, style, and expected demand. In other instances manufacturers design products for different price points, and retailers apply approximately the same markup percentages to achieve the three or four different price points offered to consumers. Sellers often feel that a limited number (such as three or four) of price points is preferable to 8 or 10 different ones, which may only confuse prospective buyers.[8]

www.sears.ca

Odd-Even Pricing Sears Canada offers a Craftsman radial saw for $499.99, the suggested retail price for a MACH 3 razor set (razor and two blades) is $6.99, and Kmart sells Windex glass cleaner on sale for 99 cents. Why not simply price these items at $500, $7, and $1, respectively? These firms are using **odd-even pricing,** which involves setting prices a few dollars or cents under an even number. The presumption is that consumers see the Sears radial saw as priced at "something over $400" rather than "about $500." In theory, demand increases if the price drops from $500 to $499.99. There is some evidence to suggest that this does happen. However, consumers may interpret these odd-ending prices as meaning lower quality.[9]

Target Pricing Manufacturers will sometimes estimate the price that the ultimate consumer would be willing to pay for a product. They then work backward through markups taken by retailers and wholesalers to determine what price they can charge wholesalers for the product. This practice, called **target pricing,** results in the

CROSS FUNCTIONAL

MARKETING NEWSNET

Achieving a Target Price: Cross-Functional Planning Pays a Customer Value Dividend to Compaq Computer

Personal computer buyers today demand better hardware and more software and expect to pay less for computer power and reliability. It is therefore understandable that creating and sustaining customer value in the PC industry is a constant challenge. Compaq Computer Corporation has met the customer value challenge and sells more personal computers than any other firm in the United States. One reason for Compaq's success has been its focus on target pricing.

Target pricing at Compaq involves cross-functional planning and integration. It begins by first determining what the final retail list price to the buyer should be, followed by the subtraction of retailer markup and the company's desired profit margin. Managers of the materials, engineering, manufacturing, and marketing functions resolve among themselves how to allocate the remaining costs to make a product that provides the desired features at the desired retail price point.

Target pricing at Compaq demands discipline, teamwork, originality, and a collective commitment to develop products at prices that PC buyers are willing to pay. Does it work? With target pricing, Compaq built a $3 billion business in home computers from scratch in two years.

manufacturer deliberately adjusting the composition and features of a product to achieve the target price to consumers. Canon uses this practice for pricing its cameras, and Heinz adopted target pricing for its complete line of pet foods. Compaq Computer Corporation successfully employed target pricing when it entered the home computer market, as described in the accompanying Marketing NewsNet.[10]

www.cdnair.ca

Bundle Pricing A frequently used demand-oriented pricing practice is **bundle pricing**—the marketing of two or more products in a single "package" price. For example, Canadian Airlines offers vacation packages that include airfare, car rental, and lodging. Bundle pricing is based on the idea that consumers value the package more than the individual items. This is due to benefits received from not having to make separate purchases and enhanced satisfaction from one item given the presence of another. Moreover, bundle pricing often provides a lower total cost to buyers and lower marketing costs to sellers.[11] For example, Cantel offers an all-in-one cellular phone and service package that includes a Motorola cellular phone and a calling plan for less than $20 a month.

Yield Management Pricing Have you noticed seats on your Air Canada or Canadian Airline flights are priced differently within economy class? What you observed is **yield management pricing**—the charging of different prices to maximize revenue for a set amount of capacity at any given time.[12] As described in Chapter 13, service businesses engage in capacity management, and an effective way to do this is by varying price by time, day, week, or season. Yield management pricing is a complex approach that continually matches demand and supply to customize the price for a service. Airlines, hotels, cruise ships, and car rental companies use it. The airline industry reports that yield management pricing produces hundreds of millions of dollars of revenue each year that might not ordinarily be produced using traditional pricing practices.[13]

CONCEPT CHECK

1. What are the circumstances in pricing a new product that might support skimming or penetration pricing?
2. What is odd-even pricing?

Cost-Oriented Approaches

With cost-oriented approaches the price setter stresses the supply or cost side of the pricing problem, not the demand side. Price is set by looking at the production and marketing costs and then adding enough to cover direct expenses, overhead, and profit.

Standard Markup Pricing Managers of supermarkets and other retail stores have such a large number of products that estimating the demand for each product as a means of setting price is impossible. Therefore, they use **standard markup pricing,** which entails adding a fixed percentage to the cost of all items in a specific product class. This percentage markup varies depending on the type of retail store (such as furniture, clothing, or grocery) and on the product involved. High-volume products usually have smaller markups than do low-volume products. Supermarkets such as Sobey's Safeway, and Loblaws have different markups for staple items and discretionary items. The markup on staple items like sugar, flour, and dairy products varies from 10 percent to 23 percent, whereas markups on discretionary items like snack foods and candy range from 27 percent to 47 percent. These markups must cover all expenses of the store, pay for overhead costs, and contribute something to profits. For supermarkets, these markups, which may appear very large, result in only a one percent profit on sales revenue if the store is operating efficiently. By comparison, consider the markups on snacks and beverages purchased at your local movie theatre. The markup on soft drinks is 87 percent, 65 percent on chocolate bars, and a whopping 90 percent on popcorn! An explanation of how to compute a markup, along with operating statement data and other ratios, is given in Appendix B to this chapter.

Cost-Plus Pricing Many manufacturing, professional services, and construction firms use a variation of standard markup pricing. **Cost-plus pricing** involves summing the total unit cost of providing a product or service and adding a specific amount to the cost to arrive at a price. Cost-plus pricing generally assumes two forms. With *cost-plus percentage-of-cost pricing,* a fixed percentage is added to the total unit costs. This is often used to price one- or few-of-a-kind items, as when an architectural firm charges a percentage of the construction costs of, say, the multimillion-dollar Air Canada Centre of the Toronto Maple Leafs. In buying highly technical, few-of-a-kind products such as hydroelectric power plants or space satellites, buyers, particularly government agencies, have found that general contractors are reluctant to specify a formal, fixed price for the procurement. Therefore, they use *cost-plus fixed-fee pricing,* which means that a supplier is reimbursed for all costs, regardless of what they turn out to be, but is allowed only a fixed fee as profit that is independent of the final cost of the project. For example, suppose that the Department of National Defence agreed to pay a manufacturer $1.2 billion as the cost of a new military satellite and agreed to a $100 million fee for providing the satellite. Even if the manufacturer's cost increased to $2 billion for the satellite, its fee would remain $100 million.

The rising cost of legal fees has prompted some law firms to adopt a cost-plus pricing approach. Rather than billing clients on an hourly basis, lawyers and their clients agree on a fixed fee based on expected costs plus a profit for the law firm.[14] Many advertising agencies also use this approach. Here, the client agrees to pay the agency a fee based on the cost of its work plus some agreed-on profit, which is often a percentage of total cost.[15]

Experience Curve Pricing The method of **experience curve pricing** is based on the learning effect, which holds that the unit cost of many products and services declines by 10 percent to 30 percent each time a firm's experience at producing and selling them doubles.[16] This reduction is regular or predictable enough that the average cost per unit can be mathematically estimated. For example, if the firm estimates that costs will fall by 15 percent each time volume doubles, then the cost of the 100th

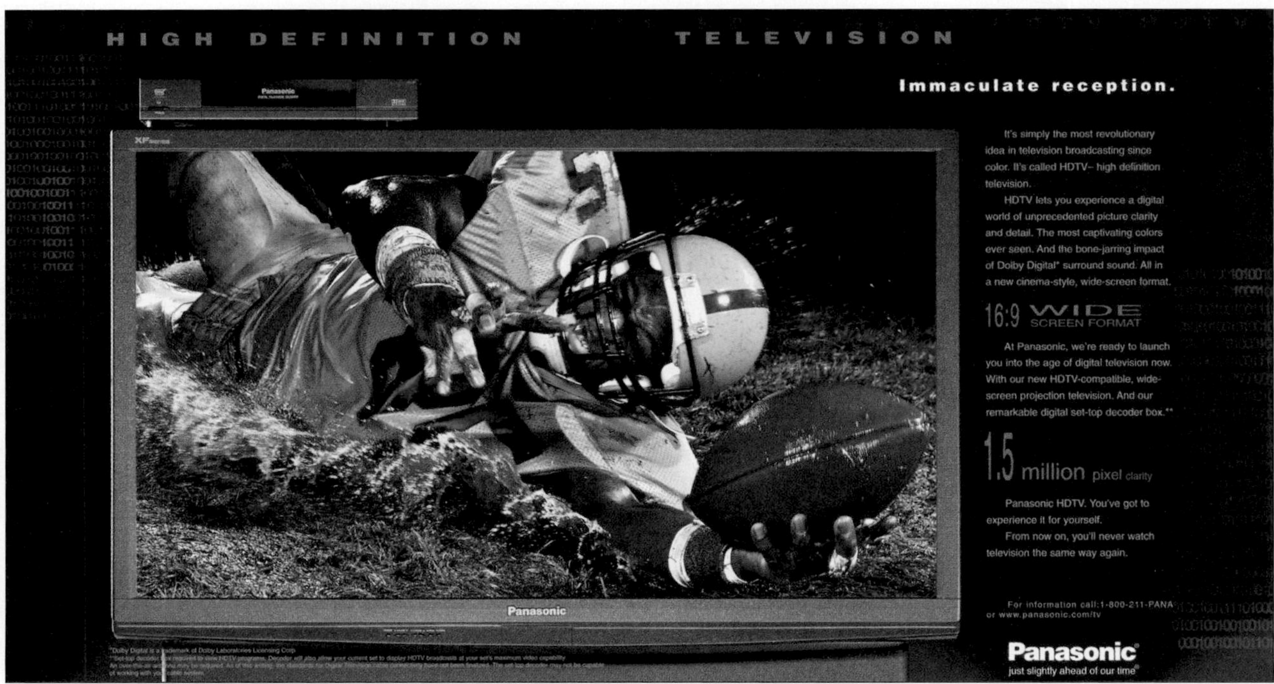

Panasonic expects to be a leader in the successful commercialization of HDTV.

Panasonic
www.panasonic.com

unit produced and sold will be about 85 percent of the cost of the 50th unit, and the 200th unit will be 85 percent of the 100th unit. Therefore, if the cost of the 50th unit is \$100, the 100th unit would cost \$85, the 200th unit would be \$72.25, and so on. Since prices often follow costs with experience curve pricing, a rapid decline in price is possible. Japanese firms in the electronics industry often adopt this pricing approach. This cost-oriented pricing approach complements the demand-oriented pricing strategy of skimming followed by penetration pricing. For example, CD player prices have decreased from \$900 to less than \$200, fax machine prices have declined from \$1000 to under \$300, and cellular telephones that sold for \$4000 are now priced below \$99. Panasonic, Sony, Samsung, Zenith, and other television manufacturers will use experience curve pricing for HDTV sets. Consumers will benefit because prices will decline as cumulative sales volume grows.[17]

Profit-Oriented Approaches

A price setter may choose to balance both revenues and costs to set price using profit-oriented approaches. These might either involve a target of a specific dollar volume of profit or express this target profit as a percentage of sales or investment.

Target Profit Pricing A firm may set an annual target of a specific dollar volume of profit, which is called **target profit pricing.** Suppose a picture framing store owner wishes to use target profit pricing to establish a price for a typical framed picture and assumes the following:

- Variable cost is a constant \$22 per unit.
- Fixed cost is a constant \$26 000.
- Demand is insensitive to price up to \$60 per unit.
- A target profit of \$7000 is sought at an annual volume of 1000 units (framed pictures).

WEB LINK Tracking the Success of MACH 3

The innovative MACH 3 shaving system is very likely to bolster the sales and operating profit for Gillette's blades and razors business. You can track the success of MACH 3 by visiting The Gillette Company Web site at http://www.gillette.com. Go to the Investors page, click business and investment profiles, and review the performance chart entitled Blades and Razors Sales and Profit from Operations.

How have sales, dollar operating profit, and operating profit margin for blades and razors changed since Gillette introduced the MACH 3 shaving system in mid-1998?

The price can be calculated as follows:

$$\text{Profit} = \text{Total revenue} - \text{Total cost}$$
$$\text{Profit} = (P \times Q) - [FC + (UVC \times Q)]$$
$$\$7000 = (P \times 1000) - [\$26\,000 + (\$22 \times 1000)]$$
$$\$7000 = 1000P - (\$26\,000 + \$22\,000)$$
$$1000P = \$7000 + \$48\,000$$
$$P = \$55$$

Note that a critical assumption is that this higher average price of a framed picture will not cause the demand to fall.

Target Return-on-Sales Pricing A difficulty with target profit pricing is that although it is simple and the target involves only a specific dollar volume, there is no benchmark of sales or investment used to show how much of the firm's effort is needed to achieve the target. Firms such as supermarket chains often use **target return-on-sales pricing** to set typical prices that will give the firm a profit that is a specified percentage, say, one percent, of the sales volume. Suppose the owner decides to use target return-on-sales pricing for the frame shop and makes the same first three assumptions shown previously. The owner now sets a target of 20 percent return on sales at an annual volume of 1250 units. This gives

$$\text{Target return on sales} = \frac{\text{Target profit}}{\text{Total revenue}}$$
$$20\% = \frac{TR - TC}{TR}$$
$$0.20 = \frac{P \times Q - [FC + (UVC - Q)]}{TR}$$
$$0.20 = \frac{P \times 1250 - [\$26\,000 + (\$22 \times 1250)]}{P \times 1250}$$
$$P = \$53.50$$

So at a price of \$53.50 per unit and an annual quantity of 1250 frames,

$$TR = P \times Q = \$53.50 \times 1250 = \$66\,875$$
$$TC = FC + (UVC \times Q) = \$26\,000 + (\$22 \times 1250) = \$53\,500$$
$$\text{Profit} = TR - TC = \$66\,875 - \$53\,500 = \$13\,375$$

As a check,

$$\text{Target return on sales} = \frac{\text{Target profit}}{\text{Total revenue}} = \frac{\$13\,375}{\$66\,875} = 20\%$$

The Gillette Company expects that its MACH 3 shaving system will increase both the dollar volume of profit and the return-on-sales for its blades and razor business. Why? The MACH 3 gross profit is three time higher than that for Gillette's Sensor-Excel shaving system![18] Visit the Web site described in the accompanying Web Link to see the effect of the MACH 3 on Gillette's blade and razor sales, dollar operating profit, and operating profit margins.

Target Return-on-Investment Pricing Firms such as GM and many public utilities set annual return-on-investment (ROI) targets such as ROI of 20 percent. **Target return-on-investment pricing** is a method of setting prices to achieve this target.

Suppose the store owner sets a target ROI of 10 percent, which is twice that achieved the previous year. She considers raising the average price of a framed picture to $54 or $58—up from last year's average of $50. To do this, she might improve product quality by offering better frames and higher-quality matting, which will increase the cost but will probably offset the decreased revenue from the lower number of units that can be sold next year.

To handle this wide variety of assumptions, today's managers use computerized spreadsheets to project operating statements based on a diverse set of assumptions. Figure 15–4 shows the results of computerized spreadsheet simulation, with assumptions shown at the top and the projected results at the bottom. A previous year's operating statement results are shown in the column headed "Last Year," and the assumptions and spreadsheet results for four different sets of assumptions are shown in columns A, B, C, and D.

FIGURE 15–4
Results of computer spreadsheet simulation to select price to achieve a target return on investment

			SIMULATION			
ASSUMPTIONS OR RESULTS	**FINANCIAL ELEMENT**	**LAST YEAR**	**A**	**B**	**C**	**D**
Assumptions	Price per unit (P)	$50	$54	$54	$58	$58
	Units sold (Q)	1 000	1 200	1 100	1 100	1 000
	Change in unit variable cost (UVC)	0%	+10%	+10%	+20%	+20%
	Unit variable cost	$ 22.00	$ 24.20	$ 24.20	$ 26.40	$ 26.40
	Total expenses	$ 8 000	Same	Same	Same	Same
	Owner's salary	$18 000	Same	Same	Same	Same
	Investment	$20 000	Same	Same	Same	Same
	Provincial and federal taxes	50%	Same	Same	Same	Same
Spreadsheet simulation results	Net sales (P × Q)	$50 000	$64 800	$59 400	$63 800	$58 000
	Less: COGS (Q × UVC)	22 000	29 040	26 620	29 040	26 400
	Gross margin	$28 000	$35 760	$32 780	$34 760	$31 600
	Less: total expenses	8 000	8 000	8 000	8 000	8 000
	Less: owner's salary	18 000	18 000	18 000	18 000	18 000
	Net profit before taxes	$ 2 000	$ 9 760	$ 6 780	$8 760	$ 5 600
	Less: taxes	1 000	4 880	3 390	4 380	2 800
	Net profit after taxes	$ 1 000	$ 4 880	$ 3 390	$ 4 380	$ 2 800
	Investment	$20 000	$20 000	$20 000	$20 000	$20 000
	Return on investment	5.0%	24.4%	17.0%	21.9%	14.0%

In choosing a price or another action using spreadsheet results, the decision maker must (1) study the results of the computer simulation projections and (2) assess the realism of the assumptions underlying each set of projections. For example, the store owner sees from the bottom row of Figure 15–4 that all four spreadsheet simulations exceed the after-tax target ROI of 10 percent. But, after more thought, she judges it to be more realistic to set an average price of $58 per unit, allow the unit variable cost to increase by 20 percent to account for more expensive framing and matting, and settle for the same unit sales as the 1000 units sold last year. She selects simulation D in this computerized spreadsheet approach to target ROI pricing and has a goal of 14 percent after-tax ROI. Of course, these same calculations can be done by hand, but this is far more time consuming.

Competition-Oriented Approaches

Rather than emphasize demand, cost, or profit factors, a price setter can stress what competitors or "the market" is doing.

Customary Pricing For some products where tradition, a standardized channel of distribution, or other competitive factors dictate the price, **customary pricing** is used. Tradition prevails in the pricing of Swatch watches. The $40 customary price for the basic model has not changed in 10 years.[19] Chocolate bars offered through standard vending machines have a customary price of 50 cents, and a significant departure from this price may result in a loss of sales for the manufacturer. Hershey typically has changed the amount of chocolate in its chocolate bars depending on the price of raw chocolate rather than vary its customary retail price so that it can continue selling through vending machines.

Above-, At-, or Below-Market Pricing For most products it is difficult to identify a specific market price for a product or product class. Still, marketing managers often have a subjective feel for the competitors' price or market price. Using this benchmark, they then may deliberately choose a strategy of **above-, at-, or below-market pricing.**

Among watch manufacturers, Rolex takes pride in emphasizing that it makes one of the most expensive watches you can buy—a clear example of above-market pricing. Manufacturers of national brands of clothing such as Alfred Sung and Christian Dior and retailers such as Holt Renfrew deliberately set premium prices for their products.

Large mass-merchandise chains such as Sears Canada and The Bay generally use at-market pricing. These chains often establish the going market price in the minds of competitors. Similarly, Revlon generally prices its products "at market." These companies also provide a reference price for competitors that use above- and below-market pricing.

In contrast, a number of firms use a strategy of below-market pricing. Manufacturers of all generic products and retailers who offer their own private brands of products ranging from peanut butter to shampoo deliberately set prices for these products about 8 percent to 10 percent below the prices of nationally branded competitive products such as Skippy peanut butter, Vidal Sassoon shampoo, or Crest toothpaste. Below-market pricing also exists in business-to-business marketing. Hewlett-Packard, for instance, consciously priced its line of office personal computers below Compaq and IBM to promote a value image among corporate buyers.[20]

Loss-Leader Pricing For a special promotion many retail stores deliberately sell a product below its customary price to attract attention to it. For example, supermarkets will often use produce or paper goods as loss leaders. The purpose of **loss-leader pricing** is not to increase sales of that particular produce but to attract customers in hopes they will buy other products as well, particularly discretionary items carrying large markups.[21]

CONCEPT CHECK

1. What is standard markup pricing?
2. What profit-based pricing approach should a manager use if he or she wants to reflect the percentage of the firm's resources used in obtaining the profit?
3. What is the purpose of loss-leader pricing when used by a retail firm?

STEP 5: SET THE LIST OR QUOTED PRICE

The first four steps in setting price covered in Chapter 14 and in this chapter result in an approximate price level for the product that appears reasonable. But it still remains for the manager to set a specific list or quoted price in light of all relevant factors.

One-Price versus Flexible-Price Policy

A seller must decide whether to follow a one-price or flexible-price policy. A **one-price policy** is setting the same price for similar customers who buy the same product and quantities under the same conditions. For example, the regular passenger vehicle charge to use The Confederation Bridge is $35 whether you are a tourist of a resident, and whether there is one or five persons in the passenger vehicle.[22] Similarly, Saturn Corporation uses a "no haggle, one-price" policy for both new and used Saturn cars. In contrast, a **flexible-price policy** is offering the same product and quantities to similar customers but at different prices. As noted at the end of this chapter, flexible pricing carried to the extreme could be considered price discrimination and is a practice prohibited under the Competition Act.[23]

www.saturn.com

Prices paid by an ultimate consumer illustrate the differences in these two policies, although the same principles apply to manufacturers and wholesalers as well. When you buy a Wilson Sting tennis racket from a discount store, you are offered the product at a single price. You can buy it or not, but there is no variation in the price under the seller's one-price policy. But with a house, the seller generally uses a flexible-price policy, and you might negotiate a purchase at a price that lies within a range of prices. Flexible prices give sellers greater discretion in setting the final price in light of demand, cost, and competitive factors.

Company, Customer, and Competitive Effects

As the final list or quoted price is set, the effects on the company, customers, and competitors must be assessed.

Company Effects For a firm with more than one product, a decision on the price of a single product must consider the price of other items in its product line or related product lines in its product mix. Within a product line or mix there are usually some products that are substitutes for one another and some that complement each other. Frito-Lay recognizes that its tortilla chip product line consisting of Baked Tostitos, Tostitos, and Doritos brands are partial substitutes for one another and its bean and cheese chip dip line and salsa sauces complement the tortilla chip line.

A manager's challenge when marketing multiple products is **product-line pricing,** the setting of prices for all items in a product line. When setting prices, the manager seeks to cover the total cost and produce a profit for the complete line, not necessarily for each item. For example, the penetration price for Sony's PlayStation video-game player was likely below its cost, but the price of its video games (complementary products) was set high enough to cover the loss and deliver a handsome profit for the PlayStation product line.[24]

Product-line pricing involves determining (1) the lowest priced product and price, (2) the highest priced product and price, and (3) price differentials for all other products in the line.[25] The lowest and highest priced items in the product line play important roles. The highest priced item is typically positioned as the premium item in quality and features. The lowest priced item is the traffic builder designed to capture the attention of the hesitant or first-time buyer. Price differentials between items in the line should make sense to customers and reflect differences in their perceived value of the products offered. Behavioural research also suggests that the price differentials should get larger as one moves up the product line.

Customer Effects In setting price, retailers weigh factors heavily that satisfy the perceptions or expectations of ultimate consumers, such as the customary prices for a variety of consumer products. Retailers have found that they should not price their store brands 20 to 25 percent below manufacturers' brands. When they do, consumers often view the lower price as signalling lower quality and don't buy.[26] Manufacturers and wholesalers must choose prices that result in profit for resellers in the channel to gain their cooperation and support. Toro failed to do this on its lines of lawn mowers and snow throwers. It decided to augment its traditional hardware outlet distribution by also selling through big discounters such as Kmart and Wal-Mart. To do so, it set prices for the discounters substantially below those for its traditional hardware outlets. Many unhappy hardware stores abandoned Toro products in favour of mowers and snow throwers from other manufacturers.

Competitive Effects A manager's pricing decision is immediately apparent to most competitors, who may retaliate with price changes of their own. Therefore, a manager who sets a final list or quoted price must anticipate potential price responses from competitors. Regardless of whether a firm is a price leader or follower, it wants to avoid cutthroat price wars in which no firm in the industry makes a satisfactory profit. For example, price wars in the airline industry usually result in losses for all players. Similarly, in the

Frito-Lay recognizes that its tortilla chip products are partial substitutes for one another and its bean and cheese dips and salsa sauces complement tortilla chips. This knowledge is used for Frito-Lay product-line pricing.

Frito-Lay, Inc.
www.frito-lay.com

residential long-distance telephone industry, even price reductions as little as one percent can have a significant effect in a highly competitve environment. In general, each time a competitor lowers its per-minute charge and is matched by the other players, revenues tend to tumble for everyone. In the Canadian brewery industry, a recent price war between Molson and Labatt trimmed millions off the bottom lines of both companies.

Balancing Incremental Costs and Revenues

When a price is changed or new advertising or selling programs are planned, their effect on the quantity sold must be considered. This assessment, called *marginal analysis* (Chapter 14), involves a continuing, concise trade-off of incremental costs against incremental revenues.

Do marketing and business managers really use marginal analysis? Yes, they do, but they often don't use phrases such as *marginal revenue, marginal cost,* and *elasticity of demand.*

Think about these managerial questions:

- How many extra units do we have to sell to pay for that $1000 advertisement?
- How much savings on unit variable cost do we have to get to keep the break-even point the same if we invest in a $10 000 labour-saving machine?
- Should we hire three more salespeople or not?

All these questions are a form of marginal or incremental analysis, even though these exact words are not used.

Figure 15–5 shows the power—and some limitations—of marginal analysis applied to a marketing decision. Note that the frame store owner must either conclude that a simple advertising campaign will more than pay for itself in additional sales or not undertake the campaign. The decision could also have been made to increase the average price of a framed picture to cover the cost of the campaign, but the principle still applies: expected incremental revenues from pricing and other marketing actions must more than offset incremental costs.

The example in Figure 15–5 shows both the main advantage and difficulty of marginal analysis. The advantage is its common-sense usefulness, and the difficulty is obtaining the necessary data to make decisions. The owner can measure the cost quite easily, but the incremental revenue generated by the ads is difficult to measure. She could partly solve this problem by offering $2 off the purchase price with use of a coupon printed in the ad to see which sales resulted from the ad.

FIGURE 15–5
The power of marginal analysis in real-world decisions

Suppose the owner of a picture framing store is considering buying a series of magazine ads to reach her up-scale target market. The cost of the ads is $1000, the average price of a framed picture is $50, and the unit variable cost (materials plus labour) is $30.

This is a direct application of marginal analysis that an astute manager uses to estimate the incremental revenue or incremental number of units that must be obtained to at least cover the incremental cost. In this example, the number of extra picture frames that must be sold is obtained as follows:

$$\text{Incremental number of frames} = \frac{\text{Extra fixed cost}}{\text{Price} - \text{Unit variable cost}} = \frac{\$1000 \text{ of advertising}}{\$50 - \$30} = 50 \text{ frames}$$

So unless there are some other benefits of the ads, such as long-term goodwill, she should only buy the ads if she expects they will increase picture frame sales by at least 50 units.

STEP 6: MAKE SPECIAL ADJUSTMENTS TO THE LIST OR QUOTED PRICE

When you pay 50 cents for a bag of M&Ms in a vending machine or receive a quoted price of $10 000 from a contractor to build a new kitchen, the pricing sequence ends with the last step just described: setting the list or quoted price. But when you are a manufacturer of M&M candies or gas grills and sell your product to dozens or hundreds of wholesalers and retailers in your channel of distribution, you may need to make a variety of special adjustments to the list or quoted price. Wholesalers also must adjust list or quoted prices they set for retailers. Three special adjustments to the list or quoted price are (1) discounts, (2) allowances, and (3) geographical adjustments (Figure 15–6).

Discounts

Discounts are reductions from list price that a seller gives a buyer as a reward for some activity of the buyer that is favourable to the seller. Four kinds of discounts are especially important in marketing strategy: (1) quantity, (2) seasonal, (3) trade (functional), and (4) cash discounts.[27]

Quantity Discounts To encourage customers to buy larger quantities of a product, firms at all levels in the channel of distribution offer **quantity discounts,** which are reductions in unit costs for a larger order. For example, an instant photocopying service might set a price of 10 cents a copy for 1 to 25 copies, 9 cents a copy for 26 to 100, and 8 cents a copy for 101 or more. Because the photocopying service gets more of the buyer's business and has longer production runs that reduce its order-handling costs, it is willing to pass on some of the cost savings in the form of quantity discounts to the buyer.

Quantity discounts are of two general kinds: noncumulative and cumulative. *Noncumulative quantity discounts* are based on the size of an individual purchase order. They encourage large individual purchase orders, not a series of orders. This discount is used by Federal Express to encourage companies to ship a large number of packages at one time. *Cumulative quantity discounts* apply to the accumulation of purchases of a product over a given time period, typically a year. Cumulative quantity discounts encourage repeat buying by a single customer to a far greater degree than do noncumulative quantity discounts.

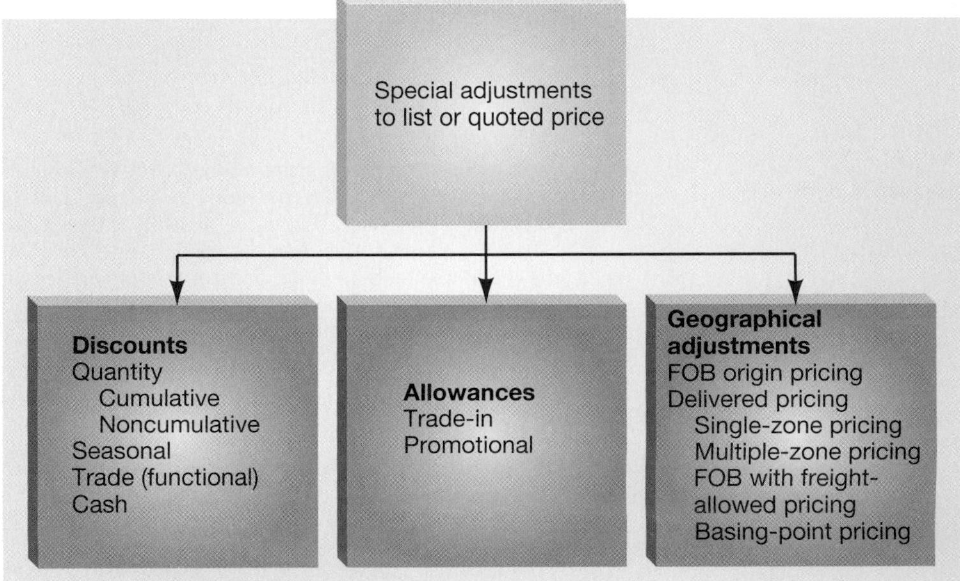

FIGURE 15–6
Three special adjustments to list or quoted price

Toro uses seasonal discounts to stimulate consumer demand and smooth out seasonal manufacturing peaks and troughs.

The Toro Company
www.toro.com

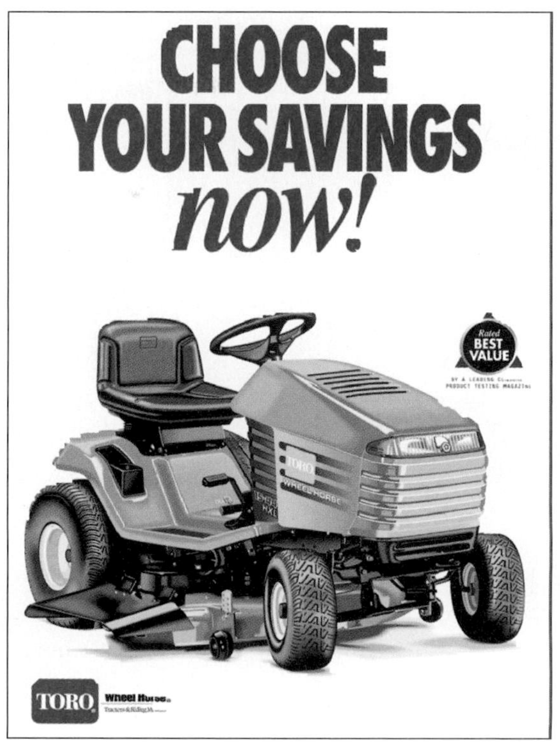

Seasonal Discounts To encourage buyers to stock inventory earlier than their normal demand would require, manufacturers often use seasonal discounts. A firm such as Toro that manufactures lawn mowers and snow throwers offers seasonal discounts to encourage wholesalers and retailers to stock up on lawn mowers in January and February and on snow throwers in July and August—five or six months before the seasonal demand by ultimate consumers. This enables Toro to smooth out seasonal manufacturing peaks and troughs, thereby contributing to more efficient production. It also rewards wholesalers and retailers for the risk they accept in assuming increased inventory carrying costs and having supplies in stock at the time they are wanted by customers.

Trade (Functional) Discounts To reward wholesalers and retailers for marketing functions they will perform in the future, a manufacturer often gives trade, or functional, discounts. These reductions off the list or base price are offered to resellers in the channel of distribution on the basis of (1) where they are in the channel and (2) the marketing activities they are expected to perform in the future.

Suppose a manufacturer quotes price in the following form: list price—$100 less 30/10/5. The first number in the percentage sequence always refers to the retail end of the channel, and the last number always refers to the wholesaler or jobber closest to the manufacturer in the channel. The trade discounts are simply subtracted one at a time. This price quote shows $100 is the manufacturer's suggested retail price; 30 percent of the suggested retail price is available to the retailer to cover costs and provide a profit of $30 ($100 × 0.3 = $30); wholesalers closest to the retailer in the channel get 10 percent of their selling price ($70 × 0.1 = $7); and the final group of wholesalers in the channel (probably jobbers) that are closest to the manufacturer get 5 percent of their selling price ($63 × 0.05 = $3.15). Thus, starting with the manufacturer's retail price and subtracting the three trade discounts shows that the manufacturer's selling price to the wholesaler or jobber closest to it is $59.85 (Figure 15–7).

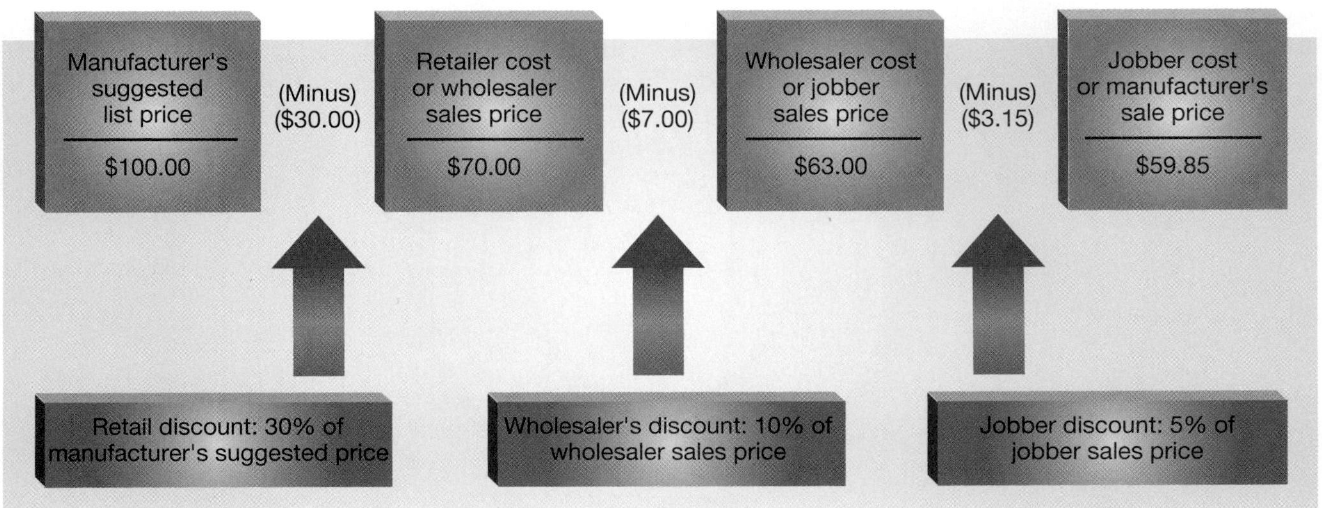

FIGURE 15–7
The structure of trade discounts

Traditional trade discounts have been established in various product lines such as hardware, food, and pharmaceutical items. Although the manufacturer may suggest the trade discounts shown in the example just cited, the sellers are free to alter the discount schedule depending on their competitive situation.

Cash Discounts To encourage retailers to pay their bills quickly, manufacturers offer them cash discounts. Suppose a retailer receives a bill quoted at $1000, 2/10 net 30. This means that the bill for the product is $1000, but the retailer can take a 2 percent discount ($1000 × 0.02 = $20) if payment is made within 10 days and send a cheque for $980. If the payment cannot be made within 10 days, the total amount of $1000 is due within 30 days. It is usually understood by the buyer that an interest charge will be added after the first 30 days of free credit.

Naive buyers may think that the 2 percent discount offered is not substantial. What this means is that the buyer pays 2 percent on the total amount to be able to use that amount an extra 20 days—from day 11 to day 30. In a 360-day business year, this is an effective annual interest rate of 36 percent (2% × 360/20 = 36%). Because the effective interest rate is so high, firms that cannot take advantage of a 2/10 net 30 cash discount often try to borrow money from their local banks at rates far lower than the 36 percent they must pay by not taking advantage of the cash discount.

Retailers provide cash discounts to consumers as well to eliminate the cost of credit granted to consumers. These discounts take the form of discount-for-cash policies. Canadian Tire is famous for its discount-for-cash policy where consumers receive 3 percent off for cash purchases in the form of cash-bonus coupons that can be used against future purchases.

Allowances

Allowances—like discounts—are reductions from list or quoted prices to buyers for performing some activity.

Trade-in Allowances A new car dealer can offer a substantial reduction in the list price of that new Ford Taurus by offering you a trade-in allowance of $500 for your 1989 Chevrolet. A trade-in allowance is a price reduction given when a used product is part of the payment on a new product. Trade-ins are an effective way to lower the price a buyer has to pay without formally reducing the list price.

Promotional Allowances Sellers in the channel of distribution can qualify for **promotional allowances** for undertaking certain advertising or selling activities to promote a product. Various types of allowances include an actual cash payment or an extra amount of "free goods" (as with a free case of pizzas to a retailer for every dozen cases purchased). Frequently, a portion of these savings is passed on to the consumer by retailers.

Some companies, such as Procter & Gamble, have chosen to reduce promotional allowances for retailers by using everyday low pricing. **Everyday low pricing** (EDLP) is the practice of replacing promotional allowances with lower manufacturer list prices. EDLP promises to reduce the average price to consumers while minimizing promotional allowances that cost manufacturers billions of dollars every year.

Geographical Adjustments

Geographical adjustments are made by manufacturers or even wholesalers to list or quoted prices to reflect the cost of transportation of the products from seller to buyer. The two general methods for quoting prices related to transportation costs are (1) FOB origin pricing and (2) uniform delivered pricing.

FOB Origin Pricing FOB means "free on board" some vehicle at some location, which means the seller pays the cost of loading the product onto the vehicle that is used (such as a barge, railway car, or truck). **FOB origin pricing** usually involves the seller's naming the location of this loading as the seller's factory or warehouse (such as "FOB Toronto" or "FOB factory"). The title to the goods passes to the buyer at the point of loading, so the buyer becomes responsible for picking the specific mode of transportation, for all the transportation costs, and for subsequent handling of the product. Buyers farthest from the seller face the big disadvantage of paying the higher transportation costs.

Uniform Delivered Pricing When a **uniform delivered pricing** method is used, the price the seller quotes includes all transportation costs. It is quoted in a contract as "FOB buyer's location," and the seller selects the mode of transportation, pays the freight charges, and is responsible for any damage that may occur because the seller retains title to the goods until delivered to the buyer. Although they go by various names, four kinds of delivered pricing methods are (1) single-zone pricing, (2) multiple-zone pricing, (3) FOB with freight-allowed pricing, and (4) basing-point pricing.

In *single-zone pricing* all buyers pay the same delivered price for the products, regardless of their distance from the seller. So although a store offering free delivery in a metropolitan area has lower transportation costs for goods shipped to customers nearer the store than for those shipped to distant ones, customers pay the same delivered price.

In *multiple-zone pricing* a firm divides its selling territory into geographic areas or zones. The delivered price to all buyers within any one zone is the same, but prices across zones vary depending on the transportation cost to the zone and the level of competition and demand within the zone. This system is also used in setting prices on long distance phone calls. As another example of multiple-zone pricing, Sable Gas is being sold to Maritime and northeast natural gas customers at prices based on their proximity to the gas pipeline. The closer the customer is to the gas, the lower the price.

With *FOB with freight-allowed pricing,* also called *freight absorption pricing,* the price is quoted by the seller as "FOB plant—freight allowed." The buyer is allowed to deduct freight expenses from the list price of the goods, so the seller agrees to pay, or "absorbs," the transportation costs.

Basing-point pricing involves selecting one or more geographical locations (basing point) from which the list price for products plus freight expenses are charged to the buyer. For example, a company might designate Montreal as the basing point and charge all buyers a list price of $100 plus freight from Montreal to their location. Basing-point pricing methods have been used in the steel, cement, and lumber industries where freight expenses are a significant part of the total cost to the buyer and products are largely undifferentiated.

ETHICS

ETHICS AND SOCIAL RESPONSIBILITY ALERT

Flexible Pricing or Price Discrimination

Many buyers dread the prospect of buying a new automobile. Why? They dread negotiating the price. Price bargaining, however, has a more serious side and demonstrates the potential pitfalls of flexible pricing: possible price discrimination based on ethnicity or gender. Research shows that some car dealers offer females higher prices on vehicles than males. Similarly, non-white buyers, male or female, may also be offered higher prices on cars than white buyers. This occurs despite the fact that all buyers used identical bargaining strategies when negotiating the price of a new car. Even if the practice cannot be proved as systematic price discrimination, it raises an ethical question: should car dealers be allowed to charge higher prices to some buyers for the identical vehicle? Some car dealers argue that the price is largely determined based on how well the consumer negotiates. They add, some buyers are simply better at haggling than others. However, there have been some indications that some dealers have taken advantage of newly arrived immigrants who do not understand the car buying process, particularly the concept of price negotiation. Similarly, some females argue that after purchasing a new car, they discovered that they paid more than a male counterpart who had purchased an identical vehicle under similar terms and conditions. Saturn Corporation has eliminated new car price negotiating and offers a no haggle, one-price policy. According to a Saturn executive, "People don't want to dicker on price, period, whether it's a house, suit of clothes, or a car. When you have to dicker, you feel uncomfortable because you always feel you paid too much." In certain instances, some consumers do. Many times, however, it tends to be female buyers and non-white purchasers. What is your feeling on this situation?

Legal and Regulatory Aspects of Pricing

Arriving at a final price is clearly a complex process. The task is further complicated by legal and regulatory restrictions. Chapter 3 described the regulatory environment of companies. Here we elaborate on the specific laws and regulations affecting pricing decisions. Five pricing practices have received the most scrutiny: (1) price fixing, (2) price discrimination, (3) deceptive pricing, (4) predatory pricing, and (5) delivered pricing.

Price Fixing A conspiracy among firms to set prices for a product is termed **price fixing.** Price fixing is illegal per se under the Competition Act (*per se* means in and of itself). When two or more competitors explicitly or implicitly set prices, this practice is called *horizontal price fixing.*

Vertical price fixing involves controlling agreements between independent buyers and sellers (a manufacturer and a retailer) whereby sellers are required not to sell products below a minimum retail price. This practice, called resale price maintenance, is also illegal under the provisions of the Competition Act.

It is important to recognize that a manufacturer's "suggested retail price" is not illegal per se. The issue of legality only arises when manufacturers enforce such a practice by coercion. Furthermore, there appears to be a movement toward a "rule of reason" in pricing cases. This rule holds that circumstances surrounding a practice must be considered before making a judgment about its legality. The "rule of reason" perspective is the direct opposite of the per se rule, which holds that a practice is illegal in and of itself.

Price Discrimination The Competition Act prohibits **price discrimination**—the practice of charging different prices to different buyers for goods of like grade and quality. The Competition Act also covers promotional allowances. To legally offer promotional allowances to buyers, sellers must do so on a proportionally equal basis to all buyers distributing the seller's products. In general, this rule of reason is applied frequently in price discrimination cases and is often applied to cases involving flexible pricing policies of firms. It is not easy to prove price discrimination has actually taken place especially when firms practise flexible-price policies.

Under the Competition Act, the legislation requres that there be a "practice" of price discrimination, implying more than one instance, or even two or three instances. However, some suggest that the use of flexible pricing may create the potentiality for some firms to engage in price discrimination. Even if the practice cannot be proved legally as price discrimination, there may be some ethical issues involved (see the Ethics and Social Responsibility Alert).[28]

www.colour-your-world.com

Deceptive Pricing Price deals that mislead consumers fall into the category of deceptive pricing. Deceptive pricing is outlawed by the Competition Act. The five most common deceptive pricing practices are described in Figure 15–8. Over the past few years, companies from Newfoundland to British Columbia have been found guilty and fined for deceptive pricing practices including Suzy Shier Ltd., Kmart, and Colour Your World. However, as you examine Figure 15–8, you should remember that it is often difficult for the government to police and enforce all these laws. So it is essential to rely on ethical standards of those making and publicizing pricing decisions.

Predatory Pricing Two types of preditory pricing are defined within the Competition Act. The first is called *geographic predatory pricing.* Sellers are prohibited from engaging in a policy of selling products or services in one region in Canada at a price

FIGURE 15–8
Five most common deceptive pricing practices

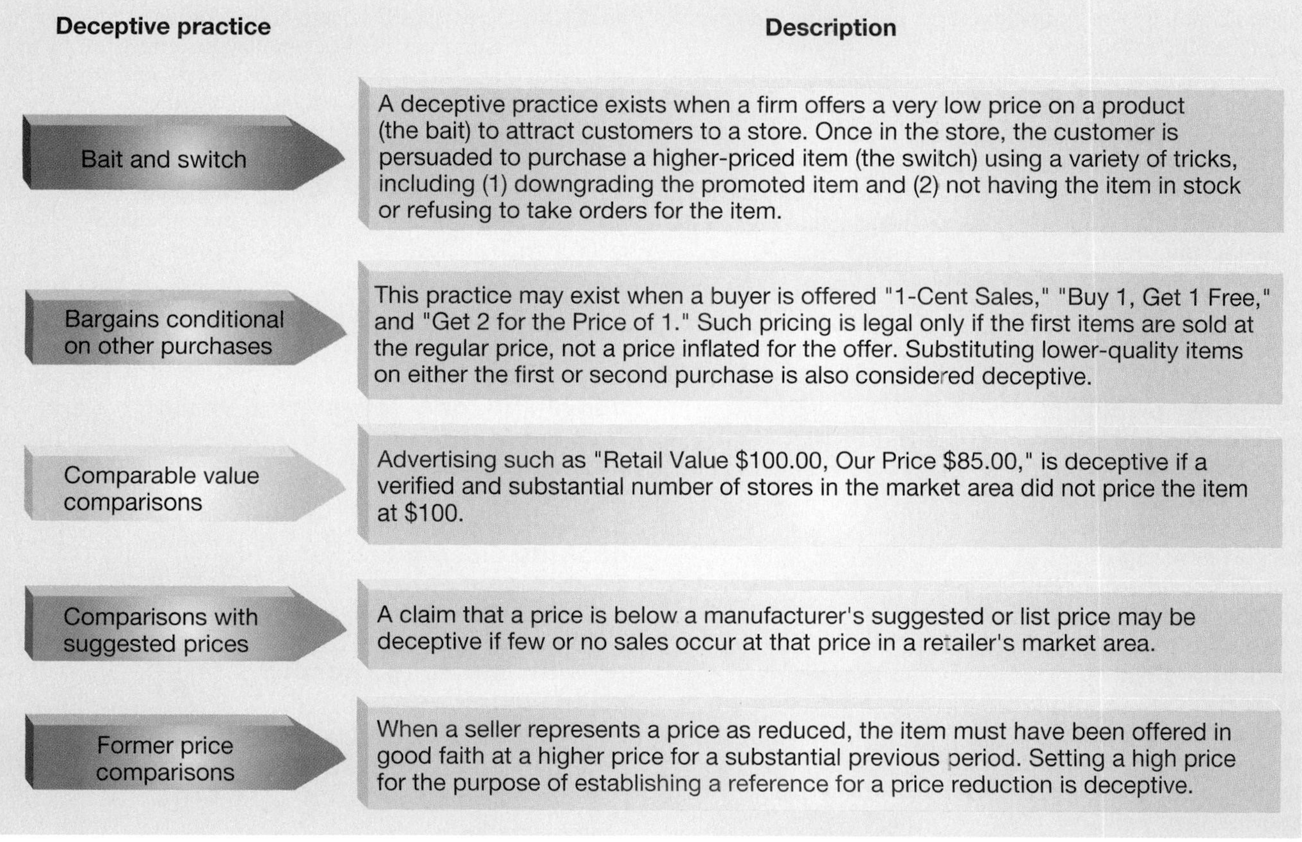

Deceptive practice	Description
Bait and switch	A deceptive practice exists when a firm offers a very low price on a product (the bait) to attract customers to a store. Once in the store, the customer is persuaded to purchase a higher-priced item (the switch) using a variety of tricks, including (1) downgrading the promoted item and (2) not having the item in stock or refusing to take orders for the item.
Bargains conditional on other purchases	This practice may exist when a buyer is offered "1-Cent Sales," "Buy 1, Get 1 Free," and "Get 2 for the Price of 1." Such pricing is legal only if the first items are sold at the regular price, not a price inflated for the offer. Substituting lower-quality items on either the first or second purchase is also considered deceptive.
Comparable value comparisons	Advertising such as "Retail Value $100.00, Our Price $85.00," is deceptive if a verified and substantial number of stores in the market area did not price the item at $100.
Comparisons with suggested prices	A claim that a price is below a manufacturer's suggested or list price may be deceptive if few or no sales occur at that price in a retailer's market area.
Former price comparisons	When a seller represents a price as reduced, the item must have been offered in good faith at a higher price for a substantial previous period. Setting a high price for the purpose of establishing a reference for a price reduction is deceptive.

lower than another region with the intent or effect of lessening competition or of eliminating a competitior.

The second type of predatory pricing offence is committed when a business engages in a policy of selling products or services at "unreasonably low" prices in an attempt to substantially lessen competition. In many cases, the very low prices are designed to drive competitiors out of business. Once competitors have been driven out, the firm raises its prices.

Delivered Pricing Delivered pricing is the practice of refusing a customer delivery of an article on the same trade terms as other customers in the same location. It is a noncriminal offence, but the Competition Tribunal can prohibit suppliers from engaging in such a practice.

CONCEPT CHECK

1. Why would a seller choose a flexible-price policy over a one-price policy?
2. If a firm wished to encourage repeat purchases by a buyer throughout a year, would a cumulative or noncumulative quantity discount be a better strategy?
3. Which pricing practices are covered by the Competition Act?

SUMMARY

1 Four general approaches of finding an approximate price level for a product or service are demand-oriented, cost-oriented, profit-oriented, and competition-oriented pricing.

2 Demand-oriented pricing approaches stress consumer demand and revenue implications of pricing and include eight types: skimming, penetration, prestige, price lining, odd-even, target, bundle, and yield management.

3 Cost-oriented pricing approaches emphasize the cost aspects of pricing and include three types: standard markup, cost-plus, and experience curve pricing.

4 Profit-oriented pricing approaches focus on a balance between revenues and costs to set a price and include three types: target profit, target return-on-sales, and target return-on-investment pricing.

5 Competition-oriented pricing approaches stress what competitors or the marketplace are doing and include three types: customary; above-, at-, or below-market; and loss-leader pricing.

6 Given an approximate price level for a product, a manager must set a list or quoted price by considering factors such as one-price versus a flexible-price policy; the effects of the proposed price on the company, customer, and competitors; and balancing incremental costs and revenues.

7 List or quoted price is often modified through discounts, allowances, and geographical adjustments.

8 Legal and regulatory issues in pricing focus on price fixing, price discrimination, deceptive pricing, predatory pricing, and delivered pricing.

KEY TERMS AND CONCEPTS

INTERNET EXERCISE

As you know, the Competition Bureau is responsible for administrating the Competition Act in Canada. As you read in this chapter, competition can be lessened and/or consumers can be harmed by unfair pricing practices. Visit the Competition Bureau's home page at http://www.strategis.ic.gc.ca/ssg/ct01250e.html

Go to the news and announcements section on the site.

1 What are the types of pricing violations involving Canadian and international companies reported on the site?

2 What types of penalties were imposed?

3 What is your opinion regarding these pricing violations?

APPLYING MARKETING CONCEPTS AND PERSPECTIVES

1 Under what conditions would a camera manufacturer adopt a skimming price approach for a new product? A penetration approach?

2 What are some similarities and differences between skimming pricing, prestige pricing, and above-market pricing?

3 A producer of microwave ovens has adopted an experience curve pricing approach for its new model. The firm believes it can reduce the cost of producing the model by 20 percent each time volume doubles. The cost to produce the first unit was $1000. What would be the approximate cost of the 4096th unit?

4 The Hesper Corporation is a leading manufacturer of high-quality upholstered sofas. Current plans call for an increase of $600 000 in the advertising budget. If the firm sells its sofas for an average price of $850 and the unit variable costs are $550, then what dollar sales increase will be necessary to cover the additional advertising?

5 Suppose executives estimate that the unit variable cost for their VCR is $100, the fixed cost related to the product is $10 million annually, and the target volume for next year is 100 000 recorders. What sales price will be necessary to achieve a target profit of $1 million?

6 A manufacturer of motor oil has a trade discount policy whereby the manufacturer's suggested retail price is $30 per case with the terms of 40/20/10. The manufacturer sells its products through jobbers, who sell to wholesalers, who sell to gasoline stations. What will the manufacturer's sale price be?

7 What are the effective annual interest rates for the following cash discount terms? (*a*) 1/10 net 30, (*b*) 2/10 net 30, and (*c*) 2/10 net 60.

8 Suppose a manufacturer of exercise equipment sets a suggested price to the consumer of $395 for a particular piece of equipment to be competitive with similar equipment. The manufacturer sells its equipment to a sporting goods wholesaler who receives a 25 percent markup and a retailer who receives a 50 percent markup. What demand-oriented pricing approach is being used, and at what price will the manufacturer sell the equipment to the wholesaler?

CASE 15–1 MY OWN MEALS

"The kids generally like the fast-food meals. I tend to not like them because I try to stay away from the high fat," says Angela Harmon, mother of three young girls. "I have to have something that is nutritious and fast," remarks Mary Champlain, mother of two. Comments like these and her own experiences led Mary Anne Jackson to conclude that there was an opportunity to provide parents with better children's food options. As Mary explains, "being a busy working mother, I knew that there was a need for this type of product in the marketplace."

THE IDEA

Mary's insight about the marketplace was supported by several socioeconomic trends. For example:

- More than 65 percent of working mothers now have school-age children, the highest percentage ever.
- About 90 percent of children under the age of 7 eat at McDonald's at least 4 times per month.
- More than 90 percent of homes in Canada now have microwave ovens.
- Women already represent almost half of the total workforce. By the year 2000, two out of three new entrants into the labour force will be women.

With this evidence, some food industry experience and business education, and a lot of entrepreneurial spirit, Mary Anne Jackson set out to satisfy the need for nutritious, convenient children's meals. Her idea: develop a line of healthy, microwaveable meals for children 2 to 10 years old.

THE COMPANY

Ms. Jackson started by founding a company, My Own Meals, Inc., with a line of five healthy microwaveable meals. The meals were offered in shelf-stable "retort" packages, which are like flexible cans. This created a whole new category of prepared foods, and raised more than a few eyebrows among the major food companies. Mary observed that "The need for children's meals was not being addressed in the past, and I think this was because most major food companies are run by men." Eventually, however, the big companies challenged My Own Meals with their own entries into the new category. The competition reinforced Mary's efforts. "Having competitors come into the marketplace justified the existence of the category," she explains.

The product line was developed using a lot of marketing research—hundreds of busy mothers provided input about product quality, usage rates, and price. The results indicated that customers would serve their children high-quality meals between three and four times each month and that they would be willing to pay approximately $2.30 for each meal.

THE ISSUE: SETTING RETAIL PRICES

"We were trying to decide if we were priced appropriately and competitively for the marketplace, and we decided that we would look at the price elasticity for our product line," observes Mary Anne Jackson. "We found that the closer we came to $3.00 a unit, the lower the volume was, and overall we were losing revenues and profits," said Jackson.

To arrive at final retail prices for her company's products Mary Anne Jackson considered factors related to demand, cost, profit, and competition. For example, because lower-quality brands had entered the market, My Own Meals needed a retail price that reflected the superior quality of its products. "We're premium priced because we're a higher quality product than any of our competitors. If we weren't, our quality image would be lowered to the image that they have," explains Jackson. At some stores, however, prices approached $3.00 and consumer demand decreased.

To estimate the prices consumers would see on their shelves, Jackson needed to estimate the cost of producing the meals and add My Own Meal's markup. Then she determined the markup that each of the distribution channels—retail grocery stores, mass merchants, day care centres, and military commissaries—would add to reach the retail price. The grocery stores were very concerned about profitability and used a concept called direct product profitability (DPP) to determine prices and shelf space. "They want to know how much money they make on each square foot of the shelf dedicated to each product line. I had to do a DPP analysis to show them why they were making more on our products for our space than the competition," remarks Mary Anne Jackson. Finally, Mary considered competitors' prices, which were:

- Looney Toons (Tyson) $2.49
- Kid Cuisine (Banquet) $1.89
- Kid's Kitchen (Hormel) $1.19

Mary knew that it was important to consider all of these factors in her pricing decisions. The price would influence the interest of consumers and retailers, the reactions of competitors, and ultimately the success of My Own Meals!

Questions

1 In what ways are the demand factors of (*a*) consumer tastes, (*b*) price and availability of substitute products, and (*c*) consumer income important in influencing consumer demand for My Own Meals products?

2 How can (*a*) demand-oriented, (*b*) cost-based, (*c*) profit-oriented, and (*d*) competition-based approaches be used to help My Own Meals arrive at an approximate price level?

3 Why might the retail price of My Own Meal's products be different in grocery stores, mass merchants, day care centres, and cafeterias?

APPENDIX B

FINANCIAL ASPECTS OF MARKETING

B

Basic concepts from accounting and finance provide valuable tools for marketing executives. This appendix describes an actual company's use of accounting and financial concepts and illustrates how they assist the owner in making marketing decisions.

THE CAPLOW COMPANY

An accomplished artist and calligrapher, Jane Westerlund, decided to apply some of her experience to the picture framing business. She bought an existing retail frame store, The Caplow Company, from a friend who owned the business and wanted to retire. She avoided the do-it-yourself end of the framing business and chose three kinds of business activities: (1) cutting the frame, mats, and glass for customers who brought in their own pictures or prints to be framed; (2) selling prints and posters that she had purchased from wholesalers; and (3) restoring high-quality frames and paintings.

To understand how accounting, finance, and marketing relate to each other, let's analyze (1) the operating statement for her frame shop, (2) some general ratios of interest that are derived from the operating statement, and (3) some ratios that pertain specifically to her pricing decisions.

The Operating Statement

The operating statement (also called an *income statement* or *profit-and-loss statement*) summarizes the profitability of a business firm for a specific time period, usually a month, quarter, or year. The title of the operating statement for The Caplow Company shows it is for a one-year period (Figure B–1). The purpose of an operating statement is to show the profit of the firm and the revenues and expenses that led to that profit. This information tells the owner or manager what has happened in the past and suggests actions to improve future profitability.

The left side of Figure B–1 shows that there are three key elements to all operating statements: (1) sales of the firm's goods and services, (2) costs incurred in making and selling the goods and services, and (3) profit or loss, which is the difference between sales and costs.

Sales Elements The sales element of Figure B–1 has four terms that need explanation:

- *Gross sales* are the total amount billed to customers. Dissatisfied customers or errors may reduce the gross sales through returns or allowances.
- *Returns* occur when a customer gives the item purchased back to the seller, who either refunds the purchase price or allows the customer a credit on subsequent purchases. In any event, the seller now owns the item again.
- *Allowances* are given when a customer is dissatisfied with the item purchased and the seller reduces the original purchase price. Unlike returns, in the case of allowances the buyer owns the item.
- *Net sales* are simply gross sales minus returns and allowances.

The operating statement for The Caplow Company shows that

Gross sales	$80 500
Less: Returns and allowances	500
Net sales	$80 000

The low level of returns and allowances shows the shop generally has done a good job in satisfying customers, which is essential in building the repeat business necessary for success.

Cost Elements The *cost of goods sold* is the total cost of the products sold during the period. This item varies according to the kind of business. A retail store purchases finished goods and resells them to customers without reworking them in any way. In contrast, a manufacturing firm combines raw and semifinished materials and parts, uses labour and overhead to rework these into finished goods, and then sells them to customers. All these activities are reflected in the cost of goods sold item on a manufacturer's operating statement. Note that the frame shop has some features of a pure retailer (prints and posters it buys that are resold without alteration) and a pure manufacturer (assembling the raw materials of moulding, matting, and glass to form a completed frame).

FIGURE B–1
Examples of an operating statement

THE CAPLOW COMPANY
Operating Statement
For the Year Ending December 31, 1999

Sales	Gross sales			$80 500
	Less: Returns and allowances			500
	Net sales			$80 000
Costs	Cost of goods sold:			
	Beginning inventory at cost		$ 6 000	
	Purchases at billed cost	$21 000		
	Less: Purchase discounts	300		
	Purchases at net cost	20 700		
	Plus freight-in	100		
	Net cost of delivered purchases		20 800	
	Direct labour (framing)		14 200	
	Cost of goods available for sale		41 000	
	Less: Ending inventory at cost		5 000	
	Cost of goods sold			36 000
	Gross margin (gross profit)			$44 000
	Expenses:			
	Selling expenses:			
	Sales salaries	2 000		
	Advertising expense	3 000		
	Total selling expense		5 000	
	Administrative expenses:			
	Owner's salary	18 000		
	Bookkeeper's salary	1 200		
	Office supplies	300		
	Total administrative expense		19 500	
	General expenses:			
	Depreciation expense	1 000		
	Interest expense	500		
	Rent expense	2 100		
	Utility expenses (heat, electricity)	3 000		
	Repairs and maintenance	2 300		
	Insurance	2 000		
	Canada Pension Plan	2 200		
	Total general expense		13 100	
	Total expenses			37 600
Profit or loss	Profit before taxes			$ 6 400

Some terms that relate to cost of goods sold need clarification:

- *Inventory* is the physical material that is purchased from suppliers, may or may not be reworked, and is available for sale to customers. In the frame shop inventory includes moulding, matting, glass, prints, and posters.
- *Purchase discounts* are reductions in the original billed price for reasons such as prompt payment of the bill or the quantity bought.
- *Direct labour* is the cost of the labour used in producing the finished product. For the frame shop this is the cost of producing the completed frames from the moulding, matting, and glass.
- *Gross margin (gross profit)* is the money remaining to manage the business, sell the products or services, and give some profit. Gross margin is net sales minus cost of goods sold.

The two right-hand columns in Figure B–1 between "Net sales" and "Gross margin" calculate the cost of goods sold:

Net sales		$80 000
Cost of goods sold		
Beginning inventory at cost	$ 6 000	
Net cost of delivered purchases	20 800	
Direct labour (framing)	14 200	
Cost of goods available for sale	41 000	
Less: ending inventory at cost	5 000	
Cost of goods sold		36 000
Gross margin (gross profit)		$44 000

This section considers the beginning and ending inventories, the net cost of purchases delivered during the year, and the cost of the direct labour going into making the frames. Subtracting the $36,000 cost of goods sold from the $80 000 net sales gives the $44,000 gross margin.

Three major categories of expenses are shown in Figure B–1 below the gross margin:

- *Selling expenses* are the costs of selling the product or service produced by the firm. For The Caplow Company there are two such selling expenses: sales salaries of part-time employees waiting on customers and the advertising expense of simple newspaper ads and direct-mail ads sent to customers.
- *Administrative expenses* are the costs of managing the business, and, for The Caplow Company, include three expenses: the owner's salary, a part-time bookkeeper's salary, and office supplies expense.
- *General expenses* are miscellaneous costs not covered elsewhere; for the frame shop these include seven items: depreciation expense (on her equipment), interest expense, rent expense, utility expenses, repairs and maintenance expense, insurance expense, and employment insurance and Canada Pension plan.

As shown in Figure B–1, selling, administrative, and general expenses total $37 600 for The Caplow Company.

Profit Element What the company has earned, the *profit before taxes,* is found by subtracting cost of goods sold and expenses from net sales. For The Caplow Company, Figure B–1 shows that profit before taxes is $6400.

General Operating Ratios to Analyze Operations

Looking only at the elements of Caplow's operating statement that extend to the right column highlights the firm's performance on some important dimensions. Using operating ratios such as *expense-to-sales ratios* for expressing basic expense or profit elements as a percentage of net sales gives further insights:

ELEMENT IN OPERATING STATEMENT	DOLLAR VALUE	PERCENTAGE OF NET SALES
Gross sales	$80 500	
Less: Returns and allowances	500	
Net sales	80 000	100%
Less: Cost of goods sold	36 000	45
Gross margin	44 000	55
Less: Total expenses	37 600	47
Profit (or loss) before taxes	$ 6 400	8%

Westerlund can use this information to compare her firm's performance from one time period to the next. To do so, it is especially important that she keep the same definitions for each element of her operating statement, also a significant factor in using the electronic spreadsheets discussed in Chapter 15. Performance comparisons between periods are more difficult if she changes definitions for the accounting elements in the operating statement.

She can use either the dollar values or the operating ratios (the value of the element of the operating statement divided by net sales) to analyze the firm's performance. However, the operating ratios are more valuable than the dollar values for two reasons: (1) the simplicity of working with percentages rather than dollars and (2) the availability of operating ratios of typical firms in the same industry, which are published by Dun & Bradstreet and trade associations. Thus, Westerlund can compare her firm's performance not only with that of *other* frame shops but also with that of *small* frame shops that have annual net sales, for example, of under $100 000. In this way she can identify where her operations are better or worse than other similar firms. For example, if trade association data showed a typical frame shop of her size had a ratio of cost of goods sold to net sales of 37 percent, compared with her 45 percent, she might consider steps to reduce this cost through purchase discounts, reducing inbound freight charges, finding lower-cost suppliers, and so on.

Ratios to Use in Setting and Evaluating Price

Using The Caplow Company as an example, we can study four ratios that relate closely to setting a price: (1) markup, (2) markdown, (3) stockturns, and (4) return on investment. These terms are defined in Figure B–2 and explained below.

Markup Both markup and gross margin refer to the amount added to the cost of goods sold to arrive at the selling price, and they may be expressed either in dollar or percentage terms. However, the term *markup* is more commonly used in setting retail prices. Suppose the average price Westerlund charges for a framed picture is $80. Then in terms of the first two definitions in Figure B–2 and the earlier information from the operating statement,

FIGURE B–2
How to calculate selling price, markup, markdown, stockturn, and return on investment

NAME OF FINANCIAL ELEMENT OR RATIO	WHAT IT MEASURES	EQUATION
Selling price ($)	Price customer sees	Cost of goods sold (COGS) + Markup
Markup ($)	Dollars added to COGS to arrive at selling price	Selling price – COGS
Markup on selling price (%)	Relates markup to selling price	$\frac{\text{Markup}}{\text{Selling price}} \times 100 = \frac{\text{Selling price} - \text{COGS}}{\text{Selling price}} \times 100$
Markup on cost (%)	Relates markup to cost	$\frac{\text{Markup}}{\text{COGS}} \times 100 = \frac{\text{Selling price} - \text{COGS}}{\text{COGS}} \times 100$
Markdown (%)	Ability of firm to sell its products at initial selling price	$\frac{\text{Markdowns}}{\text{Net sales}} \times 100$
Stockturn rate	Ability of firm to move its inventory quickly	$\frac{\text{COGS}}{\text{Average inventory at cost}}$ or $\frac{\text{Net sales}}{\text{Average inventory at selling price}}$
Return on investment (%)	Profit performance of firm compared with money invested in it	$\frac{\text{Net profit after taxes}}{\text{Investment}} \times 100$

ELEMENT OF PRICE	DOLLAR VALUE
Cost of goods sold	$36
Markup (or gross margin)	44
Selling price	$80

The third definition in Figure B–2 gives the percentage markup on selling price:

$$\text{Markup on selling price (\%)} = \frac{\text{Markup}}{\text{Selling price}} \times 100$$

$$= \frac{44}{80} \times 100 = 55\%$$

And the percentage markup on cost is obtained as follows:

$$\text{Markup on cost (\%)} = \frac{\text{Markup}}{\text{Cost of goods sold}} \times 100$$

$$= \frac{44}{36} \times 100 = 122.2\%$$

Inexperienced retail clerks sometimes fail to distinguish between the two definitions of markup, which (as the preceding calculations show) can represent a tremendous difference, so it is essential to know whether the base is cost or selling price. Marketers generally use selling price as the base for talking about "markups" unless they specifically state that they are using cost as a base.

Retailers and wholesalers that rely heavily on markup pricing (discussed in Chapter 15) often use standardized tables that convert markup on selling price to markup on cost, and vice versa. The two equations below show how to convert one to the other:

$$\text{Markup on selling price (\%)} = \frac{\text{Markup on cost (\%)}}{100\% + \text{Markup on cost (\%)}} \times 100$$

$$\text{Markup on cost (\%)} = \frac{\text{Markup on selling price (\%)}}{100\% - \text{Markup on selling price (\%)}}$$

Using the data from The Caplow Company gives

$$\text{Markup on selling price (\%)} = \frac{\text{Markup on cost (\%)}}{100\% + \text{Markup on cost (\%)}} \times 100$$

$$= \frac{122.2}{100 + 122.2} \times 100 = 55\%$$

$$\text{Markup on cost (\%)} = \frac{\text{Markup on selling price (\%)}}{100\% - \text{Markup on selling price (\%)}} \times 100$$

$$= \frac{55}{100 - 55} \times 100 = 122.2\%$$

The use of an incorrect markup base is shown in Westerlund's business. A markup of 122.2 percent on her cost of goods sold for a typical frame she sells gives 122.2% × $36 = $44 of markup. Added to the $36 cost of goods sold, this gives her selling price of $80 for the framed picture. However, a new clerk working for her who erroneously priced the framed picture at 55 percent of cost of goods sold set the final price at $55.80 ($36 of cost of goods sold plus 55% × $36 = $19.80). The error, if repeated, can be disastrous: frames would be accidentally sold at $55.80, or $24.20 below the intended selling price of $80.

Markdown A markdown is a reduction in a retail price that is necessary if the item will not sell at the full selling price to which it has been marked up. The item might not sell for a variety of reasons: the selling price was set too high or the item is out of style or has become soiled or damaged. The seller "takes a markdown" by lowering the price to sell it, thereby converting it to cash to buy future inventory that will sell faster.

The markdown percentage cannot be calculated directly from the operating statement. As shown in the fifth item of Figure B–2, the numerator of the markdown percentage is the total dollar markdowns. Markdowns are reductions in the prices of goods that are purchased by customers. The denominator is net sales.

Suppose The Caplow Company had a total of $700 in markdowns on the prints and posters that are stocked and available for sale. Since the frames are custom made for individual customers, there is little reason for a markdown there. Caplow's markdown percent is then

$$\begin{aligned}\text{Markdown}(\%) &= \frac{\text{Markdowns}}{\text{Net sales}} \times 100 \\ &= \frac{\$700}{\$80\,000} \times 100 \\ &= 0.875\%\end{aligned}$$

Other kinds of retailers often have markdown ratios several times this amount. For example, women's dress stores have markdowns of about 25 percent, and menswear stores have markdowns of about 2 percent.

Stockturn Rate A business firm is anxious to have its inventory move quickly, or "turn over." Stockturn rate, or simply stockturns, measures this inventory movement. For a retailer a slow stockturn rate may show it is buying merchandise customers don't want, so this is a critical measure of performance. When a firm sells only a single product, one convenient way to measure stockturn rate is simply to divide its cost of goods sold by average inventory at cost. The sixth item in Figure B–2 shows how to calculate stockturn rate using information in the following operating statement:

$$\text{Stockturn rate} = \frac{\text{Cost of goods sold}}{\text{Average inventory at cost}}$$

The dollar amount of average inventory at cost is calculated by adding the beginning and ending inventories for the year and dividing by 2 to get the average. From Caplow's operating statement, we have

$$\begin{aligned}\text{Stockturn rate} &= \frac{\text{Cost of goods sold}}{\text{Average inventory at cost}} \\ &= \frac{\text{Cost of goods sold}}{\dfrac{\text{Beginning inventory} + \text{Ending inventory}}{2}} \\ &= \frac{\$36\,000}{\dfrac{\$6000 + \$5000}{2}} \\ &= \frac{\$36\,000}{\$5500} \\ &= 6.5 \text{ stockturns per year}\end{aligned}$$

A customer discusses choices of framing and matting for her print with Jane Westerlund.

What is considered a "good stockturn" varies by the kind of industry. For example, supermarkets have limited shelf space for thousands of new products from manufacturers each year, so they watch stockturn carefully by product line. The stockturn rate in supermarkets for breakfast foods is about 17 times per year, for pet food about 22 times, and for paper products about 25 times per year.

Return on Investment A better measure of the performance of a firm than the amount of profit it makes in a year is its ROI, which is the ratio of net income to the investment used to earn that net income. To calculate ROI, it is necessary to subtract income taxes from profit before taxes to obtain net income, then divide this figure by the investment that can be found on a firm's balance sheet (another accounting statement that shows the firm's assets, liabilities, and net worth). While financial and accounting experts have many definitions for "investment," an often-used definition is "total assets."

For our purposes, let's assume that Westerlund has total assets (investment) of $20 000 in The Caplow Company, which covers inventory, store fixtures, and framing equipment. If she pays $1000 in income taxes, her store's net income is $5400, so her ROI is given by the seventh item in Figure B–2:

$$\begin{aligned}\text{Return on investment} &= \text{Net income/investment} \times 100 \\ &= \$5400/\$20\,000 \times 100 \\ &= 27\%\end{aligned}$$

If Westerlund wants to improve her ROI next year, the strategies she might take are found in this alternative equation for ROI:

ROI = Net sales/investment × Net income/net sales

= Investment turnover × Profit margin

This equation suggests that The Caplow Company's ROI can be improved by raising turnover or increasing profit margin. Increasing stockturns will accomplish the former, whereas lowering cost of goods sold to net sales will cause the latter.

Gateway
COUNTRY

A PC Built For You
Monthly Payment Plan
Trade It In After 2 Years

CHAPTER SIXTEEN

MARKETING CHANNELS AND WHOLESALING

16

AFTER READING THIS CHAPTER YOU SHOULD BE ABLE TO:

- Explain what is meant by a marketing channel of distribution and why intermediaries are needed.
- Recognize differences between marketing channels for consumer and industrial products and services in domestic and global markets.
- Describe the types and functions of firms that perform wholesaling activities.
- Distinguish among traditional marketing channels, electronic marketing channels, and different types of vertical marketing systems.
- Describe factors considered by marketing executives when selecting and managing a marketing channel, including channel conflict and legal restrictions.

GATEWAY: ADDING HIGH TOUCH TO HIGH-TECH MARKETING CHANNELS

Just when conventional wisdom says that virtual stores will replace the brick-and-mortar kind, the world's second-largest direct marketer of personal computers is investing in real, not electronic storefronts! Gateway (www.gateway.com), which began selling personal computers directly to consumers in 1985, now operates 58 Gateway Country showrooms. But why would Gateway want to open by these storefronts? Because Gateway has found that many personal computer buyers still prefer browsing in a store and talking with a salesperson.

The showrooms blend high tech with high touch. At Gateway Country showrooms, customers can see, touch, test, and custom-configure a computer system to meet their needs with the help of highly trained representatives. Customers are encouraged to surf the Internet, watch movie clips using a DVD drive, or visit with Gateway personnel or other customers in a comfortable setting. The showrooms' decor includes tractor seats, mock silos, and grain bins.

However, Gateway does not stock personal computers at its showrooms. Customers who want to buy a computer must still order one from Gateway, which will custom-build the system to the customer's specifications at its factories and ship it directly to a customer's home or business. In this way, Gateway retains the economic benefits of direct selling. The rapid expansion of Gateway Country showrooms attests to the success of this venture. In the final analysis, "The stores will be measured largely by whether they help Gateway build relationships with its customers," says Joseph J. Burke, the company's senior vice president for global business development.[1]

The novel approach to marketing channels evidenced by Gateway Country showrooms has already paid a handsome sales dividend to the company. Computer industry analysts estimate that 80 percent of Gateway's sales growth can be attributed to its showrooms.

This chapter focuses on marketing channels of distribution and why they are an important component in the marketing mix. It then shows how such channels benefit consumers and the sequence of firms that make up a marketing channel. Finally, it describes factors that influence the choice and management of marketing channels, including channel conflict and legal restrictions.

NATURE AND IMPORTANCE OF MARKETING CHANNELS

Reaching prospective buyers, either directly or indirectly, is a prerequisite for successful marketing. At the same time, buyers benefit from distribution systems used by firms.

Defining Marketing Channels of Distribution

You see the results of distribution every day. You may have purchased Lay's Potato Chips at the 7-Eleven store, a book through amazon.com, and Levi's jeans at Sears. Each of these items was brought to you by a marketing channel of distribution, or simply a **marketing channel,** which consists of individuals and firms involved in the process of making a product or service available for use or consumption by consumers or industrial users.

Marketing channels can be compared with a pipeline through which water flows from a source to terminus. Marketing channels make possible the flow of goods from a producer, through intermediaries, to a buyer. Intermediaries go by various names (Figure 16–1) and perform various functions.[2] Some intermediaries actually purchase items from the seller, store them, and resell them to buyers. For example, Sunshine Biscuits produces cookies and sells them to food wholesalers. The wholesalers then sell the cookies to supermarkets and grocery stores, which, in turn, sell them to consumers. Other intermediaries such as brokers and agents represent sellers but do not actually take title to products—their role is to bring a seller and buyer together. Century 21 real estate agents are examples of this type of intermediary. The importance of intermediaries is made even clearer when we consider the functions they perform and the value they create for buyers.

www.century21.com

FIGURE 16–1
Terms used for marketing intermediaries

TERM	DESCRIPTION
Middleman	Any intermediary between manufacturer and end-user markets
Agent or broker	Any intermediary with legal authority to act on behalf of the manufacturer
Wholesaler	An intermediary who sells to other intermediaries, usually to retailers; usually applies to consumer markets
Retailer	An intermediary who sells to consumers
Distributor	An imprecise term, usually used to describe intermediaries who perform a variety of distribution functions, including selling, maintaining inventories, extending credit, and so on; a more common term in industrial markets but may also be used to refer to wholesalers
Dealer	An even more imprecise term that can mean the same as distributor, retailer, wholesaler, and so forth

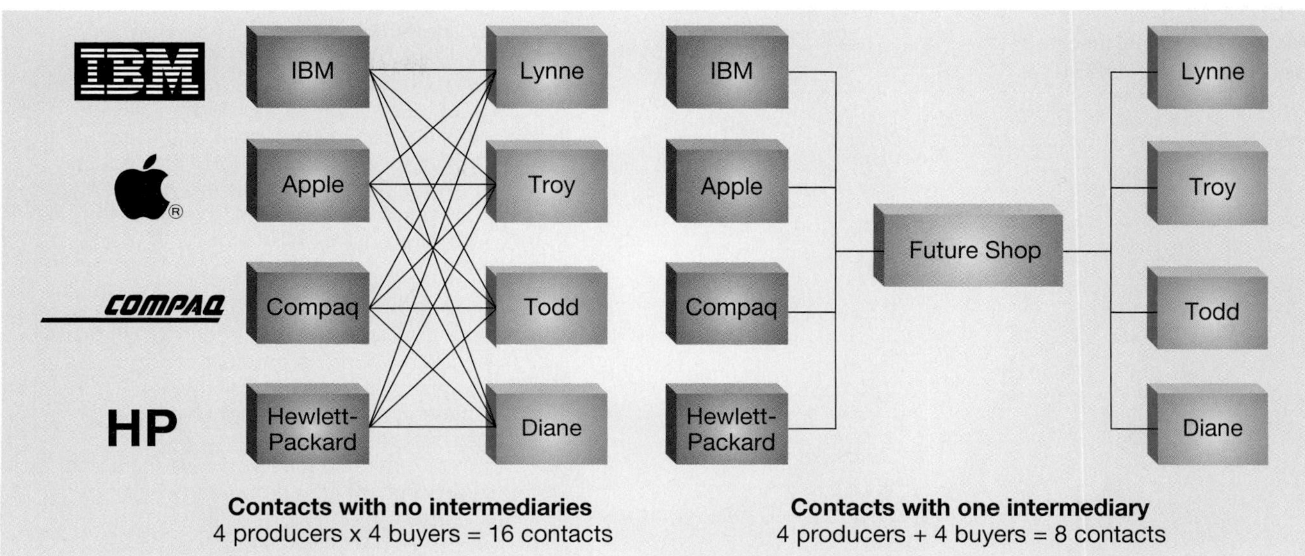

FIGURE 16–2
How intermediaries minimize transactions

Value Created by Intermediaries

Few consumers appreciate the value created by intermediaries; however, producers recognize that intermediaries make selling goods and services more efficient because they minimize the number of sales contacts necessary to reach a target market. Figure 16–2 shows a simple example of how this comes about in the personal computer industry. Without a retail intermediary (such as Future Shop), IBM, Apple, Compaq, and Hewlett-Packard would each have to make four contacts to reach the four buyers shown who are in the target market. However, each producer has to make only one contact when Future Shop acts as an intermediary. Equally important from a macromarketing perspective, the total number of industry transactions is reduced from 16 to 8, which reduces producer cost and hence benefits the consumer. This simple example also illustrates why computer manufacturers constantly compete with each other to gain access to computer retailers such as Future Shop, Circuit City and Business Depot.

Functions Performed by Intermediaries Intermediaries make possible the flow of products from producers to buyers by performing three basic functions (Figure 16–3).[3] Most prominently, intermediaries perform a transactional function that involves buying, selling, and risk taking because they stock merchandise in anticipation of sales. Intermediaries perform a logistical function evident in the gathering, storing, and dispersing of products (see Chapter 17 on supply chain and logistics management). Finally, intermediaries perform facilitating functions, which assist producers in making goods and services more attractive to buyers.

All three groups of functions must be performed in a marketing channel, even though each channel member may not participate in all three. Channel members often negotiate about which specific functions they will perform. Sometimes disagreements result, and a breakdown in relationships among channel members occurs. This happened recently when PepsiCo's bottler in Venezuela switched to Coca-Cola. Because all marketing channel functions had to be performed, PepsiCo either had to set up its own bottling operation to perform the marketing channel functions, or find another bottler, which it did.[4]

Consumer Benefits from Intermediaries Consumers also benefit from intermediaries. Having the goods and services you want, when you want them, where you want them, and in the form you want them is the ideal result of marketing channels.

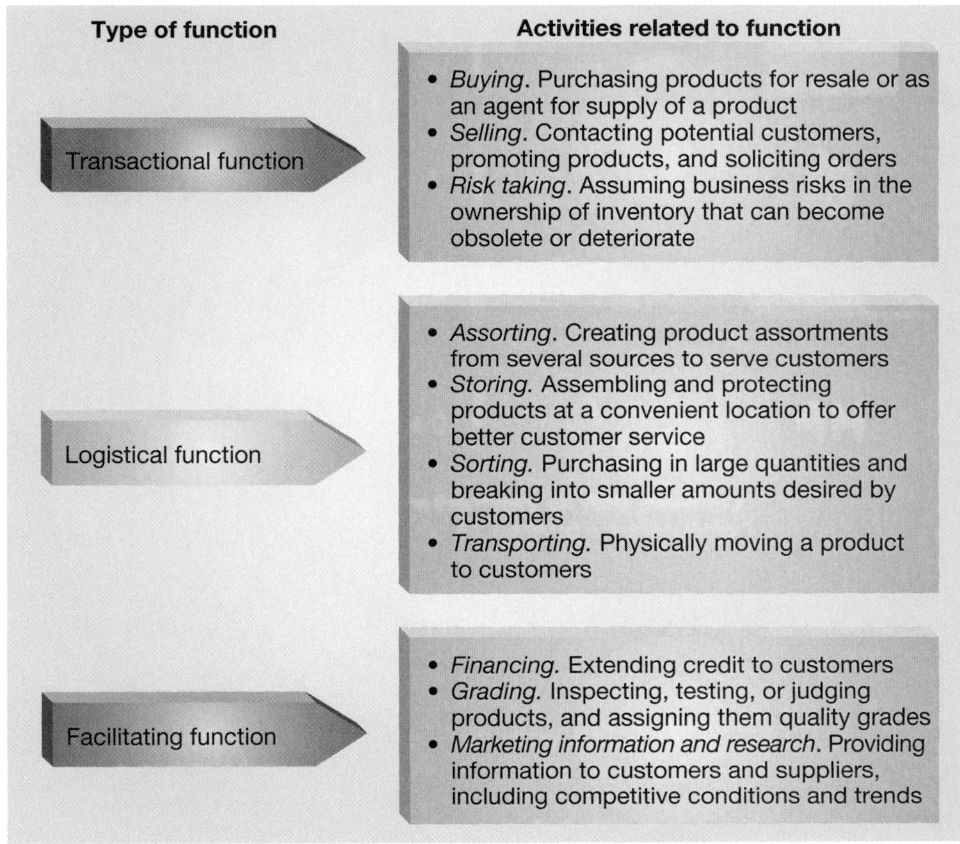

Type of function
Activities related to function
Transactional function
• Buying. Purchasing products for resale or as an agent for supply of a product
• Selling. Contacting potential customers, promoting products, and soliciting orders
• Risk taking. Assuming business risks in the ownership of inventory that can become obsolete or deteriorate
Logistical function
• Assorting. Creating product assortments from several sources to serve customers
• Storing. Assembling and protecting products at a convenient location to offer better customer service
• Sorting. Purchasing in large quantities and breaking into smaller amounts desired by customers
• Transporting. Physically moving a product to customers
Facilitating function
• Financing. Extending credit to customers
• Grading. Inspecting, testing, or judging products, and assigning them quality grades
• Marketing information and research. Providing information to customers and suppliers, including competitive conditions and trends

FIGURE 16–3
Marketing channel functions performed by intermediaries

In more specific terms, marketing channels help create value for consumers through the four utilities described in Chapter 1: time, place, form, and possession. Time utility refers to having a product or service when you want it. For example, FedEx provides next-morning delivery. Place utility means having a product or service available where consumers want it, such as having an Esso gas station located on a long stretch of lonely highway. Form utility involves enhancing a product or service to make it more appealing to buyers. For example, Compaq Computer delivers unfinished PCs to dealers, which then add memory, chips, modems, and other parts, based on consumer specifications.[5] Possession utility entails efforts by intermediaries to help buyers take possession of a product or service, such as having airline tickets delivered by a travel agency.

CONCEPT CHECK

1. What is meant by a marketing channel?
2. What are the three basic functions performed by intermediaries?

CHANNEL STRUCTURE AND ORGANIZATION

A product can take many routes on its journey from a producer to buyers, and marketers search for the most efficient route from the many alternatives available.

Marketing Channels for Consumer Goods and Services

Figure 16–4 shows the four most common marketing channels for consumer goods and services. It also shows the number of levels in each marketing channel, as

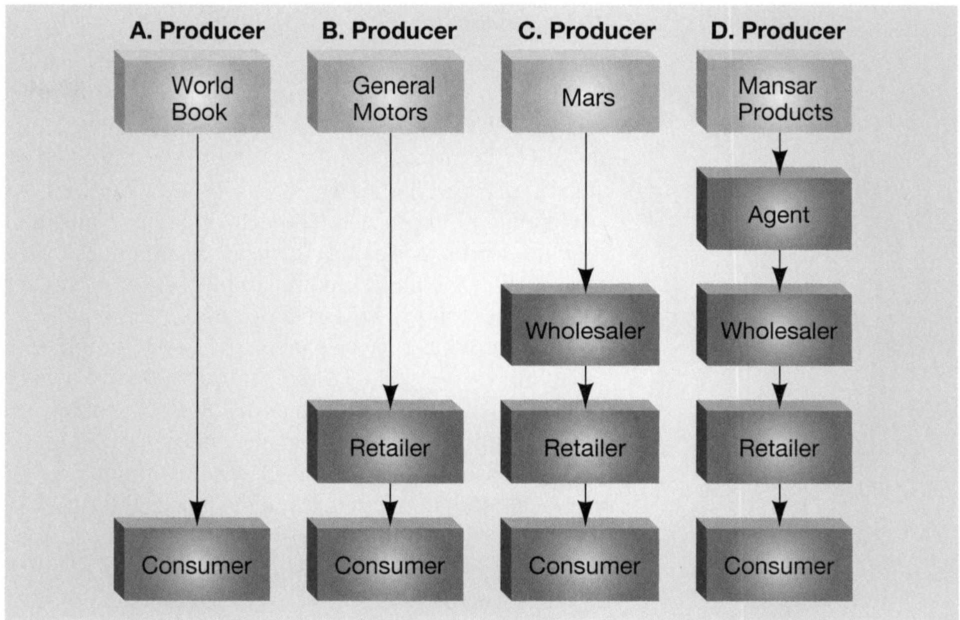

FIGURE 16–4
Common marketing channels for consumer goods and services

evidenced by the number of intermediaries between a producer and ultimate buyers. As the number of intermediaries between a producer and buyer increases, the channel is viewed as increasing in length. Thus the producer → wholesaler → retailer → consumer channel is longer than the producer → consumer channel.

Channel A represents a **direct channel** because a producer and ultimate consumers deal directly with each other. Many products and services are distributed this way. A number of insurance companies sell their financial services using a direct channel and branch sales offices, and World Book Educational Products sells its encyclopedias direct to consumers. Schwan's Sales Enterprises markets a full line of frozen foods using door-to-door salespeople who sell from refrigerated trucks. Because there are no intermediaries with a direct channel, the producer must perform all channel functions.

The remaining three channel forms are **indirect channels** because intermediaries are inserted between the producer and consumers and perform numerous channel functions. Channel B, with a retailer added, is most common when a retailer is large and can buy in large quantities from a producer or when the cost of inventory makes it too expensive to use a wholesaler. Manufacturers such as General Motors, Ford, and Chrysler use this channel, and a local car dealer acts as a retailer. Why is there no wholesaler? So many variations exist in the product that it would be impossible for a wholesaler to stock all the models required to satisfy buyers; in addition, the cost of maintaining an inventory would be too high. However, large retailers such as Sears Canada, 7-Eleven, Safeway, and The Bay buy in sufficient quantities to make it cost effective for a producer to deal with only a retail intermediary.

www.hbc.com

Adding a wholesaler in Channel C is most common for low-cost, low-unit value items that are frequently purchased by consumers, such as candy, confectionary items, and magazines. For example, Mars sells its line of candies to wholesalers in case quantities; then they can break down (sort) the cases so that individual retailers can order in boxes or much smaller quantities.

Channel D, the most indirect channel, is employed when there are many small manufacturers and many small retailers and an agent is used to help coordinate a large supply of the product. Mansar Products, Ltd. is a Belgian producer of specialty jewellery that uses agents to sell to wholesalers, which then sell to many small retailers.

Marketing Channels for Industrial Goods and Services

The four most common channels for industrial goods and services are shown in Figure 16–5. In contrast with channels for consumer products, industrial channels typically are shorter and rely on one intermediary or none at all because industrial users are fewer in number, tend to be more concentrated geographically, and buy in larger quantities (see Chapter 7).

Channel A, represented by IBM's large, mainframe computer business, is a direct channel. Firms using this channel maintain their own salesforce and perform all channel functions. This channel is employed when buyers are large and well defined, the sales effort requires extensive negotiations, and the products are of high unit value and require hands-on expertise in terms of installation or use.

Channels B, C, and D are indirect channels with one or more intermediaries to reach industrial users. In Channel B an **industrial distributor** performs a variety of marketing channel functions, including selling, stocking, and delivering a full product assortment and financing. In many ways, industrial distributors are like wholesalers in consumer channels. Caterpillar relies on industrial distributors to sell its construction and mining equipment in almost 200 countries. In addition to selling, Caterpillar distributors stock 40 000 to 50 000 parts and service equipment using highly trained technicians.[6]

Channel C introduces a second intermediary, an *agent,* who serves primarily as the independent selling arm of producers and represents a producer to industrial users. For example, Stake Fastener Company, a producer of industrial fasteners, has an agent call on industrial users rather than employing its own salesforce.

Channel D is the longest channel and includes both agents and distributors. For instance, Culligan, a producer of water treatment equipment, uses agents to call on distributors who sell to industrial users.

Electronic Marketing Channels

These common marketing channels for consumer and industrial goods and services are not the only routes to the marketplace. Advances in electronic commerce have opened new avenues for reaching buyers and creating customer value as described in Chapter 8.

Interactive electronic technology has made possible **electronic marketing channels** that employ the Internet to make goods and services available for consumption or use by consumers or industrial buyers. A unique feature of these channels

FIGURE 16–5
Common marketing channels for industrial goods and services

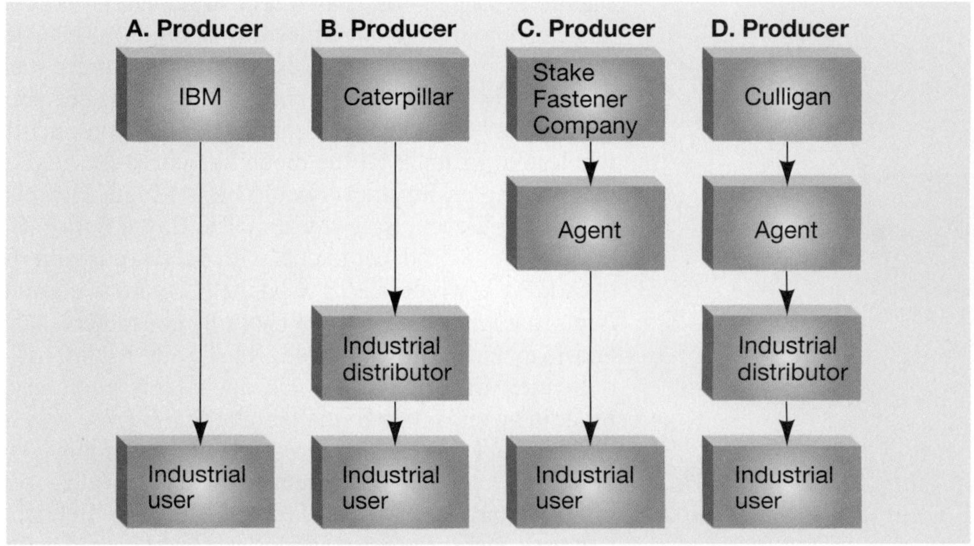

FIGURE 16–6
Representative electronic marketing channels

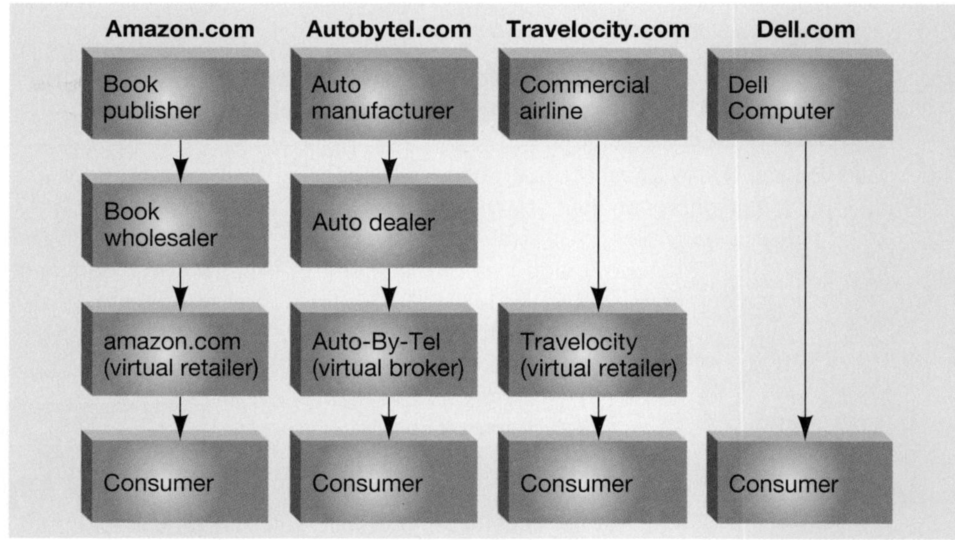

is that they combine electronic and traditional intermediaries to create time, place, form, and possession utility for buyers.[7]

Figure 16–6 shows the electronic marketing channels for books (Amazon.com), automobiles (Auto-By-Tel.com), reservation services (Travelocity.com), and personal computers (Dell.com). Are you surprised that they look a lot like common marketing channels? An important reason for the similarity resides in channel functions detailed in Figure 16–3. Electronic intermediaries can and do perform transactional and facilitating functions effectively and at a relatively lower cost than traditional intermediaries because of efficiencies made possible by information technology. However, electronic intermediaries are incapable of performing elements of the logistical function, particularly for products such as books and automobiles. This function remains with traditional intermediaries or with the producer, as evident with Dell Computer Corporation and its direct channel.

Many services can be distributed through electronic marketing channels, such as travel reservation marketed by Travelocity.com, financial securities by Schwab.com, and insurance by MetLife.com. Software too can be marketed this way. However, many other services such as health care and auto repair still involve traditional intermediaries.

Direct Marketing Channels

Many firms also use direct marketing channels to reach buyers. **Direct marketing channels** allow consumers to buy products by interacting with various advertising media without a face-to-face meeting with a salesperson. Direct marketing includes mail-order selling, direct-mail sales, catalogue sales, telemarketing, interactive media, and televised home shopping (for example, the Canadian Home Shopping Network).[8]

Some firms sell products almost entirely through direct marketing channels. These firms include L.L. Bean (apparel), Sharper Image (expensive gifts and novelties), and Egghead.com (personal computers). Manufacturers such as Nestlé and Sunkist, in addition to using traditional channels composed of wholesalers and retailers, employ direct marketing through catalogues and telemarketing to reach more buyers. At the same time, retailers such as Sears Canada use direct marketing techniques to augment conventional store merchandising activities. Some experts believe that direct marketing will account for 20 percent of all retail transactions in North America and 10 percent of retail transactions in Europe by 2002. Direct marketing is covered in greater depth in Chapter 19.

GLOBAL

MARKETING NEWSNET

Nestlé and General Mills: Cereal Partners Worldwide

Can you say Nestlé Cheerios *miel amandes?* Millions of French start their day with this European equivalent of General Mills' Honey Nut Cheerios, made possible by Cereal Partners Worldwide (CPW). CPW is the food industry's first strategic alliance designed to be a global business; it joined the cereal manufacturing and marketing capability of General Mills with the worldwide distribution clout of Nestlé. From its headquarters near Lake Geneva, Switzerland, CPW first launched General Mills cereals under the Nestlé label in France, the United Kingdom, Spain, and Portugal in 1991. Today, CPW competes in 70 markets worldwide and expects to achieve its goal of $1.4 billion in profitable sales by 2000.

The General Mills–Nestlé strategic alliance is also likely to increase the ready-to-eat worldwide market share of these companies, which are already rated as the two best-managed firms in the world. CPW is on track to reach its goal of a 20 percent worldwide share by 2000.

Multiple Channels and Strategic Alliances

www.hallmark.com

In some situations producers use **dual distribution,** an arrangement whereby a firm reaches different buyers by employing two or more different types of channels for the same basic product. For example, GE sells its large appliances directly to home and apartment builders but uses retail stores to sell to consumers. In some instances, firms use multiple channels when a multibrand strategy is employed (see Chapter 12). Hallmark sells its Hallmark greeting cards through Hallmark stores and select department stores, and its Ambassador brand of cards through discount and drugstore chains. In other instances, a firm will distribute modified products through different channels. Zoecon Corporation sells its insect control chemicals to professional pest-control operators such as Orkin and Terminex. A modified compound is sold to the Boyle-Midway for use in its Black-Flag Roach Ender brand.

www.generalmills.com

A recent innovation in marketing channels is the use of **strategic channel alliances,** whereby one firm's marketing channel is used to sell another firm's products.[9] An alliance between Kraft Foods and Starbucks is a case in point. Kraft distributes Starbucks coffee in supermarkets. Strategic alliances are popular in global marketing, where the creation of marketing channel relationships is expensive and time consuming. For example, General Motors distributes the Swedish Saab through its Saturn dealers in Canada. General Mills and Nestlé have an extensive alliance that spans 70 international markets. Read the accompanying Marketing NewsNet so you won't be surprised when you are served Nestlé (not General Mills) Cheerios in Europe, Mexico, and parts of Asia.[10]

A Closer Look at Channel Intermediaries

Channel structures for consumer and industrial products assume various forms based on the number and type of intermediaries. Knowledge of the roles played by these intermediaries is important for understanding how channels operate in practice.

The terms *wholesaler, agent,* and *retailer* have been used in a general fashion consistent with the meanings given in Figure 16–1. However, on closer inspection, a variety of

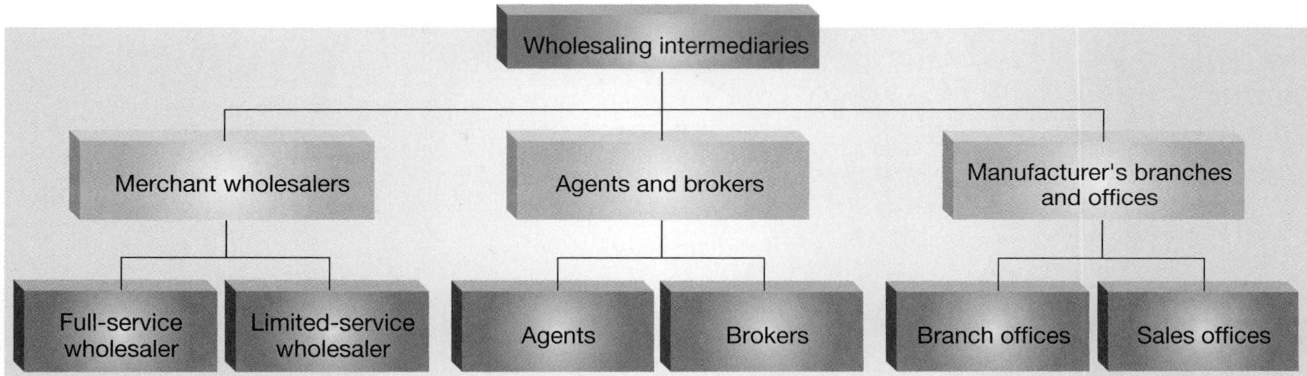

FIGURE 16–7
Types of wholesaling intermediaries

specific types of intermediaries emerges. Figure 16–7 shows a common classification of intermediaries that engage in wholesaling activities—those activities involved in selling products and services to those who are buying for the purposes of resale or business use. Intermediaries engaged in retailing activities are discussed in detail in Chapter 18. Figure 16–8 describes the functions performed by major types of independent wholesalers.[11]

Merchant Wholesalers Merchant wholesalers are independently owned firms that take title to the merchandise they handle. They go by various names, including industrial distributor (described earlier). About 83 percent of the firms engaged in wholesaling activities are merchant wholesalers.

Merchant wholesalers are classified as either full-service or limited-service wholesalers, depending on the number of functions performed. Two major types of full-service wholesalers exist. **General merchandise** (or *full-line*) **wholesalers** carry a broad assortment of merchandise and perform all channel functions. This type of wholesaler is most prevalent in the hardware, drug, and clothing industries. However, these wholesalers do not maintain much depth of assortment within specific product lines. **Specialty merchandise** (or *limited-line*) **wholesalers** offer a relatively narrow range of products but have an extensive assortment within the product lines carried. They perform all channel functions and are found in the health foods, automotive parts, and seafood industries.

Four major types of limited-service wholesalers exist. **Rack jobbers** furnish the racks or shelves that display merchandise in retail stores, perform all channel functions, and sell on consignment to retailers, which means they retain the title to the products displayed and bill retailers only for the merchandise sold. Familiar products such as hosiery, toys, housewares, and health and beauty aids are sold by rack jobbers. **Cash and carry wholesalers** take title to merchandise but sell only to buyers who call on them, pay cash for merchandise, and furnish their own transportation for merchandise. They carry a limited product assortment and do not make deliveries, extend credit, or supply market information. This wholesaler is common in electric supplies, office supplies, hardware products, and groceries. **Drop shippers,** or *desk jobbers,* are wholesalers who own the merchandise they sell but do not physically handle, stock, or deliver it. They simply solicit orders from retailers and other wholesalers and have the merchandise shipped directly from a producer to a buyer. Drop shippers are used for bulky products such as coal, lumber, and chemicals, which are sold in extremely large quantities. **Truck jobbers** are small wholesalers who have a small warehouse from which they stock their trucks for distribution to retailers. They usually handle limited assortments of fast-moving or perishable items that are sold for cash directly from trucks in their original packages. Truck jobbers handle products such as bakery items, dairy products, and meat.

Agents and Brokers Unlike merchant wholesalers, agents and brokers do not take title to merchandise and typically provide fewer channel functions. They make

FUNCTIONS PERFORMED	MERCHANT WHOLESALERS						AGENTS AND BROKERS		
	FULL SERVICE		LIMITED SERVICE						
	GENERAL MERCHANDISE	SPECIALTY MERCHANDISE	RACK JOBBERS	CASH AND CARRY	DROP SHIPPERS	TRUCK JOBBERS	MANUFACTURER'S AGENTS	SELLING AGENTS	BROKERS
TRANSACTIONAL FUNCTIONS									
Buying	Yes ★	Yes	Yes	Yes	Yes	Yes	No	No	No
Sales calls on customers	Yes	Yes	Yes	No	Yes	Yes	Yes	Yes	Yes
Risk taking (taking title to products)	Yes	Yes	Yes	Yes	Yes	Yes	No	No	No
LOGISTICAL FUNCTIONS									
Creates product assortments	Yes	Yes	Yes	Yes	No	Yes	Sometimes	No	Yes
Stores products (maintains inventory)	Yes	Yes	Yes	Yes	No	Yes	No	No	Sometimes
Sorts products	Yes	Yes	Yes	Yes	Yes	Yes	No	No	No
Transports products	Yes	Yes	Yes	No	No	Yes	Sometimes	Sometimes	Sometimes
FACILITATING FUNCTIONS									
Provides financing (credit)	Yes	Yes	Yes	No	Yes	No	No	Sometimes	No
Provides market information and research	Yes	Yes	Sometimes	No	Sometimes	No	Sometimes	Sometimes	Yes
Grading	Yes	Yes	Sometimes	No	Sometimes	No	No	Sometimes	Yes

★ Key: ●, Yes; ●, Sometimes; ●, No.

FIGURE 16–8
Functions performed by independent wholesaler types

their profit from commissions or fees paid for their services, whereas merchant wholesalers make their profit from the sale of the merchandise they own.

Manufacturer's agents and selling agents are the two major types of agents used by producers. **Manufacturer's agents,** or *manufacturer's representatives,* work for several producers and carry non-competitive, complementary merchandise in an exclusive territory. Manufacturer's agents act as a producer's sales arm in a territory and are principally responsible for the transactional channel functions, primarily selling. They are used extensively in the automotive supply, footwear, and fabricated steel industries. However, Swank Jewelry, Japanese computer firms, and Apple have used manufacturer's agents as well. By comparison, **selling agents** represent a single producer and are responsible for the entire marketing function of that producer. They design promotional plans, set prices, determine distribution policies, and make recommendations on product strategy. Selling agents are used by small producers in the textile, apparel, food, and home furnishing industries.

Brokers are independent firms or individuals whose principal function is to bring buyers and sellers together to make sales. Brokers, unlike agents, usually have no continuous relationship with the buyer or seller but negotiate a contract between two parties and then move on to another task. Brokers are used extensively by producers of seasonal products (such as fruits and vegetables) and in the real estate industry.

A unique broker that acts in many ways like a manufacturer's agent is a food broker, representing buyers and sellers in the grocery industry. Food brokers differ from conventional brokers because they act on behalf of producers on a permanent basis and receive a commission for their services. For example, Nabisco uses food brokers to sell its candies, margarine, and Planters peanuts, but it sells its line of cookies and crackers directly to retail stores. Manufacturer's agents sell Mr. Coffee coffee makers to appliance and mass merchandisers and food brokers sell its replacement coffee filters to supermarkets.

Manufacturer's Branches and Offices Unlike merchant wholesalers, agents, and brokers, manufacturer's branches and sales offices are wholly owned extensions of the producer that perform wholesaling activities. Producers assume wholesaling functions when there are no intermediaries to perform these activities, customers are few in number and geographically concentrated, or orders are large or require significant attention. A *manufacturer's branch office* carries a producer's inventory and performs the functions of a full-service wholesaler. A *manufacturer's sales office* does not carry inventory, typically performs only a sales function, and serves as an alternative to agents and brokers.

Vertical Marketing Systems and Channel Partnerships

The traditional marketing channels described so far represent a loosely knit network of independent producers and intermediaries brought together to distribute goods and services. However, new channel arrangements have emerged for the purpose of improving efficiency in performing channel functions and achieving greater marketing effectiveness. These new arrangements are called vertical marketing systems and channel partnerships. **Vertical marketing systems** are professionally managed and centrally coordinated marketing channels designed to achieve channel economies and maximum marketing impact.[12] Figure 16–9 depicts the major types of vertical marketing systems: corporate, contractual, and administered.

FIGURE 16–9
Types of vertical marketing systems

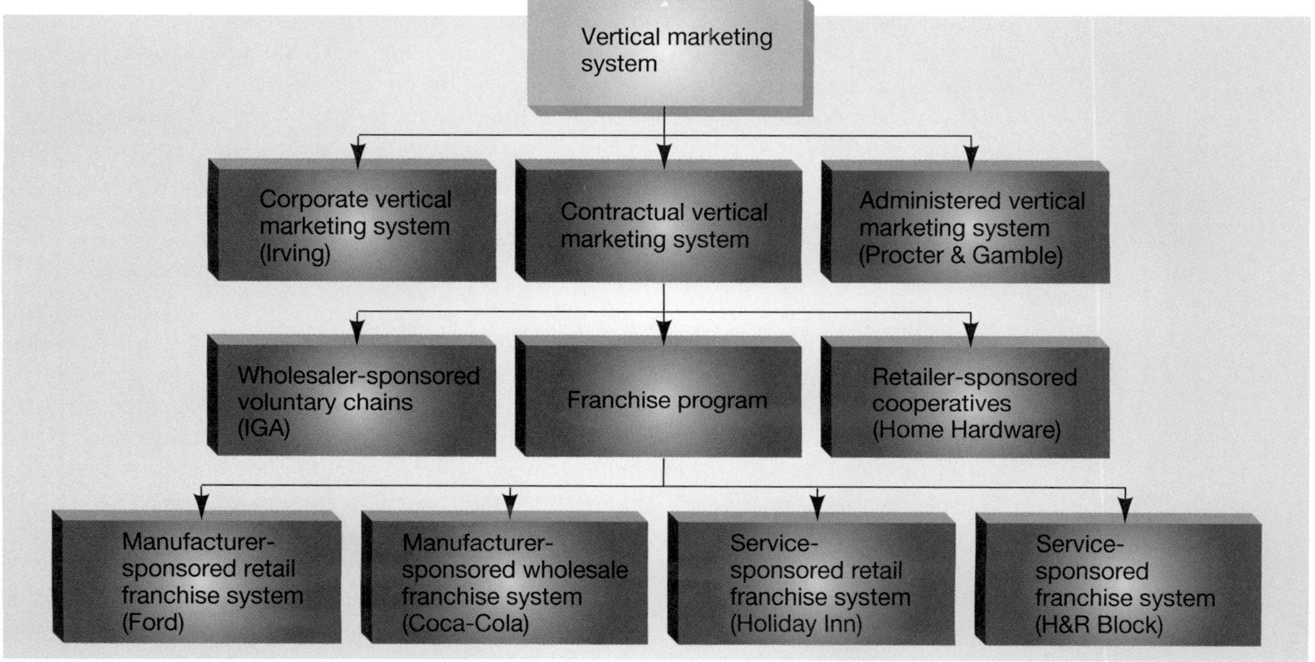

Corporate Systems The combination of successive stages of production and distribution under a single ownership is a *corporate vertical marketing system.* For example, a producer might own the intermediary at the next level down in the channel. This practice, called *forward integration,* is exemplified by Irving Oil, which refines gasoline and also operates retail gasoline stations. Other examples of forward integration include Goodyear, Singer, Sherwin Williams, and the building materials division of Boise Cascade. Alternatively, a retailer might own a manufacturing operation, a practice called *backward integration.* For example, Safeway supermarkets operate their own bakeries.

Contractual Systems Under a *contractual vertical marketing system,* independent production and distribution firms integrate their efforts on a contractual basis to obtain greater functional economies and marketing impact than they could achieve alone. Contractual systems are the most popular among the three types of vertical marketing systems. They account for about 40 percent of all retail sales.

Three variations of contractual systems exist. *Wholesaler-sponsored voluntary chains* involve a wholesaler that develops a contractual relationship with small, independent retailers to standardize and coordinate buying practices, merchandising programs, and inventory management efforts. With the organization of a large number of independent retailers, economies of scale and volume discounts can be achieved to compete with chain stores. IGA stores represent wholesaler-sponsored voluntary chains. *Retailer-sponsored cooperatives* exist when small, independent retailers form an organization that operates a wholesale facility cooperatively. Member retailers then concentrate their buying power through the wholesaler and plan collaborative promotional and pricing activities. Examples of retailer-sponsored cooperatives include Home Hardware.

The most visible variation of contractual systems is **franchising,** a contractual arrangement between a parent company (a franchisor) and an individual or firm (a franchisee) that allows the franchise to operate a certain type of business under an established name and according to specific rules.[13] Four types of franchise arrangements are most popular. Manufacturer-sponsored retail franchise systems are prominent in the automobile industry, where a manufacturer such as Ford licenses dealers to sell its cars subject to various sales and service conditions. Manufacturer-sponsored wholesale systems are evident in the soft-drink industry, where Pepsi-Cola licenses wholesalers (bottlers) who purchase concentrate from Pepsi-Cola and then carbonate, bottle, promote, and distribute its products to supermarkets and restaurants. Service-sponsored retail franchise systems are provided by firms that have designed a unique approach for performing a service and wish to profit by selling the franchise to others. Holiday Inn, Avis, and McDonald's represent this franchising approach. Service-sponsored franchise systems exist when franchisors license individuals or firms to dispense a service under a trade name and specific guidelines. An example is H&R Block tax services. Service-sponsored franchise arrangements are the fastest-growing type of franchise. Franchising is discussed further in Chapter 18.

Administered Systems In comparison, *administered vertical marketing systems* achieve coordination at successive stages of production and distribution by the size and influence of one channel member rather than through ownership. Procter & Gamble, given its broad product assortment ranging from disposable diapers to detergents, is able to obtain cooperation from supermarkets in displaying, promoting, and pricing its products. Wal-Mart can obtain cooperation from manufacturers in terms of product specifications, price levels, and promotional support, given its position as the world's largest retailer.

Channel Partnerships Increasingly, channel members are forging channel partnerships akin to supply partnerships described in Chapter 7. A **channel partnership**

consists of agreements and procedures among channel members for ordering and physically distributing a producer's products through the channel to the ultimate consumer.[14] A central feature of channel partnerships is the collaborative use of modern information and communication technology to better serve customers and reduce the time and cost of performing channel functions.

The partnership Levi Strauss & Company has with Modell's Sporting Goods is a case in point.[15] By using point-of-sale scanning equipment and direct electronic linkage to Levi Strauss, Modell's can instantaneously inform Levi Strauss what styles and sizes of jeans are needed, create purchase orders, and convey shipping instructions without any human involvement. The result? The costs of performing transaction, logistic, and facilitating functions are substantially reduced, and the customer is virtually assured of having his or her preferred 501 Levi jeans in stock. The role of information and communication technology in supply chain and logistics management is discussed further in Chapter 17.

CONCEPT CHECK

1. What is the difference between a direct and an indirect channel?
2. Why are channels for industrial products typically shorter than channels for consumer products?
3. What is the principal distinction between a corporate vertical marketing system and an administered vertical marketing system?

CHANNEL CHOICE AND MANAGEMENT

Marketing channels not only link a producer to its buyers but also provide the means through which a firm implements various elements of its marketing strategy. Therefore, choosing a marketing channel is a critical decision.

Factors Affecting Channel Choice and Management

The final choice of a marketing channel by a producer depends on a number of factors that often interact with each other.

www.avon.com

Environmental Factors The changing environment described in Chapter 3 has an important effect on the choice and management of a marketing channel. For example, the Fuller Brush Company and Avon, names synonymous with door-to-door selling, now use catalogues and telemarketing to reach customers. Rising employment among women, resulting in fewer being at home during working hours, prompted this action. Advances in the technology of growing, transporting, and storing perishable cut flowers has allowed many retailers such as Home Depot to eliminate flower wholesalers and buy direct from flower growers.[16] Additionally, the Internet has created new marketing channel opportunities for on-line marketing of flowers as well as children's toys, sporting goods and equipment, and music and video products.[17]

Consumer Factors Consumer characteristics have a direct bearing on the choice and management of a marketing channel. Determining which channel is most appropriate is based on answers to fundamental questions such as: Who are potential customers? Where do they buy? When do they buy? How do they buy? What do they buy? These answers also indicate the type of intermediary best suited to reaching target buyers. For example, Ricoh Company, Ltd. studied the serious (as opposed to recreational) camera user and concluded that a change in marketing channels was necessary. The company

The Internet has created new marketing channel opportunities for the distribution of children's toys.

FAO Schwarz
www.faoschwarz.com

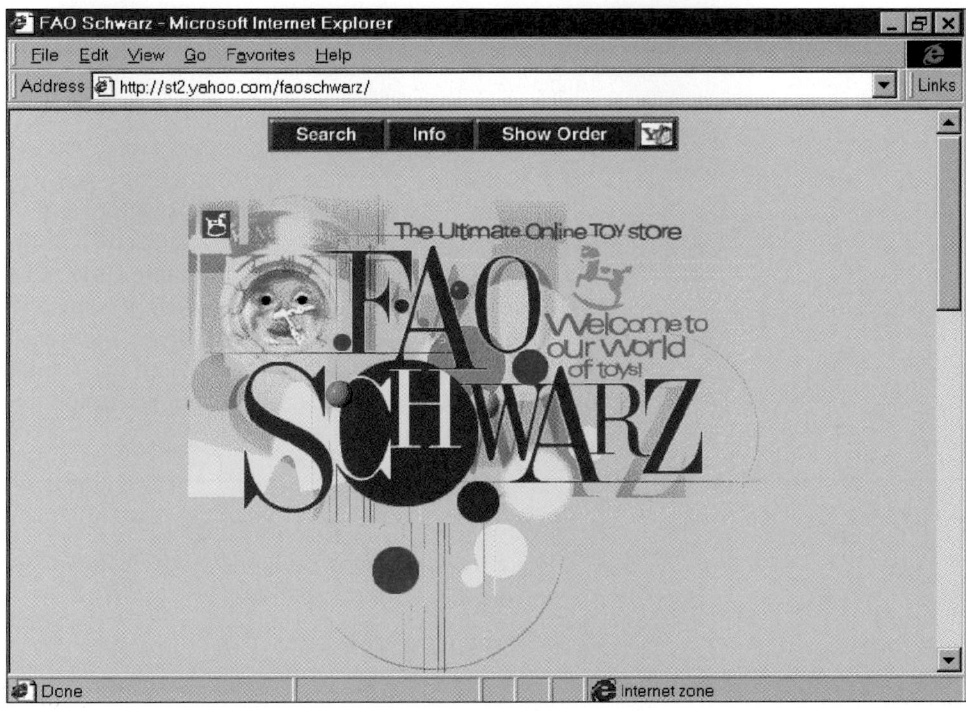

terminated its contract with a wholesaler who sold to mass merchandise stores and began using manufacturer's agents who sold to photo specialty stores. These stores agreed to stock and display Ricoh's full line and promote it prominently. Sales volume tripled within 18 months. Recognizing that car buyers now comparison shop on the Internet, Ford, General Motors, Chrysler, and Mercedes Benz now have their own Web sites to provide price and model information.[18]

www.chrysler.com

Product Factors In general, highly sophisticated products such as large, scientific computers, unstandardized products such as custom-built machinery, and products of high unit value are distributed directly to buyers. Unsophisticated, standardized products with low unit value, such as table salt, are typically distributed through indirect channels. A product's stage in the life cycle also affects marketing channels. This was shown in the description of the fax machine product life cycle in Chapter 12.

Company Factors A firm's financial, human, or technological capabilities affect channel choice. For example, firms that are unable to employ a salesforce might use manufacturer's agents or selling agents to reach wholesalers or buyers. If a firm has multiple products for a particular target market, it might use a direct channel, whereas firms with a limited product line might use intermediaries of various types to reach buyers.

Company factors also apply to intermediaries. For example, personal computer hardware and software producers wishing to reach business users might look to value-added resellers such as Future Shop, which has its own salesforce and service staff that calls on businesses.

www.futureshop.com

Channel Design Considerations

Recognizing that numerous routes to buyers exist and also recognizing the factors just described, marketing executives typically consider three questions when choosing a marketing channel and intermediaries:

Need Cash Fast? Check the VISA ATM Locator

Short of cash? VISA offers a valuable Web resource in its ATM Locator that can be accessed at www.visa.com. VISA has some 460 000 automatic teller machines in 120 countries. One is probably in your neighbourhood, wherever that is in the world! To find the nearest VISA ATM, follow the easy ATM Locator directions and request a site map. You'll be in the money in no time. Here's the map for McGraw-Hill Higher Education's neighbourhood.

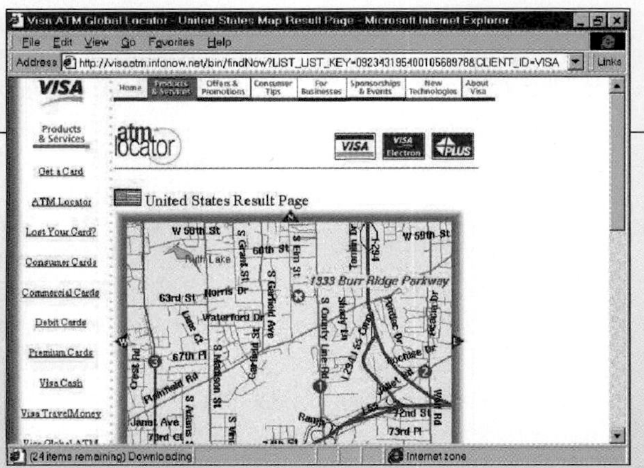

1. Which channel and intermediaries will provide the best coverage of the target market?
2. Which channel and intermediaries will best satisfy the buying requirements of the target market?
3. Which channel and intermediaries will be the most profitable?

Target Market Coverage Achieving the best coverage of the target market requires attention to the density and type of intermediaries to be used at the retail level of distribution. Three degrees of distribution density exist: intensive, exclusive, and selective. **Intensive distribution** means that a firm tries to place its products and services in as many outlets as possible. Intensive distribution is usually chosen for convenience products or services; for example, candy, fast food, newspapers, and soft drinks. Increasingly, medical services are distributed in this fashion. Cash, yes cash, is also distributed intensively by VISA. Visit VISA's Web site described in the Web Link, to locate the nearest VISA automatic teller machine.

Exclusive distribution is the extreme opposite of intensive distribution because only one retail outlet in a specified geographical area carries the firm's product. Exclusive distribution is typically chosen for specialty products or services; for example, automobiles, some women's fragrances, men's suits, and yachts. Sometimes retailers sign exclusive distribution agreements with manufacturers. For instance, Radio Shack now sells only Compaq's Presario home computers in its 7000 stores.[19]

Selective distribution lies between these two extremes and means that a firm selects a few retail outlets in a specific area to carry its products. This is the most common form of distribution intensity and is usually associated with shopping goods or services such as Rolex watches, and Ping golf clubs.

The type or availability of a retail outlet will also influence whether a target market is reached. For example, the L'eggs division of the Hanes Corporation distributes fashionable white pantyhose to nurses through catalogues because supermarkets and department stores do not typically carry these items.

Satisfying Buyer Requirements A second consideration in channel design is gaining access to channels and intermediaries that satisfy at least some of the interests buyers might want fulfilled when they purchase a firm's products or services. These interests fall into four categories: (1) information, (2) convenience, (3) variety, and (4) attendant services.

Information is an important requirement when buyers have limited knowledge or desire specific data about a product or service. Properly chosen intermediaries communicate with buyers through in-store displays, demonstrations, and personal selling. Computer stores originally grew in popularity as a source for small computers because they provided such information. Similarly, direct sales firms such as Amway, Avon, and Tupperware have been able to identify the unique information needs of Japanese women and successfully communicate the benefits of their products and method of selling. Amway is one of the fastest-growing firms in Japan, and Avon records millions of dollars in Japanese sales each year through direct selling.

Convenience has multiple meanings for buyers, such as proximity or driving time to a retail outlet. For example, 7-Eleven stores with outlets nationwide satisfy this interest for buyers, and candy and snack food firms benefit by gaining display space in these stores. For other consumers, convenience means a minimum of time and hassle. Jiffy Lube and Minit-Lube, which promise to change engine oil and filters quickly, appeal to this aspect of convenience.

Variety reflects buyers' interest in having numerous competing and complementary items from which to choose. Variety is evident in both the breadth and depth of products and brands carried by intermediaries, which enhances their attraction to buyers. Thus, manufacturers of pet food and supplies seek distribution through pet superstores such as Petco and PetsMart, which offer a wide array of pet products.

Attendant services provided by intermediaries are an important buying requirement for products such as appliances that require delivery, installation, and credit. Therefore, Whirlpool seeks dealers that provide such services.

Profitability The third consideration in designing a channel is profitability, which is determined by the margins earned (revenues minus cost) for each channel member and for the channel as a whole. Channel cost is the critical dimension of profitability. These costs include distribution, advertising, and selling expenses associated with different types of marketing channels. The extent to which channel members share these costs determines the margins received by each member and by the channel as a whole.

Global Dimensions of Marketing Channels

For the answer to how Schick became a razor and blade market share leader in Japan read the text.

Warner-Lambert Company
www.warner-lambert.com

Marketing channels around the world reflect traditions, customs, geography, and the economic history of individual countries and societies. Even so, the basic marketing channel functions must be performed. But differences do exist and are illustrated by highlighting marketing channels in Japan—the world's second-largest economy.

Intermediaries outside Western Europe and North America tend to be small, numerous, and often owner operated. Japanese marketing channels tend to include many intermediaries based on tradition and lack of storage space. As many as five intermediaries are involved in the distribution of soap in Japan compared with one or two in North America.

Understanding marketing channels in global markets is often a prerequisite to successful marketing. For example, Gillette attempted to sell its razors and blades through company salespeople in Japan as it does in North America, thus eliminating wholesalers traditionally involved in marketing toiletries. Warner-Lambert Company sold its Schick razors and blades through the traditional Japanese channel involving wholesalers. The result? Schick achieved a commanding lead over Gillette in the Japanese razor and blade market.[20]

Channel relationships also must be considered. In Japan, the distribution *keiretsu* (translated as "alignments") bonds producers and intermediaries together.[21] The bond, through vertical integration and social and economic ties, ensures that each channel member benefits from the distribution alignment. The dominant member of the distribution *keiretsu,* which is typically a producer, has considerable influence over channel member behaviour, including which competing products are sold by other channel members. Well-known Japanese companies such as Matsushita (electronics), Nissan and Toyota (automotive products), Nippon Gakki (musical instruments), and Kirin (and other brewers and distillers) employ the distribution *keiretsu* extensively. Shiseido and Kanebo, for instance, influence the distribution of cosmetics through Japanese department stores.[22]

Channel Relationships: Conflict, Cooperation, and Law

Unfortunately, because channels consist of independent individuals and firms, there is always potential for disagreements concerning who performs which channel functions, how profits are allocated, which products and services will be provided by whom, and who makes critical channel-related decisions. These channel conflicts necessitate measures for dealing with them. Sometimes they result in legal action.

Conflict in Marketing Channels Channel conflict arises when one channel member believes another channel member is engaged in behaviour that prevents it from achieving its goals. Two types of conflict occur in marketing channels: vertical conflict and horizontal conflict.

Vertical conflict occurs between different levels in a marketing channel; for example, between a manufacturer and a wholesaler or retailer or between a wholesaler and a retailer. Three sources of vertical conflict are most common. First, conflict arises when a channel member bypasses another member and sells or buys products direct, a practice called **disintermediation.** This conflict emerged when Jenn-Air, a producer of kitchen appliances, decided to terminate its distributors and sell direct to retailers. Second, disagreements over how profit margins are distributed among channel members produce conflict. This happened when Compaq Computer Corporation and one of its dealers disagreed over how price discounts were applied in the sale of Compaq's products. Compaq Computer stopped selling to the dealer for 13 months until the issue was resolved. A third conflict situation arises when manufacturers believe wholesalers or retailers are not giving their products adequate attention. For example, H. J. Heinz Company found itself in a conflict situation with its supermarkets in Great Britain when the supermarkets promoted and displayed private brands at the expense of Heinz brands.

Horizontal conflict occurs between intermediaries at the same level in a marketing channel, such as between two or more retailers (Zellers and Kmart) or two or more wholesalers that handle the same manufacturer's brands. Two sources of horizontal conflict are common. First, horizontal conflict arises when a manufacturer increases its distribution coverage in a geographical area. For example, a franchised Cadillac dealer might complain to General Motors that another franchised Cadillac dealer has located too close to its dealership. Second, dual distribution causes conflict when different types of retailers carry the same brands. For instance, the launch of Elizabeth Taylor's Black Pearls fragrance by Elizabeth Arden was put on hold when some upscale department store chains refused to stock the item once they learned that mass merchants would also carry the brand. Elizabeth Arden subsequently introduced the brand only through department stores.[23]

Cooperation in Marketing Channels Conflict can have destructive effects on the workings of a marketing channel, so it is necessary to secure cooperation among channel members. One means is through a **channel captain,** a channel member that coordinates, directs, and supports other channel members. Channel captains can be producers, wholesalers, or retailers. P&G assumes this role because it has a strong consumer following in brands such as Crest, Tide, and Pampers. Therefore, it can set policies or terms that supermarkets will follow. Wal-Mart and Home Depot are retail channel captains because of their strong consumer image, number of outlets, and purchasing volume.

A firm becomes a channel captain because it is typically the channel member with the ability to influence the behaviour of other members.[24] Influence can take four forms.

ETHICS

ETHICS AND SOCIAL RESPONSIBILITY ALERT

The Ethics of Slotting Allowances

How firms acquire and use influence in marketing channels has often prompted legal restrictions. Nevertheless, influence gained through the economic strength, expertise, identification with others, and legitimate rights of channel members can be used in numerous ways.

Some supermarket chains demand slotting allowances from manufacturers, paid in the form of money or free goods, to stock and display products. The allowances, which can range from $100 for a single store to upwards of $25 000 for a supermarket chain, have been labelled "ransom" and "extortional allowances" by manufacturers. Supermarket operators see these allowances as a reasonable cost of handling business for manufacturers.

Is the practice of charging slotting allowances unethical behaviour?

First, economic influence arises from the ability of a firm to reward other members given its strong financial position or customer franchise. Microsoft Corporation and Toys "Я" Us have such influence. Expertise is a second source of influence over other channel members. Third, identification with a particular channel member may also create influence for that channel member. For instance, retailers may compete to carry the Ralph Lauren line, or clothing manufacturers may compete to be carried by Eaton's or the Bay. In both instances the desire to be associated with a channel member gives that firm influence over others. Finally, influence can arise from the legitimate right of one channel member to direct the behaviour of other members. This situation would occur under contractual vertical marketing systems where a franchisor could legitimately direct how a franchisee behaves. Other means for securing cooperation in marketing channels rest in the different variations of vertical marketing systems.

Channel influence can be used to gain concessions from other channel members. For instance, some large supermarket chains expect manufacturers to pay allowances, in the form of cash or free goods, to stock and display their products. Some manufacturers call these allowances "extortion" as described in the Ethics and Social Responsibility Alert.[25]

Legal Considerations Conflict in marketing channels is typically resolved through negotiation or the exercise of influence by channel members. Sometimes conflict produces legal action. Therefore, knowledge of legal restrictions affecting channel strategies and practices is important. Some restrictions were described in Chapter 15, namely vertical price-fixing and price discrimination. However, other legal considerations unique to marketing channels warrant attention.[26]

In general, suppliers have the right to choose the intermediaries who carry or represent their products. However, suppliers can run into legal difficulty over *refusing to deal* with customers who can meet the usual trade terms offered by the supplier. The *Competition Act* looks seriously at cases where a supplier withholds or withdraws products from a customer if such behaviour will adversely affect that customer.

Dual distribution is a situation where a manufacturer distributes through its own vertically integrated channel in direct competition with wholesalers and retailers that also sell its products. If the manufacturer's behaviour is viewed as an attempt to unduly lessen competition by eliminating wholesalers or retailers, then such action may violate the *Competition Act* and would be examined by the Bureau of Competition Policy.

Vertical integration is viewed in a similar light. Like dual distribution, it is not illegal, but the practice could be subject to legal action if such integration were designed to eliminate or lessen competition unduly.

Exclusive dealing and tied selling are prohibited under the *Competition Act* if they are found to unduly lessen competition or create monopolies. *Exclusive dealing* exists when a supplier requires channel members to sell only its products or restricts distributors from selling directly competitive products. *Tied selling* occurs when a supplier requires a distributor purchasing some products to buy others from the supplier. These arrangements often arise in franchising. Tied selling would be investigated by the Bureau of Competition Policy if the tied products could be purchased at fair market value from other suppliers at desired standards of the franchisor and if the arrangements were seen as restricting competition. Full-line forcing is a special kind of tied selling. This is a supplier's requiring that a channel member carry its full line of products to sell a specific item in the supplier's line.

Resale or market restrictions refer to a supplier's attempt to stipulate to whom distributors may resell the supplier's products and in what specific geographical areas or territories they may be sold. These practices could be subject to review under the *Competition Act* if such restrictions were deemed to be restraining or lessening competition.

CONCEPT CHECK

1. What are the three degrees of distribution density?
2. What are the three questions marketing executives consider when choosing a marketing channel and intermediaries?
3. What is meant by "exclusive dealing"?

SUMMARY

1 A marketing channel consists of individuals and firms involved in the process of making a product or service available for use by consumers or industrial users.

2 Intermediaries make possible the flow of products and services from producers to buyers by performing transactional, logistical, and facilitating functions. At the same time, intermediaries create time, place, form, and possession utility.

3 Channel structure describes the route taken by products and services from producers to buyers. Direct channels represent the shortest route because producers interact directly with buyers. Indirect channels include intermediaries between producers and buyers.

4 In general, marketing channels for consumer products and services contain more intermediaries than do channels for industrial products and services. In some situations, producers use Internet, direct marketing, multiple channels and strategic channel alliances to reach buyers.

5 Numerous types of wholesalers can exist within a marketing channel. The principal distinction between the various types of wholesalers lies in whether they take title to the items they sell and the channel functions they perform.

6 Vertical marketing systems are channels designed to achieve channel function economies and marketing impact. A vertical marketing system may be one of three types: corporate, administered, or contractual.

7 Marketing managers consider environmental, consumer, product, and company factors when choosing and managing marketing channels.

8 Channel design considerations are based on the target market coverage sought by producers, the buyer requirements to be satisfied, and the profitability of the channel. Target market coverage comes about through one of three levels of distribution density: intensive, exclusive, and selective distribution. Buyer requirements are evident in the amount of information, convenience, variety, and service sought by consumers. Profitability relates to the margins obtained by each channel member and the channel as a whole.

9 Marketing channels in the global marketplace reflect traditions, customs, geography, and the economic history of individual countries and societies. These factors influence channel structure and relationships among channel members.

10 Conflicts in marketing channels are inevitable. Vertical conflict occurs between different levels in a channel. Horizontal conflict occurs between intermediaries at the same level in the channel.

11 Legal issues in the management of marketing channels typically arise from six practices: refusal to deal, dual distribution, vertical integration, exclusive dealing, tied selling, and resale or market restrictions.

KEY TERMS AND CONCEPTS

marketing channel p. 414
direct channel p. 417
indirect channels p. 417
industrial distributor p. 418
electronic marketing channels p. 418
direct marketing channels p. 419
dual distribution p. 420
strategic channel alliances p. 420
general merchandise wholesalers p. 421
specialty merchandise wholesalers p. 421
rack jobbers p. 421
cash and carry wholesalers p. 421
drop shippers p. 421
truck jobbers p. 421
manufacturer's agents p. 422
selling agents p. 422
brokers p. 422
vertical marketing systems p. 423
franchising p. 424
channel partnership p. 424
intensive distribution p. 427
exclusive distribution p. 427
selective distribution p.427
disintermediation p. 429
channel captain p. 429

INTERNET EXERCISE

Franchising is a large and growing industry. For many individuals, franchising offers an opportunity to operate one's own business.

The Internet provides a number of Web sites that feature franchising opportunities. The International Franchise Association (www.franchise.org) features an extensive array of information, including answers to questions about franchising. The Franchise Opportunity Story (www.franchise.com) lists franchise opportunities for the aspiring franchisee.

1 Visit the Franchise Opportunity Store Web site, and go to How Much Franchises Cost. In what category of business is the franchise investment the highest and the lowest?

2 Visit the International Franchise Association Web site, and go to Frequently Asked Questions About Franchising. What is the business failure rate among franchises? Is the business failure rate better or worse than the failure rate for new businesses in general?

APPLYING MARKETING CONCEPTS AND PERSPECTIVES

1 A distributor for Celanese Chemical Company stores large quantities of chemicals, blends these chemicals to satisfy requests of customers, and delivers the blends to a customer's warehouse within 24 hours of receiving an order. What utilities does this distributor provide?

2 Suppose the president of a carpet manufacturing firm has asked you to look into the possibility of bypassing the firm's wholesalers (who sell to carpet, department, and furniture stores) and selling direct to these stores. What caution would you voice on this matter, and what type of information would you gather before making this decision?

3 What type of channel conflict is likely to be caused by dual distribution, and what type of conflict can be reduced by direct distribution? Why?

4 How does the channel captain idea differ among corporate, administered, and contractual vertical marketing systems with particular reference to the use of the different forms of influence available to firms?

5 Comment on this statement: "The only distinction among merchant wholesalers and agents and brokers is that merchant wholesalers take title to the products they sell."

6 How do specialty, shopping, and convenience goods generally relate to intensive, selective, and exclusive distribution? Give a brand name that is an example of each goods-distribution match-up.

CASE 16–1 CRESTON VINEYARDS

Larry Rosenbloom's customers include individuals, retail stores, restaurants, and hotels. Because of the many types and large numbers of customers, distribution is as important as production at Creston Vineyards. As Larry explains, "We need distributors in our business . . . as most other [businesses] do, to get the product to the end user, to the consumer."

THE COMPANY

In 1980, Stephanie and Larry Rosenbloom purchased an abandoned ranch and started Creston Vineyards. Because it takes several years for vines to grow and produce grapes, Creston did not sell its first wine until 1982. Today, the 220-hectare ranch has 70 hectares of planted vineyards and produces over 55 000 cases of eight varieties of wines. The production facilities include a 1650-square-metre winery and 15 square metres of laboratory and office space.

Since 1982 Creston wines have won over 500 awards in wine-tasting events and competitions.

THE INDUSTRY AND DISTRIBUTION CHANNELS

The wine industry is undergoing several very interesting changes. First, sales have increased in recent years after a general decline since 1984. The decline was attributed to changing consumer demographics, shifting buying habits, and concerns about the economy. At least some of the recent interest in wine is related to the press reports suggesting the possible health benefits of red wine. A second change is the significant increase in the price of wine due to a low supply of good international wines and changing exchange rates, and an infestation of vine-eating insects (phylloxera). Finally, many wine producers are trying to change the image of wine from a beverage only for special occasions and gourmet foods to a beverage for any occasion.

The industry also faces several distribution challenges. The large number of wine producers and the variety of consumers requires a sophisticated system of distribution channels. By combining different types of intermediaries, the industry is able to meet the requirements of many customers. In addition, because the sale of wine is regulated, the use of multiple distribution channels facilitates the sale of wine in many locations.

One of the most common channels of distribution involves a distributor buying wine directly from the vineyard and reselling it to retail stores and restaurants within a geographic area. Some distributors, however, may not need quantities large enough to warrant purchasing directly from the vineyard. They usually purchase several brands at the same time from a warehouse. A broker may facilitate sales by providing information to distributors, training the distributor's salesforce, and even assisting in sales calls to retailers. John Drady, one of 12 brokers for Creston Vineyards, explains: "It's very important that we translate our knowledge and our selling skills to the distributor's salespeople so they can, in turn, go out and [sell] more readily on their own."

Other channels are also used by Creston. For example, in some markets Creston can sell directly to any customer. The vineyard also sells directly to some large retailers. Another channel of distribution is through wine clubs that provide club members with information about wines and an average of six wines per year. The popularity of wine clubs has been increasing and they now account for 15 percent of Creston's sales. The newest type of distribution channel is through on-line services. Creston now has a page on the World Wide Web (www.wines.com) that provides information about its wines and allows orders to be shipped directly to consumers. Customers will also find greetings from Alex Trebek, the Canadian-born game-show host, who is now the current owner of Creston Vineyards.

THE ISSUES

In an industry with thousands of products and hundreds of producers, Creston is relatively new and small. Selecting and managing its distribution channels to best meet the needs of many constituents is a key task. Providing marketing assistance, product information, and appropriate assortment, transportation, storage, and credit are just a few of the functions the warehouse, brokers, distributors, and retailers may provide as the product moves from the vineyard to the end user.

Creston also faces a situation where new, and possibly more efficient, channels are becoming available. Direct sales, wine clubs, and on-line services have generated substantial sales for Creston. Other channels, or new variations of existing channels, may also be available in the future. Overall, Creston must continue to utilize distribution channels to provide value to customers ranging from large retailers, to hotels and restaurants, and to individuals.

Questions

1 What functions must be performed by intermediaries in the wine industry?

2 What intermediaries and distribution channels are currently used by Creston Vineyards?

3 How do different channels of distribution reach different segments? Are there any segments Creston does not reach with its current channels?

Supply Chain:

Managing Logistics For the 21st Century

CHAPTER SEVENTEEN

SUPPLY CHAIN AND LOGISTICS MANAGEMENT

17

AFTER READING THIS CHAPTER YOU SHOULD BE ABLE TO:

- Explain what supply chain and logistics management are and how they relate to the marketing mix.
- Understand the nature of logistics trade-offs among transportation, inventory, and other logistics functions.
- Explain how managers trade off different "logistics costs" relative to customer service in order to reach a logistics decision.
- Recognize how customer service in logistics decisions contributes to customer value and successful marketing programs.
- Describe the key logistics functions of transportation, warehousing and materials handling, order processing, and inventory management and the emerging role of third-party logistics providers.

OUCH! EVEN THE BEST COMPANIES CAN FEEL THE STING OF THE BULLWHIP

Bad things can happen to great companies. Just ask Boeing, Hewlett-Packard, Bristol-Myers Squibb, and Procter & Gamble. Each of these industry leaders has experienced the bullwhip's sting at one time or another for one or more of their products.

What is the bullwhip, and why does its sting hurt so bad? Companies define the bullwhip as too much or too little inventory to satisfy customer needs, missed production schedules, and ineffective transportation or delivery caused by miscommunication among material suppliers, manufacturers, and resellers of consumer and industrial goods. Its sting is poor customer service and lost revenue and profit opportunities.

Suppliers, manufacturers, and resellers know that to get a handle on the bullwhip, attention needs to focus on the technology and coordinated activities that make possible the physical flow and transformation of goods from the raw materials stage to the final consumer or industrial user. They also recognize that accurate, timely, and shared information can soften the bullwhip's sting, thereby benefiting customers and companies alike.[1]

Welcome to the unglamorous—but critical—world of supply chain and logistics management. The essence of the problem is simple: It makes no sense to have brilliant marketing programs to sell world-class products if the products aren't available at the right time, at the right place, and in the right form and condition that customers want them. It's finding the continuing solutions through time that's always the problem. This chapter describes the role of supply chains and logistics management in marketing and how a firm balances distribution costs against the need for effective customer service.

SIGNIFICANCE OF SUPPLY CHAIN AND LOGISTICS MANAGEMENT

We often use the term *physical distribution,* but rarely consider its significance in marketing. Canadian companies spend billions of dollars transporting raw materials and finished goods each year and billions of dollars more on material handling, warehousing, storage, and holding inventory. Worldwide, these activities cost companies hundreds of billions of dollars annually.[2] In this section, we describe contemporary approaches to physical distribution, including supply chains and logistics management and illustrate how each affect elements of the marketing mix.

Relating Marketing Channels, Logistics, and Supply Chain Management

A marketing channel relies on logistics to actually make products available to consumers and industrial users—a point emphasized in the previous chapter. **Logistics** involves those activities that focus on getting the right amount of the right products to the right place at the right time at the lowest possible cost. The performance of these activities is **logistics management,** the practice of organizing the *cost-effective flow* of raw materials, in-process inventory, finished goods, and related information from point of origin to point of consumption to satisfy *customer requirements.*[3]

Three elements of this definition deserve emphasis. First, logistics deals with decisions needed to move a product from the source of raw materials to consumption, or the *flow* of the product. Second, those decisions have to be made in a *cost-effective* manner. While it is important to drive down logistics costs, there is a limit—the third point of emphasis. A firm needs to drive down logistics costs as long as it can deliver expected *customer service,* which means satisfying customer requirements. The role of management is to see that customer needs are satisfied in the most cost-effective manner. When properly done, the results can be spectacular. Procter & Gamble is a case in point. Beginning in the early 1990s, the company set out to meet the needs of consumers more effectively by collaborating and partnering with its suppliers and retailers to ensure that the right products reached store shelves at the right time and at a lower cost. The effort was judged a success when, during an 18-month period in the late 1990s, P&G's retail customers recorded a $65 million savings in logistics costs while customer service increased.[4]

The Procter & Gamble experience is not an isolated incident. Today, logistics management is embedded in a broader view of physical distribution, consistent with the emphasis on supply and channel partnering described in Chapters 7 and 16. Companies now recognize that getting the right items needed for consumption or production to the right place at the right time in the right condition at the right cost is often beyond their individual capabilities and control. Instead, collaboration, coordination, and information sharing among manufacturers, suppliers, and distributors are necessary to create a seamless flow of goods and services to customers. This perspective is represented in the concept of a supply chain and the practice of supply chain management.

A **supply chain** is a sequence of firms that perform activities required to create and deliver a good or service to consumers or industrial users.[5] It differs from a marketing channel in terms of membership. A supply chain includes suppliers who provide raw material inputs to a manufacturer as well as the wholesalers and retailers who deliver finished goods to you. The management process is also different. **Supply chain management** is the integration and organization of information and logistics activities *across firms* in a supply chain for the purpose of creating and delivering goods and services that provide value to consumers. The relationship among marketing channels, logistics management, and supply chain management is shown in Figure

FIGURE 17–1
Relating marketing channels, logistics management, and supply chain management

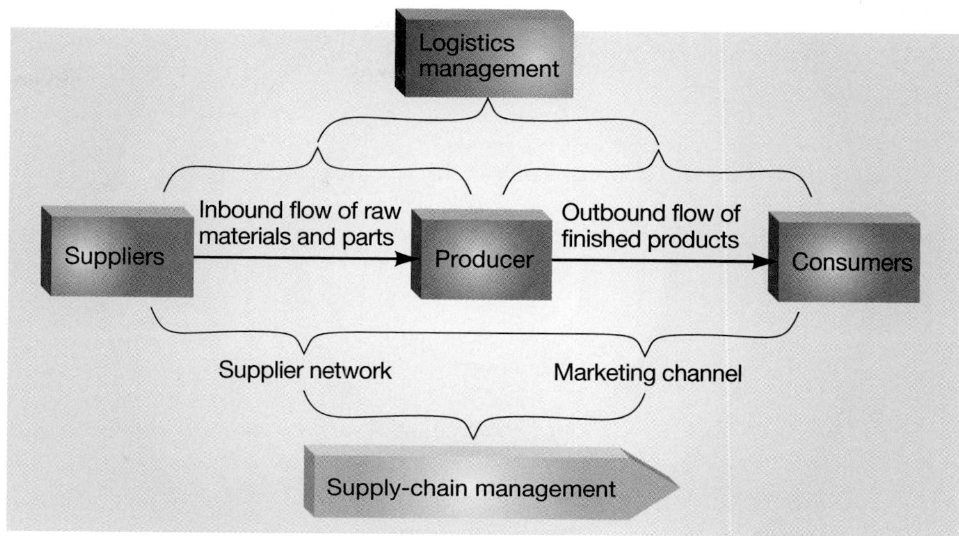

17–1. An important feature of supply chain management is its application of electronic commerce technology. Computers, bar coding, point-of-sale scanners, electronic data interchange (EDI), Extranets, and electronic funds transfer (EFT) allow companies to share and operate systems for order processing, transportation scheduling, and inventory management.

Sourcing, Assembling, and Delivering a New Car: The Automotive Supply Chain

All companies are members of one or more supply chains. A supply chain is essentially a sequence of linked suppliers and customers in which every customer is, in turn, a supplier to another customer until a finished product reaches the final consumer. Even a simplified supply chain diagram for Canadian car makers shown in Figure 17–2 illustrates how complex a supply chain can be.[6] A Canadian car maker's supplier network includes hundreds of firms. They provide items ranging from raw materials such as steel and rubber to components, including transmissions, tires, brakes, and seats, to complex subassemblies and assemblies evident in chassis and suspension systems that make for a smooth, stable ride. Coordinating and scheduling material and component flows for their assembly into actual automobiles by car makers is heavily dependent on logistical activities, including transportation, order processing, inventory control, materials handling, and information technology. A central link is the car maker's supply chain manager, who is responsible for translating customer requirements into actual orders and arranging for delivery dates and financial arrangements for automobile dealers. This is not an easy task given different consumer preferences and the amount consumers are willing to pay. To appreciate the challenge facing supply chain managers, visit the Saturn Web site described in the accompanying Web Link, and assemble your own car based on your preferences and price point.

Logistical aspects of the automobile marketing channel are also an integral part of the supply chain. Major responsibilities include transportation [which involves the selection and oversight of external carriers (trucking, airline, railway, and shipping companies) for cars and parts to dealers], the operation of distribution centres, the management of finished goods inventories, and order processing for sales. Supply chain managers also play an important role in the marketing channel. They work with extensive car dealer networks to ensure that the right mix of automobiles are delivered

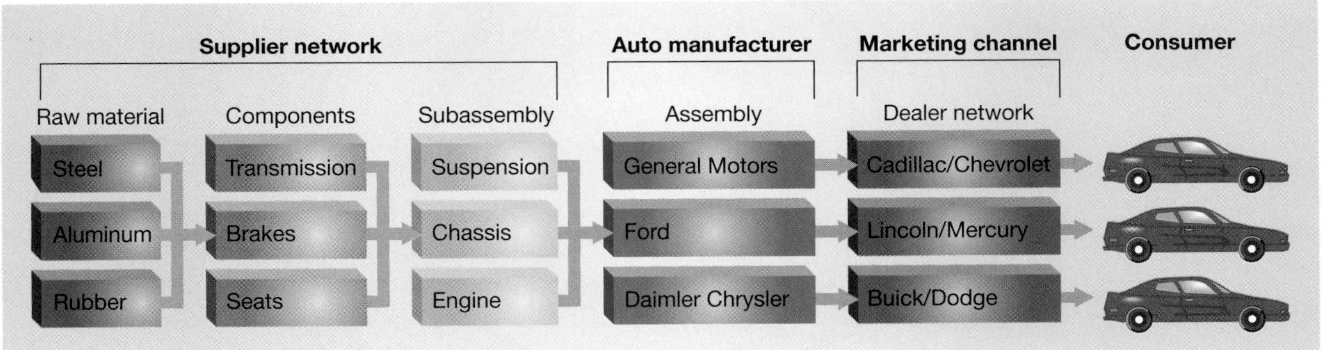

FIGURE 17–2
The automotive supply chain

to different locations. In addition, they make sure that spare and service parts are available so that dealers can meet the car maintenance and repair needs of consumers. All of this is done with the help of Internet and Extranet technology that links the entire automotive supply chain. What does all of this cost? It is estimated that logistics costs represent 25 percent to 30 percent of the retail price of a typical new car.

www.compaq.com

Supply Chain Management and Marketing Strategy

Recalling your own shopping experiences can show the critical relationship between marketing and supply chains. Consider your disappointment after travelling to a store—in response to an advertised sale—only to find that the items were out of stock or had been lost or damaged in transit. Imagine how a manufacturer such as Compaq Computer reacts upon learning that the product was not on the shelf, after spending huge sums on its extensive promotional campaign. The bottom line is that poor supply chain management practices can do serious damage to an otherwise excellent marketing strategy. To demonstrate the importance of supply chain management to marketing, consider how a supply chain impacts elements of the marketing mix—product factors, pricing factors, promotional factors, and place factors.

A supply chain manager's nightmare: how to get this dual-pack on a retailer's shelf while balancing logistics and marketing benefits and costs.

Product Factors The physical characteristics of the product, as well as its raw materials, will often dictate what kinds of transportation can be used, the length of time inventory can be accumulated, and whether markets can be served from one or many locations. One physical characteristic that has important implications is the perishability of the product, or its *shelf life.* For example, the distribution of fresh foods requires timely transportation and low inventories to minimize spoilage. Time-dated food materials must be kept fresh on the store shelves and not allowed to spoil in the warehouse. These products may require specialized transport and storage facilities, such as refrigerated vehicles. Other products have a very short time frame in which to retain their freshness, such as fresh cut flowers, fresh seafoods, or out-of-

WEB LINK Saturn: Have It Your Way

Supply chain managers are responsible for having the right products at the right place at the right time at the right price for customers. In the automotive industry, this task is complex given the variety of car options available. To appreciate the challenge, visit the Saturn Web site at www.saturn.com, click pricing centre, assemble your own Saturn, immediately obtain the manufacturer's suggested retail price (MSRP), and compare *your* assembled Saturn with a friend's Saturn.

This easy task for you represents a sizeable undertaking for a Saturn supply manager. You may not have realized it, but a Saturn comes in some 3000 versions, including the retailer-installed accessories you might want. A supply of these accessories must be available at the Saturn retailer for installation when you want to pick up your new car.

www.globeandmail.com

town newspapers. These require premium transportation, such as air freight, and, in some cases, they can only be distributed to a regional market. For example, newspapers such as *The Globe & Mail* are printed in a number of cities around the country for regional distribution the same day.

One of the most important links between a product's physical characteristics and logistics is the product package. On the one hand, the marketer views the package as an important point-of-purchase promotional device. On the other hand, there are many logistical implications associated with the packaging decision. Does the protective packaging reduce the density of the products so that less product can be loaded into the transport vehicle or warehouse? If so, logistics costs will increase. Does the product's package require it to be placed in an exterior package or carton? In this case, additional handling will be required at the retail level to prepare the product for sale. As described in the accompanying Ethics and Social Responsibility Alert, package features can make handling, stacking, filling, or disposing of the package more difficult, and once again logistics costs will increase.[7]

Pricing Factors Pricing interacts with a supply chain in several ways. As mentioned in the discussion of geographical pricing adjustments in Chapter 15, price quotations such as FOB origin assign responsibility for arranging and paying for transportation services to the buyer. Logistics costs are also important for determining quantity discounts. Transportation rate structures generally contain a quantity discount provided by the carrier such that lower rates are available for larger shipments.

Promotional Factors Promotion interacts with logistics in the areas of advertising, sales promotion, and personal selling. Advertising and promotional campaigns must be planned and coordinated with the logistics system to ensure product availability at the appropriate time. For example, General Motors learned that an eight-week wait was a big turn-off for some customers thinking about buying a Cadillac, 11 percent of whom then bought a car from a competitor rather than wait for delivery. Cadillac is

ETHICS AND SOCIAL RESPONSIBILITY ALERT

What Are the Social Costs of Packaging?

ETHICS

Some experts believe that the logistic systems of many firms depend too heavily on packaging. While efficient packaging materials allow a firm to use cheaper modes of transportation or less specialized warehouse services, these benefits are offset by costs imposed on society in general. Specifically, what should society do with the excessive packaging that comes with the product? In many cases, the packaging material is difficult to dispose of or is quickly filling landfills. Further, the focus on recycled products is a complicated issue and has its own costs and benefits. For example, Procter & Gamble has just introduced a plastic bottle for its Ultra Downy fabric softener that is made of 100 percent recycled plastic. However, because P&G will colour the bottle as part of its marketing program, the bottle will be difficult to recycle once it is used.

What are the benefits and costs to society of such packaging trends? What should communities do to counter the trend of overpackaging? What are the responsibilities of global citizens to counteract the trend of overpackaging?

testing the feasibility of customer responsiveness as a competitive differentiator with the objective of delivering popularly configured Cadillacs to customers immediately from dealers' lots, with overnight delivery if the vehicle isn't available on site. For those customers who desire a more custom configuration, Cadillac is taking their orders, assembling and delivering their exact Cadillacs within three weeks under the "Cadillac Custom Rapid Delivery" process.[8] So distribution can and must be synchronized to ensure timely and efficient handling of orders.

Place Factors It is the responsibility of logistics to get the product to the right place at the right time in usable conditions. Logistics also plays an important part in determining where a firm locates its plants and distribution centres relative to markets. Such decisions must consider transportation costs as well as the ability of the product to be transported long distances and be stored for long periods of time.

Effective logistics can also help gain access to key distribution outlets. In the Nike-Reebok "sneaker war," two critical market segments are teens and Generation X buyers, who are often willing to pay $80, $90, or more for a pair of shoes. These segments are core customers of the Foot Locker chain. Recently, Nike has been winning in Foot Locker sales because—among other things—Reebok needs to overhaul its information-tracking system and fix its distribution snags, which have resulted in limited customer exposure to its lines in Foot Locker outlets.[9]

CONCEPT CHECK

1. What is the principal difference between a marketing channel and a supply chain?
2. How does logistics interact with the product element of the marketing mix?

LOGISTICS MANAGEMENT OBJECTIVE IN A SUPPLY CHAIN

The objective of logistics management in a supply chain is to minimize relevant logistics costs while delivering maximum customer service. Realizing this objective often requires assistance from outside logistics specialists and consultants and highly specialized computer programming and software to track cost and service variables.

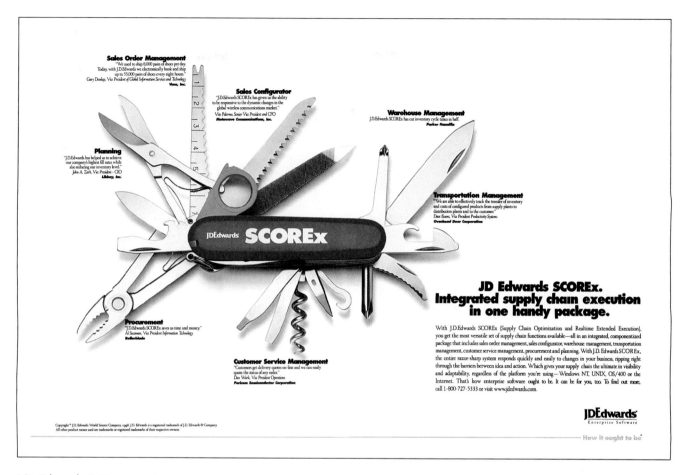

J.D. Edwards & Company is an internationally recognized supply chain management consulting firm.

www.jdedwards.com

This becomes apparent in the description of logistics costs and customer service that follows.

Total Logistics Cost Concept

For our purposes **total logistics cost** includes expenses associated with transportation, materials handling and warehousing, inventory, stockouts (being out of inventory), and order processing. A more complete list of decisions that are associated with the flow of product and make up total logistics cost includes the following: [10]

- Transportation.
- Warehousing and storage.
- Packaging.
- Materials handling.
- Inventory control.
- Order processing.
- Customer service level.
- Plant and warehouse site location.
- Return goods handling.

Note that many of these costs are interrelated so that changes in one will impact the others. For example, as the firm attempts to minimize its transportation costs by shipping in larger quantities, it will also experience an increase in inventory levels. Larger inventory levels will not only increase inventory costs but should also reduce stockouts. It is important, therefore, to study the impact on all of the logistics decision areas when considering a change.

FIGURE 17–3
How total logistics cost varies with number of warehouses used

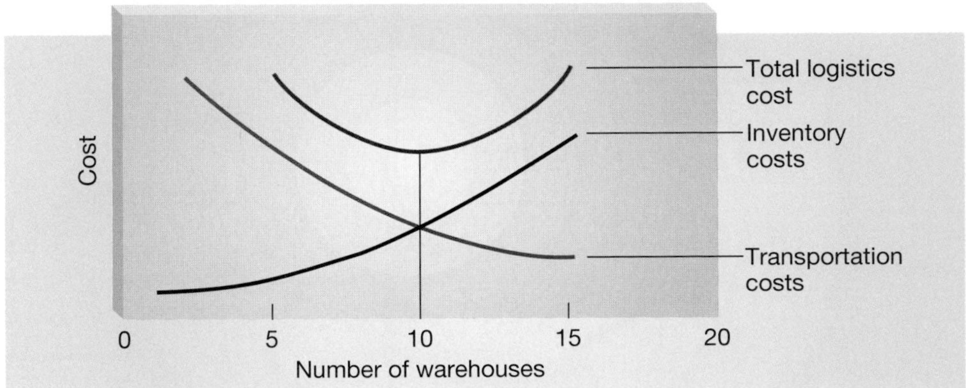

Figure 17–3 provides a graphic example. An oft-used supply chain strategy is for a firm to have a number of warehouses, which receive shipments in large quantities and then redistribute smaller shipments to local customers. As the number of warehouses increases, inventory costs rise and transportation costs fall. That is, more inventory is warehoused, but it is transported in volume closer to customers. The net effect is to minimize the total costs of logistics shown in Figure 17–3 by having 10 warehouses. This means the total cost curve is minimized at a point where neither of the two individual cost elements is at a minimum but the overall system is.

Studying its total logistics cost has had revolutionary consequences for National Semiconductor, which produces computer chips. In two years it cut its standard delivery time 47 percent, reduced distribution costs 2.5 percent, and increased sales 34 percent by shutting down six warehouses around the world and air-freighting its microchips from its huge distribution centre in Singapore. It does this even though it has six factories around the world. National also discovered that a lot of its chips were actually profit-losers, and it cut the number of products it sells by 45 percent, thereby simplifying logistics and increasing profits.[11]

Customer Service Concept

If a supply chain is a *flow,* the end of it—or *output*—is the service delivered to customers. However, service can be expensive. One firm found that to increase on-time delivery from a 95 percent rate to a 100 percent rate tripled total logistics costs. Higher levels of service require tactics such as more inventory to reduce stockouts, more expensive transportation to improve speed and lessen damage, and double or triple checking of orders to ensure correctness. A firm's goal should be to provide adequate customer service while controlling logistics costs. Customer service is now seen not merely as an expense but as a means to increase customer satisfaction and sales. For example, a 3M survey about customer service among 18 000 European customers in 16 countries revealed surprising agreement in all countries about the importance of customer service. Respondents stressed factors such as condition of product delivered, on-time delivery, quick delivery after order placement, and effective handling of problems.[12]

Within the context of a supply chain, **customer service** is the ability of logistics management to satisfy users in terms of time, dependability, communication, and convenience.[13] As suggested by Figure 17–4, a supply chain manager's key task is to balance these four customer service factors against total logistics cost factors.

Time In a supply chain setting, time refers to **lead time** for an item, which means the lag from ordering an item until it is received and ready for use or sale. This is also referred to as *order cycle time* or *replenishment time* and may be more important to

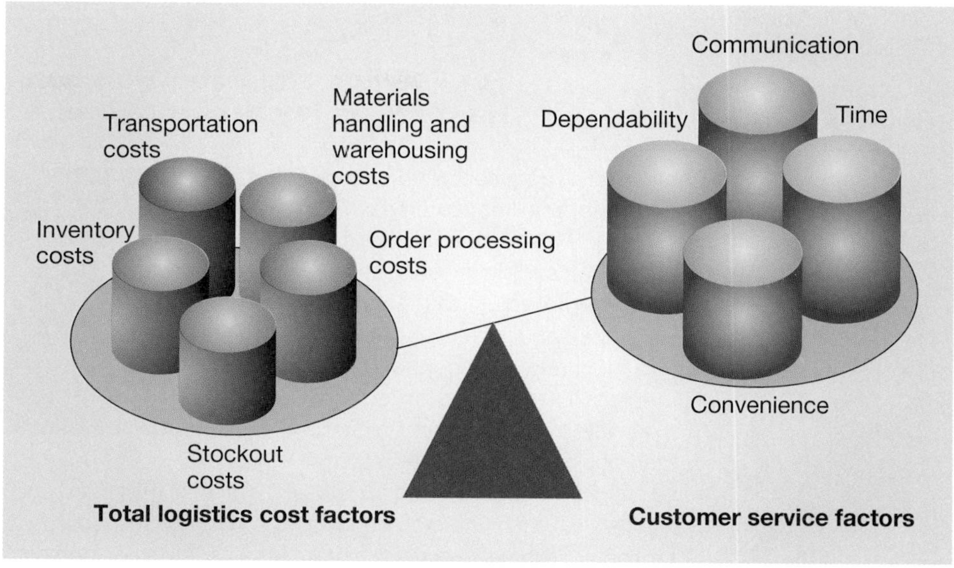

FIGURE 17–4
Logistics managers balance total logistics cost factors against customer service factors

retailers or wholesalers than consumers. The various elements that make up the typical order cycle include recognition of the need to order, order transmittal, order processing, documentation, and transportation. A current emphasis in supply chain management is to reduce lead time so that the inventory levels of customers may be minimized. Another emphasis is to make the process of reordering and receiving products as simple as possible, often through electronic data and inventory systems called **quick response** and **efficient consumer response** delivery systems.[14] These inventory management systems are designed to reduce the retailer's lead time for receiving merchandise, thereby lowering a retailer's inventory investment, improving customer service levels, and reducing logistics expense (see the accompanying Marketing NewsNet).[15] The order processing portion of lead time will be discussed later in this chapter.

Dependability Dependability is the consistency of replenishment. This is important to all firms in a supply chain and to consumers. It can be broken into three elements: consistent lead time, safe delivery, and complete delivery. Consistent service allows planning (such as appropriate inventory levels), whereas inconsistencies create surprises. Intermediaries may be willing to accept longer lead times if they know about them in advance and can thus make plans. While surprise delays may shut down a production line, early deliveries will be almost as troublesome because of the problems of storing the extra inventory. Dependability is essential for the just-in-time strategies discussed at the end of the chapter.

Communication Communication is a two-way link between buyer and seller that helps in monitoring service and anticipating future needs. Status reports on orders are a typical example of improved communication between buyer and seller. The increased communication capability of transportation carriers has enhanced the accuracy of such tracing information and improved the ability of buyers to schedule shipments. Note, however, that such information is still reactive and is not a substitute for consistent on-time deliveries. Therefore, some firms have partnered with firms specializing in logistics in an effort to institutionalize a more proactive flow of useful information that, in turn, improves on-time deliveries. Hewlett-Packard (HP), a high-tech computer printer manufacturer, recently turned its inbound raw materials over to a logistics firm. HP lets this firm manage the warehousing and coordinate parts delivery so that HP can focus on its printer business. In the process, HP estimates it has cut its warehouse operating costs by about 10 percent.[16]

www.hewlett-packard.com

TECHNOLOGY

MARKETING NEWSNET

For Fashion and Food Merchandising, Haste Is as Important as Taste

Fashion and food have a lot in common. Both depend a lot on taste and both require timely merchandising. By its nature, fashion dictates that suppliers and retailers be able to adjust to new styles, colours, and different seasons. Fashion retailers need to identify what's hot so it can be ordered quickly and what's not to avoid markdowns. Many fashion retailers have employed *quick response* delivery systems for fashion merchandise since the mid-1990s. They use point-of-sale scanner systems to record each day's sales. When stock falls below a minimum level, the system automatically generates a replenishment order. Vendors of fashion merchandise, such as Donna Karan, receive an electronic order, which is processed within 48 hours.

Food marketers and retailers use the term *efficient consumer response* to describe their replenishment systems. All major food companies, including General Mills, Del Monte, Heinz, Nestlé, and Kraft Canada, rely on EDI technology to minimize stockouts of popular items and overstocks of slow-moving items. Lowered retailer inventories and efficient logistics practices save Canadian grocery shoppers money on the food they purchase.

Convenience The concept of convenience for a supply chain manager means that there should be a minimum of effort on the part of the buyer in doing business with the seller. Is it easy for the customer to order? Are the products available from many outlets? Does the buyer have to buy huge quantities of the product? Will the seller arrange all necessary details, such as transportation? The seller must concentrate on removing unnecessary barriers to customer convenience. This customer service factor has promoted the use of vendor-managed inventory practices discussed later in the chapter.

Customer Service Standards

Firms that operate effective supply chains usually develop a set of written customer service standards. These serve as objectives and provide a benchmark against which results can be measured for control purposes. In developing these standards, information is collected on customers' needs. It is also necessary to know what competitors offer as well as the willingness of customers to pay a bit more for better service. After these and similar questions are answered, realistic standards are set and an ongoing monitoring program is established. Note that the examples in Figure 17–5 suggest that customer service standards will differ by type of firm.

FIGURE 17–5
Examples of customer service standards

TYPE OF FIRM	CUSTOMER SERVICE STANDARD
Wholesaler	At least 98% of orders filled accurately
Manufacturer	Order cycle time of no more than 5 days
Retailer	Returns accepted within 30 days
Airline	At least 90% of arrivals on time
Trucker	A maximum of 5% loss and damage per year
Restaurant	Lunch served within 5 minutes of order

CONCEPT CHECK

1. What is a current strategy adopted by firms attempting to squeeze costs from their logistics system while delivering customer service?
2. In what ways do key customer service factors differ between a manufacturer and a retailer?
3. What is the relationship between transportation costs and volume shipped? What impact does it have on the pricing of the firm?

KEY LOGISTICS FUNCTIONS IN A SUPPLY CHAIN

The four key logistic functions in a supply chain include (1) transportation, (2) warehousing and materials handling, (3) order processing, and (4) inventory management. These functions have become so complex and interrelated that many companies have outsourced them to third-party logistics providers. **Third-party logistics providers** are firms that perform most or all of the logistics functions that manufacturers, suppliers, and distributors would normally perform themselves.[17] Today, many of Canada's top manufacturers outsource one or more logistics functions, at least on a limited basis. UPS Worldwide Logistics and FedEx are just two of the companies that specialize in handling logistics functions for their clients. For example, UPS Worldwide Logistics manages the distribution of Allied Signal's FRAM, Bendix, and Autolite products made in North America to 10 000 customers across the continent. Roadway Logistics Services handles the inbound and outbound shipments of Dell computers. The four major logistics functions and the involvement of third-party logistics providers are described in detail next.

www.fedex.com

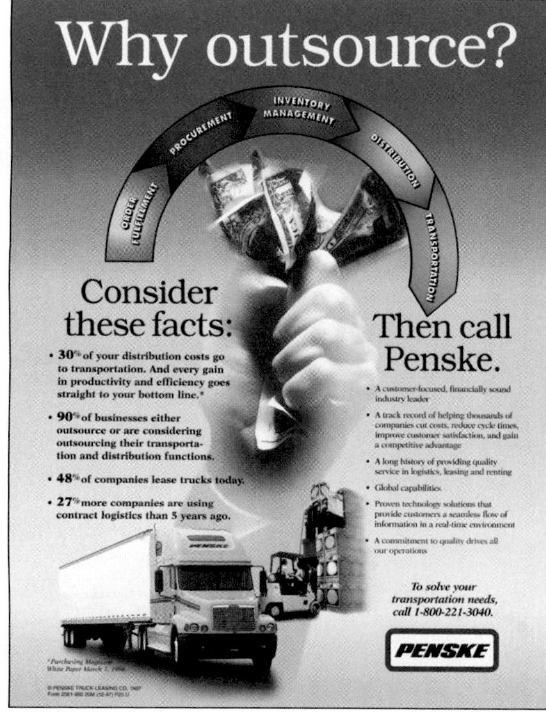

Transportation

Transportation provides the movement of goods necessary in a supply chain. There are five basic modes of transportation: railways, motor carriers, air carriers, pipelines, and water carriers, and modal combinations involving two or more modes, such as highway trailers on a rail flatcar.

All transportation modes can be evaluated on six basic service criteria:

- *Cost.* Charges for transportation.
- *Time.* Speed of transit.
- *Capability.* What can be realistically carried with this mode.
- *Dependability.* Reliability of service regarding time, loss, and damage.
- *Accessibility.* Convenience of the mode's routes (such as pipeline availability).
- *Frequency.* Scheduling.

Figure 17–6 summarizes service advantages and disadvantages of five of the modes of transportation available.

Railways Railways carry heavy, bulky items over long distances. Of the commodities tracked by the rail industry, coal, farm products, chemicals, and nonmetallic minerals represent the bulk of the total tonnage. Railways have the ability to carry larger shipments than trucks (in terms of total weight per vehicle), but their routes are less extensive. Service innovations include unit trains and intermodal service. A *unit train* is dedicated to one commodity (often coal), using permanently coupled cars that run a continuous loop from a single origin to a single destination and back. Even though the train returns empty, the process captures enough operating efficiencies to make it one of the lowest-cost transportation alternatives available. Unit trains are held to a specific schedule so that the customers can plan on reliable delivery and usually carry products that can be loaded and unloaded quickly and automatically.

Railways have been able to apply the unit train concept to **intermodal transportation,** which involves combining different transportation modes to get the best features of each. The result is a service that attracts high-valued freight, which would normally go by truck. The most popular combination is truck-rail, also referred to as *piggyback* or *trailer on flatcar (TOFC).* The other popular use of an intermodal combi-

FIGURE 17–6
Advantages and disadvantages of five modes of transportation

MODE	RELATIVE ADVANTAGES	RELATIVE DISADVANTAGES
Rail	Full capability Extensive routes Low cost	Some reliability, damage problems Not always complete pickup and delivery Sometimes slow
Truck	Complete pickup and delivery Extensive routes Fairly fast	Size and weight restrictions Higher cost More weather sensitive
Air	Fast Low damage Frequent departures	High cost Limited capabilities
Pipeline	Low cost Very reliable	Limited routes (accessibility) Slow
Water	Low cost Huge capacities	Slow Limited routes and schedules More weather sensitive

Export/import shippers such as Maersk Line use containers to move a wide variety of products, including perishable ones.

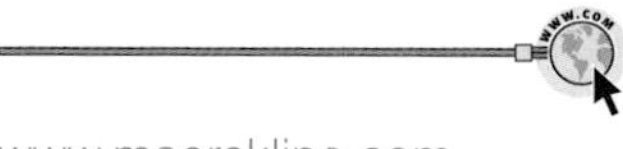

www.maerskline.com

nation is associated with export/import traffic and uses containers in place of trailers. These containers can be loaded on ships, trains, and truck trailers, so in terms of the on-land segment of international shipments, a container is handled the same way as a trailer. Containers are used in international trade because they take up less space on ocean-going vessels.

Motor Carriers In contrast to the railway industry, the for-hire motor carrier industry is composed of many small firms, including many independent truckers and firms that own their own trucks for transporting their own products.

The greatest advantage of motor carriers is the complete door-to-door service. Trucks can go almost anywhere there is a road, and with the design of specialized equipment they can carry most commodities. Their physical limitations are size and weight restrictions enforced by the states. Trucks have the reputation for maintaining a better record than rail for loss and damage and providing faster, more reliable service, especially for shorter distances. As a result, trucks carry higher-valued goods that are time-sensitive and expensive to carry in inventory. The trade-off is that truck rates are substantially higher than rail rates.

Air Carriers and Express Companies Air freight is costly, but its speed may create savings in lower inventory. The items that can be carried are limited by space constraints and are usually valuable, time-sensitive, and lightweight, such as perishable flowers, clothing, and electronic parts. Products moved in containers are especially amenable to this mode of shipment. Specialized firms provide ground support in terms of collecting shipments and delivering them to the air terminal. When air freight is handled by the major airlines—such as Air Canada and Canadian Airlines—it is often carried as cargo in the luggage space of scheduled passenger flights. This strategy allows the airline to utilize excess capacity that would otherwise be lost.

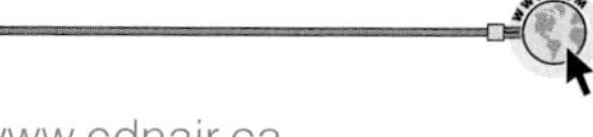

www.cdnair.ca

Canadian AirCargo provides fast, global delivery.

Freight Forwarders **Freight forwarders,** already mentioned a number of times, are firms that accumulate small shipments into larger lots and then hire a carrier to move them, usually at reduced rates. Recall that transportation companies provide rate incentives for larger quantities. Forwarders collect many small shipments consigned to a common destination and pay the carrier the lower rate based on larger volume, so they often convert shipments that are less-than-truckload (LTL) into full truckloads, thereby receiving better shipping rates. The rates charged by the forwarder to the individual shippers, in turn, are somewhat less than the small quantity rate, and the difference is the forwarder's margin. In general, the shipment receives improved service at lower cost. While forwarders may specialize in a particular mode—such as air freight—they are available for all modes of transportation. International freight forwarders play an equally important role in the export/import trades.

Air freight forwarders are an example of specialization in one transportation mode. In some cases, airlines will subcontract excess space to *air freight forwarders* or *express companies,* which are firms that market air express services to the general public. Where markets are large enough, major airlines have responded with pure air freight service between specific airports—often involving international destinations.

Warehousing and Materials Handling

Warehouses may be classified in one of two ways: (1) storage warehouses and (2) distribution centres. In *storage warehouses* the goods are intended to come to rest for some period of time, as in the aging of products or in storing household goods. *Distribution centres,* on the other hand, are designed to facilitate the timely movement of goods and represent a very important part of a supply chain. They represent the second most significant cost in a supply chain after transportation.

Distribution centres not only allow firms to hold their stock in decentralized locations but are also used to facilitate sorting and consolidating products from different plants or different suppliers. Some physical transformation can also take place in distribution centres such as mixing or blending different ingredients, labelling, and repackaging. Paint companies such as Sherwin-Williams and Benjamin Moore use distribution centres for this purpose. In addition, distribution centres may serve as manufacture sales offices, described in Chapter 16, and order processing centres.

Materials handling, which involves moving goods over short distances into, within, and out of warehouses and manufacturing plants, is a key part of warehouse operations. The two major problems with this activity are high labour costs and high rates of loss and damage. Every time an item is handled, there is a chance for loss or damage. Common materials handling equipment includes forklifts, cranes, and conveyors. Recently, materials handling in warehouses has been automated by using computers and robots to reduce the cost of holding, moving, and recording the inventories of stores.

Order Processing

There are several stages in the processing of an order, and a failure at any one of them can cause a problem with the customer. The process starts with transmitting the order by a variety of means such as the Internet, an Extranet, or electronic data interchange (EDI). This is followed by entering the order in the appropriate databases and sending the information to those needing it. For example, a regional warehouse is notified to prepare an order. After checking inventory, a new quantity may need to be reordered from the production line, or purchasing may be requested to reorder from a vendor. If the item is currently out of stock, a "backorder" is created, and the whole process of keeping track of a small part of the original order must be managed. In addition, credit may have to be checked for some customers, all documentation associated with the order must be prepared, transportation must be arranged, and a confirmation of the order must be sent. Order processing systems are generally evaluated in terms of speed and accuracy.

Electronic order processing has replaced manual processing for most large companies.[18] For example, IBM expects to be doing business electronically with all of its suppliers, either on the Internet or through EDI by 2000. Kiwi Brands, the marketer of

Materials handling through automation.

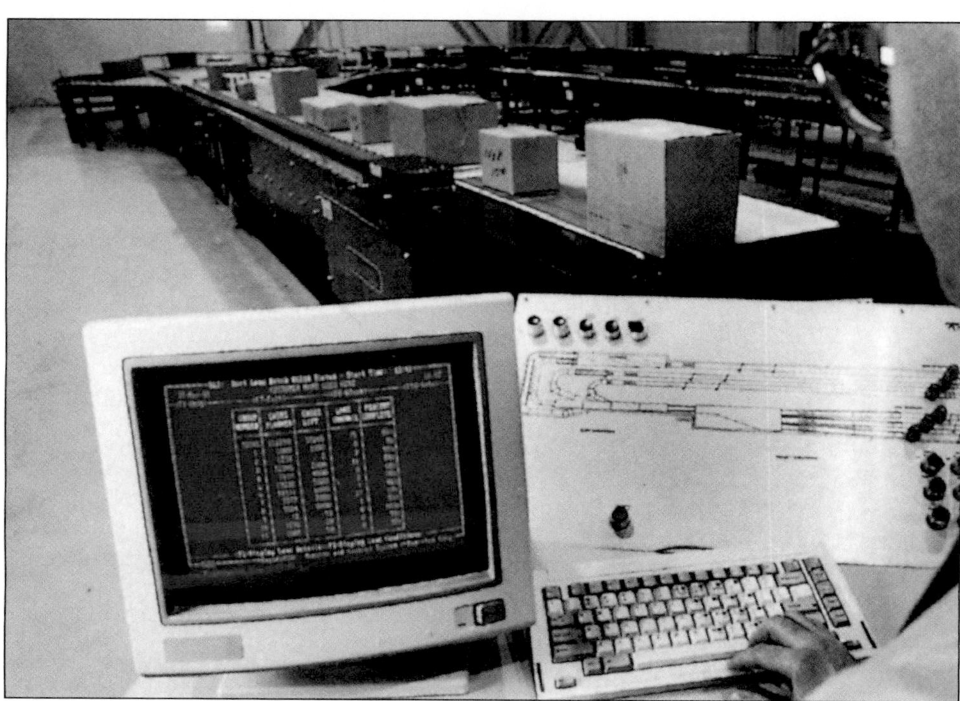

Kiwi shoe polish, Endust, and Behold, receives 75 percent of its retailers' purchase orders via EDI. The company has also implemented financial EDI, sending invoices to retailers and receiving payment order/remittance advice documents and electronic funds transfer (EFT) payments. Shippers are also linked to the system, allowing Kiwi to receive shipment status messages electronically.

Inventory Management

Inventory management is one of the primary responsibilities of the supply chain manager. The major problem is maintaining the delicate balance between too little and too much. Too little inventory may result in poor service, stockouts, brand switching, and loss of market share; too much leads to higher costs because of the money tied up in inventory and the chance that it may become obsolete. Remember the sting of the bullwhip described at the beginning of the chapter?

Creative inventory management practices can make possible cost savings in the supply chain. For example, IBM has begun closing many of its parts warehouses because Federal Express' reliable overnight delivery (see the Marketing NewsNet box) enables FedEx to inventory high-priced IBM parts at its sorting hubs and deliver them quickly to IBM customers.[19]

Reasons for Inventory Traditionally, carrying inventory has been justified on several grounds: (1) to offer a buffer against variations in supply and demand, often caused by uncertainty in forecasting demand; (2) to provide better service for those customers who wish to be served on demand; (3) to promote production efficiencies; (4) to provide a hedge against price increases by suppliers; (5) to promote purchasing and transportation discounts; and (6) to protect the firm from contingencies such as strikes and shortages.

Inventory Costs Specific inventory costs are often hard to detect because they are difficult to measure and occur in many different parts of the firm. A classification of inventory costs includes the following:

- *Capital costs.* The opportunity costs resulting from tying up funds in inventory instead of using them in other, more profitable investments; these are related to interest rates.
- *Inventory service costs.* Items such as insurance and taxes that are present in many provinces.
- *Storage costs.* Warehousing space and materials handling.
- *Risk costs.* Possible loss, damage, pilferage, perishability, and obsolescence.

Storage costs, risk costs, and some service costs vary according to the characteristics of the item inventoried. For example, perishable products or highly seasonal items have higher risk costs than a commodity-type product such as lumber. Capital costs are always present and are proportional to the *values* of the item and prevailing interest rates. The costs of carrying inventory vary with the particular circumstances but quite easily could range from 10 to 35 percent for different firms.

Supply Chain Inventory Strategies Conventional wisdom a decade ago was that a firm should protect itself against uncertainty by maintaining a reserve inventory at each of its production and stocking points. This has been described as a "just-in-case" philosophy of inventory management and led to unnecessary high levels of inventory. In contrast is the **just-in-time (JIT) concept,** which is an inventory supply system that operates with very low inventories and requires fast, on-time delivery. When parts are needed for production, they arrive from suppliers "just in time," which means neither before nor after they are needed. Note that JIT is used in

GLOBAL

MARKETING NEWSNET

Fly-by-Night Idea + Customer Service + KISS = Federal Express

Armed with one of his college term papers, which got a C– grade, Frederick W. Smith didn't build a better mousetrap and wait for the world to beat a path to his door. Instead, he set out to show the world that with his simple new innovation *he* could beat a path to everybody else's door.

He gave the name *Federal Express* to his door-to-door parcel service that uses orange, white, and purple jets. And he advertised "absolutely, positively overnight" delivery for his small-parcel service—limited to 30 kilograms, the weight one person can carry. "I figured we had to be enormously reliable," says Smith, "since our service is frequently used for expensive spare parts, live organs, or other emergency shipments."

But Federal Express (FedEx) isn't your typical "fly-by-night" outfit. After all, Smith *did* write his term paper at Yale, and he *did* use a family trust of $4 million to get started—and Federal Express *did* lose $27 million in its first 26 months of operation.

What Smith had was a good idea, a good understanding of customer service, and the tenacity and resources to stick with it. First, Smith reasoned, he had to own his own jet aircraft so *all* parcels could be picked

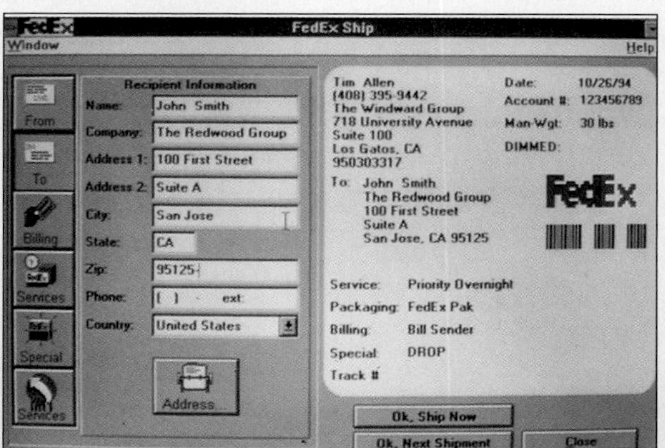

up early in the evening, flown to a single sorting centre (Memphis), and rerouted to their final destination before dawn. The KISS (keep it simple, stupid) concept worked to the company's advantage in the early years. Always looking for a better idea, FedEx introduced "FedEx Ship"—a shipping software solution in both Mac and Windows™ versions that lets any customer order pickups, print their shipping labels, and track their express deliveries without touching a telephone. Of course, FedEx benefits, too, by cutting telephone traffic and package pickup costs, and also eliminating paperwork errors that might impact sorting.

situations where demand forecasting is reliable, such as when supplying an automobile production line, and is not suitable for inventories that are to be stored over significant periods of time.

Saturn uses a sophisticated JIT system. A central computerized system directs trucks to deliver pre-inspected parts at specific times 21 hours a day, six days a week to one of the plant's 56 receiving docks. Incredibly, the JIT system must coordinate Saturn's suppliers, many of whom are located hundreds of kilometres from the Saturn facility. Does the JIT system work for Saturn? The answer is a resounding yes. The Saturn production line has been shut down only once—for 18 minutes!—because the right part was not delivered at the right place and time.

Ryder Integrated Logistics is charged with making Saturn's JIT system work smoothly. Ryder long-haul trucks and their drivers are the most expensive part of the system. The key—very literally—to this JIT system is a computer disk in the form of a plastic key that drivers plug into an on-truck computer. The computer screen then tells the driver where to go, the route to use, and how much time to spend getting there.[20]

Electronic data interchange and electronic messaging technology coupled with the constant pressure for faster response time in replenishing inventory have also changed the way suppliers and customers do business in a supply chain. The approach, called

The key to Saturn's JIT system: a Ryder truck driver downloads a key-shaped floppy disk from an on-board computer to get delivery instructions.

Ryder System, Inc.
www.ryder.com

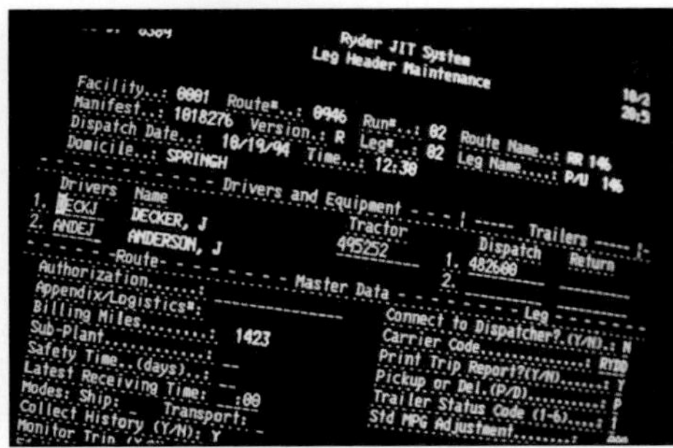

vendor-managed inventory (VMI), is an inventory-management system whereby the *supplier* determines the product amount and assortment a customer (such as a retailer) needs and automatically delivers the appropriate items.[21]

Campbell Soup's system illustrates how VMI works.[22] Campbell first establishes EDI links with retailers. Every morning, retailers electronically inform the company of their demand for all Campbell products and the inventory levels in their distribution centres. Campbell uses that information to forecast future demand and determine which products need replenishment based on upper and lower inventory limits previously established with each retailer. Trucks leave the Campbell shipping plant that afternoon and arrive at the retailer's distribution centres with the required replenishments the same day.

Closing the Loop: Reverse Logistics

The flow of goods in a supply chain does not end with the consumer or industrial user. Companies today recognize that a supply chain can work in reverse.[23] **Reverse logistics** is a process of reclaiming recyclable and reusable materials, returns, and reworks from the point of consumption or use for repair, remanufacturing, or disposal. The effect of reverse logistics can be seen in the reduced amount of waste in landfills and lowered operating costs for companies.

Companies such as Eastman Kodak (reusable cameras) and Hewlett-Packard (printer toner cartridges returned for filling) have implemented successful reverse logistics programs. Other firms have enlisted third-party logistics providers to handle this process along with other supply chain functions. GNB Technologies, Inc., a manufacturer of lead-acid batteries for automobiles and boats, has outsourced much of its supply chain activity to UPS Worldwide Logistics (WWL).[24] The company contracts with WWL to manage its shipments between plants, distribution centres, recycling centres, and retailers. This includes movement of both new batteries and used products destined for recycling and covers both truck and railway shipments. This partnership along with the initiatives of other battery makers has paid economic and ecological dividends. By recycling 90 percent of the lead from used batteries, manufacturers have kept the demand for new lead in check, thereby holding down costs to consumers. Also, solid waste management costs and the environmental impact of lead in landfills is reduced.

CONCEPT CHECK

1. What are the basic trade-offs between the modes of transportation?
2. What types of inventory should use storage warehouses and which type should use distribution centres?
3. What are the strengths and weaknesses of a just-in-time system?

SUMMARY

1 Logistics involves those activities that focus on getting the right amount of the right products to the right place at the right time at the lowest possible cost. Logistics management includes the coordination of the flows of both inbound and outbound goods, an emphasis on making these flows cost-effective, and customer service.

2 A supply chain is a sequence of firms that perform activities required to create and deliver a good or service to consumers or industrial users. Supply chain management is the integration and organization of information and logistics across firms for the purpose of creating value for consumers.

3 Although some marketers may pay little attention to logistics, they do so at their own peril. Logistics directly affects the success of the marketing program and all elements of the marketing mix.

4 The total logistics cost concept suggests that a system of interrelated costs is present such as transportation, materials handling and warehousing, inventory, and stockout costs.

5 Minimizing total logistics cost is irrelevant without specifying an acceptable customer service level that must be maintained. Although key customer service factors depend on the situation, important elements of the customer service program are likely to be time-related dependability, communications, and convenience.

6 Four key logistics in a supply chain include (*a*) transportation, (*b*) warehousing and material handling, (*c*) order processing, and (*d*) inventory management. Third-party logistics perform most or all of the logistics functions that manufacturers, suppliers, and distributors would normally perform themselves.

7 The modes of transportation (e.g., railways, motor carriers, air carriers, and trucks) offer shippers different service benefits. Better service often costs more, although it should result in savings in other areas of the logistics system.

8 The function of warehousing and material handling in a supply chain is to facilitate storage and movement of goods. Distribution centres provide flexibility and facilitate sorting and consolidating products from different plants or different suppliers.

9 Inventory management and order processing go hand in hand in a supply chain. Both functions have benefited from the technology of electronic commerce. Two popular supply chain inventory management practices are just-in-time and vendor-managed inventory management systems.

10 Reverse logistics closes the loop in a supply chain. Reverse logistics is the process of reclaiming recyclable and reusable materials, returns, and reworks from the point of consumption or use for repair, remanufacturing, or disposal.

KEY TERMS AND CONCEPTS

logistics p. 436
logistics management p. 436
supply chain p. 436
supply chain management p. 436
total logistics cost p. 441
customer service p. 442
lead time p. 442
quick response p. 443
efficient consumer response p. 443
third-party logistics providers p. 445
intermodal transportation p. 446
freight forwarders p. 448
materials handling p. 449
just-in-time (JIT) concept p. 450
vendor-managed inventory p. 452
reverse logistics p. 452

INTERNET EXERCISE

Third-party logistics providers play an important role in supply chain management. Their numbers continue to increase as marketers look to their expertise and experience in implementing key logistics functions.

The Virtual Logistics Directory (www.logisticdirectory.com) lists many third-party logistics providers and supply chain management consulting firms. Visit the Directory and select the Integrated Logistics category. Go through the listing with an eye toward answering the following two questions:

1 Which of the four key logistics functions described in the chapter are provided most often and second most often by companies listed in the Directory?

2 What percentage of the listed companies offers services outside North America?

APPLYING MARKETING CONCEPTS AND PERSPECTIVES

1 List several companies to which logistical activities might be unimportant. Also list several whose focus is only on the inbound or outbound side.
2 Give an example of how logistical activities might affect trade promotion strategies.
3 What are some types of businesses in which order processing may be among the paramount success factors?
4 What behavioural problems might arise to negate the logistics concept within the firm?
5 List the customer service factors that would be vital to buyers in the following types of companies: (*a*) manufacturing, (*b*) retailing, (*c*) hospitals, and (*d*) construction.
6 Name some cases when extremely high service levels (e.g., 99 percent) would be warranted.
7 Name the mode of transportation that would be the best for the following products: (*a*) farm machinery, (*b*) cut flowers, (*c*) frozen meat, and (*d*) coal.
8 The auto industry is a heavy user of the just-in-time concept. Why? What other industries would be good candidates for its application? What do they have in common?
9 Look again at Figure 17–3. Explain why as the number of warehouses increases, (*a*) inventory costs rise and (*b*) transportation costs fall.

CASE 17–1 NAVISTAR INTERNATIONAL

How important is supply chain and logistics management in today's business environment? Just ask managers at the Navistar International Corporation (www.navistar.com), which produces up to 400 customized trucks each day!

THE COMPANY

Navistar International is one of the largest manufacturers of medium and heavy trucks in the world. Much of its success can be attributed to the sophisticated use of micromarketing actions that deliver a customized truck equipped with features designed to improve the productivity of each specific customer. This strategy, however, created a problem—a huge inventory of parts. Tailoring a truck to the unique needs of each buyer requires that Navistar keep 80 000 parts, some of which are needed by only one or just a few customers.

Navistar's success is also the result of superior product quality. The manufacturing department focuses much of its effort on ensuring that there are few defects in Navistar trucks. This attention to quality, however, slowed the manufacturing process so that Navistar's order cycle time reached 100 days. In fact, one measure of manufacturing efficiency, the percentage of trucks delivered to the customer on time, indicated that 40 percent of Navistar's deliveries were late.

Managers at Navistar realized that to satisfy customer requirements they needed to reduce order cycle time and inventory costs while maintaining high-quality customized products. Logistics management approaches, which balance the needs of the sales, engineering, and manufacturing departments, were an obvious potential solution.

LOGISTICS MANAGEMENT AT NAVISTAR

In response to these issues, Navistar developed an elaborate material requirement planning (MRP) system to manage the purchase of parts and components from its many suppliers. Navistar also developed an electronic data interchange (EDI) with its major suppliers that allowed specifications, quotes, purchase orders, invoices, and even payments to be made electronically. The system was responsible for the elimination of millions of pieces of paper and the errors and inefficiencies caused by the manual processing of thousands of orders. Finally, a just-in-time system (JIT) was added to match deliveries of supplies with its manufacturing requirements.

These systems have helped Navistar begin to integrate the many complex tasks of producing custom-built trucks. In addition, the systems have helped dealers to improve their customer service. Dealers can now submit their orders electronically and receive information about the lead time of the specified components and the probable delivery date of the completed truck. In the future, as Navistar continues to improve its systems, current status of orders, delivery schedule adjustments, and other important information should be available to dealers.

Navistar has set challenging goals for its logistics management systems. First, it hopes to achieve 100 percent on-time delivery ("slot credibility"). Second, managers hope that Navistar can reduce its order cycle time to 30 from 45 days. Finally, the company is determined to minimize inventory. Overall, Navistar believes these changes will represent increased value for its customers and allow Navistar to maintain its dominant position in the truck market.

Questions

1 What factors helped Navistar managers realize that logistics management approaches might help them better satisfy customer requirements?

2 What systems did Navistar develop to improve its production process? How can Navistar measure their impact?

3 Explain how the new systems have improved Navistar's customer service.

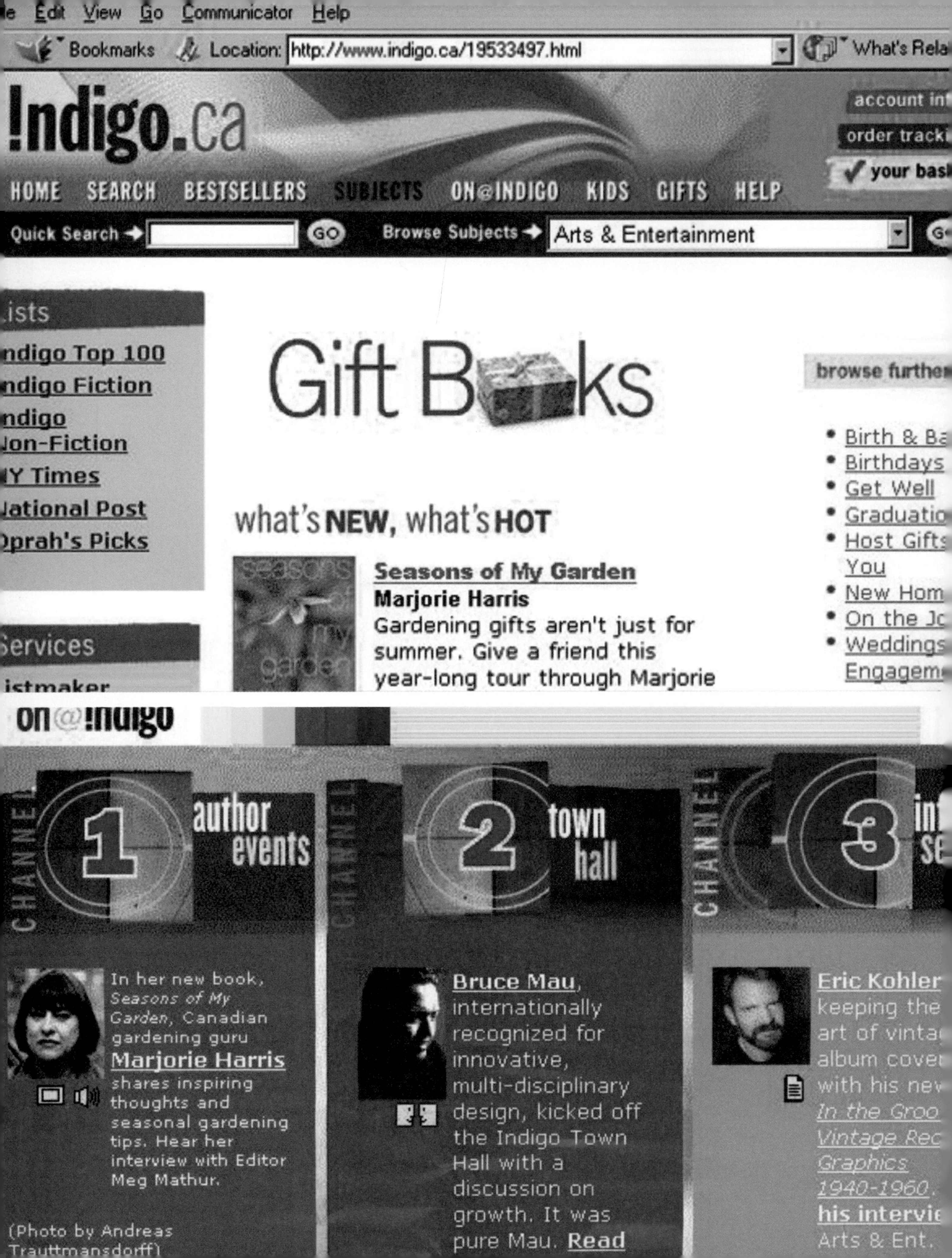

le Edit View Go Communicator Help
Bookmarks Location: http://www.indigo.ca/19533497.html
What's Rela
Indigo.ca
account in
order track
your bas
HOME SEARCH BESTSELLERS SUBJECTS ON@INDIGO KIDS GIFTS HELP
Quick Search GO Browse Subjects Arts & Entertainment
Lists
Indigo Top 100
Indigo Fiction
Indigo Non-Fiction
NY Times
National Post
Oprah's Picks
Services
Gift Books
browse further
Birth & Ba
Birthdays
Get Well
Graduatio
Host Gifts
You
New Hom
On the Jo
Weddings
Engagem
what's NEW, what's HOT
Seasons of My Garden
Marjorie Harris
Gardening gifts aren't just for summer. Give a friend this year-long tour through Marjorie
on@indigo
CHANNEL 1 author events
CHANNEL 2 town hall
CHANNEL 3
In her new book, Seasons of My Garden, Canadian gardening guru Marjorie Harris shares inspiring thoughts and seasonal gardening tips. Hear her interview with Editor Meg Mathur.
(Photo by Andreas Trauttmansdorff)
Bruce Mau, internationally recognized for innovative, multi-disciplinary design, kicked off the Indigo Town Hall with a discussion on growth. It was pure Mau. Read
Eric Kohler keeping the art of vinta album cove with his ne In the Groo Vintage Rec Graphics 1940-1960. his intervie Arts & Ent.

CHAPTER EIGHTEEN

RETAILING

18

AFTER READING THIS CHAPTER YOU SHOULD BE ABLE TO:

- Identify retailers in terms of the utilities they provide.
- Explain the alternative ways to classify retail outlets.
- Understand the many methods of nonstore retailing.
- Classify retailers in terms of the retail positioning matrix.
- Develop retailing mix strategies over the life cycle of a retail store.

RETAILING IN CYBERSPACE

Curling fans worldwide can purchase Labatt Brier souvenirs and memorabilia without ever leaving their home. All they have to do is use their computer and visit the Web site at www.brier99.com. Once they arrive at the site, they simply click on the "General Store" to view products and purchase them easily and securely. In addition, fans can select seats and buy tickets to the Brier through a link to Ticketmaster online.

This is just one example of retailing in cyberspace, or sometimes referred to as e-tailing. In cyberspace you may find individual virtual storefronts such as www. indigo.ca, where you can view and buy merchandise. Or, you may find 30 to 100 e-tailers grouped together in cybermalls such as Canadian Internet Mall (www.cdn-mall.com). And, e-tailing doesn't just involve the selling of tangible goods, but also e-services such as banking and travel services. With a few computer keystrokes, a virtual world of goods and services can be at your fingertips. In fact, retailing in cyberspace is one of the hottest topics in retailing today. To learn more about e-tailing and its impact on the Canadian retail landscape, visit The Retail Information Centre, a service from the Eaton Chair of Retailing, Ryerson Polytechnic University at www.ecr.ryerson.ca. This Web site has been designed for retailers, researchers, and students of retailing and includes links to more than 200 Canadian retail sites.[1]

What types of products will consumers buy directly through catalogues, the mail, computers, or telephone? In what type of store will consumers look for products they don't buy directly? How important is the location of the store? Will customers expect services such as alterations, delivery, installation, or repair? What price should be charged for each product? These are difficult and important questions that are an integral part of retailing. In the channel of distribution, retailing is where the customer meets the product. It is through retailing that exchange (a central aspect of marketing) occurs. **Retailing** includes all activities involved in selling, renting, and providing goods and services to ultimate customers for personal, family, or household use.

THE VALUE OF RETAILING

Retailing is an important marketing activity. Not only do producers and consumers meet through retailing actions, but retailing also creates customer value and has a significant impact on the economy. To consumers, the value of retailing is in the form of utilities provided. Retailing's economic value is represented by the people employed in retailing as well as by the total amount of money exchanged in retail sales.

Consumer Utilities Offered by Retailing

The utilities provided by retailers create value for consumers. Time, place, possession, and form utilities are offered by most retailers in varying degrees, but one utility is often emphasized more than others. Look at Figure 18–1 to see how well you can match the retailer with the utility being emphasized in the description.

Providing ATMs and banking by phone, as the Royal Bank does, puts the bank's products and services close to the consumer, providing place utility. By providing financing or leasing and taking used cars as trade-ins, Saturn makes the purchase easier and provides possession utility. Form utility—production or alteration of a product—is offered by Levi Strauss & Co. as it creates "Original Spin" jeans to meet each customer's specifications. Finding toy shelves stocked in May is the time utility dreamed about by every child (and many parents) who enters Toys "Я" Us. Many retailers offer a combination of the four basic utilities. Some supermarkets, for example, offer convenient locations (place utility) and are open 24 hours (time utility). In addition, consumers may seek additional utilities such as entertainment, recreation, or information.[2]

FIGURE 18–1
Which company best represents which utilities?

Royal Bank www.royalbank.com	One of the leaders in automated banking, the Royal Bank provides customers with convenience and 24 hour access to their banking services.
Saturn www.saturncars.com	Saturn dealers have adopted a one-price strategy that eliminates the need for negotiating. Instead, all customers are offered the same price. Test drives, financing, trade-ins, leasing are all offered to encourage customers to purchase a Saturn.
Levi Strauss www.levi.com	Levi Strauss & Co. now offers the Levi's Original Spin program, which allows customers to create their own jeans by selecting from three models, five leg types, two flys, and many colour and fabric options. The jeans are delivered in two to three weeks for $55.
Toys "Я" Us www.toysrus.com	A distinctive toy store with a backwards R, this company is what every kid dreams about. Walking into a Toys "Я" Us store is like living under a Christmas tree. Unlike most stores, which reduce their space allotted to toys after the holiday season, a huge selection of toys is always available at Toys "Я" Us.

Can You Match Them:

Time	Place	Possession	Form
________	________	________	________

The Global Economic Impact of Retailing

Retailing is important to the Canadian and global economies. Retail sales in Canada were estimated at $250 billion in 2000.[3] The retail sector also employs over 1.8 million people in Canada, or approximately 15 percent of the total employed labour force. Just three major retail categories—food stores, automotive, and clothing stores represent over 65 percent of the total retail trade in Canada (see Figure 18–2).[4]

The magnitude of retail sales is hard to imagine. Some of Canada's top retailers, for example, have annual sales revenues that surpass the GDP of several small nation-states. A study on global retailing found that the top 100 retailers in the world take in more than $1 trillion (US) in sales annually. These global retail companies operate more than 185 000 stores and have their head offices based in 15 countries. Just the top 10 global retailers, including Wal-Mart and Metro-Kaufhof International, have annual sales of over $270 billion.[5] The Marketing NewsNet describes the incredible expansion of retailers on a global scale.[6] In the Arabian Gulf, Dubai is promoting itself as a gateway to the Middle East with the "Dubai Shopping Festival." More than 3000 retail outlets participate by offering sales, discounts, special offers and other promotions. Each day the festival also holds a free drawing for a $16 000 bar of gold and a raffle for two Lexus automobiles. Because the event attracts more than two million shoppers, retailers are eager to expand their global participation in Dubai and other growing markets.[7]

CONCEPT CHECK

1. When Levi Strauss makes jeans cut to a customer's exact preferences and measurements, what utility is provided?
2. Two measures of the importance of retailing in the global economy are __________ and __________.

CLASSIFYING RETAIL OUTLETS

For manufacturers, consumers, and the economy, retailing is an important component of marketing that has several variations. Because of the large number of alternative forms of retailing, it is easier to understand the differences among retail institutions by recognizing that outlets can be classified in several ways:

- **Form of ownership.** Who owns the outlet.
- **Level of service.** The degree of service provided to the customer.
- **Merchandise line.** How many different types of products a store carries and in what assortment.

FIGURE 18–2
Retail sales, by type of business

	SALES ($BILLIONS)	% OF TOTAL
Automotive	94 500.8	38.4
Food	57 664.6	23.4
General Merchandise	27 956.2	11.4
Clothing	13 915.6	5.6
Drug stores	12 944.2	5.3
Furniture	12 536.1	5.1
Other	26 642.8	10.8
	246 161.3	100%

GLOBAL

MARKETING NEWSNET

The World Has Become a Shop Window

Around the world, customer tastes are converging, trade restrictions are disappearing, and retailers are responding with frenzied global expansion. Experts estimate that retailers will spend billions during the next two years opening new stores in foreign countries. Wal-Mart, for example, has plans to open 75 to 80 new stores in Argentina, Brazil, China, Korea, Mexico, and Puerto Rico. Gap plans to add 50 stores to its current international division of 249 stores. Eddie Bauer, Toys "Я" Us, and Home Depot also have expansion plans. Italy's Benetton already has stores in 120 countries, and Britain's Marks & Spencer has grown to 150 stores around the world.

Why are retailers expanding so rapidly? One reason is that many markets are saturated with retailers. Therefore, large merchants are looking for new places to invest. A second reason, however, is that retailers would like to transform their store names into global brands—a move that will allow them to sell higher-margin private-label goods, avoid price wars, and better negotiate with suppliers. Keith Oates of Marks & Spencer says, "we'll be a global brand in time, like Coca-Cola."

Within each method of classification there are several alternative types of outlets, as shown in Figure 18–3 and explained in the following pages.

Form of Ownership

Independent Retailer One of the most common forms of retail ownership is the independent business, owned by an individual. Small retailers tend to dominate employment in hardware, sporting goods, jewellery, and gift stores. They are also popular retailers of auto supplies, books, paint, cameras, and women's accessories. The advantage of this form of ownership for the owner is that he or she can be his or her own boss. For customers, the independent store can offer convenience, quality, personal service, and lifestyle compatibility.[8]

Corporate Chain A second form of ownership, the corporate chain, involves multiple outlets under common ownership. If you've ever shopped at The Bay, Zellers, or Loblaw's, you've shopped at a chain outlet.

In a chain operation, centralization in decision making and purchasing is common. Chain stores have advantages in dealing with manufacturers, particularly as the size of the chain grows. A large chain can bargain with a manufacturer to obtain good service or volume discounts on orders. Kmart's large volume makes it a strong negotiator with manufacturers of most products. The power of chains is seen in the retailing of computers: Small independents buy at 75 percent of list price, but large chains may pay only 60 to 65 percent of list price.[9] Consumers also benefit in dealing with

FIGURE 18–3
Classifying retail outlets

METHOD OF CLASSIFICATION	DESCRIPTION OF RETAIL OUTLET
Form of ownership	Independent retailer Corporate chain Contractual system • Retailer-sponsored cooperative • Wholesaler-sponsored voluntary chain • Franchise
Level of service	Self-service Limited-service Full-service
Merchandise line	Depth • Single line • Limited line Breadth • General merchandise • Scrambled merchandising

chains because there are multiple outlets with similar merchandise and consistent management policies.

Retailing has become a high-tech business for many large chains. Wal-Mart, for example, has developed a sophisticated inventory management and cost control system that allows rapid price changes for each product in every store. Although the technology requires a substantial investment, it is a necessary competitive tool today—a lesson illustrated by Mexico's largest drugstore chain. When Wal-Mart and other discounters opened stores in Mexico, Formacias Benavides used its state-of-the-art computer system to match prices on popular pharmaceutical products that were also available in the new competitors' stores.[10]

www.acehardware.com

Contractual System Contractual systems involve independently owned stores that band together to act like a chain. The three kinds described in Chapter 16 are retailer-sponsored cooperatives, wholesaler-sponsored voluntary chains, and franchises. One retailer-sponsored cooperative is Guardian Drugs, which consists of neighbourhood pharmacies that all agree to buy their products from the same wholesaler. In this way, members can take advantage of volume discounts commonly available to chains and also give the impression of being a large chain, which may be viewed more favourably by some consumers. Wholesaler-sponsored voluntary chains such as Ace Hardware and Independent Grocers' Alliance (IGA) try to achieve similar benefits.

As noted in Chapter 16, in a franchise system an individual or firm (the franchisee) contracts with a parent company (the franchisor) to set up a business or retail outlet. McDonald's, Holiday Inn, Midas, and H&R Block all involve some level of franchising. The franchisor usually assists in selecting the store location, setting up the store, advertising, and training personnel. The franchisee pays a one-time franchise fee and an annual royalty, usually tied to the store's sales. Although this might be seen as a relatively new phenomenon, this ownership approach has been used with gas stations since the early 1900s.[11] Franchising is attractive because of the opportunity for people to enter

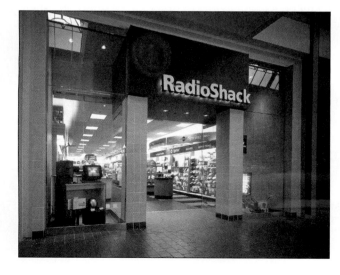

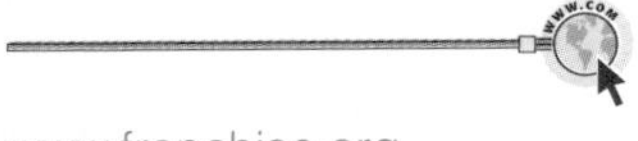

www.franchise.org

a well-known, established business where managerial advice is provided. Also, the franchise fee may be less than the cost of setting up an independent business. The International Franchise Association recently reported that franchising is one of the strongest segments of the economy.[12]

Franchise fees paid to the franchisor can range from as little as $7500 for a Radio Shack franchise to $45 000 for a McDonald's restaurant franchise. When the fees are combined with other costs such as real estate and equipment, however, the total investment can be substantial. Figure 18–4 shows some businesses that can be entered through franchise, along with the total costs of becoming a franchisee. By selling franchises, an organization reduces the cost of expansion but loses some control. A good franchisor, however, will maintain strong control of the outlets in terms of delivery and presentation of merchandise and try to enhance recognition of the franchise name.[13]

Level of Service

Even though most customers perceive little variation in retail outlets by form of ownership, differences among retailers are more obvious in terms of level of service. In some department stores very few services are provided. Some grocery stores, such as Lo Foods, have customers bag the food themselves. Other outlets, such as Holt Renfrew, provide a wide range of customer services from gift wrapping to wardrobe consultation.

Self-Service Self-service is at the extreme end of the level of service continuum because the customer performs many functions and little is provided by the outlet. Home building supply outlets and gas stations are often self-service. Warehouse stores, usually in buildings several times larger than a conventional store, are self-service with all nonessential customer services eliminated. Several new forms of self-service include Federal Express' placement of hundreds of self-service package shipping stations in retail stores such as Sam's Club and a self-service scanning system called the Portable Personal Shopper now used by some grocery stores in The Netherlands.[14]

Limited Service Limited-service outlets provide some services, such as credit, and merchandise return, but not others, such as custom-made clothes. General merchandise stores such as Wal-Mart, Kmart, and Zellers are usually considered limited service outlets. Customers are responsible for most shopping activities, although salespeople are available in departments such as consumer electronics, jewellery, and lawn and garden.

Full-Service Full-service retailers, which include most specialty stores and some department stores, provide many services to their customers. Services can include more salespeople on the floor or delivering purchases to customers' homes. Often this full-service strategy is a competitive advantage for such stores.[15]

FIGURE 18–4
The possibilities and costs of franchising

FRANCHISE	TYPE OF BUSINESS	TOTAL STARTUP COST
McDonald's	Fast-food restaurant	$385 000–$520 000
Merry Maids	Cleaning service	$27 500–$40 500
Jiffy Lube	Automobile fluid service	$208 000–$229 000
Duds'N Suds	Laundry and snack bar	$60 000
Radio Shack	Electronic accessories	$67 500
Barbizon	School of modelling	$69 500–$124 000

Merchandise Line

Retail outlets also vary by their merchandise lines, the key distinction being the breadth and depth of the items offered to customers (Figure 18–5). **Depth of product line** means that the store carries a large assortment of each item, such as a shoe store that offers running shoes, dress shoes, and children's shoes. **Breadth of product line** refers to the variety of different items a store carries.

Depth of Line Stores that carry a considerable assortment (depth) of a related line of items are limited-line stores. Black's photography stores carry considerable depth in photography equipment. Stores that carry tremendous depth in one primary line of merchandise are single-line stores. Victoria's Secret carries great depth in women's lingerie. Both limited- and single-line stores are often referred to as *specialty outlets*.

Specialty discount outlets focus on one type of product, such as electronics, business supplies, or books at very competitive prices. These outlets are referred to in the trade as *category killers* because they often dominate the market. Toys "Я" Us, for example, controls a significant share of the toy market.[16]

Breadth of Line Stores that carry a broad product line, with limited depth, are referred to as *general merchandise stores*. For example, large department stores carry a wide range of different types of products but not unusual sizes. The breadth and depth of merchandise lines are important decisions for a retailer. Traditionally, outlets carried related lines of goods. Today, however, scrambled merchandising, offering several unrelated product lines in a single store, is common. The modern drugstore carries food, camera equipment, magazines, paper products, toys, small hardware items, and pharmaceuticals. Supermarkets rent video tapes, develop film, and sell flowers.

A form of scrambled merchandising, the **hypermarket,** has been successful in Europe since the late 1960s. These hypermarkets are large stores (more than 200 000 square feet) offering a mix of 40 percent food products and 60 percent general merchandise. Prices are typically 5 to 20 percent below discount stores. The general concept behind the stores is simple: Offer consumers everything in a single outlet, eliminating the need to stop at more than one location.

Despite their success in Europe, hypermarkets have not been popular in North America. Many consumers are uncomfortable with the huge size of these stores. In addition, the competitive environment is tough: warehouse stores beat hypermarkets on price, category killers beat them on selection, and discounters beat them on location.

FIGURE 18–5
Breadth versus depth of merchandise lines

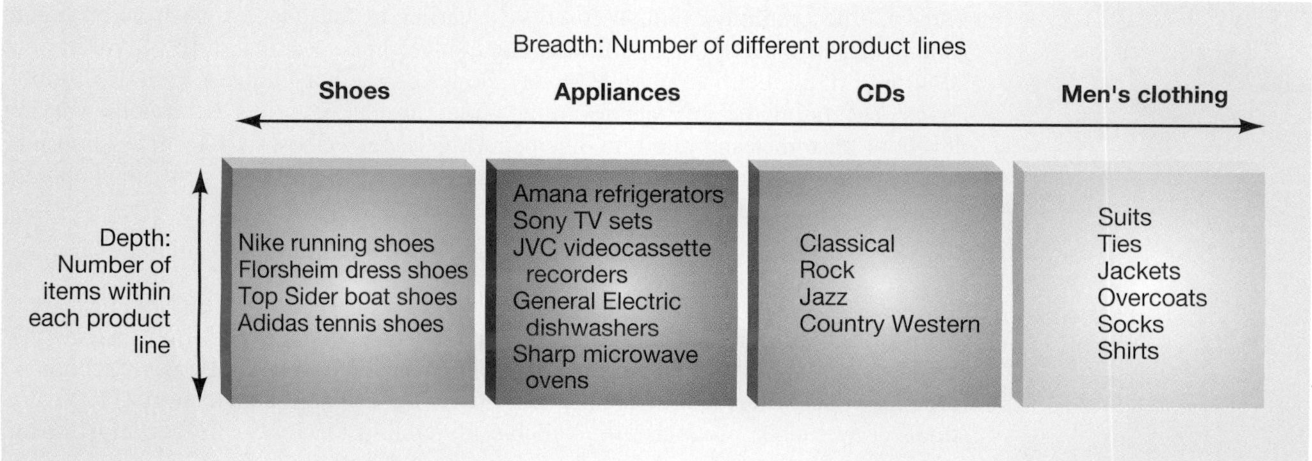

FIGURE 18–6
Differences in store concepts

	DISCOUNT STORE	SUPERCENTRE	HYPERMARKET
Average size (in square feet)	70 000	150 000	230 000
Number of employees	200–300	300–350	400–600
Annual sales ($ millions per store)	$10–$20	$20–$50	$75–$100
Gross margin	18%–19%	15%–16%	7%–8%
Number of items stocked	60 000–80 000	100 000	60 000–70 000

www.provigo.ca

Searching for a better concept, some retailers are trying new stores, called *supercentres*, which combine a typical merchandise store with a full-size grocery. Quebec grocery giant Provigo Inc. operates Maxi & Co., a combination of grocery and department store. The stores offer a complete selection of groceries as well as stationery items, hardware, linens, kitchen items, videos, books, computer programs, beauty products, etc.[17] Figure 18–6 shows the differences among discount stores, supercentres, and hypermarkets.[18]

Scrambled merchandising is convenient for consumers because it eliminates the number of stops required in a shopping trip. However, for the retailer this merchandising policy means there is competition between very dissimilar types of retail outlets, or **intertype competition.** A local bakery may compete with a department store, discount outlet, or even a local gas station. Scrambled merchandising and intertype competition make it more difficult to be a retailer.

CONCEPT CHECK

1. Centralized decision making and purchasing are an advantage of __________ ownership.
2. What are some examples of new forms of self-service retailers?
3. Would a shop for big men's clothes carrying pants in sizes 40 to 60 have a broad or deep product line?

NONSTORE RETAILING

Most of the retailing examples discussed earlier in the chapter, such as corporate chains, department stores, and limited- and single-line specialty stores, involve store retailing. Many retailing activities today, however, are not limited to sales in a store. Nonstore retailing occurs outside a retail outlet through activities that involve varying levels of customer and retail involvement. Figure 18–7 shows six forms of nonstore retailing: automatic vending, direct mail and catalogues, television home shopping, online retailing, telemarketing, and direct selling.

Automatic Vending

Nonstore retailing includes vending machines, which make it possible to serve customers when and where stores cannot. Maintenance and operating costs are high, so product prices in vending machines tend to be higher than those in stores. Typically, small convenience products are available in vending machines. In fact, most of the

FIGURE 18–7
Forms of nonstore retailing

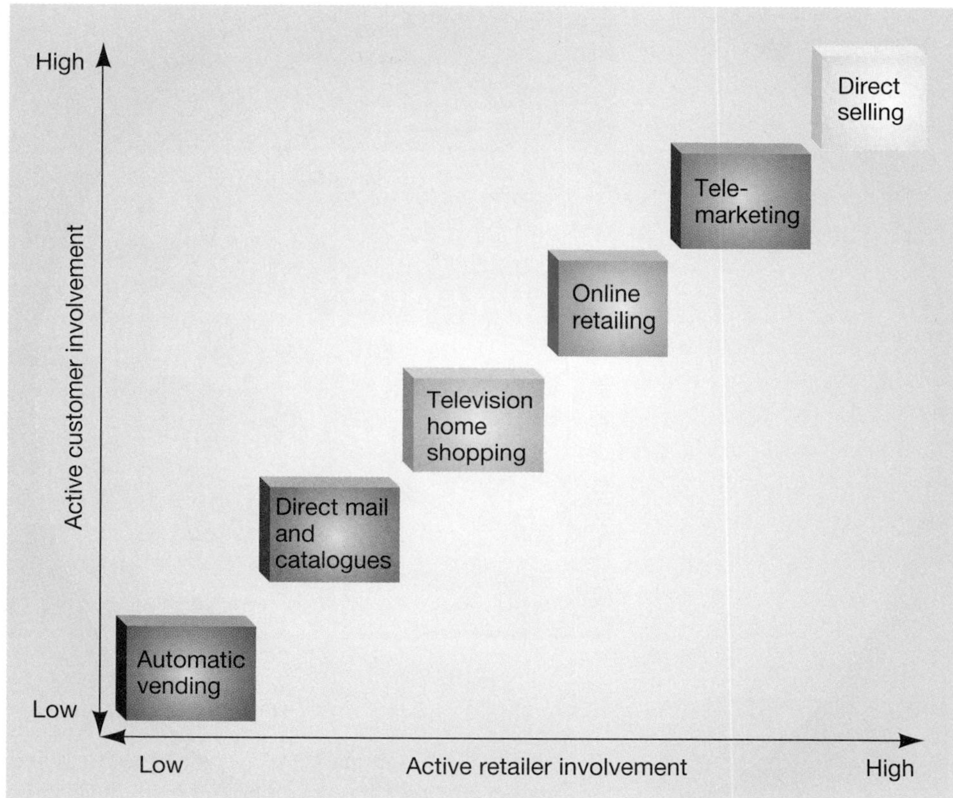

machines currently in use are soft drink machines. However, improved technology now allows vending machines to accept credit cards, which permits more expensive items to be sold through this form of retailing. Some airports, for example, now have vending machines that sell software to commuters with laptop computers. Some fitness centres have vending machines that dispense Joe Boxer underwear, and several supermarkets are testing vending machines that dispense music CDs! Another improvement in vending machines—the use of modems to notify retailers when their machines are empty—is one reason automatic merchandising sales are expected to double in the next five years.[19]

Direct Mail and Catalogues

Direct mail and catalogue retailing is attractive because it eliminates the cost of a store and clerks. In addition, it improves marketing efficiency through segmentation and targeting and creates customer value by providing a fast and convenient means of making a purchase. Canadians have been increasing the amount they spend on direct mail catalogue merchandise. Internationally, spending is also increasing.[20] Direct marketers, for example, offer rural Japanese farmers outdoor gear at discount prices through direct mail campaigns—and deliver within 72 hours![21]

As consumers' direct mail and catalogue purchases have increased, the number of direct mailings and number of catalogues as well as the number of products sold has skyrocketed. A typical household now receives more dozens of catalogues per year. The competition combined with higher paper and postal costs, however, have hurt large catalogue merchants. A successful approach now used by many catalogue retailers is to send

Vending machines serve customers when and where stores cannot.

specialty catalogues to market niches identified in their databases. L.L. Bean, a longstanding catalogue retailer, has developed an individual catalogue for fly fishing enthusiasts.[22]

Creative forms of catalogue retailing are also being developed. Hallmark, for example, offers cards for businesses in their colourful 32-page "Business Expressions" catalogue. Victoria's Secret mails as many as 45 catalogues a year to its customers to generate mail-order and 800-number business and to increase traffic in its 600 stores. Many catalogue retailers such as the Sharper Image now allow telephone orders, mail orders, and e-mail orders![23]

Television Home Shopping

Television home shopping is possible when consumers watch a shopping channel on which products are displayed; orders are then placed over the telephone. Two popular programs, the Canadian Home Shopping Network and QVC, reach millions of Canadian households. Because these programs have traditionally attracted 40- to 50-year-old women, other programs such as MTV Network's "House of Style," with host Rebecca Romijn-Stamos, is designed to attract a younger audience. A limitation of TV shopping has been the lack of buyer–seller interaction and the inability of consumers to control the items they see. But new technologies will soon

allow consumers to choose from as many as 500 channels and interact with the program source.[24]

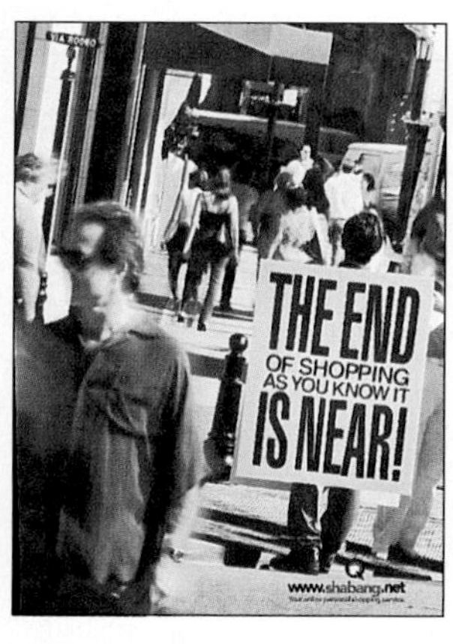

Online Retailing

Online retailing allows consumers to search for, evaluate, and order products through the Internet. For many consumers the advantages of this form of retailing are the 24-hour access, the ability to comparison-shop, privacy, and variety. The appeal varies among consumer groups, however. Studies of online shoppers have shown that while men and women are equally likely to browse Web sites, men are currently more likely to buy something online. As online retailers improve their Web offerings, though, sales are expected to increase.[25]

Online retail purchases can be the result of several very different approaches. First, consumers can pay dues to become a member of an online discount service such as CUC International's www.netMarket.com. The service offers more than one million items at very low prices to its two million subscribers. Another approach to online retailing is to use a shopping "bot" such as www.mysimon.com. This site searches the Web for a product specified by the consumer, and provides a report on the locations of the best prices available. Consumers can also use the Internet to go directly to online malls (www.fashionmall.com), apparel retailers (www.gap.com), book stores (www.amazon.com), computer manufactures (www.dell.com), grocery stores (www.peapod. com), music and video stores (www.cdnow.com), and travel agencies (www.travelocity.com). A final, and quickly growing approach, to online retailing is the online auction, such as www.ebay.com, where consumers bid on more than 1000 categories of products.[26]

To increase interest in online retailing, many retailers are adding "experiential" or interactive activities to their Web sites. The Web Link on the following page describes how apparel stores use virtual models and virtual dressing rooms to involve consumers in the purchase process and help with product selection.[27] Other changes on the horizon include the availability of very fast Internet connections through satellite services, high-speed digital telephone lines, and new-generation cable modems that run 50 to 100 times faster than current telephone lines. The merger of television home shopping and online retailing began with the introduction of WebTV, an Internet access service that uses an "Internet appliance" attached to a television to connect to the Internet. Experts predict the emergence of a new format called Interactive Home Shopping (IHS) as technology increases the interactivity between consumers and retailers. Owning a computer or a television isn't a necessity for online retailing, however, as many "online cafes" now provide guests with access to computer stations linked to the Internet.[28]

Telemarketing

Another form of nonstore retailing, called **telemarketing,** involves using the telephone to interact with and sell directly to consumers. Compared with direct mail, telemarketing is often viewed as a more efficient means of targeting consumers, although the two techniques are often used together. Information Management Network, a Dallas-based company, for example, sends direct mail to 30 million names each year to generate 650 000 responses from people who are then contacted by telemarketers. At Ryder Consumer Truck Rental, well-trained agents talk to 15 prospective customers each hour, while the staff of 24 at Lens Express makes 100 000 calls each month. Telemarketing has grown in popularity as companies search for ways to cut costs but still provide convenient access to their customers.[29]

WEB LINK Dress (Your Virtual Model) for Success!

Shopping online has many advantages: the convenience of 24-hour access, easy price comparisons, no parking hassles, and trying clothes on in the privacy of your home. That's right, now you can "build" a virtual model that reflects your body type and try on any clothing combination to see how they would look and fit. Want to try it? Go to www.landsend.com, click on My Personal Model, answer a few questions, and pick out some clothes. Or, go to www.eddiebauer. com, and click on the virtual dressing room. So . . . how do you look?!

As the use of telemarketing grows, consumer privacy has become a topic of discussion among consumers, Congress, the federal and provincial governments, and businesses. Issues such as industry standards, ethical guidelines, and new privacy laws are evolving to provide a balance between the varying perspectives.[30]

Direct Selling

Direct selling, sometimes called door-to-door retailing, involves direct sales of goods and services to consumers through personal interactions and demonstrations in their home or office. A variety of companies, including familiar names such as Fuller Brush, Avon, World Book, and Mary Kay Cosmetics, have created a multi-billion-dollar industry by providing consumers with personalized service and convenience. In Canada, however, sales have been declining as retail chains such as Wal-Mart begin to carry similar products at discount prices and as the increasing number of dual-career households reduces the number of potential buyers at home.

In response to the changes, many direct selling retailers are expanding into other markets. Avon, for example, already has 1.3 million sales representatives in 26 countries including Mexico, Poland, Argentina, and China. Similarly, other retailers such as Amway, Herbalife, and Electrolux are rapidly expanding. More than 70 percent of Amway's $7 billion in sales now comes from outside North America, and sales in Japan alone exceed sales in North America.[31] Direct selling is likely to continue to grow in markets where the lack of effective distribution channels increases the importance of door-to-door convenience and where the lack of consumer knowledge about products and brands will increase the need for a person-to-person approach.[32]

CONCEPT CHECK

1. Successful catalogue retailers often send __________ catalogues to __________ markets identified in their databases.
2. How are retailers increasing consumer interest and involvement in online retailing?
3. Where are direct selling retail sales growing? Why?

RETAILING STRATEGY

This section identifies how a retail store positions itself and describes specific actions it can take to develop a retailing strategy.

Positioning a Retail Store

The classification alternatives presented in the previous sections help determine one store's position relative to its competitors.

Retail Positioning Matrix The **retail positioning matrix** is a matrix developed by the MAC Group, Inc., a management consulting firm.[33] This matrix positions retail outlets on two dimensions: breadth of product line and value added. As defined previously, breadth of product line is the range of products sold through each outlet. The second dimension, *value added*, includes elements such as location (as with 7-Eleven stores), product reliability (as with Holiday Inn or McDonald's), or prestige (as with Birk's).

The retail positioning matrix in Figure 18–8 shows four possible positions. An organization can be successful in any position, but unique strategies are required within each quadrant. Consider the four stores shown in the matrix:

1. The Bay has high value added and a broad product line. Retailers in this quadrant pay great attention to store design and product lines. Merchandise often has a high margin of profit and is of high quality. The stores in this position typically provide high levels of service.
2. Kmart has low value added and a broad line. Kmart and similar firms typically trade a lower price for increased volume in sales. Retailers in this position focus on price with low service levels and an image of being a place for good buys.
3. Birk's has high value added and a narrow line. Retailers of this type typically sell a very restricted range of products that are of high status quality. Customers are also provided with high levels of service.
4. Kinney has low value-added and a narrow line. Such retailers are specialty mass merchandisers. Kinney, for example, carries attractively priced shoes for the entire family. These outlets appeal to value-conscious consumers. Economies of scale are achieved through centralized advertising, merchandising, buying, and distribution. Stores are usually the same in design, layout, and merchandise; hence they are often referred to as "cookie-cutter" stores.

www.birks.com

Keys to Positioning To successfully position a store, it must have an identity that has some advantages over the competitors yet is recognized by consumers.[34] A company can have outlets in several positions on the matrix, but this approach is usually done with different store names. Hudson's Bay Company, for example, owns The Bay department stores (with high value added and a broad line) and Zellers stores (low value added and a broad line). Shifting from one box in the retail positioning matrix to another is also possible, but all elements of retailing strategy must be re-examined.[35]

FIGURE 18–8
Retail positioning matrix

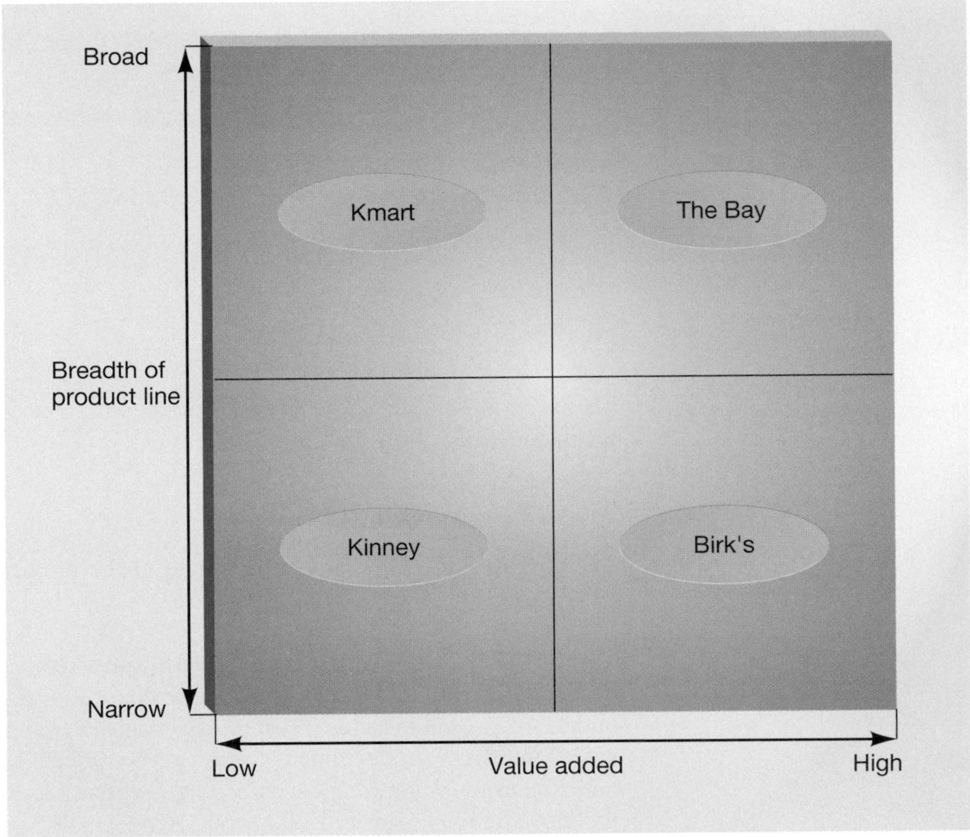

Retailing Mix

In developing retailing strategy, managers work with the **retailing mix,** which includes the (1) goods and services, (2) physical distribution, and (3) communications tactics chosen by a store (Figure 18–9).[36] Decisions relating to the mix focus on the consumer. Each of the areas shown is important, but we will cover only three basic areas: (1) pricing, (2) store location, and (3) image and atmosphere. The communications and promotion components are discussed in Chapter 20 on advertising and Chapter 21 on personal selling.

Retail Pricing In setting prices for merchandise, retailers must decide on the markup, markdown, and timing for markdowns. As mentioned in the appendix to Chapter 15 (Appendix B), the *markup* refers to how much should be added to the cost the retailer paid for a product to reach the final selling price. Retailers decide on the *original markup,* but by the time the product is sold, they end up with a *maintained markup*. The original markup is the difference between retailer cost and initial selling price. When products do not sell as quickly as anticipated, their price is reduced. The difference between the final selling price and retailer cost is the maintained markup, which is also called the *gross margin*.

Discounting a product, or taking a *markdown,* occurs when the product does not sell at the original price and an adjustment is necessary. Often new models or styles force the price of existing models to be marked down. Discounts may also be used to increase demand for complementary products.[37] For example, retailers might take a markdown on stereos to increase sales of CDs or reduce the price of cake mix to generate frosting purchases. The *timing* of a markdown can be important. Many retailers take a markdown as soon as sales fall off to free up valuable selling space and cash.

However, other stores delay markdowns to discourage bargain hunters and maintain an image of quality. There is no clear answer, but retailers must consider how the timing might affect future sales.

Although most retailers plan markdowns, many retailers use price discounts as part of their regular merchandising policy. Emphasizing consistently low prices and eliminating most markdowns or sales has become a successful strategy for retailers like Wal-Mart and Home Depot.[38] Because consumers often use price as an indicator of product quality, however, the brand name of the product and the image of the store become important decision factors in these situations.[39]

A special issue for retailers trying to keep prices low is **shrinkage,** or theft of merchandise by customers and employees. Who do you think steals more? For the answer see the accompanying Ethics and Social Responsibility Alert.[40]

Off-price retailing is a retail pricing practice that has become quite common. **Off-price retailing** involves selling brand-name merchandise at lower than regular prices. The difference between the off-price retailer and a discount store is that off-price merchandise is bought by the retailer from manufacturers with excess inventory at prices below wholesale prices, while the discounter buys at full wholesale price (but takes less of a markup than do traditional department stores). Because of

FIGURE 18–9
The retailing mix

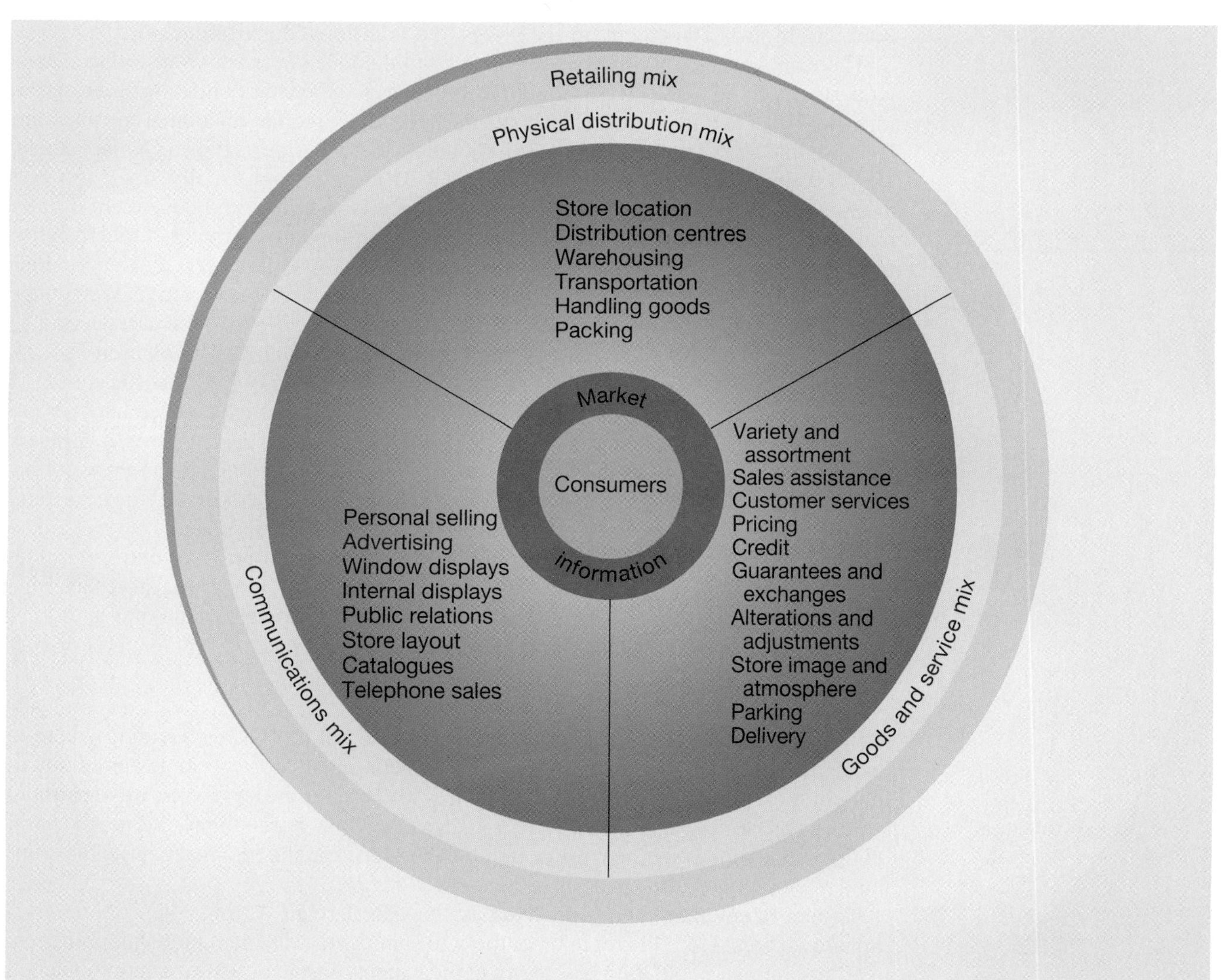

ETHICS

ETHICS AND SOCIAL RESPONSIBILITY ALERT

Who Takes the Five-Finger Discount? You'll Be Surprised

Retailers lose almost two percent of their sales to theft each year. To combat the problem, many stores attempt to discourage consumers from shoplifting with magnetic detectors, locked cases, and other deterrents. What you may find surprising, though, is that more than 50 percent of the thefts are not made by consumers but by employees! The most popular items to steal are candy from convenience stores, shirts from department stores, batteries from discount stores, and cigarettes from drug stores. When does this happen? The most popular time is between 3 and 6 P.M. Why do you think shoplifting is such a large problem? What recommendations would you make to retailers?

this difference in the way merchandise is purchased by the retailer, selection at an off-price retailer is unpredictable, and searching for bargains has become a popular activity for many consumers. Savings to the consumer at off-price retailers are reported as high as 70 percent off the prices of a traditional department store.[41]

There are several variations of off-price retailing. One is the warehouse club. These large stores (more than 100 000 square feet) began as rather stark outlets with no elaborate displays, customer service, or home delivery. They require an annual membership fee (usually $25) for the privilege of shopping there. While a typical Kmart stocks 100 000 items, warehouse clubs carry about 3500 items and usually stock just one brand name of appliance or food product. Service is minimal, and customers usually must pay by cash or check. However, the extremely competitive pricing of merchandise makes warehouse clubs attractive.[42] Some major warehouse clubs you may be familiar with include Wal-Mart's Sam's Club, BJ's Wholesale Club, and Costco's Warehouse Club. Sales of these off-price retailers have grown dramatically over the past decade.[43]

www.costco.com

A second variation is the outlet store. Factory outlets, such as Van Heusen Factory Store, Bass Shoe Outlet, and Oneida Factory Store, offer products for 25 to 30 percent off the suggested retail price. Manufacturers use the stores to clear excess merchandise and to reach consumers who focus on value shopping. Retail outlets such as Brooks Brothers Outlet Store allow retailers to sell excess merchandise and still maintain an image of offering merchandise at full price in their primary store. Some experts expect the next trend to combine the various types of off-price retailers in "value-retail centres."[44]

A third variation of off-price retailing is offered by single-price, or extreme value, retailers such as Family Dollar, Dollar General, and Dollar Tree. These stores average about 6000 square feet in size and attract customers who want value and a "corner store" environment rather than a large supercentre experience. Some experts predict extraordinary growth of these types of retailers.[45]

Store Location A second aspect of the retailing mix involves deciding where to locate the store and how many stores to have. Department stores, which started downtown in most cities, have followed customers to the suburbs, and in recent years more stores have been opened in large regional malls. Most stores today are near several others in one of five settings: the central business district, the regional centre, the community shopping centre, the strip, or the power centre.

The **central business district** is the oldest retail setting, the community's downtown area. Until the regional outflow to suburbs, it was the major shopping area, but the suburban population has grown at the expense of the downtown shopping area.

Regional shopping centres are the suburban malls of today, containing 50 to 150 stores. The typical drawing distance of a regional centre is 8 to 16 kilometres from the mall. These large shopping areas often contain two or three *anchor stores,* which are well-known national or regional stores such as Sears and The Bay. The largest variation of a regional centre is the West Edmonton Mall in Alberta. The shopping centre is a conglomerate of 600 stores, six amusement centres, 110 restaurants, and a 355-room Fantasyland hotel.[46]

A more limited approach to retail location is the **community shopping centre,** which typically has one primary store (usually a department store branch) and often about 20 to 40 smaller outlets. Generally, these centres serve a population of consumers who are within a 10- to 20-minute drive.

Not every suburban store is located in a shopping mall. Many neighbourhoods have clusters of stores, referred to as a **strip location,** to serve people who are within a 5- to 10-minute drive. Gas station, hardware, laundry, grocery, and pharmacy outlets are commonly found in a strip location. Unlike the larger shopping centres, the composition of these stores is usually unplanned. A variation of the strip shopping location is called the **power centre,** which is a huge shopping strip with multiple anchor (or national) stores. Power centres are seen as having the convenient location found in many strip centres and the additional power of national stores. These large strips often have two to five anchor stores and often contain a supermarket, which brings the shopper to the power centre on a weekly basis.[47]

Several new types of retail locations include carts, kiosks, and wall units. These forms of retailing have been popular in airports and mall common areas because they provide consumers with easy access and rental income for the property owner. Retailers benefit from the relatively low cost compared with a regular store.

Retail Image and Atmosphere Deciding on the image of a retail outlet is an important retailing mix factor that has been widely recognized and studied since the late 1950s. Pierre Martineau described image as "the way in which the store is defined in the shopper's mind," partly by its functional qualities and partly by an aura of psychological attributes.[48] In this definition, *functional* refers to mix elements such as price ranges, store layouts, and breadth and depth of merchandise lines. The psychological attributes are the intangibles such as a sense of belonging, excitement, style, or warmth. Image has been found to include impressions of the corporation that operates the store, the category or type of store, the product categories in the store, the brands in each category, merchandise and service quality, and the marketing activities of the store.[49]

Closely related to the concept of image is the store's atmosphere or ambiance. Many retailers believe that sales are affected by layout, colour, lighting, and music in the store as well as by how crowded it is. In addition, the physical surroundings that influence customers may affect the store's employees.[50] In creating the right image and atmosphere, a retail store tries to identify its target audience and what the target audience seeks from the buying experience so the store will fortify the beliefs and the emotional reactions buyers are seeking.[51] Sears, for example, is attempting to shift from its appliance and tool image by targeting middle-income women with its "Softer Side of Sears" campaign, and it recently announced a plan to sell merchandise from Benetton.[52]

CONCEPT CHECK

1. What are the two dimensions of the retail positioning matrix?
2. How does original markup differ from maintained markup?
3. A huge shopping strip with multiple anchor stores is a __________ centre.

THE CHANGING NATURE OF RETAILING

Retailing is the most dynamic aspect of a channel of distribution. Stores such as factory outlets show that new retailers are always entering the market, searching for a new position that will attract customers. The reason for this continual change is explained by two concepts: the wheel of retailing and the retail life cycle.

The Wheel of Retailing

The **wheel of retailing** describes how new forms of retail outlets enter the market.[53] Usually they enter as low-status, low-margin stores such as a drive-in hamburger stand with no indoor seating and a limited menu (Figure 18–10, box 1). Gradually these outlets add fixtures and more embellishments to their stores (in-store seating, plants, and chicken sandwiches as well as hamburgers) to increase the attractiveness for customers. With these additions, prices and status rise (box 2). As time passes, these outlets add still more services and their prices and status increase even further (box 3). These retail outlets now face some new form of retail outlet that again appears as a low-status, low-margin operator (box 4), and the wheel of retailing turns as the cycle starts to repeat itself.

In the 1950s, McDonald's and Burger King had very limited menus of hamburgers and french fries. Most stores had no inside seating for customers. Over time, the wheel of retailing for fast-food restaurants has turned. These chains have changed by altering their stores and expanding their menus. Today, McDonald's is testing new products such as McDeli sandwiches, new formats such as the McDonald's Cafe, and new decor options such as a 50s-style store. The changes are leaving room for new forms of outlets that offer only the basics—burgers, fries, and cola, a drive-through window, and no inside seating.[54] For still others, the wheel has come full circle. Taco Bell is now

FIGURE 18–10
The wheel of retailing

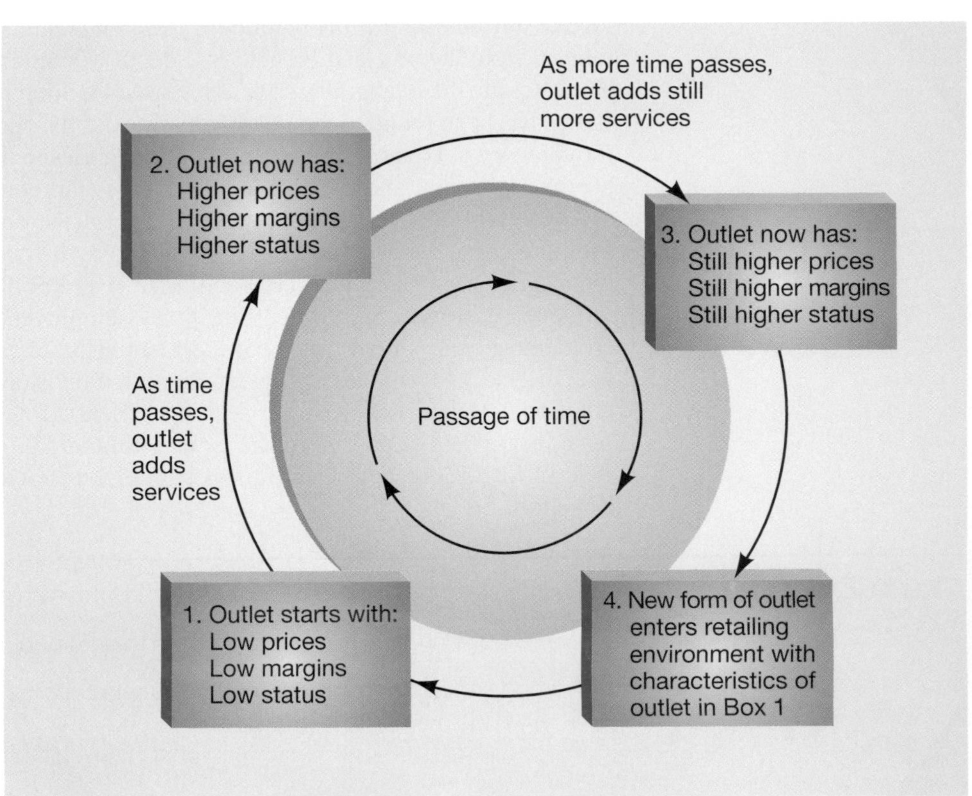

opening small, limited-offering outlets in gas stations, discount stores, or "wherever a burrito and a mouth might possibly intersect."[55]

Discount stores were a major new retailing form in the 1960s and priced their products below those of department stores. As prices in discount stores rose, in the 1980s they found themselves overpriced compared with a new form of retail outlet—the warehouse retailer. Today, off-price retailers and factory outlets are offering prices even lower than warehouses!

The Retail Life Cycle

The process of growth and decline that retail outlets, like products, experience is described by the **retail life cycle.**[56] Figure 18–11 shows the retail life cycle and the position of various current forms of retail outlets on it. Early growth is the stage of emergence of a retail outlet, with a sharp departure from existing competition. Market share rises gradually, although profits may be low because of startup costs. In the next stage, accelerated development, both market share and profit achieve their greatest growth rates. Usually multiple outlets are established as companies focus on the distribution element of the retailing mix. In this stage some later competitors may enter. Wendy's, for example, appeared on the hamburger chain scene almost 20 years after McDonald's had begun operation. The key goal for the retailer in this stage is to establish a dominant position in the fight for market share.

The battle for market share is usually fought before the maturity phase, and some competitors drop out of the market. New retail forms enter in the maturity phase, stores try to maintain their market share, and price discounting occurs. In the early 1990s, major fast-food chains such as Wendy's and McDonald's began to aggressively

FIGURE 18–11
The retail life cycle

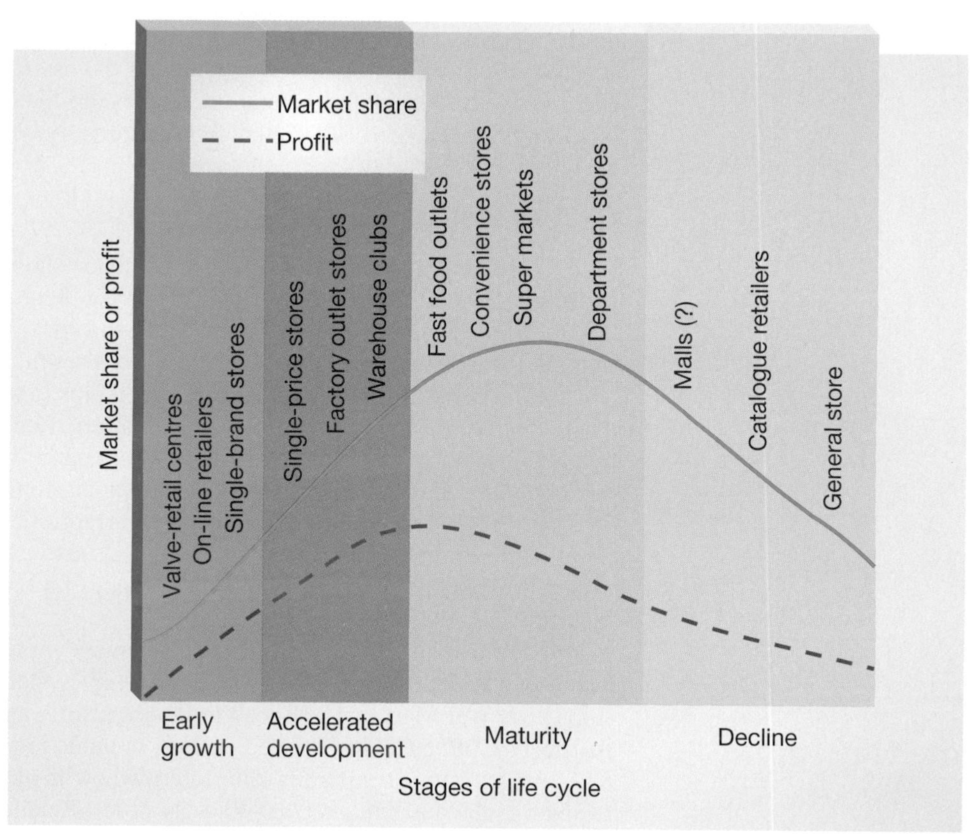

discount their prices. McDonald's introduced its Extra Value Meal, a discounted package of burger, fries, and drink, while Wendy's followed with a kid's Value Menu.

The challenge facing retailers is to delay entering the decline stage in which market share and profit fall rapidly. Specialty apparel retailers, such as The Gap, Limited, Benetton, and Ann Taylor, have noticed a decline in market share after a decade of growth. To prevent further decline, these retailers will need to find ways of discouraging their customers from moving to low-margin, mass-volume outlets or high-price, high-service boutiques.[57]

FUTURE CHANGES IN RETAILING

Three exciting trends in retailing—the increasing impact of technology, the dramatic changes in the way we shop, and the growing importance of brands—are likely to lead to many changes for retailers and consumers in the future.

The Impact of Technology

In addition, to the advent of electronic commerce or e-tailing, one of the other significant changes retailers may face in the future is the way consumers pay for purchases. In anticipation of a cashless society, some supermarkets and even some taxis now accept credit cards. But credit cards themselves are likely to be replaced by smart cards, which look the same as credit cards but store information on computer chips instead of magnetic strips. They hold information about bank accounts and amounts of available funds, and contain customer purchase information such as airline seat preferences and clothing sizes. Smart cards are already popular in Europe and Asia. Benefits for consumers include faster service—a smart card transaction is much faster than having a checque or credit card approved—and they are a convenient method of paying for small dollar-amount transactions. Merchants will also benefit because they will save the five to seven percent usually paid to credit card companies or lost in handling. Currently the absence of processing equipment is slowing the use of smart cards in North America. But recent investments by several companies are likely to help. Microsoft has developed software, called MSFDC, that lets consumers pay bills through the Internet.[58]

Changing Shopping Behaviour

In recent years consumers have become precision shoppers. The number of stores consumers visit and the number of times they visit those stores each month is declining. Shoppers are demanding convenient hours and locations, outstanding service, selection, and reasonable prices from retailers. As a result, familiar forms of retailers such as supermarkets, travel agencies, car dealerships, and hardware stores are likely to change or be replaced by new types of retailers. For example, local car dealers and neighbourhood hardware stores will be challenged by what are reffered to as "big-box" retailers. Car Canada Group, for example, is considered a big-box car dealer that offers over 400 reconditioned vehicles, warranties, financing, and fast transaction times. Big-box home improvement centres are also experiencing growth. Some retail experts suggest that consumers like these types of retailers because they are often fast, focused, and flexible.

www.chapters.ca

Another response to the changes in consumers' preferences is a form of co-branding where two retailers share a location. For example, McDonald's has developed partnerships with Wal-Mart that will lead to thousands of satellite outlets in the retail stores. Starbucks Coffee Co. has opened cafes in conjunction with Chapters Bookstores. And KFC, which attracts a strong dinner crowd, will partner with Taco Bell, which is stronger in the lunch market, at 800 of its stores. Retailers hope that consumers will appreciate the convenience of the new locations.[59]

The Importance of Brands

The use of brands is also changing dramatically. Many retailers have developed their own private-label brands to increase customer loyalty. As a result, many manufacturers have opened their own stores. Single-brand, or company, stores such as Nike Town allow manufacturers to display their entire product line in a controlled "showcase." Other company stores include Speed Authentic Fitness Stores, Original Levi's Stores, OshKosh B'Gosh Stores, and Reebok Concept Stores. Many other manufacturers are showing interest in the concept.

Two of the most successful variations of the company store trend are the Disney and Warner studio stores. The Disney stores and Warner stores market characters such as Mickey Mouse, Peter Pan, Bugs Bunny, and the Tasmanian Devil directly to the public. While both companies are fortunate to have several characters to promote, they have discovered that preferences vary throughout the world. In British stores, for example, Winnie the Pooh is the top seller, while Bambie and Thumper are preferred in France, and Mickey and Minnie are the first choices in Japan![60]

Most consumers associate strong brand names with specific products such as Coke or Tide, or particular companies such as Microsoft or Motorola. In the future, however, many large merchants will be trying to turn their store names into world brands. The changing role of products, stores, and manufacturers as popular, well-known brands is likely to generate many more changes in the dynamic practice of retailing!

CONCEPT CHECK

1. According to the wheel of retailing, when a new retail form appears, how would you characterize its image?
2. Market share is usually fought out before the _________ stage of the retail life cycle.
3. What is a smart card?

SUMMARY

1 Retailing provides customer value in the form of various utilities: time, place, possession, and form. Economically, retailing is important in terms of the people employed and money exchanged in retail sales.

2 Retailing outlets can be classified along several dimensions: the form of ownership, level of service, or merchandise line.

3 There are several forms of ownership: independent, chain, retailer-sponsored cooperative, wholesaler-sponsored chain or franchise.

4 Stores vary in the level of service they provide. Three levels are self-service, limited service, or full service.

5 Retail outlets vary in terms of the breadth and depth of their merchandise lines. Breadth refers to the number of different items carried, and depth refers to the assortment of each item offered.

6 Nonstore retailing includes automatic vending, direct mail and catalogues, television home shopping, online retailing, telemarketing, and direct selling.

7 A retail store positions itself on two dimensions: breadth of product line and value added, which includes elements such as location, product reliability, and prestige.

8 Retailing strategy is based on the retailing mix, consisting of goods and services, physical distribution, and communication tactics.

9 In retail pricing, retailers must decide on the markup, markdown, and timing for the markdown. Off-price retailers offer brand-name merchandise at lower than regular prices. This retailing form includes warehouse clubs, outlet stores, and single-price retailers.

10 Retail store location is an important retail mix decision. The common alternatives are the central business district, a regional shopping centre, a community shopping centre, or a strip location. A variation of the strip location is the power centre, which is a strip location with multiple national anchor stores and a supermarket.

11 Retail image and atmosphere help retailers create the appropriate buying experience for their target market.

12 New retailing forms are explained by the wheel of retailing. Stores enter as low-status, low-margin outlets. Over time, they add services and raise margins, which allows a new form of low-status, low-margin retailing outlet to enter.

13 Like products, retail outlets have a life cycle consisting of four stages: early growth, accelerated development, maturity, and decline.

14 Technology will change the way consumers pay for purchases in the future. Smart cards may lead to a cashless society.

KEY TERMS AND CONCEPTS

retailing p. 458
form of ownership p. 459
level of service p. 459
merchandise line p. 459
depth of product line p. 463
breadth of product line p. 463
hypermarket p. 463
intertype competition p. 464
telemarketing p. 467
retail positioning matrix p. 469
retailing mix p. 470
shrinkage p. 471
off-price retailing p. 471
central business district p. 472
regional shopping centres p. 473
community shopping centre p. 473
strip location p. 473
power centre p. 473
wheel of retailing p. 474
retail life cycle p. 475

INTERNET EXERCISE

As the chapter opener indicated, retailing in cyberspace, or e-tailing, is one of the hottest topics in retailing today. But along with new and exciting business opportunities, e-tailing brings with it a whole new set of challenges for Canadian retailers. Visit The Retail Information Centre located at www.ecr.ryerson.ca. From the information you find there, describe the Canadian retail landscape. Also, what are some of the key challenges facing Canadian retailers in light of the emergence of e-tailing?

APPLYING MARKETING CONCEPTS AND PERSPECTIVES

1 Discuss the impact of the growing number of dual-income households on (*a*) nonstore retailing and (*b*) the retail mix.
2 How does value added affect a store's competitive position?
3 In retail pricing, retailers often have a maintained markup. Explain how this maintained markup differs from original markup and why it is so important.
4 What are the similarities and differences between the product and retail life cycles?
5 How would you classify Kmart in terms of its position on the wheel of retailing versus that of an off-price retailer?
6 Develop a chart to highlight the role of each of the three main elements of the retailing mix across the four stages of the retail life cycle.
7 In Figure 18–8 Kinney was placed on the retail positioning matrix. What strategies should Kinney follow to move itself into the same position as Birk's?
8 Breadth and depth are two important components in distinguishing among types of retailers. Discuss the breadth and depth implications of the following retailers discussed in this chapter: (*a*) Levi Strauss, (*b*) Wal-Mart, (*c*) L.L.Bean, and (*d*) Future Shop.
9 According to the wheel of retailing and the retail life cycle, what will happen to factory outlet stores?
10 The text discusses the development of online retailing. How does the development of this retailing form agree with the implications of the retail life cycle?

CASE 18–1 IKEA

IKEA began as a mail-order firm in Sweden in the 1940s. Today it is one of the largest retail home furnishings chains with outlets in more than two dozen countries and sales exceeding $5 billion. IKEA has 19 stores in North America, 7 in Canada and 12 in the United States. Sales in these outlets totalled more than $550 million in 1999.

THE IKEA CONCEPT

Founded by Swedish catalogue king Ingvar Kamprad, IKEA is an acronym for his name and hometown, Elmtaryd Agunnaryd. IKEA is guided by a corporate philosophy spelled out in Kamprad's "Testament of a

Furniture Retailer." The basic philosophy can be summed up as "form, function, price = attractive, useful and affordable furniture." Specifically, IKEA's promise is "to offer a wide range of home furnishing items of good design and function, at prices so low, that the majority of people can afford to buy them." The corporate values of thrift, inventiveness, informality, and hard work are deeply rooted in the company.

Instead of traditional stores, IKEA stores are a combination of gallery and warehouse. Sales staff on the floor are kept to a minimum. Products are displayed in rooms that are fully furnished, allowing consumers to visualize how they would look in a home setting. Products are stored in flat cartons, which the consumer picks up and takes home for final assembly. In essence, IKEA's consumers are really "prosumers" (half producers, half consumers) since they assume responsibility for assembly of the products. The consumers are also active players in the distribution process since they must transport the products to their homes.

While the key to the IKEA concept is self-service and self-assembly, IKEA does offer its customers some services. For example, home delivery is available in most stores at an extra charge. If delivery is not available, IKEA will refer customers to a delivery service company in the area. IKEA will even rent out automobile roof racks to the customers to transport their purchases home. Many IKEA stores offer a home decoration service if customers wish to furnish an entire room or home, and most also offer a kitchen planning service. Using computer simulations, trained kitchen planners work with the customer to plan and choose the right kitchen. IKEA's products are easy to assemble and require no skills or tools. But if customers desire, IKEA will refer them to assembly companies who will come to the customer's home to assemble the products.

There are about 12 000 products in the total IKEA product range. Each store carries a selection of the products depending on store size. The core products are the same worldwide. IKEA contracts more than 2000 suppliers in over 60 countries to manufacture their products. The manufacturers ship the components to large warehouses or distribution centres which, in turn, supply the various stores. The suppliers must provide well-designed and high-quality products that are distinctively Scandinavian. They must also be able to provide the product at a low price and ensure continuity of supply.

IKEA's key promotion vehicle is its catalogue. The catalogue is produced in 30 editions, in 17 languages for 31 countries. The company also uses attention-getting and often provocative advertising designed to generate additional word-of-mouth publicity. For example, the company was the first to feature gay consumers in mainstream TV ads. The company also uses quirky and humorous ad appeals to reach customers. And, of course, IKEA also has its own World Wide Web site to communicate with its customers (www.IKEA.com).

The primary target market of IKEA are young (if not in age, at least in thought), educated, liberal-minded professionals who are not overly concerned with status symbols. This target market is similar across countries and regions where IKEA is located. However, because of changing demographics, especially the aging of the population in many countries, IKEA is attempting to broaden its target market to include the "older customer." IKEA is also offering a line of business furnishings for the first time in North America in an attempt to reach out to the commercial market segment.

IKEA takes a managed growth perspective in terms of retail expansion. Globally, only a few new stores are planned for each year.

Questions

1 Outline IKEA's basic marketing mix.

2 Why do you think IKEA has been successful in a highly competitive retail furnishings market?

3 From the consumer's perspective, what makes IKEA's approach to retailing an attractive alternative to traditional furniture shopping?

Tom Hanks

Meg Ryan

Someone you pass on the street may already be the love of your life.

You've Got Mail

CHAPTER NINETEEN

INTEGRATED MARKETING COMMUNICATIONS AND DIRECT MARKETING

19

AFTER READING THIS CHAPTER YOU SHOULD BE ABLE TO:

- Explain the communication process and its elements.
- Understand the promotional mix and the uniqueness of each component.
- Select the promotional approach appropriate to a product's life-cycle stage and characteristics.
- Differentiate between the advantages of push and pull strategies.
- Appreciate the value of an integrated marketing communications approach.
- Understand the value of direct marketing for consumers and sellers.

HOW DO MEG AND TOM GET MAIL?

It's Friday night and you are considering taking in a movie. Meg Ryan and Tom Hanks are back together again in a new romantic comedy, so you head for the theater. The name of the movie, *You've Got Mail*, sounds familiar, but it's not until the scenes with Tom and Meg logging on to the Internet and exchanging e-mail that you realize they are using the same online service that you use—America Online. Just a coincidence? Not a chance.

The visibility of America Online in the movie is the result of a promotional agreement between the online service and Warner Bros. movie studios. In exchange for the on-screen exposure, America Online compensated the studio—reportedly between $3 and $6 million. The agreement provided benefits for both partners: Warner Bros. defrayed some of the production and marketing expenses of the movie and added to the realism of the film, and America Online reached an important audience in an extraordinarily long form of communication.

Other movies have also used brand-name products. It was Steven Spielberg's placement of Hershey's Reese's Pieces in *E.T.* that brought a lot of interest to the candy. Similarly, when Tom Cruise wore Bausch and Lomb's Ray-Ban sunglasses in *Risky Business* and its Aviator sunglasses in *Top Gun*—and sales skyrocketed from 100 000 to 7 000 000 pairs in five years—the potential impact of "product placement" was recognized. You might remember that James Bond drove a BMW Z3 roadster in *Goldeneye*, Mel Gibson and Danny Glover ate at Dunkin Donuts in *Lethal Weapon 4*, and Matthew McConaughey and Jenna Elfman used Motorola cell phones in *EdTV*. In *The Horse Whisperer*, the Web site Equisearch.com, which provides information for equestrians, was catapulted from obscurity when the movie showed the page on screen.

It's not just movies, though. Other outlets include music videos, television shows, game shows, and even other companies' commercials. NBC's *Seinfeld* included Junior Mints, Snapple, Colombo frozen yogurt, Rold Gold pretzels, H&H Bagels, and Diet Coke in its episodes. The *Seventh Heaven* cast receives Duck Head brand clothes. *Home Improvement* actors have modelled Logo Athletic jackets, and *ER* actors use Compaq computers. Mazda recently placed a Miata in a gasoline ad.[1]

Placement of products in the many media alternatives available today is becoming an important part of marketing and promotion. Applications of the technique demonstrate the importance of creativity in communicating with potential customers. In addition, to ensure that a consistent message is delivered through product placement and all promotional activities, a process that integrates marketing communications is a necessity.

Promotion represents the fourth element in the marketing mix. The promotional element comprises a mix of tools available for the marketer called the *promotional mix*, which consists of advertising, personal selling, sales promotion, public relations, and direct marketing. All of these elements can be used to (1) inform prospective buyers about the benefits of the product, (2) persuade them to try it, and (3) remind them later about the benefits they enjoyed by using the product. This chapter first gives an overview of the communication process and the promotional elements used in marketing and then discusses direct marketing. Chapter 20 covers advertising, sales promotion, and public relations, and Chapter 21 discusses personal selling.

THE COMMUNICATION PROCESS

Communication is the process of conveying a message to others and requires six elements: a source, a message, a channel of communication, a receiver, and the processes of encoding and decoding[2] (Figure 19–1). The **source** may be a company or person who has information to convey. The information sent by a source, such as a description of a new weight reduction drink, forms the **message.** The message is conveyed by means of a **channel of communication** such as a salesperson, advertising media, or public relations tools. Consumers who read, hear, or see the message are the **receivers.**

FIGURE 19–1
The communication process

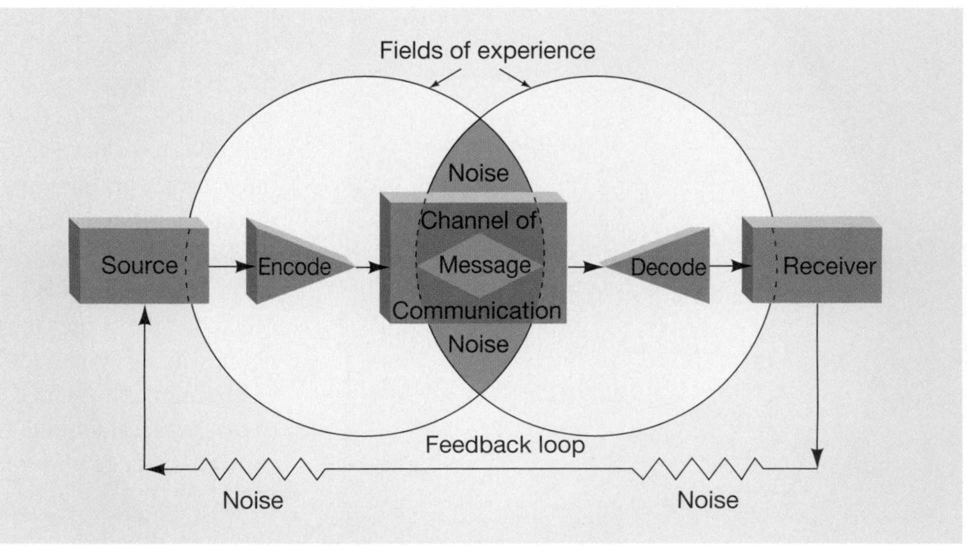

Encoding and Decoding

Encoding and decoding are essential to communication. **Encoding** is the process of having the sender transform an abstract idea into a set of symbols. **Decoding** is the reverse, or the process of having the receiver take a set of symbols, the message, and transform them back to an abstract idea. Look at the accompanying automobile advertisement: Who is the source, and what is the message?

Decoding is performed by the receivers according to their own frame of reference: their attitudes, values, and beliefs.[3] In the ad, Hummer is the source and the message is this advertisement, which appeared in *Wired* magazine (the channel). How would you interpret (decode) this advertisement? The picture and text in the advertisement show that the source's intention is to generate interest in a vehicle in which "it's not a matter of no one else being able to keep up, it's a matter of no one else being able to follow"—a statement the source believes will appeal to the readers of the magazine.

The process of communication is not always a successful one. Errors in communication can happen in several ways. The source may not adequately transform the abstract idea into an effective set of symbols, a properly encoded message may be sent through the wrong channel and never make it to the receiver, the receiver may not properly transform the set of symbols into the correct abstract idea, or finally, feedback may be so delayed or distorted that it is of no use to the sender. Although communication appears easy to perform, truly effective communication can be very difficult.

For the message to be communicated effectively, the sender and receiver must have a mutually shared **field of experience**—similar understanding and knowledge. Figure 19–1 shows two circles representing the fields of experience of the sender and receiver, which overlap in the message. Some of the better-known communication problems have occurred when Canadian companies have taken their messages to cultures with different fields of experience. Many misinterpretations are merely the result of bad translations. For example, General Motors made a mistake when its "Body by Fisher" claim was translated into Flemish as "Corpse by Fisher."[4]

A source and a message.

Hummer
www.hummer.com

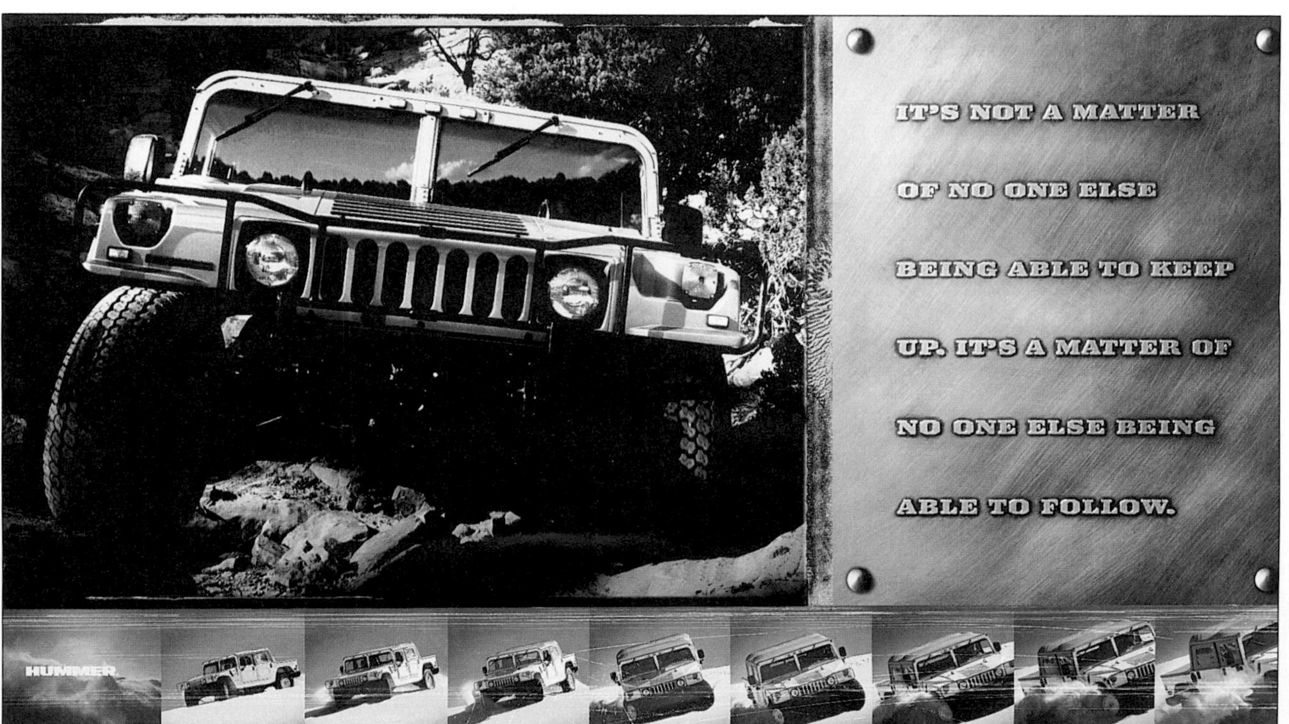
IT'S NOT A MATTER
OF NO ONE ELSE
BEING ABLE TO KEEP
UP. IT'S A MATTER OF
NO ONE ELSE BEING
ABLE TO FOLLOW.
HUMMER

Feedback

Figure 19–1 shows a line labelled *feedback loop*. **Feedback** is the communication flow from receiver back to sender and indicates whether the message was decoded and understood as intended. Chapter 20 reviews approaches called *pretesting* that ensure that messages are decoded properly.

Noise

Noise includes extraneous factors that can work against effective communication by distorting a message or the feedback received (Figure 19–1). Noise can be a simple error, such as a printing mistake that affects the meaning of a newspaper advertisement, or using words or pictures that fail to communicate the message clearly. Noise can also occur when a salesperson's message is misunderstood by a prospective buyer, such as when a salesperson's accent, use of slang terms, or communication style make hearing and understanding the message difficult.

CONCEPT CHECK

1. What are the six elements required for communication to occur?
2. A difficulty for Canadian companies advertising in international markets is that the audience does not share the same _________.
3. A misprint in a newspaper ad is an example of _________.

THE PROMOTIONAL ELEMENTS

To communicate with consumers, a company can use one or more of five promotional alternatives: advertising, personal selling, sales promotion, public relations, and direct marketing. Figure 19–2 summarizes the distinctions among these five elements. Three of these elements—advertising, sales promotion, and public relations—are often said to use

FIGURE 19–2
The promotional mix

PROMOTIONAL ELEMENT	MASS VERSUS CUSTOMIZED	PAYMENT	STRENGTHS	WEAKNESSES
Advertising	Mass	Fees paid for space or time	• Efficient means for reaching large numbers of people	• High absolute costs • Difficult to receive good feedback
Personal selling	Customized	Fees paid to salespeople as either salaries or commissions	• Immediate feedback • Very persuasive • Can select audience • Can give complex information	• Extremely expensive per exposure • Messages may differ between salespeople
Public relations	Mass	No direct payment to media	• Often most credible source in the consumer's mind	• Difficult to get media cooperation
Sales promotion	Mass	Wide range of fees paid, depending on promotion selected	• Effective at changing behaviour in short run • Very flexible	• Easily abused • Can lead to promotion wars • Easily duplicated
Direct marketing	Customized	Cost of communication through mail, telephone, or computer	• Messages can be prepared quickly • Facilitates relationship with customer	• Declining customer response • Database management is expensive

mass selling because they are used with groups of prospective buyers. In contrast, personal selling uses *customized interaction* between a seller and a prospective buyer. Personal selling activities include face-to-face, telephone, and interactive electronic communication. Direct marketing also uses messages customized for specific customers.

Advertising

www.chatelaine.com

Advertising is any paid form of nonpersonal communication about an organization, good, service, or idea by an identified sponsor. The *paid* aspect of this definition is important because the space for the advertising message normally must be bought. An occasional exception is the public service announcement, where the advertising time or space is donated. A full-page, four-colour ad in *Chatelaine* magazine, for example, costs over $30 000 and over $12 000 in *L'Actualite'*. The *nonpersonal* component of advertising is also important. Advertising involves mass media (such as TV, radio, and magazines), which are nonpersonal and do not have an immediate feedback loop as does personal selling. So before the message is sent, marketing research plays a valuable role; for example, it determines that the message is understood by the target market and that the target market will actually see the medium chosen.

An attention-getting advertisement.

There are several advantages to a firm using advertising in its promotional mix. It can be attention-getting—as with this Eastpak ad—and also communicate specific product benefits to prospective buyers. By paying for the advertising space, a company can control *what* it wants to say and, to some extent, to *whom* the message is sent. If an electronics company wants university students to receive its message about CD players, advertising space is purchased in a university campus newspaper. Advertising also allows the company to decide *when* to send its message (which includes how often). The nonpersonal aspect of advertising also has its advantages. Once the message is created, the same message is sent to all receivers in a market segment. If the message is properly pretested, the company can trust that the same message will be decoded by all receivers in the market segment.

Advertising has some disadvantages. As shown in Figure 19–2 and discussed in depth in Chapter 20, the costs to produce and place a message are significant, and the lack of direct feedback makes it difficult to know how well the message was received.

Personal Selling

The second major promotional alternative is **personal selling,** defined as the two-way flow of communication between a buyer and seller, designed to influence a person's or group's purchase decision. Unlike advertising, personal selling is usually face-to-face communication between the sender and receiver (although telephone and electronic sales are growing). Why do companies use personal selling?

There are important advantages to personal selling, as summarized in Figure 19–2. A salesperson can control to *whom* the presentation is made. Although some control is available in advertising by choosing the medium, some people may read the university newspaper, for example, who are not in the target audience for CD players. For the CD-player manufacturer, those readers outside the target audience are *wasted coverage*.

Wasted coverage can be reduced with personal selling. The personal component of selling has another advantage over advertising in that the seller can see or hear the potential buyer's reaction to the message. If the feedback is unfavourable, the salesperson can modify the message.

The flexibility of personal selling can also be a disadvantage. Different salespeople can change the message so that no consistent communication is given to all customers. The high cost of personal selling is probably its major disadvantage. On a cost-per-contact basis, it is generally the most expensive of the five promotional elements.

Public Relations

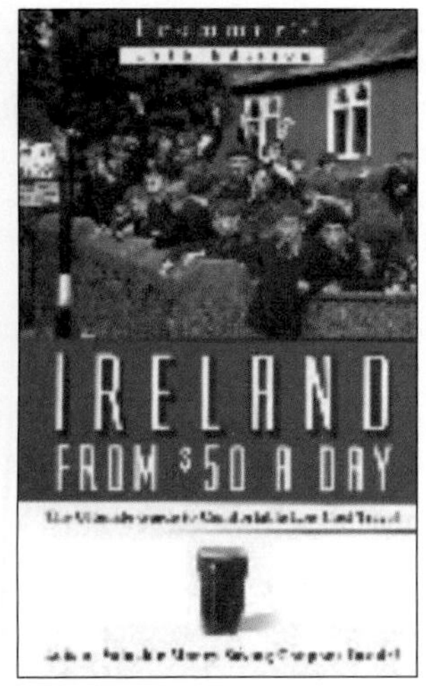

www.frommers.com

Public relations is a form of communication management that seeks to influence the feelings, opinions, or beliefs held by customers, prospective customers, stockholders, suppliers, employees, and other publics about a company and its products or services.[5] Many tools such as special events, lobbying efforts, annual reports, and image management may be used by a public relations department, although publicity often plays the most important role. **Publicity** is a nonpersonal, indirectly paid presentation of an organization, good, or service. It can take the form of a news story, editorial, or product announcement. A difference between publicity and both advertising and personal selling is the "indirectly paid" dimension. With publicity a company does not pay for space in a mass medium (such as television or radio) but attempts to get the medium to run a favourable story on the company. In this sense there is an indirect payment for publicity in that a company must support a public relations staff.

An advantage of publicity is credibility. When you read a favourable story about a company's product (such as a glowing restaurant review), there is a tendency to believe it. Travellers throughout the world have relied on Arthur Frommer's guides such as *Ireland from $50 a Day*. These books outline out-of-the-way, inexpensive restaurants, hotels, inns, and bed-and-breakfast rooms, giving invaluable publicity to these establishments. Such businesses do not (nor can they) buy a mention in the guide, which in recent years has sold millions of copies.

The disadvantages of publicity relate to the lack of the user's control over it. A company can invite a news team to preview its innovative exercise equipment and hope for a favourable mention on the 6 P.M. newscasts. But without buying advertising time, there is no guarantee of any mention of the new equipment or that it will be aired when the target audience is watching. The company representative who calls the station and asks for a replay of the story may be told, "Sorry, it's only news once." With publicity there is little control over what is said, to whom, or when. As a result, publicity is rarely the main component of a promotional campaign.

Sales Promotion

A fourth promotional element is **sales promotion,** a short-term inducement of value offered to arouse interest in buying a good or service. Used in conjunction with advertising or personal selling, sales promotions are offered to intermediaries as well as to ultimate consumers. Coupons, rebates, samples, and sweepstakes are just a few examples of sales promotions discussed later in this chapter.

The advantage of sales promotion is that the short-term nature of these programs (such as a coupon or sweepstakes with an expiration date) often stimulates sales for their duration. Offering value to the consumer in terms of a cents-off coupon or rebate provides an incentive to buy.

Sales promotions cannot be the sole basis for a campaign because gains are often temporary and sales drop off when the deal ends.[6] Advertising support is needed to convert the customer who tried the product because of a sales promotion into a long-term buyer.[7] If sales promotions are conducted continuously, they lose their effectiveness. Customers begin to delay purchase until a coupon is offered, or they question the product's value. Some aspects of sales promotions also are regulated by the federal and provincial governments. These issues are reviewed in detail later in Chapter 20.

Direct Marketing

Another promotional alternative, **direct marketing,** uses direct communication with consumers to generate a response in the form of an order, a request for further information, or a visit to a retail outlet.[8] The communication can take many forms including face-to-face selling, direct mail, catalogues, telephone solicitations, direct response advertising (on television and radio and in print), and online marketing. Like personal selling, direct marketing often consists of interactive communication. It also has the advantage of being customized to match the needs of specific target markets. Messages can be developed and adapted quickly to facilitate one-to-one relationships with customers.

While direct marketing has been one of the fastest-growing forms of promotion, it has several disadvantages. First, most forms of direct marketing require a comprehensive and up-to-date database with information about the target market. Developing and maintaining the database can be expensive and time-consuming. In addition, growing concern about privacy has led to a decline in response rates among some customer groups. Companies with successful direct marketing programs are sensitive to these issues and often use a combination of direct marketing alternatives together, or direct marketing combined with other promotional tools, to increase value for customers.

CONCEPT CHECK

1. Explain the difference between advertising and publicity when both appear on television.
2. Which promotional element should be offered only on a short-term basis?
3. Cost per contact is high with the __________ element of the promotional mix.

INTEGRATED MARKETING COMMUNICATIONS—DEVELOPING THE PROMOTIONAL MIX

A firm's **promotional mix** is the combination of one or more of the promotional elements it chooses to use. In putting together the promotional mix, a marketer must consider several issues. First, the balance of the elements must be determined. Should advertising be emphasized more than personal selling? Should a promotional rebate be offered? Would public relations activities be effective? Several factors affect such decisions: the target audience for the promotion,[9] the stage of the product's life cycle, characteristics of the product, decision stage of the buyer, and even the channel of distribution. Second, because the various promotional elements are often the responsibility of different departments, coordinating a consistent promotional effort is necessary. A promotional planning process designed to ensure integrated marketing communications can facilitate this goal.

The Target Audience

Promotional programs are directed to the ultimate consumer, to an intermediary (retailer, wholesaler, or industrial distributor), or to both. Promotional programs directed to buyers of consumer products often use mass media because the number of potential buyers is large. Personal selling is used at the place of purchase, generally the retail store. Direct marketing may be used to encourage first-time or repeat purchases.

Advertising directed to industrial buyers is used selectively in trade publications, such as *Fence* magazine for buyers of fencing material. Because industrial buyers often have specialized needs or technical questions, personal selling is particularly important. The salesperson can provide information and the necessary support after sales.

Intermediaries are often the focus of promotional efforts. As with industrial buyers, personal selling is the major promotional ingredient. The salespeople assist intermediaries in making a profit by coordinating promotional campaigns sponsored by the manufacturer and by providing marketing advice and expertise. Intermediaries' questions often pertain to the allowed markup, merchandising support, and return policies.

The Product Life Cycle

All products have a product life cycle (see Chapter 12), and the composition of the promotional mix changes over the four life-cycle stages, as shown for Purina Puppy Chow in Figure 19–3.

www.purina.com

Introduction Stage Informing consumers in an effort to increase their level of awareness is the primary promotional objective in the introduction stage of the product life cycle. In general, all the promotional mix elements are used at this time, although the use of specific mix elements during any stage depends on the product and situation. Stories on Purina's new nutritional food are placed in *Dog World* magazine, trial samples are sent to registered dog owners in 10 major cities, advertisements are placed during reruns of the TV show "Lassie," and the salesforce begins to approach supermarkets to get orders. Advertising is particularly important as a means of reaching as many people as possible to build up awareness and interest. Publicity may even begin slightly before the product is commercially available.

Growth Stage The primary promotional objective of the growth stage is to persuade the consumer to buy the product—Purina Puppy Chow—rather than substitutes, so the marketing manager seeks to gain brand preference and solidify distribution. Sales promotion assumes less importance in this stage, and publicity is not a factor because it depends on novelty of the product. The primary promotional element is advertising,

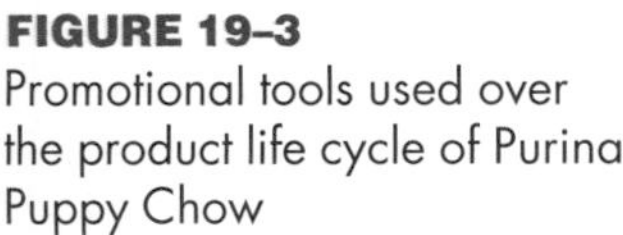

FIGURE 19–3
Promotional tools used over the product life cycle of Purina Puppy Chow

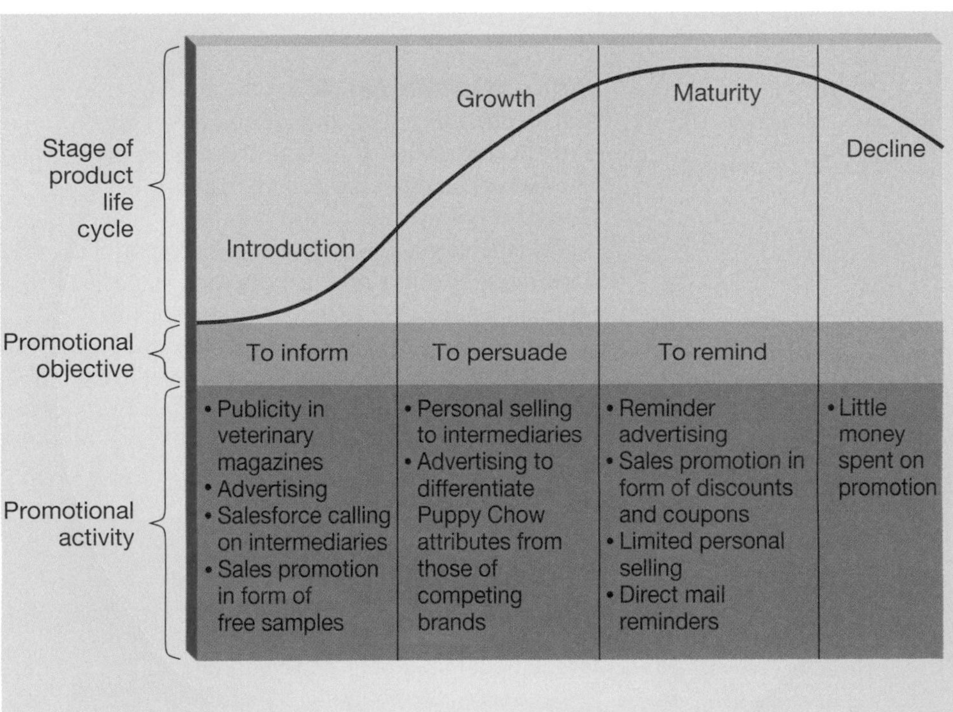

Purina Puppy Chow: a product in the maturity stage of its life cycle.

Puppy Chow

which stresses brand differences. Personal selling is used to solidify the channel of distribution. For consumer products such as dog food, the salesforce calls on the wholesalers and retailers in hopes of increasing inventory levels and gaining shelf space. For industrial products, the salesforce often tries to get contractual arrangements to be the sole source of supply for the buyer.

Maturity Stage In the maturity stage the need is to maintain existing buyers, and advertising's role is to remind buyers of the product's existence. Sales promotion, in the form of discounts and coupons offered to both ultimate consumers and intermediaries, is important in maintaining loyal buyers. In a test of one mature consumer product, it was found that 80 percent of the product's sales at this stage resulted from sales promotions.[10] Direct marketing actions such as direct mail are used to maintain involvement with existing customers and to encourage repeat purchases. Price cuts and discounts can also significantly increase a mature brand's sales. The salesforce at this stage seeks to satisfy intermediaries. An unsatisfied customer who switches brands is hard to replace.

Decline Stage The decline stage of the product life cycle is usually a period of phaseout for the product, and little money is spent in the promotional mix.

IBM
www.canibm.com

IBM must consider product characteristics such as complexity, risk, and ancillary services when designing its promotional mix.

Product Characteristics

The proper blend of elements in the promotional mix also depends on the type of product. Three specific characteristics should be considered: complexity, risk, and ancillary services. *Complexity* refers to the technical sophistication of the product and hence the amount of understanding required to use it. It's hard to provide much information in a

intel inside
pentium
i have
ramen noodles for dinner
a flat with a view of nothing in particular
callbacks tomorrow
a thinkpad
ThinkPad i Series personal ownable yours
IBM
it's new. it starts at $1499. it's available at CompUSA, Circuit City and other select retailers.

one-page magazine ad or 30-second television ad, so the more complex the product, the greater the emphasis on personal selling.

A second element is the degree of *risk* represented by the product's purchase. Risk for the buyer can be assessed in terms of financial risk, social risk, and physical risk. A hair transplant procedure, for example, might represent all three risks—it may be expensive, people can see and evaluate the purchase, and there may be a chance of physical harm. Although advertising helps, the greater the risk, the greater the need for personal selling.

The level of *ancillary services* required by a product also affects the promotional strategy. Ancillary services pertain to the degree of service or support required after the sale. This characteristic is common to many industrial products and consumer purchases. Who will repair your automobile or VCR? Advertising's role is to establish the seller's reputation. Direct marketing can be used to describe how a product or service can be customized to individual needs. However, personal selling is essential to build buyer confidence and provide evidence of customer service.

Stages of the Buying Decision

Knowing the customer's stage of decision making can also affect the promotional mix. Figure 19–4 shows how the importance of the promotional elements varies with the three stages in a consumer's purchase decision.

Prepurchase Stage In the prepurchase stage advertising is more helpful than personal selling because advertising informs the potential customer of the existence of the product and the seller. Sales promotion in the form of free samples also can play an important role to gain low-risk trial. When the salesperson calls on the customer after heavy advertising, there is some recognition of what the salesperson represents. This is particularly important in industrial settings in which sampling of the product is usually not possible.

Purchase Stage At the purchase stage the importance of personal selling is highest, whereas the impact of advertising is lowest. Sales promotion in the form of coupons, deals, point-of-purchase displays, and rebates can be very helpful in encour-

FIGURE 19–4
How the importance of promotional elements varies during the consumer's purchase decision

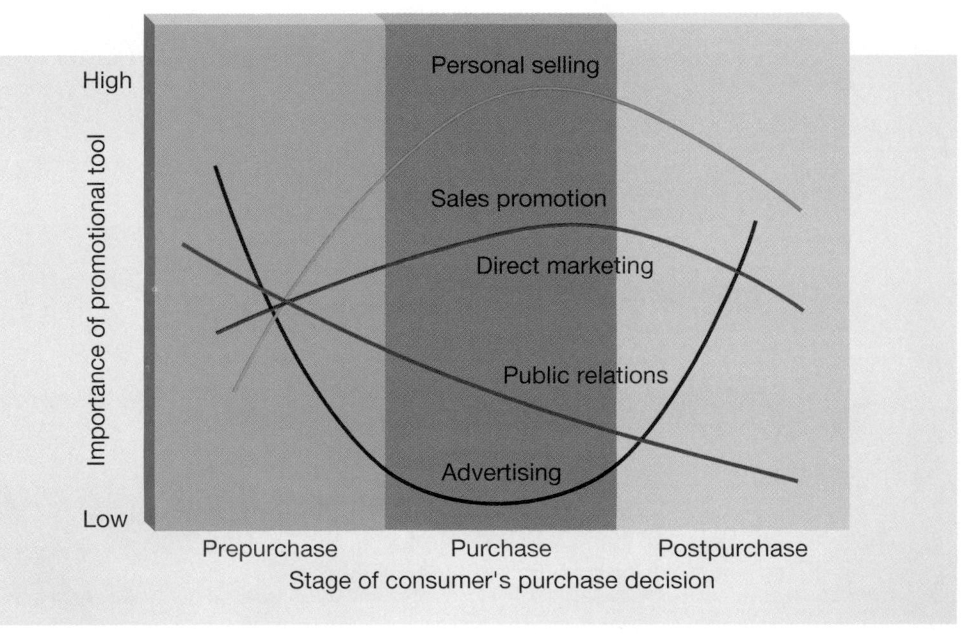

aging demand. In this stage, although advertising is not an active influence on the purchase, it is the means of delivering the coupons, deals, and rebates that are often important.

Postpurchase Stage In the postpurchase stage the salesperson is still important. In fact, the more personal contact after the sale, the more the buyer is satisfied. Advertising is also important to assure the buyer that the right purchase was made. Advertising and personal selling help reduce the buyer's postpurchase anxiety.[11] Sales promotion in the form of coupons and direct marketing reminders can help encourage repeat purchases from satisfied first-time triers. Public relations plays a small role in the postpurchase stage.

Channel Strategies

Chapter 16 discussed the channel flow from producer to intermediaries to consumer. Achieving control of the channel is often difficult for the manufacturer, and promotional strategies can assist in moving a product through the channel of distribution. This is where a manufacturer has to make an important decision about whether to use a push strategy, pull strategy, or both in its channel of distribution.[12]

Push Strategy Figure 19–5A shows how a manufacturer uses a **push strategy,** directing the promotional mix to channel members to gain their cooperation in ordering and stocking the product. In this approach, personal selling and sales promotions play major roles. Salespeople call on wholesalers to encourage orders and provide sales assistance. Sales promotions, such as case discount allowances (20 percent off the regular case price), are offered to stimulate demand. By pushing the product through the channel, the goal is to get channel members to push it to their customers.

www.pepsico.com

Canadian firms such as Pepsi-Cola Canada and Clearly Canadian Beverages spend a significant amount of their marketing resources on maintaining their relationships with their distributors, and through them, with retailers. In general, Canadian consumer goods firms are allocating greater percentages of their promotional budgets

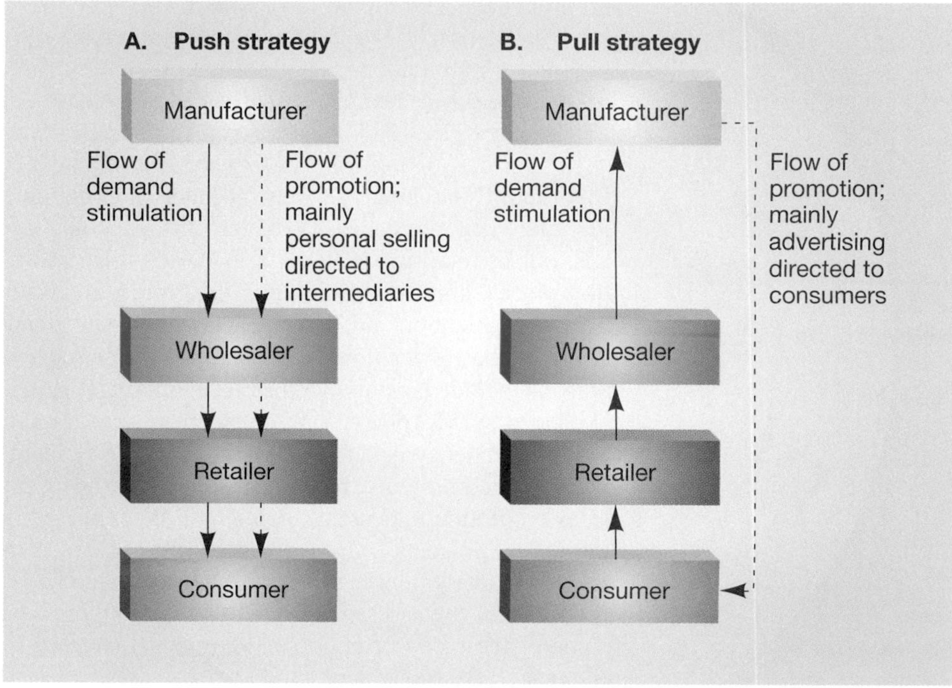

FIGURE 19–5
A comparison of push and pull promotional strategies

toward intermediaries. In some cases, as much as 60 percent of the promotional budget is being allocated to personal selling and sales promotions designed to reach intermediaries, while 40 percent is spent on promotional activities directed toward ultimate consumers.[13]

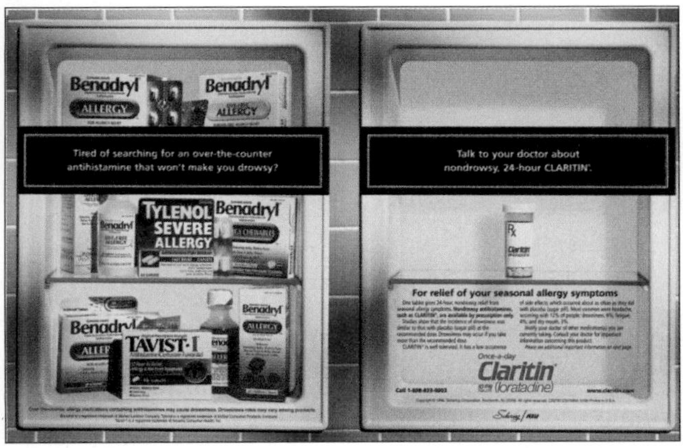

Claritin
www.claritin.com

Pull Strategy In some instances manufacturers face resistance from channel members who do not want to order a new product or increase inventory levels of an existing brand. As shown in Figure 19–5B, a manufacturer may then elect to implement a **pull strategy** by directing its promotional mix at ultimate consumers to encourage them to ask the retailer for the product. Seeing demand from ultimate consumers, retailers order the product from wholesalers and thus the item is pulled through the intermediaries. Pharmaceutical companies, for example, historically marketed only to doctors. They now spend millions annually to advertise prescription drugs directly to consumers. The strategy is designed to encourage consumers to ask their physicians for a specific drug by name—pulling it through the channel. Successful advertising strategies, such as Claritin's "Talk to your doctor . . ." campaign, can have dramatic effects on the sales of a product.[14]

Integrated Marketing Communications

www.reebok.com

In the past the promotional elements were regarded as separate functions handled by experts in separate departments. The salesforce designed and managed its activities independently of the advertising department, and sales promotion and public relations were often the responsibility of outside agencies or specialists. The result was often an overall communication effort that was uncoordinated and, in some cases, inconsistent. Reebok, for example, had to quickly change its promotion program when a scene involving Cuba Gooding and Reebok products was cut by Sony from its movie *Jerry Maguire*.[15] Today the concept of designing marketing communications programs that coordinate all promotional activities—advertising, personal selling, sales promotion, public relations, and direct marketing—to provide a consistent message across all audiences and to maximize the promotional budget is referred to as **integrated marketing communications** (IMC).

The key to developing successful IMC programs is to create a process that facilitates their design and use. A tool used to evaluate a company's current process is the IMC audit. The audit analyzes the internal communication network of the company, identifies key audiences, evaluates customer databases, assesses messages in recent ads, public relations releases, packaging, video news releases, signage, sales promotion pieces, and direct mail, and determines managers' knowledge of IMC.[16] While many organizations are interested in improving their IMC process, a recent survey suggests that fewer than one third have been successful at implementing IMC. The reasons include lack of expertise, lack of budget, and lack of management approval.[17]

Once the IMC process is implemented, most organizations want to assess its benefits. The tendency is to try to determine which element of promotion "works" better. In an integrated program, however, media advertising might be used to build awareness, sales promotion to generate an inquiry, direct mail to provide additional information to individual prospects, and a personal sales call to complete the transaction. The tools are used for different reasons, and their combined use creates a synergy that should be the focus of the assessment.[18] The accompanying Marketing NewsNet box describes some of the many promotional activities Taco Bell integrated to become the leading Mexican fast-food restaurant.[19]

CROSS FUNCTIONAL

MARKETING NEWSNET Yo Quiero IMC!

Taco Bell's promotional strategy is to attract the fickle 18- to 24-year-old crowd with interactivity, differentiation from other products, challenges, and things that are "cool." Their advertising and promotion budget last year was approximately $250 million and included a variety of integrated communication activities such as

- Advertising campaigns featuring a talking chihuahua, including the campaign introducing Taco Bell's Grande Meal package.
- Movie tie-ins such as the sweepstakes game "Feel the Force," linked to the *Star Wars* movies.
- In-store premiums such as talking Chihuahua dolls. Their lines include "Here lizard, lizard," "Viva Gorditas," "You're Getting Hungry, Very Hungry," and "Yo Quiero Taco Bell!"
- A Web page with nutritional information, restaurant locations, Taco Bell career opportunities, games, and photos from the TV ads, which are available to download.
- A Valentine's Day contest asking consumers to send a video or photo of how they would use a chihuahua toy that says "I Think I'm in Love" in a wedding proposal. The winner receives a $10 000 engagement ring from Taco Bell.
- Licensing agreements to sell backpacks, keychains, hats, and T-shirts, and deals with stores such as Wal-Mart to sell a full-size version of the dog.

The integrated campaign has been a huge success. Sales at Taco Bell now exceed $5 billion, some of the toys are selling on the Internet for as much as $100, and, according to Taco Bell spokesperson Laurie Gannon, "Our customers have asked to see more of the dog." "It appeals to an incredible cross-section—young and old, male and female. His determination makes him a hero that everybody seems to love."

CONCEPT CHECK

1. For consumer products, why is advertising emphasized more than personal selling?
2. Explain the differences between a push strategy and a pull strategy.
3. Integrated marketing communications programs provide a __________ message across all audiences.

DEVELOPING THE PROMOTION PROGRAM

Because media costs are high, promotion decisions must be made carefully, using a systematic approach. Paralleling the planning, implementation, and control steps described in the strategic marketing process (Chapter 2), the promotion decision process is divided into (1) developing, (2) executing, and (3) evaluating the promotion program (Figure 19–6). Development of the promotion program focuses on the four *W*s:

- *Who* is the target audience?
- *What* are (1) the promotion objectives, (2) the amounts of money that can be budgeted for the promotion program, and (3) the kinds of promotion to use?

FIGURE 19–6
The promotion decision process

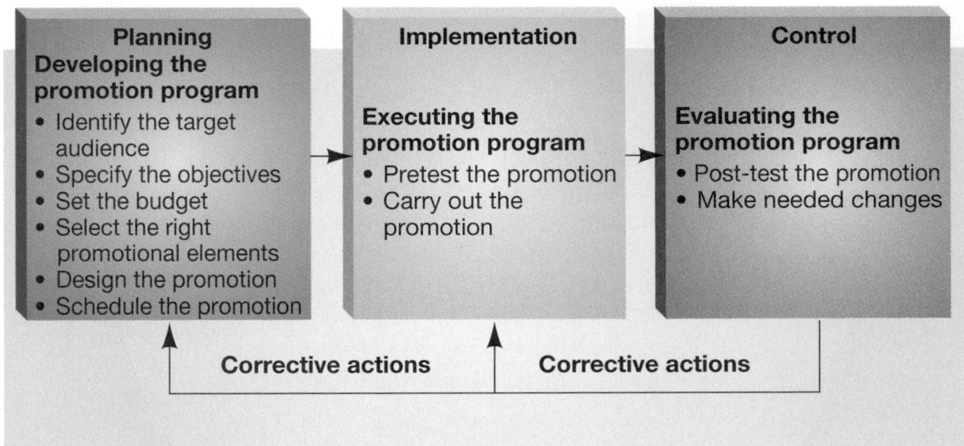

- *Where* should the promotion be run?
- *When* should the promotion be run?

Identifying the Target Audience

The first decision in developing the promotion program is identifying the *target audience*, the group of prospective buyers toward which a promotion program is directed. To the extent that time and money permit, the target audience for the promotion program is the target market for the firm's product, which is identified from marketing research and market segmentation studies. The more a firm knows about its target audience's profile—including their lifestyle, attitudes, and values—the easier it is to develop a promotion program. If a firm wanted to reach you with television and magazine ads, for example, it would need to know what TV shows you watch and what magazines you read.

Specifying Promotion Objectives

After the target audience is identified, a decision must be reached on what the promotion should accomplish. Consumers can be said to respond in terms of a **hierarchy of effects,** which is the sequence of stages a prospective buyer goes through from initial awareness of a product to eventual action (either trial or adoption of the product).[20]

- *Awareness*. The consumer's ability to recognize and remember the product or brand name.
- *Interest*. An increase in the consumer's desire to learn about some of the features of the product or brand.
- *Evaluation*. The consumer's appraisal of the product or brand on important attributes.
- *Trial*. The consumer's actual first purchase and use of the product or brand.
- *Adoption*. Through a favourable experience on the first trial, the consumer's repeated purchase and use of the product or brand.

For a totally new product the sequence applies to the entire product category, but for a new brand competing in an established product category it applies to the brand itself. These steps can serve as guidelines for developing promotion objectives.

Although sometimes an objective for a promotion program involves several steps in the hierarchy of effects, it often focuses on a single stage. Regardless of what the specific objective might be, from building awareness to increasing repeat purchases,[21] promotion objectives should possess three important qualities. They should (1) be designed for a well-defined target audience, (2) be measurable, and (3) cover a specified time period.

Setting the Promotion Budget

www.royalbank.com

After setting the promotion objectives, a company must decide on how much to spend. The promotion expenditures needed to reach millions of Canadian households are enormous. Canadian companies spent over $8 billion in 1999 on advertising, and by some estimates, double that amount on sales promotion and direct marketing to reach these households.[22] Some companies such as McDonald's Canada, Procter & Gamble, General Motors of Canada, and the Royal Bank spend hundreds of millions of dollars each year.

Determining the ideal amount for the budget is difficult because there is no precise way to measure the exact results of spending promotion dollars. However, several methods are used to set the promotion budget.[23]

Percentage of Sales In the **percentage of sales budgeting** approach, funds are allocated to promotion as a percentage of past or anticipated sales, in terms of either dollars or units sold. A common budgeting method,[24] this approach is often stated in terms such as, "Our promotion budget for this year is three percent of last year's gross sales." The advantage of this approach is obvious: it's simple and provides a financial safeguard by tying the promotion budget to sales. However, there is a major fallacy in this approach, which implies that sales cause promotion. Using this method, a company may reduce its promotion budget because of a downturn in past sales or an anticipated downturn in future sales—situations where it may need promotion the most.

Competitive Parity A second common approach, **competitive parity budgeting,** is matching the competitor's absolute level of spending or the proportion per point of market share. This approach has also been referred to as *matching competitors* or *share of market*. It is important to consider the competition in budgeting.[25] Consumer responses to promotion are affected by competing promotional activities, so if a competitor runs 30 radio ads each week, it may be difficult for a firm to get its message across with only five messages.[26] The competitor's budget level, however, should not be the only determinant in setting a company's budget. The competition might have very different promotional objectives, which require a different level of promotion expenditures.

All You Can Afford Common to many small businesses is **all-you-can-afford budgeting,** in which money is allocated to promotion only after all other budget items are covered. As one company executive said in reference to this budgeting process, "Why, it's simple. First, I go upstairs to the controller and ask how much they can afford to give us this year. He says a million and a half. Later, the boss comes to me and asks how much we should spend, and I say 'Oh, about a million and a half.' Then we have our promotion appropriation."[27]

Fiscally conservative, this approach has little else to offer. Using this budgeting philosophy, a company acts as though it doesn't know anything about a promotion–sales relationship or what its promotion objectives are.

Objective and Task The best approach to budgeting is **objective and task budgeting,** whereby the company (1) determines its promotion objectives, (2) outlines the tasks to accomplish these objectives, and (3) determines the promotion cost of performing these tasks.[28]

This method takes into account what the company wants to accomplish and requires that the objectives be specified.[29] Strengths of the other budgeting methods are integrated into this approach because each previous method's strength is tied to the objectives. For example, if the costs are beyond what the company can afford, objectives are reworked and the tasks revised. The difficulty with this method is the judgment required to determine the tasks needed to accomplish objectives. Would two or four insertions in *Time* magazine be needed to achieve a specific awareness level? Figure 19–7 shows a sample media plan with objectives, tasks, and budget outlined. The total amount to be budgeted is $430 000. If the company can only afford $300 000, the objectives must be reworked, tasks redefined, and the total budget recalculated.

Selecting the Right Promotional Tools

www.olympics.com

Once a budget has been determined, the combination of the five basic IMC tools—advertising, personal selling, sales promotion, public relations, and direct marketing—can be specified. While many factors provide direction for selection of the appropriate mix, the large number of possible combinations of the promotional tools means that many combinations can achieve the same objective. Therefore, an analytical approach and experience are particularly important in this step of the promotion decision process. The specific mix can vary from a simple program using a single tool to a comprehensive program using all forms of promotion. The Olympics have become a very visible example of a comprehensive integrated communication program. Because the Games are repeated every two years, the promotion is almost continuous. Included in the program are advertising campaigns, personal selling efforts by the Olympic committee and organizers, sales promotion activities such as product tie-ins and sponsorships, public relations programs managed by the host cities, and direct marketing efforts targeted at a variety of audiences including governments, organizations, firms, athletes, and individuals.[30] At this stage, it is also important to assess the relative importance of the various tools. While it may be desirable to utilize and integrate several forms of promotion, one may deserve emphasis. The Olympics, for example, place exceptional importance on public relations and publicity.

Designing the Promotion

The central element of a promotion program is the promotion itself. Advertising consists of advertising copy and the artwork that the target audience is intended to see or hear. Personal selling efforts depend on the characteristics and skills of the salesperson. Sales promotion activities consist of the specific details of inducements such as coupons, samples, and sweepstakes. Public relations efforts are readily seen in tangible elements such as news releases, and direct marketing actions depend on written, verbal, and electronic forms of delivery. The design of the promotion will play a primary role in determining the message that is communicated to the audience. This design activity is frequently viewed as the step requiring the most creativity. In addition,

FIGURE 19–7
The objective and task approach

OBJECTIVE

To increase awareness among university students for a new video game. Awareness at the end of one semester should be 20 percent of all students from the existing 0 percent today.

TASKS	COSTS
Advertisements once a week for a semester in 500 university papers	$280 000
Direct-mail samples to student leaders on 500 university campuses	50 000
Sponsor a national contest for video-game players	100 000
Total budget	$430 000

successful designs are often the result of insight regarding consumer's interests and purchasing behaviour. All of the promotion tools have many design alternatives. Advertising, for example, can utilize fear, humour, or other emotions in its appeal. Similarly, direct marketing can be designed for varying levels of personal or customized appeals. One of the challenges of IMC is to design each promotional activity to communicate the same message.

Scheduling the Promotion

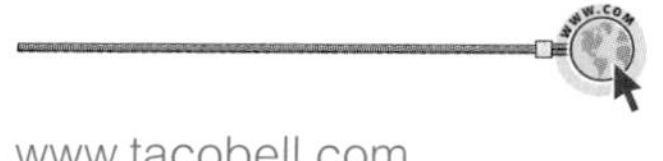

www.tacobell.com

Once the design of each of the promotional program elements is complete, it is important to determine the most effective timing of their use. The promotion schedule describes the order in which each promotional tool is introduced and the frequency of its use during the campaign. The movie *Godzilla*, for example, used an instant-win sweepstakes at Taco Bell to generate interest in the movie months before its release. The sweepstakes was followed by advertising that did not actually show Godzilla. Finally, once the movie was in theatres, product tie-ins and licence agreements began.[31] Overall, the scheduling of the various promotions was designed to generate interest, bring consumers into theatres, and then encourage additional purchases after seeing the movie. Several factors such as seasonality and competitive promotion activity can also influence the promotion schedule. Businesses such as ski resorts, airlines, and professional sports teams are likely to reduce their promotional activity during the "off" season. Similarly, restaurants, retail stores, and health clubs are likely to increase their promotional activity when new competitors enter the market.

EXECUTING AND EVALUATING THE PROMOTION PROGRAM

As shown earlier in Figure 19–6, the ideal execution of a promotion program involves pretesting each design before it is actually used to allow for changes and modifications that improve its effectiveness. Similarly, posttests are recommended to evaluate the impact of each promotion and the contribution of the promotion toward achieving the program objectives. The most sophisticated pretest and posttest procedures have been developed for advertising and are discussed in Chapter 20. Testing procedures for sales promotion and direct marketing efforts currently focus on comparisons of different designs or responses of different segments. To fully benefit from IMC programs, companies must create and maintain a test-result database that allows comparisons of the relative impact of the promotional tools, and their execution options, in varying situations. Information from the database will allow informed design and execution decisions and provide support for IMC activities during internal reviews by financial or administrative personnel. The Montreal Expos baseball team, for example, developed a database of information relating attendance to its integrated campaign using special events, merchandise sales, and a loyalty program.

Carrying out the promotion program can be expensive and time-consuming. One researcher estimates that "an organization with sales less than $10 million can successfully implement an IMC program in one year, one with sales between $200 million and $500 million will need about three years, and one with sales between $2 billion and $5 billion will need five years." To facilitate the transition there are approximately 200 integrated marketing communications agencies in operation. In addition, some of the largest advertising agencies are adopting approaches that embrace "total communications solutions." J. Walter Thompson, for example, now has a 35-person Total Solutions Group that is responsible for designing integrated programs such as the "It's best to be direct" campaign it developed for Dell Computer. While most agencies still have departments dedicated to promotion, direct marketing, and other specialties, the trend today is clearly toward a long-term perspective in which all forms of promotion are integrated.[32]

CONCEPT CHECK

1. What are the characteristics of good promotion objectives?
2. What are the weaknesses of the percentage of sales budgeting approach?
3. How have advertising agencies changed to facilitate the use of IMC programs?

DIRECT MARKETING

Direct marketing has many forms and utilizes a variety of media. The most popular forms of direct marketing—direct mail and catalogues, television, telemarketing, and direct selling—were discussed as methods of nonstore retailing in Chapter 18. In addition, interactive or online marketing is discussed in detail in Chapter 8. In this section the growth of direct marketing; its benefits; and key global, technological, and ethical issues are discussed.

The Growth of Direct Marketing

The increasing interest in customer relations is reflected in the dramatic growth of direct marketing. The ability to customize communication efforts and create one-to-one interactions is appealing to most marketers, particularly those with IMC programs. While direct marketing methods are not new, the ability to design and use them has increased with the availability of computers and databases. In recent years direct marketing growth—in terms of spending, revenue generated, and employment—has outpaced total economic growth. As mentioned earlier, expenditures on direct marketing are estimated at double the amount spent on advertising in Canada, or about $20 billion. The accompanying Web Link describes how to find local direct marketing clubs and associations where employment opportunities may be posted.

WEB LINK **Is There a Direct Marketing Club Near You?**

As one of the fastest-growing areas of marketing, there are now a large number of associations and clubs to help marketing students and professionals enhance their direct marketing knowledge and skills. To find out if there is one near you, go to the Direct Marketing Association Web site at www.the-dma.org. Click on "services" and "Local DM Clubs" or "Int'l DM Clubs," and then click on a province or country to find the club or association nearest you! Many of the listings have Web sites where you can obtain information or register to become a member!

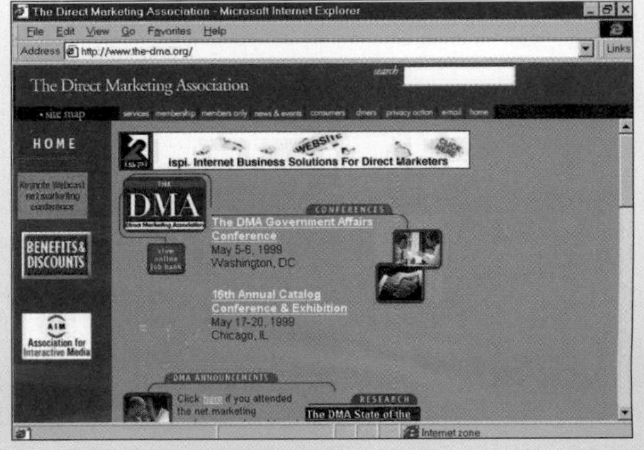

Columbia House is one example of the kinds of companies fueling the growth in direct marketing. You may have received the company's letters in the mail offering 12 free music CDs if you agree to buy four additional CDs over the next two years. In the past, the CDs were automatically delivered unless the customer tells the company not to send them. Today, through a new program called "Play," customers decide when to order. Columbia House views the change in strategy as an investment in a long-term relationship with their customers. According to Sharon Kuroki, executive vice president of music marketing, "What happens with these members is that they don't buy as much initially, but they stay in the club longer," and "they eventually buy as much" as members did with the old plan.[33]

Another component of the growth in direct marketing is the increasing popularity of the newest direct marketing channel—the Internet. Continued growth in the number of consumers with Internet access and the number of businesses with Web sites and electronic commerce offerings is likely to contribute to the future growth of direct marketing.

The Value of Direct Marketing

One of the most visible indicators of the value of direct marketing for consumers is the level of use of various forms of direct marketing. For example, about half of the Canadian population has ordered merchandise or services by phone or mail; millions have purchased items from a television offer; millions spend hours accessing online services; and about 20 percent of adults purchase from a catalogue each year. Consumers report many benefits, including the following: they don't have to go to a store, they can usually shop 24 hours a day, buying direct saves time, they avoid hassles with

Mitsubishi Motors
www.mitsubishi-motors.co.jp

Mitsubishi uses a direct-mail offer to generate traffic for dealers.

salespeople, they can save money, it's fun and entertaining, and direct marketing offers more privacy than in-store shopping. Many consumers also believe that direct marketing provides excellent customer service.[34] Toll-free telephone numbers, customer service representatives with access to information regarding purchasing preferences, overnight delivery services, and unconditional guarantees all help create value for direct marketing customers.

www.clubmed.com

The value of direct marketing for sellers can be described in terms of the responses it generates.[35] **Direct orders** are the result of offers that contain all the information necessary for a prospective buyer to make a decision to purchase and complete the transaction. Club Med, for example, uses direct e-mail offers to sell "last-minute specials" to people in its database. The messages, which are sent mid-week, describe rooms and air transportation available at a 30 to 40 percent discount if the customer can make the decision to travel on such short notice.[36] **Lead generation** is the result of an offer designed to generate interest in a product or service and a request for additional information. Insurance provider Fireman's Fund uses direct mail and direct-response TV ads to generate leads for its agents and brokers. Both offers emphasize possible savings for middle-income, middle-age households and provide an 800 number for prospective customers to call for an insurance quote.[37] Finally, **traffic generation** is the outcome of an offer designed to motivate people to visit a business. Mitsubishi recently mailed a sweepstakes offer to one million prospective buyers to encourage them to visit a Mitsubishi dealer and test drive the new Galant. The names of prospects who take test drives were entered in the sweepstakes, which included a Galant, a trip to Hawaii, and large-screen TVs as prizes.[38]

Technological, Global, and Ethical Issues in Direct Marketing

The information technology and databases described in Chapter 9 are key elements in any direct marketing program. Databases are the result of organizations' efforts to collect demographic, media, and consumption profiles of customers so that direct marketing tools—such as catalogues—can be directed at specific customers. [39]

While most companies try to keep records of their customers' past purchases, many other types of data are needed to use direct marketing to develop one-to-one relationships with customers. Data, however, have little value by themselves. To translate data into information, the data must be unbiased, timely, pertinent, accessible, and organized in a way that helps the marketing manager make decisions that lead to direct marketing actions. Some data, such as lifestyles, media use, and consumption behaviour, must be collected in consumers' homes. Other types of data can be collected from the businesses where purchases are made. Today, technology such as optical scanners helps collect data with as little intrusion on the customer as possible. Pizza Hut, for example, uses scanners to read bar codes on coupons and track the millions of customers currently in its database.[40]

Technology may also prove to be important in the global growth of direct marketing. Compared with Canada and the United States, other countries' direct marketing systems are undeveloped. The mail and telephone systems in many countries are likely to improve, however, creating many new direct marketing opportunities. Developments in international marketing research and database management will also facilitate global growth. In Argentina, for example, mail service is very slow, telephone service is poor, and response to some forms of direct marketing such as coupons is negligible. The country is the first, however, to fully deregulate its postal service and expects rapid improvement from the private company, Correo Argentino. In Mexico direct marketing activities are more advanced. Pond's recently

ETHICS

ETHICS AND SOCIAL RESPONSIBILITY ALERT

Is Personal Privacy for Sale?

MasterCard International recently asked people for their views about direct marketing and discovered that 75 percent agreed, "We need to find ways to stop business and government from collecting information about the average person." The federal government and provincial governments are concerned and have tightened regulations on direct marketers. Some of the issues and questions involved with enacting newer rules include the following:

- *Disclosure*. Should companies be required to disclose to consumers that information about them is being collected?
- *Knowledge*. Should businesses be limited in the types and amount of information collected about individuals?
- *Suppression*. Should consumers be able to remove themselves from databases?

Many businesses advocating self-regulation have adopted privacy principles to guide their marketing practices. The Canadian Direct Marketing Association also provides a means for consumers to remove their names from mailing lists. Finally, consumers in the MasterCard survey indicated that they would be more willing to disclose personal information in exchange for an incentive. What were the incentives most preferred by respondents? Better protection against fraud and lower finance charges.

What is your opinion about these privacy issues?

mailed 20 000 direct-mail offers within Mexico and was surprised by a 33 percent response.[41] Another issue for global direct marketers is payment. Because fewer consumers have credit cards, alternatives such as C.O.D. and bank deposits are needed.

Global and domestic direct marketers both face challenging ethical issues today. Of course there has been considerable attention given to some annoying direct marketing activities such as telephone solicitations during dinner and evening hours. Recent concerns about privacy, however, have led to various attempts to provide guidelines that balance consumer and business interests. The European Union recently passed a consumer privacy law, called the Data Protection Directive, after several years of discussion with the Federation of European Direct Marketing and the U.K.'s Direct Marketing Association. In Canada, Consumer and Corporate Affairs Canada and most provincial legislatures are also concerned about privacy.[42] The accompanying Ethics and Social Responsibility Alert offers some of the details of the debate.[43]

CONCEPT CHECK

1. The ability to design and use direct marketing programs has increased with the availability of _________ and _________.
2. What are the three types of responses generated by direct marketing activities?

SUMMARY

1 Communication is the process of conveying a message to others and requires a source, a message, a channel of communication, a receiver, and the processes of encoding and decoding.

2 For effective communication to occur, the sender and receiver must have a shared field of experience. Feedback from receiver to sender helps determine whether decoding has occurred or noise has distorted the message.

3 The promotional elements consist of advertising, personal selling, sales promotion, public relations, and direct marketing. These tools vary according to whether they are personal; can be identified with a sponsor; and can be controlled with regard to whom, when, where, and how often the message is sent.

4 In selecting the appropriate promotional mix, marketers must consider the target audience, the stage of the product's life cycle, characteristics of the product, decision stage of the buyer, and the channel of distribution.

5 The target for promotional programs can be the ultimate consumer, an intermediary, or both. Ultimate consumer programs rely more on advertising, whereas personal selling is more important in reaching industrial buyers and intermediaries.

6 The emphasis on the promotional tools varies with a product's life cycle. In introduction, awareness is important. During growth, creating brand preference is essential. Advertising is more important in the former stage and personal selling in the latter. Sales promotion helps maintain buyers in the maturity stage.

7 The appropriate promotional mix depends on the complexity of the product, the degree of risk associated with its purchase, and the need for ancillary services.

8 In the prepurchase stage of a customer's purchase decision, advertising and public relations are emphasized; at the purchase stage personal selling, sales promotion, and direct marketing are most important; and during the postpurchase stage advertising, personal selling, and sales promotion are used to reduce postpurchase anxiety.

9 When a push strategy is used, personal selling and sales promotions directed to intermediaries play major roles. In a pull strategy, advertising and sales promotions directed to ultimate consumers are important.

10 Integrated marketing communications programs coordinate all promotional activities to provide a consistent message across all audiences and to maximize the promotion budget.

11 The promotion decision process involves developing, executing, and evaluating the promotion program. Developing the promotion program focuses on determining who is the target audience, what to say, where the message should be said, and when to say it.

12 Setting promotion objectives is based on the hierarchy of effects. Objectives should be measurable, have a specified time period, and state the target audience.

13 Budgeting methods often used are percentage of sales, competitive parity, and the all-you-can-afford approaches. The best budgeting approach is based on the objectives set and tasks required.

14 Selecting, designing, and scheduling promotional elements requires experience and creativity because of the large number of possible combinations of the promotion mix.

15 Direct marketing offers consumers convenience, entertainment, privacy, time savings, low prices, and customer service. Sellers benefit from direct orders, lead generation, and traffic generation.

16 Global opportunities for direct marketing will increase as mail and telephone systems improve worldwide. Consumers' concerns about privacy will be a key issue for direct marketers in the future.

KEY TERMS AND CONCEPTS

communication p. 482
source p. 482
message p. 482
channel of communication p. 482
receivers p. 482
encoding p. 483
decoding p. 483
field of experience p. 483
feedback p. 484
noise p. 484
advertising p. 485
personal selling p. 485
public relations p. 486
publicity p. 486
sales promotion p. 486
direct marketing p. 487
promotional mix p. 487
push strategy p. 491
pull strategy p. 492
integrated marketing communications p. 492
hierarchy of effects p. 494
percentage of sales budgeting p. 495
competitive parity budgeting p. 495
all-you-can-afford budgeting p. 495
objective and task budgeting p. 495
direct orders p. 500
lead generation p. 500
traffic generation p. 500

INTERNET EXERCISE

Several large advertising agencies have described shifts in their philosophies to include IMC approaches to communication. In many cases the outcome has been campaigns that utilize a combination of the five promotional elements. Go to J. Walter Thompson's Web site at www.jwt.com, and review its integrated campaigns.

1 Describe the promotional elements of one of the campaigns. Why were these elements selected? How are they integrated?

2 How would you evaluate the effectiveness of each of the promotional elements used? How would you evaluate the effectiveness of the entire campaign?

APPLYING MARKETING CONCEPTS AND PERSPECTIVES

1 After listening to a recent sales presentation, Mary Smith signed up for membership at the local health club. On arriving at the facility, she learned there was an additional fee for racquetball court rentals. "I don't remember that in the sales talk; I thought they said all facilities were included with the membership fee," complained Mary. Describe the problem in terms of the communication process.

2 Develop a matrix to compare the five elements of the promotional mix on three criteria—to *whom* you deliver the message, *what* you say, and *when* you say it.

3 Explain how the promotional tools used by an airline would differ if the target audience were (*a*) consumers who travel for pleasure and (*b*) corporate travel departments that select the airlines to be used by company employees.

4 Suppose you introduced a new consumer food product and invested heavily both in national advertising (pull strategy) and in training and motivating your field salesforce to sell the product to food stores (push strategy). What kinds of feedback would you receive from both the advertising and your salesforce? How could you increase both the quality and quantity of each?

5 Fisher-Price Company, long known as a manufacturer of children's toys, has introduced a line of clothing for children. Outline a promotional plan to get this product introduced in the marketplace.

6 Many insurance companies sell health insurance plans to companies. In these companies the employees pick the plan, but the set of offered plans is determined by the company. Recently Blue Cross–Blue Shield, a health insurance company, ran a television ad stating, "If your employer doesn't offer you Blue Cross–Blue Shield coverage, ask why." Explain the promotional strategy behind the advertisement.

7 Identify the sales promotion tools that might be useful for (*a*) Tastee Yogurt—a new brand introduction, (*b*) 3M self-sticking Post-it notes, and (*c*) Wrigley's Spearmint Gum.

8 Design an integrated marketing communications program—using each of the five promotional elements—for Music Boulevard, the online music store.

9 BMW recently introduced its first sport-utility vehicle, the X5, to compete with other popular SUV vehicles such as the Mercedes-Benz M-class and Jeep Grand Cherokee. Design a direct marketing program to generate (*a*) leads, (*b*) traffic in dealerships, and (*c*) direct orders.

10 Develop a privacy policy for database managers that provides a balance of consumer and seller perspectives. How would you encourage voluntary compliance with your policy? What methods of enforcement would you recommend?"

CASE 19–1 AIRWALK, INC.

To effectively communicate with the youth audience," observes Sharon Lee, "it is important to earn their respect by knowing what they think and how they think. You must stay one step ahead of them by constantly studying what they are reading, doing, listening to, playing, and watching."

Sharon Lee speaks from experience. She is an account director at Lambesis, the advertising agency whose integrated marketing communications (IMC) program launched Airwalk shoes into the stratosphere. Lee's job is to be the key link between Airwalk and Lambesis. Her special insights into the youth market have helped make Airwalk's recent success possible. But it wasn't always so easy.

EARLY DAYS: THE STRUGGLE

George Yohn founded the company in 1986—searching for a piece of the fast-growing athletic shoe craze headed by Nike and Reebok. His first efforts marketing an aerobic shoe hit the wall, so he had to find a new product and marketing strategy. Then one of his designers found a sport that other sneaker manufacturers hadn't yet discovered: skateboarding. Yohn watched skateboarders drag their feet to turn and brake, so he developed a special athletic shoe that had extra layers of leather, more rubber in the sole, and double stitching to add longer life. Watching skateboarders do a popular trick of popping the board into the air, he named his new company "Airwalk."

The colourful skateboard shoes almost jumped off the surf and skate shops stocking them, so Airwalk moved into other freestyle segments like snowboarding and BMX and mountain bike riding. Airwalk sales hit $20 million in 1990, but an anti-snowboarding movement soon closed many slopes to skateboarders and sales fell $8 million in 1992.

REPOSITIONING AIRWALK: TARGETING MAINSTREAM YOUTHS

At this point Yohn got his great insight: if basketball shoes aren't just worn by basketball players, why should skateboarding shoes just be worn by skateboarders? This gave Yohn his new challenge in 1992: reposition Airwalk to bring its hotdogger image to mainstream youths who were looking for stylish shoes but weren't into skateboarding.

While this repositioning looked great on paper, making it actually happen was a big, big order! Although Airwalk was well known among action-sport enthusiasts, the brand name was almost unknown among mainstream youths. It was at this point that Airwalk introduced its active/casual line of sneakers targeted at these youths, mainly teens.

RESEARCH: FINDING WHAT'S COOL!

Looking back on the early 1990s, it's now possible to find some key elements that have led to Airwalk's success today. One example is the huge effort it puts into "trend spotting" research, discussed earlier in Chapter 9. Dee Gordon, a nationally known expert in trend spotting, is on the staff of Lambesis. She authors the *L Report,* published quarterly by Lambesis, that surveys 18 000 trendsetter and mainstream respondents from ages 14 to 30 and touches on every aspect of their lives. Gordon's research gives other Lambesis employees like Sharon Lee and its clients in-depth insights into what the trendsetters and cool kids are thinking, doing, and buying. Dee Gordon also studies trends around the world as a foundation for global marketing strategies developed by Lambesis clients.

MAKING IT HAPPEN: THE IMC STRATEGY

Airwalk and Lambesis recognized that much of Nike's and Reebok's success is that they recognize their business is no longer simply about selling shoes—it's about creating a cool image for their shoes. Mastering the marketing of the hard-to-define concept known as "cool" was the task that Airwalk dropped in the lap of Lambesis when Airwalk launched its first active/casual footwear line, targeted at the youth market.

The special challenge for Lambesis was to expand the market for Airwalk shoes by reaching the new, broader cool segments for its shoes without diluting their image among the existing core segments. Chad Farmer, the creative director at Lambesis who is charged with coming up with ideas for Airwalk ads, saw an opportunity to position Airwalk to the youth market as the harbinger of style in casual footwear. At the same time, Airwalk's integrated marketing communications program must retain its shoes' reputation for quality and durability while featuring their original designs and colours.

Chad Farmer's IMC program illustrates the diversity of media and strategies available to creative agencies and clients trying to break through the media clutter. This clutter is reflected in today's youths often seeing about 3000 advertising messages in a typical day. Airwalk's TV commercials and print ads are alive with humor, irreverence, and unrestrained attitude. In many of the 14 countries where Airwalks are sold, youths steal its outdoor posters to hang in their rooms. Airwalk's Web site (www.airwalk.com) not only displays its latest line of shoes, but also provides graphics, animation, and recent TV commercials that can be downloaded.

Airwalk's IMC strategy doesn't stop with conventional media. Airwalk team "riders" include the best competitive skateboarders, snowboarders, mountain bike riders, and surfers who represent the company in major competitions globally. Bands and musicians such as the Beastie Boys, Green Day, Pearl Jam, and R.E.M. wear Airwalks—gaining great visibility for the brand. Lambesis gets product placement everywhere from movies and music videos to skateboard/BMX camps and fashion magazine photos.

What has resulted from all of this? In the mid-1990s, sales increased 400 percent in a single year. Today's sales are more than $300 million. And Teen Research Unlimited, a marketing research group, reports that Airwalk is among the top 20 percent of "coolest" brands and still climbing.

Questions

1 What were Airwalk's promotional objectives when it decided to target mainstream youths with its line of shoes in its IMC program?

2 Airwalk has developed what it calls a "tripod" strategy to stress three simple one-word concepts to communicate to the youth it targets and to stress in its IMC program. From reading the case and from what you know about the youth market, what might these be?

3 Describe how Airwalk and Lambesis might use the following media or promotional elements in their IMC strategy to target the notoriously difficult-to-reach target market of youths: (*a*) TV, (*b*) billboards, (*c*) product placements in movies, (*d*) special events, and (*e*) Web site. Explain your answers.

4 As Airwalk sells its shoes around the world, it has chosen to use a *global* marketing strategy, as defined in Chapter 5. (*a*) What are the advantages and disadvantages for Airwalk of this strategy? (*b*) For example, in print ads how might Airwalk take advantage of this strategy?

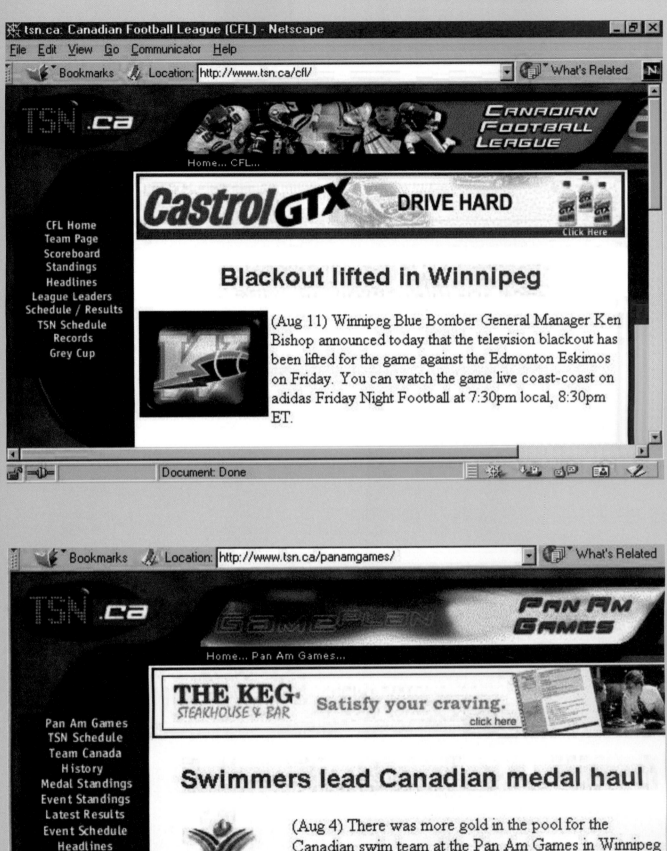

tsn.ca: Canadian Football League (CFL) - Netscape

File Edit View Go Communicator Help

Bookmarks Location: http://www.tsn.ca/cfl/ What's Related

TSN.ca

CANADIAN FOOTBALL LEAGUE

Home... CFL...

CFL Home
Team Page
Scoreboard
Standings
Headlines
League Leaders
Schedule / Results
TSN Schedule
Records
Grey Cup

Castrol GTX DRIVE HARD Click Here

Blackout lifted in Winnipeg

(Aug 11) Winnipeg Blue Bomber General Manager Ken Bishop announced today that the television blackout has been lifted for the game against the Edmonton Eskimos on Friday. You can watch the game live coast-coast on adidas Friday Night Football at 7:30pm local, 8:30pm ET.

Document: Done

Bookmarks
Location: http://www.tsn.ca/panamgames/
What's Related
TSN.ca
PAN AM GAMES
Home... Pan Am Games...
THE KEG STEAKHOUSE & BAR
Satisfy your craving.
click here
Pan Am Games
TSN Schedule
Team Canada
History
Medal Standings
Event Standings
Latest Results
Event Schedule
Headlines
Swimmers lead Canadian medal haul
Winnipeg '99
(Aug 4) There was more gold in the pool for the Canadian swim team at the Pan Am Games in Winnipeg on Wednesday, and some increasingly familiar faces stood atop the podium when the waves had calmed.
The women's 4x100 metre freestyle squad earned gold in that event with a

CHAPTER TWENTY

ADVERTISING, SALES PROMOTION, AND PUBLIC RELATIONS 20

AFTER READING THIS CHAPTER YOU SHOULD BE ABLE TO:

- Explain the differences between product advertising and institutional advertising and the variations within each type.
- Understand the steps used to develop, execute, and evaluate an advertising program.
- Explain the advantages and disadvantages of alternative advertising media.
- Understand the strengths and weaknesses of consumer-oriented and trade-oriented sales promotions.
- Recognize public relations as an important form of communication.

THE WILD WORLD OF WEB ADVERTISING

If you've been on the Internet you've been exposed to a form of advertising that did not exist only a few years ago. Now advertisers spend millions on Web advertising each year and some experts predict triple digit growth in expenditures in the next few years. Why the rapid growth? Of course the growing number of businesses and households on the Internet is appealing to advertisers. Other reasons, however, also contribute to the trend. First, advertising on the Web allows an advertiser to assess the success of the ad. Web technology allows advertisers to count the number of people who see an ad, the number of people who "click through" to the advertiser's own Web page, and, in many cases, the number of people who made a purchase. Such data are appealing because they allow advertisers to design effective ads and to target receptive audiences.

Another reason Web advertising is receiving so much attention is its potential for creating value for customers. By making the ads interactive, advertisers can provide consumers with specific, useful information. For example, TSN's popular Web site—www.tsn.ca—allows advertisers or sponsors to appear on its Web pages. You can also go to an interactive Claritin ad and find out what the pollen count is in your location. This information may help you decide if and how much Claritin to take. As technology evolves, more interactivity with audio and video elements will be possible. In addition, because Web advertising has the ability to take consumers through the entire purchase process—from creating awareness, to providing information, to placing an order, to customer service—many experts believe it will encourage integrated marketing programs that are consumer friendly.

To facilitate the development of Web advertising, Procter & Gamble (P&G)—one of the world's largest advertisers—recently hosted a "summit" for marketers, Web technology companies, and advertising agencies. The objectives of the summit were to foster collaboration, to discuss common formats for the technological developments, and to improve Web advertising's effectiveness. According to Denis Beausejour, advertising vice president for P&G, a sharp increase in Internet spending "will happen, but not if we don't make some evolutionary and related changes to bring it along." So what does the future hold? According to Beausejour and others, the Net may soon become a mass medium that rivals television![1]

Online advertising is one example of the many exciting changes taking place in the field of advertising today. Chapter 19 described **advertising** as any *paid* form of *nonpersonal* communication about an organization, good, service, or idea, by an identified sponsor. This chapter describes alternative types of advertisements, the advertising decision process, sales promotion, and public relations.

TYPES OF ADVERTISEMENTS

As you look through any magazine, watch television, listen to the radio, or browse on the Web, the variety of advertisements you see or hear may give you the impression that they have few similarities. Advertisements are prepared for different purposes, but they basically consist of two types: product and institutional.

Product Advertisements

Focused on selling a good or service, **product advertisements** take three forms: (1) pioneering (or informational), (2) competitive (or persuasive), and (3) reminder. Look at the ads by Iridium, Tylenol, and Godiva, and determine the type and objective of each ad.

Used in the introductory stage of the life cycle, *pioneering* advertisements tell people what a product is, what it can do, and where it can be found. The key objective of a pioneering ad (such as that for the Iridium global satellite phone) is to inform the target market. Informative ads have been found to be interesting, convincing, and effective.[2]

Advertising that promotes a specific brand's features and benefits is *competitive*. The objective of these messages is to persuade the target market to select the firm's

Advertisements serve varying purposes. Which ad would be considered (1) pioneering, which is (2) competitive, and which is used as a (3) reminder?

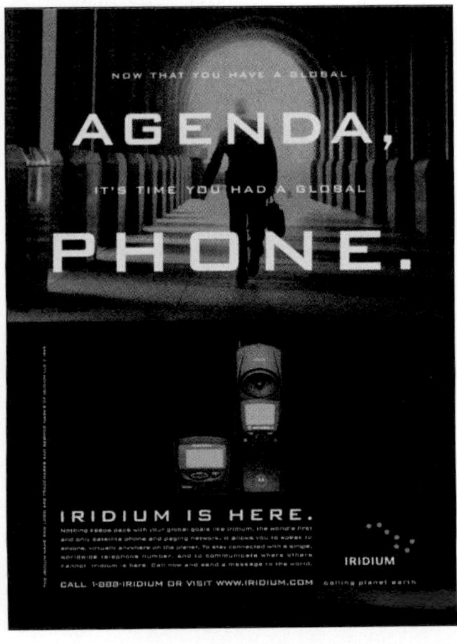

Dial soap uses reinforcement ads to encourage consumers to keep using the product.

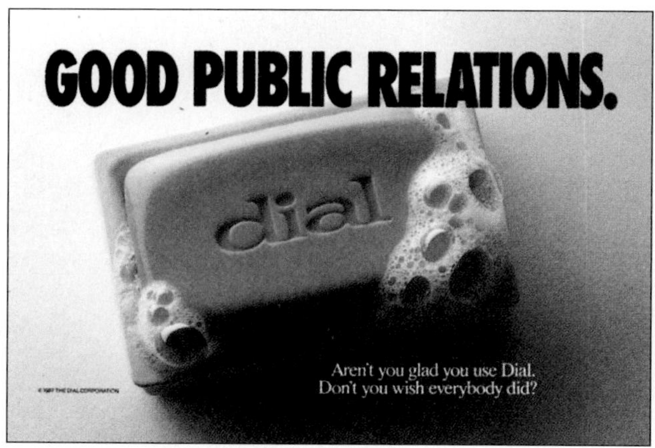

brand rather than that of a competitor. An increasingly common form of competitive advertising is *comparative* advertising, which shows one brand's strengths relative to those of competitors.[3] The Barnes and Noble ad, for example, highlights the competitive advantage of Barnes and Noble over its primary competitor, amazon.com. Studies indicate that comparative ads attract more attention and increase the perceived quality of the advertiser's brand.[4] Firms that use comparative advertising need market research and test results to provide legal support for their claims.[5]

Reminder advertising is used to reinforce previous knowledge of a product. The Godiva ad shown reminds consumers about the association between its product and a special event—in this case, your birthday. Reminder advertising is good for products that have achieved a well-recognized position and are in the mature phase of their product life cycle. Another type of reminder ad, *reinforcement*, is used to assure current users they made the right choice. One example: "Aren't you glad you use Dial? Don't you wish everybody did?"

Institutional Advertisements

www.ibm.ca

The objective of **institutional advertisements** is to build goodwill or an image for an organization, rather than promote a specific good or service. Institutional advertising has been used by companies such as the Royal Bank, Pfizer, and IBM Canada to build confidence in the company name.[6] Often this form of advertising is used to support the public relations plan or counter adverse publicity. Four alternative forms of institutional advertisements are often used:

1. *Advocacy* advertisements state the position of a company on an issue. Molson places ads encouraging the responsible use of alcohol, as shown on the next page.
2. *Pioneering institutional* advertisements, like the pioneering ads for products discussed earlier, are used for announcement about what a company is, what it can do, or where it is located. Recent Bayer ads stating "We cure more headaches than you think" are intended to inform consumers that the company produces many products in addition to aspirin.
3. *Competitive institutional* advertisements promote the advantages of one product class over another and are used in markets where different product classes compete for the same buyers. The Steel Alliance, for example, made up of major North American steel producers, including Stelco, Dofasco, and Ipsco, are spending $100 million on a TV and print campaign promoting steel's many uses.
4. *Reminder institutional* advertisements, like the product form, simply bring the company's name to the attention of the target market again.

An advocacy advertisement about the responsible use of alcohol by Molson.

"Planning every run
is the mark of a good skier,
even the run home. So think ahead,
and don't drink and drive."
Brian Stemmle
NATIONAL SKI TEAM MEMBER
Take Care.
MOLSON

CONCEPT CHECK

1. What is the difference between pioneering and competitive ads?
2. What is the purpose of an institutional advertisement?

DEVELOPING THE ADVERTISING PROGRAM

The promotion decision process described in Chapter 19 can be applied to each of the promotional elements. Advertising, for example, can be managed by following the three steps (developing, executing, and evaluating) of the process.

Identifying the Target Audience

The first decision in developing the advertising program is identifying the *target audience,* the group of prospective buyers toward which an advertising program is directed. To the extent that time and money permit, the target audience for the advertising program is the target market for the firm's product, which is identified from marketing research and market segmentation studies. The more a firm knows about its target audience's profile—including their lifestyle, attitudes, and values—the easier it is to develop and advertising program. If a firm wanted to reach you with its ads, it would need to know what TV shows you watch and what magazines you read.

Specifying Advertising Objectives

The guidelines for setting promotion objectives described in Chapter 19 also apply to setting advertising objectives. This step helps advertisers with other choices in the promotion decision process such as selecting media and evaluating a campaign. Advertising with an objective of creating awareness, for example, would be better matched with a magazine than a directory such as the Yellow Pages.[7] Similarly, an advertiser looking to induce consumers to trial or to take other direct action like visit a store location would use a direct response form of advertising like direct mail. The Canadian Advertising Foundation believes that establishing advertising objectives is so important that they established the CASSIE Awards where advertisers are recognized for achieving ad campaign objectives. Experts believe that factors such as product category, brand, and consumer involvement in the purchase decision may change the importance—and, possibly, the sequence—of the stages of the hierarchy of effects. Snickers, for example, knew that its consumers were unlikely to engage in elaborate information processing when it designed a recent campaign. The result was ads with simple humorous messages rather than extensive factual information.[8]

www.media-awareness.ca

Setting the Advertising Budget

The methods used to set the overall promotion budget as outlined in Chapter 19 can be used to establish a specific advertising budget. As with the promotional or IMC budget, the best approach to setting the ad budget is the objective and task approach. There are numerous advertising options available to the advertiser and most of the alternatives require substantial financial commitments. A formal budgeting process that involves matching the target audience to the available advertising options, evaluating the ability of those options to achieve specified objectives, and weighing the relative costs of the advertising options is definitely a requirement for effective advertising.

Designing the Advertisement

An advertising message usually focuses on the key benefits of the product that are important to a prospective buyer in making trial and adoption decisions. The message depends on the general form or appeal used in the ad and the actual words included in the ad.

Message Content Most advertising messages are made up of both informational and persuasional elements. These two elements, in fact, are so intertwined that it is sometimes difficult to tell them apart. For example, basic information contained in many ads such as the product name, benefits, features, and price are presented in a way that tries to attract attention and encourage purchase. On the other hand, even the most persuasive advertisements must contain at least some basic information to be successful.

Information and persuasive content can be combined in the form of an appeal to provide a basic reason for the consumer to act. Although the marketer can use many different types of appeals, common advertising appeals include fear appeals,[9] sex appeals, and humorous appeals.

Fear appeals suggest to the consumer that he or she can avoid some negative experience through the purchase and use of a product or through a change in behaviour. Insurance companies often try to show the negative effects of premature death on the relatives of those who don't carry enough life or mortgage insurance. Food producers encourage

CUSTOMER VALUE

MARKETING NEWSNET

Designing Ads That Deal with Negative Issues

Have you ever developed anxiety over a message you've received from an advertisement? If your answer is yes, chances are that your reaction was the result of what advertisers call a *fear appeal*. Examples you may be familiar with include fire or smoke detector ads that depict a family home burning, political candidate endorsements that warn against the rise of other unpopular ideologies, or social cause ads warning of the serious consequences of drug use, alcoholism, or AIDS. This approach is based on three steps—the creation of a fearful situation by giving the audience information about the severity of the threat and the probability of its occurrence, describing the effectiveness of a solution or coping response, and suggesting how the solution can be implemented.

How individuals react to fear appeals, though, varies significantly with their prior knowledge and experience. Indeed, the varying levels of anxiety that result from the ads suggest several ethical concerns for the psychological well-being of consumers. Therefore, advertisers need to consider four guidelines when developing their ads:

1. Whenever possible, use low or moderate (rather than high) levels of fear.
2. Offer more than one alternative as a solution.
3. Avoid deceptive implications (e.g., that a product will completely eliminate a fearful condition).
4. Pretest each ad to ensure a balance between the message and the associated level of anxiety.

the purchase of low-fat, high-fibre products as a means of reducing cholesterol levels and the possibility of a heart attack.[10] When using fear appeals, the advertiser must be sure that the appeal is strong enough to get the audience's attention and concern, but not so strong that it will lead them to "tune out" the message. The accompanying Marketing NewsNet suggests some guidelines for developing an ad with a fear appeal.[11]

In contrast, *sex appeals* suggest to the audience that the product will increase the attractiveness of the user. Sex appeals can be found in almost any product category, from automobiles to toothpaste. Victoria's Secret, for example, used this form of advertising on the Super Bowl to generate traffic for a live Web fashion show.[12] Unfortunately, many commercials that use sex appeals are only successful at gaining the attention of the audience; they have little impact on how consumers think, feel, or act. Some advertising experts even argue that such appeals get in the way of successful communication by distracting the audience from the purpose of the ad.

Humorous appeals imply either directly or more subtly that the product is more fun or exciting than competitors' offerings. As with fear and sex appeals, the use of humour is widespread in advertising and can be found in many product categories. Unfortunately for the advertiser, humour tends to wear out quickly, thus boring the consumer. Eveready ads, featuring the Energizer battery bunny, frequently change to avoid this advertising "wearout." Another problem with humorous appeals is that their effectiveness may vary across cultures if used in a global campaign.[13]

Creating the Actual Message The "creative people" in an advertising agency—copywriters and art directors—have the responsibility to turn appeals and features such as quality, style, dependability, economy, and service into attention-getting, believable advertisements.

Advertising agency TBWA Chiat/Day was recently designated as *Advertising Age* magazine's advertising Agency of the Year for "talking with the consumer rather than

A creative advertisement by agency TBWA Chiat/Day for Nissan.

Nissan North America
www.nissan-na.com

at the consumer." One example of the agency's approach is the "Think Different" campaign for Apple Computer. The commercials salute "the crazy ones, the rebels, the trouble makers, and the ones who see things differently." As the ads show personalities such as Albert Einstein, Pablo Picasso, and Jim Hensen, the voice-over claims, "You can disagree with them . . . the only thing you can't do is ignore them. They change things." Other successful campaigns include the Nissan dog-driving-an-armchair ads and the Taco Bell "Yo Quiero" ads.[14]

TBWA Chiat/Day's use of well-known personalities in the "Think Different" campaign is an example of a very popular form of advertising today—the use of a celebrity spokesperson. In homes across Canada, sports heros, rock stars, movie stars, and many other celebrities are talking directly to consumers through ads in all of today's many media options. Advertisers who use a celebrity spokesperson believe that the ads are more likely to influence sales. Long-running campaigns may also encourage consumers to associate a product with a celebrity. For example, when consumers see or hear Bill Cosby, they may think of Jello or Kodak.[15]

Translating the copywriter's ideas into an actual advertisement is a complex process. Designing quality artwork, layout, and production for the advertisements is costly and time-consuming. High-quality TV commercials typically cost over $200 000 to produce a 30-second ad. High-visibility commercials can be even more expensive: two 15-second Rolaids commercials involved $500 000 and 75 people over a six-month period. About 70 "takes" are necessary, and typical, to get things "right."[16]

CONCEPT CHECK

1. What are characteristics of good advertising objectives?
2. What is the weakness of the percentage of sales budgeting approach?

Selecting the Right Media

Every advertiser must decide where to place its advertisements. The alternatives are the *advertising media*, the means by which the message is communicated to the target audience. Newspapers, magazines, radio, and TV are examples of advertising media. This "media selection" decision is related to the target audience, type of product, nature of the message, campaign objectives, available budget, and the costs of the alternative media. Figure 20–1 shows the distribution of the over $8 billion spent on advertising in Canada among the many media alternatives.[17]

FIGURE 20–1
Canadian advertising expenditures by medium, as percentage of total ad spending

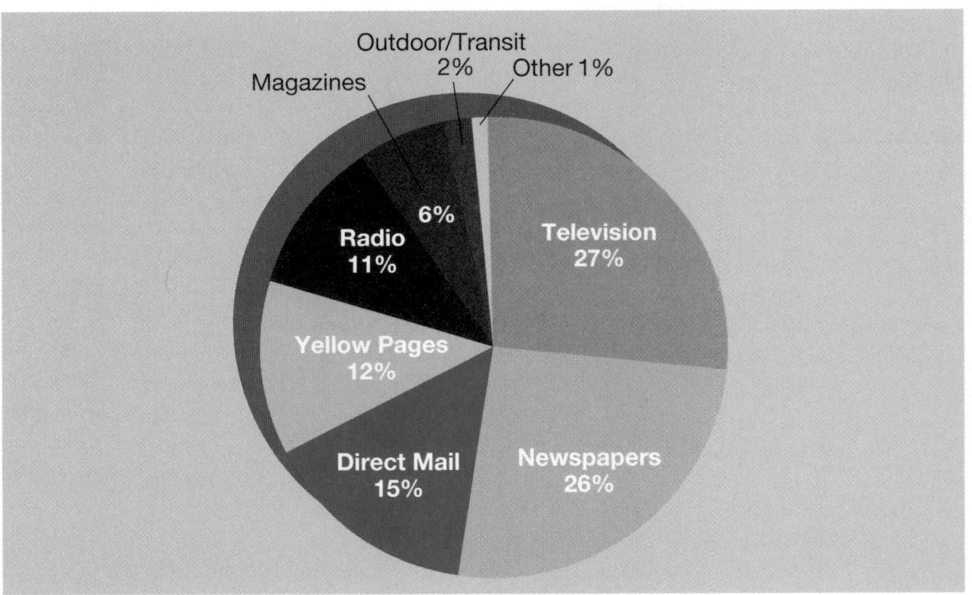

Choosing a Medium and a Vehicle within That Medium In deciding where to place advertisements, a company has several media to choose from and a number of alternatives, or vehicles, within each medium. Often advertisers use a mix of media forms and vehicles to maximize the exposure of the message to the target audience while at the same time minimizing costs. These two conflicting goals of (1) maximizing exposure and (2) minimizing costs are of central importance to media planning.

Basic Terms Media buyers speak a language of their own, so every advertiser involved in selecting the right media for their campaigns must be familiar with some common terms used in the advertising industry. Figure 20–2 shows the most common terms used in media decisions.

Because advertisers try to maximize the number of individuals in the target market exposed to the message, they must be concerned with reach. **Reach** is the number of different people or households exposed to an advertisement. The exact definition of reach sometimes varies among alternative media. Newspapers often use reach to describe their total circulation or the number of different households that buy the paper. Television and radio stations, in contrast, describe their reach using the term **rating**—the percentage of households in a market that are tuned to a particular TV show or radio station. In general, advertisers try to maximize reach in their target market at the lowest cost.

Although reach is important, advertisers are also interested in exposing their target audience to a message more than once. This is because consumers often do not pay close attention to advertising messages, some of which contain large amounts of relatively complex information. When advertisers want to reach the same audience more than once, they are concerned with **frequency,** the average number of times a person in the target audience is exposed to a message or advertisement. Like reach, greater frequency is generally viewed as desirable.[18]

When reach (expressed as a percentage of the total market) is multiplied by frequency, an advertiser will obtain a commonly used reference number called **gross rating points** (GRPs). To obtain the appropriate number of GRPs to achieve an advertising campaign's objectives, the media planner must balance reach and frequency. The balance will also be influenced by cost. **Cost per thousand** (CPM) refers to

The use of celebrity spokespersons is a popular form of advertising.

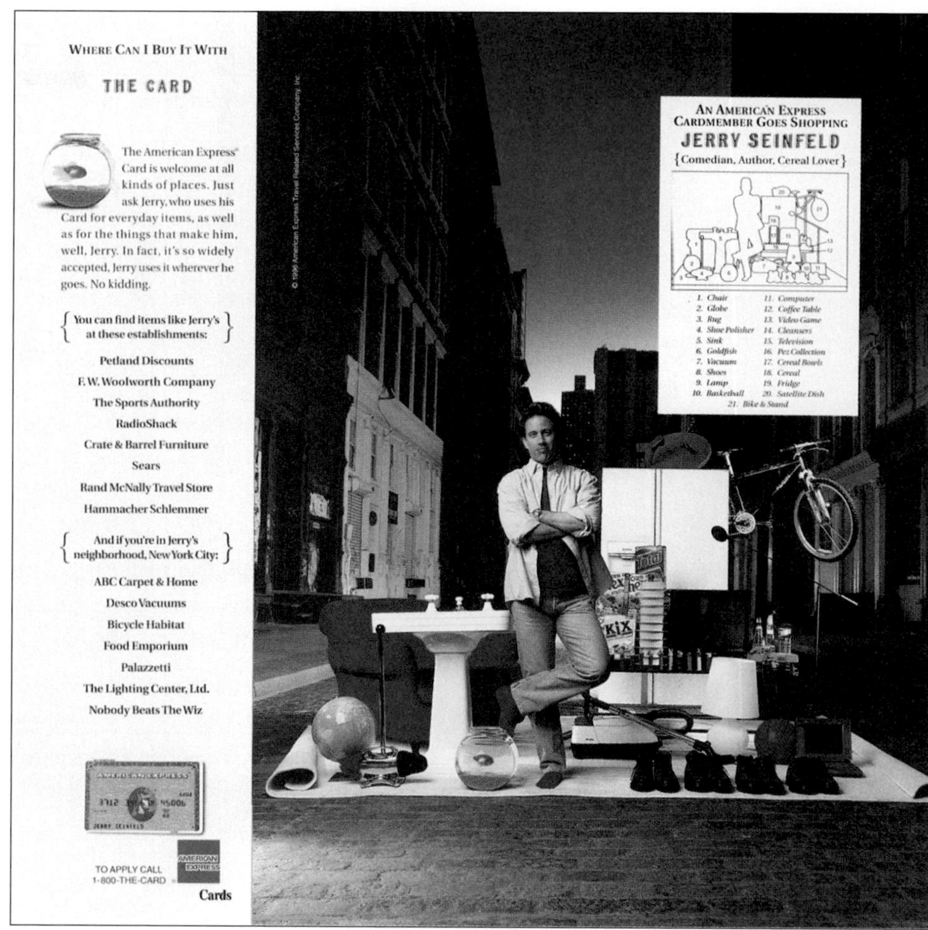

the cost of reaching 1000 individuals or households with the advertising message in a given medium (*M* is the Roman numeral for 1000).

Different Media Alternatives

Figure 20–3 summarizes the advantages and disadvantages of the important advertising media, which are described in more detail below.

FIGURE 20–2
The language of the media buyer

TERM	WHAT IT MEANS
Reach	The number of different people or households exposed to an advertisement.
Rating	The percentage of households in a market that are tuned to a particular TV show or radio station.
Frequency	The average number of times an individual is exposed to an advertisement.
Gross rating points (GRPs)	Reach (expressed as a percentage of the total market) multiplied by frequency.
Cost per thousand (CPM)	The cost of advertising divided by the number of thousands of individuals or households who are exposed.

FIGURE 20–3
Advantages and disadvantages of major advertising media

MEDIUM	ADVANTAGES	DISADVANTAGES
Television	Reaches extremely large audience; uses picture, print, sound, and motion for effect; can target specific audiences.	High cost to prepare and run ads; short exposure time and perishable message; difficult to convey complex information.
Radio	Low cost; can target specific audiences; ads can be placed quickly; can use sound, humour, and intimacy effectively.	No visual excitement; short exposure time and perishable message; difficult to convey complex information.
Magazines	Can target specific audiences; high-quality colour; long life of ad; ads can be clipped and saved; can convey complex information.	Long time needed to place ad; limited control of ad position; relatively high cost; competes for attention with other magazine features.
Newspapers	Excellent coverage of local markets; ads can be placed and changed quickly; ads can be saved; quick consumer response; low cost.	Ads compete for attention with other newspaper features; can't control ad position on page; short life span; can't target specific audiences.
Direct mail	Best for targeting specific audiences; very flexible (3-D, pop-up ads); ad can be saved; measurable.	Relatively high cost; audience often sees it as "junk mail"; no competition with editorial matter.
Internet	Video and audio capabilities; animation can capture attention; ads can be interactive and link to advertiser.	Animation and interactivity require large files and more time to "load." Effectiveness is still uncertain.
Outdoor	Low cost; local market focus; high visibility; opportunity for repeat exposures.	Message must be short and simple; low selectivity of audience; criticized as a traffic hazard, eyesore.

Sources: William F. Arens, *Contemporary Advertising,* 7th ed. (New York: McGraw-Hill/Irwin, 1999), pp. 268, R20; and William G. Nickels, James M. McHugh, and Susan M. McHugh, *Understanding Business,* 4th ed. (Homewood, IL: Richard D. Irwin, 1996), p. 495.

Television Television is a valuable medium because it communicates with sight, sound and motion. Print advertisements alone could never give you the sense of a sports car cornering at high speed or communicate Ford's excitement about its new Mustang. In addition, network television is the only medium that can reach 99 percent of the homes in Canada.[19]

Television's major disadvantage is cost: the average price of a prime-time 30-second sport on a Canadian national network can cost $30 000.[20] Because of these high charges, many advertisers have reduced the length of their commercials from 30 seconds to 15 seconds. This practice, referred to as *splitting 30s,* reduces costs but severely restricts the amount of information and emotion that can be conveyed. Research indicates, however, that two different versions of a 15-second commercial, run back-to-back, will increase recall over long intervals.[21]

Another problem with television is the likelihood of *wasted coverage*—having people outside the market for the product wee the advertisement. In recent years the cost and wasted coverage problems of TV have been reduced through the introduction of cable TV. Advertising time is often less expensive on cable channels than on the major networks. In addition, there are currently many cable channels—such as TSN, Much Music, and CNN—that reach very narrowly defined audiences.[22]

www.muchmusic.com

Other forms of television may soon change television advertising. Pay-per-episode channels such as DirecTV's Channel 199, pay-per-view movie services, and digital VCRs offer the potential of commercial-free viewing.

A relatively new, and increasingly popular, form of television advertising is the infomercial. **Infomercials** are program-length (30-minute) advertisements that take an educational approach to communication with potential customers. Volvo, Club Med, General Motors, Mattel, Revlon, and many other companies are using infomercials as a means of providing information that is relevant, useful, and entertaining to prospective customers.[23] Volvo's recent infomercial generated 4000 inquiries for additional information after airing just 13 times during a two-week period.[24]

Radio There are approximately 700 radio stations in Canada.[25] The major advantage of radio is that it is a segmented medium. There are jazz stations, classic music stations. all-talk shows, and hard rock stations, all listened to by different market segments. The average university or college student is a surprisingly heavy radio listener and spends more time during the day listening to radio than watching network television—2.2 hours versus 1.6 hours. Thus, advertisers with university and college students as their target market must consider radio.

The disadvantage of radio is that it has limited use for products that must be seen. Another problem is the ease with which consumers can tune out a commercial by switching stations. Radio is a medium that competes for people's attention as they do other activities such as driving, working, or relaxing. Peak radio listening time is during the drive times (6 to 10 A.M. and 4 to 7 P.M.).

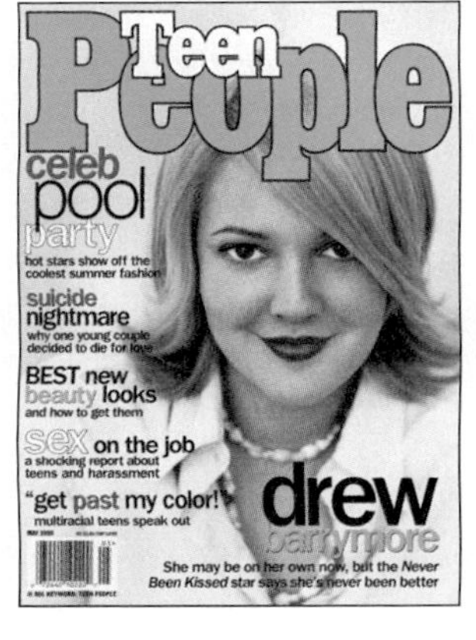

Magazines Magazines are becoming a very specialized medium. There are about 500 consumer magazines in Canada.[26] The marketing advantage of this medium is the great number of special-interest publications that appeal to narrowly defined segments. Runners read *Runner's World*, sailors buy *Sail*, gardeners subscribe to *Gardening Life,* and children peruse *Sports Illustrated for Kids*. Each magazine's readers often represent a unique profile. Take the *Rolling Stone* reader, who tends to travel, backpack, and ski more than most people—so a manufacturer of ski equipment that places an ad in *Rolling Stone* knows it is reaching the desired target audience. In addition to the distinct audience profiles of magazines, good colour production is an advantage that allows magazines to create strong images.

The cost of advertising in national magazines is a disadvantage, but many national publications publish regional and even metro editions, which reduce the absolute cost

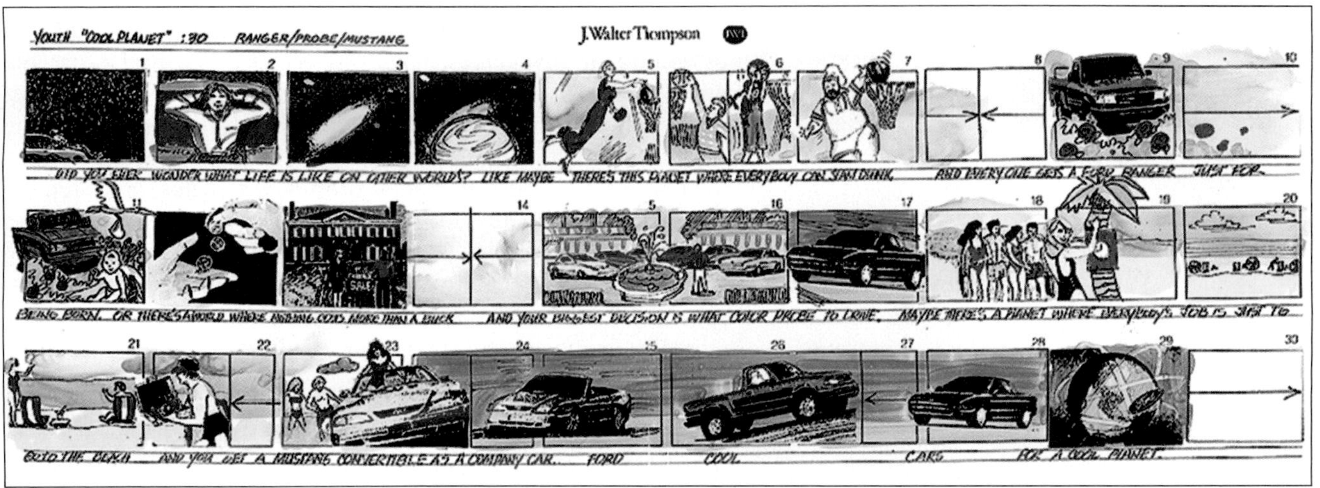

TV storyboards lead to commercials, which communicate with sight, sound, and motion.

and wasted coverage. In addition to cost, a limitation to magazines is their infrequency. At best, magazines are printed on a weekly basis, with many specialized publications appearing only monthly or less often.

Newspapers Newspapers are an important local medium with excellent reach potential. Because of the daily publication of most papers, they allow advertisements to focus on specific current events, such as a "24-hour sale." Local retailers often use newspapers as their sole advertising medium.

Newspapers are rarely saved by the purchaser, so companies are generally limited to ads that call for an immediate customer response (although customers can clip and save ads they want). Companies also cannot depend on newspapers for colour reproduction as good as that in most magazines.

www.globeandmail.ca

National advertising campaigns rarely include this medium except in conjunction with local distributors of their products. In these instances both parties often share the advertising costs using a cooperative advertising program, which is described later in this chapter. Another exception is the use of newspapers such as *The Globe and Mail*, which has national distribution.

In an effort to deliver timely news coverage, many newspapers are delivering online and this is opening up new advertising potential for such newspapers.

Direct Mail Direct mail allows the greatest degree of audience selectivity. Direct-mail companies can provide advertisers with a mailing list of their target market, such as students who live within two kilometres of the store, product managers in Toronto, or people who own mobile homes. Direct mail has an advantage in providing complete product information, compared with that provided in 15-second, 30-second, or 60-second television or radio spots. Many advertisers now use direct mail in combination with other media to create *integrated marketing communications programs.* Mass media are used to create awareness, while direct mail builds a relationship and facilitates a purchase.

One disadvantage of direct mail is that rising postal costs are making it more expensive. In fact, many direct-mail advertisers are beginning to use private delivery services, which sometimes charge less than Canada Post for catalogues and other mailers. The major limitation is that people often view direct mail as junk, and the challenge is to get them to open a letter. Databases, which help marketers send their target market only mail that is relevant to them, are improving consumers' response to advertising they receive in the mail.

Internet The Internet represents a relatively new medium for advertisers, although the growth of online advertising has been dramatic and has already attracted a wide variety of industries. Online advertising is similar to print advertising in that it offers a visual message. It has additional advantages, however, because it can also use the audio and video capabilities of the Internet. Movement and sound may simply attract more attention from viewers, or they may provide an element of entertainment to the message. Online advertising also has the unique feature of being interactive. Called *rich media*, these interactive ads have built-in games, drop-down menus, or search engines to engage viewers. Buy.com banner ads, for example, allow selection from a menu and a search for keywords. Online ads also allow viewers to "click-through" to the sponsor's Web site, where additional information or online purchases are available. Online advertising has become increasingly sophisticated in the past few years, and many experts expect the content and style to become similar to television advertising in the near future.[27]

One disadvantage of online advertising is that ads with audio and video elements take time to "load," so a viewer may click to another page before the ad becomes visible. Because the medium is new, there are some difficulties as the industry agrees on technical and administrative standards. Finally, another disadvantage of online advertising is the difficulty of measuring traffic. Current measurement techniques lead to very different ratings, which make it difficult for advertisers to know if their expenditures were a good value. According to Norman Lehoullier, managing director of ad agency Grey Interactive Worldwide, "It affects ad spending when you see wide discrepancies in numbers."[28]

A catchy billboard ad for eggs.

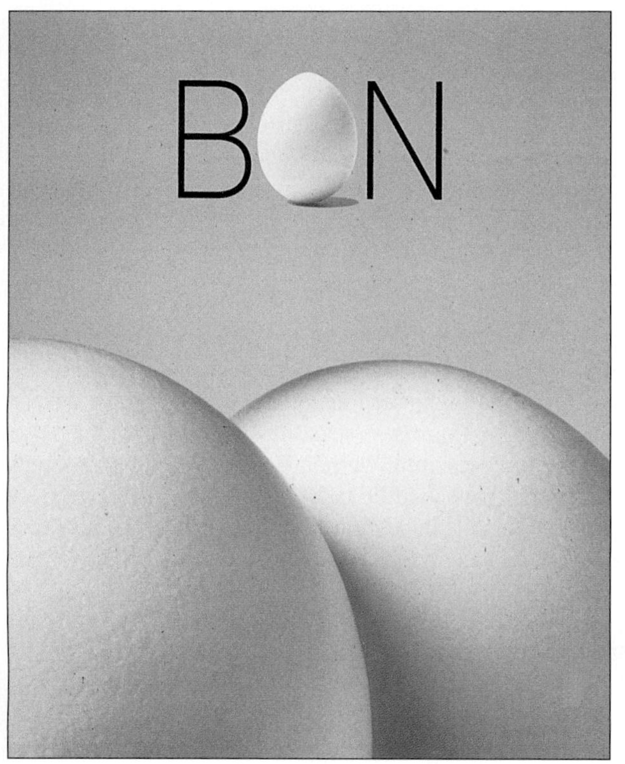

Outdoor A very effective medium for reminding consumers about your product is outdoor advertising. The most common form of outdoor advertising, called *billboards*, often results in good reach and frequency and has been shown to increase purchase rates.[29] The visibility of this medium is good supplemental reinforcement for well-known products, and it is a relatively low-cost, flexible alternative. A company can buy space just in the desired geographical market. A disadvantage to billboards, however, is that no opportunity exists for lengthy advertising copy. Also, a good billboard site depends on traffic patterns and sight lines. In many areas environmental laws have limited the use of this medium.

If you have ever lived in a metropolitan area, chances are you might have seen another form of outdoor advertising, transit advertising. This medium includes messages on the interior and exterior of buses, subway cars, and taxis. As use of mass transit grows, transit advertising may become increasingly important. Selectivity is available to advertisers, who can buy space by neighbourhood or bus route. For example, Shoppers Drug Mart of Toronto used two Toronto Transit Commission buses wrapped with Life labels and slogans and selected Toronto-area bus routes with possible high-traffic morning and evening rush hours. One disadvantage to this medium is that the heavy travel times, when the audiences are the largest, are not conducive to reading advertising copy. People are standing shoulder to shoulder on the subway, hoping not to miss their stop, and little attention is paid to the advertising.

Other Media As traditional media have become more expensive and cluttered, advertisers have been attracted to a variety of nontraditional advertising options, called *place-based media*. Messages are placed in locations that attract a specific target audience such as airports, doctors' offices, health clubs, theatres (where ads are played on the screen before the movies are shown), even bathrooms of bars, restaurants, and nightclubs![30]

Selection Criteria Choosing between these alternative media is difficult and depends on several factors. First, knowing the media habits of the target audience is essential to deciding among the alternatives. Second, occasionally product attributes necessitate that certain media be used. For example, if colour is a major aspect of product appeal, radio is excluded. Newspapers allow advertising for quick actions to confront competitors, and magazines are more appropriate for complicated messages because the reader can spend more time reading the message. The final factor in selecting a medium is cost. When possible, alternative media are compared using a common denominator that reflects both reach and cost—a measure such as CPM.

Scheduling the Advertising

There is no correct schedule to advertise a product, but three factors must be considered. First is the issue of *buyer turnover*, which is how often new buyers enter the market to buy the product. The higher the buyer turnover, the greater is the amount of advertising required. A second issue in scheduling is the *purchase frequency;* the more frequently the product is purchased, the less repetition is required. Finally, companies must consider the *forgetting rate*, the speed with which buyers forget the brand if advertising is not seen.

Setting schedules requires an understanding of how the market behaves. Most companies tend to follow one of three basic approaches:

1. *Continuous (steady) schedule.* When seasonal factors are unimportant, advertising is run at a continuous or steady schedule throughout the year.
2. *Flighting (intermittent) schedule.* Periods of advertising are scheduled between periods of no advertising to reflect seasonal demand.
3. *Pulse (burst) schedule.* A flighting schedule is combined with a continuous schedule because of increases in demand, heavy periods of promotion, or introduction of a new product.

For example, products such as dry breakfast cereals have a stable demand throughout the year and would typically use a continuous schedule of advertising. In contrast, products such as snow skis and suntan lotions have seasonal demands and receive flighting-schedule advertising during the seasonal demand period. Some products such as toys or automobiles require pulse-schedule advertising to facilitate sales throughout the year and during special periods of increased demand (such as holidays or new car introductions). Some evidence suggests that pulsing schedules are superior to other advertising strategies.[31]

CONCEPT CHECK

1. You see the same ad in *Time* and *Maclean's* magazines and on billboards and TV. Is this an example of reach or frequency?
2. Why has the Internet become a popular advertising medium?
3. What factors must be considered when choosing among alternative media?

EXECUTING THE ADVERTISING PROGRAM

Executing the advertising program involves pretesting the advertising copy and actually carrying out the advertising program. An advertiser once remarked, "I know half my advertising is wasted, but I don't know what half." By evaluating advertising efforts marketers can try to ensure that their advertising expenditures are not wasted.[32] Evaluation is done usually at two separate times: before and after the advertisements are run in the actual campaign. Several methods used in the evaluation process at the stages of idea formulation and copy development are discussed below. Post-testing methods are reviewed in the section on evaluation.

Pretesting the Advertising

To determine whether the advertisement communicates the intended message or to select among alternative versions of the advertisement, **pretests** are conducted before the advertisements are placed in any medium.

Portfolio Tests Portfolio tests are used to test copy alternatives. The test ad is placed in a portfolio with several other ads and stories, and consumers are asked to read through the portfolio. Afterward subjects are asked for their impressions of the ads on several evaluative scales, such as from "very informative" to "not very informative."

Jury Tests Jury tests involve showing the ad copy to a panel of consumers and having them rate how they liked it, how much it drew their attention, and how attractive they thought it was. This approach is similar to the portfolio test in that consumer reactions are obtained. However, unlike the portfolio test, a test advertisement is not hidden within other ads.

Theatre Tests Theatre testing is the most sophisticated form of pretesting. Consumers are invited to view new television shows or movies in which test commercials are also shown. Viewers register their feelings about the advertisements either on hand-held electronic recording devices used during the viewing or on questionnaires afterward.

Carrying Out the Advertising Program

www.sears.ca

The responsibility for actually carrying out the advertising program can be handled in one of three ways, as shown in Figure 20–4. The **full-service agency** provides the most complete range of services, including market research, media selection, copy development, artwork, and production. Agencies that assist a client by both developing and placing advertisements have traditionally charged a commission of 15 percent of media costs. As corporations have reorganized and cut costs, however, new methods of paying agencies have been introduced. About 45 percent of advertisers now pay less than 15 percent, while other pay preset fees. A small but growing number of advertisers pay performance-based fees. Advertising agency Young and Rubicam, Inc., for example, actually earned more than 15 percent from Sears because its "Softer Side of Sears" campaign has been so successful. Wrigley also uses a performance-based system to compensate its agency, BBDO.[33] **Limited-service agencies** specialize in one aspect of the advertising process such as providing creative services to develop the advertising copy or buying previously unpurchased media space. Limited-service agencies that deal in creative work are compensated by a contractual agreement for the services performed. Finally, **in-house agencies** made up of the company's own advertising staff may provide full services or a limited range of services.

FIGURE 20–4
Alternative structures of advertising agencies used to carry out the advertising program

TYPE OF AGENCY	SERVICES PROVIDED
Full-service agency	Does research, selects media, develops copy, and produces artwork
Limited-service agency	Specializes in one aspect of creative process; usually provides creative production work; buys previously unpurchased media space
In-house agency	Provides range of services, depending on company needs

EVALUATING THE ADVERTISING PROGRAM

The advertising decision process does not stop with executing the advertising program. The advertisements must be post-tested to determine whether they are achieving their intended objectives, and results may indicate that changes must be made in the advertising program.

Post-testing the Advertising

An advertisement may go through **post-tests** after it has been shown to the target audience to determine whether it accomplished its intended purpose. Five approaches common in post-testing are discussed here.[34]

Aided Recall (Recognition-Readership) After being shown an ad, respondents are asked whether their previous exposure to it was through reading, viewing, or listening. The Starch test shown in the accompanying photo uses aided recall to determine the percentage (1) who remember seeing a specific magazine ad (*noted*), (2) who saw or read any part of the ad identifying the product or brand (*seen-associated*), and (3) who read at least half of the ad (*read most*). Elements of the ad are then tagged with the results, as shown in the picture.

Starch scores an advertisement

Unaided Recall A question such as, "What ads do you remember seeing yesterday?" is asked of respondents without any prompting to determine whether they saw or heard advertising messages.

Attitude Tests Respondents are asked questions to measure changes in their attitudes after an advertising campaign, such as whether they have a more favourable attitude toward the product advertised.[35]

Inquiry Tests Additional product information, product samples, or premiums are offered to an ad's readers or viewers. Ads generating the most inquiries are presumed to be the most effective.

Sales Tests Sales tests involve studies such as controlled experiments (e.g., using radio ads in one market and newspaper ads in another and comparing the results) and consumer purchase tests (measuring retail sales that result from a given advertising campaign). The most sophisticated experimental methods today allow a manufacturer, a distributor, or an advertising agency to manipulate an advertising variable (such as schedule or copy) through cable systems and observe subsequent sales effects by monitoring data collected from checkout scanners in supermarkets.[36]

Making Needed Changes

Results of post-testing the advertising copy are used to reach decisions about changes in the advertising program. If the post-test results show that an advertisement is doing poorly in terms of awareness or cost efficiency, it may be dropped and other ads run in its place in the future. On the other hand, sometimes an advertisement may be so successful it is run repeatedly or used as the basis of a larger advertising program, as with Colgate's "White on White" laundry detergent commercials now used in 30 countries.

CONCEPT CHECK

1. Explain the difference between pretesting and post-testing advertising copy.
2. What is the difference between aided and unaided recall post-tests?

SALES PROMOTION

The Importance of Sales Promotion

At one time, sales promotion was considered by many to be a supplemental ingredient of the promotionla mix. But more recently the use of sales promotion has increased, and so has its perceived importance to marketers. In fact, in Canada, more money is now spent on sales promotion than on advertising.[37]

There are several reasons for the growth in importance of sales promotion. For one, many marketers are looking for measurable results from their promotional efforts. Sales promotion is viewed as an effective tool in this regard. Second, consumers and the trade (e.g., retailers) have become more value-conscious and tus more responsive to sale spromotion activites. Third, some suggest that the use of sales promotion has grown because it has become contagious. In short, many marketers are simply responding to the increased use of sales promotion by competitors. Finally, the availability of information technology such as computeriezed scanning equipment has also served as a stimulus for the growth of sales promotion.

While sales promotion techniques have grown in use and in stature, they are rarely used in isolation or as a stand-alone promotional tool. With the trend towards integrated marketing communications, sales promotion techniques are used more commonly in conjunction with other promotional activities. However, the selection and integration of the many sales promotion techniques requires a good understanding of the relative advantages and disadvantages of each kind of sales promotion.[38]

Consumer-Oriented Sales Promotions

Directed to ultimate consumers, **consumer-oriented sales promotions,** or simply consumer promotions, are sales tools used to support a company's advertising and personal selling efforts. The alternative consumer-oriented sales promotion tools include coupons, deals, premiums, contests, sweepstakes, samples, continuity programs, point-of-purchase displays, rebates, and product placement (see Figure 20–5).

Coupons Coupons are typically printed certificates that give the bearer a saving or a stated price reduction when they purchase a specific product. Coupons can be used to stimulate demand for mature products, or promote the early trial of a new brand. In 1999, an estimated 2.7 billion direct-to-consumer coupons were distributed in Canada. Consumers redeemed over 130 million of these coupons having an average face value of 86 cents. This means that Canadians saved about $112 million on products as a result of using coupons.[39]

Studies show that when coupons are used, a company's market share does increase during the period immediately after they are distributed.[40] There are indications, however, that couponing can reduce gross revenues by lowering the price paid by already-loyal consumers.[41] Therefore, manufacturers and retailers are particularly interested in coupon programs directed at potential first-time buyers. One means of focusing on

KIND OF SALES PROMOTION	OBJECTIVES	ADVANTAGES	DISADVANTAGES
Coupons	Stimulate demand	Encourage retailer support	Consumers delay purchases
Deals	Increase trial; retaliate against competitor's actions	Reduce consumer risk	Consumers delay purchases; reduce perceived product value
Premiums	Build goodwill	Consumers like free or reduced-price merchandise	Consumers buy for premium, not product
Contests	Increase consumer purchases; build business inventory	Encourage consumer involvement with product	Require creative or analytical thinking
Sweepstakes	Encourage present customers to buy more; minimize brand switching	Get customer to use product and store more often	Sales drop after sweepstakes
Samples	Encourage new product trial	Low risk for consumer	High cost for company
Continuity programs	Encourage repeat purchases	Help create loyalty	High cost for company
Point-of-purchase displays	Increase product trial; provide in-store support for other promotions	Provide good product visibility	Hard to get retailer to allocate high-traffic space
Rebates	Encourage customers to purchase; stop sales decline	Effective at stimulating demand	Easily copied; steal sales from future; reduce perceived product value
Product placement	Introduce new products; demonstrate product use	Positive message in a noncommercial setting	Little control over presentation of product

FIGURE 20–5
Sales promotion alternatives

these potential buyers is through electronic in-store coupon machines that match coupons to your most recent purchases.[42]

Deals Deals are short-term price reductions, commonly used to increase trial among potential customers or to retaliate against a competitor's actions. There are two basic types of deals: cents-off deals and price-pack deals. Cents-off deals offer a brand at less than a regular price, and the reduced prices are generally marked directly on the label or package. Cents-off deals can be very effective, even more so than coupons in stimulating short-term sales.

Price-pack deals offer consumers something extra such as "20 percent more for the same price," or "Two packages for the price of one." Price-pack deals can be very effective in retaliating against or preempting a competitor's actions. For example, if a rival manufacturer introduces a new cake mix, the company could respond with the price-pack deal (e.g., 2 for 1) building up the stock on the kitchen shelves of cake mix buyers and making the competitor's introduction more difficult. Marketers must be careful, however, of overusing deals. If consumers expect a deal they may delay a purchase until the deal occurs. Moreover, frequent deals may erode the perceived value of the brand to the consumer.

Premiums Premiums are items offered free or at a significant savings as incentives to buy a product. A premium offered at below its normal price is known as *self-liquidating* because the cost charged to the consumers covers the cost of the item. For example, Burger King recently offered sunglasses like those worn by Will Smith in the movie *The Wild, Wild West* at a nominal price to their customers. Offering premiums at no-cost or at low-cost encourage customers to return frequently or to use more of the product. However, the company must be careful that the consumer doesn't just buy the premium.

Contests A fourth sales promotion in Figure 20–5, the contest, is where consumers apply their analytical aor creative thinking to try to win a prize. Most often a consumer submits an entry to be judged by a panel. Many companies use contests not only to increase consumer purchases, but to obtain the names and addresses of consumers for use in database marketing purposes. Gillette's Cavalcade of Sports 25-week hockey pool contest awarded a $1 million weekly cash prize to each week's winner. If you like contests, read the accompanying Web Link to learn how to enter contest online!

www.readersdigest.ca

Sweepstakes A sweepstakes requires participants to submit some kind of entry form but are purely games of chance requiring no analytical or creative effort by the consumer. *Reader's Digest* and Publisher's Clearing House are two of the better-known sweepstakes. Canada has federal and provincial regulations covering sweepstakes, contests, and games regarding fairness, to ensure that the chance of winning is represented honestly and to guarantee that the prizes are awarded.

www.shoppersdrugmart.ca

Samples Another common consumer sales promotion is sampling, or offering the product free or at a greatly reduced price. Often used for new products, sampling puts the product in the consumer's hands. a trial size is generally offered that is smaller than the regular package size. If he consumers like the sample, it is hoped they will remember and buy the product. Kimberly-Clark used sampling to promote its UltraTrim diapers. It undertook a personally addressed sample mailing to 235 000 Canadian households using a database of mothers provided by Welcome Wagon. The sampling program was backed by TV advertising developed specifically for the Canadian market, as well as newspaper and magazine ads with coupons. Shoppers Drug Mart of Toronto handed out 18 000 samples of Life brand health & beauty products on Toronto Transit Commission buses, while EMI Music Canada is offering customers a free CD sampler featuring new Canadian bands.

Continuity Programs Continuity programs, sometimes referred to as loyalty programs, are a sales promotion tool used to encourage and reward repeat purchases by acknowledging each purchase made by a consumer and offering a premium as purchases accumulate. Airlines' and hotels' frequent-flyer and frequent-guest programs are examples. Even General Motors of Canada has a continuity program—a credit card that allows consumers to accumulate points that can be used to reduce the purchase price of a new GM vehicle. Of course, you might also be familiar with The Second Cup's "buy X, get one free" cards, or Chapters Inc.'s Chapter One Card that offers discounts and gift certificates to loyal customers.[43]

Point-of-Purchase Displays In a store aisle, you often encounter a sales promotion called a point-of-purchase display. These product displays take the form of adver-

WEB LINK You're In Luck—Contests Galore!

If you like taking your chances in sweepstakes or if you're a skilled contest participant then this is the place for you! Go to www.playhere.com, and click on "Games and Giveaways." The site lists many contests and sweepstakes designed to attract consumers. Choose one that sounds appealing, and click again. In many cases, you can enter directly over the Internet. Good luck!

A gravity-feed bin that doubles as a point-of-purchase display.

tising signs, which sometimes actually hold or display the product, and are often located in high-traffic areas near the cash register or the end of an aisle. The accompanying picture shows gravity-feed bins that Nabisco uses for its animal crackers; it helps ensure product freshness, provides storage, and captures the consumer's attention as an end-aisle, point-of-purchase display.

Some studies estimate that two thirds of a consumer's buying decisions are made in the store. This means that grocery product manufacturers want to get their message to you at the instant you are next to their brand in your supermarket aisle—perhaps through a point-of-purchase display. At many supermarkets this may be done through Actmedia's in-store marketing network. Supermarket shopping cart displays, video screens in the aisles, and audio messages remind shoppers about products they might consider buying. The advantage of these methods of promotion is that they do not rely on consumers' ability to remember the message for long periods of time. Other in-store promotions such as interactive kiosks are also becoming popular.[44]

Rebates Another consumer sales promotion in Figure 20–5, the cash rebate, offers the return of money based on proof of purchase. This tool has been used heavily by car manufacturers facing increased competition. For example, Cadillac increased its sales to maintain its number one position over Lincoln by offering $3000 rebates.[45] When the rebate is offered on lower-priced items, the time and trouble of mailing in a proof-of-purchase to get the rebate check means that many buyers—attracted by the rebate offer—never take advantage of it. However, this "slippage" is less likely to occur with frequent users of rebate promotions.[46]

Product Placement A final consumer promotion, **product placement,** involves the use of a brand-name product in a movie, television show, video, or a commercial for another product. Companies are usually eager to gain exposure for their products, and the studios believe that product placements add authenticity to the film or program. The studios also receive fees—usually $40 000—although merchandise may be offered instead of cash. Ford Explorers appeared in *Jurassic Park* because Ford agreed to supply 10 of the vehicles and sell them at wholesale to the production company members after the filming was completed. How are product placements arranged? Many companies simply send brochures and catalogues to the studio resource departments; others are approached by agents who review scripts to find promising scenes where a product might be used.[47]

Trade-Oriented Sales Promotions

Trade-oriented sales promotions, or simply trade promotions, are sales tools used to support a company's advertising and personal selling directed to wholesalers, retailers, or distributors. Some of the sales promotions just reviewed are used for this purpose, but there are three other common approaches targeted uniquely to these intermediaries: (1) allowances and discounts, (2) cooperative advertising, and (3) training of distributors' salesforces.

Allowances and Discounts Trade promotions often focus on maintaining or increasing inventory levels in the channel of distribution. An effective method for encouraging such increased purchases by intermediaries is the use of allowances and discounts. However, overuse of these "price reductions" can lead to retailers changing their ordering patterns in the expectation of such offerings. Although there are many variations that manufacturers can use with discounts and allowances, three common approaches include the merchandise allowance, the case allowance, and the finance allowance.[48]

Reimbursing a retailer for extra in-store support or special featuring of the brand is a *merchandise allowance*. Performance contracts between the manufacturer and trade member usually specify the activity to be performed, such as a picture of the product in a newspaper with a coupon good at only one store. The merchandise allowance then consists of a percentage deduction from the list case price ordered during the promotional period. Allowances are not paid by the manufacturer until it sees proof of performance (such as a copy of the ad placed by the retailer in the local newspaper).

A second common trade promotion, a *case allowance*, is a discount on each case ordered during a specific time period. These allowances are usually deducted from the invoice. A variation of the case allowance is the "free goods" approach, whereby retailers receive some amount of the product free based on the amount ordered, such as one case free for every 10 cases ordered.[49]

A final trade promotion, the *finance allowance*, involves paying retailers for financing costs or financial losses associated with consumer sales promotions. This trade promotion is regularly used and has several variations. One type is the floor stock protection program—manufacturers give retailers a case allowance price for products in their warehouse, which prevents shelf stock from running down during the promotional period. Also common are freight allowances, which compensate retailers that transport orders from the manufacturer's warehouse.

Cooperative Advertising Resellers often perform the important function of promoting the manufacturer's products at the local level. One common sales promotional activity is to encourage both better quality and greater quantity in the local advertising efforts of resellers through **cooperative advertising.** These are programs by which a manufacturer pays a percentage of the retailer's local advertising expense for advertising the manufacturer's products.

Usually the manufacturer pays a percentage, often 50 percent, of the cost of advertising up to a certain dollar limit, which is based on the amount of the purchases the retailer makes of the manufacturer's products. In addition to paying for the advertising, the manufacturer often furnishes the retailer with a selection of different ad executions, sometimes suited for several different media. A manufacturer may provide, for example, several different print layouts as well as a few broadcast ads for the retailer to adapt and use.[50]

Training of Distributors' Salesforces One of the many functions the intermediaries perform is customer contact and selling for the producers they represent. Both retailers and wholesalers employ and manage their own sales personnel. A manufacturer's success often rests on the ability of the reseller's salesforce to represent its products.

Thus, it is in the best interest of the manufacturer to help train the reseller's salesforce. Because the reseller's salesforce is often less sophisticated and knowledgeable about the products than the manufacturer might like, training can increase their sales performance. Training activities include producing manuals and brochures to educate the reseller's salesforce. The salesforce then uses these aids in selling situations. Other activities include national sales meetings sponsored by the manufacturer and field visits to the reseller's location to inform and motivate the salesperson to sell the products. Manufacturers also develop incentive and recognition programs to motivate reseller's salespeople to sell their products.

CONCEPT CHECK

1. Which sales promotional tool is most common for new products?
2. What's the difference between a coupon and a deal?
3. Which trade promotion is used on an ongoing basis?

PUBLIC RELATIONS

As noted in Chapter 19, public relations is a form of communication management that seeks to influence the image of an organization and its products and services. Public relations efforts may utilize a variety of tools and may be directed at many distinct audiences. While public relations personnel usually focus on communicating positive aspects of the business, they may also be called on to minimize the negative impact of a problem or crisis. Intel, for example, had already shipped millions of its Pentium microprocessor chips when it was revealed that the chip had a flaw that caused mathematical errors.[51] Unfortunately, the company initially denied the seriousness of the problem, creating a more difficult situation for the public relations department.

Public Relations Tools

In developing a public relations campaign, several tools and tactics are available to the marketer. The most frequently used public relations tool is publicity, which we defined in Chapter 19 as a nonpersonal, indirectly paid presentation of an organization, good, or service. Publicity usually takes the form of a *news release,* consisting of an announcement regarding changes in the company, or the product line.

The objective of a news release is to inform a newspaper, radio station, or other medium of an idea for a story. A study found that more than 40 percent of all free mentions of a brand name occur during news programs.[52] A second common publicity tool is the *news conference.* Representatives of the media are all invited to an informational meeting, and advance materials regarding the content are sent. This tool is often used when negative publicity—as in the cases of the Tylenol poisonings and the Audi 5000 acceleration problem—requires a company response.[53]

www.redcross.ca

Nonprofit organizations rely heavily on publicity to spread their messages. PSAs (*public service announcements*), where free space or time is donated by the media, is a common use of publicity for these organizations. The Canadian Red Cross, for example, depends on PSAs on radio and television to announce their needs.

A growing area of public relations involves the creation, or support, and publicizing of *special events* such as company-sponsored seminars, conferences, sports competitions, entertainment events, or other celebrations. The goal of events sponsorship is to create a forum to disseminate company information or to create brand identification to members of the target audience. College sports events such as the CIAU hockey and football championships are sponsored by Coca-Cola and General Motors, while AT&T Canada is the official sponsor of the Calgary Stampede, and the Canadian Senior Golf Championship. Western Union, EMI's Beat Factory, Loblaw's and the Toronto Raptors sponsor Toronto's Caribana Caribbean Music Festival, and Chrysler Canada, Canada Trust and others sponsor the development of the Canadian Trail project.[54]

www.nba.com/raptors/

Another public relations tool is for the organization to engage in *public-service activities* such as establishing or supporting community-based initiatives that benefit the

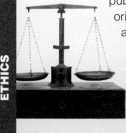

ETHICS

ETHICS AND SOCIAL RESPONSIBILITY ALERT

Public Relations: What Should We Believe?

Many organizations realize that most consumers view public relations, particularly news-oriented publicity as more credible than advertising per se. As such, many organizations have turned to well-managed public relations programs in order to influence the perceptions that relevant publics have toward them or their causes. Many organizations disseminate information that will cast them only in the best possible light or to ensure that their view on a particular issue is conveyed to the public. However, there is a growing concern that the public relations battle being waged between PETA (People for the Ethical Treatment of Animals) and the Canadian Cattlemen's Association. PETA is using a public relations campaign to persuade men to stop eating meat. Their message: eating meat causes impotence. But doctors claim that while there may be some truth in the claim, it's only a small part of the story. The Canadian Cattlemen's Association, which represents beef producers, dismisses PETA's claims as "ludicrous." This campaign by PETA follows on the heels of another campaign titled "Jesus was a Vegetarian," that encourages Christians to give up meat.

What are the dangers when organizations with conflicting views on an issue market their positions via public relations activities? What role does the media have in this situation?

well-being of society. For example, Ciba-Geigy Canada sponsors Health & Welfare Canada's Quit 4 Life Program, which encourages teens to quit smoking.

Finally, the development of *collateral materials* such as annual reports, brochures, newsletters, or video presentations about the company and its products are also basic public relations tools. These materials provide information to target publics and often generate publicity.

Good public relations activities should be planned and made part of an organization's integrated marketing communications effort. However, public relations activities must be used wisely and in an ethical and socially responsible manner (see the accompanying Ethics and Social Responsibility Alert).[55]

CONCEPT CHECK

1. What is a news release?
2. A growing area of public relations is ______________________.

SUMMARY

1 Advertising may be classified as either product or institutional. Product advertising can take three forms: pioneering, competitive, or reminder. Institutional ads are one of these three or advocacy.

2 The promotion decision process described in Chapter 19 can be applied to each of the promotional elements such as advertising.

3 Copywriters and art directors have the responsibility of identifying the key benefits of a product and communicating them to the target audience with attention-getting advertising. Common appeals include fear, sex, and humor.

4 In selecting the right medium, there are distinct trade-offs among television, radio, magazines, newspapers, direct mail, outdoor, and other media. The decision is based on media habits of the target audience, product characteristics, message requirements, and media costs.

5 In determining advertising schedules, a balance must be made between reach and frequency. Scheduling must take into account buyer turnover, purchase frequency, and the rate at which consumers forget.

6 Advertising is evaluated before and after the ad is run. Pretesting can be done with portfolio, jury, or theatre tests. Posttesting is done on the basis of aided recall, unaided recall, attitude tests, inquiry tests, and sales tests.

7 To execute an advertising program, companies can use several types of advertising agencies. These firms can provide a full range of services or specialize in creative or placement activities. Some firms use their own in-house agency.

8 More money is spent on sales promotion than on advertising. Selecting sales promotions requires a good understanding of the advantages and disadvantages of each option.

9 There is a wide range of consumer-oriented sales promotions: coupons, deals, premiums, contests, sweepstakes, samples, continuity programs, point-of-purchase displays, rebates, and product placements.

10 Trade-oriented promotions consist of allowances and discounts, cooperative advertising, and training of distributors' salesforces. These are used at all levels of the channel.

11 The most frequently used public relations tool is publicity—a nonpersonal, indirectly paid presentation of an organization, good, or service conducted through new releases, news conferences, or public service announcements.

12 Efforts to improve the value of promotion include emphasizing long-term relationships and increasing self-regulation.

KEY TERMS AND CONCEPTS

advertising p. 508
product advertisements p. 508
institutional advertisements p. 509
reach p. 514
rating p. 514
frequency p. 514
gross rating points p. 514
cost per thousand p. 514
infomercials p. 517
pretests p. 520
full-service agency p. 521
limited-service agencies p. 521
in-house agencies p. 521
post-tests p. 522
consumer-oriented sales promotions p. 523
product placement p. 526
trade-oriented sales promotions p. 526
cooperative advertising p. 527

INTERNET EXERCISE

Most Web pages accept some form of advertising. If you were to advise your college or university to advertise on the Web, what three Web pages would you recommend? You can use the information at www.adhome.com to help make your recommendation.

1 What is the monthly rate for a full banner ad at each of the Web sites?

2 Describe the profile of the audience for each of the Web sites.

3 Calculate the CPM for each Web site.

WEB SITE	MONTHLY RATE	AUDIENCE PROFILE	CPM
1.			
2.			
3.			

APPLYING MARKETING CONCEPTS AND PERSPECTIVES

1 How does competitive product advertising differ from competitive institutional advertising?

2 Suppose you are the advertising manager for a new line of children's fragrances. Which form of media would you use for this new product?

3 You have recently been promoted to be director of advertising for the Timkin Tool Company. In your first meeting with Mr. Timkin, he says, "Advertising is a waste! We've been advertising for six months now and sales haven't increased. Tell me why we should continue." Give your answer to Mr. Timkin.

4 A large life insurance company has decided to switch from using a strong fear appeal to a humorous approach. What are the strengths and weaknesses of such a change in message strategy?

5 Some national advertisers have found that they can have more impact with their advertising by running a large number of ads for a period and then running no ads at all for a period. Why might such a flighting schedule be more effective than a steady schedule?

6 Which medium has the lowest cost per thousand?

MEDIUM	COST	AUDIENCE
TV show	$5000	25 000
Magazine	2200	6000
Newspaper	4800	7200
FM radio	420	1600

7 Each year managers at Bausch and Lomb evaluate the many advertising media alternatives available to them as they develop their advertising program for contact lenses. What advantages and disadvantages of each alternative should they consider? Which media would you recommend to them?

8 What are two advantages and two disadvantages of the advertising post-tests described in the chapter?

9 The Royal Bank is interested in consumer-oriented sales promotions that would encourage senior citizens to direct deposit their Canada pension cheques with the bank. Evaluate the sales promotion options, and recommend two of them to the bank.

CASE 20–1 LYSOL

L&F is a North American business unit of the Kodak Corporation. An important brand for L&F is the Lysol product line. Most Canadian consumers are familiar with Lysol Spray, but L&F wants to increase sales of not only the spray product, but also the entire line of Lysol products. It is attempting to develop a strategy in Canada in order to market more of the entire line of Lysol products.

Lysol, primarily the spray, has a long brand heritage in Canada. The disinfectant benefit of the product is very distinctive. In the early 1990s, Lysol spray had 44 percent household penetration in Canada, but the other Lysol products—Lysol Basin, Tub & Tile Cleaner; Lysol Toilet Bowl Cleaner; and Lysol Liquid (All-Purpose) Cleaner—had much lower penetration. With little existing synergy between the products within the line, L&F wanted to bring these disparate products together. In doing so, L&F could achieve economies of scale in terms of marketing expenses. The company believed that by combining the marketing budgets for the four separate products, it could achieve a greater impact on the market. It was felt that one way to link the products together was through the unifying benefit of disinfection.

L&F wanted to achieve a greater market penetration with all four products. However, the overall household cleaning product category was not growing and in some areas was actually declining. Some industry people felt that one reason for this was that many households were cleaning less. They also felt that the recession was impacting on sales in the category. Therefore, new growth for Lysol would have to come at the expense of existing competitors.

While all competitors were using advertising and couponing, the intensity of the battle was at the shelf level. Competitive firms were literally battling it out for shelf space in order to capture market share. This meant that trade sales promotions were being used extensively, often in the form of price discounting. L&F felt it shouldn't get more involved in trade discounts because of the squeeze it put on margins. It did believe, however, that limited use of consumer coupons should be part of its overall consumer-focused marketing communications activity.

L&F believed that the Lysol brand probably had a rather tired personality. The company wanted to give it a 1990s contemporary, interesting, and even provocative image. The problem was that to most consumers, household cleaning products were really an uninteresting category. As such, building consumer awareness of the entire line would not be possible without increasing the level of consumer involvement. The question was how to create interest or involvement with the product line. A way had to be found to demonstrate the line and to have consumers pay attention.

L&F knew that timing would be important. For example, interest in the category would be highest just before or during traditional spring cleaning time in Canada, which ran between late February to early May. Interest would also be high again in late fall or early winter. But if the product line itself could not be made interesting or more involving, even good timing wouldn't help.

L&F had to determine an appropriate creative message for the consumer, select an appropriate communications medium, and consider other ways to build sales and market share for the line.

Questions

1 What would be the most appropriate advertising medium for L&F to use in order to communicate with its market?

2 What would be a creative way to build consumer involvement with the product line? What would be the specific message and execution?

3 Besides the specific advertising medium you recommended to L&F in question 1, what other promotional activities would you recommend to build sales and market share for the Lysol line?

4 What type of advertising schedule would you recommend L&F use during the year?

HOME

CHAPTER TWENTY-ONE

PERSONAL SELLING AND SALES MANAGEMENT

21

AFTER READING THIS CHAPTER YOU SHOULD BE ABLE TO:

- Recognize different types of personal selling.
- Describe the stages in the personal selling process.
- Specify the functions and tasks in the sales management process.
- Determine whether a firm should use manufacturer's representatives or a company salesforce and the number of people needed in a company's salesforce.
- Understand how firms recruit, select, train, motivate, compensate, and evaluate salespeople.
- Describe recent applications of salesforce automation.

DUN & BRADSTREET: SELLING DATA IN THE INFORMATION AGE

Dun & Bradstreet (www.dnbcorp.com) is a master of database management and marketing. D&B's database of companies is unrivalled, and its sterling reputation for reliability should make D&B's sales effort easy. If only this were so.

Selling information in the information age is a demanding task. "It's difficult to relay the benefits of our services before customers actually start using them," says Joan Rothman, senior vice president of marketing for D&B (shown on the opposite page). "Also, our market has become more competitive, especially with the onslaught of the Internet. Customers are able to gather so much raw data for free."

Among D&B's customers are company credit managers, who desire data on the creditworthiness of their customers, and marketing departments that wish to gather information on present and future customers. D&B's field salespeople must demonstrate how much better off credit managers and marketing executives would be had they already been using D&B's information. This sales process is time consuming. It recently took D&B 15 weeks of weekly meetings to sell a new service for the small-business sector to a major bank—with a seven-person sales and technical support team involved to get the account. "We had to sit down and show the bank, step by step, how much more information we had on their small-business customers and prospects than our competitors did," said Mike Archer, D&B's vice president of financial services. The effort paid off. This account now represents a multimillion-dollar business for D&B.[1]

This chapter examines the scope and significance of personal selling and sales management in marketing. It first highlights the many forms of personal selling and outlines the selling process. The functions of sales management are then described, including recent advances in salesforce automation.

SCOPE AND SIGNIFICANCE OF PERSONAL SELLING AND SALES MANAGEMENT

Chapter 19 described personal selling and management of the sales effort as being part of the firm's promotional mix. Although it is important to recognize that personal selling is a useful vehicle for communicating with present and potential buyers, it is much more. Take a moment to answer the questions in the personal selling and sales management quiz in Figure 21–1. As you read on, compare your answers with those in the text.

Nature of Personal Selling and Sales Management

Personal selling involves the two-way flow of communication between a buyer and seller, often in a face-to-face encounter, designed to influence a person's or group's purchase decision. However, with advances in telecommunications, personal selling also takes place over the telephone, through video teleconferencing and interactive computer links between buyers and sellers. For example, customers of Haggar Apparel Company can enter purchase orders into their computer, have it contact Haggar's computer, and find out when the requested products can be shipped.

Personal selling remains a highly human-intensive activity despite the use of technology. Accordingly, the people involved must be managed. **Sales management** involves planning the selling program and implementing and controlling the personal selling effort of the firm. Numerous tasks are involved in managing personal selling, including setting objectives; organizing the salesforce; recruiting, selecting, training, and compensating salespeople; and evaluating the performance of individual salespeople.

Pervasiveness of Selling

"Everyone lives by selling something," wrote author Robert Louis Stevenson a century ago. His observation still holds true today. In Canada, more than one million people are employed in sales positions.[2] Included in this number are manufacturing sales personnel, real estate brokers, stockbrokers, and salesclerks who work in retail stores. In reality, however, virtually every occupation that involves customer contact has an element of personal selling. For example, lawyers, accountants, bankers, and company personnel recruiters perform sales-related activities, whether or not they acknowledge it.

Many executives in major companies have held sales positions at some time in their careers. For example, Victor Kiam, the flamboyant chair and chief executive officer of Remington Products, Inc., previously held a sales position at Lever Brothers. It might be said that today Kiam is Remington's most visible salesperson. It is no accident that

FIGURE 21–1
Personal selling and sales management quiz

1. About how much does it cost for a manufacturer's sales representative to make a single personal sales call? (check one)

$100 _____	$200 _____	$300 _____
$150 _____	$250 _____	$350 _____

2. "A salesperson's job is finished when a sale is made." True or false? (circle one)

   True   False

3. About what percent of companies include customer satisfaction as a measure of salesperson performance? (check one)

10% _____	30% _____	50% _____
20% _____	40% _____	60% _____

Could this be a salesperson in the operating room? Read the text to find why salespeople visit hospital operating rooms to find better ways to create customer value.

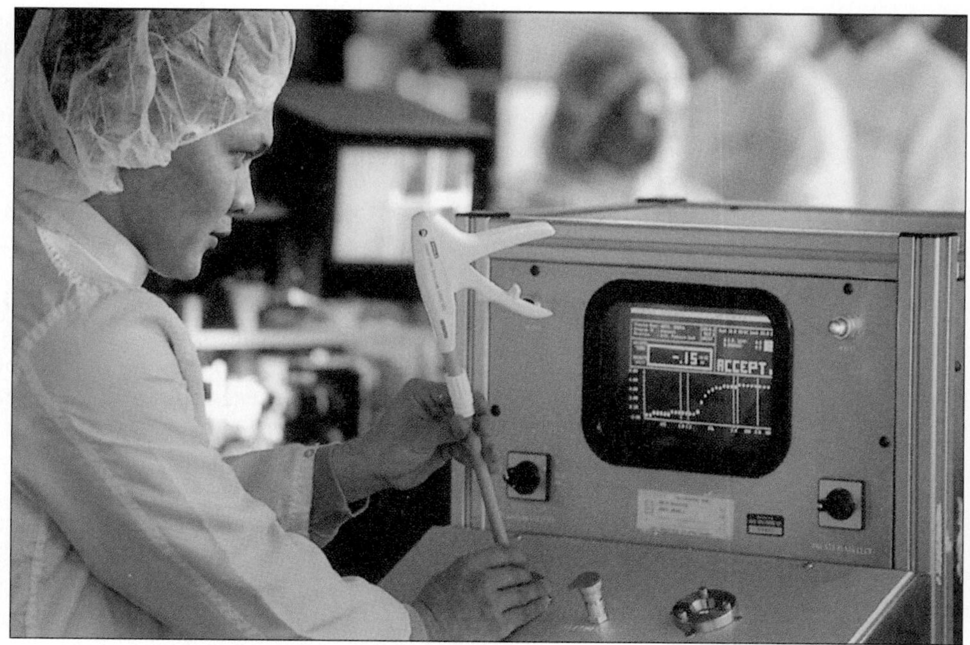

these individuals rose from sales and marketing positions to top management. Thus, selling often serves as a stepping-stone to top management, as well as being a careeer path in itself.

Personal Selling in Marketing

Personal selling serves three major roles in a firm's overall marketing effort. First, salespeople are the critical link between the firm and its customers. This role requires that salespeople match company interests with customer needs to satisfy both parties in the exchange process. Second, salespeople *are* the company in a consumer's eyes. They represent what a company is or attempts to be and are often the only personal contact a customer has with the company. For example, the "look" projected by salespeople for Avon Products, Inc. is an important factor in communicating the benefits of the company's cosmetic line. Third, personal selling may play a dominant role in a firm's marketing program. This situation typically arises when a firm uses a push marketing strategy, described in Chapter 19. Avon, for example, pays almost 40 percent of its total sales dollars for selling expenses. Pharmaceutical firms and office and educational equipment manufacturers also rely heavily on personal selling in the marketing of their products.

Creating Customer Value Through Salespeople: Relationship and Partnership Selling

As the critical link between the firm and its customers, salespeople can create customer value in many ways.[3] For instance, by being close to the customer, salespeople can identify creative solutions to customer problems. Salespeople at surgical-supply companies observe hospital surgical practices and devote hours to questioning surgeons on how surgeries can be improved. One result of this activity was the creation of a new product that makes gallbladder surgery safer, cheaper, and less painful. The product is now used in a majority of gallbladder surgeries. Salespeople can create value by easing the customer buying process. This happened at AMP, Inc., a producer of electrical products. Salespeople and customers had a difficult time getting product specifications and performance data on AMP's 70 000 products quickly and accurately. The company now records all information on CD-ROM disks that can be scanned instantly by salespeople and customers. Customer value is also created by salespeople who follow through after the sale. At Jefferson Smurfit Corporation, a multibillion-dollar supplier of packaging products, one of its salespeople juggled production from three of the company's plants to satisfy an unexpected demand for boxes from General Electric. This person's action led to the company being given GE's "Distinguished Supplier Award."

Customer value creation is made possible by **relationship selling,** the practice of building ties to customers based on a salesperson's attention and commitment to customer needs over time. Relationship selling involves mutual respect and trust among buyers and sellers. It focuses on creating long-term customers, not a one-time sale.[4] A survey of senior sales executives revealed that 96 percent consider "building long-term relationships with customers" to be the most important activity affecting sales performance. Companies such as Merck Frosst Canada, IBM Canada, National Bank, Bell Canada, and Kraft-General Foods Canada have made relationship building a core focus of their sales effort.[5]

www.merckfrosst.ca

Some companies have taken relationship selling a step further and forged partnerships between buyer and seller organizations. With **partnership selling,** buyers and sellers combine their expertise and resources to create customized solutions; commit to joint planning; and share customer, competitive, and company information for their mutual benefit, and ultimately the customer.[6] As an approach to sales, partnership selling relies on cross-functional business specialists who apply their knowledge and expertise to achieve higher productivity, lower cost, and greater customer value. Partnership selling complements supplier and channel partnering described in Chapters 7, 16, and 17. This practice is embraced by business-to-business marketers such as IBM Canada, 3M, DuPont, and Honeywell, which have established partnerships with customers such as Air Canada, Ford, and McDonald's.[7]

CONCEPT CHECK

1. What is personal selling?
2. What is involved in sales management?

THE MANY FORMS OF PERSONAL SELLING

Personal selling assumes many forms based on the amount of selling done and the amount of creativity required to perform the sales task. Broadly speaking, three types of personal selling exist: order taking, order getting, and sales support activities.[8] While some firms use only one of these types of personal selling, others use a combination of all three.

Order Taking

Typically, an **order taker** processes routine orders or reorders for products that were already sold by the company. The primary responsibility of order takers is to preserve an ongoing relationship with existing customers and maintain sales. Two types of order takers exist. *Outside order takers* visit customers and replenish inventory stocks of resellers, such as retailers or wholesalers. For example, Frito-Lay salespeople call on supermarkets, neighbourhood grocery stores, and other establishments to ensure that the company's line of snack products (such as Lay's and Ruffles potato chips) is in adequate supply. In addition, outside order takers typically provide assistance in

A Frito-Lay salesperson takes inventory of snacks for the store manager to sign. In this situation, the manager will make a straight rebuy decision.

Frito-Lay, Inc.
www.fritolay.com

arranging displays. *Inside order takers,* also called *order* or *salesclerks,* typically answer simple questions, take orders, and complete transactions with customers. Many retail clerks are inside order takers. Inside order takers are often employed by companies that use *inbound telemarketing,* the use of toll-free telephone numbers that customers can call to obtain information about products or services and make purchases. In industrial settings, order taking arises in straight rebuy situations. Order takers, for the most part, do little selling in a conventional sense and engage in only modest problem solving with customers. They often represent products that have few options, such as confectionary items, magazine subscriptions, and highly standardized industrial products. Inbound telemarketing is also an essential selling activity for more "customer service" driven firms, such as Dell Computer. Order takers in such firms undergo extensive training so that they can better assist callers with their purchase decisions.

Order Getting

An **order getter** sells in a conventional sense and identifies prospective customers, provides customers with information, persuades customers to buy, closes sales, and follows up on customers' use of a product or service. Like order takers, order getters can be inside (an automobile salesperson) or outside (a D&B salesperson). Order getting involves a high degree of creativity and customer empathy and is typically required for selling complex or technical products with many options, so considerable product knowledge and sales training are necessary. In modified rebuy or new buy purchase situations in industrial selling, an order getter acts as a problem solver who identifies how a particular product may satisfy a customer's need. Similarly, in the purchase of a service, such as insurance, a Metropolitan Life insurance agent can provide a mix of plans to satisfy a buyer's needs depending on income, stage of the family's life cycle, and investment objectives.

Order getting is not a 40-hour-per-week job. Industry research indicates that outside order getters, or field service representatives, work about 47 hours per week. As shown in Figure 21–2, 56 percent of their time is spent selling and another 11 percent is devoted to customer service calls. The remainder of their work is occupied by getting to customers and performing numerous administrative tasks.[9]

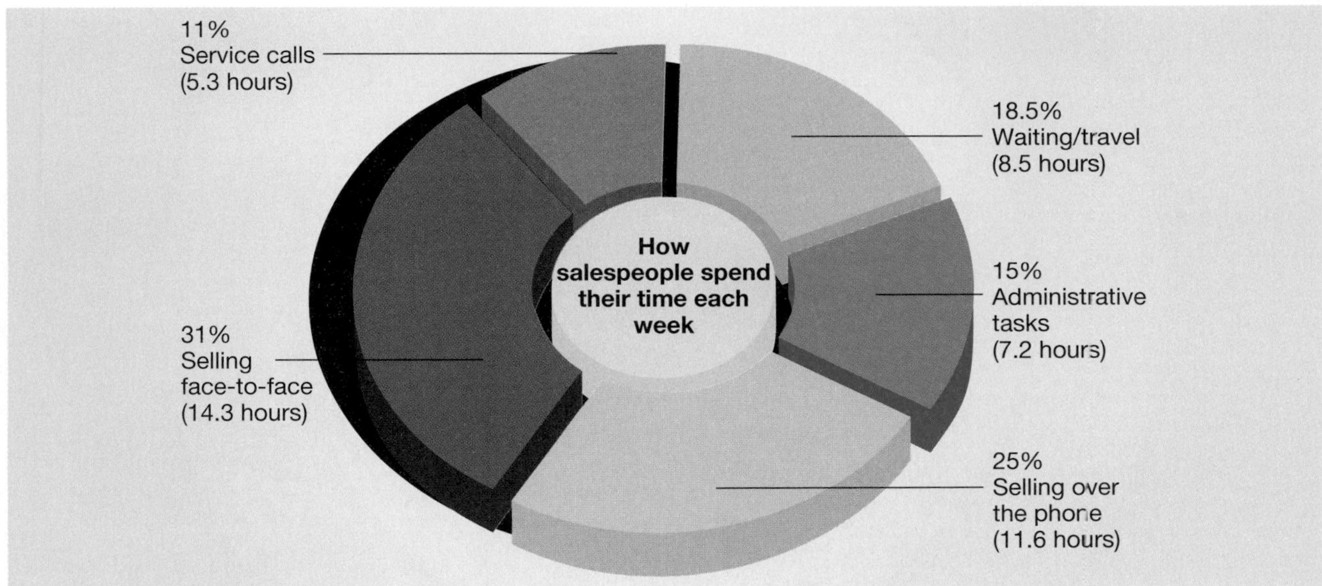

FIGURE 21–2
How outside order-getting salespeople spend their time each week

Order getting by outside salespeople is also expensive. It is estimated that the average cost of a single sale by a manufacturer's sales representative is $218.00. The cost is $184.34 in service industries.[10] (What amount did you check for question 1 in Figure 21–1?) These costs illustrate why outbound telemarketing is so popular today. *Outbound telemarketing* is the practice of using the telephone rather than personal visits to contact customers. A significantly lower cost per sales call (in the range of $20 to $25) and little or no field expense accounts for its widespread appeal. Accordingly, outbound telemarketing has grown significantly over the past decade.[11]

Sales Support Personnel

Sales support personnel augment the selling effort of order getters by performing a variety of services. For example, **missionary salespeople** do not directly solicit orders but rather concentrate on performing promotional activities and introducing new products. They are used extensively in the pharmaceutical industry, where they persuade physicians to prescribe a firm's product. Actual sales are made through wholesalers or directly to pharmacists who fill prescriptions. A **sales engineer** is a salesperson who specializes in identifying, analyzing, and solving customer problems and brings know-how and technical expertise to the selling situation but often does not actually sell products and services. Sales engineers are popular in selling industrial products such as chemicals and heavy equipment.

In many situations firms engage in cross-functional **team selling,** the practice of using an entire team of professionals in selling to and servicing major customers.[12] Team selling is used when specialized knowledge is needed to satisfy the different interests of individuals in a customer's buying centre. For example, a selling team might consist of a salesperson, a sales engineer, a service representative, and a financial executive, each of whom would deal with a counterpart in the customer's firm. Selling teams have grown in popularity due to partnering and take different forms. In **conference selling,** a salesperson and other company resource people meet with buyers to discuss problems and opportunities. In **seminar selling,** a company team conducts an educational program for a customer's technical staff, describing state-of-the-art developments. IBM and Xerox Corporation pioneered cross-functional team

CROSS FUNCTIONAL

MARKETING NEWSNET

Creating and Sustaining Customer Value Through Cross-Functional Team Selling

The day of the lone salesperson calling on a customer is rapidly becoming history. Many companies today are using cross-functional teams of professionals to work with customers to improve relationships, find better ways of doing things, and, of course, create and sustain value for their customers.

Xerox and IBM pioneered cross-functional team selling, but other firms were quick to follow as they spotted the potential to create and sustain value for their customers. Recognizing that corn growers needed a herbicide they could apply less often, a Du Pont team of chemists, sales and marketing executives, and regulatory specialists created just the right product that recorded sales of $80 million in its first year. Procter & Gamble uses teams of marketing, sales, advertising, computer systems, and distribution personnel to work with its major retailers, such as Wal-Mart, to identify ways to develop, promote, and deliver products. Pitney Bowes, Inc., which produces sophisticated computer systems that weigh, rate, and track packages for firms such as UPS and Federal Express, also uses sales teams to meet customer needs. These teams consist of sales personnel, "carrier management specialists," and engineering and administrative executives who continually find ways to improve the technology of shipping goods across town and around the world.

Efforts to create and sustain customer value through cross-functional team selling will become more popular as customers also seek greater value for their money. According to the vice president for procurement of a Fortune 500 company, "Today, it's not just getting the best price but getting the best value—and there are a lot of pieces to value."

selling in working with prospective buyers. Other firms have embraced this practice and created and sustained value for their customers, as described in the accompanying Marketing NewsNet.[13]

CONCEPT CHECK

1. What is the principal difference between an order taker and an order getter?
2. What is team selling?

THE PERSONAL SELLING PROCESS: BUILDING RELATIONSHIPS

Selling, and particularly order getting, is a complicated activity that involves building buyer–seller relationships. Although the salesperson–customer interaction is essential to personal selling, much of a salesperson's work occurs before this meeting and continues after the sale itself. The **personal selling process** consists of six stages: (1) prospecting, (2) preapproach, (3) approach, (4) presentation, (5) close, and (6) follow-up (Figure 21–3).

FIGURE 21–3
Stages and objectives of the personal selling process

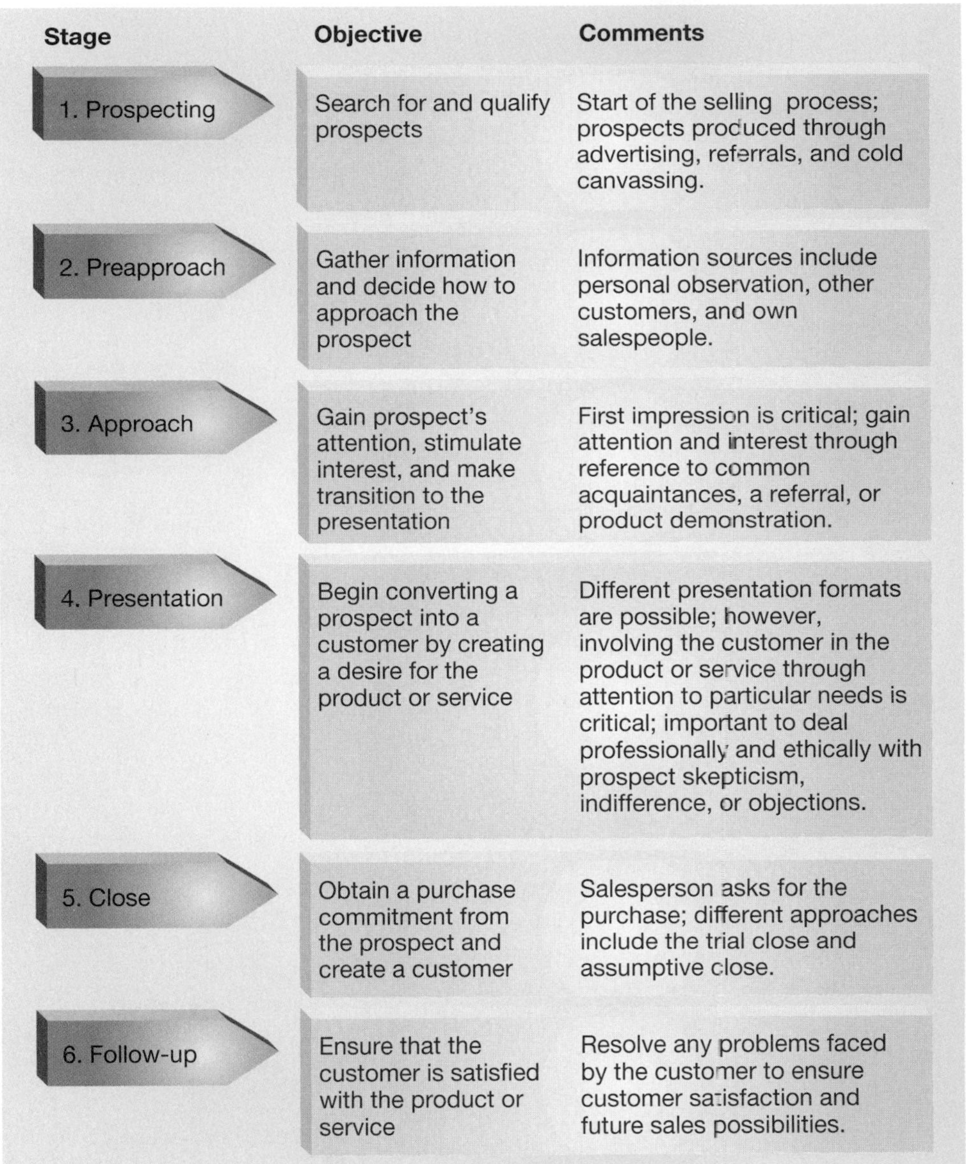

Stage	Objective	Comments
1. Prospecting	Search for and qualify prospects	Start of the selling process; prospects produced through advertising, referrals, and cold canvassing.
2. Preapproach	Gather information and decide how to approach the prospect	Information sources include personal observation, other customers, and own salespeople.
3. Approach	Gain prospect's attention, stimulate interest, and make transition to the presentation	First impression is critical; gain attention and interest through reference to common acquaintances, a referral, or product demonstration.
4. Presentation	Begin converting a prospect into a customer by creating a desire for the product or service	Different presentation formats are possible; however, involving the customer in the product or service through attention to particular needs is critical; important to deal professionally and ethically with prospect skepticism, indifference, or objections.
5. Close	Obtain a purchase commitment from the prospect and create a customer	Salesperson asks for the purchase; different approaches include the trial close and assumptive close.
6. Follow-up	Ensure that the customer is satisfied with the product or service	Resolve any problems faced by the customer to ensure customer satisfaction and future sales possibilities.

Prospecting

Personal selling begins with *prospecting*—the search for and qualification of potential customers.[14] For some products that are one-time purchases such as encyclopedias, continual prospecting is necessary to maintain sales. There are three types of prospects. A *lead* is the name of a person who may be a possible customer. A *prospect* is a customer who wants or needs the product. If an individual wants the product, can afford to buy it, and is the decision maker, this individual is a *qualified prospect.*

Leads and prospects are generated using several sources. For example, advertising may contain a coupon or a toll-free number to generate leads. Some companies use exhibits at trade shows, professional meetings, and conferences to generate leads or prospects. Staffed by salespeople, these exhibits are used to attract the attention of prospective buyers and disseminate information. Others use lists and directories. Another approach for generating leads is through *cold canvassing* in person or by

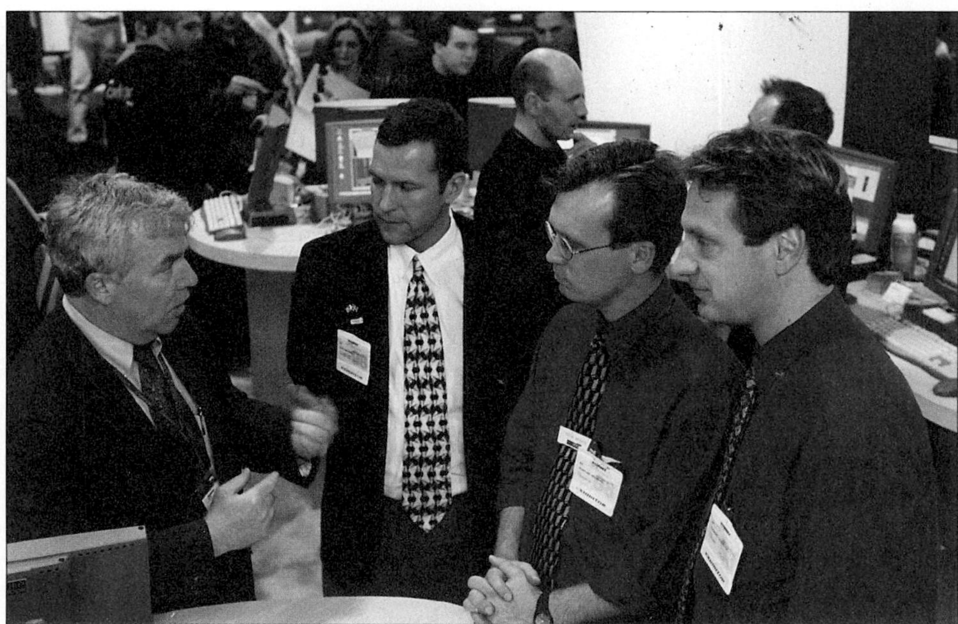

COMDEX, the largest computer trade show in the world, is viewed as a valuable source of leads and prospects in the computer industry.

COMDEX
www.comdex.com

telephone. This approach simply means that a salesperson may open a directory, pick a name, and visit or call that individual or business. Although the refusal rate is high with cold canvassing, this approach can be successful. For example, 41 brokers at a major brokerage firm identified 18 004 prospects, qualified 1208 of them, made 659 sales presentations, and opened 40 new accounts in four working days.[15] However, cold canvassing is frowned upon in most Asian and Latin American societies. Personal visits, based on referrals, are expected.[16]

Cold canvassing is also often criticized by Canadian consumers. Many consumers see cold canvassing as an intrusion to their privacy, and many find it simply distasteful.[17] Many trade associations have codes of ethics for dealing with this issue such as adhering to consumers' "do not call," "do not mail," or "do not visit" requests. The Canadian government has also attempted to more closely regulate cold canvassing with the Canadian Radio-television and Telecommunications Commission requiring telemarketers to inform consumers that they have the right to say no to such solicitations.[18]

Preapproach

Once a salesperson has identified a qualified prospect, preparation for the sale begins with the preapproach. The *preapproach* stage involves obtaining further information on the prospect and deciding on the best method of approach. Knowing how the prospect prefers to be approached, and what the prospect is looking for in a product or service, is essential regardless of cultural setting. For example, a Merrill Lynch stockbroker will need information on a prospect's discretionary income, investment objectives, and preference for discussing brokerage services over the telephone or in person. For industrial product companies such as Texas Instruments, the preapproach involves identifying the buying role of a prospect (for example, influencer or decision maker), important buying criteria, and the prospect's receptivity to a formal or informal presentation. Identifying the best time to contact a prospect is also important. For example, insurance companies have discovered the best times to call on people in different occupations: dentists before 9:30 A.M., lawyers between 11:00 A.M. and 2:00 P.M., and university professors between 7:00 and 8:00 P.M.

This stage is very important in international selling where customs dictate appropriate protocol. In many South American countries, for example, buyers expect salespeople to be punctual for appointments. However, prospective buyers are routinely 30 minutes late. South Americans take negotiating seriously and prefer straightforward presentations, but a hard-sell approach will not work.[19]

Approach

The *approach* stage involves the initial meeting between the salesperson and prospect, where the objectives are to gain the prospect's attention, stimulate interest, and build the foundation for the sales presentation itself and the basis for a working relationship. The first impression is critical at this stage, and it is common for salespeople to begin the conversation with a reference to common acquaintances, a referral, or even the product or service itself. Which tactic is taken will depend on the information obtained in the prospecting and preapproach stages.

The approach stage is very important in international settings. In many societies outside Canada, considerable time is devoted to non-business talk designed to establish a rapport between buyers and sellers. For instance, it is common for two or three meetings to occur before business matters are discussed in the Middle East and Asia. Gestures are also very important. The initial meeting between a salesperson and a prospect in Canada customarily begins with a firm handshake. Handshakes also apply in France, but they are gentle, not firm. Forget the handshake in Japan. A bow is appropriate. What about business cards? Business cards should be printed in English on one side and the language of the prospective customer on the other. Knowledgeable Canadian salespeople know that their business cards should be handed to Asian customers using both hands, with the name facing the receiver. In Asia, anything involving names demands respect.[20]

Presentation

The *presentation* is at the core of the order-getting selling process, and its objective is to convert a prospect into a customer by creating a desire for the product or service. Three major presentation formats exist: (1) stimulus-response format, (2) formula selling format, and (3) need-satisfaction format.

Stimulus-Response Format The **stimulus-response presentation** format assumes that given the appropriate stimulus by a salesperson, the prospect will buy. With this format the salesperson tries one appeal after another, hoping to "hit the right button." A counter clerk at McDonald's is using this approach when he or she asks whether you'd like an order of french fries or a dessert with your meal. The counter clerk is engaging in what is called *suggestive selling.* Although useful in this setting, the stimulus-response format is not always appropriate, and for many products a more formalized format is necessary.

Formula Selling Format A more formalized presentation, the **formula selling presentation** format, is based on the view that a presentation consists of information that must be provided in an accurate, thorough, and step-by-step manner to inform the prospect. A popular version of this format is the *canned sales presentation,* which is a memorized, standardized message conveyed to every prospect. Used frequently by firms in telephone and door-to-door selling of consumer products (for example, Hoover vacuum cleaners), this approach treats every prospect the same, regardless of differences in needs or preference for certain kinds of information. Canned sales presentations can be advantageous when the differences between prospects are unknown or with novice salespeople who are less knowledgeable about the product and selling process than experienced salespeople. Although it guarantees a thorough presentation, it often lacks flexibility and spontaneity and, more important, does not provide for feedback from the prospective buyer—a critical component in the communication process and the start of a relationship.

Need-Satisfaction Format The stimulus-response and formula selling formats share a common characteristic: the salesperson dominates the conversation. By comparison, the **need-satisfaction presentation** format emphasizes probing and listening by the salesperson to identify needs and interests of prospective buyers. Once these are identified, the salesperson tailors the presentation to the prospect and highlights product benefits that may be valued by the prospect. The need-satisfaction format, which emphasizes problem solving, is the most consistent with the marketing concept and relationship building. Two selling styles are associated with this format. **Adaptive selling** involves adjusting the presentation to fit the selling situation, such as knowing when to offer solutions and when to ask for more information. **Consultative selling** focuses on problem identification, where the salesperson serves as an expert on problem recognition and resolution.[21] Both styles are used for industrial products such as computers and heavy equipment. Many consumer service firms such as brokerage and insurance firms and consumer product firms like AT&T Canada and Gillette also subscribe to these selling styles.

Handling Objections A critical concern in the presentation stage is handling objections. *Objections* are excuses for not making a purchase commitment or decision. Some objections are valid and are based on the characteristics of the product or service or price. However, many objections reflect prospect skepticism or indifference. Whether valid or not, experienced salespeople know that objections do not put an end to the presentation. Rather, techniques can be used to deal with objections in a courteous, ethical, and professional manner. The following six techniques are the most common:[22]

1. *Acknowledge and convert the objection.* This technique involves using the objection as a reason for buying. For example, a prospect might say, "The price is too high." The reply: "Yes, the price is high because we use the finest materials. Let me show you . . . ."
2. *Postpone.* The postpone technique is used when the objection will be dealt with later in the presentation: "I'm going to address that point shortly. I think my answer would make better sense then."
3. *Agree and neutralize.* Here a salesperson agrees with the objection, then shows that it is unimportant. A salesperson would say, "That's true and others have said the same. However, they concluded that issue was outweighed by the other benefits."
4. *Accept the objection.* Sometimes the objection is valid. Let the prospect express such views, probe for the reason behind it, and attempt to stimulate further discussion on the objection.
5. *Denial.* When a prospect's objection is based on misinformation and clearly untrue, it is wise to meet the objection head on with a firm denial.
6. *Ignore the objection.* This technique is used when it appears that the objection is a stalling mechanism or is clearly not important to the prospect.

Each of these techniques requires a calm, professional interaction with the prospect and is most effective when objections are anticipated in the preapproach

GLOBAL

MARKETING NEWSNET The Subtlety of Saying Yes in East Asia

The economies of East Asia—spanning from Japan to Indonesia—closely rival the North American and EU economics. The marketing opportunities in East Asia are great, but effective selling in these countries requires a keen cultural ear. Seasoned global marketers know that in many Asian societies it is impolite to say *no,* and *yes* has multiple meanings.

Yes in Asian societies can have at least four meanings. It can mean that listeners are simply acknowledging that a speaker is talking to them even though they don't understand what is being said, or it can mean that a speaker's words are understood, but not that they are agreed with. A third meaning of *yes* conveys that a presentation is understood, but other people must be consulted before any commitment is possible. Finally, *yes* can also mean that a proposal is understood and accepted. However, experienced negotiators also note that this *yes* is subject to change if the situation is changed.

This one example illustrates why savvy salespeople are sensitive to cultural underpinnings when engaged in cross-cultural sales negotiations.

stage. Handling objections is a skill requiring a sense of timing, appreciation for the prospect's state of mind, and adeptness in communication. Objections also should be handled ethically. Lying or misrepresenting product or service features are grossly unethical practices.

Close

The *closing* stage in the selling process involves obtaining a purchase commitment from the prospect. This stage is the most important and the most difficult because the salesperson must determine when the prospect is ready to buy. Telltale signals indicating a readiness to buy include body language (prospect re-examines the product or contract closely), statements ("This equipment should reduce our maintenance costs"), and questions ("When could we expect delivery?"). The close itself can take several forms. Three closing techniques are used when a salesperson believes a buyer is about ready to make a purchase: (1) trial close, (2) assumptive close, and (3) urgency close. A *trial close* involves asking the prospect to make a decision on some aspect of the purchase: "Would you prefer the blue or grey model?" An *assumptive close* entails asking the prospect to consider choices concerning delivery, warranty, or financing terms under the assumption that a sale has been finalized. An *urgency close* is used to commit the prospect quickly by making reference to the timeliness of the purchase: "The low interest financing ends next week," or, "That is the last model we have in stock." Of course, these statements should be used only if they accurately reflect the situation; otherwise, such claims would be unethical. When a prospect is clearly ready to buy, the final close is used, and a salesperson asks for the order.

Knowing when the prospect is ready to buy becomes even more difficult in cross-cultural buyer–seller negotiations where societal customs and language play a large role. Read the accompanying Marketing NewsNet to understand the multiple meanings of *yes* in Japan and other societies in East Asia.[23]

Follow-Up

The selling process does not end with the closing of a sale; rather, professional selling requires customer follow-up. One marketing authority equated the follow-up with courtship and marriage,[24] by observing, ". . . the sale merely consummates the courtship. Then the marriage begins. How good the marriage is depends on how well the relationship is managed." The *follow-up stage* includes making certain the customer's purchase has been properly delivered and installed and difficulties experienced with the use of the item are addressed. Attention to this stage of the selling process solidifies the buyer–seller relationship. Moreover, research shows that the cost and effort to obtain repeat sales from a satisfied customer is roughly half of that necessary to gain a sale from a new customer.[25] In short, today's satisfied customers become tomorrow's qualified prospects or referrals. (What was your answer to question 2 in the quiz?)

CONCEPT CHECK

1. What are the six stages in the personal selling process?
2. What is the distinction between a lead and a qualified prospect?
3. Which presentation format is most consistent with the marketing concept? Why?

THE SALES MANAGEMENT PROCESS

Selling must be managed if it is going to contribute to a firm's overall objectives. Although firms differ in the specifics of how salespeople and the selling effort are managed, the sales management process is similar across firms. Sales management consists of three interrelated functions: (1) sales plan formulation, (2) sales plan implementation, and (3) evaluation and control of the salesforce (Figure 21–4).

Sales Plan Formulation

Formulating the sales plan is the most basic of the three sales management functions. According to the vice president of the Harris Corporation, a global communications company, "If a company hopes to implement its marketing strategy, it really needs a detailed sales planning process."[26] The **sales plan** is a statement describing what is to be achieved and where and how the selling effort of salespeople is to be deployed. Formulating the sales plan involves three tasks: (1) setting objectives, (2) organizing the salesforce, and (3) developing account management policies.

Setting Objectives Setting objectives is central to sales management because this task specifies what is to be achieved. In practice, objectives are set for the total salesforce and for each salesperson. Selling objectives can be output related and focus on dollar or unit sales volume, number of new customers added, and profit.

FIGURE 21–4
The sales management process

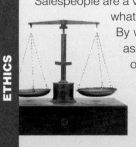

ETHICS

ETHICS AND SOCIAL RESPONSIBILITY ALERT

The Ethics of Asking Customers About Competitors

Salespeople are a valuable source of information about what is happening in the marketplace. By working closely with customers and asking good questions, salespeople often have first-hand knowledge of customer problems and wants. They also are able to spot the activities of competitors. However, should salespeople explicitly ask customers about competitor strategies such as pricing practices, product development efforts, and trade and promotion programs?

Gaining knowledge about competitors by asking customers for information is a ticklish ethical issue. Research indicates that 25 percent of North American salespeople engaged in business-to-business selling consider this practice unethical, and their companies have explicit guidelines for this practice. It is also noteworthy that Japanese salespeople consider this practice to be more unethical than do salespeople in North America.

Do you believe that asking customers about competitor practices is unethical? Why or why not?

Alternatively, they can be input related and emphasize the number of sales calls and selling expenses. Output- and input-related objectives are used for the salesforce as a whole and for each salesperson. A third type of objective that is behaviourally related is typically specific for each salesperson and includes his or her product knowledge, customer service, and selling and communication skills. Increasingly, firms are also emphasizing knowledge of competition as an objective since salespeople are calling on customers and should see what competitors are doing.[27] But should salespeople explicitly ask their customers for information about competitors? Read the accompanying Ethics and Social Responsibility Alert to see how salespeople view this practice.[28]

Whatever objectives are set, they should be precise and measurable and specify the time period over which they are to be achieved. Once established, these objectives serve as performance standards for the evaluation of the salesforce—the third function of sales management.

Organizing the Salesforce Establishing a selling organization is the second task in formulating the sales plan. Three questions are related to organization. First, should the company use its own salesforce, or should it use independent agents such as manufacturer's representatives? Second, if the decision is made to employ company salespeople, then should they be organized according to geography, customer type, or product or service? Third, how many company salespeople should be employed?

The decision to use company salespeople or independent agents is made infrequently. However, Apple Computer recently switched from using agents to its own salesforce, and Coca-Cola's Food Division replaced its salesforce with independent agents (food brokers). The Optoelectronics Division of Honeywell, Inc. has switched back and forth between agents and its own salesforce over the last 25 years and now uses both. The decision is based on an analysis of economic and behavioural factors. An economic analysis examines the costs of using both types of salespeople and is a form of break-even analysis.

Consider a situation in which independent agents would receive a five percent commission on sales, and company salespeople would receive a three percent commission, salaries, and benefits. In addition, with company salespeople, sales administration costs would be incurred for a total fixed cost of $500 000 per year. At what sales level would independent or company salespeople be less costly? This question

FIGURE 21–5
Break-even chart for comparing independent agents and a company salesforce

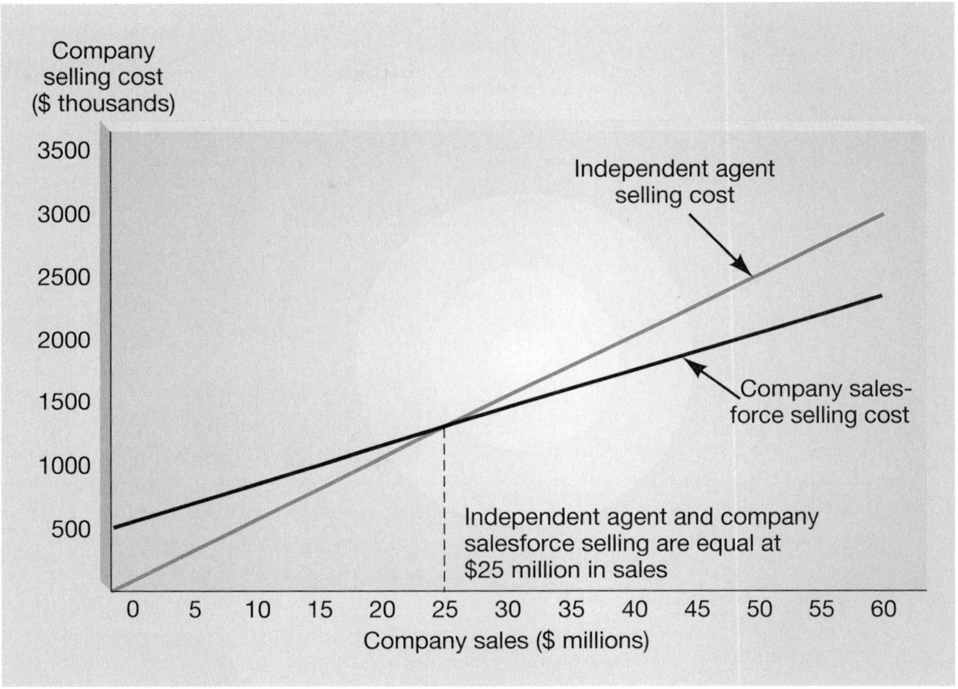

can be answered by setting the costs of the two options equal to each other and solving for the sales level amount, as shown in the following equation:

$$\frac{\text{Total cost of company salespeople}}{0.03(X) + \$500{,}000} = \frac{\text{Total cost of independent agents}}{0.05(X)}$$

where X = sales volume. Solving for X, sales volume equals $25 million, indicating that below $25 million in sales independent agents would be cheaper, but above $25 million a company salesforce would be cheaper. This relationship is shown in Figure 21–5.

Economics alone does not answer this question, however. A behavioural analysis is also necessary and should focus on issues related to the control, flexibility, effort, and availability of independent and company salespeople.[29] An individual firm must weigh the pros and cons of the economic and behavioural considerations before making this decision.

If a company elects to employ its own salespeople, then it must choose an organizational structure based on (1) geography, (2) customer, or (3) product (Figure 21–6). A geographical structure is the simplest organization, where Canada, or indeed the globe, is first divided into regions and each region is divided into districts or territories. Salespeople are assigned to each district with defined geographical boundaries and call on all customers and represent all products sold by the company. The principal advantage of this structure is that it can minimize travel time, expenses, and duplication of selling effort. However, if a firm's products or customers require specialized knowledge, then a geographical structure is not suitable.

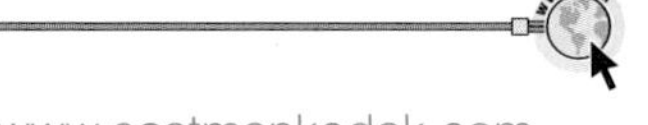

www.eastmankodak.com

When different types of buyers have different needs, a customer sales organizational structure is used. In practice this means that a different salesforce calls on each separate type of buyer or marketing channel. For example, Eastman Kodak recently switched from a geographical to a marketing channel structure with different sales teams serving specific retail channels: mass merchandisers, photo specialty outlets, and food and drug stores. The rationale for this approach is that more effective, specialized customer support and knowledge are provided to buyers. However, this structure often leads to higher administrative costs and some duplication of selling effort, because two separate salesforces are used to represent the same products.

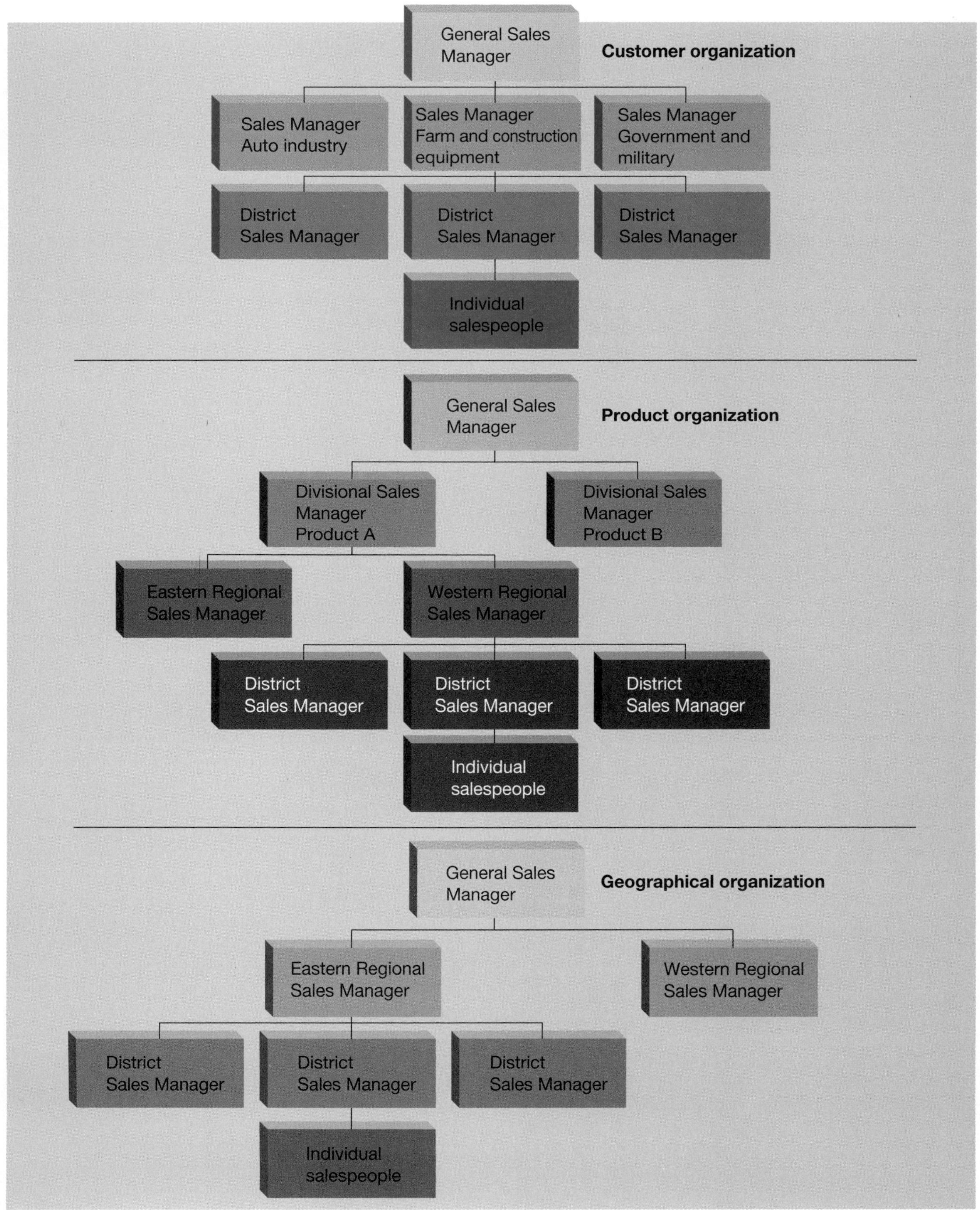

FIGURE 21–6
Organizing the salesforce by customer, product, and geography

A variation of the customer organizational structure is **major account management,** or *key account management,* the practice of using team selling to focus on important customers so as to build mutually beneficial, long-term, cooperative relationships.[30] Major account management involves teams of sales, service, and often technical personnel who work with purchasing, manufacturing, engineering, logistics, and financial executives in customer organizations. This approach, which often assigns company personnel to a customer account, results in "customer specialists" who can provide exceptional service. Procter & Gamble uses this approach with Wal-Mart as does Black & Decker with Home Depot.

When specific knowledge is required to sell certain types of products, then a product sales organization is used. For example, a steel manufacturer has a salesforce that sells drilling pipe to oil companies and another that sells specialty steel products to manufacturers. The primary advantage of this structure is that salespeople can develop expertise with technical characteristics, applications, and selling methods associated with a particular product or family of products. However, this structure also produces high administrative costs and duplication of selling effort because two company salespeople may call on the same customer.

In short, there is no one best sales organization for all companies in all situations. Rather, the organization of the salesforce should reflect the marketing strategy of the firm. Each year about 10 percent of firms change their sales organizations to implement new marketing strategies.

www.fritolay.com

The third question related to salesforce organization involves determining the size of the salesforce. For example, why does Frito-Lay have about 17 500 salespeople who call on supermarkets, grocery stores, and other establishments to sell snack foods? The answer lies in the number of accounts (customers) served, the frequency of calls on accounts, the length of an average call, and the amount of time a salesperson can devote to selling.

A common approach for determining the size of a salesforce is the **workload method.** This formula-based method integrates the number of customers served, call frequency, call length, and available selling time to arrive at a figure for the salesforce size. For example, Frito-Lay needs about 17 500 salespeople according to the following workload method formula:

$$NS = \frac{NC \times CF \times CL}{AST}$$

where:

NS = Number of salespeople

NC = Number of customers

CF = Call frequency necessary to service a customer each year

CL = Length of an average call

AST = Average amount of selling time available per year

Frito-Lay sells its products to 350 000 supermarkets, grocery stores, and other establishments. Salespeople should call on these accounts at least once a week, or 52 times a year. The average sales call lasts an average of 81 minutes (1.35 hour). An average salesperson works 2000 hours a year (50 weeks × 40 hours a week), but 12 hours a week are devoted to non-selling activities such as travel and administration, leaving 1400 hours a year. Using these guidelines, Frito-Lay would need

$$NS = \frac{350\,000 \times 52 \times 1.35}{1400} = 17\,550 \text{ salespeople}$$

The value of this formula is apparent in its flexibility; a change in any one of the variables will affect the number of salespeople needed. Changes are determined, in part, by the firm's account management policies.

	COMPETITIVE POSITION OF SALES ORGANIZATION: HIGH	COMPETITIVE POSITION OF SALES ORGANIZATION: LOW
ACCOUNT OPPORTUNITY: HIGH	1 *Attractiveness.* Accounts offer good opportunity because they have high potential and sales organization has a strong position. *Account management policy.* Accounts should receive high level of sales calls and service to retain and possibly build accounts.	3 *Attractiveness.* Accounts may offer good opportunity if sales organization can overcome its weak position. *Account management policy.* Emphasize a heavy sales organization position or shift resources to other accounts if stronger sales organization position impossible.
ACCOUNT OPPORTUNITY: LOW	2 *Attractiveness.* Accounts are somewhat attractive because sales organization has a strong position, but future opportunity is limited. *Account management policy.* Accounts should receive moderate level of sales and service to maintain current position of sales organization.	4 *Attractiveness.* Accounts offer little opportunity, and sales organization position is weak. *Account management policy.* Consider replacing personal calls with telephone sales or direct mail to service accounts. Consider dropping account.

FIGURE 21–7
Account management policy grid

Developing Account Management Policies The third task in formulating a sales plan involves developing **account management policies** specifying whom salespeople should contact, what kinds of selling and customer service activities should be engaged in, and how these activities should be carried out. These policies might state which individuals in a buying organization should be contacted, the amount of sales and service effort that different customers should receive, and the kinds of information salespeople should collect before or during a sales call.

An example of an account management policy in Figure 21–7 shows how different accounts or customers can be grouped according to level of opportunity and the firm's competitive sales position.[31] When specific account names are placed in each cell, salespeople clearly see which accounts should be contacted, with what level of selling and service activity, and how to deal with them. Accounts in cells 1 and 2 might have high frequencies of personal sales calls and increased time spent on a call. Cell 3 accounts will have lower call frequencies, and cell 4 accounts might be contacted through telemarketing or direct mail rather than in person.[32]

Sales Plan Implementation

The sales plan is put into practice through the tasks associated with sales plan implementation. Whereas sales plan formulation focuses on "doing the right things," implementation emphasizes "doing things right." The three major tasks involved in implementing a sales plan are (1) salesforce recruitment and selection, (2) salesforce training, and (3) salesforce motivation and compensation.

Salesforce Recruitment and Selection Effective recruitment and selection of salespeople is one of the most crucial tasks of sales management. It entails finding people who match the type of sales position required by a firm. Recruitment and selection practices would differ greatly between order-taking and order-getting sales positions, given the differences in the demands of these two jobs. Therefore, recruitment and selection begin with a carefully crafted job analysis and job description followed by a statement of job qualifications.[33]

A *job analysis* is a study of a particular sales position, including how the job is to be performed and the tasks that make up the job. Information from a job analysis is used to write a *job description,* a written document that describes job relationships and requirements that characterize each sales position. It explains (1) to whom a salesperson

WEB LINK What Is Your Emotional Intelligence?

A person's success at work depends on many talents, including intelligence and technical skills. Recent research indicates that an individual's emotional intelligence is also important, if not more important! Emotional intelligence (EI) has five dimensions: (1) self-motivation skills; (2) self-awareness, or knowing one's own emotions; (3) the ability to manage one's emotions and impulses; (4) empathy, or the ability to sense how others are feeling; and (5) social skills, or the ability to handle the emotions of other people.

What is your EI? Visit the Web site at www.utne.com/cgi-bin/eq to find out. Answer the 10 questions to learn what your EI quotient is and obtain additional insights.

reports, (2) how a salesperson interacts with other company personnel, (3) the customers to be called on, (4) the specific activities to be carried out, (5) the physical and mental demands of the job, and (6) the types of products and services to be sold. The job description is then translated into a statement of job qualifications, including the aptitudes, knowledge, skills, and a variety of behavioural characteristics considered necessary to perform the job successfully. Qualifications for order-getting sales positions often mirror the expectations of buyers: (1) imagination and problem-solving ability, (2) honesty, (3) intimate product knowledge, and (4) attentiveness reflected in responsiveness to buyer needs and customer loyalty and follow-up.[34] Firms use a variety of methods for evaluating prospective salespeople. Personal interviews, reference checks, and background information provided on application forms are the most frequently used methods.

Successful selling also requires a high degree of emotional intelligence. **Emotional intelligence** is the ability to understand one's own emotions and the emotions of people with whom one interacts on a daily basis. These qualities are important for adaptive selling and may spell the difference between effective and ineffective order-getting salespeople.[35] Are you interested in what your emotional intelligence might be? Read the accompanying Web Link and test yourself.

The search for qualified salespeople has produced an increasingly diverse salesforce in Canada. Women now represent half of all professional salespeople, and minority representation is growing.[36]

www.microsoft.com

Salesforce Training Whereas recruitment and selection of salespeople is a one-time event, salesforce training is an ongoing process that affects both new and seasoned salespeople. For example, Microsoft offers nearly 100 training courses annually for its experienced salespeople alone.[37] Sales training covers much more than selling practices. On average, training programs devote 35 percent of time to product information, 30 percent to sales techniques, 25 percent to market and company information, and 10 percent to other topics, including ethical practices.[38]

On-the-job training is the most popular type of training, followed by individual instruction taught by experienced salespeople. Formal classes and seminars taught by sales trainees are also popular.

Salesforce Motivation and Compensation A sales plan cannot be successfully implemented without motivated salespeople. Research on salesperson motivation suggests that (1) a clear job description, (2) effective sales management practices, (3) a sense of achievement, and (4) proper compensation, incentives, or rewards will produce a motivated salesperson.[39]

The importance of compensation as a motivating factor means that close attention must be given to how salespeople are financially rewarded for their efforts. Salespeople are paid using one of three plans: (1) straight salary, (2) straight commission, or (3) a combination of salary and commission. Under a *straight salary compensation plan* a salesperson is paid a fixed fee per week, month, or year. With a *straight commission compensation plan* a salesperson's earnings are directly tied to the sales or profit generated. For example, an insurance agent might receive a 2 percent commission of $2000 for selling a $100 000 life insurance policy. A *combination compensation plan* contains a specified salary plus a commission on sales or profit generated.

Each compensation plan has its advantages and disadvantages. A straight salary plan is easy to administer and gives management a large measure of control over how salespeople allocate their efforts. However, it provides little incentive to expand sales volume. This plan is used when salespeople engage in many non-selling activities, such as account servicing. A straight commission plan provides the maximum amount of selling incentive but can detract salespeople from providing customer service. This plan is common when non-selling activities are minimal. Combination plans are most preferred by salespeople and attempt to build on the advantages of salary and commission plans while reducing potential shortcomings of each.[40] Today, 85 percent of companies use combination plans, 12 percent use straight salary, and 8 percent rely solely on commissions. The popularity of combination plans is evident in the decision by Compaq Computers to convert its computer salespeople from straight salary to a salary plus commission plan.

Non-monetary rewards are also given to salespeople for meeting or exceeding objectives. These rewards include trips, honour societies, distinguished salesperson awards, and letters of commendation. Some unconventional rewards include the new pink Cadillacs and Pontiacs, fur coats, and jewellery given by Mary Kay Cosmetics to outstanding salespeople. Mary Kay, with 10 000 cars, has the largest fleet of General Motors cars in the world![41]

Mary Kay Cosmetics recognizes a top salesperson at its annual sales meeting.

Mary Kay Cosmetics, Inc.
www.marykay.com

Effective recruitment, selection, training, motivation, and compensation programs combine to create a productive salesforce. Ineffective practices often lead to costly salesforce turnover. Canadian and American firms experience an annual 9.6 percent turnover rate, which means that about 1 of every 10 salespeople are replaced each year.[42] The expense of replacing and training a new salesperson, including the cost of lost sales, can be high. Moreover, new recruits are often less productive than established salespeople.

Salesforce Evaluation and Control

The final function in the sales management process involves evaluating and controlling the salesforce. It is at this point that salespeople are assessed as to whether sales objectives were met and account management policies were followed. Both quantitative and behavioural measures are used.[43]

Quantitative Assessments Quantitative assessments, called quotas, are based on input- and output-related objectives set forth in the sales plan. Input-related measures focus on the actual activities performed by salespeople such as those involving sales calls, selling expenses, and account management policies. The number of sales calls made, selling expense related to sales made, and the number of reports submitted to superiors are frequently used input measures.

Output measures focus on the results obtained and include sales produced, accounts generated, profit achieved, and orders produced compared with calls made. Dollar sales volume, last year/current year sales ratio, the number of new accounts, and sales of specific products are frequently used measures when evaluating salesperson output.

Behavioural Evaluation Behavioural measures are also used to evaluate salespeople. These include assessments of a salesperson's attitude, attention to customers, product knowledge, selling and communication skills, appearance, and professional demeanor. Even though these assessments are sometimes subjective, they are frequently considered, and, in fact, inevitable, in salesperson evaluation. Moreover, these factors are often important determinants of quantitative outcomes.

Almost 30 percent of companies now include customer satisfaction as a behavioural measure of salesperson performance.[44] (What percentage did you check for question 3 in Figure 21–1?) IBM Canada has been the most aggressive in using this behavioural measure. Forty percent of an IBM salesperson's evaluation is linked to customer satisfaction; the remaining 60 percent is linked to profits achieved. Eastman Chemical Company surveys its customers with eight versions of its customer satisfaction questionnaire printed in nine languages. Some 25 performance items are studied, including on-time and correct delivery, product quality, pricing practice, and sharing of market information. The survey is managed by the salesforce, and salespeople review the results with customers. Eastman salespeople know that "the second most important thing they have to do is get their customer satisfaction surveys out to and back from customers," says Eastman's sales training director. "Number one, of course, is getting orders."[45]

Salesforce Automation

Personal selling and sales management are undergoing a technological revolution in the form of salesforce automation. **Salesforce automation** (SFA) is the use of technology designed to make the sales function more effective and efficient. SFA applies to a wide range of activities, including each stage in the personal selling process and management of the salesforce itself. Computer and communication technologies have and will continue to play a central role in salesforce automation.[46]

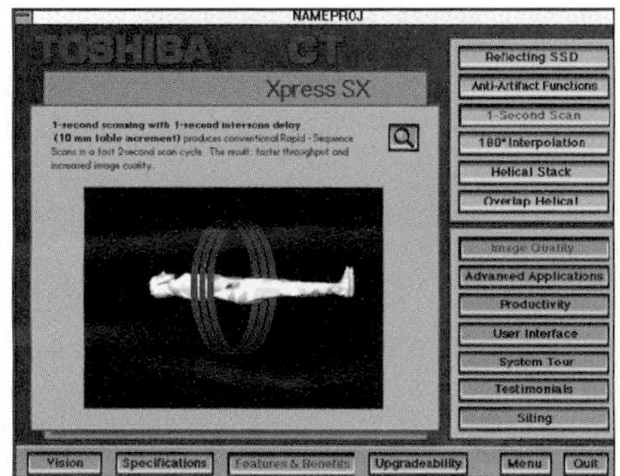

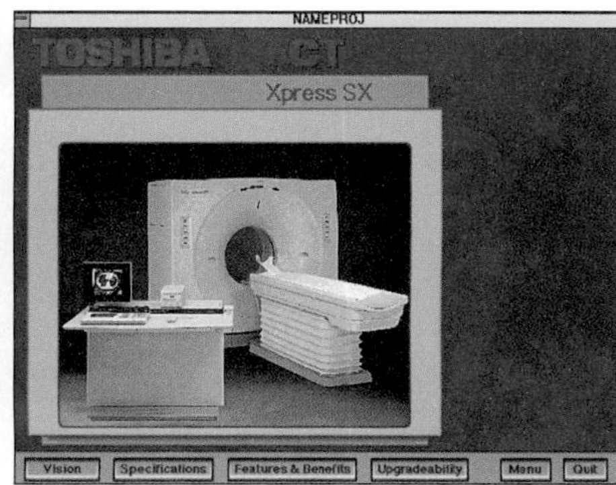

Toshiba Medical System salespeople have found computer technology to be an effective sales tool and training device.

Toshiba Medical Systems
ww.toshiba.com

Salesforce Computerization Computer technology has become an integral part of field selling through innovations such as laptop, notebook, palmtop, pad, and tablet computers. For example, salespeople for Godiva Chocolates use their laptop computers to process orders, plan time allocations, forecast sales, and communicate with Godiva personnel and customers. While in a department store candy buyer's office, a salesperson can calculate the order cost (and discount), transmit the order, and obtain a delivery date within minutes using the buyer's telephone and the computer to communicate with Godiva's order processing department.[47]

Toshiba Medical System salespeople now use laptop computers with built-in CD-ROM capabilities to provide interactive presentations for their computerized tomography (CT) and magnetic resonance imaging (MRI) scanners. In it the customer sees elaborate three-dimensional animations, high-resolution scans, and video clips of the company's products in operation as well as narrated testimonials from satisfied customers. Toshiba has found this application to be effective both for sales presentations and for training its salespeople.[48]

Salesforce Communication Technology also has changed the way salespeople communicate with customers, other salespeople and sales support personnel, and management. Facsimile, electronic mail, and voice mail are three common communication technologies used by salespeople today. Cellular (phone) technology, which now allows salespeople to exchange data as well as voice transmissions, is equally popular. Whether travelling or in a customer's office, these technologies provide information at the salesperson's fingertips to answer customer questions and solve problems.

Advances in communication and computer technologies have made possible the mobile sales office. Some salespeople now equip minivans with a fully functional desk, swivel chair, light, computer, printer, fax machine, cellular phone, and a satellite dish. If a prospect can't see the salesperson right away, he or she can go outside to work in the mobile office until the prospect is available.[49]

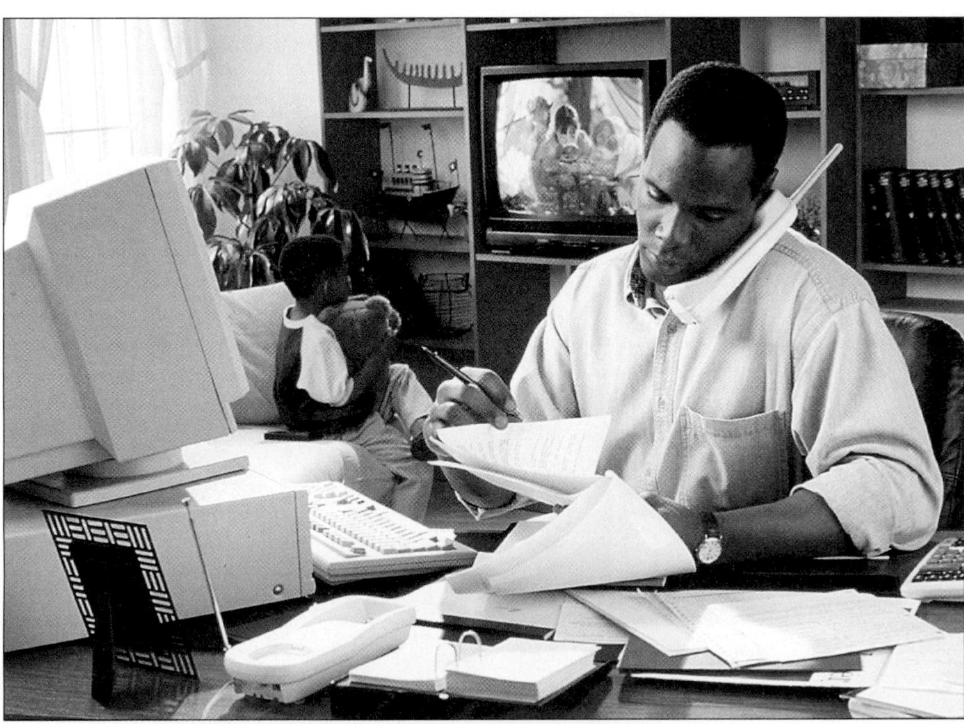

Computer and communication technologies have made it possible for IBM salespeople to work out of their homes.

IBM
www.can.ibm.com

Sales Management in the Age of Automation Salesforce automation represents both an opportunity and a challenge for sales management. Examples of SFA applications include computer hardware and software for account analysis, time management, order processing and follow-up, sales presentations, proposal generation, and product and sales training. But, applications are not free. It is estimated that equipment, software, and training costs for automating a salesforce ranges from $2500 to $5000 or more per person. However, companies such as Tandem Computer report that savings from SFA by its 1700 national and international field salespeople amount to $3 million annually.[50]

www.compaq.com

Some companies are using SFA to eliminate the need for field sales offices. Compaq Computer Corporation is a case in point. The company recently shifted its entire salesforce into home offices, closed three regional sales offices, and saved $14 million in staff salaries and office rent. A fully equipped home office for each salesperson costs the company about $11 000 and includes a notebook computer, fax/copier, cellular phone, two phone lines, and office furniture.[51]

Salesforce automation is clearly changing how selling is done and how salespeople are managed. Its numerous applications promise to boost selling productivity, improve customer service, and decrease selling cost. As applications increase, SFA has the potential to transform selling and sales management in the twenty-first century.

CONCEPT CHECK

1. What are the three types of selling objectives?
2. What three factors are used to structure sales organizations?
3. How does emotional intelligence tie to adaptive selling?

SUMMARY

1 Personal selling involves the two-way flow of communication between a buyer and a seller, often in a face-to-face encounter, designed to influence a person's or group's purchase decision. Sales management involves planning the sales program and implementing and controlling the personal selling effort of the firm.

2 Personal selling is pervasive since virtually every occupation that involves customer contact has an element of selling attached to it.

3 Personal selling plays a major role in a firm's marketing effort. Salespeople occupy a boundary position between buyers and sellers; they *are* the company to many buyers and account for a major cost of marketing in a variety of industries; and they can create value for customers.

4 Three types of personal selling exist: order-taking, order-getting, and sales support activities. Each type differs from the others in terms of actual selling done and the amount of creativity required to perform the job.

5 The personal selling process, particularly for order getters, is a complex activity involving six stages: (1) prospecting, (2) preapproach, (3) approach, (4) presentation, (5) close, and (6) follow-up.

6 The sales management process consists of three interrelated functions: (1) sales plan formulation, (2) sales plan implementation, and (3) evaluation of the salesforce.

7 A sales plan is a statement describing what is to be achieved and where and how the selling effort of salespeople is to be deployed. Sales planning involves setting objectives, organizing the salesforce, and developing account management policies.

8 Effective salesforce recruitment and selection efforts, sales training that emphasizes selling skills and product knowledge, and motivation and compensation practices are necessary to successfully implement a sales plan.

9 Salespeople are evaluated using quantitative and behavioral measures that are linked to selling objectives and account management policies.

10 Salesforce automation involves the use of technology designed to make the sales function more effective and efficient. It applies to a wide range of activities, including each stage in the personal selling process and management of the salesforce itself.

KEY TERMS AND CONCEPTS

personal selling p. 534
sales management p. 534
relationship selling p. 536
partnership selling p. 536
order taker p. 536
order getter p. 537
missionary salespeople p. 538
sales engineer p. 538
team selling p. 538
conference selling p. 538
seminar selling p. 538
personal selling process p. 539
stimulus-response presentation p. 542
formula selling presentation p. 542
need-satisfaction presentation p. 543
adaptive selling p. 543
consultative selling p. 543
sales plan p. 545
major account management p. 549
workload method p. 549
account management policies p. 550
emotional intelligence p. 551
salesforce automation p. 553

INTERNET EXERCISE

A unique resource for the latest developments in personal selling and sales management is the Sales Marketing Network (SMN) at www.info-now.com. SMN provides highly readable reports on a variety of topics including many discussed in this chapter, such as telemarketing, motivation, sales training, and sales management. These reports contain concise overviews, definitions, statistics, and reviews of critical issues. They also include references to additional information and links to related material elsewhere on the SMN site. Registration (at no cost) is required to view some of the reports.

Visit the SMN site and do the following:

1 Select a chapter topic, and update the statistics, for, say, sales training costs or the popularity of different salesforce incentives.

2 Select a topic covered in the chapter such as telemarketing, and summarize the critical issues identified for this practice.

APPLYING MARKETING CONCEPTS AND PERSPECTIVES

1 Jane Dawson is a new sales representative for the Charles Schwab brokerage firm. In searching for clients, Jane purchased a mailing list of subscribers to *The Financial Post* and called them all regarding their interest in discount brokerage services. She asked if they have any stocks and if they have a regular broker. Those people without a regular broker were asked their investment needs. Two days later Jane called back with investment advice and asked if they would like to open an account. Identify each of Jane Dawson's actions in terms of the steps of selling.

2 For the first 50 years of business the Johnson Carpet Company produced carpets for residential use. The salesforce was structured geographically. In the past five years a large percentage of carpet sales has been to industrial users, hospitals, schools, and architects. The company also has broadened its product line to include area rugs, Oriental carpets, and wall-to-wall carpeting. Is the present salesforce structure appropriate, or would you recommend an alternative?

3 Where would you place each of the following sales jobs on the order-taker/order-getter continuum shown below? (*a*) Burger King counter clerk, (*b*) automobile insurance salesperson, (*c*) IBM computer salesperson, (*d*) life insurance salesperson, and (*e*) shoe salesperson.

Order taker ———————————— **Order getter**

4 Listed here are two different firms. Which compensation plan would you recommend for each firm, and what reasons would you give for your recommendations? (*a*) A newly formed company that sells lawn care equipment on a door-to-door basis directly to consumers; and (*b*) the Nabisco Company, which sells heavily advertised products in supermarkets by having the salesforce call on these stores and arrange shelves, set up displays, and make presentations to store buying committees.

5 The TDK tape company services 1000 audio stores throughout Canada. Each store is called on 12 times a year, and the average sales call lasts 30 minutes. Assuming a salesperson works 40 hours a week, 50 weeks a year, and devotes 75 percent of the time to actual selling, how many salespeople does TDK need?

6 A furniture manufacturer is currently using manufacturer's representatives to sell its line of living room furniture. These representatives receive an 8 percent commission. The company is considering hiring its own salespeople and has estimated that the fixed cost of managing and paying their salaries would be $1 million annually. The salespeople would also receive a 4 percent commission on sales. The company has sales of $25 million dollars, and sales are expected to grow by 15 percent next year. Would you recommend that the company switch to its own salesforce? Why or why not?

7 Suppose someone said to you, "The only real measure of a salesperson is the amount of sales produced." How might you respond?

CASE 21–1 REEBOK INTERNATIONAL LTD.

"I think face-to-face selling is the most important and exciting part of this whole job. It's not writing the sales reports. It's not analyzing trends and forecasting. It's the two hours that you have to try to sell the buyer your products in a way that's profitable for both you and the retailer," relates Robert McMahon, key account sales representative. McMahon's job encompasses a myriad of activities, from supervising other sales representatives to attending companywide computer training sessions to monitoring competitors' activities. But it's the actual selling that is most appealing to McMahon. "That's the challenging, stimulating part of the job. Selling to the buyer is a different challenge every day. Every sales call, as well as you may have preplanned it, can change based on shifts and trends in the market. So you need to be able to react to those changes and really think on your feet in front of the buyer."

REEBOK—HOT ON NIKE'S HEELS IN THE ATHLETIC SHOE AND APPAREL MARKET

Reebok is the second largest athletic shoe manufacturer behind the market leader, Nike. In addition to its athletic shoes, Reebok also sells Rockport, Greg Norman Collection, and Ralph Lauren Footwear shoes. The Reebok sporting goods line remains the flagship brand, though, and distinguishes itself on the market through the DMX cushioning technology in its footwear. Reebok concentrates its resources on getting its footwear and sporting goods gear into a diversified mix of distribution channels such as athletic footwear specialty stores, department stores, and large sporting goods stores. Reebok is unique in that it emphasizes relationships with the retailers as an integral part of its marketing strategy. As an employee at MVP Sports, one of Reebok's major retailers, puts it, "Reebok is the only company that comes in on a regular basis and gives us information. Nike comes in once in a great while. New Balance comes in every six months. Saucony has come in twice. That's been it. Reebok comes in every month to update us on new information and new products. They tell us about the technology so we can tell the customers." Says Laurie Sipples, "vector" representative for Reebok, "There's a partnership that exists between Reebok and an account like MVP Sports that sets us apart. That relationship is a great asset that Reebok has because the retailer feels more in touch with us than other brands."

THE SELLING PROCESS AT REEBOK

Selling at Reebok includes three elements—building trust between the salesperson and the retailer, providing enough information to the retailer for them to be successful selling Reebok products, and finally supporting the retailer after the sale. Sean Neville, senior vice president and general manager of Reebok North America, explains, "Our goal is not to sell to the retailer, our goal is ultimately to sell to the consumer, and so we use the retailer as a partner. The salespeople are always keeping their eyes open and thinking like the retailer and selling to the consumer."

Reebok sells in teams that consist of the account representatives, who do the actual selling to the retailer, and the "vector" representatives, who spend their time in the stores training the store salespeople and reporting trends back to the account manager. The selling teams are organized geographically so that the salespeople live and work in the area they are selling in. This allows the sales team to understand the consumer intuitively. Neville explains, "If you have someone from one city fly to another and try to tell someone on the streets of that city what's happening from a trends standpoint and what products to purchase, it's very difficult."

On average, Reebok salespeople spend 70 percent of their time preparing for a sale and 30 percent of their time actually selling. The sales process at Reebok typically follows the six steps of the personal selling process identified in Figure 21–3: (1) Reebok identifies the outlets it would like to carry its athletic gear; (2) the salesforce prepares for the a presentation by familiarizing themselves with the store and its customers; (3) a Reebok representative approaches the prospect and suggests a meeting and presentation; (4) as the presentation begins, the salesperson summarizes relevant market conditions and consumer trends to demonstrate Reebok's commitment to a partnership with the retailer, states what s/he hopes to get out of the sales meeting, explains how the products work, and reinforces the benefits of Reebok products; (5) the salesperson engages in an action close (gets a signed document or a firm confirmation of the sale); and (6) later, various members of the salesforce frequently visit the retailer to provide assistance and monitor consumer preferences.

THE SALES MANAGEMENT PROCESS AT REEBOK

The sales teams at Reebok are organized based on Reebok's three major distribution channels: athletic specialty stores, sporting goods stores, and department stores. The smaller stores have sales teams assigned to them based on geographical location. The salesforce is then further broken down into footwear and apparel teams. The salesforce is primarily organized by distribution channel because this is most responsive to customer needs and wants. The salesforce is compensated on both a short-term and long-term basis. In the short-term, salespeople are paid based on sales results and profits for the current quarter as well as forecasting. In the long-term, salespeople are compensated based on their teamwork and teambuilding efforts. As Neville explains, "Money is typically fourth or fifth on the list of pure motivation. Number one is recognition for a job well done. And that drives people to succeed." Management at Reebok is constantly providing feedback to the salesforce acknowledging their success, not just during annual reviews, and Neville feels this is the key to the high level of motivation, energy, and excitement that exists in the salesforce at Reebok.

WHAT'S NEW ON THE HORIZON FOR THE SALESFORCE AT REEBOK?

Reebok has recently issued laptop computers to its entire salesforce that enable the salespeople to check inventories in the warehouses, make sure orders are being shipped on time, and even enter orders while they're out

in the field. Reebok is also focusing more on relationship selling. McMahon describes his relationship with a major buyer as, "one of trust and respect. It's gotten to the point now where we're good friends. We go to a lot of sporting events together, which I think really helps." Another recent innovation is for the salesforce to incentivize the stores sales clerks. For instance, whoever sells the most pairs of Reebok shoes in a month will get tickets to a concert or a football game.

Questions

1 How does Reebok create customer value for its major accounts through relationship selling?
2 How does Reebok utilize team selling to provide the highest level of customer value possible to its major accounts?
3 Is Reebok's salesforce organized based on geography, customer, or product?
4 What are some ways Reebok's selling processes are changing due to technical advancements?

PART IV CASE MARKETING OPPORTUNITIES IN INTERESTING TIMES

Numerous market opportunities are emerging due to e-commerce and the Internet as innovative companies explore the ability to effectively use the technology. Amazon.com has reinvented the retail game. This does not mean, however, that the end of the story for brick-and-mortar companies has been written. There are still major retail players responding to this new competitor in their field. Amazon.com can claim the honour of creating unbelievable interest in e-commerce even though there is no evidence that e-commerce is profitable for amazon.com or anyone else. There is some evidence, however, that late movers in a market can outsell pioneers in a product category if they are innovative.[1] This means that although amazon.com was first to market with its form of online purchasing, there will likely be a battle of company brands, pitting amazon.com against traditional book retailers who had created strong brand names long before anyone knew anything about amazon.com. The branded traditional book sellers may be entering the online purchasing environment late, but that doesn't mean they aren't prepared to fight. Leaders in Canadian book retailing such as Chapters and Indigo will be able to leverage their brands, giving them a strong chance of holding back the advances of amazon.com.[2]

OPPORTUNITIES FOR CANADIAN CONSUMERS

Six years ago, book publishing and retailing was considered a mature market, complete with the images of dusty bookshelves and old book jackets. Today, the book business in Canada is in transition and the activity generated at the retail level has provided new opportunities for Canadian publishers and new experiences for Canadian book buyers. The reasons for the excitement in the industry can be attributed to both the introduction of amazon.com as an interloper as well as the battle of the book superstores. This battle of the bookstores comes complete with décor to encourage people to relax and read a book. Shopping on the Net versus shopping in person gives consumers different experiences and fulfills different needs. Buying a book online is a fast, convenient way to browse titles, topics, and authors at any time of the day or night. However, it cannot provide the experience of picking up a book and reading it while sipping a mocha latte, which is what book buyers can do in a Chapters or Indigo store. The environments created by each superstore encourages buyers to take their time to find the perfect book or selection of music instead of rushing through cyberspace.

Amazon.com has been able to make significant inroads in capturing a share of the growing online buying market due in part to the fact that Americans have embraced the opportunity to purchase online faster than Canadians. Canadians are interested in buying Canadian items online but are restricted in their choices. This has happened because Canadian retailers were slow to recognize that American online retailers could actually present a threat to their business. This reason together with the lack of capital to support the development of the technology and the absence of a high-traffic Canadian Web site has caused Canadian retailers to move cautiously with the development of online purchasing opportunities for Canadians.[3] The Retail Council of Canada together with IBM Canada and IDC have found that online sales in Canada in 1998 grew to $690 million. This is more than an 200 percent increase compared with online sales in 1997. Unfortunately, however, this only represents 3.1 percent of total North American sales. According to an e-commerce consultant, U.S. sites significantly outnumber Canadian sites well beyond the 10-to-1 ratio normally considered typical in terms of American-to-Canadian population comparisons.[4]

E-Commerce Revenues—Business to Consumer
($billion)

	CANADA	U.S.	NORTH AMERICAN TOTAL	CANADA'S SHARE
1997	$0.27	$5.96	$6.23	4.3%
1998	0.69	21.66	22.35	3.1
1999	1.14	53.76	54.90	2.1

Source: Retail Council of Canada, IBM Canada Ltd., IDC[5]

[1] Venkatesh Shankar, Gregory, Carpenter, and Lakshman Krishnamurthi, "Late Mover Advantage: How Innovative Late Entrants Outsell Pioneers," *Journal of Marketing Research*, (February 1998), p. 54–70.
[2] Mark Tebbe, "Don't count out the brick-and-mortar companies yet," *InfoWorld*, (June 29, 1999), p. 27.
[3] Mark Evans, "Canadians trail U.S. in e-commerce," *The Globe and Mail*, (Tuesday, July 20, 1999), p. B5.
[4] Cynthia Reynolds, "Take the e-train," *Canadian Business*, (June 11, 1999), p. 84–90.
[5] Mark Evans, "Canadians trail U.S. in e-commerce," *The Globe and Mail*, (Tuesday, July 20, 1999), p. B5.

PREPARED TO KEEP THEIR CUSTOMERS

There is one Canadian company that is not waiting for amazon.com to take away its customers. Toronto-based Chapters Inc. began its journey into the cyberspace battlefield in 1998 with the launch of its first Web site, www.chaptersglobe.com. A second Web site (www.chapters.ca) was introduced in April 1999. Chapters claim that it is appealing to two different market segments. "Chaptersglobe.com is a site that is focused on book lovers who want to get additional information about authors and literary news," comments the president of Chapters Internet, Rick Segal. "Chapters.ca is an extension of the Chapters brand."[6] The executives at Chapters believe they can offer something different compared to their largest cyberspace competitor, amazon.com, by offering book buyers something special. Chapters.ca contains author talks, book reviews, and includes a variety of product lines such as videos, CDs, DVDs, and software. How is this different from amazon.com? Canadian book readers and audiophiles can do business in Canadian currency, a bonus when the difference between the U.S. and Canadian dollar is taken into consideration. Segal discovered other interesting differences between a Canadian book reader and an American. Through focus groups, Chapters found that Canadians are attracted to book-reading events, which are now integrated into Chapters' promotion plans of their main street stores. As well, Canadians are more protective of their privacy than American Internet users, creating an opportunity for Chapters to provide options for their customer base. This includes giving Internet shoppers the option of declining "cookies" (customized electronic identifiers) sent to their hard drive. An online customer is also given a choice to opt-in or opt-out of targeted direct e-mails of special offers.

Since the merger in 1995 of Coles and SmithBooks, Chapters has been the largest book retailer in Canada. To hold the top spot, Chapters has 29 Superstores and 305 traditional stores in almost every region of the country under the banner names Coles, SmithBook/LibraireSmith, Classic Bookstores, and The Book Company.[7] By the end of 1999, Chapters plans to open 50 Superstores across the country. Chapters also manages the McGill University Bookstore, wanting it to be a flagship for its Campus Bookstore Division. Even before online retailing, Chapters was busy creating a store inventory management system (SIMS) and a state-of-the-art distribution facility to provide cost savings and efficiencies in managing book titles and other related merchandise requiring careful management to keep inventory costs under control.

When Chapters went online, it cost the company $1.5 million, with a portion of the expense invested to support the development of the logistics infrastructure to handle Internet orders.[8] The new 306 000-square-foot-distribution centre located just outside of Toronto in Brampton, Ontario is considered crucial to the future success of Chapters. Larry Stevenson, Chapters' president and CEO, believes that "retailing is the business of getting a product to the right customer at the right place at the right time."[9] Warehousing and distribution are a major part of that formula. Having new book titles in stores across the country when people are ready to buy is one part of the distribution challenge. With online purchasing, however, there is a different challenge in managing consumer expectations of availability, pricing, packaging, and delivery. The new facility keeps 300 000 titles available for delivery the next day if an online order is received before one o'clock in the afternoon. Where distribution of merchandise to stores across the country can be done with large batches, Internet distribution is done one or two items at a time. Chapters is determined to compete with Amazon.com using technology and building a loyal Canadian customer base.

Not far behind Chapters in the race to compete in the $2-billion Canadian book-selling market is Indigo Books, Music & Café. Indigo opened its storefront doors in 1996 and after successfully capturing interest from book readers, went online in late 1998. This happened with the acquisition of the majority stock in Bookshelf.ca. The name of the site was quickly changed to indigo.ca. Heather Reisman, Indigo's president and CEO, recognized from the beginning that online retailing would be a necessity for them. "For us, it was just an issue of timing and pacing; we had to get our core physical business and our infrastructure going."[10] Since 1996, Reisman has opened seven superstores, with plans to open another 25 at the turn of the new millennium.[11] The president of Indigo believes that the people attracted to her stores are those who are "passionate about books and words on paper."[12]

Both Chapters and Indigo have created their superstores to include a growing number of amenities. Chapters' stores have Starbucks coffee shops, where Indigo offers a coffee bar with a café feel. Reisman is trying to create a boutique feel in Indigo stores. There are a growing number of people who want to spend a weekend afternoon browsing through bookshelves, enjoying a cappuccino, perhaps listening to some music and generally just relaxing. Creating the right environment for purchasing is believed to increase sales. Chapter's Larry Stevenson believes that the longer the customer stays in a store, the more money will be spent. Research shows that a Chapters' customer will linger for 62 to 75 minutes per visit, which is five times the amount of time spent in a traditional bookstore such as SmithBooks or Coles. The average amount spent per

[6]Cynthia Reynolds, "Take the e-train," *Canadian Business,* (June 11, 1999), p. 84–90.

[7]Chapters Inc, *Fiscal 1998 Annual Report.*

[8]Paul Briggs, "A New Chapter," *Canadian Transportation and Logistics,* (November/December 1998), p. 46–52.

[9]IBID.

[10]Mikala Folb, "Digital Marketing—Online Book," *Marketing Magazine,* (January 25, 1999), p. 15–16.

[11]Leah Eichler, "The great Canadian superstore contest," *Publishers Weekly,* (May 31, 1999), p. 55.

[12]IBID.

transaction in a Chapters' store is $20, almost twice the average transaction of $11 to $12 spent at a mall store.[13] The battle between Chapters and Indigo has stimulated not only sales in the book retailing market, but has also rejuvenated the Canadian publishing industry.

REJUVENATING AN INDUSTRY

The early 1990s were bleak for Canadian book publishers. Canada is a small market and it was difficult to profitably publish even well-known Canadian authors.[14] David Kent, president of Random House Canada, attributes some of the woes of the Canadian book publishing industry to Canada's small market size, but points out that Canada is "like a mouse living next door to an elephant."[15] Canadian publishers, unlike their southern neighbours, have had difficulty staying profitable because there are many distribution challenges due to the tremendous distances and scattered population pockets across the country. The United States does not have that problem, which is why it is the largest and most profitable book market in the world. However, Kent observes, this once-bleak picture of the Canadian publishing industry is turning around with all of the changes in book retailing. Online book buying combined with the two ambitious major Canadian book retailers has created demand for Canadian literature. This is good for the authors and the publishers. With demand for new Canadian fiction increasing, says Anna Porter of Key Porter, "American titles seem very expensive now and people seem to be buying more Canadian-produced books as a result."[16] Canadian storefront and online book retailers can offer something that even amazon.com cannot—Canadian book titles from Canadian publishers at Canadian dollars.

AMAZON.COM—RENEGADE OR SAVIOUR?

Amazon.com began its cyberspace journey with books and since the beginning has approached the business of online selling as any front street store, continually adding products and services to its core business. CDs, videos, DVDs, and computer software games appeared to be natural extensions as the product lines have certain similarities. The same higher-educated, higher income group prepared to browse the Internet looking for their favourite topics and authors is also the group who looks for and purchases other forms of entertainment online. That could be amazon.com's strength in its market strategy. The strategy adopted by amazon.com in the first five years of business was to strengthen its brand name by building customer loyalty and repeat purchases. Repeat purchases come from positive experiences as well as the promise of adding new products and services to keep their attention. This has been accomplished through a commitment to customer support and service as well as a plan to both develop and acquire products and services to enhance the online purchasing experience for its customers.

As any retailer understands, there are cycles in businesses and particularly in businesses with an entertainment focus. It has been important to amazon.com, when creating its pioneer position, to pay attention to a well-designed, customer centred Web site. However, that is not the only investment amazon.com has made in its attempt to be competitive in this new channel it has been instrumental in creating. As Larry Stevenson of Chapters attests, distribution is important in delivering the right product to the right customer. Amazon.com has invested in its future success by developing relationships with key companies that help to form amazon.com's infrastructure. The company carries inventory and actually purchases some of it from manufacturers. At the same time, amazon.com also depends on distributors and wholesalers that carry a wide selection of book titles to support the rapid order fulfillment requirements. Not only does amazon.com need the help of its distributors, but it also relies on a selection of publishers, labels, and manufacturers to support its ever-increasing product expansion.[17]

Included in its arsenal of market-ready weapons, amazon.com has developed sophisticated, automated interfaces for helping to sort and process orders as quickly as they promise. A number of the systems and software that help amazon.com to process orders cost effectively and within their own delivery terms are proprietary. A major investment continues to keep these systems operating at peak performance. They have developed custom information systems to track site activity, customer interactions, and order monitoring. Should amazon.com not have a title or other merchandise in stock, the system is designed to fill the portion of the order that it can with automatic ordering of any item not in stock. The customer knows immediately what he or she will be receiving and when. The system is designed to make it as easy as possible for a customer to browse, order, and wait for delivery. For those purchasing gifts online, gift wrapping is also included.

Amazon.com is an integral part of the new online commerce market, having played a role in generating the interest in risk-free online purchasing. The retail book, music, and video industries were competitive before e-commerce and before amazon.com. Now, however, as companies are seeing that a new competitor is in their midst, they are not sitting back and ignoring the new kid on the block. Competition is intense. Amazon.com, as the anointed pioneer of e-commerce is under

[13]Sean Silcoff, "Secrets of a best seller," *Canadian Business,* (June 26-July 10, 1999), p. 90-93.
[14]John F. Baker, "Northern lights," *Publishers Weekly,* (May 31, 1999), p. 52–54.
[15]John F. Baker, "Canada: If you can make it here, you'll make it anywhere," *Publishers Weekly,* (May 25, 1998), p. 41–52.
[16]John F. Baker, "Northern lights," *Publishers Weekly,* (May 31, 1999), p. 52–54.

[17]Amazon.com, *Form 10K,* 1998.

pressure to actually make a profit in cyberspace, not just sell entertainment.

SITES WORTH A VISIT

www.chaptersglobe.com
www.chapters.ca
www.indigo.com

Discussion Questions

1 From what you know about the Canadian book publishing industry, identify the following as either consumer or industrial products/services: *a)* McGraw Hill Publishing; *b)* software for order tracking; *c)* Indigo's card and gift section. Discuss the rationale for your classification choices.

2 Demonstrate your understanding of distribution channels by drawing a diagram of the relationships among the companies as discussed in the case. Draw the channel to the end consumer. What does your diagram tell you about the nature of this industry?

3 In relation to the companies and products mentioned in the case, identify the major brand personalities. Are they distinctly different? Explain. In your opinion, what is the brand equity for Chapters, Indigo and Amazon.com?

4 Discuss the major pricing issues for Canadian book retailers when competing with American companies like Amazon.com. In this case, what role does price play in this market?

5 If you were the new product development manager for Indigo Books, Music & Café, what would you recommend to Heather Reisman as the next addition to the product portfolio? Why?

Part Five

5

Managing the Marketing Process

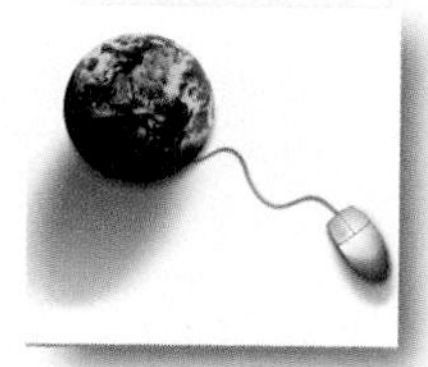

CHAPTER 22
The Strategic Marketing Process

Part Five discusses issues and techniques related to the planning, implementation, and control phases of the strategic marketing process. Chapter 22 explains how marketing executives search for a competitive advantage and allocate the firm's resources to maximize the effects of marketing efforts. Frameworks for improving marketing planning, guidelines for creating an effective marketing plan, and alternatives for organizing a marketing department are also discussed. In addition, General Mills's launch of its Frosted Cheerios breakfast cereal illustrates the planning activities of a successful marketing organization.

Betty
Crocker

CHAPTER TWENTY-TWO

THE STRATEGIC MARKETING PROCESS

22

AFTER READING THIS CHAPTER YOU SHOULD BE ABLE TO:

- Explain how marketing managers allocate their limited resources, both in theory and in practice.
- Describe three marketing planning frameworks: Porter's generic strategies, profit enhancement options, and market-product synergies.
- Describe what makes an effective marketing plan and some problems that often exist with them.
- Describe the alternatives for organizing a marketing department and the role of a product manager.
- Schedule a series of tasks to meet a deadline using a Gantt chart.
- Understand how sales and profitability analyses and marketing audits are used to evaluate and control marketing programs.

MARKETING STRATEGY AT GENERAL MILLS: SEGMENTS, SHARES, SPIN-OFFS, SYNERGIES

Assume you are a marketing manager at General Mills responsible for introducing successful new brands of cereal. Here are some facts to tell you how difficult your life is:

- Only one out of five new brands succeed, "success" here meaning achieving 0.5 percent market share—half of 1 percent—of the $9 billion-a-year North American cereal industry.
- A new product launch typically costs up to $40 million.[1]
- Busy Canadians on the run are increasingly likely to eat a bagel, muffin, or Pop-Tart for breakfast, causing cold cereal sales to fall, so your new cereal must steal sales from existing brands.

Further, the ready-to-eat cereal market is seeing smaller competitors introduce "bagged" versions of well-known General Mills and Kellogg's brands for about $1 less than their branded counterparts.[2] On the other hand, in your marketing manager position at General Mills you have some good news:

- More young adults are scarfing dry cereal by the handfuls at work or at night a la Jerry Seinfeld; remember Fingo's from Chapter 11?[3]
- The biggest consumers of ready-to-eat cereals—those under 18 and over 44—are both growing segments.[4]
- Because synergies never materialized between General Mills' food and restaurant business and their corporate cultures were far different, it spun off its Red Lobster, Olive Garden, and China Coast chains as Darden, Inc., so you don't have to compete for resources with them.

Following the spin-off of Darden, marketing strategists at General Mills hoped that the company would now be able to focus its marketing efforts to achieve higher growth in sales revenues and profits than in the past. So in your marketing manager position, you'd face touch challenges. We'll visit the launch of one new brand—Frosted Cheerios—in a few pages.

This chapter discusses issues and techniques related to planning, implementation, and control phases of the strategic marketing process, the kind of topics marketing strategists at General Mills face in achieving growth. The individual elements of the strategic marketing process were introduced in Chapter 2.

STRATEGIC MARKETING'S GOAL: EFFECTIVE RESOURCE ALLOCATION

As noted in Chapter 2, corporate and marketing executives search continuously to find a competitive advantage—a unique strength relative to competitors, often based on quality, time, cost, innovation, or customer intimacy. Having identified this competitive advantage, they must allocate their firm's resources to exploit it.[5] The timing of product and market actions may also influence the magnitude and duration of a firm's competitive advantage.[6]

Allocating Marketing Resources Using Sales Response Functions

A **sales response function** relates the expense of marketing effort to the marketing results obtained.[7] For simplicity in the examples that follow, only the effects of annual marketing effort on annual sales revenue will be analyzed, but the concept applies to other measures of marketing success—such as profit, units sold, or level of awareness—as well.

Maximizing Incremental Revenue Minus Incremental Cost Economists give managers a specific guideline for optimal resource allocation: allocate the firm's marketing, production, and financial resources to the markets and products where the excess of incremental revenues over incremental costs is greatest. This parallels the marginal revenue–marginal cost analysis of Chapter 14.

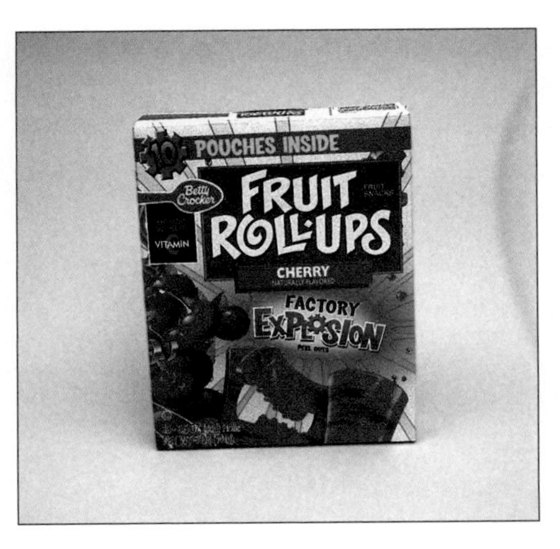

Figure 22–1 illustrates this resource allocation principle. The firm's annual marketing effort, such as sales and advertising expenses, is plotted on the horizontal axis. As this annual marketing effort increases, so does the resulting annual sales revenue. The relationship is assumed to be S-shaped, showing that an additional $1 million of marketing effort results in far greater increases of sales revenue in the mid-range (such as $4 million) than at either end (such as $2 million or $7 million).

A Numerical Example of Resource Allocation Suppose Figure 22–1 shows the situation for a General Mills product such as Fruit Roll-Ups. Also assume the sales revenue response function doesn't change through time. Point *A* shows the position of the firm in year 1, and point *B* shows it three years later in year 4. Marketing effort in the form of advertising and other promotions has increased from $3 million to $6 million a year, while sales revenue has increased from $30 million to $70 million a year.

Let's look at the major resource allocation question: what are the probable increases in sales revenue for Fruit Roll-Ups in years 1 and 4 for an extra $1 million of marketing effort? As Figure 22–1 reveals:

Year 1

Increase in marketing effort from $3 million to $4 million = $1 million

Increase in sales revenue from $30 million to $50 million = $20 million

Ratio of incremental sales revenue to effort = $20 000 000:$1 000 000 = 20:1

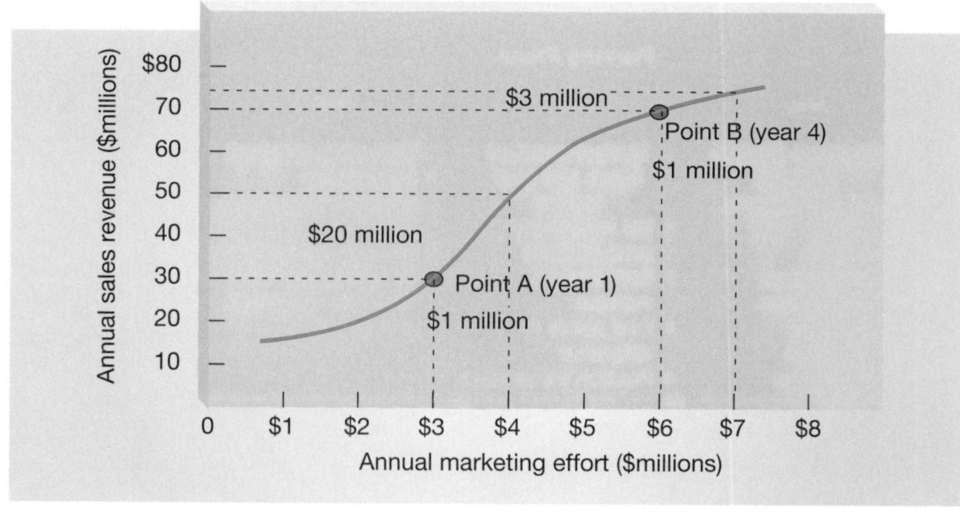

FIGURE 22–1
Sales response function showing the situation for two different years

Year 4
Increase in marketing effort from $6 million to $7 million = $1 million
Increase in sales revenue from $70 million to $73 million = $3 million
Ratio of incremental sales revenue to effort = $3 000 000:$1 000 000 = 3:1

Thus, in year 1 a dollar of extra marketing effort returned $20 in sales revenue, whereas in year 4 it returned only $3. If no other expenses are incurred, it might make sense to spend $1 million in year 4 to gain $3 million in incremental sales revenue. However, it may be far wiser for General Mills to invest the money in products in one of its other business units, such as its new Frosted Flakes cereal or its new Betty Crocker Stir 'n Bake desserts, prepared by just adding water.[8] The essence of resource allocation is simple: put incremental resources where the incremental returns are greatest over the foreseeable future.

Allocating Marketing Resources in Practice

General Mills, like many firms in these businesses, does extensive analysis using **share points,** or percentage points of market share, as the common basis of comparison to allocate marketing resources effectively. This allows it to seek answers to the question "How much is it worth to us to try to increase our market share by another 1 (or 2, or 5, or 10) percentage point?"

This also enables higher-level managers to make resource allocation trade-offs among different kinds of business units owned by the company. To make these resource allocation decisions, marketing managers must estimate (1) the market share for the product, (2) the revenues associated with each point of market share (the present-day $72 million for a share point in breakfast cereals may be five times what it is in cake mixes), and (3) the contribution to overhead and profit (or gross margin) of each share point.

The resource allocation process helps General Mills choose wisely from among the many opportunities that exist in its various products and markets.

Resource Allocation and the Strategic Marketing Process

Company resources are allocated effectively in the strategic marketing process by converting marketing information into marketing actions. Figure 22–2 summarizes the strategic marketing process introduced in Chapter 2, along with some details of the marketing actions and information that compose it. Figure 22–2 is really a simplification of the actual strategic marketing process: while the three phases of the strategic marketing process have distinct separations in the figure and the marketing actions are separated from the marketing information, in practice these blend together and interact.

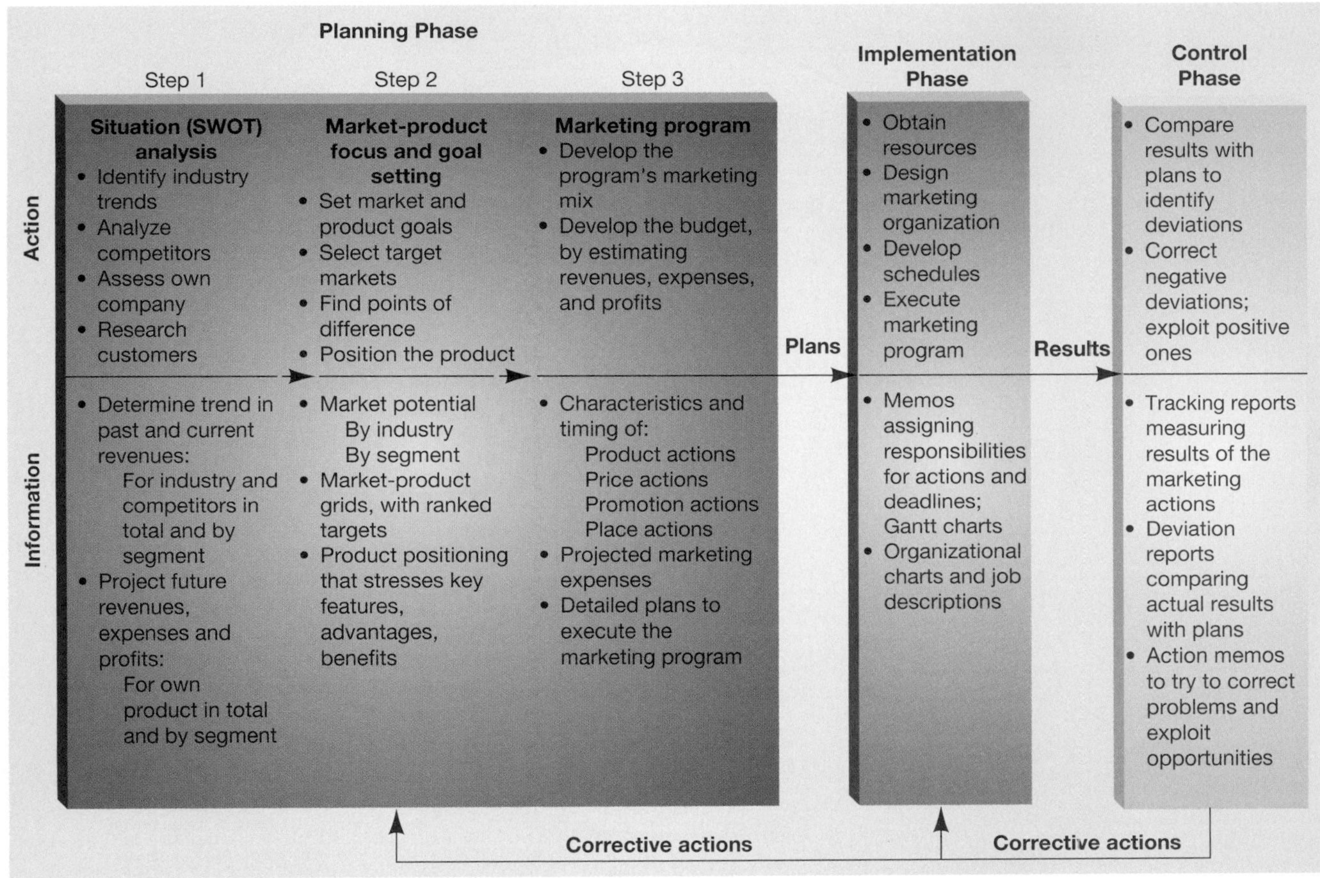

FIGURE 22–2
The strategic marketing process; actions and information

The upper half of each box in Figure 22–2 highlights the actions involved in that part of the strategic marketing process, and the lower half summarizes the information and reports used. Note that each phase has an output report:

PHASE	OUTPUT REPORT
Planning	Marketing plans (or programs) that define goals and the marketing mix strategies to achieve them
Implementation	Results (memos or computer outputs) that describe the outcomes of implementing the plans
Control	Corrective action memos, triggered by comparing results with plans, that (1) suggest solutions to problems and (2) take advantage of opportunities

The corrective action memos become "feedback loops" in Figure 22–2 that help improve decisions and actions in earlier phases of the strategic marketing process.

THE PLANNING PHASE OF THE STRATEGIC MARKETING PROCESS

Three aspects of the strategic marketing process deserve special mention: (1) the varieties of marketing plans, (2) marketing planning frameworks that have proven useful, and (3) some marketing planning and strategy lessons.

The Variety of Marketing Plans

The planning phase of the strategic marketing process usually results in a marketing plan that sets the direction for the marketing activities of an organization. As noted earlier in Appendix A, a marketing plan is the heart of a business plan. Like business plans, marketing plans aren't all from the same mould; they vary with the length of the planning period, the purpose, and the audience. Let's look briefly at three kinds: long-range, annual, and new-product marketing plans.

Long-Range Marketing Plans Typically, long-range marketing plans cover marketing activities from two to five years into the future. Except for firms in industries such as autos, steel, or forest products, marketing plans rarely go beyond five years into the future because the tremendous number of uncertainties present make the benefits of planning less than the effort expended. Such plans are often directed at top-level executives and the board of directors.

Annual Marketing Plans Usually developed by a product manager (discussed later in the chapter) in a consumer products firm such as General Mills, annual marketing plans deal with marketing goals and strategies for a product, product line, or entire firm for a single year. Typical steps that firms such as Kellogg's, Coca-Cola, and Johnson & Johnson take in developing their annual marketing plans for their existing products are shown in Figure 22–3.[9] This annual planning cycle typically starts with a detailed marketing research study of current users and ends after 48 weeks with the

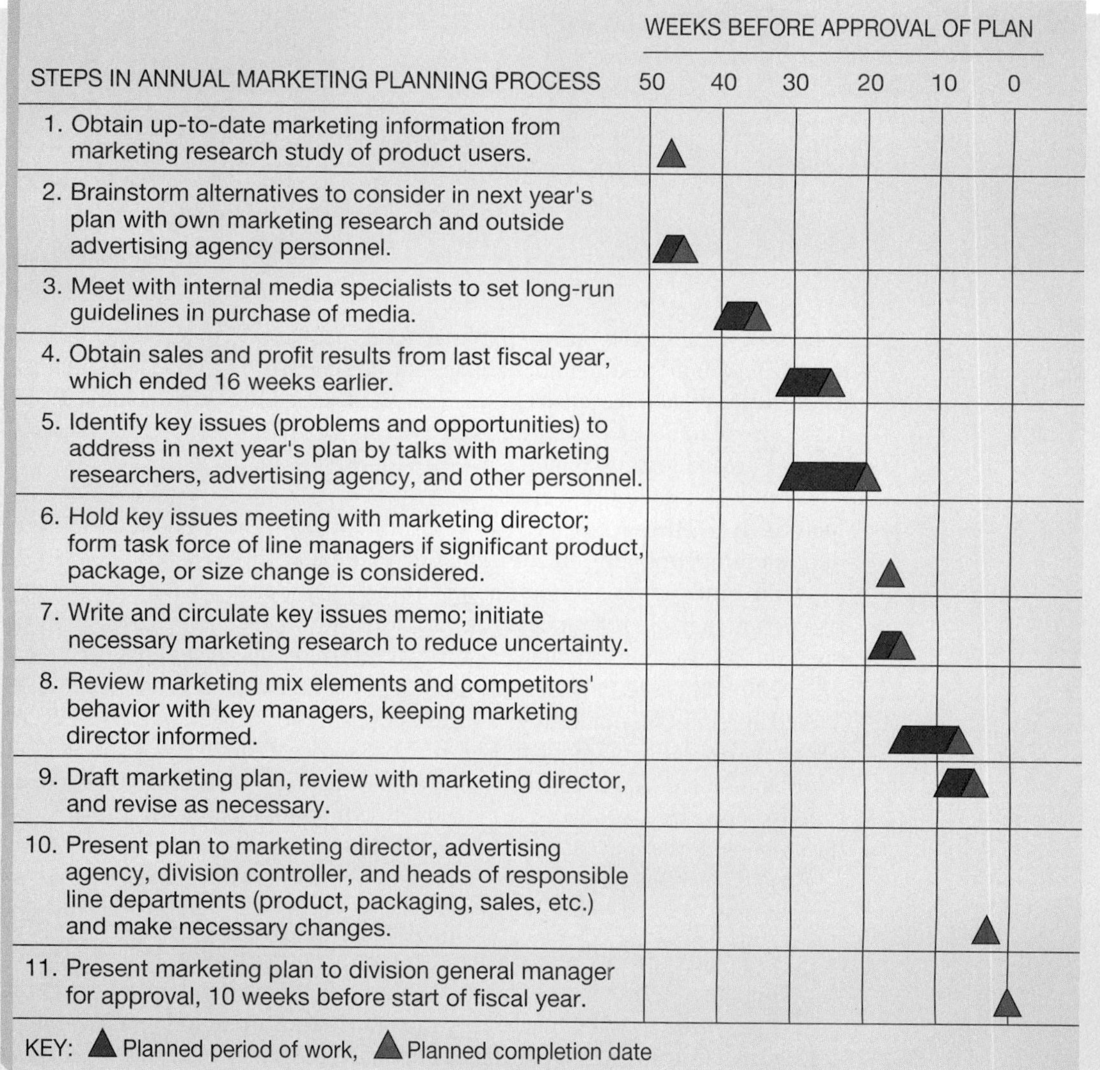

WEEKS BEFORE APPROVAL OF PLAN
STEPS IN ANNUAL MARKETING PLANNING PROCESS
50 40 30 20 10 0
1. Obtain up-to-date marketing information from marketing research study of product users.
2. Brainstorm alternatives to consider in next year's plan with own marketing research and outside advertising agency personnel.
3. Meet with internal media specialists to set long-run guidelines in purchase of media.
4. Obtain sales and profit results from last fiscal year, which ended 16 weeks earlier.
5. Identify key issues (problems and opportunities) to address in next year's plan by talks with marketing researchers, advertising agency, and other personnel.
6. Hold key issues meeting with marketing director; form task force of line managers if significant product, package, or size change is considered.
7. Write and circulate key issues memo; initiate necessary marketing research to reduce uncertainty.
8. Review marketing mix elements and competitors' behavior with key managers, keeping marketing director informed.
9. Draft marketing plan, review with marketing director, and revise as necessary.
10. Present plan to marketing director, advertising agency, division controller, and heads of responsible line departments (product, packaging, sales, etc.) and make necessary changes.
11. Present marketing plan to division general manager for approval, 10 weeks before start of fiscal year.
KEY: Planned period of work, Planned completion date

FIGURE 22–3
Steps a large consumer package goods firm takes in developing its annual marketing plan

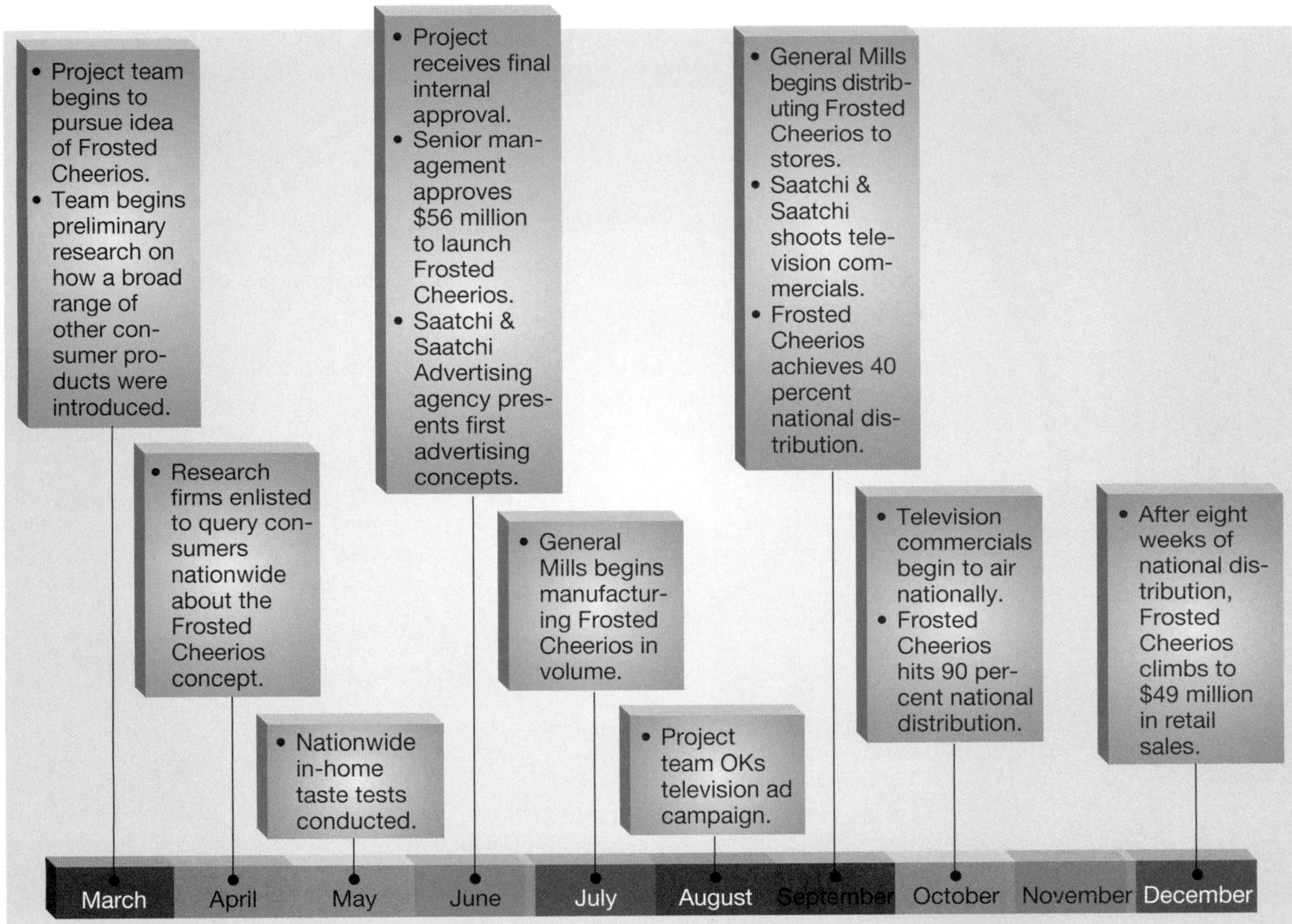

FIGURE 22–4
Frosted Cheerios: from idea to grocery shelf in six months

approval of the plan by the division general manager—10 weeks before the fiscal year starts. Between these points there are continuing efforts to uncover new ideas through brainstorming and key-issues sessions with specialists both inside and outside the firm. The plan is fine-tuned through a series of often excruciating reviews by several levels of management, which leaves few surprises and little to chance.

Marketing Plans for New-Product Launches: Frosted Cheerios Planning and implementing the introduction of Frosted Cheerios by a General Mills team shows the interactions of marketing strategy and tactics with the information, actions, and people needed for success. Central to all of this activity is a new-product marketing plan. As noted in Chapter 11, during 1993 and 1994 General Mills introduced a series of breakfast cereals that did poorly in the market. So when Mark Addicks was named director of marketing for new cereal products in March 1995, he knew the company needed a big winner. Figure 22–4 shows a time line of actions in the marketing plan that led to the shipment of Frosted Cheerios to stores in September 1995. The time from the new-product idea in March 1995 to first shipment in September took six months—half the normal new launch time for a new cereal product at General Mills.[10]

Figure 22–4 illustrates many key marketing concepts developed throughout this book:

- *Cross-functional teams.* The first thing Addicks did was recruit a team with a representative from every pertinent department: marketing, sales, research and development (R&D), marketing research, product development, and manufacturing.
- *Corporate goals.* Frosted Cheerios must contribute to General Mills's corporate targets of increasing earnings per share 12 percent annually and growth of unit volume 5 percent annually.

- *Marketing goals.* The new product must not cannibalize sales of the existing brands of Cheerios or hurt their images. Also, as noted earlier, 0.5 percent market share is considered a success.
- *Marketing budget.* Top management allocated $56 million for the launch, the most of any product in its history.
- *Target market.* The target market is kids (60 percent) and baby-boomer adults (40 percent) who do not have the sugared-cereals hang-up that their parents do.
- *Benchmarking.* The team studied successful product launches of all kinds, including Disney movies and Nickelodeon TV programs, to learn lessons for its cereal launch.
- *Marketing research on consumers.* In April (see Figure 22–4) consumers were asked about the Frosted Cheerios concept; 88 percent of the kids said they would eat them. In-home taste tests in May bore this out and identified the best from among three formulations.
- *Competitive advantages/points of difference.* A big concern was copycat imitations. So Addicks's team targeted these unique elements: complex enough to avoid copying, sweet enough to appeal to the target market, and grainy enough to maintain the Cheerios taste and image.
- *Product strategy.* Manufacturing Frosted Cheerios was a lot more complex than dipping regular Cheerios in sugar. R&D scientists found they had to blend corn flour in with the regular oat flour to give their new product the proper Cheerios "crunch." The final package, shown in Figure 22–5, was selected from seven competing designs. The figure shows the detailed planning needed to position the product favourably in the eyes and minds of consumers.
- *Pricing strategy.* The team set a price consistent with other Cheerios brands and competitive with other sugared cereals, such as Kellogg's Frosted Flakes.
- *Promotion strategy.* Working with the team, its advertising agency shot the TV commercials in September (Figure 22–5), using contemporary and campy characters such as Underdog, rap artist Queen Latifah, and loud-mouth comedian Gilbert Gottfried.[11]
- *Place strategy.* As shown in Figure 22–5, General Mills started shipping to stores in September and had 90 percent distribution the next month.

FIGURE 22–5
The cross-functional team's thinking behind the Frosted Cheerios new package

General Mills, Inc.
www.generalmills.com

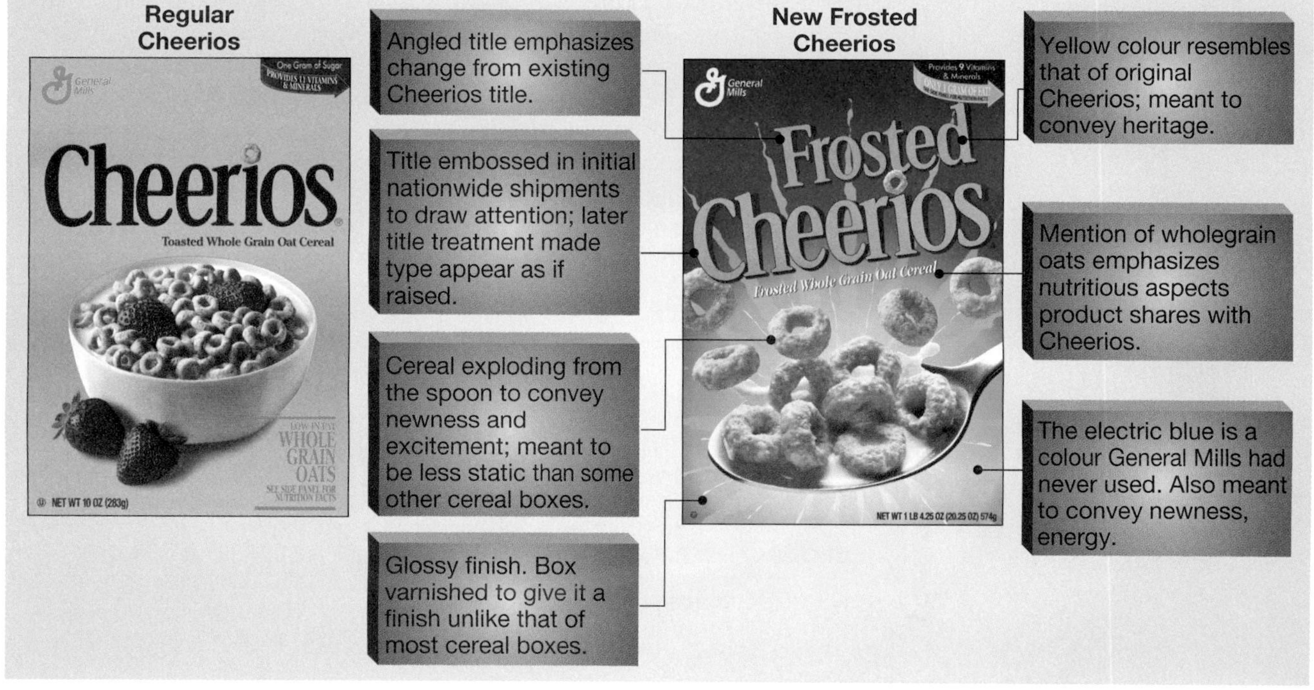

In terms of implementation, Frosted Cheerios was on retailer shelves when the TV ad campaigns started, always a huge concern with new grocery product introductions. Industry analysts have called it the most successful product launch of a ready-to-eat cereal in history.[12] Clearly Frosted Cheerios is a huge success by any standard—a success attributable to a cohesive cross-functional team's attention to detail and deadlines in its new-product marketing plan.

CONCEPT CHECK

1. What is the significance of the S-shape of the sales response function in Figure 22–1?
2. What are the main output reports from each phase of the strategic marketing process?
3. What are three kinds of marketing plans?

Frameworks to Improve Marketing Planning

Marketing planning for a firm with many products competing in many markets—a multiproduct, multimarket firm—is a complex process. Three techniques that are useful in helping corporate and marketing executives in such a firm make important resource allocation decisions are (1) Porter's generic business strategies, (2) profit enhancement options, and (3) market-product synergies. All of these techniques are based on elements introduced in earlier chapters.

Porter's Generic Business Strategies As shown in Figure 22–6, Michael E. Porter has developed a framework in which he identifies four basic, or "generic," strategies.[13] A **generic business strategy** is one that can be adopted by any firm, regardless of the product or industry involved, to achieve a competitive advantage. Some current research suggests that a firm needs several major competencies, not just one, to sustain its competitive advantage over longer periods;[14] other research suggests that the preferred strategy is to focus on a single discipline—such as operational excellence, product leadership, or customer intimacy.[15]

Although all of the techniques discussed here involve generic strategies, the phrase is most often associated with Porter's framework. In this framework the columns identify the two fundamental alternatives firms can use in seeking competitive advantage: (1) becoming the low-cost producer within the markets in which it competes or (2) differentiating itself from competitors through developing points of difference in its product offerings or marketing programs. In contrast, the rows identify the competitive scope: (1) a broad target by competing in many market segments or (2) a narrow target by competing in only a few segments or even a single segment. The columns and rows result in four business strategies, any one of which can provide a competitive advantage among similar business units in the same industry:

1. A **cost leadership strategy** (cell 1) requires a serious commitment to reducing expenses that, in turn, lowers the price or the items sold in a relatively

FIGURE 22–6
Porter's four generic business strategies

COMPETITIVE SCOPE	SOURCE OF COMPETITIVE ADVANTAGE: LOWER COST	DIFFERENTIATION
BROAD TARGET	1. Cost leadership	2. Differentiation
NARROW TARGET	3. Cost focus	4. Differentiation focus

Which of Porter's generic strategies is Volkswagen using? For the answer and a discussion of the strategies, see the text.

broad array of market segments. Sometimes significant investments in capital equipment may be necessary to improve the production or distribution process to give these low unit costs. The cost leader still must have adequate quality levels. Wal-Mart's sophisticated systems of regional warehouses and electronic data interchange with its suppliers have led to huge cost savings and its cost leadership strategy.

2. A **differentiation strategy** (cell 2) requires innovation and significant points of difference in product offerings, higher quality, advanced technology, or superior service in a relatively broad array of market segments. This allows a price premium. Delphi Automobile Systems has used this strategy to use satellite communications to connect you and your car to 24-hour-a-day emergency services, directions to a destination, and the opportunity to order a movie while on the road.
3. A **cost focus strategy** (cell 3) involves controlling expenses and, in turn, lowering prices, in a narrow range of market segments. Retail chains targeting only a few market segments in a restricted group of products—such as Office Max in office supplies—have used a cost focus strategy successfully. Similarly, some airlines have been very successful in offering low fares between very restricted pairs of cities.
4. Finally, a **differentiation focus strategy** (cell 4) utilizes significant points of difference to one or only a few market segments. Volkswagen has achieved spectacular success by targeting the "nostalgia segment," 35- to 55-year-old baby boomers, with its technology-laden Beetle.[16]

These strategies also form the foundation for Michael Porter's theory about what makes a nation's industries successful, as discussed in Chapter 5.

Profit Enhancement Options If a business wants to increase, or "enhance," its profits, it can (1) increase revenues, (2) decrease expenses, or (3) do both. Among these "profit enhancement options," let's look first at the strategy options of increasing revenues and then at those for decreasing expenses.

The strategy option of increasing revenues can only be achieved by using one or a combination of four ways to address present or new markets and products (Figure 22–7): (1) market penetration, (2) product development, (3) market development, and (4) diversification (which are described in Chapter 2).

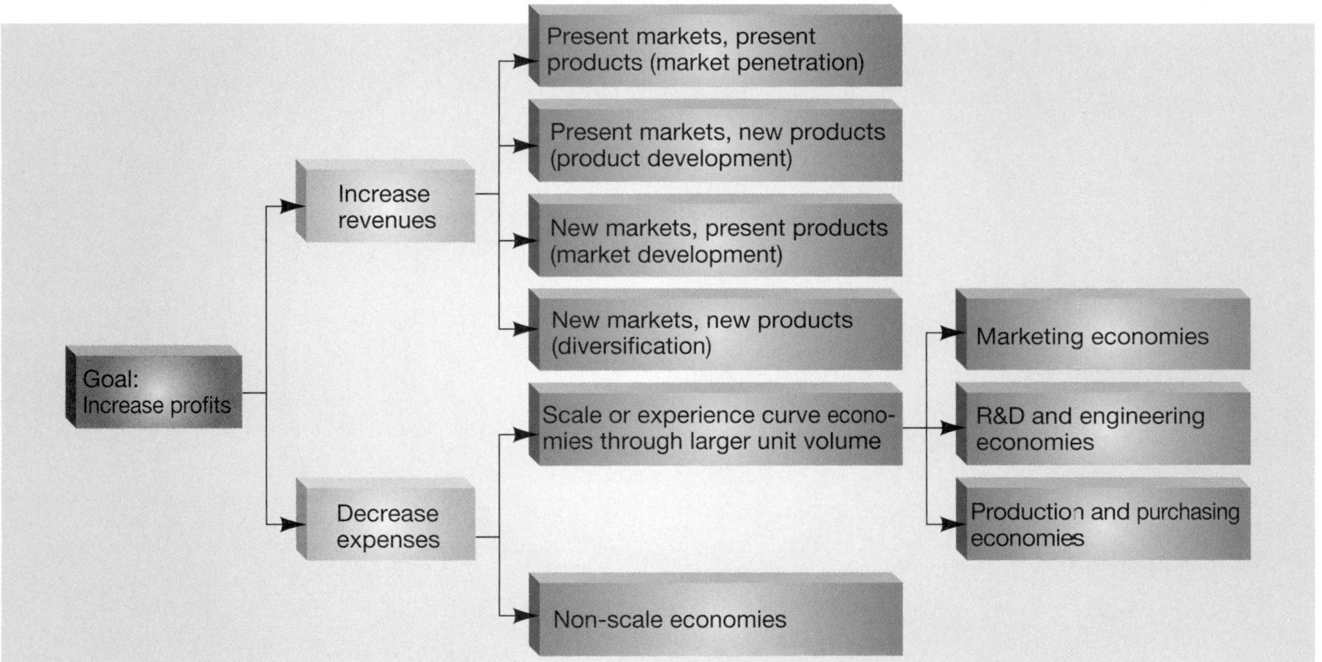

FIGURE 22–7
Profit enhancement options for increasing a firm's profits

Procter & Gamble has followed a successful strategy of market penetration (present markets, present products) by concentrating its effort on becoming the market leader in each of its more than 30 product categories. It is currently first in market share in more than half these product categories. Recent research, however, suggests that while market share may be directly related to profitability in some industries, this is not true for all. Corporate goals such as increasing customer satisfaction may be more successful than simply maximizing market share.[17]

In contrast, Johnson & Johnson has succeeded with a product development strategy—finding new products for its present markets—to complement popular brands such as Tylenol pain reliever and Accuvue contact lenses. To compete with Bristol-Meyers and other companies, Johnson & Johnson developed Tylenol PM—a combination pain killer and sleeping pill—and Surevue—a long-lasting disposable contact lens.

Walt Disney Co. pursued a market development strategy (new market, present product) following the success of the original Disneyland in Anaheim, California. The first market expansion, of course, was to Orlando, Florida, and more recently Disney built theme parks in Tokyo and Paris. Disney has also pursued a diversification strategy by entering into the motion picture business with the development of Touchstone Pictures, and by buying and operating an NHL franchise, the Mighty Ducks.

Strategy options for decreasing expenses fall into two broad categories (Figure 22–7). One is relying on scale economies or experience curve benefits from an increased volume of production to drive unit costs down and gross margins up, the best-known examples being electronic devices such as fax or voice-mail machines whose prices fell by half in a few years. Scale economies may occur in marketing, as well as in R&D, engineering, production, and purchasing.

The other strategy option to decrease expenses is simply finding other ways to reduce costs, such as cutting the number of managers, increasing the effectiveness of the salesforce through more training, or reducing the product rejects by inspectors. In an effort to decrease costs, IBM Canada and Xerox Canada had both downsized in the past through layoffs. Procter & Gamble concluded the world didn't really need 31 varieties of Head &

CUSTOMER VALUE

MARKETING NEWSNET

The Strategy Issue of the 1990s: Finding Synergies

Compaq Computer acquires Digital Equipment "to get synergy." Ford buys Volvo "to get synergy." With the current go-go days of giant mergers and acquisitions, the partners in these ventures are looking for synergies.

The recent merger of Alcan Aluminum of Montreal, Pechiney of France, and Algroup of Switzerland demonstrates some of the benefits of finding synergy: economies of scale; increasing efficiency and productivity; increased market coverage; and improved quality to customers.

The new company is expected to achieve synergies of $600 million each year.

To try your hand in this multibillion-dollar synergy game, let's assume you are vice president of marketing for Great Lawns Corporation, whose product lines are non-powered lawnmowers and powered walking mowers. A market-product grid for your business is shown at right. You distribute your non-powered mowers in the three market segments shown and your powered, walking mowers in suburban markets—but you don't yet sell your powered walking mowers in cities or rural areas.

Here are your strategy dilemmas:

1. Where are the marketing synergies (efficiencies)?
2. Where are the R&D and manufacturing synergies (efficiencies)?
3. What would a market-product grid look like for an ideal company for Great Lawns to merge with?

For the answers to these questions, read the text and study Figures 22–8 and 22–9.

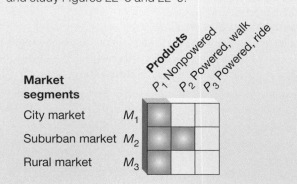

Market segments		P_1 Nonpowered	P_2 Powered, walk	P_3 Powered, ride
City market	M_1	■		
Suburban market	M_2	■	■	
Rural market	M_3	■		

Shoulders shampoo. Cutting the number of packages, sizes, and formulas in hair care alone, P&G has slashed the varieties almost in half—reducing expenses and increasing profits in the bargain.[18]

Market-Product Synergies Let's use the market-product grid framework introduced in Chapter 10 to extend the profit-enhancement structure in the last section. There are two kinds of synergy that are critical in developing corporate and marketing strategies: (1) marketing synergy and (2) R&D–manufacturing synergy. While the following example involves external synergies through mergers and acquisitions, the concepts apply equally well to internal synergies sought in adding new products or seeking new markets.

A critical step in the external analysis is to assess how these merger and acquisition strategies provide the organization with **synergy,** the increased customer value achieved through performing organizational functions more efficiently. The "increased customer value" can take many forms: more products, improved quality on existing products, lower prices, improved distribution, and so on. But the ultimate criterion is that customers should be better off as a result of the increased synergy. The firm, in turn, should be better off by gaining more satisfied customers.

A market-product grid helps identify important trade-offs in the strategic marketing process. As noted in the Marketing NewsNet, assume you are vice president of marketing for Great Lawns Corporation's line of non-powered lawnmowers and powered walking mowers sold to the consumer market. You are looking for new product and new market opportunities to increase your revenues and profits.

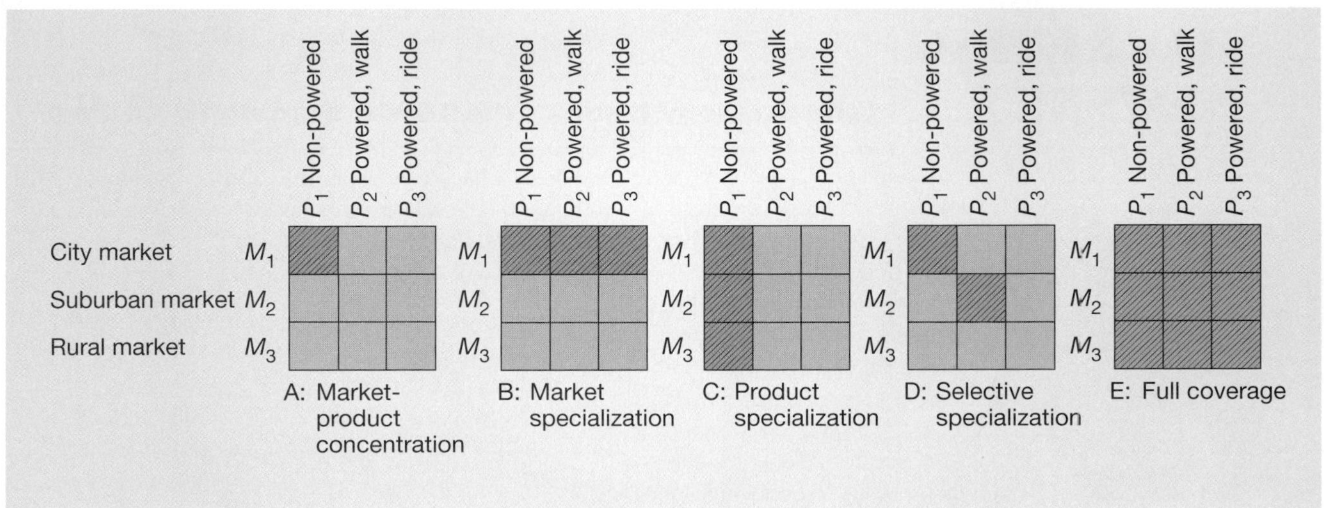

FIGURE 22–8
Market-product grid of alternative strategies for a lawnmower manufacturer

You conduct a market segmentation study and develop a market-product grid to analyze future opportunities. You identify three major segments in the consumer market based on geography: (1) city, (2) suburban, and (3) rural households. These market segments relate to the size of lawn a consumer must mow. The product clusters are (1) non-powered, (2) powered walking, and (3) powered riding mowers. Five alternative marketing strategies are shown in the market-product grids in Figure 22–8. As mentioned in Chapter 10, the important marketing efficiencies—or synergies—run horizontally across the rows in Figure 22–8. Conversely, the important R&D and production efficiencies—or synergies—run vertically down the columns. Let's look at the synergy effects for the five combinations in Figure 22–8:

A. *Market-product concentration.* The firm benefits from "focus" on a single product line and market segment, but it loses opportunities for significant synergies in both marketing and R&D–manufacturing.

B. *Market specialization.* The firm gains marketing synergy through providing a complete product line, but R&D–manufacturing have the difficulty of developing and producing two new products.

C. *Product specialization.* The firm gains R&D–manufacturing synergy through production economies of scale, but gaining market distribution in the three different geographic areas will be costly.

D. *Selective specialization.* The firm doesn't get either marketing or R&D–manufacturing synergies because of the uniqueness of the market-product combinations.

E. *Full coverage.* The firm has the maximum potential synergies in both marketing and R&D–manufacturing. The question: Is it spread too thin?

The Marketing NewsNet posed the question of what the ideal partner would be, given the market-product combinations shown in the box. If, as vice president of marketing, you want to follow a full-coverage strategy, then the ideal merger partner is shown in Figure 22–9. This would give the maximum potential synergies—if you are not spreading your merged companies too thin. Marketing gains by having a complete product line in all regions, and R&D–manufacturing gains by having access to new markets that can provide production economies of scale through producing larger volumes of its existing products.

FIGURE 22-9
An ideal merger for Great Lawns to obtain full market-product coverage

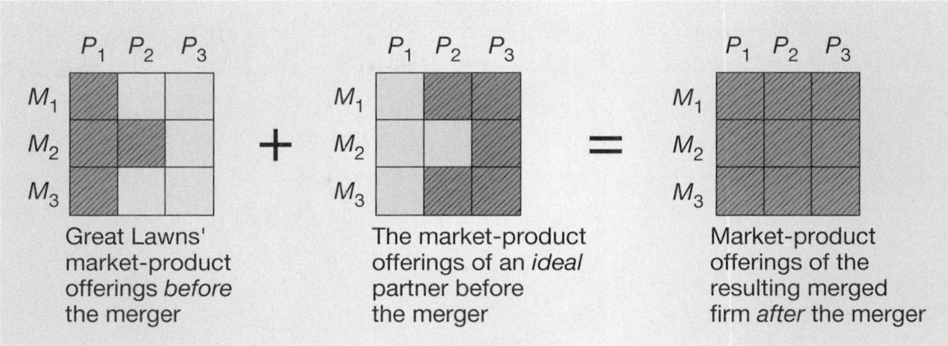

CONCEPT CHECK

1. Describe Porter's four generic business strategies.
2. What are four alternative ways to increase a firm's profits when considering profit enhancement options strategies?
3. Where do (*a*) marketing synergies and (*b*) R&D–manufacturing synergies appear in a market-product grid framework?

Some Planning and Strategy Lessons

Applying these frameworks is not automatic but requires a great deal of managerial judgment. Common-sense requirements of an effective marketing plan are discussed next, followed by problems that can arise.

Guidelines for an Effective Marketing Plan Dwight D. Eisenhower, when he commanded Allied armies in World War II, made his classic observation, "Plans are nothing; planning is everything." It is the process of careful planning that focuses an organization's efforts and leads to success. The plans themselves, which change with events, are often secondary. Effective planning and plans are inevitably characterized by identifiable objectives, specific strategies or courses of action, and the means to execute them. Here are some guidelines in developing effective marketing plans:

- *Set measurable, achievable goals.* Ideally, goals should be quantified and measurable in terms of what is to be accomplished and by when. So, "Increase market share from 18 percent to 22 percent by December 31, 2002" is preferable to "Maximize market share given our available resources." Also, to motivate people the goals must be achievable.
- *Use a base of facts and valid assumptions.* The more a marketing plan is based on facts and valid assumptions, rather than guesses, the less uncertainty and risk are associated with executing it. Good marketing research helps.
- *Utilize simple, but clear and specific, plans.* Effective execution of plans requires that people at all levels in the firm understand what, when, and how they are to accomplish their tasks.
- *Have complete and feasible plans.* Marketing plans must incorporate all the key marketing mix factors and be supported by adequate resources.
- *Make plans controllable and flexible.* Marketing plans must enable results to be compared with planned targets, which allows replanning—the flexibility to update the original plans.

"Better ingredients, better pizza"—and better planning and attention to detail: Papa John's!

Papa John's International, Inc.
www.papajohns.com

Problems in Marketing Planning and Strategy From postmortems on company plans that did work and on those that did not work, a picture emerges of where problems occur in the planning phase of a firm's strategic marketing process. The following list explores these problems:

1. Plans may be based on very poor assumptions about environmental factors, especially changing economic conditions and competitors' actions. Canadians used to equate the name Listerine with mouthwash. But Scope started an anti-Listerine campaign and successfully convinced Canadians that mouthwash didn't have to taste bad to work. The result? Listerine lost its position as market leader.
2. Planners and their plans may have lost sight of their customers' needs. The "better ingredients, better pizza" slogan makes the hair stand up on the back of the necks of Pizza Hut executives. The reason is that this slogan of Papa John's International pizza chain reflects the firm's obsessive attention to detail, which is stealing market share from five-times-bigger Pizza Hut! Sample detail: If the cheese on the pizza shows a single air bubble or the crust is not golden brown, the offending pizza is not served to the customer![19]
3. Too much time and effort may be spent on data collection and writing the plans. Westinghouse has cut its planning instructions for operating units "that looked like an auto repair manual" to five or six pages.
4. Line operating managers often feel no sense of ownership in implementing the plans. Andy Grove, when he was CEO of Intel, observed, "We had the very ridiculous system . . . of delegating strategic planning to strategic planners. The strategies these [planners] prepared had no bearing on anything we actually did."[20] The solution is to assign more planning activities to line operating managers—the people who actually carry them out.

It is easier to talk about planning than to do it well. Try your hand as a consultant to help Hugo's Ski Shack make some marketing plans, as described in the Web Link box.

WEB LINK Marketing 101 Final Exam: Solve the BCG's Hugo Ski Shack Online Case

The Boston Consulting Group, or BCG, is probably best known for its "growth-share" portfolio matrix discussed in Chapter 2. As a very active and respected management consulting organization, BCG maintains a Web site to describe its services. Included in its Web site is an interactive strategy case that asks you to address a dilemma faced by Hugo's Ski Shack, which rents water skis to vacationers. Should Hugo's expand its water ski rentals based on a possible increase in demand? Access the case at www.bcg.com/case, read the case carefully, solve it within the time limits, and consider becoming a BCG consultant after graduation!

Balancing Value and Values in Strategic Marketing Plans Two important trends are likely to influence the strategic marketing process in the future. The first, value-based planning, combines marketing planning ideas and financial planning techniques to assess how much a division or strategic business unit (SBU) contributes to the price of a company's stock (or shareholder wealth). Value is created when the financial return of a strategic activity exceeds the cost of the resources allocated to the activity.

The second trend is the increasing interest in value-driven strategies, which incorporate concerns for ethics, integrity, employee health and safety, and environmental safeguards with more common corporate values such as growth, profitability, customer service, and quality. Some experts have observed that although many corporations cite broad corporate values in advertisements, press releases, and company newsletters, they have not yet changed their strategic plans to reflect the stated values.[21]

THE IMPLEMENTATION PHASE OF THE STRATEGIC MARKETING PROCESS

The Monday morning diagnosis of a losing football coach often runs something like "We had an excellent game plan: we just didn't execute it."

Is Planning or Implementation the Problem?

The planning-versus-execution issue applies to the strategic marketing process as well: a difficulty when a marketing plan fails is determining whether the failure is due to a poor plan or poor implementation. Figure 22–10 shows the outcomes of (1) good and bad marketing planning and (2) good and bad marketing implementation.[22] Good

FIGURE 22–10
Results of good and bad marketing planning and implementation

MARKETING IMPLEMENTATION	MARKETING PLANNING AND STRATEGY: GOOD (APPROPRIATE)	BAD (INAPPROPRIATE)
GOOD (EFFECTIVE)	1 *Success:* Marketing program achieves its objectives.	2 *Trouble:* Solution lies in recognizing that only the strategy is at fault and correcting it.
BAD (INEFFECTIVE)	3 *Trouble:* Solution lies in recognizing that only implementation is at fault and correcting it.	4 *Failure:* Marketing program flounders and fails to achieve its objectives.

Swatch watches have benefited from having both good marketing planning and implementation.

planning and good implementation in cell 1 spell success, as with the Swiss firm that combined a strong product—its Swatch brand watches—with excellent advertising, distribution, and pricing. NeXT Computer, Inc. fell into the "bad-bad" cell 4 with its workstation that used a proprietary hardware strategy that discouraged many potential customers and a salesforce "just too small and strapped for cash to reach many prospects." NeXT has now closed its computer factory to focus on its software business, which Apple bought in 1997.

Cells 2 and 3 indicate trouble because either the marketing planning *or* marketing implementation—not both—is bad. A firm or product does not stay permanently in cell 2 or 3. If the problem is solved, the result can be success (cell 1); if not, it is failure (cell 4).

Toyota used good implementation on a bad marketing strategy (cell 2) when it applied its superior automobile marketing skills to the introduction of its T100 pickup truck. Consumer response was well below forecasts because the truck was too big to compete with smaller "compact" pickups and too small and underpowered to compete with full-size options. Goodyear Tire and Rubber Co. found itself in cell 3 after it successfully developed all-season radial tires but created problems with the 640 dealer distribution network by raising wholesale prices. The poor implementation led to a two-point decline in market share—a drop of three million tires.

Increasing Emphasis on Marketing Implementation

In the 1990s, the implementation phase of the strategic marketing process has emerged as a key factor to success by moving many planning activities away from the duties of planners to those of line managers.

CROSS FUNCTIONAL

MARKETING NEWSNET Implementation in the Organization of Tomorrow

In today's global marketplace, corporations struggle to reduce their response time to windows of opportunity. One of the reasons is that few companies have the complete expertise necessary to quickly launch new products in diverse and changing markets. To excel at implementation of marketing strategies, the organization of tomorrow will emphasize adaptability by taking advantage of information technology and acting, as Peter Drucker suggests, like a symphony orchestra.

Frank Ostroff and Doug Smith at the consulting firm McKinsey & Co. have suggestions for firms making the transition, including:

1. Organize around process, not task.
2. Flatten the hierarchy.
3. Give leaders responsibility for process performance.
4. Link performance to customer satisfaction.
5. Create teams that have managerial and nonmanagerial responsibilities.
6. Reward team performance.

In addition, companies will need to utilize networks of suppliers, customers, and even competitors to create *strategic alliances.*

These developments are described by many terms today, including the *boundaryless company,* the *virtual corporation,* and *capabilities-based competition,* but, regardless of the terminology, you can bet that the future will bring exciting changes in the way marketing plans are implemented. Organizations as diverse as GE, Hallmark Cards, Eastman Kodak, and Clearly Canadian Beverages are already trying many of these ideas!

GE reorganized to reduce the size of its corporate strategic planning staff and also reduced the number of layers of middle managers and pushed decision-making authority lower in the organization. Some experts argue that in the future "boundaryless organizations" in which technology, information, managers, and managerial practices are shared across traditional organizational structures will be necessary.[23] The Marketing NewsNet box describes how implementation activities may occur in tomorrow's organizations.[24]

Improving Implementation of Marketing Programs

No magic formula exists to guarantee effective implementation of marketing plans. In fact, the answer seems to be equal parts of good management skills and practices, from which have come some guidelines for improving program implementation.

Communicate Goals and the Means of Achieving Them Those called on to implement plans need to understand both the goals sought and how they are to be accomplished. Everyone in Papa John's—from founder John Schnatter to telephone order takers and make-line people—is clear on what the firm's goal is: to deliver better pizzas using better ingredients. The firm's orientation packet for employees lists its six "core values" that executives are expected to memorize. Sample: Core value no. 4 is "PAPA," or "People Are Priority No. 1, Always."[25]

Have a Responsible Program Champion Willing to Act Successful programs almost always have a **product or program champion** who is able and willing to cut red tape and move the program forward. Such people often have the uncanny ability to move back and forth between big-picture strategy questions and specific details when the situation calls for it. Program champions are notoriously brash in overcoming organizational hurdles. In many cases, they adhere to the axiom,

"Better to ask forgiveness than permission." Using this strategy, 3M's Art Fry championed Post-it Notes to success, an idea he got when looking for a simple way to mark his hymnal while singing in his church choir.

Reward Successful Program Implementation When an individual or a team is rewarded for achieving the organization's goal, they have maximum incentive to see a program implemented successfully because they have personal ownership and a stake in that success. At a General Electric surge protector plant, employees receive a bonus each quarter that the facility meets plantwide performance goals.

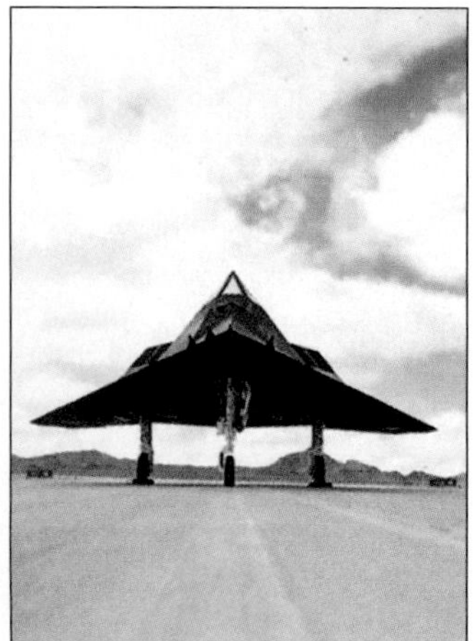

Take Action and Avoid "Paralysis by Analysis" Management experts warn against paralysis by analysis, the tendency to excessively analyze a problem instead of taking action. To overcome this pitfall, they call for a "bias for action" and recommend a "do it, fix it, try it" approach.[26] Conclusion: Perfectionists finish last, so getting 90 percent perfection and letting the marketplace help in the fine tuning makes good sense in implementation.

Lockheed Aircraft's Skunk Works got its name from the comic strip *L'il Abner* and its legendary reputation from achieving superhuman technical feats with a low budget and ridiculously short deadlines by stressing teamwork. Under the leadership of Kelly Johnson, in 35 years the Skunk Works turned out a series of world-class aircraft from the world's fastest (the SR-71 Blackbird) to the nation's most untrackable aircraft (the F-117 Stealth fighter). Two of Kelly Johnson's basic tenets: (1) make decisions promptly and (2) avoid paralysis by analysis. In fact, one study showed that Johnson's Skunk Works could carry out a program on schedule with 126 people, whereas a competitor in a comparable program was behind schedule with 3750 people.[27] Some of Johnson's other rules for running Skunk Works projects—adapted for managing marketing programs—appear in Figure 22–11.[28]

Foster Open Communication to Surface the Problems Success often lies in fostering a work environment that is open enough so employees are willing to speak out when they see problems without fear of recrimination. The focus is placed on trying to solve the problem as a group rather than finding someone to blame. Solutions are solicited from anyone who has a creative idea to suggest—from the caretaker to the president—without regard to status or rank in the organization.

FIGURE 22–11
Kelly Johnson's rules for managing projects at Lockheed's Skunk Works, adapted for managing marketing programs effectively

1. Delegate the marketing program manager practically complete control of the program—the authority for quick decisions on marketing, financial, or operational matters.
2. Provide strong—but *small*—project offices on both the customer and supplier sides.
3. Restrict project personnel *viciously* to use a *small* number of *good* people.
4. Utilize a very simple planning and reporting system with the flexibility to make schedule recovery in the face of failures.
5. Minimize the number of required reports—but record important work meticulously.
6. Schedule monthly cost reviews covering both (*a*) actual expenditures and commitments and (*b*) projected costs to program conclusions—avoiding cost overrun surprises.
7. Agree on performance specifications in *advance* of contracting.
8. Achieve absolute trust through day-to-day communication and cooperation—thereby minimizing misunderstanding and correspondence.
9. Control access of outsiders to the project and its personnel.
10. Reward good performance by pay—not by number of people supervised—thereby keeping the number of project personnel to a minimum.

For the unusual way General Motors avoided the "NIH syndrome" to help develop the Saturn, see the text.

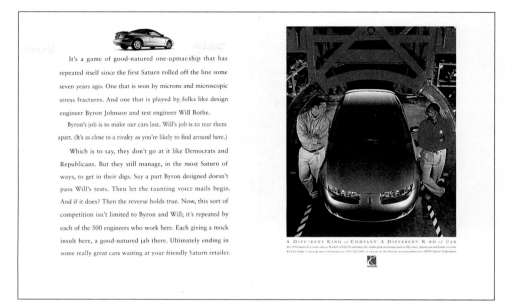

Two more Kelly Johnson axioms from Lockheed's Skunk Works apply here: (1) When trouble develops, surface the problem immediately, and (2) get help; don't keep the problem to yourself. This latter point is important even if it means getting ideas from competitors.

Saturn is General Motors' attempt to create a new company where participatory management and improved communications lead to a successful product. For example, to encourage discussion of possible cost reductions, each employee receives 100 to 750 hours of training, including balance sheet analysis. To avoid the "NIH syndrome"—the reluctance to accept ideas "not invented here" or not originated inside one's own firm—Saturn engineers bought 70 import cars to study for product design ideas and selected options that would most appeal to their target market.

Schedule Precise Tasks, Responsibilities, and Deadlines Successful implementation requires that people know the tasks for which they are responsible and the deadline for completing them. To implement the tasks required to carry out its marketing plans, the Royal Canadian Mint prepares an **action item list** that has three columns: (1) the task, (2) the name of the person responsible for accomplishing that task, and (3) the date by which the task is to be finished. Action item lists are forward looking, clarify the targets, and put strong pressure on people to achieve their designated tasks by the deadline.

Related to the action item lists are formal *program schedules,* which show the relationships through time of the various program tasks. Scheduling an action program involves (1) identifying the main tasks, (2) determining the time required to complete each, (3) arranging the activities to meet the deadline, and (4) assigning responsibilities to complete each task.

Suppose, for example, that you and two friends are asked to do a term project on the problem, "How can the university increase attendance at its performing arts concerts?"[29] And suppose further that the instructor limits the project in the following ways:

1. The project must involve a mail survey of the attitudes of a sample of students.
2. The term paper with the survey results must be submitted by the end of the 11-week quarter.

FIGURE 22–12
Tasks in complete a term project

Shown below are the tasks you might face as a member of a student team to complete a marketing research study using a mail questionnaire. Elapsed time to complete all the tasks is 15 weeks. How do you finish the project in an 11-week quarter? For an answer, see the text.

TASK	TIME (WEEKS)
1. Construct and test a rough-draft questionnaire for clarity (in person, not by mail) on friends.	2
2. Type and copy a final questionnaire.	2
3. Randomly select the names of 200 students from the school directory.	1
4. Address and stamp envelopes; mail questionnaires.	1
5. Collect returned questionnaires.	3
6. Tabulate and analyze data from returned questionnaires.	2
7. Write final report.	3
8. Type and submit final report.	1
Total time necessary to complete all activities.	15

To begin the assignment, you need to identify all the project tasks and then estimate the time you can reasonably allocate to each one. As shown in Figure 22–12, it would take 15 weeks to complete the project if you did all the tasks sequentially; so to complete it in 11 weeks, your team must work on different parts at the same time, and some activities must be independent enough to overlap. This requires specialization and cooperation. Suppose that of the three of you (A, B, and C), only student C can type. Then you (student A) might assume the task of constructing the questionnaire and selecting samples, and student B might tabulate the data. This division of labour allows each student to concentrate on and become expert in one area, but you should also cooperate. Student C might help A and B in the beginning, and A and B might help C later on.

You must also figure out which activities can be done concurrently to save time. In Figure 22–12 you can see that task 2 must be completed before task 4. However, task 3 might easily be done before, at the same time as, or after task 2. Task 3 is independent of task 2.

Scheduling production and marketing activities—from a term project to a new product rollout to a space shuttle launch—can be done efficiently with Gantt charts. Figure 22–13 shows one variation of a Gantt chart used to schedule the class project, demonstrating how the concurrent work on several tasks enables the students to finish the project on time. Developed by Henry L. Gantt, this method is the basis for the scheduling techniques used today, including elaborate computerized methods. The key to all scheduling techniques is to distinguish tasks that *must* be done sequentially from those that *can* be done concurrently. As in the case of the term project, scheduling tasks concurrently often reduces the total time required for a project.

CONCEPT CHECK

1. Why is it important to include line operating managers in the planning process?
2. What is the meaning and importance of a program champion?
3. Explain the difference between sequential and concurrent tasks in a Gantt chart.

Organizing for Marketing

A marketing organization is needed to implement the firm's marketing plans. Basic issues in today's marketing organizations include understanding (1) how line versus staff positions and divisional groupings interrelate to form a cohesive marketing organization and (2) the role of the product manager.

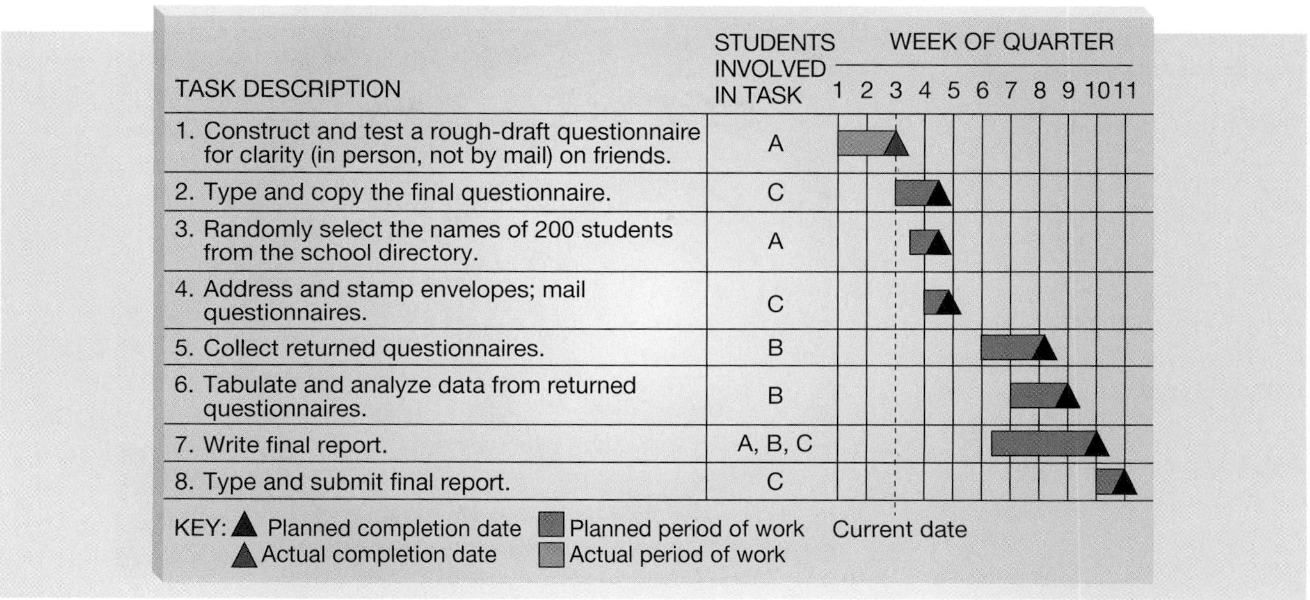

TASK DESCRIPTION
STUDENTS INVOLVED IN TASK
WEEK OF QUARTER
1 2 3 4 5 6 7 8 9 10 11
1. Construct and test a rough-draft questionnaire for clarity (in person, not by mail) on friends.
A
2. Type and copy the final questionnaire.
C
3. Randomly select the names of 200 students from the school directory.
A
4. Address and stamp envelopes; mail questionnaires.
C
5. Collect returned questionnaires.
B
6. Tabulate and analyze data from returned questionnaires.
B
7. Write final report.
A, B, C
8. Type and submit final report.
C
KEY: Planned completion date
Actual completion date
Planned period of work
Actual period of work
Current date

FIGURE 22–13
Gantt chart for scheduling the term project

Line versus Staff and Divisional Groupings Although simplified, Figure 22–14 shows the organization of Pillsbury's Prepared Dough Products Business Unit in detail and highlights the distinction between line and staff positions in marketing. People in **line positions,** such as group marketing managers, have the authority and responsibility to issue orders to the people who report to them, such as marketing managers. In this organizational chart, line positions are connected with solid lines. Those in **staff positions** (shown by dotted lines) have the authority and responsibility to advise people in line positions but cannot issue direct orders to them.

FIGURE 22–14
Organization of the Pillsbury Company

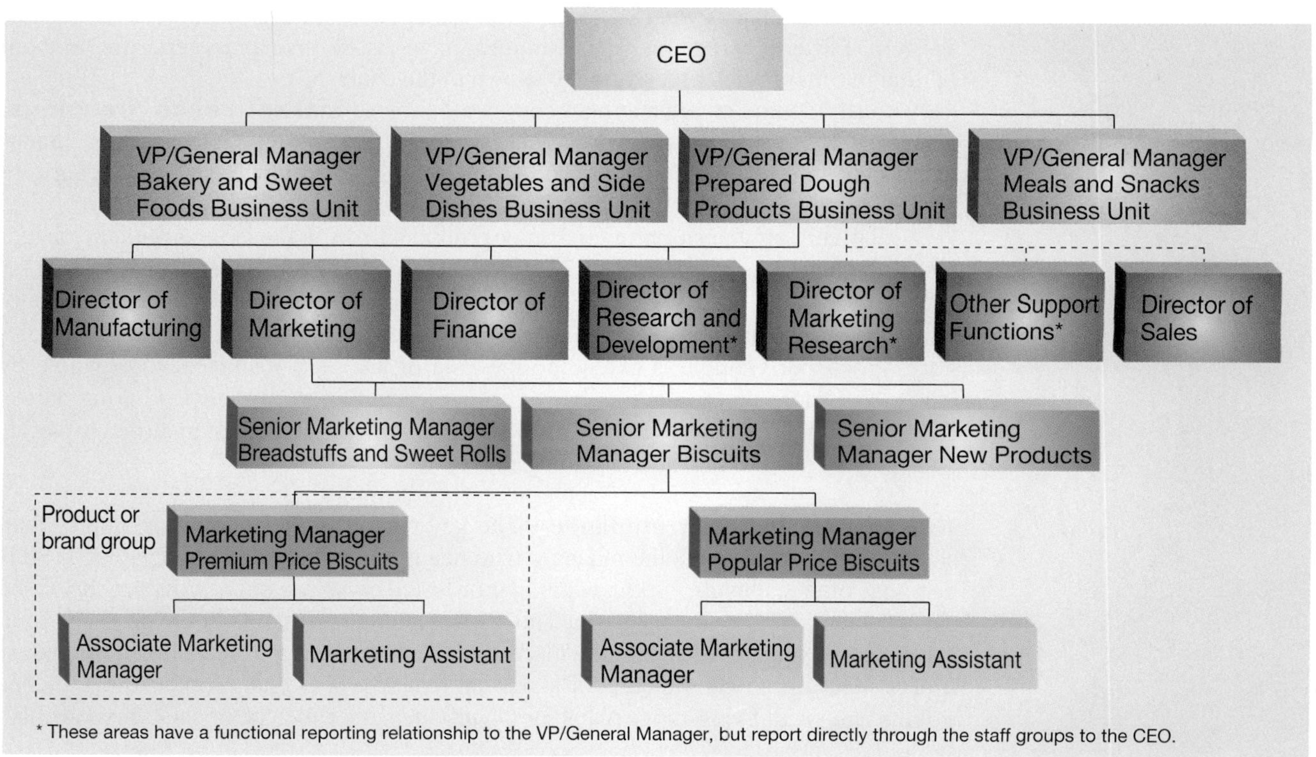

Other Support Functions*

* These areas have a functional reporting relationship to the VP/General Manager, but report directly through the staff groups to the CEO.

Products from Pillsbury's line of prepared dough products.

The Pillsbury Company
www.pillsbury.com

Most marketing organizations use divisional groupings—such as product line, functional, geographical, and market-based—to implement plans and achieve their organizational objectives. Three of these appear in some form in Pillsbury's organizational chart in Figure 22–14. At the top of its organization, Pillsbury organizes by **product line groupings,** in which a unit is responsible for specific product offerings. For example, Pillsbury has four main product lines: Bakery & Sweet Foods, Vegetables & Side Dishes, Prepared Dough Products, and Meals & Snacks.

The Prepared Dough Products Business Unit is organized by **functional groupings** such as manufacturing, marketing, and finance, which are the different business activities within a firm.

Pillsbury uses **geographical groupings** for its field sales representatives. Each director of sales has several regional sales managers reporting to him or her, such as Western, Eastern, and so on. These, in turn, have district managers reporting to them (although for simplicity these are not shown in the chart).

A fourth method of organizing a company is to use **market-based groupings,** which utilize specific customer segments, such as the banking, health care, or manufacturing segments. When this method of organizing is combined with product groupings, the result is a *matrix organization.*

A relatively new position in consumer products firms is the *category manager* (senior marketing manager in Figure 22–14). Category managers have profit-and-loss responsibility for an entire product line—all biscuit brands, for example. They attempt to reduce the possibility of one brand's actions hurting another brand in the same category. Procter & Gamble is extending the idea of category managers to organize by "global business units" such as baby care and beauty care by 2001. Cutting across country boundaries, these global business units will implement standardized worldwide pricing, marketing, and distribution.[30]

Role of the Product Manager The key person in the product or brand group shown in Figure 22–15 is the manager who heads it. As mentioned in Chapter 11, this person is often called the *product manager* or *brand manager,* but in Pillsbury he or she carries the title *marketing manager.* This person and the assistants in the product group are the basic building blocks in the marketing department of most consumer and industrial product firms. The function of a product manager is to plan, implement, and control the annual and long-range plans for the products for which he or she is responsible.

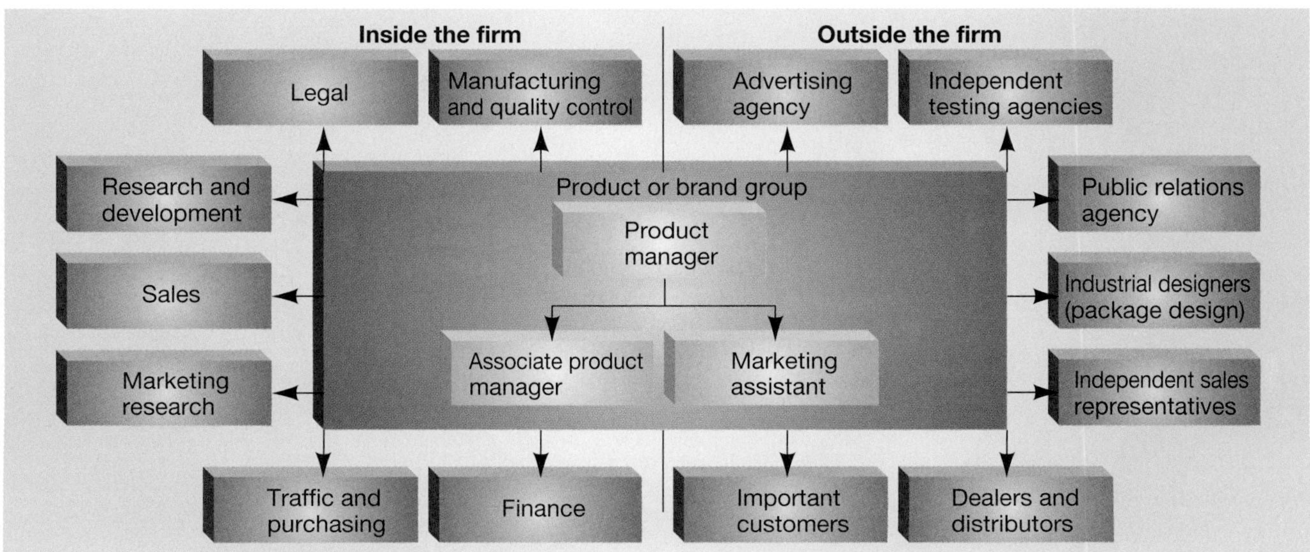

FIGURE 22–15
Units with which the product manager and product group work

There are both benefits and dangers to the product manager system. On the positive side, product managers become strong advocates for the assigned products, cut red tape to work with people in various functions both inside and outside the organization (Figure 22–15), and assume profit-and-loss responsibility for the performance of the product line. On the negative side, even though product managers have major responsibilities, they have relatively little direct authority, so most groups and functions shown in Figure 22–15 must be coordinated to meet the product's goals.[31] To coordinate the many units, product managers must use persuasion rather than orders.

But as Canadian firms move toward more customer-intimacy and relationship marketing strategies, product managers are no longer the only ones responsible for managing the product or customer base. Some Canadian firms have created new positions such as "manager of student segment" or "VP of financial services clients," which shadow the traditional product manager roles. These firms have divided their organizations into "customer-facing roles" (such as a segment manager). More and more often it is the segment managers, not the product managers, who make the final decisions on product, price, promotion, and place (distribution).[32]

THE CONTROL PHASE OF THE STRATEGIC MARKETING PROCESS

The essence of control, the final phase of the strategic marketing process, is comparing results with planned goals for the marketing program and taking necessary actions.

The Marketing Control Process

Ideally, quantified goals from the marketing plans developed in the planning phase have been accomplished by the marketing actions taken in the implementation phase (Figure 22–16) and measured as results in the control phase. A marketing manager then uses *management by exception,* which means identifying results that deviate from plans to diagnose their causes and take new actions. Often results fall short of plans, and a corrective action is needed. For example, after 50 years of profits Caterpillar accumulated losses of $1.4 billion. To correct the problem, Caterpillar focused its marketing efforts on core products and reduced its manufacturing costs. At other times the

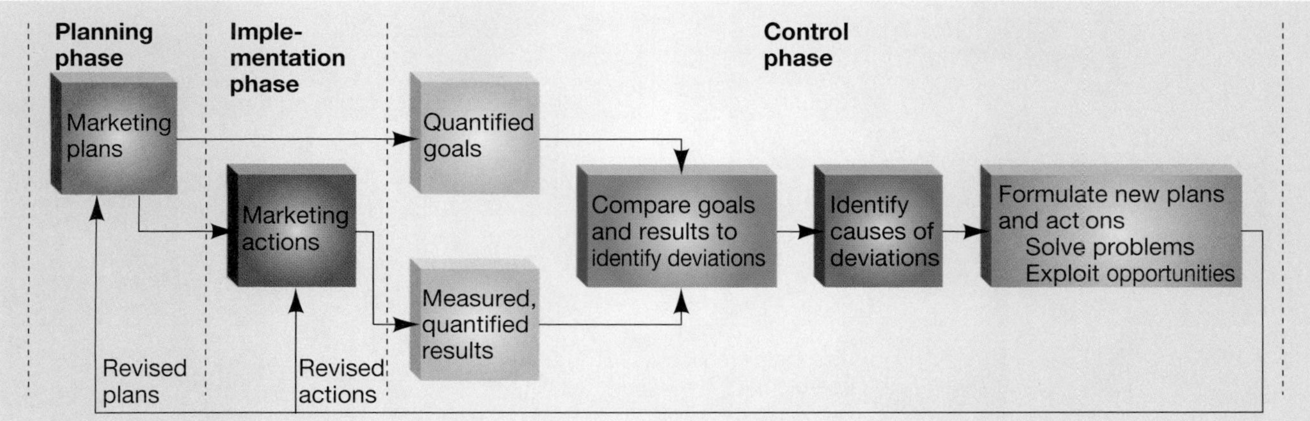

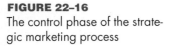

FIGURE 22–16
The control phase of the strategic marketing process

comparison shows that performance is far better than anticipated, in which case the marketing manager tries to identify the reason and move quickly to exploit the unexpected opportunity.

Measuring Results Without some quantitative goal, no benchmark exists with which to compare actual results. Manufacturers of both consumer and industrial products are increasingly trying to develop marketing programs that have not only specific action programs but also specific procedures for monitoring key measures of performance. Today marketing executives are measuring not only tangible financial targets such as sales revenues and profits, but also less tangible ones such as customer satisfaction, new-product development cycle time, and salesforce motivation.

Taking Marketing Actions When results deviate significantly from plans, some kind of action is essential. Deviations can be the result of the process used to specify goals or can be due to changes in the marketplace. Beaten badly for years in the Canadian toothpaste market by P&G's Crest, Colgate went on the offensive. It took aggressive marketing action to introduce its Total toothpaste. Not only does Total clean teeth, but it also helps heal gingivitis, one of the bleeding-gum diseases of increasing concern to aging baby boomers. For the first time in 30 years, Colgate usurped P&G's Crest to take the number one spot.[33]

Sales Analysis

For controlling marketing programs, **sales analysis**—using the firm's sales records to compare actual results with sales goals and identify areas of strength and weakness—is critical. All the variables that might be used in market segmentation may be used in **sales component analysis** (also called *microsales analysis*), which traces sales revenues to their sources, such as specific products, sales territories, or customers. Common breakdowns include the following:

- Customer characteristics: demographics, NAICS, size, reason for purchase, and type of reseller (retailer or wholesaler).
- Product characteristics: model, package size, and colour.
- Geographical region: sales territory, city, province, and region.
- Order size.
- Price or discount class.
- Commission to the sales representative.

Today's computers can easily produce these breakdowns, provided the input data contain these classifications. Therefore, it is critical that marketing managers specify the breakdowns they require from the accounting and information systems departments.

The danger is that marketing managers or chief executive officers get overwhelmed by the volume of computerized reports. To avoid this problem, each Tuesday, Ken Iverson carefully inputs into the computer numbers on the tons of steel each of Nucor's "minimills" produced the previous week. What makes the situation unique is that Iverson is chief executive officer of Nucor. Saving money is *not* the reason he does his own computer analysis. His explanation, "By keying in the numbers, you're forced to look at every figure for every week. That's the value."[34]

Profitability Analysis

To their surprise, marketing managers often discover the 80/20 principle the hard way, on the job. **Profitability analysis** enables the manager to measure the profitability of the firm's products, customer groups, sales territories, channels of distribution, and even order sizes. This leads to decisions to expand, maintain, reduce, or eliminate specific products, customer groups, or channels.

For example, following the 80/20 principle, a marketing manager will try to find the common characteristics among the 20 percent of the customers (or products, brands, sales districts, salespeople, or kinds of orders) that are generating 80 percent (or the bulk) of revenues and profits to find more like them to exploit competitive advantages. Conversely, the 80 percent of customers, products, brands, and so on that are generating few revenues and profits may need to be reduced or even dropped entirely unless a way is found to make them profitable.

The Marketing Audit

Often a broader marketing perspective is needed than is given by sales or profitability analyses, one that covers a longer time horizon and relates the marketing mix factors to environmental variables. This is the role of a **marketing audit,** which is a comprehensive, unbiased, periodic review of the strategic marketing process of a firm or SBU. The purpose of the marketing audit, which serves as both a planning and control technique, is to identify new problems and opportunities that warrant an action plan to improve performance.

Many firms undertaking a marketing audit use a checklist such as that shown in Figure 22–17 as a part of their situation analysis in their strategic marketing process. The checklist used covers factors ranging from the marketing mix factors and customer profiles to markets and competitors.

For a meaningful, comprehensive marketing audit, the individual or team conducting the audit must have a free rein to talk to managers, employees, salespeople, distributors, and customers, as well as have access to all pertinent internal and external reports and memoranda. They need to involve all levels of the organization in the process to ensure that resulting action recommendations have widespread support.

CONCEPT CHECK

1. What is the difference between a line and a staff position in a marketing organization?
2. What are four groupings used within a typical marketing organization?
3. What two components of the strategic marketing process are compared to control a marketing program?

PRODUCTS/SERVICES: THE REASON FOR EXISTENCE

1. Is the product/service free from deadwood?
2. What is the life-cycle stage?
3. How will user demands or trends affect you?
4. Are you a leader in new-product innovation?
5. Are inexpensive methods used to estimate new product potentials before consideration amounts are spent on R&D and market introduction?
6. Do you have different quality levels for different markets?
7. Are packages/brochures effective salespeople for the products/services they present?
8. Do you present products/services in the most appealing colours (formats) for markets being served?
9. Are there features or benefits to exploit?
10. Is the level of customer service adequate?
11. How are quality and reliability viewed by customers?

CUSTOMER: USER PROFILES

1. Who is the current and potential customer?
2. Are there geographic aspects of use: regional, rural, urban?
3. Why do people buy the product/service; what motivates their preferences?
4. Who makes buying decisions; when; where?
5. What is the frequency and quantity of use?

MARKETS: WHERE PRODUCTS/SERVICES ARE SOLD

1. Have you identified and measured major segments?
2. Are small potential market segments overlooked in trying to satisfy the majority?
3. Are the markets for the products/services expanding or declining?
4. Should different segments be developed; are there gaps in penetration?

COMPETITORS: THEIR INFLUENCE

1. Who are the principal competitors, how are they positioned, and where are they headed?
2. What are their market shares?
3. What features of competitors' products/services stand out?
4. Is the market easily entered or dominated?

PRICING: PROFITABILITY PLANNING

1. What are the objectives of current pricing policy: acquiring, defending, or expanding?
2. Are price policies set to produce volume or profit?
3. How does pricing compare with competition in similar levels of quality?
4. Does cost information show profitability of each item?
5. What is the history of price deals, discounts, and promotions?

FIGURE 22–17
Marketing audit questions

SUMMARY

1 Marketing managers use the strategic marketing process to allocate their resources as effectively as possible. Sales response functions help them assess what the market's response to additional marketing effort will be.

2 The planning phase of the strategic marketing process usually results in a marketing plan that sets the direction for the marketing activities of an organization. Three kinds of marketing plans are long-range, annual, and new-product plans.

3 Three useful frameworks to improve marketing planning are (*a*) Porter's generic business strategies, (*b*) profit enhancement options, and (*c*) market-product synergies.

4 An effective marketing plan has measurable, achievable goals; uses facts and valid assumptions; is simple, clear, and specific; is complete and feasible; and is controllable and flexible.

5 The implementation phase of the strategic marketing process is concerned with executing the marketing program developed in the planning phase and has achieved increased attention the past decade.

6 Essential to good scheduling is separating tasks that can be done concurrently from those that must be done sequentially. Gantt charts are a simple, effective means of scheduling.

7 Organizing marketing activities necessitates recognition of two different aspects of an organization: (*a*) line and staff positions and (*b*) product line, functional, geographical, and market-based groupings.

8 The product manager performs a vital marketing role in both consumer and industrial product firms, interacting with numerous people and groups both inside and outside the firm.

9 The control phase of the strategic marketing process involves measuring the results of the actions from the implementation phase and comparing them with goals set in the planning phase. Sales analyses, profitability analyses, and marketing audits are used to control marketing programs.

KEY TERMS AND CONCEPTS

sales response function p. 568
share points p. 569
generic business strategy p. 574
cost leadership strategy p. 574
differentiation strategy p. 575
cost focus strategy p. 575
differentiation focus strategy p. 575
synergy p. 577

product or program champion p. 583
action item list p. 585
line positions p. 587
staff positions p. 587
product line groupings p. 588
functional groupings p. 588
geographical groupings p. 588
market-based groupings p. 588
sales analysis p. 590
sales component analysis p. 590
profitability analysis p. 591
marketing audit p. 591

INTERNET EXERCISE

The Walt Disney Company's main Web site (www.disney.com) is splashy, interactive, and links to other Disney Web sites. These other sites enable the Web user to subscribe to various Disney online services or order other Disney products or services such as movies, theme park reservations, and music. Access the Disney Web site and click on the "Shopping" Web link to go to "The Disney Store Online." To purchase a video, go to the left side of the Web page. Under the "Store Directory," scroll down to the "Video Collection" link. Click on the "New Releases" link. Then, click on a video of your choice (such as *A Bug's Life*). Select either the "DVD" or "VHS" format of the video. Next, select the quantity you want (presumably "1"). Click on the "Add Items to Shopping Basket" button and then click on the "Begin Checkout" button at the top of the page to purchase the video. After you have viewed your order, click on the "Continue to Checkout" button. Enter the personal and credit card information that Disney requires to process your order (be sure to click the button that calculates the shipping and tax) and then click on the "Click Here to Complete Your Purchase" button **ONLY IF** you want to finalize the purchase.

1 Is the process for ordering merchandise from "The Disney Store Online" convenient to you as a consumer?
2 How likely are *you* to make a purchase from any company with an online store now or in the near future? Why or why not? What should companies do to get people to use their online stores instead of retail stores, catalogs, or other distribution outlets for their merchandise or services?

APPLYING MARKETING CONCEPTS AND PERSPECTIVES

1 Assume a firm faces an S-shaped sales response function. What happens to the ratio of incremental sales revenue to incremental marketing effort at the (*a*) bottom, (*b*) middle, and (*c*) top of this curve?
2 What happens to the ratio of incremental sales revenue to incremental marketing effort when the sales response function is an upward-sloping straight line?
3 In 2000 General Mills invested millions of dollars in expanding its cereal and cake mix businesses. To allocate this money between these two businesses, what information would General Mills like to have?
4 Suppose your Great Lawns mower company has the market-product concentration situation shown in Figure 22–8A. What are both the synergies and potential pitfalls of following expansion strategies of (*a*) market specialization and (*b*) product specialization?
5 Are value-driven strategies inconsistent with value-based planning? Give an example that supports your position.
6 The first Domino's Pizza restaurant was near a university campus. What implementation problems are (*a*) similar and (*b*) different for restaurants near a university campus versus a military base?
7 A common theme among managers who succeed repeatedly in program implementation is fostering open communication. Why is this so important?
8 Parts of tasks 6 and 7 in Figure 22–12 are done both concurrently and sequentially. How can this be? How does it help the students meet the term paper deadline?
9 In Pillsbury's organizational chart in Figure 22–14, where do product line, functional, and geographical groupings occur?
10 Why are quantified goals in the planning phase of the strategic marketing process important for the control phase?

CASE 22–1 CLEARLY CANADIAN

Clearly Canadian Beverage Corporation, based in Vancouver, is a leading producer of premium alternative beverages, including Clearly Canadian Sparkling Flavoured Water, Clearly Canadian O+2, REfresher and Orbitz. The company is considered one of the pioneers of the estimated $8 billion alternative beverage industry and distributes its portfolio of beverages throughout Canada, the United States, and numerous countries around the world.

HISTORY

When Clearly Canadian entered the beverage market in the late 1980s, it was an instant success with consumers looking for something different. Clearly Canadian Sparkling Flavoured Water may not have been the first alternative beverage, but it was the first product referred to as an alternative beverage. If it did not create the category, it did define it, and opened the doors for countless other players such as Snapple, Mistic, and Arizona. The company went against the grain when it started out. It wanted to carve out a niche using a premium product, a very sophisticated image, and distinctive packaging.

The company entered the market early and capitalized on the emerging consumer trend toward flavoured waters. Innovative packaging allowed the product to stand out on crowded retail shelves. Premium pricing also helped position Clearly Canadian as a high-quality product. The company also achieved widespread distribution for its product in Canada and the United States which was integral to its early success. The company also pursued an aggressive market development strategy and expanded its distribution to Mexico, England, Ireland, Japan, and other countries. By 1992, the company was selling about 22 million cases of its beverage.

However, by 1993, growth in the alternative beverage category began to slow and company sales declined. In fact, sales of Clearly Canadian dropped to 7 million cases. Experts suggested that consumers' capricious tastes and the growing competition were the primary reasons for the decline. Others insisted that with the growing number of new brands, the so-called upscale alternative beverages could no longer command premium prices. Many new brands, in fact, did use low-price strategies to undermine the premium niche positioning of the entire category. Clearly Canadian found itself losing market share to "knock off" products as well as to new beverage types such as iced tea.

CLEARLY CANADIAN REACTS

Clearly Canadian Beverage Corporation recognized that it too had contributed to its decline by being content to react to the market rather than being proactive. Whereas competitors continued to innovate in terms of packaging, image, and new products, Clearly Canadian atrophied. The company realized it had to get back to its innovative roots. By 1994, the company had added new flavours to the line and introduced a multiserving bottle as well as a four-pack concept.

It also launched a 200 ml bottle for the hospitality industry. The company also undertook new consumer promotional activities and a systemwide sales incentive program for its sales representatives. Still, these efforts did not significantly boost sales, and Clearly Canadian appeared to be a company whose time had passed.

But undaunted, the company established a five-year strategic plan and moved quickly to implement it. The company restructured internally and emerged with a new portfolio of products. The company transformed itself from a company that sold a beverage to a beverage com-

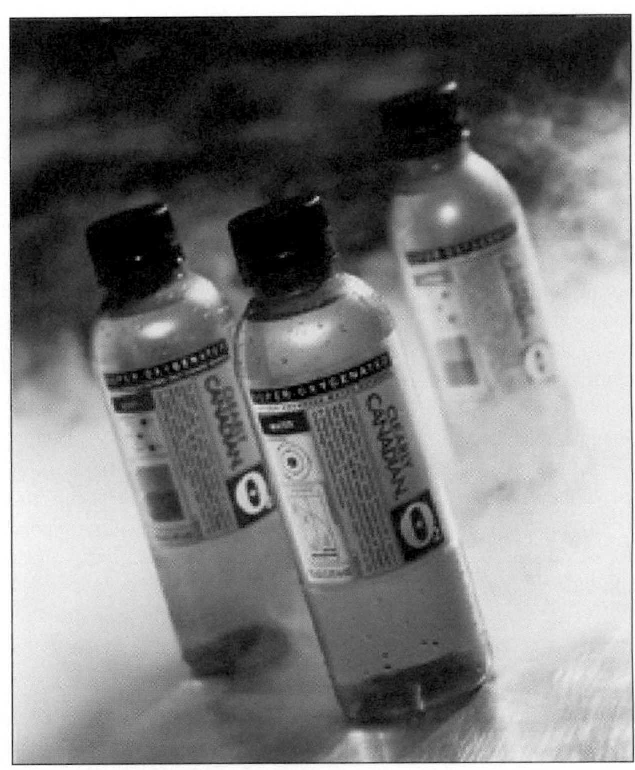

pany. It introduced a premium still water (Clearly Canadian Natural Artesian Water), and Quenchers, a line of preservative-free sparkling fruit beverages. In 1996, it also launched Orbitz, a textually modified beverage that featured fruit-flavoured gel spheres suspended in a clear fruit drink. In 1997, it relaunched its flagship brand, Clearly Canadian Sparkling Flavoured Water, in a bolder, more colourful bottle and with three new flavours. By the end of 1997, the company had retained its status as one of the top 10 ranked alternative beverage companies in terms of sales revenue.

CONTINUING THE PATH TO GROWTH

In 1998, Clearly Canadian acquired Cascade Clear Water Co. which not only added a much needed mainstream product—bottled water—to its brand portfolio but also gained manufacturing capabilities. At the end of 1998, Clearly Canadian merged its two U.S. subsidiaries, Clearly Canadian Beverage (U.S.) Corporation, and Cascade Clear Water Co., creating one-wholly-owned subsidiary called CC Beverage (U.S.) Corporation ("CC Beverage"). CC Beverage produces Clearly Canadian products for retail sale in North America and the Pacific Rim. Operating out of its state-of-the-art manufacturing facility, CC Beverage also co-packs for regional grocery store chains, bottled water companies, and other domestic and international beverage manufacturers and distributors. Additionally, CC Beverage operated a home/office bottled water delivery business in the U.S. under the Cascade Clear brand.

The company also reached distribution arrangements to sell its products at some of the largest food and beverage retailers in the U.S. and at the same time regained its distribution rights back from master distributors allowing it to control its entire North American distribution system.

Clearly Canadian also decided to focus more of its promotional initiatives at the local level, working closely with customers and distributors to execute value-added promotions in key markets. The company is relying on "guerilla marketing" techniques, such as product sampling on the street and at special events, rather than paying for expensive television and print advertising. In 1999, Clearly Canadian partnered with Warner–Lambert in on a joint sampling program where consumers received a free package of Trident sugarless gum with each purchase of a 1-litre bottle of Clearly Canadian Sparkling Flavoured Water.

The company has also reached agreements to distribute its products in key European markets such as France, Spain, Portugal, and Turkey. These agreements are in addition to its strong presence in England and Sweden. The company is also controlling costs in the areas of distribution, marketing, and production without sacrificing customer service or product quality.

Y2K AND BEYOND

After more than a decade in business, Clearly Canadian has sold more than 1.4 billion bottles of its product. Company efforts are now focused on selling the next billion bottles. To achieve this goal, the company believes it must follow its pioneer spirit and innovate in order to stay current with consumers' needs and ahead of its competition. The company now has a dramatic new product portfolio including Clearly Canadian O+2, an oxygen-enhanced beverage for active individuals, and Battery, a refreshing energy drink, as well as the Cascade Clear line of products. Its challenge for 2000 and beyond is to generate volume growth as a multibranded company with half of its sales coming from non-Clearly Canadian products. But the company's focus will remain the same: to build premium niche brands and reach more customers in more places, more profitably.

Questions

1 What generic business strategy (see Figure 22–6) was Clearly Canadian Beverage Corporation pursuing when it first entered the alternative beverage market, and what strategy does it appear to be pursuing today?

2 Discuss the basic generic marketing strategies (see Figure 22–7) that Clearly Canadian has pursued and continues to pursue today.

3 Examine Figure 22–8. Which of the five alternative marketing strategies in the market-product grids depicts Clearly Canadian's current strategy?

PART V CASE THE STRATEGY IN E-BUSINESS

Whenever e-business is discussed, amazon.com is usually mentioned as Jeff Bezos, founder and chairman has created a strong brand name for his Net-based company. June 1999 was a milestone for the company based in Seattle. Amazon.com made its 10 millionth online sale after opening its virtual door in 1995.[1] Although Bezos launched his company with his vision of a cyberspace bookstore, amazon.com is becoming much more than a techno-bookstore. Bezos' company has grown from a one-product virtual store to an international multi-product virtual corporation.

HIGH SPEED GROWTH

The growth of amazon.com has caused a ripple effect in more than one industry and there seems to be no stopping the momentum that may turn into a ground swell. There are many reasons amazon.com is considered a wonder in the e-commerce trade, but the most astounding fact is that even though the sales are staggeringly high with a growing customer base, the company has yet to make a profit. The pretax loss for fiscal 1998 is US$124.5 million with US$605.0 million in net sales revenue, a healthy increase from the 1997 loss of US$31.0 million on US$147.8 million net sales revenue.[2] Sales keep rising, as do the losses. However, this has not stopped amazon.com from charging ahead with plans to move beyond selling books and music to become the dominant portal of online selling. For now the Internet company losses do not appear to be worrying investors and amazon.com is free to pursue an aggressive growth strategy. The strategy is a risky one, but Bezos is prepared to take the gamble. There are many uncertainties in this emerging business venue as amazon.com moves into markets where established, branded companies will fight intensely to ward off the advances of this newcomer.

Building a strong customer base is not easy, but David Risher, senior VP, product development, has something to say about amazon.com's ability to keep customers coming back: "You just don't get to 10 million customers strong without creating a great service that's met the needs of so many people."[3] The key to their approach is a customer who will return. Sixty-four percent of all orders are from those online buyers who have already established a relationship with amazon.com. Risher believes that "in cyberspace, branding is important, but it's not as important as building the right service. If you build something the customers love, it creates the brand. Word-of-mouth experiences become your best advocate."[4]

Amazon.com was the brainchild of founder Jeff Bezos in 1994 and after raising US$1 million from family and friends for developing software and negotiating with suppliers, the virtual bookstore went online in 1995. Selling books began the saga of the company that is now attributed as the leader in online selling. And this story is not about to end on a bookshelf. Bezos expanded the product line to include music and other related entertainment products such as videos. With each step expanding the product portfolio offered at amazon.com, the company found itself competing within several established industries, up against a number of well-known companies.

PUTTING PRESSURE ON THE ESTABLISHMENT

In book retailing, amazon.com caught the attention of at least two large American book chains—Barnes & Noble and Borders. Barnes & Noble Inc. is still America's largest bookstore chain, with 521 Barnes & Noble stores and 466 B. Dalton stores. After amazon.com began selling books online, Barnes & Noble set up a new subsidiary to compete with amazon.com head-to-head on the Net. The subsidiary, barnesandnoble.com, lost US$42 million for the parent company by the end of fiscal 1998, demonstrating that online business is an expensive undertaking, even for those experienced companies savvy in marketing and branding. However, Barnes & Noble is in a strong position to compete with amazon.com due to the broad base of its business. In addition to its storefront and online bookstores, Barnes & Noble owns a direct-mail book selling business and a book publisher.[5] All of this will provide Barnes & Noble with the resources to defend its market from amazon.com. Armed with a strong brand name and marketing savvy, Barnes & Noble is scouting the Memphis area looking for space for a new distribution centre in Memphis, Tennessee.[6] With the addition of a new facility, Barnes & Noble is investing in an improved infrastructure to handle its inventory needs and online orders. The introduction of a Barnes & Noble web site has forced the company to evaluate its approach to order processing if it wants to compete with amazon.com.

Another amazon.com competitor in book-selling is Borders. Borders, the second-largest book chain in the United

[1]Ann Saccomano, "Not the same old story," *Traffic World*, (June 21, 1999), p. 19.

[2]Amazon.com, *Form 10K*, 1998.

[3]Kim Cleland, "Amazon.com: David Risher," *Advertising Age*, (June 28 1999), p. S16.

[4]IBID.

[5]Barnes & Noble Inc., *The Industry Standard*, www.thestandard.net, May 6, 1999.

[6]James Overstreet, "Barnes & Noble plans 600-employe Memphis center," *Birmingham Business Journal*, (June 28, 1999), p. 9.

States, has been slow to respond to the amazon.com threat. However, Borders is not out of the race yet. Borders not only has stores in the U.S. but it also has a presence in the United Kingdom, Australia, and Singapore. They have more than 1100 bookstores, including 250 book and music superstores and 900 Waldenbooks stores found mostly in malls. Borders' philosophy is similar to that of the two top Canadian book retailers, Chapters and Indigo Books, Music and Café. Borders, with its store layouts, encourage a laid-back approach to shopping for books, complete with snack bars and comfortable seating.[7] However, this may not be enough to hold off both amazon.com online and Barnes & Noble on the street.

MUSIC AND THE INTERNET

When amazon.com added music to its product offering, CDNow took notice. Another online marketer, CDNow was started by twins Jason and Matthew Olim and boasts a loyal customer following, with the more than 300 000 items on their Web site. Most of the items are CDs but they also sell music videos, T-shirts, and movies. The interesting aspect of this Web site is that there is a selection of obscure CDs catering to the eclectic audiophile. The value of the site is enhanced with music reviews and an option for a customer to create custom CDs through its supersonic BOOM unit.[8] CDNow was well on its way as the pioneer providing music online when amazon.com added CDs to its cyberspace shelves in June 1998.[9] Since then, CDNow began losing market share, causing problems for the company. In July 1999, Sony Corporation and Time Warner Inc. announced that their jointly owned Columbia House music and video would merge with CDNow.[10] This bargain is intended to help the struggling pioneer in digital music as well as provide Columbia House with access to CDNow's database of 16 million customers. Columbia House is a direct marketer of music and video recordings using mainly direct mail and the Internet. CDNow is now associated with two of the world's largest record companies, Warner Music and Sony Music, which, together control 35 percent of recording sales in the United States. CDNow's technology, which allows customers to download songs from an Internet connection, has transformed the music industry. Sony and Time Warner are interested in this segment, as there still seems to be great growth potential. The Columbia House and CDNow relationship will provide Sony and Time Warner with access to this segment of entertainment commerce. Amazon.com is now competing with two new competitors for recording sales.

Whatever challenges amazon.com is facing from some powerful and determined competitors, the company continues to charge forward with new products and new ventures. The break-neck speed with which amazon.com is growing does not appear to be slowing. Changes in the company reflect amazon.com's commitment to growing the company. In June 1999, Jeff Bezos appointed Joseph Galli as president and chief operating officer of amazon.com.[11] Galli reports to Jeff Bezos, who remains the CEO. Galli's experience has been with Black & Decker, where he was responsible for new product development and improving customer service. He is well known for creating Black & Decker's worldwide product development system and instrumental in implementing a world-class manufacturing and purchasing infrastructure. With Bezos and his new president, more changes are in order as the company continues to move from being an entrepreneurial business to a large international institution.[12]

From its beginnings in online book retailing, amazon.com has grown significantly since 1995. Not only is amazon.com known as the number one Internet company selling music, video, and books but it now also offers free electronic greeting cards and computer game titles. Gift wrapping also is part of their service, as is the 1-Click shopping for regular customers, making the buying experience online as convenient and secure as possible. In addition to contacting previous buyers with personalized purchasing recommendations, in April 1999 Bid-Click was added to the web site to make it as interactive as possible.[13] Bid-Click allows amazon.com's customers to bid on merchandise of their choice, engaging them in a unique shopping experience.

Amazon.com also operates two international sites: www.amazon.com.uk in the United Kingdom and www.amazon.com.de in Germany. Beyond its branded sites, amazon.com operates a Web-based address book, calendar, and reminder service called www.planetall.com. Other sites under the amazon.com operation are www.imbd.com the Internet Movie Database, and www.livebid.com, a site of live-event auctions on the Internet. Amazon.com's influence in cyberspace goes beyond its own sites with investments in other online retailers such as drugstore.com, Pets.com, and HomeGrocer.com. There appears to be little that the company doesn't want in its attempt to achieve its business objective to "become the best place to buy, find and discover any product or service available online."[14] The company believes that in order to succeed, amazon.com must continue to invest in marketing and promotion at the same time as developing existing products, technology, and infrastructure.

[7]Borders Group, Inc., *The Industry Standard*, www.thestandard.net, May 6, 1999.

[8]CDNow, Inc., *The Industry Standard*, www.thestand.net, May 6, 1999.

[9]Anonymous, "Amazon.world," *Newsweek*, (April 12, 1999), p. 14.

[10]Anonymous, "Sony and Time Warner make music deal," *Weekly Corporate Growth Report*, (July 26, 1999), p. 10293.

[11]Anonymous, "Amazon.com Names Joseph Galli President and Chief Operating Officer," *PR Newswire*, (June 25, 1999), p. 6246.

[12]Financial, "Amazon Adds New President," *The Washington Post*, (June 26, 1999), p. E02.

[13]Anonymous, "Amazon.com Names Joseph Galli President and Chief Operation Officer", *PR Newswire*, (June 25, 1999), p. 6246.

[14]Amazon.com, *Form 10k*, 1998.

CONTINUING TO EXPAND

There was a great deal of activity in the summer of 1999 as amazon.com again made bold moves in extending its interests by entering a number of new deals. Amazon.com and Liquid Audio have agreed on a mutually beneficial Internet advertising deal. Liquid Audio Inc. is a provider of Internet software and services for delivering music online.[15] The agreement allows amazon.com to use Liquid Audio software for its customers to download music. Another deal that amazon.com has struck is a 10-year contract with Sotheby's auction house. The prestigious auction house is working with amazon.com to develop and launch a joint online auction site planned for late 1999. Amazon.com invested US$45 million in the 255-year-old auction house. Sotheby's plans to keep its own Web site, and the jointly owned Web site will focus on "lower end merchandise including coins, stamps, sports and Hollywood memorabilia."[16] In addition to these two deals, amazon.com has entered into a product information licence with fashionmall.com, Inc.[17] The relationship between the two Internet giants grants amazon.com the right to product listings sold by the fashion web portal. However, fashionmall.com gains access to amazon.com's huge customer base, with direct links to pages on the fashionmall.com Web site. These joint ventures are part of amazon.com's plan to continually add new products to its core business.

Not only has amazon.com been busy with joint ventures, but it also announced the opening of an additional mega-distribution centre, bringing the total number of distribution centres across the United States to seven.[18] Adding a seventh distribution centre in southeastern United States gives amazon.com total distribution capacity nationwide of 3.5 million square feet.

Although amazon.com receives great reviews from the business press on its Web site design and its aggressive growth strategy, the company does face problems at this early stage in its relatively short existence. Its performance in the stock market demonstrates that investors are uncertain about the company, with shares trading up and down between US$19.50 to US$221 in one year. Business writer and observer Heather Clancy says, "I don't get the Amazon phenomenon, although I am myself a regular user of their services. Perhaps I'm just naïve about the stock market. Or perhaps we've just entered some new phase of valuation in which the company that spends the most hedging its bets for E-commerce and E-business will be rewarded the most on the stock market."[19] Losses continue mounting even as sales keep rising. There may come a time when this fast growth will hurt rather than help the company.

Once a company starts attracting attention and maintains an aggressive stance in the market, other companies may take exception. In October 1998, for example, Wal-Mart filed a lawsuit against amazon.com for violating trade secrets by hiring a large number of Wal-Mart employees considered information technology experts.[20] Wal-Mart contended that amazon.com, by hiring former employees who were knowledgeable about Wal-Mart's distribution and computer systems, was guilty of stealing trade secrets. Amazon.com countersued.[21] An undisclosed settlement was reached in spring 1999, just when another suit was filed by amazon Bookstore alleging trademark infringement.[22] The Minneapolis bookstore has owned the name since 1970 and feels that the success of amazon.com is creating confusion for them. Being on top comes with a price as amazon.com is discovering. Their visibility makes them targets for criticism. In February 1999, amazon.com was criticized for accepting advertising dollars from publishers for granting editorial reviews on certain books. This may not seem ethical to some, but Jeff Bezos defended the action by saying it was similar to the practice of book retailers accepting money to promote books in Main street stores.[23]

The future of amazon.com is uncertain. The company has been able to achieve incredible growth. The status of being the pioneer of e-commerce has come in a relatively short period of time. This has taken some companies by surprise, at the same time placing amazon.com in the spotlight for others to attack. The losses the company has accumulated would make most investors nervous, but for some reason in this case they are standing by this fledgling company. There doesn't seem to be much getting in the way of amazon.com continuing to expand. Those watching amazon.com are like spectators watching Wayne Gretzky on the ice. It's better to watch where the puck is going rather than where it is.

SITES WORTH A VISIT

www.barnesandnoble.com
www.borders.com
www.cdnow.com
www.sothebys.amazon.com
www.fashionmall.com

[15]Marc Pollack, "Amazon flows with Liquid Audio," *Hollywood Reporter*, (June 18, 1999), p. 4.
[16]Anonymous, "Amazon sells coins," *New Media Age*, (June 24, 1999), p. 4.
[17]Anonymous, "fashionmall.com, Inc. Inks Deal with Amazon.com," *PR Newswire*, (June 30, 1999), p. 2816.
[18]Anonymous, "Amazon to open Southeastern DC.," *Discount Store*, (June 21, 1999), p. 6.
[19]Heather Clancy, "The Engines of E-Business," *Computer Reseller News*, (June 21, 1999), p. 15.
[20]Michael Gannon, "Amazon.com, Wal-Mart Settle Suit," *Venture Capital Journal*, (May 1, 1999), p. 1
[21]Robert Preston, "IT Innovation Is A Fragile Thing Indeed," *Internetweek*, (April 12, 1999), p. 7.
[22]Dominick Callicchio, "Amazon.com: Back on the defensive?," *Informationweek*, (April 19, 1999), p. 14.
[23]Owen Thomas, "Amazon builds a wall," *Red Herring The Business of Technology*: www.redherring.com/insider, (February 11, 1999).

Discussion Questions

1 How would you define amazon.com's business strategy? Does this company suffer from paralysis by analysis? Explain.

2 In your opinion, what does it mean for amazon.com that Jeff Bezos has hired a product development expert as the new president?

3 When looking at amazon.com's product lines and new ventures, can you identify any synergies? Do you think the new ventures support the company's overall objectives?

4 Discuss your views on amazon.com's potential future success if they continue with the strategic approach they are now using.

APPENDIX C

CAREER PLANNING IN MARKETING

GETTING A JOB: THE PROCESS OF MARKETING YOURSELF

Getting a job is usually a lengthy process, and it is exactly that—a *process* that involves careful planning, implementation, and control. You may have everything going for you: a respectable grade point average (GPA), relevant work experience, several extracurricular activities, superior communication skills, and demonstrated leadership qualities. Despite these, you still need to market yourself systematically and aggressively; after all, even the best products lie dormant on the retailer's shelves unless marketed effectively.

The process of getting a job involves the same activities marketing managers use to develop and introduce products into the marketplace.[1] The only difference is that you are marketing yourself, not a product. You need to conduct marketing research by analyzing your personal qualities (performing a self-audit) and by identifying job opportunities. Based on your research results, select a target market—those job opportunities that are compatible with your interests, goals, skills, and abilities—and design a marketing mix around that target market. *You* are the "product"; you must decide how to "position" yourself in the job market. The price component of the marketing mix is the salary range and job benefits (such as health and life insurance, vacation time, and retirement benefits) that you hope to receive. Promotion involves communicating with prospective employers through written correspondence (advertising) and job interviews (personal selling). The place element focuses on how to reach prospective employers—at the campus placement centre or job fairs, for example.

This appendix will assist you in career planning by (1) providing information about careers in marketing and (2) outlining a job search process.

CAREERS IN MARKETING

The diversity of marketing opportunities is reflected in the many types of marketing jobs, ranging from purchasing to marketing research to public relations to product management. The growing interest in marketing by service and nonprofit organizations—such as hospitals, financial institutions, the performing arts, and government—has added to the numerous opportunities offered by traditional employers such as manufacturers, retailers, consulting firms, and advertising agencies. In addition, as high-tech firms become more consumer-oriented, their demand for employees with marketing skills has soared.[2] Examples of Canadian companies that have opportunities for graduates with degrees in marketing include Ford of Canada, Royal Bank, Nortel, Procter & Gamble, Cisco, IBM Canada, Pillsbury Canada, Deloitte Consulting, Angus Reid Group, and many others. Most of these career opportunities offer the chance to work with interesting people on stimulating and rewarding problems.

Studies of career paths and salaries suggest that marketing careers can also provide an excellent opportunity for advancement and substantial pay. Surveys of chief executive officers (CEOs) of publicly held companies reveal that marketing and finance were the most common career paths to their positions. Similarly, reports of average starting salaries of university graduates indicate that salaries in marketing compare favourably with those in many other fields. The future is likely to be even better. A recent Canadian survey has pegged marketing as well as information technology departments as the areas where most of the hiring will occur over the next few years. In fact, the survey revealed that 65 percent of hiring by for-profit companies will be in marketing.[3]

Figure C–1 describes marketing occupations in six major categories: product management and physical distribution, advertising, retailing, sales, marketing research, and nonprofit marketing. One of these may be right for you! (Additional sources of marketing career information are provided at the end of this appendix.)

PRODUCT MANAGEMENT AND PHYSICAL DISTRIBUTION

Product manager for consumer goods develops new products that can cost millions of dollars, with advice and consent of management—a job with great responsibility.
Supply chain manager oversees the organization within a company that transports products to consumers and handles customer service.
Operations manager supervises warehousing and other physical distribution functions and often is directly involved in moving goods on the warehouse floor.
Traffic and transportation manager evaluates the costs and benefits of different types of transportation.
Inventory control manager forecasts demand for stockpiled goods, coordinates production with plant managers, and keeps track of current levels of shipments to keep customers supplied.
Administrative analyst performs cost analyses of physical distribution systems.
Customer service manager maintains good relations with customers by coordinating sales staffs, marketing management, and physical distribution management.
Physical distribution specialist is an expert in the transportation and distribution of goods.

SALES

Direct salesperson (door-to-door) calls on consumers in their homes to make sales.
Trade salesperson calls on retailers or wholesalers to sell products for manufacturers.
Industrial or semitechnical salesperson sells supplies and services to businesses.
Complex or professional salesperson sells complicated or custom-designed products to business. This requires understanding of the technology of a product.

NONPROFIT MARKETING

Marketing manager for nonprofit organizations develops and directs mail campaigns, fundraising, and public relations.

ADVERTISING

Account executive maintains contact with clients while coordinating the creative work among artists and copywriters. In full-service ad agencies, account executives are considered partners with the client in promoting the product and helping to develop marketing strategy.
Media buyer deals with media sales representatives in selecting advertising media and analyzes the value of media being purchased.
Copywriter works with art director in conceptualizing advertisements and writes the text of print or radio ads or the storyboards of television ads.
Art director handles the visual component of advertisements.
Sales promotion manager designs promotions for consumer products and works at an ad agency or a sales promotion agency.
Public relations manager develops written or filmed messages for the public and handles contacts with the press.
Specialty advertising manager develops advertising for the sales staff and customers or distributors.

RETAILING

Buyer selects products a store sells, surveys consumer trends, and evaluates the past performance of products and suppliers.
Store manager oversees the staff and services at a store.

MARKETING RESEARCH

Project manager for the supplier coordinates and oversees the market studies for a client.
Account executive for the supplier serves as a liaison between client and market research firm, like an advertising agency account executive.
In-house project director acts as project manager (see above) for the market studies conducted by the firm for which he or she works.
Marketing research specialist for an advertising agency performs or contracts for market studies for agency clients.

Source: David W. Rosenthal and Michael A. Powell, *Careers in Marketing,* ©1984, pp. 352–54. Adapted by permission of Prentice Hall, Englewood Cliffs, NJ.

FIGURE C–1
Twenty-six marketing occupations

Product Management and Physical Distribution

Many organizations assign one manager the responsibility for a particular product. For example, Procter & Gamble (P&G) has separate managers for Tide, Cheer, Gain, and Bold. Product or brand managers are involved in all aspects of a product's marketing program, such as marketing research, sales, sales promotion, advertising, and pricing, as well as manufacturing. Managers of similar products typically report to a category manager and may be part of a *product management team.*[4]

College graduates with bachelor's and master's degrees—often in marketing and business—enter P&G as brand assistants, the only starting position in its product or brand group. Each year students from campuses across Canada accept positions with

P&G. As brand assistants, their responsibilities consist primarily of selling and sales training.

After one to two years of good performance, the brand assistant is promoted to assistant brand manager and after about the same period to brand (product) manager. These promotions often involve several brand groups. For example, a new employee might start as brand assistant for P&G's soap products, be promoted to assistant brand manager for Crest toothpaste, and subsequently become brand manager for Folger's coffee, Charmin, or Pampers. The reason, as recruiter Henry de Montebello explains, is that "in the future everybody will have strategic alliances with everybody else, and the executives who thrive will be well-rounded."[5]

Several other jobs related to product management (Figure C–1) deal with physical distribution issues such as storing the manufactured product (inventory), moving the product from the firm to the customers (transportation), maintaining good relations with customers (customer service), and engaging in many other aspects of the manufacture and sale of goods. Prospects for these jobs are likely to increase as wholesalers increase their involvement with selling and distribution activities and begin to take advantage of overseas opportunities.[6]

Advertising

Although we may see hundreds of advertisements in a day, what we can't see easily is the fascinating and complex advertising profession. The entry-level advertising positions filled every year include jobs with a variety of firms. Advertising professionals often remark that they find their jobs appealing because the days are not routine and they involve creative activities with many interesting people.

Advertising positions are available in three kinds of organizations: advertisers, media companies, and agencies. Advertisers include manufacturers, retail stores, service firms, and many other types of companies. Often they have an advertising department responsible for preparing and placing their own ads. Advertising careers are also possible with the media: television, radio stations, magazines, and newspapers. Finally, advertising agencies offer job opportunities through their use of account management, research, media, and creative services.

Starting positions with advertisers and advertising agencies are often as assistants to employees with several years of experience. An assistant copywriter facilitates the development of the message, or copy, in an advertisement. An assistant art director participates in the design of visual components of advertisements. Entry-level media positions involve buying the media that will carry the ad or selling air time on radio or television or page space in print media. Advancement to supervisory positions requires planning skills, a broad vision, and an affinity for spotting an effective advertising idea. Students interested in advertising should develop good communication skills and try to gain advertising experience through summer employment opportunities or internships.

Retailing

There are two separate career paths in retailing: merchandise management and store management (Figure C–2). The key position in merchandising is that of a buyer, who is responsible for selecting merchandise, guiding the promotion of the merchandise, setting prices, bargaining with wholesalers, training the salesforce, and monitoring the competitive environment. The buyer must also be able to organize and coordinate many critical activities under severe time constraints. In contrast, store management involves the supervision of personnel in all departments and the general management of all facilities, equipment, and merchandise displays. In addition, store managers are responsible for the financial performance of each department and for the store as a whole. Typical positions beyond the store manager level include district manager, regional manager, and divisional vice president.[7]

FIGURE C–2
Typical retailing career paths

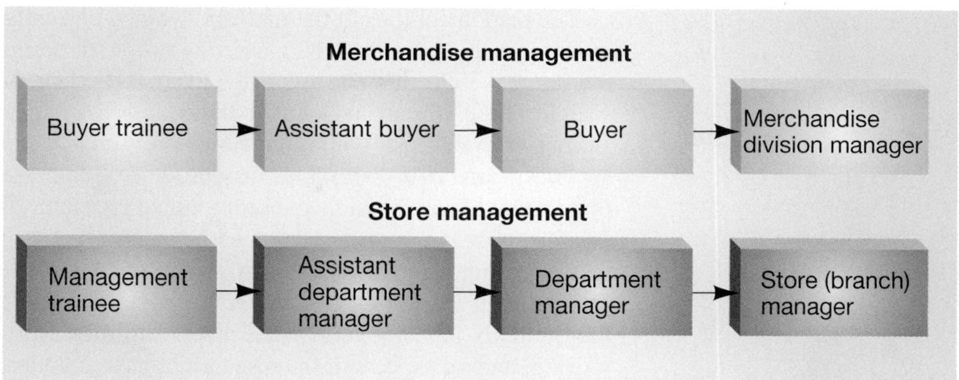

Most starting jobs in retailing are trainee positions. A trainee is usually placed in a management training program and then given a position as an assistant buyer or assistant department manager. Advancement and responsibility can be achieved quickly because there is a shortage of qualified personnel in retailing and because superior performance of an individual is quickly reflected in sales and profits—two visible measures of success.

Sales

University graduates from many disciplines are attracted to sales positions because of the increasingly professional nature of selling jobs and the many opportunities they can provide. A selling career offers benefits that are hard to match in any other field: (1) the opportunity for rapid advancement (into management or to new territories and accounts); (2) the potential for extremely attractive compensation; (3) the development of personal satisfaction, feelings of accomplishment, and increased self-confidence; and (4) independence—salespeople often have almost complete control over their time and activities. Many companies now offer two sales career paths—one for people who want to go into management, and another for those who want to remain in sales for their entire career.

Employment opportunities in sales occupations are found in a wide variety of organizations, including insurance agencies, retailers, and financial service firms. Activities in sales jobs include *selling duties*, such as prospecting for customers, demonstrating the product, or quoting prices; *sales-support duties*, such as handling complaints and helping solve technical problems; and *nonselling duties*, such as preparing reports, attending sales meetings, and monitoring competitive activities. Salespeople who can deal with these varying activities are critical to a company's success.

One of the fastest areas of growth in sales positions is in the direct marketing industry. Interest in information technology, relationship marketing, and integrated marketing has increased the demand for contact with customers. For many firms this means new or additional telemarketing efforts; for other firms it means increasing the amount of time salespeople spend with clients.

Marketing Research

Marketing researchers play important roles in many organizations today. They are responsible for obtaining, analyzing, and interpreting data to facilitate making marketing decisions. This means marketing researchers are basically problem solvers. Success in the area requires not only an understanding of statistics and computers but also a broad base of marketing knowledge[8] and an ability to communicate with management. Individuals who are inquisitive, methodical, analytical, and solution oriented find the field particularly rewarding.

The responsibilities of the men and women currently working in the market research industry include defining the marketing problem, designing the questionnaire, selecting the sample, collecting and analyzing the data, and, finally, reporting the results of the research. These jobs are available in three kinds of organizations. *Marketing research consulting firms* contract with large companies to provide research about their products or services.[9] *Advertising agencies* may provide research services to help clients with questions related to advertising and promotional problems. Finally, some companies have an *in-house research staff* to design and execute their research projects. Typical positions would include director, statistician, analyst, field work director, and interviewer.[10]

Although marketing researchers may start as assistants performing routine tasks, they quickly advance to broader responsibilities. Survey design, interviewing, report writing, and all aspects of the research process create a challenging career. In addition, research projects typically deal with such diverse problems as consumer motivation, pricing, forecasting, and competition. A survey of research organizations suggested that, to be successful in marketing research positions, students should develop skills in written, oral, and interpersonal communication; statistics and analysis; research design; and logic. The survey also suggested that practical work experience (e.g., internships) provides a useful supplement to classroom education.[11]

International Careers

Many of the careers just described can be found in international settings—in multinational Canadian corporations, small- to medium-sized firms with export business, and franchises. The international public relations firm Burson-Marstellar, for example, has offices in New York, Sydney, Copenhagen, and Bangkok. Similarly, franchises such as Blockbuster Entertainment are expanding in many other markets outside of North America. The dramatic changes in Europe and the need to rebuild the economies of the former Soviet republics may provide other opportunities. Variations of the permanent international career are also possible—for example, some companies may alternate periods of work at "headquarters" with "field" assignments in foreign countries. Finally, a domestic international career—working for a foreign-owned company with an office in Canada—may be appealing.

Applicants for international positions should first develop a skill that can be applied in an international setting. In addition, however, internationally competent employees will need language and cultural skills. A Conference Board description illustrates the point:

> The successful managers of the future will probably be those who speak both Japanese and English, who have a strong base in Brussels and contacts in the Pacific Rim, and who know the cafés and bars of Singapore.

Further, in many organizations, international experience has become a necessity for promotion and career advancement.[12]

THE JOB SEARCH PROCESS

Activities you should consider during your job search process include assessing yourself, identifying job opportunities, preparing your résumé and related correspondence, and going on job interviews.

Assessing Yourself

You must know your product—you—so that you can market yourself effectively to prospective employers. Consequently, a critical first step in your job search is conducting a self-analysis, which involves critically examining yourself on the following dimensions: interests, abilities, education, experience, personality, desired job

INTERESTS
How do I like to spend my time?
Do I enjoy being with people?
Do I like working with mechanical things?
Do I enjoy working with numbers?
Am I a member of many organizations?
Do I enjoy physical activities?
Do I like to read?

ABILITIES
Am I adept at working with numbers?
Am I adept at working with computers?
Do I have good verbal and written communication skills?
What special talents do I have?
At which abilities do I wish I were more adept?

EDUCATION
How have my courses and extracurricular activities prepared me for a specific job?
Which were my best subjects? My worse? The most fun? The least?
Is my GPA an accurate picture of my academic ability? Why?
Do I aspire to a graduate degree? Before beginning my job?
Why did I choose my major?

EXPERIENCE
What previous jobs have I held? What were my responsibilities in each?
What internships or co-op positions have I held? What were my responsibilities?
What volunteer positions have I held? What were my responsibilities?
Were any of my jobs or positions applicable to positions I may be seeking? How?
What did I like the most about my previous jobs? Like the least?
Why did I work in the jobs I did?
If I had it to do over again, would I work in these jobs? Why?

PERSONALITY
What are my good and bad traits?
Am I competitive?
Do I work well with others?
Am I outspoken?
Am I a leader or a follower?
Do I work well under pressure?
Do I work quickly, or am I methodical?
Do I get along well with others?
Am I ambitious?
Do I work well independently of others?

DESIRED JOB ENVIRONMENT
Am I willing to relocate? Why?
Do I have a geographical preference? Why?
Would I mind traveling in my job?
Do I have to work for a large, nationally known firm to be satisfied?
Must the job I assume offer rapid promotion opportunities?
If I could design my own job, what characteristics would it have?
How important is high initial salary to me?

PERSONAL GOALS
What are my short-term and long-term goals? Why?
Am I career oriented, or do I have broader interests?
What are my career goals?
What jobs are likely to help me achieve my goals?
What do I hope to be doing in 5 years? In 10 years?
What do I want out of life?

FIGURE C–3
Questions to ask in your self-analysis

environment, and personal goals.[13] The importance of performing this assessment was stressed by a management consultant:[14]

> Many graduates enter the world of work without even understanding the fact that they are specific somebodies, much less knowing the kinds of competencies and motivations with which they have been endowed. . . . The tragedy of not knowing is awesome. Ignorant of who they are, most graduates are doomed to spend too much of their lives in work for which they are poorly suited. . . . Self-knowledge is critical to effectively managing your career.

Asking Key Questions A self-analysis, in part, entails asking yourself some very important and difficult questions (Figure C–3). It is critical that you respond to the questions honestly, because your answers ultimately will be used as a guide in your job selection.[15] A less-than-candid appraisal of yourself might result in a job mismatch.

Identifying Strengths and Weaknesses After you have addressed the questions posed in Figure C–3, you are ready to identify your strengths and weaknesses. To do so, draw a vertical line down the middle of a sheet of paper and label one side of the paper "strengths" and the other side "weaknesses." Based on your answers to

FIGURE C–4
Hypothetical list of job candidate's strengths and weaknesses

STRENGTHS	WEAKNESSES
Enjoy being with people	Am not adept at working with computers
Am an avid reader	Have minimal work experience
Have good communication skills	Have a mediocre GPA
Am involved in many extracurricular activities	Am sometimes impatient
Work well with others	Resent close supervision
Work well independently	Work methodically (slowly)
Am honest and dependable	Will not relocate
Am willing to travel in the job	Anger easily sometimes
Am a good problem solver	Lack of customer orientation
Have a good sense of humor	
Am a self-starter, have drive	

the questions, record your strong and weak points in their respective column. Ideally this cataloging should be done over a few days to give you adequate time to reflect on your attributes. In addition, you might seek input from others who know you well (such as parents, close relatives, friends, professors, or employers) and can offer more objective views. They might even evaluate you on the questions in Figure C–3, and you can compare the results with your own evaluation. A hypothetical list of strengths and weaknesses is shown in Figure C–4.

What skills are most important? The answer, of course, varies by occupation and employer. Recent studies, however, suggest that problem-solving skills, communication skills, interpersonal skills, analytical and computer skills, and leadership skills are all valued by employers. Personal characteristics employers seek in a job candidate include honesty, integrity, motivation, initiative, self-confidence, flexibility, and enthusiasm. Finally, most employers also look for work experience, internship experience, or co-op experience.[16]

Taking Job-Related Tests Personality and vocational interest tests, provided by many colleges and universities, can give you other ideas about yourself. After tests have been administered and scored, test takers meet with testing service counselors to discuss the results. Test results generally suggest jobs for which students have an inclination. The most common tests at the college level are the Strong Interest Inventory and the Campbell Interest and Skill Survey. Some counseling centres also administer the Myers-Briggs Type Indicator—a personality measure that helps identify professions you may enjoy.[17] If you have not already done so, you may wish to see whether your school offers such testing services.

Identifying Your Job Opportunities

To identify and analyze the job market, you must conduct some marketing research to determine what industries *and* companies offer promising job opportunities that relate to the results of your self-analysis. Several sources that can help in your search are discussed below.

College Placement Office Your college placement office is an excellent source of job information. Personnel in that office can (1) inform you about which companies will be recruiting on campus, (2) alert you to unexpected job openings, (3) advise you about short-term and long-term career prospects, (4) offer advice on résumé construction, (5) assess your interviewing strengths and weaknesses, and (6) help you evaluate a job offer. In addition, the office usually contains a variety of written materials focusing on different industries and companies and tips on job hunting.

Online Career and Employment Services Many companies no longer make frequent on-campus visits. Instead, they may use the many on-line services available to advertise an employment opportunity or to search for candidate information. Human Resources Development Canada also has a special employment web site. The Electronic Labour Exchange matches work to people and people to work faster than traditional methods. You can use this service to search for job opportunities all across Canada (www.ele-spe.org). If you are not on-line, often your college placement office has a computer available to access this web site.

Library The public or college library can provide you with reference material that, among other things, describes successful firms and their operations, defines the content of various jobs, and forecasts job opportunities. For example, *The Financial Post* magazine publishes a report on the 500 largest Canadian companies and their respective sales and profits; Dun & Bradstreet also publishes directories of companies in Canada. A librarian can indicate reference materials that will be most pertinent to your job search.

Advertisements Help-wanted advertisements provide an overview of what is happening in the job market. Local (particularly Sunday editions) and school newspapers, trade press (such as *Marketing*), and business magazines contain classified advertisement sections that generally have job opening announcements, often for entry-level positions. Reviewing the want ads can help you identify what kinds of positions are available and their requirements and job titles, which firms offer certain kinds of jobs, and levels of compensation.

Employment Agencies An employment agency can make you aware of several job opportunities very quickly because of its large number of job listings available through computer databases. Many agencies specialize in a particular field (such as sales and marketing). The advantages of using an agency include that it (1) reduces the cost of a job search by bringing applicants and employers together, (2) often has exclusive job listings available only by working through the agency, (3) performs much of the job search for you, and (4) tries to find a job that is compatible with your qualifications and interests. Employment agencies are much maligned because some engage in questionable business practices, so check with the Better Business Bureau or your business contacts to determine the quality of the various agencies.

Personal Contacts An important source of job information that students often overlook is their personal contacts. People you know often may know of job opportunities, so you should advise them that you're looking for a job. Relatives and friends might aid your job search. Instructors you know well and business contacts can provide a wealth of information about potential jobs and even help arrange an interview with a prospective employer. They may also help arrange "informational interviews" with employers who do not have immediate openings. These interviews allow you to collect information about an industry or an employer and give you an advantage if a position does become available. It is a good idea to leave your résumé with all your personal contacts so they can pass it along to those who might be in need of your services. Student organizations (such as the student chapter of the American Marketing Association) may be sources of job opportunities, particularly if they are involved with the business community. Local chapters of professional business organizations (such as the American Marketing Association) also can provide job information; contacting their chapter president is a first step in seeking assistance from these organizations. In the past decade, small employers have provided the greatest growth in employment, and their most common source of new employees is through personal referrals.[18]

Direct Contact Another means of obtaining job information is direct contact—personally communicating to prospective employers (either by mail or in person) that you would be interested in pursuing job opportunities with them. Often you may not even know whether jobs are available in these firms. If you correspond with the companies in writing, a letter of introduction and an attached résumé should serve as your initial form of communication. Your major goal in direct contact is ultimately to arrange a job interview.

Writing Your Résumé

A résumé is a document that communicates to prospective employers who you are. An employer reading a résumé focuses on two key questions: (1) What is the candidate like? and (2) What can the candidate do for me? It is imperative that you design a résumé that addresses these two questions and presents you in a favorable light. Personnel in your campus placement office can provide assistance in designing résumés.

The Résumé Itself A well-constructed résumé generally contains up to nine major sections: (1) identification (name, address, and telephone number), (2) job or career objective, (3) educational background, (4) extracurricular activities, (5) work experience or history, (6) skills or capabilities (that pertain to a particular kind of job for which you may be interviewing), (7) accomplishments or achievements, (8) personal interests, and (9) personal references. There is no universally accepted format for a résumé, but three are more frequently used: chronological, functional, and targeted. A *chronological* format presents your work experience and education according to the time sequence in which they occurred (i.e., in chronological order). If you have had several jobs or attended several schools, this approach is useful to highlight what you have done. With a *functional* format, you group your experience into skill categories that emphasize your strengths. This option is particularly appropriate if you have no experience or only minimal experience related to your chosen field. A *targeted* format focuses on the capabilities you have for a specific job. This alternative is desirable if you know what job you want and are qualified for it. In any of the formats, if possible, you should include quantitative information about your accomplishments and experience, such as "increased sales revenue by 20 percent" for the year you managed a retail clothing store. A résumé that illustrates the chronological format is shown in Figure C–5.[19]

Technology is creating a need for a new type of résumé—the electronic résumé. While traditional versions of résumés may be easily delivered through fax machines, today most career experts suggest that a second electronic version be available. The reason? Computers read differently than people. To fully utilize on-line opportunities, an electronic résumé with a popular font and relatively large font size—and without italic text, graphics, shading, underlining or vertical lines—must be available. In addition, because on-line recruiting starts with a key-word search, it is important to include key words and avoid abbreviations.[20]

Letter Accompanying a Résumé The letter accompanying a résumé, or cover letter, serves as the job candidate's introduction. As a result, it must gain the attention and interest of the reader or it will fail to give the incentive to examine the résumé carefully. In designing a letter to accompany your résumé, address the following issues:[21]

- Address the letter to a specific person.
- Identify the position for which you are applying and how you heard of it.
- Indicate why you are applying for the position.
- Summarize your most significant credentials and qualifications.
- Refer the reader to the enclosed résumé.
- Request a personal interview, and advise the reader when and where you can be reached.

A sample letter comprising these six factors is presented in Figure C–6. Some students have tried creative approaches to making their letter stand out—sending a gift with

FIGURE C–5
Chronological résumé

SALLY WINTER

Campus address (until 6/1/00): Elm Street Apartments #2B College Town, ON M1B 0A7 Phone: (416) 555-1648 swinter@ou.edu	Home address: 123 Front Street Vancouver, BC V6C M1B Phone: (613) 555-4995

EDUCATION
B.S. in Business Administration, Omega University, 2000, 3.3 overall GPA—3.6 GPA in major

WORK EXPERIENCE
Paid for 70 percent of my college expenses through the following part-time and summer jobs:

Legal Secretary, Smith, Lee & Jones, Law Firm, Burnaby, BC—summer 1998
- Took dictation and transcribed tapes of legal proceedings
- Typed contracts and other legal documents
- Reorganized client files for easier access
- Answered the phone and screened calls for the partners

Salesclerk, College Varsity Shop, College Town, 1997–1999 academic years
- Helped customers with buying decisions
- Arranged stock and helped with window displays
- Assisted in year-end inventories
- Took over responsibilities of store manager when she was on vacation or ill

Assistant Manager, Treasure Place Gift Shop, Vancouver—summers and Christmas vacations—1996–1999
- Supervised two salesclerks
- Helped select merchandise at trade shows
- Handled daily accounting
- Worked comfortably under pressure during busy seasons

CAMPUS ACTIVITIES
- Elected captain of the women's varsity tennis team for two years
- Worked as a reporter and night editor on campus newspaper for two years

PERSONAL INTERESTS
- Collecting antique clocks, listening to jazz, swimming

REFERENCES AVAILABLE ON REQUEST

their letter or using creative packaging, for example. Although these tactics may gain a recruiter's attention, most hiring managers say that a frivolous approach makes for a frivolous employee. As a general rule, nothing works better than an impressive cover letter and good academic credentials.[22]

Interviewing for Your Job

The job interview is a conversation between a prospective employer and a job candidate that focuses on determining whether the employer's needs can be satisfied by the candidate's qualifications. The interview is a "make-or-break" situation: If the interview goes well, you have increased your chances of receiving a job offer; if it goes poorly, you probably will be eliminated from further consideration.

Preparing for a Job Interview To be successful in a job interview, you must prepare for it so you can exhibit professionalism and indicate to a prospective employer that you are serious about the job. When preparing for the interview, several critical activities need to be performed.

FIGURE C–6
Sample letter accompanying a résumé

Sally Winter
Elm Street Apartments, #2B
College Town, Ontario MIB 0A7
January 31, 2000

Mr. J. B. Jones
Sales Manager
Hilltop Manufacturing Company
Markham, Ontario LIN 9B6

Dear Mr. Jones:

Dr. William Johnson, Professor of Business Administration at Omega University, recently suggested that I write to you concerning your opening and my interest in a sales position. With a B.S. degree in business administration and courses in personal selling and sales management, I am confident that I could make a positive contribution to your firm.

During the past four years I have been a salesclerk in a clothing store and an assistant manager in a gift shop. These two positions required my performing a variety of duties including selling, purchasing, stocking, and supervising. As a result, I have developed an appreciation for the viewpoints of the customer, salesperson, and management. Given my background and high energy level, I feel that I am particularly well qualified to assume a sales position in your company.

My enclosed résumé better highlights my education and experience. My extracurricular activities should strengthen and support my abilities to serve as a sales representative.

I am eager to talk with you because I feel I can demonstrate to you why I am a strong candidate for the position. I have friends in Markham with whom I could stay on weekends, so Fridays or Mondays would be ideal for an appointment. I will call you in a week to see if we can arrange a mutually convenient time for a meeting. I am hopeful that your schedule will allow this.

Thank you for your kind consideration. If you would like some additional information, please feel free to contact me. I look forward to talking with you.

Sincerely,

Sally Winter

enclosure

Before the interview, gather facts about the industry, the prospective employer, and the job. Relevant information might include the general description for the occupation; the firm's products or services; the firm's size, number of employees, and financial and competitive position; the requirements of the position; and the name and personality of the interviewer.[23] Obtaining this information will provide you with additional insight into the firm and help you formulate questions to ask the interviewer. This information might be gleaned, for example, from corporate annual reports, *The Globe and Mail, The Financial Post,* or trade publications. If information is not readily available, you could call the company and indicate that you wish to obtain some information about the firm before your interview.

Preparation for the job interview should also involve role playing, or pretending that you are in the "hot seat" being interviewed. Before role playing, anticipate questions interviewers may pose and how you might address them (Figure C–7). Do not memorize your answers, though, because you want to appear spontaneous, yet logical and intelligent. Nonetheless, it is helpful to practice how you might respond to the

FIGURE C–7
Question frequently asked by interviewers

INTERVIEWER QUESTIONS

1. What can you tell me about yourself?
2. What are your strengths? Weaknesses?
3. What do you consider to be your most significant accomplishment to date?
4. What do you see yourself doing in 5 years? In 10 years?
5. Are you a leader? Explain.
6. What do you really want out of life?
7. How would you describe yourself?
8. Why did you choose your college major?
9. In which extracurricular activities did you participate? Why?
10. What jobs have you enjoyed the most? The least? Why?
11. How has your previous work experience prepared you for a job?
12. Why do you want to work for our company?
13. What qualifications do you think a person needs to be successful in a company like ours?
14. What do you know about our company?
15. What criteria are you using to evaluate the company for which you hope to work?
16. In what kind of city would you prefer to live?
17. What can I tell you about our company?
18. Are you willing to relocate?
19. Are you willing to spend at least six months as a trainee? Why?
20. Why should we hire you?

FIGURE C–8
Question frequently asked by interviewees

INTERVIEWEE QUESTIONS

1. Why would a job candidate want to work for your firm?
2. What makes your firm different from its competitors?
3. What is the company's promotion policy?
4. Describe the typical first-year assignment for this job.
5. How is an employee evaluated?
6. What are the opportunities for personal growth?
7. Do you have a training program?
8. What are the company's plans for future growth?
9. What is the retention rate of people in the position for which I am interviewing?
10. How can you use my skills?
11. Does the company have development programs?
12. What kind of image does the firm have in the community?
13. Why do you enjoy working for your firm?
14. How much responsibility would I have in this job?
15. What is the corporate culture in your firm?

questions. In addition, develop questions you might ask the interviewer that are important and of concern to you (Figure C–8).

When role playing, you and someone with whom you feel comfortable should engage in a mock interview. Afterward, ask the stand-in interviewer to candidly appraise your interview content and style. You may wish to videotape the mock interview; ask the personnel in your campus placement office where videotaping equipment can be obtained for this purpose.

Before the job interview you should attend to several details. Know the exact time and place of the interview; write them down—do not rely on your memory. Get the full company name straight. Find out what the interviewer's name is and how to pronounce it. Bring a notepad and pen along on the interview, in case you need to record anything. Make certain that your appearance is clean, neat, professional, and conservative. And be punctual; arriving tardy to a job interview gives you an appearance of being unreliable.

Succeeding in Your Job Interview You have done your homework, and at last the moment arrives and it is time for the interview. Although you may experience some apprehension, view the interview as a conversation between the prospective employer and you. Both of you are in the interview to look over the other party, to see whether there might be a good match. You know your subject matter (you); furthermore, because you did not have a job with the firm when you walked into the interview, you really have nothing to lose if you don't get it—so relax.[24]

When you meet the interviewer, greet him or her by name, be cheerful, smile, and maintain good eye contact. Take your lead from the interviewer at the outset. Sit down after the interviewer has offered you a seat. Do not smoke. Sit up straight in your chair, and look alert and interested at all times. Appear relaxed, not tense. Be enthusiastic.

During the interview, be yourself. If you try to behave in a manner that is different from the "real" you, your attempt may be transparent to the interviewer or you may ultimately get the job but discover that you aren't suited for it. In addition to assessing how well your skills match those of the job, the interviewer will probably try to assess your long-term interest in the firm. William Kucker, a recruiter for General Electric, explains, "We're looking for people to make a commitment."[25]

As the interview comes to a close, leave it on a positive note. Thank the interviewer for his or her time and the opportunity to discuss employment opportunities. If you are still interested in the job, express this to the interviewer. The interviewer will normally tell you what the employer's next step is. Rarely will a job offer be made at the end of the initial interview. If it is and you want the job, accept the offer; if there is any doubt in your mind about the job, however, ask for time to consider the offer.

Following Up on Your Job Interview After your interview, send a thank-you note to the interviewer and indicate whether you are still interested in the job. If you want to continue pursuing the job, "polite persistence" may help you get it. According to one expert, "Many job hunters make the mistake of thinking that their career fate is totally in the hands of the interviewer once the job interview is finished."[26] You *can* have an impact on the interviewer *after* the interview is over.

The thank-you note is a gesture of appreciation and a way of maintaining visibility with the interviewer. (Remember the adage, "Out of sight, out of mind.") Even if the interview did not go well, the thank-you note may impress the interviewer so much that his or her opinion of you changes. After you have sent your thank-you note, you may wish to call the prospective employer to determine the status of the hiring decision. If the interviewer told you when you would hear from the employer, make your telephone call *after* this date (assuming, of course, that you have not yet heard from the employer); if the interviewer did not tell you when you would be contacted, make your telephone call a week or so after you have sent your thank-you note.

As you conduct your follow-up, be persistent but polite. If you are too eager, one of two things could happen to prevent you from getting the job: the employer might feel that you are a nuisance and would exhibit such behaviour on the job, or the employer may perceive that you are desperate for the job and thus are not a viable candidate.

Handling Rejection You have put your best efforts into your job search. You developed a well-designed résumé and prepared carefully for the job interview. Even the interview appears to have gone well. Nevertheless, a prospective employer may send you a rejection letter. ("We are sorry that our needs and your superb qualification don't match.") Although you will probably be disappointed, not all interviews lead to a job offer because there normally are more candidates than there are positions available.

If you receive a rejection letter, you should think back through the interview. What appeared to go right? What went wrong? Perhaps personnel from your campus placement office can shed light on the problem, particularly if they are in the custom of having interviewers rate each interviewee. Try to learn lessons to apply in future interviews. Keep interviewing and gaining interview experience; your persistence will eventually pay off.

SELECTED SOURCES OF MARKETING CAREER INFORMATION

The following is a selected list of marketing information sources that you should find useful during your academic studies and professional career.

Business and Marketing Publications

Peter D. Bennett, ed., *Dictionary of Marketing Terms*, 3d ed. (Lincolnwood, IL: NTC Publishing 1998). This dictionary contains definitions of more than 3000 marketing terms.

Victor P. Buell, ed., *Handbook of Modern Marketing,* 2nd ed. (New York: McGraw-Hill, 1986). This handbook was designed to provide a single authoritative source of information on marketing to aid the reader in overall understanding, followed by "how-to" information.

Canadian Business Index. This is available on-line (CAN/OLE) and covers 200 business periodicals.

Jill Cousins and Lesley Robinson, eds., *The Online Manual*, 2nd ed. (Cambridge, Mass.: Blackwell Publishers, 1993). This manual is a practical tool to help both the experienced and inexperienced information user select from the thousands of databases now available on-line.

Jeffrey Heilbrunn, ed., *Marketing Encyclopedia* (Lincolnwood, IL: NTC Publishing, 1995). This book provides a collection of essays by professional and academic marketing experts on issues and trends shaping the future of marketing.

Jerry M. Rosenberg, *Dictionary of Business and Management,* (New York: John Wiley & Sons, 1995). This dictionary contains more than 5,500 concise definitions of marketing and advertising terms.

Career Planning Publications

Richard N. Bolles, *The 1999 What Color Is Your Parachute?: A Practical Manual for Job-Hunters and Career-Changers,* (Berkeley, CA: Ten Speed Press, 1998). A companion workbook is also available. See www.tenspeedpress.com/parachute.

Karmen Crowther, *Researching Your Way to a Good Job* (New York: John Wiley & Sons, 1993). See www.wiley.com.

Fred E. Jardt and Mary B. Nemnich, *Cyberspace Resume Kit: How to Make and Launch a Snazzy Online Resume* (Indianapolis, IN: JIST Works, Inc., 1998). See www.jist.com.

Ronald L. Krannich and Caryl Rae Krannich, *The Best Jobs for the 21st Century,* 3rd ed., (1998); *Interview for Success: A Practical Guide to Increasing Job Interviews, Offers, and Salaries,* 7th ed., (1998); *Find a Federal Job Fast,* 4th ed., (1998); *Jobs and Careers with Non Profit Organizations,* (1998); and *The Complete Guide to International Jobs and Careers,* 2nd ed. (1992), (Manassas Park, VA: Impact Publications). See www.impactpublications.com/career.

Margaret Riley, Frances Roehm, and Steve Oserman, *The Guide to Internet Job Searching: 1998–1999 Edition,* (Lincolnwood, IL: NTC Publishing Group, 1998). See www.ntc-cb.com or www.rileypress.com.

Martin Yate, *Knock 'Em Dead: 1999 Edition; Cover Letters That Knock 'Em Dead; and Resumes That Knock 'Em Dead,* (Holbrook, MA: Adams Media Corporation, 1999). See www.adamsmedia.com or www.knockemdead.com.

Selected Periodicals

Advertising Age, Crain Communications, Inc. (semiweekly). www.adage.com

Business Horizons, Indiana University (bimonthly). www.jaipress.com

Business Week, McGraw-Hill (weekly). www.businessweek.com

eCommerce Times, eMarketer.com (daily). www.emarketer/enews.com

Fortune, Time, Inc. (biweekly).

Harvard Business Review, Harvard University (bimonthly). www.hbsp.harvard.edu/products/hbr

Industrial Marketing Management, Elsevier Science Publishing Co., Inc. (quarterly). www.elsevier.com

Internet Marketing & Technology Report, Internet Marketing Resources (monthly). www.intermarketing.com

Journal of Advertising Research, Advertising Research Foundation (bimonthly). www.amic.com/arf

Journal of Business and Industrial Marketing, MCB University Press (quarterly). www.mcb.co.uk

Journal of Consumer Research, Journal of Consumer Research, Inc. (quarterly).

Journal of Health Care Marketing, American Marketing Association (quarterly).

Journal of Marketing, American Marketing Association (quarterly). www.ama.org/pubs/jm

Journal of Marketing Research, American Marketing Association (quarterly). www.ama.org/pubs/jmr

Journal of Retailing, Institute of Retailing Management, JAI Press (quarterly). www.jaipress.com

Marketing, McLean Hunter (weekly). www.marketingmag.ca

Marketing News, American Marketing Association (biweekly). www.ama.org/pubs/mn

Sales and Marketing Management, Bill Communications, Inc. (16 per year). www.salesandmarketing.com

Professional and Trade Associations

American Marketing Association
250 S. Wacker Dr.
Chicago, IL 60606-5819
(312) 648-0536
www.ama.org
Toronto Chapter
100 University Avenue
Toronto, Ontario M5W 1V8
(416) 367-3573

Canadian Advertising Foundation
350 Bloor St. E. #402
Toronto, Ontario M4W 1H5
(416) 961-6311

Canadian Advertising Research Foundation
175 Bloor St. E., South Tower #307
Toronto, Ontario M4W 3R8
(416) 964-3832

Canadian Association of Broadcasters
350 Sparks Street #306
P.O. Box 627 Stn. B
Ottawa, Ontario K1P 5S2
(613) 233-4035
e-mail: CAB-ACR.ca

Canadian Direct Marketing Association
1 Concorde Gate #607
Don Mills, Ontario M3C 3N6
(416) 391-2362

Canadian Federation of Business and Professional Women's Clubs
56 Sparks Street #308
Ottawa, Ontario K1P 5A9
(613) 234-7619

Canadian Federation of Independent Business
4141 Yonge Street #401
Willowdale, Ontario M2P 2A6
(416) 222-8022

Canadian Institute of Marketing
41 Capital Drive
Nepean, Ontario K2G 0E7
(613) 727-0954

Conference Board of Canada
255 Smyth Road
Ottawa, Ontario K1H 8M7
(613) 526-3280
www.ConferenceBoard.ca

Institute of Canadian Advertising
Yonge-Eglinton Centre
2300 Yonge St.
Box 2350—Suite 500
Toronto, Ontario M4P 1E4
www.goodmedia.com/ica/

Purchasing Management Association of Canada
2 Carlton Street #1414
Toronto, Ontario M5B 1J3
(416) 977-7111

Professional Marketing Research Society
2323 Yonge Street #806
Toronto, Ontario M4P 2C9
(416) 493-4080

Retail Council of Canada
121 Bloor St. E #1210
Toronto, Ontario M4W 3M5
(416) 922-6678
www.retailcouncil.org

Retail Merchants Association of Canada
1780 Birchmount Road
Scarborough, Ontario M1P 2H8
(416) 291-7903

ALTERNATE CASES

CASE D–1 BURTON SNOWBOARDS

THE COMPANY

At the age of 23, Jack Burton Carpenter quit a well-paid financial position to pursue his passion for snowboarding. He founded Burton Snowboards with a $20 000 inheritance.

Carpenter first became interested in snowboarding when he received a Snurfer for Christmas in the late 1960s. The Snurfer was essentially two skis bound together with a rope for steering. Although the Snurfer was never a commercial success, Carpenter never forgot the product, and it became the basis for the Burton snowboard. The early years were rough. He sold fewer than 1500 boards in his first three years in business. The big break came in 1983 when Vermont's Stratton Mountain became the first ski resort to allow snowboarding. Burton (he dropped the Carpenter to avoid confusion) sent employees out to more than 300 ski resorts to lobby to allow boarders on the hills. Burton Snowboarding has grown to be the leading snowboard maker in the world with offices in Japan, Austria, and Vermont. Estimated 1997 sales were $150 million.

THE INDUSTRY

Snowboarding is a wintertime sport that resembles surfing on a ski hill. The modern snowboard industry began around 20 years ago. Snowboarding is currently considered one of the hottest sports around, with an annual growth rate of 30 percent. Snowboarders represent more than 25 percent of all ski passes and are the fastest growing part of the ski industry. The number of snowboarders is expected to exceed the number of skiers by 2010.

Snowboarding is achieving worldwide attention and acceptance. The International Olympic Committee and the International Ski Federation first accepted snowboarding as a medal sport in the 1998 Winter Olympics, held in Nagano, Japan.

THE COMPETITION

Estimates are that there are 300 snowboarding companies. Barriers to entry are relatively low, so new entrants can be expected. Industry giants such as Burton, Sims, and Nitro account for the bulk of the market, but Solomon and Forum are becoming very popular.

Burton is not only the pioneer but has also been the trendsetter for snowboarding. Burton has the product line with the greatest depth and breadth with racing, free riding, park, and pipe boards. Burton's line appeals to novice as well as professional boarders. Prices range from $300 to $800. In addition to boards, Burton offers helmets (through its wholly owned subsidiary, Red), bags, bindings, and boots. For information on Burton's product line, visit them at www.burton.com.

THE ISSUES

Burton uses print advertisements in such magazines as *Snowboarder* and *transworld SNOWboarding*. The ads are often tied in with reader service cards at the back of the magazine so that additional information can be requested. Burton also sponsors riders—a very important promotional tool and vital to the sport's success. These team members are often role models for young boarders. Among Burton's celebrity riders are Terje Haakonsen, Jim Rippey, Shannon Dunn, and Johan Olafsson. Even well-known celebrity boarders couldn't survive financially without such sponsorship. Burton also sponsors snowboarding events such as the 1999 U.S. Open. Other promotional items include posters and stickers.

Snowboard design is constantly changing. Currently boards are becoming longer (for better landings), are trending toward unidirectional styles (rather than the blunt nosed boards that can ride in both directions), and now have more sidecuts and narrower stances than in the past.

Burton has been very loyal to the distributors that have helped them build the business. While Burton tends to be distributed primarily in specialty shops, there may be increasing pressure to offer the boards at national chains.[1]

Questions

1 What are the environmental forces influencing the snowboarding industry?

2 What are the differences in marketing goals for Burton Snowboarding in (*a*) its early years while developing the industry and (*b*) today with growing competition?

3 Identify the elements of the marketing mix for Burton currently. What marketing mix would you recommend for Burton, given the changes occurring in the snowboarding marketplace?

CASE D-2 CALLAWAY GOLF

The popularity of golf in the 1990s has skyrocketed for a number of reasons—aging baby boomers looking for a quality way to enjoy precious leisure time, the Tiger Woods phenomenon, and probably, to some degree the increased wealth of the middle class during an extended period of unprecedented economic growth. This economic prosperity, the Bull Market Factor, might also explain the increased practice of business entertainment and conferencing on and around the golf course. Technological improvements in golf clubs, components, and equipment have made the game easier and more enjoyable to play. Also, the construction of more golf courses has increased the opportunity for many people to play golf.

THE COMPANY

Callaway Golf Company was formed in 1982 when Ely Callaway, a former president of Burlington Industries, purchased a hickory-shafted golf club company. Originally named Callaway Hickory Stick, the company was renamed Callaway Golf, and the seeds were planted for one of the golf industry's greatest stories. Callaway Golf struggled as a small equipment company in an extremely competitive arena against such giants as Wilson, Titleist, Spalding, Ping, McGregor, Taylor Made, and others that had dominated the club market for years. Taylor Made golf clubs were fast becoming popular as they had recently introduced, with much success, the first metal wood or driver. Callaway's club sales took off in 1991 with the introduction of the first popular oversized driver, the Big Bertha.

Focusing on the use of high technology and aerospace materials, the Big Bertha driver, named after a WWI German cannon, quickly became popular with golfers of all abilities. The Big Bertha driver provided a larger sweet spot for an increased effective hitting area. This large sweet spot, through design and material technology, made the Big Bertha driver one of the most forgiving clubs manufactured to date. It became extremely popular, and Callaway experienced phenomenal sales growth shortly after its introduction. Sales at Callaway more than doubled from 1990 to 1991 from $22 million to $55 million. As word spread among golfers, sales for 1992 to 1993 more than doubled again from $55 million to $132 million.

Callaway quickly followed up its Big Bertha driver introduction with a full line of metal fairway woods that also proved to be very well designed, very forgiving, and easier to hit than long irons for many men and women golfers. These clubs were given cute and clever names such as The Deuce, Heaven Wood, and Divine Nine, which also became popular with the average golfer.

Sales continued to explode at Callaway Golf. In 1993 sales increased to $255 million, and in 1994 sales hit $449 million. With the huge success of the Big Bertha oversized driver and the equally popular and cleverly marketed fairway woods, Callaway planted the seeds or ideas for other new startup companies to enter the market.

Most golfers, pros and amateurs alike, probably experiment more with new drivers, fairway woods, and putters than any other clubs. In fact many top professionals and amateurs choose to play with their old favourite irons for years and years before changing. Callaway Golf was smart to enter the club market the way it did and then follow it up with specialty clubs that golfers enjoy to tinker with more than irons. Callaway sales continued to increase, reaching $843 million in 1997, following the introduction of its most popular titanium club, the Great Big Bertha driver. Metal woods and drivers make up 64 percent of Callaway Golf's total product sales. Its entry into the market with high-quality, premium-priced metal woods and drivers allowed Callaway to expand into putter and iron sales. However, Callaway's bread and butter was market entry via premium-quality fairway woods and drivers of superior design and technology. To learn more about Callaway and its products, visit the company Web site at www.callawaygolf.com.

THE GLOBAL GOLF INDUSTRY

The golf industry has a strong worldwide appeal and, in many respects, has links across the globe. Golf is extremely popular in many countries around the world, including Scotland (golf's birthplace), England, Sweden, Spain, South Africa, Australia, New Zealand, and Japan, where golf enthusiasm rises to unheard-of levels. Many countries and continents from around the world are represented both professionally and at the amateur level in local and worldwide competitions. The professional golf tours from around the world have done much to link golf as a global sport. The most recent international golf competition is the newly formed World Golf Championships, which pit the best players from around the world in match play and stroke play competitions. The five world professional golf tours—the PGA, the European PGA, the Japan PGA, the Australasian PGA, and the South African PGA—are all represented in the newly formed World Golf Championships.

Golf enthusiasts around the world follow the sport through televised tournaments, golf magazines, coverage in newspapers and sports reports, as well as through Internet Web sites. Many of the golf-related Web sites are very popular, and their prevalence on the Internet continues to grow.

Golf is truly a global sport. Courses and competition are held in many countries and on almost every continent—except Antarctica. Professional and amateur players from around the world compete and interact with a high degree of etiquette and sportsmanship. Professional players represent equipment manufacturers from around the world. Golfers, at both the professional and amateur levels, share ideas and experiences from the game they play. When it comes to the equipment they use, golfers for the most part choose the clubs and equipment that works for them. For any equipment manufacturer, the world is the market, and the market is the world.

CALLAWAY'S INTERNATIONAL MARKETING

For Callaway Golf, one of the largest golf club equipment manufacturers, the world market is a very big part of its total market for clubs. About 35 percent of the company's 1997 sales came from outside North America. Sales from Japan alone represented 10 percent of all 1997 product sales. International golf professionals, from England's Colin Montgomerie to Sweden's Annika Sorenstam, represent Callaway Golf. At the same time, Callaway claims hundreds of pros and more than seven million amateurs worldwide as players and representatives of their clubs. For Callaway Golf, golf is truly a global sport, and the market is truly a global market.

THE GOLF EQUIPMENT MARKET

The golf equipment market is highly congested and very competitive. Many players exist, large and small, and the field is constantly changing with new startups, mergers, and acquisitions. Major players include Fortune Brands (Titleist), Adams Golf, Karsten (Ping), Taylor Made Golf, Orlimar Golf, Spalding Holdings, Mizuno, and many others.

Two of these club manufacturers in particular have recently followed the Callaway plan to the marketplace. Adams Golf and Orlimar Golf have successfully launched and captured a significant share of the fairway wood and specialty club market. Both companies offer unique technological innovations and premium products that deliver, and both companies make claims to be the number one fairway wood on one pro tour or another. Other club manufacturers followed Callaway's "bigger is better" philosophy. Taylor Made Golf, Titleist, Ping, and many others have designed popular oversized drivers. Many oversized premium golf clubs exist today, offering technical innovation, forgiveness, power, distance, and accuracy that golfers look for in a driver. The club market is crowded, and Callaway's market share is under attack, but Callaway

Golf still claims to be the number one club manufacturer and one of the most popular golf clubs in use today.

ISSUES

In sports, it is often said that getting to the top is easier than staying there. Callaway Golf is faced with this challenge. Callaway Golf became so big so fast, rising from nowhere in 1990 to becoming one of the largest golf club equipment manufacturers at the end of the decade, that in many respects, it is challenged with sustaining its phenomenal growth and protecting its market share. Now it seems every competitor, new and old, is after a piece of the Callaway's pie because Callaway has the largest piece to share.

For Callaway Golf, one of the largest current issues is the status of global economic prosperity. As countries from Japan to Europe experience struggling economies, golf—an expensive leisure luxury—becomes an activity people partake of less or learn to enjoy with the equipment at hand. Golf equipment can last for many years. If times are tough, people can still play, but they'll probably play with the equipment they already own. Other issues for Callaway include the fast followers, Orlimar and Adams. Both companies have developed products that cut into Callaway's bread and butter—the fairway wood and specialty wood market. The Adams Tight Lies fairway woods and the Orlimar Tri-metal woods are both popular clubs with pros and amateurs. Both companies have also launched High-Tech drivers that could capture some of Callaway's driver market share. The other Big Players in the equipment business are also after Callaway's market share and may pose a greater threat to Callaway's business. These companies are large and strong enough to survive any market slump and also have the resources to buy up smaller successful companies that may provide them with popular products and technology. Finally, Callaway's biggest problem might be coming up with new products that are as popular as the ones that took them to the top in the early 1990s.[2]

Questions

1 What are the pros and cons of a global versus a multidomestic approach to marketing golf clubs for Callaway? Which approach do you feel would have more merit and why?

2 What are some of the significant environmental factors that could have a *major* impact on the marketing of golf clubs internationally? Describe each factor and the nature of its possible effect.

3 What marketing mix recommendations would you have for Callaway as they attempt to increase international market share?

CASE D–3 HONEYWELL, INC.: OPTOELECTRONICS DIVISION

After several years of developing fibre-optic technology for military projects, executives in the Optoelectronics Division of Honeywell, Inc. decided to pursue commercial applications for their products and technology. The task would not be easy because fibre optics was a new technology that many firms would find unfamiliar. Fibre optics is the technology of transmitting light through long, thin, flexible fibres of glass, plastic, or other transparent materials. When it is used in a commercial application, a light source emits infrared light flashes corresponding to data. Millions of light flashes per second send streams through a transparent fibre. A light sensor at the other end of the fibre "reads" the data transmitted. It is estimated that sales of fibre-optic technology could exceed $3 billion in 1997. Almost half the dollar sales volume would come from telecommunications, about 25 percent from government or military purchases, and about 25 percent from commercial applications in computers, robotics, cable TV, and other products.

Interest in adapting fibre-optic technology and products for commercial applications had prompted Honeywell executives to carefully review buying behaviour associated with the adoption of a new technology. The buying process appeared to contain at least six phases: (1) need recognition, (2) identification of available products, (3) comparison with existing technology, (4) vendor or seller evaluation, (5) the decision itself, and (6) follow-up on technology performance. Moreover, there appeared to be several people within the buying organization who would play a role in the adoption of a new technology. For example, top management (such as the president and executive vice presidents) would certainly be involved. Engineering and operations management (e.g., vice presidents of engineering and manufacturing) and design engineers (e.g., persons who develop specifications for new products) would also play a major role. Purchasing personnel would have a say in such a decision and particularly in the vendor-evaluation process. The role played by each person in the buying organization was still unclear to Honeywell. It seemed that engineering management personnel could slow the adoption of fibre optics if they did not feel it was appropriate for the products made by the company. Design engineers, who would actually apply fibre optics in product design, might be favourably or unfavourably disposed to the technology depending on whether they knew how to use it. Top management personnel would participate in any final decisions to use fibre optics and could generate interest in the technology if stimulated to do so.

This review of buying behaviour led to questions about how to penetrate a company's buying organization and have fibre optics used in the company's products. Although Honeywell was a large, well-known company with annual sales exceeding $8 billion, its fibre-optic technology capability was much less familiar. Therefore the executives thought it was necessary to establish Honeywell's credibility in fibre optics. This was done, in part, through an advertising image campaign that featured Honeywell Optoelectronics as a leader in fibre optics.[3] For more information about Honeywell and its fibre-optics products, visit the company Web site at www.honeywell.com.

Questions

1 What type of buying situation is involved in the purchase of fibre optics, and what will be important buying criteria used by companies considering using fibre optics in their products?

2 Describe the purchase decision process for adopting fibre optics, and state how members in the buying centre for this technology might play a part in this process.

3 What effect will perceived risk have on a company's decision of whether to use fibre optics in its products?

4 What role does the image advertising campaign play in Honeywell Optoelectronics' efforts to market fibre optics?

CASE D–4 XOOM.COM

Xoom.com, Inc. is a leading Internet-based direct electronic commerce company that attracts members to its site by offering them a variety of free Web-based services including Web page hosting, chat rooms, message boards, e-mail, and online greeting cards. The company gets its revenue from two main streams—electronic commerce (selling products to its member database) and advertising (charging other companies to place banners and links on its often-visited site).

Xoom.com was started in September 1996. The company had 1998 sales of $8.3 million, with a phenomenal one-year growth rate of 937.5 percent. Its Web properties reached almost one out of every three people on the Web during December 1998 (29.5 percent unduplicated Web site reach) and, according to Media Metrix, is adding new members at a rate of approximately 23 000 per day.

Xoom.com competes with Web portals such as Yahoo! and Lycos for advertising customers and firms such as GeoCities for both advertisers and members.

THE IDEA

Xoom.com offers a variety of free services to attract Web surfers to its site. To become a member, you must register and provide Xoom.com with your e-mail address and other demographic information and agree to receive product offers from the company via e-mail. This database of users is one of Xoom.com's most valuable assets. Not only does it allow Xoom.com to expose its users to targeted advertising on site, but it also allows the company to send customized retail offers and newsletters to its members on a regular basis. Xoom.com members can purchase such products as computer modems, DVD players, digital cameras, and collectibles. Because the free services that attracted members to Xoom.com are Web-based services such as Web page hosting and chat rooms, these members tend to be more receptive to buying on the Internet. Users are obviously using the Internet for more than just work. Members are fairly evenly divided between male and female (52.6 percent male versus 47.4 percent female) but more than 70 percent have at least some college. Less than 2 percent of members classified their occupation as being "factory worker or labourer," while administrative/clerical, technical, and professional profession accounted for almost 35 percent of members.

Xoom.com's Buyer's Club Partner Program is a turnkey direct marketing platform for firms with Web sites to sell products directly to Xoom.com visitors and customers. Companies that are just developing a customer database can benefit from participation in the Xoom.com Buyer's Club Partner Program as it provides an opportunity to learn not only how to sell direct but also what types of products and services are desired. Xoom.com has a number of co-branded Web sites with firms such as Phillips Publishing, ZD Net, eBay, GoTo.com, and BUYDIRECT.COM, among others.

By partnering with other companies, Xoom.com can benefit consumers by targeting product offers to the particular needs of the members. Partnering companies also benefit from this access to a carefully targeted group of consumers who are most likely to be interested in their product. By creating a model that outsources the functions of physical fulfillment, inventory, and customer service, Xoom.com is moving its business closer to a "zero gravity" model of electronic commerce.

Xoom.com's Internet-based direct marketing model is also based on speed. Sending product offers to targeted consumers via e-mail not only eliminates mailing and printing costs but also allows for rapid testing. Using the Internet, Xoom.com can achieve campaign results with lower working capital and greater profitability with lower response rates.

THE ISSUES

The challenge for Xoom.com is to develop and hold a loyal group of subscribers in the face of an ever-increasing number of competitors. This will be critical for attracting and holding advertisers and partners. Some users also tire of the regular e-mail solicitations. However, Xoom.com continuously upgrades its free services to provide members with a reason to stay loyal. Xoom.com also uses very advanced modeling systems and market testing to estimate member responses to various special offers. For example, it may send out a "test mailing" of an offer at several different price points to decide on the optimal price point for an offer. Responses are also tracked by the minute to forecast sales on an ongoing basis. Because of the low cost of mailings, Xoom.com can afford to send their "test" mailing to several hundred thousand members, which allows for accurate forecasting of final campaign results.

The fact that Xoom.com's electronic commerce model is based exclusively on the Internet and their resulting expertise in the domain has given it a decided edge as companies take advantage of the international reach of the Internet. In March 1999, Xoom.com announced the launch of Xoom Italy at www.Xoom.com.it with localized content and local partners. This is just a first step in its aggressive expansion into Europe and then the rest of the world.[4]

Questions

1 How does Xoom.com create customer value (*a*) for its advertisers and partners and (*b*) for consumers?

2 Xoom.com has two revenue streams—electronic commerce and advertising. What is the relationship between these two revenue streams? What kind of marketing environment does the company face for each of these streams?

3 Profile the typical Xoom.com subscriber. Who are they, and what are they looking for?

4 What are the problems and issues electronic commerce companies such as Xoom.com face as they take full advantage of the global reach of the Internet?

CASE D–5 THE APPLE iMAC

TIME Digital called it the 1998 Machine of the Year—Apple's revolution in a box. It has been touted as a design and technology breakthrough. Andy Grove, chairman of Intel, has said of the iMac, "Not for the first time something Apple is doing is electrifying the entire industry."

THE PRODUCT/IDEA

"Is it a landmark work of industrial design or a bizarre curiosity that looks like a 1960s vintage TV set?" Steve Jobs, one of the original founders of Apple and interim CEO, wanted the company to develop a computer "like the Jetsons would use." British designer, Jonathon Ive, Apple's 31-year-old vice president of design, and his largely international design team were responsible for translating Jobs' vision into a computer people could relate to.

The product is the Apple iMac. The "i" in iMac stands for Internet, and the iMac is designed to be a Web cruiser. It is described as a "very nice, fast computer for a decent price." The iMac has built-in stereo speakers, a CD-ROM drive conveniently located below the screen, and a mouse that is round rather than elongated. Like the original Macintosh, the iMac combines the computer and monitor in one unit. Unlike the original Macintosh, the iMac has a curvy, translucent appearance. The iMac takes up less space and is very simple to set up. Originally the iMac was offered in Bondi blue—funky blue-green and off-white two-tone. The iMac is now available in different "flavors" including blueberry, grape, tangerine, lime, and strawberry. Perhaps most compelling is the iMac's tactile appeal. Customers want to touch the machine and feel a connection with it.

Apple has been criticized for abandoning old technology too soon. The biggest perceived drawbacks to the iMac are that it doesn't have a built-in floppy disk drive and it depends on next-generation plugs for peripherals such as printers. These shortcomings can be overcome easily but will raise the price. Other best-selling computers in 1998 included the Hewlett-Packard 6355 and Compaq's three Presario computer models. While these machines have many of the same functions, they don't deliver the speed and style of the iMac.

MARKETING OF THE IMAC

Apple launched the iMac with a $100 million marketing blitz in television and print advertising. Apple's tagline "Think Different" was used across all Apple products as well as for the iMac.

Apple's iMac computer was the number-one-selling PC through retail and mail-order channels during the 1998 holiday season. Since its introduction in mid-August 1998, it has been the number-one-selling PC, capturing six percent of total unit sales in addition to leading overall sales in the fourth quarter, according to Stephen Baker, senior hardware analyst at PC Data. Sales of the iMac also helped Apple boost its overall share from retail and mail-order channels from 6.7 percent to 9.6 percent in six months. Overall unit sales growth for first quarter of 1999 were up 49 percent over the previous year to date. All this comes on the heels of 3 years of losses at Apple.

The iMac is primarily aimed at the educational and consumer markets. Apple claims that about 30 percent of iMac sales are from "newbies," first-time computer buyers, and 12 percent are converts from Windows.[9]

Check out the latest on Apple and the iMac at www.apple.com.[5]

Questions

1 From a consumer's standpoint, what type of innovation is the iMac? Would this be any different for consumers who already own other Apple products?

2 What are the different types of consumers that Apple is trying to target with the iMac? Discuss the implication for Apple as it markets the iMac in terms of the other marketing mix elements of channel, price, and promotion.

3 Evaluate Apple's iMac on the following five factors that are common reasons for new product failure: (*a*) size of market, (*b*) significant points of difference, (*c*) product quality, (*d*) access to consumers, and (*e*) timing.

CASE D–6 STARBUCKS COFFEE

What'll you have? Skinny latte, espresso, almond truffle mocha? Increasingly coffee drinkers are turning to Starbucks to quench a growing thirst for specialty coffee.

THE COMPANY

Starbucks Coffee has been hugely successful. Net sales have grown from $65 309 000 in 1991 to $465 213 000 in 1995. Starbucks got its start in 1971 as a gourmet coffee bean store. In 1987, Starbucks' current chief executive, Howard Schultz, opened the first stylish Starbucks coffee bar. The focus then and now has been on high-end gourmet coffees. Customers can buy fresh roasted beans from around the world, gift packs, Starbucks coffee cups and sweets, as well as freshly brewed coffees. All coffee beans are roasted in-house to maintain quality. The company prides itself on buying top-quality beans, vacuum packs the beans two hours after roasting, and donates to charity any beans that go unsold seven days after opening the bag.

Starbucks employees are recruited from college campuses and community groups and given more than 24 hours of coffee-making training and lore. Starbucks maintains designers and architects in-house to develop, maintain, and update the hip, upscale image of the stores. All of this has led to the high-quality service that has built Starbucks' brand loyalty.

Citing concern about maintaining quality, Starbucks has turned down lucrative franchising agreements. All stores are company owned. Starbucks had more than 1900 stores in place in early 1999. The company purposely opens stores near one another, even if it involves some cannibalization, to ensure intensive distribution coverage.

Airports, hotels, and malls are all locations for Starbucks coffee bars. Another unique approach to distributing the product is developing special coffee blends for others. For example, Barnes and Noble bookstores have their own coffee bars in many locations, and these coffee bars exclusively sell the Starbucks "Barnes and Noble Coffee Blend." Canadian Airlines also runs advertising touting the fact that it now serves Starbucks coffee on its flights.

Research also is a key part of Starbucks' success. A sophisticated point-of-sale systems allows the company to track store and regional buying trends. The Starbucks real estate division sifts through data on potential markets and market characteristics for at least nine months prior to a store opening.

THE COFFEE MARKET

The coffee market wasn't always perking along. As recently as 10 years ago, the National Coffee Association was concerned about declining coffee consumption among younger adults. However, the growth of specialty coffees has not only boosted coffee consumption (nationally, 47 percent of consumers consider themselves coffee drinkers today) but has repositioned a product category that had little differentiation. Coffee was coffee, almost a generic product.

There are still concerns about the long-term trend in coffee consumption. While specialty brews have increased, consumers now drink an average of 1.87 cups a day, a decline from the early 1960s when the average per-capita consumption was more than three cups per day.

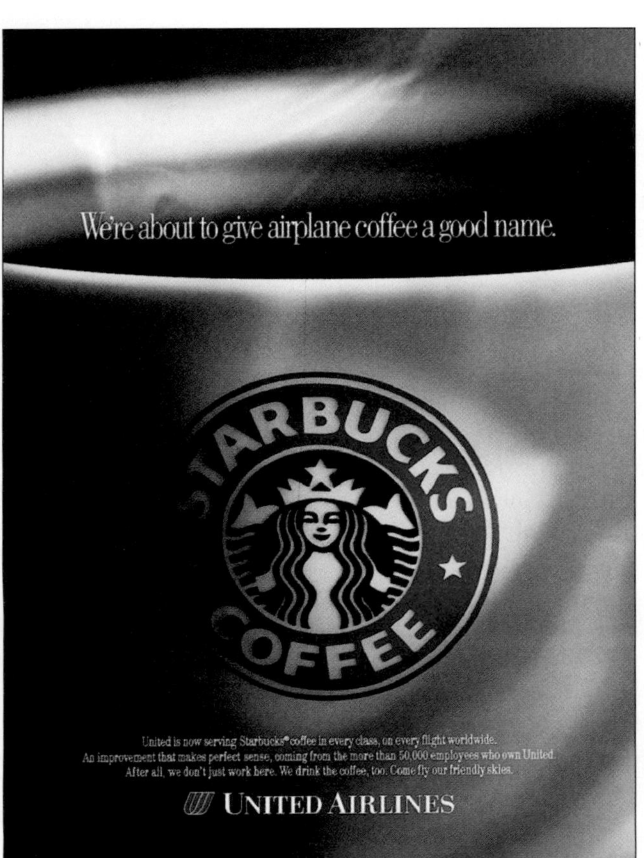

We're about to give airplane coffee a good name.
STARBUCKS COFFEE
United is now serving Starbucks® coffee in every class, on every flight worldwide.
An improvement that makes perfect sense, coming from the more than 50,000 employees who own United.
After all, we don't just work here. We drink the coffee, too. Come fly our friendly skies.
UNITED AIRLINES

THE COMPETITION

Today, Starbucks faces competition from a number of national, regional, and even local coffee bars and houses. Starbucks is credited with helping to educate the public about specialty coffee, creating the opening for large and small competitors. Chock Full O-Nuts has developed drive-through coffee outlets called Quickava. Even fast-food outlets such as Tim Horton's and Dunkin Donuts are improving their coffee offerings.

Starbucks' CEO Schultz views supermarkets as Starbucks' main competition. Supermarkets sell about 70 percent of all coffee and are increasingly going upscale, selling whole beans to be ground in the store. Starbucks has turned down opportunities to distribute its coffee through supermarkets until recently. In 1998 Starbucks began test sales of ground and whole bean coffee in supermarkets. Kraft Foods has entered into a licensing agreement with Starbucks to place coffee in grocery stores.

THE ISSUES

A major issue for Starbucks is the price of coffee, which can fluctuate wildly. Frost in Brazil, the world's largest coffee producer, can damage coffee plants for years. New bushes can take five years to mature. Commodity coffee prices doubled while specialty premium coffees briefly tripled in price as recently as the mid-1990s.

With increasing domestic competition, Starbucks has expanded to Europe and Asia. Starbucks has retail locations in Japan, Singapore, the Philippines, Taiwan, Thailand, the United Kingdom, New Zealand, and Malaysia. Starbucks opened its first store in Beijing, China, in 1999, partnering with Beijing Mei Da Coffee Co. Ltd., its distributor for wholesale operations in Beijing since 1994. Starbucks also opened its first outlet in the Middle East in Kuwait.

Frappucino, a blended coffee and milk drink served chilled or over ice, is a product developed by Starbucks in conjunction with PepsiCo. In spite of the fact that few consumers drank cold coffee prior to Frappucino's introduction as well as General Foods' market failure with a cold cappucino product called Cappio, Frappucino appears to be gaining acceptance. Pepsi's venture with Lipton Tea Company produced the number one product in the ready-made iced tea category. Starbucks' has also developed Starbucks' coffee-flavoured ice cream in partnership with Dryer's Grand Ice Cream, Inc. These products have made Starbucks a more significant brand within the grocery store channel. Starbucks also sells coffee and products such as espresso machines, coffee presses, music, and books through its coffee bars and its Web site at www.starbucks.com.[6]

Questions

1 What type of distribution strategy is Starbucks employing? How does this distribution strategy fit in with Starbucks' product and positioning?

2 What is Starbucks' competitive advantage? Discuss whether you feel this is a sustainable competitive advantage.

3 Starbucks' current distribution system can be described as a corporate vertical marketing system (VMS) for its coffee bars. In addition, Starbucks uses channel partnerships for some of its ventures (such as its relationships with Barnes and Noble and with Dryer's Grand Ice Cream). Starbucks has turned down lucrative franchising agreements that would create a contractual VMS. What are the pros and cons of continuing the present distribution system versus a contractual (franchising) VMS as Starbucks continues to grow and expand? What recommendations would you make to Starbucks concerning changes in its distribution strategy given its growth objectives?

CASE D–7 DELL COMPUTER CORPORATION

THE COMPANY

Dell is the largest direct seller of computers in the world and one of the top global PC manufacturers. Dell had more than $12.3 billion in sales in 1998, a 58.9 percent annual increase in sales. Dell offers PCs, notebooks, network servers, peripherals, and software. More than 90 percent of Dell's sales are to businesses and governmental customers. Dell's success is attributed in large part to its effective use of supply chain management.

SUPPLY CHAIN MANAGEMENT AT DELL

"Supply chain management is what it's all about. It's velocity," according to Tom Meredith, chief financial officer of Dell Computer Corporation. "The customer is interested in speed when it comes to innovation, pricing, configuration, delivery, and support."

Dell has closely aligned its suppliers with its direct channel strategy, resulting in dramatic improvements in inventory management and control. Inventories are down from 45 days worth of supply for production and operations to less than 11 days worth of supplies from five years ago. The newest Dell manufacturing plant is running with seven hours worth of inventory! This is important in an industry where component costs can decline 30 percent to 35 percent per year. This helps Dell take advantage of lower anticipated inventory costs in the future as well as minimizing the risk of holding obsolete parts in inventory. Meredith states that Dell "went negative in our cash conversion cycle for the last several quarters. In other words, we get paid faster than we pay."

No less significant have been Dell's efforts to work with vendors to reduce vendor cycle times—the time that elapses from Dell placing an order to receiving that order in a Dell manufacturing facility. Dell has reduced its supplier base from more than 300 suppliers to well under 100 over the last five years. Dell communicates with its suppliers and supply chain partners through "platinum supplier" Web pages. These pages provide each vendor with information on Dell's forecasted demand for the vendor's products, share production schedules, and allow for e-mail communication to make adjustments and changes.

The Dell web site (www.dell.com) allows customers to shop online. Different online "stores" are available for different types of customers such as education, government, home/home office, and businesses. Shoppers can select the items they want and place them in their shopping basket. Once the order has been submitted, the Web site has the capability to check delivery dates and even to monitor the status of the order with its online tracking system. Meredith states that Dell sees more than $3 million in sales per day over the Internet.

Dell works closely with its customers. Dell achieves customer intimacy with daily contact, and because of these relationships and customer input, the company is able to develop products on schedules that anticipate customer demand. Currently, Dell's more than 9,000 "elite customers" have personalized Web pages, and the top 40 corporate customers that represent about $1 billion in sales have "premier pages" for communication and information exchange.

Dell uses an architectural approach called G2 to integrate all its electronic commerce and communication systems. Dell's G2 uses browser and Internet/Intranet technology as the interface for all applications. This makes it possible for every PC in the world to interact with Dell.

Dell utilizes decision support applications for modeling and simulating materials and factory scheduling to improve supply chain efficiency. For example, Dell can look out hours or days in advance, match this up with materials flow, and, based on this information, optimize a manufacturing plan to execute in the factory.

What does this all mean for the customer? Better services and lower costs—value that gives Dell an edge in the marketplace.[7]

Questions

1 Explain how Dell's approach to supply chain management satisfies the logistical objectives of minimizing logistics costs while maximizing customer service.

2 What are the supply chain management implications for Dell's competitors that primarily utilize an indirect channel strategy? What supply chain and marketing recommendations do you suggest for Dell, given the competitive environment?

3 How does supply chain management relate to the marketing concept at Dell?

CASE D–8 THE NEW VOLKSWAGEN BEETLE

"Hug it? Drive it? Hug it? Drive it?" It's new, it's old. It's nostalgia. It's cutting edge. It's the New Volkswagen Beetle, reintroduced to the North American market after a 19-year absence. Consumer reaction has been overwhelming. People stop to look at the car, honk at the driver, and give a "thumbs up." People can't help but smile when they see one. It's the renewal of an automobile love affair that has resulted in astonishing success for the New Beetle as well as for other VW products such as the Cabriolet, Jetta, Golf, and Passat. The automotive industry has taken note and attempted to take advantage of "retro" designs in other new cars such as the Ford Thunderbird in 2000.

THE PRODUCT AND MARKET

Volkswagen originally designed the Beetle in pre–World War II Germany as a people's car—*volks* (people) *wagen* (car). It provided dependable, reliable, and economical transportation. The car was first sold in North America in 1949 for under $1000. The car was a commercial success around the world with more than 21 million built, more than any other car in history. However, VW all but discontinued manufacturing the car by 1986. The original Bug was last sold here in 1979. In Brazil the product was discontinued in 1986, but there was such an emotional outpouring of support and cries for the return of the *Fusca* (Portuguese for "beetle") that the company reintroduced the Bug in 1993. No less than the president of Brazil called for the return of the Beetle. His name was the first on a waiting list of more than 18 000 Brazilians waiting to buy the car. Mexico was the only market where the original Beetle continued to be produced without interruption. *Vocho*, the pet name for the Bug in Mexico, is the most popular car in the country—and the most affordable at about $8000.

"The original Volkswagen Beetle was the biggest-selling and best-loved car in North American history," according to *Adweek*. Why then did Volkswagen discontinue the product? Why not reintroduce the original product to the North American market? Why redesign a New Beetle? There are a number of theories. The vintage Beetle probably would not meet government-mandated safety standards for new automobiles. In addition, VW seemingly attempted to reposition the company and its newer products as more upscale than the unpretentious Beetle. The New Beetle has a water-cooled engine in the front of the car, more horsepower, dual front- and side-impact airbags, and new features that even include a bud vase within the familiar Beetle silhouette.

Research conducted by Volkswagen's advertising agency, Arnold Communications, showed that the car appealed to a broad audience. Instead of targeting a market segment based on demographics such as age and income, Arnold targeted a psychographic profile. Customers for the New Beetle were confident, unique, and not afraid of being the centre of attention.

THE PROMOTIONAL LAUNCH

The New Beetle promotional campaign was designed around very simple silhouettes of the car against stark backgrounds with short, witty tag lines. Some examples include

"If you were really good in a past life (photo of the original Beetle), you can come back as something better" (photo of the New Beetle).

"If you sold your soul in the '80s, here's your chance to buy it back."

"The engine's in the front, but its heart's in the same place."

"Less flower, more power."

"A work of art with side-impact airbags, and a bud vase."

Print advertising; television advertising on such shows as "X-Files," "The Practice," and "Ally McBeal"; and point-of-purchase brochures all conveyed the same designs and appeal. Volkswagen's Web page carries information about the New Beetle as well as other Volkswagen products at www.vw.com. The "Drivers wanted" tag line used across all VW products is also included in Beetle advertising. Publicity came from stories in the media written about the car and about the advertising awards won by Arnold Communications for its work on the campaign.

The results of the promotional campaign were impressive. There was up to 3-month-long waiting lists for the New Beetle. Buyers were paying full price for the car, and then some.[8]

Questions

1 What are the primary promotional objectives for the launch of the New Beetle? How do you expect these objectives to change after the New Beetle has been on the market for 5 years?

2 How did Volkswagen use integrated marketing communications to launch the New Beetle? What are the strengths and weaknesses of each element of the promotional mix, and how do they correspond to Volkswagen's promotional objectives for the New Beetle?

3 Volkswagen's launch of the New Beetle program heavily emphasized a pull promotional strategy versus a push promotional strategy. Why? Is this emphasis likely to change over time?

CASE D–9 TIMEX: CHANGING AN IMAGE

"Takes a licking and keeps on ticking." For years this is the image that has been associated with Timex watches—dependable, reliable, almost indestructible. Timex's advertising was closely associated with the Timex image. The advertising campaign featured different attempts to destroy Timex watches that failed to stop the Timex from ticking. One memorable ad showed a Timex watch strapped to the propeller of a motor boat before being driven across the lake. The dripping watch was proudly displayed as the second hand swept past the face of the watch.

THE COMPANY

Timex has been the industry leader since 1960. In fact, Timex's share of the of the North American watch market was 50 percent by the late 1960s and as much as 20 percent worldwide. However, Timex missed several important environmental trends that changed the industry. For one thing, Timex stuck to analog technology, losing money and market share to competitors that adopted digital technology in the 1970s. By the time Timex caught on to the importance of the electronic watch, competitors had already developed and marketed far-superior products. Timex employees dubbed the first Timex electronic watches "quarter pounders" because of their clumsy, clunky appearance. In 1982, a Swiss company approached Timex and asked it to do the worldwide marketing for a new product. Timex turned down the offer, believing the garish plastic watches would be a flop. It was a major blunder for Timex. The Swatches that Timex turned down became a fashion success around the globe. By 1983, North American market share for Timex had fallen to about 17 percent, with operating losses approaching $100 million.

THE MARKET

Times changed and so did consumer needs and wants for watches. Timex's biggest mistake was failing to keep up with the watch's evolution from a functional object to a fashion accessory. Coordinating watches with clothing, changing watch bands for different occasions, and wearing designer watches that convey status and prestige are increasingly important to consumers. According to the Jewellery Experts, the average consumer today owns five watches compared with 1.5

about 30 years ago. Timex was left behind as the rest of the industry moved from watches as a functional tool to watches as fashion statements.

THE PRODUCT

Timex appears to have learned from its mistakes. Fashion consultants now visit twice a year from New York and Paris to provide insight to Timex on trends and interests that can translate into new watch styles. Timex executives travel to retailers and other trade shows to spot fashion trends. Timex took advantage of consumer interest in sport watches to develop the Indiglo watch. Indiglo patented technology uses energy from the watch battery to excite electrons in the watch face. Unlike other watches that require exposure to the sun or lamp, the Timex Indiglo does not need to be "charged" to emit light.

Timex was also very successful advertising the Indiglo watches when the technology was introduced in 1992. Its introductory commercial effectively conveyed the simple message about the glowing watch face while hinting at the "takes a licking and keeps on ticking" theme. In the background, Sinatra sings "strangers in the night . . ." as a smitten firefly hovers over the glowing watch dial. Smack! A huge hand suddenly swats at the infatuated firefly but misses, hitting the watch. *Time* magazine called this campaign "the best television campaign of 1992." The 1992 Gallup Watch Brand Survey found that 98 percent of consumers knew the Timex brand, followed by Seiko (87 percent).

Recognizing that simply introducing a unique product with a patented technology is insufficient to gain market share, Timex boosted its ad budget significantly in the mid-1990s. Timex also faced increasing competition from major competitors. Hearing that Seiko, Armitron, and Citizen planned to add watches to their lines with a lighting technology similar to Indiglo, Timex initially responded with advertising blitzes, especially at the holiday season. Additionally, Timex has made a major change in its advertising strategy. Watch companies traditionally focused their advertising campaigns in the spring and fall. In what industry executives call a first, Timex Corporation began advertising continuously throughout the year. Given its success, it is not surprising that Timex put almost its entire advertising budget into campaigns for Indiglo in the mid-1990s. Timex was fortunate enough to get some impressive testimonials from customers that rolled in along with sales. These stories provided some fascinating material for potential ad campaigns. Consider the following:

- A man led a group of people down 34 unlit flights of stairs in the bombed World Trade Centre in New York City by the light of an Indiglo.
- A Los Angeles couple lit their way to safety after an earthquake with an Indiglo watch.
- Four people clung to a capsized fishing boat overnight, comforted by the reassuring blue beam of a Timex Indiglo.

The Indiglo technology is "making ho-hum Timex kind of hip." In fact, earlier attempts to upscale the product line and develop more fashionable products were hampered by perceptions that the products have "got a $12.95 name on them." In fact, Timex was named the top fashion brand by the Fairchild 100—the fashion industry's version of the *Fortune* 100. Timex was named the number one brand in jewelry and watches category, surpassing Swatch, a distant second.

Currently more than 65 percent of Timex watches are equipped with Indiglo technology, part of a product line that includes 1500 styles, up from 300 in 1970. Indiglo technology has been improved and refined, making it available on both analog and digital watches. All Day Indiglo technology, using holographic film, now makes it easier to read your Timex in low light conditions when the night light is not activated.

THE COMPETITION

Competitors are taking two positions with respect to the popularity of the Timex Indiglo. Some are attempting to imitate the technology. For example, Seiko's LumiBrite watch has dials coated with a nonradioactive compound that absorbs light during the day and re-emits it for up to 5 hours in the dark. Others suggest that the light-up dial is a novelty that will not appeal to the masses. Bulova's marketing vice president, Philip Shaw, does not feel that night-lighting technology will become a watch standard, unlike water resistance. Shaw states, "People buy our watches for style."

THE ISSUES TODAY

Industry observers expect the next big technological trend in watches will be two-way voice communication timepieces—Dick Tracy style. Prototypes have been too large and do not easily fit on the wrist. However, early test models of the Indiglo were too large as well. The next best thing right now may be Beepwear, a Timex partnership with Motorola to combine pager and watch technology.

Timex also scored a critical hit with its high-tech Data-Link watch. The Data-Link watches allowed users to download a variety of information from their personal computers, such as phone numbers, appointments, birthdays, etc., to their Timex watches simply by pointing the face of their watches to a flashing PC screen. These products are targeted toward business executives, professionals, managers, salespeople, and students.

Timex has also launched new products such as the Humvee watch line based on a licensing agreement between Timex and AM General, the manufacturer of the Humvee and Hummer. Timex has also been very successful with its Disney licensing agreement. The Pooh and Pooh Adult watches are among its most popular, including models that have a three-dimensional effect making it appear that a swarm of bees or leaves rotate around the dial and one model that plays the "Winnie the Pooh" theme song with the touch of a button. The Timex Pulse Timing Watch for medical personnel was developed based on customer requests. The Timex Ironman Triathalon, the best selling watch for 11 years running, has been given a total make-over. Timex also has finger watches and 12 unique watch styles inspired by ancient civilizations. To learn more about the latest from Timex, visit it at www.timex.com.[9]

Questions

1 How did Timex change its image through advertising? What role did new product development play in this image change?

2 What advertising objectives should Timex have for the Indiglo today? How do objectives for the Indiglo affect advertising objectives for other Timex products?

3 Discuss what sort of promotional message should be emphasized in Timex ads. (Emphasize the technology, the styling, and competitive advantages.)

4 What type of advertisements, media, and scheduling would you recommend for Timex?

CASE D–10 FIELD FURNITURE ENTERPRISES

Edward Meadows, president of Field Furniture Enterprises, met with representatives of Kelly, Astor, & Peters Advertising (KAP) and Andrew Reed, Field's vice president of marketing and sales, to discuss the company's advertising program for 2000. The KAP representatives recommended that Field Furniture increase its advertising in shelter magazines (such as *Good Housekeeping* and *Better Homes and Gardens*, which feature home improvement ideas and new ideas in home decorating) by $250 000 and maintain the expenditures for other promotional efforts at a constant level during 2000. The rationale given for the increase in advertising was that Field Furniture had low name recognition among prospective buyers of furniture, and it intended to introduce new styles of living and dining room furniture. Reed, however, had a different opinion as to how Field Furniture should spend the $250 000. He thought it was necessary to (1) hire additional salespeople to call on the 30 new retail stores to be added by the company in 2000, (2) increase the funds devoted to cooperative advertising, and (3) improve the selling aids given to retail stores and salespeople.

THE COMPANY

Field Furniture is a medium-sized manufacturer of medium- to high-priced living and dining room furniture. Sales in 1999 were $50 million. The company sells its furniture through 1000 furniture specialty stores nationwide, but not all stores carry the company's entire line. This fact bothered Meadows because, in his words, "If they ain't got it, they can't sell it!" The company employs 10 full-time salespeople, who receive a $40,000 base salary annually and a small commission on sales. A company salesforce is atypical in the furniture industry because most furniture manufacturers use selling agents or manufacturer's representatives who carry a wide assortment of noncompeting furniture lines and receive a commission on sales. "Having our own sales group is a policy my father established 30 years ago," noted Meadows, "and we've been quite successful having people who are committed to our company. Our people don't just take furniture orders. They are expected to motivate retail salespeople to sell our line, assist in setting up displays in stores, coordinate cooperative advertising plans, and give advice on a variety of matters to our retailers and their salespeople."

In 1999, Field spent $2.45 million for total promotional expenditures, excluding the salary of the vice president of marketing and sales. Promotional expenditures were categorized into four groups: (1) sales expense and administration, (2) cooperative advertising programs with retailers, (3) trade promotions, and (4) consumer advertising. Cooperative advertising allowances are usually spent on newspaper advertising in a retailer's city and are matched by the retailer's funds on a dollar-for-dollar basis. Trade promotion is directed toward retailers and takes the form of catalogues, trade magazine advertisements, booklets for consumers, and point-of-purchase materials such as displays for use in retail stores. Also included in this category is the expense of trade shows. Field Furniture is represented at two trade shows a year. Consumer advertising is directed to potential consumers through shelter magazines. The typical format used in consumer advertising is to highlight new furniture and different living and dining room arrangements. Dollar allocation for each program in 1999 was as follows:

PROMOTIONAL PROGRAM	EXPEDITURE
Sales expense and administration	$ 612 500
Cooperative advertising	1 102 500
Trade advertising	306 250
Consumer advertising	428 750
Total	$2 450 000

THE INDUSTRY

The household wooden furniture industry is composed of hundreds of firms, but no one firm captured more than 3 percent of the total household wooden furniture market.

The buying and selling of furniture to retail outlets centres around manufacturers' expositions at selected times and places around the country. At these marts, as they are called in the furniture industry, retail buyers view manufacturers' lines and often make buying commitments for their stores. However, Field's experience has shown that sales efforts in the retail store by company representatives account for as much as half the company's sales in a given year. The major manufacturer expositions are held in October and April. Regional expositions are also scheduled in June through August.

Company research on consumer furniture-buying behaviour indicated that people visit several stores when shopping for furniture, and the final decision is made jointly by a husband and wife in about 90 percent of furniture purchases. Other noteworthy findings are as follows:

- Eighty-four percent of buyers believe "the higher the price, the higher the quality" when buying home furnishings.
- Seventy-two percent of buyers browse or window shop in furniture stores even if they don't need furniture.
- Eighty-five percent read furniture ads before they actually need furniture.
- Ninety-nine percent agreed with the statement, "When shopping for furniture and home furnishings, I like the salesperson to show me what alternatives are available, answer my questions, and let me alone so I can think about it and maybe browse around."
- Ninety-five percent get redecorating ideas from shelter magazines.
- Forty-one percent have written off for a manufacturer's booklet.
- Sixty-three percent feel they need decorating advice for "putting it all together."

BUDGETARY ISSUES

After the KAP Advertising representatives made their presentation, Reed again emphasized that the incremental $250 000 should not be spent for consumer advertising. He noted that Field Furniture had set as an objective that each salesperson would make 6 calls per year at each store and spend at least 4 hours at each store on every call. "Given that our salespeople work a 40-hour week, 48 weeks per year, and devote only 80 percent of their time to selling due to travel time between stores, we already aren't doing the sales job," Reed added. Meadows agreed but reminded Reed that the $250 000 increment in the promotional budget was a maximum the company could spend, given other cost increases.[10]

Questions

1 How might you describe furniture buying using the purchase decision process described in Chapter 6?

2 How might each of the elements of the promotional program influence each stage in the purchase decision process?

3 What should Field's promotional objectives be?

4 How many salespeople does Field need to adequately service its accounts?

5 Should Field Furniture emphasize a push or pull promotional strategy? Why?

CASE D–11 SECOND HARVEST

Second Harvest is a charitable, nonprofit organization that began in Toronto in 1985. Its mission: to locate and collect surplus perishable food and deliver it to social security agencies and community organizations in Metro Toronto that feed the hungry. Second Harvest is not a food bank; it handles perishable food only and it does not warehouse food. It serves as a link between surplus food—food which would otherwise go to waste—and organizations that provide food to people in need. Many social service agencies and community organizations have difficulty keeping up with the demand for emergency food assistance. In Toronto it is estimated that over 154 000 people depend on emergency food programs each month. Most of the people are single women with children. Ironically, while people are going hungry more than 20 percent of food produced in North America is wasted.

Second Harvest's basic day-to-day operation are conducted out of a small office under the direction of an executive director, working with a small staff, and primarily a core group of volunteers. Using a small fleet of trucks, donated by good corporate citizens, Second Harvest retrieves surplus food from any industry, group, or individual who regularly or occasionally has excess food, including food producers, farmers, retailers, wholesalers, restaurants, hospitals, production houses, and organizers of special events. It then delivers this food to a variety of agencies or organizations including drop-ins or soup kitchens, food pantries or food banks, residences or shelters, and subsidized housing developments. In 1997 Second Harvest picked up and delivered more than 1 million pounds of food. This food consisted of bread, baked goods, dairy products, produce, beverages, meat, snack foods, and prepared foods.

Second Harvest has also been involved with several self-help initiatives, including the publication of a cookbook which contains inexpensive, easy-to-prepare recipes designed to help those on fixed incomes who need to stretch their food dollars. Second Harvest also plays a role as an advocate for change in public policy as it pertains to hunger and poverty.

In order to achieve its objectives, Second Harvest attempts to create awareness of the organization and its efforts through public relations activities, including PSAs, news releases, newsletters, and special events. One of its major events is an annual fund raiser called Toronto Taste, where attendees pay to sample the food dishes created by Toronto chefs. Second Harvest also participates in hospitality industry trade shows where it hopes to create greater awareness of its activities, and to increase its food donor base. It also has a public relations firm that donates its time and talent in order to help heighten Second Harvest's profile in the community.[11]

Questions

1 How can Second Harvest motivate more individuals and organizations to donate to their cause?

2 What specific marketing communication tools would you recommend that Second Harvest use to reach those prospective donors?

3 What are some unique sources of surplus food that Second Harvest could tap into?

CASE D–12 NATIONAL COMMUNITY TREE FOUNDATION

In the 1990 Green Plan, the Government of Canada made clear its commitment to providing a safe and healthy environment for present and future generations. A key part of the Green Plan is a program called Tree Plan Canada. It recognizes the fundamental importance of our rural and urban forests in addressing the problem of global warming and improving the quality of life for all Canadians. The National Community Tree Foundation (NCTF) was formed as a nonprofit (nongovernmental) organization to manage the Tree Plan Canada program and to ensure that its objectives became realities. The fundamental purpose of the NCTF is "to foster and encourage the planting and care of trees in and around more than 5000 cities, towns, and villages by 1998."

Tree planting is certainly not a new idea in this country. THe forestry sector plants millions of trees each year. But virtually all of these trees are planted to compensate for the effects of timber harvesting or forest fires. So the first hurdle facing the foundation was to educate Canadians that they too had an important role to play in planting new trees in urban and rural areas. If NCTF's objectives were to be achieved within the timeframe specified, then average Canadians would have to be motivated to plant trees in and around their communities. But Canadians would only plant trees if they understood the benefits of trees as an integral part of the ecosystem. The public's affinity for trees and forests was a good starting point, with the aesthetic appreciation and a belief in the "goodness of green."

What was still needed was crystal-clear communication of the solid science that makes trees vital to human survival. Canadians needed to know, or be reminded, that trees are the lungs of the earth, filtering the air we breathe and removing pollutants. NCTF wanted Canadians to appreciate that a mature tree keeps on cleaning and cleaning, at no charge, for many decades. But if the message was only seen as a lesson, NCTF would lose its audience—just providing boring facts about an issue that people believed they already understand simply would not work. The challenge would be to create broad awareness, if not change a mindset, with regard to the value and benefits of trees, and, in doing so, prompt Canadians to take action in planting our urban and rural forests. NCTF allocated an initial $420 000 for promotional activities designed to accomplish these objectives.[12]

Questions

1 Given the challenges facing NCTF, what promotion techniques would you recommend the foundation use?

2 Besides the initial target audience of "average adults Canadians," who else should NCTF target for involvement in the program?

3 What type of creative theme would prompt Canadians to action?

CASE D–13 METRO TORONTO WORKS DEPARTMENT

In recent years there has been a pronounced increase in the public's awareness of environmental issues. Yet the perceived magnitude of some of the problems was so overwhelming that many people weren't modifying their behaviour, thinking that one person could hardly make a difference. Moreover, in Metro Toronto, there was both ignorance and uncertainty as to the range of environmental or waste management services offered by the Metro Toronto Works Department. While the Blue Box Recycling program had high visibility (a walk though the neighbourhood on collection days would show many blue containers by the curbside), other initiatives of the Works Department were less well known.

Metro Toronto Works Department wanted Metro residents to become part of the solution. This meant continuous education about what was and what wasn't recyclable through the Blue Box program, and raising awareness of other less familiar programs. But increased participation in waste management programs would only happen if residents perceived them to be simple and convenient rather than time-consuming and complex.

The department determined an advertising and public relations campaign would be necessary to generate awareness and encourage increased household participation in the waste management programs. The campaign would focus on all waste management programs including the Blue Box Recycling, Backyard Composting, Water Efficiency, and Household Hazardous Waste Dis posal. Seasonal projects (such as summer lawn watering reduction, and Christmas tree recycling) and special events (such as Environmental Days and Waste Reduction Week) also had to be highlighted. The department decided no scare tactics would be used. The campaign would be a positive one. Citizens would be encouraged to participate and shown that their cooperation was necessary, easy, and meaningful. The thrust of the campaign would rest on the premise that, although the magnitude of environmental waste was huge, every single one of us, every single day, could make small contributions that, when added together, become significant.[13]

Questions

1 Given the campaign's objective, what would you recommend as the primary advertising media choice for Metro Works?

2 What would be the basic message appeal you would recommend to encourage residents to participate?

3 What public relations activities would you recommend for Environmental Days and Waste Reduction Week?

CASE D–14 BMW

"We're fortunate right now at BMW in that all of our products are new and competitive," says Jim McDowell, vice president of marketing at BMW, as he explains BMW's product life cycle. "Now, how do you do that? You have to introduce new models over time. You have to logically plan out the introductions over time, so you're not changing a whole model range at the same time you're changing another model range."

BMW's strategy is to keep its products in the introduction and growth stages by periodically introducing new models in each of its product lines. In fact, BMW does not like to have any products in the maturity or decline stage of the product life cycle. Explains McDowell, "If a product is declining, we would prefer to withdraw it from the market, as opposed to having a strategy for dealing with the declining product. We're kind of a progressive, go get 'em company, and we don't think it does our brand image any good to have any declining products out there. So that's why we work so hard at managing the growth aspect."

BMW—THE COMPANY AND ITS PRODUCTS

BMW is one of the preeminent luxury car manufacturers in Europe, North America, and the world today. BMW produces several lines of cars, including the 3 series, the 5 series, the 7 series, the Z line (driven by Pierce Brosnan as James Bond in *Goldeneye*), and the new X line, BMW's "sport activity" vehicle line. In addition, BMW is now selling Rovers, a British car line anchored by the internationally popular Land Rover sport utility vehicle, and will begin selling Rolls Royce vehicles in 2003. Sales of all the BMW, Rover, and Land Rover vehicles have been on the rise globally. High-profile image campaigns (such as the James Bond promotion) and the award-winning BMW Web site (where users can design their own car) continue to increase the popularity of BMW's products.

PRODUCT LIFE CYCLE

BMW cars typically have a product life cycle of seven years. To keep products in the introductory and growth stages, BMW regularly introduces new models for each of its series to keep the entire series "new." For instance, with the 3 series, it will introduce the new sedan model one year, the new coupe the next year, then the convertible, then the station wagon, and then the sport hatchback. That's a new product introduction for five of the seven years of the product life cycle. McDowell explains, "So, even though we have seven-year life cycles, we constantly try and make the cars meaningfully different and new about every three years. And that involves adding features and other capabilities to the cars as well." How well does this strategy work? BMW often sees its best sales numbers in either the sixth or seventh year after the product introduction.

As global sales have increased, BMW has become aware of some international product life cycle differences. For example, it has discovered that some competitive products have life cycles that are shorter or longer than seven years. In Sweden and Britain automotive product life cycles are eight years, while in Japan they are typically only four years long.

BRANDING

"BMW is fortunate—we don't have too much of a dilemma as to what we're going to call our cars." McDowell is referring to BMW's trademark naming system that consists of the product line number and the motor type. For example, the designation "328" tells you the car is in the 3 series and the engine is 2.8-litres in size. BMW has found this naming system to be clear and logical and can be easily understood around the world. The Z and X series don't quite fit in with this system. BMW

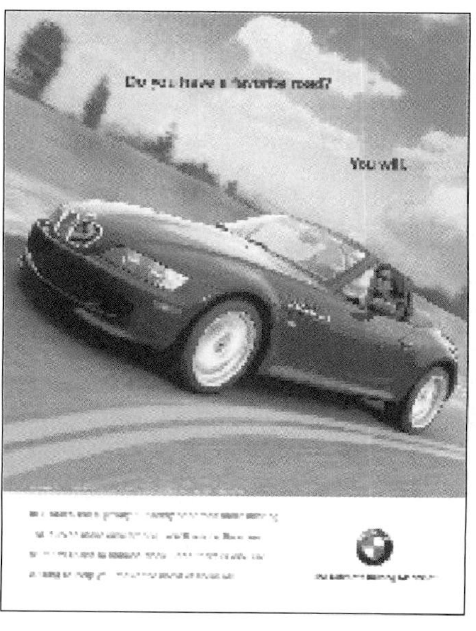

had a tradition of building experimental, open-air cars and calling them Z's, and hence when the prototype for the Z3 was built, BMW decided to continue with the Z name. For the sport activity vehicle, BMW also used a letter name—the X series—since the four-wheel drive vehicle didn't fit with the sedan-oriented 3, 5, and 7 series. Other than the Z3 (the third in the Z series) and the X5 (named 5 to symbolize its mid-sized status within that series), the BMW branding strategy is quite simple, unlike the evocative names many car manufacturers choose to garner excitement for their new models.

MANAGING THE PRODUCT THROUGH THE WEB—THE WAVE OF THE FUTURE

One of the ways BMW is improving its product offerings even further is through its innovative Web site (www.bmw.ca). At the site, customers can learn about the particular models, e-mail questions, and request literature or test-drives from their local BMW dealership. What really sets BMW's Web site apart from other car manufacturers, though, is the ability for customers to configure a car to their own specifications (interior choices, exterior choices, engine, packages, and options) and then transfer that information to their local dealer. As Carol Burrows, product communications manager for BMW, explains, "The BMW Web site is an integrated part of the overall marketing strategy for BMW. The full range of products can be seen and interacted with online. We offer pricing options online. Customers can go to their local dealership via the Web site to further discuss costs for purchase of a car. And it is a distribution channel for information that allows people access to the information 24 hours a day at their convenience."[14]

Questions

1 Compare the product life cycle described by BMW for its cars to the product life cycle shown in Figure 12–1. How are they (*a*) similar and (*b*) dissimilar?

2 Based on BMW's typical product life cycle, what marketing strategies are appropriate for the 3 series? The X5?

3 Which of the three ways to manage the product life cycle does BMW utilize with its products—modifying the product, modifying the market, or repositioning the product?

4 How would you describe BMW's branding strategy (manufacturer branding, private branding, or mixed branding)? Why?

5 Go to the BMW Web site (www.bmw.ca) and design a car to your own specifications. How does this enable you as a customer to evaluate the product differently than would be otherwise possible?

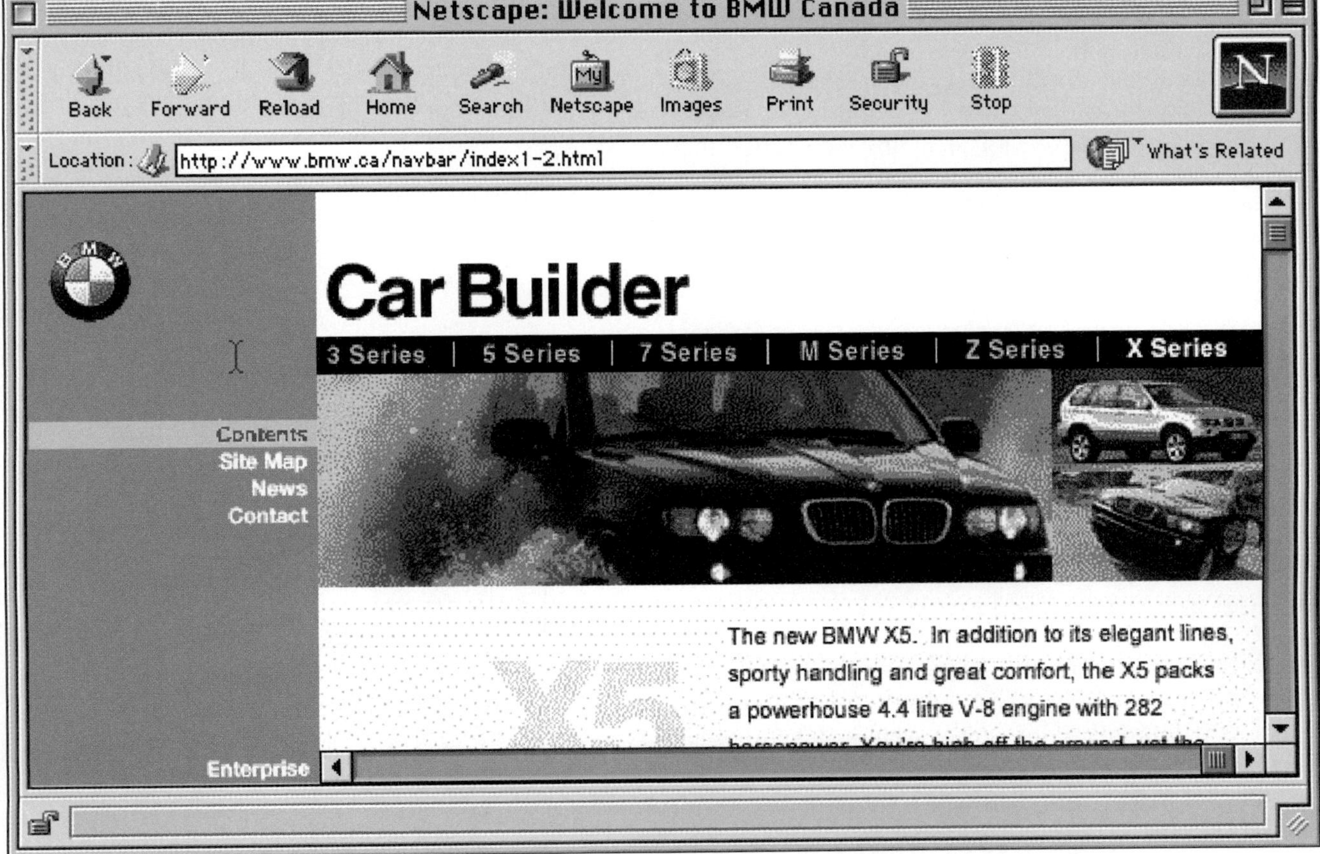

GLOSSARY

80/20 rule The principle that 80 percent of sales (and costs) are generated by 20 percent of the items or customers.
above-, at-, or below-market pricing Pricing based on what the market price is.
accelerated development The second stage of the retail life cycle, characterized by rapid increases in market share and profitability.
account management policies Policies that specify whom sales people should contact, what kinds of selling and customer service activities should be engaged in, and how these activities should be carried out; in advertising agency, refers to policies used by an account executive in dealing with clients.
action item list An aid to implementing a market plan, consisting of three columns: (1) the task, (2) the name of the person responsible for completing the task, and (3) the date by which the task is to be finished.
adaptive selling A need-satisfaction sales presentation involving adjusting the presentation to fit the selling situation.
advertising Any paid form of nonpersonal communication about an organization, good, service, or idea by an identified sponsor.
advocacy advertisements Institutional advertisements that state the position of a company on an issue.
all you can afford budgeting Allocating funds to advertising only after all other budget items are covered.
anchor stores Well-known national or regional stores that are located in regional shopping centres.
approach stage In the personal selling process, the initial meeting between the salesperson and prospect where the objectives are to gain the prospect's attention, stimulate interest, and build the foundation for the sales presentation.
atmosphere A store's ambience or setting.
attitudes Learned predispositions to respond to an object or class of objects in a consistent manner.
average revenue The average amount of money received for selling one unit of a product.

baby boomlet The generation of children born in 1977 and later.
baby boomers The generation of children born between 1946 and 1964.
back translation The practice of retranslating a word or phrase into the original language by a different interpreter to catch errors.
bait-and-switch advertising An advertising practice in which a company shows a product that it has no intention of selling to lure the customer into the store and sell him a higher-priced item.
balance of trade The difference between the monetary value of a nation's exports and imports.
banner ads Strip ads in online advertising that usually contain a company or product name or some kind of promotional offer.
barriers to entry Business practices or conditions that make it difficult for a new firm to enter the market.
barter The practice of exchanging goods and services for other goods and services rather than for money.
basing-point pricing Selecting one or more geographic locations (basing point) from which the list price for products plus freight expenses are charged to buyers.
beliefs A consumer's subjective perception of how well a product or brand performs on different attributes; these are based on personal experience, advertising, and discussions with other people.
benchmarking Discovering how other organizations do something better than yours so your firm can imitate or leapfrog competition.
bidder's list A list of firms believed to be qualified to supply a given item.
blended family Two families from prior marriages merged into a single household as spouses remarry.
bots Electronic shopping agents or robots that comb Web sites to compare prices and product or service features.
brand equity The added value a given brand name provides a product.
brand extension The practice of using a current brand name to enter a completely different product class.
brand loyalty A favourable attitude toward and consistent purchase of a single brand over time.
brand manager (*see* product manager)
brand name Any word or device (design, shape, sound, or colour) that is used to distinguish one company's products from a competitor's.
branding Activity in which an organization uses a name, phrase, design, or symbol, or a combination of these, to identify its products and distinguish them from those of a competitor.
brand personality A set of human characteristics associated with a brand name.
breadth of product line The variety of different items a store or wholesaler carries.
break-even analysis An analysis of the relationship between total revenue and total cost to determine profitability at various levels of output.
break-even chart A graphic presentation of a break-even analysis.
break-even point (BEP) Quantity at which total revenue and total cost are equal and beyond which profit occurs.
brokers Channel intermediaries that do not take title to merchandise and make their profits from commissions and fees by negotiating contracts or deals between buyers and sellers.
buildup forecast Summing the sales forecasts of each of the components to arrive at a total forecast.
bundle pricing The marketing of two or more products in a single "package" price.
business analysis Involves specifying the features of the product and the marketing strategy needed to commercialize it and making necessary financial projections.
business analysis stage Step 4 of the new-product process, which involves specifying the product features and marketing strategy and making necessary financial projections to commercialize a product.

business culture Comprises the effective rules of the game, the boundaries between competitive and unethical behaviour, and the codes of conduct in business dealings.
business firm A privately owned organization that serves its customers in order to earn a profit.
business marketing The marketing of goods and services to commercial enterprises, governments, and other profit and nonprofit organizations for use in the creation of goods and services that they then produce and market to other business customers as well as individuals and ultimate consumers.
business plan A roadmap for the entire organization for a specific future period of time, such as one year or five years.
business portfolio analysis Analysis of a firm's strategic business units (SBUs) as though they were a collection of separate investments.
business unit Element of a firm that markets a set of related products to a clearly defined group of customers.
business unit competencies Special capabilities resulting from the business unit's personnel, resources, or functional units.
business unit goal A performance target the business unit seeks to reach to achieve its mission.
business unit level Level at which business unit managers set directions for their products and markets.
business unit mission A statement specifying the markets and product lines in which a business unit will compete.
buy classes Groups of three specific buying situations organizations face: new buy, straight rebuy, and modified rebuy.
buyer turnover The frequency with which new buyers enter the market to buy a product.
buying centre The group of persons within an organization who participate in the buying process and share common goals, risks, and knowledge important to that process.
buying criteria The factors buying organizations use when evaluating a potential supplier and what it wants to sell.

capacity management Managing the demand for a service so that it is available to consumers.
case allowance A trade-oriented sales promotion in which retailers receive a discount on each case ordered during a specific time period.
cash and carry wholesaler A limited-service merchant wholesaler that takes title to merchandise but sells only to buyers who call on it and pay cash for and transport their own merchandise.
category killers Specialty discount outlets that focus on one product category such as electronics or business supplies at very competitive prices
cause-related marketing Tying the charitable contributions of a firm directly to the customer revenues produced through the promotion of one of its products.
caveat emptor A Latin term that means "let the buyer beware."
census metropolitan area Geographic labour market areas having a population of 100 000 persons or more.
central business district The oldest retail setting; the community's downtown area.
channel captain A marketing channel member that coordinates, directs, and supports other channel members; may be a manufacturer, wholesaler, or retailer.
channel of communication The means (e.g., a salesperson, advertising media, or public relations tools) of conveying a message to a receiver.
channel partnering Agreements and procedures among channel members for ordering and physically distributing a producer's product through the channel to the ultimate consumer.
closed-end question (*see* fixed alternative question)
closing stage The stage in the personal selling process that involves getting a purchase commitment from a prospect.
co-branding The pairing of two brand names of two manufacturers for joint marketing purposes.
code of ethics A formal statement of ethical principles and rules of conduct.
cognitive dissonance The feeling of postpurchase psychological tension or anxiety a consumer often experiences.
combination compensation plan A compensation plan whereby a salesperson is paid a specified salary plus a commission based on sales or profit.
commercialization The final phase of the new-product process in which the product is positioned and launched into full-scale production and sale.
commercial online services Companies that provide electronic information and marketing services to subscribers who are charged a monthly fee.
communication The process of conveying a message to others. Six elements—a source, a message, a channel of communication, a receiver, and the processes of encoding and decoding—are required for communication to occur.
community shopping centre A retail location that typically has one primary store (usually a department store branch) and 20 to 40 smaller outlets and serves a population base of about 100 000.
company forecast (*see* sales forecast)
comparative advertisements Advertisements that show one brand's strengths relative to those of competitors.
competition The set of alternative firms that could provide a product to satisfy a specific market's needs.
Competition Act Key legislation designed to protect competition and consumers in Canada.
competitive advantage A unique strength relative to competitors, often based on quality, time, cost, innovation, or customer intimacy.
competitive advertisements Advertisements that promote a specific brand's features and benefits.
competitive institutional advertisements Institutional advertisements that promote the advantages of one product class over another and are used in markets where different product classes compete for the same buyer.
competitive parity budgeting Matching the competitors' absolute level of spending or the proportion per point of market share.
computer-assisted retailing A retailing method whereby customers order products over computer linkups from their home after viewing items on the TV or on their computer monitor.
computer-mediated buying The use of Internet technology to seek information, evaluate alternatives, and make purchase decisions.
concept tests External evaluations of a product idea that consist of preliminary testing of the new product idea (rather than the actual product) with consumers.

conference selling A form of team selling where a salesperson and other company resource people meet with buyers to discuss problems and opportunities.
consultative selling A need-satisfaction sales presentation where the salesperson focuses on problem definition and serves as an expert on problem recognition.
consumer behaviour Actions of a person to purchase and use products and services, including the mental and social processes that precede and follow these actions.
consumer ethnocentrism The tendency to believe that it is inappropriate, indeed immoral, to purchase foreign-made products.
consumer goods Products purchased by the ultimate consumer.
consumer socialization The process by which people acquire the skills, knowledge, and attitudes necessary to function as consumers.
consumer-oriented sales promotion Sales tools used to support a company's advertising and personal selling efforts directed to ultimate consumers; examples include coupons, sweepstakes, and trading stamps.
consumerism A movement to increase the influence, power, and rights of consumers in dealing with institutions.
contest A sales promotion in which consumers apply their analytical or creative thinking to win a prize.
continuity programs Sales promotions used to encourage and reward repeat purchases by acknowledging each purchase made by a consumer and offering a premium as purchases accumulate.
continuous innovations New products that require no new learning to use.
contracting A strategy used during the decline stage of the product life cycle in which a company contracts the manufacturing or marketing of a product to another firm.
contractual vertical marketing system A channel arrangement whereby independent production and distribution firms integrate their efforts on a contractual basis to obtain greater economies and marketing impact.
convenience goods Items that the consumer purchases frequently and with a minimum of shopping effort.
cookies Computer files that a marketer can download onto the computer of an online shopper who visits the marketer's Web site.
cooperative advertising Advertising programs in which a manufacturer pays a percentage of the retailer's local advertising expense for advertising the manufacturer's products.
corporate chain A type of retail ownership in which a single firm owns multiple outlets.
corporate culture A system of shared attitudes and behaviours held by the employees that distinguish an organization from others.
corporate goals Strategic performance targets that the entire organization must reach to pursue its vision.
corporate level Level at which top management directs overall strategy for the entire organization.
corporate philosophy The values and "rules of conduct" for running an organization.
corporate takeover The purchase of a firm by outsiders.
corporate vertical marketing system A channel arrangement whereby successive stages of production and distribution are combined under a single owner.
corporate vision A clear word picture of the organization's future, often with an inspirational theme.
corporate Web site A Web site designed to accommodate interactive communication initiated by a company's employees, investors, suppliers, and customers.
cost of goods sold Total value of the products sold during a specified time period.
cost focus strategy Involves controlling expenses and, in turn, lowering prices, in a narrow range of market segments.
cost leadership strategy Using a serious commitment to reducing expenses that, in turn, lowers the price of the items sold in a wide range of market segments.
cost per thousand (CPM) The cost of reaching 1000 individuals or households with an advertising message in a given medium. (*M* is the Roman numeral for 1000.)
cost plus fixed-fee pricing A pricing method where a supplier is reimbursed for all costs, regardless of what they may be, plus a fixed percentage of the production or construction costs.
cost plus percentage-of-cost pricing Setting the price of a product or service by adding a fixed percentage to the production or construction costs.
cost-plus pricing The practice of summing the total unit cost of providing a product or service and adding a specific amount to the cost to arrive at a price.
countertrade Using barter rather than money in making global sales.
coupons Printed certificates that give the bearer a saving or a stated price reduction when they purchase a specific product.
cross-cultural analysis The study of similarities and differences between consumers in two or more nations or societies.
cross-functional teams A small number of people from different departments in an organization who are mutually accountable to a common set of performance goals.
cross-tabulation Method of presenting and relating data on two or more variables to display summary data and discover relationships in the data.
cue A stimulus or symbol perceived by the consumer.
cultural ethnocentricity The belief that aspects of one's culture are superior to another's.
cultural symbols Things that represent ideas and concepts.
culture The sets of values, ideas, and attitudes of a homogeneous group of people that are transmitted from one generation to the next.
cumulative quantity discounts The discount given to a buyer based on the accumulation of purchases of a product over a given time period, typically a year.
customary pricing A method of pricing based on a product's tradition, standardized channel of distribution, or other competitive factors.
customer contact audit A flow chart of the points of interaction between a consumer and a service provider.
customer service The ability of a logistics system to satisfy users in terms of time, dependability, communications, and convenience.
customer value The unique combination of benefits received by targeted buyers that includes quality, price, convenience, on-time delivery, and both before-sale and after-sale service.
customs Norms and expectations about the way people do things in a specific country.

database marketing An organization's effort to collect demographic, media, and consumption profiles of customers in order to target them more effectively.
deal A sales promotion that offers a short-term price reduction.
deceptive pricing A practice by which prices are artificially inflated and then marked down under the guise of a sale.
decision making The act of consciously choosing from alternatives.
decline stage The fourth and last stage of the product life cycle when sales and profitability decline.
decoding The process of having the receiver take a set of symbols, the message, and transform them back to an abstract idea.
deletion A strategy of dropping a product from the product line, usually in the decline stage of the product life cycle.
delivered pricing Practice of refusing a customer delivery of an article on the same terms as other customers in the same location.
demand curve The summation of points representing the maximum quantity of a product consumers will buy at different price levels.
demand factors Factors that determine the strength of consumers' willingness and ability to pay for goods and services.
demand-backward pricing Setting a price by estimating the price consumers would be willing to pay for goods and services.
demographics The study of the characteristics of the population.
depth interviews Detailed individual interviews with people relevant to the research project.
depth of product line The assortment of each item a store or wholesaler carries.
derived demand Sales of a product (typically industrial) that result from the sales of another item (often consumer).
desk jobber (*see* drop shipper)
development Phase of the new product process in which the idea on paper is turned into a prototype; includes manufacturing and laboratory and consumer tests.
dichotomous question A fixed alternative question that allows only a "yes" or "no" response.
differentiation focus strategy Using significant points of difference in the firm's offerings to reach one or only a few market segments.
differentiation positioning avoiding direct (head-to-head) competition by stressing unique aspects of the product.
differentiation strategy Using innovation and significant points of difference in product offerings, higher quality, advanced technology, or superior service in a wide range of market segments.
diffusion of innovation The process by which people receive new information and accept new ideas and products.
direct channel A marketing channel where a producer and ultimate consumer interact directly with each other.
direct exporting A firm selling its domestically produced goods in a foreign country without intermediaries.
direct forecast An estimate of the value to be forecast without the use of intervening steps.
direct investment In global marketing, a domestic firm actually investing in and owning a foreign subsidiary or division.
direct marketing A promotional alternative that uses direct communication with consumers to generate a response in the form of an order, a request for further information, or a visit to a retail outlet.
direct marketing channels Allow consumers to buy products by interacting with various advertising media without a face-to-face meeting with a salesperson.
direct orders The result of direct marketing offers that contain all the information necessary for a prospective buyer to make a decision to purchase and complete the transaction.
direct ownership In international trade, a domestic firm actually investing in and owning a foreign subsidiary or division.
discontinuous innovations New products that require totally new consumption patterns.
discounts Reductions from list price that a seller gives a buyer as a reward for some buyer activity favourable to the seller.
discretionary income The money that remains after taxes and necessities have been paid for.
disintermediation The practice whereby a channel member bypasses another member and sells or buys products direct.
disposable income The money a consumer has left after taxes to use for food, shelter, and clothing.
diversification A strategy of developing new products and selling them in new markets.
downsizing The practice of reducing the content of package without changing package size and maintaining or increasing the package price.
drive A stimulus that moves an individual to action.
drop shipper A merchant wholesaler that owns the merchandise it sells but does not physically handle, stock, or deliver; also called a desk jobber.
dual distribution An arrangement by which a firm reaches buyers by employing two or more different types of channels for the same basic product.
dumping When a firm sells a product in a foreign country below its domestic price.
durable good An item that lasts over an extended number of uses.
dynamically continuous innovations Products that disrupt the consumer's normal routine but do not require learning totally new behaviours.

early adopters The 13.5 percent of the population who are leaders in their social setting and act as an information source on new products for other people.
early growth The first stage of the retail life cycle, when a new outlet emerges as a sharp departure from competitive forms.
early majority The 34 percent of the population who are deliberate and rely on personal sources for information on new products.
economic infrastructure A country's communication, transportation, financial, and distribution systems.
economy The income, expenditures, and resources that affect the cost of running a business and household.
efficient consumer response (see quick response)
elastic demand A situation where a percentage decrease in price produces a larger percentage increase in quantity demanded, thereby actually increasing sales revenue.
electronic commerce Any activity that uses some form of electronic communication in the inventory, exchange, advertisement, distribution, and payment of goods and services.

electronic data interchange (EDI) Computers linked in two different firms to transmit documents such as purchase orders, bills of lading, and invoices.
elements of the marketing mix (*see* marketing mix)
emotional intelligence The ability to understand one's own emotions and the emotions of people with whom one interacts on a daily basis.
encoding The process of having the sender transform an abstract idea into a set of symbols.
environmental factors The uncontrollable factors involving social, economic, technological, competitive, and regulatory forces.
environmental scanning Acquiring information on events occurring outside the company and interpreting potential trends.
ethics The moral principles and values that govern the actions and decisions of an individual or group.
euro-branding The strategy of using the same brand name for the same product across all countries in the European Community.
evaluative criteria Both the objective and subjective attributes of a brand important to consumers when evaluating different brands or products.
everyday low pricing The practice of replacing promotional allowances given to retailers with lower manufacturer list prices.
evoked set The group of brands a consumer would consider acceptable out of the set of brands in the product class of which he or she is aware.
exchange The trade of things of value between buyer and seller so that each is better off after the trade.
exclusive dealing An arrangement a manufacturer makes with a reseller to handle only its products and not those of competitors.
exclusive distribution A distribution strategy whereby a producer sells its products or services in only one retail outlet in a specific geographical area.
exclusive territorial distributorship A manufacturer grants a reseller sole rights to sell a product in a specific geographic area.
experience curve pricing A method of pricing where price often falls following the reduction of costs associated with the firm's experience in producing or selling a product.
experiment Manipulation of an independent variable (cause) and measuring its effect on the dependent variable (effect) under controlled conditions.
exporting Producing goods in one country and selling them in another country.
express warranties Written statements of a manufacturer's liabilities for product deficiencies.
Extranet An Internet/Web-based network that permits private business-to-business communications between a company and its suppliers, distributors, and other partners.

facilitators Intermediaries that assist in the physical distribution channel by moving, storing, financing, or insuring products.
fad A product whose life cycle has two stages consisting of rapid introduction and equally quick decline.
failure fees A penalty payment made to retailers by manufacturers if a new product does not reach predetermined sales levels.
family branding (*see* multiproduct branding)
family life cycle The concept that each family progresses through a number of distinct phases, each of which is associated with identifiable purchasing behaviours.
fashion product A product whose life cycle curve may decline, then return through another life cycle.
feedback The communication flow from receiver back to sender; indicates whether the message was decoded and understood as intended.
field experiment A test of marketing variables in actual store or buying settings.
field of experience A person's understanding and knowledge; to communicate effectively, a sender and a receiver must have a mutually shared field of experience.
finance allowance A trade-oriented sales promotion in which retailers are paid for financing costs or financial losses associated with consumer sales promotions.
fixed alternative question A question in which the respondent merely checks an answer from predetermined choices.
fixed cost An expense of the firm that is stable and does not change with the quantity of product that is produced and sold.
flexible-price policy Offering the same product and quantities to similar customers, but at different prices.
flighting schedule A scheduling approach in which periods of advertising are scheduled between periods of no advertising to reflect seasonal demand.
FOB (free on board) Refers to the point at which the seller stops paying transportation costs.
FOB origin pricing A method of pricing where the title of goods passes to the buyer at the point of loading.
FOB with freight-allowed pricing A method of pricing that allows the buyer to deduct freight expenses from the list price of the product sold; also called freight absorption pricing.
focus groups Informal interview sessions of 6 to 10 persons relevant to the research project, brought together in a room with a moderator to discuss topics surrounding the marketing research problem.
follow-up stage The phase of the personal selling process that entails making certain that the customer's purchase has been properly delivered and installed and that any difficulties in using the product are promptly and satisfactorily addressed.
forced distribution markets (*see* selected controlled markets)
forgetting rate The speed with which buyers forget a brand if advertising is not seen.
form of ownership Who owns a retail outlet. Alternatives are independent, corporate chain, cooperative, or franchise.
form utility The value to consumers that comes from production or alteration of a good or service.
formula selling presentation The selling format that consists of providing information in an accurate, thorough, and step-by-step manner to persuade the prospect to buy.
forward buying A response to discounts offered by manufacturers in which supermarkets purchase more merchandise than they plan to sell during the promotion. The remaining stock is sold at regular price later, or diverted to another store.
four I's of service Four unique elements to services: intangibility, inconsistency, inseparability, and inventory.
four P's (*see* marketing mix)
franchising The contractual agreement between a parent company and an individual or firm that allows the franchisee to

operate a certain type of business under an established name and according to specific rules.
freight consolidators (*see* freight forwarders)
freight forwarders Firms that accumulate small shipments into larger lots and then hire a carrier to move them, usually at reduced rates.
frequency The average number of times a person in the target audience is exposed to a message or advertisement.
full warranty A statement of liability by a manufacturer that has no limits of noncoverage.
full-service agency An advertising agency providing a complete range of services, including market research, media selection, copy development, artwork, and production.
full-service retailer A retailer that provides a complete list of services to cater to its customers.
functional groupings Organizational groupings in which a unit is subdivided according to the different business activities within a firm, such as manufacturing, marketing, and finance.
functional level Level at which groups of specialists create value for the organization.

gap analysis An evaluation tool that compares expectations about a particular service to the actual experience a consumer has with the service.
General Agreement on Tariffs and Trade (GATT) An international treaty intended to limit trade barriers and promote world trade through the reduction of tariffs.
general merchandise stores General merchandise stores carry a broad product line with limited depth.
general merchandise wholesaler A full-service merchant wholesaler that carries a broad assortment of merchandise and performs all channel functions.
Generation X The generation of children born between 1965 and 1976.
generational marketing The use of marketing programs designed for the distinct attitudes and consumer behaviour of the cohorts, or generations, that make up the marketplace.
generic brand A branding strategy that lists no product name, only a description of contents.
generic business strategy Strategy that can be adapted by any firm, regardless of the product or industry involved, to achieve a competitive advantage.
geographical groupings Organization groupings in which a unit is subdivided according to geographical location.
global competition A competitive situation that exists when firms originate, produce, and market their products and services worldwide.
global consumers Customer groups living in many countries or regions of the world who have similar needs or seek similar features and benefits from products and services.
global marketing strategy The practice of standardizing marketing activities when there are cultural similarities and adapting them when cultures differ.
goal A targeted level of performance set in advance of work.
government units The federal, provincial, and local agencies that buy goods and services for the constituents they serve.
grey market A situation in which products are sold through unauthorized channels of distribution; also called parallel importing.
green marketing Marketing efforts to produce, promote, and reclaim environmentally sensitive products.
gross domestic product The monetary value of all goods and services produced in a country during one year.
gross income The total amount of money earned in one year by a person, family, or household.
gross margin Net sales minus cost of goods sold.
gross rating points (GRPs) A reference number for advertisers, created by multiplying reach (expressed as a percentage) by frequency.
growth stage The second stage of the product life cycle characterized by rapid increases in sales and by the appearance of competitors.

harvesting A strategy used during the decline stage of the product life cycle in which a company continues to offer a product but reduces support costs.
head-to-head positioning Competing directly with competitors on similar product attributes in the same target market.
hierarchy of effects The sequence of stages a prospective buyer goes through from initial awareness of a product to eventual action (either trial or adoption of the product). The stages include awareness, interest, evaluation, trial, and adoption.
high learning product A product that has a long introductory phase to its life cycle because significant education is required for consumers to use the item or appreciate its benefits.
horizontal conflict Disagreements between intermediaries at the same level in a marketing channel.
horizontal price fixing The practice whereby two or more competitors explicitly or implicitly collaborate to set prices.
hypermarket A large store (over 200 000 square feet) offering a mix of food products and general merchandise.

idea generation A phase of the new product process, in which a firm develops a pool of concepts as candidates for new products.
idle production capacity A situation where a service provider is available but there is no demand.
implied warranties Warranties assigning responsibility for product deficiencies to a manufacturer even though the item was sold by a retailer.
inbound telemarketing The use of toll-free telephone numbers that customers can call to obtain information about products or services and make purchases.
inconsistency A unique element of services; variation in service quality because services are delivered by people with varying capabilities.
independent retailer A retail outlet for which there is an individual owner.
indirect channel A marketing channel where intermediaries are situated between the producer and consumers.
indirect exporting A firm selling its domestically produced goods in a foreign country through an intermediary.
industrial distributor A specific type of intermediary between producers and consumers that generally sells, stocks, and delivers a full product assortment.
industrial espionage The clandestine collection of trade secrets or proprietary information about a company's competitors.

industrial firms Organizational buyers that in some way reprocess a good or service it buys before selling it again.
industrial goods Products used in the production of other items for ultimate consumers.
industry A group of firms offering products that are close substitutes for each other.
industry potential (*see* market potential)
inelastic demand A situation where a small percentage decrease in price produces a smaller percentage increase in quantity demanded.
information technology Involves designing and managing computer and communication systems to satisfy an organization's needs for data storage, processing and access.
infomercials Program length advertisements, often 30 minutes long, that take an educational approach to communicating with potential customers.
in-house agency A company's own advertising staff which may provide full services or a limited range of services.
innovators The 2.5 percent of the population who are venturesome and highly educated, use multiple information sources, and are the first to adopt a new product.
inseparability A unique element of services; the fact that a service cannot be separated from the deliverer of the service or the setting in which the service occurs.
institutional advertisement Advertisements designed to build goodwill or an image for an organization, rather than promote a specific good or service.
intangibility A unique element of services; the fact that services cannot be held, touched, or seen before the purchase decision.
integrated marketing communications The concept of designing marketing communications programs that coordinate all promotional activities—advertising, personal selling, sales promotion, direct marketing and public relations—to provide a consistent message across all audiences and to maximize the promotional budget.
intensive distribution A distribution strategy whereby a producer sells products or services in as many outlets as possible in a geographic area.
interactive marketing Buyer–seller electronic communications in a computer-mediated environment in which the buyer controls the kind and amount of information received from the seller.
intermodel transportation Combining different transportation modes in order to get the best features of each.
internal marketing The notion that a service organization must focus on its employees, or internal market, before successful programs can be directed at customers.
Internet An integrated global network of computers that gives users access to information and documents.
Internet marketing channels Channels that employ the Internet to make goods and services available for consumption or use by consumers or industrial buyers.
intertype competition Competition between dissimilar types of retail outlets brought about by scrambled merchandising.
Intranet An Internet/Web-based network used within the boundaries of an organization.
introductory phase The first stage of the product life cycle in which sales grow slowly and profit is low.
inventory (1) Physical material purchased from suppliers, which may or may not be reworked and is available for sale to customers. (2) A unique element of services; the need for and cost of having a service provider available.
involvement The personal, social, and economic significance of the purchase to the consumer.
ISO 14000 Worldwide standards for environmental quality and green marketing practices.
ISO 9000 International standards for registration and certification of a manufacturer's quality management and quality assurance system.

job analysis A written description of what a salesperson is expected to do.
job description Written document that describes job relationships and requirements that characterize each sales position.
joint venture An arrangement in which a foreign company and a local firm invest together to create a local business.
jury of executive opinion forecast Asking knowledgeable executives inside the firm about likely sales during a coming period.
jury test A pretest in which a panel of customers is shown an advertisement and asked to rate its attractiveness, how much they like it, and how much it draws their attention.
just-in-time (JIT) concept An inventory supply system that operates with very low inventories and requires fast, on-time delivery.

laboratory experiment A simulation of marketing-related activity in a highly controlled setting.
laggards The 16 percent of the market who have fear of debt, use friends for information sources, and accept ideas and products only after they have been long established in the market.
late majority The 34 percent of the population who are skeptical, below average in social status, and rely less on advertising and personal selling for information than do innovators or early adopters.
laws Society's values and standards that are enforceable in the courts.
lead generation The result of a direct marketing offer designed to generate interest in a product or a service, and a request for additional information.
lead time Lag from ordering an item until it is received and ready for use.
learning Those behaviours that result from (1) repeated experience and (2) thinking.
level of service The degree of service provided to the customer by the retailer: self, limited, or full.
licensing A contractual agreement whereby a company allows another firm to use its brand name, patent, trade secret, or other property for a royalty or fee.
lifestyle A mode of living that is identified by how people spend their time and resources (activities), what they consider important in their environment (interests), and what they think of themselves and the world around them (opinions).
Likert scale A fixed alternative question in which the respondent indicates the extent to which he agrees or disagrees with a statement.

limited-coverage warranty A manufacturer's statement indicating the bounds of coverage and noncoverage for any product deficiencies.
limited-line store A retail outlet, such as a sporting goods store, that offers considerable assortment, or depth, of a related line of items.
limited-service agency An agency that specializes in one aspect of the advertising process such as providing creative services to develop the advertising copy or buying previously unpurchased media space.
limited-service retailer A retailer that provides selected services such as credit or merchandise return to customers.
line extension The practice of using a current brand name to enter a new market segment in its product class.
line positions People in line positions, such as group marketing managers, have the authority and responsibility to issue orders to the people who report to them, such as marketing managers.
logistics management Organizing the cost-effective flow of raw materials, in-process inventory, finished goods, and related information from point of origin to point of consumption to satisfy customer requirements.
loss-leader pricing Deliberately pricing a product below its customary price to attract attention to it.
lost-horse forecast Starting with the last known value of the item being forecast, listing the factors that could affect the forecast, assessing whether they have a positive or negative impact, and making the final forecast.
low-learning product A product that has an immediate gain in sales in the introductory phase because the benefits are easily observed by consumers and little education is required to use it.

macromarketing The study of the aggregate flow of a nation's goods and services to benefit society.
mail-order retailer A retailing operation in which merchandise is offered to customers by mail.
maintained markup The difference between the final selling price and retailer cost; also called gross margin.
major account management The practice of using team selling to focus on important customers to build mutually beneficial long-term, cooperative relationships.
make-buy decision An evaluation of whether a product or its parts will be purchased from outside suppliers or built by the firm.
management by exception A tool used by a marketing manager that involves identifying results that deviate from plans, diagnosing their cause, making appropriate new plans, and taking new actions.
manufacturer branding A branding strategy in which the brand name for a product is designated by the producer, using either a multiproduct or multibranding approach.
manufacturer's agents Individuals or firms that work for several producers and carry noncompetitive, complementary merchandise in an exclusive territory; also called manufacturer's representatives.
manufacturer's branch office A wholly owned extension of a producer that performs channel functions, including carrying inventory, generally performed by a full-service merchant wholesaler.
marginal analysis Principle of allocating resources that balances incremental revenues of an action against incremental costs.
marginal cost The change in total cost that results from producing and marketing one additional unit.
marginal revenue The change in total revenue obtained by selling one additional unit.
markdown Reduction in retail price usually expressed as a percentage equal to the amount reduced, divided by the original price and multiplied by 100.
market People with the desire and ability to buy a specific product.
market-based groupings Organizational groupings that assign responsibility for a specific type of customer to a unit.
market development Selling existing products to new markets.
market growth rate The annual rate of growth of the specific market or industry in which a firm or SBU is competing; often used as the vertical axis in business portfolio analysis.
market modification Attempts to increase product usage by creating new-use situations or finding new customers.
market orientation Focusing organizational efforts on (1) continuously collecting information about customers' needs and competitors' capabilities, (2) sharing this information across departments, and (3) using the information to create customer value.
market penetration A strategy of increasing sales of present products in their existing markets.
market potential Maximum total sales of a product by all firms to a segment under specified environmental conditions and marketing efforts of the firms (also called industry potential).
market segmentation Aggregating prospective buyers into groups, or segments, that (1) have common needs and (2) will respond similarly to a marketing action.
market segments The groups that result from the process of market segmentation; a relatively homogeneous collection of prospective buyers.
market share The ratio of sales revenue of the firm to the total sales revenue of all firms in the industry, including the firm itself.
market testing A phase of the new product process, in which prospective consumers are exposed to actual products under realistic purchase conditions to see if they will buy.
market-product grid Framework for relating market segments to products offered or potential marketing actions by a firm.
marketing The process of planning and executing the conception, pricing, promotion, and distribution of ideas, goods, and services to create exchanges that satisfy individual and organizational objectives.
marketing audit A comprehensive, unbiased, periodic review of the strategic marketing process of a firm or a strategic business unit (SBU).
marketing channel People and firms involved in the process of making a product or service available for use or consumption by consumers or industrial users.
marketing concept The idea that an organization should (1) strive to satisfy the needs of consumers (2) while also trying to achieve the organization's goals.
marketing mix The marketing manager's controllable factors of product, price, promotion, and place he or she can take to solve a marketing problem.
marketing orientation When an organization focuses its efforts on (1) continuously collecting information about customers' needs and competitors' capabilities, (2) sharing this

information across departments, and (3) using the information to create customer value.

marketing plan A roadmap for the marketing activities of an organization for a specified future period of time, such as one year or five years.

marketing program A plan that integrates the marketing mix to provide a good, service, or idea to prospective consumers.

marketing research The process of defining a marketing problem and opportunity, systematically collecting and analyzing information, and recommending actions to improve an organization's marketing activities.

marketing strategy The means by which a marketing goal is to be achieved, characterized by (1) a specified target market and (2) a marketing program to reach it.

marketing tactics The detailed day-to-day operational decisions essential to the overall success of marketing strategies.

marketing Web site A Web site designed to engage consumers in interactive communication or dialogue that will result in the sale of a company's product or service or move the consumer closer to a purchase.

marketspace An information- and communication-based electronic exchange environment mostly occupied by sophisticated computer and telecommunication technologies and digitized offerings.

markup The amount added to the cost of goods sold to arrive at a selling price, expressed in dollar or percentage terms.

mass customization Tailoring goods or services to the tastes of individual customers in high volumes at a relatively low cost.

materials handling Moving goods over short distances into, within, and out of warehouses and manufacturing plants.

mature households Households headed by people over age 50.

maturity phase The third stage of the product or retail life cycle in which market share levels off and profitability declines.

merchandise allowance A trade-oriented sales promotion in which a retailer is reimbursed for extra in-store support or special featuring of the brand.

merchandise line The number of different types of products and the assortment a store carries.

message The information sent by a source to a receiver in the communication process.

micromarketing How an organization directs its marketing activities and allocates its resources to benefit its customers.

missionary salespeople Sales support personnel who do not directly solicit orders but rather concentrate on performing promotional activities and introducing new products.

mixed branding A branding strategy in which the company may market products under their own name and that of a reseller.

modified rebuy A buying situation in which the users, influencers, or deciders change the product specifications, price, delivery schedule, or supplier.

monopolistic competition A competitive setting in which a large number of sellers offer unique but substitutable products.

monopoly A competitive setting in which there is a single seller of a good or service.

moral idealism A personal moral philosophy that considers certain individual rights or duties as universal regardless of the outcome.

motivation Motivation is the energizing force that causes behaviour that satisfies a need.

multibranding A manufacturer's branding strategy in which a distinct name is given to each of its products.

multidomestic marketing strategy A firm's worldwide marketing strategy that offers as many different product variations, brand names, and advertising programs as countries in which it does business.

multiple-zone pricing Pricing products the same when delivered within one of several specified zones or geographical areas, but with different prices for each zone depending on demand, competition, and distance: also called zone-delivered pricing.

multiproduct branding A branding strategy in which a company uses one name for all products; also called blanket or family branding.

national character A distinct set of personality characteristics common among people of a country or society.

need That which occurs when a person feels deprived of food, clothing, or shelter.

need-satisfaction presentation A selling format that emphasizes probing and listening by the salesperson to identify needs and interests of perspective buyers.

new buy The first-time purchase of a product or service, characterized by greater potential risk.

new-product concept A tentative description of a product or service a firm might offer for sale.

new-product process The sequence of activities a firm uses to identify business opportunities and convert them to a saleable good or service. There are seven steps: new-product strategy, idea generation, screening and evaluation, business analysis, development, testing, and commercialization.

new-product strategy development The phase of the new-product process in which a firm defines the role of new products in terms of overall corporate objectives.

news conference A publicity tool consisting of an informational meeting with representatives of the media who received advanced materials on the meeting content.

news release A publicity tool consisting of an announcement regarding changes in the company or product line.

noise Extraneous factors that work against effective communication by distorting a message or the feedback received.

noncumulative quantity discounts Price reductions based on the size of an individual purchase order.

nondurable good An item consumed in one or a few uses.

nonprobability sampling Using arbitrary judgments to select the sample so that the chance of selecting a particular element may be unknown or zero.

nonprofit organization A nongovernmental organization that serves its customers but does not have profit as an organizational goal.

nonrepetitive decisions Those decisions unique to a particular time and situation.

North American Industry Classification System (NAICS) A system for classifying organizations on the basis of major activity or the major good or service provided used by the three NAFTA countries—Canada, Mexico, and the United States.

objective and task budgeting A budgeting approach whereby the company (1) determines its advertising objectives,

(2) outlines the tasks to accomplish the objectives, and (3) determines the advertising cost of performing these tasks.
objectives Specific, measurable performance targets and deadlines.
observation Watching, either mechanically or in person, how people actually behave.
odd-even pricing Setting prices a few dollars or cents under an even number, such as $19.95.
off-peak pricing Charging different prices during different times of the day or days of the week to reflect variations in demand for the service.
off-price retailing Selling brand name merchandise at lower than regular prices.
oligopoly A competitive setting in which a few large companies control a large amount of an industry's sales.
one-price policy Setting the same price for similar customers who buy the same product and quantities under the same conditions.
one-price stores A form of off-price retailing in which all items in a store are sold at one low price.
open-end question A question that a respondent can answer in his or her own words.
opinion leaders Individuals who exert direct or indirect social influence over others.
order cycle time (*see* lead time)
order getter A salesperson who sells in a conventional sense and engages in identifying prospective customers, providing customers with information, persuading customers to buy, closing sales, and following on customer experience with product or service.
order taker A salesperson who processes routine orders and reorders for products that have already been sold by the company.
organizational buyers Units such as manufacturers, retailers, or government agencies that buy goods and services for their own use or for resale.
organizational buying behaviour The decision-making process that organizations use to establish the need for products and identify, evaluate, and choose among alternative brands and suppliers.
organizational buying criteria The objective attributes of the supplier's products and services and the capabilities of the supplier itself.
organizational goals Specific objectives a business or nonprofit unit seeks to achieve and by which it can measure its performance.
original markup The difference between retailer cost and initial selling price.
outbound telemarketing Use of the telephone rather than personal visits to contact customers.
outsourcing Contracting work that formerly was done in-house by employees such as those in marketing research, advertising, and public relations departments to small, outside firms.

Pacific Rim The area of the world consisting of countries in Asia and Australia.
packaging The container in which a product is offered for sale and on which information is communicated.
panel A sample of consumers or stores from which researchers take a series of measurements.
parallel development An approach to new product development that involves the simultaneous development of the product and production process.
partnership selling The practice whereby buyers and sellers combine their expertise and resources to create customized solutions, commit to joint planning, and share customer, competitive, and company information for their mutual benefit, and ultimately the customer.
penetration pricing Pricing a product low in order to discourage competition from entering the market.
perceived risk The anxieties felt because the consumer cannot anticipate the outcome but sees that there might be negative consequences.
percent of sales budgeting Allocating funds to advertising as a percentage of past or anticipated sales, in terms of either dollars or units sold.
perception The process by which an individual selects, organizes, and interprets information to create a meaningful picture of the world.
perceptual map A graph displaying consumers' perceptions of product attributes across two dimensions.
personal selling The two-way flow of communication between a buyer and seller, often in a face-to-face encounter, designed to influence a person's or group's purchase decision.
personal selling process Sales activities occurring before and after the sale itself, consisting of six stages: (1) prospecting, (2) preapproach, (3) approach, (4) presentation, (5) close, and (6) follow-up.
personality A person's consistent behaviours or responses to recurring situations.
physical distribution management Organizing the movement and storage of finished product to the customer.
piggyback franchising A variation of franchising in which stores operated by one chain sell the products or services of another franchised firm.
pioneering advertisements Advertisements that tell what a product is, what it can do, and where it can be found.
pioneering institutional advertisements Institutional advertisements about what a company is or can do or where it is located.
place-based media Advertising media alternative that places messages in locations that attract a specific target audience such as airports, doctor's offices, and health clubs.
place utility The value to consumers of having a good or service available where needed.
point-of-purchase displays Displays located in high-traffic areas in retail stores, often next to checkout counters.
points of difference Those characteristics of a product that make it superior to competitive substitutes.
portals Electronic gateways to the World Wide Web that supply a broad array of news and entertainment, information resources and shopping services.
portfolio test A pretest in which a test ad is placed in a portfolio with other ads and consumers are questioned on their impressions of the ads.
possession utility The value of making an item easy to purchase through the provision of credit cards or financial arrangements.
posttests Tests conducted after an advertisement has been shown to the target audience to determine whether it has accomplished its intended purpose.

power centre Large strip malls with multiple anchor (or national stores), a convenient location, and a supermarket.
preapproach stage The stage of the personal selling process that involves obtaining further information about a prospect and deciding on the best method of approach.
precycling Efforts by manufacturers to reduce waste by decreasing the amount of packaging they use on products.
premium A sales promotion that consists of offering merchandise free or at significant savings over retail.
presentation stage The core of the personal selling process in which the salesperson tries to convert the prospect into a customer by creating a desire for the product or service.
prestige pricing Setting a high price so that status-conscious consumers will be attracted to the product.
pretests Tests conducted before an advertisement is placed to determine whether it communicates the intended message or to select between alternative versions of an advertisement.
price The money or other considerations exchanged for the purchase or use of the product, idea, or service.
price discrimination The practice of charging different prices to different buyers for goods of like trade and quality.
price elasticity of demand The percentage change in quantity demanded relative to a percentage change in price.
price fixing A conspiracy among firms to set prices for a product.
price lining Setting the price of a line of products at a number of different specific pricing points.
pricing constraints Factors that limit a firm's latitude in the price it may set.
pricing objectives Goals that specify the role of price in an organization's marketing and strategic plans.
primary data Data gathered and assembled specifically for the project at hand.
primary demand Desire for a product class rather than for a specific brand.
private branding When a company manufactures products that are sold under the name of a wholesaler or retailer.
proactive strategies New product strategies that involve an aggressive allocation of resources to identify opportunities for product development.
probability sampling Using precise rules to select the sample such that each element of the population has a specific known chance of being selected.
product A good, service, or idea consisting of a bundle of tangible and intangible attributes that satisfies consumers and is received in exchange for money or other unit of value.
product advertisements Advertisements that focus on selling a good or service and take three forms: (1) pioneering (or informational), (2) competitive (or persuasive), and (3) reminder.
product (program) champion A person who is able and willing to cut red tape and move a product or program forward.
product class An entire product category or industry.
product counterfeiting Low cost copies of a popular brand, not manufactured by the original producer.
product development A strategy of selling a new product to existing markets.
product differentiation A strategy having different but related meanings; it involves a firm's using different marketing mix activities, such as product featuring and advertising, to help consumers perceive the product as being different and better than other products.
product form Variations of a product within a product class.
product item A specific product noted by a unique brand, size, and price.
product life cycle The life of a product over four stages: introduction, growth, maturity, and decline.
product line A group of products closely related because they satisfy a class of needs, are used together, are sold to the same customer group, are distributed through the same outlets, or fall within a given price range.
product line groupings Organizational groupings in which a unit is responsible for specific product offerings.
product line pricing The setting of prices for all items in a product line.
product manager A person who plans, implements, and controls the annual and long-range plans for the products for which he or she is responsible.
product mix The number of product lines offered by a company.
product modifications Strategies of altering a product characteristic, such as quality, performance, or appearance.
product placement Advertising media alternative in which the manufacturer pays for the privilege of having a brand name product used in a movie.
product positioning The place an offering occupies in consumers' minds on important attributes relative to competitive offerings.
product repositioning Changing the place an offering occupies in a consumer's mind relative to competitive products.
production goods Products used in the manufacturing of other items that become part of the final product.
profit A business firm's reward for the risk it undertakes in offering a product for sale; the money left over after a firm's total expenses are subtracted from its total revenues.
profit equation Profit = Total revenue – Total cost.
profit responsibility The view that companies have a single obligation, which is to maximize profits for its owners or shareholders.
profitability analysis A means of measuring the profitability of the firm's products, customer groups, sales territories, channels of distribution, and order sizes.
program schedule A formal time-line chart showing the relationships through time of the various program tasks.
promotional allowance The cash payment or extra amount of "free goods" awarded sellers in the channel of distribution for undertaking certain advertising or selling activities to promote a product.
promotional mix The combination of one or more of the promotional elements a firm uses to communicate with consumers. The promotional elements include: advertising, personal selling, sales promotion, and public relations.
prospecting stage In the personal selling process, the search for and qualification of potential customers.
protectionism The practice of shielding one or more sectors of a country's economy from foreign competition through the use of tariffs, or quotas.
protocol In the new product development process, an early statement that identifies a well-defined target market; specifies customers' needs, wants, and preferences; and states what the product will be and do.

psychographics Characteristics represented by personality and lifestyle traits (activities, interests, and opinions).
public relations A form of communication management that seeks to influence the feelings, opinions, or beliefs held by customers, shareholders, suppliers, employees, and other publics about a company and its products or services.
public service announcement (PSA) A publicity tool that uses free space or time donated by the media.
publicity A nonpersonal, indirectly paid presentation of an organization, good, or service.
publicity tools Methods of obtaining nonpersonal presentation of an organization, good, or service without direct cost. Examples include news releases, news conferences, and public service announcements.
pull strategy Directing the promotional mix at ultimate consumers to encourage them to ask the retailer for the product.
pulse schedule The combination of a steady schedule and a flighting schedule because of increases in demand, heavy periods of promotion, or introduction of a new product.
purchase decision process Steps or stages a buyer passes through in making choices about which products to buy.
purchase frequency The frequency of purchase of a specific product.
pure competition A competitive setting in which a large number of sellers compete with similar products.
push strategy Directing the promotional mix to channel members or intermediaries to gain their cooperation in ordering and stocking a product.

quality Those features and characteristics of a product that influence its ability to satisfy customer needs.
quantity discounts Reductions in unit costs for a larger order quantity.
questionnaire data Facts and figures obtained by asking people about their attitudes, awareness, intentions, and behaviours.
quick response An inventory management system designed to reduce the retailer's lead time for receiving merchandise.
quota A restriction placed on the amount of a product allowed to enter or leave a country.

rack jobber A merchant wholesaler that furnishes racks or shelves to display merchandise in retail stores, performs all channel functions, and sells on consignment.
rating (TV or radio) The percentage of households in a market that are tuned to a particular TV show or radio station.
reach The number of different people or households exposed to an advertisement.
reactive strategies New product strategies are defensive approaches in response to competitors' new items by developing new products.
rebate A sales promotion in which money is returned to the consumer based on proof of purchase.
receivers The consumers who read, hear, or see the message sent by a source in the communication process.
reciprocity An industrial buying practice in which two organizations agree to purchase products from each other.
recycling The use of technological developments to allow products to go through the manufacturing cycle several times.
reference group People to whom a person turns as a standard of self-appraisal or source of personal standards.
regional marketing A form of geographical segmentation that develops marketing plans to reflect specific area differences in taste preferences, perceived needs, or interests.
regional rollouts Introducing a new product sequentially into geographical areas to allow production levels and marketing activities to build up gradually.
regional shopping centres Suburban malls with up to 100 stores that typically draw customers from a 8 to 16-km radius, usually containing one or two anchor stores.
regulation The laws placed on business with regard to the conduct of its activities.
reinforcement A reward that tends to strengthen a response.
relationship marketing Linking the organization to its individual customers, employees, suppliers, and other partners for their mutual long-term benefits.
relationship selling The practice of building ties to customers based on a salesperson's attention and commitment to customer needs over time.
relative market share The sales of a firm or SBU divided by the sales of the largest firm in the industry; often used as a horizontal axis in business portfolio analysis.
reminder advertisements Advertisements used to reinforce previous knowledge of a product.
reminder institutional advertisements Institutional advertisements that bring a company's name to the attention of the target market.
repeat purchasers People who tried the product, were satisfied, and buy again.
repetitive decisions Decisions repeated at standard intervals during the work year.
replenishment time (*see* lead time)
repositioning Changing the place an offering occupies in a consumer's mind relative to competitive offerings.
requirements contract A contract that requires a buyer to meet all or part of its needs for a product from one seller for a period of time.
reseller A wholesaler or retailer that buys physical products and resells them again without any processing.
restructuring (reengineering or streamlining) Striving for more efficient corporations that can compete globally by reducing duplicate efforts in multiple company locations, closing or changing unprofitable plants and offices, and laying off employees.
retail life cycle A concept that describes a retail operation over four stages: early growth, accelerated development, maturity, and decline.
retailer-sponsored cooperative chain A contractual system involving independently owned stores that bind together to act like a chain.
retailing All the activities that are involved in selling, renting, and providing goods and services to ultimate consumers for personal, family, or household use.
retailing mix The strategic components that a retailer manages, including goods and services, physical distribution, and communication tactics.
retailing positioning matrix A framework for positioning retail outlets in terms of breadth of product line and value-added.

return on investment (ROI) The ratio of after-tax net profit to the investment used to earn that profit.
returns Refunds or credit granted a customer for an item returned to the seller.
reverse logistics The process of reclaiming recyclable and reusable materials, returns, and reworks from the point-of-consumption or use for repair, remanufacturing, or disposal.
reverse marketing The effort by organizational buyers to build relationships that shape suppliers' products, services, and capabilities to fit a buyer's needs and those of its customers.
rich media Online promotion, such as banner advertising, that utilizes the audio, video, and interactive capabilities of the Internet to attract more attention from viewers and to provide an element of entertainment to the message.

sales analysis A tool for controlling marketing programs where sales records are used to compare actual results with sales goals and to identify strengths and weaknesses.
sales component analysis A tool for controlling marketing programs that traces sales revenues to their sources such as specific products, sales territories, or customers.
sales engineer A salesperson who specializes in identifying, analyzing, and solving customer problems and who brings technological expertise to the selling situations, but does not actually sell goods and services.
salesforce automation The use of technology designed to make the sales function more effective and efficient.
salesforce survey forecast Asking the firm's salespeople to estimate sales during a coming period.
sales forecast What one firm expects to sell under specified conditions for the uncontrollable and controllable factors that affect the forecast.
sales management Planning, implementing, and controlling the personal selling effort of the firm.
sales plan A statement describing what is to be achieved and where and how the selling effort of salespeople is to be deployed.
sales promotion A short-term inducement of value offered to arouse interest in buying a good or service.
sales response function The relationship between the expense of marketing effort and the marketing results obtained. Measures of marketing results include sales revenue, profit, units sold, and level of awareness.
samples A sales promotion consisting of offering a product free or at a greatly reduced price.
sampling The process of gathering data from a proportion of the total population rather than from all members of that particular population.
scrambled merchandising Offering several unrelated product lines in a single retail store.
screening and evaluation The phase of the new product process in which a firm uses internal and external evaluations to eliminate ideas that warrant no further development effort.
seasonal discounts Price reductions granted buyers for purchasing products and stocking them at a time when they are not wanted by customers.
secondary data Data previously collected and assembled for some project other than the project at hand.
selected controlled markets These sites also referred to as forced distribution markets are where a market test for a new product is conducted by an outside agency and retailers are paid to display the new product.
selective demand Demand for a specific brand within a product class.
selective distribution A distribution strategy whereby a producer sells its products in a few retail outlets in a specific geographical area.
selective perception The tendency for humans to filter or choose information from a complex environment so they can make sense of the world.
self-concept The way people see themselves and the way they believe others see them.
self-liquidating premium A sales promotion offering merchandise at a significant cost savings to the customer, its price covering the cost of the premium for the company.
self-regulation An industry policing itself rather than relying on government controls.
selling agent A person or firm that represents a single producer and is responsible for all marketing functions of that producer.
semantic differential scale A seven-point scale in which the opposite ends have one- or two-word adjectives with opposite meanings.
seminar selling A form of team selling where a company team conducts an educational program for a customer's technical staff describing state-of-the-art developments.
semiotics The field of study that examines the correspondence between symbols and their role in the assignment of meaning for people.
sensitivity analysis Asking "What if . . . " questions to determine how changes in a factor like pricing or advertising affect marketing results like sales revenues or profits.
service continuum A range from the tangible to the intangible or good-dominant to service-dominant offerings available in the marketplace.
services Activities, deeds, or other basic intangibles offered for sale to consumers in exchange for money or something else of value.
share points Percentage points of market share; often used as the common basis of comparison to allocate marketing resources effectively.
shelf life The time a product can be stored before it spoils.
shopping goods Products for which the consumer will compare several alternatives on various criteria.
shrinkage A term used by retailers to describe theft of merchandise by customers and employees.
single-line store A store that offers tremendous depth in one primary line of merchandise; for example, a running shoe store.
single-source data Information provided by a single firm on household demographics and lifestyle, purchases, TV viewing behaviour, and responses to promotions like coupons and free samples.
single-zone pricing Pricing policy in which all buyers pay the same delivered product price, regardless of their distance from the seller; also known as uniform delivered pricing or postage stamp pricing.
situation analysis Taking stock of where the firm or product has been recently, where it is now, and where it is headed in terms of the organization's plans and the external factors and trends affecting it.

situational influences A situation's effect on the nature and scope of the decision process. These include (1) the purchase task, (2) social surroundings, (3) physical surroundings, (4) temporal effects, and (5) antecedent states.
skimming pricing A high initial price attached to a product to help a company recover the cost of development.
slotting fees Payment by a manufacturer to place a new product on retailer's shelf.
social audit A systematic assessment of a firm's objectives, strategies, and performance in the domain of social responsibility.
social classes The relatively permanent and homogeneous divisions in a society of people or families sharing similar values, interests, and behaviour.
social forces The characteristics of the population, its values, and its behaviour in a particular environment.
social responsibility The idea that organizations are part of a larger society and are accountable to society for their actions.
societal marketing concept The view that an organization should discover and satisfy the needs of its customers in a way that also provides for society's well-being.
societal responsibility The view that firms have obligations to preserve the ecological environment and benefit the general public.
source A company or person who has information to convey.
special merchandise wholesaler A full-service merchant wholesaler that offers a relatively narrow range of products but has an extensive assortment within the products carried.
specialty outlet Retailers that offer large selections in a narrow range of products.
specialty goods Products that a consumer will make a special effort to search out and buy.
splitting 30s Reducing the length of a standard commercial from 30 seconds to 15 seconds.
staff positions People in staff positions have the authority and responsibility to advise people in the line positions but cannot issue direct orders to them.
stakeholder responsibility The view that an organization has an obligation only to those constituencies that can affect achievement of its objectives.
standard markets Sites where companies test market a product through normal distribution channels and monitor the results.
standard markup pricing Setting prices by adding a fixed percentage to the cost of all items in a specific product class.
Starch test A posttest that assesses the extent of consumers' recognition of an advertisement appearing in a magazine they have read.
statistical inference Drawing conclusions about a population from a sample taken from that population.
steady schedule A scheduling approach in which advertising is run at a steady schedule throughout the year; sometimes called "drip" scheduling.
stimulus discrimination The ability to perceive differences in stimuli.
stimulus generalization When a response elicited by one stimulus (cue) is generalized to another stimulus.
stimulus-response presentation A selling format that assumes the prospect will buy if given the appropriate stimulus by a salesperson.
stock keeping unit (SKU) A distinct ordering number to identify a product item.
store audits Measurements of the sales of the product in stores and the number of cases ordered by a store from the wholesaler.
straight commission compensation plan A compensation plan where the salesperson's earnings are directly tied to his sales or profit generated.
straight rebuy The reordering of an existing product or service from the list of acceptable suppliers, generally without checking with the various users or influencers.
straight salary compensation plan A compensation plan where the salesperson is paid a fixed amount per week, month, or year.
strategic alliances Agreements between two or more independent firms to cooperate for the purpose of achieving common goals.
strategic business unit (SBU) A decentralized profit centre of a large firm that is treated as though it were a separate, independent business.
strategic channel alliances A practice whereby one firm's marketing channel is used to sell another firm's products.
strategic marketing process The activities whereby an organization allocates its marketing mix resources to reach its target markets.
strip location A cluster of stores that serves people who live within a 5- to 10-minute drive in a population base of under 30 000.
subcultures Subgroups within the larger or national culture with unique values, ideas, and attitudes.
subliminal perception Means that a person sees or hears messages without being aware of them.
supply chain A sequence of firms that perform activities required to create and deliver a good or service to consumers or industrial users.
supply chain management The integration and organization of information and logistic activities across firms in a supply chain for the purpose of creating and delivering goods and services that provide value to customers.
supply partnerships A relationship between an organizational buyer and its supplier created to adopt mutually beneficial efforts to lower the cost and/or increase value delivered to the ultimate consumer.
support goods Items used to assist in the production of other goods.
survey A research technique used to generate data by asking people questions and recording their responses on a questionnaire.
survey of buyers' intentions forecast A method of forecasting sales that involves asking prospective customers whether they are likely to buy the product or service during some future time period.
survey of experts forecast Asking experts on a topic to make a judgment about some future event.
sustainable competitive advantage A strength, relative to competitors, in the markets served and the products offered.
sweepstakes Sales promotions consisting of a game of chance requiring no analytical or creative effort to win a prize.
SWOT analysis An acronym describing an organization's appraisal of its internal strengths and weaknesses and its external opportunities and threats.

synergy The increased customer value achieved through performing organizational functions more efficiently.

target market One or more specific groups of potential consumers toward which an organization directs its marketing program.
target pricing The practice of deliberately adjusting the composition and features of a product to achieve the target price to consumers.
target profit pricing Setting a price based on an annual specific dollar target volume of profit.
target return-on-investment pricing Setting a price to achieve a return-on-investment target.
target return-on-sales pricing Setting a price to achieve a profit that is a specified percentage of the sales volume.
tariff A government tax on goods or services entering a country.
team selling Using a group of professionals in selling to and servicing major customers.
technological forecast Estimating when scientific breakthroughs will occur.
technology An environmental force that includes inventions or innovations from applied science or engineering research.
telemarketing Involves the use of the telephone to interact with and sell directly to consumers.
test marketing The process of offering a product for sale on a limited basis in a defined area to gain consumer reaction to the actual product and to examine its commercial viability and the marketing program.
theatre test A pretest in which consumers view test ads in new television shows or movies and report their feelings on electronic recording devices or questionnaires.
third-party logistics providers Firms that perform most or all of the logistics functions that manufacturers, suppliers, and distributors would normally perform themselves.
time utility The value to consumers of having a good or service available when needed.
timing The issue of deciding when to discount the price of merchandise.
top-down forecast Subdividing an aggregate forecast into its principal components.
total cost The total expense a firm incurs in producing and marketing a product, which includes fixed cost and variable cost; in physical distribution decisions, the sum of all applicable costs for logistical activities.
total logistics cost Expenses associated with transportation, materials handling and warehousing, inventory, stockouts, and order processing.
total revenue The total amount of money received from the sale of a product.
trade (functional) discounts Price reductions granted to wholesalers or retailers on the basis of future marketing functions they will perform for the manufacturer.
trade feedback effect A country's imports affect its exports and exports affect imports.
trade name The commercial, legal name under which a company does business.
trade-oriented sales promotions Sales tools used to support a company's advertising and personal selling efforts directed to wholesalers, distributors, or retailers. Three common approaches are allowances, cooperative advertising, and salesforce training.
trademark Legal identification of a company's exclusive rights to use a brand name or trade name.
trading down Reducing the number of features, quality, or price of a product.
trading up Adding value to a product by including more features or higher-quality materials.
traffic generation The outcome of a direct marketing offer designed to motivate people to visit a business.
trend extrapolation Extending a pattern observed in past data into the future.
trial The initial purchase of a product by the consumer.
truck jobber Small merchant wholesalers that usually handle limited assortments of fast-moving or perishable items that are sold directly from trucks for cash.

ultimate consumers People who use the goods and services purchased for a household; sometimes also called ultimate users.
uncontrollable factors (*see* environmental factors)
uniform delivered pricing A geographical pricing practice where the price the seller quotes includes all transportation costs.
unit train A train that is dedicated to one commodity, is loaded and unloaded with sophisticated equipment, and runs from origin to destination at high speed.
unit variable cost Variable cost expressed on a per unit basis.
unitary demand elasticity A situation where the percentage change in price is identical to the percentage change in quantity demanded.
universal product code (UPC) A number assigned to identify each product, represented by a series of bars of varying widths for scanning by optical readers.
unsought goods Products that the consumer does not know about or knows about and does not initially want.
usage rate Refers to quantity consumed or patronage during a specific period, and varies significantly among different customer groups.
utilitarianism A personal moral philosophy that focuses on the "greatest good for the greatest number" by assessing the costs and benefits of the consequences of ethical behaviour.
utility The benefits or customer value received by users of the product.

value Specifically, value can be defined as the ratio of perceived quality to price (Value = Perceived benefits/Price).
value added In retail strategy decisions, a dimension of the retail positioning matrix that refers to the service level and method of operation of the retailer.
value analysis A systematic appraisal of the design, quality, and performance requirements of a product to reduce purchasing costs.
value consciousness Consumer concern for obtaining the best quality, features, and performance of a product or service for a given price.
value pricing The practice of simultaneously increasing service and product benefits and maintaining or decreasing price.
values Personally or socially preferable modes of conduct or states of existence that are enduring.

variable cost An expense of the firm that varies directly with the quantity of product produced and sold.
vending machines A retailing operation in which products are stored in and sold from machines.
vendor-managed inventory An inventory management system whereby the supplier determines the product amount and assortment a customer (such as a retailer) needs and automatically delivers the appropriate items.
venture teams Multidisciplinary groups of marketing, manufacturing, and R&D personnel who stay with a new product from conception to production.
vertical conflict Disagreement between different levels in a marketing channel.
vertical marketing systems Professionally managed and centrally coordinated marketing channels designed to achieve channel economies and maximum marketing impact.
vertical price fixing The practice whereby sellers are required to not sell products below a minimum retail price, sometimes called resale price maintenance.

want A need that is shaped by a person's knowledge, culture, and individual characteristics.
warehouse A location, often decentralized, that a firm uses to store, consolidate, age, or mix stock; house product-recall programs; or ease tax burdens.
warehouse clubs Large retail stores (over 100 000 square feet) that require a yearly fee to shop at the store.
warranty A statement indicating the liability of the manufacturer for product deficiencies.
wasted coverage People outside a company's target audience who see, hear, or read the company's advertisement.
webcasting The practice of pushing out corporate and marketing Web site information to online consumers rather than waiting for them to find the site on their own.
Web communities Web sites that cater to a particular group of individuals who share a common interest.
wheel of retailing A concept that describes how new retail outlets enter the market as low-status, low-margin stores and change gradually in terms of status and margin.
whistleblowers Employees who report unethical or illegal actions of their employers.
wholesaler-sponsored voluntary chain A contractual system involving independently owned wholesalers who band together to act like a chain.
word of mouth People influencing each other during their face-to-face conversations.
workload method A formula-based method for determining the size of a salesforce that integrates the number of customers served, call frequency, call length, and available time to arrive at a salesforce size.
World Trade Organization An institution that sets rules governing trade among its members through a panel of experts.
World Wide Web A part of the Internet that supports a retrieval system that formats information and documents into Web pages.

yield management pricing The charging of different prices to maximize revenue for a set amount of capacity at a given time.

CHAPTER NOTES

CHAPTER 1

1. Personal interview with David Samuels, February 1999.
2. Information supplied by Bauer Canada, May 1999.
3. Steven A. Meyerowitz, "Surviving Assaults on Trademarks," *Marketing Management* (no. 1, 1994), pp. 44–46; and Carrie Goerne, "Rollerblade Reminds Everyone That Its Success Is Not Generic," *Marketing News* (March 2, 1992), pp. 1–2.
4. Peter D. Bennett, *Dictionary of Marketing Terms,* 2nd ed. (Lincolnwood, IL: NTC Publishing Group, 1995), p. 166.
5. Frederick E. Webster, Jr., "The Changing Role of Marketing in the Corporation," *Journal of Marketing* (October 1992), pp. 1–17; and Jagdish N. Sheth and Rajendra S. Sisodia, "Feeling the Heat," *Marketing Management* (Fall 1995), pp. 9–23.
6. Richard P. Bagozzi, "Marketing as Exchange," *Journal of Marketing* (October 1975), pp. 32–39; and Gregory T. Gundlach and Patrick E. Murphy, "Ethical and Legal Foundations of Relational Marketing Exchanges," *Journal of Marketing* (October 1993), pp. 35–46.
7. E. Jerome McCarthy, *Basic Marketing: A Managerial Approach* (Homewood, IL: Richard D. Irwin, 1960); and Walter van Waterschoot and Christophe Van den Bulte, "The 4P Classification of the Marketing Mix Revisited," *Journal of Marketing* (October 1992), pp. 83–93.
8. James Surowiecki, "The Return of Michael Porter," *Fortune* (February 1999), pp. 135–38; and Kathleen M. Eisenhardt and Shona L. Brown, "Time Pacing: Competing in Markets That Won't Stand Still," *Harvard Business Review* (March–April 1998), pp. 59–69.
9. Rahul Jacob, "The Struggle to Create an Organization for the 21st Century," *Fortune* (April 3, 1995), pp. 90–99; and "Putting a Price on Customer Loyalty," *Dallas Morning News* (June 26, 1994), p. 2H. See also "What's a Loyal Customer Worth?" *Fortune* (December 11, 1995), p. 182.
10. Michael Treacy and Fred D. Wiersema, *The Discipline of Market Leaders* (Reading, MA: Addison-Wesley, 1995); Michael Treacy and Fred Wiersema, "How Market Leaders Keep Their Edge," *Fortune* (February 6, 1995), pp. 88–98; and Michael Treacy, "You Need a Value Discipline—But Which One?" *Fortune* (April 17, 1995), p. 195.
11. "Faded Blues: Levi Struggles to Fit in Again," *Star Tribune* (February 23, 1999), pp. A1, A6.
12. Susan Fournier, Susan Dobseha, and David Glen Mick, "Preventing the Premature Death of Relationship Marketing," *Harvard Business Review* (January–February 1998), pp. 42–51.
13. The material on Rollerblade's current marketing strategy is based on a personal interview with David Samuels, information from the Rollerblade Web site, and Rollerblade sales materials.
14. Joseph Pereira, "Your Inner Skateboard: 'Grinding Shoes,' " *The Wall Street Journal* (November 9, 1998), pp. B1, B4.
15. Robert F. Keith, "The Marketing Revolution," *Journal of Marketing* (January 1960), pp. 35–38.
16. *1952 Annual Report* (New York: General Electric Company, 1952), p. 21.
17. John C. Narver, Stanley F. Slater, and Brian Tietje, "Creating a Market Orientation," *Journal of Market Focused Management* (no. 2, 1998), pp. 241–55; Stanley F. Slater and John C. Narver, "Market Orientation and the Learning Organization," *Journal of Marketing* (July 1995), pp. 63–74; and George S. Day, "The Capabilities of Market-Driven Organizations," *Journal of Marketing* (October 1994), pp. 37–52.
18. Minnette E. Drumwright, "Socially Responsible Organizational Buying: Environmental Concern as a Noneconomic Buying Criterion," *Journal of Marketing* (July 1994), pp. 1–19; Michael E. Porter and Claas van er Linde, "Green and Competitive Ending the Stalemate," *Harvard Business Review* (September–October 1995), pp. 120–34; Jacquelyn Ottman, "Edison Winners Show Smart Environmental Marketing," *Marketing News* (July 17, 1995), pp. 16, 19; and Jacquelyn Ottman, "Mandate for the '90s: Green Corporate Image," *Marketing News* (September 11, 1995), p. 8.
19. Shelby D. Hunt and John J. Burnett. "The Macromarketing/Micromarketing Dichotomy: A Taxonomical Model," *Journal of Marketing* (Summer 1982), pp. 9–26.
20. Philip Kotler and Sidney J. Levy, "Broadening the Concept of Marketing," *Journal of Marketing* (January 1969), pp. 10–15.
21. C. K. Prahalad and Kenneth Lieberthal, "The End of Corporate Imperialism," *Harvard Business Review* (July–August 1998), pp. 69–79.

Rollerblade, Inc.: This case was written by Giana Eckhardt of the University of Minnesota.

CHAPTER 2

1. Information supplied by Gulf Canada, August 1999.
2. Ibid.
3. Roger A. Kerin, Vijay Mahajan, and P. Rajan Varadarajan, *Contemporary Perspectives on Strategic Marketing Planning* (Boston: Allyn & Bacon, 1990), Chapter 1; and Orville C. Walker, Jr., Harper W. Boyd, Jr., and Jean-Claude Larreche, *Marketing Strategy* (Burr Ridge, IL: Richard D. Irwin, 1992), Chapters 1 and 2.
4. Charles W. L. Hill and Gareth R. Jones, *Strategies Management: An Integrated Approach,* 4th ed. (Boston: Houghton-Mifflin, 1998).
5. Gary Hamel and C. K. Prahalad, "Strategic Intent," *Harvard Business Review* (May–June 1989), pp. 63–76.
6. "Coca-Cola Co. Restructures Itself into Units Covering Globe," *Star Tribune* (January 13, 1996), p. D2.
7. Lesley Dow, "Pillsbury Turnover," *Marketing* (July 14, 1997)—www.marketingmag.ca, July 17, 1997.
8. Jeffrey Abrams, *The Mission Statement Book* (Berkeley, CA: Ten Speed Press, 1995), p. 41.
9. www.marketingmag.ca, July 4, 1999.
10. Robert S. Kaplan and David P. Norton, "The Balanced Scoreboard Measures That Drive Performance," *Harvard Business Review* (January–February 1992), pp. 71–79.
11. Mark Fawcett, "Getting with the Program," *The Financial Post Magazine* (March 1996), pp. 48–49.

12. Adapted from "The Experience Curve Reviewed, IV. The Growth Share Matrix of the Product Portfolio," (Boston: The Boston Consulting Group, 1973).
13. Kerin, Mahajan, and Vardarajan, p. 52.
14. Strengths and weaknesses of the BCG technique are based largely on Derek F. Abell and John S. Hammond, *Strategic Market Planning: Problem and Analytic Approaches* (Englewood Cliffs, NJ: Prentice Hall, 1979); and Yoram Wind, Vijay Mahajan, and Donald Swire, "An Empirical Comparison of Standardized Portfolio Models," *Journal of Marketing* (Spring 1983), pp. 89–99.
15. Rich Brown, "Making the Product Portfolio a Basis for Action," *Long Range Planning* (February 1991), pp. 102–10.
16. J. Scott Armstrong and Roderick J. Brodie, "Effects of Portfolio Planning Methods on Decision Making: Experimental Results," *International Journal of Research in Marketing* (Winter 1994), pp. 73–84.
17. George Stalk, Phillip Evans, and Lawrence E. Shulman, "Competing on Capabilities: The New Rules of Corporate Strategy," *Harvard Business Review* (March–April 1992), pp. 57–69.
18. Roger A. Kerin and Robert A. Peterson, *Strategic Marketing Problems: Cases and Comments,* 8th ed. (Englewood Cliffs, NJ: Prentice Hall, 1997), pp. 2–3; and Derek F. Abell, *Defining the Business* (Englewood Cliffs, NJ: Prentice Hall, 1980), p. 18. See also Doug McCuain and Christopher Holt, "Getting Intimate with Customers," *Marketing* (July 14, 1997)—www.marketingmag.ca, July 17,1997.
19. Christopher Meyer, *East Cycle Time* (New York: Free Press, 1993); and Michael E. Porter, *Competitive Advantage* (New York: Free Press, 1985).
20. Loyd Eskildson, "TQM's Role in Corporate Success: Analyzing the Evidence," *National Productivity Review* (Autumn 1995), pp. 25–38.
21. Mark Maremont, "Kodak's New Focus," *Business Week* (January 30, 1995), pp. 63–68.
22. Claudia H. Deutsch, "There's Gold in These Old Photos in the Attic," *The New York Times* (June 30, 1998), p. C6.
23. Michael J. Himowitz, "Kodak's Cool Digital Pix Site," *Fortune* (September 28, 1998), p. 285; The ads were provided by Ogilvy & Mather, Atlanta, GA.
24. Laura Johannes, "Kodak Looks for Another Moment with Film for Pros," *The Wall Street Journal* (March 13, 1998), pp. B1, B6.
25. Emily Nelson, "For Kodak's Advantix, Double Exposure as Company Relaunches Camera System," *The Wall Street Journal* (April 23, 1998), pp. B1, B11; and Linda Grant, "Why Kodak Still Isn't Fixed," *Fortune* (May 11, 1998), pp. 179–81.
26. Tony Walker, "Kodak Focuses on China for Enlarged Growth," *Financial Times* (May 21, 1998), p. 16.
27. Roger O. Crockett and Peter Elstrom, "How Motorola Lost Its Way," *Business Week* (May 4, 1998), pp. 140–48; and Daniel Roth, "Burying Motorola," *Fortune* (July 6, 1998), pp. 28–29.
28. Peter Nulty, "Kodak Grabs for Growth Again," *Fortune* (May 16, 1994), pp. 76–78.
29. Ibid.

Specialized Bicycle Components, Inc.: This case was written by Giana Eckardt of the University of Minnesota.

CHAPTER 3

1. Don Tapscott, *Growing Up Digital* (New York: McGraw-Hill, 1998); Melinda Beck, "Generation Y: Next Population Bulge Shows Its Might," *The Wall Street Journal* (February 3, 1997), p. B1; and Faye Rice, "Making Generational Marketing Come of Age," *Fortune* (June 26, 1995), pp. 110–14.
2. "U.S. Consumption of Coffee Drops to Record Low," *Food and Drink Weekly* (April 20, 1998); and "Gourmet Coffee Craze Bucks National Decline in Coffee Consumption," *PR Newswire* (September 29, 1998); Shannon Dortch, "Coffee at Home," *American Demographics* (August 1995), pp. 4–6; and Marcia Mogelonsky, "Instant's Last Drop," *American Demographics* (August 1995), p. 10.
3. Seanna Browder and Emily Thornton, "Reheating Starbucks," *Business Week* (September 28, 1998), pp. 66, 70.
4. "American Marketing Association Special Report on Trends and Forces Shaping the Future of Marketing," (Chicago: American Marketing Association), May 19, 1998; James Heckman, Maricris G. Briones, and Michelle Wirth Fellman, "Outlook 99: A Look at What the Year Ahead Will Bring," *Marketing News* (December 7, 1998); p. 1; Brent Schlender, "Peter Drucker Takes the Long View," *Fortune* (September 28, 1998), pp. 162–73; Michael J. Mandel, "The 21st Century Economy," *Business Week* (August 31, 1998), pp. 58–67; Statistics Canada, CANSIM matrix 6231; and Goldfarb Consultants, Toronto, 1998; Nina Munk, "The New Organization Man," *Fortune* (March 16, 1998), pp. 63–74; and Harry S. Dent, Jr., *The Roaring 2000s* (New York: Simon and Schuster, 1998).
5. Statistics Canada, CANSIM matrices 6367-6379; and 6367-6900.
6. Ibid.
7. D. Allan Kerr, "Where There's Gray There's Green," *Marketing News* (June 22, 1998), p. 2.
8. Patricia Braus, "The Baby Boom at Mid-Decade," *American Demographics* (April 1995), pp. 40–45; and Cheryl Russell, "On the Baby-Boom Bandwagon," *American Demographics* (May 1991), pp. 24–31.
9. Marcy Magiera and Pat Sloan, "Levis, Lee Loosen Up for Baby Boomers," *Advertising Age* (August 3, 1992), p. 9.
10. Toddi Gutner, "Generation X: To Be Young, Thrifty, and in the Black," *Business Week* (July 21, 1997), p. 76; Howard Gleckman, "Generation $ Is More Like It," *Business Week* (November 3, 1997), p. 44; Karen Ritchie, "Marketing to Generation X," *American Demographics* (April 1995), pp. 34–39; and Diane Crispell," Generations to 2025," *American Demographics* (January 1995), p. 4.
11. Beck, "Generation Y: Next Population Bulge Shows Its Might"; and Susan Mitchell, "The Next Baby Boom," *American Demographics* (October 1995), pp. 22–31.
12. Statistics Canada, cat. 97-213-XPB (Ottawa, 1998).
13. Information supplied by Goldfarb Consultants, Toronto, 1998.
14. Statistics Canada, cat. 13-207-XPB.
15. Statistics Canada, Market Research Handbook, cat. 63-224 (Ottawa, 1999).
16. www.angus.reid.ca
17. Douglas Bell, "Immigration Trends Shape Demand," *Marketing* (May 21, 1993), p. 29.
18. "Grizzlies Capitalize on Asian Fan Interest in NBA," *Marketing* (August 5, 1996), p. 2.
19. Chad Rubel, "Parents Magazines Make Room for Daddy," *Marketing News* (February 27, 1995), pp. 1, 5, 14.
20. Information supplied by Clearly Canadian Beverage Corporation, June 11, 1999.
21. Donalee Moulton, "Sobeys Takes Low Road in Food Pricing," *Marketing* (August 5, 1996), p. 2.
22. "Banks Poach Credit Card Business with Lower Rates," *Marketing* (August 5, 1996), p. 4.
23. Statistics Canada, *Income Distribution by Size in Canada*, cat. 13-207 (Ottawa, 1997).
24. Robert D. Hof, Gary McWilliams, and Gabrielle Saveri, "The 'Click Here' Economy," *Business Week* (June 22, 1998), pp. 122–28; Rochelle Garner, "The Ecommerce Connection," *Sales and Marketing Management* (January 1999), pp. 40–46; Clint Willis, "25 Cool Things You Wish You Had and Will," *Forbes ASAP* (June 1, 1998), pp. 49–60; and Rebecca Piirto, "Cable TV," *American Demographics* (June 1995), pp. 40–43.
25. Neil Gross, Peter Coy, and Otis Post, "The Technology Paradox," *Business Week* (March 6, 1995), pp. 76–84.
26. Leon Jaroff, "Smart's the Word in Detroit," *Time* (February 6, 1995), pp. 50–52.
27. Clint Willis, "25 Cool Things You Wish You Had and Will," *Forbes ASAP* (June 1, 1998), pp. 49–60.
28. Stephanie Anderson, "There's Gold in Those Hills of Soda Bottles," *Business Week* (September 11, 1995), p. 48; Maxine Wilkie, "Asking

Americans to Use Less Stuff," *American Demographics* (December 1994), pp. 11–12; and Jacquelyn Ottman, "New and Improved Won't Do," *Marketing News* (January 30, 1995), p. 9.

29. Don Peppers, Martha Rogers, and Bob Dorf, "Is Your Company Ready for One-to-One Marketing?" *Harvard Business Review* (January–February 1999), pp. 151–60; and Peter Burrows, "Instant Info Is Not Enough," *Business Week* (June 22, 1998), p. 144.

30. Mark Campbell, "Dial a Bank," *Canadian Banker* (September/October, 1996), pp. 18–23.

31. "Rural Phone Firm Takes Aim at Giant Rival," *The Chronicle Herald* (July 15, 1997), p. C3.

32. Michael Porter, *Competitive Advantage* (New York: Free Press, 1985); and Michael Porter, *Competitive Strategy* (New York: Free Press, 1980).

33. Cary Hamel and Jeff Sampler, "The E-Corporation," *Fortune* (December 7, 1998), pp. 80–92; Shikhar Ghosh, "Making Business Sense of the Internet," *Harvard Business Review* (March–April 1998), pp. 127–35; Ramon J. Peypoch, "The Case for Electronic Business Communities," *Business Horizons* (September–October 1998), pp. 17–20; Harry S. Dent, Jr., *The Roaring 2000s,* p. 137; and Erick Schonfeld, "Schwab Puts It All Online," *Fortune* (December 7, 1998), pp. 94–100.

34. www.marketingmag.ca, Jan. 19, 1999.

35. James B. Treece, Kathleen Kerwin, and Heidi Dawley, "Ford," *Business Week* (April 3, 1995), pp. 94–104; and Keith Hammonds, Kevin Kelly, and Karen Thurston, "The New World of Work," *Business Week* (October 17, 1994), pp. 76–87.

36. Michael Mandel, Christopher Farrell, and Catherine Yang, "Land of the Giants," *Business Week* (September 11, 1995), pp. 34–35; and Howard Chua-Eoan, "Too Big or Not Too Big?" *Time* (October 2, 1995), pp. 32–33.

Imagination Pilots Entertainment: This case was prepared by Steven W. Hartley.

CHAPTER 4

1. Information supplied by Molson Breweries, Public Affairs Department, Toronto, 1999.

2. For a discussion of the definition of ethics, see Eugene R. Lazniak and Patrick E. Murphy, *Ethical Marketing Decisions: The Higher Road* (Boston, MA: Allyn & Bacon, 1993), Chapter 1.

3. Verne E. Henderson, "The Ethical Side of Enterprise," *Sloan Management Review* (Spring 1982), pp. 37–47.

4. M. Bommer, C. Gratto, J. Grauander, and M. Tuttle, "A Behavioral Model of Ethical and Unethical Decision Making," *Journal of Business Ethics,* vol. 6 (1987), pp. 265–80.

5. F. G. Crane, "What's Ethical and What's Not with Canadian Business Students," Working Paper, 1997.

6. "The Bottom Line on Ethics," *U.S. News & World Report* (March 20, 1995), pp. 61–66; "Business Week/Harris Poll: Is an Antibusiness Business Backlash Building?" *Business Week* (July 20, 1987), p. 71.

7. "Who's Trusted, Who's Not?" *American Demographics* (June 1995), p. 55.

8. N. Craig Smith, "Marketing Strategies for the Ethics Era," *Sloan Management Review* (Summer 1995), pp. 85–97; Kenneth Labich, "The New Crisis in Business Ethics," *Fortune* (April 20, 1992), pp. 167ff.

9. For a comprehensive review on marketing ethics, see Gregory T. Gunlach and Patrick E. Murphy, "Ethical and Legal Foundations in Relational Marketing Exchanges," *Journal of Marketing* (October 1993), pp. 35–46; and John Tsalikis and David J. Fritzche, "Business Ethics: A Literature Review with a Focus on Marketing Ethics," *Journal of Business Ethics,* vol. 8 (1989), pp. 695–743. See also Lawrence B. Chonko, *Ethical Decision Making in Marketing* (Thousand Oaks, CA: Sage, 1995).

10. William Beaver, "Levi's Is Leaving China," *Business Horizons* (March–April 1995), pp. 35–40.

11. Barry R. Shapiro, "Economic Espionage," *Marketing Management* (Spring 1998), pp. 56–58; and Damon Darlin, "Where Trademarks Are Up for Grabs," *The Wall Street Journal* (December 5, 1989), pp. B1, B4.

12. "Borrowing Software," *Brandweek* (March 2, 1998), p. 20; and "Piracy Losses Top $12 Billion," *Dallas Morning News* (February 17, 1999), p. 2D.

13. Vern Terpstra and Kenneth David, *The Cultural Environment of International Business,* 3rd ed. (Cincinnati: South-Western Publishing Co., 1991), p. 12.

14. For an extended treatment of ethics in the exchange process, see Gregory T. Gundlach and Patrick E. Murphy, "Ethical and Legal Foundations in Relational Marketing Exchanges."

15. "Carnivore in the Cabbage Patch," *U.S. News and World Report* (January 20, 1997), p. 69.

16. "A Little Privacy, Please," *Business Week* (March 6, 1998), pp. 98–102; "Is Nothing Private?" *U.S. News & World Report* (June 15, 1998), p. 59; and "On-Line Groups Are Offering Up Private Plans," *The Wall Street Journal* (June 22, 1998), pp. B1, B3.

17. Lois Therrion, "Want Shelf Space at Supermarkets? Ante Up," *Business Week* (August 7, 1989), pp. 60–61.

18. William J. Holstein, "Corporate Spy Wars," *U.S. News & World Report* (February 23, 1998), pp. 46–52; and "More Spies Targeting U.S. Firms," *Dallas Morning News* (January 12, 1998), pp. 1D, 4D.

19. "P&G Expected to Get about $120 Million in Settlement of Chewy-Cookie Lawsuit," *The Wall Street Journal* (September 11, 1989), p. B10.

20. "Six Deadly Sins," *The Economist* (March 7, 1998), pp. 12–13.

21. "Good Grief," *The Economist* (April 8, 1995), p. 57. See also James Krohe, Jr., "The Big Business of Business Ethics," *Across the Board* (May 1997), pp. 23–29.

22. Savior L. S. Nwachukwu and Scott J. Vitell, Jr., "The Influence of Corporate Culture on Managerial Ethical Judgments," *Journal of Business Ethics,* vol. 17 (1997), pp. 757–76; and Ismael R. Akaah and Daulatram Lund, "The Influence of Personal Values and Organizational Values on Marketing Professionals' Ethical Behavior," *Journal of Business Ethics,* vol. 13 (1994), pp. 417–30.

23. "The Uncommon Good," *The Economist* (August 19, 1995), pp. 55–56; "Workers Who Blow the Whistle on Bosses Often Pay a High Price," *The Wall Street Journal* (July 18, 1995), p. B1.

24. For an extensive discussion on these moral philosophies, see R. Eric Reidenbach and Donald P. Robin, *Ethics and Profits* (Englewood Cliffs, NJ: Prentice Hall, 1989); Chonko, *Ethical Decision Making;* and Lazniak and Murphy, *Ethical Marketing Decisions.*

25. James Q. Wilson, "Adam Smith on Business Ethics," *California Management Review* (Fall 1989), pp. 59–72; Edward W. Coker, "Smith's Concept of the Social System," *Journal of Business Ethics,* vol. 9 (1990), pp. 139–42; and George M. Zinkhan, Michael Bisesi, and Mary Jane Saxton, "MBAs: Changing Attitudes Toward Marketing Dilemmas," *Journal of Business Ethics,* vol. 8 (1989), pp. 963–74.

26. Alix M. Freedman, "Bad Reaction: Nestlé's Bid to Crash Baby-Formula Market Ache U.S. Stirs a Row," *The Wall Street Journal* (February 16, 1989), pp. A1, A6; and Alix Freedman, "Nestlé to Drop Claim on Label of Its Formula," *The Wall Street Journal* (March 13, 1989), p. B5.

27. Robert B. Reich, "The New Meaning of Corporate Social Responsibility," *California Management Review* (Winter 1998), pp. 8–17.

28. Milton Friedman, "A Friedman Doctrine: The Social Responsibility of Business Is to Increase Profits," *New York Times Magazine* (September 13, 1970), p. 126.

29. "Beating the Odds in Biotech," *Newsweek* (October 12, 1992), p. 63.

30. "Can Perrier Purify Its Reputation?" *Business Week* (February 26, 1990), p. 45; and "Perrier Expands North American Recall to Rest of Globe," *The Wall Street Journal* (February 15, 1990), pp. B1, B4.

31. "Environment Winners Show Sustainable Strategies," *Marketing News* (April 27, 1998), p. 6; and Bennett Davis, "Whole Earth Commerce," *Ambassador Magazine* (May 1998), pp. 36–41. See also Ajay Menon and Anil Menon, "Environpreneurial Marketing Strategy: The

Emergence of Corporate Environmentalism as Market Strategy," *Journal of Marketing* (January 1997), pp. 51–67; and Cathy L. Hartman and Edwin R. Stafford, "Crafting 'Environpreneurial' Value Chain Strategies through Green Alliances," *Business Horizons* (March–April 1998), pp. 62–72.

32. See Olivier Boiral and Jean-Marie Sala, "Environmental Management: Should Industry Adapt ISO 14001?" *Business Horizons* (January–February 1998), pp. 57–64.

33. For an extended discussion on this topic, see P. Rajan Varadarajan and Anil Menon, "Cause-Related Marketing: A Coalignment of Marketing Strategy and Corporate Philanthropy," *Journal of Marketing* (July 1988), pp. 58–74. The examples given are found in this article and Daniel Kadlec, "The New World of Giving," *Time* (May 5, 1997), pp. 62–63; and "Companies Trumpet Virtues of Causes in Selling Products," *Dallas Morning News* (February 15, 1998), pp. 1J, 11J.

34. "Reinventing Cause Marketing," *Brandweek* (October 27, 1997), p. 17; "A Market For Charity," *Dallas Morning News* (February 15, 1998), pp. 1J, 11J; "Switching for a Cause," *American Demographics* (April 1997), pp. 26–27; and Kadlec, "The New World of Giving."

35. These steps are adapted from J. J. Carson and G. A. Steiner, *Measuring Business Social Performance: The Corporate Social Audit* (New York: Committee for Economic Development, 1974). See also Sandra A. Waddock and Samuel B. Graves, "The Corporate Social Performance–Financial Performance Link," *Strategic Management Journal,* vol. 18 (1997), pp. 303–19.

36. D. A. Rondinelli and G. Vastag, "International Standards and Corporate Policies: An Integrated Framework," *California Management Review* (Fall 1996), pp. 106–22.

37. "Santa's Sweatshop," *U.S. News & World Report* (December 16, 1996), pp. 50–60.

38. Cyndee Miller, "Marketers Weight Effects of Sweatshop Crackdown," *Marketing News* (May 12, 1997), pp. 1, 19. See also "Nike Battles Backlash from Overseas Sweatshops," *Marketing News* (November 9, 1998), p. 14.

39. For a listing of unethical consumer practices, see Robert E. Wilkes, "Fraudulent Behavior by Consumers," *Journal of Marketing* (October 1978), pp. 67–75. See also Catherine A. Cole, "Research Note: Determinants and Consumer Fraud,"*Journal of Retailing* (Spring 1989), pp. 107–20.

40. See, for example, "Consumers Lean Toward Green," *Marketing News* (August 31, 1998), p. 2; and Tibbett L. Speer, "Growing the Green Market," *American Demographics* (August 1997), pp. 45–49.

41. Speer, "Growing the Green Market."

42. Dicter Bradbury, "Green Forest Products Gain Marketing Niche," *Maine Sunday Telegram* (May 11, 1997), p. B1, p. B14.

Pricing in the Pharmaceutical Industry: Sources: "U.S. Has Developed an Expensive Habit; Now, How to Pay for It?" *The Wall Street Journal* (November 16, 1998), pp. A1, A10; "Drug Costs Can Leave Elderly a Grim Choice: Pills or Other Needs," *The Wall Street Journal* (November 17, 1998), pp. A1, A15; and "Why Generic Drugs Often Can't Compete Against Brand Names," *The Wall Street Journal* (November 18, 1998), pp. A1, A10; and "Who's Really Raising Drug Prices?" *Time* (March 8, 1999), pp. 46–48.

CHAPTER 5

1. Information supplied by W. K. Buckley Ltd.

2. These estimates are based on statistics from *Direction of Trade Statistics Yearbook, 1998* (Washington, DC: International Monetary Fund, 1998), and trend projections by the authors. Trade statistics reported in this chapter also come from these sources, unless otherwise indicated.

3. "American Trade Policy," *The Economist* (January 30, 1999), pp. 63–65.

4. "Bartering Gains Currency in Hard-Hit Southeast Asia," *The Wall Street Journal* (April 6, 1998), p. A10; and Beatrice B. Lund, "Corporate Barter as a Marketing Strategy," *Marketing News* (March 3, 1997), p. 8.

5. Statistics Canada, CANSIM matrix 6548; and cat. 65-001 (Ottawa, 1999).

6. Statistics Canada, CANSIM matrixes 3651 and 3685, 1999.

7. Michael E. Porter, *The Competitive Advantage of Nations* (New York: The Free Press, 1990), pp. 577–615; and Michael E. Porter, "Why Nations Triumph," *Fortune* (March 12, 1990), pp. 94–108. For another view, see David S. Landes, *The Wealth and Poverty of Nations* (New York: W. W. Norton & Company, 1998).

8. "Rougher Sailing Across the Atlantic," *Business Week* (July 27, 1998), p. 29; "Japan's Price of Protection," *Fortune* (March 6, 1995), p. 48; and "New World Trade Chief Fears Economic Nationalism," *Dallas Morning News* (March 22, 1995), p. 11D.

9. "Trade Winds," *The Economist* (November 8, 1997), pp. 85–86.

10. "The Beef Over Bananas," *The Economist* (March 6, 1999), pp. 65–66; Gary C. Hufbauer and Kimberly A. Elliott, *Measuring the Cost of Protection in the United States* (Washington, D.C.: Institute for International Economies, 1994).

11. "It Ain't Just Peanuts," *Business Week* (December 18, 1995), p. 30.

12. "The WTO Crunch," *The Economist* (April 4, 1998), pp. 78–79; Paul Magrusson, "Why the WTO Needs an Overhaul," *Business Week* (June 29, 1998), p. 35.

13. "Industrial Evolution," *Business Week* (April 27, 1998), pp. 100–101; for a comprehensive report on marketing strategy for the European Union, see Colin Egan and Peter McKiernan, *Inside Fortress Europe: Strategies for the Single Market* (Reading, MA: Addison-Wesley, 1994).

14. "Special Report: The Euro," *Business Week* (April 27, 1998), pp. 90–108.

15. Joachim Bamrud, "Setting the Agenda: From Miami to Brazil," *Latin Trade* (June 1998), pp. 3A–12A.

16. "Special Report: East Asian Economies," *The Economist* (March 7, 1998); and "Will East Asia Slam the Door?" *The Economist* (September 12, 1998), p. 88.

17. "Juniper's New-Router Shipments Kick Off Race in Internet Devices," *The Wall Street Journal* (September 16, 1998), p. 86; and General Mills, Inc., *Annual Report*, 1998.

18. For an excellent overview of different types of global companies and marketing strategies, see Warren J. Keegan, *Global Marketing Management*, 6th ed. (Upper Saddle River, NJ: Prentice Hall, Inc., 1998), pp. 43–54.

19. "Global Companies Don't Work; Multinationals Do," *Advertising Age* (April 18, 1994), p. 23.

20. For an extensive discussion on identifying global consumers, see Jean-Pierre Jeannet and H. David Hennessey, *Global Marketing Strategies*, 4th ed. (Boston: Houghton Mifflin Company, 1998).

21. "Ready to Shop Until They Drop," *Business Week* (June 22, 1998), pp. 104 ff; Chip Walker, "Can TV Save the Planet?" *American Demographics* (May 1996), pp. 21–29; *Global Teenager Is a Myth, But Asian Teenagers Are Going Global* (New York: McCann-Erickson, 1997); "Teens Seen as the First Truly Global Consumers," *Marketing News* (March 27, 1995), p. 9; Shawn Tully, "Teens: The Most Global Market of All," *Fortune* (May 16, 1994), pp. 90–97; and Dan S. Acuff, *What Kids Buy and Why* (New York: The Free Press, 1997).

22. For comprehensive references on cross-cultural aspects of marketing, see Paul A. Herbig, *Handbook of Cross-Cultural Marketing* (New York: The Halworth Press, 1998); and Jean-Claude Usunier, *Marketing Across Cultures*, 2nd ed. (London: Prentice Hall Europe, 1996). Unless otherwise indicated, examples found in this section appear in these excellent references.

23. "McDonald's Adapts Mac Attack to Foreign Tastes with Expansion," *Dallas Morning News* (December 7, 1997), p. 3H; and "Taking Credit," *The Economist* (November 2, 1996), p. 75.

24. Roger E. Axtell, *Do's and Taboos Around the World,* compiled by the Packer Penn Company (New York: John Wiley and Sons, 1985).
25. These examples appear in Del I. Hawkins, Roger J. Best, and Kenneth A. Coney, *Consumer Behavior*, 7th ed. (Burr Ridge, IL: Irwin/McGraw-Hill, 1998), Chap. 2.
26. "Greeks Protest Coke's Use of Parthenon," *Dallas Morning News* (August 17, 1992), p. D4.
27. Saeed Samiee, "Customer Evaluation of Products in a Global Market," *Journal of International Business Studies,* third quarter, 1994, pp. 579–604.
28. "Geo Gaffes," *Brandweek* (February 23, 1998), p. 20.
29. The following examples appear in "Global Thinking Paces Computer Biz," *Advertising Age* (March 6, 1995), p. 10; and "U.S. Firms Sometimes Lose It in the Translation," *Dallas Morning News* (August 17, 1992), pp. D1, D4.
30. Terrence A. Shimp and Subhash Sharma, "Consumer Ethnocentrism: Construction and Validation of the CETSCALE," *Journal of Marketing Research* (August 1987), pp. 280–89.
31. Jill Gabrielle Klein, Richard Ettenson, and Marlene D. Morris, "The Animosity Model of Foreign Product Purchase: An Empirical Test in the People's Republic of China," *Journal of Marketing* (January 1998), pp. 89–100; and Shimp and Sharma, "Consumer Ethnocentrism."
32. This example is based on "Global Coffee Market Share Comparisons,"*Advertising Age* (December 10, 1995), p. 47; Carla Rapoport, "Nestlé's Brand Building Machine," *Fortune* (September 19, 1995), pp. 147–56; and Nestlé Corporation, *Annual Report*, 1997.
33. "Selling in Russia: The March on Moscow," *The Economist*, March 18, 1995, pp. 65–66.
34. "Rubles? Who Needs Rubles?" *Business Week* (April 13, 1998), pp. 45–46.
35. "Russia and Central-Eastern Europe: World's Apart," *Brandweek* (May 4, 1998), pp. 30–31; "We Will Bury You . . . With a Snickers Bar," *U.S. News & World Report* (January 26, 1998), pp. 50–51; and "Selling in Russia."
36. Chip Walker, "The Global Middle Class," *American Demographics* (September 1995), pp. 40–47.
37. "Consumer Abroad: Developing Shopaholics," *U.S. News & World Report* (February 10, 1997), p. 55.
38. "Mattel Plans to Double Sales Abroad," *The Wall Street Journal* (February 11, 1998), pp. A3, A11.
39. Philip R. Cateora and John L. Graham, *International Marketing*, 10th ed. (Burr Ridge, IL: Irwin/McGraw-Hill, 1999), p. 560.
40. This discussion is based on Jean-Louis Mucchielli, Peter J. Buckley, and Victor V. Cordell, *Globalization and Regionalization: Strategies, Policies, and Economic Environments* (New York: The Halworth Press, 1998); "European Union: Europe's Mid-Life Crisis," *The Economist* (May 31, 1997), pp. 38–42; and "East Asian Economies."
41. "Small Firms Flock to Quality System," *Nation's Business* (March 1998), pp. 65–67.
42. For an extensive examination of these market entry options, see, for example, Masaaki Kotake and Kristiaan Helsen, *Global Marketing Management* (New York: John Wiley & Sons, 1998); Johny K. Johansson, *Global Marketing* (Chicago: Richard D. Irwin, 1997); Vern Terpstra and Ravi Sarathy, *International Marketing*, 7th ed. (Fort Worth, TX: The Dryden Press, 1997); Sak Onkuisit and John J. Shaw, *International Marketing*, 3rd ed. (Upper Saddle River, NJ: Prentice Hall, 1997); Keegan, *Global Marketing Management;* and Cateora and Graham, *International Marketing*.
43. Information supplied by W. K. Buckley Ltd.
44. Martin Knelman, "Mickey on the Road to Avonlea," *The Financial Post* magazine, (March 1996), pp. 22–28.
45. McDonald's *Annual Report*, 1997; and "Globalization: Get Rich Quick," *Time* (April 13, 1998), pp. 204–5.
46. Avraham Shama, "Entry Strategies of U.S. Firms to the Newly Independent States, Baltic States, and Eastern European Countries," *California Management Review* (Spring 1995), pp. 90–109.
47. Michael Hirsh, "The New China: Tricks of the Trade," *Newsweek* (June 29, 1998), pp. 40–42.
48. Masaaki Kotake and Maria Cecilia Coutinho de Arruda, "South America's Free Trade Gambit," *Marketing Management* (Spring 1998), pp. 39–46; "Going It Alone," *The Economist* (April 19, 1997), pp. 64–65; and "Mercedes: Made in Alabama," *Fortune* (July 7, 1997), pp. 150 ff.
49. Shama, "Entry Strategies of U.S. Firms."
50. The examples are found in "It's Goo, Goo, Goo, Goo Vibrations at the Gerber Lab," *The Wall Street Journal* (December 4, 1996), pp. A1, A6; Donald R. Graber, "How to Manage a Global Product Development Process," *Industrial Marketing Management* (November 1996), pp. 483–489; and Usunier, *Marketing Across Cultures.*
51. This discussion is based on John Fahy and Fuyuki Taguchi, "Reassessing the Japanese Distribution System," *Sloan Management Review* (Winter 1995), pp. 49–61.
52. Edward Tse, "The Right Way to Achieve Profitable Growth in the Chinese Consumer Market," *Strategy & Business* (Second Quarter 1998), pp. 10–21.
53. "Copyright Scope Limited for Some Firms," *The Wall Street Journal* (March 10, 1998), p. B10; "Parallel Imports: A Grey Area," *The Economist* (June 13, 1998), pp. 61–62; and "When Grey Is Good," *The Economist* (August 22, 1998), p. 17.

CNS, Inc., and 3M: Breathe Right® Nasal Strips: This case was prepared by Giana Eckardt. Sources: *CNS, Inc., 1997 Annual Report* (Minneapolis, MN: CNS, Inc., 1998); personal interview with Dr. Daniel E. Cohen, Chief Executive Officer of CNS (June 1998).

CHAPTER 6

1. Elena Scotti, "Born to be Mild, or Wild?" *BRANDWEEK* (March 16, 1998), pp. 22–23; Jon Berry, "Consumers Keep the Upper Hand," *American Demographics* (September 1998), pp. 20–22; "GM Taps Harris to Help Lure Women," *Advertising Age* (February 17, 1997), pp. 1, 37; "Dealer Dilemma," *BRANDWEEK* (March 16, 1998), p. 22; and "Elle Launches Guide for Women Car Buyers," *Advertising Age* (April 6, 1998), p. 34.
2. James F. Engel, Roger D. Blackwell, and Paul Miniard, *Consumer Behavior,* 9th ed. (Fort Worth, TX: Dryden Press, 1998). See also Gordon C. Bruner III and Richard J. Pomazal, "Problem Recognition: The Crucial First Stage of the Consumer Decision Process," *Journal of Consumer Marketing* (Winter 1988), pp. 53–63.
3. For thorough descriptions of consumer experience and expertise, see Stephen J. Hoch and John Deighton, "Managing What Consumers Learn from Experience," *Journal of Marketing* (April 1989), pp. 1–20; and Joseph W. Alba and J. Wesley Hutchinson, "Dimensions of Consumer Expertise," *Journal of Consumer Research* (March 1987), pp. 411–54.
4. For in-depth studies on external information search patterns, see Sridhar Moorthy, Brian T. Ratchford, and Debabrata Tulukdar, "Consumer Information Search Revisited: Theory and Empirical Analysis," *Journal of Consumer Research* (March 1997), pp. 263–77.
5. For an extended discussion on evaluative criteria, see Del J. Hawkins, Roger J. Best, and Kenneth A. Coney, *Consumer Behavior,* 7th ed. (New York: Irwin/McGraw-Hill, 1998), pp. 550–67.
6. John A. Howard, *Buyer Behavior in Marketing Strategy,* 2nd ed. (Englewood Cliffs, NJ: Prentice Hall, 1994), pp. 101, 128–89, and F. G. Crane and T. K. Clarke, *Consumer Behaviour in Canada: Theory and Practice,* 2nd edition (Toronto: Dryden, 1994), pp. 26–28.
7. William J. McDonald, "Time Use in Shopping: The Role of Personal Characteristics," *Journal of Retailing* (Winter 1994), pp. 345–66; Robert J. Donovan, John R. Rossiter, Gillian Marcoolyn, and Andrew Nesdale, "Store Atmosphere and Purchasing Behavior,"*Journal of Retailing* (Fall 1994), pp. 283–94; and Eric A. Greenleaf and Donald R. Lehman, "Reasons for Substantial Delay in Consumer Decision Making," *Journal of Consumer Research* (September 1995), pp. 186–99.

8. For a review of how computer-mediated buying can influence the consumer decision process, see Russell S. Winer et al., "Choice in Computer-Mediated Environments," *Marketing Letters,* vol. 8, no. 3 (1997), pp. 287–96.
9. "Future Shop," *Forbes ASAP* (April 6, 1998), pp. 37–52; "General Motors' to Take Nationwide Test Drive on Web," *The Wall Street Journal* (September 28, 1998), p. B4.
10. Ruth N. Bolton and James H. Drew, "A Multistage Model of Customers' Assessment of Service Quality and Value," *Journal of Consumer Research* (March 1991), pp. 376–84.
11. Jagdish N. Sheth, Banwari Mitral, and Bruce Newman, *Consumer Behavior* (Fort Worth, TX: Dryden Press, 1999), p. 22.
12. Rahul Jacob, "The Struggle to Create an Organization for the 21st Century," *Fortune* (April 3, 1995), pp. 90–99.
13. John E. G. Bateson and K. Douglas Hoffman, *Managing Services Marketing,* Fourth Edition (Forth Worth: Dryden, 1998).
14. For an overview of research on involvement, see John C. Mowen and Michael Minor, *Consumer Behavior,* 5th ed. (Upper Saddle River, NJ: Prentice Hall, 1998), pp. 64–68; and Frank R. Kardes, *Consumer Behavior* (Reading, MA: Addison-Wesley, 1999), pp. 256–58.
15. For an overview on the three problem-solving variations, see Hawkins, Best, and Coney, *Consumer Behavior,* pp. 498–501; Howard, *Buyer Behavior,* pp. 69–162.
16. Russell Belk, "Situational Variables and Consumer Behavior," *Journal of Consumer Research* (December 1975), pp. 157–63. Representative recent studies on situational influences are discussed in Mowen and Minor, *Consumer Behavior,* pp. 451–75.
17. A. H. Maslow, *Motivation and Personality* (New York: Harper & Row, 1970). See also Richard Yalch and Frederic Brunel, "Need Hierarchies in Consumer Judgments of Product Designs: Is It Time to Reconsider Maslow's Hierarchy?" in Kim Corfman and John Lynch, eds., *Advances in Consumer Research* (Provo, UT: Association for Consumer Research, 1996), pp. 405–10.
18. Arthur Koponen, "The Personality Characteristics of Purchasers," *Journal of Advertising Research* (September 1960), pp. 89–92; Joel B. Cohen, "An Interpersonal Orientation to the Study of Consumer Behavior," *Journal of Marketing Research* (August 1967), pp. 270–78; and Rena Bartos, *Marketing to Women Around the World* (Cambridge, MA: Harvard Business School, 1989).
19. Terry Clark, "International Marketing and National Character: A Review and Proposal for an Integrative Theory," *Journal of Marketing* (October 1990), pp. 66–79.
20. For an interesting analysis of self-concept, see Russell W. Belk, "Possessions and the Extended Self," *Journal of Consumer Research* (September 1988), pp. 139–68.
21. Myron Magnet, "Let's Go for Growth," *Fortune* (March 7, 1994), p. 70.
22. This example provided in Michael R. Solomon, *Consumer Behavior,* 4th ed. (Upper Saddle River, NJ: Prentice Hall, 1999), p. 59.
23. For further reading on subliminal perception, see Anthony G. Greenwald, Sean C. Draine, and Richard L. Abrams, "Three Cognitive Markers of Unconscious Semantic Activation," *Science* (September 1996), pp. 1699–1701; Joel Saegert, "Why Marketing Should Quit Giving Subliminal Advertising the Benefit of the Doubt," *Psychology & Marketing* (Summer 1987), pp. 107–20; Dennis L. Rosen and Surendra N. Singh, "An Investigation of Subliminal Embed Effect on Multiple Measures of Advertising Effectiveness," *Psychology & Marketing* (March/April 1992), pp. 157–173; and Kathryn T. Theus, "Subliminal Advertising and the Psychology of Processing Unconscious Stimuli: A Review of Research," *Psychology & Marketing* (May/June 1994), pp. 271–90.
24. "I Will Love This Story," *U.S. News & World Report* (May 12, 1997), p. 12; "Dr. Feelgood Goes Subliminal," *Business Week* (November 6, 1995), p. 6; and "Firm Gets Message Out Subliminally," *Dallas Morning News* (February 2, 1997), pp. 1H, 6H.
25. "Customer Loyalty: Going, Going . . . ," *American Demographics* (September 1997), pp. 20–23; *Brand-Driven Marketers Are Beating Themselves in the War Against Price-Based and Private Label Competition* (New York: Bates USA, 1994), and Jo Marney, "Building Splurchases," *Marketing* (January 27, 1997); www.marketingmag.ca, July 18, 1997.
26. Martin Fishbein and I. Aizen, *Belief, Attitude, Intention and Behavior: An Introduction to Theory and Research* (Reading, MA: Addison Wesley Publishing, 1975), p. 6.
27. Richard J. Lutz, "Changing Brand Attitudes through Modification of Cognitive Structure," *Journal of Consumer Research* (March 1975), pp. 49–59. See also Mowen and Minor, *Consumer Behavior,* pp. 287–88.
28. "Pepsi's Gamble Hits Freshness Dating Jackpot," *Advertising Age* (September 19, 1994), p. 50.
29. "The Marketing 100: Colgate Total," *Advertising Age* (June 29, 1998), p. 544.
30. "The Frontiers of Psychographics," *American Demographics* (July 1996), pp. 38–43; http://future.sri.com. See also "You Can Buy A Thrill: Chasing the Ultimate Rush," *American Demographics* (June 1997), pp. 47–51.
31. See, for example, Lawrence F. Feick and Linda Price, "The Market Maven: A Diffuser of Marketplace Information," *Journal of Marketing* (January 1987), pp. 83–97; and Peter H. Block, "The Product Enthusiast: Implications for Marketing Strategy," *Journal of Consumer Marketing* (Summer 1986), pp. 51–61.
32. "Survey: If You Must Know, Just Ask One of These Men," *Marketing News* (October 25, 1992), p. 13.
33. "Maximizing the Market with Influentials," *American Demographics* (July 1995), p. 42.
34. "Put People Behind the Wheel," *Advertising Age* (March 22, 1993), p. S-28.
35. F. G. Crane and T. K. Clarke, "The Identification of Evaluative Criteria and Cues Used in Selecting Services," *Journal of Services Marketing* (Spring 1988), pp. 53–59.
36. Representative recent work on positive and negative word of mouth can be found in Robert E. Smith and Christine A. Vogt, "The Effects of Integrating Advertising and Negative Word-of-Mouth Communications on Message Processing and Response," *Journal of Consumer Psychology,* 4 (1995), pp. 133–51; Paula Bone, "Word-of-Mouth Effects on Short-Term and Long-Term Product Judgments," *Journal of Business Research,* 32 (1995), pp. 213–23; Chip Walker, "Word of Mouth," *American Demographics* (July 1995), pp. 38–45; and Dale F. Duhan, Scott D. Johnson, James B. Wilcox, and Gilbert D. Harrell, "Influences on Consumer Use of Word-of-Mouth Recommendation Sources," *Journal of the Academy of Marketing Science* (Fall 1997), pp. 283–95.
37. "We Will Bury You . . . With a Snickers Bar," *U.S. News and World Report* (January 26, 1998), p. 50ff; "A Beer Tampering Scare in China Shows Peril of Global Marketing," *The Wall Street Journal* (November 3, 1995), p. B1; and "Pork Rumors Vex Indonesia," *Advertising Age* (February 16, 1989), p. 36.
38. For an extended discussion on reference groups, see Wayne D. Hoyer and Deborah J. MacInnis, *Consumer Behavior* (Boston: Houghton Mifflin Co., 1997), Chapter 15.
39. For an extended discussion on consumer socialization, see George P. Moschis, *Consumer Socialization* (Lexington, MA: Lexington Books, 1987).
40. "Get 'em While They're Young," *Marketing News* (November 10, 1997), p. 2.
41. This discussion is based on J. Paul Peter and Jerry C. Olson, *Consumer Behavior and Marketing Strategy,* 5th ed. (New York: Irwin/McGraw-Hill 1999), pp. 341–43; Robert E. Wilkes, "Household Life-Cycle Stages, Transitions, and Product Expenditures," *Journal of Consumer Research* (June 1995), pp. 27–42; and Jan Larson, "The New Face of Homemakers," *American Demographics* (September 1997), pp. 45–50.
42. Diane Crispell, "Dual-Earner Diversity," *American Demographics* (July 1995), pp. 32–37.

43. "Wearing the Pants," *BRANDWEEK* (October 20, 1997), pp. 20, 22; and "Look Who's Shopping," *Progressive Grocer* (January 1998), p. 18.
44. "Marketing," *BRANDWEEK* (May 18, 1998), pp. 46–52; and "Teen Green," *American Demographics* (February 1998), p. 39. See also James V. McNeal, "Tapping the Three Kids' Markets," *American Demographics* (April 1998), pp. 37–41; and "Hey Kid, Buy This," *Business Week* (June 30, 1997), pp. 62–69.
45. For a discussion of social class in Canada see Crane and Clarke, pp. 127–49.
46. Milton Yinger, "Ethnicity," *Annual Review of Sociology* (1985), pp. 151–80.
47. Francois Vary, "Quebec Consumer Has Unique Buying Habits," *Marketing* (March 23, 1992), p. 28; Louise Gagnon, "Metro Plays to Decline in Impulse Purchases," *Marketing* (May 12, 1997)— www.marketingmag.ca, July 20, 1997; Louise Gagnon, "Eaton's Quebec Ads Target Hip Shoppers," *Marketing* (June 16, 1997)—www.marketingmag.ca, July 18, 1997; Louise Gagnon, "Price Cuts Escalate Beer Battle," *Marketing* (June 30, 1997)—www.marketingmag.ca, July 17, 1997.
48. Ann Boden, "Aiming at the Right Target," *Marketing* (January 28, 1991), p. 6.

Three Sisters Cafe: This case was prepared by Frederick G. Crane.

CHAPTER 7

1. Interview with Gary Null, Honeywell, MICRO SWITCH Division, August 25, 1998.
2. Peter LaPlaca, "From the Editor," *Journal of Business and Industrial Marketing* (Summer 1992), p. 3.
3. Statistics Canada, *Market Research Handbook,* cat. 63-224 (Ottawa, 1999).
4. Ibid.
5. *1997 North American Industry Classification System* (Washington, DC: Office of Management and Budget, 1998).
6. An argument that consumer buying and organizational buying do not have important differences is found in Edward F. Fern and James R. Brown, "The Industrial/Consumer Marketing Dichotomy: A Case of Insufficient Justification," *Journal of Marketing* (Spring 1984), pp. 68–77. However, most writers on the subject do draw distinctions between the two types of buying. See, for example, Michael D. Hutt and Thomas W. Speh, *Business Marketing Management,* 6th ed. (Fort Worth, TX: Dryden Press, 1998); and H. Michael Hayes, Per V. Jenster, and Nils-Erik Aaby, *Business Marketing: A Global Perspective* (Chicago: Richard D. Irwin, 1996).
7. This listing and portions of the following discussion are based on Edward G. Brierty, Robert W. Eckles, and Robert R. Reeder, *Business Marketing,* 3rd ed. (Upper Saddle River, NJ: Prentice Hall, 1998); Frank G. Bingham, Jr., *Business Marketing Management* (Lincolnwood, IL: NTC, 1998); and Hutt and Speh, *Business Marketing Management.*
8. "Silicon Valley's Stamina," *Business Week* (August 31, 1998), pp. 88–93; "The I-Way Will Be Paved with Silicon," *Business Week* (January 9, 1995), p. 77; and "TI Introduces Smaller, Faster DSPs," *Dallas Morning News* (September 29, 1998), p. 4D.
9. "Latin Trade Connection," *Latin Trade* (June 1997), p. 72.
10. For a study of buying criteria used by industrial firms, see Daniel H. McQuiston and Rockney G. Walters, "The Evaluative Criteria of Industrial Buyers: Implications for Sales Training," *Journal of Business & Industrial Marketing* (Summer/Fall 1989), pp. 65–75. See also "What Buyers Look For," *Sales & Marketing Management* (August 1995), p. 31.
11. "Small Firms Flock to Quality System," *Nation's Business* (March 1998), pp. 66–67.
12. David L. Blenkhorn and Peter M. Banting, "How Reverse Marketing Changes Buyer-Seller Roles," *Industrial Marketing Management* (August 1991), pp. 185–90; and Michael R. Leenders and David L. Blenkhorn, *Reverse Marketing: The New Buyer-Supplier Relationship* (New York: Free Press, 1996).
13. "Chrysler's Neon," *Business Week* (May 3, 1993), p. 119.
14. For an up-to-date discussion on JIT, see Douglas M. Lambert, James R. Stock, and Lisa M. Ellram, *Fundamentals of Logistics Management* (New York: Irwin/McGraw-Hill, 1998).
15. "$35 Million Machine: Wires Not Included," *Newsweek* (April 15, 1995), p. 25.
16. This discussion is based on N. Craig Smith and John A. Quelch, *Ethics in Marketing* (Homewood, IL: Richard D. Irwin, 1993), p. 796; Nathaniel Gilbert, "The Case for Countertrade," *Across the Board* (May 1992), pp. 43–45; and Alan J. Dubinsky, Marvin A. Jolson, Masaaki Kotobe, and Che Un Lim, "A Cross-National Investigation of Industrial Salespeople's Ethical Perceptions," *Journal of International Business Studies* (Fourth Quarter 1991), pp. 651–70.
17. Pratibha A. Dabholkar, Wesley J. Johnston, and Amy S. Cathey, "The Dynamics of Long-Term Business-to-Business Exchange Relationships," *Journal of Academy of Marketing Science,* vol. 22, 2 (1994), pp. 130–45.
18. "Boeing Receives a Key Order for Airlines," *The Wall Street Journal* (March 15, 1996), pp. A3, A10.
19. This discussion is based on James C. Anderson and James A. Narus, *Business Market Management* (Upper Saddle River, NJ: Prentice Hall, 1999); Robert D. Buzzell and Gwen Ortmeyer, "Channel Partnerships Streamline Distribution," *Sloan Management Review* (Spring 1995), pp. 85–96; and Neil Rackham, Lawrence Friedman, and Richard Ruff, *Getting Partnering Right* (New York: McGraw-Hill, 1996).
20. "Log On, Link Up, Save Big," *Business Week* (June 22, 1998), pp. 132–38; and "Finally, Europeans Are Storming the Net," *Business Week* (May 11, 1998), pp. 48–49. See also Earl D. Honeycutt, Jr., Theresa B. Flaherty, and Ken Benassi, "Marketing Industrial Products on the Internet," *Industrial Marketing Management* (January 1998), pp. 63–72.
21. These examples appear in "The 'Click Here' Economy," *Business Week* (June 22, 1998), pp. 122–28; "Bringing Electronic Commerce Into Reach," *Industrial Distribution* (September 1998), pp. T12–T15; and "Log On, Link Up, Save Big," *Business Week.*
22. "To Byte the Hand That Feeds," *The Economist* (January 17, 1998), pp. 61–62; and "The 'Click Here' Economy," *Business Week.*
23. Thomas V. Bonoma, "Major Sales: Who Really Does the Buying?" *Harvard Business Review* (May–June 1982), pp. 11–19. For recent research on buying centers, see Morry Ghinghold and David T. Wilson, "Buying Center Research and Business Marketing Practices: Meeting the Challenge of Dynamic Marketing," *Journal of Business & Industrial Marketing,* vol. 13, no. 2 (1998), pp. 96–108; and Philip L. Dawes, Don Y. Lee, and Grahame R. Dowling, "Information Control and Influence in Emerging Buying Centers," *Journal of Marketing* (July 1998), pp. 55–68.
24. Paul A. Herbig, *Handbook of Cross-Cultural Marketing* (New York: The Halworth Press, 1998).
25. Jule M. Bristor, "Influence Strategies in Organizational Buying: The Importance of Connections to the Right People in the Right Places," *Journal of Business-to-Business Marketing,* vol. 1 (1993), pp. 63–98.
26. These definitions are adapted from Frederick E. Webster, Jr., and Yoram Wind, *Organizational Buying Behavior* (Englewood Cliffs, NJ: Prentice Hall, 1972), p. 6.
27. For an extensive description of 18 industrial purchases, see Arch G. Woodside and Nyren Vyas, *Industrial Purchasing Strategies: Recommendations for Purchasing and Marketing Managers* (Lexington, MA: Lexington Books, 1987). See also Joseph A. Bellizzi, "Business-to-Business Selling and the Organizatonal Buying Process," in Sidney J. Levy, George R. Frerichs, and Howard L. Gordon, eds., *Marketing Managers Handbook,* (Chicago: The Dartnell Corporation, 1994).

28. Patrick J. Robinson, Charles W. Faris, and Yoram Wind, *Industrial Buying and Creative Marketing* (Boston: Allyn & Bacon, 1967).
29. Representative studies on the buy-class framework that document its usefulness include Erin Adnerson, Wujin Chu, and Barton Weitz, "Industrial Purchasing: An Empirical Exploration of the Buy-Class Framework," *Journal of Marketing* (July 1987), pp. 71–86; Morry Ghingold, "Testing the 'Buy-Grid' Buying Process Model," *Journal of Purchasing and Materials Management* (Winter 1986), pp. 30–36; P. Matthyssens and W. Faes, "OEM Buying Process for New Components: Purchasing and Marketing Implications," *Industrial Marketing Management* (August 1985), pp. 145–57; and Thomas W. Leigh and Arno J. Ethans, "A Script-Theoretic Analysis of Industrial Purchasing Behavior," *Journal of Marketing* (Fall 1984), pp. 22–32. Studies not supporting the buy-class framework include Joseph A. Bellizi and Philip McVey, "How Valid Is the Buy-Grid Model?" *Industrial Marketing Management* (February 1983), pp. 57–62; and Donald W. Jackson, Janet E. Keith, and Richard K. Burdick, "Purchasing Agents' Perceptions of Industrial Buying Center Influences: A Situational Approach," *Journal of Marketing* (Fall 1984), pp. 75–83.
30. See, for example, R. Vekatesh, Ajay Kohli, and Gerald Zaltman, "Influence Strategies in Buying Centers," *Journal of Marketing* (October 1995), pp. 61–72; Gary L. Lilien and Anthony Wong, "An Exploratory Investigation of the Structure of the Buying Center in the Metal Working Industry," *Journal of Marketing Research* (February 1984), pp. 1–11; and Wesley J. Johnston and Thomas V. Bonoma, "The Buying Center: Structure and Interaction Patterns," *Journal of Marketing* (Summer 1981), pp. 143–56. See also Christopher P. Puto, Wesley E. Patton III, and Ronald H. King, "Risk Handling Strategies in Industrial Vendor Selection Decisions," *Journal of Marketing* (Winter 1985), pp. 89–98.

Energy Performance Systems, Inc.: This case was written by William Rudelius. Sources: Personal interviews with L. David Ostlie, Tom Kroll, and Paul Helgeson.

CHAPTER 8

1. Information supplied by MediaLinx Interactive, Toronto, June 1999.
2. International Trade Administration definition reported in A. J. Campbell, "Ten Reasons Why Your Company Should Use Electronic Commerce," *Business America* (May 1998), p. 12.
3. Unless otherwise indicated, this discussion is based on "Latest Headcount: 148 Million Online," www.cyberatlas.com, downloaded February 18, 1999; Andrew Urbaczewski, Leonard M. Jessup, and Bradley C. Wheeler, "A Manager's Primer on Electronic Commerce," *Business Horizons* (September–October 1998), pp. 5–16; Ravi Kalakota and Andrew B. Whinston, *Electronic Commerce: A Manager's Guide* (Reading, MA: Addison-Wesley 1997); Tim McCullum, "The Net Result of Computer Links," *Nation's Business* (March 1998), pp. 55–57; and "Online Population to Quadruple," www.cyberatlas.com, downloaded February 17, 1999.
4. Michael Krantz, "Click Till You Drop," *Time* (July 20, 1998), pp. 34–39. See also Paul Foley and David Sutton, "Boom Time for Electronic Commerce—Rhetoric or Reality," *Business Horizons* (September–October 1998), pp. 21–30; and "When the Bubble Bursts," *The Economist* (January 30, 1999), pp. 23–25.
5. "International Data Corporation: 133 Million Intranet Users By 2001," *Nua Internet Surveys* (www.nua.ie/surveys), downloaded January 27, 1999.
6. See "An R_x for Communication, ELVIS Saves Eli Lilly Time, Money," *PC Today Processor* (www.pctoday.com), downloaded January 28, 1999.
7. Raymond S. Bamford and Robert A. Burgelman, "Internet-Based Electronic Commerce in 1997: A Primer" (Graduate School of Business, Stanford University, 1997).
8. Shawn Tully, "How Cisco Mastered the Net," *Fortune* (August 17, 1998), pp. 207–10.
9. David Kirkpatrick, "The E-Ware War," *Fortune* (December 7, 1998), pp. 102–12; and Eryn Brown, "VF Corp. Changes Its Underware," *Fortune* (December 7, 1998), pp. 115–18.
10. Heather Green and Seanna Growder, "Cyberspace Winners: How They Did It," *Business Week* (June 22, 1998), pp. 154–60.
11. www.conquest.ca, downloaded June 12, 1999.
12. This discussion is based on *Nua Internet Surveys* (www.nua.ie/surveys), downloaded January 27, 1999, and www.angusreid.ca.
13. The source for iVALS descriptions is found at the SRI International Web site: http://future.sri.com:80/vals/ivals.index.html, downloaded February 1, 1999.
14. Russell S. Winer et al., "Choice in Computer-Mediated Environments," *Marketing Letters* (vol. 8, no. 3, 1997), pp. 287–96; and Joseph Alba et al., "Interactive Home Shopping: Consumer, Retailer, and Manufacturer Incentives to Participate in the Electronic Marketplace," *Journal of Marketing* (July 1997), pp. 38–53.
15. "Future Shop," *Forbes ASAP* (April 6, 1998), pp. 37–5; and Foley and Sutton, "Boom Time for Electronic Commerce."
16. "The E-commerce Cometh," *Brandweek* (September 21, 1998), p. 10.
17. The breakdown shown in this figure consolidates several estimates, principally from Juniper Communications and Forrester Research. See, for example, "Online Shopping Revenues by Type: 1996–2002," *Advertising Age* (October 26, 1998), p. S14.
18. "A Cybershopper's Best Friend," *Business Week* (May 4, 1998), p. 84.
19. "It's a Woman's Web," *Brandweek* (September 7, 1998), pp. 46–47.
20. Erick Schonfeld, "The Customized, Digitized, Have-It-Your-Way Economy," *Fortune* (September 28, 1998), pp. 115–21.
21. "Now It's Your Web," *Business Week* (October 5, 1998), pp. 164–74.
22. Matt Lake, "The New Megasites: All-in-One Web Supersites," *PC World Online*, www.pcworld.com, downloaded February 9, 1999; and "Portals Rethink Retail Strategies, Shopping Agents," *Advertising Age* (February 1, 1999), pp. 28, 32.
23. "Branding on the Net," *Business Week* (November 9, 1998), pp. 78–86.
24. www.angusreid.ca, downloaded June 5, 1999; and John Gustavson, "Netiquette and DM," Marketing www.marketingmag.ca, downloaded June 1, 1999.
25. "Cookies," *PC Webopaedia Definition and Links,* www.webopedia.com, downloaded February 10, 1999.
26. Clay Hathorn, "Online Business: Trying to Turn Cookies into Dough," *Microsoft Internet Magazine Archive*, www.microsoft.com, downloaded February 15, 1999.
27. For an early, but still relevant, description of how the new marketspace will influence marketing, see Jeffrey F. Rayport and John J. Sviokla, "Managing in the Marketspace," *Harvard Business Review* (November–December 1994), pp. 141–53; Jeffrey F. Rayport and John J. Sviokla, "Exploiting the Virtual Value Chain," *Harvard Business Review* (November–December 1995), pp. 75–85; and Donna L. Hoffman and Thomas P. Novak, "Marketing in a Hypermedia Computer-Mediated Environment: Conceptual Foundations," *Journal of Marketing* (July 1996), pp. 50–68. See also Robert A. Peterson, Sridhar Balasubramanian, and Bart J. Bronnenberg, "Exploring the Implications of the Internet for Consumer Marketing," *Journal of the Academy of Marketing Science* (Fall 1997), pp. 329–46.
28. This discussion is based on John Deighton, "Note on Marketing and the World Wide Web," *Harvard Business School Note #9-597-037* (Boston: Harvard Business School Publishing, 1997). See also John Deighton, "The Future of Interactive Marketing," *Harvard Business Review* (November–December 1996), pp. 151–62.
29. "Random Access: Dell's Sell," *Forbes ASAP* (February 22, 1999), p. 16; and "Online with the Operator," *American Demographics*.
30. "The Corporation of the Future," *Business Week* (August 31, 1998), pp. 102–6; "Net Sales," *Sales & Marketing Management* (April 1998), pp. 90–91; and www.cisco.com, downloaded February 10, 1999.
31. Procter & Gamble, Inc., www.pg.com, downloaded February 10, 1999.

32. These examples are found in "Met Life Backs Local Agents with Sidewalk Sponsorship," *Marketing News* (January 18, 1999), p. 38; and "Branding on the Net," *Business Week*.
33. Deighton, "Note on Marketing and the World Wide Web."
34. George E. Belch and Michael A. Belch, *Advertising and Promotion: An Integrated Marketing Communications Approach*, 4th ed. (New York: Irwin/McGraw-Hill, 1998). For extensive coverage of the different forms of online advertising, see William F. Arens, *Contemporary Advertising*, 7th ed. (New York: Irwin/McGraw-Hill, 1999), pp. 515–24.
35. "A Shameless Bribe," *Online Media Strategies for Advertising. A Supplement to Advertising Age* (Spring 1998), p. 60A.
36. acnielsen.ca, downloaded June 5, 1999.
37. Nelson Wang, "Sponsorships Popular with Web Advertisers," *Internet World*, www.internetworld.com, downloaded February 17, 1999.
38. "Berkeley Systems Finds Interstitials Beat Other Ads," *Advertising Age* (August 12, 1998), p. 3.
39. "Intermercials, Sponsorships Will Emerge as New Online Ad Models," *Advertising Age* (June 27, 1997), p. 24.
40. For an extensive discussion of webcasting, see *Webcasting and Push Technology Strategies* (Charleston, SC: Computer Technology Research Corp., 1999).
41. Point Cast, Inc., www.pointcast.com, downloaded February 15, 1999.
42. Amy Cortese, "It's Called Webcasting, and It Promises to Deliver the Info You Want, Straight to Your PC," *Business Week* (February 24, 1997), pp. 95–104.
43. Bob Donath, "Managing the Workhorses of the Web," *Marketing News* (January 18, 1999), p. 6.
44. Krantz, "Click Till You Drop."
45. Scott Woolley, "I Got It Cheaper Than You," *Forbes* (November 2, 1998), pp. 82, 84.
46. For useful reading on the challenges of interactive marketing, see Don Peppers, Martha Rogers, and Bob Dorf, "Is Your Company Ready for One-to-One Marketing?" *Harvard Business Review* (January–February 1999), pp. 151–60; and Larry Downes and Chunka Mui, *Unleashing the Killer App: Digital Strategies for Market Dominance* (Boston, MA: Harvard Business School Press, 1998).
47. Mary Beth Grover, "Lost in Cyberspace," *Forbes* (March 8, 1999), pp. 124–28.

America Online, Inc.: This case was written by Michael Vessey.

CHAPTER 9

1. John Horn, "Studios Play Name Game," *Star Tribune* (August 10, 1997), p. F11.
2. Peter Passell, "As Cost of Movie Making Rises, Hollywood Bets It All on Openings," *Star Tribune* (December 29, 1997), pp. D1, D4.
3. Thomas R. King, "How Big Will Disney's 'Pocahontas' Be?" *The Wall Street Journal* (May 15, 1995), pp. B1, B8.
4. Richard Turner and John R. Emshwiller, "Movie-Research Czar Is Said by Some to Sell Manipulated Findings," *The Wall Street Journal* (December 17, 1993), p. A1.
5. Helene Diamond, "Lights, Camera . . . Research!" *Marketing News* (September 11, 1989), pp. 10–11; and "Killer!" *Time* (November 16, 1987), pp. 72–79.
6. Jeff Strickler, "Titanic Director Was Floating on Air after Local Test," *Star Tribune* (December 26, 1997), pp. D1, D2.
7. Bruce Orwall, " 'Primary Colors' Had So Much Going for It, and Then It Just Sank," *The Wall Street Journal* (April 15, 1998), pp. A1, A10.
8. "The Business of Blockbusters," *Wharton Alumni Magazine* (Fall, 1997), pp. 8–12.
9. "New Marketing Research Definition Approved," *Marketing News* (January 2, 1987), pp. 72–79.
10. Joseph Pereira, "Unknown Fruit Takes on Unfamiliar Markets," *The Wall Street Journal* (September 9, 1995), pp. B1, B5.
11. Cyndee Miller, "Kiddi Just Fine in the U.K., But Here It's Binky," *Marketing News* (August 28, 1995), p. 8.
12. Michael J. McCarthy, "Ford Companies Hunt for a 'Next Big Thing' but Few Can Find One," *The Wall Street Journal* (May 6, 1997), pp. A1, A6.
13. "Focus on Consumers," *General Mills Midyear Report* (Minneapolis, MN: January 8, 1998), pp. 2–3.
14. Michael J. McCarthy, "Stalking the Elusive Teenage Trendsetter," *The Wall Street Journal* (November 19, 1998), pp. B1, B10.
15. Roy Furchgott, "For Cool Hunters, Tomorrow's Trend Is the Trophy," *The New York Times* (June 28, 1998), p. 10; and Emily Nelson, "The Hunt for Hip: A Trend Scout's Trail," *The Wall Street Journal* (December 9, 1998), pp. B1, B6.
16. Scott B. Dacko, "Data Collection Should not Be Manual Labor," *Marketing News* (August 28, 1995), p. 31.
17. Dale Burger, "Pushing Creativity to the Limit," *Computing Canada* (May 24, 1995), p. 37.
18. Ken Riddell, "Shoppers Adds Life to Pop Market," *Marketing* (July 26, 1993), p. 2.
19. Kenneth Wylie, "Special Report: Eager Marketers Driving New Globalism," *Advertising Age* (October 30, 1995), pp. 28–29.
20. Patrick E. Murphy and Gene R. Laczniak, "Emerging Ethical Issues Facing Marketing Researchers," *Marketing Research* (June 1992), pp. 6–11.
21. Adapted from Donald S. Tull and Del I. Hawkins, *Marketing Research: Measurement and Method,* 5th ed. (New York: Macmillan Publishing Company, 1990), Chap. 23.
22. John A. Byrne, "Virtual Management," *Business Week* (September 21, 1998), pp. 80–82.
23. Steve Alexander, "Data Mining," *Star Tribune* (August 17, 1997), pp. D1, D5.
24. James H. Gilmore and B. Joseph Pine II, "The Four Faces of Mass Customization," *Harvard Business Review* (January–February 1997), pp. 91–101; Susan Phinney, "Lenses, Levis Lead the Way in Products Made to Individual Order," *Star Tribune* (May 14, 1997), p. B2; and Erick Schonfeld, "The Customized, Digitized, Have-It-Your-Way Economy," *Fortune* (September 28, 1998), pp. 115–24.
25. Mark A. Moon, John T. Mentzer, Carlo D. Smith, and Michael S. Garver, "Seven Keys to Better Forecasting," *Business Horizons* (September–October 1998), pp. 44–52.
26. Statistics Canada, CANSIM matrices 6367, 6379, and Retail Council of Canada, Toronto, 1997.
27. Doug McCuaig and Christopher Holt, "Getting Intimate with Customers," *Marketing* (July 14, 1997)—www.marketingmag.ca, July 17, 1997.

Bookworms, Inc.: This case was prepared by James E. Nelson.

CHAPTER 10

1. Joseph Pereira, "Board-Riding Youths Take Sneaker Maker on a Fast Ride Uphill," *The Wall Street Journal* (April 16, 1998), pp. A1, A8; and Joseph Pereira, "Sneaker Company Tops Out-of-Breath Baby Boomers," *The Wall Street Journal* (January 16, 1998), pp. B1, B2.
2. James Champy, "Ending Your Company's Slump," *Sales & Marketing Management* (May 1998), p. 26; and Bill Saporito, "Can Nike Get Unstuck," *Time* (March 30, 1998), pp. 48–53.
3. Steven Greenhouse, "Groups Reach Agreement for Curtailing Sweatshops; Approve Monitoring and a Code of Conduct," *The New York Times* (November 5, 1998), p. A20.
4. Kenneth Labich, "Nike vs. Reebok: A Battle for Hearts, Minds, and Feet," *Fortune* (September 18, 1995), pp. 90–106.
5. Robert Lohrer, "Reebok in Tailored Clothing Business; Greg Norman Collection Adds Blazers, Dress Slacks," *Daily News Record* (January 29, 1997), p. 1; and "Reebok DMX Trac Golf Shoe Is Giving Retailers a Profitable Playing Partner," *PR Newswire* (July 22, 1998), p. 7.

6. Jeff Jensen, "Reebok Backs New Shoe with Anti-Nike Stance," *Advertising Age* (May 25, 1998), p. 4; and "Air Apparent," *Time* (March 2, 1998), p. 20.
7. David Leohnardt, "Two-Tier Marketing," *Business Week* (March 17, 1997), pp. 82–90.
8. Erick Schonfeld, "The Customized, Digitized, Have-It-Your-Way Economy," *Fortune* (September 28, 1998), pp. 115–24; and James H. Gilmore and B. Joseph Pine III, "The Four Faces of Mass Customization," *Harvard Business Review* (January–February 1997), pp. 91–101.
9. Issues in using marketing segmentation studies are described in William Rudelius, John R. Walton, and James C. Cross, "Improving the Managerial Relevance of Market Segmentation Studies," in Michael J. Houston, ed., *1987 Review of Marketing* (Chicago: American Marketing Association, 1987), pp. 385–404.
10. Goldfarb Consultants, Toronto, February, 1999.
11. Example supplied by Allison Scoleri, Goldfarb Consultants, Toronto, February 1, 1999.
12. Ibid.
13. James Pollock, "Ault Whips Up the Dairy Industry with Purfiltre," *Marketing* (March 13, 1995), p. 2.
14. Sanjay S. Mehta and Gurinderjit B. Mehta, "Development and Growth of the Business Class: Strategic Marketing Implications for the Airline Industry," *Journal of Customer Service in Marketing and Management,* vol. 3, no. 1 (1997), pp. 59–78.
15. The discussion of Apple's segmentation strategies through the years is based on information from its Web site: www.apple-history.com/history.html; and Michael Krantz, "Jobs' Golden Apple," *Time* (August 2, 1999), pp. 66–68.
16. Jim Carlton, "Apple to Post Profit Again on Sales Gains," *The Wall Street Journal* (January 6, 1999), pp. A3, A8.
17. Craig S. Smith and Rebecca Blumenstein, "In China, GM Bets Billions on a Market Strewn with Casualties," *The Wall Street Journal* (February 11, 1998), pp. A1, A11; and Rebecca Blumenstein, "GM Is Building Plants in Developing Nations to Wow New Markets," *The Wall Street Journal* (August 4, 1997), pp. A1, A4.
18. Gregory L. White, "GM to Crunch Five Marketing Divisions into One," *The Wall Street Journal* (August 5, 1998), p. A3, A6; and "GM Aims to Cut Time to Market with $1.5 Billion Modernization," *Star Tribune* (November 11, 1998), p. D7.
19. Angelo B. Henderson, "U-Turn on Caddy Truck Detours GM Strategy," *The Wall Street Journal* (March 26, 1998), pp. B1, B9.
20. Alex Taylor III, "Is Jack Smith the Man to Fix GM?" *Fortune* (August 3, 1998), pp. 86–92; and Bill Vlasic, "Too Many Models, Too Little Focus," *Business Week* (December 1, 1997), p. 148.
21. Kathleen Kerwin, "Why Didn't GM Do More for Saturn?" *Business Week* (March 16, 1998), p. 62.

Cantel: This case was prepared by Frederick G. Crane.

CHAPTER 11

1. Personal interview with Todd DiMartini, 3M, 1998.
2. Ibid.
3. Bob Kearney, "Joining Forces: 3M Puts Stock in Bonding," *3M Today* (January 1995), pp. 2–5.
4. Definitions within this section are from Committee on Definitions, *Marketing Definitions: A Glossary of Marketing Terms* (Chicago: American Marketing Association, 1960).
5. Frank Gibney, Jr., "A New World at Sony," *Time* (November 17, 1997), pp. 56–64; and Frank Gibney, Jr., and Sebastian Moffett, "Sony's Vision Factory," *Time Digital* (March 10, 1997), pp. 30–34.
6. Neil Gross and Paul C. Judge, "Let's Talk!" *Business Week* (February 23, 1998), pp. 61–72.
7. Greg A. Stevens and James Burley, "3,000 Raw Ideas = 1 Commercial Success!" *Research-Technology Management* (May–June 1997), pp. 16–27.
8. R. G. Cooper and E. J. Kleinschmidt, "New Products—What Separates Winners from Losers?" *Journal of Product Innovation Management* (September 1987), pp. 169–84. Copyright © 1987 by Elsevier Science Publishing Co., Inc.; and Robert G. Cooper, *Winning at New Products,* 2nd ed. (Reading, MA: Addison-Wesley Publishing, 1993), pp. 49–66.
9. An example is the Stanford Innovation Project studies of the U.S. electronics industry, whose results are reported in B. J. Zirger and M. A. Maidique, "A Model of New Product Development: An Empirical Test," *Management Science* (July 1990), pp. 867–83.
10. Greg Burns, "Has General Mills Had Its Wheaties?" *Business Week* (May 8, 1995), pp. 68–69.
11. Marcia Mogelonsky, "Product Overload?" *American Demographics* (August 1998), pp. 5–12.
12. John Gilbert, "To Sell Cars in Japan, U.S. Needs to Offer More Right-Drive Models," *Star Tribune* (May 27, 1995), p. M1.
13. Dan Morse, "High-Tech Bat Swings for Fences," *The Wall Street Journal* (July 9, 1998), pp. B1–B7.
14. Magelonsky, "Product Overload?" p. 5.
15. Larry Armstrong, "Channel-Surfing's Next Wave," *Business Week* (July 31, 1995), pp. 90–91.
16. "They're Still Talkin' about 'Team Talk'," *3M Stemwinder* (May 17, 1995), pp. 1, 4.
17. *Parade Magazine,* December 27, 1998, p. 7.
18. Gibney, and Moffett, "Sony's Vision Factory."
19. Otis Port, "Xerox Won't Duplicate Past Errors," *Business Week* (September 29, 1998), pp. 98–101.
20. Larry Armstrong, "Video: Eye-Popping TV—But It Will Cost You," *Business Week* (February 23, 1998), pp. 118–20; Janet Moore, "Television's Digital Future?" *Star Tribune* (August 8, 1998), pp. D1–D3; and Chris O'Malley, "HDTV Is Here! So What?" *Time* (October 5, 1998), p. 52.
21. William M. Bulkeley, "Scientists Try to Make Broccoli 'Fun'," *The Wall Street Journal* (July 17, 1995), pp. B1, B3.
22. Dennis Berman, "Now, Tennis Balls Are Chasing Dogs," *Business Week* (July 23, 1998), pp. 138.
23. Cynthia Clark, "We're Stuck On Magnetic Poetry," *Publisher's Weekly* (September 28, 1998), p. 27.
24. Bill Vlasic, "When Air Bags Aren't Enough," *Business Week* (June 8, 1998), pp. 84–86.
25. William M. Carley, "Engine Troubles Put GE Behind in Race to Power New 777s," *The Wall Street Journal* (July 12, 1995), pp. A1, A6.

Palm Computing, Inc.: This case was written by Michael Vessey.

CHAPTER 12

1. "Stirring Things Up at Quaker Oats," *Business Week* (March 20, 1998), p. 42; "Gatorade Frost: Sue Wellington," *Advertising Age* (June 29, 1998), p. SB; "Gatorade Re-Ups with NFL at $130M," *BRANDWEEK* (June 8, 1998), p. 4; *The Quaker Oats Company 1997 Annual Report* (Chicago: The Quaker Oats Company, 1998); and "Gatorade Gets Fierce with Next Sub-Brand," *BRANDWEEK* (October 19, 1998), p. 6.
2. For an extended discussion of the generalized product life-cycle curve, see David M. Gardner, "Product Life Cycle: A Critical Look at the Literature," in Michael Houston, ed., *Review of Marketing 1987* (Chicago: American Marketing Association, 1987), pp. 162–94.
3. "The Sun Chip Also Rises," *Advertising Age* (April 27, 1992), pp. S2, S6; and "How Gillette Brought Its MACH3 to Market," *The Wall Street Journal* (April 15, 1998), pp. B1, B8.
4. Orville C. Walker, Jr., Harper W. Boyd, Jr., and Jean-Claude Larréché, *Marketing Strategy,* 3rd ed. (New York: Irwin/McGraw Hill, 1999), p. 231.
5. Portions of the discussion on the fax machine industry are based on "Atlas Electronics Corporation," in Roger A. Kerin and Robert A. Peterson, *Strategic Marketing Problems: Cases and Comments,* 8th ed. (Upper Saddle River, NJ: Prentice Hall, 1998), pp. 494–506; "Think It's New? Think Again!" *Popular Mechanics* (December 1997), p. 32;

"The Facts on Faxes," *Dallas Morning News* (May 12, 1997), p. 20; and "The Technology that Won't Die," *Forbes* (April 5, 1999), p. 56.

6. "E-Mail, IP Transmission Will Imitate, Not Replace, Fax Machines," *News Release* (San Jose, CA: Dataquest, June 1, 1998); and "Old Champions, New Contenders," *The Economist* (October 11, 1997), pp. 78–79.
7. Glenn Rifkin, "Mach 3: Anatomy of Gillette's Latest Global Launch," *Strategy & Business* (Second Quarter 1999), pp. 34–41.
8. For more on fads, see "The Theory of Fads," *Fortune* (October 14, 1996), pp. 49, 52.
9. Based on "The Games Sony Plays," *Business Week* (June 15, 1998), pp. 128–30; "Giants of Video-Game Industry Rallying for Rebound," *The Wall Street Journal* (May 31, 1996), p. B3; "Zap, Kaboom! Video Games Sizzle for Holidays," (November 13, 1997), pp. B1, B15; "Looking for a Sonic Boom," *BRANDWEEK* (March 2, 1998), pp. 26–29; and "U.S. Retail Sales of Video Games Up 32% for Year," *The Wall Street Journal* (November 6, 1998), p. B10.
10. "Sonic Strikes Back," *BRANDWEEK* (February 16, 1998), pp. 1, 6; and "Sony Unveils 128-bit PlayStation," *Dallas Morning News* (March 3, 1999), p. 20.
11. Everett M. Rogers, *Diffusion of Innovations,* 4th ed. (New York: The Free Press, 1995).
12. S. Ram and Jagdish N. Sheth, "Consumer Resistance to Innovation: The Marketing Problem and Its Solution," *Journal of Consumer Marketing* (Spring 1989), pp. 5–14.
13. www.marketingmag.ca, downloaded March 8, 1999.
14. For an historical perspective on the product/brand manager system, see George S. Low and Ronald A. Fullerton, "Brands, Brand Management, and the Brand Manager System: A Critical-Historical Evaluation," *Journal of Marketing Research* (May 1994), pp. 173–90.
15. "Haggar, Farah, Levi's Iron Out the Wrinkles," *Advertising Age* (March 6, 1995), p. 12; and Nancy Boomer, "Frozen Iced Tea Heats Up Summer Drink Category," *Marketing* (June 2, 1997)—www.marketingmag.ca, July 18, 1997.
16. "E-Z Rider," *BRANDWEEK* (August 18, 1997), pp. 24–28; and "Sony and Nintendo Battle for Kids Under 13," *The Wall Street Journal* (September 24, 1998), p. B4.
17. "P&G's Soap Opera: New Ivory Bar Hits the Bottom of a Tub," *The Wall Street Journal* (October 23, 1992), p. B11.
18. "Will the British Warm Up to Iced Tea? Some Big Marketers Are Counting on It," *The Wall Street Journal* (August 22, 1994), p. B1; and "Sneaker Company Tags Out-of-Breath Baby Boomers," *The Wall Street Journal* (January 16, 1998), pp. B1, B2.
19. "Food for What Ails You," *BRANDWEEK* (May 4, 1998), pp. 37–42; and "Nutri-Grain Targets Kids with Enhanced Calcium," *BRANDWEEK* (April 5, 1998), p. 6.
20. "Marketers Try to Ease Sting of Price Increases," *Marketing News* (October 9, 1995), pp. 5–6; "It's the Pits," *Consumer Reports* (February 1992), p. 203; and John G. Hinge, "Critics Call Cuts in Package Size Deceptive Move," *The Wall Street Journal* (February 5, 1991), pp. B1, B8.
21. This discussion is based on Kevin Lane Keller, *Strategic Brand Management* (Upper Saddle River, NJ: Prentice Hall, 1998); and Jennifer L. Aaker, "Dimensions of Brand Personality," *Journal of Marketing Research* (August 1997), pp. 347–56. See also Susan Fournier, "Consumers and Their Brands: Developing Relationship Theory in Consumer Research," *Journal of Consumer Research* (March 1998), pp. 343–73.
22. For an extended treatment of brand equity, see David A. Aaker, *Building Strong Brands* (New York: The Free Press, 1996); and Tom Duncan and Sandra Moriarity, *Driving Brand Value* (New York: McGraw-Hill, 1997).
23. "License to Sell," *BRANDWEEK* (June 8, 1998), pp. 37–42.
24. "Losing the Name Game," *Newsweek* (June 8, 1998), p. 44.
25. "A Good Name Should Live Forever," *Forbes* (November 16, 1998), p. 88.
26. Rob Osler, "The Name Game: Tips on How to Get It Right," *Marketing News* (September 14, 1998), p. 50; and Keller, *Strategic Brand Management*. See also "Pamela W. Henderson and Joseph A. Cote, "Guidelines for Selecting or Modifying Logos," *Journal of Marketing* (April 1998), pp. 14–30.
27. "Buying the Ranch on Brand Equity," *BRANDWEEK* (October 25, 1992), p. 6; and "Kellogg Changes Name of Controversial Cereal," *Marketing News* (August 19, 1991), p. 22.
28. "A Survey of Multinationals," *The Economist* (June 24, 1995), p. 8.
29. For an overview of brand equity and brand extensions, see Vicki R. Lane, "Brand Leverage Power: The Critical Role of Brand Balance," *Business Horizons* (January–February 1998), pp. 25–84.
30. "When Brand Extension Becomes Brand Abuse," *BRANDWEEK* (October 26, 1998), pp. 20, 22.
31. www.rogers.com/RCI, November 13, 1996; and Lara Mills, "Companies Conclude That Two Big Brands Can Market Better Than One," *Marketing* (December 23/30, 1996)—www.marketingmag.ca, July 18, 1997.
32. www.marketingmag.ca, downloaded March 8, 1999.
33. "Kodak Pursues a Greater Market Share in Japan with New Private-Label Film," *The Wall Street Journal* (March 7, 1995), p. B11.
34. "The National Peztime," *The Dallas Morning News* (October 9, 1995), pp. 1C, 2C; David Welch, *Collecting Pez* (Murphysboro, IL: Bubba Scrubba Publications, 1995); and "Pez: Dispense with Idea It's Just for Kids," *BRANDWEEK* (September 26, 1996), p. 10.
35. "Coca-Cola Finds Success Trading New for the Old," *The Wall Street Journal* (March 24, 1995), p. B5.
36. "Which Hue Is Best? Test Your Color I.Q.," *Advertising Age* (September 14, 1987), pp. 18, 20; and "Supreme Court to Rule on Colors as Trademarks," *Marketing News* (January 2, 1995), p. 28.
37. This discussion is based, in part, on Barry N. Rosen and George B. Sloane III, "Environmental Product Standards, Trade and European Consumer Goods Marketing," *Columbia Journal of World Business* (Spring 1995), pp. 74–86; "Life Ever After," *The Economist* (October 9, 1993), p. 77; and "How to Make Lots of Money, and Save the Planet Too," *The Economist* (June 3, 1995); pp. 57–58. See also Stuart L. Hart, "Beyond Greening: Strategies for a Sustainable World," *Harvard Business Review* (January–February 1997), pp. 66–77; and Ajay Menon and Anil Menon, "Enviropreneurial Marketing Strategy: The Emergence of Corporate Environmentalism as Market Strategy," *Journal of Marketing* (January 1997), pp. 51–67.
38. Paula Mergenbagen, "Product Liability: Who Sues?" *American Demographics* (June 1995), pp. 48–54; and "Bottled Up," *The Economist* (December 17, 1994), p. 69.
39. For representative research on warranties, see Joydeep Srivastava and Anusree Mitra, "Warranty as a Signal of Quality: The Moderating Effect of Consumer Knowledge on Quality Evaluations," *Marketing Letters* (November 1998), pp. 327–36; Melvyn A. Menezes and John A. Quelch, "Leverage Your Warranty Program," *Sloan Management Review* (Summer 1990), pp. 69–80; and "Broken? No Problem," *U.S. News & World Report* (January 11, 1999), pp. 68–69.

Polaroid Canada: This case was prepared by Frederick G. Crane. Adopted from *Canadian Advertising Success Stories* (Toronto: Canadian Congress of Advertising, 1995).

CHAPTER 13

1. www.nunavut.com, downloaded March 9, 1999; www.time.com, downloaded April 1, 1999; and David Crary, "New Territory of Nunavut Looking for Tourists," *Maine Sunday Telegram* (May 16, 1999), p. 4k.
2. John E. G. Bateson and Douglas Hoffman, *Managing Services Marketing,* Fourth Edition (Fort Worth: Dryden, 1999).
3. Herbert G. Grubel and Michael A. Walker, *Service Industry Growth* (Vancouver: The Fraser Institute, 1989).
4. Christopher H. Lovelock, *Services Marketing,* 3rd edition (Upper Saddle River, NJ: Prentice-Hall, 1996).
5. Valarie A. Zeithaml, "How Consumer Evaluation Processes Differ Between Goods and Services," in James H. Donnelly and William R.

George, eds., *Marketing of Services* (Chicago, IL: American Marketing Association, 1981).
6. Keith B. Murray, "A Test of Services Marketing Theory: Consumer Information Acquisition Activities," *Journal of Marketing* (January 1991), pp. 10–25; and F. G. Crane, *Professional Services Marketing: Strategy and Tactics* (New York: The Haworth Press, Inc., 1993).
7. Murray, "A Test of Services Marketing Theory."
8. Vicki Clift, "Everyone Needs Service Flow Charting," *Marketing News* (October 23, 1995), pp. 41, 43; Mary Jo Bitner, Bernard H. Booms, and Mary Stanfield Tetreault, "The Service Encounter: Diagnosing Favorable and Unfavorable Incidents," *Journal of Marketing* (January 1990), pp. 71–84; Eberhard Scheuing, "Conducting Customer Service Audits," *Journal of Consumer Marketing* (Summer 1989), pp. 35–41; and W. Earl Susser, R. Paul Olsen, and D. Daryl Wyckoff, *Management of Service Operations* (Boston: Allyn & Bacon, 1978).
9. John Ozment and Edward Morash, "The Augmented Service Offering for Perceived and Actual Service Quality," *Journal of the Academy of Marketing Science* (Fall 1994), pp. 352–63.
10. A. Parasuraman, Valarie A. Zeithaml, and Leonard L. Berry, "Reassessment of Expectations as a Comparison Standard in Measuring Service Quality: Implications for Further Research," *Journal of Marketing* (January 1994), pp. 111–24; and Leonard L. Berry, *On Great Service* (New York: Free Press, 1995).
11. A. Parasuraman, Valarie A. Zeithaml, and Leonard L. Berry, "Reassessment of Expectations as a Comparison Standard in Measuring Service Quality."
12. Amy Ostrom and Dawn Iacobucci, "Consumer Trade-Offs and the Evaluation of Services," *Journal of Marketing* (January 1995), pp. 17–28; and J. Joseph Cronin, Jr., and Steven A. Taylor, "Measuring Service Quality: A Reexamination and Extension," *Journal of Marketing* (July 1992), pp. 55–68; A. H. Kizilbash, Nessim Y. Hanna, and John S. Wagle, "Is Gap Analysis a Useful Aid for Measuring Service Quality in Industrial Product Sales Organizations?" *Journal of Customer Service in Marketing and Management,* vol. 3, no. 4 (1997), pp. 75–80; Alain Genestre and Paul Herbig, "Service Quality: An Examination of Demographic Differences," *Journal of Customer Service in Marketing and Management,* vol. 3, no. 3 (1997), pp. 65–83; and Jack Dart, "Professional Service Quality: The Practice or the Professional?" *Journal of Customer Service in Marketing and Management,* vol. 3, no. 2 (1997), pp. 7–21.
13. Stephen S. Tax and Stephen W. Brown, "Recovering and Learning from Service Failure," *Sloan Management Review* (Fall 1998), pp. 75–88; Stephen S. Tax, Stephen W. Brown, and Murali Chandrashekaran, "Customer Evaluations of Service Complaint Experiences: Implications for Relationship Marketing," *Journal of Marketing* (April 1998), pp. 60–76; Stephen W. Brown, "Service Recovery Through IT," *Marketing Management* (Fall 1997), pp. 25–27; and Leonard L. Berry and A. Parasuraman, "Listening to the Customer—The Concept of a Service-Quality Information System," *Sloan Management Review* (Spring 1997), pp. 65–76.
14. Leonard L. Berry, "Relationship Marketing of Services—Growing Interest, Emerging Perspectives," *Journal of the Academy of Marketing Science* (Fall 1995), pp. 236–45; Mary Jo Bitner, "Building Service Relationships: It's All About Promises," *Journal of the Academy of Marketing Science* (Fall 1995), pp. 246–51; Kevin P. Gwinner, Dwayne D. Gremler, and Mary Jo Bitner, "Relational Benefits in Services Industries: The Customer's Perspective," *Journal of the Academy of Marketing Science* (Spring 1998), pp. 101–14; Susan Fournier, Susan Dobscha, and David Glen Mick, "Preventing the Premature Death of Relationship Marketing," *Harvard Business Review* (January–February 1998), pp. 42–51; and John V. Petrof, "Relationship Marketing: The Wheel Reinvented?" *Business Horizons* (November–December 1997), pp. 26–31.
15. Thomas S. Gruca, "Defending Service Markets," *Marketing Management* (1994 No. 1), pp. 31–38; and Leonard L. Berry, Jeffrey S. Conant, and A. Parasuraman, "A Framework for Conducting a Services Marketing Audit," *Journal of the Academy of Marketing Science* (Summer 1991), pp. 255–68.
16. Patriya Tansuhaj, Donna Randall, and Jim McCullough, "A Services Marketing Management Model: Integrating Internal and External Marketing Functions," *Journal of Services Marketing* (Winter 1988), pp. 31–38.
17. Christian Gronroos, "Internal Marketing Theory and Practice," in Tim Bloch, G. D. Upah, and V. A. Zeithaml, eds., *Services Marketing in a Changing Environment* (Chicago, IL: American Marketing Association, 1984); and Dennis J. Cahill, *Internal Marketing* (New York: The Haworth Press Inc., 1996).
18. Ibid.
19. Hong Lee and Robert Boissoneau, "Empowering People in Modern Organizations for Improved Customer Service," *Journal of Customer Service in Marketing and Management,* vol. 3, no. 2 (1997), pp. 55–69; and Scott W. Kelly, "Developing Customer Orientation among Service Employees," *Journal of the Academy of Marketing Science* (Winter 1992), pp. 27–36.
20. Sundar G. Bharedwaj, P. Rajan Varadarajan and John Fahy, "Sustainable Competitive Advantage in Services Industries: A Conceptual Model and Research Propositions," *Journal of Marketing* (October 1993), pp. 83–99.
21. Frederick H. deB. Harris and Peter Peacock, "Hold My Place, Please," *Marketing Management* (Fall 1995), pp. 34–46.
22. Christopher Lovelock, *Services Marketing,* 3rd ed. (Upper Saddle River, NJ: Prentice Hall, 1996), pp. 204–23.
23. F. G. Crane, "The Relative Effect of Price and Personal Referral Cues on Consumers' Perceptions of Dental Services," *Health Marketing Quarterly,* vol. 13, no. 4 (1996), pp. 91–105.
24. Christopher Lovelock, *Services Marketing.*
25. Robert E. Hite, Cynthia Fraser, and Joseph A. Bellizzi, "Professional Service Advertising: The Effects of Price Inclusion, Justification, and Level of Risk," *Journal of Advertising Research* 30 (August/September 1990), pp. 23–31; and F. G. Crane, *Professional Services Marketing: Strategy and Tactics.*
26. F. G. Crane, *Professional Services Marketing: Strategy and Tactics.*
27. Thomas A. Stewart, "A New 500 for the New Economy," *Fortune* (May 15, 1995), pp. 166–78; Philip Elmer-Dewitt, "Mine, All Mine," *Time* (June 5, 1995), pp. 46–54; and James Brian Quinn and Penny C. Paquette, "Technology in Services: Creating Organizational Revolutions," *Sloan Management Review* (Winter 1990), pp. 67–78; and Joshua Quittner, "E-Book Report," *Time* (May 3, 1999), p. 84.
28. Daniel Pedersen, "Dissing Customers," *Newsweek* (June 23, 1997), pp. 56–57; and Dennis J. Cahill, "What's Wrong with Service Providers? A Customer-Service Perspective," *Journal of Customer Service in Marketing and Management,* vol. 3, no. 2 (1997), pp. 71–79.
29. Ibid; Leonard L. Berry, A. Parasuraman, and Valarie A. Zeithaml, "Improving Service Quality in America: Lessons Learned," *Academy of Management Executive,* vol. 8, no. 2 (1994), pp. 32–52.

National Hockey League: This case was prepared by Frederick G. Crane. Source: National Hockey League.

CHAPTER 14

1. www.confederationbridge.com, and interview with CBSL.
2. www.http://lamborghini.itg.net/main/diablo; and www.kelleybluebook.com.
3. Adapted from Kent B. Monroe, *Pricing: Making Profitable Decisions,* 2nd ed. (New York: McGraw-Hill, 1990), chapter 4. See also David J. Curry, "Measuring Price and Quality Competition," *Journal of Marketing* (Spring 1985), pp. 106–17.
4. Numerous studies have examined the price-quality-value relationship. See, for example, Jacob Jacoby and Jerry C. Olsen, eds., *Per-*

ceived Quality (Lexington, MA: Lexington Books, 1985); Kent B. Monroe and William B. Dodds, "A Research Program for Establishing the Validity of the Price-Quality Relationship," *Journal of the Academy of Marketing Science* (Spring 1988), pp. 151–68; Akshay R. Rao and Kent B. Monroe, "The Effect of Price, Brand Name, and Store Name on Buyers' Perceptions of Product Quality: An Integrative Review," *Journal of Marketing Research* (August 1989), pp. 351–57; William D. Dodds, Kent B. Monroe, and Dhruv Grewal, "Effects of Price, Brand, and Store Information on Buyers' Product Evaluations," *Journal of Marketing Research* (August 1991), pp. 307–19; and Roger A. Kerin, Ambuj Jain, and Daniel J. Howard, "Store Shopping Experience and Consumer Price-Quality-Value Perceptions," *Journal of Retailing* (Winter 1992), pp. 235–45. For a thorough review of the price-quality-value relationship, see Valerie A. Ziethaml, "Consumer Perceptions of Price, Quality, and Value," *Journal of Marketing* (July 1988), pp. 2–22. See also Jerry Wind, "Getting a Read on Market-Defined 'Value'," *Journal of Pricing Management* (Winter 1990), pp. 5–14.

5. These examples are from Roger A. Kerin and Robert A. Peterson, "Carrington Furniture (A)," *Strategic Marketing Problems: Cases and Comments,* 8th ed. (Englewood Cliffs, NJ: Prentice Hall, 1998), pp. 307–17; and "Software Economics 101," *Forbes* (January 28, 1985), p. 88.
6. F. G. Crane, "The Relative Effect of Price and Personal Referral Cues on Consumers' Perceptions of Dental Services," *Health Marketing Quarterly*, vol 13, no. 4, 1996, pp. 91–105.
7. N. Craig Smith and John A. Quelch, *Ethics in Marketing* (Homewood, IL:Richard D. Irwin, 1993); and F. G. Crane, "What's Ethical and What's Not with Canadian Business Students," *Working Paper,* 1997.
8. Carol VinZant, "Electronic Books Are Coming at Last," *Fortune* (July 6, 1998), pp. 119–24.
9. J. C. Conklin, "Don't Throw Out Those Old Sneakers, They're a Gold Mine," *The Wall Street Journal,* (September 21, 1998), pp. A1, A20; Richard Gibson, "Bean Market? Some Worry That Beanies Are Ripe for a Fall," *The Wall Street Journal* (September 25, 1998), pp. A1, A11; and Ken Bensinger, "Racing for Mint-Condition Toys," *The Wall Street Journal* (September 25, 1998), p. W10.
10. Daniel Levy, Mark Bergen, Shautanu Dutta, and Robert Venable, "The Magnitude of Menu Costs: Direct Evidence from Large U.S. Supermarket Chains," *The Quarterly Journal of Economics* (August 1997), pp. 791–825.
11. David Wessel, "The Price Is Wrong, and Economics Are in an Uproar," *The Wall Street Journal* (January 2, 1991), pp. B1, B6.
12. Ron Winslow, "How a Breakthrough Quickly Broke Down for Johnson & Johnson," *The Wall Street Journal* (September 18, 1998), pp. A1, A5.
13. Bruce Orwall, "Theater Consolidation Jolts Hollywood Power Structure," *The Wall Street Journal* (January 21, 1998), pp. B1, B2.
14. Jeff Lobb, "The Right (Pepsi) Stuff," *Marketing* (July 8, 1996), p. 15.
15. "Price War Is Raging in Europe," *Business Week* (July 6, 1992), pp. 44–45.
16. Michael Garry, "Dollar Strength: Publishers Confront the New Economic Realities," *Folio: The Magazine for Magazine Management* (February 1989), pp. 88–93; Cara S. Trager, "Right Price Reflects a Magazine's Health Goals," *Advertising Age* (March 9, 1987), pp. 5–8ff; and Frank Bruni, "Price of Newsweek? It Depends," *Dallas Times Herald* (August 14, 1986), pp. S1, S20.
17. Vanessa O'Connell, "How Campbell Saw a Breakthrough Menu Turn into Leftovers," *The Wall Street Journal* (October 6, 1998), pp. A1, A12.
18. For an overview of price elasticity studies, see Ruth N. Bolton, "The Robustness of Retail-Level Elasticity Estimates," *Journal of Retailing* (Summer 1989), pp. 193–219; and Gerald J. Tellis, "The Price Elasticity of Selective Demand: A Meta-analysis of Econometic Models of Sales," *Journal of Marketing Research* (November 1988), pp. 331–41.
19. See, for example, Susan L. Holak and Srinivas K. Reddy, "Effects of a Television and Radio Advertising Ban: A Study of the Cigarette Industry," *Journal of Marketing* (October 1986), pp. 219–27; and Rick Andrews and George R. Franke, "Time-Varying Elasticities of U.S. Cigarette Demand, 1933–1987," *AMA Educators' Conference Proceedings* (Chicago: American Marketing Association, 1990), p. 393.
20. Andrew E. Serwer, "Head to Head with Giants—and Winning," *Fortune* (June 13, 1994), p. 154.
21. Kent B. Monroe, *Pricing: Making Profitable Decisions,* 2nd ed. (New York: McGraw-Hill, 1990), pp. 24–26.
22. Gregory L. White, "General Motors to Take Nationwide Test Drive on Web," *The Wall Street Journal* (September 28, 1998), p. B4.

CHAPTER 15

1. Mark Moremont, "How Gillette Brought Its MACH 3 to Market," *The Wall Street Journal* (April 15, 1998), pp. B1, B8; "Taking It on the Chin," *The Economist* (April 18, 1998), pp. 60–61; and "Gillette's Edge," *Business Week* (January 19, 1998), pp. 70–77.
2. "New Gillette MACH 3 Shaving System Begins Shipping to Stores Across North America," *The Gillette Company New Release* (June 26, 1998).
3. "Sony Prices Its Advanced Game Player at $299, Near Low End of Expectations," *The Wall Street Journal* (May 12, 1995), p. B4.
4. "Sony Slashes the Price of Play Station Game by More Than 25%," *The Wall Street Journal* (March 5, 1997), p. B6.
5. For the classic description of skimming and penetration pricing, see Joel Dean, "Pricing Policies for New Products," *Harvard Business Review* (November–December 1976), pp. 141–53. See also Reed K. Holden and Thomas T. Nagle, "Kamikaze Pricing," *Marketing Management* (Summer 1998), pp. 31–39.
6. Jean-Noel Kapferer, "Managing Luxury Brands," *The Journal of Brand Management* (July 1997), pp. 251–60.
7. "Luxury Steals Back," *Fortune* (January 16, 1995), pp. 112–19. See also "Buying Time," *Fortune* (September 8, 1997), p. 192.
8. See, for example, V. Kumar and Robert P. Leone, "Measuring the Effects of Retail Store Promotions on Brand and Store Substitution," *Journal of Marketing Research* (May 1998), pp. 178–85; and "AT&T Simplifies Price Tiers," *Dallas Morning News* (November 5, 1997), p. 10.1D.
9. Robert M. Schindler and Thomas M. Kibarian, "Increased Consumer Sales Response Through Use of 99-Ending Prices," *Journal of Retailing* (Summer 1996), pp. 187–99. For further reading on odd-even pricing, see Mark Stiving and Russell S. Winer, "An Empirical Analysis of Price Endings with Scanner Data," *Journal of Consumer Research* (June 1997), pp. 57–67; and Robert M. Schindler, "Patterns of Rightmost Digits Used in Advertised Prices: Implications for Nine-Ending Effects," *Journal of Consumer Research* (September 1997), pp. 192–201.
10. "PCs: The Battle for the Home Front," *Business Week* (September 25, 1995), pp. 110–14; David Kirkpatrick, "The Revolution at Compaq Computer," *Fortune* (December 14, 1992), pp. 80–82ff; and "Compaq Worldwide PC Leadership Expands in Third Quarter," *Compaq News Release* (October 26, 1998).
11. Thomas T. Nagle and Reed K. Holder, *The Strategy and Tactics of Pricing,* 2nd ed. (Englewood Cliffs, NJ: Prentice Hall, 1995), pp. 225–28.
12. Kent B. Monroe, *Pricing: Making Profitable Decisions,* 2nd ed. (New York: McGraw-Hill, 1990), pp. 326–27.
13. Robert J. Dolan and Hermann Simon, *Power Pricing: How Managing Price Transforms the Bottom Line* (New York: The Free Press, 1996), p. 249.
14. "Lawyers Start to Stop the Clock," *Business Week* (August 17, 1995), p. 108.
15. George E. Belch and Michael A. Belch, *Introduction to Advertising and Promotion,* 4th ed. (New York: Irwin/McGraw-Hill, 1998), p. 85.
16. For a comprehensive discussion on the experience curve, see Roger A. Kerin, Vijay Mahajan, and P. Rajan Varadarajan, *Contemporary Perspectives on Strategic Market Planning* (Boston: Allyn and Bacon, 1990), chapter 4.
17. "HDTV SETS: Too Pricey, Too Late?" *The Wall Street Journal* (January 7, 1998), pp. B1, B11.

18. "Gillette Co. Sees Strong Early Sales for Its New Razor," *The Wall Street Journal* (July 17, 1998), p. B3.
19. Aimee L. Stern, "The Pricing Quandry," *Across the Board* (May 1997), pp. 16–22.
20. "Hewlett-Packard Cuts Office-PC Prices in Wake of Moves by Compaq and IBM," *The Wall Street Journal* (August 22, 1995), p. B11.
21. "Retailers Using Cut-Rate Videos as Lures," *Dallas Morning News* (October 4, 1995), p. 5H.
22. www.confederationbridge.com.
23. www.strategis.ic.gc.ca.
24. Jeffrey A. Trachtenberg, "Sony Sells 100,000 Video-Game Units on First Weekend," *The Wall Street Journal* (September 12, 1995), p. A12.
25. Monroe, *Pricing,* p. 304.
26. F. G. Crane, "The Relaive Effect of Price and Personal Referral Cues on Consumers' Perceptions of Dental Servicecs," *Health Marketing Quarterly*, vol. 13, no. 4 (1996), pp. 91–105.
27. For an extensive discussion on discounts, see Monroe, *Pricing,* chapters 14 and 15.
28. Ian Ayres and Peter Siegelman, "Race and Gender Discrimination in Bargaining for a New Car," *The American Economic Review* (June 1995), pp. 304–21; "Saturn's Uniform Pricing Extended to Used Cars," *Dallas Morning News* (August 14, 1995), p. 4D; and "Goodbye to Haggling," *U.S. News & World Report* (October 20, 1997), p. 57.

My Own Meals: Sources: Personal interview with Mary Anne Jackson; Mike Duff, "New Children's Meals: Not Just Kids Stuff," *Supermarket Business* (May 1990), p. 93; Heidi Parson, "MOM, Incorporated," *Poultry Processing* (August–September 1989); Lisa R. Van Wagner, "Kids Meals: The Market Grows Up," *Food Business* (May 20, 1991); Mary Ellen Kuhn, "Women to Watch in the 90's," *Food Business* (September 10, 1990); and Arlene Vigoda, "Small Fry Microwave Meals Become Big Business," *USA Today* (June 4, 1990).

CHAPTER 16

1. Alan Goldstein, "Off-Line Opportunity," *Dallas Morning News* (December 9, 1998), pp. 1D, 11D; "About Gateway," www.gateway.com, December 9, 1998; "Gateway to Use Its Stores to Lure Small Businesses," *The Wall Street Journal* (April 8, 1999), pp. B1, B4.
2. See, Peter D. Bennett, ed., *Dictionary of Marketing Terms,* 2nd ed. (Chicago: American Marketing Association, 1995).
3. Based on Frederick E. Webster, Jr., *Industrial Marketing Strategy,* 2nd ed. (New York: John Wiley & Sons, 1998).
4. PepsiCo, Inc., *Annual Report,* 1997.
5. "Compaq Computer Picks Dealers to Finish Assembling Its PCs," *The Wall Street Journal* (July 7, 1997), p. B6.
6. Donald V. Fites, "Make Your Dealers Your Partners," *Harvard Business Review* (March–April 1996), pp. 84–95.
7. This discussion is based on Bert Rosenbloom, *Marketing Channels: A Management View,* 6th ed. (Fort Worth, TX: Dryden Press, 1999), pp. 452–58.
8. *Economic Impact: U.S. Direct Marketing Today* (New York: The Direct Marketing Association, 1998).
9. For a discussion on strategic channel alliances, see P. Rajan Varadarajan and Margaret H. Cunningham, "Strategic Alliances: A Synthesis of Conceptual Foundations," *Journal of the Academy of Marketing Science* (Fall 1995), pp. 282–96; and Johny K. Johansson, "International Alliances: Why Now?" *Journal of the Academy of Marketing Science* (Fall 1995), pp. 301–4. The examples appear in "Pepsi, Ocean Spray Renew Deal; Fruitworks Expands," *BRANDWEEK* (April 6, 1998), p. 14; and "GM Pondering Consolidations in Field Marketing," *Advertising Age* (May 11, 1998), p. 4.
10. General Mills, Inc., *Annual Report,* 1998; and "Spoon-to-Spoon Combat Overseas," *The New York Times* (January 1, 1995), p. 17.
11. For an extensive discussion of wholesaling, see Louis W. Stern, Adel I. El-Ansary, and Anne T. Coughlan, *Marketing Channels,* 5th ed. (Upper Saddle River, NJ: Prentice Hall, 1996), chapter 3.
12. For an overview of vertical marketing systems, see Lou Peltson, David Strutton, and James R. Lumpkin, *Marketing Channels* (Chicago: Richard D. Irwin, 1997), chapter 14.
13. Statistics provided by the International Franchise Association. See also "Franchising the American Dream," *Time* (November 7, 1998), p. 178.
14. For a review of channel partnering, see Robert D. Bussell and Gwen Ortmeyer, "Channel Partnerships Streamline Distribution," *Sloan Management Review* (Spring 1995), pp. 85–96. See also Jakki J. Mohr and Robert E. Spekman, "Perfecting Partnerships," *Marketing Management* (Winter/Spring 1996), pp. 35–43.
15. Edwin R. Rigsbee, *The Art of Partnering* (Dubuque, IA: Kendall/Hunt Publishing Co., 1994), pp. 82–83.
16. Kroger, Inc., *Annual Report,* 1998.
17. "Future Shop," *Forbes ASAP* (April 6, 1998), pp. 37–53.
18. "General Motors to Take Nationwide Test Drive on Web," *The Wall Street Journal* (September 28, 1998), p. B4.
19. "Radio Shack to Sell Only Compaq PCs," *Dallas Morning News* (January 29, 1998), p. 2D.
20. "Gillette Tries to Nick Schick in Japan," *The Wall Street Journal* (February 4, 1991), pp. B3, B4.
21. This discussion is based on John Fahy and Fuyuki Taguchi, "Reassessing the Japanese Distribution System," *Sloan Management Review* (Winter 1995), pp. 49–61; Michael R. Czinkota and Jon Woronoff, *Unlocking Japanese Markets* (Chicago: Probus Publishing Co., 1991), pp. 92–97; and "Japan Keeping U.S. Products Out of Asia; Intricate Network Known as 'Keiretsu' Excludes Outsiders," *The Baltimore Sun* (November 9, 1997), p. 6F.
22. Based on an interview with Pamela Viglielmo, Director of International Marketing, Fran Wilson Cosmetics; "U.S. Firm Gives Lip (Coloring) Service to Japan," *Marketing News* (March 16, 1992), p. 6; and "At Last, a Product That Makes Japan's Subways Safe for Men," *Advertising Age* (January 16, 1995), p. I-24.
23. "Black Pearls Recast for Spring," *Advertising Age* (November 13, 1995), p. 49.
24. Studies that explore the dimensions and use of power and influence in marketing channels include the following: Gul Butaney and Lawrence H. Wortzel, "Distributor Power versus Manufacturer Power: The Customer Role," *Journal of Marketing* (January 1988), pp. 52–63; Kenneth A. Hunt, John T. Mentzer, and Jeffrey E. Danes, "The Effect of Power Sources on Compliance in a Channel of Distribution: A Causal Model," *Journal of Business Research* (October 1987), pp. 377–98; John F. Gaski, "Interrelations Among a Channel Entity's Power Sources: Impact of the Exercise of Reward and Coercion on Expert, Referent, and Legitimate Power Sources," *Journal of Marketing Research* (February 1986), pp. 62–67; Gary Frazier and John O. Summers, "Interfirm Influence Strategies and Their Application within Distribution Channels," *Journal of Marketing* (Summer 1984), pp. 43–55; Sudhir Kale, "Dealer Perceptions of Manufacturer Power and Influence Strategies in a Developing Country," *Journal of Marketing Research* (November 1986), pp. 387–93; George H. Lucas and Larry G. Gresham, "Power, Conflict, Control, and the Application of Contingency Theory in Channels of Distribution," *Journal of the Academy of Marketing Science* (Summer 1985), pp. 27–37; and F. Robert Dwyer and Julie Gassenheimer, "Relational Roles and Triangle Dramas: Effects on Power Play and Sentiments in Industrial Channels," *Marketing Letters,* vol. 3 (1992), pp. 187–200.
25. For an overview of how costly slotting allowances have become in the grocery industry, see Nancy Millman, "Grocers' Aisles the Arena in the Battle for Shelf Space," *Chicago Tribune* (July 29, 1996), p. NW1.

CHAPTER 17

1. David Bovet and Yossi Sheffi, "The Brave New World of Supply Chain Management," *Supply Chain Management Review* (Spring 1998), pp. 14–23; and H. Lee, V. Padmanabhan, and S. Whang, "The Bullwhip Effect in Supply Chains," *Sloan Management Review* (Spring 1997), pp. 93–102.
2. These estimates are based on "U.S. Logistics Closing on Trillion Dollar Mark," *Business Week* (December 28, 1998), p. 78.
3. *What's It All About?* (Oakbrook, IL: Council of Logistics Management, 1993).
4. Ken Cottrill, "Reforging the Supply Chain," *Journal of Business Strategy* (November/December 1997), pp. 35–39.
5. This discussion is based on Robert B. Handfield and Earnest Z. Nichols, *Introduction to Supply Chain Management* (Upper Saddle River, NJ: Prentice Hall 1998), chapter 1.
6. This description is based on Robert M. Monczka and Jim Morgan, "Supply Chain Management Strategies," *Purchasing* (January 15, 1998), pp. 78–85; "Survey of Manufacturing," *The Economist* (June 20, 1998), Special Report; "Restructure of Dealer Networks Will Change Retailing," *Marketing News* (October 26, 1998), p. 10; and Handfield and Nichols, *Introduction to Supply Chain Management.*
7. John Holusha, "P&G Downy Bottles Use Recycled Plastic," *The New York Times* (January 14, 1993), p. C5; and Bruce Van Voorst, "The Recycling Bottleneck," *Time* (September 14, 1992), p. 52.
8. Bovet and Sheffi, "The Brave New World of Supply Chain Management."
9. Joseph Pereira, "In Reebok-Nike War, Big Woolworth Chain Is a Major Battlefield," *The Wall Street Journal* (September 22, 1995), pp. A1, A5.
10. For an extensive description of total logistics costs, see Douglas M. Lambert, James R. Stock, and Lisa M. Ellram, *Fundamentals of Logistics Management* (New York: Irwin/McGraw-Hill, 1998), pp. 15–24.
11. Ronald Henkoff, "Delivering the Goods," *Fortune* (November 28, 1994), pp. 64–78.
12. Toby B. Gooley, "How Logistics Drive Customer Service," *Traffic Management* (January 1996), p. 46.
13. For an overview of how customer service has been viewed and defined, see "A Compendium of Research in Customer Service," *International Journal of Physical Distribution and Logistics Management,* 24, no. 4 (1994), pp. 1–68.
14. Michael Levy and Barton A. Weitz, *Retailing Management,* 3rd ed. (New York: Irwin/McGraw Hill, 1998), p. 331.
15. Ibid, p. 332; and Handfield and Nichols, *Introduction to Supply Chain Management,* p. 18.
16. Jon Bigness, "In Today's Economy, There Is Big Money to Be Made in Logistics," *The Wall Street Journal* (September 6, 1995), pp. A1, A9.
17. Robert C. Lieb and Arnold Maltz, "What's the Future for Third-Party Logistics?" *Supply Chain Management Review* (Spring 1998), pp. 71–79.
18. "IBM Moves Procurement to the Web-Big Time," *Purchasing* (December 10, 1998), p. S13; and Sherree DeCovny, "Electronic Commerce Comes of Age," *Journal of Business Strategy* (November/December 1998), pp. 38–44.
19. Scott Leibs, "Using IT to Grow," *Industry Week* (December 21, 1998), pp. 56–59; Christina Duff and Bob Ortega, "Watch Out for Flying Packages," *Business Week* (November 14, 1995), p. 40; Roy Rowan, "Business Triumphs of the Seventies," *Fortune* (December 1979), p. 34; and Lieb and Maltz, "What's the Future for Third-Party Logistics?"
20. Henkoff, "Delivering the Goods."
21. Cottrill, "Reforging the Supply Chain."
22. Marshall L. Fisher, "What Is the Right Supply Chain for Your Product?" *Harvard Business Review* (March–April 1997), pp. 105–16.
23. For an excellent overview on reverse logistics, see Edward J. Marien, "Reverse Logistics as Competitive Strategy," *Supply Chain Management Review* (Spring 1998), pp. 43–53.
24. Doug Bartholomew, "IT Delivers for UPS," *Industry Week* (December 21, 1998), pp. 60–63.

CHAPTER 18

1. www.marketingmag.ca, downloaded July 15, 1999; and www.retailcouncil.org, downloaded July 15, 1999.
2. Kenneth Cline, "The Devil in the Details," *Banking Strategies* (November/December 1997), p. 24; and Roger Trap, "Design Your Own Jeans," *The Independent* (October 18, 1998), p. 22.
3. Statistics Canada, *Market Research Handbook,* cat. 63-224 (Ottawa, 1997).
4. Canadian Markets, *The Financial Post* (Toronto, 1999).
5. World's Top Stores, *Marketing* (March 1, 1993), p. 18.
6. "Retailers Rush to Capture New Markets," *Financial Times* (March 13, 1998), p. 2; Carla Rapoport and Justin Martin, "Retailers Go Global," *Fortune* (February 20, 1995), pp. 102–8; William Symonds, "Invasion of the Retail Snatchers," *Business Week* (May 9, 1994), pp. 72–73; and Eugene Fram and Riad Ajami, "Globalization of Markets and Shopping Stress: Cross-Country Comparisons," *Business Horizons* (January– February 1994), pp. 17–23.
7. Jo Foley, "To Buy or Not to Buy in Dubai," *The Times* (March 7, 1998); and "Fly, Buy a Bigger Dubai," *The Hindu* (March 15, 1998).
8. Gene Koretz, "Those Plucky Corner Stores," *Business Week* (December 5, 1994), p. 26.
9. Alison L. Sprout, "Packard Bell Sells More PCs in the US than Anyone," *Fortune* (June 12, 1995), pp. 82–88; Marcia Berss, "We Will Not Be in a National Chain," *Forbes* (March 27, 1995), p. 50; and Steve Kichen, "Pick a Channel," *Forbes* (March 2, 1992), pp. 108, 110.
10. Christopher Palmeri, "Who's Afraid of Wal-Mart?" *Forbes* (July 31, 1995), p. 81.
11. Richard C. Hoffman and John F. Preble, "Franchising into the Twenty-First Century," *Business Horizons* (November–December 1993), pp. 35–43.
12. Allen Whitehead, "Trouble in Franchise Nation," *Fortune* (March 6, 1995), pp. 115–29; and Jennifer S. Stack and Joseph E. McKendrick, "Franchise Market Expands as Rest of Economy Slumps," *Marketing News* (July 6, 1992), p. 11.
13. LaVerne L. Ludden, *Franchise Opportunities Handbook* (Indianapolis, IN: JIST Works, Inc., 1999); and Scott Shane and Chester Spell, "Factors for New Franchise Success," *Sloan Management Review* (Spring 1998), pp. 43–50.
14. Marc Rice, "Competition Fierce in Complex Business of Delivering Packages," *Marketing News* (May 22, 1995), p. 5; Tim Triplett, "Scanning Wand Makes Checkout Lines Disappear," *Marketing News* (July 4, 1994), p. 6; and Tara Parker-Pope, "New Devices Add Up Bill, Measure Shoppers' Honesty," *The Wall Street Journal* (June 6, 1995), pp. B1, 13.
15. Cyndee Miller, "Nordstrom Is Tops in Survey," *Marketing News* (February 15, 1993), p. 12; "Daytons Is Top Retailer in Customer Satisfaction Survey," *Marketing News* (June 6, 1994), p. 8; and Richard Stevenson, "Watch Out, Macy's, Here Comes Nordstrom," *New York Times Magazine* (August 27, 1989), p. 40.
16. Hank Kim and Andrew McMains, "Games A Foot at Toys 'Я' Us," *ADWEEK* (January 11, 1999), p. 2.
17. Lesley Dow, "Maxi Advances into Loblaws' Home Turf," *Marketing* (July 14, 1997), www.marketingmag.ca, downloaded August 4, 1997.
18. Laurie M. Grossman, "Hypermarkets: A Sure-Fire Hit Bombs," *The Wall Street Journal* (June 25, 1992), p. B1.
19. Steve Scrupski, "Tiny 'Brains' Seen for Vending Machines," *Electronic Design* (December 1, 1998), p. 64F; Dan Alaimo, "Two Stores Are Recording a Hit with CD Vending Machine," *Supermarket News* (June 15, 1998), p. 65; "Scoop," *Seventeen* (January 1999), p. 28; "Vending Machine Software," *Marketing News* (May 8, 1995), p. 1;

and "Coke Machine Modems Send Distress Signals," *Marketing News* (October 9, 1995), p. 2.

20. Anne D'Innocenzio, "Getting Booked: Coping with Catalog Crunch," *WWD* (December 9, 1998), p. 8.

21. Edward Nash, "The Roots of Direct Marketing," *Direct Marketing* (February 1995), pp. 38–40; and Edith Hipp Updike and Mary Kurtz, "Japan Is Dialing 1 800 BUYAMERICA," *Business Week* (June 12, 1995), pp. 61–64.

22. Susan Chandler and Therese Palmer, "Can Spiegel Pull Out of the Spiral?" *Business Week* (August 28, 1995), p. 80; Gary McWilliams, Susan Chandler, and Julie Tilsner, "Strategies for the New Mail Order," *Business Week* (December 19, 1994), pp. 82–85; and Annetta Miller, "Up to the Chin in Catalogs," *Newsweek* (November 20, 1989), pp. 27–58.

23. Christopher Palmeri, "Victoria's Little Secret," *Forbes* (August 24, 1998), p. 58; Robert Lenzner and Philippe Mao, "Banking Pops Up in the Strangest Places," *Forbes* (April 10, 1995), pp. 72–76; and Dyan Machan, "Sharing Victoria's Secrets," *Forbes* (June 5, 1995), pp. 132–33.

24. Gail DeGeorge and Lori Bongiorno, "Polishing Up the Cubic Zirconia," *Business Week* (July 31, 1995), pp. 83–84; Chad Rubel, "Home Shopping Network Targets Young Audience," *Marketing News* (July 17, 1995), pp. 13, 26; and Kathy Haley, "Keys Are Interactive TV and Channel Expansion," *Advertising Age* (February 22, 1993), p. C16.

25. Raymond R. Burke, "Do You See What I See? The Future of Virtual Shopping," *Journal of the Academy of Marketing Science* (Fall 1997), pp. 352–60; Ellen Neuborne and Stephanie Anderson Forest, "Retailing," *Business Week* (January 12, 1998), p. 116; and Maricris G. Briones, "On-line Retailers Seek Ways to Close Shopping Gender Gap," *Marketing News* (September 14, 1998), pp. 2, 10, and www.forrester.com, June 15, 1999.

26. Mary J. Cronin, "Business Secrets of the Billion-Dollar Website," *Fortune* (February 2, 1998), p. 142; Robert D. Hof, Ellen Neuborne, and Heather Green, "Amazon.com: The Wild World of E-Commerce," *Business Week* (December 14, 1998), pp. 106–19; "Future Shop," *Forbes ASAP* (April 6, 1998), pp. 37–52; Chris Taylor, "Cybershop," *Time* (November 23, 1998), p. 142; Stephen H. Wildstrom, "'Bots' Don't Make Great Shoppers," *Business Week* (December 7, 1998), p. 14; and Jeffrey Ressner, "Online Flea Markets," *Time* (October 5, 1998), p. 48.

27. Steve Casimiro, "Shop Till You Crash," *Fortune* (December 21, 1998), pp. 267–70; De'Ann Weimer, "Can I Try (Click) That Blouse (Drag) in Blue?" *Business Week* (November 9, 1998), p. 86.

28. Chris O'Malley, "No Waiting on the Web," *Time* (November 16, 1998), p. 76; B. G. Yovovich, "Webbed Feat," *Marketing News* (January 19, 1998), p. 1, 18; Joseph Alba, John Lynch, Barton Weitz, Chris Janiszewski, Richard Lutz, Alan Sawyer, and Stacy Wood, "Interactive Home Shopping: Consumer, Retailer, and Manufacturer Incentives to Participate in Electronic Marketplace," *Journal of Marketing* (July 1997), pp. 38–53.

29. Donna Bursey, "Targeting Small Businesses for Telemarketing and Mail Order Sales," *Direct Marketing* (September 1995), pp. 18–20; "Inbound, Outbound Telemarketing Keeps Ryder Sales in Fast Lane," *Direct Marketing* (July 1995), pp. 34–36; "Despite Hangups, Telemarketing a Success," *Marketing News* (March 27, 1995), p. 19; Kelly Shermach, "Outsourcing Seen as a Way to Cut Costs, Retain Service," *Marketing News* (June 19, 1995), pp. 5, 8; and Greg Gattuso, "Marketing Vision," *Direct Marketing* (February 1994), pp. 24–26.

30. "TeleWatch to Help Control Unethical Telemarketing," *Telemarketing & Call Center Solutions* (April 1998), p. 28.

31. Bill Vlasic and Mary Beth Regan, "Amway II: The Kids Take Over," *Business Week* (February 1, 1998), pp. 60–70.

32. Mathew Schifrin, "Okay, Big Mouth," *Forbes* (October 9, 1995), pp. 47–48; Veronica Byrd and Wendy Zellner, "The Avon Lady of the Amazon," *Business Week* (October 24, 1994), pp. 93–96; and Ann Marsh, "Avon Is Calling on Eastern Europe," *Advertising Age* (June 20, 1994), p. 116.

33. The following discussion is adapted from William T. Gregor and Eileen M. Friars, *Money Merchandizing: Retail Revolution in Consumer Financial Services* (Cambridge, MA: Management Analysis Center, Inc., 1982).

34. Eva Houre, "Stores Must Get Creative to Survive," *The Chronicle Herald* (August 13, 1999), p. C-1.

35. Gail Tom, Michelle Dragics, and Christi Holdregger, "Using Visual Presentation to Assess Store Positioning: A Case Study of JCPenney," *Marketing Research* (September 1991), pp. 48–52.

36. William Lazer and Eugene J. Kelley, "The Retailing Mix: Planning and Management," *Journal of Retailing* (Spring 1961), pp. 34–41.

37. Francis J. Mulhern and Robert P. Leon, "Implicit Price Bundling of Retail Products: A Multiproduct Approach to Maximizing Store Profitability," *Journal of Marketing* (October 1991), pp. 63–76.

38. Gwen Ortmeyer, John A. Quelch, and Walter Salmon, "Restoring Credibility to Retail Pricing," *Sloan Management Review* (Fall 1991), pp. 55–66.

39. William B. Dodds, "In Search of Value: How Price and Store Name Information Influence Buyers' Product Perceptions," *Journal of Consumer Marketing* (Spring 1991), pp. 15–24.

40. "A Time To Steal," *Brandweek* (February 16, 1999), p. 24.

41. Rita Koselka, "The Schottenstein Factor," *Forbes* (September 28, 1992), p. 104, 106.

42. Rice, "Competition Fierce"; and Gary Strauss, "Warehouse Clubs Heat Up Retail Climate," *USA Today* (September 7, 1990), pp. 1B, 2B.

43. "Warehouse Clubs Fine-tune Units," *Chain Drug Review* (June 29, 1998), p. 38; James M. Degen, "Warehouse Clubs Move from Revolution to Evolution," *Marketing News* (August 3, 1992), p. 8; Dori Jones Yang, "Bargains by the Forklift," *Business Week* (July 15, 1991), p. 152; and "Fewer Rings on the Cash Register," *Business Week* (January 14, 1991), p. 85.

44. Ira P. Schneiderman, "Value Keeps Factory Outlets Viable," *Daily News Record* (July 20, 1998), p. 10; Stephanie Anderson Forest, "I Can Get It for You Retail," *Business Week* (September 18, 1995), pp. 84–8; and Adrienne Ward, "New Breed of Mall Knows: Everybody Loves a Bargain," *Advertising Age* (January 27, 1992), p. 55.

45. Anne Faircloth, "Value Retailers Go Dollar For Dollar," *Fortune* (July 6, 1998), pp. 164–66.

46. Barry Brown, "Edmonton Makes Size Pay Off in Down Market," *Advertising Age* (January 27, 1992), pp. 4–5.

47. James R. Lowry, "The Life Cycle of Shopping Centers," *Business Horizons* (January–February 1997), pp. 77–86; Eric Peterson, "Power Centers! Now!" *Stores* (March 1989), pp. 61–66; and "Power Centers Flex Their Muscle," *Chain Store Age Executive* (February 1989), pp. 3A, 4A.

48. Pierre Martineau, "The Personality of the Retail Store," *Harvard Business Review* (January–February 1958), p. 47.

49. Julie Baker, Dhruv Grewal, and A. Parasuraman, "The Influence of Store Environment on Quality Inferences and Store Image," *Journal of the Academy of Marketing Science* (Fall 1994), pp. 328–39; Howard Barich and Philip Kotler, "A Framework for Marketing Image Management," *Sloan Management Review* (Winter 1991), pp. 94–104; Susan M. Keaveney and Kenneth A. Hunt, "Conceptualization and Operationalization of Retail Store Image: A Case of Rival Middle-Level Theories," *Journal of the Academy of Marketing Science* (Spring 1992), pp. 165–75; James C. Ward, Mary Jo Bitner, and John Barnes, "Measuring the Prototypicality and Meaning of Retail Environments," *Journal of Retailing* (Summer 1992), p. 194; and Dhruv Grewal, R. Krishnan, Julie Baker, and Norm Burin, "The Effect of Store Name, Brand Name and Price Discounts on Consumers' Evaluations and Purchase Intentions," *Journal of Retailing* (Fall 1998), pp. 331–52. For a review of the store image literature, see Mary R. Zimmer and Linda L.

Golden, "Impressions of Retail Stores: A Content Analysis of Consumer Images," *Journal of Retailing* (Fall 1988), pp. 265–93.

50. Mary Jo Bitner, "Servicescapes: The Impact of Physical Surroundings on Customers and Employees," *Journal of Marketing* (April 1992), pp. 57–71.

51. Jans-Benedict Steenkamp and Michel Wedel, "Segmenting Retail Markets on Store Image Using a Consumer-Based Methodology," *Journal of Retailing* (Fall 1991), p. 300; and Philip Kotler, "Atmospherics as a Marketing Tool," *Journal of Retailing*, vol. 49 (Winter 1973–74), p. 61.

52. De'Ann Weimer, "The Softest Side of Sears," *Business Week* (December 28, 1998), pp. 60–62; Susan Chandler, "Drill Bits, Paint Thinner, Eyeliner," *Business Week* (September 25, 1995), pp. 83–84.

53. The wheel of retailing theory was originally proposed by Malcolm P. McNair, "Significant Trends and Development in the Postwar Period," in A. B. Smith, ed., *Competitive Distribution in a Free, High-Level Economy and Its Implications for the University* (Pittsburgh: University of Pittsburgh Press, 1958), pp. 1–25; see also Stephen Brown, "The Wheel of Retailing—Past and Future," *Journal of Retailing* (Summer 1990), pp. 143–49; and Malcolm P. McNair and Eleanor May, "The Next Revolution of the Retailing Wheel," *Harvard Business Review* (September–October 1978), pp. 81–91.

54. Andrew E. Serwer, "McDonald's Conquers the World," *Fortune* (October 17, 1995), pp. 103–16; Lois Therrien, "McRisky," *Business Week* (October 21, 1991), pp. 114–22; and Gail DeGeorge, "Someone Woke the Elephants," *Business Week* (April 4, 1994), p. 52.

55. Bill Saporito, "What's for Dinner?" *Fortune* (May 15, 1995), pp. 51–64.

56. William R. Davidson, Albert D. Bates, and Stephen J. Bass, "Retail Life Cycle," *Harvard Business Review* (November–December 1976), pp. 89–96.

57. Gretchen Morgenson, "Here Come the Cross-Shoppers," *Forbes* (December 7, 1992), pp. 90–101.

58. Michael Krantz, "The First Bank of Redmond," *Time* (April 27, 1998), p. 52; Russell Mitchell, "The Smart Money Is on Smart Cards," *Business Week* (August 14, 1995), p. 68; Thomas McCarroll, "No Checks. No Cash. No Fuss," *Time* (May 9, 1994), pp. 60–62; and Robert Shaw, "How the Smart Card Is Changing Retailing," *Long Range Planning* (February 1991), pp. 111–14.

59. Mary Kuntz, Lori Bongiorno, Keith Naughton, Gail DeGeorge, and Stephanie Anderson Forest, "Reinventing the Store," *Business Week* (November 27, 1995), pp. 84–96; and David Fischer, "The New Meal Deals," *U.S. News & World Report* (October 30, 1995), p. 66.

60. Mary Kuntz, "These Ads Have Windows and Walls," *Business Week* (February 27, 1995), p. 74; and Richard Corliss, "What's Hot, Doc? Retail!" *Time* (May 9, 1994), pp. 64–66.

IKEA: This case was prepared by Frederick G. Crane.

CHAPTER 19

1. Dale Buss, "You Ought to Be in Pictures," *Business Week* (June 22, 1998), p. ENT 16; Julia Fein Azoulay, "Getting Product Placed in Film and TV," *ASAP* (October 21, 1998), p. 46; T. L. Stanley and Karen Benezra, "Hollywood Creative Types Getting in on Corporate Partner Development," *BRANDWEEK* (May 19, 1998); Shinan Govani, "Product Placement in Movies—Is It Really So Bad?" *The Christian Science Monitor* (February 10, 1999), p. 11; and Blair R. Fischer, "Making Your Product the Star Attraction," *PROMO* (January 1996), pp. 42–47, 88.

2. Wilbur Schramm, "How Communication Works," in Wilbur Schramm, ed., *The Process and Effects of Mass Communication* (Urbana, IL: University of Illinois Press, 1955), pp. 3–26.

3. F. G. Crane and T. K. Clarke, *Consumer Behaviour in Canada: Theory and Practice,* 2nd. Ed. (Toronto: Dryden, 1994), pp. 287–98.

4. David A. Ricks, Jeffrey S. Arpan, and Marilyn Y. Fu, "Pitfalls in Advertising Overseas," *Journal of Advertising Research*, vol. 14 (December 1974), pp. 47–51.

5. Adapted from *Dictionary of Marketing Terms*, 2nd ed., Peter D. Bennett, ed. (Chicago: American Marketing Association, 1995), p. 231.

6. B. C. Cotton and Emerson M. Babb, "Consumer Response to Promotional Deals," *Journal of Marketing*, vol. 42 (July 1978), pp. 109–13.

7. Robert George Brown, "Sales Response to Promotions and Advertising," *Journal of Advertising Research*, vol. 14 (August 1974), pp. 33–40.

8. Adapted from *Economic Impact: U.S. Direct Marketing Today* (New York: Direct Marketing Association, 1998), p. 25.

9. Siva K. Balasubramanian and V. Kumar, "Analyzing Variations in Advertising and Promotional Expenditures: Key Correlates in Consumer, Industrial, and Service Markets," *Journal of Marketing* (April 1990), pp. 57–68.

10. Dunn Sunnoo and Lynn Y. S. Lin, "Sales Effects of Promotion and Advertising," *Journal of Advertising Research*, vol. 18 (October 1978), pp. 37–42.

11. F. G. Crane and T. K. Clarke, pp. 237–38, and 346.

12. James M. Olver and Paul W. Farris, "Push and Pull: A One-Two Punch for Packages Products," *Sloan Management Review* (Fall 1989), pp. 53–61.

13. Ken Riddell, "Advertising Sees Share of Pie Dwindling," *Marketing* (January 7, 1994), p. 2.

14. Joseph Weber, "Drug Ads: A Prescription for Controversy," *Business Week* (January 18, 1993), pp. 58–60.

15. T. L. Stanley, "The Big Biz: Place Based Media," *BRANDWEEK* (May 11, 1998).

16. Tom Duncan, "Is Your Marketing Communications Integrated?" *Advertising Age* (January 24, 1994), p. 26.

17. Kim Cleland, "Few Wed Marketing, Communications," *Advertising Age* (February 27, 1995), p. 10.

18. Don Schultz, "Objectives Drive Tactics in IMC Approach," *Marketing News* (May 9, 1994), pp. 14, 18; and Neil Brown, "Redefine Integrated Marketing Communications," *Marketing News* (March 29, 1993), pp. 4–5.

19. Betsy Spethmann, "The Nation's Top Promoted Brands," *PROMO* (December 1998), p. 50; Theresa Howard, "Taco Bell Stakes $75M on Buying Dinner," *BRANDWEEK* (February 22, 1999); T. L. Stanley and Becky Ebenkamp, "Against the Force," *BRANDWEEK* (February 15, 1999); and Theresa Howard, "Taco Bell Aims to Inspire Holiday Feeding Frenzy with Plush Chihuahuas," *BRANDWEEK* (September 14, 1998).

20. Robert J. Lavidge and Gary A. Steiner, "A Model for Predictive Measurement of Advertising Effectiveness," *Journal of Marketing* (October 1961), p. 61.

21. Brian Wansink and Michael Ray, "Advertising Strategies to Increase Usage Frequency," *Journal of Marketing* (January 1996), pp. 31–46.

22. www.marketingmag.ca/media-digest/html, downloaded July 4, 1999.

23. Don E. Schultz and Anders Gronstedt, "Making Marcom an Investment," *Marketing Management* (Fall 1997), pp. 41–49; and J. Enrique Bigne, "Advertising Budget Practices: A Review," *Journal of Current Issues and Research in Advertising* (Fall 1995), pp. 17–31.

24. John Philip Jones, "Ad Spending: Maintaining Market Share," *Harvard Business Review* (January–February 1990), pp. 38–42; and Charles H. Patti and Vincent Blanko, "Budgeting Practices of Big Advertisers," *Journal of Advertising Research*, vol. 21 (December 1981), pp. 23–30.

25. James A. Schroer, "Ad Spending: Growing Market Share," *Harvard Business Review* (January–February 1990), pp. 44–48.

26. Jeffrey A. Lowenhar and John L. Stanton, "Forecasting Competitive Advertising Expenditures," *Journal of Advertising Research*, vol. 16, no. 2 (April 1976), pp. 37–44.

27. Daniel Seligman, "How Much for Advertising?" *Fortune* (December 1956), p. 123.

28. James E. Lynch and Graham J. Hooley, "Increasing Sophistication in Advertising Budget Setting," *Journal of Advertising Research*, vol. 30 (February/March 1990), pp. 67–75.
29. Jimmy D. Barnes, Brenda J. Muscove, and Javad Rassouli, "An Objective and Task Media Selection Decision Model and Advertising Cost Formula to Determine International Advertising Budgets," *Journal of Advertising*, vol. 11, no. 4 (1982), pp. 68–75.
30. Don E. Schultz, "Olympics Get the Gold Medal in Integrating Marketing Event," *Marketing News* (April 27, 1998), pp. 5, 10.
31. Betsy Spethmann, "The Nation's Top Promoted Brands," *PROMO* (December 1998), p. 50; and Wayne Friedman, "Saying Goodbye to Hollywood," *Advertising Age* (January 11, 1999), p. 12.
32. Kate Fitzgerald, "Beyond Advertising," *Advertising Age* (August 3, 1998), pp. 1, 14; Curtis P. Johnson, "Follow the Money: Sell CFO on Integrated Marketing's Merits," *Marketing News* (May 11, 1998), p. 10; and Laura Schneider, "Agencies Show That IMC Can Be Good for Bottom Line," *Marketing News* (May 11, 1998), p. 11.
33. Carol Krol, "Columbia House Looks Down the Road for Gains from Play," *Advertising Age* (March 1, 1999), p. 20.
34. *Statistical Fact Book '98* (New York: The Direct Marketing Association, 1998).
35. Adapted from *Economic Impact: U.S. Direct Marketing Today* (New York: Direct Marketing Association, 1998), pp. 25–26.
36. Carol Krol, "Club Med Uses E-mail to Pitch Unsold, Discounted Packages," *Advertising Age* (December 14, 1998), p. 40.
37. Carol Krol, "Insurer Fireman's Fund Sees Direct as 'Channel of the Future,'" *Advertising Age* (February 15, 1999), p. 18.
38. Jean Halliday, "Taking Direct Route," *Advertising Age* (September 7, 1998), p. 17.
39. Julie Tilsner, "Lillian Vernon: Creating a Host of Spin-offs from Its Core Catalog," *Business Week* (December 19, 1994), p. 85; and Lisa Coleman, "I Went Out and Did It," *Forbes* (August 17, 1992), pp. 102–4.
40. Carol Krol, "Pizza Hut's Database Makes Its Couponing More Efficient," *Advertising Age* (November 30, 1998), p. 27.
41. Alan K. Gorenstein, "Direct Marketing's Growth Will Be Global," *Marketing News* (December 7, 1998), p. 15; Don E. Schultz, "Integrated Global Marketing Will Be the Name of the Game," *Marketing News* (October 26, 1998), p. 5; and Mary Sutter and Andrea Mandel-Campbell, "Customers Are Eager, Infrastructure Lags," *Advertising Age International* (October 5, 1998), p. 12.
42. Juliana Koranten, "European Privacy Rules Go into Effect in 15 EU States," *Advertising Age* (October 26, 1998), p. S31; and Rashi Glazer, "The Illusion of Privacy and Competition for Attention," *Journal of Interactive Marketing* (Summer 1998), pp. 2–4.
43. Laura Loro, "Downside for Public Is Privacy Issue," *Advertising Age* (October 2, 1995), p. 32; Cyndee Miller, "Concern Raised over Privacy on Infohighway," *Marketing News* (January 2, 1995), pp. 1, 7; "Telemarketing Rules OK'd," *Marketing News* (September 11, 1995), p. 1; Judithe Waldrop, "The Business of Privacy," *American Demographics* (October 1994), pp. 46–55; and Mag Gottlieb, "Telemarketing and the Law," *Direct Marketing* (February 1994), pp. 22–23.

CHAPTER 20

1. Maricris G. Briones, "Plotting a Course for Internet Ads," *Marketing News* (September 28, 1998), pp. 1, 12; Kate Maddox, "P&G's Plan: Jump-Start Web as Viable Ad Medium," *Advertising Age* (August 17, 1998), pp. 1, 14; and Jane Hodges, "P&G Tries to Push Online Advertising," *Fortune* (September 28, 1998), p. 280, and www.marketingmag.ca/media-digest/html, July 4, 1999.
2. David A. Aaker and Donald Norris, "Characteristics of TV Commercials Perceived as Informative," *Journal of Advertising Research*, vol. 22, no. 2 (April–May 1982), pp. 61–70.
3. Larry D. Compeau and Dhruv Grewal, "Comparative Price Advertising: An Integrative Review," *Journal of Public Policy & Marketing* (Fall 1998), pp. 257–73; and William Wilkie and Paul W. Farris, "Comparison Advertising: Problems and Potentials," *Journal of Marketing* (October 1975), pp. 7–15.
4. Jennifer Lawrence, "P&G Ads Get Competitive," *Advertising Age* (February 1, 1993), p. 14; Jerry Gotlieb and Dan Sorel, "The Influence of Type of Advertisement, Price, and Source Credibility on Perceived Quality," *Journal of the Academy of Marketing Science* (Summer 1992), pp. 253–60; and Cornelia Pechman and David Stewart, "The Effects of Comparative Advertising on Attention, Memory, and Purchase Intentions," *Journal of Consumer Research* (September 1990), pp. 180–92.
5. Bruce Buchanan and Doron Goldman, "Us vs. Them: The Minefield of Comparative Ads," *Harvard Business Review* (May–June 1989), pp. 38–50; Dorothy Cohen, "The FTC's Advertising Substantiation Program," *Journal of Marketing* (Winter 1980), pp. 26–35; and Michael Etger and Stephen A. Goodwin, "Planning for Comparative Advertising Requires Special Attention," *Journal of Advertising*, vol. 8, no. 1 (Winter 1979), pp. 26–32.
6. Lewis C. Winters, "Does It Pay to Advertise to Hostile Audiences with Corporate Advertising?" *Journal of Advertising Research* (June/July 1988), pp. 11–18; and Robert Selwitz, "The Selling of an Image," *Madison Avenue* (February 1985), pp. 61–69.
7. Bob Donath, "Match Your Media Choice and Ad Copy Objective," *Marketing News* (June 8, 1998), p. 6.
8. Demetrios Vakratsas and Tim Ambler, "How Advertising Works: What Do We Really Know?" *Journal of Marketing* (January 1999), pp. 26–43.
9. Michael S. LaTour and Herbert J. Rotfeld, "There Are Threats and (Maybe) Fear-Caused Arousal: Theory and Confusions of Appeals to Fear and Fear Arousal Itself," *Journal of Advertising* (Fall 1997), pp. 45–59.
10. Bob Garfield, "Allstate Ads Bring Home Point about Mortgage Insurance," *Advertising Age* (September 11, 1989), p. 120; and Judann Dagnoli, "'Buy or Die' Mentality Toned Down in Ads," *Advertising Age* (May 7, 1990), p. S-12.
11. Hank Kim and Scott Hume, "Positioning: Blue Cross, Kaiser Permanente Ads Play Big on HMO Trust Factor," *BRANDWEEK* (September 14, 1998); Jeffrey D. Zbar, "Fear!" *Advertising Age* (November 14, 1994), pp. 18–19; John F. Tanner, Jr., James B. Hunt, and David R. Eppright, "The Protection Motivation Model: A Normative Model of Fear Appeals," *Journal of Marketing* (July 1991), pp. 36–45; Michael S. LaTour and Shaker A. Zahra, "Fear Appeals as Advertising Strategy: Should They Be Used?" *The Journal of Consumer Marketing* (Spring 1989), pp. 61–70; and Joshua Levine, "Don't Fry Your Brain," *Forbes* (February 4, 1991), pp. 116–17.
12. Bob Garfield, "Chauvinist Pigskin," *Advertising Age* (February 1, 1999), pp. 1, 45.
13. Dana L. Alden, Wayne D. Hoyer, and Chol Lee, "Identifying Global and Culture-Specific Dimensions of Humor in Advertising: A Multinational Analysis," *Journal of Marketing* (April 1993), pp. 64–75; and Johny K. Johansson, "The Sense of 'Nonsense': Japanese TV Advertising," *Journal of Advertising* (March 1994), pp. 17–26.
14. Alice Z. Cuneo and Laura Petrecca, "The Best Agencies: Different Thinking and Business Wins Make TBWA Chiat/Day Agency of the Year," *Advertising Age* (March 30, 1998), pp. S-1, 4.
15. Brian D. Till and Terence A. Shimp, "Endorsers in Advertising: The Case of Negative Celebrity Information," *Journal of Advertising* (March 22, 1998), pp. 67.
16. Kim Cleland, "More Advertisers Put Infomercials into Their Plans," *Advertising Age* (September 18, 1995), p. 50; and John Pfeiffer, "Six Months and a Half a Million Dollars, All for 15 Seconds," *Smithsonian* (October 1987), pp. 134–35.
17. www.marketingmag.ca/media-digest/html, downloaded July 4, 1999.

18. Giles D'Souza and Ram C. Rao, "Can Repeating an Advertisement More Frequently than the Competition Affect Brand Preference in a Mature Market?" *Journal of Marketing* (April 1995), pp. 32–42.
19. www.marketingmag.ca/media-digest/html, downloaded July 4, 1999.
20. Ibid.
21. Surendra N. Singh, Denise Linville, and Ajay Sukhdial, "Enhancing the Efficacy of Split Thirty-Second Television Commercials: An Encoding Variability Application," *Journal of Advertising* (Fall 1995), pp. 13–23; Scott Ward, Terence A. Oliva, and David J. Reibstein, "Effectiveness of Brand-Related 15-Second Commercials," *Journal of Consumer Marketing*, no. 2 (1994), pp. 38–44.
22. J. William Gurley, "How the Web Will Warp Advertising," *Fortune* (November 9, 1998), pp. 119–20; and Joe Mandese, "In New Growth Phase, Cable Feeding on Itself," *Advertising Age* (March 27, 1995), pp. S-1, 2, 10.
23. Jacqueline M. Graves, "The Fortune 500 Opt for Infomercials," *Fortune* (March 6, 1995), p. 20; and William McCall, "Infomercial Pioneer Becomes Industry Leader," *Marketing News* (June 19, 1995), p. 14.
24. Jean Halliday, "Volvo Ready to Act on Leads after Infomercial Success," *Advertising Age* (January 25, 1999), p. 61.
25. www.marketingmag.ca/media-digest/html, downloaded July 4, 1999.
26. Ibid.
27. Judy Strauss and Raymond Frost, *Marketing on the Internet: Principles of Online Marketing* (Englewood Cliffs, NJ: Prentice Hall, 1999), pp. 196–249; and Maricris G. Briones, "Rich Media May Be Too Rich for Your Blood," *Marketing News* (March 29, 1999), p. 4.
28. Strauss and Frost, *Marketing on the Internet;* and Heather Green, "The New Ratings Game," *Business Week* (April 27, 1998), pp. 73–78.
29. Arch G. Woodside, "Outdoor Advertising as Experiments," *Journal of the Academy of Marketing Science*, 18 (Summer 1990), pp. 229–37.
30. Ed Brown, "Advertisers Skip to the Loo," *Fortune* (October 26, 1998), p. 64; and Brian Dunn, "Zooming in on the Target," *Marketing* (November 17, 1997), www.marketingmag.ca, downloaded July 5, 1998.
31. Sehoon Park and Minhi Hahn, "Pulsing in a Discrete Model of Advertising Competition," *Journal of Marketing Research* (November 1991), pp. 397–405.
32. Rob Norton, "How Uninformative Advertising Tells Consumers Quite a Bit," *Fortune* (December 26, 1994), p. 37; and "Professor Claims Corporations Waste Billions on Advertising," *Marketing News* (July 6, 1992), p. 5.
33. Pat Sloan and Judann Pollack, "Wrigley to Compensate BBDO on Performance: Gum Marketer Exec Says Plan in Works for U.S. Advertising," *Advertising Age* (April 14, 1997), p. 4; and Mary Kuntz, "Now Mad Ave Really Has to Sing for Its Supper," *Business Week* (December 18, 1995), p. 43.
34. The discussion of posttesting is based on William F. Arens, *Contemporary Advertising*, 6th ed. (Burr Ridge, IL: Richard D. Irwin, 1996), pp. 181–82.
35. David A. Aaker and Douglas M. Stayman, "Measuring Audience Perceptions of Commercials and Relating Them to Ad Impact," *Journal of Advertising Research*, vol. 30 (August/September 1990), pp. 7–17; and Ernest Dichter, "A Psychological View of Advertising Effectiveness," *Marketing Management*, vol. 1, no. 3 (1992), pp. 60–62.
36. David Kruegel, "Television Advertising Effectiveness and Research Innovation," *Journal of Consumer Marketing* (Summer 1988), pp. 43–51; and Laurence N. Gold, "The Evolution of Television Advertising-Sales Measurement: Past, Present, and Future," *Journal of Advertising Research* (June/July 1988), pp. 19–24.
37. Keith McIntyre, "Sometimes Smaller is Better," *Marketing* (November 28, 1994), p. 14.
38. Magid M. Abraham and Leonard M. Lodish, "Getting the Most Out of Advertising and Promotion," *Harvard Business Review* (May–June 1990), pp. 50–60; Steven W. Hartley and James Cross, "How Sales Promotion Can Work for and against You," *Journal of Consumer Marketing* (Summer 1988), pp. 35–42; Robert D. Buzzell, John A. Quelch, and Walter J. Salmon, "The Costly Bargain of Trade Promotion," *Harvard Business Review* (March–April 1990), pp. 141–49; and Mary L. Nicastro, "Break-Even Analysis Determines Success of Sales Promotions," *Marketing News* (March 5, 1990), p. 11.
39. *The 1998 Review of Couponing Trends* (Markham: Ontario: NCH Promotional Services, January 1999).
40. Kapil Bawa and Robert W. Shoemaker, "Analyzing Incremental Sales from a Direct-Mail Coupon Promotion," *Journal of Marketing* (July 1998), pp. 66–78.
41. Roger A. Strang, "Sales Promotion—Fast Growth, Faulty Management," *Harvard Business Review*, vol. 54 (July–August 1976), pp. 115–24; and Ronald W. Ward and James E. Davis, "Coupon Redemption," *Journal of Advertising Research*, vol. 18 (August 1978), pp. 51–58. Similar results on favorable mail-distributed coupons were reported by Alvin Schwartz, "The Influence of Media Characteristics on Coupon Redemption," *Journal of Marketing*, vol. 30 (January 1966), pp. 41–46.
42. "Competing with Coupons," *Marketing News* (March 15, 1999), p. 2; and Larry Armstrong, "Coupon Clippers, Save Your Scissors," *Business Week* (June 20, 1994), pp. 164–66.
43. www.marketingmag.ca, downloaded January 17, 1999.
44. Kathleen Deveny, "Displays Pay Off for Grocery Marketers," *The Wall Street Journal* (October 15, 1992), pp. B1, B5; "VideOcart Is Rolling Again," *Promo* (August 1991), pp. 1, 36; and Bradley Johnson, "Retailers Check Out In-Store," *Advertising Age* (December 16, 1991), p. 23.
45. Bradley Johnson, "How Rebates Saved Cadillac," *Advertising Age* (January 11, 1999), p. 8.
46. Marvin A. Jolson, Joshua L. Wiener, and Richard B. Rosecky, "Correlates of Rebate Proneness," *Journal of Advertising Research* (February–March 1987), pp. 33–43.
47. Danon Darlin, "Junior Mints, I'm Going to Make You a Star," *Forbes* (November 6, 1995), pp. 90–94.
48. This discussion is drawn particularly from John A. Quelch, *Trade Promotions by Grocery Manufacturers: A Management Perspective* (Cambridge, MA: Marketing Science Institute, August 1982).
49. Michael Chevalier and Ronald C. Curhan, "Retail Promotions as a Function of Trade Promotions: A Descriptive Analysis," *Sloan Management Review*, vol. 18 (Fall 1976), pp. 19–32.
50. G. A. Marken, "Firms Can Maintain Control over Creative Co-op Programs," *Marketing News* (September 28, 1992), pp. 7, 9.
51. Leon Reinstein, "Intel's Pentium: A Study in Flawed Public Relations," *Business Week* (January 23, 1995), p. 13; and David Kirkpatrick, "Intel's Tainted Tylenol?" *Fortune* (December 26, 1994), pp. 23–24.
52. Scott Hue, "Free 'Plugs' Supply Ad Power," *Advertising Age* (January 29, 1990), p. 6.
53. Marc Weinberger, Jean Romeo, and Azhar Piracha, "Negative Product Safety News: Coverage, Responses, and Effects," *Business Horizons* (May–June 1991), pp. 23–31.
54. "AT&T Saddles Up with Stampede," *Marketing* (July 14, 1997)—www.marketingmag.ca, July 17, 1997; "News in Brief," *Marketing* (July 7, 1997)—www.marketingmag.ca, July 17, 1997; "Marketers Warning to the Caribana Festival," *Marketing* (June 30, 1997)—www.marketingmag.ca, July 17, 1997.
55. Martin O'Hanlon, "Meat Lovers Not Complete Lovers," *The Chronicle-Herald* (August 11, 1999), p. A1, A2.
56. Michael Treacy and Fred Wiersema, "Customer Intimacy and Other Value Disciplines," *Harvard Business Review* (January–February 1993), pp. 84–93.
57. Scott Hume and Ricardo Davis, "Successful Promos Stress Value-Added," *Advertising Age* (September 21, 1992), p. 35; Zachary Schiller, "Not Everyone Loves a Supermarket Deal," *Business Week* (February 17, 1992), pp. 64–68; and Patricia Sellers, "The Dumbest Marketing Ploy," *Fortune* (October 5, 1992), pp. 88–94.

58. Herbert J. Rotfeld, Avery M. Abernathy, and Patrick R. Parsons, "Self-Regulation and Television Advertising," *Journal of Advertising*, 19, no. 4 (1990), pp. 18–26.

CHAPTER 21

1. This discussion is based on Geoffrey Brewer, "Selling an Intangible," *Sales & Marketing Management* (January 1998), pp. 52–58; and Dun & Bradstreet, *www.dnb.com.*
2. Statistics Canada, Canada Year Book, cat. 11-402 E (Ottawa 1999).
3. Jaclyn Fierman, "The Death and Rebirth of the Salesman," *Fortune* (July 25, 1994), pp. 80–91; "Teaming Up," *Sales & Marketing Management* (October 1993), pp. 98–104; "Getting Hot Ideas from Customers," *Business Week* (May 18, 1992), pp. 86–87; and Brian Tracy, "Stop Talking and Start Asking Questions," *Sales & Marketing Management* (February 1995), pp. 79–87.
4. For recent research and commentary on relationship selling, see John R. DeVincentis and Neil Rackham, "Breadth of a Salesman," *The McKinsey Quarterly,* no. 4 (1998), pp. 32–43; Michael J. Swenson and Greg Link, "Relationship Selling: New Challenges for Today's Salesperson," and Kenneth R. Evans, David Good, and Theodore W. Hellman, "Relationship Selling: New Challenges for Today's Sales Manager," in Gerald J. Bauer et al., eds., *Emerging Trends in Sales Thought and Practice* (Westport, CT: Quorum Books, 1998); and Marvin A. Jolson, "Broadening the Scope of Relationship Selling," *Journal of Personal Selling & Sales Management* (Fall 1997), pp. 75–88; and Barton A. Weitz and Kevin D. Bradford, "Personal Selling and Sales Management: A Relationship Marketing Perspective," *Journal of the Academy of Marketing Science* (Spring 1999), pp. 241–254.
5. David W. Cravens, "The Changing Role of the Sales Force," *Marketing Management* (Fall 1995), pp. 49–57.
6. F. Robert Dwyer and John F. Tanner, Jr., *Business Marketing* (New York: Irwin/McGraw-Hill, 1999), p. 376.
7. Douglas J. Dalrymple and William L. Cron, *Sales Management*, 6th ed. (New York: John Wiley & Sons, Inc., 1998), p. 45.
8. For a perspective on types of selling, see Thomas R. Wotruba, "The Evolution of Personal Selling," *Journal of Personal Selling & Sales Management* (Summer 1991), pp. 1–12. See also René Y. Darmon, "A Conceptual Scheme and Procedure for Classifying Sales Positions," *Journal of Personal Selling & Sales Management* (Summer 1998), pp. 31–46.
9. Christen Heide, *Dartnell's 29th Salesforce Compensation Survey 1996–1997* (Chicago: The Dartnell Corporation, 1996), p. 117. See also "Give Me Two Weeks and We'll Give You a New Salesforce," *Sales & Marketing Management* (December 1998), pp. 31–43.
10. "What a Sales Call Cost," *Sales & Marketing Management* (December 1998), pp. 42–43.
11. "Critical Issues in Research Must Be Faced Now," *Marketing News* (June 8, 1998), p. 15.
12. For recent research and commentary on team selling, see Keith A. Chrzanowski and Thomas W. Leigh, "Customer Relationship Strategy and Customer-Focused Teams," in Gerald J. Bauer et al. *Emerging Tends;* Mark A. Moon and Susan Forquer Gupta, "Examining the Formation of Selling Centers: A Conceptual Framework," *Journal of Personal Selling & Sales Management* (Spring 1997), pp. 31–41.
13. Neil Rackham, Lawrence Friedman, and Richard Ruff, *Getting Partnering Right* (New York: McGraw-Hill, 1996), pp. 47–48; and "The Selling Game," *The Wall Street Journal* (March 29, 1994), p. A1.
14. For an interesting overview on prospecting, see "Give Us Leads! Give Us Leads!" *Sales & Marketing Management* (July 1997), pp. 67–72; and "The Best Way to Prospect," *Sales & Marketing Management* (January 1998), p. 80.
15. Carol J. Loomis, "Have You Been Cold-Called?" *Fortune* (December 16, 1991), pp. 109–15.
16. "Corporate Cultures: Clearing Customs," *SKY Magazine* (July 1995), pp. 35–40.
17. These results are reported in Irma Zandl and Richard Leonard, *Targeting the Trendsetting Consumer* (Homewood, IL: Business One Irwin, 1992), p. 141.
18. James Pollock, "In Pursuit of Privacy," *Marketing* (June 4, 1993), pp. 1, 4.
19. Paul A. Herbing, *Handbook of Cross-Cultural Marketing* (New York: The Holworth Press, 1998).
20. "French Connections," *Dallas Morning News* (December 28, 1998), p. 2D.
21. For an extensive treatment of adaptive and consultative selling, see Bart A. Weitz, Stephen B. Castleberry, and John F. Tanner, *Selling: Building Relationships* (New York: Irwin/McGraw-Hill, 1998), chapter 6.
22. For an extensive discussion of objections, see Charles M. Futrell, *Fundamentals of Selling* (New York: Irwin/McGraw-HIll, 1999), chapter 10.
23. Philip R. Cateora and John L. Graham, *International Marketing,* 10th ed. (New York: Irwin/McGraw-Hall, 1999), p. 128, 131; and Herbing, *Handbook of Cross-Cultural Marketing,* p. 60.
24. Theodore Levitt, *The Marketing Imagination* (New York: Free Press, 1983), p. 111.
25. "Leading Edge," *Sales & Marketing Management* (July 1995), p. 13. See also "Focus on the Customer," *Fortune* (September 7, 1998), Special Advertising Section.
26. *Management Briefing: Sales and Marketing* (New York: The Conference Board, October 1996), pp. 3–4.
27. "Why It Pays to Be Curious," *Sales & Marketing Management* (August 1998), p. 76.
28. Alan J. Dubinsky, Marvin A. Jolson, Ronald E. Michaels, Masaaki Katobe, and Chae Un Lim, "Ethical Perceptions of Field Sales Personnel: An Empirical Assessment," *Journal of Personal Selling & Sales Management* (Fall 1992), pp. 9–21; and Alan J. Dubinsky, Marvin A. Jolson, Masaaki Katobe, and Chae Un Lim, "A Cross-National Investigation of Industrial Salespeople's Ethical Perceptions," *Journal of International Business Studies* (Fourth Quarter 1991), pp. 651–70.
29. See Gilbert A. Churchill, Neil M. Ford, and Orville C. Walker, J., *Sales Force Management,* 5th ed. (New York: Irwin/McGraw-Hall 1997), pp. 112–13.
30. Dalrymple and Cron, *Sales Management,* p. 44. See also Arun Sharma, "Who Prefers Key Account Management Programs? An Investigation of Business Buying Behavior and Buying Firm Characteristics," *Journal of Personal Selling & Sales Management* (Fall 1997), pp. 27–39; Dan C. Weilbaker and William A. Weeks, "The Evolution of National Account Management: A Literature Perspective," *Journal of Personal Selling & Management* (Fall 1997), pp. 49–50; and Paul Dishman and Philip S. Nitse, "National Accounts Revisited," *Industrial Marketing Management* (January 1998), pp. 1–9.
31. Several variations of the account management policy grid exists. See, for example, Dalrymple and Cron, *Sales Management,* pp. 183–89; Churchill, Ford, and Walker, *Sales Force Management,* pp. 203–8.
32. Patricia Sellers, "How to Remake Your Sales Force," *Fortune* (May 4, 1992), p. 103. See also "Look Who's Calling," *Sales & Marketing Management* (May 1998), pp. 43–46.
33. This discussion is based on Dalrymple and Cron, *Sales Management,* pp. 332–36.
34. See, for example, "What Buyers Look For," *Sales & Marketing Management* (August 1995), p. 31; and "The Best Sales Reps Will Take on Their Bosses for You," *Purchasing* (November 7, 1996), p. 81.
35. Weitz, Castleberry, and Tanner, *Selling,* p. 22. For further reading see, Daniel Goleman, "What Makes a Leader?" *Harvard Business Review* (November–December 1998), pp. 93–102; and A. Fisher, "Success Secret: A High Emotional IQ," *Fortune* (October 26, 1998), pp. 293–98.

36. www.statcan.ca, downloaded July 15, 1999.
37. "Is There a Payoff?" *Sales & Marketing Management* (June 1995), pp. 64–71.
38. Earl D. Honeycutt, Jr., Clyde E. Harris, Jr., and Stephen B. Castleberry, "Sales Training: A Status Report," *Training and Development Journal* (May 1987), pp. 42–47.
39. See, for example, Melanie Berger, "When Their Ship Comes In," *Sales & Marketing Management* (April 1997), pp. 60–65; William L. Cron, Alan J. Dubinsky, and Ronald E. Michaels, "The Influence of Career Stages on Components of Salesperson Motivation," *Journal of Marketing* (January 1988), pp. 78–82; Pradeep K. Tyagi, "Relative Importance of Key Job Dimensions and Leadership Behaviors in Motivating Salesperson Work Performance," *Journal of Marketing* (Summer 1985), pp. 76–86; Richard C. Beckerer, Fred Morgan, and Lawrence Richard, "The Job Characteristics of Industrial Salespersons: Relationship of Motivation and Satisfaction," *Journal of Marketing* (Fall 1982), pp. 125–35; and Walter Kiechel III, "How to Manage Salespeople," *Fortune* (March 14, 1988), pp. 179–80.
40. Churchill, Ford, and Walker, *Sales Force Management,* p. 508.
41. "Mary Kay's Off-Road Bonus," *Business Week* (April 6, 1998), p. 8.
42. Michele Marchetti, "Effective Recruiting Means Cloning Your Sales Force's Heavyweights," *Sales & Marketing Management* (December 1998), p. 32.
43. For further reading, see Goutam N. Challagolla and Tassadduq A. Shervani, "A Measurement Model of the Dimensions and Types of Output and Behavior Control: An Empirical Test in the Salesforce Context," *Journal of Business Research* (July 1997), pp. 159–72.
44. "More Companies Link Sales Pay to Customer Satisfaction," *The Wall Street Journal* (March 29, 1994), p. A1; and "IBM Leans on Its Sales Force," *Business Week* (February 7, 1994), p. 110. For further reading on this topic, see Arun Sharma and Dan Sarrel, "The Impact of Customer Satisfaction Based Incentive Systems on Salespeople's Customer Service Response," *Journal of Personal Selling & Sales Management* (Summer 1995), pp. 17–29.
45. Melissa Campanelli, "Eastman Chemical: A Formula for Quality," *Sales & Marketing Management* (October 1994), p. 88; William Keenan, Jr., "What's Sales Got to Do with It?" *Sales & Marketing Management* (March 1994), pp. 66–70; and Cravens, "The Changing Role of the Sales Force."
46. Ginger Conlon, "Automating Your Sales Force," *Sales & Marketing Management* (December 1998), pp. 63–71. See also George W. Colombo, *Sales Force Automation* (New York: McGraw-Hill, 1994). For additional insight into the adoption and implementation, see two articles in *The Journal of Business & Industrial Marketing,* vol. 12, number 3/4, 1997: Madhavan Parthasarathy and Ravipreet S. Sohgi, "Salesforce Automation and the Adoption of Technological Innovations by Salespeople: Theory and Implications"; and Bruce D. Keillor, R. Edward Bashaw, and Charles E. Pettijohn, "Salesforce Automation Issues Prior to Implementation: The Relationship between Attitudes toward Technology, Experience, and Productivity."
47. Cravens, "The Changing Role of the Sales Force."
48. Robert L. Lindstrom, "Training Hits the Road," *Sales & Marketing Management,* part 2 (June 1995), pp. 10–14.
49. "Going Mobile, Part 2," *Sales & Marketing Management* (June 1994), p. 5.
50. Cravens, "The Changing Role of the Sales Force."
51. "Supercharged Sell," *Inc. Tech* (November 1998), pp. 42–50.

Reebok International Ltd.: This case was written by Giana Eckardt.

CHAPTER 22

1. Richard Gibson, "A Cereal Maker's Quest for the Next Grape-Nuts," *The Wall Street Journal* (January 23, 1997), pp. B1, B7.
2. David Leonhardt, "Cereal-Box Killers Are on the Loose," *Business Week* (October 12, 1998), pp. 74–77.
3. Ellen Neuborne, "MMM! Cereal for Dinner," *Business Week* (November 24, 1997), pp. 105–106.
4. *1997 General Mills Annual Report* (Minneapolis: General Mills, Inc., 1997), p. 5.
5. Pankaj Ghemawat, "Sustainable Advantage," *Harvard Business Review* (September–October 1986), pp. 53–58.
6. Roger A. Kerin, P. Rajan Varadarajan, and Robert A. Peterson, "First-Mover Advantage: A Synthesis, Conceptual Framework, and Research Propositions," *Journal of Marketing* (October 1992), pp. 33–52.
7. Murali K. Mantrala, Prabhakant Sirha, and Andris A. Zoltners, "Impact of Resource Allocation Rules on Marketing Investment-Level Decisions and Profitability," *Journal of Marketing Research* (May 1992), pp. 162–75.
8. *1998 General Mills Annual Report* (Minneapolis: General Mills, Inc., 1998), p. 7.
9. This discussion and Figure 22–3 are adapted from Stanley F. Stasch and Patricia Longtree, "Can Your Marketing Planning Procedures Be Improved?" *Journal of Marketing* (Summer 1980), p. 82; by permission of the American Marketing Association.
10. Terry Fledler, "Soul of a New Cheerios," *Star Tribune* (January 28, 1996), pp. D1, D4; and Tony Kennedy, "New Cheerios about to Sweeten Cereal Market," *Star Tribune* (July 25, 1995), pp. 1D, /2/d.
11. Ibid.
12. Fledler, "Soul of a New Cheerios," p. 1D.
13. Adapted with permission of The Free Press, a Division of Macmillan, Inc., from *Competitive Advantage: Creating and Sustaining Superior Performance,* by Michael E. Porter. Copyright 1985 by Michael E. Porter.
14. William B. Wertner, Jr., and Jeffrey L. Kerr, "The Shifting Sands of Competitive Advantage," *Business Horizons* (May–June, 1995), pp. 11–17.
15. Michael Treacy and Fred Wiersema, "How Market Leaders Keep Their Edge," *Fortune* (February 6, 1995), pp. 88–89.
16. Keith Naughton and Bill Vlasic, "The Nostalgia Boom," *Business Week* (March 23, 1998), pp. 58–64; and David Woodruff and Keith Naughton, "Hard Driving Boss," *Business Week* (October 5, 1998), pp. 82–90.
17. J. Martin Fraering and Michael S. Minor, "The Industry-Specific Basis of the Market Share-Profitability Relationship," *Journal of Consumer Marketing,* vol. 11, no. 1 (1994), pp. 27–37.
18. Zachary Schiller, Greg Burns, and Karen Lowry Miller, "Make It Simple," *Business Week* (September 9, 1996), pp. 96–104.
19. John Greenwald, "Slice, Dice, and Devour," *Time* (October 26, 1998), pp. 64–66.
20. Stratford Sherman, "How Intel Makes Spending Pay Off," *Fortune* (February 22, 1993), pp. 57–61.
21. Lee Ginsburg and Neil Miller, "Value-Driven Management," *Business Horizons* (May–June 1992), pp. 23–27; Richard L. Osborn, "Core Value Statements: The Corporate Compass," *Business Horizons* (September–October 1991), pp. 28–34; and Charles E. Watson, "Managing with Integrity: Social Responsibilities of Business as Seen by America's CEOs," *Business Horizons* (July–August 1991), pp. 99–109.
22. Reprinted by permission of the *Harvard Business Review.* An exhibit from "Making Your Marketing Strategy Work" by Thomas V. Bonoma (March/April 1984). Copyright ©1984 by the President and Fellows of Harvard College; all rights reserved.
23. Larry Hirschhorn and Thomas Gilmore, "The New Boundaries of the 'Boundaryless' Company," *Harvard Business Review* (May–June 1992), pp. 104–15.
24. Hans Hinterhuber and Wolfgang Popp, "Are You a Strategist or Just a Manager?" *Harvard Business Review* (January–February 1992), pp. 105–13; Thomas Steward, "The Search for the Organization of Tomorrow," *Fortune* (May 18, 1992), pp. 92–98; George Stalf, Philip Evans, and Lawrence Shulman, "Competing on Capabilities: The New Rules of Corporate Strategy," *Harvard Business Review* (March–April

1992), pp. 57–69; and Jon Katzenbach and Douglas Smith, *The Wisdom of Teams* (Boston: Harvard Business School Press, 1992).

25. Daniel Roth, "This Ain't No Pizza Party," *Fortune* (November 9, 1998), pp. 158–64.
26. Thomas J. Peters and Robert H. Waterman, Jr., *In Search of Excellence: Lessons from America's Best-Run Companies* (New York: Harper & Row, 1982).
27. Ralph Vartabedian, "Built for the Future," *Minneapolis Star Tribune* (April 7, 1992), pp. 1D, 7D; Roy J. Harris, Jr., "The Skunk Works: Hush-Hush Projects Often Emerge There," *The Wall Street Journal* (October 13, 1980), p. 1; and Tom Peters, "Winners Do Hundreds of Percent over Norm," *Minneapolis Star Tribune* (January 8, 1985), p. 5B.
28. Ben Rich and Leo Janos, *Skunk Works* (Boston: Little Brown and Company, 1994), pp. 51–53.
29. The scheduling example is adapted from William Rudelius and W. Bruce Erickson, *An Introduction to Contemporary Business,* 4th ed. (New York: Harcourt Brace Jovanovich, 1985), pp. 94–95.
30. Peter Galuska, Ellen Neuborne, and Wendy Zellner, "P&G's Hottest New Product: P&G," *Business Week* (October 5, 1998), pp. 92–96.
31. Robert W. Ruekert and Orville W. Walker, Jr., "Marketing's Interaction with Other Functional Units: A Conceptual Framework and Empirical Evidence," *Journal of Consumer Marketing* (Spring 1987), pp. 1–19; and Steven Lysonski, Alan Singer, and David Wilemone, "Coping with Environmental Uncertainty and Boundary Spanning in the Product Manager's Role," *Journal of Consumer Marketing* (Spring 1989), pp. 33–43.
32. Doug McCuaig and Christopher Holt, "Getting Intimate with Customers," *Marketing* (July 14, 1997)—www.marketingmag.ca, July 17, 1997.
33. Linda Grant, "Outmarketing P&G," *Fortune* (January 12, 1998), pp. 150–52.
34. John Grossman, "Ken Iverson: Simply the Best," *American Way* (August 1, 1987), pp. 23–25; Thomas Moore, "Goodbye, Corporate Staff," *Fortune* (December 21, 1987), pp. 65–76; and Michael Schroeder and Walecia Konrad, "Nucor: Rolling Right into Steel's Big Time," *Business Week* (November 19, 1990), pp. 76–81.

Clearly Canadian: This case was prepared by Frederick G. Crane based on information supplied by Clearly Canadian Beverage Corporation.

APPENDIX A

1. Personal interview with Arthur R. Kydd, St. Croix Venture Partners.
2. Examples of guides to writing marketing plans include: William A. Cohen, *The Marketing Plan* (New York: John Wiley & Sons, Inc., 1995); Mark Nolan, *The Instant Marketing Plan* (Santa Maria, CA: Puma Publishing Company, 1995); and Roman G. Hiebing, Jr., and Scott W. Cooper, *The Successful Marketing Plan,* 2nd ed. (Lincolnwood, IL: NTC Business Books, 1997).
3. Examples of guides to writing business plans include the following: Rhonda M. Abrahms, *The Successful Business Plan: Secrets & Strategies,* 2nd ed. (Grants Pass, OR: The Oasis Press/PSI Research, 1993); Joseph A. Covello and Brian J. Hazelgren, *The Complete Book of Business Plans* (Naperville, IL: Sourcebooks, Inc., 1995); Joseph A. Covello and Brian J. Hazelgren, *Your First Business Plan,* 3rd ed. (Naperville, IL: Sourcebooks, Inc., 1998); and Angela Shupe, ed., *Business Plans Handbook,* vols. 1–4 (Detroit: Gale Research, 1997).
4. Abrahms, *The Successful Business Plan,* p. 30.
5. Some of these points are adapted from Abrahms, pp. 30–38; others are adapted from William Rudelius, *Guidelines for Technical Report Writing* (Minneapolis, MN: University of Minnesota, undated).
6. The authors are indebted to Randall F. Peters and Leah Peters for being allowed to adapt elements of a business plan for Paradise Kitchens, Inc. for the sample marketing plan and for their help and suggestions.

APPENDIX C

1. Denny E. McCorkle, Joe F. Alexander, and Memo F. Diriker, "Developing Self-Marketing Skills for Student Career Success," *Journal of Marketing Education* (Spring 1992), pp. 57–67.
2. James Heckman, "Marketers Making $$$ in High Tech," *Marketing News* (November 23, 1998), pp. 1, 20; and Michael J. Mandel and Toddi Gutner, "Your Next Job," *Business Week* (October 13, 1997), pp. 64–70
3. "Jobs, jobs, jobs," *Marketing* (June 30, 1997)—www.marketingmag.ca, July 17, 1997.
4. Linda M. Gorchels, "Traditional Product Management Evolves," *Marketing News* (January 30, 1995), p. 4.
5. David Kirkpatrick, "Is Your Career on Track?" *Fortune* (July 2, 1990), pp. 38–48.
6. Robin T. Peterson, "Wholesaling: A Neglected Job Opportunity for Marketing Majors," *Marketing News* (January 15, 1996), p. 4.
7. "The Climb to the Top," *Careers in Retailing* (January 1995), p. 18; and www.simslatham.com/retail, downloaded July 15, 1999; and www.cirass.com, downloaded July 15,1999.
8. Michael R. Wukitsch, "Should Researchers Know More about Marketing?" *Marketing Research* (Winter 1993), p. 50.
9. "Market Research Analyst," in Les Krantz, ed., *Jobs Rated Almanac,* 3rd ed. (New York: John Wiley & Sons, 1995).
10. Cyndee Miller, "Marketing Research Salaries Up a Bit, But Layoffs Take Toll," *Marketing News* (June 19, 1995), pp. 1, 3.
11. Joby John and Mark Needel, "Entry-Level Marketing Research Recruits: What Do Recruiters Need?" *Journal of Marketing Education* (Spring 1989), pp. 68–73.
12. Kathryn Petras and Ross Petras, *Jobs 95* (New York: Fireside, 1994), pp. 100–18.
13. "Your Job Search Starts with You," *Job Choices: 1996,* 39th ed. (Bethlehem, PA: National Association of Colleges and Employers, 1995), pp. 6–9.
14. Arthur F. Miller, "Discover Your Design," in *CPC Annual,* vol. 1 (Bethlehem, PA: College Placement Council, Inc., 1984), p. 2.
15. Robin T. Peterson and J. Stuart Devlin, "Perspectives on Entry-Level Positions by Graduating Marketing Seniors," *Marketing Education Review* (Summer 1994), pp. 2–5.
16. Callum J. Floyd and Mary Ellen Gordon, "What Skills Are Most Important? A Comparison of Employer, Student, and Staff Perceptions," *Journal of Marketing Education* (August 1998), pp. 103–9; "What Employers Want," *Job Outlook '98* (Bethlehem, PA: National Association of Colleges and Employers); and Andrew Marlatt, "Demand for Diverse Skills Is On Upswing," *Internet World* (January 4, 1999).
17. Diane Goldner, "Fill in the Blank," *The Wall Street Journal* (February 27, 1995), pp. R5, R11.
18. Constance J. Pritchard, "Small Employers—How, When & Who They Hire," *Job Choices: 1996,* 39th ed. (Bethlehem, PA: National Association of Colleges and Employers, 1995), pp. 66–69.
19. Adapted from C. Randall Powell, "Secrets of Selling a Résumé," in Peggy Schmidt, ed., *The Honda How to Get a Job Guide* (New York: McGraw-Hill, 1985), pp. 4–9.
20. Joyce Lain Kennedy, "Computer-Friendly Resume Tips," *Planning Job Choices: 1999,* 42nd ed. (Bethlehem, PA: National Association of Colleges and Employers, 1998), p. 49.
21. Arthur G. Sharp, "The Art of the Cover Letter," *Career Futures,* vol. 4, no. 1 (1992), pp. 50–51.

APPENDIX D

1. This case was prepared by Linda Rochford from the following sources: Burton Web site at www.burton.com; www.hoovers.com/capsules/51732.html; Burton Snowboards, Hoover's Online Profile, 1999; 1998 State of the Industry Report, Sporting Goods Manufacturers Associa-

tion (SGMA); www.sportlink.com/research/1998research/industry/98soti.html; Sports Participation Trends Report 1997; www.sportlink.com/research.1998r...ch/industry/98participationtrends.html; and interview with Ben Gustafson, snowboarding competitor and enthusiast.

2. This case was prepared by Paul H. Sandholm and Linda Rochford from the following sources:
www.hoovers.com/capsules/15521.html;
wysiwyg://9/http://www.hoovers.com/annuals/15521af.html;
wysiwyg://4/http:www.hoovers.com/capsules/15521af.html; and
http:www.golfweek.com.
3. This case was prepared by Linda Rochford and Rajiv Vaidyanathan, University of Minnesota–Duluth, from the following sources: www.xoom.com; www.hoovers.com/capsules/57391.html; and personal interviews with Xoom.com executives.
4. This case was prepared by Linda Rochford from the following sources: Alan Goldstein, "The iMac: Funny Look, Serious PC," *Dallas Morning News* (August 25, 1998), Personal Technology Section, p. 1F; "Apple's Revolution in a Box," *TIME Digital,* cgi.pathfinder.com/time/digital/feature/0,2955,18248,00.html (January 1999), pp. 1–5; "iMac Tops Fourth Quarter US Retail/Mail Order PC Sales," *PRNewsletter,* www.prnewswire.com/cgi-bin/stories.pl?ACCT=104&STORY=/www/story/01-21-1999/0000850728& (January 21, 1999); "Apple Reports Fiscal First Quarter Profits of $152 Million," www.apple.com/pr/library/199/jan/13earnings.html (January 13, 1999); and "The Mac: Then and Now," www.cnet.com/Content/Reports/Special/ Mac/ (1999).
5. This case was prepared by Linda Rochford from the following sources: John Welbes, "Coffee Connoisseurs," *Duluth News Tribune* (September 25, 1995), pp. 1B, 3B, 5B; Dori Jones Yang, "The Starbucks Enterprise Shifts into Warp Speed," *Business Week,* (October 24, 1994), pp. 76–77; Rhonda Brammer, "Grounds for Caution," *Barrons* (August 15, 1994), p. 20; www.hoovers.com/capsules/15745.html; and www.starbucks.com.
6. This case was prepared by Linda Rochford from the following sources: David E. Kalish, "Secret of Success: Enterpreneur Michael Dell Had a Better Idea and Decided to Stick With It," *Chicago Tribune, Business News* (August 30, 1998); www.dell.com; www.hoovers.com/capsules/13193.html; and "Supply Chain Management Is Velocity: The Manufacturer's View," www.sun.com/products-n-solutions/manufacturing/pubs/om-3/.
7. This case was prepared by Linda Rochford from the following sources: "New VW Beetle Ads to Bow This Week," *Ad Week,* vol. 9, no. 10 (1998), p. 76; "Snyder's Arnold Communications Awarded Top International Advertising Honors," *Business Wire* (July 10, 1998); "Beetlemania," *Ad Week,* vol. 39, no. 28 (July 13, 1998), p. 24; Alison Fahey and Eleftheria Parpis, "Lion Roars for Arnold, VW Hub Shop Wins Top Print Prize at International Fete," *Ad Week* (June 29, 1998); Debra Goldman, "Bug Redux: the New Volkswagen Beetle," *Ad Age,* vol. 39, no. 12 (March 23, 1998), p. 38; Judy Warner, "Arnold Unveils New Beetle TV Spots for Volkswagen of America," *Ad Week,* vol. 39, no. 11 (March 16, 1998), p. 5; and Craig Wilson, "VW's New Beetle Becomes a National Obsession," *USA Today* (April 22, 1998), pp. 1A–2A, 76.
8. This case was prepared by Linda Rochford and Rajiv Vaidyanathan, University of Minnesota–Duluth, from the following sources: "Image-conscious Consumers Wear Social Ambitions on Wrist," *Duluth News Tribune* (August 2, 1995), p. 6; "Timex Plans $10M Push in 4th Quarter," *Advertising Age* (September 6, 1993), p. 23; "Timex Swatch Campaigns Set for Battle," *The Wall Street Journal* (May 31, 1995), p. B9; "The Best Advertising of 1992," *Time* (January 4, 1993), p. 70; Riccardo A. Davis, "More Ads to Watch," *Advertising Age* (February 7, 1994), p. 50; Elaine Underwood, "Indiglo Watch Lights Up, Better Times for Timex," *Brandweek,* (April 25, 1994), pp. 30–32; Neal McGrath, "Timex, After a Licking, They're Back Ticking," *Asian Business* (December 1994), pp. 18, 20; Chris Roush, "At Timex, They're Positively Glowing," *Business Week* (July 12, 1993), p. 141; Swatch Web site at www.swatch.com; Seiko Web site www. SeikoUSA.com; and Timex Web site www.timex.com.
9. This case was written by Gina Eckardt.

CREDITS

CHAPTER 1

p. 4, Courtesy of Rollerblade, Inc.; p. 8, Courtesy Rollerblade, Inc.; p. 11, New Product Showcase and Learning Center, Inc., photograph by Robert Haller; p. 13 (left), Courtesy Wal-Mart Stores, Inc.; p. 13 (right), Reprinted with permission of Lands' End, Inc.; p. 17, Courtesy of Rollerblade, Inc.; p. 18; All photos courtesy of Rollerblade, Inc.; p. 22, Courtesy of Alberta Health; Photograph by Larry Marcus.

CHAPTER 2

p. 28, Courtesy of Gulf Canada Resources Limited; p. 37 (left), Reproduced by permission of Intel Corporation, Copyright 1998 Intel Corporation; p. 37 (right), Duncan Hines ad: Courtesy of Aurora Foods; p. 38, "The HP information, logo and copyrighted information contained within this textbook is reproduced with the permission of Hewlett-Packard (Canada) Ltd. Hewlett-Packard expressly reserves its copyright interest in all Hewlett-Packard reproduced material in this textbook and is not to be reproduced without the expressed written consent of Hewlett-Packard (Canada) Ltd."; p. 44, ©1996 Paradise Kitchens, Inc. Reprinted with permission; p. 46, Courtesy of Eastman Kodak Co.: agency: Ogilvy & Mather/Atlanta; p. 51, Courtesy of Specialized Bicycles.

APPENDIX A

pp. 55, 62, 64, 66, 67 (left), 67 (right), ©1996 Paradise Kitchens, Inc. All photos and ads reprinted with permission.

CHAPTER 3

p. 72, Courtesy Microsoft Corporation; p. 77, Courtesy of Club Med Sales, Inc.; p. 79, Courtesy of Benetton; p. 81, Courtesy of Sobey's Ltd.; p. 83, Courtesy Westin Hotels & Resorts, agency: Cole & Weber, Seattle, photographers: Kathleen Norris Cook and Tim Bieber/Image Bank Northwest and Tony Stone Images; p. 84 (left), Courtesy IBM; p. 84 (center), Courtesy Diamond Multimedia Systems, Inc.; p. 84 (right), Courtesy of USSB; p. 85 (left), Courtesy Young & Rubicam/Frankfurt; p. 85 (right), Courtesy of Lever Brothers Company; p. 94, Both courtesy of Imagination Pilots Entertainment; p. 95, Courtesy of Imagination Pilots Entertainment.

CHAPTER 4

p. 96, Courtesy of Molson Breweries; p. 101, Rex USA Ltd.; p. 102, Courtesy Transparency International; p. 104, Photograph by Sharon Hoogstraten; p. 107 (top), Photograph by Sharon Hoogstraten; p. 107 (bottom), Courtesy Irwin Professional Publishing; p. 108, Courtesy McDonald's Corporation.

CHAPTER 5

p. 118, Courtesy of W. K. Buckley Ltd.; p. 123 (left), Courtesy of Sony Electronics, Inc.; p. 123 (right), Courtesy of Bruno Magli; p. 128, Courtesy ALMAP/BBDO, Sao Paulo; p. 129, Levi ad: Courtesy Harrod & Mirlin/ FCB, Toronto; p. 131, Travelpix/FPG International; p. 132, Courtesy Nestlé S.A.; p. 133, Reprinted with permission of Reader's Digest/photograph by Richard Hong; p. 134, Courtesy of The Coca-Cola Company; p. 136, Courtesy The PRS Group; p. 138, James Schnepf; p. 139, Courtesy of McDonald's Corporation; p. 141, Courtesy, The Gillette Company; p. 145, Copyright ©1997 Universal Press Syndicate. All rights reserved.

CHAPTER 6

p. 146, Courtesy Campbell Ewald, Warren, MI; p. 150, Courtesy Grey Advertising; p. 151, Courtesy of Eddie Bauer, Inc.; p. 156, Courtesy inscape for Time Warner Interactive; p. 157 (left), ©1998 National Fluid Milk Processor Promotion Board; agency: Bozell Worldwide/ New York; p. 157 (right), Photograph by Greg Wolff; p. 159 (left), Courtesy of Colgate-Palmolive Company; p. 159 (right), The Bayer Company; p. 161 (left), Courtesy, The Gillette Company; p. 161 (right), Courtesy Omega U.S./Bide Quervain; p. 162, Les Stone/Sygma; p. 163, The *Sports Illustrated for Kids* cover is reprinted courtesy of *Sports Illustrated for Kids* December 1998 issue. Copyright ©1998, Time, Inc. All rights reserved; p. 165, Courtesy of Haggar Clothing Co. ©1997 Haggar Clothing Co.

CHAPTER 7

p. 172, ©1999 Endacott Ltd.; p. 175, Courtesy of Marvo USA, New York, NY; p. 176, Reprinted with permission of the Census Bureau; p. 179, Courtesy of SGS-Thomson Microelectronics; p. 180, Courtesy of Sylvania/GTE Products Corporation; p. 181, Courtesy of Chrysler Corporation; p. 183, Reproduced by permission of Intel Corporation, Copyright 1998 Intel Corporation; p. 184, Courtesy of GE Information Services; p. 185, Dan Bosler/Tony Stone Images; p. 189, Courtesy of Allen-Bradley Company, Inc; p. 193, Courtesy Energy Performance Systems, Inc.

CHAPTER 8

p. 200, Courtesy Sympatico™; p. 202 (top), Michael J. Hruby; p. 202 (bottom), Courtesy Toys "Я" Us; p. 206, iVALS Internet User Segments, SRI Consulting; p. 208, Courtesy SRI Consulting; p. 210, ©Matt Mahurin Inc.; p. 212, Courtesy Cisco Systems, Inc.; p. 213 (left), Advertising created for Onsale, Inc. by USWEB/CKS; p. 213 (right), Courtesy Women.Com Networks, Inc.; p. 214, Courtesy of Praco, Ltd.; p. 215, Reprinted with permission of The Gap; p. 218, Courtesy of America Online; p. 219, Courtesy of America Online.

CHAPTER 9

p. 220, Shooting Star; p. 224, Courtesy The Dairy Farmers of Canada; p. 227, Courtesy Ocean Spray; p. 231, Courtesy of Binky-Griptight; p. 232, Courtesy Campbell's Soup Company; p. 234, Courtesy Wendy's International Inc.; p. 237, Courtesy of Shoppers Drug Mart; p. 238, Courtesy Fisher-Price.

CHAPTER 10

p. 252, Brent Jones; p. 254 (top), Courtesy New Balance Athletic Shoe, Inc.; p. 254 (bottom), Courtesy Vans, Inc.; p. 262, Courtesy of Ault Foods; p. 263 (top), Courtesy of Genova & Partners; p. 263 (bottom), DILBERT reprinted by permission of United Features Syndicate, Inc.; p. 266, Courtesy of Wendy's International, Inc.; p. 268, Courtesy of Apple Computer, Inc.; p. 273 (left), Courtesy of Buick Motor Division; p. 273 (right), Courtesy of Oldsmobile; agency: Leo Burnett.

CHAPTER 11

p. 284, Courtesy of 3M Company; p. 287, Courtesy of Nike, Inc.; p. 288, Courtesy Rolex Watch USA, Inc.; p. 291 (top), Courtesy Sony Computer Entertainment America Inc.; p. 291 (bottom), Breathe Right™ nasal strips are manufactured by CNS, Inc., Minneapolis, MN/Advertising agency: Seitsema, Engeland Partners, Minneapolis, MN; p. 294 (left), New Product Showcase and Learning Center, Inc./Photograph by Robert Haller; p. 294 (right), Courtesy of the Original Pet Drink Co., Inc.; p. 296, Sharon Hoogstraten; p. 298, Courtesy of 3M Company; p. 299, Courtesy Penn Racquet Sports; Agency: Veritas Advertising, Inc.; p. 301, Courtesy of Frito-Lay, Inc.; p. 303, Jose Azel/Aurora; p. 304, John Madere/The Stock Market; p. 306, Churchill & Klehr/Tony Stone Images; p. 307, Courtesy of Hewlett-Packard Company; p. 310, 3Com, the 3Com logo, and Palm Computing are registered trademarks, and Palm V and the Palm V logo are trademarks of Palm Computing, Inc., 3Com Corporation, or its subsidiaries.

CHAPTER 12

p. 312, Courtesy Clearly Canadian Beverage Corporation; p. 317 (left), Courtesy American Honda Motor Company, Inc.; agency: Rubin Postaer and Associates; p. 317 (right), Courtesy of Canon USA, Inc.; p. 323, Courtesy of Mars Inc.; p. 327, Courtesy of Elite Foods, Inc.; p. 329, Courtesy Louis Vuitton; p. 330 (left), Courtesy of Black & Decker (U.S.), Inc.; p. 330 (right), Courtesy of DeWalt Industrial Tool Company; p. 331, Courtesy of Pez Candy, Inc.; p. 332, Courtesy of The Coca-Cola Company; p. 333, ©The Procter & Gamble Company. Used with permission.

CHAPTER 13

p. 338, The Nunavut Handbook, 1999 Commemorative Edition. Published by Nortext Media Inc., Iqaluit NT; p. 341, Courtesy of Canadian Pacific Hotels and Harrod and Mirlin; p. 342, Courtesy of Oxford Properties; p. 346, Figure 13–4: Adapted from W. Earl Sasser, R. Paul Olsen, and D. Daryl Wyckoff, *Management of Service Operations: Text, Cases, and Readings* (Boston: Allyn & Bacon, 1978); p. 349 (left), Courtesy of McDonald's Corporation; p. 349 (center), Courtesy of Sprint; p. 349 (right), Courtesy of Canadian Red Cross.

CHAPTER 14

p. 356, ©John Sylvester Photography; p. 358, ©Kohler Company; p. 362 (left), Michael J. Hruby; p. 362 (right), Courtesy of Nike, Inc.; p. 364, Michael J. Hruby; p. 365, Courtesy of Fiat USA, Inc.; p. 366, Sharon Hoogstraten; p. 370, Courtesy of Luigines, Inc.

CHAPTER 15

p. 380, Courtesy, The Gillette Company; p. 387, Courtesy Grey Advertising; p. 392, Sharon Hoogstraten; p. 395, Courtesy of The Toro Company.

APPENDIX B

pp. 410, Courtesy of The Caplow Company.

CHAPTER 16

p. 412, Courtesy Gateway 2000; p. 414, Figure 16–1: Reprinted by permission of the publisher from *Dictionary of Marketing Terms,* Peter D. Bennett, Editor, ©1996 by the American Marketing Association; p. 420, Courtesy Nestlé S.A.; p. 426, Courtesy FAO Schwartz; p. 427, Courtesy VISA; p. 428, Courtesy of Dai-Ichi Kikaku Co., Ltd. and Warner Lambert.

CHAPTER 17

p. 434, Reprinted with permission of *Business Week;* illustration by David Cale; p. 438, Sharon Hoogstraten; p. 439, Courtesy Saturn Corporation; p. 441, Courtesy of J.D. Edwards World Solutions Company; p. 444, Mark Richards/ PhotoEdit; p. 445 (left), Courtesy of Penske Truck Leasing Co. ©1997; p. 445 (right), Courtesy Emery Worldwide; p. 447, Courtesy of Maersk, Inc.; p. 448, Courtesy of Canadian Airlines, Canadian Air Cargo; p. 449, Courtesy of Rapistan Demag Corporation; p. 451, Courtesy of Federal Express Corporation; p. 452, Both photos Fritz Hoffmann/ Imageworks.

CHAPTER 18

p. 456, Courtesy Indigo.ca; p. 460, Corbis/ Bettmann; p. 461, Reprinted with permission of Tandy Corporation; p. 466 (top), Paul Chesley/Tony Stone Images; p. 466 (middle), Courtesy of L.L. Bean, Inc.; p. 466 (bottom), Courtesy of QVC Network, Inc.; p. 467 (top), Courtesy of Shabang; p. 467 (bottom), Courtesy of amazon.com; p. 468 (left), Reprinted with permission of Lands' End, Inc.; p. 468 (right), Courtesy of Cybersmith, Cambridge, MA; p. 475, Courtesy Taco Bell; p. 477, Courtesy of Nike, Inc.

CHAPTER 19

p. 480, Shooting Star; p. 483, Courtesy of Pyro; p. 485, Courtesy of East Pak; p. 486, Reprinted with permission of Macmillan General References USA, a division of Ahsuog, Inc. from *Frommer's Ireland from $50 a Day,* by Mark Meagher, Elizabeth Neave, Susan fro Poole, Robert Emmet Meagher. Copyright ©1998 by Simon & Schuster, Inc.; p. 487, Courtesy Fence Magazine; p. 489 (top), Photography by Greg Wolff; p. 489 (bottom), Courtesy IBM; p. 492, Courtesy The Quantum Group; p. 493, Courtesy Taco Bell; p. 498, Courtesy the Direct Marketing Association; p. 499, ©Mitsubishi Motors Corporation: agency: Direct Partners/Los Angeles; photographers: ©Vincent Dente, ©Bob Stevens, and ©Tim Baur.

CHAPTER 20

p. 506, Courtesy TSN; p. 508 (left), Courtesy Iridium North America; agency: Ammirati Puris Lintas; p. 508 (center), Courtesy barnesandnoble.com; p. 508 (right), Courtesy of Godiva Chocolatier; p. 509, Courtesy of DDB Needham Worldwide and The Dial Corporation; p. 510, Courtesy of Molson Breweries; p. 513, Copyright, Nissan 1997; Nissan, Frontier, and the Nissan logo are registered trademarks of Nissan; p. 515, Courtesy American Express; p. 517 (top), People Magazine Syndication; p. 517 (bottom), Courtesy of Ford Motor Company; p. 519 , Federation des producteurs d'oeufs de consommation du Quebec; p. 522, Courtesy Ford Motor Company; p. 526, Ray Marklin.

CHAPTER 21

p. 532, ©Arnold Adler; p. 535, ©John Madere; p. 537, ©Jay Brousseau; p. 539, Courtesy Xerox Corporation; p. 541, Courtesy ZD Events; p. 542, CB Productions/The Stock Market; p. 544, Ken Ross/FPG International; p. 551, Courtesy UTNE Reader; p. 552, Courtesy of Mary Kay; p. 553, Courtesy of Toshiba America Medical Systems and Interactive Media; p. 554, Jose Pelaez/The Stock Market; p. 558, Courtesy Reebok International Ltd.

CHAPTER 22

p. 566, Michael J. Hruby; p. 566, Michael J. Hruby; p. 574, Figure 22–6: Reprinted with permission from The Free Press, a division of Simon & Schuster, from Competitive Advantage: Creating and Sustaining Superior Performance by Michael E. Porter. Copyright ©1985 by Michael E. Porter; p. 575, Courtesy Volkswagen of America, Inc. and Arnold Communications, Inc.; p. 580, Courtesy of Papa John's International; p. 581, Figure 22–10: Reprinted by permission of Harvard Business Review. An exhibit from "Making Your Marketing Strategy Work," by Thomas V. Bonoma, March–April 1984. Copyright ©1984 by the President and Fellows of Harvard College, all rights reserved; p. 582, Courtesy Swatch Group (U.S.) Inc.; p. 584, Courtesy of Lockheed Advanced Development Company; p. 585, Courtesy of Saturn Corporation; p. 586, Figure 22–12: Figure from *An Introduction to Contemporary Business,* Fourth Edition by William Rudelius and W. Bruce Erickson, copyright ©1985 by Harcourt Brace & Co., reproduced by permission of the publisher; p. 587, Figure 22–13: Figure from *An Introduction to Contemporary Business,* Fourth Edition by William Rudelius and W. Bruce Erickson, copyright ©1985 by Harcourt Brace & Co., reproduced by permission of the publisher; p. 588, Sharon Hoogstraten; p. 594, Courtesy Clearly Canadian Beverages.

APPENDIX C

p. 612, Thatch cartoon by Jeff Shesol/Reprinted with permission of Vintage books.

APPENDIX D

p. 615, Courtesy of Kingpin Snowboarding; p. 622, Courtesy of United Airlines; p. 631, 633, Courtesy BMW.

NAME INDEX

COMPANY/PRODUCT INDEX

D

H

I

J

K

L

SUBJECT INDEX

D

T